A TREASURY OF NEW ENGLAND FOLKLORE

STORIES, BALLADS, AND TRADITIONS OF THE YANKEE PEOPLE

Edited by B. A. BOTKIN

There is more than humor in the saying that New England is a state of mind. There is New England, wherever New Englanders go. —William Chauncy Langdon

CROWN PUBLISHERS NEW YORK

PRINTED IN THE UNITED STATES OF AMERICA

ACKNOWLEDGMENTS

The editor and publishers wish to thank the following authors or their representatives, publishers, publications, historical societies and committees, for their kind permission to use material in this book. Full copyright notices are given on the pages on which the material appears.

Abingdon-Cokesbury Press; John Allison; The Altrurian Club (Vt.); D. Appleton-Century Co., Inc.; A. S. Barnes & Co., Inc.; Mrs. Phillips Barry; Bobbs-Merrill Co.; *The Boston Traveler;* The Town of Buckland Committee; Thomas and Joseph Butterworth; The Colonial Press; Miss Jennie F. Copeland; Cornell Maritime Press; Coward-McCann, Inc.; Creative Age Press; Danvers Historical Society; F. A. Davis Co.; Dial Press, Inc.; Dodd, Mead & Co., Inc.; Doubleday, Doran Co., Inc.; Duell, Sloan & Pearce, Inc.; E. P. Dutton & Co., Inc.; Flanders Ballad Collection, Middlebury College; Funk & Wagnalls Co.; Miss Lisabel Gay; *Gourmet* Magazine; Harcourt, Brace & Co., Inc.; Walter and Margaret Hard; Harper & Bros.; Harvard University Press; Henry Holt & Co., Inc.; Franz J. Horch; Houghton Mifflin Co.; Idlewild Press; Mrs. Clifton Johnson; Herbert G. Jones; *Journal of American Folklore;* Keynote Recordings, Inc.; Alfred A. Knopf, Inc.; John K. Lagemann; Freeman Lincoln; J. B. Lippincott Co.; Little, Brown & Co.; The Macmillan Co.; The Marine Research Society; Marshall Jones Co.; Marshfield Tercentenary Committee; Musicraft Records, Inc.; *New England Quarterly; The New Yorker; The New York Times;* Northampton Historical Society; W. W. Norton & Co., Inc.; G. P. Putnam's Sons; Random House, Inc.; Reynal & Hitchcock, Inc.; Rinehart & Co., Inc.; Rutgers University Press; G. Schirmer, Inc.; Charles Scribner's Sons; Edward Rowe Snow; *Southern Folklore Quarterly;* Sigmund Spaeth; Mrs. Guy E. Speare; Stephen Daye Press; Donald G. Trayser; Charles E. Tuttle Co.; University of California Press; University of Michigan Press; Vanguard Press; Vermont Historical Society; Viking Press, Inc.; Ives Washburn, Inc.; Waverly House; Wehman Bros.; Weymouth Historical Society; Dr. B. J. Whiting; Whittlesey House; The Williams & Wilkins Co.; Willis Kingsley Wing; Yale University Press; Yankee, Inc. (*The Old Farmer's Almanac*); Yankee Publishing Co.

CONTENTS

PART ONE: FABULOUS YANKEES

I. YANKEE PEDDLERS AND TRICKSTERS

II. LOCAL CHARACTERS

III. STOUT FELLOWS AND HARD LIARS

PART TWO: MYTHS, LEGENDS, AND TRADITIONS

I. WONDERS OF THE INVISIBLE WORLD

II. THE POWERS OF DARKNESS

III. PLACE LORE

IV. HISTORICAL TRADITIONS

PART THREE: BELIEFS AND CUSTOMS

I. THE POWER OF FAITH

II. THE FORCE OF CUSTOM

PART FOUR: WORD LORE

I. YANKEEISMS

II. FOLK-SAY

PART FIVE: SONGS AND RHYMES

I. BALLADS AND SONGS

II. RHYMES AND JINGLES

NEW ENGLAND AS A FOLKLORE COUNTRY

As a folklore country, New England has an advantage over other regions in that its lore is part of a well-defined, well-documented tradition. A tradition derives its strength and being from a sense of group identity, on the one hand, and a sense of historical continuity, on the other. And since local history, legend, speech, and folkways give what Whitman calls "that taste of identity and locality which is so dear in literature," they are basic to a regional tradition. This is especially true in New England.

As a "finished place," in Bernard De Voto's phrase, New England has a finished culture, one of the attributes of which is the desire to recapture, if not to perpetuate, the past in the present. The "Yankee race," moreover, is a "race of readers," who, perhaps more than any other regional group, like to read about themselves. Local and ancestral pride and curiosity about the local past meet in a body of historical and local color writings unsurpassed anywhere else in the country. "In the broadest and most enlightened sense," wrote Samuel Adams Drake in 1899, "we, of to-day, are but the passing custodians of those visible and authentic memorials which Time and Progress have yet spared to us. They belong not to us, but to History. We can tear down, but who shall build up again?" This is the truly conservative attitude, which, without tearing down or building up, seeks to select and conserve those aspects and values of the past deemed worthy of preservation. The result is tradition—a "limited part of life to-day," according to Albert Guérard, as it is a "limited part of history."

Besides the "visible and authentic memorials" of the past, a tradition consists of the invisible memorials of folklore. The folklore of a region is made up, first, of the common heritage of migratory traditions, and, secondly, of a more or less indigenous development. In the sense of having accumulated about itself a body of superstitions, prejudices, myths, and legends regarding traditional or "old New England," New England not only *has* but *is* folklore—folklore *of* as well as *in* New England.

All tradition, including folklore, is a matter of living memory plus written record. "All through my childhood," writes Wilbur Cross, "I learned of the past not from books but from the lips of men and women." In this way Yankees make good folklorists. For the conditions of New England life have fostered not only folklore but the folkloristic along with the historical impulse. These conditions include relative homogeneity and healthy provincialism. In the "indigenous environment" of the small farm, the small factory, the village, the local church, and the family circle (all characteristic of the small-scale, closely-knit topography, economy, and culture of the region), the provincialism of New England (a product of cultural isolation, clannishness, and exclusiveness) has grown rather than declined through the years.

For all these reasons, New England is more than a section of the country, more than a province; it is a country in itself, with a strong sense of "nationality" rooted in "racial remembrance." Within the New England country are contained many smaller countries (including sub-regions, states, communities, and ethnic groups), each with its own traditions and provincialism. "Conditions," writes Clifton Johnson of Northampton folk, "made them conservative; and it became almost proverbial among them that if a man owned a strip of meadow land, belonged to the First Church, bought his clothes of Deacon Daniel Kingsley, and was a subscriber to the Hampton *Gazette,* he surely would go to heaven when he died."

Since folklore is universal in diffusion and local in adaptation, there is no such thing as a purely regional folklore any more than there is a purely national folklore. The nearest approach to it is place lore. Here belong local place-name stories, local foods, local anecdotes, and local characters—guaranteed to awaken nostalgia in all New Englanders as well as any one who has ever lived or vacationed in the region. Here, too, belong the characteristic tales and traditions (many of them local in origin but national in scope) of the land and the people, and their struggle for freedom and survival.

As immortalized in history and enshrined in literature, the local patriotism of New England folklore has become part of national patriotism. Longfellow's "epic of the Indian" and his poems dealing with the "life of the first settlers, the fortunes of the men of Plymouth, the tranquil joys and tragic end of the French at Acadie" (which, along with the works of his fellow New England writers, constitute for many of us our first and only contact with New England folklore) have made him, in a sense, our national poet. The historic shrines of Boston, as the "cradle of liberty," are no less national than regional sacred symbols.

"Who cares for the growth of New England," declared Rev. E. Frank Howe, in his historical oration at the Centennial Celebration of Grafton, Mass., on July 4, 1876, "so long as it can continue to give principles, and institutions, and men to the nation? Who cares for the growth of New England if the entire nation becomes New Englandized?" The New Englandizing of the country was accomplished not only through educational, religious, and political ideas and forms, but also through speech, literature, and lore. Wherever Yankees went, they carried with them as part of their cultural baggage the folk songs and tales, beliefs and customs, which linked them with old England and became part of the American cultural heritage. In spite of the inevitable changes, additions, and losses suffered in the diffusion and acculturation process, in spite even of New England's loss of cultural leadership, the region has always stood in much the same relation to the rest of the country as England has to America—that of a spiritual homeland.

In still another sense the New England legend is national. This is the sense in which outsiders have contributed their own versions (not entirely unbiased) of the Yankee character (*e.g.*, the peddler) and Yankeeland; and the local prejudices and rivalries that diversify the regional picture also complicate the interregional one. And cutting across regional and national lines, the mindskills and handskills that belong to the folk everywhere form the broad universal base of New England folklore, whose variants provide points of comparison and contrast with those of other regions.

The world of New England folklore, finally, belongs to the present as well as the past. If much of it resembles the yellowed, time-stained pages of a volume of old newspapers which crumble at the touch, much of it still has vitality and relevance for the living. Here is the eternal conflict between Merry England, with its gay sinners, and Puritanism, with its grisly saints. Here are the common people, "daily covered by the dust of the farm or shop or the spray of the ocean," with "good common sense, and big warm hearts." Here are the time-hallowed rituals of work and play, food and drink, festival and faith, love and death. And here are the timeless phenomena of the soil, the sea, the sky, and the elements.

In the proverbial weather descriptions of the *Old Farmer's Almanac* are the elemental poetry and magic of the signs and seasons whose influence underlies the power of faith and custom—"stormy with raw winds," "slippery going," "look for a thaw," "blustery and rough," "falling weather," "windy and shivery," "more comfortable indoors." And in the sayings of Josh Billings the irreverence and incongruity of native American humor are mixed with just the right proportion of crackerbox sageness and Yankee skepticism. "If yu trade horses with a jockey yu kant git cheated but *once* —but if yu trade with a deakon, yu may git cheated *twice*—once in the horse, and once in the deakon."

Out of the homely epic of Yankee toil, ingenuity, and enterprise; out of the human comedy of Yankee idiosyncrasies and expedients; out of the local mythology of Yankee heroes, eccentrics, monsters, sprites, witches, and demons (whose antics remind us of the wild rout of mummers in Hawthorne's story of "The Maypole of Merry Mount") emerges a portrait (in the national picture) of an admirable rather than a lovable people, whose virtues and faults are distinctly American.

Somewhere among these Yankee faces may be the fulfilment of the prophecy, in Hawthorne's allegory of "The Great Stone Face," of the coming of the great man who would resemble the Old Man of the Mountains. As one prospect after another, hailed by the people, proved disappointing to Ernest—Mr. Gathergold, the rich merchant with the Midas touch; Old Stony Phiz, the Presidential candidate; General Blood-and-Thunder, the illustrious commander; the great poet; and even Ernest himself, so we may look for the likeness of the Great Stone Face of the Fabulous Yankee in individual heroes—Ethan Allen, Daniel Webster, Barnum—only to find his true image in our own collective face of Uncle Sam, who began as Uncle Jonathan.

As the first of a series of projected regional folklore collections, this book follows the pattern of its predecessor, *A Treasury of American Folklore*, differing principally in the addition of a section of "Beliefs and Customs."

None of the considerable body of New England material in the earlier volume has been duplicated here, with the exception of a variant of "Thar She Blows."

I want to thank my publishers for their continuing co-operation, encouragement, and constructive criticism. I admire the efficiency and dispatch with which Bertha Krantz has handled the final responsibility of seeing the book (and me) through the press. Of the many other people who have helped make the work possible and feasible, I am especially indebted, for courteous service, to the Library of Congress, the New York Public Library, the Boston Public Library, the Harvard University Library, the Massachusetts Historical Society, the American Antiquarian Society, the Croton Free Library, the Ossining Public Library, and the Field Library of Peekskill; to the booksellers (especially the Pageant Book Store) who have helped me build up my New England library; to Frances Kurland, who transcribed and edited a number of tunes; to the many friends who have furnished suggestions and assistance of one kind or another; and, above all, to my wife, Gertrude Botkin, who performed the heroic task of preparing the typescript (which has here been reduced by one third), assisted with the music, and once more shared with me the labor of putting a book into shape.

In addition to the credits given under "Acknowledgments" and in the source notes, I want to acknowledge here the many contributions, published and unpublished, of my former colleagues of the Federal Writers' Project and two original anecdotes of Mrs. Grace Partridge Smith.

The title-page and cover decoration is based on a print of "Brother Jonathan before He Became Uncle Sam" in the New York *Times*, by way of the Picture Collection of the New York Public Library.

At this point, mindful of the book's limitations and omissions, of the wealth of sources provided by the many story-tellers and researchers who have preceded me, and of the thin and shifting line that separates a good from a poor version, I take comfort in Josh Billings' distinction between a mistake and a blunder: "When a man sets down a poor umbreller, and takes up a good one, he makes a *mistake*, but when he sets down a good umbreller, and takes up a poor one, he makes a *blunder*."

B. A. B.

Croton-on-Hudson, New York
October, 1947

PART ONE

FABULOUS YANKEES

If one of the main products of the region was the New England conscience, another, at least according to the popular belief in other districts, was the wooden nutmeg.

—ODELL SHEPARD

Even Cotton Mather could not avoid a tone of pious boastfulness when he narrated the doings of New England. Everything was remarkable. New England had the most remarkable providences, the most remarkable painful preachers, the most remarkable heresies, the most remarkable witches. Even the local devils were in his judgment more enterprising than those of the old country. They had to be in order to be a match for the New England saints.

—SAMUEL MCCHORD CROTHERS

But what I chiefly lament is the disappearance of the Yankee—not the conventional Yankee of the theatre, for he had never an existence elsewhere; but the hearty yet suspicious, "cute" though green, drawling, whittling, unadulterated Yankee, with his broad humor, delicious patois, *and large-hearted patriotism. . . . Railway and telegraph, factory and work-shop, penetrating into the most secluded hamlets, have rubbed off all the crust of an originality so pronounced as to have become the type, and often the caricature too, of American nationality the world over.*

—SAMUEL ADAMS DRAKE

I predict that on the last day of this planet, when the sun hangs cold in the sky, only two men will be left to face it. One will be a Chinaman, and if you ask the other he will say, "O yes, I was born at Cohasset."

—VAN WYCK BROOKS

I. YANKEE PEDDLERS AND TRICKSTERS

"Yankee" has become almost a synonym for ingeniousness, thrift, and "cuteness." . . . He is a born arguer, and a born peddler, and a born whittler, a Jack-at-all-trades and good at them all.
—CLIFTON JOHNSON

. . . trading and swapping was more than a livelihood there. It was an emotional safety valve, perhaps—maybe the Yankee Puritan's substitute for gambling.—R. E. GOULD

Mankind luv to be cheated, but they want to hav it dun bi an artist.—JOSH BILLINGS

1. THE FABULOUS YANKEE

IN THE fabulous country of Yankeeland, Yankeedom, or Down East lives a fabulous creature known as the Yankee. The oldest and best known of American traditional types, this generic folk hero of New England is not to be confused with actual New Englanders any more than the legendary Backwoodsman, Hoosier, etc., are to be mistaken for the original. Yet, no mere symbol, the fabulous Yankee has a folk reality and humanity that make him more than a local or even national figure.

Perhaps no regional type has attracted to itself more myths and libels than the sensible, self-dependent, God-fearing, freedom-loving conservative, stubborn, practical, thrifty, industrious, inventive, and acquisitive Yankee. One reason for this is the fact that "The individual whom they call Yankee is very difficult to find, because you hardly know what to accept for a definition of him." [1] Another reason is to be sought in the sectional pride and prejudice, the local solidarities and loyalties, which have helped to shape popular conceptions of the Yankee. These conflicts and changes are reflected in the origin and growth of the word "Yankee" itself, through its varying connotations, favorable and unfavorable.

As a result, the history of the fabulous Yankee is the history not of a single type but of many sub-types—the Connecticut Yankee, the Vermont Yankee, the Yankee countryman, the Yankee peddler, the Yankee storekeeper, the comic Yankee, the sage Yankee, etc.—in which history and tradition are inextricably mixed. Many Yankee types, necessarily vanished or vanishing, survive largely in folklore.

---

[1] Mark Miles, "The Yankee," *The Mirror of the Philomathean Society*, Phillips Academy, Andover, Vol. 5 (July, 1859), No. 3, p. 17.

2. The Yankee Clown

The fabulous Yankee is first of all the comic countryman—the Yorkshire clown [1] and the English Hodge of the jest books transplanted to American soil. With them he belongs to the tradition of the "countryman in the great world" or the "rustic set in a complicated environment." Under the guise of Jonathan—the simple, awkward rustic, agape and agog at the world—the comic Yankee makes his bow in "Yankee Doodle." This song of uncertain origin and authorship, half British satire and half American self-burlesque, gave rise to many folk versions and parodies, such as "The Yankee's Return from Camp" and "Corn Cobs Twist Your Hair," and is said to have begun and ended the Revolution.

> "Yankee Doodle" is the tune
> Americans delight in;
> 'Twill do to whistle, sing, or play
> And just the thing for fightin'.

Thereafter, the character of Jonathan, like the song, was identified with the homespun pose of the provincial American—raw, bumptious, inquisitive—and associated with the development of national and regional consciousness.

After the Revolution, the comic Yankee became a stock figure on the stage, beginning with Jonathan, in the first American comedy, *The Contrast* (1787) by Royall Tyler (a Boston-born Harvard lawyer, later chief justice of the Vermont Supreme Court) and continuing down to the Civil War through such characters as Jonathan Ploughboy, Hiram Dodge, Solomon Swop, and Sam Patch, acted by George Handel ("Yankee") Hill, James H. Hackett, and Dan Marble. For the vogue of the stage Yankee, these and other comedians' Yankee impersonations and monologues, drawing upon oral tradition, were even more directly responsible.

The history of the comic Yankee is thus the history of a folk legend and a literary stereotype, in which oral yarns and popular songs rub shoulders with jest books, almanacs, newspaper sketches, travel books, local color novel, poems, and plays, and professional humorous writings.

3. Yankee Wits and Sages

Like the Yorkshire clown the comic Yankee was not all fool but more rogue than fool. Although his brash greenness made him the natural butt of jokes and practical jokes, his deceptive simplicity (as in Royall Tyler's Jonathan) concealed a heart of gold and native wit and sagacity, which served as a convenient vehicle for social and political satire.

---

[1] The name Yorkshire has become a synonym for acuteness, not unmixed with a touch of unscrupulousness. In Lincolnshire, for example, when anything is done which is very clever, sharp, or unscrupulous, they say: That's real Yerksheer. To put Yorkshire on a person means in Lancashire to cheat, trick or overreach him; in Lancashire and Lincolnshire, a sharp overreaching person is called a Yorkshire bite. Even in his own country the Yorkshireman has this reputation.—Elizabeth Mary Wright, *Rustic Speech and Folklore* (London, 1913), pp. 2–3.

The possibilities of the comic Yankee as a homely critic were more fully realized in the 1830's, when the homespun Yankee, originally the spokesman of American democracy, became the mouthpiece of conservative politics. As the original cracker-box philosopher, the Yankee has always stood for sound common sense and the good old days as against radical and newfangled notions. In January, 1830, Seba Smith inaugurated in the Portland *Daily Courier* (the first Maine daily) his thirty-year series of Jack Downing letters. These were written in Down East language to the folks back home in Downingville by a "green, unsophisticated lad from the country," who blundered into the halls of the Maine legislature (then the scene of intense party rivalry) and so into national politics as the friend and critic of President Andrew Jackson.

In creating a new comic type, the cracker-box or rustic philosopher, Smith remained true to Down East character, background, and vernacular, and gave us the first real Yankee in American humor, in contrast to the more artificial stage Yankee. Jack Downing had many imitators of the same and other names, including Davy Crockett of anti-Jackson, anti-Federalist propaganda, and became a popular figure in political cartoons—the prototype of Uncle Sam, with his beaver hat, swallow-tailed coat, and striped trousers. As political hanger-on and commentator, he continued the tradition of the "countryman in the great world"—a "talkative, prying, speculative jimcrack of a fellow."

Like many another successful Yankee, Jack Downing, characteristically, began as a peddler, coming to Portland with a wagonload of ax handles, hoop poles, and other notions to sell. He thus foreshadows the droll, glib figure of the Yankee peddler, picaresque and pawky, who was destined to become the masterpiece of the comic Yankee—the beatinest fellow on earth.

4. Sharp Yankees

The Yankee peddler, hawking first his own handiwork and then other "notions," originated in the household and jackknife industries and small manufactures of New England. Here a hard land and climate, coupled with a middle-class, mercantile heritage and ingrained habits of thrift, diligence, and handiness, produced an industrious and restless tribe of spinning, weaving, whittling, contriving, swapping Yankees. Beginning as a neighborhood swapper, the Yankee spilled over into the roads and sea-lanes of commerce (just as the home craftsman spilled over into the factories) to become roving merchant to the country and the world.

As Marjorie Barstow Greenbie points out, the Yankee (perpetual motion incarnate) had a genius not only for making things but also for placing them. "Moving about, setting things to rights, actively using his hands, the New Englander constantly observed that the great trouble with the world is that things are not in the right place. By simple locomotion you can turn a deficit into an asset, and turn misfortune into a gift from the gods. Take ice, for example. There is altogether too much of it in winter. . . . But move the ice to the tropics. . . ." [1]

It remained for a Nova Scotia judge, Thomas Chandler Haliburton, to

[1] *American Saga* (New York, 1939), p. 33.

immortalize the Yankee peddler in literature by combining the picaresque pattern of the peddler's travels with the character of the crackerbox philosopher, thus making him a peddler of intellectual as well as wooden wares. Although *The Clockmaker; or, The Sayings and Doings of Sam Slick, of Slickville* (1836), originated in the author's desire to promote the development of Nova Scotia's natural resources and to preach provincial Toryism and Imperialism, it is remembered chiefly for the character of Sam Slick and the latter's wise saws and droll anecdotes.

Sam Slick (whom James Russell Lowell declared to be a "libel on the Yankee character, and a complete falsification of Yankee modes of speech") was half Yankee and half backwoodsman. In thus making him a composite of Jack Downing and Davy Crockett, Haliburton revealed, consciously or unconsciously, the close connection that existed between the peddler and the frontier. For, like the Indian trader and fur trader before him, the peddler followed the shifting fringe of settlement in pursuit of a livelihood and was an active force in the extension of the frontier. To the folks back home he brought valuable information about the new country. And many a peddler gladly exchanged his pack for land and a home in the South or the West.

As a picaresque character, combining rascality with humor, the peddler was at home on the frontier, where, in Simon Suggs's words, "It is good for a man to be shifty in a new country," and where it was said that "You might as well try to hold a greased eel as a live Yankee!" As the comic Yankee became a hero-legend, so the "scheming Yankee" was erected into a symbol of sectional prejudice climaxed by the Civil War.

The peddler's proverbial unscrupulousness in taking advantage of a situation and even creating a situation to sharpen his wits on was reflected in the language of the time. A "Yankee trick" became a "common name for anything very smart, done in the way of trade, no matter in which of the States the doer was born."[1] To *yankee* and *out-Yankee* meant to cheat and outcheat. The peddler also carried over the folklore motif of the comic contest of wits between the merchant and his customer, with the tables frequently turned on the former. And just as the peddler's audience enjoyed the spectacle of good-natured roguery, of a trap being set and the victim walking into it, so the New Englander, however much he may have deplored the peddler's shady reputation, began to enjoy the joke on himself and joined in the laughter at the countless stories of "cute" Yankee tricksters and "biters bit," told in village stores and taverns and circulated in newspapers, almanacs, and jokebooks.

5. Village Store and Tavern Humor

With the passing of the Yankee peddler, by the time of the Civil War, his mantle fell on the Yankee storekeeper. Since in many cases the latter started as a peddler, he retained many of the peddler's characteristics and tricks and perpetuated much of the lore of peddling. Stationary trade, however, made it necessary for the storekeeper to steer a middle course between the peddler's *caveat emptor* and the merchant's ingratiating motto,

[1] Cornelius Mathews, *Writings* (1846), II, 308, cited by Thornton in *An American Glossary* (Philadelphia, 1912), II, 961.

"The customer is always right." At the same time the calculating ethics of "Honesty is the best policy" permitted a wide margin of haggling, chiseling, and hoodwinking on the part of both merchant and customer; and stories of Yankee storekeepers, tavernkeepers, and other tradesmen stress the petty, legalistic side of small business in contrast to the freebooting, swindling methods of the footloose peddler and the "merchant adventurer." There is still a comic contest of wits between buyer and seller, but the chief contestants are the storekeeper who is a "little nigh on a trade" and the snug customer, who tries to get something for nothing. The storekeeper also had to keep his weather eye open and his sails trimmed for the lazy or dishonest clerk and the high-pressure drummer.

The nature of the general store as a social center put the storekeeper further on his mettle and on his guard. Along with the tavern the store served as a resort for village loafers, gossips, jesters, story-tellers, and pundits. In the atmosphere of easy sociability and fun-making thus created, customers and hangers-on indulged in petty pilfering, shop-lifting, sophistries, and ruses, which put a strain on the storekeeper's pocketbook and bookkeeping as well as on his vigilance and good humor. Favorite themes of store and tavern humor are "skunking" and "skinning" hoaxes; the detection and punishment of petty thieves; the hypocritical greed and ice-water charity of deacons; the pranks, forfeits, kangaroo courts, and boasting and lying contests of the store and tavern "clubs"; and the chicanery of horse-jockeys.

In the folkways of village humor the tavern occupied a special place. Here the native and the stranger, the countryman and the great world, met on the jousting ground of wit and story-telling. Here the commercial traveler followed in the peddler's footsteps; local politicians brought the affairs of the state and nation closer to home; and the city slicker and the farmer come to town matched wits with each other and with the landlord and the tavern-haunters.

6. Practical Jokers

In village store and tavern humor we find Yankee tricks of the trade generalized into Yankee tricks, and sharpness and greenness interchangeable, with tricksters tricked and the tricked turning trickster. And when the comic contest of wits is transferred to the realm of practical jokes, "sharp practice spiced with good humor" becomes good humor spiced with sharp practice. But, more than mere fun-making or mischief-making, Yankee pranks and sells were thought to serve a useful purpose by affording the victim a "surplus fund of experience."

The greatest and most practical "practical wag" that ever came out of a country store was the Connecticut Yankee, P. T. Barnum. As a clerk in his father's store in Bethel, he learned that "sharp trades, tricks, dishonesty, and deception are by no means confined to the city." [1] And as the world's greatest showman, he capitalized on the "perfect good nature with which the American public submit to a clever humbug," [2] while indulging the "jocose element" in his character, for any excess of which, he says, part of

---

[1] *Struggles and Triumphs* (Buffalo, 1873), p. 33.
[2] *Ibid.*, p. 148.

the blame must attach to his early surroundings of the store—the "theatre of village talk, and the scene of many practical jokes."

B. A. B.

Josh Billings on Live Yankees

LIVE Yankees are chuck full of karakter and sissing hot with enterprize and curiosty.

In bild we find them az lean az a hunter's dorg, with a parched countenance, reddy for a grin, or for a sorrow; ov elaastick step: thortful, but not abstrakted; pashunt, bekauze cunnin; ever watchful; slo to anger; avoiding a fight; but rezolute at bay.

In dress alwuz slik, but not stuck up; their harness alwuz betrays them wherever they go.

The oil ov their langwidge iz their dezire tew pleze, and their greezy words foreshadder a proffit.

They are natral mechanicks; the histry ov man's necessitys iz the histry ov their invenshuns.

The Live Yankee haz no hum; hiz luv ov invenshun breeds a luv ov change, and wharever a human trail shows itself we find him pantin on the trak.

He never gits sick at the stummuk in a furrin land, or grows sentermental; the buty ov a river tew him iz its capacity for a steambote; its sloping banks checker into bildin lots, and its poetry waters might do the drudgery ov a cottin mill.

He looks at a marble pyramid, guesses at its height, calkulates the stone by the perch, and sells the magnifisent relick in Boston at a proffit.

He climbs the Alpin hights, crossed by conkerin heroes, and iz struk with the proprierty ov tunneling it.

He sits, cross-legged, beneath the sheltring vine and listens to the oneazy sea, sees the warm promise ov the grape, and forgettin the holy memrys ov the land ov song, grinds the smilin vintage into wine and maiks a happy bargin.

You can meet him in Constanternopel, makin up in grimace what he lacks in langwidge, spreadin a plaster with hiz tounge, for the man ov Mahomet.

Go where you will, from the numb palsied North tew the swetting limberness ov the South, from the top ov earth's mornin tew half past eleven at night, and the everlastin Yankee you will find, either vehement in an argue, or purswazive in a swop.

From *Josh Billings on Ice, and Other Things*, pp. 20–22. Entered according to Act of Congress in the year 1868, by G. W. Carleton & Co., in the Clerk's Office of the District Court of the United States, for the Southern District of New York. New York: Carleton, Publisher. London: S. Low, Son & Co. 1870.

Hiz religion iz praktikal; he mourns over the heathen, and iz reddy tew save them by the job.

He luvs liberty with a red pepper enthuziasm, and fully beleafs Nu England kan whip the universe.

If the phlegmatick Englishman brags about roast beef and hiz ansesters, Jonathan haz a pumpkin pie and a grandpop tew match them.

If the Frenchman grows crazy over a frigazee ov frog's hind legs, Jonathan pulls out a donut and a Rhode Island greening.

If the dusky Italian talks about the mad vomits ov vesuvius, Jonathan turns in the water power ov Niagara.

In argument alwuz ernest, and in reazoning alwuz specius, this progressive phenomena tramps the world with the skeleton ov a pattent right in hiz carpet bag, and, in his ever open hand and face a pleasant "Heow air yer?"

If you would save your pride from being sandpapered, risk it not in a dicker with Jonathan.

His razor is the true Damascus, strapped on the wand ov Midas for a golden harvest; hiz sanctity iz often shrewdness, and hiz sweet savor iz often the reflekted halo ov the comin shillin.

Constitushunaly and by edukashun honest, he iz alwuz reddy tew cry for the deeds dun in the boddy; hiz hospitalitys and charities are cerimonial dutys, and if hiz religion iz sometimes only the severitys ov a sabbath, it iz bekauze hiz bias iz the thursting impulse of a creatin genius chained tew the more sordid pashun for lucre.

Factotum for the World

No other man is like him. It has been said of him, that he is made for all situations, and manages to work his way in all places. Place him upon a rock in the midst of the ocean, and, with his pen-knife and a bunch of shingles, he would work his way on shore. He sells salmon from the Kennebec to the people of Charleston; haddock, fresh from Cape Cod, to the planters of Matanzas; raises coffee in Cuba; swaps mules and horses for molasses, in Porto Rico; retails ice from Cumming's and Alden's pond, in South Reading, in the East Indies; takes mutton from Brighton to New Orleans and South America; raises multicaulis for the Governor of Jamaica; becomes an admiral in a foreign nation; builds railroads for the Autocrat of Russia; starts in a cockleshell craft of fifteen tons, loaded with onions, mackerel, and "notions," for Valparaiso; baits his traps on the Columbia river; catches wild beasts in Africa for Macomber's caravan; sells granite, on contract, to rebuild San Juan de Ulloa; is ready, like Ledyard, to start for Timbuctoo "tomorrow morning"; exiles himself for years from home, to sketch, in their own wilderness, the wild men of the woods, and astonishes

---

From *The (Old) Farmer's Almanack,* Calculated on a New and Improved Plan, for the Year of Our Lord 1851, by Robert B. Thomas, p. 45. Entered, according to Act of Congress, in the year 1850, by J. H. Jenks and G. W. Palmer, in the Clerk's Office of the District Court of the District of Massachusetts. Boston: Jenks, Palmer & Co.

refined Europe with the seeming presence of the untutored savage; prescribes sarsaparilla and eye-water to the mandarins of China, and, if he pleases, makes his Southern brethren rich with cotton inventions. He is found foremost among those who sway the elements of society—is the schoolmaster for his country, and missionary for the whole heathen world. He is unequalled in tact, and instead of going over round-about ways, starts across lots for any desired point. If perpetual motion is ever to be discovered, he will be sure to be the lucky contriver, for he is the factotum for the world.

YANKEES AND ENGLISHMEN

Corn Cobs Twist Your Hair

There was a man in our town,
  I'll tell you his condition.
He sold his oxen and his plough,
  To buy him a commission.

Chorus:
  Corn Cobs twist your hair,
    Cart wheel run round you,
  Fiery dragons take you off,
    And mortar pestal pound you.

When this man a commission got,
  He prov'd to be a coward,
He wouldn't go to Canada,
  For fear he'd get devour'd.

But he and I we went to town,
  Along with Captain Goodin,
And there we saw the Yankee boys,
  As thick as hasty puddin.

Now there was General Washington,
  With all the folks about him,
He swore they got so tarnal proud,
  They couldn't do without him.

And there they had a great big thing,
  Big as a log of maple,
And ev'ry time they wheel'd it round,
  It took two yoke of cattle.

And when they went to fire it off,
  It took a horn of powder,
It made a noise like Daddy's gun,
  Only a nation louder.

And there they had a little thing,
  All bound round with leather,
With little sticks to beat upon,
  To call the men together.

And there we saw a hollow stick,
  With six holes bor'd right in it,
And ev'ry time they blow'd upon,
  We thought the devil was in it.

And there we saw them with
    big knives,
  Stuck in a piece of leather,
And when the Captain he cri'd draw,
  They all draw'd out together.

From "Corn Cobs Twist Your Hair," A Favorite National Melody, Arranged to a Comic Song and Chorus and Sung by Little Yankee Hill, Written, Selected, and Arranged for the Pianoforte. Entered according to the Act of Congress, in the Year 1836, by George Endicot, in the Clerk's Office of the District Court, of the Southern District of New York. In *Series of Old American Songs,* Reproduced in Facsimile from Original or Early Editions in the Harris Collection of American Poetry and Plays, With Brief Annotations, by S. Foster Damon, Curator, No. 19. Providence, Rhode Island: Brown University Library. 1936.

This song is a folk development of the earliest version of "Yankee Doodle," with a Tom o' Bedlam refrain.—S. F. D.

Facsimile of the Original Sheet Music, 1836.

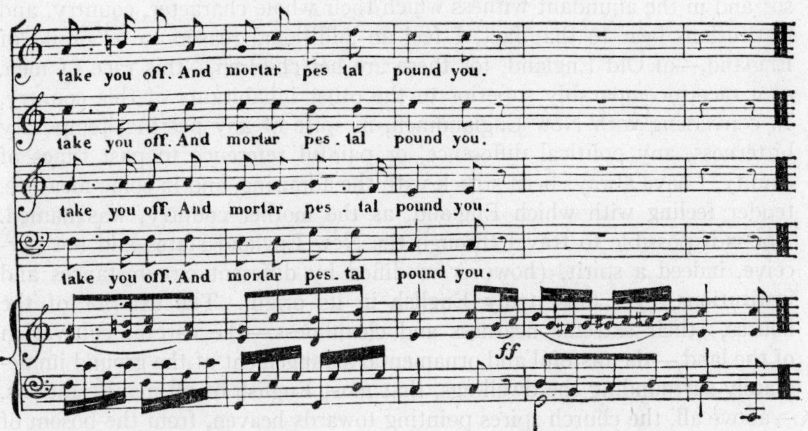
take you off. And mortar pes tal pound you.
take you off. And mortar pes . tal pound you.
take you off. And mortar pes - tal pound you.
take you off, And mortar pes . tal pound you.
ff

Now brother Ike was very bold,
 As bold as Captain Crocket,
For he sneak'd round on t'other side,
 And held on Daddy's pocket.

Now I and brother Ike goes hum,
 We wasn't fraid of powder,
For Daddy said he'd learn us both,
 To scream a little louder.

Our cousin Jim he went to town,
 With a pair of striped trowses,
He swore the town he couldn't see,
 There was so many houses.

Our Aunt Jemima climb'd a tree,
 She had a stick to boost her,
And there she sat a throwing corn,
 At our old bob tail rooster.

Now cousin Sal she went to town,
 And got upon a steeple,
She took a frying pan of grog,
 And pour'd it on the people.

Our Uncle Ben he lost his cow,
 And didn't know where to find her,
And when the cow she did cum hum,
 She had her tail behind her.

Now Sister Sue grows very thin,
 And no one knows what ails her,
She us'd to eat nine pound of pork,
 But now her stomach fails her.

And now I've sung you all my song,
 I've told you all the causes,
And all that I do want of you,
 Is all your kind applauses.

The Noble Yankee Race

To THE English traveller, around whose heart the love of country and the influences of early association may yet cling, New England appears to me, of all the portions of the United States which I have visited, most likely to afford gratification; and the *Yankees,*—properly so called,—the Americans with whom he will find, and towards whom he will feel most sympathy. They do us the honour to call themselves *purely English* in their origin; they alone, of the whole population of the United States, undoubtedly were

From *Journal*, by Frances Anne Butler, Vol. II, pp. 145–147 n. Entered, according to the Act of Congress, in the year 1835, by Carey, Lea & Blanchard, in the Clerk's Office of the District Court for the Eastern District of Pennsylvania. Philadelphia.

so; and in the abundant witness which their whole character, country, and institutions bear to that fact, I feel an additional reason to be proud of England,—of Old England, for these are her children,—this race of men, as a race incomparably superior to the other inhabitants of this country. In conversing with New Englandmen, in spite of any passing, temporary bitterness, any political difference, or painful reference to past times of enmity, I have always been struck with the admiring, and in some measure, tender feeling with which England, as the mother country, was named. Nor is it possible to travel through the New England states and not perceive, indeed a spirit, (however modified by different circumstances and institutions,) yet most truly English in its origin. The exterior of the houses,—their extreme neatness and cleanliness,—the careful cultivation of the land,—the tasteful and ornamental arrangement of the ground immediately surrounding the dwellings, that most English of all manifestations, —above all, the church spires pointing towards heaven, from the bosom of every village,—recalled most forcibly to my mind my own England, and presented images of order, of industry, of taste, and religious feeling, nowhere so exhibited in any other part of the Union. I visited Boston several times, and mixed in society there, the tone of which appeared to me far higher than that of any I found elsewhere. A general degree of cultivation exists among its members, which renders their intercourse desirable and delightful. Nor is this superior degree of education confined to Boston; the zeal and the judgment with which it is being propagated throughout that part of the country, is a noble national characteristic. A small circumstance is a good illustration of the advance which knowledge has made in these states. Travelling by land from New Haven to Boston, at one of the very smallest places where we stopped to change horses, I got out of the carriage to reconnoitre our surroundings. The town, (if town it could be called,) did not appear to contain much more than fifty houses: amongst the most prominent of these, however, was a bookseller's shop. The first volumes I took up on the counter, were Spurzheim's volume on education, and Dr. Abercrombie's works on the intellectual and moral faculties. I saw more pictures, more sculptures, and more books in private houses in Boston than I have seen any where else. I could name more men of marked talent that I met with there than any where else. Its charitable and literary institutions are upon a liberal scale, and enlightened principles. Among the New Englanders I have seen more honour and reverence of parents, and more witnesses of a high religious faith, than among any other Americans with whom I have lived and conversed.

Comic Yankee Servants

MANY anecdotes are current about the manners of the young people who come down from the retired parts of the country to domestic service in

From *Society in America*, by Harriet Martineau, Vol. II, pp. 253–254. New York and London: Saunders and Otley. 1837.

Boston. A simple country girl obeyed her instructions exactly about putting the dinner upon the table, and then summoning the family. But they delayed a few minutes, from some cause; and when they entered the dining-room, found the domestic seated and eating. She had helped herself from a fowl, thinking that "the folk were so long a-coming, the things would get cold." A young man from Vermont was hired by a family who were in extreme want of a footman. He was a most friendly personage, as willing as he was free and easy; but he knew nothing of life out of a small farm-house. An evening or two after his arrival, there was a large party at the house. His mistress strove to impress upon him that all he had to do at tea-time was to follow, with the sugar and cream, the waiter who carried the tea; to see that every one had cream and sugar; and to hold his tongue. He did his part with an earnest face, stepping industriously from guest to guest. When he had made the circuit, and reached the door, a doubt struck him whether a group in the furthest part of the room had had the benefit of his attentions. He raised himself on his toes with, "I'll ask"; and shouted over the heads of the company, "I say, how are ye off for sweetenin' in that ere corner?"

Captain Basil Hall and the Countryman

[CAPTAIN HALL] was walking up and down the veranda of a country tavern in Massachusetts, while the coach changed horses. A thunder-storm was going on, and, with that pleasant European air of indirect self-compliment in condescending to be surprised by American merit, which we find so conciliating, he said to a countryman lounging against the door, "Pretty heavy thunder you have here." The other, who had divined at a glance his feeling of generous concession to a new country, drawled gravely, "Waal, we *du,* considerin' the number of inhabitants."

The Road to Walpole

THE next town we wished to reach was Walpole, but the roads offered by no means easy travelling. The inhabitants of Vermont, noted for their industry, their honesty, and their stationary character, are also distinguished for a peculiar turn of humor in their remarks and some oddities of manner, being in the latter respect even more primitive than the Penn-

---

From Introduction to "The Biglow Papers, Second Series," in *The Poetical Works of James Russell Lowell,* p. 225. Copyright, 1848, 1857, 1866, 1868, 1869, 1876, and 1885, by James Russell Lowell. Boston and New York: Houghton, Mifflin and Company.

From *Retrospections of America, 1797–1811,* by John Bernard, Edited from the Manuscript by Mrs. Bayle Bernard, With an Introduction, Notes, and Index, by Laurence Hutton and Brander Matthews, pp. 319–320. Copyright, 1886, by Harper & Brothers. New York. 1887.

sylvanians. Their neighbors of Massachusetts (by some termed the Scotch of North America), in passing continually through this state on their way to and from Canada and the back countries, are frequently exposed to the ridicule of the inhabitants. One of the many stories in circulation bearing on this subject was that of a Bostonian travelling through Vermont, and overtaken by night on a lonely road, who at length saw a youngster some distance ahead, and apprehensive that he had mistaken his way, called out to the lad:

"Jack! Jack! I want to know which is the way to Chesterfield?"

"How did you know my name was Jack?" responded the youth.

"Why, I guessed it," replied the traveller.

"Oh, then you may guess your way to Chesterfield!"

Fearful of being nonplussed in a similar way myself, I was very particular each morning before I quitted the tavern to learn all I could of the road we were to pursue throughout the day, as there were few opportunities afterwards of ascertaining anything on the subject. Notwithstanding this caution, I lost my track one day, and was actually retracing my steps to Boston. I learned this in a characteristic manner when I pulled up to inquire of a countryman who was felling a tree by the roadside—

"My good friend," said I, "am I on the right road to Walpole?"

"Yes," replied the man; "you are on the right road; but I reckon you must turn your horse's head or you'll never get there!"

Provincial Phraseology and Hospitality

THE inn most esteemed in Providence is kept by one Amidon, and there I was accordingly advised to go. Arriving about the hour of nine in the forenoon, I asked for breakfast. Mr. Amidon replied by saying, "Breakfast is almost through"; and on my pressing the question, he added, that "He did not know how it would operate." Both these answers were given with a slow utterance and even tone of voice, such as greatly increased what I thought their ridicule. Reduced into English, they meant, first, that breakfast was almost over; and secondly, that he did not know whether the house could or could not conveniently afford me a breakfast.

I had already acquired so much acquaintance with this provincial phraseology, and provincial manner of answering questions, as to be at no loss for the meaning of my host; and passing into the house, where I found a large table, with the wreck of the breakfast that was *through,* I was at length courteously indulged with a breakfast for myself.

My wants were equally ill-timed on the morning of my departure. It was about six o'clock when I prepared to leave Mr. Amidon's; and I confess

---

From *Travels through the Northern Parts of the United States, in the Years 1807 and 1808,* by Edward Augustus Kendall, Esq., Vol. II, pp. 2–3. New York: Printed and published by I. Riley. 1809.

that I had not promised myself (what nevertheless is most agreeable to me) to breakfast before setting out. Discovering, however, in the kitchen, while I was paying Mrs. Amidon her bill, that two or three kettles were already boiling, I became unreasonable enough to ask, whether or not I could have some tea? but I received for answer the words, "Not at *this* time of the day!"

A Yankee in London: Buying Gape-Seed

A YANKEE, walking the streets of London, looked through a window upon a group of men writing very rapidly; and one of them said to him in an insulting manner, "Do you wish to buy some gape-seed?" Passing on a short distance the Yankee met a man, and asked him what the business of those men was in the office he had just passed. He was told that they wrote letters dictated by others, and transcribed all sorts of documents; in short, they were writers. The Yankee returned to the office and inquired if one of the men would write a letter for him, and was answered in the affirmative. He asked the price, and was told one dollar. After considerable talk, the bargain was made; one of the conditions of which was that the scribe should write just what the Yankee told him to, or he should receive no pay. The scribe told the Yankee he was ready to begin; and the latter said,—

"Dear marm:" and then asked, "Have you got that deown?"

"Yes," was the reply, *"go on."*

"I went to ride t'other day: have you got that deown?"

"Yes; go on, go on."

"And I harnessed up the old mare into the wagon: have you got that deown?"

"Yes, yes, long ago; *go on.*"

"Why, how fast you write! And I got into the wagon, and sat deown, and drew up the reins, and took the whip in my right hand: have you got that deown?"

"Yes, long ago; *go on.*"

"Dear me, how fast you write! I never saw your equal. And I said to the old mare, *'Go 'long,'* and jerked the reins pretty hard: have you got that deown?"

"Yes; and I am impatiently waiting for more. I wish you wouldn't bother me with so many foolish questions. Go on with your letter."

"Well, the old mare wouldn't stir out of her tracks, and I hollered, *'Go 'long, you old jade! go 'long.'* Have you got that deown?"

"Yes, indeed, *you pestersome fellow; go on.*"

By John B. Gough. From *Brilliant Diamonds of Poetry and Prose,* Comprising the Most Unique, Touching, Pithy, and Beautiful Literary Treasures. . . , edited by Rev. O. H. Tiffany, pp. 57–58. Copyright, 1883, by O. H. Tiffany. Union Publishing Company. 1893.

"And I licked her, and licked her, and licked her [continuing to repeat these words as rapidly as possible].

"Hold on there! I have written two pages of 'licked her,' and I want the rest of the letter."

"Well, and she kicked, and she kicked, and she kicked—[continuing to repeat these words with great rapidity].

"Do go on with your letter; I have several pages of '*she kicked.*'"

[The Yankee clucks as in urging horses to move, and continues the clucking noise with rapid repetition for some time.]

The scribe throws down his pen.

"Write it deown! write it deown!"

"I can't!"

"Well, then, I won't pay you."

[The scribe, gathering up his papers.] "What shall I do with all these sheets upon which I have written your nonsense?"

"You may use them in doing up your *gape-seed.* Good-by!"

The Yorkshireman of America

THIS is, perhaps, the most appropriate place for some observations on him who plays the "title-rôle" in this part of the States; though the prevalent absurdity in England of calling an American of whatever state by the general title of Yankee is not greater than the misapplication of the title in America to all classes of New-Englanders. The origin of the name, indeed, as stated by Heck Welder,[1] is the Indian pronunciation of "English"—"Yengeese"—by which appellation they distinguished the New-Englanders from the Virginians, or Southern people, whom they called the "Long-knives." Yankee, however, is really now a term denoting character rather than locality, and represents a certain set of qualities in a particular grade of society. The Yankee is a man of the lower orders, sometimes a farmer, more often a mechanic (the very spirit of mechanism embodied), and yet more usually a travelling trader. The Yankee is the Yorkshireman of America; the same cunning, calculating, persevering personage, with an infusion of Scotch hardiness and love of wandering. Like him, he goes upon the principle that all men are rogues, and like him he is instanced by his customers as the best illustration of the doctrine. He has the same talent for expedients; the same keen eye to character and to expedite a sale; the same want of nicety in regard to means, so long as they are not legally offensive (going to jail he considers not so much a disgrace as a

---

From *Retrospections of America, 1797–1811,* by John Bernard, Edited from the Manuscript by Mrs. Bayle Bernard, With an Introduction, Notes, and Index by Laurence Hutton and Brander Matthews, pp. 36–37. Copyright, 1886, by Harper & Brothers. New York. 1887.

[1] Rev. John Gottlieb Ernestus Heckewelder. See "Yankee" below.

waste of time), so that it would be just as appropriate to call the refined gentry and enlightened manufacturers of the County of York "regular Yorkshiremen," as to cite any man who moves in the respectable circle of Boston as "a regular Yankee."

Yorkshire Stories

I'm Yorkshire [1]

The Rev. Robert Collyer tells a good story about a Yorkshireman. He says they are much like the Yankees in some respects; for instance, they are always sharp at bargaining, and also full of curiosity, and, like Yankees, are given to asking questions on every occasion where information can be gained thereby, on any subject however trivial. But sharp as they are at bargains, when they once agree to make a trade and shake hands on it, they stick to it, although subsequently one of the parties may discover that he has been overreached by the other. He said that on one occasion a Yorkshire farmer was ploughing with his horse, and the animal suddenly dropped dead in the furrow. The farmer let him lie there, and instantly drove over to the house of another farmer about five miles away. He dismounted and walked into the house on the invitation of his farmer friend, and they talked on various subjects. At last the visitor said:—

"You know my white horse?"

"Oh, yes, very well," was the reply.

"How will you trade your bay horse for him?"

"Even," said his friend.

"Shake hands on it," and they shook hands.

Whereupon the visitor remarked:—

"My horse lies dead in the furrow, where he fell while ploughing this afternoon."

"All right," said the other, "mine died last Thursday, and his skin is hanging in the barn."

My Dog Is Yorkshire, Too [2]

A Yorkshire boy visited Liverpool one day, taking his dog along with him. He never had been in so large a city before, and consequently stared into all the store-windows and gazed around, as nearly every object was new to him, keeping up a run of questions to passers-by.

---

[1] From *Funny Stories*, Told by Phineas T. Barnum, pp. 123–124. Copyright, 1890, by Phineas T. Barnum. New York, London, Glasgow and Manchester: George Routledge and Sons, Limited.

[2] *Ibid.*, pp. 124–125.

"What be that?" was his question continually repeated. Entering the large fish-market, whenever he saw a fish that was new and strange to him the question was immediately put, "What be that?" He came to a barrel full of live lobsters. "What be they?" he asked in astonishment, pointing his finger to the barrel.

"Lobsters," was the reply; "and you may take hold of them if you like."

"Nay, nay, I be Yorkshire, I be."

"Well, put your dog's tail in the barrel."

"Ay, I will do that"; upon which he lifted up his dog and let his tail drop in among the lobsters. One large-sized one caught his tail, upon which the dog jumped from its master and ran yelping down the street, the lobster holding on firmly. The fishermen all screamed with delight, and ran to the door to hear the dog yelp and see him run.

The young Yorkshireman looked on with astonishment and open mouth. Presently the dog turned the corner of the street and was out of sight.

"Hold on!" cried the fisherman; "your dog has run away with my lobster; call him back."

"Nay," said the boy, "my dog is Yorkshire, too; call back your lobster!"

Yorkshire [3]

A Yorkshire boy asked a gentleman for some salt, who gave it [to] him, and asked why he wanted it. "Perhaps," said the boy, "you may give me an egg, and I wish to be ready to eat it." "Then take an egg," replied the gentleman. "Are there not many horse stealers in Yorkshire?" "My father," quoth the boy, "is a Yorkshireman, and is thought to be an honest man, but would no more mind stealing a horse, than I would drinking your ale" (turning the gentleman's ale down his throat at the same time). "That will do: I see you are Yorkshire."

PULLING SOME GOOD ONES

Yankee Trader Types

The Swapper

This curious class of mammalia, the "Down-Easter" as it is often called, is divisible into three species—the swapper, the jobber, and the peddler,

[3] From *The Laughing Philosopher:* or Fun, Humour, and Wit; Being a Collection of Choice Anecdotes, Many of Which, Never Before in Print, Originated in or about "The Literary Emporium," p. 92. Pittsburgh, Pennsylvania: Published by Cook and Schoyer. Louisville, Kentucky: Maxwell, Cook and Company. 1834.

From *Retrospections of America, 1797–1811,* by John Bernard, Edited from the

all agreeing in one grand characteristic—love of prey—but varying in many striking particulars. The swapper claims precedence in point of antiquity, his character and name being a direct importation from Yorkshire. The word to "swap," meaning to exchange, is still current there and possesses a high historic interest, some local historians having proved, I believe, that it was this peculiarity in the Northern Saxons which for so many years drove the hordes of invaders to the South. The swapper is the only division of the tribe that may be called stationary, though he is not more peculiar in this respect than in the mode he adopts to make a fortune. He thinks neither of buying, nor selling, nor growing, nor manufacturing; the key to his El Dorado is—exchange. With most this practice is a passion, with many a disease; some are inoculated with the virus, but the majority have it in the natural way, and it has then all the precocity of genius, with the tenacity of faith. It shows itself in childhood, when the infant swaps its milk for marbles; and at school, when the boy swaps everything but floggings. As his possessions increase he puts all he owns into a state of transition; house, land, and cattle are drawn into the whirlpool; even coat, hat, and boots. He soon loves swapping for its own sake; the means becomes the end; the mere act and business of exchanging seems essential to his existence. If now analyzed the feeling would be found pure; if it is no love of lucre, it is much less envy of his fellow-creatures' possessions; it is neither desire of profit nor of accumulation; it is simply the love of novelty.

The swapper is, of all men, the least affected by relics, the least concerned about memorials. Turning his back upon his father's wisdom, he has full faith in the instruction and resources of the future. With him everything old is useless, he keeps nothing long enough to prove its value by experience, but puts all his trust in the excellences of new inventions. The swapper is a fine moral symbol, no man illustrating more directly the vanity of human wishes, or the evanescence of all things. Again, he is a moral warning, no man displaying more of the spirit of a gambler, or more often meeting the fate of one. Yet his is a kind of madness which ought to be harmless from its singularity, for there is nothing even analogous to it, except that domestic evil in England—a buyer of bargains. Thus he spends his days as everybody's agent or anybody's market. If poor, he exchanges to become rich; if rich, to become poor; till, having swapped wealth for want, ease for anxiety, and youth for age, he at last swaps this world for the next.

I made these discoveries principally during my residence at a country-box near Boston, where my nearest neighbor was a specimen of this class, in the last stage of the disorder. Every morning that he heard I was at home he was sure to pay me a visit in order, as he termed it, to "make a

---

Manuscript by Mrs. Bayle Bernard, With an Introduction, Notes, and Index by Laurence Hutton and Brander Matthews, pp. 37–47. Copyright, 1886, by Harper & Brothers. New York, 1887.

trade." Whatever object his eye rolled upon it roused "that one dear thought"—to barter; my plough for his cart, my horse for his cow, or my dog for his cat. If I proved obdurate to the advantages proposed on one point, he attacked me on another. Not an inch of my property but suggested some article of exchange on his own premises. Would I swap my peaches for plums? my carrots for cabbages? I verily believe, had I not agreed to gratify him on some occasions, he would have proposed to swap the rats in our barns, or the snails in our orchards. At times I endeavored to soften my refusal by inviting him to dinner, but the mania still clung to him as his real hunger and thirst. On pouring out some brandy he remembered that he had a keg at home he should like to trade away; and the sight of my mutton suggested the idea of a score of sheep which he would make over to me for two oxen.

The appearance of my friend was in strict keeping with his ruling propensity. His dress was constantly undergoing mutations in which the variety of colors and textures precluded the monotonous impression of a suit. He was half nankeen one day, half leather the next. Every market morning furnished some novelty, particularly in his hats, which were enthroned and deposed with all the despatch of Grand Turks. A pair of homespun trousers seemed to stick to him the longest, though their history, I've little doubt, resembled that which the Virginians (to whom a swapper was a perpetual source of satire) were in the habit of relating. They said that a farmer who had not had a "trade" for some time, feeling rather dull one Sunday, resolved to "go to meeting." On his way there he saw a young man hoeing in a field, so he stopped and began to lecture him on the immorality of his conduct. Finding that he would not attend to him, the farmer at last bawled out, "I say, young man, you won't listen to religion, but you've got on an awful strong pair of trousers, will you swap?"

I remember a pendant to this from the same source. A Connecticut dealer who was "down" with a fever, in a very dangerous state, had had a particular medicine sent to him, to be taken four times a day. A friend, calling in, smelt the mixture and pronounced it to be excellent; it had cured his grandmother. "It is worth a dollar a bottle," said he. At these electrifying words the dying man opened his eyes, raised himself an inch, and faltered out, "A dollar a bottle, Enoch! there are three bottles of it, and, if you've no objection, I'll swap the whole lot for your black terrier."

The Jobber

The second species of "Down-Easter," a jobber, is a man of genius, mechanical it may be, but still a genius. He has probably been taught a trade, shoemaking for instance, which being conducive to reflection, leads him into a view of the varied wants of man from the foot upwards, from the bed he requires to rest upon, to the roof that must cover him. All arts agree in requiring certain qualities, such as solidity, convenience, proportion, and durability, whence it is obvious if a man thoroughly understands the craft of shoemaking (to say nothing of its philosophy, the giving neatness to an ugly foot, which will restore enjoyment to a sensitive mind), he has a guide and handmaid to the sister arts, a pass-key to the cells of mechanism, in whose works practice will give proficiency. Thus he superadds to his original vocation carpentry, cabinet and coffin making, bricklaying, and farriery; and as soon as his mind is sufficiently stored he collects his tools (for knowledge, with him, is action), crams them into a basket, and strides off to the Western States, where in every new-formed settlement he proves a welcome visitor, supplying to each house that slight assistance which their comfort may require. Joking apart, there is not a doubt that this class of men are among the most useful in the Union. They unite to a rough expertness, in all they undertake, the temperance and industry demanded by the state of things about them, and virtue, in this case, meets with its reward. The man that can turn his hand to anything, generally turns everything into his hand; his leather pouch soon exhibits the appearance of a tumor, till he is at length enabled to eschew vagrancy, buy a plot of ground, and build a shop in some fast-rising settlement, which he opens in "the general line"; when, as the increasing wants of the community call for the introduction of regular trades, they also introduce customers to consume his cheese and bacon.

A jobber is generally a red-faced, yellow-haired man, with light-blue eyes and a capacious mouth, dressed in a nankeen suit which was made for him when a lad, and from whose expressive restrictions his republican frame is now freeing itself at back, elbows and waistband.

The Peddler

But the grand division of the tribe is the New England peddler, who, unlike the last described, has no inventive ingenuity, save in the art of puffing, and still less like the first, not the slightest taste for swapping. He considers his own goods so much superior to his customers' that nothing but hard cash can represent their value. To buy cheap and sell high comprehends for him the whole cycle of human knowledge; the supreme excellence of north-country stuffs is his religion; and science has taught him to believe that the world itself would not go round but to the tick of a New England clock. The same spirit which carried his ancestors into the backwoods with their train of teams and children sends him every spring on a voyage of discovery to the South. This visit is regarded by the Southern trader in the light of a visitation; he may be truly said to have Yankeephobia, and to look upon a "Connecticut chap" as a commercial Scythian, a Tartar of the North whose sole business in life is to make inroads on his peace and profit. He ranks him in the list of plagues next to the yellow fever, and before locusts, taxation, and a wet spring; indeed, some go so far as to suppose that a shower of Yankees was the crowning pestilence which made Pharaoh give up the Israelites.

The panic they occasion is not more from a terror of their cleverness than of their singularly indomitable spirit. There is no getting rid of them. None of the usual similes of a burr, or sticking-plaster, give any idea of a peddler's tenacity; he has the gripe of a crab with the suction of a mosquito; you can't deny, you can't insult, you can't fatigue him; you can only dismiss him by a purchase. Such a character must be particularly obnoxious to an indolent and relaxed community. A tornado could not create greater havoc in the ease and enjoyment of a Carolinian evening than the buzzing and humming of such a wasp. In some places his mere appearance is the sounding of a tocsin to bar doors and windows, while many even double lock drawers, to prevent a conjuration over the counter by which the money seems to leap out of the till into the peddler's pocket. It may be amusing to pause for an instant on such a scene.

Suppose a village in one of the rich Virginian or Carolinian valleys, clustering round a road that climbs up a hill so almost perpendicular that it seems to realize the idea of Jacob's ladder. From the gate of the planter's lawn run, or, rather, stagger off, the sheds of the butcher, the baker, and the blacksmith, terminated by that arena for cock-fighting and politics, a tavern. About sunset labor has ceased and the inhabitants are leaning or lying out of their doors, the cows are wandering home, the children are playing about, and the "niggers" are laughing loud in the distant sugar-houses. In this sweet hour of calm all hearts are disposed to indulge in Christian emotions. Look at the group and you'd take them for a colony of Moravians, with all enemies pardoned and all cares forgotten; when suddenly a pedestrian is seen wending down the hill, his legs, in the slanting sunbeams, sending their shadows half a mile before him. By his length of staff he might be taken for a pilgrim, but the sprawl of his walk awakens anything but sacred associations. Gradually his hull looms into distinctness, they perceive he is a long-backed man, with a crouching head and loaded shoulders; suspicions are excited; and at length one who may have suffered more than the rest, perhaps, from the endemic, recognizes its symptoms and exclaims, "I'll be shot if it ain't a Yankee!" At these words if there is not a general rout, or springing up, and banging-to of doors, it must be because their faculties are prostrated by the surprise, and they lie spell-bound, as cattle are said to do on the approach of the anaconda. As the enemy advances at a swinging pace among them, his keen gray eye rolling round in selection of a victim, they remember the strange man who first found out their quiet hiding-place, and the wonder and contempt this curious species of fellow-creature at first excited—a fellow who could neither drink, bet, nor talk politics, but kept prying into holes and corners to prove the extent of their needs, and who ultimately walked away with all the silver of the settlement. Whatever may have been their former experiences, one of the number is a doomed man. If he doesn't want a clock which ticks loud enough to scare away the rats, or a razor so keen that if you but strop it overnight and put it under your pillow you'll wake up clean shaved in the morning, yet—"Sure alive, missis wants a new cap," and he's got a small stock, "jest such as the squires' wives wear at the camp-meetin's"; or, "The young gals need some gowns," and he has "all kinds of cotton that are all the better for bein' turned—for the inside gets fresh as t'other's wearin' out."

The "Down-Easter's" system of attacking a stubborn antagonist displays great generalship. He begins by resting his pack upon the half-hatch of the door; its numerous contents presently require a field of display; nowhere so fitting as on the counter within, if it be a shop; he begs leave but to show them; "Look at them, mister, they won't sting you." The outworks once carried, his shot (caps and combs, "hankychers," etc.) fly about in all directions and take deadly effect on some of the family. By a singular fatality everything that is tried on seems to be made expressly for the wearer; she never looked so well in anything before. And equally strange is the discovery that, up to that moment, they had been living without a solitary convenience. Every one but the father perceives the necessity of Sally having a pair of shoes, Enoch a jackknife, and the parlor a timepiece. From the shop Jonathan fights his way into the backroom, and there his victim, driven into a corner, is beaten into an acknowledgment of his wants and deficiencies, and the capitulation that ensues is a discussion of their number and the expense of supplying them. When the campaign is over in one house he proceeds to another, and so on to all in succession, till he arrives at the tavern, where he usually succeeds in trading the landlord out of bed and breakfast.

Smarting under this infliction, it can be no wonder that the Virginians indulge in occasional vituperations, insist that the Yankee cheats them in every transaction, and that, however he may vary his commodities from the traditionary wooden nutmegs and red-flannel sausages, swindling is still his talent, his stimulus, and local distinction. In proof of this they point to the fact that there are no Jews in New England, the competition being too great for them to exist.

I was told a story of a "Down-Easter" mode of creating a demand for a supply which, amid all the ingenuities of modern commerce, may fairly claim originality. One of the class called a "hickory dealer," or seller of wooden ware, came down to the South in summer-time with a well-laden wagon, but was destined to encounter a sweeping opposition in the yellow fever, which had commenced business about a week previous in such a wholesale way that the only wooden ware in requisition was a coffin. The ravages of the plague were at this time so dreadful that it will be supposed there was a general tendency to try the most desperate and absurd expedients to avert it, though many such proved but pioneers to its progress. This the peddler was aware of, so resolved, as regarded his own fortunes, to extract good from evil. Dressing himself as respectably as possible, he mounted his horse and rode up to a printing-office in Williamsburgh, where, under an assumed name, he had a hundred bills struck off to this effect:

"WANTED IMMEDIATELY,

"Wooden ware in any quantity for the fever hospital at Philadelphia, such being found not to convey the infection.

"By order of the Board of Health, Seth Adams.

"N.B.—All persons are cautioned how they use crockery, which is the cause of plague to thousands."

Fifty of these placards he sent his boy to stick round the streets of a village lying in his road, where the fever had begun to show itself. A discovery so important, so simple, and apparently in such close connection with a remedy, created an instant sensation. The doom of crockery was pronounced. Jugs, bowls, basins, teapots, and other utensils most esteemed or necessary were hurled out of the windows in showers. No grandmother's gift, no ancestor's relic, survived this fall of China; the streets soon exhibited a series of domestic tumuli, and looked like a pottery after an earthquake. About noon, when the work of destruction was at its height, a wagon made its way into the village, with a man vociferating with all the power of his lungs, "Wooden ware!" His arrival was hailed as a God-send; a crowd collected round him as to a magician who brought talismans; and in less than two hours his plague-averting platters were all disposed of at exorbitant prices.

A more defensible piece of cleverness was that of a Passamaquoddy captain who, arriving in the port of London soon after the peace, was inveigled into a low tavern by some sharpers, with the intention of plundering him at cards. Failing, however, in every endeavor to draw him into play, they drank three bottles of wine with him and then went out. The landlord, coming in, expressed his surprise. "Are your friends gone?" he asked. "My friends?" replied the captain; "they brought me here, but I don't know them." "Ah," said the landlord, "I see you are not much acquainted with our London blades." "No, I ain't." "Well, you'll grow wiser in time; you must pay the reckoning." "What, for all four?" "Certainly, for all four." "Well, if that's the case," rejoined Jonathan, drawing out a handful of silver, "I may as well have another bottle." The landlord stepped out eagerly to get it from the cellar, when the captain, taking a piece of chalk from the mantelpiece, wrote on the table, "I leave you a Yankee handle for your London blades," and quickly walked off also.

Peddler's Progress

The Tin Peddler [1]

About the year 1740, William Pattison, a native of Ireland, came to this country, and settled in this town [Berlin, Conn.]. His trade was that of a

[1] From *Travels in New England and New York* (1796–1815), by Timothy Dwight, Vol. II, pp. 53–55. New Haven, Connecticut: T. Dwight. 1821–22.

tinner; and soon after his arrival, he commenced manufacturing tinware, and continued in that business until the revolutionary war. He was then under the necessity of suspending it, as the raw material could not be obtained. After the war, this manufacture was carried on at Berlin, by those young men who had learned the art from Mr. Pattison; and these persons have since extended the business over a number of the neighboring towns.

For many years, after tinned plates were manufactured in this place into culinary vessels, the only method used by the pedlar for conveying them to distant towns, for sale, was by means of a horse and two baskets, balanced on his back. After the war, carts and wagons were used for this purpose, and have, from that time to the present, been the only means of conveyance which have been adopted.

The manner in which this ware is disposed of puts to flight all calculation. A young man is furnished by the proprietor with a horse, and a cart covered with a box containing as many tin vessels as the horse can conveniently draw. This vehicle within a few years has, indeed, been frequently exchanged for a wagon; and then the load is doubled. Thus prepared, he sets out on an expedition for the winter. A multitude of these young men direct themselves to the Southern States; and in their excursions travel wherever they can find settlements. Each of them walks, and rides, alternately, through this vast distance, till he reaches Richmond, Newbern, Charleston, or Savannah; and usually carries with him to the place of his destination no small part of the gain, which he has acquired upon the road. Here he finds one or more workmen, who have been sent forward to co-operate with him, furnished with a sufficient quantity of tinned plates to supply him with all the ware which he can sell during the season. With this he wanders into the interior country; calls at every door on his way; and with an address, and pertinacity, not easily resisted, compels no small number of the inhabitants to buy. At the commencement of summer they return to New York; and thence to New Haven, by water; after selling their vehicles and their horses. The original load of a single horse, as I am told, is rarely worth more than three hundred dollars; or of a wagon, more than six hundred. Yet this business is said to yield both the owner and his agent valuable returns; and the profit to be greater than that, which is made by the sale of any other merchandise of equal value. Even those who carry out a single load, and dispose of it in the neighboring country, find their employment profitable. . . .

Every inhabited part of the United States is visited by these men. I have seen them on the peninsula of Cape Cod, and in the neighborhood of Lake Erie; distant from each other more than six hundred miles. They make their way to Detroit, four hundred miles further; to Canada; to Kentucky; and, if I mistake not, to New Orleans and St. Louis.

All the evils, which are attendant upon the bartering of small wares, are incident to this, and every other mode of traffic of the same general nature. Many of the young men employed in this business part at an early period with both modesty, and principle. Their sobriety is exchanged for cunning, their honesty for imposition; and their decent behavior for coarse impudence. Mere wanderers, accustomed to no order, control or worship; and directed solely to the acquisition of petty gains; they soon fasten upon this object; and forget every other, of a superior nature. The only source of their pleasure or their reputation is gain; and that, however small, or however acquired, secures both. No course of life tends more rapidly, or more effectually, to eradicate every moral feeling.

Berlin has, I suspect, suffered not a little from this source. Were their manufactures sold like other merchandise the profits would undoubtedly be lessened: but the corruption of a considerable number of human beings would be prevented.

* * * * *

The business of selling tin ware has within a few years undergone a considerable change. Formerly the pedlar's load was composed exclusively of this manufacture: now he has an assortment of merchandise to offer to his customers. He carries pins, needles, scissors, combs, coat and vest buttons, with many other trifling articles of hardware; and children's books, and cotton stuffs made in New England. A number set out with large wagons loaded with dry goods, hats and shoes; together with tin ware, and the smaller articles already mentioned. These loads will frequently cost the proprietor from one to two thousand dollars; and are intended exclusively for the Southern and Western states.

It is frequently the fact that from twenty to thirty persons are employed by a single house in the manufacturing and selling of tin ware and other articles. The workmen, furnished with a sufficient quantity of the raw materials to employ them for six months, are sent on by water, in the autumn, to Virginia, North and South Carolina, or Georgia. They station themselves at some town in the interior, where the employer, or his agent, has a store, well furnished with such articles as the pedlars require. As the stock of each pedlar is exhausted, he repairs to the store for a supply. In this way, a large amount of goods are vended during the six or eight months they are absent.

Some idea may be formed of the extent to which this business is sometimes carried from the fact that immediately after the late war with Great Britain, which terminated in 1815, ten thousand boxes of tinned plates were manufactured into culinary vessels in the town of Berlin, in one year.

The Peddler's Reputation [2]

Western Connecticut, where the soil was thin and the waters were swift, was beginning to pour her surplus of young men into the trails and tote-roads, turnpikes and highways of America. They went South and West

---

[2] From *Pedlar's Progress,* The Life of Bronson Alcott, by Odell Shepard, pp. 42–44. Copyright, 1937, by Odell Shepard. Boston: Little, Brown and Company.

and even "way down East," carrying in handbags, valises, carts, and wagons everything portable that they thought might sell. They carried news from the seaboard towns into faraway farmsteads and huddles of huts whither, without their help, it would never have come. They carried last year's fashions, public opinion of a decade gone by, and the prejudices that never die out, together with assorted heartbreak for many an uplandish maiden. One fears that they were not always well-bred or perfectly well-behaved. They could not shave often. Their baths were mostly those that they took perforce while fording unbridged streams. Country dogs regarded them with strong and well-founded dislike. When they slept at inns and taverns, as they were sometimes allowed to do, the rate was usually fourpence a night, with two pence added for supper or breakfast; and it was occasionally stipulated—or so we are told—that not more than five pedlars were to sleep in a bed and that all boots were to be removed before retiring. More frequently they slept in barns.

A virile lot, bold, carefree, and adventurous, the Yankee pedlars of a hundred and more years ago made up one of the most picturesque classes of men that America has ever produced. They stood halfway between the merchant and the gipsy, with a faint touch added of the mountebank. One might term them the "commercial gentlemen" of those days if one remembered that they carried the goods they sold, that they seldom returned on their own tracks, and that they did not even try to secure what is nowadays called "the confidence of their buyers."

To say that the Yankee pedlar was a consummate liar was considered, in Bronson Alcott's youth-time, an assertion of the obvious. To have called him "dishonest" would have been thought a violent understatement. In estimating these opinions, however, we should consider that pedlars had been going up and down the land for more than a century, spreading a reputation about themselves which was not in all instances entirely deserved. It was the kind of reputation that a wandering people or class, or even individual, will always acquire among those who stay at home and peer suspiciously through the narrow crack of the door. There was something in it of *caveat emptor,* "let the purchaser be cautious," but there was rather more of the homebody's fear of the homeless, foot-loose man. Moreover, people had come to delight in the pedlar's real or alleged iniquities. He was an institution, a treasure, something to be proud of, like the town fool of New England, the champion liar of the Middle West, or the cowboy who wins a prize belt for profane vituperation. If a pedlar from Connecticut was only moderately dishonest and had "taken them in" rather less than they had expected, people liked to help him out by asserting that the desiccated and wormy nutmegs he had sold them were made of wood. Thus he became the hero of a legend, and eventually filled an honorable place in the "tall tales" with which the popular imagination was seething from the Atlantic to the Mississippi. He enjoyed these tales as much as anyone, and used them in his business.

In considering the Connecticut pedlar's reputation, furthermore, one needs to see it in historical perspective. Barter, trade, commerce, business, merchandising, have never been a whit more "honest" than the conditions about them have compelled them, or made it profitable for them, to be. They have given up seeking a profit of a thousand per cent. only when, by taking only half as much, they could hope, in the long run, to make more money; and this would be only when they expected to deal with the same customers year after year. There is, in fact, one scale of commercial "honesty" for the established and stationary business serving a settled community, and quite another for the merchant who needs to think only of the single transaction. Benjamin Franklin, when he said that "honesty is the best policy," spoke like the city-bred shopkeeper that he essentially was. It was not that he and other members of his comparatively respectable class were really more honest than pedlars, but only that they had found it profitable to seem so.

Peddlers' Tricks of the Trade

THE reputation the early peddler won was enjoyed by chapmen of even so late a date as the Civil War. In fact, it was shrewdly turned to account as a bit of humour in the introductory remarks that preceded the bargaining. A peddler would drive up to a house and blithely address his prospective customer in some such patter as this: "Madam, are you in need of any pocket saw-mills? Horn gun flints? Basswood hams? Wooden nutmegs? White oak cheeses? Tin bungholes? Or calico hog troughs?" And having gained the smile of the lady of the house, he proceeded to recite what he actually did have in his wagon—tinware, mats, glassware, brooms, washboards, clothes pins, rolling pins, matches, paddy irons, kettles, and pots.

The yarns about Yankee clock peddlers are legion. Perhaps the most amusing is the one about the peddler who always sold a clock on the understanding that he would return in a few weeks, and, if the clock did not run satisfactorily, would replace it with another. It was also his rule to sell all the clocks in his stock but one. When he reached the end of his route he turned back with his one remaining clock. At the first house, the clock he had sold did not run, so he replaced it with the one that remained. At the second house, he replaced the unsatisfactory clock with the one he had taken from the first house. And so on, he went, selling and replacing clocks that never would work, and waxing fat on the proceeds!

From *Hawkers & Walkers in Early America*, Strolling Peddlers, Preachers, Lawyers, Doctors, Players, and Others, from the Beginning to the Civil War, by Richardson Wright, pp. 22, 84, 254. Copyright, 1927, by J. B. Lippincott Company. Philadelphia.

One of the Yankee maritime peddling tricks was this: The New England crew would buy corn of the plantation owners. The grain was measured on the quarter deck near the centre. When the measuring commenced, one of the crew began playing a jig on a violin, and all the spare hands started dancing vehemently. As the deck was springy, some of the corn would spill into the scuppers. The percentage of corn gained by this operation was considerable.

A Watch Trade

AFTER seeing your letter to Ephraim, as I said before, I concluded it wouldn't be a bad scheme to tackle up and take a load of turkeys, some apple-sass, and other notions that the neighbors wanted to get to market, and as your Uncle Nat would be in Boston with the ax-handles, we all thought best to try our luck there. Nothing happened worth mentioning on the road, nor till next morning after I got here and put up in Elm street. I then got off my watch pretty curiously, as you shall be informed. I was down in the bar-room, and thought it well enough to look pretty considerable smart, and now and then compared my watch with the clock in the bar, and found it as near right as ever it was, when a feller stept up to me and ask'd how I'd trade? and says I, for what? and says he, for your watch, and says I, any way that will be a fair shake; upon that says he, I'll give you *my* watch and five dollars; says I, it's done! He gave me the five dollars, and I gave him my watch. Now, says I, give me *your* watch; and, says he, with a loud laugh, I han't got none, and that kind a turned the laugh on me. Thinks I, let them laugh that lose. Soon as the laugh was well over the feller thought he'd try the watch to his ear; why, says he, it don't go; no, says I, not without it's carried; then I began to laugh. He tried to open it and couldn't start it a hair, and broke his thumb nail into the bargain. Won't she open, says he? Not's I know on, says I, and then the laugh seemed to take another turn.

Razor-Strop Trade

"I RECKON I couldn't drive a trade with you to-day, Square," said a "ginooine" specimen of a Yankee peddler, as he stood at the door of a merchant in St. Louis.

From *My Thirty Years Out of the Senate,* by Major Jack Downing, pp. 46–49. Entered, according to Act of Congress, in the Clerk's Office of the District Court of the Southern District of New York, by Seba Smith. New York: Oaksmith & Company. 1859.

From *Cyclopaedia of Commercial and Business Anecdotes* . . . by Frazar Kirkland, Vol. II, p. 555. Entered, according to Act of Congress, in the year 1864, by D. Appleton and Company, in the Clerk's Office of the District Court of the United States for the Southern District of New York. New York and London.

"I reckon you calculate about right, for you *can't*," was the sneering reply.

"Well, I guess you needn't git huffy 'beout it. Now here's a dozen ginoooine razor-strops—worth $2.50; you may have 'em for $2.00."

"I tell you I don't want any of your traps—so you may as well be going along."

"Wal, now look here, Square, I'll bet you five dollars, that if you make me an offer for them 'ere strops, we'll have a trade yet."

"Done!" replied the merchant, placing the money in the hands of a bystander. The Yankee deposited a like sum.

"Now," said the merchant, "I'll give you a picayune [sixpence] for the strops."

"They're your'n!" said the Yankee as he quietly pocketed the stakes.

"But," said he, after a little reflection, and with great apparent honesty, "I calculate a joke's a joke; and if you don't *want* them strops, I'll trade back."

The merchant's countenance brightened.

"You are not so bad a chap, after all," said he; "here are your strops, give me the money."

"There it is," said the Yankee, as he received the strops and passed over the sixpence. "A trade is a trade; and, now you are wide awake, the next time you trade with that 'ere sixpence, you'll do a little better than to buy razor strops."

And away walked the peddler with his strops and his wager, amidst the shouts of the laughing crowd.

Sam Tolman's Bonnets

In the early days, when work in the shop lasted only during the winter and early spring months, some men found occupation by going out on the road with bonnets to sell. Many of these were seconds from the shop, or bonnets that were slightly out of style, and were disposed of in the back country places by selling them from house to house, Yankee peddler fashion. The first John Rogers himself used to make such trips down on Cape Cod. In 1840 Lloyd Allen and Avery Dunham went into Maine. These were contrasting characters; Lloyd Allen, short, round and pink-cheeked; Avery Dunham, tall and spare. Avery it was who probably did the most talking and joking; Lloyd was the keen observer and gave the most accurate report of the trip when they got back.

Sam Tolman, a handflatter, and incidentally a practical joker, was perhaps the truest Yankee peddler. In the spring, he started off on foot

---

From *Every Day but Sunday, The Romantic Age of New England Industry,* by Jennie F. Copeland, pp. 54–55. Copyright, 1936, by Jennie F. Copeland. Brattleboro, Vermont: Stephen Daye Press.

with two big boxes, 3 x 2½ x 2, one under each arm. The bonnets of that period were so small and light that he could carry a supply to last a couple of weeks. If the stock did not hold out, he used the last as samples and took orders. One of his most profitable fields was Martha's Vineyard. There the women had little chance to learn what was being worn on the mainland, and less opportunity to buy when they did hear the style news. In this way Tolman's visits were a real boon, for he always told them just what women were wearing and how to wear it. One year, when the bonnets were flat and the size of small saucers, he told the island women that it was the fashion that year for a woman to wear two, one on the front of the head and one on back over the bob, or in the speech of today, bun. Consequently, every customer bought two. How he laughed over it when he got back to Our Town!

The Peddler in Reverse

THERE was a brisk demand for sewing silk manufactured in the Gurleyville district, which was run off on spools by pretty girls who easily found husbands. These girls were nicknamed "spoolers." Down to the time of the Civil War and somewhat later sewing silk from the Gurleyville mills was distributed by local pedlars, many of whom were young men who wanted to see the world outside of Mansfield as well as to make a little money. I can imagine them as they set out on foot, with flowered carpetbags filled with silk, one in each hand, for neighboring towns within the State or across the borders. Their customers were housewives and small country stores. . . . So easy was it to sell silk thread that a young man who failed to make good was called a "good-for-nothing" for the rest of his life. One such fellow came back from a fortnight's trip with his carpetbags as well stuffed as when he started out. "What," his father asked him, "have you got in them bags?" "Silk," was the reply. "Didn't you sell any of that silk?" "No," replied John. "Were there no inquiries?" "One man," replied John, "asked me what I had got in them bags, and I told him it was none of his damn business." Everybody laughed whenever that story was told.

Gollywhoppers' Eggs

A YEAR or two [later] . . . , when roads began to be better, the first tin-peddler with his cart penetrated to that remote new settlement in the

From *Connecticut Yankee,* An Autobiography, by Wilbur L. Cross, p. 15. Copyright, 1943, by Yale University Press. New Haven.

From *My Folks in Maine,* by C. A. Stephens, pp. 28–35. Copyright, 1934, by The Old Squire's Book Store. Published by The Old Squire's Book Store. Norway, Maine.

wilds. Falmouth was his place of hail; and it chanced that he arrived on a day when all the menfolks had gone to a "muster" of the militia at New Gloucester, twenty miles away.

The settlers' wives were delighted to see him. He was a smiling fellow, possessed of engaging ways with womenfolks—afterwards known as Wily Swift. It was rumored that he had been in jail once or twice for crooked dealing. He brought what those pioneer women most needed; namely, tinware, pins, needles, thread, and many other small useful articles which their remote situation rendered difficult to procure.

But money—nearly all silver then—was painfully scarce, and indeed their wherewithal to pay consisted largely of goose feathers, lambskins and a few cured peltries of wild animals which their husbands had been able to trap.

It appears that just before Wily Swift had left Falmouth for this ambitious journey to the northward, a Spanish brig had docked there, molasses-laden, from Cuba; and it also brought a quantity of coconuts, then somewhat a novelty in that young seaport. For this was long before the United Fruit Company had begun to bring tropical fruits in such abundance that the tables of our people are now as well supplied as if lemons, oranges, bananas and coconuts were growing at our doors.

If coconuts were a rarity at Falmouth, much less had settlers far inland made their acquaintance; and by way of introducing them, Peddler Swift had been led to invest in a few dozens which he hoped to sell at a sixpence apiece. But for some reason the brown spheres had not gone off well. Either on account of their novelty, or because of the scarcity of money, our enterprising itinerant of traffic found himself likely to have much of his stock left on his hands and hence had recourse to an unusual device for disposing of it.

His first effort in this direction was made at the log house of the Eastman family, not far from the similar habitation over which Great-grandmother Betty presided. With a great show of impressiveness he exhibited one of the coconuts; and perceiving that Aunt Nabby Eastman had never seen one and asked wonderingly what it could be, he immediately unloosed the tides of his easy mendacity, assuring her that it was the egg of a gorgeously beautiful bird, called a gollywhopper, not as large as an ostrich, but twice the size of a turkey.

"But you can hatch one of these eggs under a goose," he affirmed. "Or if a goose is loath to set, the egg can be wrapped in a blanket, kept moist and placed in a warm corner of your fireplace. They hatch in twenty-two days."

"But what do I want of a gollywhaker?" the practical-minded young Aunt Nabby demanded.

"You mean gollywhopper," Swift corrected gravely. "Every new farm where poultry and lambs are raised ought to have one. Their peculiar cries keep off hawks, owls, foxes, wild cats and even bears. None of these destructive pests have ever been known to come round a farm where a gollywhopper was kept. Why, Ma'am, a gollywhopper will chase a fox for miles! They live on mice, grasshoppers and rabbits. They pick up all their own food out in the fields and woods. It costs nothing to feed them. It is better to have a pair, for you can always sell their eggs. My present idea is that it is more profitable to raise gollywhoppers than geese or turkeys. Their long green and red feathers are very beautiful. Southern women use them to trim their hats."

This and much more, as he saw Aunt Nabby's eyes opening wide; and the upshot of his fallacious loquacity was that at length he succeeded in parting with two coconuts in return for four lambs' pelts and one otter skin.

Thereupon he drove to the next house, the Hobbs place, and opened similar negotiations with Aunt Sophrony, first informing her incidentally that he had just sold two of the marvelous eggs at the Eastmans', who undoubtedly would soon be in profitable possession of a large flock of lovely gollywhoppers.

It was an old saying among tinpeddlers that when one woman in a rural community had been induced to make a purchase, far less persuasion was required to effect sales among her neighbors. The garrulous faker finally succeeded in disposing of another coconut at Aunt Sophrony Hobbs', this time in exchange for three pounds of live geese feathers; and then he departed for the next clearing, that of Uriah Holt. There again he expatiated on the incomparable advantages of gollywhoppers as live stock on new farms, and at last got rid of another coconut at Sarah Holt's place, receiving in payment twenty weight of retted flax.

Trade, in fact, continued fairly brisk, and as the noon hour approached he arrived at Great-grandmother Elizabeth's primitive abode in good season to find her busily preparing her solitary midday meal.

"I have only one of these valuable eggs now remaining in my cart, Ma'am!" he cried. "All your neighbors have bought one, and some of them two. This is your last chance. You shall have this one at a bargain"; and with vast impressiveness he exhibited the treasure, fondling it in his hands.

It happened, however, that young Great-grandmother Betty's girlhood had been passed in old Salem, then the commercial rival of Boston.

Many ships from foreign ports docked there; and great-grandmother knew a coconut when she saw it.

"What sort of an egg did you say that was?" she asked quietly.

"A gollywhopper's egg, Ma'am," quoth the wily one, and thereupon entered on his now stereotyped account of the potential advantages of gollywhopper farming and the wellnigh necessity for the pioneers to own a flock of them.

Wimble Betty lay low, and heard him through without comment. She then inquired how many eggs he had sold and to whom, also what had been paid for them. In fact she led him on to tell his whole story without airing her knowledge by even a smile. The truth was that she had by no means forgotten nor forgiven the way those neighbor women had snitched on her in the matter of that barrel of West India [she had bored a hole in].

"I had a good mind to let them set those coconuts under their geese, and say nothing," she afterwards declared. But the rascal's unblushing falsehoods so roused her indignation that she finally determined to expose him and force him to relinquish his ill-gotten gains.

"Now, seeing it is you, Ma'am, and that this is my only egg left," he went on, "if you'll give me some dinner and bait my horse, I'll let you have it for one-and-six" (one shilling and sixpence, equal to three or four dollars at the present time).

Great-grandmother Elizabeth listened guilefully, laying plans.

"But I haven't the money," she confessed with assumed pensiveness.

"Perhaps some of your neighbors would lend it to you," the peddler suggested craftily.

"Maybe,"—and Great-grandmother Betty brightened visibly. "But," she added, "you will have to wait till I can run around and see. Put your horse in the barn. Open the great door, drive right in and feed him. I will lay out some food. You can eat and have a smoke while I am gone."

She set off, running, and on reaching the Hobbs farm informed young Aunt Sophrony, with proper sarcasm, how many kinds of imbecile she had shown herself, buying gollywhoppers' eggs of a rascal!

"They are nothing in the world but coconuts!" cried young great-grandmother. "Not worth a thrippence apiece! But hurry! The scamp is at my house. We will trap him yet," quoth she.

They hastened to the Eastman clearing and roused out Aunt Nabby. In short, Great-grandmother Betty went the rounds of the settlement, denouncing the imposture and exhorting each and all to follow her home.

"But our menfolks are away at Muster and have taken their guns," Sarah Holt remonstrated. "He is a great strong fellow! We can't handle him alone!"

"Yes, we can!" cried Great-grandmother Elizabeth. "Get a hayfork from your barn and come on quick!" She heartened up seven of the settlers' wives to join her on the warpath.

It must have been an amusing spectacle, those seven housewives each with a hayfork over her shoulder, stivering along the new road through the woods.

Great-grandsir's log house had no windows at the back, and his new barn was in the rear, distant twenty or thirty yards. Our Wimble Betty, like a good strategist, led her little army of Amazons round about to the barn and, entering it unobserved, secured possession of the peddler's horse and cart, and then drew up her forces just inside the open doorway.

"He may tackle us," she warned. "If he does, punch him with your forks!"

Meantime the unsuspecting Swift, having concluded his homely repast, was taking matters easy at the house, enjoying a pipe and waiting for his ingenuous hostess to return with the silver. He felt that he had done a pretty good stroke of business and had no suspicion of the war cloud that was enveloping his rear. His first intimation of this change in his prosperity was a coconut flung in at the door and the voice of his late hostess bidding him come forth and hand over all that which he had obtained under false pretenses. He dashed out, then rushed to the barn —only to be met by the tines of seven hay-forks guarding the doorway.

It is said that he indulged in remarks of the most unseemly nature. But the fourteen tines confronted him steadily. Those were sturdy young pioneer women accustomed to handling hay-forks. Any attempt to rush the garrison meant perforation.

His wiliness returning, he at first attempted to parley, but at length capitulated.

"Let me get my horse and I'll give you back your stuff," he promised.

"Oh, no!" Great-grandmother Betty retorted. "A fellow that will tell one lie will tell two! You stay outside. I'll get it myself," and while her myrmidons held the doorway she opened the cart and secured the lambskins, peltries, packs of feathers and the retted flax. The coconuts were contemptuously tossed back into the cart, which was then pushed out over the threshold into the yard.

"There, now, you gollywhopper!" cried our militant young ancestress. "Take your old cart and eggs! But you owe me for a dinner, and when you have handed over two papers of pins, two papers of needles and three hanks of linen thread, we will pass out your horse—not before!"

And family tradition has it that Swift complied, then went his ways, wiser perhaps and more cautious for the future.

Barnum and the Cherry-Colored Cat

One day in the early '80's Barnum was dozing in his New York office, when there came a rap on the outer door. At his command "Come in," there stepped through the door as perfect a specimen of Yankee as was ever seen off the stage. After he was seated, he spat out about a yard of amber juice, and eyed P. T. with a humorous squint.

"You're P. T. Barnum, ain't ye?" began the Yankee.

"Right the first time," rejoined the famous showman.

"Wal naow," said his caller, "I've heerd you've got a right smaht passel o' cur'ous animiles in this show of yours, but I bet a buckeye I've got a critter up on my farm in Connecticut that beats any animile cur'osity inside this buildin'."

Mr. Barnum was canny, but showed a willingness to be convinced. Would his caller be a bit more specific in regard to this wonderful "critter."

From *Hold Yer Hosses!* The Elephants Are Coming, by "Uncle" Bob Sherwood, pp. 79–80. Copyright, 1932, by The Macmillan Company. New York.

"Wal naow, what'ud you say ef I was to tell ye that I had on my place a beautiful cat?"

"Well, there's nothing new or strange in that. Ten thousand people in New York could claim the same thing."

"Yaas, but my cat is of a beautiful cherry color." The instinct of the professional showman was reflected instantly in Mr. Barnum's smile of incredulity. But he held his interest in check.

"Well, in that event you have something the public might pay to see," he remarked. "How much do you want for your cherry-colored cat?"

"That's for you to say, Mr. Barnum. My old woman is mighty sweet on the animile and she wouldn't sell him for a song. Tell you what I'll do, if he's all I say he is, you're to pay me three hundred dollars for him on delivery to you in New York."

"Done," said P. T.

One week later, a crate arrived at the museum by express collect. Tacked to the box was a bill for three hundred dollars "for one cherry-colored cat as agreed." The bill was paid. The crate was opened. The creature found inside was undoubtedly a cat—but such a cat as can be found in any alley, its color a rusty black.

"What do you mean," Barnum wired angrily, "by sending me a black cat, when it was agreed it should be a cherry-colored one?"

Back came the answer:

"Dear Mr. Barnum: Did you never see a black cherry? We have loads of them up here in Connecticut."

Barnum acknowledged himself beaten. The hoax leaked out, perhaps through P. T.'s help, and the cherry-colored cat was the means of a big advertisement for the museum.

Raising the Wind

A GOOD story is told by somebody—we don't recollect who—of a couple of Yankees who chanced to be travelling at the South, and had run short of funds. Out of "tin," and out at the toes, they hit upon the following expedient to raise the rhino.

By dint of address they contrived to come it over the printer, and procured a quantity of hand-bills, giving notice to the denizens of the town where they were stopping, that "*a monster* Guyuscutus," of the genus "*humm,*" would be exhibited on the following day, at a certain place—admittance 25 cents, children half price. A curtain was obtained, which was drawn across one end of the apartment where the show was to come off, and the time having arrived, one of the worthy pair performed the part of

By "The Young 'Un" (George P. Burnham). From *The Spirit of the Times,* XV (1845), 370. Cited in "Guyuscutus, Royal Nonesuch and Other Hoaxes," by B. J. Whiting, *Southern Folklore Quarterly,* Vol. VIII (December, 1944), No. 4, p. 265.

doorkeeper and receiver-general, while his companion in sin was busy behind the screen (which was so arranged as to prevent discoveries) where he kept up an incessant and most unearthly moaning, while the company were entering and being seated. The hour having at last arrived for the show to commence, the doorkeeper left his post, and marching across the hall, which was crowded with men, women and children, he disappeared behind the curtain. Immediately after his exit a terrific howling, barking, and chaffering commenced, in the midst of which the clattering of chains and a heavy fall or two, were distinctly heard. A terrific struggle appeared to be going on behind the green baize, and an occasional "Oh! ah—hold hard, Jim"—"hit him on the head"—"that's it"—"no it isn't," etc., were heard for some minutes by the audience in front, who by this time had become greatly excited, and not a little alarmed. Amidst the call for the "manager" the exclamations were heard—"he'll break his chains"—*"there he goes!"*—and the doorkeeper rushes from behind the scenes, hatless and breathless, his hair on end, while he shouts at the top of his lungs—"Save yourselves, gentlemen! Save your children! *The Guyuscutus is loose!!"*

It needs hardly to be added that the immediate rush for the door was "immense," and that in the *melee,* the overturning of chairs and settees—the shrieks of the women, and the yelling of the children, our Yankees mizzle—while the audience, upon recovering their feet and their senses, only learn, too late, that the "proprietors" of the exhibition have eloped, and that, individually and collectively—*they had been done brown!*

Grandma Willey's Chair

I TOOK a party once from Black Mountain House over to Crawford Notch. They wanted to visit the old Willey House. I remember it was kept at the time by Azariah Moore. You've heard about the Willey Slide, how the whole family was destroyed by rushing out doors when the slide came, and how if they'd stayed in the house they'd have been saved. The slide split behind up the house and went both sides of it—never touched the house. Lots of legends clustered about the old house. One was that there was a crippled old Grandma Willey who couldn't run out when the rest did and sat in her wooden rocking chair while the slide went by on her both sides.

At the time my crowd was up there they were very curious about an old wooden rocking chair which stood in the middle of the room. It was pretty dilapidated, chopped up, pieces hacked out of it. "What's that chair?" one of them asked. "Why," said Azariah Moore, "that's old Grandma Willey's rocking chair. One she sat in time of the slide, and was saved. Ain't you never heard about it?" They never had, so he told 'em. Nothing will do with these summer people but they must have a souvenir

---

As told by Mr. Willis to Mr. Pratt. Manuscripts of the Federal Writers' Project of the Works Progress Administration for the State of New Hampshire.

from every place they visit, and as Azariah explained that the condition of the chair was due to the hunger of visitors for souvenirs, my people asked if they might have a chip. "Oh, certainly," he consented. "Everybody teased me so for chips along back—they even whittled 'em out of the chair when I wa'n't looking. Go ahead. And I even furnish the hatchet to cut out the chips with. Here 'tis, if you want to use it."

They did, and as they were busy using it, Azariah slyly crooked his finger at me from the door to come out into the kitchen toward the bar room. "You see, Willie," he told me in a low voice, "when I found the summer folks was so possessed to lug away souvenirs of every curiosity in the mountains I got to providing 'em. I provide 'em old Grandma Willey's chair in there. I buy 'em new, scratch and bang 'em up, hack 'em up, till they look pretty old, for a starter, and then turn 'em over to the summer folks, and they do the rest. That's the third old Grandma Willey chair they've had this season. Oh, of course, they give me a little something—a quarter a chip—standard price."

A Deal in Timberland

I MADE my money from lumber and real estate mostly. I got started young and I worked hard. First I used my hands and muscles; then I started using my brain and letting other men work with their hands. A lot more strong backs in this country than there are sharp minds. Didn't take me long to figger it out neither. I was a young feller, in my twenties, and doing pretty well. I owned a sawmill and a store and a lot of land. I had some good timberlands, some of the best around. I always knew my lumber. I took to lumber like a redheaded woodpecker.

This big New York company wanted to buy some of my timberland. They sent men up here to look it all over, and they liked the looks of it first-rate. I made sure they saw the best stuff standing. Well, after fussing and fooling around they went back to New York to report. Had some correspondence with the company. I was supposed to go to New York to close the deal. I knew them fellers thought I was pretty green, so I thought I'd have some fun with 'em.

I bought a whole new outfit for the trip down to New York. I bought some overalls, a jumper, boots, sheepskin, leggings, and I dressed up in 'em and wore 'em down. Them city fellers liked to died when they see me come in the office!

I says to 'em: "Had a tarnation of a time finding this place. So many big high buildings and so many people. You're way up in the air here, ain't you? How fur you s'posed it is down to the ground? I ain't used to all this commotion. Almost wish I had stayed to home!"

As told by "Hank" Davis to Roaldus Richmond. Manuscripts of the Federal Writers' Project of the Works Progress Administration for the State of Vermont.

I says to 'em: "This is my best outfit I got on here. Only wear it to dress up for something special. Couple of years I'll buy me a new one, and I'll put this right on for everyday. Up home we have to be sparing of our clothes."

I says: "What be them cars that run up on top of them tall poles and make such an awful racket. I wouldn't dare to walk under 'em, let alone ride in 'em. I never see such contraptions as you got here in the city."

Well, by God, them city fellers was having more fun with me, you know —but not half so much fun as I was having with them. Finally we got round to talking business. They wanted to give me three thousand dollars, down payment. I held out for five thousand. They begin to sweat and squirm a little then. After quite a spell they got ready to write me off a check for five thousand. I stalled 'em off some more, said I'd promised my wife not to close the deal till I talked with her. They wanted me to use the office phone, but I said I had to have a private telephone booth when I talked to my wife on account she had such a loud voice it might rupture folks's eardrums that wa'n't used to listening to it. So they let me go out. I stopped in a place I knew before and got a couple of drinks. I gave the bartender some more of that farmer lingo, and the fellers in there liked to died laughing at me. What I really went out for was to go to a bank and see if their check was any good. I found out it was and I went back to the office and picked it up. Them fellers didn't appear none too happy!

Then I asks 'em how I'm going to get back to the depot.

I told 'em I was pretty apt to get lost in all the crowds and traffic and noise. I said I couldn't keep from looking up at the high buildings and it made me dizzy and I was apt to fall down and get run over. Well, by God, you know what they did? They sent a man right along with me clear up as far as White River Junction!

Well, in the spring them city fellers came up to take over, you know, and I collected the rest on the land. After they talked to some of the local lumbermen, they begun to think maybe they hadn't made such a good deal as they thought. They found out they hadn't stung Hank Davis a whole hell of a lot. And here's the best part of it all now. That company went *bankrupt* trying to get the lumber out of there!

HORSE JOCKEYS

Tricks of Horses and Men

It is a late summer afternoon. A man nicknamed Toot drives up before the group seated on the veranda, cutting as he does so a wide circle, with

From *Connecticut Yankee*, An Autobiography, by Wilbur L. Cross, pp. 29-31.

reins held tight. As he jumps from his buggy someone says: "I see, Toot, you've got a new hoss." "Yes, sir." "Where did you get him?" "None of your damn business." Another asks: "How old is he?" "Going on nine." Everybody laughs. And another asks: "May I look into his mouth?" "You may look into him anywhere you damn please. But look out that he don't bite you." After inspecting the horse's teeth the man shakes his head and smiles; and as he walks slowly back into the crowd, someone inquires: "What did you find?" The inspector of the horse's teeth directs his reply to the whole company: "I guess he is of age all right. I guess Toot has to cut his hay pretty fine for them teeth." Toot's retort is that the horse is nearer eight than nine years old and that he sold his feedcutter long ago. Still another man asks: "Any objection, Toot, to my feeling that off hind leg? Unless I am blind there is a spavin there." "You may feel of his legs or of his tail if you want to get kicked in the guts." The man rubs his right hand along both hind legs for a long while and soberly announces that the horse is badly spavined in both hind legs. With a profusion of profanity Toot gives him the lie and offers to poke him in the face. As soon as quiet is restored, a newcomer who has hitched his horse and buggy near Toot's and has listened in without yet saying anything, turns to Toot with "How about a trade?" "No more hoss trades for me," Toot replies in a decisive tone. "I've got here just the kind of hoss I have been looking for all my life. Young. Sound as a dollar. With no outs except that he is rather hard on the bit. I'll keep the cuss until he dies on my hands." By this time everybody is laughing. Soon the newcomer breaks in again: "Any objection, Toot, to my taking a little turn with the hoss down the road and back?" After a minute's hesitation Toot replies to the courteous request: "Not alone. I'll go along with you. I'll drive and you set on the seat with me." In fifteen minutes they return. Not a word is spoken by anybody. The crowd is just looking on to see what may happen. Toot and the newcomer alight. Each begins to take the harness off his own horse to transfer him to the thills of the other buggy. That was one kind of a horse trade. No cash, of course, was involved. It was clearly an even swap.

It did not take me long to make the acquaintance of most of the horses within several miles of the village as I observed them and heard tales about them. Many of them had tricks which a driver had to guard against for his safety on the road. My brother George had his troubles with horses of this kind. His first horse on beginning business was a mare which he kept in a stable behind the store. Whenever I went into the stall to lead her out she started to kick and bite unless handled very gently. A year or so afterwards she caught the "epizootic," a violent and nasty influenza, and at the same time developed a bad case of scratches on two legs, which lamed her terribly. On a day when a trade was imminent it was my job to curry her off and to loosen up her legs by running her round the back-yard while the terms of the trade were being discussed in the store. After I had finished with her she looked pretty well as she stood in the shed with the scratches partly concealed by the hair of her fetlocks. My brother and the other man came out to take a view of her. In reply to several questions indicating some suspicion on the part of the other man, we assured him that the epizootic was disappearing and that the application of arnica for another week on her sore legs would effect a perfect cure. He appeared to be fairly well satisfied with this prognosis, and the trade was made after some haggling over what my brother should pay to boot—whether it should be $15 or $20. When the transaction was over, each party seemed to be the happiest man in the world. Each thought he had fooled the other. And it was so in a sense neither anticipated.

My brother had got in exchange for the old mare, who went to the boneyard a year later, a young Canuck, a name then common for a rather small horse bred in French Canada. He had taken him on a wild gamble, having never seen him before the trader appeared. As soon as the old mare was out of sight my brother asked me if I thought the Canuck had any outs. I told him that when I led the horse towards the stable he acted as if he didn't want to go there and that when I finally coaxed him into the stall he was so nervous that he shook all over. That was so bad an omen that my brother shook all over like the horse. He proposed that we go out and hitch the Canuck into the buggy for a trial of his speed. With great difficulty we got the Canuck, who kept whirling around, between the thills and at last we were able to fasten the traces to the whippletree. Then we jumped into the buggy, my brother holding the reins. The Canuck reared, plunged forward, and then backed us round all over the yard, while George kept exclaiming, "Sold again, by God."

In course of time the Canuck was swapped for a large and beautiful horse who had the trick of throwing his tail over one of the reins and then running at full speed. In turn he was swapped for a very gentle horse who, while trotting along, stepped on a rolling stone and fell to the ground breaking a thill and throwing me over the dashboard among his heels. These were the kind of horses I associated with. In a boy's way I tried to train them out of their tricks, which, however, I kept as secret as I kept the size of shoes worn by girls in the community. Also I used to ride bareback and always rode my father's mare in that way. I loved horses of all sorts and learned from them characteristics of behavior not very remote from the characteristics of some men and women I have had to deal with in private and public life. There is very little difference between tricks of horses and tricks of men.

From Nags to Riches

A CLASSIC story of New England horse trading is one told about the Vermont Yankee who set out from his home in the northern part of the state

From *The Horse & Buggy Age in New England,* by Edwin Valentine Mitchell, p. 193. Copyright, 1937, by Coward-McCann, Inc. New York.

driving a sorry nag hitched to a decrepit buggy. At the first opportunity he swapped the horse and buggy and then traded again and again as he proceeded southward through his native state. When he reached Brattleboro he was driving a fine span of horses hitched to a splendid new carriage.

The Horse Had Two Faults

My father once sold a horse. The horse was absolutely worthless, and he dressed up the window like this: He said, "Now you see that horse. He looks all right; got a good mouth, legs all right, nice color, clever as a sheep. But he's got faults and I don't like him, and I am selling him on account of them. Now I might have lied to you and told you he was all right and maybe fooled you. But I won't lie. Now this horse has got two faults. I'll tell you one before we trade, and if we trade I'll tell you the other."

The other man asked what the first fault was, and father said, "He's awful hard to catch." If the horse was turned out to pasture, it took all the neighbors to get a hand on him. The answer to this was easy—don't turn him out; and as the price was reasonable the man agreed to trade. After he had paid his money he asked father what the second fault was. Father shoved the bills into his pocket and said, "He ain't good for nothin' when you catch him."

Evening the Score

It happened back in 'eighty-five or 'eighty-six, when hoss-tradin' was a reg'lar test of a man's intelligence. Jeff Newcomb was one o' the young sports around Riverdale, them days. Drove fast hosses an' was always lookin' fer a trade. He heard I wanted a good steady roader, so one day he stopped me in the square.

"Got just the animal you're after, Judge," says he. "Six-year-old, handsome as they come." I looked the hoss over pretty careful. He was just six, all right, an' seemed to be as sound as a nut. I drove him twice around the square an' liked his action, so I bought him fer $200 cash. Halfway

---

From *Yankee Storekeeper*, by R. E. Gould, pp. 1–2. Copyright, 1946, by Curtis Publishing Co. and R. E. Gould. New York and London: Whittlesey House, McGraw-Hill Book Company, Inc.

Cf. "Only Two Faults," by Phineas T. Barnum, *Funny Stories* (London, 1890), pp. 102–103, where the horse-jockey is a Dutchman.

From *Lumberjack*, by Stephen W. Meader, pp. 188–191. Copyright, 1934, by Harcourt, Brace and Company, Inc. New York.

Told for generations in my own family.—S. W. M.

home I found he was a breather. Trot him three mile an' he'd start whistlin' an' blowin' like a busted locomotive.

Couple o' weeks later a gang o' gypsies come through. I walked my hoss down to their camp an' had a look at their string. There was only one I liked real well, an' o' course I knew there was somethin' wrong with every hoss they had fer sale. Jest the same, this partic'lar mare was a beauty. Built fer speed—pretty bay color—goin' on five. They had her hitched up to a road-cart, an' after I'd looked at all the rest I asked 'em, casual-like, if she could travel. One of 'em hopped to the seat an' took her 'round the lot at as sweet a two-forty clip as ever I see. When he come up alongside again he asked how I'd trade. 'Course, I didn't let on to be much interested. Thought I'd find out what was the trouble with her, if I could. So I strolled up to her head, pretendin' I wanted to look at her teeth again. Put my hand on the bridle an' backed her up a step or two. Minute I did that, durned if she didn't set square down 'tween the shafts. Jest a natural born setter.

Them gypsies was sore as pups. Couldn't imagine I'd still be willin' to trade, but I acted dumb an' said I was sorry, an' s'posed it was jest an accident. Finally I give 'em my whistler fer the mare an' got $75 to boot.

Next day I hitched her up to the cut-under buggy—bein' mighty careful not to back her—an' drove down to Riverdale. Some o' the boys were out on the river road, brushin' their trotters. I jogged along on the grass, watchin' out o' the corner o' my eye. Pretty soon I spotted what I'd been lookin' fer. Jeff Newcomb was comin' up the line. He had a hoss I knew—a big brown youngster, with a fair turn o' speed—a good stayer. I touched up the mare an' she come dancin' out alongside jest as he passed. "Hi, Jeff," I grinned, an' waved my whip, friendly as could be. The road was clear, ahead. He let out the brown, an' we was at it. I passed him inside of a quarter mile, and then we turned 'round an' come down again, goin' fer all we was wuth. That mare was a caution. She give his good brown hoss the prettiest lickin' y' ever see, an' when we reached the square he was four or five lengths behind. I 'most forgot her bad habits, drivin' her, an' I could see Jeff had fell plumb in love with her.

"Where'd ye git her?" says he, soon as he pulls up with me. I jest laughed an' told him I had to be gittin' along. "Hold on," he says, "I could use a stepper like that." "Ain't fer sale," I told him. But he wanted to trade so bad I finally weakened. Took his brown hoss—as honest a roader as I ever owned—an' two sets o' harness, an' $50 in trade.

. . . Last thing I seen as I drove off . . . was Jeff tryin' to back the mare into the shafts of his buggy. She was settin', an' Jeff was swearin'.

So you see . . . I know him an' he knows me. Next time we met we shook hands, to show we was all square. An' we've trusted each other ever since.

The Cribbing Horse

Some years ago there lived in town an old horse trader known for miles around for his knack of swapping horses and always coming out the winner. Although he was over seventy years of age, his mind was as keen as a knife, and he always kept two or three old horses in his barn, and it pleased him immensely if any of the younger generation tried to get the best of him in a horse trade.

A young neighbor had a cribbing [1] horse and it was necessary to keep a cribbing strap on the horse's neck while in the stable. Getting tired of this, the young man decided to trade; so he went to the old man's house, and after a long session of dickering, in which nothing was said about the cribbing, the trade was made. When he got home, his wife was so pleased with the appearance of the new horse that she said, "It's a shame that you cheated the old man so. You had better go right back and tell him what you did and give him the cribbing strap." So back he went and told the old man about it, apologetically, and said, "I'm ashamed that I got the best of you, but you know, when a man like you ages, he—er—kind of overlooks things, don't he?"

The old man with a twinkle in his eye said, "Ned, how long has that horse I swapped with you been in the barn?" With a look of astonishment the young man said, "Oh, about an hour. Why?" "Why?" the old man said, with a grin from ear to ear. "Son, if you want to save your barn, I'd advise you to hustle back home with that strap because that horse was the worst cribber I ever had in my life."

A First-Rate Setter

The story about the mule I think I have seen in print; it was about a farmer who wanted to buy a mule for his own use on his farm, which was several miles outside of the village in which he lived. A neighbour in the village owned a mule, and offered him for sale. The two men talked the matter over, the owner of the mule assuring the other that the animal was perfectly sound and good in every respect. The farmer purchased the animal, and while riding him out to his farm the next day, after going a

---

By Mrs. Walter Whitney, Gray, Maine. Manuscripts of the Federal Writers' Project of the Works Progress Administration for the State of Maine.

[1] Cribbing, crib-biting: "A vice of horses, in which they grasp the manger with the incisor teeth, arch the neck, and swallow large quantities of air."—*Webster's Collegiate Dictionary,* Fifth Edition.

From *Funny Stories,* Told by Phineas T. Barnum, pp. 103–105. Copyright, 1890, by Phineas T. Barnum. New York, London, Glasgow, and Manchester: George Routledge and Sons, Limited.

mile or two, the mule suddenly stopped, sat down on his haunches, and would not budge. The usual mode of pulling, kicking and coaxing was resorted to, and at last the animal got on his feet again and went on. At night the farmer took the mule to his former owner, and said:—

"I have had enough of that animal. You said he was gentle and well-broken in every way; but to-day, while riding him toward my farm, he suddenly stopped, sat down, and would not budge an inch."

"Did you see a rabbit?" the mule-seller asked.

"Rabbit? No! What has that got to do with it?"

"Well, were you near any woods?"

"Let me see—yes, there were some woods close by; but what has that got to do with the mule?"

"I forgot to mention to you that he is a setter, and he must have seen a rabbit somewhere, and sat down, as he always does."

"I never heard of such a thing," exclaimed the purchaser.

"Well, I can't help that. He is a first-rate setter, and in all other respects is an excellent mule."

"Then I shall not often go where there are rabbits; so if this is all that ails him, I will keep him."

The next day, while riding the mule in the country, he attempted to cross a stream, and in the middle of the river the mule sat down as before, half-drowning the farmer. During the struggle to get him on his feet again, the farmer grew very indignant, and used some emphatic language not often heard in those parts. On his return to the village, he took the mule again to his former owner, and said:—

"There, you can take this animal back; I have had enough of him in the last two days."

"What is the matter now?"

"Why, I was nearly drowned to-day; the confounded beast sat down with me on his back in the middle of the stream!"

"Oh, that is all right; he is just as good on fish as he is on rabbits."

The Horse That Didn't Look So Good

SOME years ago in Clark's Falls, a village north of Stonington, a newcomer to the locality walked into the stable of Brown, the horsetrader. The man wanted to buy a horse suitable for driving in a light rig.

After Brown had showed him the stock he had, the customer scanned them and finally decided upon a certain bay.

"How much for that bay?"

Manuscripts of the Federal Writers' Project of the Works Progress Administration for the State of Connecticut.

For a discussion and variants of the "Ill-Looking Horse" motif, see Richard M. Dorson, *Jonathan Draws the Long Bow* (Cambridge, 1946), pp. 21, 82.

"Waal," drawled Brown, "I'll take a hunderd an' a quarter for her—but she don't look so good!"

"Why yes she does!" said the customer. "She looks as good to me as the rest of them animals!"

Brown was willing to sell, but he further allowed that the horse didn't look so good. At any rate the deal was completed. The buyer hitched up the bay to his buggy, and started home.

Just after nightfall, the horse landed the buggy in the ditch. After extricating himself, the buggy, and the horse, the enraged man drove back to Brown.

"What's the matter with this horse?" he yelled. "She ran me into the ditch!"

"Waal," said Brown, "you bought her, and she's yourn. But don't say I didn't warn ye. I said she don't look so good; she be nigh blind fer a year."

Reason for Sale

THERE was once a shrewd lawyer who lived on Mason's Island, a small village on the Connecticut coast reached by a connecting bridge from the mainland. The lawyer, desiring to sell a saddle horse, inserted an advertisement in the paper which read thus:

Saddle horse for sale. Reason for sale,
owner wants to leave town.

In reply to this advertisement, a prospective buyer travelled to the island. He inspected the horse, and after some talk, bought the animal for seventy-five dollars. The new owner saddled the horse and started for the mainland. When they came to the bridge, the horse balked, and no amount of coercion would get him across. In anger, the man drove back to the lawyer. After he explained the difficulty at the bridge, the lawyer chuckled.

"Well," said he, "I said that the reason for sale was that I wanted to leave town, and I just couldn't leave town with that horse!"

Willing Horses

A HORSE trader named Luther Perkins in Mechanic Falls was so smooth of tongue and wit that no one could get the better of him. He sold a man

---

Manuscripts of the Federal Writers' Project of the Works Progress Administration for the State of Connecticut.

From Poland, Maine. Manuscripts of the Federal Writers' Project of the Works Progress Administration for the State of Maine.

a pair of horses guaranteed to be willing horses. The horses were very poor at working and the buyer complained to him.

"I thought you said these horses were willing."

"So I did," replied Perkins, "and so they are. One's willing to stop and the other one's willing to let him."

SMART MERCHANTS AND CUSTOMERS

Sam Temple's Store: A Rhyming Advertisement

Salt Pork and Powder, Shot and Flints,
Cheese, Sugar, Rum and Peppermints,

Tobacco, Raisins, Flour and Spice,
Flax, Wool, Cotton and sometimes Rice,

Old Holland Gin and Gingerbread,
Brandy and Wine, all sorts of Thread,

Segars I keep, sometimes on bunch;
Materials all for making Punch,

Biscuit and Butter, Eggs and Fishes.
Molasses, Beer and Earthen Dishes.

Books on such subjects as you'll find
A proper food to feast the mind.

Hard Soap and Candles, Tea and Snuff,
Tobacco Pipes—perhaps enough,

Shells, Chocolate, Stetson's Hoes
As good as can be (I suppose),

Straw Hats, Oats, Baskets, Oxen Muzzles,
A thing which many people puzzles,

Knives, Forks, Spoons, Plates, Mugs, Pitchers, Platters,
A Gun with shot wild geese bespatters,

Spades, Shovels, Whetstone, Scythes and Rakes,
As good as any person makes,

Shirts, Frocks, Shoes, Mittens, also Hose,
And many other kinds of Clothes,

Shears, Scissors, Awls, Wire, Bonnet Paper,
Old Violin and Cat Gut Scraper,

Tubs, Buckets, Pails and Pudding Pans,
Bandana Handkerchiefs and Fans,

Shagbarks and Almonds, Wooden Boxes,
Steel Traps (not stout enought for Foxes,

But excellent for holding Rats
When they elude the Paws of Cats),

From *Norfolk Repository,* Dedham, 1805. In *Grandfather Was Queer,* Early American Wags and Eccentrics from Colonial Times to the Civil War, by Richardson Wright, pp. 36–37. Copyright, 1939, by Richardson Wright. Philadelphia, New York, Toronto and London: J. B. Lippincott Company.

Samuel Temple, who harried the youth of his day by writing "Temple's Arithmetic," was also a rhymester of sorts. When he went into storekeeping, at Dedham, Mass., he set forth his stock in verse—and saw that it was printed in the local paper. —R. W.

I've more than Forty kinds of Drugs,
Some good for Worms and some for
Bugs,

Lee's, Anderson's and Dexter's Pills,
Which cure at least a hundred ills,

Astringents, Laxatives, Emetics,
Cathartics, Cordials, Diuretics,

Narcotics, Stimulants and Pungents,
With half a dozen kinds of Unguents.

Perfume most grateful to the Nose
When mixed with Snuff or dropped on
clothes,

One Medicine more (not much in
fame),
Prevention is its real name,

An ounce of which, an author says
Outweighs a Ton of Remedies.

The many things I shall not mention
To sell them cheap is my intention.

Lay out a dollar when you come
And you shall have a glass of Rum.

N.B. Since man to man is so unjust,
'Tis hard to say whom I can trust.

I've trusted many to my sorrow:
Pay me today: I'll trust tomorrow.

Cordwood

. . . SKIN JUBB landed a load of cordwood at Jim's store a few weeks ago, small stuff, and half of it crookeder'n a dog's hind leg. Skin took his pay and started to hurry off as Jim went out to look it over. But 'fore Skin got out of hearin' Jim called him back—then handed him a quarter extry and a fi'-cent cigar. "Wut's all this for?" says Skin.

"Waal," says Jim, "the quarter is for the extry time you must-a spent huntin' up the smallest, crookedest sticks you could find—and the cigar's a prize for stackin' 'em up into a cord o' wood you could chase a cat through from any p'int of the compass!" [1]

Back in the days when bartering was more common, a man agreed to deliver a load of cordwood for a new pair of boots. He brought a load of poplar wood, which is very poor firewood. He received his pair of boots, but after he had worn them a couple of weeks the stitches began to come out and the eyelets to rip out and tear. He hurried into the shoemaker's and started to complain. The shoemaker silenced him with, "Wal, what do you expect of popple boots." [2]

---

[1] From *Village Down East*, Sketches of Village Life on the Northeast Coast of New England before "Gas-Buggies" Came, from Conversations with Zackary Adams, Duck Trap Cove, Maine, by John Wallace, p. 42. Copyright, 1943, by Stephen Daye Press, Inc. Brattleboro, Vermont.

[2] From "Whitefield" by Ola G. Veazie. Manuscripts of the Federal Writers' Project of the Works Progress Administration for the State of New Hampshire.

There's Odds in Deacons

TALES have been handed down of an elder who was a "leetle nigh" on a trade. To a would-be purchaser said he, "Waal, I'll allow that you'll be pleased to see that horse go up hill." The man bought the horse, soon returning. "The pesky critter balked at the first rise; tho't you sed she was a prime goer!" "Not jes so," answered the elder, "I said you'd be pleased to see her go up hill: naow wouldn't you?"

Expecting a customer for a cow, and wishing to keep the bargain on his side, Elder C. selected the most undesirable cow and placed her in his best stall; the farmer was affably told that he might choose any from the herd except Mammy's pet butter cow. "Couldn't part with her no ways." The customer got the pet cow. There is a saying in New England, "All deacons are good, but there's odds in deacons." [1]

The customers of a certain Deacon ——, who sold milk, complained after a while that the article furnished was blue and poor; to which he replied, "Do you think I would cheat you? I say upon my honor that I never put a drop of water in my milk in all my life." This answer satisfied his customers, till a certain hired man of his got mad, and left his service, when he let out the secret. He said, "The Deacon told you the truth when he said he never put a drop of water in his milk in all his life; but I'll tell you what he did do. He put water in his milk pail, and then milked into it." [2]

It reminded me of the good old deacon in Connecticut who was in the habit of selling milk to his neighbors on all days in the week. One Sunday, however, his parson came home with him to tea, and while they were at the table a little girl came in for a quart of milk. The deacon was afraid of being scandalized in the presence of the parson, and so he told the girl he did not sell milk on Sunday. The girl, who had been accustomed to buy on that day as on other days, was much surprised and turned to go away, when the sixpence in her hand was too much of a temptation for the deacon, who called out:

---

[1] From *Old Paths and Legends of the New England Border:* Connecticut, Deerfield, Berkshire, by Katharine M. Abbott, pp. 265–266. Copyright, 1907, by Katharine M. Abbott. New York and London: G. P. Putnam's Sons.

[2] From *Legends of Woburn,* Now First Written and Preserved in Collected Form . . . by Parker Lindall Converse, p. 129. Copyright, 1892, by Parker L. Converse. Woburn, Mass.: Printed for Subscribers Only.

"Here, little girl! you can leave the money now, and call and get the milk to-morrow!"[3]

The tobacco had to be kept from drying and this furnished the occasion of the wicked slander on the deacon, who was supposed to have said to his clerk, "John, have you wet down the tobacco?" "Yes, sir." "Have you sanded the sugar?" "Yes, sir." "Then come in to prayers!"[4]

One season had been very dry and the mill yard of Deacon Joel's saw mill was full of logs. The water to saw them was exhausted. The day before Fast Day, observed by the Orthodox as Sunday, there came a big rain. The pond began to run over into the spillway. This was too much for the Deacon. He lifted the gate and sawed away all day. Meeting Parson Leonard a few days later, he was surprised to be upbraided for what he had done. He answered with some acrimony: "Now, Parson, which is the more sinful, for me to work on Fast Day and give the money to the poor, or for you and Parson Sewall to swap horses at Little's Bridge twice every Sunday when you exchange pulpits and defraud the Bridge Company of its tolls?"[5]

Deaconing

In preparing and packing fruit for the market, the practice of "deaconing," as it is called, is very extensively followed—that is, topping off a barrel of apples with the best specimens; the rather irreverent term "deaconing" having its origin, probably, from some one holding that office having been unfortunately distinguished for his frequent adoption of the

---

[3] From *Struggles and Triumphs: or, Forty Years' Recollections of P. T. Barnum, Written by Himself*, pp. 731–732. Entered according to Act of Congress, in the year 1871, by P. T. Barnum, in the Office of the Librarian of Congress, at Washington. Entered also at Stationer's Hall, London, England. Buffalo, New York: Warren, Johnson & Co. 1873.

[4] From *Black Tavern Tales, Stories of Old New England*, by Charles L. Goodell, p. 102. Copyright, 1932, by Charles L. Goodell. Brooklyn: Willis McDonald & Co.
Other versions refer to watering the rum, dusting the pepper, chicorying the coffee, larding the butter, and flouring the ginger.

[5] From *Marshfield, 70°–40′ W: 42°–5′ N, The Autobiography of a Pilgrim Town*, Being an Account of Three Hundred Years of a New England Town; Founded by the Pilgrims; Lived in and Developed by the Royalists; Adopted by Daniel Webster & Beloved by Many of the Ancestors of Those Who Today Make It Their Home, 1640–1940, p. 167. Copyright, 1940, by Marshfield Tercentenary Committee. Marshfield, Massachusetts.

From *Cyclopaedia of Commercial and Business Anecdotes . . .* , by Frazar Kirkland, Vol. I, p. 206. Entered, according to Act of Congress, in the year 1864, by D. Appleton and Company, in the Clerk's Office of the District Court of the United States for the Southern District of New York. New York and London.

plan, so as to put an inviting show on his fruit. A dealer down East, who happened to be "posted," sold a barrel of apples to a customer, at the same time recommending them as the choicest apples that had been raised in the town. In due time the barrel was opened, and found to contain a very inferior quality; whereupon the customer, feeling that he had been imposed upon, made complaint to the seller, who in turn very coolly made answer, that he guessed he must have opened the barrel at the wrong end! The only change this little episode was known to produce in the seller's practice was to make him careful afterward to "deacon" *both* ends.

As Good as His Word

In an interior town in old Connecticut lives a shaky character, named Ben Hayden. Ben has some good points, but he will run his face when and where he can, and never pay. In the same town lives Mr. Jacob Bond, who keeps the store at the corners. Ben had a "score" there, but to get his pay was more than Mr. Bond was equal to, as yet. One day Ben made his appearance with a bag and wheelbarrow, and said, "Mr. Bond, I want to buy two bushels of corn, and *I want to pay cash for it.*" "Very well," replied Mr. Bond, "all right"; and so they both ascended the loft, and when the necessary operations were gone through with, they respectively returned. But by the time the trader had got down and looked around him, old Ben had got some distance from the door, and was rapidly making for home. "Halloo, halloo, Ben!" cried out the trader lustily; "you said you wanted to pay cash for that corn." Old Ben deliberately sat down on one handle of his barrow, and cocking his head on one side, said, "That's all true, Mr. Bond. I *do* want to pay you the cash for the corn, but I can't!"

The Power of Imagination

A lady in Springfield went into a store one day to buy some dress goods. She asked the clerk to show her some blue silk. He couldn't find blue, so he took down a bolt of green.

"But this is *green,*" objected the customer. "I want *blue.*"

"Oh, never mind," replied the clerk. "Just *imagine* it's blue and it *will* be blue!"

After a moment's hesitation, the lady said she would take *twenty* yards. The clerk measured off the amount desired, wrapped it up and handed it over the counter. Without a word, the lady walked calmly down the aisle

Ibid., 262.

From "A Yankee Tale—Fact or Folksay?", by Grace Partridge Smith, *Journal of American Folklore,* Vol. 58 (October–December, 1945), No. 230, p. 344.

with the package. As she neared the door, the clerk called: "But, madam, you haven't paid for the silk yet!" Over her shoulder as she passed out the door, she called, "Just *imagine* it's paid for and it *will be* paid for!"[1]

The Draper and the Bible

A VERY pious man, who set up in the dry goods business, told his clerks always to deal with a customer in such a way that they could quote scripture to justify the deal. One day a woman came in to buy some material for a dress. A clerk waited on her and said, pointing to a bale of cloth on the counter: "I have been showing this silk-and-wool goods to one of our customers. It is the color they are wearing this season, and ought to be very popular."

The cloth did not suit her. The clerk put it back on the shelf and showed her everything else he had. Then he laid on the counter the goods he had first shown her and said, "Now *this* seems to be a real favorite." It seemed to be just what she wanted; so she bought it and left.

The owner had overheard the conversation and seen the trouble the clerk had gone to in order to please her. Coming up to the clerk, he asked: "Now what quotation from the Bible could you apply to her?" To which the clerk promptly replied: "She was a stranger, and I took her in."

Turning Water into Grog

A WELL known old sea captain of Searport, when about sixty years of age, nearly lost his shipping business and five schooners as a result of his taste for liquor. His eldest son was appointed conservator of his estate, and allowed the old captain to take a voyage now and then. The captain of the schooner on which he sailed was always instructed never to let the old gentleman have any money when on shore.

On the occasion of one of his trips, while anchored at T Wharf in Boston, the captain sat on deck looking the length of Atlantic Avenue, viewing the many saloon signs with a parched throat. After speculating

---

[1] . . . The story in question was told to the writer by a nonagenarian [Mrs. James Otis Partridge (Arvilla Pauline Kimball); born in Moretown, Vt., 1838, died in Iowa City, 1938; the writer's mother] who heard it some eighty-odd years ago in Springfield, Massachusetts. It was always emphasized by my informant that the incident related actually happened; she gave the name of the store where the affair took place and that of the owner or manager. It was one of a number of stories about that eastern city, often listened to by her audience with a lift of the eyebrow. Since it was repeated to me "time without number" during the narrator's lifetime, I am able to record it in very nearly the exact words used. . . . G. P. S.

By Mrs. Elva Kimball Walker, Mascoma, New Hampshire. Contributed by Mrs. Grace Partridge Smith, Carbondale, Illinois.

for hours as to how he could obtain a drink, he became inspired. Going to the cabin he filled a gallon demijohn half full of water, and hurried to the nearest saloon. Entering, he informed the bartender that he wanted the demijohn filled with rum, and said he thought that it would take about two quarts as it was already half full. When the bartender had filled the demijohn and demanded his pay the captain told him to charge it. Whereupon the bartender reclaimed his two quarts of rum. Repeating this at the next five saloons along the avenue, the captain returned to his ship with two quarts of excellent rum.[1]

. . . A new liquor warehouse opening at Boston on a ready-money and low-price system, Jonathan walked in one day with a two-gallon keg on his shoulder, and asked for a gallon of the best brandy. The liquor having been poured through a funnel into his keg the money was demanded. Pretending ignorance of their mode of doing business, the Yankee said that he would pay the next time he came into town. The shopman demurred, saying that he did not intend to give any credit. "But," asked the Yankee in mock surprise, "do you intend to take back the brandy?"

"To be sure," replied the other, "if you don't pay for it."

"Then," said he, "you must bring your measure, for I had some liquor of my own in the keg."

This was done, a gallon of the contents measured back, and the fellow marched off with another gallon of fine grog, having half filled his keg beforehand with *water*.[2]

Paying for the Cider

AFTER I had walked about three or four hours I come along towards the upper end of the town where I found there were stores and shops of all sorts and sizes. And I met a feller, and says I, what place is this? Why this, says he, is Huckler's Row. What, says I, are these the stores where the traders in Huckler's Row keep? And says he, yes. Well then, thinks

---

[1] From *The (Old) Farmer's Almanack,* Calculated on a New and Improved Plan for the Year of Our Lord 1934, No. 142, by Robert B. Thomas, p. 49. Copyright, 1933, by Carroll J. Swan. Boston, Massachusetts.

[2] From *Retrospections of America, 1797–1811,* by John Bernard, Edited from the Manuscript by Mrs. Bayle Bernard, With an Introduction, Notes, and Index by Laurence Hutton and Brander Matthews, p. 343. Copyright, 1886, by Harper & Brothers. New York. 1887.

From *The Life and Writings of Major Jack Downing,* of Downingville, Away Down East in the State of Maine, Written by Himself, Second Edition, pp. 31–33. Entered, according to Act of Congress, in the year 1834, by Lilly, Wait, Colman, & Holden, in the Clerk's Office of the District Court of the District of Massachusetts. Boston.

I to myself, I have a pesky good mind to go in and have a try with one of these chaps, and see if they can twist my eye teeth out. If they can get the best end of a bargain out of me, they can do what there aint a man in Downingville can do, and I should jest like to know what sort of stuff these ere Portland chaps are made of. So in I goes into the best looking store among 'em. And I see some biscuit lying on the shelf, and says I, Mister, how much do you ax apiece for them are biscuit? A cent apiece, says he. Well, says I, I shant give you that, but if you 've a mind to, I 'll give you two cents for three of 'em, for I begin to feel a little as though I should like to take a bite. Well, says he, I would n't sell 'em to any body else so, but seeing it's you I don't care if you take 'em. I knew he lied, for he never see me before in his life. Well he handed down the biscuits and I took 'em, and walked round the store awhile to see what else he had to sell. At last, says I, Mister, have you got any good new cider? Says he, yes, as good as ever you see. Well, says I, what do you ax a glass for it? Two cents, says he. Well, says I, seems to me I feel more dry than I do hungry now. Aint you a mind to take these ere biscuit again and give me a glass of cider? And says he, I dont care if I do; so he took and laid 'em on the shelf again, and poured out a glass of cider. I took the cider and drinkt it down, and to tell the truth it was capital good cider. Then, says I, I guess it 's time for me to be a going, and I stept along towards the door. But, says he, stop Mister. I believe you have n't paid me for the cider. Not paid you for the cider, says I, what do you mean by that? Did n't the biscuit that I give you jest come to the cider? Oh, ah, right, says he. So I started to go again; and says he, but stop, Mister, you did n't pay me for the biscuit. What, says I, do you mean to impose upon me? do you think I am going to pay you for the biscuit and let you keep 'em tu? Aint they there now on your shelf, what more do you want? I guess sir, you dont whittle me in that way. So I turned about and marched off, and left the feller staring and thinking and scratching his head, as though he was struck with a dunderment. Howsomever, I did n't want to cheat him, only jest to show 'em it wan't so easy a matter to pull my eye teeth out, so I called in next day and paid him his two cents.

The Egg, the Darning-Needle, and the Treat

. . . A TRADE at a store was an occasion for drinking; and I have an anecdote at command which illustrates how strong the obligation of the custom was upon the merchant to treat his customer after trading with him. (The occurrence is said to have taken place on the New York side of the lake; though, if the story is true, I think one of the parties must certainly have been a Yankee.) According to the account, the patronizing customer took an egg, and went to the store to buy a darning-needle. The purchase was made, and the egg taken in payment. The purchaser remained some time as if waiting for something; but the merchant seemed rather disposed to take no notice of the common rule, in such case made and provided. At length the customer seemed to suspect a design to dodge, and getting somewhat out of patience, he turned and popped the momentous question: "An't ye goin' to treat?" "O certainly," said the merchant, and the decanter of brandy, a bowl of sugar, a pitcher of water and a tumbler were set on. The mixture was made, when the customer again looked up and said, "I guess I'll take an egg to put into it." The same egg that had just been bought was accordingly handed on. But, on breaking it the customer exclaimed: "Here, see! the egg I let ye have had *two yelks,* and I guess you ought to let me have two darning-needles." And the darning-needle was accordingly handed over, and thus the trade was closed.[1]

Money was scarce in the early settlement. Business was conducted by a system of barter. The following illustrates the method and also some of the tricks of the shyster.

A raw country bumpkin away down East,
A pretty cute chap, in his own eyes, at least,
Walked in one day to a small country store
Which it happened he'd never been into before.
Too honest to steal and too well off to beg,
He had brought in his pocket a newly laid egg.
When the storekeeper asked him what goods he was arter,
He didn't know hardly, he wanted to barter.
He said his old woman could get him his meals,
But she couldn't go out 'cause she'd holes in her heels.
And a well-to-do woman, as every one knows,
Is ashamed of her heels tho' she's proud of her toes,
A good darning needle he wanted to buy,
That was warranted never to cut in the eye.
So the egg was laid down and the needle passed out,
When the purchaser, finding it bright, sharp, and stout,
At once stuck it into his satinette sleeve,
And, then, looking round before taking his leave,
His eye caught a signboard, gilt-lettered and neat,
Where were printed in capitals, BARTER & TREAT.
"Oh! I see by your sign that you treat when you trade." *
"Why, yes, sometimes; but then, you see,
When we make such a very small barter, we—"
"Oh, well, never mind, if you ain't goin' to do't,
You go put up a signboard to suit."

[1] From Gov. Eaton's Temperance Address—an Extract, Delivered before the Young Men's Temperance Association, at Enosburgh in 1855, in *The Vermont Historical Gazetteer:* A Magazine Embracing a History of Each Town, Civil, Ecclesiastical, Biographical and Military, edited by Abby Maria Hemenway, Vol. II, p. 161. Entered according to Act of Congress, in the year 1871, by Abby Maria Hemenway, in the Office of the Librarian of Congress, at Washington. Burlington, Vermont.

* A line seems to have been omitted here.

"Hold on," said the trader, "now, seein' it's you,
We'll do as you say, we'll make our word true.
What liquor'll you have, for we've everything handy."
"Oh, Sir! I never takes any but brandy."
The trader reached under the counter *instanter*
And drew out a glass and the brandy decanter.
Then the man who had come for the purpose of dicker
Poured into the tumbler four fingers of liquor,
He sweetened it, stirred it, and then set it down,
While he stood for a moment scratching his crown.
Then, while he looked straight at the trader a minute,
Said, "I never take brandy without an egg in it."
So he took up the egg, he'd just passed off in dicker,
Cracked it and broke it right into the liquor,
When he found out a fact which the hen never knew—
Instead of one yolk in the egg there were two.
"I swanny, by golly, now, Cap'n, see here,
It's a great double yolker, now isn't that queer?
I didn't know 'twas a two yolker, did you?"
"Why, no," said the trader, "I didn't, 'tis true."
"Now, Cap'n, you seem like a pretty fair man,
And I mean to patronize you when I can.
You've done well so far, and I don't want to wheedle,
But couldn't you give us another good needle?"
The storekeeper stood and most horribly grinned,
As any man would, who had found himself skinned.
Then he took out a needle, gave it a toss,
And charged the transaction to Profit and Loss.[2]

Paying for the Stolen Butter

No other class of men in any country possess that facetious aptness of inflicting a good-humored revenge which seems to be innate with a Green Mountain boy. Impose upon or injure a Vermonter, and he will seem the drollest and best-natured fellow you ever knew in all your life, until suddenly he pounces upon you with some cunningly devised offset for your duplicity; and even while he makes his victim smart to the core, there is that manly open-heartedness about him which infuses balm even while the wound is opening, and renders it quite impossible that you should hate

[2] From *History of Weymouth, Massachusetts,* in Four Volumes, Vol. 2, p. 821. Published by the Weymouth Historical Society, Howard H. Joy, President, Under Direction of the Town. 1923.

From *Wehman's Idle Hours with the Humorists,* Brimful of Fun about Yankee Yarns, Western Sports, Boarding-House Hash, Rich College Scrapes, Wild Widows' Wit, and Tall Tales of Sailors and Marines, pp. 28–30. New York: Published by Henry J. Wehman. [n. d.]

him, however severe may have been the punishment he dealt out to you. These boys of the Green Mountains seem to possess a natural faculty of extracting fun from every vicissitude and accident that the changing hours can bring; even what are bitter vexations to others, these happy fellows treat in a manner so peculiar as to completely alter their former character and make them seem to us agreeable, or at least endurable, which was before in the highest degree offensive. Another man will repay an aggravation or an insult by instantly returning injury, cutting the acquaintance and shutting his heart for ever against the offender; but a Vermonter, with a smile upon his face, will *amuse* himself while obtaining a far *keener* revenge, cracking a joke in conclusion, and making his former enemy forgive him and even love him after chastisement.

One winter evening, a country store-keeper in the Mountain State was about closing his doors for the night, and while standing in the snow outside putting up his window shutters, he saw through the glass, a lounging worthless fellow within grab a pound of fresh butter from the shelf and hastily conceal it in his hat.

The act was no sooner detected than the revenge was hit upon, and a very few moments found the Green Mountain store-keeper at once indulging his appetite for fun to the fullest extent, and paying off the thief with a facetious sort of torture for which he might have gained a premium from the old inquisition.

"I say, Seth!" said the store-keeper, coming in and closing the door after him, slapping his hands over his shoulders and stamping the snow off his shoes.

Seth had his hand upon the door, his hat upon his head, and the roll of new butter in his hat, anxious to make his exit as soon as possible.

"I say, Seth, sit down; I reckon, now, on such an *e-tar*-nal night as this a little something warm wouldn't hurt a fellow; come and sit down."

Seth felt very uncertain; he had the butter, and was exceedingly anxious to be off, but the temptation of "something warm" sadly interfered with his resolution to go. This hesitation, however, was soon settled by the right owner of the butter taking Seth by the shoulders and planting him in a seat close to the stove, where he was in such a manner cornered in by barrels and boxes and while the country grocer sat before him there was no possibility of his getting out, and right in this very place sure enough the store-keeper sat down.

"Seth, we'll have a little warm Santa Cruz," said the Green Mountain grocer, as he opened the stove door, and stuffed in as many sticks as the space would admit. "Without it you'd freeze going home such a night as this."

Seth already felt the butter settling down closer to his hair, and jumped up, declaring he must go.

"Not till you have something warm, Seth; come, I've got a story to tell you, too; sit down, now"; and Seth was again pushed into his seat by his cunning tormentor.

"Oh! It's too darn'd hot here," said the petty thief, again attempting to rise.

"Set down—don't be in such a plaguey hurry," retorted the grocer, pushing him back in his chair.

"But I've got the cows to fodder, and some wood to split, and I *must* be agoin'," continued the persecuted chap.

"But you mustn't tear yourself away, Seth, in this manner. Set down; let the cows take care of themselves, and keep yourself *cool,* you appear to be fidgetty," said the roguish grocer, with a wicked leer.

The next thing was the production of two smoking glasses of hot rum toddy, the very sight of which, in Seth's present situation, would have made the hair stand erect upon his head, had it not been well oiled and kept down by the butter.

"Seth, I'll give you a *toast* now, and you can *butter* it yourself," said the grocer, yet with an air of such consummate simplicity that poor Seth still believed himself unsuspected. "Seth, here's—here's a Christmas goose—[it was about Christmas time]—here's a Christmas *goose,* well *roasted* and *basted* eh? I tell you, Seth, it's the greatest eatin' in creation. And, Seth, don't you never use hog's fat or common cooking butter to baste with; fresh pound butter, just the same as you see on that shelf yonder, is the only proper thing in natur to baste a goose with—come take your *butter* —I mean, take your toddy."

Poor Seth now began to *smoke,* as well as to *melt,* and his mouth was as hermetically sealed up as though he had been born dumb. Streak after streak of the butter came pouring from under his hat, and his handkerchief was already soaked with the greasy overflow. Talking away, as if nothing was the matter, the grocer kept stuffing the wood into the stove, while poor Seth sat bolt upright, with his back against the counter, and his knees almost touching the red-hot furnace before him.

"Darnation cold night this," said the grocer. "Why, Seth, you seem to perspire as if you was warm! Why don't you take your hat off? Here, let me put your hat away!"

"No!" exclaimed poor Seth at last, with a spasmodic effort to get his tongue loose, and clapping both hands upon his hat, "No! I must go; let me out; I ain't well; let me go!" A greasy cataract was now pouring down the poor fellow's face and neck, and soaking into his clothes, and trickling down his body into his very boots, so that he was literally in a perfect bath of oil.

"Well, good night, Seth," said the humorous Vermonter, "if you *will* go"; adding, as Seth got out into the road, "Neighbor, I reckon the fun I've had out of you is worth a shilling, so I shan't charge for that *pound of butter*!"

The Soap Cure

An old lady who used to come to town to sell butter and eggs was a pest and a sort of a thief. She'd hit my store about noon and make some small purchase such as a pound of tea. Then she would grab a couple of pilot biscuits and run for the cheese case. She'd grab a knife and jab it into the cheese and cut out at least a half pound, and this made her lunch. When she got through we'd have to trim away another half pound to satisfy the next customer—who couldn't be blamed for disliking twice the amount of rind he should have had.

I studied the case of the cheese-swiping old woman for a long time, and then one day my heart lit up and radiated joy all over. We had a very firm cheese of light yellow color. We also had some Goodwill soap about the same color. The next time I saw the old lady on her way to my place, I took a bar of Goodwill soap and cut out a wedge of it. I also cut a wedge out of the cheese, and inserted the soap wedge daintily. I cleaned up all the scraps and hid the knife. In she came, and she fell for it. She gagged and sputtered and coughed and hid behind a pile of canned goods until the spasm passed. She finally came out, paid for her pound of tea, and I never saw her in my store again.

The Stolen Cheese

. . . One day, after selling a customer a few pounds of wool and putting it into the bag, he went into his counting room, and looking into a glass which reflected the counter, he saw the man slip in a small skim cheese. Mr. S. on returning said, he thought he had by mistake put in more wool than was ordered, and would just place the bag in the scale again. The man objected, as he said the weight was all right—but Mr. S. threw it in, and finding it some eight pounds heavier, offered to take back a part of the contents. The customer however concluded that he would take the whole, and so to save exposure paid between two and three dollars for a cheese which might have been bought for twenty-five cents.

From *Yankee Storekeeper,* by R. E. Gould, p. 124. Copyright, 1946, by Curtis Publishing Co. and R. E. Gould. New York and London: Whittlesey House, McGraw-Hill Book Company, Inc.

From *Rambles about Portsmouth,* Second Series. Sketches of Persons, Localities and Incidents of Two Centuries: Principally from Tradition and Unpublished Documents, by Charles W. Brewster, p. 131, with a Biographical Sketch of the Author, by Wm. H. Y. Hackett. Entered according to Act of Congress, in the year 1869, by Lewis W. Brewster, in the Clerk's Office of the District Court of the District of New Hampshire. Portsmouth, New Hampshire.

Who Stole the Pork?

On another occasion, after missing a barrel of pork some months, a man said to him one day, Mr. Sheafe, did you ever find out who stole that pork? O yes, said Mr. S. Indeed, who was it? Nobody but you and I ever knew it was stolen: so pay for it at once, if you wish nobody else to know about it. The man paid for the pork.

A Cure for Shop-Lifting

Samuel Moses, Jr.'s shop was on the lot directly south of Mrs. Alexander Ladd's residence. On the opposite side of the street, where the Messrs. Sise's crockery ware store now is, was also an eccentric man, Mr. John Allcock, who dealt in hardware, groceries, provisions, hats, etc., as his father had on the same spot many years before him. It was John who endeavored to make a speedy sale of chalk on hand, by announcing that it would soon become scarce, as the *chalkmaker* in England was *dead*. One day as he was in his counting-room, looking in a glass which reflected the position of his customers at the counter, he saw a young lady, whom he left selecting needles, put several of them slyly in her mouth. After receiving pay for the few she exhibited, he suddenly clapped both hands against her cheeks, saying he liked to pat a pretty girl, bringing the points of the needles to the surface of the skin! It was a rash act, but was doubtless effectual in curing the girl of petty shop-lifting.

Mending the Needle

There is one little story illustrative of sailor character, which occurred in this neighborhood. A sailor once called on a female friend in the tailor's shop of Mr. Nathaniel Fernald on the east, and chanced to break the eye

---

Ibid., p. 132.

From *Rambles about Portsmouth,* Sketches of Persons, Localities, and Incidents of Two Centuries: Principally from Tradition and Unpublished Documents, by Charles W. Brewster, pp. 185–186. Entered according to Act of Congress, in the year 1859, by C. W. Brewster & Son, in the Clerk's Office of the District Court of the District of New Hampshire. Portsmouth, New Hampshire.

From *Rambles about Portsmouth,* Second Series, Sketches of Persons, Localities and Incidents of Two Centuries: Principally from Tradition and Unpublished Documents, by Charles W. Brewster, pp. 217–218, with a Biographical Sketch of the Author, by Wm. H. Y. Hackett. Entered according to Act of Congress, in the year 1869, by Lewis W. Brewster, in the Clerk's Office of the District Court of the District of New Hampshire. Portsmouth, New Hampshire.

of a needle. He made inquiry where he could have it mended, and was pointed over the way to the blacksmith shop of a wag named George Plaisted, who was asked if he could do the job. Plaisted looked at it, pronounced it rather difficult, but thought it might be done for ten cents. So he sent George Beck to the next shop for a cent's worth of needles, blued the eye of one of them over the fire, rubbed it, and handed it over to the tar. He examined it, said it could not have been done better in England, paid the price and half a pint of rum for his skill, and restored the needle to its owner. The little story has been so often told, we think it has enough of interest now to have a locality.

Hoist With His Own Petard

At Norwalk a comb-maker, more alive to interest than principle, hinted one day to John as follows:—

"John, a good many horns for country comb-makers come on sloops and are stored in the warehouse of Munson, Hoyt, and Co., on the dock. Now, if you can manage to 'hook' some occasionally I'll give you a shilling apiece for 'em."

This was less than half their value, but to John it would be clear profit on the proposed investment. So the next night he brought four fine ox-horns and received a half-dollar. The night following he brought four more. The comb-maker cautioned him not to get caught, and John promised to be careful. Night after night, for weeks, Haight brought horns, and regularly received the proceeds of his plunder. One night John brought a dozen horns in one lot and demanded three dollars.

"They are larger than any I have before hooked, and are worth three times what I ask for them," said John.

The astonished comb-maker looked at them and exclaimed:—

"Why, these are the largest and finest Spanish horns! Where did you get them?"

"At the storehouse on the wharf, of course," John replied.

"Well, I'll give you two dollars on account, and tomorrow I'll go down to the storehouse and examine the lot."

John pocketed the two dollars; but it was the last money he earned in that way. For, next morning, the comb-maker discovered that there were no such horns in the warehouse, and made another discovery that he had paid John Haight more than one hundred dollars for stealing horns from the pile in his own back shop, and bringing them to the front door to sell to their owner!

From *Funny Stories,* Told by Phineas T. Barnum, pp. 18–19. Copyright, 1890, by Phineas T. Barnum. New York, London, Glasgow, and Manchester: George Routledge and Sons, Limited.

Asking the Lord

An old woman, one Hepsibah Brewer, lived in one of his [Samuel Arnold's] buildings, and was a frequent object of his charity. One day she came into his store, in a hurry, and said: "Uncle Sam, I want a cod-fish." "Go and get it then," said he. She started for his back room, and he cried out,—"Not there! not there! I've no cod-fish for you!" "Yes, you have got cod-fish, too, and I want one. It's late!" "Well," said he, "I think we'll ask the Lord about it." "Now, Mr. Arnold, what do you want to be so foolish for? I'm in a hurry for it." "Very well; if you can't wait on the Lord, go where you can do better! But, Hepsy, no prayer, no cod-fish!" Aunt Hepsy threw herself down upon her aged knees, exclaiming, in no very reverential tones, "If you want to pray, pray then!" Uncle Sam knelt down beside her, and his prayer ran in this wise: "O, Lord, here is Hepsy again after another fish! It seems to us, you know, that she comes rather often! But I don't know that we had not better let her have one this time, as she seems to be in a hurry, and the next time she must go to 'Lijah's or some of the neighbors." As he arose from his knees, he said, "Well, Hepsy, the Lord says you may have some fish; but don't take the whole ones; pick out the broken fish; they are just as good for you, and they don't sell as well."

Store Justice

The old "Red Store" was a favorite gathering place for the men folk each evening. For entertainment a story had to be told or a song sung or a jig danced; otherwise a penalty was exacted. Either a drink had to be purchased for the crowd or the man himself was forced to take a long drink of salt and water. One of the habitués liked snuff very much but did not like to buy his own. He learned where the snuff was kept in the store and upon coming in usually helped himself from the jar. The owner of the store got tired of this, and so one night he filled the jar with molasses drippings and tipped off the rest of the assembled crowd. They were talking and laughing as per usual when this man arrived, and he walked over and stuck his arm into the jar nearly up to his elbow, for the snuff jar had

From *The Westfield Jubilee:* A Report of the Celebration at Westfield, Mass., on the Two Hundredth Anniversary of the Incorporation of the Town, October 6, 1869, with the Historical Address of the Hon. William G. Bates, and other Speeches and Poems of the Occasion, with an Appendix, Containing Historical Documents of Local Interest, pp. 195–196. Westfield, Massachusetts: Clark & Story, Publishers. 1870.

From "Littleton," by Ola G. Veazie. Manuscripts of the Federal Writers' Project of the Works Progress Administration for the State of New Hampshire.

been nearly empty. A roar from the group nettled him so that he did not join them again for a long time.

Another storekeeper sold one of his regular customers a "white oak" cheese for a new milk cheese and then made it up to him by selling him a razor that would not cut, charging him $1.50 for it. This case received a mock-trial by the gang around the store, and the case was decided against the plaintiff on the ground that, having known the storekeeper for a great many years, he should have known better than to have trusted him in the first place and therefore ought to suffer the consequences.

Hazing New Clerks

THERE was fun in the old store, though. The old man never remonstrated so long as customers were not inconvenienced. One gag was to give a new clerk a hammer and nail, and point out a post where he was to drive the nail to hang his coat on. One swat with the hammer revealed that the post was iron, and it would ring about fifteen minutes. I'd been there about four days when I came back and found my frock pockets full of lard, a discovery that amused the older clerks more than it did me. I improved on the trick, and got revenge, by varying with some molasses.

A favorite trick was to let a new clerk take an order from a good-looking girl customer. He would be writing down the order, putting his best foot forward after the manner of his kind, and she would often be coyly assisting his maneuvers. It would look like a romance for sure, when one of the older clerks would walk by and say, in passing, "Your wife wants you to bring home a pound of butter when you come to supper." . . .

TRAVELERS AND TAVERNERS

The Rival Coach Lines

THE fare on these coaches was three dollars for the trip between Providence and Boston. This exorbitant sum was a sore annoyance to all thrifty men, and indignantly did they rail and protest against it. At last a union was formed, and a line of rival coaches was established, on which the fare

---

From *Yankee Storekeeper*, by R. E. Gould, pp. 34–35. Copyright, 1946, by Curtis Publishing Co. and R. E. Gould, New York and London: Whittlesey House, McGraw-Hill Book Company, Inc.

From *Customs and Fashions in Old New England*, by Alice Morse Earle, pp. 211–212. Copyright, 1893, by Charles Scribner's Sons. New York.

was to be two dollars and a half a trip. This caused great dismay to the regular coach company, who at once reduced their fare to two dollars. The rival line, not to be outdone, announced their reduction to a dollar and a half. The regulars then widely advertised that their fare would thenceforth be only one dollar. The rivals then sold seats for the trip for fifty cents apiece; and in despair, after jealously watching for weeks the crowded coaches of the new line, the conquered old line mournfully announced that they would make trips every day with their vehicle filled with the first applicants who chanced to be on time at the starting-place, and that these lucky dogs would be carried for nothing.

The new stage-coaches were now in their turn deserted, and the proprietors pondered for a week trying to invent some way to still further cut down the entirely vanished rates. They at last placarded the taverns with announcements that they would not only carry their patrons free of expense, but would give each traveller on their coaches a good dinner at the end of his journey. The old coach-line was rich and at once counter-advised a free dinner and a good bottle of wine too, to its patrons—and there, for a time, the fierce controversy came to a standstill, both lines having crowded trips each day.

Mr. Shaffer, who was a fashionable teacher of dancing and deportment in Boston, and a well-known "man about town," a jolly good fellow, got upon the Providence coach one Monday morning in Boston, had a gay ride to Providence and a good dinner and bottle of wine at the end of the journey, all at the expense of the coach company. On Tuesday he rode more gayly still back to Boston, had his dinner and his wine, and was up on Wednesday morning to mount the Providence coach for the third ride and dinner and bottle. He returned to Boston on Thursday in the same manner. On Friday the fame of his cheap fun was thoroughly noised all over Boston, and he collected a crowd of gay young sparks who much enjoyed their frolicking ride and the fine Providence dinners and wine. All returned in high spirits with Shaffer to Boston on Saturday to meet the sad, sad news that the rival coach lines had made a compromise and had both signed a contract to carry passengers thereafter for two dollars a trip.

A Good Trade

"UNCLE" Lyman Upham used to tell of going to Boston with a load of pork and taking some dressed poultry also. On his way he stopped at a tavern, and sold a turkey for fifty cents. On his return, he stopped at the

From Historical Celebration of the Town of Brimfield, Hampden County, Mass., Wednesday, October 11, 1876, with the Historical Address of Rev. Charles M. Hyde, D.D. and Other Addresses, Letters, Documents, etc., Relating to the Early History of the Town. Published by Vote of the Town. Springfield, Massachusetts: The Clark W. Bryan Co., Printers. 1879.

same tavern, needing dinner a little in advance of the regular hour. The same turkey, stuffed and roasted, was set before him. Riding always gives one a good appetite, and "Uncle" Lyman soon left nothing but bones. He paid fifty cents for his dinner, and thought that for once in his life he had got the best of a bargain.

I'll Thank You for It

WELL, one night a wayfarer came along to A. Nourse's house and asked to be put up. As they sat around the fire the subject of gratitude came up. "I tell you," says Nourse, "the words, 'I thank you,' are worth 12½ cents. 'I thank you kindly' are worth 25 cents. 'I thank you very, very kindly' are worth 37½ cents." The next morn as the stranger started to go on his way, old gentleman Nourse cried, "Twenty-five cents, if you please." "Sir!" smiled the traveller, "for your hospitality I thank you. For your bed and board I thank you very, very kindly and—" "Hold!" cried his host, "I'm in your debt already. Say no more, but get you gone quickly or I'll be bankrupt." [1]

I just remember a sort of half-witted man, who straggled about Danbury and Bethel, when I was a boy, and who was called "General" Hubbard. He was a good-natured, easy-going fellow, who, notwithstanding his lack of brains, sometimes made a witty remark. He dressed in an old military suit of clothes with a cocked hat which a general in the Revolutionary War had presented to him. He was a favorite with everybody who would joke with him or extend to him any favors he might want in the way of food, clothing, &c. One day "General" Hubbard called upon Major Hickok, who carried on the business of shoemaking, and asked him whether he would sole his boots for him. "Oh, yes," replied the major, "with pleasure." So Hubbard put off his boots, handed them to a couple of workmen, and waited until they were finished. When he had drawn the boots on his feet again he rose, and making a graceful bow to Major Hickok, said, "I am very much obleeged to you, major." "Oh, that's more than I ask!" said the major. "I only ask two shillings, and 'very much obliged' is two shillings, and sixpence." "I will take the rest in cider!" said the "General." The cider was forthcoming, and the bill was settled in that way.[2]

---

[1] From Historical Reminiscences of the Early Times in Marlborough, Massachusetts, and Prominent Events from 1360 to 1910, Including Brief Allusions to Many Individuals and an Account of the Celebration of the Two Hundred and Fiftieth Anniversary of the Incorporation of the Town, by Ella A. Bigelow, p. 174. Copyright, 1910, by City of Marlborough. Marlborough, Massachusetts: Times Publishing Company.

[2] From *Funny Stories,* Told by Phineas T. Barnum, p. 34. Copyright, 1890, by Phineas T. Barnum. New York, London, Glasgow, and Manchester: George Routledge and Sons, Limited.

The Unwilling Guest

. . . Chet Cadwell . . . used to run the Mansion House tavern times. One evenin' in February, a city feller driv in an' took lodgin's fur the night.

"I've gut to leave airly in the mornin'," says he.

"How airly?" says Chet.

"Four o'clock," says the feller. "Not a minute later." Wal, Chet set up all night an' kept a fire goin'. At half past three exactly, he had a big breakfast ready o' pounded steak, fried pertaters, pie, johnny cake, an' fixin's—an' called the feller. Wal', it had been an awful cold night an' frost was a cracklin' an' the feller says, "I guess I'll change my mind an' not git up."

"I guess you won't," says Chet. "You'll git up an' have your breakfast."

The feller begged off fur all he was wuth.

"Can't I stay on with ye," says he, "an' take things reg'lar?"

"I don't care what ye do," says Chet, "arter you've had your breakfast."

Chet made the feller git up and eat that breakfast an' charged him thutty-five cents fur it.

Outstaying His Welcome

We must not omit an anecdote, respecting one of the Deweys, who removed to the Black River country, and who was accustomed to come down every fall or winter, and spend the gloomy months—gloomy to him in Lewis county—with his well-to-do relations. After a somewhat prolonged stay, he was surprised, one morning, to see his host, in the corner, crying. "Why cousin Tim," said he, "what ails you?" The host replied,—"You'll never come down to see me any more!" "O yes I will, cousin Tim; I'll surely come down next fall!" "No you won't! Something tells me you *won't*!" "Nonsense," said the visitor; "why do you think so? What has put such a notion into you head? Haven't we *always* come down, and spent the winter with ye? Come, cheer up, cousin Tim! cheer up, and tell me what makes you think so." The grieved host blew his nose, wiped his eyes, and turning his solemn face to his sympathizing guest, said—" 'Cause you'll never go away!" The hint was not given in vain.

From *Bubblin's an' B'ilin's at the Center,* by Merle Dixon Graves, p. 71. Copyright, 1934, by Merle Dixon Graves. Rutland, Vermont: The Tuttle Company.

From *The Westfield Jubilee:* A Report of the Celebration at Westfield, Mass., on the Two Hundredth Anniversary of the Incorporation of the Town, October 6, 1869, with the Historical Address of the Hon. William G. Bates, and other Speeches and Poems of the Occasion, with an Appendix, Containing Historical Documents of Local Interest, p. 200. Westfield, Massachusetts: Clark & Story, Publishers. 1870.

Cape Cod Humor

RETURNING late one night from a long and hard day's fishing, Cleveland lost his way in the woods, and became a victim of Cape Cod humor. A heavy rain finally forced him to seek shelter at a lonely house in a clearing, and upon knocking at the door, an occupant above asked him what he wanted. "I want to stay here tonight," requested the President. "Well, stay there," replied the voice in the darkness.[1]

Daniel Webster went shooting one fall along the Scusset marshes, and when it grew dark the inn where he was stopping seemed very far away. He walked for miles—cold and hungry—until he came to a farmhouse. It was a raw night and the family had gone to bed. Webster pounded on the door, and at last a window was raised, and a man's voice asked,

"What do you want?"

"I want to stay here all night."

"All right—stay there." And down went the window.[2]

The Jesting Traveler

LONE travellers often sought the companionship of the "post rider," feeling sure of good company, and a safe guidance in unmarked ways. Riding one dark night between Springfield and Hartford, with a jolly companion, the "postman" was much to his disgust called upon to wait, while his companion rode up to the door of a house beside the road, and with his whip pounded on the door, shouting "Hallo! the house!" Soon a night-capped head appeared at an upper window, and answered the call. The joker says, "Have you lost a knife?" "No, have you found one?" "No, but I didn't know but I should."

[1] From *Cape Cod Ahoy!* A Travel Book for the Summer Visitor, by Arthur Wilson Tarbell, p. 51. Copyright, 1932, by Arthur Wilson Tarbell. Boston: A. T. Ramsay & Company.

[2] From *And This Is Cape Cod!* by Eleanor Early, p. 3. Copyright, 1936, by Eleanor Early. Boston and New York: Houghton Mifflin Company.

From *History of Greenfield,* Shire Town of Franklin County, Massachusetts (1682–1900), by Francis M. Thompson, Vol. II, p. 978. Entered according to an Act of Congress in the year 1904 by Francis M. Thompson, in the office of the Librarian of Congress at Washington. Greenfield, Massachusetts: Press of T. Morey and Son.

The Projecting Oven

THE oven projected out on the west side of the house. I am not aware that there is a single specimen of these old chimneys and projecting ovens now remaining in this County. Mr. Oris Bacon's was the last I recollect in Barnstable. A man passing a house of this construction, and thinking to pass a good joke on the lady thereof, knocked at the door; on her appearance, he said: "Madam, do you know your oven has got out of doors?" She replied, "Will you have the kindness to bring it in, it is too hot for me to handle?"

The Squire and the Peddler

. . . I WILL just here say for the benefit of such readers as may not be acquainted with the reach of ground that was some fifty years ago called Apple Tree Plain, that it lies a little south-east of the narrow causeway that passes over a western arm of the Peace Dale mill-pond on which the late Hon. Elisha R. Potter once chanced to meet a pedlar with his tin cart near the centre of the causeway. It being impossible to pass each other, and neither party seeming disposed to back out, Mr. Potter took a newspaper from his pocket and settled himself back in his seat as if he had the design of staying until the pedlar gave ground to him. After continuing to read for an hour or so, the pedlar at length broke silence and commenced conversation by ejaculating in an interrogatory tone, "I say, Squire?" "Well," said Mr. Potter, "what have you got to propose?" "Nothing," replied the pedlar, "only to remark that when your honor has committed that newspaper to heart, you will please allow me a chance to peruse it!" Mr. Potter thought it was no use to contend with such a customer and so backed his horse to the other end of the causeway and let the pedlar pass on his way.

From *Genealogical Notes of Barnstable Families,* Being a Reprint of the Amos Otis Papers, Originally Published in The Barnstable Patriot, revised by C. F. Swift, Largely from Notes Made by the Author, Vol. I, p. 490 n. Entered according to Act of Congress, in the year 1885, by F. B. Goss, in the office of the Librarian of Congress, at Washington. Barnstable, Mass.: F. B. & F. P. Goss, Publishers and Printers. 1888.

From *The Jonny-Cake Papers of "Shepherd Tom,"* Together With Reminiscences of Narragansett Schools of Former Days, by Thomas Robinson Hazard, With a Biographical Sketch and Notes by Rowland Gibson Hazard, p. 82. Copyright, 1915, by Rowland G. Hazard. Boston: Printed for the Subscribers.

Borrowing a Horse

A YANKEE, performing a journey through the back countries on foot, saw two horses in a field as he passed along, one of which he determined to borrow for a few miles, as he was feeling very weary. Accordingly, writing in pencil on a slip of paper that he would leave the beast at the next town on the road, he tied the note to one horse's fetlock, and, mounting the other, with merely a halter for a bridle, rode off with him. This transaction happening to be observed, an alarm was given to the owner of the animals, who, saddling the remaining one, without paying any attention to the note attached to its leg, rode away after the unknown borrower, or, as he considered him, perhaps, thief. Unluckily for the Yankee, he was mounted on a slow traveler compared with the steed he had left behind, and he soon descried with some consternation a rider behind urging a powerful beast along the road at full speed, evidently in pursuit of him. Having neither whip nor spur, he found it a difficult matter to impel the horse he rode beyond its usual pace, and his pursuer, therefore, had every chance of coming up with him directly. At this moment he perceived a cottage by the roadside at no great distance, towards which, by blows and kicks, he urged his steed somewhat faster, the farmer gaining on him nevertheless at every step. Reaching the door, he dismounted, and went in. The farmer, riding up immediately after in a tremendous passion, threw himself off his horse, leaving it by the side of its fellow, and ran into the cottage to seize and secure the thief. The Yankee, however, was prepared for him. Having slipped up-stairs, he opened the front window, which looked out upon the road, and as the farmer ran into the house let himself down outside, mounted the saddled horse, seized the other by the halter, and rode off securely with both. . . .

A Profitable Violation

. . . AS, HOWEVER, the next day was Sunday, and, according to the laws of Connecticut, it was criminal to violate Sabbath rest by putting one's self in motion, we were constrained to abide there until the Monday morning. Our host at the inn was a very communicative and humorous kind of man, not at all of a piece with the inhabitants in general, and, though obliged to submit to the laws of the place in which he lived, by no means backward in expressing his opinion of them to his customers. From this

---

From *Retrospections of America, 1797–1811*, by John Bernard, Edited from the Manuscript by Mrs. Bayle Bernard, With an Introduction, Notes, and Index by Laurence Hutton and Brander Matthews, pp. 342–343. Copyright, 1886, by Harper & Brothers. New York. 1887.

Ibid., pp. 332–333, 335–336.

oracle I gathered some further information as to the working of the famous Blue Laws. As is well known, they entirely forbade trade or travelling upon the Sabbath; so that by the letter of the law all goods bought or sold upon that day were forfeited to the state, while not, on the most urgent plea of necessity, might an animal be permitted to clink his profane hoof upon the Sabbatical stones of New Haven. From the growing spirit of commerce in the country at large, and the unlucky situation of Connecticut, which rendered it the thoroughfare for business, it was found, however, to be every day—or rather every seventh day—a more difficult task to carry these regulations into effect. Accordingly a multitude of peace-officers under the various titles of beadles, constables, and street-keepers, were posted all day in the streets and avenues, to enforce strict maintenance of that quietude which the statutes enjoined. It was their business to take care that no person appeared without-doors during "meeting time," and on the entry of a traveller into the town, immediately to stop him, lead his horse to a stable and himself to the "meeting."

* * * * *

In latter years, when beginning to find it impossible to restrain altogether the current of intercourse which flowed through their state, these puritanical worthies resolved to convert the restriction into a source of pecuniary profit, and accordingly permitted a man to pursue his journey on payment of a fine, proportioned, I believe, either to the number of his horses or of his family. A sharp-witted Yankee, returning home through Connecticut, was stopped, therefore, at a little village, and requested to pay the fine, which he consented to do if he were taken before the magistrate who was to receive it, and who was a man of great property and extensive mercantile connections. The Yankee, tearing a leaf from his pocket-book, wrote thereon a few words, and presenting it to the magistrate with the money, requested him to sign a receipt for the few shillings, in order that he might not be called on to pay the fine twice over, should he be stopped again before the morrow. So reasonable a request being unhesitatingly complied with, the traveller put the paper in his pocket and departed, apparently in no worse humor for the interruption he had encountered. About ten days afterwards, business calling the magistrate to Boston, he took occasion to step into his banker's to look over his account, when they informed him that they had duly honored his last week's draft for one hundred dollars. He stared in surprise. They produced it for him, and he immediately recognized the handwriting of the Yankee, with his signature plainly attached.

Escaping the Trap

The War of 1812 put a stop to navigation and compelled all transfers to property to be made by wagons. It was said to cost six thousand dollars to transport a piece of ordnance from New York to Buffalo. A great number of teams bearing produce from Vermont and New Hampshire, and smuggled goods from Canada, passed through Andover. In the absence of mercantile news, the arrival of these wagons was announced under the head of "Horsemarine news." One of the humors of the war was an amusing parody upon the "Mariners of England" entitled the "Wagoners of Freedom," a ditty of which I can still repeat several verses. These teamsters had, however, adopted one article of the sailors' faith that was by no means acceptable to the people of Andover. They held that "there was no Sunday off soundings," and continued their progress on that day greatly to the scandal of the righteous town. It was plain that the law must be enforced, and accordingly tithing-men lay in wait on Sunday at the tavern, and at the corners of the public roads. They succeeded in stopping the heavy teams, but horsemen and light carriages slipped through their fingers. But a way was soon devised to meet this difficulty. A deacon was joined to the tithing-men the very next Sunday, and the party were put in command of the tollgate, about a mile out of the town on the road leading to Boston. It was known about the school that a trap had been set which no Sunday traveler could hope to escape, and great was the interest in waiting for a victim. At length a gentleman driving a fine horse passed along the street, and, all unconscious of his fate, proceeded towards the tollgate. The excitement was now intense, for we expected to see him brought back by the deacon in ignominious captivity. But the spectators were disappointed, for this part of the programme was not carried out. In what wonderful way the traveler had managed to elude the deacon and his guard we could not divine. The return of the party at sunset brought the explanation, and a doleful tale of depravity passed from mouth to mouth. It appeared that the gentleman had been duly stopped at the tollgate and informed that he could go no farther. But instead of showing the indignation which his captors had expected, he expressed himself as delighted to find that Andover was bent on enforcing the admirable Sunday laws, and had selected agents so prompt and capable as to preclude all chance of their evasion. "But the law, gentlemen," he went on to say, "as you well know, excepts those who travel upon errands of necessity or mercy; and I assure you that my mother is lying dead in Boston." Upon this statement the gate was reluctantly opened, and the traveler allowed to proceed.

From *Figures of the Past,* from the Leaves of Old Journals, by Josiah Quincy, New Edition, with an Introduction and Notes by M. A. DeWolfe Howe, pp. 11–13.

But no sooner was he fairly out of danger than he reined in his horse and delivered himself of these heartless words: "Good-by, Deacon; tell the busybodies of Andover that my mother is lying dead in Boston,—and you may add, if you like, that she has been lying dead there *for the last twenty years!*"

Franklin and the Oysters

IT WAS on one of these annual journeyings that Dr. Franklin happened to arrive at a tavern near New London on a cold evening, where he found every place around the blazing wood fire closely occupied. No one offering to relinquish his seat, the doctor called upon the landlord to give his horse a peck of raw oysters, which order was repeated in a more decided tone upon the host hesitating to comply with his request. The oysters were accordingly carried out by the landlord, followed by the individuals who had monopolized the seats around the fire, they all being curious to see a horse eat oysters. The landlord soon returned and told the doctor, who, by this time, was comfortably ensconced in the armchair in the warmest corner, that his horse refused to eat the oysters. "Poor, foolish beast!" said the doctor; "he don't know what is good; bring them to me, and see if I will refuse them!"

Franklin Forestalling Inquiry

THE late Dr. Franklin, in the early part of his life, followed the business of a printer, and had occasion to travel from Philadelphia to Boston. In his journey he stopped at one of their inns, the landlord of which possessed the true disposition of his countrymen, which is, to be inquisitive, even to impertinence, into the business of every stranger. The Doctor, after the fatigue of the day's travel, had set himself down to supper, when his landlord began to torment him with questions. The Doctor well knew the disposition of those people; he apprehended, that, after having answered his questions, others would come in, and go over the same ground, so he

From *Recollections of Olden Times:* Rowland Robinson of Narragansett and His Unfortunate Daughter, with Genealogies of the Robinson and Hazard Families of Rhode Island, by Thomas R. Hazard, "Shepherd Tom," in His Eighty-First and Eighty-Second Years, Also Genealogical Sketch of the Hazards of the Middle States, by Willis P. Hazard, of Westchester, Pa., p. 38. Entered according to Act of Congress, in the year 1879, by John P. Sanborn, in the office of the Librarian of Congress, at Washington, D. C. Newport, Rhode Island.

From *Weatherwise's Almanack,* for the Year of Our Lord 1797. Printed at Boston, and Sold by J. Boyle, C. Bingham, B. Larkin, Wm. Pelham, E. Larkin, J. Nancrede, J. West, J. Bumstead, and other Booksellers in Town and Country.

determined to stop him. Have you a wife, landlord? Yes, Sir. Pray let me see her. Madam was introduced with much form. How many children have you? Four, Sir. I should be happy to see them. The children were sought and introduced. How many servants have you? Two, Sir, a man and woman. Pray fetch them. When they came the Doctor asked if there were any other persons in the house; and being answered in the negative addressed them with much solemnity: My good friends, I sent for you here to give you an account of myself. My name is BENJAMIN FRANKLIN; I am a printer, of —— years of age, reside at Philadelphia, and am going from thence to Boston. I sent for you all, that if you wish for any further particulars, you may ask, and I will inform you, which done, *I flatter myself you will permit me to eat my supper in peace.*

Completing the Poem

FROM Lincoln we give the only specimen of versification obtained. For many years there resided in this town one of those eccentric beings, compounded of shiftlessness and oddity, spiced with a knack at extempore rhyming. One time, McComber, our present hero, was lounging around a new tavern, recently fitted up from an old building where meetings had been formerly held. The landlord, preferring his departure before dinner, plainly hinted his room would be better than his custom, whereupon, a waggish friend present, knowing McComber's talent, suggested that he should make a verse in honor of the new house, and the proprietor should give him a dinner. The landlord, having no objection to a poetical compliment upon his stand, consented to the arrangement; but demanded the verse before dinner. The poet claimed the dinner first. At length they compromised,—half the verse before dinner, and the other half after, and McComber at once recited,—

> There swings a sign,—'tis made of pine,
> And hangs among the trees;

Adjourning the completion till he had devoured the waiting dinner, with a facetious smile he readily repeated and concluded,—

> There swings a sign,—'tis made of pine,
> And hangs among the trees;
> This house was once a house of prayer,
> But now a den of thieves.

From "Lincoln," by James T. Gove, in *The Vermont Historical Gazetteer:* A Magazine, Embracing A History of Each Town, Civil, Ecclesiastical, Biographical and Military, edited by Abby Maria Hemenway, in Three Volumes, Vol. I, p. 49. Entered according to Act of Congress, in the year 1859, by Abby Maria Hemenway, in the Clerk's Office of the District Court of the District of Vermont. Burlington, Vermont: Published by Miss A. M. Hemenway. 1867.

The Yankee and the Stolen Spoons

In a quiet little Ohio village, many years ago, there was a tavern where the stages always changed, and the passengers expected to get breakfast. The landlord of said hotel was noted for his tricks upon travellers, who were allowed to get fairly seated at the table, when the driver would blow his horn, (after taking his horns) and sing out, "Stage ready, gentlemen"; whereupon the passengers were obliged to hurry out and take their seats, leaving a scarcely-tasted breakfast behind them for which, however, they had to fork over fifty cents. One day when the stage was approaching the house of this obliging host, a passenger said he was afraid they would not be able to get any breakfast.

"What?—how? No breakfast!" exclaimed the rest. "Don't they expect passengers to breakfast?"

"Oh, yes! they expect you to it, but not to eat it. I am under the impression that there is an understanding between the landlord and driver, that for sundry and various drinks, etc., the latter starts before you can scarcely commence eating."

"Why, wot on airth are yew talkin' 'bout? Ef yew kalkerlate I'm goin' to pay 'four ninepences' fur my breakfuss and not git the valee on't, you are mistakin'!" said a voice from the back seat, the owner of which was Hezekiah Spaulding—though "tew hum" they call him "Hez," for short. "I'm goin' to git my breakfuss here, and not pay nary thing till I dew."

"Then you'll be left."

"Not as you knows on, I won't."

"Well, we'll see," said the other, as the stage drove up to the door, and the landlord, ready to "do the hospitable," says—

"Breakfast just ready, gents! Take a wash, gents? Here's water, basins, towels and soap."

After performing their ablutions, they all proceeded to the dining-room, and commenced a fierce onslaught upon the edibles, though Hez took his time. Scarcely had they tasted their coffee, when they heard the unwelcome sound of the horn, and the driver exclaim, "Stage ready!" Up rise eight grumbling passengers, pay their fifty cents, and take their seats.

"All aboard, gents?" inquires the host.

"One missing," said they.

Proceeding to the dining-room, the host finds Hez very coolly helping himself to an immense piece of steak, the size of a horse's lip.

"You'll be left, sir! Stage is going to start!"

"Wal, I hain't got nothin' tew say agin' it!" drawls out Hez.

From *Comic Metamorphoses,* Being a Perfect Encyclopedia of Fun and Humor . . . , by Dr. W. Valentine, pp. 187–190. Entered according to an Act of Congress, in the year 1855, by Garrett & Company, in the Clerk's Office of the District Court for the Southern District of New York. New York: Dick and Fitzgerald.

"Can't wait, sir; better take your seat."

"I'll be gaul-darned ef I dew, nuther, till I've got my breakfuss! I paid for it, and I'm goin' to git the valee on't! and ef yew kalkalate I ain't, yew air mistaken."

So the stage did start, and left Hez, who continued his attack on the edibles. Biscuits, coffee, steaks, &c. &c., disappeared rapidly before the eyes of the astonished landlord.

"Say, Squire, them there cakes is 'bout eat; fetch us nuther grist on 'em. You, [to the waiter,] 'nuther cup uv that air coffee. Pass them eggs. Raise yewre own pork, Squire?—this is 'mazin' nice ham. Land about yere is tolerable cheap, Squire? Hain't got much maple timber in these parts, have ye?" and thus Hez kept quizzing the landlord, until he had made a hearty meal.

"Say, Squire, now I'm bound to conclude payin' my devowers tew this ere table, but ef yew'd jist give us a bowl o' bread and milk tew sorter top off with, I'd be much obleeged tew ye."

So out goes landlord and waiter for the bowl, milk and bread, and set them before Hez.

"Spewn, tew, ef you please?"

But no spoons could be found. Landlord was sure he had plenty of silver ones laying on the table when the stage stopped.

"Say, yew! dew yew think them passengers is going to pay yew for a breakfuss and not git *no compensashun*?"

"Ah! what! Do you think any of the passengers took them?"

"Dew I THINK! No. I don't think, but I'm sartin. Ef they air all as green as you 'bout here, I'm goin' tew locate immediately and tew wonst."

The landlord rushed out to the stable, and starts a man off after the stage, which had gone about three miles. The man overtakes the stage and says something to the driver in a low tone. He immediately turns back, and on arriving at the hotel, Hez comes to take his seat, and says—

"Heow air ye, gents? I'm rotten glad to see yew!"

"Can you point out the man you think has got the spoons?" asked the landlord.

"Pint him out? Sartinly, I ken. Say, Squire, I paid you four ninepences fur a breakfuss, and I kalkalate I GOT THE VALEE ON'T! You'll find the spoons in the coffee pot!"

Go ahead, ALL ABOARD, driver!

Shoe-Pegs Meigs

A LITTLE money might be earned by cutting heel-pegs for shoemakers. These were made of a maple trunk sawed across the grain, making the

---

From *Home Life in Colonial Days*, by Alice Morse Earle, pp. 315–316. Copyright, 1898, by The Macmillan Company. New York and London. 1919.

circular board thin enough—a half inch or so—for the correct length of the pegs. The end was then marked in parallel lines, then grooved across at right angles, then split as marked into pegs with knife and mallet. A story is told of a farmer named Meigs, who, on the winter ride to market in company with a score or more of his neighbors, stole out at night from the tavern fireside where all were gathered to the barn where the horses were put up. There he took an oat-bag out of a neighbor's sleigh and poured out a good feed for his own horse. In the morning it was found that his horse had not relished the shoe-pegs that had been put in his manger; and their telltale presence plainly pointed out the thief. These shoe-pegs were a venture of two farmer boys which their father was taking to town to sell for them, and in indignation the boys thrust on the thief the name of Shoe-pegs Meigs, which he carried to the end of his life.

PRACTICAL WAGS

The Biter Bit

SOME few years since, in the County of Penobscot, there lived a man by the name of H——, whose greatest pleasure was in tormenting others. His own family was generally the butt of his sport.

One cold and blustering night, he retired to bed at an early hour, his wife being absent at a neighbor's. Some time after, she returning, finding the door closed, she demanded admittance.

"Who are you?" cried Mr. H——.

"You know who I am. Let me in; it's very cold."

"Begone, you strolling vagabond! I want nothing of you here."

"But I must come in."

"What is your name?"

"You know my name—it is Mrs. H——."

"Begone! Mrs. H—— is a very likely woman; she never keeps such late hours as this."

Mrs. H—— replied, "If you don't let me in, I will drown myself in the well."

"Do, if you please," he replied.

She then took a log and plunged it into the well, and returned to the side of the door.

Mr. H——, hearing the noise, rushed from the house to save, as he supposed, his drowning wife. She at the same time slipped in and closed

From *The Farmer's and Mechanic's Almanac,* for the Year of Our Lord 1853. New York: Moffat's Vegetable Life Pills and Phoenix Bitters.

the door after her. Mr. H——, almost naked, in turn demanded admittance.

"Who are you?" she demanded.

"You know who I am; let me in, or I shall freeze."

"Begone, you thievish rogue! I want nothing of you here."

"But I must come in."

"What is your name?"

"You know my name—it is Mr. H——."

"Mr. H—— is a very likely man; he don't keep such late hours."

Suffice it to say, she, after keeping him in the cold until she was satisfied, opened the door and let him in.

Caught in His Own Trap

QUABBIN, like other towns, had its stormy meetings; sometimes it was the town party, and sometimes the country party that won; but in the long run justice was generally done. An instance of sharp practice may be mentioned:—

A wealthy and prominent citizen, who was a leading church-member, and vehemently disliked by the people of the outlying districts, made a motion at one meeting that the authorities be instructed to close a certain road which was little used. He said nothing in support of his motion, and preserved an impassive look. A leading man in the country party was quick to see that the mover really wanted the road kept open, as it led to his own land. This man, therefore, promptly seconded the motion, looking round keenly at his supporters in the rear of the hall. They were in full force that day, and the motion was carried by show of hands. The truth was, the mover had found that whatever he proposed was defeated, and, desiring to have this road maintained for his personal convenience, moved to discontinue it, and was caught in his own trap. It was a pity he resorted to a trick by which his influence was so much impaired; for he had been one of the most liberal and enlightened friends of the public schools, and in favor of most projects of reform..

The Hunter and the Dutchman

. . . A HUNTER in the Green Mountains took his dogs and gun and strolled off at a season when to kill deer was forbidden by the law under a heavy

From *Quabbin, The Story of a Small Town, with Outlooks upon Puritan Life,* by Francis H. Underwood, pp. 139–140. Copyright, 1892, by Lee and Shepard. Boston. 1893.

From the Historical Address of Joseph Griswold, Buckland Centennial, September 10, 1879, in *The History of Buckland, 1779–1935,* by Fannie Shaw Kendrick, with Genealogies by Lucy Cutler Kellogg, p. 225. Buckland, Massachusetts: Published by the Town of Buckland Committee. 1937.

fine. He followed his dogs who had started a deer till he found himself in a Dutchman's yard. Calling back his dogs he peeped into the barn and found the owner dressing flax. The Dutchman had just spied the deer, and he raised his swingling knife and pointing with it exclaimed, "Mine Gott, how I could shoot that deer if only I had my gun?" The hunter, overhearing this speech, fired himself, and the deer fell, when he rushed in and told the Dutchman he had caught him killing deer contrary to law. Dutchy scratched his head. Said he, "Tell you what I do; you take the deer and say nothing." So the man took it over his shoulder, whistled to his dogs, slyly picked up his gun and started for home. He had not gone far when he was shouted at to stop, and coming up to him the Dutchman laid his hand on his shoulder and said: "Mr. Hunter, who would have thought the damn old swingling knife would have gone off so!"

Filling the Bottle

Mr. Gibbon liked to tell a story, particularly that of being beaten by sharp old Sock Moores who one day entered Mr. Gibbon's little store which he "set up" near his house after moving here from Dedham, and handing over one of those large bottles having the bottom driven up through the center, called for a quart of rum. "Why, Sock, this bottle won't hold a quart," cried Mr. Gibbon. "Well, now Sam, 'twill. If it won't, I'll pay for it. If it will you shall make no charge." Agreed. The bottle was filled, and a gill or more was left in the measure. Sock took the bottle, drove the cork in, turned the bottle over and ordered the balance to be poured into the bottom. "Do you know," cried Gibbon, "there was room enough and to spare for every bit left, and I sent Sock home happy," and tilting back his chair, Mr. Gibbon would laugh and laugh.

A Yankee Sell: Poking a Hat Through a Ring

I was quite amused a short time since, at the following incident which took place in a downtown shipping office. The conversation was on betting, each person in the office relating in turn some one operation of the kind that he had some time been engaged in. Finally it came to Captain Jack, who

From *Historical Reminiscences of the Early Times in Marlborough, Massachusetts, and Prominent Events from 1860 to 1910,* Including Brief Allusions to Many Individuals and an account of the Celebration of the Two Hundred and Fiftieth Anniversary of the Incorporation of the Town, by Ella A. Bigelow, p. 25. Copyright, 1910, by City of Marlborough. Marlborough, Massachusetts: Times Publishing Company.

From *Comic Metamorphoses,* Being a Perfect Encyclopedia of Fun and Humor, . . . by Dr. W. Valentine, pp. 267–268. Entered according to an Act of Congress, in the year 1855, by Garrett & Company, in the Clerk's Office of the District Court for the Southern District of New York. New York: Dick and Fitzgerald.

opened, by saying, "That he never made a bet of any consequence, or did not recollect one just now—but would bet any one in the room five dollars that he would poke that hat [pointing to one] through a ring which he had on his first finger, and not injure the hat."

"That can't be did, no how," said some one in the room.

"Will you bet?" asked the captain.

"I don't care if I do," said number two, his eyes glistening at the prospect of making five dollars on such a "sure thing," as he termed it.

The money was deposited, and all hands gathered around to see some one "did brown." Capt. Jack slowly takes off the ring, and passes it round to show that all is fair. Every one is satisfied. Then he deliberately wipes and polishes the inside, and announces that he is ready.—Number two advances to the "pile" to be in readiness. Now the captain holds the ring between his fore finger and thumb, and marches towards the hat, holding the ring an inch from it; he ran his small finger through the ring, which struck the hat and won him the bet, as he had "poked the hat through the ring."

All turned to see how number two enjoyed it, but the tails of a coat disappearing through the doorway told the story.

How Samuel Moses, Jr., Raised a Treat

One morning the change was short, and the means for a treat with a friend did not appear at hand. There was hanging in the shop a fresh cod fish for dinner. He told his companion to retire, and to return after he saw the next person enter, and to call it a *cusk*. Mr. Hill, soon coming in to get shaved, remarked to Mr. Moses, "This is a fine cod." "Cod—cod! why sir, that is a cusk!" "No, it's certainly a cod." "A bottle of spirit on it," said Mr. Moses, "and we will leave it to the first man who comes in." "Agreed," said Mr. Hill, confident in his correctness. Now enters the companion, as though it was his first appearance, wishing them good morning. "What fish is this?" asked Mr. Moses. "This is a cusk—and capital eating it is too." The treat was paid by Mr. Hill, and the joke as well as the spirit was enjoyed by the confederates.

Curing a Man of Stealing Wood

In a hard and long winter, when wood was very scarce in Boston, a man gave him [Governor Winthrop] private information that a needy person in

From *Rambles about Portsmouth*, Sketches of Persons, Localities, and Incidents of Two Centuries: Principally from Tradition and Unpublished Documents, by Charles W. Brewster, pp. 184–185. Entered according to Act of Congress, in the year 1859, by C. W. Brewster & Son, in the Clerk's Office of the District Court of the District of New Hampshire. Portsmouth, New Hampshire.

the neighborhood sometimes stole wood from his pile; upon which the governor, in a seeming anger, replied, *Does he so? I'll take a course with him; go, call that man to me; I'll warrant you, I'll cure him of stealing.* When the man came, the governor, considering that if he had stolen, it was more out of necessity than disposition, said to him, *Friend, it is a severe winter, and I doubt you are but meanly provided with wood; wherefore I would have you supply yourself at my wood-pile, till this cold season be over.* And he then merrily asked his friends *whether he had not effectually cured this man of stealing his wood?* [1]

In the neighborhood of Hinsdale lived an easy-going individual, who found it less troublesome to borrow wood from the schoolhouse pile, already chopped by the boys, than to chop his own wood. The larger boys soon suspected who was taking such an interest in their wood pile, and they determined to fix the old gentleman. Accordingly, they bored holes in a few of the larger sticks, filled them with powder, and drove in tightly fitting wooden plugs. This scheme worked to perfection. The old gentleman got some of the loaded sticks that very night and put them on his fire under a boiling pot. When the explosion came, it is said that the pot shot up through the great chimney flue into the clear sky and landed on top of the barn.[2]

Piling the Wood

Dr. Beecher held his big family together in a fabulous solidarity of love for him. Nevertheless, he had trouble getting his battalion of strong sons to pile the wood which the parish supplied. At length he resorted to a low stratagem. He had an annual, spring contest with a New Haven minister as to who could produce the first cucumbers in his cold frame. This was the sort of thing in which the family would present an unbreakably united front to the enemy. Dr. Beecher instructed those parishioners who drew in his wood to dump it on top of the cold frames where the cucumbers were to grow. Then, at cucumber planting time, he would discover the location of the wood, to his dismay. Instantly the whole family—including the

---

[1] From *The Early History of New England,* Illustrated by Numerous Interesting Incidents, by Rev. Henry White, p. 299. Entered according to an Act of Congress, in the year 1841, by Rev. Henry White, in the Clerk's Office of the District Court of New Hampshire. Boston: Sanborn, Carter, Bazin & Co. [n. d.]

[2] By T. J. Winn, Jr. Manuscripts of the Federal Writers' Project of the Works Progress Administration for the State of New Hampshire.

From *The Housatonic,* Puritan River, by Chard Powers Smith, p. 228. Copyright, 1946, by Chard Powers Smith. New York and Toronto: Rinehart & Company, Incorporated.

girls, who were forbidden to do it—flew at the wood and had it piled in a few hours.

The Elder and the Rum

. . . WHEN in Sandwich the men of one church clubbed together to buy a hogshead of rum and, on its arrival from the coast, left it in the church shed for the night, all through his long sermon next day the presiding elder smiled to himself, for one by one the men in the church went softly out but soon returned coughing and with looks of alarm. The elder on the night before had secretly broached the hogshead and replaced the rum with water and beet juice and enough pepper to make it hot. For the good of his friends he had transferred the original rum in casks to his cellar and so made the sin they had planned his own!

Doctor Hillman's Prescription

WHEN old Doctor Hillman called on a patient and left some medicine he'd say: "If the dose I've prescribed doesn't have any effect take a double dose. Then you'll either be better or worse, or you'll be about the same."

Joe Marsh Taken In

ONE cold day, Joe sat by his warm bar-room stove, indulging at once his indolence and literary taste—the former in the natural way, and the latter in reading a History of Napoleon.

Joe read a page or two, when he yielded to a desire to sleep. Some of those roguish boys (of which Bennington has not a few), who were making Joe one of their regular calls, conceived the idea of turning back the leaves to where he first commenced. Joe wakes up in the process of time, and renews his reading; reads as far as it continues interesting, when he again

---

From *The Great White Hills of New Hampshire,* by Ernest Poole, p. 129. Copyright, 1946, by Ernest Poole. Garden City, New York: Doubleday & Company, Inc.

From *Highways and Byways of New England,* Including the States of Massachusetts, New Hampshire, Rhode Island, Connecticut, Vermont and Maine, Written and Illustrated by Clifton Johnson, p. 295. Copyright, 1915, by The Macmillan Company. New York and London. 1916.

From *Wit and Humor,* A Choice Collection, by Marshall Brown, pp. 257–258. Entered according to the Act of Congress, in the year 1877, by Marshall Brown and J. W. Kreps, in the office of the Librarian of Congress, at Washington. Copyright, 1879, by S. C. Griggs and Company. Chicago.

falls asleep, and the boys turn back the leaves as before. This is repeated *four* times, when a bright idea effectually wakes Joe up.

"Gosh, boys! that Napoleon's the smartest feller ever lived; *crossed the Alps four times in one day, and dragged a heavy cannon after him*!"

To his bar he adds a store of candies, in which the boys invest all the cents and eggs, etc., they can hook for the purpose of trade. Joe winks at their wickedness, and puts their pilferings into his till. One evening a big boy brought in a hen and sold it to Joe for a pound of candy. Joe gave him the candy, and told him to put the hen in the barn, which he did. Soon another boy, encouraged by the success, brought in a hen, and got the same price, and this set the thing going—the boys always carrying the hen to the barn at Joe's direction. In the morning he found he had been sold badly, having bought the same hen six times, and one of his own at that!

Plupy: A New Hampshire Boy of the Sixties

Church Sociable

December 19 [, 186–]. Cold as time. Went to a sosiable tonite at the Unitarial vestry. cant go again becaus Keene told mother i was impident to the people. i want impident. you see they was making poetry and all sitting around the vestry. they wanted to play copenhagin and post office and clap in and clap out, but Mister Erl woodent let them because it was in church. so they had to play poetry. one person wood give a word and then the oppisite person wood give a word that rimed with it. it was auful silly. a girl wood give the word direxion and then a stewdcat wood say affexion and waul his eyes towards the girl. and then another wood say miss, and another stewdcat wood say kiss and then he wood waul his eyes, and when it came my turn i said what rimes with jellycake, and the girls turned red and the stewdcats looked funny, and Mister Burley said if i coodent behave i had better go home. Keene needent have told mother anyway. You jest wait Keene, and see what will happen some day.

A Cure for Warts

April 2. been trying to get rid of some warts. Pewt says if you hook a piece of pork after dark, rub it on the warts and say arum erum irum orum urum and nurum 3 times turn round twice and throw the pork thru a

From *The Real Diary of a Real Boy*, by Henry A. Shute, pp. 20–21, 76–80, 146–149. Copyright, 1902, 1903, by Henry A. Shute; 1906, by The Everett Press Co. Chicago: The Reilly & Lee Co. Also from *"Sequil"* or Things Whitch Aint Finished in the First, by Henry A. Shute, pp. 18–21, 30–37, 37–39, 45–46, 56–57, 69–74, 86–87, 117–122, 127–130. Copyright, 1904, by Henry A. Shute. Entered at Stationers' Hall. Boston, Massachusetts: Published by The Everett Press.

window, then the warts will all be gone the next day. me and Beany is going to try it tomorrow.

* * * * *

April 6. dident wright anything last nite, was too scart. i never was so scart in all my life before. me and Beany came awful near getting in jale. we dident know where to hook the pork. i went to our cellar but father was down there making vinigar all the evening, then we went to Beanys cellar but Mister Watson was sitting on the cellar door. so Beany told his father that a man was looking for him to see about a horse and Mister Watson started down to the club stable. then Beany hooked the pork and rubbed it over his warts and then i rubbed it over my warts and we said arum erum irum orum urum and nurum 3 times jest as Pewt said, turned round twice and i plugged the pork right threw a gaslite jest then the gasman came along, he yelled at us and jumped out of his wagon and went for us. we ran down threw the school yard as fast as we cood hiper. there is a hollow in the corner of the school yard by Bill Morrills back yard and there is a little hole in the bottom of the fence where the fellers crawl threw when the football goes into his garden. we skinned threw that hole jest in time. the gasman tried to crawl threw but he coodent, then he clim the high fence but while he was doing that we ran across the carrige factory yard and down by the old brewery up Bow street and home. i went to bed pretty lively and so did Beany. gosh but we was scart.

April 7. One of Beanys warts has gone.

April 8. brite and fair. my warts have not gone.

April 9. brite and fair. my warts have not gone.

April 10. clowdy but no rane. my warts have not gone.

April 11. rany. i have got 2 more warts. i gess i hadent ought to have broke that gasiite.

April 12. i have got another.

Lead the Old Blind Horse

Aug. 3, 186– brite and fair. the fellers played a pretty mean trick on me tonite. they played it on Nibby Hartwell last nite. Nibby is visiting his aunt and comes from the city and is pretty green like most folks from the city. you see if i hadent got sent to bed becaus Cele told on me i wood have been there and seen them play it on Nibby. well last nite all the fellers was out. Whack and Boog and Pozzy and Pewt and Beany and Nipper and Cawcaw and Pile and Chick and Micky and Pricilla and Fatty. Nibby he was there too. they wanted to play lead the old blind horse to water and i was to be the blind horse. they said they had some fun playing it the nite before, that was when they played it on Nibby but I dident know that. Well you blindfole a feller and give him a rope and a swich and the other fellers get on the other end of the rope and the feller nearest you has a bell and rings it and you pull and if you can pull him up to you, you can paist time out of him with your swich, only if you pull off your blindfole all the fellers can paist time out of you. well they blindfoled me and hollered ready and i began to yank and pull and the feller rung his bell and he came pretty hard at first but i kept yanking and bimeby he come so quick that i nearly fell over back wards and i felt him and grabed him and began to paist time out of him when he grabed away my swich and began to paist me, and that wasent fair and i pulled off my blindfole and who do you suppose it was, well it was William Perry Molton and he was mad. they had tied me to his door bell and i had yanked out almost ten feet of wire. when i saw who it was gosh i began to holler and he stoped licking me. i gess he never licked anyone before becaus he dident know just how to lay it on. well when he found out how it was he let me go but he said he shood have to do something about the boys distirbing him so. it was a pretty mean trick to play on a feller. we are going to try and play it on Pop Clark tomorrow nite.

A Horse Trade

Sept. 28. Rany as time. father has sold Nelly to old Si Smith. she was lame in her hind leg and when she stands in the stable she holds her hind leg up in the air all the time, and when she goes out she limps auful but after she goes a whil she aint lame. so last nite father hitched her up and took me and we drove over to Wire Shaws in Kensington and when we came back he took out the whip and hit her under the belly with it 2 times and you aught to see her go. when we came to old Si Smiths she was going like old Billy Robinsons troter. then father turned round and drove up to Sis and old Si and Shep Hodgden and Gimmy Biddle and Charles Fifield was there and father said this will make jest the horse you want for your store and old Si said she aint biger than a rat and father said i gess she is big enuf to carry out all your lodes unless you put down your price, and then they all laffed at Si, and then Si said she was a puller and father said what do you want Josiar one that you have to push, and then they laffed agen and when father called him Josiar i know Si had better look out for when father calls me Henry i know i am in for a liking. then Si said she is lame in every leg and father said you get in here and drive her and if she goes a lame step i will give her to you, and old Si said to Shep and Gimmy you get in and drive her and they got in and drove off and father said he wood take 50 dolars for her and old Si said he wood give 35 dolars for her and they talked and talked and then Shep and Gimmy came back and said she went all rite and old Si said he wood give father 40 dolars and father said she was worth 50 but as Si was a nabor he wood like to acomodate him. well old Si was counting out the money when he said he bet she was a kicker father said she is kind as a kitten and dont bite or kick dont she Harry and i said she cant kick becaus she always holds up one leg in the stall, and old Si said whats that and i told him how she coodent kick becaus she held up one leg, and then Gimmy and Shep and Charlie Fifield and old Mister Page all laffed and hollered and stamped round and slaped their legs and said that is a good one, and old Si stoped counting his money and swore aufully and father looked auful mad for a minit and then he said she is wirth every cent of 50 dolars and asked Si what he wood give and Si said 15 dolars and they talked and talked and after a while he give father 25 dolars. then we went home and father looked prety mad. i dident know what i had done but when we got home he said Harry you go to bed, so i went up about scart to deth but by and by i crep to the stairs and lissened and he was telling about it to mother and he said if he had sence enuf not to ask me about it he cood had got 15 dolars more out of old Si and he was mad enuf to lick me, and then he began to laff and mother laffed and said it served you jest rite George to try and cheet a old man, and father said Nelly was wirth 50 dolars and the last baril of flour that Si sold him was older then Methooselas gread granfather and he wood have got square with Si if it hadent been for that boy. well mother said you cant whip him for telling the truth and father said thunder no i aint going to lick him but i was mad enuf to. so i felt prety good and crep back to bed.

The Ministers' Visit

Oct. 16, 186– today the hole town was full of ministers, most of them had long tailed coats and white necktis. Deekon Gooch came down to the house with 2 of them. aunt Sarah was wating in her best dress and when she saw them coming she said Murder Joanna they is 2 of them, what shall we do, and mother said, mercy sakes what will George say. well the bell rung and i went to the door and asked them in and Deekon Gooch said they was Mister Fernald and Mister Robinson, he said they was his brothers. then Deekon he went off and i showed them to the front room up stairs and one of them asked me if i loved the lord and i said yes sir and he said i was a good boy. and then he asked me if i went to church and sunday school and i said yes sir and he asked me what was the tex last sunday and i said i dident know what tex ment and he said what did he prech from and i said he preeched from the pulpit in church and from the platform in sunday school, and Mister Fernald he began to laff and Mister Robinson he said i woodent laff if i was you brother, and then he said what does the minister say after the first prair and i said o yes i know now, he says we will now take up the usual colection and then Mister Fernald laffed again, then Mister Robinson he asked me how many sisters i had and i said 4 and he asked if they went to church and i said Keene and Cele sing in the quire and Georgie goes but Annie and Frankie and the baby was two little and then he asked if father went to church and i said not very often, only when Keene and Cele had to sing a duet, and then he asked me what else he did sundays and i said sometimes he made viniger down celler and sometimes he went over to see John Adams hens or down to Gim

Melchers shop or up to Hirum Gilmores, and he said it is very deploorible is it not, brother and Mister Fernald he laffed again and said he gessed he better not ask me any more questions, and perhaps my father woodent like to have me tell all about him, and i said father wasent afrade, and he said he dident give much for ministers ennyway and then Mister Fernald laffed as hard as he cood and Mister Robinson looked mad, then we went down stairs and they shook hands with mother and aunt Sarah and Mister Robinson he set down by aunt Sarah and asked her about the church and prair meetings a why she dident always go and lots of things like that and Mister Fernald he got the baby in his lap and he talked to mother about the children and told us stories and he was jest buly. then bimeby father he came home and he shook hands with them and he said he was glad to see them whitch was a auful lie. then mother said super was ready and we all went in to super and father kept talking and telling stories until mother said George and looked at him, and he shet up and turned red and then Mister Robinson began to pray and all of us kept still but Georgie who began to gigle, and mother looked scowly at her and she shet up two. then father looked at mother and winked and i had to put my hand over my mouth. mother she almost laffed to, and Mister Robinson he kept on praying till bimeby Frankie he said Mama i wish that man wood stop and Mister Fernald he began to coff i bet he wanted to laff. well ennyway Mister Robinson he stoped. then father helped them to chicking and bisket and gelly and coffy and everything and then he helped us and we all begun to eat and bimeby Annie said we have got some napkins tonite, and Frankie said we have got some little plates to put the butter on, and i saw them first, and Annie said we have got some new goblets two, so there, and Frankie run his tung out at Annie and she made up a face at him, and then father told them to stop and they stoped and mother and aunt Sarah turned red and Mister Robinson he looked auful sollum and Mister Fernald looked funny and then he looked at father an begun to laff and father laffed and then we all laffed as hard as we cood, and Mister Fernald he said, dont mind a bit Missis Shute, i have got children of my own, i like Mister Fernald. after super Frankie and Annie were sent to bed and we went into the parlor and father kept us all laffing telling stories, and then Keene and Cele sung now i lay me down to sleep, and there is a bank on which the wild time grows, and Cele sung flow gently sweet Afton and Georgie sung i wood i were a fary queen, and then Mister Robinson wanted us to sing a religious song and we sung shall we gather at the river. then they asked me to sing and i said i coodent and father said before he thought, that boy is bedeviled to play a cornet, then Mister Fernald he said let him play it, it wont hurt him, then father begun to tell some more stories and kept us laffin fit to die, and Mister Fernald he said he hadent laffed so much for years, and he said, to mother, Missis Shute i gess you have a prety good natured husband, and she said yes, and father he said he most never got mad and jest then the bell rung, and Keene went to the door and said that Mister Swane the poliseman wanted to see father and father he went to the door and in a minit we herd him swaring and herd him say it is a dam lie Swane and you know it and then Swane went away and father came in and said that someone had ridden horseback over the concreek sidewalk and they tride to lay it on me. then it was bedtime and Mister Robinson he prayed some more and he prayed for those who took the name of the lord in vane, and then we went to bed.

Oct. 17. Brite and fair, the old ministers has gone. i am glad of it. i liked Mister Fernald but i hated old Robinson. i gess he wont get invited here again. this morning at brekfast he prayed again untl the brekfast was most cold and he prayed a good deal about takin the name of the lord in vane and i cood see that mother looked mad but she dident say anything. bimeby he begun to talk to mother about father having a unfortunate temper, and said his langage was shocking, and Cele she up and said, i gess my father is as good as you are and Keene stuck out her tung and mother sent them away from the table, and then old Robinson he said i am afrade your children are not well brought up, and mother looked rite at him a minit and then she said, i shood feel very badly if my children shood xcept hospitality from another person and crittisise that person to his face, at all events i cannot submit to have my husband or my children crittisised, and Mister Robinson he dident say ennymore you bet. after brekfast they went away, and Mister Fernald he shook hands with us all and he asked mother to let Cele and Keene come down to shake hands and she did. after they had went mother she gave us a peace of mince pie apeace and we all hoorayed for mother. none of us went to church today.

Greasing the Wheel

Oct. 18. brite and fair. tonite father borowed Gim Loverings horse and wagun to go riding. Gim said it aught to be greesed, so father asked me to greese the wheals, and then he said i will do it myself, and then i will be sure it will be done rite. so he got the munky rench and the lantern and some lard and went out to greese the wheals, and when he had greesed them he come in and washed his hands and then he went out and told mother not to set up for him and he unhitched the horse and hollered gitap and when the horse started one side of the wagun went down whack and out came father. well he held on to the ranes and stoped the horse and mother said what is the matter, and father said that infernal boy dident screw up the nut and the wheal come of and nearly broke my neck, and as soon as i tie this horse i will give him a good whaling and aunt Sarah said George you greesed the wheals yourself and father said by thunder so i did. then i got the lantern and we looked for the wheal and it was leaning up against the apple tree and father said jest look at that, the wheal ran up to the tree and stoped, and then we hunted round for the nut and we coodent find it and i got down on my nees and father held the lantern, and Cele and Keene came out and hunted and we coodent find it. bimeby father said he could put on the wheal and hold it on till he got back to Gims and he lifted up the ex and i went to put on the wheal and there was the nut all screwed on the ex. father had put on the nut but had forgot to put on the wheal and had left the ex resting on the jack. i gess he hadent better say mutch about me.

Making Up Poetry about the Fellows

Nov. 5. Brite and fair. i have been sick today. i gess i et two much spare rib. when i think of it it makes me sick. so i have been thinking over the poitry about the fellers. some of it is prety good.

Ed Tole fell in a hole
and coodent get out to save his sole

i made that up.

Plupy Shute
is a dirty brute.
and never will fite
if they is a chance to scoot.

Pewt he made that up.

Old Tim Calahan
he was a hell of a man.

Fatty Melcher he made that up.

Frank Hanes aint got enny branes
and dont know enuf to go in when it ranes.

Beany he made that up.

Nipper Brown tumbled down
and busted his head and cracked his crown.

i made that up too.

Granvil Miller the barber
went to shave his father
the razer sliped and cut his lip
becaus he forgot the lather.

Skinny Bruce he made that up.

i tell you they is some pretty good poits among the fellers. but any feller whitch gets poitry made up about him gets mad.

Whacking Cat's Head

Feb. 4. it snowed hard all day all the fellers are whacking cats head on each others back. you take some chorck and chorck the inside of your hand and your ferst and last finger and then you wet your fingers and make eyes and nose and mouth in your chorcky hand and then you wate til a feller comes along and then you lam him one on the back and it makes the funniest cats head on his back you ever see with eyes and nose and mouth and 2 long ears whitch your fingers made. i got 5 on my back today and i got 1 on Beany and 2 on Pewt and 1 on Pop Clark and 1 on Nipper Brown.

Exhibition Day at School

Mar. 3. Brite and fair. tomorow is exibision day. today we rehersed. Pricilla sung puling hard agenst the streem and played the organ. Potter read a composition and Nipper xplaned the sum about the hundred geese the one i never cood do. Good morow farmer with your hundred geese sir i have not a hundred but if i had as many more and half as many more and 2½ geese i shood have a hundred, how many geese had he. well Nipper can do that sum and so he has got to show of. i havent got to do ennything xcept to say my speach when old Francis gives me my prise, whitch is prety good for me.

Mar. 4. Brite and fair. i am not fealing very well tonite. father dident go to boston this morning but staid to home. this morning in school we rehersed for exibision. Pricilla sung and plaid and Nipper rote down the geese sum on the blackboard and rote his name under it jest as good as he cood. i wanted to rite Nipper under it but old Francis wood paist time out of me if he found out who rote it. you aught to hear Pricil play and sing. he sings do your best for one another making life a plesent dream, help a poor and weried brother puling hard agenst the streem, and the old organ goes boom ya, boom ya, boom ya ya ya, that is a prety song for a feller to sing whitch never will give the fellers the core of his apple but always eats it hisself. well this afternoon i put on my best close and my plad neckti and a new paper coller and went to school erly. prety soon the people begun to come in. they was old Perry Molton and old Nat Shute and Gewett Swazie the committy, and old Bil Morrill with his hair curled under behind and Chick Chickerings father and mother and doctor Goram, Nippers father and mother and Pricillas father and mother and lots of people and i thought father wasent coming but bimeby he come in with his new britches that he made Erl and Cutts give him and his boots blacked and aunt Sarah and Keene and Cele. Aunt Sarah had got her best earings and her dolman with beeds and Keene and Cele had on their bronze boots and there plad dresses and they got a seet on the platform. Keene and Cele felt prety big becaus they was in the seminary and Aunt Sarah felt prety big becaus she had on her earings and her dolman and father felt prety big becaus i was going to get a prise. well first old Francis said a prayer and everyone bowed there heads and father bowed his two but i saw him peek out under his hand. well then we all sung and Mary Emery plaid the organ. then our class resited and Nipper xplained his sum about the geese and then Potter spoke a peace and then Pricilla plaid and sung his peace. then there was a dialog and then we sung sum more. then old Francis opened his desk and took out a little riting desk and said it had been prety hard to tell whitch was the best scolar becaus they was 3 boys who were so near together. so he would give the riting desk to Arthur Goram and the glass inkstand to Johnny Brown and the stamp colecters book to Charly Hobbs. so when he give them Potter and Nipper and

Pricilla stood up and bowd and said thank you. if they had been so smart they aught to have a speach ready. ennyway i had my speach all ready. then old Francis said there was one boy who had grate talents and was a very brite boy but owing to his fondness for play had not done as well as he shood. but he had showed such talent that he aught to be menshioned espesially as he had been studying much better laitly. when old Francis said that aunt Sarah and Keene and Cele set up strate and father tride to look as if he dident know who he meant and i said my speach over soft, to be sure i had it rite. then old Francis said i have selected as a present for this boy a book, and the name of this boy is, and then he stoped a moment and i cood almost hear my heart thumping, and then he said Johnny Chickering. Gosh i had forgotten all about Chick Chickering living on Coart Street. when he said that aunt Sarah and Keene and Cele sat rite back in there chairs and father turned auful red and looked at me as if he wanted to nock my head rite of and then he droped his hat on the floor and it fell of the platform and roled way out under Medo Thirstons seet and then he blew his nose with a auful toot. then old Francis give Chick the book and then he read the names of the 10 next best scolars and my name wasent there eether. and then father looked mad enuf to bust, and Aunt Sarah and Keene and Cele looked prety sick. then we all sung happy school Ah from the never shall our hearts long time be turning, and then school was dismissed. doctor Goram and Nippers father and mother and Pricillas father and mother and Chicks father and mother and lots of the people staid to shake hands with old Francis, but father marched rite out and Aunt Sarah and the girls two. well when i got home you aught to have heard father. he said i was the laziest and most wirthless boy there ever was, and i was a disgrace to him and he sent me to bed lively. i dident want the old book ennyway.

Playing April Fools

Apr. 1. today i had a good one to get on Beany. i rung the doorbell of our house and mother came to the door and i stood there laffin and she laffed and said i am glad to see you sir because i want you to fill the woodbox and get me 5 pails of water. gosh i dident think it was so funny. at school old Francis woodent let us play april fools on each other but in the afternoon i went over to get Beany to come with me to get a 4 foot yardstick down to Lyfords. i was going to get Beany to ask for it and then they wood lam him, becaus they isent enny 4 foot yardstick. i jest laffed to think of Beany getting licked well when i asked Beany he said he wood go only his father wanted him to go down to old Kellogs harness shop to get a pint of strap oil to oil some harnes, and if i wood go with him ferst he would go with me. so i said yes and we went. jest before we got there Beany said you go in and ask for it, and i will wait becaus old Kellog dont like me very well. so i went in and old Kellog was sitting straddle of a seet with big wooden nippers on it and he was sowing on a harness and he said cross like what do you want and i said i want a pint of strap oil and he said o yes i have got some good strap oil and he got down and grabed me by the coller and took down a strap and licked me till i hollered. then he let me go and when i went out rubing my legs Beany was jest laffing fit to die and he said you thought you was prety smart old Plupy to get me to go down for a 4 foot yard stick dident you. and then he ran his tung out and run of down town. i will pay Beany for that.

Trading for a Cow

May 24. brite and fair. tonite me and father went down to old man Collins. he wants to sell father his cow. he says she gives 20 quats of milk a day. father says the milk we get of the milk man is all chork and water.

May 25. rany as time. father ofered 30 dolars for old man Collins cow. he wants 35 dollars. she has got auful long horns. old man Collins said she had auful big milk vanes. father said they was varycose vanes and she want wirth 30 dolars but he wood give it to help out a old man. old man Collins he said if she kep on giving milk the way she was a giving it they wood have to milk her in a tub. then father he said he gessed she give so mutch milk that it want good for ennything and old man Collins he said you cood take the creem up by one corner and lift it out like a old pair of linen britches. they dident trade tonite.

May 26. brite and fair. tonite me and father went down to old man Collins agen. father said he was going to trade for that cow only i must shet up and not say ennything. he said you jest wach me and you will lern sumthing about trading. so i wached him. well we went down and father said well mister Collins how do you feel about trading tonite. and old man Collins he said, i gess you are two late George fer i have sold her to a man in Hamton Falls. and father said what did you get for her and old man Collins he said i told him he could have her for 35 dolars and he ofered me 33 dolars and 50 cents and i said the first man whitch ofers me 35 dolars gets her, and i gess he will be up tomorow morning. then father he said have you made the trade and old man Collins he said he hadent made enny trade but he had kind of let the man understand he cood have her for 35 dolars. then father he said he wood give 35 dolars and old man Collins he said he dident know about selling her xcept to the Hamton Falls man but if father wood give him 37 dolars he cood give the Hamton Falls man 2 dolars if he came up and was disapointed. so father he give old man Collins 37 dolars and we got a roap and tide it round her horns and led her home. when we got home we tried to get her in the barn, father he went ahead and she folowed him in and all of a suddin she backed out lively and father came out jest fluking, holding on to the roap and taking feerful long stradles. he looked so mad that i dident dass to laff. well father held on like a good feller and bimeby she stoped. then father said so so and held out sum meal in a pail and got her in the barn and tide her to a post. then he give her sum hay and we went in and he told mother she had beter make sum araingments to sell sum milk for we was going to have 20 quats every day. then mother she said if the cow gives milk like my hens lade egs they woodent be mutch milk to sell, and father said you jest wait til morning. then we went down to old Gechels store and father he bougt the bigest milk pail he cood find.

May 27. brite and fair. this morning me and father got up erly and we went out to feed the cow and i piched down the hay and father he set down and begun to milk her, he brought out the big pail and a little one to use after he had filled the big one. well the ferst thing he did was to aim a streem rite in my eye. then he milked in the pail and it made a funy sound, well he kep milking and bimeby it stoped coming, and he squeazed away as hard as he cood and he coodent get a drop and bimeby he give up and said he gessed it was becaus she was in a new place and was loansum. when we went into the house and straned it thrugh a siv they wasent quite 2 quats. mother she laffed and asked what he had done with the other 8 quats and father he said you wait til tonite. then he et his brekfast and went to boston and i et mine and drove the old cow to pasture. i found a robins nest in a pine tree and took one eg. it is all rite to take one becaus the old bird cant count.

May 28, 186– brite and fair. last nite after super father milked the old cow again. he only got 2 quats and a half. he was prety mad and he said he wood get even with old man Collins sum day. tonite he met old man Collins and he asked father if she milked esy and father said yes and he asked father how mutch she give and father said she give more than he wanted. that want a lie for father dont like milk. i bet father will get even with him sum day. nothing else today but church.

Getting Vaccinated

June 11. i hate to go to church. we have all got to be vaxinated. sum peeple in the next town have got the small pocks. Beany has been and Pewt two. Beany says the doctor takes a nife and cuts a hole in your arm and then puts on a big scab whitch has come of somebodys arm whitch has been vaxinated, and that stops the blud. but he says that if the scab dont fit you bleed to deth. so i asked father about it tonite and he said that Beany lied about it, but he says if you are vaxinated with the scab of a redheaded person your hair will turn red, and if he has warts or frekles you will have warts two and frekles. father said once when he was a boy he knew a feller whitch was vaxinated with a scab of a cock-eyed man and bimeby the feller began to squint and he kep on squinting wirse and wirse and bimeby he was cock-eyed two. and father he said he knew another feller whitch had a wooden leg and he sent his scab to another feller to be vaxinated and that feller began to limp and he always walked stifleged. i gess father was fooling. ennyway i hope i shant be vaxinated with Skinny Bruces scab, becaus he is redheaded. father he said he was going to get a scab of Horis Cobb for me and perhaps i wood have a little fat on me and not be so spindel shanked. i wish i cood get a scab of Gim Erly or Tady Finton and i cood lick time out of Pewt.

June 12. brite and fair. Beany has a auful sore arm. he dont dass to rassle or fite or do ennything.

June 13. brite and fair. Pewt has got one two. tomorrow nite the doctor is coming.

June 15. brite and fair. last nite after super the doctor come and he went into the parlor and father and mother and Cele and Keene and me and Georgie and Annie and Frank and the baby was all in the setting room. well ferst father went in and he was only in there a few minits and he dident holler enny and then he come out laffing, and i asked him whose scab he had and he said he dident know but it must have been from sum minister becaus he had been thanking the lord it was all over. then mother she went in and father told her he had got the scab of old Mike Casey for her. mother is english and she dont like the irish and father said it to plage her. well she went in and then Aunt Sarah went in and Keene and Cele and they dident holler eether. then my tern came and i went in and it dident hurt a bit only sort of smarted tickly like. i asked the doctor whose scab i had and he said Bruce Brigams. buly. Bruce Brigam is the best cornet player in town. i bet i can play like time if i ever get a cornet. then the rest of them went in and none of them hollered xcept the baby and he always hollers when ennything is the matter. . . .

The Devil Is Dead

One Sabbath morning, unknown to his father, he [Moses Ingalls] joined his companions and started a hunt. They followed down the Androscoggin a few miles, when they espied a large moose in the river eating watergrass. Ingalls gave him a shot. The moose escaped, as they supposed, uninjured. On his return home, being asked by his father where he had been, he replied that he had been out hunting, seen a moose, and had shot at him, but did not kill him. To this his father replied, with false discretion we think, "No, Moses! that was the devil you shot at, instead of a moose. How dare you so break the Sabbath?" Some few days after this, Moses, passing down the river, found the moose dead, killed by the shot he had given him the previous Sabbath. Returning home, with exultation marked on his countenance, he said, "Father, the devil is dead!"—"What do you say?" replied his father. "Why, Moses, what do you mean?"—"Mean,

---

From *Incidents in White Mountain History:* Containing Facts Relating to the Discovery and Settlement of the Mountains, Indian History and Traditions, A Minute and Authentic Account of the Destruction of the Willey Family, Geology and Temperature of the Mountains; Together with Numerous Anecdotes Illustrating Life in the Back Woods, by Rev. Benjamin G. Willey, pp. 250–251. Entered, according to Act of Congress, in the year 1855, by Benjamin G. Willey, in the Clerk's Office of the District Court of the District of Massachusetts. Boston: Published by Nathaniel Noyes. 1856.

father!" said he in return, "mean, why I mean as I said the devil is dead. You said the creature I shot at the other day was the devil, and, if so, he is dead, because I have just found the creature I know to be the one I shot at, and he is dead enough." Long after that the report went, Moses *shot* the devil.

Kit Potter and the Fourteen Cats

. . . THERE were living at my grandfather's house, in Narragansett, fifteen full-grown cats all told, besides some litters of kittens. One first-day forenoon, when all the great-room folks had gone to Quaker meeting, excepting me, who had torn my breeches purposely that morning so that I might be left at home, Abe and I arranged to have a good time. So we shut the inside shutters of the great-room, thus excluding the light, all but what got through a little heart-shaped hole at the top of each pair of shutters, and then set ourselves to catch the cats and shut them in the dark room. After an hour's work, we succeeded in grabbing and shutting up fourteen of the number, including the great yaller tom-cat, which was nigh upon as big as a catamountain. There was, however, an old black cat that took to the cock-loft of the garret, which Abe finally declared the Devil himself couldn't get if he tried to. The cock-loft was very dark, and we could see nothing but the old sarpent's eyes looking like two balls of fire, and when we went softly to the place, they showed themselves in another corner of the cock-loft. So we gave her up, and went down to the great-room, into which we shut ourselves with the fourteen cats, which were of all the colors of the rainbow, including several other shades to boot. Next, Abe and I each got a window-stick and went to chasing the cats like mad around the room, occasionally hitting one on the head or wherever came handiest. After racing round and round a few times, the great yaller cat darted into the fireplace and up the chimney, followed by the whole drove.

Just at this time old Kit Potter, the Tower Hill cooper, chanced to be coming down the lane, and seeing the cats pouring out of the top of the chimney, he hurried back to his house and told his wife that she needn't dispute with him any longer about Hazard's house being haunted, for he had just seen more than five hundred witches sitting on the roof, and more coming out of the chimney.

From *The Jonny-Cake Papers of "Shepherd Tom,"* Together with Reminiscences of Narragansett Schools of Former Days, by Thomas Robinson Hazard, With a Biographical Sketch and Notes by Rowland Gibson Hazard, pp. 88–89. Copyright, 1915, by Rowland G. Hazard. Boston: Printed for the Subscribers.

The Corpse That Talked

. . . IN A certain locality the village graveyard was being constantly robbed of its dead; so frequently were the graves disturbed that two of the young men of the village were set to watch the graveyard. The night was dark and gloomy, so the two young men easily secreted themselves from the sight of whomsoever the robbers of the dead might be. Soon there came two men with spade and shovel and at once began their nefarious work. When they had removed the coffin and placed it on the bier, one of the young men, all unobserved, laid himself upon the coffin under the white sheet. Almost immediately, after starting to make their exit with the corpse, one of the men said to the other, "How d——d heavy this body is!" Whereupon the living voice under the sheet exclaimed, "Well, you dastardly robbers, if I am too heavy to be carried, I can walk!" From that date on, there was no more robbing the graveyard in that neighborhood.

Diving for the Bean

BEAN-PORRIDGE was among the good healthful regulation diets. Hence:—

Bean-porridge hot and bean-porridge cold. Some of the skippers were charged with ordering the bean-soup thinner than the law allowed. One day when dinner was announced, the bean-soup placed upon the table, and the skipper had taken his place at the head according to custom, a funny little Frenchman began to peel off his jacket. "What in creation are you going to do?" said the skipper. "To pull off my jacket and tive for pean, by Cot!" said the Frenchman. Thereafter, they had no occasion to complain of their bean-soup on that voyage.

Stone Soup

. . . HE WAS a-travelin' an' got short o' money, or mebby he was a reg'lar beggar, I do' know, but ary way, he stopped tu a haouse an' ast for somethin' tu eat, an' they wouldn't give him nothin'. So he ast 'em if they

---

From *Reminiscences of Candia,* by Wilson Palmer, pp. 271–272. Copyright, 1905, by Wilson Palmer. Cambridge: Printed at The Riverside Press.

From *Truro—Cape Cod, or Land Marks and Sea Marks,* by Shebnah Rich, p. 343. Second Edition, Revised and Corrected. Copyright, 1883, by D. Lothrop and Company. Boston. 1884.

From *Uncle Lisha's Outing,* by Rowland E. Robinson, pp. 177–178. Copyright, 1897, by Rowland E. Robinson. Boston and New York: Houghton, Mifflin and Company.

wouldn't lend him a kittle a spell an' a spwun, so 's 't he c'ld make hisself a kittle o' stun soup, an' so they did just tu see what he 'd du. Wal, he built him a fire side o' the rwud an' sot a kittle o' water a-b'ilin', an' he took an' washed a stun 'baout 's big as his fist an' popped it int' the kittle, an' sot an' watched it b'ile a spell, an' then he dipped up a spoo'f'l an' tasted on 't.

"It's proper good," says he, "but it's kinder fraish, an' I wish 't I hed a leetle grain o' salt tu put into 't," an' they went an' fetched him a han'f'l an' he put that in.

"That 's a gre't improvement," says he, a-tastin' ag'in, "but it wouldn't hurt it none if the' was a hunk o' meat in 't; any sort of a scrap 'at you was a-goin' tu heave away. I hain't partic'lar." An' so they fetched him a good hunk o' meat an' he hove that int' the kittle, an' then says he, "I s'pose you 'd jes' 's live 's I'd pull one o' them 'ere turnips over there? This 'ere soup 's goin' tu be putty strong o' stun if it don't ha' some vegetables in 't."

So he went an' got him a turnip, an' whilst he was abaout it he got an onion, an' cut 'em up an' chucked 'em in. An' when he got it b'iled he eat 'nough tu last him tew days, an' says he, a-rubbin' of his stomerk, "The' hain't nothin' 'at makes better soup 'n a good stun, wi' a few leetle additions, an' I'm much obleeged tu ye for the use o' your kittle," says he.

One Pea Soup

You see, dar was one mans ant very good up, an' he 'll ant gat not'in' for heat on his haouse 'cep' one pea for all his waf an' ten chillens. He tol' hees hwomans for put de pot on de stofe an' full him up wid water an' put dat pea on it. Den bambye w'en he beegin fo' bile he 'look on de pot an' see dat pea jomp raoun' all 'lone, he say, "Dat leetly pea was look lonesick, an' Ah 'll goin' see 'f Ah can fin' somet'ings for hees company."

So he go in de naght to nudder man's barn, where dey was keel bif critter an' hang it for cold off, an' he was cut good chonk an' take it on his haouse an' t'row it in de pot 'long to de pea w'en his waf he 'll ant see. Bambye w'en de pea was bile plenty an' his waf beegin tas'e for heat, he say:

"Bah gosh, Ah'll ant never see so pea lak dat for mek soup, me." An de mans tol' him:—

"You 'll ant never gat raght kan' o' pea 'fore."

Ibid., pp. 178–179.

The Price of a Dinner

Upon Tremont Street, near Winter Street, in Boston, there stood at that time in a garden a fine old house which was kept as a restaurant, and was a pleasant summer lounging-place for all gay cits. One day a very portly, aldermanic man presented himself at the entrance of the restaurant and asked the price of a dinner. Shaffer, who was present, immediately assumed all the obsequious airs of a waiter, and calling for a tape-measure, proceeded to measure the distance around the protuberant waist of the astonished and insulted inquirer, who could hardly believe his sense of hearing when the impudent Shaffer very politely answered, "Price of dinner, sir!—about four dollars, sir!—for that size, sir!"

The Minister's Revenge

It appears an old Minister came there once, to hold a meetin' at his house—well, after meetin' was over, the Elder took the minister all over his farm, which is pretty tidy, I tell you; and he showed him a great Ox he had, and a swinging big Pig, that weighed some six or seven hundred weight, that he was plaguy proud of, but he never offered the old minister any thing to eat or drink. The preacher was pretty tired of all this, and seeing no prospect of being asked to partake with the family, and tolerably sharp set, he asked one of the boys to fetch him his horse out of the barn. When he was taking leave of the Elder (there were several folks by at the time), says he, Elder Thomson, you have a fine farm here, a very fine farm, indeed; you have a large Ox too, a very large Ox; and I think, said he, I've seen to day, (turning and looking him full in the face, for he intended to hit him pretty hard), *I think I have seen to-day the greatest Hog I ever saw in my life.* The neighbors snickered a good deal, and the Elder felt pretty streaked. I guess he'd give his great Pig or his great Ox either, if that story hadn't got wind.

The Constable and the Pigs

There is an old story told about a New Gloucester farmer named Bildad Arnold who lived at the foot of a hill now known as Rowe's Hill. Bildad

---

From *Customs and Fashions in Old New England*, by Alice Morse Earle, p. 213. Copyright, 1893, by Charles Scribner's Sons. New York.

From *The Clockmaker; or, The Sayings and Doings of Samuel Slick of Slickville*. Philadelphia: Carey, Lea, and Blanchard. 1837.

By Mrs. Flora Berry and Annie Berry, New Gloucester, Maine. Manuscripts of the Federal Writers' Project of the Works Progress Administration for the State of Maine.

always allowed his pigs to run without fences, in spite of the fact that any animal running loose at that time could be taken to the New Gloucester pound (no longer in existence) and the owner must pay a certain sum to liberate them. He always called the pigs at feeding time by rapping with a stick on the side of the house.

One day Ben Loring, constable, finding the pigs loose, started to drive them to the pound. Bildad watched him drive the pigs up the hill and then started rapping on the house with his stick. Down came the pigs, squealing and hooting, and down came Loring after them. Up he drove them again, Bildad watching quietly, stick in hand, until they reached the top. Rap, rap, rap. Down they came again, and behind them the sweating, exasperated constable. The process was repeated, until the constable retired, more or less gracefully.

Swearing Out the Balance

My store had much to do in giving shape to my future character as well as career, in that it became a favorite resort; the theatre of village talk, and the scene of many practical jokes. For any excess of the jocose element in my character, part of the blame must attach to my early surroundings as a village clerk and merchant. In that true resort of village wits and wags, the country store, fun, pure and simple, will be sure to find the surface. My Bethel store was the scene of many most amusing incidents, in some of which I was an immediate participant, though in many, of course, I was only a listener or spectator.

The following scene makes a chapter in the history of Connecticut, as the State was when "blue-laws" were something more than a dead letter. To swear in those days was according to custom, but contrary to law. A person from New York State, whom I will call Crofut, who was a frequent visitor at my store, was a man of property, and equally noted for his self-will and his really terrible profanity. One day he was in my little establishment engaged in conversation, when Nathan Seelye, Esq., one of our village justices of the peace, and a man of strict religious principles, came in, and hearing Crofut's profane language he told him he considered it his duty to fine him one dollar for swearing.

Crofut responded immediately with an oath, that he did not care a d——n for the Connecticut blue-laws.

"That will make two dollars," said Mr. Seelye.

This brought forth another oath.

"Three dollars," said the sturdy justice.

From *Struggles and Triumphs: or, Forty Years' Recollections of P. T. Barnum,* Written by Himself, Author's Edition, pp. 52–54. Entered according to Act of Congress, in the year 1871, by P. T. Barnum, in the Office of the Librarian of Congress, at Washington. Entered also at Stationer's Hall, London, England. Buffalo, New York: Warren, Johnson & Co. 1873.

Nothing but oaths were given in reply, until Esquire Seelye declared the damage to the Connecticut laws to amount to fifteen dollars.

Crofut took out a twenty-dollar bill, and handed it to the justice of the peace, with an oath.

"Sixteen dollars," said Mr. Seeley, counting out four dollars to hand to Mr. Crofut, as his change.

"Oh, keep it, keep it," said Crofut, "I don't want any change, I'll d——d soon swear out the balance." He did so, after which he was more circumspect in his conversation, remarking that twenty dollars a day for swearing was about as much as he could stand.

Little Rest Laughter

. . . In the olden time when Providence, Bristol, and Grinnage were nowhere, Newport, Tower Hill, and Little Rest [1] were the chief compact towns in Rhode Island. After the Revolution, Little Rest became one of the capitals of the state, where the county courts, removed from Tower Hill, sat, and the General Assembly held an annual session. The origin of its unique name is uncertain. Some hold that it originated from the multitude of lawyers that used to reside and assemble there, who made it their chief business to involve everybody they came in contact with in quarrels and lawsuits, that they might profit thereby, thus giving their clients Little Rest. Others say that the name was not conferred on the village until after the General Assembly held its annual session, at which time the public accommodations were so limited, that the members of both houses were obliged to sleep four in a bed, heads and points, to make better stowage. Of course there could be but little rest under such circumstances, and hence the name Little Rest. From all I can learn, I think, however, the name was of earlier date than the creation of the General Assembly of the State of Rhode Island and Providence Plantations, and grew out of the fact that in the olden time, Little Rest was the home and headquarters of a class of men who were peculiarly addicted to inflicting practical jokes not only on one another, but upon all temporary visitors to the village, and thereby giving their victims but little rest. I could fill many volumes with scores of Little Rest anecdotes of this kind that rival in "bodily wit," as lawyer Joe Aplin would designate it, and humor, anything to be found in Cervantes, Smollett, Fielding, or Scott, had I their genius to relate them with fitting terms and accompaniments. . . .

* * * * *

From *The Jonny-Cake Papers of "Shepherd Tom,"* Together with Reminiscences of Narragansett Schools of Former Days, by Thomas Robinson Hazard, With a Biographical Sketch and Notes by Rowland Gibson Hazard, pp. 111–112, 113–118. Copyright, 1915, by Rowland G. Hazard. Boston: Printed for the Subscribers.

[1] Kingston Village.—R. G. H.

There used to live in the north-west corner of the town of Exeter, in Washington county, one Willard, who was held by the Narragansetters to be the loudest laugher in the state, if not in New England. It so happened that some Tivertoners from Newport county attended the court on some occasion, who contended with the Little Resters that one Durfee, of their town, and not Willard, was the champion laugher of Rhode Island. It was finally agreed by the rival contestants that at the next term of court, Willard and Durfee should be induced to meet unbeknown to each other, under some convenient pretext, at the Tom Potter red house, then a tavern, that still stands on the south-west corner of the cross-roads, some fifty or more rods from the court-house. Accordingly, at the next term of court, the two disciples of Democritus were on the spot, each attended by his special friends and backers, who understood exactly how to draw their respective *protégés* out. After the glass had circulated freely, a story was told by a friend of Willard's to suit the occasion, that caused an explosion from his lungs that fairly shook the house. When Willard had subsided, a Tiverton man told another appropriate story that caused Durfee to explode in a key that fully equaled Willard's outburst. Judge Wilcox was then holding a term of the Common Pleas, and when he heard the two loud reports from Willard and Durfee, thinking it must be the rumbling of distant thunder, he beckoned Sheriff Sam Allen to his side, and whispered in his ear to go out and see from whence the thunder came from apparently a clear sky. Allen quickly returned and told the judge that there was not the least speck of a cloud to be seen in any part of the heavens. Just at that moment the object was revealed to Willard and Durfee that was had in view in bringing them together—on which announcement such a concurrent burst of laughter broke from both of them in union, that the court-house shook and Judge Wilcox, panic-stricken, supposing an earthquake to be on hand, informally adjourned the court and darted out of the house, fearing it was about to fall on his head.

I remember when there used to live, some forty or fifty years ago, in a tenement belonging to the late Hon. E. R. Potter, that stood on the west side of the road leading south a short distance from the aforementioned Tom Potter house, an old Irishman by the name of Benjamin Storer, a day laborer. Storer kept a pig, of course, and the finest, in his own estimation, of any on Little Rest Hill. So proud was Storer of the beauty of his pig that wherever he went he made it the chief subject of conversation, so that Storer and his pig became a by-saying in the village. Storer worked a great deal for his landlord, in his garden and otherwise, and often interceded with him to bring some of his friends to his house, that they might admire his pig. So one day, whilst the General Assembly was sitting at Little Rest, Mr. Potter announced to Storer that Governor Fenner and some half a dozen or more of the most distinguished members were to dine with him on the next day, and that he would invite them after dinner to go over and look at his pig. Storer, of course, was highly gratified at this announcement, and so soon as the sun set, the then limit of a day's work, he went through the village, telling everybody he met of the honor that was to be bestowed on his pig by the Governor and his friends. Among others, Storer imparted a knowledge of his good luck to Squire Matthew Waite and Deputy Sheriff E. R. Gardner. When the morrow arrived, the services of both Storer and his wife Hannah were required at Mr. Potter's, so that the pig was left alone. After dinner Mr. Potter called Storer from the garden, and told him the Governor and his friends had concluded to go over and look at his pig. So the delighted old man started off a few minutes before his distinguished visitors to make all things ready. Soon after, Mr. Potter accompanied by Governor Fenner and his other guests arrived on Storer's premises, where a most extraordinary sight met their vision. There they beheld the usually courteous, staid, and self-poised old man, storming with rage as he tore the hat from his head and stamped it into the ground. "What," said Mr. Potter, "is the matter, Storer; are you crazy?" To this query no intelligible answer could be got from Storer, who tried to reply, but could only give utterance to a jumble of unintelligible words, in which "Gardner," "Waite," "Lunt," "shave," and "pig" were the chief burthen. On looking into the pen, the mystery was quickly explained. There stood Storer's beautiful pig, shaved from his snout to the tip of his tail as clean as the palm of a baby's hand. Not a hair nor the ninth part of a hair, nor the stump of a hair, was left upon the animal's body, head, ears, limbs, or tail. The provocative to laughter was irresistible, and such a roar went forth from all the company present, that soon every man, woman, and child within a mile, including the members of both houses of Assembly, rushed to the spot to find out what was the matter with Storer and his pig.

I suppose some may think that it was not possible anybody should laugh loud enough to be heard a mile off. Such ignorant persons should remember that the men of that day, especially in Rhode Island, were not such weak-lunged creatures as those of the present degenerate times. Mr. Potter was a man of full six feet high, and weighed more than two hundred and fifty pounds, whilst old Fenner, though not quite so tall as Potter, was more than twice as big round, and of course held twice as much wind, whilst they were both gifted with stentorian lungs. Some faint idea of Potter's power of blowing, and consequently of loud laughing, may be guessed at by the fact that one day whilst a little snipper-snapper who sat about ten feet back of him, in the General Assembly, then in session at Little Rest, was speaking, he made some saucy remarks touching the South County, when Potter, without leaving his seat, merely turned his head round, and at one puff blew the little fellow clean out of an open window, although the impertinent chap could not have weighed much less than seventy-five pounds avoirdupois. It was a two-story window, and the poor fellow might have cracked his skull were it not that in his fall he lighted directly on top of old Prince Robinson's gingerbread and apple stand. Prince said that when he first came down he thought it was the Demerara monkey that had just arrived on the hill in the show, but on observing his pate, he said he saw at once he had not enough brains for a monkey, and was only a Providence-county lawyer.

In the sequel it came out that when Storer, the evening before, revealed to Squire Waite and Sheriff Gardner the fact that the chief dignitaries of the state were to make his pig a complimentary visit the next day, they thought it a good time to have a little sport at the old man's expense. As if to favor Waite and Gardner in their wicked design, there lived at the time a little west of the Corners, on the north side of the main street of the village, old William Lunt, who held two responsible offices during the Revolutionary War, being a major in the army and General Washington's barber, both at the same time. After the war, the major settled in Little Rest and made a very comfortable living by his trade, as every man who came to the village was willing to pay for at least one shave by Washington's barber, especially when it was done with the identical razor that Major Lunt took especial care to inform his customer had smoothed the face of the Father of his Country hundreds of times. It so chanced that the major, though an honorable and honest man—my brother Joseph erected a monument over his remains—was somewhat jealous of his neighbor Storer's pig, because he took great pride in one he himself possessed, regarding which Storer had been heard to make invidious comparisons when contrasting it with his own beautiful animal. The consequence was that when Waite and Gardner went over to the shop and tempted Washington's old barber with a ninepence, the price of four shaves, to go with them and denude Storer's pig, he readily consented. So the three conspirators went over to Storer's house whilst he and his wife Hannah were doing a day's work at Mr. Potter's, and after dosing his pig with a delicious mixture of milk and molasses, sweetened with a pint of new rum, Waite and Gardner seized the unconscious animal and held him handy, whilst Lunt, with his George Washington razor, shaved him from the tip of his snout to the end of his tail, as clean and smooth, as before said, as the palm of a baby's hand.

II. LOCAL CHARACTERS

The running of the first train over the Eastern Road from Boston to Portsmouth . . . was attended by a serious accident . . . this initial train . . . ran over and killed—LOCAL CHARACTER.

—THOMAS BAILEY ALDRICH

Ice and granite, it is said, are the chief products of New England; and they fitly symbolize the hardy character of her sons.

—GEORGE R. RUSSELL, in *The (Old) Farmer's Almanack*, 1855

A strange hybrid, indeed, did circumstance beget, here in the New World, upon the old Puritan stock, and the earth never before saw such mystic-practicalism, such niggard-geniality, such calculating-fanaticism, such cast-iron-enthusiasm, such sour-faced-humor, such close-fisted-generosity.

—James Russell Lowell

The people of the region think of themselves as reticent, and as given to dry humor and understatement; as having a strong sense of lineage and of relationship to their past; as being unusually aware of their past and influenced by it; as keeping a tenacious grip on possessions, either land or heirlooms; as having a certain suspicion of the outsider; as being ingenious and inventive in dealing with physical problems; as having a strong sense of individual responsibility and an almost complete inability to play or to take things lightly; as having their emotions constantly suppressed but expressed for all in an assumed belief in the little white church, the public school, and the savings bank. Now people scarcely hold to these beliefs. The traits they ascribe to themselves are not real but accredited characteristics fostered by literary treatments of the region.

—Conference on the Eastern Maritime Region, August 29–31, 1942, Rockland, Maine, Summary of the Discussion

1. "Characters"

"What is a 'character'?" asks Joseph C. Lincoln, and answers: "Why, he or she is, apparently, an individual who speaks and acts and, perhaps, thinks in a manner different from that in which you, yourself, speak and act and think. And it is just possible that he, because of that difference, may consider you a character; he has that privilege, of course. . . . It depends on the point of view, doesn't it? And there is another point to be considered. A 'character' may not be a character at all in his own environment and become one when he steps outside of it."[1]

Thomas Bailey Aldrich emphasized the localism of local characters. To him a local character was an indigenous "individual built on plans and specifications of its [the community's] own, without regard to the prejudices and conventionalities of outlying districts." With the coming of the railroad, he adds, local character "was not instantly killed," but "died a lingering death." And by a process of attrition it gradually disintegrated, dissolving into "certain bits of color, certain half obsolete customs and scraps of the past."[2]

Continuing the Puritan emphasis on character, New England localism bred "characters" and a distinct feeling for "characters." New England provincialism (in the best sense of the word) rests on the twin pillars of family tradition and the tradition of the New England town or village and self-government (symbolized by the town meeting). Both traditions, espe-

[1] *Cape Cod Yesterdays* (Boston, 1935), pp. 258–259.
[2] *An Old Town by the Sea* (Boston, 1894), pp. 105–106, 108–109.

cially in rural communities, foster respect for strong characters and distinctive traits and talents, which become part of the social heritage. Thus the Yankee ideal of a hard-working, efficient, upright, democratic citizenry includes the tough and hardy builders of pioneer New England; the stern, self-sufficient patriarchs of the farm; and the charmingly crotchety villagers that inhabit places like Harriet Beecher Stowe's "Oldtown" (Natick, Massachusetts).

New England also had its rebels and non-conformists who carried the Yankee spirit of self-dependence—the right to be one's self—to extremes. Violating the sense of order inherent in the neat, tight pattern of New England farm and village life, their revolt broke through the surface of New England constraint to give us erratic geniuses like Margaret Fuller, Thoreau, and Melville, as well as a host of minor recluses, cranks, self-constituted prophets, reprobates, vagrants, and ne'er-do-wells. The very ideals of hard work, thrift, and duty produced a reaction in the form of the village-do-nothing, typified by Mrs. Stowe's Sam Lawson, who nevertheless possessed the virtue of handiness or "faculty," while complete inability or unwillingness to make adjustment to social norms or personal tragedy resulted in pathetic schizophrenics and vagrants like the Old Darnman and the Leatherman.

2. Droll Yankees

The discovery of the comic Yankee—half clown, half rogue—came about, as we have seen, as part of the discovery of national and regional traits and showed the forces of local patriotism and sectional rivalry at work—another instance of localism in New England character. In the course of this discovery, the Yankee, from the laughable "countryman in the great world," became a homely critic of the outside world and a sharp trader engaged in a comic contest of wits with the world at large. And in the composite portrait of the fabulous Yankee that grew up in oral and written tradition, we find the comic (green), sage, and "cute" Yankee gradually fusing into the droll Yankee—the indigenous countryman (a truly local character), at home in his own little world.

The droll Yankee, whose lineaments may first be traced in James Russell Lowell's Hosea Biglow (1848) is chiefly distinguished by his matter-of-fact or "reluctant" wit and eloquence, superimposed upon moral earnestness and down-to-earth common sense. He is a man of few words and many notions, of strong principles and decided opinions, expressed in odd behavior, observations, and speech. Farmer, old salt, workman, the droll Yankee is closer to New England than the simple yokel or slick peddler—a "character" in his idiosyncrasies and a "local character" in the sense of being strongly colored and flavored by locality and localisms of speech.

3. Yankee Wit

The hallmark of the droll Yankee is wit. Dry, homely, sharp, shrewd, salty, quaint, crabbed, sly, pithy, engimatic, Yankee wit is essential wit—saying much in little—"enlivened with many curious twists and turns and out-of-the-way notions." These qualities are externalized by the Yankee's habit of slow speaking, of turning a question "over in his mind once or twice before he gives answer, often improving the interval to spit seriously and meditatively."

These tricks of expression have become familiar as the stock-in-trade of the humorist and humorous lecturer of the crackerbox philosopher variety. As devices for telling a humorous story, it will be remembered, Mark Twain recommended the grave manner, the studied silences, and the casually dropped, absent-minded, often irrelevant and incongruous remarks dealt in by Artemus Ward.[1] What Mark Twain calls the story-teller's "soliloquizing way" is simply the Yankee's habit of talking as if he were thinking aloud or talking to himself; and what he calls the "pause" is the Yankee's habit or trick of slow timing. According to Charles Edward Crane, the Yankee "loves to bait his listener" and "He lights a slow fuse and with a poker face he watches that fuse burn to the setting off of a little bomb of the unexpected."[2]

Thus the droll Yankee's apparently unconscious humor, slow speech, twangy drawl, and eloquent silence involve a considerable element of artifice. "Silent Cal" Coolidge's public silence was both deliberate and natural, for "in private Coolidge was garrulity itself."[3] Crane testifies that he knows many Vermonters "who have little in common with 'Silent Cal' and who can talk the 'handle off the pump,' or the 'tin ear off an iron dog.'"[4] If this seems like a paradox, it is related to and borne out by that other Yankee paradox of inquisitiveness and curiosity with respect to strangers in contrast to suspicious distrust of outsiders.

Finally, Yankee wit is characterized by understatement—"triple-X in dryness," according to Crane, or underemphasis, according to Joseph C. Lincoln, appropriate to the "reluctant or rustic philosophic style" of eloquence which George Philip Krapp contrasts with the "expansive" eloquence of the hyperbolical orator and the exuberant eloquence of the back-

---

[1] In the character of the itinerant showman, which Charles Farrar Browne added to the gallery of American folk types, Jennette Tandy sees him aiming "at the presentation of a national, not a local type." Yet in his rôle as lecturer, Browne, like that other Yankee humorist and lecturer, Henry Wheeler Shaw (Josh Billings), retained many Yankee traits. And the following description of Artemus Ward, the genial showman, clearly relates him to the tradition of the droll Yankee: "The shrewdness of a Barnum was to be united with the stupidity of an uneducated itinerant exhibitor. . . . The old showman was to have the smartness of a Yankee, combined with the slowness of one whose time had been chiefly spent among the backwoods; he was to blend humorous stupidity with unscrupulous mendacity, to have very little of the reverential about him, a modicum of the philosophical, and a large amount of the broadly comic."—E. P. Hingston, *The Genial Showman* (1870), Vol. I, pp. 136, 137. Cited by Jennette Tandy, *Crackerbox Philosophers in American Humor and Satire* (New York, 1925), p. 136.

[2] *Let Me Show You Vermont* (New York, 1937), p. 29.

[3] Stewart H. Holbrook. See "The Enigma of Silent Cal" below. Cf. Horace Green, *The Life of Calvin Coolidge* (New York, 1924), p. 20: "But particularly in the habit of reticence, broken by slaty epigrams, does he reveal traits of the soil; for the smaller the community, the less is small talk honored."

[4] *Op. cit.*, p. 29.

woods Southerner and Westerner.[1] Lowell also notes a love of incongruity, which he defines as "that humorous quality of the mind which delights in finding an element of identity in things seemingly the most incongruous, and then again in forcing an incongruity upon things identical."[2] There is further incongruity between the "sober treatment of comic things and comic treatment of sober matters" (such as death)—a source of quaintness traced by John Camden Hotten to the Puritans.[3] The result is that dry utterance of funny things in an unfunny, commonsensical fashion and what Lincoln calls the "unsmiling gravity with which the point of the joke is delivered," combining the right proportions of greenness, sageness, and "cuteness" in the droll Yankee.

B. A. B.

Artemus Ward on New England

THIS is the happy land of baked beans and pure religion. Here "I guess I can dew it!" Here men get rich on farms which at first sight look as if they could produce nothing but crops of rocks. Here land which an Illinois farmer wouldn't have on his premises at any rate is held at an elevated figure. Here when a man don't clearly understand you, he says, "Hay?" and when he is astonished, "Sho!" Here people talk through their noses to a great and sometimes alarming extent, nature having kindly provided some of them with noses like covered bridges, each nostril being large enough to let a double team of words go through. Here the people have just eccentricities enough to be interesting. Here they can invent, chop, swap, work, and (if necessary) fight. Here there is maple sugar, virtue, shrewdness, strong arms and big chests, pickerel, rosy cheeks and true hearts, ever-busy knitting needles, cream, an undying love for Bunker Hill, honey, patriotism, stocking yarn, mountains, ponds, hoop-poles, churches, schoolhouses, pine logs, scenery that knocks Switzerland into a disordered chapeau, and air so pure that the New Yorker is sorry he can't bottle some of it and carry it to the metropolis for daily use.

---

[1] *The English Language in America* (New York, 1925), Vol. I, pp. 324 ff.

[2] Introduction to *The Biglow Papers: Second Series, The Poetical Works of James Russell Lowell* (Boston, 1885), p. 225.

[3] Introduction to *The Complete Works of Charles F. Browne* (London, 1865), p. 27.

From "Maine in March," by Artemus Ward ("Alphonso the Brave"), *Vanity Fair,* April 20, 1861, p. 181, reprinted in *Artemus Ward, (Charles Farrar Browne),* A Biography and Bibliography, by Don C. Seitz, p. 297.

YANKEEDOM AGAINST THE WORLD

The Yankee and the Stranger

. . . A YOUNG man who had gone away from a New England village with his family at an early age returned after an absence of many years for the purpose of measuring the family wood-lot. On his arrival he went to the post-office to make certain inquiries of the postmaster, and on emerging from the post-office he paused to pass the time of day with four or five old residents who were sitting on the post-office steps, apparently allowing their minds to turn over silently in neutral, as one might say.

"Looks a little like rain," he remarked by way of an opening wedge.

His words were greeted with a rich silence on the part of the old residents.

"I say," he repeated, after something of a wait, "it looks as though it might rain."

After another long and eloquent silence, one of the natives removed his pipe from his mouth, neatly deluged an adjacent fly, turned his head slowly, gazed blankly at the young man, and finally asked:

"What you say yuh name wuz?"

"Why," said the young man, "my name's Eldridge. My family used to live over at Baxter's Dam Corners. Looks a little like rain, doesn't it?"

At this the silence again settled down over the post-office steps, but eventually the same inquisitive native once more turned his head and looked coldly at the stranger. "Any relation to Eben Eldridge?" he asked carelessly.

"Yes, indeed," said the young man. "Eben Eldridge was my uncle. We'll probably get a little rain, don't you think so?"

"Then your father wuz Herb Eldridge, wa'n't he?" asked the native.

"Yes, Herbert Eldridge was my father," the young man replied.

"Oh, that so!" said the native, deftly favoring another fly with a shower bath. "Eben Eldridge's nephew and Herb Eldridge's boy, hey? Hm! Well, well!"

He and his companions studied the toes of their shoes intently for a few moments, and finally the native looked up at the sky dubiously. "Well," he admitted with some reluctance, "it *may* rain."

From *Concentrated New England.* A Sketch of Calvin Coolidge, by Kenneth L. Roberts, pp. 8–10. Copyright, 1924, by the Bobbs-Merrill Company. Indianapolis.

A Great Little State

You know, Connecticut is a great little state. More things are made here and were invented here than any other state in the Union. Well, I was sittin' on the verandy of a hotel in St. Louis and there was a lot of other fellers there. It was a warm day and the lobby was crowded and a bunch of us was sittin' out on the verandy.

We got talkin' back and forth and tellin' where we come from and all, and there was a feller there from Kansas. He started to lay it into me for comin' from such a little bit of a state. I says, "Listen here, Mister. You come from Kansas, don't you?" I says, "My brother is a land broker out there. He's a Connecticut boy. He's lent money to half the people in his county," I says. "Why, your whole goddam state is mortgaged to New England," I says, "and Connecticut is holdin' half the mortgages.

"Look at the buttons on your coat," I says. "Ten to one they were made in Waterbury. You're smokin' a cigar right now that was manufactured in Hartford. You got a dollar watch in your pocket. Where was that made? Waterbury." I says, "The bed you slept on last night had a mattress that was made down in Bridgeport." I kept givin' it to him like that for ten minutes. "Don't go braggin' to me about that God-forsaken mud-hole you call a state," I says. "I come from a real state." Well, that feller finally got up and walked into the hotel. The other fellers were laughin' to beat the band.

The Iowan and the Vermonter

Once a visitor from the West came to Vermont and fell in with one of the natives and the following conversation took place. Said the Iowa man, "I am from Iowa. That is a wonderful state. You can raise anything. No mountains, no stones, the soil twenty feet thick. I cannot understand how you folks can get a living on these rocky hill-sides." The Vermonter answered with a drawl, "Waal, it is hard. We keep a few chickens, a pig, a hoss, a cow and maybe a few sheep, and have a garden, and a good many of us have some Iowa 6 per cent mortgages, so we get along after a fashion."

From "Connecticut Clockmakers," as told by Arthur Botsford, Thomaston, Connecticut, to Francis Donovan, in *Living Lore of New England*. Manuscripts of the Federal Writers' Project of the Works Progress Administration for the State of Connecticut.

From *The Boyhood Days of President Calvin Coolidge*, or From The Green Mountains to the White House, Original Sketches of Plymouth Life, by Ernest C. Carpenter, pp. 77–78. Copyright, 1925, by the Marble City Press. Rutland, Vermont: The Tuttle Company.

The Yankee and the Southerner

"Down East," observed a Southerner to a Yankee, "a cow and a calf, and a calico frock, is said to be a girl's portion; and that's the place you come from." "Well," replied the Yankee, "people have to be born pretty much where other folks say, barrin' accidents. An' you're from that place, ain't ye? where a potato patch [that] has cracks in [it] so wide that the grasshoppers are picked up at the bottom by handfuls—all their necks broke tryin' to jump over—is a portion of the eldest son. My father told me," continued the Down Easter, "he was ridin' by one of your great farms, and observin' the wretchedness of the land, he said, 'The fellow that owns this must be plaguy poor.' 'Not so poor as you think,' answered a voice from the blackberry bushes, 'for I don't own but a third on't. My father gin away one third to a man to take t'other.' "

The Vermonter in Texas

Speaking of the scarcity of Democrats in Plymouth—it was probably from this town that a certain man migrated to Texas, and there one day found himself in an enthusiastic gathering of Democrats. One got up and made a noisy harangue, and then asked the Democrats to stand up as witnesses to their political faith. Practically everyone arose but this Vermonter. Then derisively the speaker said, "If there is any Republican here, let him stand." This man stood up alone and of course everyone laughed at him. The speaker said, "Why are you a Republican?" The man replied, "Well, I am from Vermont. My father was a Republican, and I suppose that is the reason I am a Republican." But the speaker said, "That is no reason at all. Suppose your father or your grandfather had been a horse thief. Would that make you one?" And the Vermonter replied, "No, probably in that case I would have been a Democrat."

CONSERVATIVE YANKEES

Exhuming the Remains

An incident told in many Vermont communities for two generations and always as a local occurrence has to do with the transfer of an ancient ceme-

---

From *Turner's Comick Almanack for 1840,* Correctly Calculated for the Whole United States and Territories, [n. p.]. Boston: James Fisher. New York and Philadelphia: Turner & Fisher.

From *The Boyhood Days of President Calvin Coolidge,* or From The Green Mountains to the White House, Original Sketches of Plymouth Life, by Ernest C. Carpenter, pp. 128–129. Copyright, 1925, by the Marble City Press. Rutland, Vermont: The Tuttle Company.

tery to a new location. All consents had been obtained except in the case of a comparatively recent grave. The occupant had been buried only seventy years and had two elderly grandnephews still living. One of them refused consent for a long time, but finally gave in, though he would have nothing whatever to do with the business of transfer. After it was over the two old brothers were sitting on the front porch and the following dialogue ensued:

"Did they?"

"Yep."

"Were you thar?"

"Yep."

"How was the box?"

"Purty nigh gone."

"Coffin?"

"Sorta moldy."

"D'ja look in?"

"Yep."

"How was Uncle John?"

"Kinda poorly." [1]

A Bristol man, having put by substantial economies, erected a family monument and assembled the remains of his immediate forebears in one plot. This entailed the exhumation of the remains of his grandmother, which had been reposing some thirty-seven years at Salisbury. The trying operation being achieved, the man entered his home, noticeably subdued. The women of the household were a-twitter with curiosity.

"Tell us, Pa," coaxed his daughter. "How did Grandma look?"

"Mmmmm-m-m." An interval of determined silence.

"Don't set there like a stump, Elmer," insisted his wife. "It won't hurt y' t' talk. How did Grandma look?"

"H'm-m-m-mm. Well, Grandma didn't look what you'd call real rugged." [2]

Bringing in the Log

Sam Slick tells the following story:—

Squire Peleg Sandford and all his family were all of them the most awful

---

[1] From *As Much As I Dare,* A Personal Recollection by Burges Johnson, p. 32. Copyright, 1944, by Ives Washburn, Inc. New York.

[2] From "Some Characteristics of Northern Vermont Wit," by Robert Davis, *Proceedings of the Vermont Historical Society,* New Series, Vol. V (December, 1937), pp. 322–323.

From *Comic Metamorphoses,* Being a Perfect Encyclopedia of Fun and Humor . . . , by Dr. W. Valentine, pp. 176–177. Entered according to an Act of Congress, in the year 1855, by Garrett & Company, in the Clerk's Office of the District Court for the Southern District of New York. New York: Dick and Fitzgerald.

passionate folks that ever lived, when they chose; and then they could keep in their temper, and be as cool as cucumbers. One night old Peleg, as he was called, told his son Gucom, a boy of fourteen years old, to go and bring in a back-log for the fire. Back-log, you know, Squire, in a wood-fire, is always the biggest stick that one can find or carry. It takes a stout junk of a boy to lift one.

Well, as soon as Gucom goes to fetch the log, the old squire drags forward the coals, and fixes the fire so as to leave a bed for it, and stands by, ready to fit it in its place. Presently in comes Gucom with a little cut-stick, no bigger than his leg, and throws it on. Uncle Peleg got so mad, he never said a word, but just seized his riding-whip, and gave him an awful whippin'. He tanned his hide properly for him, you may depend.

"Now," says he, "go, sir, and bring in a proper back-log."

Gucom was clear grit as well as the old man, for he was a chip of the old block, and no mistake; so out he goes without so much as sayin' a word, but instead of goin' to the wood-pile, he walks off altogether, and stayed away eight years, till he was one-and-twenty and his own master.—Well, as soon as he was a man grown, and lawfully on his own hook, he took it in his head one day he'd go home and see his father and mother agin, and show them that he was alive and kicking; for they didn't know whether he was dead or not, never havin' heard of or from him one blessed word all that time. When he arrived at the old house, daylight was down, and the lights lit, and as he passed the keepin' room winder, he looked in, and there was the old Squire sittin' in the chair he was eight years afore, when he ordered in the back-log, and gave him such an unmerciful whippin'. So what does Gucom do but stop at the wood-pile, and pick up a most hugaceous log, (for he had grow'd to be a whappin' big fellow then,) and openin' the door, marches in and lays it down upon the hearth, and then lookin' up, says he—

"Father, I've brought you in the back-log."

Uncle Peleg was struck up all of a heap; he couldn't believe his own eyes, that the six-footer was the boy he had cowhided, and he couldn't believe his own ears when he heard him call him father; a man from the grave wouldn't have surprised him more; he was quite onfakalized and bedumbed for a minute. But he came to right off, and iced down to a freezin' point in no time.

"What did you say?" said he.

"That I have brought you in the back-log, sir, you sent me out for."

"Well then, you've been an amazin' long time a fetchin' it," said he, "that's all I can say. Draw the coals forward, put it on, and then go to bed."

Now that's a fact, Squire; I know the parties myself and that's what I do call coolness, and no mistake!

Sylvester and John

. . . SYLVESTER had a younger brother named John, between whom and himself a coolness had existed for many years, so intense that they never spoke to each other. Old Jimmy Helme, who delighted in making peace among his neighbors, had often sought to reconcile the brothers, but without effect. One day as Jimmy was standing at the Four Corners with Sylvester, he saw John coming along on the other side. "Now," said Jimmy, "do speak to John, and I know he will speak to you." "I would do so, Mr. Helme, to oblige you," said Sylvester, "but I know he won't speak to me!" "Well, now," rejoined Jimmy, "do just try and see." So when John got opposite to where they stood, Sylvester halloaed across the street, "John!" John stopped, and Sylvester continued, "When are you going to bring home that iron bar you stole from me, you thief?" Without saying a word John passed on. "There, Mr. Helme," said Sylvester, "I told you it would be no use!"

When on his death-bed, Sylvester relented and sent for his brother John. When John came to his bed-side, Sylvester told him he would like to make up with him before he died, to which John readily assented, whereupon they shook hands and exchanged many friendly greetings. The interview lasted for an hour or more, when John shook his brother's hand, bidding him an affectionate good-bye. Just as John was closing the door behind him, Sylvester called him back and said, "Now, John, we are good friends, ain't we, just as if nothing had ever happened?" "Yes, brother Sylvester," replied John, "that is just as I feel." "Just so," said Sylvester, "but remember, John, this is only in case I don't get well again. If I do, why then we are to be just as we were before." "Yes, brother Sylvester," said John, "that is just as I understand it, and should have said so before, only I didn't think there was any chance of your ever leaving your bed again alive." . . .

How the Old Lady Beat John

ONE stormy winter night, after midnight, I was sitting here reading, the

---

From *The Jonny-Cake Papers of "Shepherd Tom,"* Together With Reminiscences of Narragansett Schools of Former Days, by Thomas Robinson Hazard, with a Biographical Sketch and Notes by Rowland Gibson Hazard, pp. 165–166. Copyright, 1915, by Rowland G. Hazard. Boston: Printed for the Subscribers.

From *Among the Northern Hills,* by W. C. Prime, pp. 124–127. Copyright, 1895, by Harper & Brothers. New York.

Of the many . . . stories that lawyers tell, I think the one that takes the prize is the yarn about an old widow in a little town not far from our home . . . such is the power that hatred can bring to some of these people in the hills.—Ernest Poole, *The Great White Hills* (Garden City, 1946), pp. 230–231.

rest of the family having gone to sleep long before, when old Dr. Strong thundered at the door-knocker, and made noise enough to wake the Seven Sleepers. It is a way he has, and neither my wife nor the girls, who were roused out of slumber, nor I myself, had any question who was at the door. I let him in myself, and a tempest of wind and snow with him. The blast that drove him into my arms also put out the hall lights, whirled into the library, and flared the reading-lamp so that it broke the chimney and blazed up to a colored tissue-paper affair which Susie had put over the shade, set it on fire, and for a moment threatened a general conflagration of papers and books on the table.

"Shut the door yourself!" I shouted, and rushed in here to put out the fire. That done, I went back and found the old doctor out of breath, in the dark, trying to shut the door against the wind. It took the strength of both of us to do it. Then I told him to find his way to the library, for he knew it, and I went off in search of another lamp.

When I came back he was just recovering his wind, and, after a gasp or two, told me his errand. "Old Mrs. Norton is dying. She can't live till morning. She's alive now only on stimulants. She wants to make a will, and I have come for you."

"A nice night," I said, "for a two-mile drive, to make a will for a woman who hasn't a cent in the world to leave. Why didn't you tell her so, and have done with it."

"Now look here," said the doctor, "this is a case of an old woman and old neighbor and friend, and she wants you to do something for her, and you'll do it, if it's only to comfort her last hours. Get your things and come with me. We shall not find her alive if you don't hurry, and you'll be sorry if that happens."

The upshot of it was that I went. We had a fearful drive out to the farm-house on the flat, which you are asking about. Mrs. Norton was the widow of John Norton, who had died forty odd years before this. John Norton when he married her was a widower with one son—John. He was a man of considerable property, and when he died left a widow, that son John by his first wife, and two sons by his second wife. The elder son, John, had never been on very warm terms with his step-mother, and for some years had had no intercourse with the family.

I found the old lady lying in the big room, on a great bedstead on one side of the room, opposite to the broad chimney, in which was a roaring fire, the only light in the room. After the doctor had spoken to her and administered something—a stimulant, I suppose—he came over to me and said in a whisper: "Hurry up; she's very weak."

I had brought paper and pen and ink with me. I found a stand and a candle, placed them at the head of the bed, and, after saying a few words to her, told her I was ready to prepare the will, if she would now go on and tell me what she wanted to do. I wrote the introductory phrase rapidly, and, leaning over towards her, said: "Now go on, Mrs. Norton." Her voice was quite faint, and she seemed to speak with an effort. She said:

"First of all I want to give the farm to my sons Harry and James; just put that down." "But," said I, "you can't do that, Mrs. Norton; the farm isn't yours to give away."

"The farm isn't mine?" she said, in a voice decidedly stronger than before.

"No; the farm isn't yours. You have only a life interest in it."

"This farm, that I've run for goin' on forty-three year next spring, isn't mine to do what I please with it! Why not, Judge? I'd like to know what you mean!"

"Why, Mr. Norton, your husband, gave you a life estate in all his property, and on your death the farm goes to his son John, and your children get the village houses. I have explained that to you very often before."

"And when I die John Norton is to have this house and farm, whether I will or no?"

"Just so. It will be his."

"Then I ain't going to die!" said the old woman, in a clear and decidedly ringing and healthy voice. And, so saying, she threw her feet over the front of the bed, sat up, gathered a blanket and coverlet about her, straightened up her gaunt form, walked across the room, and sat down in a great chair before the fire.

The doctor and I came home. That was fifteen years ago. The old lady's alive to-day. And she accomplished her intent. She beat John, after all. He died four years ago, in Boston, and I don't know what will he left. But whoever comes into the farmhouse when she goes out, it will not be John. And since John's death the farm has been better kept, and everything about it is in vastly better condition for strangers than it would have been for John.

Getting at the Right Tooth

. . . "Big Joe" is in his seventies now, but back when Cornish was still a logging center, his brawn and skill with an ax made him the local Paul Bunyan. One day he stomped into George Hunt's general store with a terrible toothache.

"Yank out this 'un right here, George," he said, placing his finger on a tooth.

Hunt looked. The bad tooth was obviously the third back from the one the patient indicated, and Hunt said so.

"Are you tryin' to tell me I don't know my own mind?" roared Big Joe. So Hunt pulled a perfectly sound tooth. As he expected, the patient was back half an hour later for another anesthetic.

From "Democracy in Our Town," by John Kord Lagemann, *Collier's,* Vol. 119 (March 8, 1947), No. 10, p. 13. Copyright, 1947, by The Crowell-Collier Publishing Company. Springfield, Ohio.

"Pull the next one."

This time there was no argument. "I figure to get at the right one directly," Hunt told the boys around the stove.

Sure enough, Big Joe came back to have it pulled. "Reckon I lost a couple o' good teeth," he said, spitting out the shreds, "but, damn it, I still got my principles."

Out of Bibles

. . . A VERY well-meaning, but unfortunately illiterate man, in a neighboring town, was called upon a short time since by the village parson, a devout individual who had never before met with the other. The minister had but recently entered upon his clerical duties in the place, and in the course of his visit he took occasion to converse at length with his parishioner, whom he found to be a very worthy citizen, well disposed and apparently honest, but who was remarkably religious, who had read (according to his own ideas) a great deal, and who had done his share towards the good of the village generally, and of his own household more especially.

"You practise family service, I trust?" asked the Dominie.

"Wal, yes. Yes, sir," replied the man, at a venture, though he had not the slightest idea of the parson's meaning.

"And you have a few books here, I see."

"Yes, sir. Only the useful and the moral."

"Yes," continued the clerical gentleman, and he turned to the little table, looked over the sparse library, found a copy of Robinson Crusoe, an odd volume of Paul and Virginia, Murray's Grammar, and a few others—and at length the parson proposed to read with the family if the man would hand him the Bible.

"Yes, yes, sir," replied the other, considerably disconcerted. But, putting his spectacles on his nose, he immediately advanced to the table and commenced examining the backs of the scattered volumes; there was no such work in sight!

He was in a temporary dilemma, but his good wit instantly came to his aid, for, turning quickly, he added,

"Wal, sir—we've allers had 'em—but, fact is—to tell the treuth—*we're abaout aout o' Bibles*!" And the good soul sat down again, at once, greatly relieved.

The parson sighed, vouchsafed a few words of kindly advice, and left his honest-meaning parishioner to himself.

From *Gleanings from the Portfolio of the "Young 'Un,"* A Series of Humorous Sketches, Third Edition, [by George P. Burnham], pp. 111–112. Entered according to Act of Congress, in the year 1849, by R. B. Fitts and G. P. Burnham, in the Clerk's Office of the District Court of the District of Massachusetts. Boston: Published by R. B. Fitts & Co.

SALT WATER YANKEES

The Seven Jurors and the Harbor of Hawaii

DANIEL WEBSTER, in a letter to a friend in West Dennis, said in 1851:

"Gentlemen, the nature of your population is somewhat peculiar. I have often been struck by the very great number of sea captains as well as other mariners which the County of Barnstable and the neighboring islands furnish. . . . I was once engaged in the trial of a case in your district, in which a question arose respecting the entrance into the harbor of Owohyhee [Hawaii] between reefs of coral rock guarding it on either side. The counsel for the opposite party proposed to call witnesses to give information to the jury concerning this entrance. I saw at once a smile, which I thought I understood, and suggested to the judge that very probably some of the jurors had seen the entrance themselves; upon which, seven out of the twelve jurors arose and said that they were quite familiarly acquainted with it, having seen it often."

Ma'am Hackett's Garden

FISHING on the Banks is largely carried on by fast-sailing well-equipped schooners. They carry fresh vegetables, frozen meats, and canned goods to eat, and the crew has the best of fare. It requires three or four months to lay in a cargo of cod. The decision as to just where a schooner shall fish depends a great deal on the depth of the water and the character of the bottom. By constant sounding with the lead line an expert captain gets to know the realm beneath the waters very thoroughly. The lead has a hollow at its lower extremity in which a little grease is inserted, so that a sample of the sea bottom may be secured. The story is told of a certain old Nantucket skipper who could invariably tell just where his vessel was by examining the soil his lead brought up. In order to perplex him his crew once put some garden loam from the home island in the cup of the lead, made a pretence of sounding, and then asked the skipper to name the position of the schooner. The old fisherman tasted the dirt on the lead—his favorite method of determining its individuality—and suddenly exclaimed, "Nantucket's sunk, and here we are right over Ma'am Hackett's garden!"

From *Cape Cod Pilot*, by Jeremiah Digges, with Editorial and Research Assistance of the Members of the Federal Writers' Project, p. 101. American Guide Series, Federal Writers' Project, Works Progress Administration for the State of Massachusetts. Copyright, 1937, by Poor Richard Associates. Provincetown and New York: Modern Pilgrim Press and the Viking Press.

From *New England, A Human Interest Geographical Reader*, by Clifton Johnson, pp. 84–86. Copyright, 1917, by The Macmillan Company. New York and London

How Squire Fearing Piloted the Sloop

THE Woonkinco River entered the bay by a deep channel, and the harbor was often lively with sloops, schooners, and ships arriving and departing. Small sailing vessels from the bay passed up the Weweantet River to the "brickkiln landing," where sloops loaded firewood and timber, and farmers landed crops gathered on the bay shores. Squire Fearing's farm included lands in Agawame, and as they were six or seven miles from his dwelling-house, the crops were brought to this landing, and carted thence to his barns. One autumn, as the story goes, he had corn to be harvested on the island off Fearing Neck, and his neighbor, Captain Uriah Savery, had a sloop which the Squire hired to bring home the corn; having assured the captain that he knew the channels and could pilot the way to the island. They started from the landing and easily ran down the river to Great Hill. After passing this promontory the Squire lost the way. Looking across the bay, all the headlands and coves appeared alike to him, and he could recognize no landmark by which to direct a course. He gave the captain orders to steer in so many diverse directions that the old mariner was convinced that this justice of the peace, who dispensed the laws of the Commonwealth from Fearing Hill, was more of a farmer than a navigator. In his humiliation the Squire confessed that he did not know the marine way to the island, but he had often gone to it by land and swum his carts and oxen across the channel. The captain put the sloop before the wind, and running her towards Tempest Knob had the good fortune to make Fearing Neck. As they passed along the shores not a landmark was recognized by the Squire. Suddenly he vindicated his claim to be a pilot by exclaiming: "Uriah! Uriah! I told ye I knew the way; there's old Macmanaman and his striped oxen on the shore for sartin!"

Following the Wrong Gulls

"IT's shutting in thick over the whole of the bay," Cap'n Eldad told the lad at the wheel, who was a green hand and off-Cape at that. "Better let her go for home." And he started down the companionway.

"But what course shall I steer?" the youth called after him; for "home" was in Truro, and the vessel was in the middle of Cape Cod Bay.

From *Colonial Times on Buzzard's Bay,* by William Root Bliss, pp. 156–157. Copyright, 1888, by William Root Bliss. Boston and New York: Houghton, Mifflin and Company.

From *Cape Cod Pilot,* by Jeremiah Digges, with Editorial and Research Assistance of the Members of the Federal Writers' Project, p. 206. American Guide Series, Federal Writers' Project, Works Progress Administration for the State of Massachusetts. Copyright, 1937, by Poor Richard Associates. Provincetown and New York: Modern Pilgrim Press and the Viking Press.

"Follow the gulls," replied Cap'n Eldad. "They'll take you straight into Pamet Harbor."

The skipper turned in. He awoke six hours later—long beyond any reasonable running time—came on deck, and found the vessel off the Back Shore of the Cape. What in 'tarnity's name, he wanted to know, was his helmsman trying to do—go a furrin viage?

"I've been following the gulls, like you told me," the lad replied.

"Why, you fog-brained farmer! You've been following Chatham gulls, not Truro gulls!"

The Captain's Hat

THEIR knowledge of the weather comes of lifelong study. There is the story, for instance, of old Cap'n Phineas Eldridge, retired skipper who took to growing turnips on a farm in Eastham, but who had grown weatherwise through many years in command of a coasting schooner. One evening the Cap'n was late for supper, and his wife, glancing out the window, saw a light flitting about the turnip field. Then the Cap'n dashed in, spun the telephone crank and shouted, "Give me Chatham, quick! Hello, Chatham? I want Sam Paine, the postmaster. Hey, Sam! My hat's just blowed off and got clear of me, but she's scudding due south in this breeze, and allowing for the reef in the brim, I calculate she'll just about make it to your place in fourteen minutes more. Mail her back to me, will you, Sam?"

The hat, of course, fetched up on the specified doorstep in Chatham, in exactly fourteen minutes after the Cap'n hung up the receiver, and was sent back to him next morning by parcel post.

How Long from Port?

A SIX months' North Atlantic voyage, officially called a " 'tween seasons" voyage, unofficially called a "plum-pudding voyage," was much scorned by the sturdy old-timers of New Bedford. Such a voyage was generally carried on by Provincetown brigs and schooners. One old New Bedford skipper, who had been coerced against his inclination to make such a voyage, was busily engaged casting off from the wharf when his agent approached and whispered in his ear, "Captain Jones, you've forgotten to kiss your wife good-bye!" Without shifting his gaze from aloft, the captain demanded—

Ibid., pp. 10–11.

From *The Yankee Whaler*, by Clifford W. Ashley, p. 103. Boston: Houghton Mifflin Company.

"What's ailin' her? I'm only going to be gone six months."

There have been many yarns told illustrative of the extreme length and precarious nature of a whaleman's voyages. One captain reported upon his return from a four years' fruitless search that he hadn't a single barrel of oil or a single pound of bone aboard, but he'd "had a damn fine sail!" A California clipper is said to have once hailed a whaler in the neighborhood of the Horn and to have asked, "How long from port?" One of a row of ragged and long-bearded men, who were lined up at the rail, answered, "We don't remember, but we were young men when we started!"

Counting the Children

WHEN the vessels left, the wives assembled on the wharves to say good-by, and it was a convention that everyone keep a stiff upper lip.

"We Provincetown women," one banker's wife told me, "would watch an off-Cape bride sharp to see she didn't show a tear. That's no way to see a man off when he's going to be away for months maybe."

"How many children have you, Captain Davis?" I asked an old-timer.

"Wife," he said, "how many times have I been bankin' since we was married?"

Whalers' Bastards

THERE were transgressions. There were occasional sons and daughters born to couples while the husband had been at sea for a couple of years. One such occasion was the cause of a visit to the mother by a committee of neighbors from the village church.

"Mrs. Jones." began the elder solemnly, "there is something that ought to be explained. You have just given birth to a son, and yet your husband has been at sea for the past two years and over. Have you anything to say in explanation?"

"Why, yes," replied the mother, with evident sincerity. "John has written to me several times since he has been away."

From *Time and the Town, A Provincetown Chronicle,* by Mary Heaton Vorse, p. 114. Copyright, 1942, by Mary Heaton Vorse. New York: The Dial Press.

From *Tales and Trails of Martha's Vineyard,* by Joseph C. Allen, p. 66. Copyright, 1938, by Joseph C. Allen. Boston: Little, Brown and Company.

Captain Peleg's Letter

"Now then, Arathusy," Captain Peleg told his wife, "it's twenty minutes to sailing-hour. Better start your crying and get it over with, so's I won't be holding up the vessel."

As he pursed his lips and began tidying up his ditty-box, an obedient sob escaped his wife.

"Oh, Peleg, 'twouldn't be so hard, if you'd only write me a letter while you're away on these etarnal long v'yages! Promise me, Peleg, you'll write this time—just one letter!"

The Captain groaned and promised. And eighteen months later, Arathusy, all a-tremble, tore open an envelope and read:

Hong Kong, China,
May 21, 1854.

Dear Arathusy:

I am here and you are there.

P. Hawes.

Captain Eleazer's *Bulldog*

THERE is no question but that these men loved a good ship, a fast ship. Among the thousand Cape Cod yarns that are variations on this theme is the one about Captain Eleazer, skipper of one of the trimmest schooners in the "Injies trade." His vessel, the *Bulldog*, was "built to split a drop of water into a half moon while she heeled," and he had let the town know he was proud of her. He married a girl name Abigail Bangs, and townsfolk began asking him if he planned to change the name of the vessel to the *Abigail S* as a token of affection for his bride. His reply was, "No, I don't see fitten for to change the vessel's name. But if Abigail keeps on steady being a good girl like she is, I've been thinking I might have her rechristened Bulldog."

From *Cape Cod Pilot*, by Jeremiah Digges, with Editorial and Research Assistance of the Members of the Federal Writers' Project, p. 65. American Guide Series, Federal Writers' Project, Works Progress Administration for the State of Massachusetts. Copyright, 1937, by Poor Richard Associates. Provincetown and New York: Modern Pilgrim Press and the Viking Press.

Ibid., p. 69.

The Captain's Prescription

Many old-time ships carried in the medicine chest what was called the "symptom book," in which were detailed such symptoms as were likely to develop in certain diseases. The diagnosis being thus disclosed, instructions were given to administer such and such a dose of remedy number so and so from the medicine chest. One day a sick sailor having developed the symptoms calling for number eleven, the captain found to his dismay that the bottle supposed to contain that number was empty. However, not to be stumped by a little thing like that, he administered equal parts of number six and number five to the amount of the dose directed for number eleven. The story has it that the man was pretty sick for a time, but that he finally pulled through, though whether owing to a strong constitution or to the captain's ingenuity, deponent sayeth not.

The Captain's Shirts

. . . Some Cape Cod captains were the *cleanest* men. Captain Zenas Marston, of Hyannisport, wore a clean shirt and shaved every day he was at sea. When he went on a long voyage, he took over three hundred shirts with him—and every one of them had been made by his wife. Captain Sumner Pierce, of Barnstable, came home one June with seven hundred shirts to be laundered. They were "boiled shirts," too. It was cheaper, the captains said, to buy new ones than to get soiled shirts washed. The women washed in wooden tubs and heated their irons on cook stoves, and it took Mrs. Pierce all summer to get Sumner's shirts out of the way.

Thar She Blows!

We was cruising down the Mozambique Channel under reefed tops'ls and the wind blowin' more'n half a gale, two years outer New Bedford an' no ile. An' the masthead lookout shouts, "Thar she blows!"

From *The Nantucket Scrap Basket,* Being a Collection of Characteristic Stories and Sayings of the People of the Town and Island of Nantucket, Massachusetts. Compiled, Edited and Arranged by William F. Macy and Roland B. Hussey and Published for the Benefit of "The Sons and Daughters of Nantucket," pp. 13–14. Copyright, 1916, by William F. Macy and Roland B. Hussey. Nantucket: The Inquirer and Mirror Press. 1916.

From *And This Is Cape Cod!,* by Eleanor Early, p. 153. Copyright, 1936, by Eleanor Early. Boston and New York: Houghton Mifflin Company.

From *History of New Bedford,* by Zephaniah Pease. Cited in *Sea Language Comes Ashore,* by Joanna Carver Colcord, p. 190. Copyright, 1945, by Cornell Maritime Press. New York.

An' I goes aft.

"Cap'n Simmons," sez I (his being the same name as mine, but no kith or kin, thank God!) "the man at the masthead sez, 'Thar she blows!' Shall I lower?"

"Mr. Simmons," sez the cap'n, "it's blowin' a little too peart an' I don't see fittin' fer to lower."

An' I goes forrard.

An' the man at the masthead sings out, "Thar she blows an' breaches!"

An' I goes aft.

"Cap'n Simmons," sez I, "the lookout at the masthead sez, 'Thar she blows an' breaches!' Shall I lower?"

"Mr. Simmons," sez the cap'n, "it's blowin' too peart an' I don't see fittin' fer to lower."

An' I goes forrard.

An' the lookout at the masthead sings out, "Thar she blows an' breaches, an' sparm at that!"

An' I goes aft.

"Cap'n Simmons," sez I, "the lookout sez, 'Thar she blows an' breaches, an' sparm at that!' Shall I lower?"

"Mr. Simmons," sez he, "it's blowin' too peart an' I don't see fittin' fer to lower, but if so be you sees fittin' fer to lower, Mr. Simmons, why lower, an' be good an' God damned to ye."

An' I lowers an' goes on the whale, an' when I comes within seventy-five foot of her I sez, "Put me jest three seas nearer, fer I'm hell with the long harpoon." An' I darted the iron an' it tuk.

When I comes alongside the ship, Cap'n Simmons stands in the gangway. "Mr. Simmons," sez he, "you are the finest mate that ever sailed in this ship. Below in the locker on the port side there's rum and seegars at your sarvice."

"Cap'n Simmons," sez I, "I don't want your rum, no more your seegars. All I want of you, Cap'n Simmons, is plain seevility, an' that of the commonest, God damndest kind."

An' I goes forrard.

The Stammering Sailor

The circumstances are thus told: When he fell overboard there was only one other man on deck—a man who stammered, but a good singer. When Capt. Bacon fell overboard he attempted to call the crew, but could not articulate a word. One said to him "sing it," and he commenced and sung "John Bacon's overboard."[1]

---

[1] From *Genealogical Notes of Barnstable Families,* Being a Reprint of the Amos Otis Papers, Originally Published in The Barnstable Patriot. Revised by C. F. Swift, Largely from Notes Made by the Author, Vol. I, p. 35 n. Entered according to Act of Congress, in the year 1885, by F. B. Goss, in the Office of the Librarian of Congress, at Washington. Barnstable, Mass.: F. B. & F. P. Goss, Publishers and Printers. 1888.

A stuttering foremast hand, seeing a shipmate fall overboard, rushed aft to tell the captain, but so terrified and excited was he that he could only mouth helplessly, "B-b-b-b—!" "Sing it, man," roared the captain, "sing it!" Whereupon the sailor (for 'tis well known that stutterers can always sing) chanted:

"Overboard goes Barnabas—
Half a mile astarn of us." [2]

The generation of Cape Codders who could remember the packets is gone. But the story of Elnathan Annable, the stammering sailor, survives the ages. According to the legend, the skipper of a Truro packet falls overboard while the vessel is scudding before the wind, and only one man is on deck to witness the accident. But poor Elnathan Annable stammers, and when he is excited, cannot speak a word. Elnathan is a good singer, however, and can overcome his stammering by singing the reluctant words. He manages to call all hands on deck, but cannot tell them what has happened. At last one of the crew shouts, "Sing it!" And Elnathan, pale and horrified, sings out:

"O, you'll forgive these tears,
For now you all must learn
John Nickerson is overboard
Half a mile astern! [3]

I'm His Man

. . . A Hyannis captain remembered that an owner once said to him when he was looking for a berth: "The new clipper ship Spit-fire is lading for San Francisco and the cap'n's a driver. He wants a mate can jump over the fore-yard every morning before breakfast." "I'm his man," retorted the seaman, "if it's laid on the deck." He shipped forthwith, and had a passage of one hundred and two days to San Francisco.

---

[2] From *The Nantucket Scrap Basket,* Being a Collection of Characteristic Stories and Sayings of the People of the Town and Island of Nantucket, Massachusetts. Compiled, Edited and Arranged by William F. Macy and Roland B. Hussey and Published for the Benefit of "The Sons and Daughters of Nantucket," p. 15. Copyright, 1916, by William F. Macy and Roland B. Hussey. Nantucket: The Inquirer and Mirror Press. 1916.

[3] From *Cape Cod Pilot,* by Jeremiah Digges, with Editorial and Research Assistance of the Members of the Federal Writers' Project, p. 210. American Guide Series, Federal Writers' Project, Works Progress Administration for the State of Massachusetts. Copyright, 1937, by Poor Richard Associates. Provincetown and New York: Modern Pilgrim Press and the Viking Press.

From *Old Cape Cod; The Land, The Men, The Sea,* by Mary Rogers Bangs, p. 238. Copyright, 1920 and 1931, by Mary Rogers Bangs. Boston and New York: Houghton Mifflin Company.

The Seagoing Coffin

It was characteristic of Cotton Mather and his followers that they enjoyed the contemplation of death; their descendants have not changed the subject matter, but they have a lighter touch. As proof of this, Joe Lincoln once told me of his effort to find the source of a story that is told in nearly every town on the Cape. In each place the oldest inhabitants can tell you the exact spot where the incident occurred, and the names of the *dramatis personae*.

Aunt Emma, it seems, was near her end, and the only maker of caskets in the vicinity was Cap'n Zeke, the boat builder. He had promised to have a coffin ready, but each time the family inquired he had done nothing about it. Finally they went to him with anxious insistence, for Aunt Emma was fading fast.

"I'm mighty sorry," said Cap'n Zeke; "fact is I've been so busy with this thu'ty-footer I just couldn't put my mind to anythin' else. But I'll have her for ye day-after-t'morrer mornin'."

Cap'n Zeke was as good as his word. The coffin got to the house as he had promised and just in time. But he had been a little bit absent-minded and had put a centerboard in it.

This same story is ancient folklore along the Maine coast, but down there they tell you that the Cap'n added a rudder.

She Sleeps Six

. . . Cape fishermen, you are to know, rate the size of their boats not by their length but by the number of men they can sleep. "She sleeps four" or "she sleeps five" is the way they phrase it. One day a certain distant rich man died who had loved this land, and his last request was to be buried in a mausoleum at a Cape cemetery by the sea. Not long afterwards an old fishing skipper, looking into it one morning through the finely grilled doors, was accosted by a passerby with the remark:

"That's a grand tomb, Cap'n Jim."

"Yes, sir, this is a mighty good 'un," was the captain's reply, "she's here for keeps, and she sleeps six."

From *As Much As I Dare,* A Personal Recollection, by Burges Johnson, p. 31. Copyright, 1944, by Ives Washburn, Inc. New York.

From *Cape Cod Ahoy!,* A Travel Book for the Summer Visitor, by Arthur Wilson Tarbell, p. 102. Copyright, 1932, by Arthur Wilson Tarbell. Boston: A. T. Ramsay & Company.

Cap'n Tibbett and the Body

ALONG the Maine coast—I have been told several places where it occurred—two farmers were gathering kelp along the beach for fertilizer, when they came upon a corpse. Neither recognized it, but one said he thought it might be old Cap'n Tibbett who lived alone in a cabin down on the point. They thought they had better go out to the cabin and see, before reporting their discovery.

They reached the cabin, knocked on the door and old Cap'n Tibbett opened it.

"Well," said one of them, "we're mighty relieved. We found a body down in the kelp and thought it might be you."

"H'm," said Cap'n Tibbett, rolling his quid. "Found a body, did you? Was it wearing a pea-jacket?"

"Yep, had on a pea-jacket!"

"Corduroy pants?"

"Yep."

"Boots?"

"Yep."

"Was they knee-boots or these here thigh-boots?"

"They was knee-boots."

"Well, then—'twan't me."

A Wreck's a Wreck

. . . OLD Chrissy was an old rascal of a woman that was the head of a gang of [Block Island] wreckers. They lured ships in with false lights, and they killed the sailors and passengers, so there wouldn't be any tales told. Old Chrissy took charge of the killing. She had a big club and she'd hist her skirt and wade out in the surf and clout the people on the head as they swam in or floated in. She called a wreck a wrack, the way the Block Islanders do. That's the way she pronounced it. One night, she and her gang lured a ship up on the reef, and the sailors were floating in, and old Chrissy was out there clouting them on their heads. One poor fellow floated up, and it was one of old Chrissy's sons, who'd left the island and gone to the mainland to be a sailor. He looked up at old Chrissy and said, "Hello, Ma." Old Chrissy didn't hesitate. She gave him a clout on the head with her club. "A son's a son," she said, "but a wrack's a wrack."

From *As Much As I Dare,* A Personal Recollection, by Burges Johnson, pp. 32–33. Copyright, 1944, by Ives Washburn, Inc. New York.

As told by Charlie Brayman. From "Dragger Captain," by Joseph Mitchell in *The New Yorker,* Vol. XXII (January 11, 1947), No. 48, p. 42. Copyright, 1947, by The F-R. Publishing Corporation. New York.

A Long Wreck Hook for the Preacher

. . . I HEARD a Block Island [1] the other day. Johnny Bindloss told it. Johnny had it years ago from his grandfather, old man William Park Bindloss. He was a stone mason who specialized in lighthouses. He built South East Light on Block Island, and he lived over there a year or two and got acquainted. In those days, according to the general talk, the islanders got the better part of their bread and butter salvaging off wrecks. There'd be wrecks on the reefs all during the winter, coasting vessels mostly, and the stuff in them would wash up on the beach. The islanders would stand on the beach all day and all night, hooking for the stuff with poles that had bent nails on the ends of them. They were called wreck hooks. Everybody would line up down there and hook—little children, great-grandmothers, *every*body that could walk. The competition got so thick that they all agreed on a standard-length hook. Everybody had to use the same length. Around that time, a preacher from the mainland came over and settled on the island to preach the word of God and make a living for himself. The islanders listened to him, but they didn't offer to pay him anything. Along about February, he got real lean and raggedy. He was nothing but skin and bones. The islanders didn't want him to starve to death over there. For one thing, they'd have to bury him. So they held a meeting and argued the matter back and forth. One man made a motion they should take up a collection for the preacher, but this man had a reputation for being simple and his motion was so idiotic they didn't even discuss it. Some wanted each family to give the preacher a peck of potatoes or a turnip or two, and some were for giving him a fish whenever there was a good big catch. They couldn't agree. They argued until late that night. Finally, they decided they'd let him have a wreck hook an inch and a half longer than all the rest. If he couldn't get a living with that, he could starve to death.

Anecdote Characteristic of Sailors

SOON after the last war [of 1812], one of our frigates, bound into Boston, anchored for a few days off Salem. The inhabitants of the town, having ascertained that the ship would remain over Sunday, sent an invitation to the officers and crew to attend service on shore. They accepted it; and on Sunday morning, about meeting time, arrived at the wharf in gallant trim; the officers in the usual naval uniform, and the sailors in that of

---

As told by Ellery Franklin Thompson. From "Dragger Captain," by Joseph Mitchell in *The New Yorker,* Vol. XXII (January 11, 1947), No. 48, pp. 41–42. Copyright, 1947, by The F-R. Publishing Corporation. New York.

[1] They also collect Block Island stories, or Block Islands.—J. M.

theirs. From the wharf, where they were met by the authorities of the church, they marched to the meeting house, the sailors under the command of the boatswain. On reaching the house, the officers were conducted to seats on the lower floor; but the sailors, choosing, as they expressed it, "to sit aloft," were shown into the gallery, where, after going through various evolutions, by order of the boatswain, for purpose as he said of making "handsome stowage," they were finally all comfortably seated. The services commenced and were continued without interruption until the minister had got pretty well advanced in his sermon. He had chosen a text adapted to the occasion, and being very anxious for the spiritual welfare of these sons of the ocean, was uncommonly warm and eloquent in his discourse. The sailors, not used to preaching, began to grow uneasy, and the boatswain in particular; but no great insubordination had as yet shown itself. The minister, observing the commotion in the gallery, and thinking it to be the genuine signs of conviction, now directed his sermon more particularly to this portion of his "sea-faring brethren," and that they might the better understand his meaning, he framed his language in similes and figures adapted to their comprehension. He compared a sinner in this life, without religion, to a ship of war in a violent gale, without sufficient strength to enable her to ride it out—the first was as surely on his course to hell as the ship was to be wrecked. He then proceeded to describe a ship in this condition—her rigging broken—her sails lost, or torn in pieces by the furious wind—her groaning masts expected every moment to go by the board—her rudder unshipped, and the unmanageable vessel drifting at the mercy of the winds and waves. "What appalling cry is that which now rises on the blast, benumbing all as with the fear of death? Hark! 'We're lost—the ship is running on a lee shore, and in a few minutes' "—"Avast, there," cried the boatswain, who, throughout the description, had been up and down in his seat at least a dozen times, thinking all the while it was the ship that was going to hell, and being so much carried away by the excitement of the moment, that fancying himself on shipboard, he blew his whistle with tremendous energy, and cried out in a stentorian voice, "Tumble up, tumble up, my lads, and furl every d——d rag, loose the foretop-most-staysail, double reef the mizzen-topsail, jump into the chains, one of you, with the lead—cheerily, men, cheerily, *and we'll weather hell in spite of damnation*!" [1]

. . . I like better this story of the stout old fisherman who in church so unexpectedly answered his pastor's thrilling exhortation, "Supposing, my brethren, that any of you should be overtaken in the bay by a north-

[1] From *The Old American Comic Almanac,* with Whims, Scraps and Oddities from the Land of Johnny Bull, Brother Jonathan and Mons. Nontongpaw, New Series, Whole Number IX, Number I, p. 33. Entered, according to an Act of Congress in the year 1838, by Samuel N. Dickinson, in the Clerk's Office of the District Court of Massachusetts. Boston. 1839.

east storm, your hearts trembling with fear, and nothing but death before, whither would your thoughts turn? what would you do?"—with the instant inspiration of common-sense, "I'd hoist the foresail and scud away for Squam!" [2]

YANKEE PREACHERS

Fisherman's Reward

To ILLUSTRATE and Demonstrate the Providence of God our Saviour over the Business of the Fisherman, I will Entertain you with Two short Modern Histories. . . . When our Mr. Brock lived on the Isles of Shoals, he brought the Fishermen into an Agreement that besides the Lord's Day they would Spend one Day every Month together in the Worship of the Glorious Lord. A certain day which by their Agreement belonged unto the Exercises of Religion being arrived, they came to Mr. Brock, and asked him, that they might put by their Meeting and go a Fishing, because they had Lost many Days by the Foulness of the Weather. He, seeing that without and against his consent they resolved upon doing what they asked of him, replied, "If you will go away I say unto you, 'Catch Fish if you can!' But as for you that will tarry, and Worship our Lord Jesus Christ this day, I will pray unto Him for you that you may afterwards take Fish till you are weary." Thirty Men went away from the Meeting and Five tarried. The Thirty that went away from the Meeting with all their Craft could Catch but four Fishes. The Five which tarried went forth afterwards and *they* took *five Hundred.* The Fishermen were after this Readier to hearken unto the Voice of their Teacher.

Prayer for Rain

ONE summer, in the early years of the town [of Goshen], there was a worse drouth than any other in the memory of the oldest inhabitant. The grass fields became brown and crisp, the brooks dried, and the highways sent up clouds of dust with every scurry of wind. Several farmers consulted and decided to ask their pastor to pray in the pulpit for more favorable weather conditions.

---

[2] From *Among the Isles of Shoals*, by Celia Thaxter, p. 45. Entered according to Act of Congress, in the year 1873, by James R. Osgood & Co., in the Office of the Librarian of Congress, at Washington. Boston.

From *The Fisherman's Calling*, A Brief Essay to Serve the Great Interests of Religion among Our Fishermen, by Cotton Mather, pp. 22–24. Boston: T. Green. 1712.

The following Sunday, as the old pastor was reading notices handed in on slips of paper, he came to the request that a special prayer be made for rain. After glancing at it, he looked through a window at the cloudless, unrelenting blue sky, and observed the direction of a light wind that was blowing. Then he said to his congregation: "I have been asked to pray for rain and will make the prayer if you wish; but I do not think it will do much good as long as the wind remains in the northwest." [1]

Of the local clerics the best-remembered was Aaron Kinne, a preacher of the old type, who lived in Egremont in 1803 and for twenty years sermonized in the various towns of southern Berkshire. During a severe drought a special meeting was called that all members of the church might pray for rain. The crops were drying up and the meadows looked as if they had been scorched by fire. Mr. Kinne was asked to lead the meeting, and when the congregation had gathered, he called loud and long upon the Almighty to send rain to the Berkshires, especially to Egremont and the adjoining town of Alford. Then, closing his prayer, he paused and added as an afterthought, "But after all our petitions, O God, we would not presume to dictate, but we would advise." [2]

In the long ago, there lived an old man who believed, firmly, in the efficacy of prayer and during a season of pronounced drought, at the weekly meetin', rose to pray and said, "Oh Lord, we need rain bad, send us rain. We don't want a rippin', rarin', tearin' rain that'll harrer up the face of Natur, but a drizzlin', drozzlin', sozzlin' rain, one that'll last all night and putty much all day, Oh Lord." [3]

. . . It is narrated of him that on one of these occasions, there had been for a long time no rain, and the earth was dry and parched. "Master John"

---

[1] From *Historic Hampshire in the Connecticut Valley,* Happenings in a Charming Old New England County from the Time of the Dinosaur Down to About 1900, by Clifton Johnson, pp. 298–299. Copyright, 1932, by The Northampton Historical Society. Springfield, Massachusetts: Milton Bradley Company.

[2] From *The Berkshire Hills,* Compiled and Written by Members of the Federal Writers' Project of the Works Progress Administration for Massachusetts, p. 179. Copyright, 1939, by The Berkshire Hills Conference, Inc. New York: Duell, Sloan and Pearce.

[3] By Carrie Ordway. From *More New Hampshire Folk Tales,* collected by Mrs. Moody P. Gore and Mrs. Guy E. Speare, p. 238. Copyright, 1936, by Mrs. Guy E. Speare. Plymouth, New Hampshire: Compiled and published by Mrs. Guy E. Speare.

Confer the anecdote of the Scotch minister cited from Dean Ramsay's *Reminiscences of Scottish Life and Character* in *Old New England Traits,* by George Lunt (1873, p. 126): "At one time when the crops were much laid by continuous rains, and wind was earnestly desired in order to restore them to a condition fit for the sickle,—'A minister,' he says, 'in his Sabbath services expressed their wants in prayer, as follows: "O Lord, we pray thee to send us wind, no a rantin' tantin', tearin' wind, but a noohin' (noughin?), soughin', winnin' wind."' "

[Ballantine] prayed earnestly for the dews upon the mown grass, and showers that water the earth; and after several weekly petitions, his prayers were answered. The windows of heaven were opened, and down came the torrents, that made up the Jefferson flood. The river rose to an unprecedented height. The meadows were overflowed, and still the waters increased so as really to alarm the people. Sunday came, and with it, "Master John," in the sacred desk, indicating by his manner that something was to be done, and that quickly. He modestly referred to the earnest petitions he had offered up for the "cisterns of the sky," and the discharge of their contents upon "the thirsty ridges of the field," and how abundantly that petition had been answered; and in view of the fact, that apparently a deluge was impending, he broke out into the following eloquent supplication: "Lord, Lord, stay thy hand! O, stay thy hand! Enough! enough! art thou a going to drown us out?" * It is said that the rain ceased, the water subsided, and the woodchucks, and other dwellers in the holes of the earth, who had been drowned out, as "Master John" feared the people would have been, returned to their burrows, or dug new holes above high water mark. . . .[4]

. . . The Van Dyke yarn most often heard is of a spring when his drive was hung up by low water. With a crew of over two hundred idle, their French-Canadian boss came and asked him:

"Well, Mister Van Dyke, maybe you t'ink pretty good plan I go ask Padre say mass for some rain, so river he rise and we go along."

"Here's ten dollars," said Van Dyke, "and tell that priest to pray like hell!"

That was Friday night. The priest said mass and next day it rained. All over the week end the rain poured down and from upriver came such an angry flood that the huge long logs were carried by thousands up creeks and out onto meadows, to bring Van Dyke only damage suits in place of a whole year's profit in logs. In a frenzy he called in his river boss and gave him a hundred-dollar bill.

"Now tell that Goddamned son of a bitch to shut off the water up there!" he roared.[5]

---

* "Lord, Lord, stay thy hand! Oh, stay thy hand! Enough! Enough! Art thou goin' to drown us out like woodchucks?"—Merle Dixon Graves, *Bubblin's an' B'ilin's at the Center* (Rutland, 1934), p. 15.

[4] From *The Westfield Jubilee:* A Report of the Celebration at Westfield, Mass., on the Two Hundredth Anniversary of the Incorporation of the Town, October 6, 1869, with the Historical Address of the Hon. William G. Bates, and other Speeches and Poems of the Occasion, with an Appendix, Containing Historical Documents of Local Interest, p. 178. Westfield, Massachusetts: Clark & Story, Publishers. 1870.

[5] From *The Great White Hills of New Hampshire,* by Ernest Poole, pp. 35–36. Copyright, 1946, by Ernest Poole. Garden City, New York: Doubleday & Company, Inc.

Prayer for Wind

In the early part of his ministry particularly, it was the custom of the fishermen to make two trips during the season to the Banks. So that during the summer months, some of the vessels were going and coming at the same time. If the wind was west, it would be fair only for those going down to the Banks; and if east, only fair for those coming home, and dead ahead for the return fleet. Mr. Damon understood this, and his benevolent heart shaped his prayers to the contingency by introducing the following passage:

"We pray, O Lord, that thou wilt watch over our mariners that go down to do business upon the mighty deep, keep them in the hollow of thy hand; and we pray thee, that thou wilt send a side-wind so that their vessels may pass and repass."

Hurrying Grace

In the same neighborhood [Hillsboro] lived Deacon William Conn, a thrifty farmer, sturdy Whig and pillar of the church, who invariably asked the blessing at table summer and winter, in which he loyally mentioned the women of his family.

Sometimes in the midst of haying, black clouds came rolling up in the west as he and his hired men sat down to the noonday meal, and the good deacon, fearful of the impending shower, would endeavor to speed up the service as he closed his eyes and intoned, "Wilt thou, O Lord, bless these portions of food Marm has prepared and Susan made ready (pass the potatoes, Charles) for Christ's sake, Amen."

Minister and Fish

Bluefish are more abundant during some years than during others. They dislike cool water; but whenever the temperature of the sea ranges from sixty to seventy-five degrees, the bay is likely to be full of them. Their coming and going have been mysterious. From the year 1659 to the year 1763, they were recorded as plentiful about Nantucket and the south shore of Barnstable County during the summers; but in the year 1764 they dis-

---

From *Truro—Cape Cod, or Land Marks and Sea Marks,* by Shebnah Rich, p. 292. Second Edition, Revised and Corrected. Copyright, 1883, by D. Lothrop and Company. Boston. 1884.

From *More New Hampshire Folk Tales,* collected by Mrs. Moody P. Gore, and Mrs. Guy E. Speare, p. 207. Copyright, 1936, by Mrs. Guy E. Speare. Plymouth, New Hampshire: Compiled and published by Mrs. Guy E. Speare.

appeared suddenly, and it is stated that they were not seen again in northern waters, except in small schools, until the year 1810; when and thereafter they returned in large numbers annually to Buzzard's Bay. There is a tradition that during their absence their return was annually expected and watched for all along the shore. At last a large school came into the bay on a Sunday morning in June, and the lads who discovered them hurried to the meeting-house to proclaim the glad tidings. The doors were wide open, the preacher was expounding, when a shrill cry rang in: "Bluefish in the bay!" In a twinkling the meeting-house was emptied, and every boat belonging to the village was soon spreading its sails for the open water. This action was not without precedent. I have read in the annals of Truro, on Cape Cod, that in February, 1755, the people were assembled in their meeting-house for the ordination of the town's minister; when, on account of certain news received at the door, it was "Voted that as many of the inhabitants are called away from the meeting by news of a whale in the bay, this meeting be adjourned." They wanted a whale before they wanted a preacher. There are many people who have the same want now.[1]

"[The blackfish are] something like small whales," the fisherman responded, "and I've seen 'em that'd weigh a ton. They're no good to eat, but we cut off the fat and boil it in great big kittles by the shore for the oil. We used to get 'em every year, but now only once in a long time. The biggest capture we ever made numbered fourteen hundred and five. They go just like a flock of sheep, and all you have to do is to get behind 'em with your boats and drive 'em up on shore and lance 'em. When it was known that this school of blackfish was in the bay every boat in town went out to drive 'em. The minister was there with the rest of us, and he give a little girl a Bible afterward for tellin' him about the blackfish in time so he could go. We all hollered and pounded the sides of the boats and made as much noise as we could. Everybody but the minister was swearing and ripping out the toughest words they knew. You'd thought they'd been ashamed to use such language before him, but he was so excited he didn't notice it. Besides, he was making such a racket himself that he had no chance to hear the rest. Well, he had a good strong voice and was a great hollerer anyway. He was shouting: 'Praise the Lord! *Bless* the Lord for so great a gift to this little place.'

"In two hours the fish was all run up on the shore and killed, and when the time come to divide profits there was fifty dollars for every man who had a hand in the job, and that was most all the men in town."[2]

---

[1] From *The Old Colony Town and Other Sketches,* by William Root Bliss, pp. 61–62. Copyright, 1893, by William Root Bliss. Boston and New York: Houghton, Mifflin and Company.

[2] From *Highways and Byways of New England,* Including the States of Massachusetts, New Hampshire, Rhode Island, Connecticut, Vermont and Maine, Written and

During the winter of 1816,* hunger for people and starvation for beasts brought sickness and death in many parts of the state. As the spring gradually appeared and the ice was melting in Lake Winnepesaukee, the people who lived around this sheet of water eagerly watched for the annual arrival of the schools of fish that came to the shores during the spawning season.

One Sunday as the preacher was expounding the Word of God to his parish, suddenly a figure rushed into the church without ceremony and joyfully shouted, "The Shad have come! The Shad have come!"

Instantly and without the usual displeasure when the Sunday service was disturbed, the preacher said, "This is no time for sermons. Let everyone seek for food." Leading the congregation, the good man rushed from the church and soon he and all the village now known as Center Harbor were fishing on Sunday and for the first time that winter, a feast was enjoyed.[3]

The World, the Flesh, and the Devil

A CERTAIN minister, who had some unpleasantness with the church, took as his text, "The world, the flesh, and the devil," and said, "I shall touch lightly upon the world, hasten to the flesh, and pass on to the devil, when I will give it to you hot as you can sup it."

A Timely Text

A "good sermonizer" was the Reverend Timothy Alden, of Old Yarmouth, with a nice eye for timeliness in the choice of his texts. For fifty years his little flock had faithfully supplied firewood for the parsonage, in accordance with his salary agreement, and for fifty years the Reverend Alden sermonized in return, ever finding the word of God that best befitted the occasion. But one cold winter in the 1790's, the day set for delivery of his firewood passed, and it appeared that this little item had been let to

---

Illustrated by Clifton Johnson, pp. 195–196. Copyright, 1915, by The Macmillan Company. New York and London. 1916.

* The Corn Famine Year.

[3] From *New Hampshire Folk Tales,* Compiled by Mrs. Moody P. Gore and Mrs. Guy E. Speare, p. 235. Copyright, 1932, by New Hampshire Federation of Women's Clubs.

From *Truro—Cape Cod, or Land Marks and Sea Marks,* by Shebnah Rich, p. 314. Second Edition, Revised and Corrected. Copyright, 1883, by D. Lothrop and Company. Boston. 1884.

From *Cape Cod Pilot,* by Jeremiah Digges, with Editorial and Research Assistance of the Members of the Federal Writers' Project, p. 66. American Guide Series, Federal Writers' Project, Works Progress Administration for the State of Massachusetts. Copyright, 1937, by Poor Richard Associates. Provincetown and New York: Modern Pilgrim Press and the Viking Press.

lapse. The following Sabbath, the pastor announced his text from Proverbs XXVI, 20:

"Where no wood is, there the fire goeth out."

The Rev. Mr. Bulkley's Advice

THE following humorous story, in which Mr. Bulkley the first minister in this town was concerned, is from an ancient publication.

"The Rev. Mr. Bulkley of Colchester, Conn., was famous in his day as a casuist and sage counsellor. A church in his neighborhood had fallen into unhappy divisions and contentions, which they were unable to adjust among themselves. They deputed one of their number to the venerable Bulkley, for his services; with a request that he would send it to them in writing. The matters were taken into serious consideration, and the advice, with much deliberation, committed to writing. It so happened, that Mr. Bulkley had a farm in an extreme part of the town, upon which he entrusted a tenant; in superscribing the two letters, the one for the church was directed to the tenant, and the one for the tenant to the church. The church was convened to hear the advice which was to settle all their disputes. The moderator read as follows: *You will see to the repair of the fences, that they be built high and strong, and you will take special care of the old black bull.* This mystical advice puzzled the church at first, but an interpreter among the more discerning ones was soon found, who said, Brethren, this is the very advice we most need; the directions to repair the fences is to admonish us to take good heed in the admission and government of our members: we must guard the church by our master's laws, and keep out strange cattle from the fold. And we must in a particular manner set a watchful guard over the *Devil,* the old black bull, who has done so much hurt of late. All perceived the wisdom and fitness of Mr. Bulkley's advice, and resolved to be governed by it. The consequence was, all the animosities subsided and harmony was restored to the long afflicted church. What the subject of the letter sent to the tenant was, and what good effect it had upon him, the story does not tell."

The Missionary's Success

YEARS ago the Songo Locks was peopled by a hard-drinking, hard-fighting, unlawful group that had much intermarried. A missionary, hearing of this

---

From *Connecticut Historical Collections,* Containing a General Collection of Interesting Facts, Traditions, Biographical Sketches, Anecdotes, &c., Relating to the History and Antiquities of Every Town in Connecticut, with Geographical Descriptions, by John Warner Barber, p. 308. Entered according to the Act of Congress, in the year 1836, by John W. Barber and A. Willard, in the Clerk's Office of the District Court of Connecticut. New Haven and Hartford.

As told by Dr. J. P. Dodge to Percy A. Allen, Naples, Maine. Manuscripts of the Federal Writers' Project of the Works Progress Administration for the State of Maine.

hard-boiled tribe, decided to visit them and conduct a campaign. After the campaign he was approached by a Naples business man who inquired if the parson had saved many souls, to which the good man replied: "I had some success. Anyway, I left Jesus Christ with them, but I've been worried sick since I did so, for fear they'll crucify him again."

Jonny-Cake under the Stove

LIKE all Berkshire towns, Washington has a story or two worth telling. One concerns the Reverend Braman Ayers, possibly the last of the old-time "A-h-men!" Methodist ministers who preached here, a man who mixed wit and ingenuity with religion to the disparagement of neither. One fine spring day he paid a visit to his brother's home. Driving past, he sniffed the smell of his sister-in-law's tasty johnny-cake, and quite designedly he reined his horse into his brother's yard at high noon. Invited to eat dinner with the family, the minister seated himself at the table, apparently oblivious of the dismay on his sister-in-law's face.

"Johnny-cake indeed!" she probably muttered to herself as she deftly slid the cake out of the oven. "If Brother Ayers eats one piece, he'll eat two; and if he eats two, he'll certainly eat three; and if he eats three—"

Silently imploring the Lord to remember her virtues and be as lenient as possible with her transgression, she shoved the fragrant yellow cake out of sight. In its place, wheat bread was set in prominence on the red tablecloth, while the parson's hostess reminded him, in somewhat of a hurry, "Brother, it's time to say grace."

"Oh Lord," began the Reverend, sniffing for direction, "bless this food prepared for our use, and bless the johnny-cake"—sniffing triumphantly—"*under the stove!* A-h-men!"

The Camel and the Needle's Eye

THIS story was told by a descendant of an old Lancaster family. In the rural district one Sunday, a minister took for his text this passage, "It is easier for a camel to go through the eye of a needle than for a rich man to enter into the Kingdom of Heaven." He said, "You all know what a

---

From *The Berkshire Hills,* Compiled and Written by Members of the Federal Writers' Project of the Works Progress Administration for Massachusetts, pp. 224–225. Copyright, 1939, by The Berkshire Hills Conference, Inc. New York: Duell, Sloan and Pearce.

By Mrs. Emma Weeks Roberts. From *More New Hampshire Folk Tales,* collected by Mrs. Moody P. Gore and Mrs. Guy E. Speare, pp. 284–285. Copyright, 1936, by Mrs. Guy E. Speare. Plymouth, New Hampshire: Compiled and published by Mrs. Guy E. Speare.

needle is, it has a very small eye, now a camel is a large animal, a beast of burden, and there couldn't be a needle large enough for a camel to go through, but there could be a cable small enough to go through a large needle, so brethren, after due deliberation, I have come to this opinion, that the text is a misprint, meaning cable, instead of camel."

The Dominie and the Horse

THE longest pastorate in the church was that of Charles Gleason, the second pastor, who was ordained October, 1744 and died May, 1790. The next pastorate in point of years was the fourth, Abiel Williams, reaching from 1799 to 1831. The people of the town called him "Priest Williams" and a more genial, kindly pastor never rejoiced the hearts of his parishioners. He was past master in his knowledge of cattle, horses and land. There is a story, probably apocryphal, that one Sabbath when a farmer drove up with a fine horse, the good old dominie laid his hand upon the horse's side and said, "If it was not Sunday, how much would you take for that horse?"

YANKEES AND INDIANS

Indians and Rum

THE Indians seem to have a born love for rum. Mr. Stone, the settled preacher at Provincetown, used often to preach to the Mashpees, who were quite devotional. One of the deacons was asked how he liked Mr. Stone. He said: "Mr. Stone one very good preacher, but he preach too much about rum. When he no preach about rum, Injun think nothing 'bout it; but when he tells how Injun love rum, and how much they drunk, then I think how good it is, and think no more 'bout the sermon, my mouth waters all the time so much for rum." When asked whether he liked Mr. Stone or blind Joe (a Baptist minister) best, he said: "Mr. Stone, he make best sermons, but blind Joe he make best Christians." [1]

Some years since, Mr. C——, a respectable clergyman in Litchfield county, was reproving an old Indian for his cruel and revengeful conduct towards those who had offended him. "You should love your enemies," con-

From *Black Tavern Tales, Stories of Old New England*, by Charles L. Goodell, p. 36. Copyright, 1932, by Charles L. Goodell. Brooklyn: Willis McDonald & Co.

[1] From *Truro—Cape Cod, or Land Marks and Sea Marks*, by Shebnah Rich, pp. 85–86. Second Edition, Revised and Corrected. Copyright, 1883, by D. Lothrop and Company. Boston. 1884.

cluded the parson, "and preserve an affection for those that hurt you." "I do love my enemies," retorted the son of nature, "and have a great affection for them that hurt me." "No such thing," returned Mr. C——; "you don't love your enemies." "I do!" "Who are the enemies you love?" "RUM and CIDER."[1]

An Indian, who lived near the Connecticut River, called at a tavern in the fall of the year and had a dram, for which he paid two coppers. The next spring, happening at the same house, he called for a dram and had to pay three coppers for it. "How is this, Landlord," said he, "last fall you asked but two coppers for a glass of rum, now you ask three." "Oh, it costs me a good deal to keep rum over winter; it is as expensive to keep a hogshead of rum over winter as a horse." "Ah!" said the Indian, "I can't see through that; he won't eat so much hay; maybe though he drink as much water."[2]

A certain clergyman said to an Indian, "I am sorry to see you drink rum." The Indian replied, "Yes, we Indians do *drink* rum; but we do not *make* it."[3]

I heerd an Indian one day ax a tavern keeper for some rum; why, Joe Spawdeeck, said he, I reckon you have got too much already. Too much of any thing, said Joe, is not good, but too much rum is jist enough.[4]

Wickhegan

[*Wickhegan* is] an Indian word meaning in general an official document, more particularly the written permission granted by a chief to hunt on his

[1] From *The Farmer's Almanac,* Calculated on a New and Improved Plan, for the Year of Our Lord, 1815, No. XXIII, by Robert B. Thomas. Boston: Printed for West & Richardson, Proprietors of the Copy-Right.

[2] From *The (Old) Farmer's Almanack,* Calculated on a New and Improved Plan for the Year of Our Lord 1905, No. 113, by Robert B. Thomas, p. 49. Entered, according to Act of Congress, in the year 1904, by Horace E. Ware, in the Office of the Librarian of Congress, at Washington. Boston: William Ware & Co.

[3] From *History of the Town of Medford, Middlesex County, Massachusetts,* from Its First Settlement, in 1630, to the Present Time, 1855, by Charles Brooks, p. 486. Boston: Published by James M. Usher. 1855.

[4] From *The Clockmaker; or The Sayings and Doings of Samuel Slick of Slickville,* p. 52. Philadelphia: Carey, Lea, and Blanchard. 1837.

From "A Word-List from Aroostook," by J. W. Carr and G. D. Chase, in *Dialect Notes,* Vol. III (Part V, 1909), p. 418. Publication of the American Dialect Society. New Haven, Connecticut.

tribe's territory; also a fine or the price of a permit. The story is that an Old Town Indian got drunk and was arrested and brought before the municipal court in Bangor. The judge fined him ten dollars but remitted the fine on condition that he would not get drunk again. The Indian began to fumble in his pocket and produce money. The judge started to explain that he need not pay now. But the Indian answered, "No judge, I pay *wickhegan.* I might die and go to Happy Hunting Ground and the Great Spirit would ask me if I owed anybody. Then I would remember my fine and would have to hunt all over hell, judge, to find you."

When the Powder Grows

A WHITE trader sold a quantity of powder to an Indian, and imposed upon him by making him believe it was a grain which grew like wheat, by sowing it upon the ground. He was greatly elated by the prospect, not only of raising his own powder, but of being able to supply others, and thereby becoming immensely rich. Having prepared his ground with great care, he sowed his powder with the utmost exactness in the spring. Month after month passed away, but his powder did not even sprout, and winter came before he was satisfied that he had been deceived. He said nothing; but some time after, when the trader had forgotten the trick, the same Indian succeeded in getting credit of him to a large amount. The time set for payment having expired, he sought out the Indian at his residence, and demanded payment for his goods. The Indian heard his demand with great complaisance; then looking him shrewdly in the eye, said, *"Me pay you when my powder grow."* This was enough. The guilty white man quickly retraced his steps.

Head Work

As Gov. JOSEPH DUDLEY, of Massachusetts, observed an able-bodied Indian, half naked, come and look on, as a pastime, to see his men work, he asked him why he did not work, *and get some clothes to cover himself.* The Indian answered by asking him why *he* did not work. The governor, pointing with his finger to his head, said, "*I work head work,* and so have no need to work with my hands as you should." The governor told him he wanted a calf killed, and that if he would go and do it, he would give him a shilling. He accepted the offer, and went immediately and killed the

---

From *The Early History of New England,* Illustrated by Numerous Interesting Incidents, by Rev. Henry White, p. 238. Entered according to an Act of Congress, in the year 1841, by Rev. Henry White, in the Clerk's Office of the District Court of New Hampshire. Boston: Sanborn, Carter, Bazin & Co. [n. d.]

Ibid., pp. 236–237.

calf, and then went sauntering about as before. The governor, on observing what he had done, asked him why he did not dress the calf before he left it. The Indian answered, "*No, no, Coponoh,* (governor,) that was not in the bargain. I was to have a shilling for killing him. Am he no dead, Coponoh?" The governor, seeing himself outwitted, told him to dress it and he would give him another shilling.

This Indian having several times outwitted the governor, he, falling in with him some time after, asked him by what means he had cheated and deceived him so many times. He answered, pointing with his finger to his head, "*Head work, Coponoh, head work!*"

Indian Taverns

As ELSEWHERE, the early settlers here became involved in many land disputes. One such quarrel was settled by an Indian; and in the story was born a curious tradition that survives in the South Sea country to this day.

Indian John Horton had seen the first white man come to Suckanesset. He had watched them measure off the earth, and then dispute their own measurements. He had helped them build fences. He had come to understand many of their ways.

One day, when Indian John was a very old man, there came to him Jonathan Hatch, Isaac Robinson, Peter Blossom and eleven other white men. This time they were arguing over a boundary line between Five-Mile River and Coonamesset Pond.

Years before, they said, the boundary had been set "from the edge of one high hill to another"; and some now contended that the "edge" of the hill was at the bottom, and others said it was at the top. Did Indian John remember exactly what was meant by the "edge of the hill?"

Indian John felt weary as the fourteen men gathered around him for his answer. Then he said:

"Yes, I remember. It went neither by the top of the hill nor the bottom, but halfway between."

But then they wanted to know what marker had been used, to show *exactly* where the line should run; and when Indian John said the marker was a great rock, they declared that he was lying, that there was no rock midway on the hill.

"Come with me," Indian John said.

Along the hill he searched, running now and then to a bush, a tree, a

---

From *Cape Cod Pilot,* by Jeremiah Digges, with Editorial and Research Assistance of the Members of the Federal Writers' Project, pp. 375–377. American Guide Series, Federal Writers' Project, Works Progress Administration for the State of Massachusetts. Copyright, 1937, by Poor Richard Associates. Provincetown and New York: Modern Pilgrim Press and the Viking Press.

See "Halfway Rock and Other Sacrifice Rocks" below.

dead bough. And at last under a pile of brush, he uncovered a great rock. "Here," he told the white men, "is the rock where the people set their bound. Each time they passed it, to show their good faith they put on a bough. In time it became covered with boughs, and that is why you could not see it."

Because he was the only living witness, the white men believed him and were satisfied. Each of them put a bough on the heap. And Indian John was very thankful that he had found a large rock—for they are rare in the hills of Suckanesset.

Ever after that, the Indians sealed their own agreements with piles of brush, to which each passerby added a stick, as a symbol of accord. As time went on, there were many brush-heaps in the South Sea country, and new generations carried on the custom without knowing why.

White men have misnamed the piles of sticks, calling them "Indian taverns" and giving strange explanations for them. But the story of Indian John Horton is on record, and near the Falmouth-Mashpee town line at Waquoit, there is a pile of sticks where, to this day, the people of Mashpee add their sticks when they pass by.

A New Way to Make People Happy

Mr. Winslow, returning from Connecticut to Plymouth, left his bark at Narragansett, and intending to return home by land, took the opportunity to make a visit to Massasoit, who, with his accustomed kindness, offered to conduct him home. But before they sat out, Massasoit secretly despatched one of his men to Plymouth with a message, signifying that Mr. Winslow was dead, carefully directing his courier to tell the place where he was killed, and the time of the fatal catastrophe. The surprise and joy produced by Mr. Winslow's return must have satisfied even Massasoit's ardent affection, when the next day he brought him home to his weeping family. When asked why he had sent this account, both false and distressing, he answered that it was their manner to do so, to heighten the pleasure of meeting after an absence.

From *The Early History of New England,* Illustrated by Numerous Interesting Incidents, by Rev. Henry White, pp. 225–226. Entered according to an Act of Congress, in the year 1841, by Rev. Henry White, in the Clerk's Office of the District Court of New Hampshire. Boston: Sanborn, Carter, Bazin & Co. [n. d.]

Indian Justice

[In 1720] Jacob [Spalding] one day purchased of an Indian a deer skin, for which he paid him a *tenor bill.* The latter, somewhat intoxicated, forgot soon after that he had received it, and asked for the money a second time. Jacob of course paid no attention to such an unwarrantable demand, and the Indian went away muttering revenge. The next day while shingling a barn, Jacob saw him returning with two companions. He leaped from the roof, met them, and was again asked to pay the price of the deer skin. He refused to comply, till one of the company, who appeared to be the Sachem of his tribe, said he had come to see "fair play," and avowed it to be honorable for two Indians to contend with one white man. Jacob therefore imagined he would have a rather difficult task to accomplish, but plucking up courage, he exerted himself to the utmost, and on the very first encounter, *laid them both* upon the ground and gave them a "sound drubbing." The other who was looking on, was not at all disposed to assist his brethren, and gave them no other encouragement than, "Poor dogs, poor dogs; me hope he kill you both!!" However, Jacob, after "pounding them" a short time, suffered them to escape. But the next day he saw them coming again, and the individual who imagined himself his creditor, bearing a rifle which he was in the act of loading. But in thrusting his hand into his pocket to find the ball, he drew out the identical *bill* which he had received two days before! Conscience-struck, he said to Jacob, who was coming to meet him, "Me believe now, Jacob, you paid me de tenor bill." After this confession, Jacob addressed the person who had come to see "fair play." "You," said he, "that have come to see fair play, what do you advise us to do with him?" "Tie him to de tree and whip him," was the reply, which was done accordingly. And here a circumstance occurred which shows to what extent the Indians carried their principle of honor. The individual in question, after this humiliating treatment, became so dejected that he fled from his tribe and was never heard of afterwards.

The Englishman with Two Heads

About the *15th* of *August*, Captain *Mosely* with sixty Men, met with a company, judged about three hundred *Indians*, in a plain place where few

---

From *Connecticut Historical Collections,* Containing a General Collection of Interesting Facts, Traditions, Biographical Sketches, Anecdotes, &c., Relating to the History and Antiquities of Every Town in Connecticut, with Geographical Descriptions, by John Warner Barber, p. 427. Entered according to the Act of Congress, in the year 1836, by John W. Barber and A. Willard, in the Clerk's Office, of the District Court of Connecticut. New Haven and Hartford.

From *The Present State of New-England* . . . faithfully composed by a Merchant of Boston, and communicated to his Friend in London (London, 1675), p. 12. In *The Old Farmer and His Almanack,* by George Lyman Kittredge, p. 354. Copyright, 1904, by Horace E. Ware. Boston: William Ware and Company.

Trees were, and on both sides preparations were making for a Battle; all being ready on both sides to fight, Captain *Moseley* plucked off his Periwig, and put it into his Breeches, because it should not hinder him in fighting. As soon as the *Indians* saw that, they fell a Howling and Yelling most hideously, and said, *Umh, umh, me no stawmerre fight Engis mon, Engis mon get two hed, Engis mon got two hed; if me cut off un hed, he got noder, a put on beder as dis;* with such like words in broken *English*, and away they all fled and could not be overtaken, nor seen any more afterwards.

Justice Waban

THE following is handed down as a true copy of a warrant issued by an Indian magistrate.—"You, you big constable, quick you catchum Jeremiah Offscow, strong you holdum, safe you bringum afore me.

"Thomas Waban, Justice peace."

When Waban became superannuated, a younger magistrate was appointed to succeed him. Cherishing that respect for age and long experience, for which the Indians are remarkable, the new officer waited on the old one for advice. Having stated a variety of cases and received satisfactory answers, he at length proposed the following:—"when Indians get drunk and quarrel and fight and act like Divvil, what you do dan?"—"Hah! tie um all up, and whip um plaintiff, whip um fendant and whip um witness."

YANKEE HUSBANDS AND WIVES

Abraham Underhill's Wife

. . . ABRAHAM UNDERHILL . . . owned a tavern here in the early days. It seems he was a rare old tippler but he had a smart and thrifty wife. She was also deeply pious. She bore her lot uncomplainingly despite Abraham's jovial ways. One time, after she had risen in the middle of the night to set out a hot meal for him and some of his cronies, who had returned to the tavern none too sober, a friend condoled with her. "Oh, well," said Mrs. Underhill, "all of Abraham's enjoyment will have to be in this world, and I mean to see that he gets as much as possible."

From *History of the Town of Natick, Mass.*, from the Days of the Apostolic Eliot, MDCL, to the Present Time, MDCCCXXX, by William Biglow, p. 85. Boston: Published by Marsh, Capen, & Lyon. 1830.

For a discussion of Waban and this anecdote and its variants, see George Lyman Kittredge, *The Old Farmer and His Almanack* (Boston, 1904), pp. 333–350.

As told by Zephine Humphrey. From *This Is Vermont*, by Walter and Margaret Hard, p. 79. Copyright, 1936, by Walter Hard and Margaret Hard. Brattleboro, Vermont: Stephen Daye Press.

The Reformed Wife

THE following pleasant and unusual circumstance is said to have taken place in Newington many years since. Mr. A—— of this place, who was a very religious and conscientious man, married for a wife, one of the most ill natured and troublesome women which could be found in the vicinity. This occasioned universal surprise wherever he was known, and one of his neighbors ventured to ask him the reasons which governed his choice. Mr. A—— replied, that having had but little or no trouble in the world, he was fearful of becoming too much attached to things of time and sense. And he thought by experiencing some afflictions, he should become more weaned from the world, and that he married such a woman as he thought would accomplish the object. The best part of the story is, that the wife hearing of the reasons why he married her, was much offended, and *out of revenge,* became one of the most pleasant and dutiful wives in the town, declaring that she was not going to be made a *pack horse,* to carry her husband to heaven.

The Will of the Lord

AMONG the Morse stories is that a certain deacon Morse, having lost his first wife some time previous, rode early one morning to the chosen one's door and without dismounting knocked, and inquired of the father for his daughter Betsey who hurried to the door. The Deacon without even saying good morning cried: "Betsey, it has been revealed to me that you are to become my wife."—"The will of the Lord be done!" exclaimed the maiden with corresponding taste and congeniality of feeling, anticipating her reward in the richest husband in New London Co. The marriage was a happy one and the brevity of the above courtship saved time to serve their generation.[1]

The Lees owned all the land along Bride Brook as far as the eye could see, but there was an ancient dispute as to whether the territory came

From *Connecticut Historical Collections,* Containing a General Collection of Interesting Facts, Traditions, Biographical Sketches, Anecdotes, &c. Relating to the History and Antiquities of Every Town in Connecticut, with Geographical Descriptions, by John Warner Barber, p. 116. Entered according to the Act of Congress, in the year 1836, by John W. Barber and A. Willard, in the Clerk's Office, of the District Court of Connecticut. New Haven and Hartford.

[1] From Historical Reminiscences of the Early Times in Marlboro, Massachusetts, and Prominent Events from 1860 to 1910, Including Brief Allusions to Many Individuals and an Account of the Celebration of the Two Hundred and Fiftieth Anniversary of the Incorporation of the Town, by Ella A. Bigelow, pp. 210–211. Copyright, 1910, City of Marlborough. Marlborough, Massachusetts: Times Publishing Company.

under the authority of Lyme or New London. Finally it was decided to settle the matter by the time-honored method of trial by combat. Lyme's gladiators won. Their chief, one Reynold Marvin, claimed young Betty Lee's hand as a reward. The maiden was standing, like Rebecca, at the well when the swain made known his desires in most unorthodox fashion.

"The Lord," began the pious suitor," has commanded me to marry you." Betty dropped her eyes. It has been said she also dropped a plate she was wiping; and said, demurely:

"Then the Lord's will be done!"[2]

Thomas Hatch's Courtship

A PLEASANT story is told respecting his courtship. It is said that he was son of a farmer and served his father before learning the trade of a tailor. His wife was also a farmer's daughter, and in time of harvest assisted him in the fields, and was very expert in the use of the sickle. Two young men asked her hand in marriage and it was agreed that the one who should reap the larger piece in a given time should win the prize. The land was marked off and an equal proportion assigned to Miss Grace. She was the best reaper, and having decided that she would marry Thomas Hatch, she slyly cut over on the part set off to him, and in consequence Thomas came out ahead, claimed and received her hand in marriage.

Pulling the Rope

AT AN unknown time previous to 1762 Samuel and his brother Elisha appeared in Canaan. In 1770 Samuel built a house on the Blackberry River near the modern Samuel Forbes Bridge on the Lower Road to East Canaan. At an unknown time, possibly before he built his house, he became smitten of Lucy, daughter of Amos Peirce, a young lady who is said to have been his equal in physiognomy, physique and strength of will. On one point they seem to have agreed from the start, the desirability of getting married. Since Papa Peirce held a different view, an elopement was arranged, and the two coy titans rode off on the same unhappy horse into New York State where they were duly hitched. On returning to the homestead, Samuel pitched a rope over his new barn. "Now, my sweet," said he, "do

---

[2] From *Connecticut Trilogy,* by Marguerite Allis, with Drawings by the Author, p. 142. Copyright, 1934, by Marguerite Allis. New York: G. P. Putnam's Sons.

From *Genealogical Notes of Barnstable Families,* Being a Reprint of the Amos Otis Papers, Originally Published in The Barnstable Patriot, revised by C. F. Swift, Largely from Notes Made by the Author, Vol. I, p. 462. Entered according to Act of Congress, in the year 1885, by F. B. Goss, in the Office of the Librarian of Congress, at Washington. Barnstable, Mass.: F. B. & F. P. Goss, Publishers and Printers. 1888.

you draw down on your end and I will draw on mine, and whichever draws the other over the roof is to rule this roost." They both pulled with no effect. "Now, my sweet," proposed Samuel, "do you come around on this side, and let us draw together." The sweet Lucy complied, and together they pulled the rope over the barn. "Let that be the way this house will be run," quoth Samuel.[1]

Weddings were the grand exhibitions of fashion and occasions for the display of rank; to have a great wedding was to win a name in society. A story is told of one George Babcock, who was as shrewd as he was eccentric. Wishing to enforce the idea of family concord among the people, he at a certain time threw a rope over his house, and stationing his wife on the side opposite to himself, called to her, "Pull, Betty, pull!" Both pulled, but nothing was gained. He then asked Betty to join him at his end of the rope, remarking, "See now, my dear, how easily two can accomplish, when united, what is impossible to them when divided." The story has been a legacy of good to the town.[2]

Don't Hit That Post Again

ON THE western slope of Monument Mountain once stood the Pelton Farm, whose stone gatepost led to a tragi-comic episode. The wife and mother of the family occupying the house had died; as the funeral cortege was leaving the yard, the conveyance carrying the body hit the post. The force of the collision was so great that the corpse was thrown to the ground and the shock revived the woman, who not only showed signs of life but lived five years before she again passed away. Once more the funeral party started on its way, but this time when the hearse approached the post, the husband suddenly stopped the procession and solemnly warned the driver, "Be careful now, don't hit that post again!"

---

[1] From *The Housatonic, Puritan River,* by Chard Powers Smith, p. 258. Copyright, 1946, by Chard Powers Smith. New York and Toronto: Rinehart & Company, Incorporated.

[2] From *Westerly (Rhode Island) and Its Witnesses,* For Two Hundred and Fifty Years, 1626–1876, Including Charlestown, Hopkinton, and Richmond, Until Their Separate Organization, with the Principal Points of Their Subsequent History, by Frederic Denison, A.M., pp. 142–143. Entered according to Act of Congress, in the year 1878, by Frederic Denison, in the Office of the Librarian of Congress, at Washington, D. C. Providence: Published by J. A. & R. A. Reid.

From *The Berkshire Hills,* Compiled and Written by Members of the Federal Writers' Project of the Works Progress Administration for Massachusetts, p. 162. Copyright, 1939, by The Berkshire Hills Conference, Inc. New York: Duell, Sloan and Pearce.

For mutations of this jest, see W. Carew Hazlitt, *Studies in Jocular Literature* (London, 1890), pp. 120–121. Mrs. Clifton Johnson (in a letter) relates the same story of Molly Webster, the Hadley witch.

Breaking the Pitcher

THE following story seems to be told in about every town in the North Country and always about some rather vain and pompous gentleman. The man goes down cellar for a pitcher of cider and somehow stumbles. His wife hears him and calls down, "Did you break the pitcher?" This so angers the man, for he thinks that the good wife should ask him if he hurt himself, that he calls back, "No, by thunder, but I will," at which he hurls the precious pitcher at the cellar wall.

Rat or Mouse

. . . DER was hol' man an' hol' hwomans in Canada gat maree togedder w'en dey was hol' an' in t'ree day dey was set heat dinny, an' leetly maouse run on de haouse, an' hol' hwomans say, "See dat maouse." Hol' mans say, "It was rats," an' hol' hwomans say, "No, it was maouse." "Ah tol' you it was rats," he 'll said. "Maouse," she 'll said, an' dey holler "Rat," "Maouse," an' get so mad he 'll go 'way an' stay t'ree year. Den he 'll come back, an' she 'll was veree glad fer see it. "It was too bad you 'll go 'way so, jes' for leetly maouse." "Ant Ah 'll tol' you it was rats?" he 'll holler, and he 'll go, an' never come some more. . . .

The Old Couple and the Bear

. . . I'VE hearn tell o' tew ol' critters 'at got sot aidgeways an' come aout better 'n you tell on. They'd lived together thirty year, but bimeby they fell aout an' they'd mump raound all day 'thaout speakin', an' when it come night they'd turn the' backs tow-ards one other an' snore, an' purtend tu be asleep, each one wishin' 't t' other 'd speak, but nary one would n't fust. An' so it run on till one night in the fall o' the year they heered a turrible rumpus 'mongst the sheep in the yard, an' he ups an' dresses him an' goes aout. Arter quite a spell, an' he did n't come back, she slips on her gaownd an' shoes an' aout she goes tu see what's the matter ailded him, an' lo an' behol', he was clinched in with an almighty gret bear, the bear a-chawin' at him an' him a-huggin' as hard as the bear tu keep him f'm gittin' his hind claws intu his in'ards, which is onpleasant, as I know.

From "Lancaster," by Ola G. Veazie. Manuscripts of the Federal Writers' Project of the Works Progress Administration for the State of New Hampshire.

From *Danvis Folks,* by Rowland E. Robinson, pp. 297–298. Copyright, 1894, by Rowland E. Robinson. Boston and New York: Houghton Mifflin Company.

Ibid., pp. 298–299.

"Go it, ol' man, go it, bear," says she, "it's the fust fight ever I see 'at I did n't keer which licked."

She stood lookin' on a leetle spell, with her fists on her hips, till she see the ol' man was a-gittin' tuckered, an' the bear a-hevin' the best on 't, an' then she up with a sled stake an' gin the bear a wollop on the head 't knocked him stiffer 'n a last, and then they hed a huggin' match over the carkis of the bear, an' lived tu gether as folks ortu, tu the eend of the' days.

Yankee Diligence

TO WASTE either time or money was to a Yankee the breaking of the Ten Commandments. When a good old deacon had passed away, his relict, waiting in the darkened room for the funeral to begin, whispered to her daughter, "Hand me my knitting. I might knit a few bouts while the folks are gathering."

The Parsimonious Widower

IN VERMONT there is a story told me by old citizens in different communities, and in each place it is passed along as local history.

Henry Pease had been a widower for going on a year, and had tried to do for himself, but without much success. He was a parsimonious old fellow, or as the neighbors phrased it, "jest a mite near," and he would not afford hired help. So finally he began calling on the Widow Perkins, reputed to be an excellent cook. But the widow was cagey; she would not commit herself in any way until she had seen Henry's home. Properly chaperoned, she visited it and was quite outspoken about the untidiness and lack of repair, and especially the state of the old-fashioned oven which needed a new soapstone lining. When things were fixed up, she said, she'd like to see it again.

Henry busied himself about cleaning and simple repairs, but he could not bring himself to buy a new lining for the oven. Then he thought of the fine headstone on his late consort's grave, so he went up to the cemetery one night and carried away the slate stone. It split and sawed up nicely and the oven was as good as new.

When the widow came again she was greatly pleased by the look of

---

From *Black Tavern Tales, Stories of Old New England,* by Charles L. Goodell, p. 138. Copyright, 1932, by Charles L. Goodell. Brooklyn: Willis McDonald & Co.

From *As Much As I Dare,* A Personal Recollection, by Burges Johnson, pp. 31–32. Copyright, 1944, by Ives Washburn, Inc. New York.

everything, especially the oven, and agreed to bake a batch of biscuit in it and stay to lunch. Everything went smoothly for Henry until the slab of hot biscuit came to the table. On the bottom of the slab in reversed but sharply defined capitals the assembled company read: "Sacred to the memory of my beloved wife Mathilda."

YANKEE DROLLERIES

The Secret of True Economy

Two men met on the street one day, and in the course of conversation the one said to the other: "How do you manage to feed your large family with your small income?" "Well," he responded, "I'll tell you. I find out what they don't like and give 'em plenty of it."

Poor Butter

I REMEMBER once a man came in and asked, "Have you any poor butter?" I looked him straight in the eye, and he stared back. I said, with extreme truthfulness, "Yes, sir, I have." He said he'd take a pound, and I wrapped up some butter that almost threw me while I was tying the string. The next night the man came in again, and casually stated, "I'll take two more pounds of that butter."

While I held it down and reached for the wrapping paper I said, "I wish you'd tell me why you want this—I've been ripped up the back plenty of times for selling stuff like this."

He told me the secret. "My wife has two big booby boys by her first husband, and they're visiting us. They'll put a quarter of a pound of butter on a biscuit and swallow it, but by God this butter makes 'em stand back."

From *The Nantucket Scrap Basket,* Being a Collection of Characteristic Stories and Sayings of the People of the Town and Island of Nantucket, Massachusetts, Revised, Expanded, and Rearranged by William F. Macy, p. 91. Copyright, 1916, by William F. Macy and Roland B. Hussey; 1930, by William F. Macy. Boston and New York: Houghton Mifflin Company.

From *Yankee Storekeeper,* by R. E. Gould, p. 74. Copyright, 1946, by Curtis Publishing Co. and R. E. Gould. New York and London: Whittlesey House, McGraw-Hill Book Company, Inc.

He Gave His Note

A CERTAIN Nantucket Micawber, whose promise to pay was as good for a dollar as it was for a thousand (and no better) came home one day and announced to his wife that he had bought a horse. "What did you give for it?" asked the wife. "Oh, I gave my note," he answered, blandly. "Cheap enough," quoth the wife. "Why didn't you get a span?"

Selling the Dog

BENJAMIN GORHAM, son of Benjamin, (called Young Fiddler) resided in the house that formerly stood where Capt. John T. Hall's now stands. He had not the business capacity of his brothers; but was a man of wit and a boon companion. The following story is told of him, and illustrates his general character: When a boy he had a dog that was very troublesome, and annoyed his mother very much. One day he went home and with a serious air said, "Mother, I have sold my dog." "I am very glad, Benjamin, she was so troublesome—how much did you get for her?" "$500." "Did you, Benjamin!" "Yes, mother, I did, most certainly." "What did you get your pay in, Benjamin?" "Aye, that's it,—in bitch pups, at $50 apiece." This story is the origin of the common saying, applied to a man who makes a bad barter trade: "He got his pay in bitch pups."

Jim Edwards' Galluses and the Stump

THERE was a pair of brothers out back here, name of John and Jim Edwards. One time they was breaking up with three yoke oxen. John was holding the plow and Jim was toting the gad stick. The oxen was big fellers and my, how they could pull. They come along to a great big stump

---

From *The Nantucket Scrap Basket,* Being a Collection of Characteristic Stories and Sayings of the People of the Town and Island of Nantucket, Massachusetts, Compiled, Edited and Arranged by William F. Macy and Roland B. Hussey, and published for the benefit of "The Sons and Daughters of Nantucket," p. 94. Copyright, 1916, by Wm. F. Macy and Roland B. Hussey. Nantucket: The Inquirer and Mirror Press.

From *Genealogical Notes of Barnstable Families,* Being a Reprint of the Amos Otis Papers, Originally Published in The Barnstable Patriot, revised by C. F. Swift, Largely from Notes Made by the Author, Vol. I, p. 441. Entered according to Act of Congress, in the year 1835, by F. B. Goss, in the Office of the Librarian of Congress, at Washington. Barnstable, Mass.: F. B. & F. P. Goss, Publishers and Printers. 1888.

As told by Arthur A. Carleton, West Newbury, Vermont, to Mrs. Rebecca M. Halley. Manuscripts of the Federal Writers' Project of the Works Progress Administration for the State of Vermont.

and them oxen went right over it. 'Fore John could salt molasses that plow went clean through the stump like a hot knife through butter. They was going so fast that John sailed right up over the top and when the plow left the stump it snapped shet and caught him right by the seat of the britches. The oxen kep' a-pulling, the britches held, the stump stayed shet, an' John hollared to Jim, "Hy-ar, give 'em th' gad, Jim! It's comin' out, b'God! Mother made these galluses!" The boys got ten cord of wood out of that stump!

Prohibition Whale Oil

While the anguish produced by prohibition is of recent date in most states, in one or two New England states it befell to an earlier generation to endure this form of privation a good many years ago.

In this region prohibition made its entrance about the time that whale oil was in its last stages of usefulness for illuminating purposes.

It had been a long established custom to include, among other necessities at the grocery store, the refilling of the family jug with Medford rum. And when, owing to meddlesome tactics of certain teetotalers, storekeepers became somewhat shy about replenishing these jugs, there was much dismay.

However, there were exceptional dealers who not only had a stock of old Medford on hand, but felt a deep sympathy for old reliable customers who were thus subjected to such inconvenience, and who would "find a way." One of these ways was to have the customer call for oil and at the same time give a certain signal. When this plan was working well, the customer would find the contents of the jug to be entirely satisfactory.

One Saturday afternoon, two worthy citizens who lived on adjacent farms back on the hills, started to go to the country store to do a little "trading" for their wives. Incidentally one of them took along the faithful old jug which had been refilled several times in a very satisfactory way since the prohibition edict was supposed to be in full working order.

Entering the store, the man with the jug approached the counter and gave his order for a few small articles needed by the housekeeper at home. As there were people standing about and the clerk was a new recruit, the customer asked that the clerk fill the jug with "oil," at the same time giving him the usual signal, a broad wink. After a brief chat with acquaintances regarding crops, the weather, etc., the customer gathered up his parcels and his jug and accompanied by his neighbor, who had also made some moderate purchases, went outside, placed the parcels in the buggy and started for home.

It is quite likely that they would not have started for home nearly so soon but for anticipations associated with the jug. A half mile or so out of

---

From *New England Joke Lore,* The Tonic of Yankee Humor, by Arthur G. Crandall, pp. 267–270.

the village there was a bend in the road, an old-time covered bridge being the only building in sight. The team was brought to a halt and while the horse started to browse by the roadside, the jug was brought out by the owner, uncorked and passed over to his friend, who, relieving himself of a "chew," lifted the jug to his lips and took a large mouthful of the contents. Controlling himself by violent effort, he passed the jug back to the owner who was waiting with as much patience as he could muster, leaned over the side of the buggy and succeeded in relieving his mouth of its unwelcome contents. The owner of the jug, however, was not so fortunate, as in his eagerness he swallowed a good-sized mouthful of the whale oil before he discovered his horrible mistake.

Tradition has it that these two worthies were never quite so friendly after that unfortunate incident. What happened to the store clerk is unknown.

Kerosene oil would doubtless prove to be a very enticing beverage compared with whale oil, perhaps as nauseous as any oleaginous substance yet discovered.

Walking on the Water

A MAN named Isaac Edwards, quite a church-goer, was struck one Sunday by the idea that he could walk on the water as Christ had done. He was returning home from church with his ten-year-old son. At a section of water near Beaver Dam, West Poland, where the water wasn't very deep, he plunged in and immediately sank. He stood up in the water, a bit chagrined.

"Well, Rol," he said to his son, "I went two or three steps 'fore I went down."

He Didn't Kick

DR. ISAAC S. THOMPSON, who was a relative of the first minister in Standish, was a hard, intemperate character. He was a small man who rode horseback and carried his medicines in saddle bags. It is said that he once told his drunken companions, while on a spree at the tavern, that if they would hang him by the neck he "wouldn't kick." They procured a rope and hung him up until nearly dead. "Squire" Dean happened to come on, cut him down, and saved his life. As soon as he recovered speech, he said, "Well, I didn't kick."

From South Poland, Maine. Manuscripts of the Federal Writers' Project of the Works Progress Administration for the State of Maine.

By Solon Brackett, Sebago Lake, Maine. Manuscripts of the Federal Writers' Project of the Works Progress Administration for the State of Maine.

The Wrong Man

YEARS ago there used to be stopping places along the road to Portland where a teamster could bait [feed] his oxen or horses and get a drink or so of rum for himself. There was one near East Deering, Portland. A man from Pownal, Gersham Libby, stopped there once, took his oxen out of the shafts, and baited them. Then, having had a few drinks, he lay out in his cart and went to sleep. Some practical jokers took the oxen around back of the building and hitched them there. When Gersham awoke and saw the oxen gone, he rubbed his eyes and said:

"If I'm Gersham Libby, I've lost a yoke of oxen; if I'm not, I've found a cart."

Misfits

IT'S turrible resky a-gittin' one thing 'at 's a leetle cuter 'n the rest o' yer belongin's. . . . Oncet I got me a new awl 'at put me clean aout 'n consait o' my ol' kit, an' cost me more 'n a month's airnin's a-buyin' new tools 'at I didn't need, an' some on 'em jest useless consarns.

I've knowed a feller tu git a patch sot on a boot 'at looked so much better 'n the rest on 't 'at he hed tu git a new pair an' then a suit o' clo's tu match, an' then his womern must up an' hev a new caliker gaownd. But the beatinest was Ros'l Drake's door, a bran new front door 'at he bid off tu Amos Wilkinses vandue. Do' know haow Amos come tu hev it, but he hed it, an' Ros'l he bid it off, an' took it hum an' sot it in the barn, and at fust his womern sputtered 'baout his buyin' of it, an' they hed a notion o' puttin' on 't in the place o' their ol' front door, but it wouldn't fit, an' they cal'lated ef it did it 'ould make the hul haouse look humblier 'n ever. But it would n't du to waste that aire door, 'at was paneled an' hed a big brass knocker, an' so what d' they du finally but turn tu an' build them a new haouse tu fit that aire door, which the ol' one was plenty good 'nough.

Wal . . . they hed tu mortgage the' place, an' finally lost it, ol' haouse, new haouse, front door an' all, an' went off over intu Adam's Gore tu live in a lawg haouse, an' glad 'nough tu git sech shelter.

By Fred Marston, Pownal, Maine. Manuscripts of the Federal Writers' Project of the Works Progress Administration for the State of Maine.

From *Danvis Folks,* by Rowland E. Robinson, pp. 254–255. Copyright, 1894, by Rowland E. Robinson. Boston and New York: Houghton Mifflin Company.

Getting More for His Money

. . . [A] MAN . . . complained because a Boston dentist charged him $5.00 for pulling his tooth.

He complained that the Boston dentist had pulled his tooth in about one second, and he thought $5.00 was an overcharge because a few years before a New Hampshire dentist had dragged him all over his office for about ten minutes to pull one tooth and had only charged him $7.50.

He said the New Hampshire dentist had given him a lot more for his money.

Too Cold to Freeze

. . . IT IS also stated, that about the first settlement of the town, one of the inhabitants by the name of Tufts, a singular sort of a man, became so weary of life, that he determined to freeze himself to death. Going out in the severity of winter, he seated himself down where a cold "northwester" blew fair upon him, and awaited the accomplishment of his purpose. After sitting awhile, he found the severity of the weather so uncomfortable that he was induced to go in the house, declaring that it was actually *too cold* to freeze to death, and wished for a great coat and mittens, in order to make his exit in a more comfortable manner.

The Stupid Hired Man

THE hired man was sent by the owner of a farm to see if the cattle had gotten into an upper field. He was back very soon and reported that they were in the field. It was so soon that the owner did not see how he had had time to drive them back into the pasture and fix the fence and upon inquiry found that he had not. The man said, "Why, you only asked me to see if they were there."

This same man was sent to mow the upper field, meaning, of course, to

---

From *The Story of a Father and Son* or "Unscrewing the Inscrutable," Third Edition, p. 51. Cambridge, Massachusetts: Elliott Addressing Machine Company.

From *Connecticut Historical Collections,* Containing a General Collection of Interesting Facts, Traditions, Biographical Sketches, Anecdotes, &c. Relating to the History and Antiquities of Every Town in Connecticut, with Geographical Descriptions, by John Warner Barber, pp. 106–107. Entered according to the Act of Congress, in the year 1836, by John W. Barber and A. Willard, in the Clerk's Office, of the District Court of Connecticut. New Haven and Hartford.

By Ola G. Veazie. Manuscripts of the Federal Writers' Project of the Works Progress Administration for the State of New Hampshire.

mow only the hay there. He was gone such a long time that he was taken to task about it and said, "Wal, the hay mowed fine, the corn fair, but the potatoes were devilish."

Recognizing the Broom

ONE of Poland's queer characters was Hanson Orr, the hired man of some of Mrs. Keen's people. He had a number of quips that he got off occasionally, such as, when trying to establish what day it was: "Is it Thursday or Friday or some day next week?"

On most occasions he was somewhat dull. Once some visitors took a picture of him as he was sweeping in the barn doorway, unknown to him. They showed him the picture and asked him if he recognized the man. Hanson studied it; no, he didn't know as he did.

"Why, it's you, Hanson!" the jokers cried.

Hanson looked disgruntled, and said: "Thought that broom looked familiar."

Better Than That

"ZEKE," in North Stonington, was a farm hand who "hired out" to various farms. One afternoon he participated in an afternoon of hog-slaughtering. One especially large hog was dressed off, so big that the farmer asked his helpers to make a guess as to the weight of it. Zeke also ventured a guess. When the carcass was put on the scale, the farmer turned to the group, with the announcement: "Why, Zeke, you guessed it just exactly right. How'd you do it?" "Humph, 'tain't nothing," drawled Zeke, shifting his tobacco quid from one cheek to the other. "Sometimes I can do considerable better'n that."

Borrowing the Saddle

YEARS ago in Old Town, Maine, there lived an old Frenchman who could speak very little English. One day he was sent to borrow a saddle. On the way to the neighbor's house he forgot the name of what he was after, so on

---

By Elsie Keen, Poland, Maine. Manuscripts of the Federal Writers' Project of the Works Progress Administration for the State of Maine.

From "Stonington." Manuscripts of the Federal Writers' Project of the Works Progress Administration for the State of Connecticut.

By Frank Landry, Old Town, Maine. Manuscripts of the Federal Writers' Project of the Works Progress Administration for the State of Maine.

approaching the man he was going to ask the favor of, he said, "I'd like to borrow your iddi giddi and the iddi giddi, the belli woggen, giggin hoggin, long thing, poppin thing, thing a man sits upon." The man got him to repeat this a number of times, and was about to give up when the idea came to him to have the Frenchman show him what he wanted. So the Frenchman led him to the barn and showed the saddle.

A Cure for the Glanders

. . . NATE JEFFERS from over East . . . [is] cousin o' Cy Hendricks, who used to run stage over t' the Center. One mornin' the both of 'em met on the Blandford road.

"Mornin' Cy," says the fust.

"Mornin' Nate," says the secunt.

"What did you give your hoss fur glanders?"

"Croton iyle," says the secunt.

A few days later they met agin.

"Mornin' Cy," says the fust.

"Mornin' Nate," says the secunt.

"What you say you give your hoss fur glanders?"

"Croton iyle," say the secunt.

"Kilt mine," says the fust.

"Kilt mine," says the secunt.

The Man from Monkton

TO THOSE of rural districts who seldom travel far from the home fireside, there are suggestions of possible interest and entertainment in conversing with strange frequenters of the highway. This was especially true of earlier days when, because of frugal habits and rather unsatisfactory public roads, unfamiliar faces in the highways were few indeed.

It is not surprising therefore that when a real old gentleman who had served his community and even his state acceptably in his more active days, observed an absolute stranger walking rapidly up the road, he should have meandered out to the front gate for a little closer inspection.

The traveler was evidently in haste, but was brought up to a short turn with an interrogation from the old gentleman that it would have been very impolite to have ignored. Then followed a conversation which is yet occasionally referred to after more than half a century.

From *Bubblin's an' B'ilin's at the Center,* by Merle Dixon Graves, pp. 69–70. Copyright, 1934, by Merle Dixon Graves. Rutland, Vermont: The Tuttle Company.

From *New England Joke Lore,* The Tonic of Yankee Humor, by Arthur G. Crandall, pp. 252–254. Copyright, 1922, by F. A. Davis Company. Philadelphia.

"You seem to be in a hurry today."

"Yes, I am."

"Where did you come from?"

"I came from Monkton."

"When did you leave there?"

"Day before yesterday."

"Where did you stay last night?"

"I stayed in Goshen."

"Where are you going today?"

"I am going to Jericho."

"What are you going to Jericho for?"

"I am going to school."

"A man as old as you going to school! What are you going to school for?"

"I am going to school to see if I can't learn how to mind my own business."

Taunton's Seasons

The plenty in season, the scarcity when the run of fish was gone, has passed into the myths of a town of the Old Colony. A traveler in the frozen winter, meeting an emaciated villager, asks the name of the place; a weak voice drawls out, "Taunton, Good Lord!" Returning in the genial spring, the sun shining, the streams unlocked, the herring in full run, he meets the same person, now erect, plump, and audacious. To the same question the renovated citizen answers, "Taunton!! and be d——d to you!"

Jim Eldredge's Old Mill

A discriminating lady from Baltimore, with an indulgent eye for Dutch effects, sallied forth one May morning to buy an old windmill. She was the first to conceive the idea that such an interesting annex to her cottage would make unique quarters for her guests. As old windmills, however, are not to be acquired off-hand at any chain store, the pursuit led her many a mile

---

From *Economic and Social History of New England, 1620–1789,* by William B. Weeden, Vol. I, p. 133. Copyright, 1890, by William B. Weeden. Boston and New York: Houghton, Mifflin and Company. 1890.

From *Cape Cod Ahoy!,* A Travel Book for the Summer Visitor, by Arthur Wilson Tarbell, p. 103. Copyright, 1932, by Arthur Wilson Tarbell. Boston: A. T. Ramsay & Company.

from one end of the Cape to the other. Success came in the end. She chanced upon a fine old specimen in Falmouth, had it transported tenderly to Chatham, and then carried through her attractive plan to its least detail, which was roses rambling over the arms of the mill. Imagine her surprise when shortly afterwards a veteran character of the neighborhood strolled around, and exclaimed, "Well, well, I'm glad to see Jim Eldredge's old mill back in Chatham. You know, a man from Falmouth came here fifteen or twenty years ago and took it away. Sort of wanted to decorate his grounds."

More Bacon

CONGDON's tavern was also associated with a pleasant anecdote in connection with the famous "John Randolph, of Roanoke." Edmund Randolph, Secretary of State under Washington, accompanied by his kinsman, John Randolph, of Roanoke, and John R. Smith, of Philadelphia, left the city of New York on horseback and hastened to Newport to see the French minister on official business. From the time the travelers left New York until they reached Wickford, they had been unable to get scarce a thing to eat but fried bacon and eggs. Wherever they stopped for the night and inquired what was to be had for supper, the reply of the host of the tavern was uniformly the same—"fried ham and eggs!"—greatly to the distaste of the wearied travelers and more especially to the disgust of John of Roanoke.

Wickford has ever been celebrated for both its soft and hard shelled clams, the latter being then called by the Indian name "quahog."[1] On the arrival of the guests at Congdon's tavern, in answer to the usual question, the landlord replied "that he could give them clams for supper." At this announcement John of Roanoke was so pleased that he absolutely rubbed the palms of his hands together through gleeful emotion. This lasted, however, but a few moments, when "mine host" again opened the door to say to his guests "that he was sorry the tide was too high to allow of getting clams, but that he could give them some capital quahogs. "Good God!" exclaimed John of Roanoke, "more bacon!"

From *Recollections of Olden Times:* Rowland Robinson of Narragansett and His Unfortunate Daughter, with Genealogies of the Robinson and Hazard Families of Rhode Island, by Thomas R. Hazard, "Shepherd Tom," in His Eighty-First and Eighty-Second Years, Also Genealogical Sketch of the Hazards of the Middle States, by Willis P. Hazard, of Westchester, Pa., pp. 65–66. Entered according to Act of Congress, in the year 1879, by John P. Sanborn, in the Office of the Librarian of Congress, at Washington, D. C. Newport, Rhode Island.

[1] Pronounced "ko-hog."

A Severe Punishment

A STRANGER came one day to Lonetown Tavern long ago, and stayed day after day, and week after week. He did no work, and seemed to have no business; he did not even let his name be known. This was all very puzzling to the townsfolk, and they were entirely at sea in their conjectures as to why he was there.

At length the people of the village sent a delegation to the man to get some information as to who and what he was. He would give them no satisfaction then; but after some talk back and forth he consented to name a time when he would answer their various questions plainly and fully.

On the appointed night the delegation presented itself, and was thus enlightened: "Gentlemen," said the stranger, "I am a criminal. I had my choice at the bar of justice, to be hung or to spend six months in Lonetown. I chose to come here, but I wish now that I had chosen to be hung."

With that the stranger bade the company "Good-evening," and bowed himself out of the room.

The Thief's Defense

I THINK it was Jonathan N. Hazard who missed his axe, and on meeting black Jim Tefft (a noted thief, whom he suspected), asked him when he was going to bring back the axe he stole from him. Jim seemed horrified at the charge and defended himself stoutly. Jonathan expressed surprise at Jim's alleged innocence, and remarked that he could not think of any one else who would steal it! But Jim got in the last word when he rejoined. "Mr. Hazard, you may depend upon it, there is a great deal stole around here on my credit!" . . .

Keeping Out the Deer

WINDSOR DRURY was a famous bear trapper. One time a deer got into one of his traps and he was haled into court over the matter. The case had been

From *What They Say in New England,* A Book of Signs, Sayings, and Superstitions, collected by Clifton Johnson, p. 247. Copyright, 1896, by Lee and Shepard. Boston.

From *The Jonny-Cake Papers of "Shepherd Tom,"* Together with Reminiscences of Narragansett Schools of Former Days, by Thomas Robinson Hazard, with a Biographical Sketch and Notes by Rowland Gibson Hazard, p. 333. Copyright, 1915, by Rowland G. Hazard. Boston: Printed for the Subscribers.

From "Easton," by Ola G. Veazie. Manuscripts of the Federal Writers' Project of the Works Progress Administration for the State of New Hampshire.

argued without his having to say much during a whole day. When the court was finally adjourned without any decision, as a parting verbal shot he said, "I have written notices near my traps that these are bear traps and not for deer, so if you want to keep them out you had better teach the deer to read."

Not Bright

A FARM-HAND who had not been considered very bright was accidentally killed, and his family took the matter to court to try to get some damages from his employer. During the questioning in court, the judge asked the employer if the laborer was foolish. The employer replied, "No." When asked if he was bright, he replied, "No." The judge asked him to explain, and he said: "Wal, Judge, I ain't bright and you ain't bright, but if any one called us foolish we'd be madder'n hell."

Chandler's Thumb

SOME time between the years 1780 and 1800 a man named Chandler ran a store in Lower Gloucester where, among other things, he sold rum to the team drivers on their way through. Chandler had unusually large thumbs, and being a penurious man, he thrust a large thumb into the mug when filling it and serving his customers, thus saving a little rum on each drinker. A big Irish teamster, who had stopped there many times, one day seized the mug, thumb and all, at the same time drawing a knife. "I've paid for that thumb over and over," he shouted, "and now I'm going to have it."

Clagett and the Teamster

WYSEMAN CLAGETT was a most persevering searcher out of petty offences against the dignity of the crown and peace of the province. There was no escape for the violator of the law, and the statutes against small offences

From "Littleton," by Ola G. Veazie. Manuscripts of the Federal Writers' Project of the Works Progress Administration for the State of New Hampshire.

By Lewis P. True, New Gloucester, Maine. Manuscripts of the Federal Writers' Project of the Works Progress Administration for the State of Maine.

From *Rambles About Portsmouth,* Sketches of Persons, Localities, and Incidents of Two Centuries: Principally from Tradition and Unpublished Documents, by Charles W. Brewster, pp. 234–235. Entered according to Act of Congress, in the year 1859, by C. W. Brewster & Son, in the Clerk's Office of the District Court of the District of New Hampshire. Portsmouth, New Hampshire.

were executed in their utmost rigor. In common parlance the word "Clagett" became synonymous with the word "prosecute," and "to be Clagetted" meant the same thing as "to be prosecuted."

There is one anecdote related of the King's Attorney which would seem to indicate, that however just he might be in administering for the King, he could swerve a little when self-interest and irritation prompted. There was one day a load of wood on the parade for sale. The man would not part with it for the sum offered. The Attorney, in a state of irritation, went home, and told one of his servants to go and insult that man, and report what he said or did. The man did as he was told—for none who lived with him dared do otherwise. The irritated teamster, with an oath and a threat, shook his goad at the man. A complaint was at once made, the man summoned before the King's Attorney, charged with using profane language. He appeared trembling before the throne which Clagett had erected in his office, on which, in his judicial wig, he presided with magisterial dignity, with the clerk's seat on one side and the sheriff's on the other. The poor man begged his honor's pardon and asked forgiveness. "I heartily forgive you," was the reply. The man began to retire. "Stop, stop, sir—*I* forgive you, but the *law* don't. You are found guilty of profanity, and fined five dollars." "Oh dear, sir, my load of wood, which I brought in to raise the means for paying my taxes, will not sell for so much, and I have nothing else—what shall I do!" "Your case," said the King's Attorney, "is indeed a hard one, and in pity for you, you may drive the load of wood into my yard, and I will make up the balance of the fine myself." The *favored* man left his wood as directed.

The Dancing Sheriff

FOLLOWING the shore of the lake less than a mile from this point south, we come to the first bridge that was built in Narragansett, on which Deputy Sheriff Cranston, of North Kingstown, was in the olden time compelled to dance under the following circumstances. The constable had in his possession an execution for some three or four dollars against one Elias Wilbour, and called at the Rowland Robinson farm—then owned and occupied by the late Peleg Gardiner—, where the old man was at work in the hay field, to collect it. The debtor, pleading inability to meet the demand, was told that he must then go to jail. To this arrangement Elias readily consented, merely stipulating that he should be allowed first to see

From *Recollections of Olden Times:* Rowland Robinson of Narragansett and His Unfortunate Daughter, with Genealogies of the Robinson and Hazard Families of Rhode Island, by Thomas R. Hazard, "Shepherd Tom," in His Eighty-First and Eighty-Second Years, Also Genealogical Sketch of the Hazards of the Middle States, by Willis P. Hazard, of Westchester, Pa., pp. 68–70. Entered according to Act of Congress, in the year 1879, by John P. Sanborn, in the Office of the Librarian of Congress, at Washington, D. C. Newport, Rhode Island.

his employer. The two proceeded to the house where Wilbour obtained from Mr. Gardiner five dollars due him for past work. The debtor, thereupon expressing his readiness to proceed to jail, was told by his custodian that it was now unnecessary to take him from his work, as he had in his possession more than enough money to discharge the execution. Elias, however, who was something of a wag in his way, could not be made to understand the officer's logic, and insisted that he could not part with any of his money, as he should want it all to pay his jail board! "But," said Cranston, "pay the execution with a part of the money only, and I won't take you to jail." The force of such reasoning, however, old Wilbour could not be made to appreciate, and they proceeded on their way towards the jail, the constable trying his utmost in the meantime to induce his prisoner to discharge the debt and return to his work, but without success. From the first, Cranston had no intention of taking Elias to jail, only meaning to frighten him into paying the debt, and when they arrived at the bridge, finding he could do nothing with the stupid or obstinate old man and his own way thereafter not lying in the direction of the jail, he told Elias he might go back to his work and let the debt remain unpaid. This proposition, however, was repeatedly declined by Wilbour, who reminded Cranston that he had told him "he would take him to jail, and to jail he meant to go, even if obliged to go alone!" After a good deal of colloquy on the subject Wilbour finally consented to go back on the condition that he himself should be permitted to sing "Old Charmany [Chalmouny] Fair" whilst the deputy sheriff danced it out to his tune on the bridge. The latter's business being urgent, he finally dismounted, and throwing off his coat complied with Wilbour's demands to the letter, after which Cranston went on his way rejoicing that he had got rid of his ugly customer, who then went back to the hay field and resumed work.

Robinson and the Governor's Sheep

Wm. T. Robinson, son of Thomas and father of Mrs. Mary Hunter, used to relate an amusing anecdote of one of the early Robinsons who, it appears, had joined the Quaker Meeting. Governor Brenton had placed him on a farm belonging to him, situated on the south end of the island, adjacent to Brenton's Point, and stocked it largely with sheep. In a violent snowstorm, such as used to prevail more frequently than of late in New England—though I have known several in my day, perhaps equally destructive—, these sheep having been left in an exposed position, were driven by the inclement tempest of wind and sleet off the rocks into the sea, where they perished. When Robinson communicated the loss of the sheep to Brenton, the Governor being a man of hasty temper, as most of the early settlers of Newport and King's—now Washington—counties in Rhode

Ibid., pp. 11-12.

Island seem to have been, he flew into a towering rage with his tenant, and reproached him in unmeasured terms for the loss of the sheep through, as he charged, gross neglect. To all the abuse heaped upon him Robinson answered not a word, which submissiveness seemed only to increase Brenton's ire, who at last, in his frenzy, declared that Robinson should pay for the lost sheep, and bid him choose a man to arbitrate their value, while he chose another, which Brenton did on his part *instanter*. It was now Robinson's turn to choose his man. "Friend Brenton," said he, "I know of no one whom I should prefer to trust my interest with than thou! I think I will choose thee for my man." This was too much for the governor, who, after bursting into a fit of laughter, told his unmanageable tenant to go back to the farm and he would venture to trust one more flock of sheep to his care.

Nighest the Fire

Some years ago up in Connecticut, a long, lean Yankee dropped into the old Franklin hotel. The weather was cold, and a knot of lawyers were in the bar-room sitting around the fire, smoking, drinking, and chatting.

A young sprig spoke to him and said:

"You look like a traveler."

"Wall, I 'spose I am; I come from Wisconsin afoot, 'tany rate."

"From Wisconsin! that is quite a distance to come on one pair of legs. I say, did you ever pass through the 'lower regions' in your travels?"

"Yes, sir," he answered, a kind of wicked look stealing over his ugly phizmahogany, "I 'ben through the outskirts."

"I thought it likely. Well, what is it like down there?"

"Oh," said the Yankee, deliberately, half shutting his eyes, and drawing around the corner of his mouth, "you'll find it much the same as in this region—*the lawyers sit nighest the fire.*"

A Dirty Fellow

An example of the merits of dress was somewhat ludicrously presented by a colloquy between two Harvard men who arrived at eminence, and who were as wide apart as the poles in their attention to personal appearance.

From *Wit and Humor, A Choice Collection,* by Marshall Brown, pp. 61–62. Entered according to the Act of Congress, in the year 1877, by Marshall Brown and J. W. Kreps, in the office of the Librarian of Congress, at Washington. Copyright, 1879, by S. C. Griggs and Company. Chicago.

From *Historic Fields and Mansions of Middlesex,* by Samuel Adams Drake, pp. 236–237. Entered according to Act of Congress, in the year 1873, by James R. Osgood and Company, in the Office of the Librarian of Congress, at Washington. Boston. 1874.

Theophilus Parsons was a man very negligent of his outward seeming while Harrison Gray Otis was noted for his fine linen and regard for his apparel. The elegant Otis, having to cross-examine a witness in court whose appearance was slovenly in the extreme, commented upon the man's filthy exterior with severity, and spoke of him as a "dirty fellow," because he had on a dirty shirt. Parsons, whose witness it was, objected to the badgering of Otis.

"Why," said Otis, turning to Parsons, with ill-concealed irony, "how many shirts a week do you wear, Brother Parsons?"

"I wear one shirt a week," was the reply. "How many do you wear?"

"I change my shirt every day, and sometimes oftener," said Otis.

"Well," retorted Parsons, "you must be a 'dirty fellow' to soil seven shirts a week when I do but one."

There was a sensation in the court-room, and Mr. Otis sat down with his plumage a little ruffled.

Too Late

YEARS ago—, and for aught we know, it still exists—there was a statute in vogue in New-Hampshire legalizing the annual election of hog-reeves throughout the towns in that State. The office was a lucrative one in some places, though it was generally made opprobrious, and the most obnoxious individuals in the community were usually selected to fill this post. Some good jokes occurred, in various ways, in connection with the office, however.

Farmer Thorow resided in a small town above Nashua, and prided himself upon the neatness of his cattle, the cleanliness of his fields, the symmetry of his fences, and the thriftiness of his orchards; but Farmer T. was a nervous man, penurious and close-fisted.

Waking early one morning, he discovered on a sudden from his chamber-window that four large hogs had broken into a nice young orchard of his just below the house, and in his usual excitable manner he hurried on his clothes and made the best of his way down to 'Squire Looksharp, (the hog-reeve was called " 'Squire,") whom he very quickly aroused, with his vociferous complaint.

"Now, 'Squire," he said, "hurry up. There's four o' my neighbor's hogs got into my little apple-orchard, and 'f you'll hurry it'll be a good job for you; there're nice, fat ones, an' no mistake."

"Be right straight along," said the 'Squire, who remembered the details of the law relating to this sort of seizure—one-half to the hog-reeve, and the other half to the poor of the town—and, within half an hour, he had

From *Gleanings from the Portfolio of the "Young 'Un,"* A Series of Humorous Sketches, Third Edition, [by George P. Burnham], pp. 10–13. Entered according to Act of Congress, in the year 1849, by R. B. Fitts and G. P. Burnham, in the Clerk's Office of the District Court of the District of Massachusetts. Boston: Published by R. B. Fitts & Co.

peaceable possession of four animals such as the neighborhood couldn't otherwise boast of!

The seized hogs were quickly slaughtered by the town-official, and were shortly "hung up to dry," in the 'Squire's storehouse. Farmer T. righted up his broken fence, and then repaired to his yard to see that all was snug at the pig-pen; he had no idea that his hogs should trouble his neighbors—not he—when lo! he found that a board had been forced from the side of the enclosure, and the sty was empty!

In the meantime, 'Squire Looksharp had had the seized hogs dressed; and now he sent for his good wife, who appeared at the storehouse door.

"Betty," said the 'Squire, "the statoot pervides, in case of seizure, that one haff the pigs shall go to the official, an' the other haff to the poor. Now, Betty, who's poorer than yeou are?"

"Sure enough," said the 'Squire's wife, obediently, "sure enough! If anybody's poorer 'n *I* am, I'd like to hear about it."

"Well, so I cal'late, Betty. An' thairfore, one haff these pigs goes to the poor, (that's *yeou,*) and the other haff, as I said afore, goes to the officer, an' that's *me!*" and the four hogs very soon found their way into 'Squire Looksharp's pork-barrels.

An hour afterwards, Farmer Thorow arrived at the 'Squire's, sprang over the stile, into the house, through the back kitchen, out again into the yard, where he encountered the 'Squire, quietly at work.

"I say, 'Squire!"

"Hello!"

"What'n thunder you doin'!"

"'Baout what?"

"Where's the pigs?"

"Distributed 'cording to law."

"What!"

"Haff to the hog-reeve, haff to the poor."

"They're mine!" shouted Farmer T., half-crazed at his loss. "They're mine, 'Squire—broke out o' *my* pen."

"You made the complaint, yourself."

"I know—but"—

"An' it's tew late, Farmer; the property's dewly divided—can't go behind the statoot."

The farmer squirmed, threatened to be revenged on somebody at the first opportunity, but seeing his mistake at length returned home; and from that day forward had no occasion for a similar lesson. He never afterwards complained of his neighbors' hogs!

The Medford Fisheries

MEDFORD was represented in the General Court by a conscientious and trustworthy man, who had fallen into the habit of sleeping after dinner. Sleep he must, and sleep he would. Medford had petitioned the Legislature for a grant of certain rights touching the fishery in Mystic River. This gentleman had presented the petition; and the day was fixed for its consideration by the house. That day had arrived; and the Medford representative was all alive to the question, and had prepared his speech for the decisive moment, in defence of the petition. Two sessions were held that day; and the Medford fisheries were to come up immediately after dinner! How, then, could our representative get his nap? He went to his seat in the house at a very early moment; and soon his next neighbor came and sat beside him. It now occurred to him that he might safely secure a short nap, by asking his neighbor to wake him when the subject of Medford fisheries was called up. His friendly neighbor promised to do so: therefore Medford went to sleep. The house soon came to order; and it was then proposed to pass another bill first, because no debate would be needed upon it. The bill was for the suppression of houses of ill-fame. It was not debated; and the vote upon it was about to be taken, when our representative's next neighbor thought that his friend would like to vote on the occasion, and therefore awoke him suddenly. He had hardly got his eyes and wits fairly open before the speaker cried out, in the usual phrase, "Is the house ready for the question?" Medford sprang upon his feet in an instant, exclaiming, "Mr. Speaker! I must ask the attention of the house for a few moments to some remarks on this important and interesting question; because, Mr. Speaker, many of my constituents get their living by this very business." A roar of laughter burst from every quarter of the house. The Medford representative stood aghast in raw wonder. As soon as quiet could be restored, the speaker said to him, "Do you know what the question before the house is?" "Why, yes: it's fishing in the Mystic River, ain't it?" Another peal of laughter convulsed the assembly.

Mr. Doe's Brains

. . . IT IS told how a man by the name of Doe had at one time so serious a brain difficulty that the family physician was called. The doctor, after a thorough diagnosis of the case, said to Mr. Doe, "You must take to your

---

From *History of the Town of Medford, Middlesex County, Massachusetts,* from Its First Settlement, in 1630, to the Present Time, 1855, by Charles Brooks, p. 490. Boston: Published by James M. Usher. 1855.

From *Reminiscences of Candia,* by Wilson Palmer, pp. 225–226. Copyright, 1905, by Wilson Palmer. Cambridge: Printed at The Riverside Press.

bed, that I may perform an operation on your brain." But Mr. Doe was an exceedingly busy man, so much so that he could not spare the time for the proposed operation, so he suggested to the doctor that he take the brains out of his cranium, carry them home and fix them up. Meanwhile he could keep on with his work. The doctor did as his patient advised, and in a little time had Mr. Doe's brains in their normal condition; so he, without any undue delay, sent word to Mr. Doe that his brains were as good as new, and he could have them by calling. Mr. Doe at once sent back word to the doctor, "Never mind, do what you will with my brains,—I shall not need them again, for since you took them home, I have been elected to the legislature." . . .

Bounding North Weymouth

AT THE time of the removal of tolls from the Hingham and Quincy turnpike and bridges there was a big fight in the Legislature on the question. Hon. Elias S. Beals was the representative from Weymouth, and a strong advocate of the measure. In order to make the situation clear to the committee he exhibited a map showing the boundaries of North Weymouth,—the bay on the north, Hingham bridge east, Quincy bridge west, and the only road to the South passing through the Old North Cemetery.

Mr. Beals in his speech explained the matter somewhat after this manner. Pointing to his map he said: "Gentlemen, I wish to call your attention to the location of the village of North Weymouth. On the north the boundless Atlantic Ocean, on the east a toll bridge, on the west a toll bridge, and on the south death stares us in the face."

Lone Wolves

. . . I HAVE often heard my grandmother tell with great interest the proceedings of former years. One instance, I recollect, was this: that at one time when the State Legislature met, a man of rather ordinary appearance presented himself. The members viewed him and then asked him if he was the choice of the people? His answer was this: Sirs, I am the only man in my town; of course there was no one to set up against me; therefore I considered it my privilege to come here, and I have made my appearance. This caused some glee, but the honest man was not refused a seat. At another

From *History of Weymouth, Massachusetts,* Published by the Weymouth Historical Society, Howard H. Joy, President, Under Direction of the Town, 1923, Vol. 2, p. 810.

From *The History of the White Mountains from the First Settlement of Upper Coos and Pequaket,* by Lucy, Wife of Ethan Allen, Crawford, pp. 14–15. Entered according to Act of Congress, in the year 1845, by Lucy Crawford, in the Clerk's Office of the District Court of New Hampshire. White Hills. 1846.

time, as the military laws were in those days similar to ours, a neighboring town legally warned a meeting for the purpose of choosing military officers and to have a training. After the officers were chosen there was but one remaining soldier: and he looking wishfully upon his superiors said: Gentlemen, I have one request to make, that is, as I am the only soldier, I hope your honors will not be too severe in drilling me, but will spare me a little as I may be needed another time. He could form a column, he said, but it racked him shockingly to display.

No Eagle

SOME years ago in the town of New Boston, after the meeting-house was built and a cupola added, the town fathers conceived the idea that a nice gilt eagle on top of the cupola would be a fine thing. Accordingly they sent to Massachusetts to get an estimate of the expense so as to be ready at town meeting time to support the proposition. The town was poor, the debts were many, and the question of a gilt eagle was discussed and "cussed" for weeks. On town meeting day it seemed as though the selectmen would carry their point and the eagle might soon adorn the spire of the church, but finally farmer Joseph Dunbar arose and said, "Gentlemen—and others —I always reckoned the voters of New Boston were big fools, and probably always would be, but if they are willing to give five honest to goodness gold eagles for one gilt one, they are darn sight bigger fools than I had supposed." No eagle ever adorned the spire of the meeting-house.

An Honest Man

SOME time ago there lived in Stonington a farmer with political aspirations. The reputation he acquired in the course of satisfying his ambitions was not altogether savory. One day a colleague of his met an old farmer who came from the politician's district and asked: "What do you think of the man out your way?"

The old gentleman stroked his beard and looked wise, but said nothing. "Would you call him an honest man, or a liar?" persisted the colleague.

After more stroking of the beard the old man replied slowly, "We-ell, I wouldn't go so fur as to call him a liar—but I heared tell by them as knows him that when he wants his pigs to come for their feed, he has to git somebody else to call 'em."

Manuscripts of the Federal Writers' Project of the Works Progress Administration for the State of New Hampshire.

Manuscripts of the Federal Writers' Project of the Works Progress Administration for the State of Connecticut.

CLEVER RETORTS AND ENIGMATIC REMARKS

Sleeping in Church

In a certain town not more than fifty miles from Boston, as the clergyman was holding forth in his usual drowsy manner, one of the deacons, probably influenced by the narcotic qualities of the discourse, fell into a doze. The preacher happening to use the words, "What is the price of all earthly pleasures?" the good deacon, who kept a small store, thinking the inquiry respecting some kind of merchandise, immediately answered, "Seven and sixpence a dozen." [1]

It used to be the custom to hold a classmeeting every week in churches as well as a mid-week prayer meeting. At East Columbia, where there was formerly a settled minister, a farmer had driven into the class meeting after a hard day's work in the open and soon settled down into sleep. It was the usual procedure of these class meetings to have a brief sermon by the pastor and then turn the meeting into an experience meeting, at which each one present was expected to say something. After all the others had spoken, the minister tapped this farmer on the shoulder and asked him if he did not love the Lord. "Some," was the very brief answer before the tired farmer lapsed back into his slumber.[2]

A man who went to sleep in church suddenly awakened to ask how long the minister had been preaching. When told "thirty or forty years," he remarked: "Well I guess I'll stay. He must be most through." [3]

A clergyman, having in the course of a dull sermon preached all his audience to sleep except an idiot, suddenly exclaimed, "What, will you not keep awake one hour? What a shame! You are all asleep except this poor idiot!" The idiot, looking him in the face, said, "Yes, and if I hadn't been a poor idiot I should have been asleep too." [4]

---

[1] From *The New-England Almanac,* for the Year of Our Lord 1833, by Anson Allen, Philo., p. 17. Hartford: Published and Sold by Andrus and Judd.

[2] By Ola G. Veazie. Manuscripts of the Federal Writers' Project of the Works Progress Administration for the State of New Hampshire.

[3] By Mrs. C. A. Weston, Portland, Maine. Manuscripts of the Federal Writers' Project of the Works Progress Administration for the State of Maine.

[4] From *The Old Farmer's Almanack,* Calculated on a New and Improved Plan for the Year of Our Lord 1904, No. 112, by Robert B. Thomas, p. 51. Entered, according to Act of Congress, in the year 1903, by Horace E. Ware, in the Office of the Librarian of Congress, at Washington. Boston: William Ware & Co.

"Why," said a country clergyman to one of his flock, "do you always snore in your pew when I am in the pulpit, while you are all attention to every stranger I invite?" "Because, Sir, when you preach I am sure all is right; but I can't trust a stranger, without keeping a good lookout." [5]

Eggs Is Eggs

ONE day a man brought in a dozen of extra large eggs and so tried to get a fancy price for them. The storekeeper refused, saying "Eggs is eggs." The next week he brought in a dozen bantam eggs, and when the storekeeper started to object, quietly remarked, "Eggs is eggs."

Super Is Dead

THEY used to laugh at one of our jocose broom manufacturers who took a two-horse load of brooms to Albany, of course selling his wares as he had opportunity by the way. He closed out the end of his load to a wide-awake man in Albany, taking his pay in flour. He wasn't much acquainted with handling flour and the barrels were marked "fine flour." When he arrived home with his flour that he hoped to sell at a profit the people asked him why he didn't buy "superfine" instead of fine. He replied that they told him that "Old Super" was dead so they could not use his name on that flour any more. He never outgrew that.

Clock Oil

MERRICK [Butler, the miller] had a brother Hamilton, who was a clock tinker. He used to travel about the country plying his trade. Someone

---

[5] From *The New-England Farmer's Almanac,* for the Year of the Christian Era, 1842, No. XXVIII, by Truman Abell. Claremont, New Hampshire: Published and Sold at the Claremont Bookstore.

From "Littleton," by Ola G. Veazie. Manuscripts of the Federal Writers' Project of the Works Progress Administration for the State of New Hampshire.

From *History of the Town of Whately, Mass.* Including a Narrative of Leading Events from the First Planting of Hatfield: 1661–1899, as Revised and Enlarged by James M. Crafts, with Family Genealogies, pp. 274–275. Entered according to Act of Congress in 1899 by James M. Crafts in the Office of the Librarian of Congress. Orange, Mass.: Printed for the Town by D. L. Crandall. 1899.

From *The Boyhood Days of President Calvin Coolidge,* or From The Green Mountains to the White House, Original Sketches of Plymouth Life, by Ernest C. Carpenter, p. 50. Copyright, 1925, by the Marble City Press. Rutland, Vermont: The Tuttle Company.

once asked him the secret of his success in mending clocks. He replied in a confidential way, "I usually oil my clocks with cricket's oil, but for my best customers I use an oil made out of the feet of bumblebees."

Without a Cow

IN EARLY days there were three potato distilleries in Colebrook. The price was 25¢ for a single gallon of whisky. The surplus was taken to Portland for trading purposes. A large family lived near one of the distilleries, and every day and sometimes oftener they sent a little boy over with a jug to be filled. The proprietor remarked one time that the boy came rather often, and the boy in defense replied, "What's a gallon of whisky in a family without a cow?"

Twenty-five Hour Day

WE DO not have to go away from the [straw] shop to find something to laugh about. There was the handy man about the shop, who did odd jobs when the men were at work and after they had gone home. He was not paid high wages and was allowed to keep his own time sheet, which was seldom questioned, until one day he handed in, "One day, 25 hours." Asked how he could get twenty-five hours in one day, he replied,

"Why, I worked the noon hour."

Weather Predictions

AN OLD resident of the North country, when questioned about the weather in early spring, said. "It will be cold weather as long as there is snow on the mountains, and there will be snow on the mountains as long as it is cold weather."[1]

Henry Heywood, the Lancaster lawyer, was met on the street one spring morning and greeted with, "Chilly morning, isn't it?" He replied: "Why,

---

By Ola G. Veazie. Manuscripts of the Federal Writers' Project of the Works Progress Administration for the State of New Hampshire.

From *Every Day but Sunday, The Romantic Age of New England Industry*, by Jennie F. Copeland, p. 56. Copyright, 1936, by Jennie F. Copeland. Brattleboro, Vermont: Stephen Daye Press.

---

[1] By Mrs. Emma Weeks Roberts. From *More New Hampshire Folk Tales*, collected by Mrs. Moody P. Gore and Mrs. Guy E. Speare, p. 284. Copyright, 1936, by Mrs. Guy E. Speare. Plymouth, New Hampshire: Compiled and published by Mrs. Guy E. Speare.

yes, I've always noticed that it never seems to warm up until the snow goes off the mountains and that the snow does not leave the mountains until it warms up." [2]

Weather Lore

An old man was told by a younger man that there was going to be a spell of settled weather and the old man replied, "Gad, we shan't have it, for the equinoctial hain't crossed the horizontal." This referred to the belief that there is always a "line" storm as the sun travels north or south in the spring and fall.

Winter Before Last's Snow

. . . An early summer visitor driving through a deep gorge, scarcely touched at any part of the day by sunshine, found a man busily shoveling snow which had evidently drifted deep across the road.

"You must have had lots of snow here last winter," he remarked as he drove by.

"Oh! no," was the reply, "this is winter before last's snow."

Dried Apple Trees

Back in 1860 Simon was working in the orchard when an apple tree salesman called and asked him if he wanted to buy some young apple trees.

Simon replied, "Nope, I have enough trees."

The salesman then remarked that there were three or four dead trees. "How about replacing them?"

Simon said, "Nope, they're not dead."

The salesman said, "They must be dead. They look like it."

Simon replied, "They're not dead. They're what I grow my dried apples on."

---

[2] By Ola G. Veazie. Manuscripts of the Federal Writers' Project of the Works Progress Administration for the State of New Hampshire.

From "Sugar Hill," by Ola G. Veazie. Manuscripts of the Federal Writers' Project of the Works Progress Administration for the State of New Hampshire.

From *New England Joke Lore,* The Tonic of Yankee Humor, by Arthur G. Crandall, p. 18. Copyright, 1922, by F. A. Davis Company. Philadelphia.

By G. Briggs, Wayne, Maine. Manuscripts of the Federal Writers' Project of the Works Progress Administration for the State of Maine.

God and the New Hampshire Farmer

A FARMER was working his small rocky plot on a back road when a curate who was new to the district came along. He stopped to talk and in the course of the conversation remarked, "You and God certainly have done a nice piece of work here." "Yeah," the man answered, "you ought to have seen it when God had it all alone."

A Natural Death

. . . YOU must remember old Gardiner Kenyon, who lived on Point Judith and died at the age of ninety. He had been in bed some days with illness, when, on hearing his wife direct a daughter to send for a doctor, he cried out, "Wife, don't bring any doctor into my room: I have concluded to die a natural death."

Gallows Wit

. . . WHEN the last public hanging took place in Windham County in 1835, there was an immense crowd which "caroused most scandalously." It was on this occasion that the doomed man got off one of the best of last-minute remarks. Looking out of his cell while he waited for the cart to take him to the gallows, he saw people hurrying by.

"Why are they running?" he asked. "Nothing can happen until I get there."

An Indian's Letter to His Friends

KING DICK and Queen Daphne lived on Pine Island, so called, situated on what is now Hanover Street. Dick requested Col. John Bailey to write

---

From "Lancaster," by Ola G. Veazie. Manuscripts of the Federal Writers' Project of the Works Progress Administration for the State of New Hampshire.

From *The Jonny-Cake Papers of "Shepherd Tom,"* Together with Reminiscences of Narragansett Schools of Former Days, by Thomas Robinson Hazard, With a Biographical Sketch and Notes by Rowland Gibson Hazard, p. 334. Copyright, 1915, Rowland G. Hazard. Boston: Printed for the Subscribers.

From *Town Meeting Country,* by Clarence M. Webster, p. 125. American Folkways, edited by Erskine Caldwell. Copyright, 1945, by Clarence M. Webster. New York: Duell, Sloan & Pearce.

From *A Historical Sketch of the Town of Hanover, Mass.,* with Family Genealogies, by John S. Barry, p. 51. Boston: Published for the Author by Samuel G. Drake. 1853.

a letter for him to his friends, on the Cape, and on being asked what he should write, replied, "King Dick and Queen Daphne, ebery ting, ebery ting."

Some Kind of Rill

MILITARY titles were in high esteem, even among those who did not know one from another. For instance, there was the old woman who always was repeating proudly that her son was in the army. "He's either a ginny-rill or a corpo-rill—I can never remember which," she said, "but it is some kind of a rill."

Kit Comstock's Hair

OF KIT COMSTOCK a rural witticism is remembered. He was bald, quite completely so, but wore a flowing beard. When asked what had become of his hair, he would reply, "Oh, I pulled it through," with a tug at his beard.

Answering the Reproof

THE minister was reproving a neighbor for his profanity. In an apologetic way the man said: "Mr. Clark, you pray and I swear and we don't either of us mean anything by it."

David Dunn's Witticisms

DAVID DUNN, a man prominent in politics in Poland, speaker of the House in the Maine Legislature, and, by a peculiar coincidence, Governor

---

From *Historic Hampshire in the Connecticut Valley,* Happenings in a Charming Old New England County from the Time of the Dinosaur Down to About 1900, by Clifton Johnson, p. 168. Copyright, 1932, by The Northampton Historical Society. Springfield, Massachusetts: Milton Bradley Company.

By Rowland Gibson Hazard, in *The Jonny-Cake Papers of "Shepherd Tom," Together with Reminiscences of Narragansett Schools of Former Days,* by Thomas Robinson Hazard, With a Biographical Sketch and Notes by Rowland Gibson Hazard, p. 396. Copyright, 1915, by Rowland G. Hazard. Boston: Printed for the Subscribers.

By Augustus K. Small, Portland, Maine. Manuscripts of the Federal Writers' Project of the Works Progress Administration for the State of Maine.

From Poland, Maine. Manuscripts of the Federal Writers' Project of the Works Progress Administration for the State of Maine.

of Maine for one day, was a rather eccentric character. He always carried an umbrella, rain or shine. When asked why he did it, he replied: "A wise man carries an umbrella in good weather; any fool can take one when it rains."

David Dunn was an ardent Democrat. Once, in his Mechanic Falls office, to which he walked every day from Poland, a few friends decided to play a trick on him. Dunn had a fondness for cider and occasionally took a jug to his office. When he went for the mail, they took his jug from his cabinet. When he looked for the jug and found it gone, he said: "The Republicans have been here."

Later the jug was returned—empty. Dunn shook it, found the cider gone, and exclaimed: "The Democrats have been here. Republicans wouldn't have brought the jug back."

David Dunn was administrator for several estates in his day. The curious would sometimes try to get information out of him concerning property. When such a one had died, they would say, "I wonder how much property he left."

"Yes," David Dunn would reply, "he left all he had—all he had."

Clever Retorts

On Slippery Places [1]

. . . It was on one of those icy mornings that they have more or less frequently in Candia during the winter time, that my brother Alfred was attempting to make his way safely along the road, when, in the twinkling of an eye, down he went full length on the treacherous ice. Just at that moment Deacon French came along. Seeing my brother's somewhat ridiculous predicament, the deacon said, "Mr. Palmer, the wicked stand on slippery places," to which my brother immediately replied, "Yes, I know it, but you see, deacon, I can't stand while you are safely on your feet."

None of Mine [2]

. . . David L. Barnes, Esq., was addressing, at one time, a jury in an important case when he quoted, by way of illustration of his argument and

---

[1] From *Reminiscences of Candia,* by Wilson Palmer, p. 220. Copyright, 1905, by Wilson Palmer. Cambridge: Printed at The Riverside Press.

[2] From *Reminiscences of Taunton,* In Ye Auld Lang Syne, by Charles R. Atwood, pp. 141–142. Taunton: Republican Steam Printing Rooms. 1880.

for the purpose of making a strong impression upon the jury, the address of satan to the Lord, "Skin for skin, yea, all that a man hath will he give for his life," adding, in consequence for not being as fresh and familiar with Bible reading, perhaps, as with Coke upon Littleton, "saith our Savior." Mr. [James] Sproat was up in an instant and, solemnly addressing the court, said, "May it please your Honor—He may be brother Barnes' savior, but he is none of mine."

Laying Up Treasures in Heaven[3]

Mr. Baylies, on returning from the meeting Thanksgiving day, met Mr. Tillinghast in the sitting-room of the hotel, and in the course of conversation Mr. B. said to Mr. T. that he had deposited a ten cent piece in the contribution box to be placed on interest until he reached heaven. Mr. T. instantly replied, "Ah, yes, that will amount to a very large sum before you will be admitted there."

Painting the Meeting-House[4]

In one of the towns of New England, since the commencement of the reform in temperance, at a meeting held for the transaction of business, a proposition was introduced and carried for painting the meeting-house. Of course it was necessary to decide what color it should be painted. One gentleman proposed white; another, green; another, yellow; another, red; and reasons were offered for each. At last says one: "Mr. Moderator, I move that it be painted *rum* color, and I will give a reason. There is Captain ——, who sits near you, has had his *face* painted *rum* color these fifteen years; and it grows *brighter and brighter every year.*"

THE YANKEE JOE MILLER

Yankee Inventions

C.—"Well, Mr. Blitz, do you know there's a place called Nantucket where they make machines to manufacture nutmegs?"

B.—"What kind of machines?"

C.—"Why, you put a tree into the machine, then turn a crank, and the trunk comes out bacon, hams, and tongues; the large branches, wooden

[3] *Ibid.*, p. 121.

[4] From *The Christian Almanac, for New-England*, for the Year of Our Lord and Saviour, Jesus Christ, 1831, Vol. II, No. 3, p. 24. Boston: Published by Lincoln & Edmands, for the American Tract Society.

clocks and nutmegs; the balance is worked into cowcumber seeds, Brandreth's pills, ladies bustles, &c."

B.—"That's a great machine."

C.—"It's not half as great as the shad machine."

B.—"What's that?"

C.—"They've made a machine for eating shad."

B.—"How's that?"

C.—"Why they put the machine in the mouth, and the shad in the hopper, turn the crank, the meat goes down and the bones fly out. I like to got killed with one of 'em."

B.—"How so?"

C.—"Why, I'm left-handed, and I put it in my mouth and turned the crank the wrong way, and the bones went down my throat and the meat flew out. They took me for a Bonypart."

B.—"A Bonypart!"

C.—"Why, I was nothing but bones for a month."

B.—"I always knew the Yankees were very ingenious."

C.—"Well, did you ever see a catapiana."

B.—"No, what's that?"

C.—"Why, they take a board about six feet long, have it full of holes, then they get a lot of black and white cats, put their tails through the holes, the black tails are the flats and the sharps, and the white tails the naturals. You play on it with the feet."

B.—"With the feet!"

C.—"Yes, tread on the tails, and such music it makes you never heard in all your life, I tell you."[1]

A shoemaker in Connecticut bought some shoe pegs made of rotten wood. Not being able to use them, he took his knife and sharpened the other end of them, and sold them for oats.[2]

It is reported that a Yankee down East has invented a machine for corking up daylight, which will eventually supersede gas. He covers the interior of a flour barrel with shoemaker's wax, holds it open to the sun, then suddenly heads up the barrel. The light sticks to the wax, and at night can be cut into lots to suit purchasers.

An inventive Yankee has produced an apparatus which, he says, is a cure for snoring. He fastens upon the nose a gutta-percha tube leading to

[1] From *Comic Metamorphoses,* Being a Perfect Encyclopedia of Fun and Humor . . . , by Dr. W. Valentine, pp. 126–127. Entered according to an Act of Congress, in the year 1855, by Garrett & Company, in the Clerk's Office of the District Court for the Southern District of New York. New York: Dick and Fitzgerald.

[2] From *Fisher's Comic Almanac for 1845.* Boston: Published by James Fisher.

the tympanum of the ear. Whenever the snorer snores, he himself receives the first impression, finds how disagreeable it is, and, of course, reforms.[3]

A New Use for Niagara

A TAILOR from Nantucket exclaimed, on first beholding the Falls of Niagara, "What an almighty fine place to sponge a coat in!"

A Sharp Grocer

A SHARP grocer, when a customer who was buying a gallon of molasses observed that a good deal remained in the measure after it was turned, remarked: "There was some in the measure before I drew your gallon."

The Order of Their Going

A YANKEE pedlar with his cart, overtaking another of his class on the road, was thus addressed: "Hallo, what do you carry?" "Drugs and medicines," was the reply. "Good," returned the other, "you may go ahead; I carry grave-stones."

Yankee Industry

THE editor of the *Eglantine* says that the girls in Connecticut, who are remarkable for their industry, drink about a pint of yeast before going to bed at night, to make them *rise* early in the morning.

---

[3] From *The American Joe Miller:* A Collection of Yankee Wit and Humour, Compiled by Robert Kempt, pp. 16, 35. Entered at Stationer's Hall. London: Adams and Francis. 1865.

Ibid., p. 173.

From *The New-England Farmers' Almanac,* for the Year of the Christian Era, 1867, No. 51, by Truman W. Abell, p. 47. Entered according to Act of Congress, in the year 1863, by Abraham G. Jones, in the Clerk's Office of the District Court of the District of New Hampshire. Claremont, New Hampshire: The Claremont Manufacturing Co.

From *The American Joe Miller:* A Collection of Yankee Wit and Humour, Compiled by Robert Kempt, p. 175. Entered at Stationer's Hall. London: Adams and Francis. 1865.

Ibid., p. 1.

Whittling without a Purpose

A YOUNG Yankee had formed an attachment for the daughter of a rich old farmer, and after agreeing with the "bonnie lassie" went to the old farmer to ask his consent; and during the ceremony, which was an awkward one with Jonathan, he whittled away at a stick. The old man watched the movements of the knife, at the same time continuing to talk on the prospects of his future son-in-law, as he supposed, until the stick was dwindled down to naught. He then spoke as follows:—"You have fine property, you have steady habits; good enough looking; but you can't have my daughter. Had you made something, no matter what, of the stick you whittled away, you could have had her; as it is you cannot. Your property will go as the stick did, little by little, until all is gone, and your family reduced to want. I have read your character; you have my answer."

City Habits

A GENTLEMAN from Boston, on a visit to his friend in the country, speaking of the times, observed that his wife had lately expended $50 for a habit. His friend replied, "Here, in the country, we don't allow our wives to *get into such habits*."

The Ungallant Suitor

A CONNECTICUT Jonathan, in taking a walk with his *dearest,* came to a toll bridge, when he, as honestly as he was wont to be, said, after paying his toll (which was one cent), "Come, Suke, you must pay your own toll, for just as like 's not I shan't have you after all."

Ibid., pp. 18–19.

From *The Maine Farmers' Almanac,* for the Year of Our Lord 1860, No. 42, by Daniel Robinson. Entered, according to Act of Congress, in the year 1859, by Masters, Smith & Co., in the Clerk's Office of the District Court of Maine. Hallowell.

From *The National Comic Almanac for the Year 1836,* Calculated for Each State in the Union, With Humorous Stories and Anecdotes, [n.p.]. Entered according to Act of Congress, in the year 1835, in the Clerk's Office of the District Court of Massachusetts. Published by the President of the American Eating Club.

Saving of Fuel

Not long since, stoves were offered for sale in Boston, which the seller remarked "would save *half* the fuel." Mr. W., being present, observed, "Sir, I will buy *two* of them, and then I shall save the *whole*!"

A Couple of Reasons Too Many

. . . (A) maple-sugar man in Vermont . . . was sued for returning a borrowed sap-kettle in a damaged condition, and pleaded in defence—first, that the kettle was sound when he returned it; secondly, that it was cracked when he borrowed it; and thirdly, that he never had the sap-kettle. . . .

Yankee Curiosity

"You're from down East, I guess?" said a sharp, nasal voice behind me. This was a supposition first made in the Portland cars, when I was at a loss to know what distinguishing and palpable peculiarity marked me as a "down-easter." Better informed now, I replied, "I am."—"Going West?" "Yes"—"Travelling alone?" "No."—"Was you raised down East?" "No, in the Old Country."—"In the little old island? Well, you're kinder glad to leave it, I guess? Are you a widow?" "No."—"Are you travelling on business?" "No."—"What business do you follow?" "None."—"Well, now, what are you travelling for?" "Health and pleasure."—"Well, now, I guess you're pretty considerable rich. Coming to settle out West, I suppose?" "No, I'm going back at the end of the fall."—"Well, now, if that's not a pretty tough hickory-nut! I guess you Britishers are the queerest critters as ever was raised!" [1]

As a sailor, who had lost an arm, was traveling in the country, he stopped at a house for refreshment. The curiosity of the landlord was excited to know in what manner it was lost. "I'll tell you," said Jack, "if you won't

---

From *The Laughing Philosopher:* or Fun, Humour, and Wit; Being a Collection of Choice Anecdotes, Many of Which, Never Before in Print, originated in or about "The Literary Emporium," p. 6. Pittsburgh, Pennsylvania: Published by Cook and Schoyer. Louisville, Kentucky: Maxwell, Cook and Company. 1834.

From *The American Joe Miller:* A Collection of Yankee Wit and Humour, Compiled by Robert Kempt, p. 3. Entered at Stationer's Hall. London: Adams and Francis. 1865.

---

[1] *Ibid.*, p. 176.

ask me any other questions about it."—The landlord agreed. "Well, then," said Jack, "it was bit off!" The Yankee would not forfeit his word, but anxiously replied—"Darnation! I wish I know'd WHAT bit it off!" [2]

Curing Yankee Inquisitiveness

One of the last stories of Yankee inquisitiveness makes the victim give his tormentor a direct cut, in telling him he wished to be asked no further questions. The inquisitor fell back a moment to take breath, and change his tactics. The half-suppressed smile on the faces of the other passengers soon aroused him to further exertions; and, summoning up more resolution, he then began again. "Stranger, perhaps you are not aware how mighty hard it is for a Yankee to control his curiosity. You'll please excuse me, but I really would like to know your name and residence, and the business you follow. I expect you ain't ashamed of either of 'em, so now won't you just obleedge me?" This appeal brought out the traveller, who, rising up to the extremest height allowed by the coach, and throwing back his shoulders, replied: "My name is General Andrew Washington. I reside in the State of Mississippi. I am a gentleman of leisure, and, I am glad to be able to say, of extensive means. I have heard much of New York, and I am on my way to see it; and, if I like it as well as I am led to expect, *I intend to—buy it.*" Then was heard a shout of stentorian laughter throughout the stage-coach, and this was the last of that conversation.

Answering One Question by Asking Another

A wager was laid on the Yankee peculiarity of answering one question by asking another. To decide the bet a Down-Easter was interrogated. "I want you," said the better, "to give me a straightforward answer to a plain question." "I kin du it, mister," said the Yankee. "Then why is it New Englanders always answer a question by asking one in return?" *"Du they?"* was Jonathan's reply.

---

[2] From *Farmer's Almanac,* for the Year of Our Lord 1852, Fifty-Second Year, [n. p.] [by David Young, Philom. Upper Aquebogue, L. I.: Published by G. O. Wells (?)].

From *The American Joe Miller:* A Collection of Yankee Wit and Humour, Compiled by Robert Kempt, p. 176. Entered at Stationer's Hall. London: Adams and Francis. 1865.

This trait . . . is, I take it, a relic of the inquisitorial character of the old colonial days, when every stranger was expected to give an account of himself, or be set down as a suspicious character.—Samuel Adams Drake, *The Pine-Tree Coast* (Boston, 1891), p. 73.

Ibid., p. 32.

Yankee Laconics

"HILLO, master," said a Yankee to a teamster, who appeared in something of a hurry. "What time is it?—Where are you going?—How deep is the creek?—And what is the price of the butter?" "Past one, almost two—home—waist deep—and elevenpence," was the reply.

Sharp Answers

"BOY, your corn which you are hoeing there, appears to be quite small." "Yes, sir, we planted little corn." "But it looks yellow." "Yes, sir, dad had to go all way down to Uncle Nat's to get yellow corn to plant." "I shouldn't think you would have more than half a crop." "No, sir, we don't expect but half a crop—we plant on shares."

Fined for Smoking

THERE was a law in Boston against smoking in the street. A down-easter strutted about the city one day, puffing at a cigar. Up walked the constable. "Guess you're smokin'," he said. "You'll pay two dollars, stranger." "I ain't smokin'," was the quick response, "try the weed yourself; it ain't alight." The constable took a pull at the cigar, and out came a long puff of white smoke. "Guess you'll pay *me* two dollars," said the down-easter, quietly. "Wal," replied the constable, "I cal'late you're considerable sharp. S'pose we liquor."

The Captain's Pudding

THE following story is told of a Yankee captain and his mate:—Whenever there was a plum-pudding made, by the captain's orders, all the plums were put into one end of it, and that end placed next to the captain, who,

Ibid., p. 184.

From *The Farmer's Almanack,* Calculated on a New and Improved Plan, for the Year of Our Lord 1843, by Robert B. Thomas, pp. 39–40. Entered according to Act of Congress, in the year 1842, by Charles J. Hendee, in the Clerk's Office of the District Court of Massachusetts. Boston: Jenks & Palmer.

From *The American Joe Miller:* A Collection of Yankee Wit and Humour, Compiled by Robert Kempt, p. 185. Entered at Stationer's Hall. London: Adams and Francis. 1865.

Ibid., p. 123.

after helping himself, passed it to the mate, who never found any plums in his part of it. After this game had been played for some time, the mate prevailed on the steward to place the end which had no plums in it next to the captain. The captain no sooner perceived that the pudding had the wrong end turned towards him, than picking up the dish, and turning it round, as if to examine the china, he said: "This dish cost me two shillings in Liverpool"; and put it down, as if without design, with the plum end next to himself. "Is it possible?" said the mate, taking up the dish. "I shouldn't suppose it was worth more than a shilling." And, as if in perfect innocence, he put down the dish with the plums next to himself. The captain looked at the mate; the mate looked at the captain. The captain laughed; the mate laughed. "I tell you what, young one," said the captain, "you've found me out, so we will just cut the pudding lengthwise this time, and have the plums fairly distributed hereafter."

A Long Reason

THE reason why the Vermont and New Hampshire boys are so tall is because they are in the habit of drawing themselves up so as to peep over the mountains to see the sun rise. It is dreadful stretching work.

Old Age

THE people live uncommon long at Vermont. There are two men there so old that they have forgotten who they are, and there is nobody alive who can remember it for them.

Reckoning His Age

. . . A YOUNG man "down East" was asked his age; to which he answered —"Wal, I don't know exactly, but I have had the seven year itch three times."

From *Turner's Comic Almanack for 1838,* [n.p.]. Entered according to the Act of Congress in the year 1837, by Turner & Fisher, in the Clerk's Office of the District Court of the Eastern District of Pennsylvania. Boston: James Hoane. New York and Philadelphia: Turner & Fisher.

From *The American Joe Miller:* A Collection of Yankee Wit and Humour, Compiled by Robert Kempt, p. 188. Entered at Stationer's Hall. London: Adams and Francis. 1865.

Ibid., p. 141.

Out of Wives

A VIGOROUS old fellow in Maine who had lately buried his fourth wife was accosted by an acquaintance who, unaware of his bereavement, asked, "How is your wife, Cap'n Plowjogger?" to which the captain replied, with a perfectly grave face, "Waal, to tell ye the trewth, I'm kinder out of wives just naow."

Diploma Digging

ONE of the old herb doctors who flourished years ago in Maine would never admit his lack of any remedy. An acquaintance once said to him: "See here, doc, have you any diploma?"

"Wal, no, I ain't got none on hand, but I'm going to dig some just as soon as the ground thaws out in the spring."

Damaging the Engine

A MAN was sitting on the track of the New London road, when the train came along and pitched him head over heels into the bushes. The train stopped and backed to pick up the body, when the man coolly informed the conductor, as he brushed the dirt from his coat sleeves, that if he "had damaged the engine any he was ready to settle for it," and walked off home.

Addressing Cattle

A NEW ENGLAND man was given to addressing his cattle in rather emphatic terms. One day when the cows were more than usually frolicsome he was

---

From *Tit-Bits of American Humor,* Collected from Various Sources, p. 21. New York and London: White & Allen.

From *The (Old) Farmer's Almanack,* Calculated on a New and Improved Plan for the Year of Our Lord 1927, No. 135, by Robert B. Thomas, p. 44. Copyright, 1926, by The Old Farmer's Almanac, Incorporated. Boston, Massachusetts.

From *The American Joe Miller:* A Collection of Yankee Wit and Humour, Compiled by Robert Kempt, p. 128. Entered at Stationer's Hall. London: Adams and Francis. 1865.

From *The Concord Patriot* in *The Old Farmer's Almanack,* Calculated on a New and Improved Plan for the Year of Our Lord 1903, No. 111, by Robert B. Thomas, p. 52. Entered, according to Act of Congress, in the year 1902, by Horace E. Ware, in the Office of the Librarian of Congress, at Washington. Boston: William Ware & Co.

heard to exclaim: "Yes, scatter, will ye! Blast ye! If there warn't but one of ye, ye'd scatter!"

The Yankee's First Alligator

A DOWN east Yankee, seeing an alligator for the first time on the Mississippi, with his mouth open, exclaimed: "Wal, he ain't what yeou may call a *hansum* critter, but he's got a deal of openness when he smiles."

The Deacon's Blunder

A DEACON, not remarkable for his good eye-sight, once in giving out a psalm for the congregation to sing, when he came to the lines—

"The eastern sages shall come in,
With messages of grace"—

put the audience in a roar of laughter, by calling out in a loud voice—

"The eastern stages shall come in
With sausages and grease."

Lining Out the Hymn

IT WAS the custom of our pious ancestors to use Sternhold and Hopkins's translation of the Psalms in their churches. The minister appointed the portion to be sung, read it through, and then repeated the first line, which was sung; one of the deacons next read the remainder, line by line, giving time for the choir to sing a line between each reading. One of these Psalms begins thus:

"The Lord will come; and he will not
"Keep silence; but speak out."

A sailor happened to step into a church, just in time to hear the minister read the former of these lines, which sounded, as if punctuated thus:

"The Lord will come, and he will not."

From *The New-England Farmers' Almanac,* for the Year of the Christian Era, 1866, No. 50, by Truman W. Abell, p. 48. Entered according to the Act of Congress, in the year 1863, by Abraham G. Jones, in the Clerk's Office of the District Court of the District of New Hampshire. Claremont, New Hampshire: The Claremont Manufacturing Company.

From *The New-England Farmers' Almanac,* for the Year of the Christian Era, 1852, No. XXXVIII, by Truman Abell. Claremont, New Hampshire: Published and Sold by the Claremont Manufacturing Company.

From *The Maine Farmers' Almanac,* for the Year of Our Lord 1826, No. 8, by Daniel Robinson. Hallowell, Maine: Printed, Published and Sold by Glazier & Co.

This being sung, the deacon rose, and read the latter thus:

"Keep silence, but speak out."

"Shiver my timbers," says Jack, "if these people are not crazy!" and immediately *putting about, sheered off.*

The Minister's Grace

THE minister had dropped in just as preparations for supper were nearly finished, and the good wife felt obliged to delay the meal while she prepared something adequate for the occasion. When the meal was served, this was the minister's grace:

"The Lord be praised!
 How I'm amazed
To see how things have mended.
 Short-cake and tea
 For supper I see
Where milk and mush were intended."

Pills to Recover Strayed Cattle

A FOOLISH, idle fellow, hearing that a quack had gained great credit and wealth by the sale of small pills, undertook to make pills himself and to sell them. He gave the same pills to all patients whatever; and by chance they sometimes succeeded, and his name became famous.— A country fellow called on him, and desired to know if his pills would enable him to find his cow he had lately lost. The quack bid him swallow six pills. In his way home, the operation of the pills obliged him to retire into a wood, where he found his cow. The fellow spread a report, that he knew a doctor who sold pills which would recover strayed cattle.

Rain, Hail, and Snow

IT IS said that while the celebrated Veteran of the Type, Isaiah Thomas, of Massachusetts, was printing his Almanac, for the year 1780, one of the

---

From *The (Old) Farmer's Almanack,* Calculated on a New and Improved Plan for the Year of Our Lord 1946, No. 154, by Robert B. Thomas, p. 45. Copyright, 1945, by Mabel M. Swan. Dublin, New Hampshire: Yankee, Inc.

From *The Farmer's Almanac,* Calculated on a New and Improved Plan, for the Year of Our Lord, 1812, No. XX, by Robert B. Thomas. Boston: Printed for John West & Co., Proprietors of the Copyright.

From *National Intelligence,* in *The Rhode-Island Almanack,* for the Year of Our Lord Christ, 1824, by Isaac Bickerstaff, Esq. *Philom.,* July. Providence, Rhode Island: Printed and Sold by Brown & Danforth.

boys asked him what he should put opposite the 13th of July. Mr. T., being engaged, replied, "any thing, any thing"; the boy returned to the office, and set "rain, hail and snow." The country was all amazement—the day arrived, when it actually rained, hailed and snowed violently. From that time Thomas' Almanacs were in great demand.

Road Directions

A FRIEND who has travelled relates the following as a literal direction given to him by an inhabitant of a remote town in New England, in reply to his inquiry for the direct road to —— meeting house. "Well, ah, stranger, you go right strait ahead, till you come to a large oak tree, then you take that are tree on your right shoulder, and go on until you come to the brick school-house—then take the brick school house on your left shoulder, and keep strait on till you come to squire Wingate's, and then do you take the squire's house right on your back, and you can't miss your way."

Ready for Either Side

A COUNTRYMAN walked into the office of a lawyer the other day, and began his application.

"Sir, I have come to get your advice in a case that is giving me some trouble."

"Well, what's the matter?"

"Suppose, now," said the client, "that a man had one spring of water on his land, and his neighbor living below should build a dam across the creek running through both farms, and it was to back the water up into the other man's spring, what ought to be done?"

"Sue him, sir—sue him, by all means," said the lawyer, who always became excited in proporition to the aggravation of his clients. "You can recover heavy damages sir, and the law will make him pay well for it. Just give me the case, and I'll bring the money from him."

"But stop," cried the terrified applicant for legal advice, "it's I that have built the dam, and it's neighbor Jones that owns the spring, and he threatens to sue me."

From *The New-England Farmer's Almanac,* for the Year of the Christian Era, 1834, No. XX, by Truman Abell. Windsor: Published and Sold by Ide & Goddard.

From *The (Old) Farmer's Almanack,* Calculated on a New and Improved Plan, for the Year of Our Lord 1872, by Robert B. Thomas, p. 41. Entered, according to Act of Congress, in the year 1871, by Brewer & Tileston, in the Office of the Librarian of Congress, at Washington. Boston.

The keen lawyer hesitated a moment before he tacked his ship and kept on.

"Ah! well, sir, you say that you built a dam across that creek. What sort of a dam was it, sir?"

"It was a mill-dam."

"A mill-dam for grinding grain, is it?"

"Yes, it was just that."

"And it is a good neighboring mill, is it?"

"So it is, sir, and you may well say so."

"And all your neighbors bring their grain to be ground, do they?"

"Yes, sir; all but Jones."

"Then it is a great public convenience, is it not?"

"To be sure it is. I would not have built it but for that. It is far superior to any other mill, sir."

"And now," said the old lawyer, "you tell me that man Jones is complaining just because the water from the dam happens to put back into his little spring; and he is now threatening to sue you! Well, all I have to say is, let him sue, and he'll rue the day, as sure as my name is B——."

Wind and Water

A WINDY orator in the legislature, after a lengthy effort, stopped for a drink of water. "I rise," said Bloss, "to a point of order." Everybody stared, wondering what the point of order was. "What is it?" asked the speaker. "I think, sir," said Bloss, "it is out of order for a windmill to go by water!"[1]

There was an interesting hearing in a law suit between two neighbors some years ago in Bristol, N. H. One of the lawyers on the case was making an eloquent plea for his client and paused often to take a drink of water from a glass and pitcher on the table. After listening for some time the other lawyer on the case drily remarked, "Well, I declare, this is the first time that I ever saw a windmill run by water power."[2]

---

[1] From *The (Old) Farmer's Almanack,* Calculated on a New and Improved Plan, for the Year of Our Lord 1877, No. 85, by Robert B. Thomas, p. 40. Entered, according to Act of Congress, in the year 1876, by William Ware, in the Office of the Librarian of Congress, at Washington. Boston.

[2] By Frances Emmons. From *The (Old) Farmer's Almanack,* Calculated on a New and Improved Plan for the Year of Our Lord 1941, No. 149, by Robert B. Thomas, p. 61. Copyright, 1940, by Mabel M. Swan. Dublin, New Hampshire: Published by Yankee, Inc.

Asking a Man if He's a Liar

JOEL STEVENS and Deacon Epharium Tenney were the backbone of their little New England town. But they didn't always get along. The Deacon was hot-tempered, known to be a sharp trader, and inclined to stretch the truth. Joel wasn't one to get "haired-up" over anything.

At one selectmen's meeting an argument came up and Epharium made a statement grossly unfair and untrue, which Joel convincingly refuted. Epharium, instead of recognizing that anyone could be right except himself, demanded, "Joel, do you mean to call me a liar?" To which Joel replied in his slow drawl, "No, Deacon, I don't. But ain't ye?"

The Farmer and the Beggar

A STRONG, hearty, lazy fellow, who preferred begging for a precarious subsistence, to working for a sure one, called at the house of a blunt Massachusetts farmer, and in the usual language of his race, asked for "cold victuals and old clothes." "You appear to be a stout, hearty looking man," said the farmer, "what do you do for a living?" "Why, not much," replied the fellow, "except travelling about from one place to another." "Travelling about, ha?" rejoined the farmer, "can you travel pretty well?" "Oh yes," returned the sturdy beggar, "I am pretty good at that." "Well then," said the farmer, coolly opening the door, "let's see you travel."

He Might as Well Have Et

A CLERGYMAN was having dinner with a parishioner preceding an afternoon service. He ate very sparingly, explaining that it was not well to eat too hearty a meal before preaching.

The housewife was unable to attend the service, so when her husband returned she inquired, "And how was he?"

"Oh, well," he replied, wearily, "he might as well have et."

From *The (Old) Farmer's Almanack,* Calculated on a New and Improved Plan for the Year of Our Lord 1946, No. 154, by Robert B. Thomas, p. 45. Copyright, 1945, by Mabel M. Swan. Dublin, New Hampshire: Yankee, Inc.

From *The Christian Almanac, for New-England,* for the Year of Our Lord and Saviour, Jesus Christ, 1831, Vol. II, No. 3, p. 27. Boston: Published by Lincoln & Edmands, for the American Tract Society.

From *The (Old) Farmer's Almanack,* Calculated on a New and Improved Plan for the Year of Our Lord 1927, No. 135, by Robert B. Thomas, p. 43. Copyright, 1926, by The Old Farmer's Almanac, Incorporated. Boston, Massachusetts.

The Pilgrim Mothers

. . . The woman who had been listening to an hour's praise of the Pilgrim Fathers . . . finally interrupted to say, "What about the Pilgrim Mothers?"

"Well, what about them?" the speaker inquired.

"What about them? Why, they endured all the Pilgrim Fathers endured, and they endured the Pilgrim Fathers besides."

What the American Commander Said to His Men Before the Battle of Bunker Hill

. . . They claim he told them there was only enough powder to repulse the British three times, so if the British reformed their lines and started up the hill the fourth time they would have to retreat to Cambridge, and added, "Of course you will have to run fast to save your lives, and since I am kind of old and lame I will run along now."

ODD STICKS

The Village Do-Nothing

Every New England village, if you only think of it, must have its do-nothing as regularly as it has its school-house or meeting-house. Nature is always wide-awake in the matter of compensation. Work, thrift, and industry are such an incessant steam-power in Yankee life, that society would burn itself out with intense friction were there not interposed here and there the lubricating power of a decided do-nothing,—a man who won't be hurried, and won't work, and will take his ease in his own way, in spite of the whole protest of his neighborhood to the contrary. And there is on the face of the whole earth no do-nothing whose softness, idleness, general inaptitude to labor, and everlasting, universal shiftlessness can compare with that of this worthy, as found in a brisk Yankee village.

From *Forty Years a Country Preacher*, by George B. Gilbert, p. 93. Copyright, 1939, by Harper & Brothers. New York and London.

From *The Story of a Father and Son* or "Unscrewing the Inscrutable," pp. 24–25. Cambridge, Massachusetts: Elliott Addressing Machine Company.

From *Oldtown Folks and Sam Lawson's Oldtown Fireside Stories*, by Harriet Beecher Stowe, Vol. I, pp. 32–33, 38–39. Copyright, 1869, by Harriet Beecher Stowe; 1871, by James R. Osgood & Co.; 1896, by Houghton Mifflin & Co. Boston and New York.

Sam Lawson filled this post with ample honor in Oldtown. He was a fellow dear to the souls of all "us boys" in the village, because, from the special nature of his position, he never had anything more pressing to do than croon and gossip with us. He was ready to spend hours in tinkering a boy's jack-knife, or mending his skate, or start at the smallest notice to watch at a woodchuck's hole, or give incessant service in tending a dog's sprained paw. He was always on hand to go fishing with us on Saturday afternoons; and I have known him to sit hour after hour on the bank, surrounded by a troop of boys, baiting our hooks and taking off our fish. He was a soft-hearted old body, and the wrigglings and contortions of our prey used to disturb his repose so that it was a regular part of his work to kill the fish by breaking their necks when he took them from the hook.

"Why, lordy massy, boys," he would say, "I can't bear to see no kind o' critter in torment. These 'ere pouts ain't to blame for bein' fish, and ye ought to put 'em out of their misery. Fish hes their rights as well as any on us."

* * * * *

Sam was of respectable family, and not destitute of education. He was an expert in at least five or six different kinds of handicraft, in all of which he had been pronounced by the knowing ones to be a capable workman, "if only he would stick to it." He had a blacksmith's shop, where, when the fit was on him, he would shoe a horse better than any man in the county. No one could supply a missing screw, or apply a timely brace, with more adroitness. He could mend cracked china so as to be almost as good as new; he could use carpenter's tools as well as a born carpenter, and would doctor a rheumatic door or a shaky window better than half the professional artisans in wood. No man could put a refractory clock to rights with more ingenuity than Sam,—that is, if you would give him his time to be about it.

* * * * *

Now Sam knew everything about everybody. He could tell Mrs. Major Broad just what Lady Lothrop gave for her best parlor carpet, that was brought over from England, and just on what occasions she used the big silver tankard, and on what they were content with the little one, and how many pairs of long silk stockings the minister had, and how many rows of stitching there were on the shoulders of his Sunday shirts. He knew just all that was in Deacon Badger's best room, and how many silver tablespoons and teaspoons graced the beaufet in the corner; and when each of his daughters was born, and just how Miss Susy came to marry as she did, and who wanted to marry her and couldn't. He knew just the cost of Major Broad's scarlet cloak and shoe-buckles, and how Mrs. Major had a real *Ingy* shawl up in her "camphire" trunk, that cost nigh as much as Lady Lothrop's. Nobody had made love, or married, or had children born, or been buried, since Sam was able to perambulate the country, without his informing himself minutely of every available particular; and his unfathomable knowledge on these subjects was an unfailing source of popularity.

Besides this, Sam was endowed with no end of idle accomplishments. His indolence was precisely of a turn that enjoyed the excitement of an occasional odd bit of work with which he had clearly no concern, and which had no sort of tendency toward his own support or that of his family. Something so far out of the line of practical utility as to be in a manner an artistic labor would awaken all the energies of his soul. His shop was a perfect infirmary for decayed articles of *vertu* from all the houses for miles around. Cracked china, lame teapots, broken shoe-buckles, rickety tongs, and decrepit fire-irons, all stood in melancholy proximity, awaiting Sam's happy hours of inspiration; and he was always happy to sit down and have a long, strictly confidential conversation concerning any of these with the owner, especially if Hepsy were gone out washing, or on any other work which kept her at a safe distance.

Sam could shave and cut hair as neatly as any barber, and was always in demand up and down the country to render these offices to the sick. He was ready to go for miles to watch with invalids, and a very acceptable watcher he made, beguiling the night hours with endless stories and legends. He was also an expert in psalmody, having in his youth been the pride of the village singing-school. In those days he could perform reputably on the bass-viol in the choir of a Sunday with a dolefulness and solemnity of demeanor in the highest degree edifying,—though he was equally ready of a week-evening in scraping on a brisk little fiddle, if any of the thoughtless ones wanted a performer at a husking or a quilting frolic. Sam's obligingness was many-sided, and he was equally prepared at any moment to raise a funeral psalm or whistle the time of a double-shuffle.

But the more particular delight of Sam's heart was in funerals. He would walk miles on hearing the news of a dangerous illness, and sit roosting on the fence of the premises, delighted to gossip over the particulars, but ready to come down at any moment to do any of the odd turns which sickness in a family makes necessary; and when the last earthly scene was over, Sam was more than ready to render those final offices from which the more nervous and fastidious shrink, but in which he took almost a professional pride.

Sacred and Profane

Ezra Barber lived at East Epping near the Camp Ground. He was a Methodist—devout on Sundays and a bit profane on weekdays.

At prayer time in church when the worshipers fell upon their knees with back to the pulpit, and elbows upon the seats in front of them, Ezra's habit

---

From *More New Hampshire Folk Tales,* collected by Mrs. Moody P. Gore and Mrs. Guy E. Speare, pp. 240–241. Copyright, 1936, by Mrs. Guy E. Speare. Plymouth, New Hampshire: Compiled and published by Mrs. Guy E. Speare.

was to open his old hunting case watch and with a pin, toy with the works, more or less frequently calling out "Bless the Lord," "Amen," as the brothers and sisters one after another addressed the throne of heavenly grace.

[As I was] Sitting directly behind him one evening, he necessarily faced me upon his knees in prayer, with his watch in one hand and a pin in the other, manipulating the works and encouraging the supplicant of the moment with "Bless the Lord," and "Amen."

On this occasion I was astonished to hear the following as a single sentence—"Bless the Lord—My Gosh—God be praised—The damn mainspring is broke—Amen."

No Store for Him

NEXT north of the "brick store," was a wooden store, formerly owned by the late Bohan King, the father of Henry, William and Seth King. He was a hatter, and died many years ago. The store was once occupied by Richard Falley, who was an inveterate fisherman. He would leave the key in the door, and with his fishing rod, would take to the streams, as if fishing was the main business of his life. One of his friends remonstrated with him, alleging that his absences incommoded his friends who wished to buy goods. "Why," said Falley, "I always leave the key in the door!" "Yes, but they may omit to leave the money, or to charge for the goods taken, and so you will fail." "Well," said he, "that may be so; but if a store can't support itself, it's no store for me!"

The Lazy Shopkeeper

A STORY is told of a lazy Nantucket shopkeeper who was not inclined to give up his personal comfort or ease. Whenever he saw a customer enter the front door he would call out from his chair: "Well, what is it? What is it? Because perhaps I haven't got it." On one occasion a customer wished to buy a pail and inquired the prices of the different sizes hanging

---

From *The Westfield Jubilee:* A Report of the Celebration at Westfield, Mass., on the Two Hundredth Anniversary of the Incorporation of the Town, October 6, 1869, with the Historical Address of the Hon. William G. Bates, and Other Speeches and Poems of the Occasion, with an Appendix, Containing Historical Documents of Local Interest, p. 188. Westfield, Mass.: Clark & Story. 1870.

From *The Nantucket Scrap Basket,* Being a Collection of Characteristic Stories and Sayings of the People of the Town and Island of Nantucket, Massachusetts, Compiled, Edited and Arranged by William F. Macy and Roland B. Hussey, and published for the benefit of "The Sons and Daughters of Nantucket," pp. 60–61. Copyright, 1916, by William F. Macy and Roland B. Hussey. Nantucket: The Inquirer and Mirror Press.

in a line from the ceiling. The shopkeeper, without getting out of his chair, designated each pail with his foot, saying: "That is 50 cents; that is 62½ cents." "Well," said the customer, "I will take that one," pointing to the pail he wished to buy. The shopkeeper did not stir, and a wave of distress seemed to be passing over him. Presently, with an air of great perplexity, he said: "No, I won't sell it, for I shall only have to buy another."

Grindstone Out of Cheese

. . . A SHARP shrewd Yankee by the name of Raymond kept a general store in Ashuelot village. He was quite illiterate and his methods of bookkeeping were original. One day a customer purchased a grindstone and not being able to pay down for it, 'twas charged on a piece of paper. The account ran along quite awhile, when one day the delinquent came in and was promptly reminded of his indebtedness, but was dunned for a cheese. "I never bought a cheese of you." "Yes you did," and Mr. Raymond produced the slip of paper it was charged on, showing a circle of hieroglyphics indicating the man's identity. "I never bought a cheese, but I did buy a grindstone I have not paid for." Raymond thought a minute and then admitted that it was a grindstone and he neglected to put a hole in [the] center of the circle for the crank to distinguish it from a cheese, so it was settled.

Foony Gerrish

. . . FOONY GERRISH, a wig maker, often became the jest of the populace. Though illiterate, he evinced a desire to rank amongst the educated. On one occasion a person in the bar room of the "Wolfe Tavern" perceiving him seemingly intent upon perusing a newspaper which was held bottom upward, inquired, "What is the news, Mr. Gerrish?" "Terrible gales," hurriedly returned the old man, "terrible gales, ships all bottom upwards." Wishing to be thought a man of business Foony bought a ledger. That morning he sold a wig, for which, much to the purchaser's astonishment, he declined to take payment, "he would charge it." At night he detained one of the young clerks in the neighborhood to note it down. Having written the date the young man inquired the name of the debtor. Foony looked puzzled, scratched his head, he "never thought to inquire the name," but

---

By Mrs. Emma Gore Hale. From *More New Hampshire Folk Tales,* collected by Mrs. Moody P. Gore and Mrs. Guy E. Speare, pp. 31–32. Copyright, 1936, by Mrs. Guy E. Speare. Plymouth, New Hampshire: Compiled and published by Mrs. Guy E. Speare.

From *Reminiscences of a Nonagenarian,* Edited and Illustrated by Sarah Anna Emery, pp. 250–251. Newburyport: William H. Huse & Co., Printers. 1879.

after a moment's deliberation he added, "Never mind, put it down, one wig to a man that looked like an Amesbury man." Whether Foony received the price of the wig from this dubiously described individual I am unable to state.

A Good Job of Measuring

When a foreman in a Keene shop was requested to do a certain piece of work a few years ago, he wanted to find out first what materials he had to work with. He therefore gave a good Irishman a two-foot rule and sent him out to the stock room to measure up a strip of sheet metal.

The Irishman returned after a time, and the foreman said, "Well, Pat, how much iron did you find? How long was it?"

"Yes, and to be sure," said Pat, "it's twice the length of me rule, plus the width of me hand and the length of a brick, less the length of me arm."

A Fair Wage

"Charley" Morse, as he was affectionately called by those who knew him best, was . . . noted far and wide for his wit and pungent criticism and bluntness of speech. A fact well illustrated when he went to Lambert Bigelow years ago for a position in his general store, and when asked how much he expected to be paid for his services replied with characteristic frankness: "I want you to pay me enough so that I won't have to steal from you in order to get a living."

The Clever Blacksmith

. . . Nailer Tom served his seven years' apprenticeship at blacksmithing, in Newport, with a man named Dodge, I think, who did a good deal of ship work, sometimes by the job, at others by the pound. Dodge's shop was near

---

From "Keene," T. J. Winn, Jr. Manuscripts of the Federal Writers' Project of the Works Progress Administration for the State of New Hampshire.

From *Historical Reminiscences of the Early Times in Marlborough, Massachusetts, and Prominent Events from 1860 to 1910,* Including Brief Allusions to Many Individuals and an Account of the Celebration of the Two Hundred and Fiftieth Anniversary of the Incorporation of the Town, by Ella A. Bigelow, p. 212. Copyright, 1910, by City of Marlborough. Marlborough, Massachusetts: Times Publishing Company.

From *The Jonny-Cake Papers of "Shepherd Tom,"* Together with Reminiscences of Narragansett Schools of Former Days, by Thomas Robinson Hazard, With a Biographical Sketch and Notes by Rowland Gibson Hazard, p. 326. Copyright, 1915, by Rowland G. Hazard. Boston: Printed for the Subscribers.

Gravelly Point. When he was engaged in job work, the question would be sometimes asked, "Mr. Dodge, ain't you making that work rather light?" The reply would be: "Nobody can tell the strength of iron." When, on the other hand, he would be doing the ship work by the pound, the question would be asked, "Mr. Dodge, ain't you making that work very heavy?" The reply would be: "Nobody can tell the power of the wind and the waves." . . .

Too Good to Spoil

AT THAT time [1811] every vessel placed upon the stocks was wholly completed and equipped for sea before it sailed over the bar. This brought a multiplicity of business to the town. Along the wharves stretched lofty warehouses crowded with merchandise. Carts and drays rattled up and down, incoming and outgoing vessels came and went, the merry songs and "heave ho's" of the sailors, blended with the cheery tones and hearty jests of the stevedores, carts from the interior unloaded and loaded—at every turn was bustle, industry and activity. Here were the spacious sail and rigging lofts, pump and block makers' shops, and ship chandlers' stores, everything that pertained to maritime trade. Mr. Joshua Norton, Joseph Stanwood and the Messrs. Davis and Haynes had large sail lofts; Thomas Prichard a rigging loft on Ferry wharf; Enoch Toppan a block maker's shop on Carter's wharf. Maj. Joshua Greenleaf did most of the ship iron work at his large smithy on Liberty street. Mr. Gordon had a similar establishment at Bellevilleport. This gentleman was somewhat economical in his household. At that period cheese was a customary appendage of the dinner table, being considered an accessory to digestion. Mr. Gordon employed several workmen. One day a large cheese was placed on the table; after the meat had been disposed of, Mr. Gordon took a knife to cut the cheese; turning it over, he exclaimed, "This is a good cheese, a pretty cheese, too good to spoil!" and laying down the knife, he rose and called his men to their work. That afternoon a large anchor was to be forged, the fire was kindled, the iron heated.

"That is a good heat!" exultantly exclaimed the master.

"A good heat," with one voice responded the men.

"A grand heat," reiterated the master.

"A grand heat," again responded the men.

"Then why don't you strike?" impatiently demanded the master.

"It is a good heat?" queried the foreman.

"Yes, yes, strike, strike, I tell ye," hurriedly ordered the master in a quick authoritative tone. "Strike, strike."

"Don't you think it is too good a heat to spoil?" quietly returned the foreman, while not an arm was uplifted.

From *Reminiscences of a Nonagenarian,* Edited and Illustrated by Sarah Anna Emery, pp. 226–227. Newburyport: William H. Huse & Co., Printers. 1879.

The hint was taken; the cheese brought with a loaf of brown bread. The luncheon eaten and well washed down with grog, the anchor was forged with a will. . . .

Boots and Shoes

CALEB HAWES, when he took from the factory a case of boots (to be "made" at home as the custom was), if they ran in sizes from 6 to 10 he would always make up the 6's first. His explanation was this: "Wall, ef I wuz to die, the other fellow would hev to make the larger sizes."

The daily stent would be two to three pairs, but if Caleb was in a carefree mood he would decide upon "Two pairs and a fox hunt to-day, and four pairs to-morrow."

One day this manufacturer criticized one of his oldest hands, a man who had spent most of his life treeing boots and shoes. After some faultfinding the "boss" said, "Now I will show you how to tree a shoe," and he did so and passed it up with the remark, "There, that's the way I want a shoe treed." The workman waited until the boss had passed along, and placed the shoe in a conspicuous place, resuming his work. After dinner the boss walked into the room—and also into the trap. Picking up the same shoe, "Do you call that shoe treed?" "No," was the reply, "I don't, but that is the shoe *you* treed this forenoon."

Nathaniel Shaw, a sincere publicist, was a shoe manufacturer who always had the interests of his workmen at heart, and paid them as liberally as he could for their services. On one occasion, when he told one of his men who was getting 25 cents per case for his work that he would be increased to 26 cents, much to his astonishment the workman said, "No, Nat., leave it at twenty-five; it is easier to reckon."

One of the shop's crew on leaving his employ was asked by a friend why he left. The reply was, "Oh, Nat. kept hinting and so I quit." "Hinting?" commented the friend, "what do you mean—what did he say?" "Why, he said he didn't want me any more."

In the pioneer days of the boot and shoe industry many of the manufacturers kept a "general store" and paid their workmen in part with goods out of the store. Col. Ebenezer Humphrey of North Weymouth had an employee named Athanasius Stoddard, and times were so hard that when Mr. Stoddard brought in some shoes and wanted his pay the Colonel said, "I can't pay you in money, but have in the store some very nice satinet to

---

From *History of Weymouth, Massachusetts,* Vol. 2, pp. 789, 803, 806–807, 810. Published by the Weymouth Historical Society, Howard H. Joy, President, Under Direction of the Town. 1923.

makes clothes for yourself or family." "No, Colonel," was the response, "my family can't eat satinet all the time."

For Knowing How

"WHAT is the price of the work? he (Coolidge) asks, looking at the shoe carefully. . . . Well, Mr. Lucey, there is one thing about shoes you'll never learn!"

"And what is that?" I asked. And I wasn't so pleased—'cause I know how to make shoes. An' he told me a story. A long one, it was. About a plumber that charged twenty-five dollars for fixin' a drain, for which he said five dollars was for the drain and twenty dollars was for knowin' how.

"That's your trouble, Mr. Lucey," he said. "You don't charge enough. You don't charge for knowin' how." [1]

ONE time a man got stranded beside the road with his car, which was a large one. Along came a man with an old dilapidated Ford and offered to help. He fixed the car, and when the man offered to pay him, he said that he would accept $1.10. Curiosity prompted the man to ask why such an odd amount. The reply was, "Ten cents for the labor and a dollar for the knowledge." [2]

Save the Peavies

I WORKED on the drives from Connecticut Lake to Mt. Tom. But I generally stopped at Turner's Falls. I'd go up in the fall and spend the winter in the woods. We'd cut the logs and pile 'em on the bank of a little stream somewheres, if it warn't handy to get them to the river. We had to mark each one with the company mark, kind of a brand, I guess, cut in the end of each log. And they were piled in such a way that when the freshet came in the spring, we could yank out a couple of props, and the whole caboodle of logs would go rolling into the water.

We'd send a small gang on ahead—maybe a couple of boats—to break

[1] From *The Life of Calvin Coolidge,* by Horace Green, pp. 52–53. Copyright, 1924, by Duffield & Company. New York.

[2] From "Littleton," by Ola G. Veazie. Manuscripts of the Federal Writers' Project of the Works Progress Administration for the State of New Hampshire.

By Robert Wilder. Manuscripts of the Federal Writers' Project of the Works Progress Administration for the State of Massachusetts.

According to Mr. Wilder, who knew Van Dyke and who has heard the circumstances of the story many times, this version was written from memory after hearing it told by an old riverman named "Hop."

up the jams, and keep the drive going. Then the bunch of us would come with the horses. And last would come another small gang with maybe a team or two, to haul in the logs the farmers had stole offen us. And I guess maybe the gang changed the marking on a log once in a while, if they thought it would pay.

The idea was for the first bunch to ride the freshet. And not let the drive get held up. Of course, the water would take the logs over meadows, and when the river went down, we'd have to haul them out with horses. But we knew where it was liable to happen, so we'd have a man at the right place to keep them in the current. And sometimes two, or three. And sometimes we'd string a boom—hitch logs end to end. And hitch the ends to trees, maybe—so the boom would steer the logs for us. For the quicker we got the drive through, the cheaper it was for old Van Dyke. He didn't have so big a payroll. And that old devil was everywhere. Last part of it he had a car and chauffeur, so's he didn't have to drive, but could keep his mind on swearing.

Such sleep as we got, we got on the ground. And then be waked up by a kick from Van Dyke's boot, if he caught you at it. Guess he never slept at all. And to save time in cooking, the cook of the first gang would bury beans in bean pots in holes dug in the sand and filled with hot coals, so that the next bunch didn't need to waste any time.

I got sick of being wet and cold all the time, so I got a job cooking. Van Dyke told me that if I'd let rum alone I could stand on a log. And what the hell was I cold for? That work would keep me warm. But I told him I thought I could save him money on the grub. So I got the job.

We used to buy our supplies from little stores in the towns along the river that stood in with Van Dyke. And they used to give me a little book with what I'd bought written in it. I bought anything they had that I thought the boys would like. But I made the storekeeper write in beans so much, and codfish so much. But nothing else. I let the storekeeper charge up a pound or so extra for doing this.

One day Van Dyke came running. He'd seen some egg shells in the ashes of one of my campfires up river. "Show me your books!" he yelled. I showed 'em. He couldn't read much. But he knew beans and codfish when he seen it. He looked surprised. But he said. "That's the stuff, Hop, beans and codfish is good enough for peasoups.[1] Sock it to 'em!" But after that I buried my egg shells.

He said codfish helped a man to swim. And that beans was better than dynamite for blowing up a jam. What he meant was he liked them because they was cheap. And that men had to be well fed on something or they couldn't do their work.

One time, in the French King Rapids, the logs jammed. And when a couple of the gang went out to hunt the key log, the jam broke. The men ran for it, but it was no use. Both got knocked into the water. Of course,

---

[1] French Canadians.—R. W.

we ran out on the logs to help. But old Van Dyke yelled, "Never mind the men, save the peavies!" That was him. Never mind the men, he could get more. But the peavies—the hooks on a wooden handle, that we rolled logs with—was property. And property cost money.[1]

So maybe we didn't cheer that day at Turner's Falls, when Van Dyke had his chauffeur back his touring car to the edge of that cliff that overlooks the Falls, so's he could stand up in back and wave his arms and swear at us. I was standing on a boom out in the middle of the river, pushing logs that was branded for down the river so's they'd go over the Falls, and steering those we wanted inside the boom, and keeping one eye on Van Dyke, like everyone else. Guess the Falls was making too much noise to suit him, and he wanted to get nearer so's we wouldn't miss anything he was saying. He waved the chauffeur to back more. The chauffeur acted scared and only backed a couple of feet, and stopped so's Van Dyke almost lost his balance—he was standing in back. He turned around and said something to the chauffeur, then stood watching him fumbling with the handles. The man was badly rattled, I guess, with Van Dyke right there on his neck, almost. The car coughed once or twice, and then shot back over the cliff. And, my, didn't we cheer! "Never mind the man, save his matches!" yelled somebody. And we all cheered again.

We were awful sorry for the chauffeur, though. We'd forgotten all about him. And both of 'em were killed deader'n the codfish old Van Dyke used to make us eat.

Captain Baxter

Capt. William Baxter, who, for many years before the Nantucket railroad was built, and even for some time thereafter, drove the 'Sconset stage, was an inveterate joker and wag, and many are the good stories told of him by those who knew him. . . .

When Cap'n Baxter was conveying a party of visitors across the commons to 'Sconset on a dark and foggy night, he would frequently stop, jab the handle of his whip into the road and gravely taste the dust which clung to it. When inquiries were made as to the meaning of this eccentric performance, he responded: "Why bless you, I know this old island blind-

---

[1] "Never mind the man! Grab his cant dog! That cost the company money!" That was the old river-hogs' battle cry.—Louise Dickinson Rich, *We Took to the Woods*. (Philadelphia, 1942), p. 213.

From *The Nantucket Scrap Basket*, Being a Collection of Characteristic Stories and Sayings of the People of the Town and Island of Nantucket, Massachusetts, Compiled, Edited and Arranged by William F. Macy and Roland B. Hussey, and published for the benefit of "The Sons and Daughters of Nantucket," pp. 62–65. Copyright, 1916, by William F. Macy and Roland B. Hussey. Nantucket: The Inquirer and Mirror Press.

folded the darkest night that ever was. I just take a sounding, and I can tell to a foot where we are by the taste of the bottom." . . .

"How blue the water is!" murmured one fair passenger making her first trip to 'Sconset on the Swiftsure. "Why, there," said the Cap'n, "this must be the day." Somewhat puzzled, the passenger inquired, "Yes? what day?" "Why, we like to make things look nice for you strangers, so about once in so often we tip a couple of hogsheads of blueing overboard, so as to make the water a pretty color, and they must have just done it today."

Two young men, "coofs," who had heard of Captain Baxter's quips and jests, were most desirous of enjoying his fun at first hand, and for this purpose they drove out to 'Sconset. It chanced that the first one they met on entering the village was the Cap'n himself, and to him they expressed their wishes. "You have come at just the right time," said the Cap'n pleasantly. "Cap'n Baxter is to lecture this evening at the school-house, and you'll have a chance to hear him there. But I advise you to be on hand early so as to get good seats." As soon as the evening shades began to gather, the young men with happy anticipations, betook themselves to the school-house and sat down on the steps to await the opening of the door. And there they sat, and sat, and continued to sit while darkness settled around them, and the village quieted down for the night. At last, becoming fearful that something was wrong, they returned to the village, where again they told their tale to the first man they met. The man laughed. "I guess you've seen Cap'n Baxter," he said.

When Cap'n Bill lay on what was apparently his death bed, his old friend, Joseph Clapp, an equally incorrigible joker, went to see him and condole with him. The old man was pretty far gone and very weak, but that did not prevent Capt. Joe from having his little joke. On leaving, his parting words were: "Well, William, I wouldn't hurry about leaving this sinful world. Thee'd better stay here as long as thee can, for thee's not likely to go to any better place." Cap'n Bill took the hint, and his convalescence was rapid from that hour.

Old Man Abbott's State

. . . Up in Whitefield at that time old man Abbott, who painted houses and signs, was still what he had always been, a genial rubicund drinker overflowing with jokes and mirth. To him one day came old Mother Hutchins, whose son was later owner and manager of the Washington *Post*. A devout Methodist all her life, the old lady never lost a chance to turn upon those godless ones who abounded in merriment and sin. When she found the jolly old man perched on a ladder painting a house and she

---

From *The Great White Hills of New Hampshire,* by Ernest Poole, pp. 128–129. Garden City, New York: Doubleday & Company, Inc.

paused to figure out how to start, he feigned to take no notice but whistled as he painted on. The old lady's indignation rose.

"Mr. Abbott," she asked, "do you really feel you are willing to die in the state you're in now?"

"No, Granma," was his cheery reply, "when I git good and ready to die, I'm a-goin' over to Vermont." And as he gaily whistled on, she marched indignantly away, whispering, "Glory be to God!"

God Strike Me Down

. . . The lame old man on a farm up over Ossipee . . . denied the existence of God. After losing a son in the Civil War, so loud did he grow in such blasphemies that a devout deacon went one day to wrestle with him for his soul. While they wrestled, a mountain storm broke loose; and when three strokes of lightning crashed close to the infidel's house, the deacon promptly declared them to be signals of the wrath of Jehovah.

"Oh yeah?" the old agnostic cried. He threw open the door and waved his stick out into the thundering storm. "Oh, God," he shouted, "if you are up there strike me down! And you, Black Satan, swoop up from hell, if there is any hell, and plunge my soul into the flames and give this deacon here the bliss of hearing me yowl with the damned!"

He stood waiting, but no bolt from an angry heaven struck him down. Instead the storm broke and through a patch of blue in the clouds a shaft of warm benignant sunshine shone on the infidel's hoary head. And he chuckled, as without a word the disconsolate deacon left for home.

Quite a Storm

On a summer afternoon the Sewing Circle met at the home of Mrs. Bennett. A thunderstorm of terrific violence broke during the session and the terrified ladies cowered together. "Old Man" Bennett, who was noted for his fearlessness, undertook to calm them. With a great show of bravery he strode to the front door, flung it open and shook his fist at the sky shouting, "Durn ye! If ye're so danged powerful, come on and strike that ole hornbeam tree!" As if in answer to his challenge, there was a vivid flash accompanied by a deafening crack, and the tough wood of the hornbeam was split asunder. "Old Man" Bennett returned to the Circle and sat down meekly. "Waal," he said, " 'tis quite a storm, ain't it?"

Ibid., p. 128.

Manuscripts of the Federal Writers' Project of the Works Progress Administration for the State of Connecticut.

Old Jim and the Wind

. . . OLD Jim Phillips . . . used to live in the old house that stood just back of the sand-hills of the Narragansett Pier beach in Little Neck, near the mouth of Narrow river. Old Jim used to go fishing in a crazy, leaky boat, and one day he got caught outside in a terrible squall, accompanied with a sea that threatened every minute to swamp his boat. So the old fellow began to pray: "Easy, Lord, easy, Lord, poor old man and poor old boat!" Jim kept repeating the words until his boat luckily fetched into the mouth of the river and grounded in comparatively smooth water, when he jumped ashore, shouting, "Now blow, Devil, blow, Devil, stout old man and stout old boat."

Sylvester, the Hay, and the Rain

SYLVESTER was a character. One day he got his acre-and-a-half lot of hay all nicely made and raked into windrows, ready to draw together and stack, when there came up a sudden thunder-shower, such as, when I was a boy, most always came every afternoon in the week in mowing time, except Sunday, and wet the windrows through. Next day Sylvester got his hay dry again and raked into windrows ready to draw and stack, when up came another shower and soaked it again, until it was as wet as a drowned rat. On the next day, after a deal of turning and shaking with pitchforks, the hay was dried for the fourth time and windrowed, when a white cap on a black cloud was seen rapidly approaching from the north-west. Sylvester's patience now gave out, and swearing that he would get even with the thunder-cloud, he started on the run to the house and came back in like manner with a fire-brand in his hand and set fire to every windrow of hay, when all was burned to ashes before the rain began to fall. . . .

A Letter from General Stark

. . . WHEN a small boy, his father was a near neighbor of Gen. Stark. The General being absent in the war and help scarce, by permission of his

From *The Jonny-Cake Papers of "Shepherd Tom,"* Together with Reminiscences of Narragansett Schools of Former Days, by Thomas Robinson Hazard, With a Biographical Sketch and Notes by Rowland Gibson Hazard, p. 359. Copyright, 1915, by Rowland G. Hazard. Boston: Printed for the Subscribers.

Ibid., p. 165.

From "Maidstone," by Hon. Moody Rich, in *Vermont Historical Gazetteer:* A Magazine, Embracing a History of Each Town, Civil, Ecclesiastical, Biographical and Military, edited by Abby Maria Hemenway, in Three Volumes, Vol. I, p. 1033. Entered according to Act of Congress, in the year 1859, by Abby Maria Hemenway, in the Clerk's Office of the District Court of the District of Vermont. Burlington, Vermont: Published by Miss A. M. Hemenway. 1867.

father he went and worked for Mrs. Stark in the hay-field in company with herself, a son of about the same age as himself, the girls and two hired men. A few days before the battle of Bennington, while thus engaged a courier arrived in great haste and delivered to Mrs. Stark a letter from her husband, —and with the rake leaning on her shoulder she read it aloud, which was to the following effect:

"Dear Molly: in less than one week the British forces here will be ours. Send every man from the farm that will come, and let the haying go to hell." This was characteristic of the General.

Old Drew

SOME thirty or more rods east by south of where the old willow trees, before mentioned, formerly stood, the site of which is now marked by a buttonwood tree and a barway a rod or so from the tree, there is still to be seen the stone foundation and tumble-down chimney of a house on the border of a big bog, that was, more than a century ago, occupied by an old shoemaker by the name of Drew. In one of the periodical violent snow-storms of early times, this house with the exception of the top of the chimney was entirely buried in a snow-drift. Old Drew, happening to have a good supply of fuel inside the premises, made no effort to make a way out through the snow-bank. When some days after the storm, Christopher Robinson, son of Governor William Robinson, was informed of the circumstances, he sent his negroes to open a passage way through the snow to Drew's door. When they reached the door, the old man was found sitting contentedly at work by the light of a tallow candle; and he did not express much gratitude for being relieved, as he said it did not take so much fuel to warm his room while it was banked up as it did when the snow was away. Old Drew once went to Newport and hired himself out to do journeyman's work. The overseer came into the shop in the afternoon, and noticing for the first time the peculiar workmanship of his newly hired man, remarked that the shoe he was just finishing off was the worst looking thing that was ever made in his shop. "What will you bet on that," queried Drew. "Five dollars," was the reply. "Done," said Drew, and opening a drawer, drew out

From *Recollections of Olden Times:* Rowland Robinson of Narragansett and His Unfortunate Daughter, With Genealogies of the Robinson and Hazard Families of Rhode Island, by Thomas R. Hazard, "Shepherd Tom," in His Eighty-First and Eighty-Second Years, Also Genealogical Sketch of the Hazards of the Middle States, by Willis P. Hazard, of Westchester, Pa., pp. 124–125. Newport, Rhode Island: Published by John P. Sanborn. 1879.

the mate of the shoe he was just finishing, that he made in the forenoon. The man merely glanced at it and paid the five dollars without demur, telling Drew as he handed him the money that he might also keep the shoes he had made, in lieu of wages.

The Walking Street-Thermometer

ANOTHER character, of an original type, was Jack Agry, who was called the "Walking Street-Thermometer." This highly reputable gentleman had an unusual dread of the cold. He was a "great reader," and loved his seat by the chimney corner. When he ventured out in winter he wore a long colonial overcoat, big thick mittens, and a cloth cap pulled down over his ears. It is said that people used to tell the temperature by the manner in which Jack Agry carried his arms. In warm weather, he permitted them to hang down naturally at his side; but with increasing coldness, he raised them higher and higher, holding them sometimes akimbo, and sometimes folded at his back. At one time Jack Agry kept a store; and on one cold January morning he found the huge keyhole of the door filled with ice. After several ineffectual efforts to insert the ponderous key in order to unlock the door, this enterprising business man remarked, "I guess July will give her a sweat!" and went home to wait for a thaw. It was said that, from that frigid day, Jack Agry never went back to his place of business.

Measuring the Cold by Blankets

HE WAS abstemious, eating no animal food, and drinking no ardent spirits or wine. His diet consisted chiefly of milk and vegetables. His garments were cut after a fashion of his own, large, loose and lined with baize. His bed was the same summer and winter. It is said that the Chinese estimate the degrees of cold by *jackets*. Dr. Hersey adopted a similar rule. He had on his bed a dozen all-wool, fulled blankets. In the summer he turned down one or two. When the weather became cool in autumn, he turned down three or four, and during the coldest weather in winter he buried himself under the whole. With him the weather was from one to ten blankets cold.

From *Old Hallowell on the Kennebec,* by Emma Huntington Nason, pp. 302–303. Copyright, 1909, by Emma Huntington Nason. Augusta, Maine: Press of Burleigh and Flynt.

From *Genealogical Notes of Barnstable Families,* Being a Reprint of the Amos Otis Papers, Originally Published in The Barnstable Patriot, revised and completed by C. F. Swift, Largely from Notes Made by the Author, Vol. II, p. 7. Barnstable, Mass.: F. B. & F. P. Goss, Publishers and Printers. 1890

Weather Prophet

When one wished to be considered a true prophet on weather wisdom they have been heard to exclaim: "Well, I guess you can put me on record with Jonathan Tayntor's ancestor" who was considered infallible in weather wisdom, never having been known to prophesy wrong, and was often consulted by his neighbors when any business depended upon the weather. He was a man, too, who seldom said more than "Yes" and "No," though he looked more when occasion required. A neighbor came to him one day and asked if the weather would hold fair until tomorrow while he harvested his field of wheat. "Yes," was the reply. But noon came and with it a torrent of rain, and the wheat lay on the ground destroyed. As Mr. Tayntor had never been known thus to err in his judgment, the neighbor attributed it to malice, and he was duly arraigned before a jury for "maliciously deceiving, with intent to injure his neighbor," etc. History says, whether with the dignity attributed to the early New England fathers, or whether through the love of fun suggested by the charge, no one knows, but the jury pronounced him guilty, fining him 4 shillings and 6 pence, and it was thus recorded.

Ephraim Barber

In the bend of the road stands the house of, in olden times, Ephraim Barber, the old brass clock maker. No better eight-day clocks were ever manufactured, and even to-day they stand ticking all over the country. Only a short time ago one of Marlborough's citizens journeying abroad stepped into an old hostelry of England and much to his surprise and pleasure saw ticking before him an old grandfather's clock "made by Ephraim Barber, Marlborough, New England."

Ephraim was a gunsmith in the employ of the government for many years, and a most skilful workman. He was a great hunter, always carrying a rifle of his own manufacture; also a good pedestrian, making nothing of walking to and from Boston. At one time he was representative to General Court. Eccentric in conversation but most honest and upright. He kept no horse and was one day carried by a friend to a neighboring farmer to buy some rye. "Come, Mr. Barber, come out to the barn to see it measured." "No," was the reply, "rye is measured in Heaven." He once owned a

From *Historical Reminiscences of the Early Times in Marlborough, Massachusetts, and Prominent Events from 1860–1910,* Including Brief Allusions to Many Individuals and an Account of the Celebration of the Two Hundred and Fiftieth Anniversary of the Incorporation of the Town, by Ella A. Bigelow, pp. 303–304. Copyright, 1910, by City of Marlborough. Marlborough, Massachusetts: Times Publishing Company.

Ibid., pp. 145–146.

woodlot and arranged with Gilbert Howe, another honest old man, to let the latter cut his fire wood from this lot, and as partial return Mr. Howe was to pasture Mr. Barber's cow. After the various dicker accounts between these two men had run on for years, they met one day upon the street. Mr. Barber said, "How do we stand?" "I don't know," said Mr. Howe, "do you?" "No. Have you had what you want?" "Yes, have you?" "Yes." "Call it square." "Agreed."

Ungrateful Elisha

Nearly sixty years ago, when I was a child, Elisha called at my father's house. Addressing my father, he said, "I have no corn in my house; I pray that, out of your great abundance, you will give me only half a bushel." My father, knowing Elisha's character and habits, said, "I am busy today; if you will go to the crib and shell it yourself you may take *'only half a bushel.'*" Quoth Elisha, "I will go a *leetle* further, and if I do not get it ready shelled I will call on my return and shell it." He did not call on his return.

* * * * *

He asked the late Capt. Nathan Hallet to give him some codfish. Capt. Hallet had just bought a quintal for his own use, that were sunburnt in curing, and though they would break easy, and therefore unfit to send to market, were nice and good. He gave Elisha several. He knew that Capt. Hallet was using the same in his family, and he could not refuse to receive them. However, before leaving the yard he dropped them beside the fence. Capt. Hallet told the story. A little time after some one asked Elisha if it was true. "Yes," said Elisha, "it is true. Do you think I will eat broken fish of Capt. Hallet? I want the best. I have poor fish enough at home."

Ephraim Hazard's Perpetual Motion Machine

Some half-mile to the north-west of Aleck Gardiner's there lived, since my memory, Ephraim Hazard, a white-headed, venerable-looking old man, whom I personally knew, and who, Thomas B. Hazard—called Nailor Tom,

---

From *Genealogical Notes of Barnstable Families,* Being a Reprint of the Amos Otis Papers, Originally Published in The Barnstable Patriot, revised and completed by C. F. Swift, Largely from Notes Made by the Author, Vol. II, pp. 160–161. Barnstable, Mass.: F. B. & F. P. Goss, Publishers and Printers. 1890.

From *Recollections of Olden Times:* Rowland Robinson of Narragansett and His Unfortunate Daughter, With Genealogies of the Robinson and Hazard Families of Rhode Island, by Thomas R. Hazard, "Shepherd Tom," Also Genealogical Sketch of the Hazards of the Middle States, by Willis P. Hazard, of Westchester, Pa., pp. 60–61. Entered according to Act of Congress, in the year 1879, by John P. Sanborn, in the Office of the Librarian of Congress, at Washington, D. C. Newport, Rhode Island.

a man of inexhaustible anecdote—used to say, was the first discoverer of a machine that involved in its mechanical construction the only true principle of the then much mooted question of perpetual motion. In compliance with Ephraim's repeated solicitation, "Nailor Tom" called one day to see this wonderful invention. He was taken by Eph. into the garret, where stood an old woolen yarn spinning-wheel, some four feet in diameter. To one of the spokes of this there was tied a pair of kitchen tongs, whilst from the opposite there dangled a flat-iron. Taking hold of the rim, the old man gave the wheel a smart turn with his hand that sent it flying around with great speed until the flat-iron dropped to the floor. "There, cousin Tom," exclaimed the ingenious mechanic, "if that flat-iron had been a little weightier than them kitchen tongs, and them kitchen tongs had been a little weightier than that flat-iron, and that old tow string hadn't broke, that wheel would have gone round and round, just like the world, for ever and ever."

Saving a Fuss

It is told that the night [Uncle "Liphey" Paddock] died, he roused and inquired of the "watcher" [term used for night nurse in those days] what the hour was. It was then near midnight. He asked what time the tide changed, and was told. "Well," he said, "you go out and get the 'board' [there was always a board kept in certain households for "laying out" bodies] and bring it here, for I'll die about the time the tide turns, and I don't want you people running around all excited after a board, and ev'rybody hollerin', 'Is Liphey Paddock dead? Has Liphey Paddock died?' You jest git the board, now, and we'll save lots of that fussin'."

Timothy Crumb's Courtship

Tim had hired by the month to Squire Champlin, who lived on a farm a little north-west of where the Kingston depot is now situated. Tim had taken a shine to Sal, and after three or four sittings up with her, had engaged to wait on her to meeting the next Sunday. So Tim got up early in

---

From *The Nantucket Scrap Basket*, Being a Collection of Characteristic Stories and Sayings of the People of the Town and Island of Nantucket, Massachusetts, Compiled, Edited and Arranged by William F. Macy and Roland B. Hussey, and published for the benefit of "The Sons and Daughters of Nantucket," p. 95. Copyright, 1916, by William F. Macy and Roland B. Hussey. Nantucket: The Inquirer and Mirror Press.

From *The Jonny-Cake Papers of "Shepherd Tom,"* Together with Reminiscences of Narragansett Schools of Former Days, by Thomas Robinson Hazard, with a Biographical Sketch and Notes by Rowland Gibson Hazard, pp. 119–122. Copyright, 1915, by Rowland G. Hazard. Boston: Printed for the Subscribers.

the morning, and after getting through his chores and breakfast, he thought before dressing up to wait on Sal, he would go to the river and wash off. Accordingly he went down and undressed, hanging his red shirt, which was a little sweaty, in a swamp blueberry bush to dry while he was in the water. It so happened that Deacon Brown's old bull Wrinkle was lying on a little knoll near by, unnoticed by Tim. The sight of Tim's red shirt was not at all pleasing to old Wrinkle, who now got up and began to paw the ground and bellow. This did not, however, move Tim, as he had heard Wrinkle making pretenses of the kind several times before. Bime'by, however, old Wrinkle made for the red shirt, and before Tim could interfere, the enraged beast tossed it in the air and then stamped it into the ground, and when Tim started to the rescue of his under garment, the old sarpent, not apparently recognizing him with his clothes off, gave chase to the naked biped, following Tim on the run, bellowing and shaking his horns as he went, right into the river. Things began to look rather squally, and just as the old varmint seemed getting ready to make a dive with both horns set for action, Tim seized the branches of a swamp white oak that hung over the water, and swung himself on a big limb out of reach of old Wrinkle, who now placed himself just beneath where Tim sat, roaring at the top of his voice and making sundry other threatening demonstrations. Tim, however, felt safe where he was, so far as Wrinkle was concerned, although he had some misgivings whether or not Sal Brown might not, in consequence of his enforced neglect to keep his engagement, permit that other fellow, Jim Arlington, who, too, was after her, to wait on her to hear Elder Northup preach. All at once, Tim heard a buzzing over his head, and looking up, saw, to his horror, not more than two yards above his head, a hornets' nest, nigh upon as big as a bushel basket, covered all over with the worst kind of black hornets, who, he could readily see, were getting ready to attack him. Tim took in the situation at once, and saw plainly that there was but one chance for him, desperate as it was. So seizing, with both hands, the limb on which he sat, he lowered himself quickly down a-straddle of old Wrinkle's neck, seizing a horn in each hand at the same moment, the better to enable him to retain his uneasy position. Just as he lighted on the neck of old Wrinkle, about two quarts of hornets dropped on Tim's bare neck and shoulders, about half a pint of which slopped over and fell straight into old Wrinkle's left ear. This did not help matters at all, but made the bull madder than ever, who now started off on the run for the deacon's house, plunging and roaring as he went. Sally Brown had dressed herself to go to meeting, and was waiting in the great-room for Tim, when hearing old Wrinkle making such a catouse, she stepped to the front door to see what was the matter. Just as Sally with her arms akimbo had placed herself in the open door-way, Wrinkle and Tim reached a high chestnut rail fence that was within about two rods of where she stood. Sal recognized Wrinkle at first sight, but was somewhat doubtful of the identity of Tim, as she exclaimed: "For the Lord's sake, is that you, Tim, or the dev—" She meant to say devil, and would have done so had she been allowed time, but before Sal got the last syllable out, old Wrinkle made a desperate dive through the fence, making kindling splinters of the big chestnut rails, and ejecting Tim with such velocity from his neck and horns, that, after making three complete somersaults in the heavens, the nether parts of his body struck Sally Brown about midships, a big toe just grazing each side of her diaphragm as they passed, more like a forked thunder-bolt or streak of lightning, than anything with human legs, and knocked her clean through the kitchen door, where she fell flat with her face towards the ceiling. As for Tim, he gathered himself up without saying a word, and rushed out of the back door into the big swamp near by, and pursuing a circuitous route in the bushes, recovered his red shirt and other clothes, and then made a bee-line west. A week afterwards, Jim Knowles, who had been out West to reconnoitre, reported that on his return from the Genesee country, in crossing the Connecticut river below Hartford, he passed Tim paddling a white pine log with a piece of bark, in an opposite direction, which was the last ever heard of Timothy Crumb in Narragansett.

Anecdotes of Slaves

Tony and Cuff [1]

There are several anecdotes told of some of these slaves that may be amusing to such as have not heard them. They relate principally to two of the slaves once held by Mr. Brown, and particularly to Tony (sometimes called Antony Dwight), and Cuff. It is not always certain to which of these a particular anecdote relates.

* * * * *

One of the anecdotes told of Tony's strength and agility is that at the raising of a forty-foot barn belonging to Samuel Norton, Esq., he jumped from beam to beam, the whole length of the building. This has always been a mooted question; and it seems almost impossible that it could have been done. There must have been five beams and four spaces of ten feet each, and to accomplish the feat it would be necessary to stand on a beam fifteen or sixteen feet from the ground, to jump over each of the four spaces, and come to a stand on the last beam. The two greatest difficulties would be to leap from the first beam over the first space, and to come to a stand on the last beam. That Tony jumped over all these spaces, I have no doubt. Such a tradition is not likely to have been fabricated. It is stated in "Hobart's Sketches of Abington," without any query or comment. My solution is that Tony did his jumping whilst the frame of the barn laid

[1] From *History of the Town of Abington, Plymouth County, Massachusetts,* from Its First Settlement, by Benjamin Hobart, pp. 252, 253–256. Entered according to Act of Congress, in the Year 1866, by Benjamin Hobart, in the Clerk's Office of the District Court for the District of Massachusetts. Boston: T. H. Carter and Son. 1866.

upon the ground, put together preparatory to raising; and that by starting at a distance and running, he might do it—passing on from the last beam to the ground without stopping.

It is told also of Tony, when he complained of having to pick bones, and Mr. Torrey said to him, "the nearer the bone the sweeter the meat," that he tied Mr. T.'s horse, after a hard day's work, all night, to a stake near a large rock, where, of course, he got hardly anything to eat. In the morning, when inquired of why he did so, he answered his master, "The nearer the bone, the sweeter the meat,—the nearer the rock, the sweeter the grass."

His master complained of his wearing out his shoes too fast, and got him a pair shod with iron, telling him he thought they would last him longer. Tony put them on and danced all night on a flat rock, and wore them entirely out. In the morning he carried them to Mr. Torrey, and said he had had a dance last night and wore them all up—iron bottoms did not last so long as leather ones.

Mr. Torrey always required of Tony to remember the text at meeting, which he could never do correctly; but on one occasion he came home from meeting and said to Mr. Torrey, "I've got him; I remember the text." Mr. T. said, "Well, what was it?" The text was these words in Daniel, "Mene, mene, *tekel,* upharsin." The interpretation of one word—tekel—is, "Thou art weighed in the balance, and art found wanting." Tony said, "A tea-kettle was weighed, and it wasn't heavy enough."

Cuff, his other slave, was a very bad fellow,—malicious and crafty. He used to drive Mr. T.'s team, carting plank and lumber to Weymouth Landing. He was frequently taken up and fined for criminal acts. On one occasion he was sentenced to be whipped with a certain number of stripes, at the Whipping Post. After the clerk of the town had put them on, Mr. Torrey, who stood by, requested him to add three more for him, for he was an ugly fellow. The clerk refused, saying he had done his duty according to the sentence of the justice. Mr. T. took the lash and added three severe strokes more. Cuff, after being released, walked away muttering, and saying, "Massa shall lose three of his oxen for these three strokes"; and so he did. One ox was overheated by him in going to Weymouth, driven into the river and foundered, and died in consequence. He broke the leg of another, by throwing a stone at him. A third was killed in the woods, by "some accident done on purpose."

He was so obstinate and unmanageable that Mr. Torrey put an iron collar around his neck, with a hook riveted to it, hanging down in front. When the collar around his neck was riveted together, Cuff shed tears, which he was never known to do before. When inquired of, out of town, about the collar, he said it was put on by his master to prevent his having the throat ail, which was very common in Abington. The hook, he would conceal under his waistcoat.

On one occasion—not to mention any more—he was taken up for breaking the Sabbath, tried before Justice Joseph Greenleaf, . . . and fined. After he had paid the fine, he asked for a receipt of the justice. The justice asked him for what purpose he wanted a receipt? Cuff answered, "By-and-by you die, and go to the bad place, and after a time Cuff die, and go and knock at the good gate, and they say, 'What do you want, Cuff?' I say, 'I want to come in'; they say I can't, because I broke the Sabbath at such a time. I say, 'I paid for it.' They will say, 'Where is your receipt?' Now, Mr. Judge, I shall have to go away down to the bad place to get a receipt of you, that I mended him, before I can enter the good gate."

I received most of these traditionary statements about the slaves, from Mr. Bela Dyer, to whom they were communicated by his grandmother, the aged widow Dyer, who gave the account of the first settlers in South Abington. The account of Cuff's trial before Justice Greenleaf, I had from my brother, Nathaniel Hobart, who was contemporary with those times, and who died many years since, in the eightieth year of his age.

Prime, Cuffee and Peter [2]

Some of the blacks were good mechanics. The parlor of the house of the late Richard Hart, on Russell street, was handsomely finished by Caesar, a house slave. Prime Fowle was the pressman of the first paper printed in New Hampshire. Through long service in bending over the press, he was bent to an angle of about forty-five degrees. He mourned the loss of his mistress and called her an old fool for dying. At funerals, it was the custom for the negroes of the family to walk at the left hand of each white survivor, among the chief mourners. At the funeral of Mrs. Fowle, Prime should have gone on the left of his master, but he went on the right. His master whispered, "Go the other side." Prime did not move. His master touched him and whispered again, "Go the other side." This was too much. The old peppery negro sputtered out, as loud as he could, "Go tudder side ye sef, ye mean jade."

Cuffee Chase, brother of Dinah Whipple, was of a resentful spirit, and could not easily forgive an injury. His master's horse bit him one day, and Cuffee in return deprived him for several days of his food, and had almost starved the animal before the family discovered the cause of his failure. The slave of Rev. Joseph Stevens, of Kittery, had a better apology for a similar act. His master, as he saw him picking some bones for dinner which had been already well trimmed, said to him "Nearer the bone the sweeter the meat, Sambo." Not long after, he was sent to the pasture with the horse of a visiting clergyman, which he tied to a pile of rocks. To a reproof

---

[2] From *Rambles About Portsmouth,* Sketches of Persons, Localities, and Incidents of Two Centuries: Principally from Tradition and Unpublished Documents, by Charles W. Brewster, pp. 208–210. Entered according to Act of Congress, in the year 1859, by C. W. Brewster, & Son, in the Clerk's Office of the District Court of the District of New Hampshire. Portsmouth, New Hampshire.

for the act, Sambo replied, "Nearer the bone, the sweeter the meat—nearer the rock, the sweeter the grass, massa."

Jonathan Warner had several slaves, among them Peter. One day Peter's hat being the worse for wear, he asked his master for a better covering for his head. "If you will make a rhyme, Peter, you shall have a new hat," said his master. This was discouraging to Peter, for he was never guilty of such a thing in his life. He left in a very thoughtful mood, and at length resolved to get assistance in his difficulty. He goes to the office of Wyseman Claggett, and states his case, "What is your name?" asked the counsellor. "Peter Warner, massa."

"Peter Warner—threw his hat in the chimney corner," said Mr. C. playfully. "There is your rhyme, now go and get your new hat." Peter went home, repeating the rhyme all the way, and hastened to the parlor. "Massa, I've got the rhyme," said he, much elated. "Well, say it."

"Peter Warner—took his hat and threw it—in the fireplace."

Peter received his hat, his master remarking that it was nearer to a rhyme than he expected of him.

Fighting for Liberty [3]

. . . The anecdote of the slave of General Sullivan, of New Hampshire, is well known. When his master told him that they were on the point of starting for the army, to fight for liberty, he shrewdly suggested that it would be a great satisfaction to know that he was indeed going to fight for *his* liberty. Struck with the reasonableness and justice of this suggestion, General S. at once gave him his freedom.

III. STOUT FELLOWS AND HARD LIARS

The humor of hyperbole, as well as that of ironical understatement, is quite in accordance with the New England character.
—George Lyman Kittredge

In 1661 a man in Eastham was fined one pound for lying about a whale. This is supposed to be the original "Fish Story."
—Shebnah Rich

[3] From *Prose Works of John Greenleaf Whittier,* pp. 169–170, Vol. II. Entered according to Act of Congress, in the year 1866 by John Greenleaf Whittier, in the Clerk's Office of the District Court of the District of Massachusetts. Boson: Ticknor and Fields.

. . . there's a putty consid'able sight o' things in this world that's true; and then ag'in there's a sight o' things that ain't true. Now, my old gran'ther used to say, "Boys," says he, "if ye want to lead a pleasant and prosperous life, ye must contrive allers to keep jest the happy medium *between truth and falsehood." Now, that are's my doctrine.*

—SAM LAWSON, in *Oldtown Fireside Stories*,
by Harriet Beecher Stowe

1. "OVERPLUS OF EXPRESSION"

ALTHOUGH the Yankee is distinguished from his tall-talking Southern and Western compatriots by his "reluctant" eloquence, the others have no monopoly on either hyperbole or humorous exaggeration. Like most American folk metaphor, Yankee sayings have that "overplus of expression" which for James Russell Lowell constituted the tendency of humor as over against the "logical precision" of wit.[1] Following this distinction, it might be said that, far from being incompatible with the understatement of Yankee wit, humorous exaggeration flourishes among Yankee story-tellers no less than in more exuberant regions.

Yankee hyperbole takes the form not only of folk metaphor ("Cold as the north side of a Jenooary gravestone by starlight"[1]) but also of the intensifying extravagances of the jest books and almanacs:

> There is a man living down East whose *feet* are so *large* that he pulls his *pantaloons* over his *head.*
>
> There is a fellow down East so powerful in the arms that he is employed to *squeeze tar out of pine trees.*
>
> There is a man in Vermont so tall that whenever it rains, he gets his hat wet a quarter of an hour before the rain reaches any one else.[2]

This sort of "tall talk" is so much in the spirit of the tall tale that the latter may be described as an expanded hyperbole, built up into a tale by the use of circumstantial narrative calculated to make it plausible.[3]

Because of the prevalence of the "broad grin" in both our folk speech and story-telling, humorous exaggeration has been singled out (especially by British critics) as the distinguishing trait of American humor, correlated with American geography.

---

[1] Introduction to "The Biglow Papers: Second Series," in *The Poetical Works of James Russell Lowell* (Boston, 1885), p. 225.

[1] *Ibid.*, p. 224.

[2] *Turner's Comic Almanack*, for 1838, 1840, and 1843, respectively. See also "The Yankee Joe Miller" above.

[3] Since this was written, there has come to hand C. Grant Loomis's collection of "Jonathanisms: American Epigrammatic Hyperbole," in *Western Folklore*, Vol. VI, (July, 1947), No. 3. pp. 211–227. Dr. Loomis, an indefatigable collector of tall tales from printed sources, here attempts to establish the use of the word "Jonathanism" (originally a Yankeeism or Americanism) to mean an "American epigrammatic hyperbole" and adds: "A Jonathanism is an integral element of tall-tale lore and is, perhaps, the initiating force behind the longer, exaggerated anecdote."

> In considering the nature of American humor, it is obvious that broad exaggeration is its great characteristic. It is essentially *outré*. No people seek to raise the laugh by such extravagant means as the Yankees [*i.e.*, Americans]. Their ordinary speech is hyperbole, or tall talk. They never go out shooting unless with the long bow. . . . The humor of a people always reflects the character of that people, and character, as we all know, is influenced in no small measure by country and climate. Our American brethren are born, or as they themselves say "raised," in a country whose physical features have been planned on a scale far surpassing in magnitude—not unfrequently in beauty also—those of every other country in the world. . . . Into this Brobdingnag of our cousins Munchausen emigrated early, and the genius of the celebrated German Baron still continues to control its people.[1]

And for the reason, perhaps, that the West eclipses the East in the magnitude of its natural features, as well as of its boasting and boosting, it has been said that "It is no use for an Eastern man to try to tell a big story when there is a Western man about."[2]

2. "I Came to New England Seeking Wonders"

Besides humorous exaggeration, the tall tale involves artful mendacity. Because the deceived and deceiving imagination finds a fertile soil and a congenial atmosphere in a new country, especially as seen by the traveler, the "earliest remains (of the American tall tale) are embedded in a matrix of travelers' tales."[3] "I came to New England seeking wonders"[4] is the burden of most colonists and colonial travelers. Compounded of "folklore, mendacity, and humor," with varying degrees of accuracy of observation and falseness of hypotheses and varying proportions of misinformation and fantasy, travelers' tales share with tall tales the desire to improve on actual happenings.

> The perpetrators of such oral fictions were not mere liars. They were artists in ascertaining the limits of their victim's capacity for being deceived. If these limits could not be found, so much the better.[5]

Similarly keyed to the love of marvels and a belief in the impossible are the early histories of New England. The very titles of such books—Edward Johnson's *The Wonder-Working Providence of Sion's Saviour in New England* (1654), John Josselyn's *New England Rarities Discovered* (1672), Increase Mather's *Remarkable Providences Illustrative of the Earlier Days of American Colonisation* (1684)—show a readiness to confuse science with superstition and faith with credulousness, if not, as in

---

[1] Robert Kempt, *The American Joe Miller* (London, 1865), pp. vi–vii.

[2] "A Western Man Takes the Lead Again as Usual," *Phinney's Calendar, or Western Almanac* . . . 1880, (n. p.).

[3] James R. Masterson, "Travelers' Tales of Colonial Natural History," I, *Journal of American Folklore,* Vol. 59 (January–March, 1946), No. 231, p. 51.

[4] *The Journal of William Jefferay, Gentleman* . . . A Diary That Might Have Been, edited by John Osborne Austin (Providence, 1899), p. 18.

[5] Masterson, *op. cit.,* II, *Journal of American Folklore,* Vol. 59 (April–June, 1946), No. 232, p. 187.

Samuel Peters *General History of Connecticut* (1790), history with fiction. With grim piety and unconscious humor, these historians relate true-tall tales of hardships, plagues, storms, disasters, witchcraft, and other "singular occurrences" and "memorable accidents" as well as freaks of nature.[1]

In the same category of true-tall tales are the accounts of early settlers' experiences on the New England border, amidst the terrors of the wilderness and wild animals—bears, wolves, wild-cats, panthers. When John Strong thrust his hand into the mouth of a bear in whose embrace he was locked and held on to its tongue until he freed himself by a supreme effort, he was in the miraculous tradition of Munchausen and Davy Crockett. Such marvels are heightened by the early settlers' superstitious beliefs in the anthropomorphic intelligence or benevolence of the bear.

3. Local Pride and Prejudice

If Yankees have made any distinctive contributions to American tall tales, these are in the field of hunting and fishing. According to one old Maine guide, "The only difference between a hunter and a fisherman is that the fisherman expects to be branded a liar and therefore exercises some control over his imagination."[2] When hunting became a sport, hunters' brags were told for their own sake, as part of the sociability of the campfire; and stories of fearsome critters grew up as tales to prank tenderfeet. The sea, with its whales, cod, sea serpents, fogs, and storms, and the rivers, with their remarkable runs of fish or schools of fish frozen in the ice, rival the woods as a source of New England lying tales.

The New England country also has its strong men and giants, who perform seemingly impossible feats of lifting, toting, throwing, walking, etc.,[3] and its prodigious eaters and drinkers. Tough yarns of rich land, poor land, and hard land (symbolized by New England's stony fields and stone walls); of freaks of climate and weather; and of the folk etymology of place names match those of other regions.

Other tall tales originate in satirical hoaxes and libels, provoked by factional and regional rivalry and quarrels. In this category are the whopping brags and feuding taunts of local patriots, as in *The Jonny-Cake Papers of "Shepherd Tom" Hazard* (1880). Thus New Englanders use artful exaggeration to strengthen pride or prejudice, faith or skepticism.

When Thoreau asked a minister from Truro what the fishermen did in the winter, the other replied: "Nothing, but go a-visiting, sit about, and tell stories, though they worked hard in the summer, and it is not a long vacation they get." And wherever Yankees seek a vacation from toil, and visit and sit about, as in the country store, the "master hand at telling stories" is likely to be the one who can tell the biggest lies.

B. A. B.

---

[1] See Part Two below.

[2] Raymond R. Camp, "The Hunter Bags a Tale," *The New York Times Magazine*, December 15, 1946, p. 54.

[3] For examples see Richard M. Dorson, *Jonathan Draws the Long Bow* (Cambridge, 1946), pp. 121 ff.

HYPERBOLE INTO YARN

Monstrosities of Mirth

THE most obvious characteristic of American humor is its power of "pitching it strong," and drawing the long bow. It is the humor of exaggeration. This consists of fattening up a joke until it is rotund and rubicund, unctuous and irresistible as Falstaff himself, who was created by Shakespeare, and fed fat, so as to become for all time the very impersonation of humor in a state of corpulence. That place in the geography of the United States called "Down East" has been most prolific in the monstrosities of mirth. Only there would a tree'd coon have cried to the marksman with his gun pointed, "Don't fire, colonel! I'll come down." Only in that region do they travel at such speed that the iron rails get hot enough to serve the carriages with heat instead of hot-water bottles; and sometimes so hot that on looking back you see the irons writhing about like live snakes trying to wriggle off to the water to cool themselves. Only there do they travel so fast that the signal-whistle is of no use for their engines, because, on one occasion at least, the train was in, and smashed in a collision, long before the sound of the whistle got there. Only there can a blow be struck so "slick" as to take an animal's ear off with such ease, that the animal does not know he is one ear short until he puts his fore-foot up to scratch it. Only there, surely, are the thieves so 'cute that they drew a walnut log right out of its bark, and left five sleepy watchers all nodding as they sat astride a tunnel of walnut-wood rind.

A Yarn

A YARN is a distinctively qualified relation. While it assumes the appearance of veracity on its inception, the boldness of its progressive or final incidents must startle the incredulity of the most obtuse. Without this characteristic audacity of relation, no concatenated order of narrated particulars can legitimately claim to be a yarn. The implied characteristic of mental ingenuity being very prominent, few persons are capable of inventing a good yarn. The scarcity of the species makes a good narrator of yarns a person of local celebrity. Such a person lived years ago in this town, and, though he has gone, the memory of his yarns has not departed. We give one.

From *The World of Wit and Humour,* edited by George Manville Fenn, p. 211. London, Paris, and New York: Cassell, Petter, & Galpin. [n. d.]

From "Items and Incidents in Hopkinton," by C. C. Lord, *The Granite Monthly,* Vol. II (July, 1879) p. 307. Concord, New Hampshire: H. H. Metcalf, Publisher.

The tale includes assumed circumstances attendant upon a flood of the Contoocook river. The banks of this stream being low, a sudden rise of water often floods the adjacent meadows and intervales, sometimes also submerging the lower floors of dwellings in the vicinity. A considerable portion of Contoocook village has been thus sometimes flooded. On the occasion of one of the heaviest freshets on the Contoocook, a farm-house on one of its banks was suddenly partially engulfed. The occupants—husband and wife—were in a situation both unhappy and precarious. Their neighbors promptly determined to rescue them. Here the yarn begins.

The original narrator, who claimed to have been one of the rescuing party, stated that a boat was procured, into which a number of persons entered and pulled for the imperiled home. Having reached the house, they rowed into the front door and made their way into a room where the unfortunate inmates were found upon a bed, which supported them above the water. The boat being brought to the bedside, the relieved persons stepped gladly into it, and preparations were made to return to shore. Just then, however, one of the rescuing party suggested that a little cider would be an appropriate acknowledgment of a favor. The host was complacent. He immediately leaped from the boat, procured a light, went down cellar, drew some cider, returned and regaled the company, and then the whole party stood out for dry land. The reader will remember we have already made our comments at the beginning of this matter.

An Hyperbole

MANY years ago there lived in this town a diligent knight of the lap-stone, the products of whose skill were of sufficient reputation to ensure him a decent activity in business. That a plain shoemaker should be able to indulge in a figure of speech that should impress itself upon the memory of future generations only proves how much talent is sometimes resident in humble situations. However, one day a citizen of recognized local prominence and influence called upon our friend, the shoemaker, and discussed the subject of a pair of new boots.

"Can you make a pair of boots that won't soak water?" asked the local patrician.

"Yes, sir," replied the humble disciple of St. Crispin.

"Very well. Make me a pair of boots that won't soak water."

The measure was taken, the boots made, and the customer served. In a short time, bearing an expression of displeasure on his countenance, the citizen returned.

"Mr. Leathers, these boots are not satisfactory."

"Why not?"

Ibid., p. 308.

"They soak water badly. You agreed to furnish me a pair of tight boots."

"I think those you have must be tight ones."

"No, they are not."

The two began to argue with much earnestness. At length the customer insisted:

"They are the worst boots to soak water I ever had. You never saw such a pair of boots to soak water."

"I have seen a pair that soaked water worse than that," stoutly affirmed the shoemaker.

"I would like to know if there was ever a pair of boots that would soak water worse than this," warmly replied the customer.

"Why," said the shoemaker, "I have seen a pair that soaked so badly that it would draw the water right up out of a well."

The point taken by the shoemaker was irresistible. The boots were conveyed home again, and no further complaint was made or question asked.

A Bigger Story

A PARTY of three or four men were one day sitting in front of the tavern, and, seeing Mr. Rosebrook approaching, the following conversation, in substance, ensued: Says Mr. A., there comes the Old Duke, the man that can tell a bigger story than any body else. This remark was rather directed to Mr. B. who, by the way, thought himself a champion at that sort of play. Mr. B. replied, I'll bet I can beat him.

Mr. A.—Well, we'll see.

When Mr. R. had joined the company, the contest was commenced by Mr. B.

Mr. B. says: Mr. Rosebrook, as a number of us were passing along the road the other day, we saw an immense egg lying in the highway; as it was so large as to obstruct travel, we were obliged to remove it, and it took four men with levers to roll it out of the road!

I have no doubt of it, instantly replied Uncle James. I haven't the least doubt of it, for I saw the bird that laid that egg when she flew over, and she was so large that she darkened the sun for two hours!

From "Guildhall," by Milton Cutler, in *The Vermont Historical Gazetteer:* A Magazine, Embracing a History of Each Town, Civil, Ecclesiastical, Biographical and Military, edited by Abby Maria Hemenway, in Three Volumes, Vol. I, pp. 1000–1001. Entered according to Act of Congress, in the year 1859, by Abby Maria Hemenway, in the Clerk's Office of the District Court of the District of Vermont. Burlington, Vermont: Published by Miss A. M. Hemenway. 1867.

Hard Lying

THERE lives in New Hampshire a man called Joe, a fellow noted for the tough lies he can tell. A correspondent informs us that Joe called in at Holton's lately, and found him almost choked with smoke, when he suggested, "You don't know as much about managing smoky chimneys as I do, squire, or you'd cure 'em." "Ah! said Holton, with interest, "did you ever see a smoky chimney cured?" "Seen it?" said old Joe, "I think I have. I had the worst one in Seaboard county once, and I cured it a little too much." "How was that?" asked Holton. "Why, you see," said Joe, "I built a little house out yonder, at Wolf Hollow, ten or twelve years ago. Jim Bush, the fellow that built the chimneys, kept blind drunk three-quarters of the time, and crazy drunk the other. I told him I thought he'd have something wrong; but he stuck to it and finished the house. Well, we moved in, and built a fire the next morning to boil the tea-kettle. All the smoke came through the room and went out of the windows; not a bit went up the flues. We tried it for two or three days, and it got worse and worse. By and by it came on to rain, and the rain began to come down the chimney. It put the fire out in a minute, and directly it came down by the pailful. We had to get the baby off the floor as soon as we could, or it would have been drowned. In fifteen minutes the water stood knee-deep on the floor. I pretty soon saw what was the matter. The drunken cuss had put the chimney wrong end up, and it drawed downwards. It gathered all the rain within a hundred yards, and poured it down by bucketfuls." "Well, that was unfortunate," remarked Holton, "but what in the world did you do with the house? Surely you never cured that chimney?" "Didn't I, though?" answered old Joe; "yes, I did." "How?" asked Holton. "Turned it the other end up," said the incorrigible, "and then you ought to have seen it draw. That was the way I cured it too much." "Drew too much?" asked Holton. "Well, squire, you may judge for yourself," said old Joe. "Pretty soon after we got the chimney down the other end up, I missed one of the chairs out of the room, and directly I see'd another of 'em shooting towards the fireplace. Next the table went, and I see the back log going up. Then I grabbed the old woman under one arm and the baby under t'other and started; but just as I got to the door I see'd the cat going across the floor backwards, holding on with her claws to the carpet, yelling awfully. It wasn't no use. I just see her going over the top of the chimney, and that was the last of her." "Well, what did you do then?" asked Holton; "of course you could not live in such a house?" "Couldn't I, though?" said Joe; "but I did; I put a poultice on the jamb of the fireplace, and that drawed t'other way, so we had no more trouble." This is what we call hard lying.

From *The American Joe Miller:* A Collection of Yankee Wit and Humour, Compiled by Robert Kempt, pp. 4–5. Entered at Stationer's Hall. London: Adams and Francis. 1865.

The Man Who Bottled Up the Thunder

One evening in Mr. Smiley's baker shop the topic of thunder showers came up. A man asked Mr. Smiley to tell about the big thunder shower which he experienced last summer. Mr. Smiley's story is as follows:

"Last summer I was helping my father to get in the hay before the storm. We were almost through when it began to rain and thunder. Suddenly a big round ball of fire fell from the sky bouncing along the ground and went right plump into a wood-chuck hole. Looking around, I saw a large flat stone which I picked up and placed over the wood-chuck hole to keep the ball of fire from coming out, then thought no more about it. The other day I was up in the same field when I remembered about last summer, and sure enough there was the same rock still over the wood-chuck hole. Walking over to the rock, I removed it, when suddenly two tremendous crashes of thunder came out of the hole. I had bottled the thunder last summer and just released it the other day."

He is still referred to as "Mr. Smiley, the man who bottled up the thunder."

The Man That Cut Bread So Fast with the Shoe-Knife

. . . Wal the' was a shoemaker 't lived in Connecticut, an' my father knowed him, 'at hed a knife julluk this . . . the cutest thing t' cut bread with't ever was, but he wouldn't let nob'dy but his own self use it, so they use ter send fer him to all gret duins t' cut the' bread fer 'em. Wal, arter he'd ben a-cuttin' raoun' fer three, fo' year, they sent fer him one July to go t' Colonel Leavenworth's gret shearin'. He kep' a thousan' sheep, an' hed twenty shearers, an' made a big splonto, "wine in quart mugs an' straw-b'ries rolled in cream," he use ter brag about, but they wan't on'y pint mugs 'n not filled very often at that, an' the wine was cider, an' the' wan't more 'n tew strawb'ries apiece, 'n' they was dried apples. Wal, the shoemaker come with his knife keener 'n ever, an' the han's an' comp'ny hed all got washed up for dinner with the' clean clo's on, an' stood raound watchin' on him cut the bread, ker slice, ker slice, faster 'n a gal could pick up the slices, off 'm a loaf 't he hel' agin his breast. He done it so neat 't they cheered him, which he got kinder 'xcited, an' tried t' cut faster 'n ever, an' the next lick he gin the loaf he cut hisself clean in tew, an' the man 'at

---

By Fred Smith, Fayette, Maine. Manuscripts of the Federal Writers' Project of the Works Progress Administration for the State of Maine.

From *Uncle Lisha's Shop,* Life in a Corner of Yankeeland, by Rowland E. Robinson, p. 32. Copyright, 1910, by Forest and Stream Publishing Co. New York. 1902.

stood behind him clean in tew, an' badly waounded the next one. They sot tew an' stuck 'em together so 't they lived, but it spilte the shoemaker's bread-cuttin' business, an' he hed to go back to shoemakin' an' starvin', julluk me.

Bradley's Ax

THERE's some tales they tell about a man named Bradley who used to live in Wolcott early in the last century. He wanted an ax one time, so he collected a lot of old razor blades and had the blacksmith make him one out of these. Made a mighty good ax, and had a ring that could be heard for miles.

One morning after he hadn't used the ax for several days it was missing and Bradley hunted high and low for it, to no avail. All of a sudden he heard that familiar ring, coming from the south somewhere. He got on his horse and started after it. When he got to Long Island Sound, he could still hear that ring coming across the water. So he plunged his horse in and swam across. Still guided by the familiar sound he went right to the spot, knocked down the culprit, picked up his ax, and swam back across the Sound and got to Wolcott in time for breakfast.

One time they were using the ax on the steeple of a church they were repairing. Bradley was working on the ground. He happened to have both hands full when he looked up and saw that the ax had slipped from its handle and was coming straight for him. Quick as a flash, he opened his mouth and caught the ax in his teeth.

Sam Patch Turns Up Again

. . . THAT are man was a great diver, says the Clockmaker, and the last dive he took was off the falls of Niagara, and he was never heered of agin till tother day, when Captain Enoch Wentworth, of the Susy Ann Whaler, saw him in the South Sea. Why, says Captain Enoch to him, why Sam, says he, now on airth did you get here? I thought you was drowned at the Canadian lines. Why, says he, I didn't get *on* airth here at all, but I came right slap *through* it. In that are Niagara dive, I went so everlasting deep, I thought it was just as short to come up tother side, so out I came in those parts. If I don't take the shine off the Sea Serpent, when I get back to Boston, then my name's not Sam Patch. . . .

Manuscripts of the Federal Writers' Project of the Works Progress Administration for the State of Connecticut.

From *The Clockmaker; or, The Sayings and Doings of Samuel Slick of Slickville*, p. 46. Philadelphia: Carey, Lea, and Blanchard. 1837.

For the Sam Patch legend, see Richard M. Dorson, "Sam Patch, Jumping Hero," *New York Folklore Quarterly*, Vol. I (August, 1945), No. 3, pp. 133–151.

STRONG MEN

John Strong and the Bear

ONE fall the bears were making destructive work in his cornfield; he found where they came in, and placed his trap in their road. The second morning he found his trap gone, and plenty of signs that a large bear had taken it; he got two of his neighbors, Kellogg and Pangborn, to go with him. They had two guns and an axe, and three dogs. After following the track for some two miles, they heard the dogs, and as they came up they found the bear with her back against a large stub, cuffing the dogs whenever they came within reach. The trap was on one of her hind legs. Kellogg proposed to shoot the bear, but Strong said he could kill her with his axe as well as to waste a charge of ammunition, which was scarce and difficult to get. So taking the axe, and remembering his encounter on the lake, he turned the bit of the axe, intending to split her head open. He approached cautiously, and when near enough, gave the blow with tremendous force, but the bear, with all the skill of a practised boxer, caught the axe as it was descending; with one of her paws knocking it out of his hand, at the same time catching him with the other, she drew him up for the death-hug; as she did so, endeavoring to grab his throat in her mouth. One moment more, and he would have been a mangled corpse. The first effort, he avoided by bending his head close upon his breast; the second, by running his left hand into her open mouth and down her throat, until he could hook the ends of his fingers into the roots of her tongue. This hold he kept until the end, although every time the bear closed her mouth his thumb was crushed and ground between her grinders, her mouth being so narrow that it was impossible to put it out of the way. He now called on Kellogg for God's sake to shoot the bear, but this he dared not do, for fear of shooting Strong; for as soon as he got the bear by the tongue, she endeavored to get rid of him by plunging and rolling about, so that one moment the bear was on top, and the next Strong. In these struggles they came where the axe had been thrown at first. This Strong seized with his right hand, and striking the bear in the small of the back, severed it at a blow. This so paralyzed her that she loosened her hug, and he snatched his hand from her mouth, and cleared himself of her reach. The men then dispatched her with their guns. His mutilated thumb he carried, as a memento of the fight, to his dying day.

From "Addison," by Hon. John Strong, in *The Vermont Historical Gazetteer:* A Magazine, Embracing a History of Each Town, Civil, Ecclesiastical, Biographical and Military, edited by Abby Maria Hemenway, in Three Volumes, Vol. I, p. 8. Entered according to Act of Congress, in the year 1859, by Abby Maria Hemenway, in the Clerk's Office of the District Court of the District of Vermont. Burlington, Vermont: Published by Miss A. M. Hemenway. 1867.

A Hunter's Story

In the early day one Isaiah Preston and one Stinson, two of the early settlers of this vicinity, went out on a moose hunt. They were not fortunate until they got several miles from home. It was in the winter time, and they, on account of the depth of snow, were obliged to travel on snow-shoes.

Just at night they found and shot a large moose in a hollow near the south-west end of Mansfield mountain. The shades of night were coming on, they built a fire, dressed their moose, cooked their supper of moose meat, made a bed of evergreen boughs and laid down to pleasant dreams.

After they had made preparation for a night's lodging in the woods, it being very cold, Preston said to Stinson that he would take the moose hide and wrap himself up in that, which he did, giving Stinson both of the blankets. They slept soundly and well, and were unmolested and undisturbed, excepting by the distant howl of the wolves.

Morning dawned, and Preston thought he would unrobe himself and help Stinson build the fire and cook their breakfast; but he found his hands and legs tied so tightly by the frozen hide that he must inevitably have perished had it not been for the assistance of his companion. After being restored to liberty, they hung upon a tree the portion of the moose they could not carry, and packed the rest 8 or 10 miles on their backs to their hungry families. In this way the early settlers supplied themselves with game, it being their only meat. Many are their stories of hardships and hair-breadth escapes of these iron-sinewed pioneers.

Copp's Walk

On the last day of January, 1855, Nathaniel Copp, son of Hayes D. Copp, of Pinkham's Grant, near the Glen House, set out from home on a deer hunt, and was out four successive days. On the fifth day he again left to look for a deer killed the previous day, about eight miles from home. Having found it, he dragged the carcass (weighing two hundred and thirty pounds) home through the snow, and at one o'clock P.M. started for

---

From "Richmond," by S. H. Davis, in *The Vermont Historical Gazetteer:* A Magazine, Embracing a History of Each Town, Civil, Ecclesiastical, Biographical and Military, edited by Abby Maria Hemenway, in Three Volumes, Vol. I, p. 848. Entered according to Act of Congress, in the year 1859, by Abby Maria Hemenway, in the Clerk's Office of the District Court of the District of Vermont. Burlington, Vermont: Published by Miss A. M. Hemenway. 1867.

From *The Heart of the White Mountains, Their Legend and Scenery,* by Samuel Adams Drake, pp. 167–168. Entered according to Act of Congress, in the year 1881, by Harper & Brothers, in the Office of the Librarian of Congress, at Washington. New York. 1882.

another he had tracked near the place where the former was killed, which he followed until he lost the track, at dark. He then found that he had lost his own way, and should, in all probability, be obliged to spend the night in the woods, with the temperature ranging from 32° to 35° below zero.

Knowing that to remain quiet was certain death, and having nothing with which to light a fire, the hunter began walking for his life. The moon shone out bright and clear, making the cold seem even more intense. While revolving in his mind his unpleasant predicament he heard a deer bleat. He gave chase, and easily overtook it. The snow was too deep for the animal to escape from a hunter on snow-shoes. Copp leaped upon his back, and despatched him with his hunting-knife. He then dressed him, and, taking out the heart, put it in his pocket, not for a trophy, but, as he told me, to keep starvation at arm's-length. The excitement of the chase made him forget cold until he perceived himself growing benumbed. Rousing himself, he again pushed on, whither he knew not, but spurred by the instinct of self-preservation. Daylight found him still striding on, with no clew to a way out of the thick woods, which imprisoned him on every side. At length, at ten in the morning, he came out at or near Wild River, in Gilead, forty miles from home, having walked twenty-one consecutive hours without rest or food, the greater part of the time through a tangled growth of underbrush.

His friends at home becoming alarmed at his prolonged absence during such freezing weather, three of them, Hayes D. Copp, his father, John Goulding, and Thomas Culhane, started in search of him. They followed his track until it was lost in the darkness, and, by the aid of their dog, found the deer which young Copp had killed and dressed. They again started on the trail, but with the faintest hope of ever finding the lost man alive, and, after being out twenty-six hours in the extreme cold, found the object of their search.

No words can do justice to the heroic self-denial and fortitude with which these men continued an almost hopeless search, when every moment expecting to find the stiffened corpse of their friend. Goulding froze both feet; the others their ears.

When found, young Copp did not seem to realize in the least the great danger through which he had passed, and talked with perfect unconcern of hunts that he had planned for the next week. One of his feet was so badly frozen, from the effect of too tightly lacing his snow-shoe, that the toes had to be amputated.

Harding's Prowess

THERE is a tradition about an adventure of Stephen Harding, who kept the ferry here [at Kennebunkport] long ago, that belongs to this locality.

From *The Pine-Tree Coast,* by Samuel Adams Drake, pp. 92–93. Copyright, 1890, by Estes & Lauriat. Boston. 1891.

Harding's log-house stood on the swell of ground enclosed between Gooch's Creek and the beach and river. Tradition reports him a man of uncommon physical strength and courage,—a very giant, in fact. The Indians knew Harding well, and Harding knew them of old.

One morning, on going out of the house, he saw a band of Indians, returning doubtless from their repulse at Wells, filing across the rocks rising at the farthest end of the beach. The redskins, of course, were coming to pay him a visit.

It was now Harding's turn to be alarmed. Fortunately for him, the band was still at a distance, but there was not a moment to lose. Hurrying back to the house, Harding told his wife to take their little year-old infant, and make haste to put the creek between her and the redskins. The terrified woman snatched up the child, and ran off with it as she was told, while Harding remained behind to protect her flight, if, as he half suspected, more Indians should be lurking about there.

It turned out as he thought; for upon going into his blacksmith's shop, four Indians started up from the ground and made a rush for him. Harding now thought it time to be making his own escape. His cornfield offered the only cover at hand, so into that he plunged with rapid strides; but while running at the top of his speed, to his unspeakable dismay he suddenly came upon his wife, whom he supposed to be in safety, crouching down among the corn. The poor woman was prostrated by terror, and being no longer capable of making the least effort to save her life, had sunk down helpless within only a few rods of the house. Harding's extraordinary muscular strength was now put to the test. Taking his wife under one arm, and his babe under the other, he dashed on again for the creek, into which he plunged, getting safely over it, with his charge unharmed, too, though the savages followed him to the shore of the creek before they gave up the chase. Once across, the thick woods enabled Harding to place his wife and child in a secure hiding-place. All this time his favorite dog had followed close at his heels; but for fear that the animal's barking might betray them, his master was forced to kill him. All that night they lay in the woods. Late the next day, the fugitives, foot-sore and half-starved, reached Storer's garrison at Wells. It is probable that the Indians wished to take Harding alive, or he could hardly have escaped so easily. They showed great admiration for his prowess in this affair, often saying of him, "Much man Stephen: all same one Indian."

Kicking a Potato Home

. . . Another illustrative tale is told of a certain eccentric individual, who bought a bag of potatoes "down below," and having with the assistance of two or three able bodied men, secured the same upon his back, set out for St. Johnsbury. Unfortunately and greatly to his dismay, a small rent in the corner of the bag became so enlarged in the course of the homeward trip, as to permit the escape of one of the esculents, and how to recover this was a problem which gave ample scope to his available eccentricity. Fearing to stoop, lest the weight of the bag should prevent his subsequent perpendicularity, and unwilling to lose so dainty a morsel, he proceeded to inflict upon the said potato sundry well-directed kicks, which in due time propelled it with variable velocities to the floor of his kitchen, whence it met its appropriate fate. For the authenticity of the above we are incompetent to vouch, but we accept it as a practical treatise on the times. . . .

A Jug of Molasses

One of the first men by the name of Jackman to live in the district since known as the Jackman neighborhood was a very tall man. One day he walked to St. Johnsbury for a jug of molasses and carried it home on a stick thrown over his shoulder. It is between ten and twelve miles and would be considered quite a distance to-day. Upon arriving home, he forgot how tall he was and how low-posted the house was, and the stick with the jug of molasses above his shoulder hit the top of the door frame and threw the jug onto the stone step breaking it into a thousand small pieces. He turned right around without saying a word and walked back to St. Johnsbury and brought home another gallon.

From "St. Johnsbury," by Edward T. Fairbanks, in *Vermont Quarterly Gazetteer*, A Historical Magazine, Embracing a Digest of the History of Each Town, Civil, Educational, Religious, Geological and Literary, No. IV, October, 1862, edited by Abby Maria Hemenway, p. 395. Entered according to Act of Congress, in the year 1859, by Abby Maria Hemenway, in the Clerk's Office of the District Court of the District of Vermont. Ludlow, Vermont: Published by Miss A. M. Hemenway. Albany, New York: J. Munsell.

From "Littleton," by Ola G. Veazie. Manuscripts of the Federal Writers' Project of the Works Progress Administration for the State of New Hampshire.

Stagers' Feats

Some of the old stagers were greatly distinguished for their skill in handling a team of four and six horses, and it was an awe-inspiring sight, especially to the juvenile community, to see the smoking, high-mettled steeds dash up to the tavern door at full speed, the reins so skilfully handled that the wheels, just grazing the door-stone, would stop with the rapidity of an electric shock at exactly the right spot. Some of these veterans of the whip were remarkably expert in exercising their lash. We well remember the feat of a driver, noted for his dexterity, who wagered the "drinks"—it was customary in those days to imbibe—with a gentleman on the outside seat, that he would, on passing the first flock of fowls within reach of his lash, decapitate any bird the gentleman might select, provided the gentleman would be answerable for all damages; the other conditions being, that the driver should not relinquish his reins or seat, nor check the speed of his horses. His skill was soon put to the test, for, on passing a farm house, a flock of hens, convoyed by a stately rooster, were approached. As the coach passed at full speed, the driver was directed to try his skill on the rooster. Quick as thought, the unerring lash flashed through the air, and encircling the neck of the hapless chanticleer, his glittering head flew across the road, leaving his fluttering body with the astonished hens!

Stout Jeffrey

Less than two miles to the south-easterly from this bridge stands the Governor George Brown house, which was occupied by Geoffrey Hazard, called "Stout Jeffrey," who if the half that is told be true, must have approached nearer in physical strength to the fabled Hercules than almost any other man known in modern times. I have heard old people say that Stout Jeffrey was remarkably broad across the shoulders, and so thick through the chest that when he stood with his face fronting you his head looked as if it were set unnaturally far back on his shoulders, and that when his back was towards you, it looked as though he stooped, his head seeming to project so far in the contrary direction.

From *Waifs from the Way-Bills of an Old Expressman,* by T. W. Tucker, pp. 13–14. Entered, according to the Act of Congress, in the year 1872, by Lee and Shepard, in the Office of the Librarian of Congress, at Washington. Boston and New York.

From *Recollections of Olden Times:* Rowland Robinson of Narragansett and His Unfortunate Daughter, with Genealogies of the Robinson and Hazard Families of Rhode Island, by Thomas R. Hazard, "Shepherd Tom," in His Eighty-First and Eighty-Second Years; Also Genealogical Sketch of the Hazards of the Middle States, by Willis P. Hazard, of Westchester, Pa., pp. 70–71. Entered according to Act of Congress, in the year 1879, by John P. Sanborn, in the Office of the Librarian of Congress, at Washington, D. C. Newport, Rhode Island.

Most marvelous stories used to be told and vouched for within my memory of the feats of strength performed by Stout Jeffrey, and also those of a sister who married a Wilcox. There may now be seen on the lawn in front of Rowland Hazard's house at Peacedale, in Narragansett, a blue stone [1] weighing by the scales sixteen hundred and twenty pounds, that Mr. Hazard had drawn with oxen some years ago from Stout Jeffrey's homestead in Boston Neck, with which the following tradition is associated. Several negroes were engaged in laying a wall on the premises, when Stout Jeffrey, chancing to observe a large stone lying near by that they had neglected to build into the wall, asked why they had left it out. "Cos, massa, it be too heavy," was the reply. Thereupon Stout Jeffrey stooped down and taking the stone partly on his knees, carried it some twenty feet from the wall and dropping it on the ground said, "Let *that stone* lie there until a man is found strong enough to put it back again."

It was said that Stout Jeffrey and his sister would alternately lift in playful sport a full barrel of cider—thirty-one gallons—by the chimes and holding it up drink at its bung—a thing hard to believe in these degenerate days.

Jonas Lord

THERE was a man by the name of Jonas Lord, who was born in 1820 and died in 1900. He was a massive man, well over six feet tall, and very strong. He was so strong and powerful that he would never wind his own watch; some one else would always do it for him. His fingers were thick and without much feeling and he was apt to wind the stem right off.

In the machine shop where Jonas Lord worked it was necessary every week for each man to bring his anvil weighing 400 pounds to the blacksmith shop to be refinished. This generally required two men and the use of a wheelbarrow, but to Jonas Lord it was a simple matter. He just placed the anvil under his arm as if it were a newspaper and walked over to the blacksmith shop, had it refinished, and returned with it. One day the men in the shop waylaid him when he had the anvil under his arm and talked to him for a half an hour. Jonas Lord stood there all that time without as much as shifting the position of the anvil.

One day in the tool shop a large die used for stamping out scythes by

[1] A bronze tablet set into the surface of the stone bears this legend:

> Stout Jeffrey Hazard lifted this Stone,
> In pounds just sixteen twenty one,
> In South Kingstown he lived and died,
> God save us all from sinful Pride.
> —R. G. H., *ibid.*, p. 397.

By L. Crosberry, S. Wells, W. Richards, W. Morrill, and Mrs. J. Hart, Wayne, Maine. Manuscripts of the Federal Writers' Project of the Works Progress Administration for the State of Maine.

means of a trip hammer had to be removed. This die weighed 600 pounds and generally required several men to move it. When it was time for the die to be moved, all the men seemed to have disappeared except Jonas. He shouted for them and, receiving no answer, he moved the die by himself, carrying it about one hundred feet to the machine shop.

Shortly after Jonas Lord came to work at this machine shop and was learning the trade, there were many practical jokes played on him, until finally he informed all the men that the next man that tried to plague him would receive as good as he gave. That very afternoon the boss walked into the shop and told young Lord to clean up the mess around the boiler. As a rule in those days the ashes and clinkers were removed and placed in a big iron vat to cool off and then removed. This work was not young Lord's work, so he wasn't over-anxious to do it. The boss realized this and sarcastically said, "Come on, why don't you pick up the vat and the ashes and lug them out? You're big enough." With that young Lord got mad and picked up the vat with one arm and the boss with the other and went outside and dumped the ashes out first and then dropped the boss on top of the ashes.

The proprietor of the hardware store in Wayne was endeavoring to sell a mowing machine to a customer, who refused to buy unless the machine was demonstrated. Just at this moment Jonas Lord came into the store, and the proprietor asked Jonas to take the man out and demonstrate the machine. Jonas stepped between the two shafts of the machine and told the customer to get on. Picking up the shafts as if he were a horse, he started across the nearby field. Realizing that the man hadn't put the machine in gear, Jonas turned around and said, "What the heck is the matter with you? Put the machine in gear." He towed the machine down the field and back again with little effort. Needless to say, the machine was sold.

Jigger Johnson, River Boss

THERE were river bosses who claimed to know every rock, eddy and white-water stretch in our mountain rivers and creeks. Jim Smart knew the Androscoggin as a man knows a cantankerous wife, and on that same river Dan Bossy was called the "cattiest" man who ever drove logs. But for toughness, Jigger Johnson held first place. From Maine at the age of twelve he had come into the woods and had worked and fought his way by twenty up to a job as woods and river boss. He often drove crews to open revolt but, though only five feet six, he would face the rebels with peavy or ax and threaten to kill any man who failed to get right back on the job. Stories are still told of his battles. When stripped, his whole body showed

---

From *The Great White Hills of New Hampshire,* by Ernest Poole, pp. 55–57. Copyright, 1946, by Ernest Poole. Garden City, New York: Doubleday & Company, Inc.

the scars left by scores of calked boots; but men left his head alone, for his bite was swift and his teeth were strong. He is said to have bitten off a man's ear and spit it out when the fight was done. When once with his crew he went into Berlin and got thoroughly soused, some of his men laid for him on the dark road back to camp and "calked" him well and, with both his arms and legs broken, left him for dead. But Jigger managed to wriggle and roll to a neighboring pigsty, rolled into manure to keep warm and so slept off his drunk, was found by a forest ranger and taken to a hospital, whence a month later he emerged limping a bit but still going strong. And when one of the lads who had "calked" him met him on the street that night, the logger left Berlin on the run, for he thought he had seen Jigger's ghost!

Famed for his use of the Bible, he called one logger "dirtier than the combined britches of Mathew, Mark, Luke and John"; and [said] of another, that in Berlin with the gals he could "beat old King Solomon hisself"! In barrooms men all stopped to listen in admiration while Jigger swore; and when he bellowed logger ballads, they said it rocked the floor. Joe Dodge, who is himself some epicure in profanity, declares that never has he heard anything equal to Jigger's line. Dodge knew him well in his old age; for when Jigger quit as camp boss about twenty years ago, he took a job in the Forest Service and built part of a Carter Dome trail.

"I used to see him there," said Dodge. "He would work all summer, save four hundred bucks and then go on one hell of a bender. Now and then we used to harbor him here in Pinkham Notch Camp on his jubilees, and while he was working on the trail we often took him up cigars. Then he got a fire-lookout job on Chocorua and later on Carter Dome; and there he served well through dangerous times when the woods were dry; but in wet spells, with nothing to do, he drank himself into d.t.'s on a home brew that he called Eagle Sweat. When for that the Service fired him, down near Chocorua he trapped for years, and in wildcats he could lick his weight. He loved to take a cat alive. Trapping one fall, he found the carcass of a deer with throat and shoulder torn by a cat. Figuring that the killer would be back to feed at dusk, Jigger climbed into a hemlock close by. Dark came and then *two* cats appeared. Jigger quietly hitched himself out on a limb; and when both were well into the guts of the deer, he jumped and crashed down on the pair. The battle took him quite some time but at the end he had a cat tucked clawing and spitting under each arm. Four miles he hiked to his cabin below and, whenever a cat got restless, Jigger would bang him on the head. At home he threw one in the wood box and nailed down the lid; the other he tied with telephone wire to his bedpost and then went to sleep. He kicked the cat each time she yowled, so by morning she was dead; but the other one he shipped in a crate to Portland, to a sporting-goods firm that wanted a live cat in their window.

"He got four or five cats each fall. Catching one on the side of Madison, he hog-tied her and brought her to a Forest Service guard station near here. By that time old Jigger was all clawed up, so he threw the cat into the dynamite room and went to Gorham on a drunk. At the station the guard and his wife spent a bad night. She was soon to have a baby and it got on her nerves to hear the big cat screeching and clawing around in that room filled with dynamite and percussion caps. They flagged cars on the road till one kind soul went to Gorham and brought Jigger back. Drunker than a billy goat, he walked right in and grabbed the cat, who had scattered percussion caps over the floor!"

But in the fall of 1935, having caught and killed a six-foot lynx, he brought it to town for the bounty and spent the money on a drunk, and then, on the way back to his traps, crashed his flivver into a telegraph pole. So Jigger lived and so he died.[1]

Old Sam Hewes, River Man

Lines written some time ago to commemorate the personality and exploits of the doughty Samuel Hewes, whose grave may be seen today beside his wife's in the cemetery at South Fairlee, Vermont:

When I was a little feller, the funniest man that I ever saw
Was Old Sam Hewes.
He hadn't any palate, and he talked with a hee and a haw,
Did Old Sam Hewes.
He'd been a hard old ticket, is what the people said,
Had Old Sam Hewes.
He'd broad and brawny shoulders and a great big bushy head,
Had Old Sam Hewes.
He was the biggest and the stoutest of any man in town,
Was Old Sam Hewes.
At fighting and at wrestling he could put the strongest down,
Could Old Sam Hewes.
Across the lake at Plattsburg he had fought the British there,
Had Old Sam Hewes.
He was wounded by a bullet but he didn't seem to care,
Did Old Sam Hewes.
Our men they were retreating, and they called on him to follow,
To Old Sam Hewes.
The British tried to take him but he beat them out all hollow,
Did Old Sam Hewes.
Two red coats with their bayonets came to him on the run,
At Old Sam Hewes.
But he knocked aside those bayonets and he hit them with his gun,
Did Old Sam Hewes.

[1] Cf. "Saga of the Jigger [Jones]" in Stewart H. Holbrook's *Holy Old Machinaw* (New York, 1938), pp. 1–13.

From Fairlee, Vermont. Manuscripts of the Federal Writers' Project of the Works Progress Administration for the State of Vermont.

And then he reached and grabbed them, one under each arm,
Did Old Sam Hewes.
And he brought them into camp without suffering further harm,
Did Old Sam Hewes.
He'd taken for his wife a grim old Indian squaw,
Had Old Sam Hewes.
She hadn't any beauty that any ever saw,
But Old Sam Hewes.

They were happy and contented as any man and wife,
She and Old Sam Hewes.
And he cherished her and loved her until the end of life,
Did Old Sam Hewes.

I saw their graves to-day where they're sleeping side by side,
The brawny and mighty Samuel and his dusky Indian bride.
God rest them,
Her and Old Sam Hewes.

MEASURE OF SPEED

Fast Train

"Well, it's curous how we du git over the ground! Why, the trees all look as if they was a-dancin' a jig to double-quick time. I kin recollect ten or twelve years ago, that if I started from Bosting on a Wednesday, I cud git in Filedelphy on the next Saturday, makin' just three days. Now I kin git from Bosting to Filedelphy in one day; and I've been cal'latin' that if the power of steam increases for the *next* ten years as it has been doin' for the *last* ten years, I'd be in Filedelphy just two days before I started from Bosting!"

A Fast Horse

A Vermont horse jockey, boasting the other day of the speed of his horse, gravely asserted that he could trot seventeen miles an hour. "Seventeen miles an hour!" says a bystander, "I guess that is a thumper." "My dear friend," replied he of the Green Mountains, "seventeen miles an hour for the creature, now, is no great; for when he was but two years old, the

---

From *Cyclopaedia of Commercial and Business Anecdotes . . .*, edited by Frazar Kirkland, Vol. I, p. 365. Entered, according to Act of Congress, in the year 1864, by D. Appleton and Company, in the Clerk's Office of the District Court of the United States for the Southern District of New York. New York and London.

From *The New-England Farmer's Almanac,* for the Year of the Christian Era, 1842, No. XXVIII, by Truman Abell. Claremont, New Hampshire: Published and Sold at the Claremont Bookstore.

lightning killed the old mare, and ***chased the colt all round the field, without getting within ten rods of him.***"

Beating the Rain Storm

MAYOR COUGHLIN says that Uncle Eli once told him that while on a visit to his old home in Huntington, he noticed by the clouds that a severe rain storm was coming up, and immediately harnessed up his horse "Ripton" and started for Bridgeport. The rain commenced to fall just north of him, but his horse being a good roadster, he called on him to travel, and it was only a few minutes before he drove under his shed without a drop of water having struck him or his horse; when he looked back to see whether his dog had kept pace with him, he saw him a few rods behind swimming in water ten feet deep.[1]

The *Maine Farmer* tells a number of tough stories about a man whom it calls "Neverbeat." Here is one:—A gentleman was boasting in the presence of Neverbeat about the speed of his horse, which, he said, would trot a mile inside of three minutes, and follow it for three miles. "A mile inside of three minutes ain't much to brag about," said Neverbeat. "Why, the other day I was up to S——, sixteen miles distant; just as I started for home, a shower came sweeping on. The rain struck in the back part of the waggon; and the moment it struck, I hit old Kate a cut with the whip, away she trotted, scarcely touching her fore feet to the ground. She kept just nip and nip with the shower. ***The waggon was filled with water, but not a drop fell on me.***"[2]

Nantucket "Sleigh Ride"

A HARPOONED whale will usually "sound" at once, often going down very deep and remaining under for the better part of an hour. On rising to the surface, he will often "run," that is, swim away at high speed, dragging the

[1] From *Funny Stories,* Told by Phineas T. Barnum, p. 99. Copyright, 1890, by Phineas T. Barnum. New York, London, Glasgow, and Manchester: George Routledge and Sons, Limited.

[2] From *The American Joe Miller:* A Collection of Yankee Wit and Humour, Compiled by Robert Kempt, p. 204. Entered at Stationer's Hall. London: Adams and Francis. 1865.

From *The Nantucket Scrap Basket,* Being a Collection of Characteristic Stories and Sayings of the People of the Town and Island of Nantucket, Massachusetts, Second Edition, Revised, Expanded and Rearranged by William F. Macy, pp. 28–29. Copyright, 1916, by William F. Macy and Roland B. Hussey. Copyright, 1930, by William F. Macy. Boston and New York: Houghton Mifflin Company. 1930.

boat after him by the whale line. From time immemorial this method of marine travel has been known as a "Nantucket sleigh ride" and a very exciting trip it can be.

One old whaleman given to "drawing the long bow" once entertained an interested group of summer folks with a story the truth of which we do not vouch for, but we give it for what it is worth: "We was fast to an old bull whale, an' the minute he broke water he started off to looard lickety-split. Sufferin' cats! How that whale did travel! We fleeted aft's fur's we could git, but even then the water poured over the gunnel for'ard and kep' us all bailing's hard's we could to keep her afloat. All of a sudden I happened to look aft, an' there was an empty whale boat follerin' in our wake astarn. For a minute or so she follered us close; then we gained on her an' gradually she fell off an' swung round into the troth o' the sea. The next wave struck her, an' smash! she went, all to smithereens, an' that was the last we seen of her."

"But what was it? Where'd the other boat come from?"

"Wal, believe it or not! 'twas a mystery to *us* till we got aboard ship and h'isted our boat up on the davits. Then we see her plankin' was as clean as the day she come out o' the shop. You see that thar whale went so fast he pulled our boat clean out o' the paint, an' what we seen was jest that shell o' paint follerin' after us!"

REMARKABLE HUNTING AND SHOOTING

Sam Hyde's Single Shot

. . . SAM and Joe Hyde were brothers and their wigwams were located one west of the old Porter house at Danversport, another probably on "Lindall's Hill" and another up in the Bush. They were Indians, the only Native Americans. None of your Modern Mushroom Native Americans whose ancestors came across the big waters. They were Indians, the only Native Americans of which history gives us any account. But to my story: Sam and Joe Hyde had the reputation of being great liars, but more especially Sam, and it is a saying unto this day, both in the United States and some say across the Atlantic when any one tells what is not true, "you lie like Sam Hyde." I will relate some of his exploits. He said one day he went out gunning, when he saw sixty humming birds sitting on sixty posts, sixty feet apart; he had his gun loaded with but one shot on the top of the

From "Reminiscences of Danvers in the Forties and Fifties," by William L. Hyde, in *The Historical Collections of the Danvers Historical Society*, Vol. 5, pp. 8–9. Edited by the Committee on Publication. Danvers, Massachusetts: Published by the Society. 1917.

powder. He fired and that one shot passed through the eyes of the sixty birds, killing them all, of course. Now this may be true for aught I know, but I call it a pretty tough story.

Jonathan's Hunting Excursion

"Did you ever hear of the scrape that I and uncle Zekiel had duckin' on 't on the Connecticut?" asked Jonathan Timbertoes, while amusing his old Dutch hostess, who had agreed to entertain him under the roof of her log cottage, for and in consideration of a bran new tin milk-pan. "No, I never did; do tell it," said Aunt Pumkins. "Well—you must know that I and uncle Zeke took it into our heads on Saturday's afternoon to go a gunning after ducks, in father's skiff; so in we got and sculled down the river; a proper sight of ducks flew backwards and forwards I tell ye—and by'm-by a few on 'em lit down by the mash, and went to feeding. I catched up my powder-horn to prime, and it slipped right out of my hand and sunk to the bottom of the river. The water was amazingly clear, and I could see it on the bottom. Now I couldn't swim a jot, so sez I to uncle Zeke, you're a pretty clever fellow, just let me take your powder-horn to prime. And don't you think, the stingy critter wouldn't. Well, says I, you're a pretty good diver, 'un if you'll dive and get it, I'll give you primin. I thought he'd leave his powder-horn; but he didn't, but stuck it in his pocket, and down he went—and there he staid"—here the old lady opened her eyes with wonder and surprise, and a pause of some minutes ensued, when Jonathan added,—"I looked down, and what do you think the critter was doin?" "Lord!" exclaimed the old lady, "I'm sure I don't know." "There he was," said our hero, "setting right on the bottom of the river, pouring the powder out of my horn into hizen."

The Vermont Nimrod

Mr. Thomas,

We have frequently heard of the wonderful feats and extraordinary stories of *Simonds, old Kidder, and Sam Hyde;* but I believe neither of them have exceeded the following, related by G. H——ll, a mighty hunter, and known in that part of the country where he lived by the name of the

---

From *The Farmer's Almanack,* Calculated on a New and Improved Plan, for the Year of Our Lord 1836, by Robert B. Thomas. Entered according to Act of Congress, in the year 1835, by Carter, Hendee and Co., in the Clerk's Office of the District Court of Massachusetts. Boston.

From *The Farmer's Almanack,* Calculated on a New and Improved Plan for the Year of Our Lord, 1809, No. XVII, by Robert B. Thomas. Boston: Printed for John West & Co.

VERMONT NIMROD.—It may serve to divert some of your evening readers. A. Z.

"I was once," said he, "passing down the banks of the Hudson in search of game, and suddenly heard a crackling on the opposite bank. Looking across the river, I saw a stately buck, and instantly drew up and let fly at him. That very moment a huge sturgeon leaped from the river in the direction of my piece.—The ball went through him, and passed on. I flung down my gun—threw off my coat and hat, and swam for the floating fish, which, mounting, I towed to the bank and went to see what more my shot had done for me. I found the ball had passed through the heart of the deer, and struck into a hollow tree beyond; where the honey was running out like a river! I sprung round to find something to stop the hole with, and caught hold of a white rabbit—It squeaked just like a stuck pig; so I thrash'd it away from me in a passion at the disappointment, and it went with such force that it killed three cock partridges and a wood cock."!!!

Captain Paddock's Whale Iron

ONE of the most singular incidents in connection with the exploits of Nantucket's whalemen and whaleships was that of Peter Paddock. Captain Paddock struck a whale in the Pacific ocean and "lost his iron," the whale escaping. Thirteen years later, while on another voyage in the Pacific, he struck a whale and when it was being cut up, the iron which he lost so many years previous was found imbedded in the flesh. It bore his own initials "P. P.," and was easily identified as the lost iron. That Captain Paddock should strike the same whale after a lapse of thirteen years and thus recover his iron himself was considered most remarkable by the Nantucket whalemen.

Sharp Shooting

October 1st. It's common for the Soldiers to fire at a target fix'd in the stream at the bottom of the *common.* A countryman stood by a few days ago, and laugh'd very heartily at a whole regiment's firing, and not one being able to hit it. The officer observ'd him, and ask'd why he laugh'd? Perhaps you'll be affronted if I tell you, reply'd the countryman. No, he would not, he said. *Why then,* says he, I laugh to see how awkward they fire. *Why,* I'll be bound I hit it ten times running. Ah! will you, reply'd

---

From *The Nantucket Scrap Basket,* Being a Collection of Characteristic Stories and Sayings of the People of the Town and Island of Nantucket, Massachusetts, Second Edition, Revised, Expanded and Rearranged by William F. Macy, pp. 29–30. Copyright, 1916, by William F. Macy and Roland B. Hussey. Copyright, 1930, by William F. Macy. Boston and New York: Houghton Mifflin Company. 1930.

the officer; come try: Soldiers, go and bring five of the best guns, and load 'em for this honest man. Why, you need not bring so many: let me have any one that comes to hand, reply'd the other, but I chuse to load *myself*. He accordingly loaded, and ask'd the officer where he should fire? He reply'd, to the right—when he pull'd tricker, and drove the ball as near the right as possible. The officer was amaz'd—and said he could not do it again, as that was only by chance. He loaded again. Where shall I fire? *To the left*—when he perform'd as well as before. Come! once more, says the officer.—He prepar'd the third time.—Where shall I fire *naow?—In the Center.*—He took aim, and the ball went as exact in the middle as possible. The officers as well as soldiers *star'd,* and tho't the Devil was in the man. *Why,* says the countryman, I'll tell you *naow.* I have got a *boy* at home that will toss up an apple and shoot out all the seeds as it's coming down.[1]

The following dialogue on "sharp shooting" is reported to have taken place between a Virginee and a Yankee picket:—"I say, can you fellows shoot?" "Wall, I reckon we can some. Down in Mississippi we can knock a bumble-bee off a thistle bow at three hundred yards." "Oh, that ain't nothing to the way we seewt up in Varmount. I belonged to a military company ther', with a hundred men in the company, and we went out for practice every week. The capt'n draws us up in single file, and sets a cider-barrel rolling down the hill, and each man takes his shot at the bung-hole as it turns up. It is afterwards examined, and if there is a shot that didn't go in the bung-hole the number who missed it is expelled. I belonged to the company ten years, and there ain't been nobody expelled yet."

* * * * *

They have pretty good marksmen in Vermont. Brown was telling Smith, of New Hampshire, the skill of a Green Mountain hunter. "Why," said he, "I have seen him take two partridges and let them both go—one in front and the other behind him; and he would fire and kill the one in front, and then whirl round and kill the other." "Did he have a double-barrelled gun?" enquired Smith. "Of course he did." "Well," replied Smith, "I saw a man do the same thing with a single-barrel." Brown didn't believe the thing possible, and said so.[2]

It is said that Nicholas, one of the best gunners in the American navy, is son to a barber who formerly resided at Gay Head. His skill as a marks-

[1] From *Letters of John Andrews, Esq., of Boston, 1772–1776,* Compiled and Edited from the Original Mss., with an Introduction, by Winthrop Sargent, Reprinted from the Proceedings of the Massachusetts Historical Society, pp. 58–59. Cambridge: Press of John Wilson and Sons. 1866.

[2] From *The American Joe Miller:* A Collection of Yankee Wit and Humour, Compiled by Robert Kempt, pp. 1–2, 202. Entered at Stationer's Hall. London: Adams and Francis. 1865.

man is surprising. When about four years of age, he was awoke one night by a rat, who was leisurely gnawing his great toe, with as much gusto as though it was a piece of real old Dutch cheese. Young Nicholas cautiously took a loaded pistol from under his pillow, for even at that age the bent of his genius had become fully developed and fired at the rat, without rising from his recumbent posture. The pistol contained two buckshot only; but so true was the aim of the youngster, they both took effect, each one entering an eye of the rat, who fell dead upon the spot without a struggle.[3]

Three Foxes With One Stone

YET it were injustice not to mention the name of one no longer living, who became *celebrated in the chase.* I mean *Mr. Prosper Leffingwell,* a respected resident of this place, who, though he followed the humble occupation of hunting, yet became so expert, and enjoyed a reputation so widely extended, that I might deeply wound the feelings of all his now aged companions in the same profession, who revere him as a superior spirit, were I to omit to notice him in speaking of this town. 'Twere useless to attempt to detail all the events which marked the career of this famous sportsman. He was the terror of the *foxes* and *rabbits* for ten miles around. Many instances I might relate to illustrate the degree of skill to which he attained, but let one suffice. It is said that on one occasion, while returning home from hunting, he met *three foxes* advancing towards him "all in a row." As his gun was not loaded, he seized a stone and directed it as well as he was able in a straight line towards their heads. Wonderful to tell, he brought them all *down*! He gazed a moment in astonishment. He found he had struck the first in the nose, the second in the hip, and the third in the forehead—all with the same stone! The first was not quite dead, the second was badly lamed, but the third showed no signs of life whatever. While chasing the second, the first recovered and scampered away. Had he sprung upon them the moment he saw them fall, he might have secured all three.

---

[3] From *The Comic Token for 1835,* A Companion to the Comic Almanac, p. 30. Entered according to the Act of Congress in the year 1834, by Charles Ellms, Agent, in the Clerk's Office for the District Court of Massachusetts. Boston.

From *Connecticut Historical Collections,* Containing a General Collection of Interesting Facts, Traditions, Biographical Sketches, Anecdotes, &c., Relating to the History and Antiquities of Every Town in Connecticut, with Geographical Descriptions, by John Warner Barber, p. 432. Entered according to the Act of Congress, in the year 1836, by John W. Barber and A. Willard, in the Clerk's Office, of the District Court of Connecticut. New Haven and Hartford.

A Gone Coon

IN THE Western States, where the raccoon is plentiful, they use the abbreviation *'coon* when speaking of people. When at New York, I went into a hairdresser's shop to have my hair cut; there were two young men from the west—one under the barber's hands, the other standing by him.

"I say," said the one who was having his hair cut, "I hear Captain M—— is in this country."

"Yes," replied the other, "so they say; I should like to see the *'coon.*"

"I'm a *gone 'coon*" implies "I am distressed—*or* ruined—*or* lost." I once asked the origin of this expression, and was very gravely told as follows:—

There is a Captain Martin Scott in the United States army who is a remarkable shot with a rifle. He was raised, I believe, in Vermont. His fame was so considerable through the State, that even the animals were aware of it. He went out one morning with his rifle, and spying a raccoon upon the upper branches of a high tree, brought his gun up to his shoulder; when the raccoon, perceiving it, raised his paw up for a parley. "I beg your pardon, mister," said the raccoon, very politely; "but may I ask you if your name is *Scott?*"—"Yes," replied the captain.—"*Martin* Scott?" continued the raccoon.—"Yes," replied the captain.—"*Captain* Martin Scott?" still continued the animal.—"Yes," replied the captain, "Captain Martin Scott."—"Oh! then," says the animal, "I may just as well come down, for I'm a *gone 'coon.*"[1]

Col. Martin Scott, son of Phineas Scott, one of the early settlers of Bennington, was born here Jan. 18, 1788. His youth was spent on his father's farm during which he received only a common school education. He was fond of hunting from his boyhood and in early life became an expert and noted marksman. He was always accustomed to aim at the head of game, and considered it disgraceful to make a wound in the body. He would drive a nail into a board part way with a hammer, and then taking the farthest distance at which his eye could distinctly see it, drive it home with his unerring bullet. His skill with the rifle was such that he was excluded from the common sport of turkey shooting, no owner of a turkey being willing to risk his shot for any sum short of its full value.

In April 1814 he was appointed Second Lieutenant in the army, became Captain in 1828, and afterward rose to the rank of Lieutenant Colonel, always sustaining his character as a brave and active officer. From about

[1] From *A Diary in America*, with Remarks on Its Institutions, by Capt. [Frederick] Marryat, C. B., Vol. II, pp. 37–38. Entered according to the Act of Congress, in the year 1838, by F. Marryat, in the Clerk's Office of the District Court for the Eastern District of Pennsylvania. Philadelphia: Carey & Hart. 1839.

the year 1820 he was for 12 or 15 years stationed at Green Bay, Prairie du Chien, and other military posts on the Western frontier. Here he had great opportunities for indulging in his favorite amusement and became famous in all that region for his extraordinary success in the pursuit of all kinds of game. Like all hunters from Nimrod down he was fond of relating his field adventures, which he often did to the great entertainment of his hearers. One of his stories must be repeated here, though it loses much of its interest in attempting to put it on paper.

He said that many of the wild animals throughout the forests he had frequented had become so well acquainted with his skill as a marksman that they would surrender on being introduced to him, without requiring the waste of any powder, and that this was particularly the case with raccoons. When he discovered one on a tree he would hollo to it. "Coon come down!" to which the animal would say, "Who is that's calling me?" His answer would be, "I am Martin Scott." "What," the coon would inquire, "Captain Martin Scott of the army?" "Yes," would be the answer. "Well, Captain Scott," says the conquered animal, "you needn't fire, *I'm a gone Coon*, and may as well come down," and down he would come at once.[2]

The Double-Barreled Shotgun

Right down to this day I can't hardly think about gramp without remembering his account of the muzzle-loading, double-barreled shotgun he had when he was a young man. He said he figured on going hunting, so he put in two charges of powder. When he come to look for his shot, he found he'd used it all up, and he didn't want to take the trouble of getting out his bronze bullet mold and casting more. He scratched around in the shop and happened on a box of tacks. He shook some of the tacks into one barrel, but tacks was kind of scarce, too, and he didn't want to use them all. He saw an old broken jackknife lying around, and he just dropped that down the other barrel.

Then he took a turn around the woods, but he didn't see nothing. He walked right around the north pasture and up through the woodlot, and nary a sign of game. Finally he got disgusted and started home through the sugar bush.

And then right next to the sugarhouse, a rabbit set up on its hind legs

---

[2] From "Bennington," by Hon. Hiland Hall, in *The Vermont Historical Gazetteer: A Magazine, Embracing a History of Each Town, Civil, Ecclesiastical, Biographical and Military*, Edited by Abby Maria Hemenway, in Three Volumes, Vol. I, pp. 177–178. Entered according to Act of Congress, in the year 1859, by Abby Maria Hemenway, in the Clerk's Office of the District Court of the District of Vermont. Burlington, Vermont: Published by Miss A. M. Hemenway. 1867.

From "Grandpa Was Quite a Fellow," by Walter Needham, as recorded by Barrows Mussey, in *The Saturday Evening Post*, Vol. 219 (November 9, 1946), No. 19, p. 13. Copyright, 1946, by The Curtis Publishing Company. Springfield, Ohio.

and looked at him. He got ready to shoot, and just as the rabbit dropped down, he fired. He fired the barrel with the knife in it first. The knife was so heavy that it went low and split the rabbit's skin right down the middle. The skin flapped open and flew up just as he fired the other barrel, with the tacks. Those tacks spread the hide neat and tight on the back wall of the sugarhouse. . . .

The Crooked Gun

It is said that a man named Partridge had a gun with a crooked barrel for shooting around corners. He said humorously, "I could stand by my door and shoot a man behind the house, but I had to jump inside quick or it would get me from behind."

Hunter's Luck

A paper notorious for its veracity says "that a man in New Hampshire went out gunning one day this spring; he saw a flock of pigeons sitting on a branch of an old pine, so he dropped a ball into his gun and fired. The ball split the branch, which closed up, and caught the toes of all the birds in it. He saw that he had got them all, and so he fastened two balls together and fired, cut the branch off, which fell into the river. He then waded in and brought it on shore. On counting them there were 300 pigeons, and in his boots were two barrels of shad." [1]

The favorite boast of the hunters was that upon one occasion a young man saw twelve of these thieves [crows and blackbirds] sitting side by side on the branch of a large tree. Taking careful aim, he sent a charge of shot which split the bark of the branch lengthwise. The concussion widened the cleft for an instant, just long enough for the startled birds to spread their wings for flight, but closing quickly enough to make them prisoners, their toes being held firmly in the bark of the tree. The storyteller probably closed with the same statement as a former narrator, that he had not himself witnessed the sight.[2]

From Poland, Maine. Manuscripts of the Federal Writers' Project of the Works Progress Administration for the State of Maine.

[1] From *The American Joe Miller:* A Collection of Yankee Wit and Humour, Compiled by Robert Kempt, p. 104. Entered at Stationer's Hall. London: Adams and Francis. 1865.

[2] From *In Old South Hadley* by Sophie E. Eastman, p. 211. Copyright, 1912 by Sophie E. Eastman. Chicago: The Blakely Printing Company.

Singular Experiences

Two old fellows in a town around Keene give some singular "experiences." One of them was coming down a hill in winter on a bob-sled. Directly in his path was a barn with the door open at either end. A jolt threw him off the sled, and he sailed over the barn roof, to come down on the sled as it appeared on the snow after coming through the barn.

Another was fishing in the mountains and took five hundred trout, each tipping the scales at one pound each. He shouldered them and came down the mountain side, sinking to his knees at every step in the granite ledge.[1]

A farmer went out to drive in his young cattle one fall afternoon when it was beginning to snow. He thought he had a very difficult time to get them into the barnyard and it was after dark before he had succeeded. When he went out later with a lantern, he discovered that he had rounded up two deer which had apparently been on good terms with the cattle and feeding with them.

At the old general store the teller of a good story was always welcome. One time a man told of coming across a young deer that was lying down and how he grabbed it by its tail in an endeavor to capture it. He held on all right until the deer jumped a fence and kicked him in the stomach and then he was forced to let go and lost the deer.

Another night at the store one of the men told very solemnly how he had moved a large set of buildings on only two cartloads with his fine oxen. Another man gave the rest of the crowd the wink and said, "Why, I can vouch for that. It's absolutely true. I moved the cellar myself, walls and all and only used my light pair of horses." The first man left the company in high rage to think that his story was made sport of and not believed.[2]

Old Town Tall Tales

The Cat with the Wooden Leg

THERE was a trapper used to live out back here in the woods, and every winter he set a lot of traps. He had a tiger cat that used to follow him around and that cat got to be such a good hunter that he was able to get

[1] From "Keene," by Ola G. Veazie. Manuscripts of the Federal Writers' Project of the Works Progress Administration for the State of New Hampshire.

[2] From "Monroe," by Ola G. Veazie. Manuscripts of the Federal Writers' Project of the Works Progress Administration for the State of New Hampshire.

As told by Mike Pelletier, Old Town, Maine. Manuscripts of the Federal Writers' Project of the Works Progress Administration for the State of Maine.

all his food out in the woods. The trapper didn't have to feed him at all, in fact the cat got so that it wouldn't eat anything unless it killed it himself. One day the cat was out huntin' all alone and he got one of his front paws caught in a trap. When the trapper found him the paw was half chewed off and he got the cat out of the trap and took it home. That paw was so bad that the man had to cut it off. It healed all right, but the cat kept gettin' thinner because it couldn't enjoy the food the trapper gave it. By and by the man said, "I'll have to do something or I'll lose that cat sure," so he got a little piece of cedar and whittled out a wooden leg for the cat and he tacked some leather on the little piece of wood to make a socket to fit on the stump of the cat's leg. He made leather straps to go around the cat's body to hold the leg in place. Well, when the cat first got that wooden leg on it used to shake its paw tryin' to get the thing off, but by and by it got used to it and the cat got so it could prance around in great style. As soon as it got so it could run real well it started goin' out into the woods again to look for game. The trapper knew the cat was gettin' it, too, because it started to fatten up. That fellow got kind of interested so one day he followed the cat out to see how it managed with that wooden leg, and he saw the cat creep up on something and grab it with one paw and hit it over the head with that wooden leg.

Bringing in the Bear

There was another about a fellow that invited a couple of friends of his from New York to come up and learn something about bear huntin'. The three of them got out in the woods and this fellow told his friends that he'd go ahead and do a little scoutin'. By and by they saw their guide comin' tearin' through the woods with a bear after him. "Get out of the way, boys," the fellow hollered. "I'm takin' this one back to the camp alive."

Tagging a Deer

There was a fourteen-year-old boy shot a deer over here in Milford a few years ago. Now this story is really true: I know myself, it's a fact. This boy's father taught him to always tag a deer he shot so that no one else could claim it. Well, when the boy shot this deer he slipped his tag on to the deer's horns, but when he was turned the other way for a minute the deer jumped up and made off. Sometimes, you know, when a deer is hit it'll drop, but it's apt to get up and run away if it's able to. That deer got out of sight before the boy got over his surprise, but the boy started to follow along the tracks in the hope of catchin' up. By and by he heard a shot ahead and when he got up there he found two men skinnin' his deer.

He told the men that the deer belonged to him, and to prove it he showed them the tag on the deer's horns. One of the men looked at the tag and says, "All right, boy, the deer is yours. Anybody that can tag a deer that was goin' as fast as that one was when we saw it certainly deserves the animal."

Tying a Knot in a Panther's Tail

. . . We was go huntin' for deer. Ah guess so, an' da was leetly mite snow on de graoun'. Wal seh, we'll see it track, we ant know what he was be, an' we'll folla dat, oh, long, long tam. Bamby he'll go in hole in rock, leetly laidge, you know, 'baout tree, fo', prob'ly seex tam big dis shantee was. Wal, seh, boy, Ah'll left it ma brudder-law for watch dat holes, an' Ah'll go 'raoun' back side laidge see all what Ah'll see. Ah'll look veree caffly, an' what you tink Ah'll fin' it? Leetly crack in rock 'baout so wide ma tree finger of it, an' dat panter hees tail steek off of it 'baout so long ma arm, prob'ly, where he'll push hind fust in dat holes. An' he'll weegly hees tail so (waving his forefinger slowly). Wal, Ah'll tink for spell what Ah do. Den Ah'll go cut off strong steek so big half ma wris' and two foots long. Den Ah'll tek hol' dat tails an' tied knot in him, veree caffly, den Ah'll run steek t'rough an' pull knot hard! Oh, bah gosh! you'll oughty hear dat panters yaller an' holla! Wus as fo' honded tousan' cat! Yes, seh! Oh, he'll hugly, Ah tol' you! but he can' help it, he can' gat it loose 'less he pull up hees tails off. Wal, seh, Ah'll lafft at it, Ah can' help it, mos' Ah'll split off ma side. Den Ah'll go 'raoun' ma brudder-law, an' he'll be scare mos' dead, an' goin' runned way. Ah'll tol' heem, Ah goin' in dat holes shoot dat panters. "Oh, gosh!" he'll ax me, "he tore you dead more as forty piece!" Ah'll say, "Ah so good man Ah'll don't 'fraid me." Den Ah'll crawl in dat holes an' Ah'll shoot it, boom! raght 'tween hees head! An' bamby pooty soon he ant yaller some more, be all still as mices. Den Ah'll come off de holes an' Ah'll tol' ma brudder-law he'll crawl in an' pull off dat panters. He'll pooty 'fraid for go, but bamby he go. He touch hol' of it, he can' pull it cause hees tail tie, but he ant know. "Bah gosh!" he say, "dat panters more heavy as two ton! Ah can' pull it!" Den Ah'll go 'raoun' an' taked off dat steek, an' holla "pull!" an' ma brudder-law pull more harder he can—boom! he go tumbly on hees back, dat panters on top of it! Oh! 'f he ant scare, ma brudder-law. Yas seh! Wal, seh, boy . . . 'f you ant mek b'lieve dat stories you go Canada 'long to me Ah show you de steek. Ma brudder-law he'll saved it. Ah ant never tol' you stories so true lak dat, seh!

From *Sam Lovel's Camps,* Uncle Lisha's Friends under Bark and Canvas, A Sequel to Uncle Lisha's Shop, by Rowland E. Robinson, pp. 65–66. Copyright, 1889, by Forest and Stream Publishing Co. New York. 1899.

Duck Hunting Yarn

HAD pretty good hunting along about this time last year. 'Twas up at Cold Pond, over Tioga way. Folks sure knew what they was talking about when they named that place, Cold Pond, sure gets cold there, early too. It must have been about the first of November as I remember. That morning I had found a thin crust of ice on the watering trough in my barnyard when I led Dol out to drink.

Well, it was getting along towards nightfall, and I had been all over that god-forsaken section, clean from the Banty Place I had walked, across the swamp lands, and swinging across the side of Ragged Mountain. I was heading back to where I had started from, coming back by way of the old road that leads past this here Cold Pond. I figgered it would be shorter, and the sun was going down behind Forbes.

Hadn't shot a thing all day except a couple of "hogs"—figgered that their noses would pay for a couple boxes of shot. Well, as I was going to say, I was passing along the edge of the pond, sort of in the alders and brush when I heard a commotion. Hadn't been paying much attention to what was going on around me, was just moseying along towards home. I looked out onto the water and there was a whole flock of ducks; big fat ones, must have been nigh two hundred of them, maybe more. It was getting dusky, and they had settled for the night. 'Twas mighty cold up thereabouts, too.

I histed up my gun and took a pot shot, right into the middle of them. They looked fat and good, and I just didn't want to go home with nothing to show for my trouble. There was an awful quacking and squalling among them birds, but not a one flew off—I couldn't rightly figure out why they didn't get out of there quicker than scat.

Well, sir, to make a long story short I found that them there birds had been frozen into the ice that had formed over the northern part of the pond where they had lit. There warn't no ice near the edge of shore, but right over the deepest part, where it is so deep that no man has ever been able to plumb the bottom, the ice had formed several inches thick. I figger they must have been there since the night before, but of course, maybe the ice may have formed that night since the sun left Cold Pond. Mighty chilly place up there you know.

I climbed into a boat that some fishermen had left on the shore and rowed out to that ice patch. I kinda wanted to see if I had shot any of them ducks, and if I hadn't gotten any, why, I could walk around on the ice, wring a few necks, and cut my legal limit of birds out of the ice. But I didn't figure on how scared them ducks would be when I walked into the middle of them.

By Harry E. Flanders. Manuscripts of the Federal Writers' Project of the Works Progress Administration for the State of New Hampshire.

They put up the gol-durndest hullaballoo you ever heard and started to flap their wings real excited like. I was about in the middle of the ice cake then and the whole kit and kaboodle of them was a flapping and a quacking —they made quite a wind with their threshing around like that.

I was some surprised, now let me tell you, when that cake of ice began to lift out of the water. There were so many ducks frozen into the ice that when they got to flapping their wings, all together, they lifted the ice plumb off the pond, and the next thing I knew there I was, in the middle of a bunch of ducks, sailing over the trees. Right over Ragged Mountain and Kearsarge we went, them gol-durned birds flapping their wings to beat sixty.

Scairt? Hell no! I always had wanted to fly around up in the air and see what it was going to feel like to go to heaven, but just never had gotten around to it, and here was my chance to see what things looked like from up in the air.

Course I could have wrung their necks, one by one, and let myself down to earth again, easy like, but I was beginning to enjoy myself now. Course the ice was kind of cold, but I ain't one to ask for everything. They headed south, and we just kept on flying until the ice melted from the heat of the sun.

The Green Duck Hunter and the Live Decoys

If one can get the market gunner of yesterday talking, he will tell you many stories of the city greenhorn and his performances alongshore or on the marshes. He will enjoy telling them, too, and his sulphurous comments are as interesting as the yarns themselves. Here is one.

The hero was a young fellow who came to the village in the duck season. He was not equipped for the sport, but he overcame that obstacle by borrowing a gunning float, a gun and one live decoy duck. They told him where, at the marshy edge of one of the inlets, he might find game. He rowed to that spot, put on his lone decoy, anchored his float and prepared for slaughter. The decoy was what the townsman who had lent it to him called a "first-class quacker." The decoy quacked and swam about and the gunner crouched and shivered and waited.

His wait was not a long one. In from the sea and down toward him swooped a tremendous flock of wild fowl. It was such a huge flock that, in his frenzy of excitement, he forgot to take aim, but blazed away in the direction of everything in general. The wild fowl clamorously soared to safety, but the gunner, peeping out over the edge of his float, was thrilled by the sight of a dead duck. He had actually killed something with his very first shot. He had, but it was the decoy he had borrowed. The "first-class quacker" was noisy no longer, but its owner was talkative later on.

Jotham Stories

"My grandfather," says Jotham, "was a great hunter. On stormy days like this he would take down his old long, single-barrelled gun and go out and bring home all kinds of game, mostly ducks and geese. In his day the ducks and geese bred around here and you could get 'em any time, but the best shooting was in the early fall on a northeaster. The heavy waves down on the coast drive the birds out of their feeding grounds and they come up to the fresh-water ponds inland to drink and get a change of feed. It is the same way with the shore birds, yellow-legs and plover and the like, though in my grandfather's day they didn't care much about such small game. Bigger birds were plenty enough. Grandfather used to hate yellow-legs, though, for they are telltales.

"Once he went over to Muddy Pond loaded for duck. It is a great place for ducks. In those days they used to come in there and sometimes pack it solid full. You could hardly see the pond for the ducks in it. Grandfather always knew just the right day to go, and this time when he looked down on the pond from the hill he saw hardly any water at all, nothing much but ducks. It was the chance of his life. He slipped down the hill among the scrubs to the cedars and then began to creep carefully up. You know what the pond is like, perfectly round and only a couple of acres or so, with a rim of marsh and then another big rim of swamp cedars, then the hills all about, neither inlet nor outlet; a queer pond anyway, and queer things happen on it, same as they did that day. Grandfather had got half way through the swamp cedars when he came to a little opening which he had to cross. Just then there came up on the east wind a big flock of telltales, 762 of them, whirling over the hills without a sound till they saw him. Then they began to yelp."

"Look here, Jotham," I am always careful to say at this point, "how could he tell that there were just 762 of them? He couldn't count so many as they flew."

"Didn't have to count 'em as they flew," answers Jotham. "He counted 'em after he had shot 'em.

"Well, they began to yelp 'Look out for him! Look out for him!' and the ducks knew what that meant. All that great blanket of ducks uncovered the pond with one motion. Grandfather said it was just like a curtain rising straight up, for they were all black ducks. There is no other duck can go straight up in the air. Other ducks slide off on a slant against the wind."

How Jotham manages to put the lonely quaver of the yellow-leg's call into that phrase "Look out for him! Look out for him!" with its four-note repetition is more than I know, but he always does, and you can see the big flock swing through the mist as he says it.

From *Old Plymouth Trails*, by Winthrop Packard, pp. 204–213. Boston: Small, Maynard & Company, Publishers.

"Grandfather was pretty mad to lose that chance at good game and he made up his mind that he'd take it out of the telltales, so he began to whistle 'em back. He was a master hand at any wild call and pretty soon he lit the flock. There they were, a rim of yellow-legs all around the pond, a perfect circle except in one place, where some dogwood bushes made down to the water's edge. Then granddad had a great idea. He saw his chance to kill every one of those infernal telltales where they sat. He studied on the size of that circle for a minute. Then he put the long barrel of that old gun between two swamp cedar stumps and bent on it carefully. He kept doing this, looking at the circle, then bending the gun barrel till he had the gun bent just on the curve of the circle of yellow-legs sitting round the pond. Then he smiled for he knew he had 'em. He crept carefully into the dogwood bushes till he was in just the right place, took a good aim round that circle, and then he onlatched on 'em.

"Well, he'd figured that circle just right. The shot swung round it and killed every one of them seven hundred and sixty-two yellow-legs right where they stood. But tarnation; he'd forgotten all about himself, he was so interested in the science of it. The back of his neck was right in that circle and the shot came round true as could be and hit him right there. The force of it was pretty well spent going so far and killing so many yellow-legs, but it dented some bits of dogwood leaves right into his system and he had dogwood poisoning pretty bad. He used to have it every year after that, about the time the first northeaster set in."

Anybody who knows Muddy Pond will know that Jotham's story ought to be true, for the pond is there to prove it, just as he describes it.

"Of course," says Jotham at this point, "that was skill. Not one hunter in a hundred would have thought to bend his gun so as to throw the shot in a circle or would have been able to estimate the amount of the curve so exactly right. Another thing happened to my grandfather over at that pond that was part skill and part luck. He was on his way home from partridge shooting one day just before Thanksgiving. He found he was out of shot just before he got to the pond. His flask had leaked and let every bit of the shot out, and when he came to load up after shooting his last partridge he stopped with the powder, for there was no shot to put in. Just then he came in sight of the pond and there were seven geese swimming round in it; and that the day before Thanksgiving!

"It was a tough time to be without any shot, but grandfather was equal to the emergency. He simply left his ramrod right in the gun, put on a cap, and began to worm his way through the cedars to the shore, where he could get a good, close shot at the geese. Just as he did this another hunter who was no kind of a shot, came to the other side of the pond and saw the birds. He was one of the kind that have the buck fever at the sight of game, and he put up his gun and shot slam at the flock, too far away to do any execution, then he let out a yell and began to run down to the shore as fast as he could go.

"Of course he scared the geese and they lit out, swinging right by grandfather. Grandfather was a nervy hunter. He held his fire till he got the heads of those seven geese right in line, and then he shot and strung 'em all right through the eyes with the ramrod. Granddad couldn't quite see where he had hit 'em, but when the smoke cleared away he saw the seven geese still flying and his ramrod going off with 'em, and he was some considerable astonished and a good deal put about at losing his ramrod.

"Now here's the queer part of it: Those seven geese were blinded, of course, with a ramrod strung right through their eyes, but the life in a wild goose is powerful strong and they kept on flying just the same, until they went out of sight, right in the direction of granddad's home. But he got home and had hung up his gun without seeing anything more of them and he thought his ramrod was sure gone for good. Then grandmother came to him, kind of scared, saying she heard spirit rappings on the pantry wall. Granddad heard the noise, a sort of tapping, but he couldn't see anything until he looked out the pantry window.

"Yes, there they were seven of 'em, hung on the ramrod and the ramrod hung on a blind-hook, just outside granddad's pantry window, their wings still flapping a little and making that rapping sound, just as if they were knocking to be let in at the pantry of the man that had shot 'em. All the relations used to come to grandfather's for Thanksgiving, and thirty-five of 'em sat down to dinner that year and every one of 'em had all the roast goose they could eat."

Frightened or injured game birds do perform strange feats as many an honest huntsman will tell you. I myself have a neighbor, no relative of Jotham's who shot at a partridge in the woods a quarter of a mile from his house and saw the bird fly away. When he got home a half-hour later he found his pantry window broken and a partridge lying dead on the pantry floor, either the one he had shot at or another just as good—and as the proverb has it, one story is good until another one is told. Jotham usually caps his list with the following:

"I guess the greatest wild goose hunting grandfather ever did was the time the big flock got caught in the ice storm. It came in November, a foot of soft snow and then one of those rainstorms that freeze as soon as the rain touches anything. Every twig on the trees that storm was as big as your wrist with ice and there was an inch or two of clear ice on everything and more coming all the time, when grandfather heard a big flock of wild geese honking. They didn't seem to be going over, but their voices hung in the air right over the big steep hill from the barn up into the back pasture. After they'd been honking up there for some time grandfather went up to see what it was all about, but he didn't take his gun. As he climbed the hill through the wet snow he heard 'em plainer and plainer, and when he got to the top he saw a most 'strodinary sight. There was a good-sized flock, ninety-seven geese, to be exact, that had got so iced up that they had to settle on the top of the hill.

"The ice had formed on their feathers as they flew and they were so weighted down they couldn't fly and they were getting more and more iced up every minute. Granddad didn't care to go back for his gun for fear some of the other nimrods in the neighborhood would come on the scene and bag the game first, but there wasn't any need of a gun. All he had to do was to drive 'em home. They were terribly iced up, but their legs were still free and he chased 'em about for some time before he got 'em started down hill. But once over the edge of the hill the weight of the ice on 'em turned 'em right over and over, and so they rolled on down. It was a wet snow and as they rolled they took up more and more of it till by the time they came slap up against the side of the barn every single goose was sealed up in the middle of a hard, round snowball. They all stopped there and all that grandfather had to do was to pile them up, and there they were, in cold storage for the winter. Every time the family wanted roast goose they went out and split open a snowball. The folks in granddad's time used often to freeze their fresh meat and keep it out in the snow all winter, but he was the only one that I ever heard of that stored wild geese in that way."

FISHERMAN'S LUCK

Grant's Tame Trout

THE sage of Beaver Camp sat sunning himself on the bench beside the cook camp, the bench so widely known as the scene of countless weary hours of that perpetual toiler. He seemed to be smoking an old black pipe, whereas he was only dropping matches into its empty bowl at intervals of three minutes, agreeable to the terms of his contract with the American Match trust.

As he so sat and pondered, the writer, at the time a recent arrival, approached and said: "Mr. Grant, I wish you would give me the true history of your wonderful success in taming a trout. I have heard of it in all parts of the world but I have always longed to hear the story direct from headquarters."

"Well, it really ain't so much of a story," replied the famous chronicler. "It was this way. Nine year ago the eleventh day of last June, I was fishin' out there in the pads, and right under that third yaller leaf to the right of the channel—yes, that one with the rip in it—I ketched a trout 'bout six inches long. I never see a more intelligent lookin' little feller—

From "The Tame Trout," by Samuel T. Farquhar, *California Folklore Quarterly*, Vol. III (July, 1944), No. 3, pp. 177–178. Copyright, 1944, by the California Folklore Society. Berkeley and Los Angeles: Published for the California Folklore Society by the University of California Press. Reprinted from *The Tame Trout and Other Fairy Tales,* narrated by Ed Grant of Beaver Pond, Maine, chronicled by Francis I. Maule of Philadelphia. Phillips: Maine Woods and Woodsman Print. 1904.

high forehead, smooth face, round, dimpled chin, and a most uncommon bright, sparkling, knowin' eye.

"I always allowed that with patience and cunning a real young trout (when they gets to a heft of 10 or 15 pounds there ain't no teachin' them nothin') could be tamed jest like a dog or cat.

"There was a little water in the boat and he swims around in it all right till I goes ashore and then I gets a tub we had, made of the half of a pork barrel, fills it with water and bores a little small hole through the side close down to the bottom and stops the hole with a peg.

"I sets this tub away back in a dark corner of the camp and every night after the little fellow gets asleep I slip in, in my stockin' feet, and pulls out the peg softly and lets out jest a little mite of the water. I does this night after night so mighty sly that the little chap never suspected nothin' and he was a-livin' hale and hearty for three weeks on the bottom of that tub as dry as a cook stove, and then I knowed he was fit for trainin'.

"So I took him out o' doors and let him wiggle awhile on the path and soon got to feedin' him out of my hand. Pretty soon after that when I walked somewhat slow (I'm naturally quite a slow walker some folks think) he could follow me right good all round the clearin', but sometimes his fins did get ketched up in the brush jest a mite and I had to go back and swamp out a little trail for him; bein' a trout, of course he could easy follow a spotted line.

"Well, as time went on, he got to follerin' me most everywhere and hardly ever lost sight of me, and me and him was great friends, sure enough.

"Near about sundown one evening, I went out to the spring back of the camp, same one as you cross goin' to Little Island, to get some butter out of a pail, and, of course, he comes trottin' along behind. There was no wind that night, I remember, and I could hear his poor little fins a-raspin' on the chips where we'd been gettin' out splits in the cedar swamp. Well, sir, he follered me close up and came out onto the logs across the brook and jest as I was a-stoopin' down over the pail I heard a kee-plunk! behind me and Gorry! if he hadn't slipped through a chink between them logs and was drowned before my very eyes before I could reach him, so he was." Here a tear started from the good old man's eye on a very dusty trip down his time-stained cheek.

"Of course I was terrible cut up at first—I couldn't do a stroke of work for three weeks—but I got to thinkin' that as it was comin' on cold (it was in late November then) and snow would soon be here and he, poor little cuss, wasn't rugged enough for snow-shoein' and he couldn't foller me afoot all winter no how, and as he couldn't live without me, mebby it was jest as well after all he was took off that way. Do you know, Mister, some folks around here don't believe a word of this, but if you'll come down to the spring with me, right now, I'll show you the very identical chink he dropped through that night, so I will. I've never allowed anyone to move it. No, sir! nor I never will."

Here the old man dropped match number thirty-seven[1] into his pipe and sucked at it hard in silence, while I crept softly away on tiptoes. I never could bring myself to speak of it again, after seeing him so deeply moved—I never could.

Catching Trout by Tickling

THE biggest trout I ever caught was in the month of March, many years ago, just after the old Peace Dale milldam was carried away in a freshet. As I was sauntering along the bank of the Saucatucket river, some ten or fifteen rods below the dam, I saw a big speckled trout side of a rock, and I just thought I would try the English method of catching trout where the water is cold, by tickling! So I just put my hand down slily behind the tail of the fish, and making a sort of half-moon or rather crescent with my fingers and palm, I carried my hand beneath him and manipulated him gently with the tips of my fingers. Whether it was the warmth of my fingers, or what, I don't know, but the trout did not move otherwise than to rise gradually to the surface of the water, my hand following him all the while, with the ends of my fingers occasionally gently tickling him, until he got his back almost out of water, when with a sudden jerk I landed him on the bank. I took him home and found he just turned the steelyards at three pounds and one-half.

The Mink Story

ON A Maine Lake famous for its sporty landlocked salmon, I often listened with my son to the yarns of our guide. Charlie, sparsely built man, past middle age, a great tobacco-chewer and a first-class guide, was a good companion. Perhaps for the boy's edification he told this story.

One day, something that was said about animal life in the vicinity of Grand Lake Stream gave Charlie a lead which he promptly followed.

[1] Ed Grant's regular allowance is one pound of tobacco to each gross of matches used.—S. T. F.

From *The Jonny-Cake Papers of "Shepherd Tom,"* Together With Reminiscences of Narragansett Schools of Former Days, by Thomas Robinson Hazard, With a Biographical Sketch and Notes by Rowland Gibson Hazard, pp. 356–357. Copyright, 1915, by Rowland G. Hazard. Boston: Printed for the Subscribers.

By Charles E. Goodspeed. From *A Treasury of Fishing Stories,* compiled by Charles E. Goodspeed, pp. 391–393. Copyright, 1946, by A. S. Barnes and Company, Inc. New York. Originally printed, in a slightly different version, in *Angling in America,* Its Early History and Literature, by Charles Eliot Goodspeed, pp. 321–322. Copyright, 1939, by Charles E. Goodspeed. Boston: Houghton Mifflin Company.

"Did I ever tell you," he said, a far-away look in his eyes indicating that his powers of imagination were at work—"did I ever tell you the funny thing that happened to me last summer?

"Along the middle uv May," he began, "I'd been up the lake to see if there wuz any loose logs floatin' round in Sobsen's Bay. About the middle uv the afternoon it begun to rain real hard so I paddled ashore, got under a spruce near the head uv a cove nigh where a little brook come into the lake, an' set down an' filled my pipe fur a smoke. By'n' by, seein' trout wuz risin' towards the mouth uv the brook, I set up my rod an' put on a couple uv flies—a Silver Doctor and for the dropper a new one that I tied myself. The fish warn't much for size—most half-pounders—a few wuz bigger.

"They come along pretty good and when I took one off the hook I'd throw him back into the stern. As I stood up an' started to shove off when it stopped rainin', I looked round but there warn't a single fish in the canoe! Not one!

"I wuz stumped for sure," Charlie said, ejecting a quid into the water and taking out his knife to cut off a fresh chew. "Where in tophet hed them trout gone? It bothered me, for they warn't big enough to flop overboard themselves, and anyway I would hev heered 'em. I looked 'round but couldn't see nothin', so I set down and lighted my pipe ag'in, to think it over. Arter a while I begun to fish some more. The fust trout I lost. The next one wuz a little feller that I hedn't orter've kept but I wanted to see what in heck wuz up so I throwed him behind me in the canoe jest the way I had been doin' before. I kep' kinder quiet, didn't look back, but kep' on fishin' till I got a couple more. When I'd throwed the last one up along with the others I turned round a little so I could see what wuz goin' on, but keepin' quiet and not makin' no noise. What do you s'pose I saw? A brown head with little shiny eyes and bristlin' whiskers come up over the side uv the canoe! It wuz a mink! When he saw me he dodged back quick. I kep' still, didn't move none, and in less'n a minute Mister Mink's head popped up ag'in. Then all to onct his neck and shoulders come over th' edge an' before you could say 'scat' he picked up one uv them trout in his mouth an' wuz off like a flash. I waited and it warn't long before he come back for the other fish. This time I turned way round an' watched him, but he didn't go fur. There wuz a rotten birch stump under the trees 'bout ten foot off, an' the mink hed dug out a hole under it. When I looked in it, thar wuz eight nice trout lyin' side by side, the big ones underneath, jest as neat as my old woman'd lay 'em on a dish.

"Now," said Charlie, "here's what happened. Fust I counted them trout to see if they wuz all there. One wuz missin', so I looked round, but not seein' him nowheres, I picked the rest up out uv the hole where they wuz and went back to the canoe. Jest as I wuz goin' to step in I happened to look down, and that missin' trout wuz lyin' right on the ground. I a'most stepped on it. He wuz jest where the mink dropped him when he saw how small he wuz."

Charlie paused for a reminiscent chuckle.

"A mighty cute one that mink wuz. The little trout warn't more'n seven inches an' the mink had tried to cover him up with leaves."

Again Charlie stopped, this time to avoid what promised to be a lame conclusion of his story. "An' mebbe," he meditatively said, "mebbe that mink thought I wuz a game-ward'n!"

Why I Never Shoot Bears

Fred Jennes, veteran woods guide of Greenville, Maine, tells this tall tale and swears by all the Bibles in Piscataquis county that it is gospel truth:

"Do you know why I don't kill bears?" he asked. "No! Well, it's this way. Three years ago this June I was on a fishing trip up to Grand Lake. I had been out on the water pretty nearly all of one day and, getting tired, paddled back to camp. I hauled the canoe up on the sandy beach and started for the shack.

"When I got within about 100 feet of the place I saw the front door was open. I peeked in. There stood a big black bear just pulling the cork out of my molasses jug with his teeth. Out came the sticky syrup all over the floor. Bruin lapped up some of it and then rubbed his right paw into the rest—smeared it all over.

"So I crept around behind the camp, stuck my head in the window and yelled. He shot through the door like a bullet and headed for the lake. I never saw such an odd gait on a bear before—sort of mixture of running and galloping. And all on three legs. He was holding up the paw daubed with molasses.

"From where I stood it looked as if the critter had sat down on the shore and was holding his sweetened paw up to the air. It was June and the air was full of flies, mosquitoes and black midges. I could see that they were swarming around that molasses foot. Soon it was covered with flies feasting on that stuff.

"Suddenly he waded out in the water and stood up. He was in to his shoulders. He placed the sweetened paw down close to the surface and the next thing I saw a fine trout jump clear of the water at those flies.

"Every time a fish leaped clear of the water, Bruin would give it a cuff that sent it ashore and far up the beach.

"Finally as he saw the pile of trout on the sand he seemed to think he had enough. He waded ashore lapping off the insects and I expected he would sit down and gobble every fish. I recalled that all I had caught that day was two small fish.

"Well, sir, he had a fine feed, and when he had eaten half a dozen fine big trout, he paused, looked over at the bushes where I was and actually

---

From the *Boston Traveler*, June 1, 1938. Reprinted in *Angling in America*, Its Early History and Literature, by Charles Eliot Goodspeed, pp. 323–324. Copyright, 1939, by Charles E. Goodspeed. Boston: Houghton Mifflin Company.

laid the remaining fish in a row. Then he ambled off up the shore and oddly enough kept looking back over his shoulder.

"I walked down to the beach and true enough there were half a dozen wonderful trout. At the edge of the woods the bear stopped and was standing up. As loud as I could, I yelled, 'Thanks old man!' Do you know he actually waved a paw at me and dove into the thicket. I honestly think he left me those fish to pay for my spilled molasses. No, *sir*, I never shoot bears."

The Frozen Bass

I MAY here say that the day preceding the great fire in New York in 1835 (that consumed more than half the business portion of the city) was as warm as a half-heated baker's oven, while the night of the fire that followed was the coldest that had been known for years, in fact, so cold that the water froze solid in the hose of the fire engines. On that warm day the bass had entered the breach that leads to the sea at the southern extremity of the Salt pond, in countless myriads, and the wind being southerly and both weather and water unusually warm, the immense school of fish stopped overnight near the surface of the water, doubtless meaning to settle down into their deep winter quarters the next day. But early in the night the wind suddenly chopped round to the northwest and brought with it such an unheard-of low temperature that the lake was converted almost in an instant into a sheet of ice some foot and more in thickness, holding in its embrace nearly all of the striped bass that had entered the pond on the day before. A day or two after this I went down upon the pond and saw scores upon scores of men cutting out the bass with chopping axes. They had already piled up hundreds of thousands to all appearance in heaps as big as small hay-stacks. The whole surface of the lake looked like a huge piece of Mosaic thickly inlaid with frozen bass weighing two or three to twenty or more pounds each. New York and other markets were bountifully supplied with the finest fish from this source for weeks afterwards. . . .

Walking on Fish

AS THE evening waned, the stories grew more and more improbable, till the climax was reached when some ancient fisherman told how his grand-

---

From *The Jonny-Cake Papers of "Shepherd Tom,"* Together with Reminiscences of Narragansett Schools of Former Days, by Thomas Robinson Hazard, With a Biographical Sketch and Notes by Rowland Gibson Hazard, pp. 309–310. Copyright, 1915, by Rowland G. Hazard. Boston: Printed for the Subscribers.

From *In Old South Hadley* by Sophie E. Eastman, p. 211. Copyright, 1912 by Sophie E. Eastman. Chicago: The Blakely Printing Company.

father said that in Revolutionary days the shad were so thick in the river during the month of May that one day, wishing to cross to the island, and not being able to find a boat, he borrowed a pair of snow shoes and walked safely over upon the backs of the fishes.

Too Many Fish

. . . GREAT many tam, but one teekly tam Ah 'll go feeshins an' Ah 'll trow meh hook wid nice waum on it an' de traout was so hongry in hees belly an' so crazy in hees head dey 'll go after it so fas', de fus one git it, de nex' one touch hol' hees mouf of dat one's tail an' de nex' de sem way till dey was twenty prob' ly 'f dey ant fifteen all in string, an' Ah 'll pull it mos' so hard Ah 'll can't, an' seh, Ah 'll gat all of it honly de middlin' one was kan o' slimber, an' broke off, so Ah 'll loss de hine en' of de row. . . . W'en de traout in de water see where Ah 'll sot mah deesh of waum on de bank, he 'll beegin jomp on de bank for gat it, an' tumble top of herself for gat it. Den seh, Onc' Lasha, Ah 'll peek up mah deesh an' shook it, an' holly "caday, caday," an' dat traouts folla me home so fas' Ah 'll had to run an' shut de door for keep it from feel up de haouse.

Wal, oncet aout West, where I was in Westconstant, the' was a man went an' chopped a hole in the ice in a crik tu water his cattle, an' there was a dozen bullpaouts come up in the hole, an' he begin a-heavin' on 'em aout tu kerry 'em hum fer his dinner, but, fust he knowed, it filled up full, an' he run tu git a bushel baskit tu scoop 'em up, an' when he got back the hole was a-runnin' over wi' fish, jest a-b'ilin' over on t' the ice, an' kep' a-duin' so till they run over on t' the shore furder an' furder, till he begun tu be afeared they'd kiver up his farm an' spile it. But the folks begin tu hear on 't an' come wi' their teams f'm twenty mild off, an' hauled the bullpaouts away in reg'lar percessions, thirty forty sled-loads in a string, an' fed 'em to the' hawgs, an' m'nured the' land wi' them, till folks did n't know whether they was eatin' pork or fish, on'y fer bein' no bones, an' the hull country smelt like a fish kittle all summer.

Big Toe, Big Bass

THE old men of the last generation loved to tell about the long noonings between meetings when they were boys. There were always men who had

---

From *Danvis Folks*, by Rowland E. Robinson, pp. 263–264, 264–265. Copyright, 1894, by Rowland E. Robinson. Boston and New York: Houghton Mifflin Company.

From *Truro—Cape Cod, or Land Marks and Sea Marks*, by Shebnah Rich, pp. 255–256. Copyright, 1883, by D. Lothrop and Company. Boston.

the gift of story-telling. Perhaps some of their relations would be termed in these modern days "fish stories." Old Hutta Dyer had the reputation of being the Prince of Yarners. Whenever he seated himself to smoke his pipe, whether under the trees or the sheds, there the boys gathered also. It is doubtful if the Grecian youth listened more attentively to the wisdom of Socrates and Laches, or the sublime contemplations of Plato, than the young men and boys attending these weekly orations. It is a tradition of old Hutta, that while fishing for bass from the shore at the back side, having hard luck, he half-hitched his line around his great toe, and lay down on the soft sand. With the gentle lullaby of the rippling waves in his ears he fell asleep, but was very suddenly awakened by being dragged feet-first into the surf. An immense strain on the line half-hitched around his great toe kept his long leg as stiff as a handspike, whatever became of the rest of his body. It seemed a mile to that fatal line, and a physical impossibility to find the end of his leg. But it was not a time of much deliberation; with almost superhuman effort, he recovered the line, and landed upon the sand an immense squid-hound bass of sixty pounds. This species are now often caught from the shore; they are *alive,* and require practice to land them. Instances are known of this fish weighing nearly one hundred pounds.

Skike Fishing

One of the renowned tall-story tellers of old New England is Jack O'Donnell, a magnate in the fishing industry, who relates an extraordinary incident of the ingenuity and progressive spirit of the fishermen along the rock-bound coast of Maine. Jack tells us how the shrewd Yankee fishermen go out in a dory and take with them a big auger—you know, the kind of boring implement that you use to dig postholes. Well, they use an auger made of wood, so that it won't rust.

And with that auger they proceed to bore a hole in the ocean. Then a peculiar thing happens. They have a fish in these parts known as the skike. The skike is an impetuous fish, and when he sees that hole in the ocean he rushes right up into it. In fact, he rushes so fast that he shoots out above the surface of the water.

There he gets a deep breath of air which swells his lungs out. The skike's whole body swells, so that when he tries to get back into the hole in the ocean, he's too big. He can't get back in the hole, and the fishermen grab him.

From *Tall Stories,* The Rise and Triumph of the Great American Whopper, by Lowell Thomas, pp. 48–49. Copyright, 1931, by Funk & Wagnalls Company. New York City.

And then they have skike chowder and fried skike to go along with the baked beans for their supper that night.

The Man That Liked to Fish

. . . GREAT many while 'go, w'en de tam was hol', dar was one man Canada was lak for feesh so much he ant do mos' not'ing but dat. W'en his corn ought for be plant his waf was plant it, if he gat plant 't all, an' he go feeshin'. W'en his corn was ought for be hoe, he go feeshin'. W'en it was tam for cut off, his waf cut it off, an' de mans go feeshin' an' de sem for husk it, an' jes' de sem for rip his wheat, an' t'rash it, his waf he do it, all of it. An' w'en his hwood was ought for be cut he go feeshin' in de ice. An' w'en de Govny want it for go faght de Hinjin an' de Angleesh, he 'll run 'way an' go feeshin', so bamby de pries' he 'll gat mad at it an' he tol' it 'f he ant 'have hese'f for be so shiflin', he goin' turn it into kingfishin' an' den see 'f he 'll gat 'nough feeshin'.

De mans he some scare an' promise for be better, 'fore soon he fregit an' go feeshin' all de tam jes' de sem. Den de pries', Oh, haow he 'll was mad an' turn dat man into kingfishin' raght off. De man he was surprise prob'bly, for feel hese'f such leetly feller all cover wid fedder, but pooty soon he feel glad for t'ink he 'll ant gat for wear clo's dat was trouble for git, an' can go feeshin' all de tam.

He go up de river, "K-r-r-r-r," an' he go daown de river, "K-r-r-r-r," an' wen he see leetly feesh, 'baout so big he can swaller, "splosh," he jomp on it an' flew on a tree for heat it an' say, "T'ank you, Père Jerome, it was funs for be kingfishin'." When he was flew pas' hees hown haouse on de river an' see hees waf homp hees back hoein' an' rippin' in de sun an' hees chillren cry for hongry he 'll holler "K-r-r-r-r," jes' lak he was laught at it, he such gre't wicked.

Wal, seh, he 'll had good tam all summer an' long in de fall 'fore it come col'. Den he ant hear de sing bird yaller any more 'cause dey all gone 'cep' de jay an' de hwoodpeckit; den de river froze on top, but he 'll ant know 'nough for go to de warm wedder. He guess he was be hable for stay jes' long anybody. One morny de river was be froze on top, but he 'll ant know when he go for his breakfis' an' he go "K-r-r-r-r," lookin' for see some feesh, an' bamby he 'll see leetly feesh swim under de ice an' he holler "K-r-r-r-r" an' go firs' head raght on top of it, "Floop," an' bus' his head on de ice an' broke his brain all off an' dat was de en' of it.

From *Uncle Lisha's Outing*, by Rowland E. Robinson, pp. 217–218. Copyright, 1897, by Rowland E. Robinson. Boston and New York: Houghton Mifflin and Company.

A Gone Fish

Tom Rodman's grog was held to be the best in the County. Squire Hooper and his old crony, Gran'ther Holland, differed on this point alone, for Gran'ther Holland always upheld the peculiar merit of Elisha Watson's drink. These two rumsellers were keen rivals in the groggery business, both managing to keep their customers in debt, and in the end taking even their farms at forced sale. In short, they were a precious pair. The story runs that one foggy summer morning, Gran'ther Holland sent word to Squire Hooper that it was a likely day to go tautogin' on Peaked Rock. They often fished together, and were the best of friends, quarreling only on the point of drink. So, taking their heavy chestnut saplin peeled poles, they went down to the Peaked Rock, then still standing upright on the ledge where Whimsy Cot, now the property of Mrs. Irving Fisher, of New Haven, stands overlooking the rock. The day turned out badly—hot and hotter till the sun burned off the fog, so the tautog got shy and lay swinging in the tide waiting for the twilight; the anglers lost their bait, and their tempers also; now and then by chance they "stole" a chogset, pest of the tautog fisherman. Most of these wily thieves dropped back, and of course told their friends below, *who* was after them. A few were saved for the frying-pan. No fish has a finer flavor, when properly fried. Along about noon Gran'ther Holland growled out, "Le's give up, and go on home, no use brilin' here any longer." "All right," says Squire Hooper, "I'll jest fish up my last crab." So he tied her on good and solid, and hadn't more 'n got his line down when he felt a big one take holt, and bore down hard on his big pole, to hist him out. The big tautog, soon's he felt the pull, sung out with fright, "Chogsetties, who in hell has got hold of that thar dam pole?" "Squire Hooper! ole boy, Squire Hooper!" Hearing this, the big fish groaned out, "Good-bye, boys, I guess I'm a goner. *I'll be to Tom Rodman's afore sunset.*"

REMARKABLE ANIMAL BEHAVIOR

The Hawk Feather That Ate the Chicken Feathers

. . . One tam Ah'll was leetly boy an' leeve in Canada, mah mudder was mek it some bed fedder of geese's fedder an' she was gat it mos' all stuff up

By Rowland Gibson Hazard in *The Jonny-Cake Papers of "Shepherd Tom,"* Together with Reminiscences of Narragansett Schools of Former Days, by Thomas Robinson Hazard, With a Biographical Sketch and Notes by Rowland Gibson Hazard, pp. 399–400. Copyright, 1915, by Rowland G. Hazard. Boston: Printed for the Subscribers.

From *Uncle Lisha's Outing*, by Rowland E. Robinson, pp. 133–134. Copyright, 1897, by Rowland E. Robinson. Boston and New York: Houghton Mifflin and Company.

but leetly maght he ant gat nough fedder. Den mah fader was keel two hawk was come raoun' for ketch de chicklin, an' mah mudder was pull de fedder for feenish his bed of it. It was very nice plump beds, an' dey keep it for de bes' one for w'en company come see it, an' nex' year mah gran'pere an' gran'mere come for visit all naght, an', seh, gran'mere was gre't big hol' hwomans, an' w'en he come on de room in de morny he was r-r-r-rubby, r-r-r-rubby heself an' grunt very hard, an' w'en mah mudder ax it what de matter, she say de bed rope cut him all in chonk, 'cause de bed fedder was so t'in, an' mah mudder was supprise mos' for be mad for have it say so 'baout hees bes' bed, but w'en he ex-amine he fin' honly de hawk fedder, de res' it was all heat up. . . .

Grafting a Sheep Skin on a Horse

. . . He had an old horse unfit for duty, so one cold day in December he killed him and hung his skin on the fence to dry, and on the same day he killed several sheep and hung their skins on the same fence; . . in the evening the old horse pushed his nose through the kitchen window and whinnered as if cold and hungry, whereupon Abbey rushed out into the dark to replace his skin upon the animal, and by mistake put on the sheep skins, "and don't you think" continued Abbey, "that horse lived and the next year I sheared forty pounds of wool from him." . . .

The Remarkable Rooster

A group of men was discussing the relative strength of their animals when Mr. Judkins began telling them about a rooster which his father had raised a good many years ago, and how strong it was. One spring Mr. Judkins' father hatched out a great number of chicks. Shortly after their arrival, he began noticing one special chick that seemed to be larger and had more vitality than the others. This chick grew very fast and in a short time it was noticed, as the chick grew into a good-sized rooster, that it was remarkably strong for its size. The children would harness the rooster to a wagon and the rooster would ride them all around. A great many of the neighbors, having heard so many stories about the rooster in reference to his unusual size and remarkable strength, called to see him.

In the course of the conversation and admiration, the men requested

---

From *Proceedings* of the Orleans County, Vermont, Historical Society, November, 1889, to January 1, 1891, pp. 50–51. Cited in "Jonathan Draws the Long Bow," by Richard M. Dorson, *The New England Quarterly*, Volume XVI (June, 1943), No. 2, p. 246.

By C. Lane, Fayette, Maine. Manuscripts of the Federal Writers' Project of the Works Progress Administration for the State of Maine.

that the bird give a demonstration of its power. By chance there was an eleven-foot log lying in the yard, and the rooster was harnessed and attached to the log. Upon being told to go ahead, he walked off dragging the log behind him. Suddenly the woman of the house appeared at the door and said to the startled men, "Huh! that's no log, nothing but a cob harnessed to him. Why don't you give him something real to pull?"

Fiddling for the Wolves

Years ago there was a feller round here named Sammy Sprig, who was a great leetle fiddler. Comin' through the woods one time on the road from Sandisfield that goes past Wolf Swamp, an' with nothin' but his fiddle fur company, he see a pack o' wolves on his track. Fust off they 'd sneak up on him an' growl an' then fall back as he 'd stop an' yell at 'em. Gittin' bolder and bolder, they 'd ha' jumped him like as not, if he hadn't come to a desarted cabin side the road. Rushin' inter this, an' without waitin' to shet the door, he clim up like a squirrel an' squatted on the rafters. The wolves didn't stop to knock but dashed right in an' howled an' leaped an' strained to git at him. Wal', the moon was shinin' an' he see the cabin was full of 'em, so what does he do but inch along on a rafter, reach down an' shet the door. Then gittin' out his fiddle, he played 'em dance tunes all night till next day when some o' the neighbors come an' kilt the devlish critters.

Milking a She-Bear

. . . In Ashland over across our range, on a cold March night of 1840, a woman went out to milk Sally her cow for her starving baby in the house. As she crossed the yard, the wind blew out her lantern but on she went into the dark barn and, counting her steps down the floor till she felt she had come to Sally's stall, sat on a stool and milked the beast. She had expected scant milk, for the little old cow was starving, too; but it came in plenty and her surprise was increased by the fact that the animal's fur was thicker than Sally's winter coat and also that it stood so low. When the beast gave her a grateful muzzle with its big furred head, with a start she discovered that all this time she had been milking a huge she-bear, glad to have her aching udders emptied by her new friend. Without one scream the woman milked on and she claimed that her starving baby just loved the warm rich milk that night!

From *Bubblin's an' B'ilin's at the Center,* by Merle Dixon Graves, p. 120. Copyright, 1934, by Merle Dixon Graves. Rutland, Vermont: The Tuttle Company.

From *The Great White Hills of New Hampshire,* by Ernest Poole, pp. 366–367. Copyright, 1946, by Ernest Poole. Garden City, New York: Doubleday & Company, Inc.

The Boar That Hunted Bears

WAY back in the times when this village was first settled everybody kept pigs. They let 'em run loose in a big herd. Early in the fall they'd get 'em all together and turn 'em out up on the side of Moore Mountain. They'd make a big pen and keep 'em in it a few days and nights to get 'em used to it. Then they'd let 'em go to fatten up on acorns and berries and things.

Well, there was an old boar at the head of the outfit. He was big boss of the whole gang. He must have weighed six-seven hundred and he had tusks as long as this. He would lead that whole herd round through the woods and keep 'em mindin' their P's an' Q's.

Late one afternoon some of the young folks was up in the upper end of the village foolin' round the way young folks will and they heard a commotion up near the pig lot. They looked around and there was that old boar a-roundin' up about forty of the old sows and young stuff and shovin' 'em into the hog lot. He was ripped in a dozen places and losin' blood fast, but when he got 'em all in he told 'em to stay there if they valued their hides and then he put up over the hill a-kitin'.

The young ones rushed back to the village and told what they had seen and a bunch of men got their rifles. They back-tracked the boar clear up over the top of the mountain, and just down the other side they come onto a big bear all laid out with his insides ripped open and deader'n a door nail.

Well, sir, they kept on and pretty soon they come onto *another* bear treated just the same. They left that one and followed the boar's tracks a couple miles further to the edge of the pond. There was a tremenjous commotion going on down there and they hurried on as fast as they could. 'Twas beginning to fall dark and they couldn't do so good in the thick woods. When they got out onto the edge of the pond there in a clearin' was the old boar and he was layin' off round and round in the middle of a ring of *three* bears. He'd gored 'em some, but they was closing up on him fast. Two rifles barked and two bears died, and just as they drew on the third bear, he brought his paw smack down on the boar's back. Then they got him, too. Well, sir, there was the old boar and five bears way off in the woods scattered from there to the village. One man built a fire and stayed with the boar that night. The critter's hind quarters was paralyzed from the whack the bear gave him and he couldn't walk and he was too heavy to pack. So the other two went back to the village. In the mornin' they hitched a couple pair of oxen to a drag and cut a road through to the pond. They piled the old boar and the five bears onto the drag and took them back to the village. All the villagers had bear meat to

---

As told by Arthur A. Carleton, West Newbury, Vermont, to Mrs. Rebecca M. Halley. Manuscripts of the Federal Writers' Project of the Works Progress Administration for the State of Vermont.

eat that winter and there was several nice bear-skin rugs made out of them as weren't damaged much.

Oh, the boar? Well sir, he wa'n't much damaged except he couldn't walk no more. They kept him in ease and comfort until his tusks fell out and he died of old age.

Lemmie and the Big Fellow in a Fur Coat

. . . LEMMIE was a big man—one o' the biggest. Weighed two hundred an' fifty—mostly muscle. At least, I guess not much of it was brains. He could lift a hoss. Used to do it fer a bet at barn-raisin's an' sech.

Well, one frosty night in the spring o' the year, he was comin' home afoot from a dance. Road lay through the big woods, an' there wa'n't much moon to see by, but Lemmie he was feelin' good—full o' strength an' hard cider. He'd got within about a mile o' home when he saw a big feller in a fur coat settin' in the road right in front of him.

"Git up, ye lummox!" hollers Uncle Lemmie. "Want to freeze to death?" The other chap grunted at him sort o' scornful and Lemmie didn't like his tone o' voice. So he ups an' heaves a rock at him—catchin' him square amidships. "Woof!" says the feller, an' gits on his feet, wavin' his arms like he wanted to rassle. Rasslin', o' course, was right in Lemmie's line. "All right," he yells. "Durn ye, come on!"

He grabs him 'round the body, an' my, oh my, what a chest that feller had! Turrible strong in the arms, too, an' rough—no holts barred. Fust thing Lemmie knew he felt finger-nails diggin' right through his jacket, an' the earlap of his cap was chawed most off. Lemmie'd only been feelin' playful before. Now he got mad.

"Hey!" he shouts. "That ain't no way to fight! If ye want trouble, I'll give it to ye, by cracky!" An' he tries to trip him, but the feller's a sight too stout in the legs. Then Lemmie draws a deep breath an' starts squeezin' with his arms. The feller snorts an' twists, but he keeps his holt an' bends him backwards, huggin' tighter an' tighter all the time. His chin is over the other chap's shoulder, so he ain't seen his face, but he can't help wonderin' where sech a powerful man come from. After a while he feels the feller's wind begin to go out of him, puffin' an' wheezin'. Lemmie's pretty well tuckered himself but he won't own up. Jest squeezes harder, till his arms git numb.

All of a sudden there's a sort o' snap. The feller in the fur coat goes limp an' slips down in the road with Lemmie on top of him. "Give up?" calls Lemmie, soon as he can git his breath. No answer. "All right," says he, "we'll stay here till ye do." So they lay there on the ground a while longer.

'Bout sun-up a neighbor comes by with a team, on his way to mill. An'

From *Lumberjack,* by Stephen W. Meader, pp. 122–124. Copyright, 1934, by Harcourt, Brace and Company. New York.

there he finds Lemmie fast asleep on top of a dead bear. Pretty fair-sized bear, too. Weighed 'round four hundred pounds, if I remember right. Folks used to tell me I took after Uncle Lemmie in the strength o' my arms. . . . But then most of us Garlands was powerful men.

Trapping Bears With Rum

. . . MY PA used to tell a story . . . about maple syrup. Seems ther' was a farmer over Hopkinton way, back in the old days, an' he was troubled with bears, one spring. Lost a couple o' shoats out of his pen, an' found the tracks o' bears, but couldn't ketch up with 'em to shoot 'em. Three or four nights he heard 'em prowlin' 'round the buildin's, scarin' the stock, an' every time he'd run out with the gun, they'd be gone. Finally he thought up a smart plan. He got his boys to build some little wooden troughs, an' set 'em out, 'round the clearin'. He'd made plenty o' sugar an' syrup, so he took a mess of it an' mixed in the half of a gallon jug o' Medford rum—the kind everybody had in the house, them days. Then he put the stuff in the troughs an' went to bed. When daylight come, he looked out, an' there was a funny sight. An old she-bear an' two cubs was rollin' an' staggerin' around the place drunk as lords. Soon as he could stop laughin' he went out an' shot the big one. The boys kept the cubs fer pets.

LOCAL WONDERS

Mosquitoes

. . . NIGHT had come in earnest when I arrived at Wellfleet whose thoroughfares were brightened to some slight degree by a scattering of kerosene street lights. I found a hotel and had supper. Afterward I sat down in the office where were the landlord and one of his local friends whom he addressed familiarly as "Mac." Some mosquito bites that had been inflicted on my hands during the day were still painful, and when the landlord observed me rubbing the sore spots he divined what was the matter.

"There's mosquitoes here on the Cape the whole year round," he said, "and I do believe Wellfleet is the worst place on God's earth for 'em. I

Ibid., pp. 207–208.

From *Highways and Byways of New England,* Including the States of Massachusetts, New Hampshire, Rhode Island, Connecticut, Vermont and Maine, Written and Illustrated by Clifton Johnson, pp. 189–190. Copyright, 1915, by The Macmillan Company. New York and London. 1916.

tried to do a little gardening last summer, but I couldn't. The mosquitoes drove me into the house."

"And we only had an average crop of 'em," Mac commented.

"No matter what hour of the day or night I went to my garden they were right there waiting for me," the landlord continued. "They ain't fussy about workin' overtime."

"They have two gangs," Mac affirmed; "or perhaps there's three and they work in eight hour shifts."

"I thought they didn't sing as much as usual this year," the landlord said. "They'd get right onto you and if they found you a little bit tough they'd go off and set down in front of you and whet their bills and then come to jab again."

"I've been to some of our low meadows where they'd almost carry you off," Mac said. "Seems to me one of those meadows would make a good penitentiary. Just tie your criminal there and let 'em punish him."

"He'd go crazy and they'd kill him in a little while," the landlord declared. "Up in the Maine woods I've found 'em pretty thick along the trout brooks, but if you built a smudge they wouldn't bother you. Here, though, they are on to all those dodges. They are a useless pest and ain't even good for fertilizer. I know a feller who said he killed a lot and put 'em in the rows where he was plantin', but it didn't make things grow a bit better."

The Mosquitoes with the Canvas Britches

CAPT. JONES, of Stonington, is responsible for the following: On his passage from New York a few years ago he observed, one summer afternoon, a heavy cloud arise from the land, and, to his great surprise, approach the vessel. Suddenly it broke near him and covered the deck with millions of musquitoes, while part of the flock went through the mainsail, leaving nothing but bolt ropes hanging idly to the spars. Corroborative evidence to this astonishing tale was found in the person of a "down-east skipper," who heard the story, and who, on comparing dates with the narrator, declared that two days afterwards he was boarded by the same flock of musquitoes, and they all wore canvas breeches.

New Hampshire Rock Farms

SOME of the Western papers are having a little fun at the expense of New Hampshire. A person travelling in that state thus writes to a Toledo press:

From *Phinney's Calendar, or Western Almanac, for the Year of Our Lord 1873,* by George R. Perkins. Buffalo, New York: Published by James M. Lent.

From *The New England Farmer's Almanac,* for the Year of the Christian Era, 1858, No. XLIV, by Truman W. Abell. Boston: Published by Brown, Taggard & Chase.

—"All along the route I noticed great tracts of rocks carefully fenced in, for no other reason, that I could imagine, than to keep the cattle out, and thus prevent their starving to death."

Rocky Soil

. . . THE barren hills and pastures of some parts of Brampton . . . were so rocky that it was a common saying of the old people that the devil in going to and fro over the earth broke his apron-strings when he reached this place, and the stones which would have sufficed for many miles of country were emptied on the hills of Brampton.

The sheep, so it was said, had to have their noses sharpened, in order to nibble the wiry grass which sprang up between the thickly scattered stones.

Lean Pigs

THE Lowell News says that the farmer whose pigs were so lean that it took two of them to make a shadow has been beat by another who had several so thin that they would crawl out through the cracks in their pen. He finally stopped that "fun" by tying knots in their tails!

Poor Land

I WAS drivin' stage through this piece o' woods some years ago, when I come all to once on a rabbit settin' on the brush fence an' cryin' as if his heart would break. Bein' a good-natured man, an' fond of askin' questions, I spose,—jest as you are,—I stopt the hosses, and said, "What ails ye there? Kin a feller do anythin' to help ye through yer trouble?" The rabbit wiped his eyes with his tail as well as he could, and said to me, "Stranger, my father died last week and left me two hundred acres of this land, an' I've got to get my livin' off on it"; an' then he bust out cryin' ag'in. "G'lang," said I to the hosses, "can't do a thing to help ye, if it's as bad as that."[1]

From *Brampton Sketches, Old-Time New England Life,* by Mary B. Claflin, p. 22. Copyright, 1890, by T. Y. Crowell & Co. New York.

From *The Old Farmer's Almanack,* Calculated on a New and Improved Plan, for the Year of Our Lord 1853, by Robert B. Thomas, p. 40. Entered, according to Act of Congress, in the year 1852, by Jenks, Hickling & Swan, in the Clerk's Office of the District Court of the District of Massachusetts. Boston.

---

[1] From *The Granite Monthly,* Vol. XXXII (March, 1902), p. 162. Cited in "Jonathan Draws the Long Bow," by Richard M. Dorson, *The New England Quarterly,* Volume XVI (June, 1943), No. 2, p. 272.

. . . Speaking of Poverty Plain corn, reminds me of the testimony of a witness on this subject. He had sworn that the use of a lot on that plain was worth nothing, and less than nothing. The opposing counsel asked him, in cross examination,—"You say, Mr. D., that the use of that land is worth nothing?" "I do." "Have not you seen *rye* upon it?" "I have." "Have you not seen corn upon it?" "Coarn, coarn! I have; but good heavens! *what* coarn! why, many a time, have I seen toads, sitting up on their ends, and playing with the tassels with their fore paws!" [2]

A Steep Field

IN ONE of Uncle Eli's fields there was a steep hill. A friend calling on him asked him how it was possible that he had ploughed it. "I did it with a pair of horses," he replied, "but it was so steep in some places that one of the horses had to ride on top of the other."

The Fast Pumpkin

A TRAVELLER on a miserably looking lean steed was hailed by a Yankee who was hoeing his pumpkins by the road-side—"Hallo friend," said the farmer, "where are you bound?" "I am a-going to settle in the western country," replied the other. "Well, get off and straddle this here pumpkin vine,—it will grow and carry you faster than that ere beast."

The Giant Pumpkin

Now I can't vouch for this story. 'Twas told to me way back when I was a little shaver. I won't say as to whether it was true or not because I wasn't

---

[2] From *The Westfield Jubilee:* A Report of the Celebration at Westfield, Mass., on the Two Hundredth Anniversary of the Incorporation of the Town, October 6, 1869, with the Historical Address of the Hon. William G. Bates, and other Speeches and Poems of the Occasion, with an Appendix, Containing Historical Documents of Local Interest, p. 199. Westfield, Massachusetts: Clark & Story, Publishers. 1870.

From *Funny Stories,* Told by Phineas T. Barnum, p. 99. Copyright, 1890, by Phineas T. Barnum. New York, London, Glasgow, and Manchester: George Routledge and Sons, Limited.

From *The New England Farmer's Almanac,* for the Year of the Christian Era, 1843, No. XXIX, by Truman Abell. Claremont, New Hampshire: Published and Sold at the Claremont Bookstore.

As told by Arthur A. Carlton, West Newbury, Vermont, to Mrs. Rebecca M. Halley. Manuscripts of the Federal Writers' Project of the Works Progress Administration for the State of Vermont.

there. It all happened long 'fore I was born. My Grandsir, now, lived on a farm down on the little Ox Bow. There were nice fertile fields down there along the river same as there are now. One fall, Grandsir turned his pigs out on the little Bow same as usual. There was one big old sow about ready to farrow. She got lost and didn't come up to eat with the others and you may know there is somethin' far wrong when a pig won't come to dinner. Well, sir, my Grandsir and a couple others long about dark went huntin' that sow. They traveled all over the little Ox Bow. Finally they went down toward the bank of the river. It's forty-fifty feet wide there. On the bank was a punkin vine, a goralmighty big one, leaves like umbrellas. Out from the vine was growin' stalks, big ones, and two of them stalks had grown together. You know, the way molasses candy looks when you pull it, flat this way. Well, the old sow's tracks went right up to that vine and disappeared, just vanished into thin air. That vine stretched out right across the river. Clear over to the New Hampshire side. Warn't no other place the old sow could have gone, so Grandsir knew she must have crossed the river on the punkin vine. Wait now, that warn't all of it. The men got a canoe and crossed the river. That was way before the bridges were built. On the other side they follered up the bank. They went along and there in a little while they come to the place where the vine had hit the bank. They went along by it and there were the sow's tracks. Way back a bit they come across a big punkin, the biggest one they ever saw. Around the other side was a little hole about so big. They peeked in and there was the old sow sleepin' sound with a whole litter of little pigs cuddled up to her.

The Size of Narragansett Huckleberries

I HAVE elsewhere spoken incidentally of the Narragansett huckleberry, which is an entirely different thing when grown in the delicious Gulf Stream atmosphere of southern Rhode Island than anywhere else in either the western or eastern hemisphere. The largest and best flavored huckleberries are usually to be found on the edges of woodlands where the bushes are partially shaded by the sparse branches of old trees. In such localities the bush grows much taller and the berries much bigger than on bleak, unprotected hills. Indeed, in some instances the delicious flavored woodland berries attain to a size almost marvelous, though perhaps not quite so big as was once reported to one of the British periodicals, the *London Quarterly*, by an English tourist, who happening some years ago to be passing by an

---

From *The Jonny-Cake Papers of "Shepherd Tom,"* Together with Reminiscences of Narragansett Schools of Former Days, by Thomas Robinson Hazard, With a Biographical Sketch and Notes by Rowland Gibson Hazard, pp. 102–103. Copyright, 1915, by Rowland G. Hazard. Boston: Printed for the Subscribers.

old huckster woman in Newport who was seated by a pile of uncommonly large pumpkins she had to sell, remarked to her, "Old woman, we have bigger happles than them in Hengland." "Happles," she rejoined, "do you call them happles? Why, them ain't happles, them 's 'uckleberries!" The Henglish correspondent received the witty remark of the sarcastic old woman for gospel, and so entered it on his memorandum book and reported to his principals that huckleberries grew in the warm, salubrious Gulf Stream atmosphere of Rhode Island, the Eden of America, as big as bushel baskets.

The Doctor and the Muffins

THEN there were Phillis' muffins! It makes me fetch a long sigh to think of them even at this late day, more than seventy years, the fabled age of man, nothing being said of that of woman, after I have tasted them! But, then, such a taste! A taste that no mortal with a sign of a palate in his mouth if once tasted can ever forget! Why, I just remember when a genial, baldheaded New York doctor whose Christian and surname, if I remember, began with an F and an S, or with an S and an F, I can't say which, stopped over night at my grandfather's on his way to Newport. We chanced to have muffins for breakfast, and Phillis added a round dozen to the usual batch for fifteen members of our family, great-room and kitchen folks, all told. But such a bolting of muffins no mortal, I am sure, ever beheld before! One, two, three, four dozen were swallowed in quick succession by my grandfather's genial young friend, and he had got far into the fifth dozen when Margaret, the colored waitress, whispered to my grandmother that the mixing was clean gone! Up to this time the doctor had been the jolliest and most loquacious good fellow that ever sat down to a Narragansett breakfast table. But no sooner were the muffins all sped, than a most extraordinary change came over his spirit, and not a word could be got out of him but simply, "Muffins." Said my grandfather, "Doctor, let me recommend these hot Maryland biscuits! Our cook prides herself especially on making the best Maryland biscuits to be found in America." "Muffins!" quoth the doctor, as he stared inquiringly into my grandfather's face. "Let me help you, doctor," said my grandmother beseechingly, "to some of this cream toast; it looks very nice!" "Muffins!" retorted the doctor, "Muffins!" It was no go! Words were wasted on the doctor. Phillis' enrapturing muffins had penetrated and dislocated his brain, and until the doctor's premature death which occurred some months afterward, he was never heard to pronounce any other word than muffins. After his demise, the Manhattan Allopathic College of Physicians made a careful post-mortem examination of all of the organs of the defunct, and decided unanimously that the death

Ibid., pp. 109–111.

of their illustrious professional brother was caused by the mortal disease set down in Galen's infallible books as *muffina dislocano braineo,* which occurs they said but very seldom, and then only in the Narragansett country in Rhode Island, where colored cooks and witchery are closely allied and most bound.

The Huckleberry Jonny-Cake Smile

But above all other edibles, in the estimation of the olden-time children of Narragansett, loomed up the huckleberry jonny-cake, which, to be first-rate, must be made half and half of meal and fresh gathered ripe berries. Phillis used to say there was nothing she " 'spised" more than a huckleberry jonny-cake with no huckleberries in it. It used to be held in Narragansett that the faces of little boys and girls that were fed during the whole berry season on half and half huckleberry jonny-cake grew into the shape of a smile that remained until berries came again the next summer.

In fact, I remember when a small boy calling with my father on an errand at Mr. Stedlar's, whose wife had just mixed and put on the barrel-head board a huckleberry jonny-cake, which lay unbaked on the table, preparatory to being placed before the fire. No less than eight children of all sexes and sizes soon entered, whom I had observed making mud-pies near the sink gutter as we approached the house. Each of these by turn gave the cake several affectionate pats with their dripping hands as they looked me blandly in the face and exclaimed in triumphant tones,—Huckleberry jonny-cake! accompanied with a self-congratulatory, telling smile. On my father remarking on their happy expression of countenance, the mother told him that the year before she had fed all her children for six entire days wholly on huckleberry jonny-cakes, and that she found a smile had remained on their countenances every moment of time both when awake and asleep for just six months thereafter. Mrs. Stedlar further said that she had intended to feed her children on huckleberry jonny-cakes that summer for twelve days in succession, so that they would continue to smile the twelve months round, but that she should have to give it up after that day, which was the ninth since she began, as she found they laughed in their sleep so loud and long that they kept their old grandmother awake all night!

Ibid., pp. 52–53.

Giant Puddings

Norwich Puddings and New London Dumplings[1]

With respect to the puddings, it is reported that they were frequently made of such size and solidity as to carry ruin in their path if the pyramid chanced to fall. . . .

A sportive story was formerly current, that on a certain festive occasion, a conical pudding was set in the center of the table, in monumental dignity, but losing its balance at the first insertion of the carving-knife, it fell and knocked down *three men.* Whereupon the townsmen made a regulation that no pudding should henceforth consist of more than *twenty coombs* of corn, that is, about four bushels.

The Norwich *puddings* were played by the local humorist against the New London *dumplins.* The latter, it is said, were often made so large and hard that it was necessary to chip them up with a pick-axe. The remains of a great dinner being at one time thrown into the river, near the town, the Isle of Rocks, a noted fishing ledge in the harbor, was formed, and is still by some of their neighbors called the New London Dumplins.

The Rival Cooks[2]

In a green valley among the Berkshire hills in days gone by there lived two women in houses less than a quarter of a mile apart, who took great pride in their cooking. Each was sure she was the best cook of the two, and their rivalry at length grew so warm that they agreed to have a contest to see which could make the largest pudding. They stewed and brewed and baked with great labor and mystery. The test-day came, and a large company of old and young from all the region about gathered to see and taste the giant puddings. The crowd drew up around the festive board, and gazed and commented and ate. What the size of the puddings really was is not reported; but we get a hint of their magnitude from the fact that after slice after slice had been cut away from one side of the smallest one, the remainder fell over and killed one of the children at the table.

---

[1] From *History of Norwich, Connecticut:* From Its Possession by the Indians, to the Year 1866, by Frances Manwaring Caulkins, p. 79 and note. Entered according to Act of Congress, in the year 1866, by F. M. Caulkins, in the Clerk's Office of the District Court of the United States, for the District of Connecticut. [Hartford, Connecticut.] Published by the Author.

[2] From *What They Say in New England,* A Book of Signs, Sayings, and Superstitions, collected by Clifton Johnson, p. 248. Copyright, 1896, by Lee and Shepard. Boston.

Cape Cod Wonders

THE farm exhibits, like everything else at the fair, were in all respects the ultimate superlative. The only squash on earth that ever grew bigger than the 55-pound marrow squash that Bill Gray had brought from his Yarmouth acres was the one that Bill Gray had left at home, to keep for himself. That one was so big the oxcart started to give way when he let it down with a tackle. Then Clark Hoxie of Sandwich showed up with a squash that weighed 62 pounds, but explained that the sandy base of his farm had proved too weak to support the weight of his best specimen, which had kept sinking as it grew, until it had gone down, down, "clear to China, by Godfrey!"

There will never be another Country Fair in Barnstable, at least none under the auspices of the Society, which wound up its business in 1936, but while a turnip yet grows in Eastham, or a strawberry in Falmouth, or a haddock on Georges Banks, there will always be a tall tale to grow with it. This sandy soil, when it ceases to nourish anything else, will produce yarns while it remains above tidemark. Only the other day the newspapers carried the story of a young man of Chatham, who has discovered a new and easy way to catch fish. He merely dips his hook in molasses—"long-tail sugar," Cape folks call it—and casts it high in the air. The molasses attracts bees. Then, when the hook drops into the water, the bees are stuck and go in with it, and that makes them mad. The fish sees the hook with what look like real flies attached, and when he goes for it, the wet, angry bees sting him to death.

Housatonic River Valley Wonders

IN THE vanguard of these newcomers was Captain Joseph Crocker, riding on horseback with his aged mother on a pillion behind him, and the rest of the family trundling along in an oxcart. Captain "Joe" had learned to spin a yarn with the best of them during his dog watches at sea, and though his tales wouldn't always hold water, they held attention. Eager ears were turned to the fabulous stories about the Housatonic River Valley

From *Cape Cod Pilot,* by Jeremiah Digges, with Editorial and Research Assistance of the Members of the Federal Writers' Project, p. 61. American Guide Series, Federal Writers' Project, Works Progress Administration for the State of Massachusetts. Copyright, 1937, by Poor Richard Associates. Provincetown and New York: Modern Pilgrim Press and the Viking Press.

From *The Berkshire Hills,* Compiled and Written by Members of the Federal Writers' Project of the Works Progress Administration for Massachusetts, p. 135. Copyright, 1939, by The Berkshire Hills Conference, Inc. New York: Duell, Sloan and Pearce.

sent home by Captain Joe and his friends. Along its banks, so the tale went, the sod was so rich it dripped grease if you hung it in the sun. The hogs fattened so fast in the pastures, they ran around squealing "Kill me! Kill me!" The children grew so tanned and sturdy that the settlers mistook their own offspring for Indian youngsters strayed from the few remaining tribes—all peaceful, of course. Part of the story must be buncombe, but the other half had to be Gospel truth. Even Joe Crocker's imagination wasn't *that* good.

A Hen Plucked by the Gale

. . . AL HIGGINS, of Cape Cod, grants an interview to a reporter for the New Bedford *Standard-Times:*

I got up early to see how the hens were making it. I no sooner got the henhouse door open when my best rooster hopped out into a gust of wind that stripped him to the pin-feathers and tossed him against the chopping-block with such a thump that the axe fell and cut off his head, slick as a whistle. There he was—killed, picked, and ready to clean. I don't believe there ever was such a gale.

Goshen Cold

GOSHEN is the cold place. You never knew Jack Muller the painter did you? He was a comical kind of a lad. He used to say he'd had his ears frozen once. If you asked him where, he'd say up in Goshen, pickin' strawberries in the summer time.

Big Snow

A VERMONT paper, in giving an account of a late snow storm, states that a stage driver who found it impossible to proceed further with the vehicle

---

From *Cape Cod Pilot,* by Jeremiah Digges, with Editorial and Research Assistance of the Members of the Federal Writers' Project, p. 10. American Guide Series, Federal Writers' Project, Works Progress Administration for the State of Massachusetts. Copyright, 1937, by Poor Richard Associates. Provincetown and New York: Modern Pilgrim Press and the Viking Press.

From "Connecticut Clockmaker," as told by Mr. MacCurrie, Thomaston, Connecticut, to Francis Donovan, in *Living Lore of New England.* Manuscripts of the Federal Writers' Project of the Works Progress Administration for the State of Connecticut.

From *The Old American Comic Almanac, 1843,* with Whims, Scraps, and Oddities from the Land of Johnny Bull, Brother Jonathan, and Mons. Nontongpaw, p. 5. Entered according to an Act of Congress in the year 1842, by Thomas Groom in the Clerk's Office of the District Court of Massachusetts. Boston.

detached a horse from it, and on his return was thrown into the snow, by the animal stumbling; on getting up, he found the cause to have been the horse's stepping one foot in the *chimney* of a two-story house! The editor does not state whether the driver stopped to cook his breakfast.

Frozen Death

THE events described herewith took place within 20 miles of Montpelier, Vermont. They were first found recorded in a local diary which the author verified with an old man who vouched for their truth—and said his father was among those operated on. The practise is not commonly carried on today.

"*January 7*—I went on the mountain today and witnessed what to me was a horrible sight. It seems that the dwellers there who are unable either from age or other reasons to contribute to the support of their families are disposed of in the winter months.

"I will describe what I saw. Six persons, four men and two women, one man a cripple about thirty years old, the other five past the age of usefulness, lay on the earthy floor of the cabin drugged into insensibility, while members of the families were gathered about them in apparent indifference. In a short time the unconscious bodies were inspected by one man who said: 'They are ready.' They were then stripped of all their clothing except a single garment. The bodies were carried outside and laid on logs exposed to the bitter cold mountain air, the operation having been delayed several days for suitable weather.

"Soon the noses, ears, and fingers began to turn white, then the limbs and faces assumed a tallowy look. I could stand the cold no longer and went inside, where I found the friends in cheerful conversation. In about an hour I went out and looked at the bodies. They were fast freezing.

"Again I went inside where the men were smoking their clay pipes but silence had fallen on them. Perhaps they were thinking that the time would come when they would be carried out in the same way. I could not shut out the sight of the freezing bodies outside, neither could I bear to be in darkness, but I piled on the wood in the cavernous fireplace and, seated on a single block, passed the dreary night, terror-stricken by the horrible sights I had witnessed.

By Robert Wilson, in *The (Old) Farmer's Almanack,* Calculated on a New and Improved Plan for the Year of Our Lord 1943, by Robert B. Thomas, pp. 50, 83. Copyright, 1942, by Mabel M. Swan. Dublin, New Hampshire: Yankee, Inc.

Cf. Charles Edward Crane, *Winter in Vermont* (New York, 1941), p. 85, who cites this story (under the title, "Human Hibernation") from an old clipping in a scrapbook belonging to Elbert S. Stevens, of Bridgewater Corners. The clipping, of unknown source, date, and authorship, was reprinted in the *Rutland Herald,* May 24, 1939.

"*January 8*—Day came at length but did not dissipate the terror that filled me. The frozen bodies became visibly white on the snow that lay in huge drifts about them. The women gathered about the fire and soon began to prepare breakfast. The men awoke and affairs assumed a more cheerful aspect.

"After breakfast the men lighted their pipes and some of them took a yoke of oxen and went off into the forest, while others proceeded to nail together boards making a box about ten feet long and half as high and wide. When this was completed they placed about two feet of straw in the bottom. Then they laid three frozen bodies in the straw. Then the faces and upper part of the bodies were covered with a cloth; more straw was put in the box and the other three bodies placed on top, and covered the same as the first ones, with cloth and straw.

"Boards were then firmly nailed on top to protect the bodies from being injured by carnivorous animals that made their home on these mountains. By this time the men who had gone off with the ox team returned with a huge load of spruce and hemlock boughs which they unloaded at the foot of a steep ledge, came to the house and loaded the box containing the bodies on the sled, and drew it near the load of boughs.

"These were soon piled on and around the box and it was left to be covered with snow, which I was told would lie in drifts twenty feet deep over this rude tomb. 'We shall want our men to plant our corn next spring,' said the wife of one of the frozen men, 'and if you want to see them resuscitated, you come here about the tenth of next May.'

"With this agreement I left the mountaineers, living and frozen, to their fate and returned to my home in Boston, where it was weeks before I was fairly myself."

Turning the leaves of the diary, I came to the following entry:

"*May 10*—I arrived here at ten a.m. after riding about four hours over muddy, unsettled roads. The weather here is warm and pleasant, most of the snow is gone except where there are drifts in the fence corners and hollows. But nature is not yet dressed in green.

"I found the same parties here I left last January. They were ready to disinter the bodies, but I had no expectations of finding life there. A feeling that I could not resist, however, impelled me to come and see.

"We repaired at once to the well-remembered spot at the ledge. The snow had melted from the top of the brush, but still lay deep around the bottom of the pile. The men commenced work at once, some shoveling, and others tearing away the brush. Soon the box was visible. The cover was taken off, the layers of straw removed, and the bodies, frozen and apparently lifeless, lifted out and laid on the snow.

"Large troughs made out of hemlock logs were placed nearby filled with tepid water, into which the bodies were placed separately with the head slightly raised. Boiling water was then poured into the trough from kettles hung on poles nearby until the water was as hot as I could hold my hand in. Hemlock boughs had been put in the boiling water in such quantities that they had given the water the color of wine.

"After lying in the bath about an hour, color began to return to the bodies, when all hands began rubbing and chafing them. This continued about an hour when a slight twitching of the muscles followed by audible gasps, showed that vitality was returning.

"Spirits were then given in small quantities and allowed to trickle down their throats. Soon they could swallow and more was given them when their eyes opened and they began to talk, and finally sat up in their bath-tubs.

"They were taken out and assisted to the house where after a hearty meal they seemed as well as ever and in no wise injured, but rather, refreshed by their long sleep of four months."

Fog Yarn

THE fogs that sometimes envelop Nantucket gave rise to a pleasant fiction, which smacks of the salt. A whaling ship, outward-bound, having been caught in one of unusual density in leaving the port, the captain made a peculiar mark in it [the fog] with a harpoon, and on his return, after a three years' cruise, fell in with the harbor at the very same spot.

Fog and Fundy

I WENT over to Campobello impressed with the notion that there was quite too much "Taffy" about all those Welsh names that sound so outlandish to unaccustomed ears. Then again, this quarter of the world has always had such an unenviable reputation, on account of its fogs, that fog and Fundy have come to be synonymous terms with most people. "Why," said a man I met by the way, "you'd be a settin' there, with clear sky all around you, and in half an hour the fog would be thick enough to drive a nail into and hang your hat on it. Fog! Bah! Mount Desert's a paradise to it. I don't know but you could shovel it up and cart it off by the wheelbarrow-load if it would fetch anything."

From *Nooks and Corners of the New England Coast,* by Samuel Adams Drake, p. 349. Entered according to Act of Congress, in the year 1875, by Harper & Brothers, in the Office of the Librarian of Congress, at Washington. New York.

From *The Pine-Tree Coast,* by Samuel Adams Drake, p. 355. Copyright, 1890, by Estes and Lauriat. Boston. 1891.

Shingling Out onto the Fog

A RATHER loquacious individual was endeavoring to draw an old man into conversation, but hitherto without much success, the old fellow having sufficient discernment to see that his object was to make a little sport for the passengers at his expense. At length says loquacious individual: "I suppose you consider Down East a right smart place; but I guess it would puzzle them to get up quite so thick a fog as we are having here this morning, wouldn't it?" "Well," said the old man, "I don't know about that. I hired one of your Massachusetts chaps to work for me last summer, and one rather foggy mornin' I sent him down to the meadow to lay a few courses of shingle on a new barn I was finishin' off. At dinner-time the fellow came up, and, sez he, 'That's an almighty long barn of yourn.' Sez I, 'Not very long.' 'Well,' sez he, 'I've been to work all this forenoon, and haven't got one course laid yet.' 'Well,' sez I, 'you're a lazy fellow, that's all I've got to say.' And so after dinner I went down to see what he'd been about, and I'll be thundered ef he hadn't shingled more than a hundred foot *right out on to the fog*."

Overdoing It

BEN BLOWHARD says that one of his voyages was made under a captain who was noted for working his crew, and on the trip home, having "nothing else to do," he kept all hands at work "setting up rigging"—that is, tightening the standing rigging which supports the vessel's masts. "Well," said old Ben, "it was nothing but set up riggin' almost every day, till we hove in sight of land. We were bound to New London, and just as we were passin' Montauk P'int she grounded in five fathom. Then the captain ripped and swore till all was blue. 'Heave the lead,' says he. We hove first on stab'ard and then on the lab'ard side. There she was, stuck in thirty feet of water, and she only drawed eighteen! I guess our boys laughed some when we found we'd set up the riggin' so much that we'd hauled her masts *through the vessel's bottom twelve feet*!"

From *The American Joe Miller:* A Collection of Yankee Wit and Humour, Compiled by Robert Kempt, pp. 57–58. Entered at Stationer's Hall. London: Adams and Francis. 1865.

From *Tit-Bits of American Humor,* Collected from Various Sources, p. 19. New York and London: White & Allen. [n. d.]

Maine's Woodland Terrors

It is feared that some of the creatures which infest the woods of Aroostook, Piscataquis, and Penobscot counties, especially in the lumbering season, have had their mischievous qualities magnified in local myths for the silencing of fretful children and the stimulation of generosity on the part of green choppers. It is the newcomer in a lumber-camp who is expected to supply the occasional quart of whiskey that shall pacify Razor-shins, and to do a little more than his share of the breakfast-getting, errand-running, and so on, in order to quiet the hostility of the will-am-alones. Like the duppies and rolling calves of the West Indies, these creatures are not seen as often as they were, for they have a fixed hostility to schools, never venturing within ten miles of one.

The will-am-alone is a quick little animal, like a squirrel, that rolls in its fingers poison-lichens into balls and drops them into the ears and on the eyelids of sleeping men in camp, causing them to have strange dreams and headaches and to see unusual objects in the snow. It is the hardest drinkers in the camp who are said to be most easily and most often affected by the poison. The liquor in prohibition States is always plentiful and bad, and in combination with the pellets of the will-am-alones is nearly fatal.

More odd than this animal is the side-hill winder, a rabbit-like creature so called because he winds about steep hills in only one direction; and in order that his back may be kept level, the down-hill legs are longer than the up-hill pair. He is seldom caught; but the way to kill him is to head him off with dogs when he is corkscrewing up a mountain. As the winder turns, his long legs come on the up-hill side and tip him over, an easy prey. His fat is a cure for diseases caused by the will-am-alone, but to eat his flesh is to die a hard and sudden death.

Much to be dreaded is the ding-ball, a panther whose last tail-joint is ball shaped and bare of flesh. With this weapon it cracks its victim's skull. There is no record of a survival from the blow of a ding-ball. In older traditions it sang with a human voice, thus luring the incautious from their cabins to have their sconces broken in the dark. It is fond of human flesh, and will sing all night for a meal of Indians.

An unpleasant person is Razor-shins, a deathless red man who works for such as are kind to him, but mutilates that larger number of the ignorant who neglect to pay tribute. Keep Razor-shins supplied with fire-water,—a jug at every full moon,—and he will now and then fell a tree for you with his sharp shin-bones, if nobody is around, or will clear up a bit of road. But fail in this, and you must be prepared to give up your scalp, which he

---

From *American Myths and Legends*, by Charles M. Skinner, Vol. I, pp. 34–38. Copyright, 1903, by J. B. Lippincott. Philadelphia and London.

can slice from your head with a single kick, or he will clip off your ears and leave cuts on you that will look like sabre-strokes. When a green hand arrives in a lumber-camp it is his duty to slake the thirst of Razor-shins. He puts a jug of virulent Bangor whiskey at the door. The best proof that the Indian gets it is shown in the odor of breathed alcohol that pervades the premises all night and the emptiness of the jug in the morning.

Where French Canucks are employed at chopping, you must look to see them all quit work if a white owl flies from any tree they are felling; and they must not look back nor speak to it, for it is a ghost and will trouble them unless they leave that part of the wood for fully thirty days.

But worst of all is the windigo, that ranges from Labrador to Moosehead Lake, preferring the least populous and thickest wooded districts. A Canadian Indian known as Sole-o'-your-foot is the only man who ever saw one and lived—for merely to look upon the windigo is doom, and to cross his track is deadly peril. There is no need to cross the track, for it is plain enough. His footprints are twenty-four inches long, and in the middle of each impress is a red spot, showing where his blood has oozed through a hole in his mocassin; for the windigo, dark and huge and shadowy as he seems, has yet a human shape and many human attributes. The belief in this monster is so genuine that lumbermen have secured a monopoly of certain jobs by scaring competitors out of the neighborhood through the simple device of tramping past their camp in furcovered snow-shoes and squeezing a drop of beef blood or paint into each footprint. There was at one time a general flight of Indian choppers from a lumber district in Canada, and nothing could persuade them to return to work; for the track of the windigo had been seen. It was found that this particular windigo was an Irishman who wanted that territory for himself and his friends; but the Indians would not be convinced. They kept away for the rest of the season. The stealthy stride of the monster makes every lumberman's blood run as cold as the Androscoggin under its ice roof, and its voice is like the moaning of the pines.

The Tote-Road Shagamaw

FROM the Rangeley Lakes to the Allegash and across in New Brunswick loggers tell of an animal which has puzzled many a man, even those who were not strangers in the woods. Frequently the report is circulated that the tracks of a bear have been seen near camp, but a little later this is denied and moose tracks are reported instead. Heated arguments among

---

From *Fearsome Creatures of the Lumberwoods, With a Few Desert and Mountain Beasts,* by William T. Cox, p. 23. Copyright, 1911, by William T. Cox. Washington, D. C.: Press of Judd & Detweiler, Inc.

the men, sometimes resulting in fist fights, are likely to follow. It is rightly considered an insult to a woodsman to accuse him of not being able to distinguish the track of either of these animals. To only a few of the old timber cruisers and rivermen is the explanation of these changing tracks known. Gus Demo, of Oldtown, Maine, who has hunted and trapped and logged in the Maine woods for 40 years, once came upon what he recognized as the tracks of a moose. After following it for about 80 rods it changed abruptly into unmistakable bear tracks; another 80 rods and it changed to moose tracks again. It was soon observed by Mr. Demo that these changes took place precisely every quarter of a mile, and, furthermore, that whatever was making the tracks always followed a tote road or a blazed line through the woods. Coming up within sight of the animal, Gus saw that it had front feet like a bear's and hind feet like those of a moose, and that it was pacing carefully, taking exactly a yard at a step. Suddenly it stopped, looked all about, and swung as on a pivot, then inverting itself and walking on its front feet only, it resumed its pacing. Mr. Demo was only an instant in recognizing by the witness trees that the place where the animal changed was a section corner. From this fact he reasoned that the shagamaw must have been originally a very imitative animal, which, from watching surveyors, timber cruisers, and trappers patiently following lines through the woods, contracted the habit itself. He figures that the shagamaw can count only as high as 440; therefore it must invert itself every quarter of a mile.

Gazerium and Snydae

From Maine comes news of two extinct creatures, the *gazerium* and the *snydae*. Both, according to Richard G. Kendall, a specialist in unearthly zoölogy highly esteemed in that great State, were found only along the Kennebec river, and were favorite delicacies of the Kennebec Indians and the early white settlers. Kendall says that the *gazerium* resembled a shrimp, but had two legs forward and only one aft, and that it fed chiefly upon the *snydae,* which were minute forms of marine life. The *snydae,* in turn, fed upon the eggs of the *gazerium,* so the two species gradually exterminated each other. He adds:

The Kennebecs usually cooked the *gazerium* in deep fat. It tasted something like a French fried potato, with just a hint of the flavor of cocktail sauce imparted to it by its diet of *snydae*.[1]

From *Supplement I: The American Language,* An Inquiry into the Development of English in the United States, by H. L. Mencken, p. 251. Copyright, 1945, by Alfred A. Knopf, Inc. New York.

[1] "Journal of a Journeyman," Portland *Press Herald,* March 20, 1944.—H. L. M.

Gyascutus

DURING my boyhood on a Vermont farm the *gyascutus* or cute cuss, was not a rare barnyard animal. He or the female of the species, *gyascuta,* which we affectionately called the *cuter cuss,* were as necessary as the cow to most Vermont farmers. Indeed, without the *gyascutus,* dairy farming in Vermont would have been restricted to the narrow lowlands, the riverside meadows that probably do not account for more than one-tenth of one per cent. of Vermont's acreage. . . .

Obviously, the ordinary cow cannot clamber over Vermont pastures. The early settlers, bringing cows from other States, quickly learned this, and for several years a problem worse than the Indians . . . was that of getting cows to and from pasture. It took two men for each cow and the task was comparable to teaching her to go up and down a ladder.

But the *gyascutus* had legs shorter on one side than on the other, so it could circumambulate the Vermont hills with the greatest ease. The Vermonters immediately understood they must have cows with the *gyascutus's* running gear, so they domesticated the creature and by interbreeding developed a new breed of cattle. Today, as all Americans should know, all Vermont calves are born with legs shorter on one side than the other. . . .

Some *gyascustuses,* or *gyuscuti,* survived in an unadulterated state even as recently as the period of my boyhood. They were cherished by the farmers as evidence of Providence's concern for their welfare. We recall one especially affectionate *gyascuta* that was strongly attached to us in our early youth. How many times we have trudged to school in tears at the sight of the *cuter cuss's* attempts to follow us on a road made for legs of equal length.[1]

The Come-at-a-Body

REPORTED by Mr. B. B. Bickford of Gorham, N. H. Not found outside the White Mountains. A short, stubby, rather small animal, resembling a woodchuck but having very soft, velvety, kitten-like fur. Harmless, but surprising. Has the terrifying habit of suddenly rushing directly at you from the brush, then stopping only a few inches away and spitting like a cat. A strong mink-like scent is thrown, and the Come-at-a-Body rushes away.

From "A Cuter Cuss for a Pet," by William H. Heath, in the Haverhill (Mass.) *Gazette,* March 18, 1944, p. 4. Cited in *Supplement I: The American Language,* An Inquiry into the Development of English in the United States, by H. L. Mencken, pp. 247–248. Copyright, 1945, by Alfred A. Knopf, Inc. New York.

[1] Mr. Heath, in March, 1944, asked his father in Vermont to search the attic of the family homestead "for an old snapshot of the female of the species that was a pet of my boyhood." Unfortunately, it could not be found.—H. L. M.

From *Fearsome Critters,* by Henry H. Tryon, p. 13. Copyright, 1939, by Idlewild Press. Cornwall, New York.

PART TWO

MYTHS, LEGENDS, AND TRADITIONS

Jonathan is conscious still that he lives in the world of the Unseen as well as of the Seen.

—JAMES RUSSELL LOWELL

. . . fabulous humors naturally grow out of the very body of all surprising terrible events—as the smitten tree gives birth to its fungi.

—HERMAN MELVILLE

Tradition . . . sometimes brings down truth that history has let slip, but is oftener the wild babble of the time, such as was formerly spoken at the fireside and now congeals in newspapers.

—NATHANIEL HAWTHORNE

It may be said, then, that while History has its truth, the Legend has its own; both taking for their end the portrayal of Man as he has existed in every age,—a creature in whom the imagination is supreme, and who performs deeds terrible or heroic according as it may be aroused into action.

—SAMUEL ADAMS DRAKE

I. WONDERS OF THE INVISIBLE WORLD

Such Divine Judgements, Tempests, Floods, Earth-quakes, Thunders as are unusual, strange Apparitions, or what ever else shall happen that is Prodigious, Witchcrafts, Diabolical Possessions, Remarkable Judgements upon noted Sinners, eminent Deliverances, and Answers of Prayer, are to be reckoned among Illustrious Providences.—INCREASE MATHER

. . . these with many other stories they told me, the credit whereof I will neither impeach nor inforce, but shall satisfie my self, and I hope the Reader hereof, with the saying of a wife, learned and honourable Knight, that there are many stranger things in the world, than are to be seen between *London* and *Stanes.*

—JOHN JOSSELYN

1. PROVIDENCES AND PRODIGIES

THE early history of New England is filled with accounts of "surprising terrible events" and "fabulous rumors" no less marvelous than the local wonders of travelers' and tall tales and similarly arising out of a pious or playful belief in the impossible. For before the New Englander became a Yankee, he was a Puritan; and the superstitious seventeenth century gave credence and currency to remarkable providences and memorable accidents such as were recorded by the Mathers for the improvement of religion and by historians like Edward Johnson intent on showing the "wonder-working providence of Sion's Saviour in New England."

In their desire to found a great church and a great state in Massachusetts the Puritans were convinced that God showed a providential regard for his children by delivering them from the perils of the sea and the wilderness, protecting them from the Indians, and otherwise providing for their needs. At the same time, "*these* too were tryed with very humbling circumstances," and in answer to "fervent prayers" God often "condescended" an "extraordinary account" for the "quieting of their afflicted spirits." Such was the vision of the New Haven Specter Ship which appeared in the sky over New Haven harbor in June, 1647, and revealed to the "admiring spectators" the "tragick end" of the ship of which they had had no news for six months.

These prodigies differed from the omens of the ancients in that they were providential rather than accidental, but they invoked the same awe and dread of the shadows that coming events cast before them. Thus, in his history of King Philip's war, Increase Mather declared that "It is a common observation, verified by the experience of many ages, that great and publick calamityes seldome come upon any place without prodigious warnings to forerun and signify what is to be expected."

Two notable accounts have come down to us of public calamities that failed to materialize, with heroi-comic rather than tragic effects and implications. In April, 1775, a baseless rumor of impending British invasion swept the town of Ipswich and threw the populace into a ridiculous frenzy of terror and flight, which Whittier rationalizes as "a prudent and wholesome regard to their own comfort and safety" and the safety of their "hard-gained property." Earlier, on a July night in 1758, the alarmed residents of Windham were routed from their beds by the fiendish outcries of what they took to be attacking Indians but what proved to be bull frogs fighting for water in a nearly dried-up pond.

2. History *versus* Myth

Erroneous perception such as underlay the Ipswich and Windham frights also gave rise to legends like the *Palatine* Light. Tradition says that in the first half of the eighteenth century (1752, according to one source), the ship *Palatine* "sailed from some German port, laden with well-to-do emigrants, bound to Philadelphia; that the captain died or was killed on the passage; that the officers and crew starved and plundered the helpless emigrants, and finally, in their boats, abandoned the vessel, which drifted ashore. . . . The ship was undoubtedly burned." [1]

So much for "history." Now for myth.

> A part of her legend is that she was somehow changed into a ship of fire, rising up from the waters of Block Island Sound, which separates the Island from the main land, and gracefully sailing on this tack or that, mysteriously manned by an invisible captain and crew, until hull, spars, ropes, and sails all slowly vanished in the air or settled down into the deep. Nor was all of this a myth, or an *ignis fatuus*. For there is ample evidence that a very strange light once performed very strange freaks over those waters. . . .

Upon analyzing the legend and attempting to find a satisfactory explanation, Reverend S. T. Livermore arrived at the conclusion that there was no connection between the burning of the *Palatine* [2] (by pillaging Block Islanders, according to a tradition which Reverend Livermore stoutly denies) and the *Palatine* Light, and that possibly the latter "was fed by gas rising through the water." At the same time he admits: "Of this phenomenon no satisfactory explanation has ever been given, while much talent has been employed in making it instrumental in gratifying the taste for the marvelous."

3. Nature Faking

In 1817 a similar zeal for the truth led the Linnean Society of Boston to undertake an investigation of the Gloucester sea-serpent, taking the sworn

---

[1] For this and subsequent passages regarding the *Palatine* Light, see Rev. S. T. Livermore, *Block Island* (Hartford, 1882), pp. 92–105.

[2] The records show that the ship was wrecked in the Bay of Bengal in 1784.

depositions of twelve witnesses. Yet, for all its scientific effort in collecting testimony, the Committee fell into the vulgar and absurd error of a false hypothesis, declaring that a common land-snake, found on shore shortly after the appearance of the serpent, was "of the same species."

The history of the sea-serpent proves that, far from being killed by the historical and scientific impulse, the myth-making imagination may exist alongside of it and that in building up elaborate hypotheses based on hearsay or misinformation, myth is supplemented and often surpassed by hoaxing and practical joking. This is especially true in the realm of natural history, where attempts to establish corroborative evidence recall Defoe's method, as in "The Strange Apparition of Mrs. Veal," of employing "ingenious confirmation" to divert attention from the basis in "anonymous evidence."

Far from being limited to the common people, myth, like superstition, is also found among the learned men of early New England, often in the same breath with a scientific statement. Thus, in addition to his snake stories, Cotton Mather, in 1717, sent the Royal Society a miraculous cure for snakebite—*Ophiophuga*, Cottonis Mather.

> A *Poultiss* of this bruised and laid to the Part Bitten by the *Rattle-Snake*, it immediately fetches out the *Deadly Poyson:* it's also remarkable, that if put into the *Shoes*, no *Serpent* will dare to come near them. A *Tea* of it is a good *Ophthalmiack*.[1]

4. Ghost-Ridden and Devil-Doomed

As a corollary to the belief in providence or divine intervention (supernatural phenomena), the seventeenth century believed in "diabolical operations" (preternatural phenomena). As Melville says, "in maritime life, far more than in that of terra firma, wild rumors abound, wherever there is any adequate reality for them to cling to." Perhaps the noblest and terriblest embodiment of the maleficent forces of the universe is Moby-Dick, the white whale, the "rumors and portents" of whose savagery, ubiquitousness, immortality, and whiteness fired the apocalyptic imagination of Melville.

With the accusing ghost who returns to avenge a wrong or the devil-doomed spirit condemned to the endless repetition of a Sisyphean task, as with the doom that follows a prophetic curse, and other such miracles, we are once more in the kingdom of morality, where the sense of a divine order, as well as the taste for the marvelous, is satisfied by retributive or poetic justice.

B. A. B.

---

[1] George Lyman Kittredge, *Letters of Samuel Lee and Samuel Sewall Relating to New England and the Indians, The Publications of the Colonial Society of Massachusetts* (Cambridge, 1912), p. 184.

SINGULAR OCCURRENCES

The New Haven Specter Ship

Behold, a fourth colony of New-English Christians, in a manner *stolen* into the world, and a colony, indeed, *constellated* with many stars of the first magnitude. The colony was under the conduct of as holy, and as prudent, and as genteel persons as most that ever visited these nooks of America; and yet *these* too were tryed with very humbling circumstances.

Being Londoners, or merchants and men of traffick and business, their design was in a manner wholly to apply themselves unto *trade;* but the design failing, they found their great estates sink so fast, that they must quickly *do something.* Whereupon in the year 1646, gathering together almost all the strength which was left them, they built one ship more, which they fraighted for England with the best part of their tradable estates; and sundry of their eminent persons embarked themselves in her for the voyage. But, alas! the ship was never after heard of: she foundred in the sea; and in her were lost, not only the *hopes* of their future trade, but also the *lives* of several excellent persons, as well as divers *manuscripts* of some great men in the country, sent over for the service of the church, which were now buried in the ocean. The fuller story of that grievous matter, let the reader with a just astonishment accept from the pen of the reverend person who is now the pastor of New-Haven. I wrote unto him for it, and was thus answered:

"Reverend and Dear Sir—

"In compliance with your desires, I now give you the relation of that apparition of a ship in the air, which I have received from the most credible, judicious and curious surviving observers of it.

"In the year 1647, besides much other lading, a far more rich treasure of passengers, (five or six of which were persons of chief note and worth in New Haven) put themselves on board a new ship, built at Rhode Island, of about 150 tuns; but so walty, that the master (Lamberton) often said she would prove their grave. In the month of January, cutting their way through much ice, on which they were accompanied with the Reverend Mr. Davenport, besides many other friends, with many fears, as well as prayers and tears, they set sail. Mr. Davenport, in prayer, with an observable emphasis, used these words: 'Lord, if it be thy pleasure to bury these

---

From *Magnalia Christi Americana;* or, The Ecclesiastical History of New England, from Its First Planting, in the year 1620, unto the Year of Our Lord 1698, in Seven Books, by Cotton Mather, Volume I, pp. 83–84. Entered, according to Act of Congress, in the year 1852, by Silas Andrus & Son, in the Clerk's Office of the District Court of Connecticut. Hartford. 1853.

our friends in the bottom of the sea, they are thine; save them!' The spring following, no tidings of these friends arrived with the ships from England: New Haven's heart began to fail her: this put the godly people on much prayer, both publick and private, 'that the Lord would (if it was his pleasure) let them hear what he had done with their dear friends, and prepare them with a suitable submission to his Holy Will.' In June next ensuing, a great thunder storm arose out of the north-west; after which (the hemisphere being serene) about an hour before sun-set, a ship of like dimensions with the aforesaid, with her canvas and colours abroad (though the wind northernly) appeared in the air coming up from our harbour's mouth, which lyes southward from the town, seemingly with her sails filled under a fresh gale, holding her course north, and continuing under observation, sailing against the wind for the space of half an hour.

"Many were drawn to behold this great work of God; yea, the very children cryed out, 'There's a brave ship!' At length, crowding up as far as there is usually water sufficient for such a vessel, and so near some of the spectators, as that they imagined a man might hurl a stone on board her, her *main-top* seemed to be blown off, but left hanging in the shrouds; then her *mizzen-top;* then all her *masting* seemed blown away by the board: quickly after the *hulk* brought unto a careen, she overset, and so vanished into a smoaky cloud, which in some time dissipated, leaving, as everywhere else, a clear air. The admiring spectators could distinguish the several colours of each part, the principal rigging, and such proportions, as caused not only the generality of persons to say, 'This was the mould of their ship, and this was her tragick end,' but Mr. Davenport also in publick declared to this effect, 'That God had condescended, for the quieting of their afflicted spirits, this extraordinary account of his sovereign disposal of those for whom so many fervent prayers were made continually.' Thus I am Sir, "Your humble servant,

"JAMES PIERPONT"

Reader, there being yet living so many credible gentlemen, that were eyewitness of this *wonderful* thing, I venture to publish it for a thing as *undoubted* as 'tis wonderful.

The Moodus Noises

CONTEMPORARY ACCOUNTS [1]

FROM time immemorial, East Haddam has been the seat of uncommon subterranean noises, called Moodus noises. The Indian name of the town

[1] From *Connecticut Historical Collections,* Containing A General Collection of Interesting Facts, Traditions, Biographical Sketches, Anecdotes, &c., Relating to the History and Antiquities of Every Town in Connecticut, with Geographical Descriptions, by John Warner Barber, pp. 525–528. Entered according to the Act of Congress, in the year 1836, by John W. Barber and A. Willard, in the Clerk's Office, of the District Court of Connecticut. New Haven and Hartford.

was *Mackimoodus,* which in English is the *place of noises;* a name given with the utmost propriety to the place. The accounts given of the noises and quakings there are very remarkable. Were it not that the people are accustomed to them, they would occasion great alarm. The Rev. Mr. Hosmer, in a letter to Mr. Prince, of Boston, written August 13th, 1729, gives this account of them:—"As to the earthquakes, I have something considerable and awful to tell you. Earthquakes have been here, (and no where but in this precinct, as can be discerned; that is, they seem to have their centre, rise and origin among us,) as has been observed for more than thirty years. I have been informed, that in this place, before the English settlements, there were great numbers of Indian inhabitants, and that it was a place of extraordinary *Indian Pawaws,* or in short, that it was a place where the Indians drove a prodigious trade at worshipping the devil. Also I was informed, that, many years past, an old Indian was asked, What was the reason of the noises in this place? To which he replied, that the Indian's God was very angry because Englishman's God was come here.

"Now whether there be any thing diabolical in these things, I know not; but this I know, that God Almighty is to be seen and trembled at, in what has been often heard among us. Whether it be fire or air distressed in the subterraneous caverns of the earth, cannot be known; for there is no eruption, no explosion perceptible, but by sounds and tremors, which sometimes are very fearful and dreadful. I have myself heard eight or ten sounds successively, and imitating small arms, in the space of five minutes. I have, I suppose, heard several hundreds of them within twenty years; some more, some less terrible. Sometimes we have heard them almost every day, and great numbers of them in the space of a year. Often times I have observed them to be coming down from the north, imitating slow thunder, until the sound came near or right under, and then there seemed to be a breaking like the noise of a cannon shot, or severe thunder, which shakes the houses, and all that is in them. They have in a manner ceased, since the great earthquake. As I remember, there have been but two heard since that time, and those but moderate."

A worthy gentleman, about six years since, gave the following account of them. "The awful noises, of which Mr. Hosmer gave an account, in his historical minutes, and concerning which you desire further information, continue to the present time. The effects they produce, are various as the intermediate degrees between the roar of a cannon and the noise of a pistol. The concussions of the earth, made at the same time, are as much diversified as the sounds in the air. The shock they give to a dwelling house, is the same as the falling of logs on the floor. The smaller shocks produced no emotions of terror or fear in the minds of the inhabitants. They are spoken of as usual occurrences, and are called Moodus noises. But when they are so violent as to be felt in the adjacent towns, they are called earthquakes. During my residence here, which has been almost thirty-six years, I have invariably observed, after some of the most violent of these shocks, that an account has been published in the newspapers, of a small shock of an earthquake, at New London and Hartford. Nor do I believe, in all that period, there has been any account published of an earthquake in Connecticut, which was not far more violent here than in any other place. By recurring to the newspapers, you will find, that an earthquake was noticed on the 18th May, 1791, about 10 o'clock, P.M. It was perceived as far distant as Boston and New York. A few minutes after there was another shock, which was perceptible at the distance of seventy miles. Here, at that time, the concussion of the earth, and the roaring of the atmosphere, were most tremendous. Consternation and dread filled every house. Many chimnies[*sic*] were untopped and walls thrown down. It was a night much to be remembered; for besides the two shocks which were noticed at a distance during the night there was here a succession of shocks, to the number of twenty, perhaps thirty; the effects of which, like all others, decreased in every direction, in proportion to the distances. The next day, stones of several tons weight, were found removed from their places; and apertures in the earth, and fissures in immovable rocks, ascertained the places where the explosions were made. Since that time, the noises and shocks have been less frequent than before; though not a year passeth over us, but some of them are perceptible." *

Mount Tom is situated at the junction of Moodus with Salmon river. . . . This mountain seems to be situated about the centre from which the Moodus noises proceed. The severest shocks are felt as far N. Easterly as Boston, and as far S. West as New York, and there noticed as earthquakes. In 1816 and 1817, in the night, these noises were more than usually violent. A person was on Mount Tom about 15 years since, at the time these noises were heard. It appeared to this person as though a stone or large body fell underneath the ground directly under his feet, and grated down to a considerable distance in the depths below. The cause of these noises is explained by some to be mineral or chemical combinations, exploding at a depth of many thousand feet beneath the surface of the earth. The jar is similar to that of exploded gun powder.

* * * * *

. . . "Various have been the conjectures concerning the cause of these earthquakes or Moodus noises, as they are called. The following account has gained credit with many persons.—It is reported that, between 20 and 30 years ago, a transient person came to this town, who called himself Doctor Steel, from Great Britain, who having had information respecting those noises, made critical observation at different times and in different places, till at length he dug up two pearls of great value, which he called Carbuncles, near Salmon river;—and that he told people the noises would be discontinued for many years, as he had taken away their cause; but as he had discovered others in miniature, they would be again heard in process of time. The best evidence of the authenticity of this story is, that

* The foregoing account is from Trumbull's *History of Connecticut.*

it has happened agreeably to his prophecy. The noises did cease for many years, and have again been heard for two or three years past, and they increase—three shocks have been felt in a short space, one of which acording to a late paper was felt at New London, though it was by the account much more considerable in this and the adjacent towns." *

An Interview [2]

I inquired particularly about these noises of two men who were sitting on the post office piazza. "We still have one once in a while," the older man said. "The ground shakes and there's a noise like a cannon going off or a rumblin' like thunder. It woke me up once in the night and the dishes were rattling on the buttery shelves. You remember old Hardy, don't you, Fred?"

"Yes," the younger man replied, "he gave me a horse-whipping one time when I was a boy."

"Well," the older man resumed, "he tells of being at work on the medder one day when the ground shook so strong that it brought the cattle down on their knees. The noises are made by gas and dead air exploding underground. They start a mile and a half from here on Cave Hill. Right in the side of that high hill there's a cave you can walk into for about forty rods. You can keep going until the air gets so stagnant that your light goes out. Then it's time for you to start back."

"We use to have quite a famous drum corps here," Fred remarked, "and some one made up a piece of poetry about that and the Moodus earthquake. The words were:

"A man from Texas tall and stout
Stuck up his nose and hollered out,
'Oh, what is that infernal noise?'
'Twas nothing but the Drum Corps boys."

The Windham Frogs

Much pleasantry has been indulged at the expense of the inhabitants of Windham, on account of a singular occurrence which happened in the year

* From the *Connecticut Gazette* (New London), August 20, 1790, No. 1397, dated "East Haddam, August 5, 1790."

[2] From *Highways and Byways of New England,* Including the States of Massachusetts, New Hampshire, Rhode Island, Connecticut, Vermont and Maine, Written and Illustrated by Clifton Johnson, pp. 278–279. Copyright, 1915, by The Macmillan Company. New York and London. 1916.

From *Connecticut Historical Collections,* Containing a General Collection of Interesting Facts, Traditions, Biographical Sketches, Anecdotes, &c., Relating to the History and Antiquities of Every Town in Connecticut, with Geographical Descriptions, by John Warner Barber, pp. 446–447. Entered according to the Act of Congress, in the year 1836, by John W. Barber and A. Willard, in the Clerk's Office, of the District Court of Connecticut. New Haven and Hartford.

1758, by which the inhabitants were very much frightened. The following is from a sheet recently printed in the county, entitled "Lawyers and Bullfrogs," and will show the cause of the fright. . . .

"On a dark cloudy dismal night in the month of July, A.D. 1758, the inhabitants of Windham, a small town in the Eastern part of Connecticut, had retired to rest, and for several hours, all were wrapped in profound repose—when suddenly, soon after midnight, the slumbers of the peaceful inhabitants were disturbed by a most terrific noise in the sky right over their heads, which to many, seemed the yells and screeches of infuriated Indians, and others had no other way of accounting for the awful sounds which still kept increasing, but by supposing the day of judgment had certainly come, and to their terrified imaginations, the awful uproar in the air, seemed the immediate precursor of the clangor of the last trumpet.—At intervals, many supposed they could distinguish the calling out of the particular names, as of Cols. DYER and ELDERKIN, two eminent lawyers, and this increased the general terror. . . . But soon there was a rush from every house, the tumult in the air still increasing—old and young, male and female, poured forth into the streets, '*in puris naturalibus*,' entirely forgetful, in their hurry and consternation, of their nether habiliments, and with eyes upturned tried to pierce the almost palpable darkness.—My venerable informant, who well recollects the event, says that some daring 'spirits' concluding there was nothing supernatural in the hubbub and uproar over head, but rather, that they heard the yells of Indians commencing a midnight attack, loaded their guns and sallied forth to meet the invading foes. These valiant heroes on ascending the hill that bounds the village on the East, perceived that the sounds came from that quarter, and not from the skies, as first believed, but their courage would not permit them to proceed to the daring extremity of advancing Eastward, until they had discovered the real cause of alarm and distress, which pervaded the whole village.—Towards morning the sounds in the air seemed to die away. . . . In the morning, the whole cause of alarm, which produced such distressing apprehensions among the good people of the town, was apparent to all who took the trouble to go to a certain mill pond situated about three fourths of a mile Eastward of the village.—This pond, hereafter, in the *annals of Fame,* forever to be called the FROG POND, in consequence of a severe drought, which had prevailed many weeks had become nearly dry, and the Bull Frogs, (with which it was densely *populated,*) at the mill fought a pitched battle on the sides of the ditch which ran through it, for the possession and enjoyment of the fluid which remained.—Long and obstinately was the contest maintained; and many thousands of the combatants were found defunct, on both sides of the ditch, the next morning.—It had been uncommonly still, for several hours before the battle commenced, but suddenly, as if by a preconcerted agreement, every frog on one side of the ditch, raised the war cry, Col. Dyer, Col. Dyer, and at the same instant, from the opposite side, resounded the adverse shout of Elderkin too, Elderkin too.—Owing to some peculiar state of the atmosphere, the awful noises and cries appeared, to the distressed Windhamites, to be directly over their heads. . . ."

The Great Ipswich Fright

THE 21st of April, 1775, witnessed an awful commotion in the little village of Ipswich. Old men, and boys, (the middle aged had marched to Lexington some days before,) and all the women in the place who were not bedridden or sick, came rushing as with one accord to the green in front of the meeting-house. A rumor, which no one attempted to trace or authenticate, spread from lip to lip that the British regulars had landed on the coast and were marching upon the town. A scene of indescribable terror and confusion followed. Defence was out of the question, as the young and able-bodied men of the entire region round about had marched to Cambridge and Lexington. The news of the battle at the latter place, exaggerated in all its details, had been just received; terrible stories of the atrocities committed by the dreaded "regulars" had been related; and it was believed that nothing short of a general extermination of the patriots,—men, women, and children,—was contemplated by the British commander. Almost simultaneously the people of Beverly, a village a few miles distant, were smitten with the same terror. How the rumor was communicated no one could tell. It was there believed that the enemy had fallen upon Ipswich, and massacred the inhabitants without regard to age or sex.

It was about the middle of the afternoon of this day that the people of Newbury, ten miles farther north, assembled in an informal meeting at the town-house to hear accounts from the Lexington fight and to consider what action was necessary in consequence of that event. Parson Carey was about opening the meeting with prayer when hurried hoof-beats sounded up the street, and a messenger, loose-haired and panting for breath, rushed up the staircase. "Turn out, turn out, for God's sake," he cried, "or you will be all killed! The regulars are marching on us; they are at Ipswich now, cutting and slashing all before them!" Universal consternation was the immediate result of this fearful announcement; Parson Carey's prayer died on his lips; the congregation dispersed over the town, carrying to every house the tidings that the regulars had come. Men on horseback went galloping up and down the streets shouting the alarm. Women and children echoed it from every corner. The panic became irresistible, uncontrollable. Cries were heard that the dreaded invaders had reached Oldtown Bridge, a little distance from the village, and that they were killing all

---

From *Prose Works of John Greenleaf Whittier*, Vol. II, pp. 115–121. Entered according to Act of Congress, in the year 1866, by John Greenleaf Whittier, in the Clerk's Office of the District Court of the District of Massachusetts. Boston: Ticknor and Fields.

For an earlier account, see Joshua Coffin, *A Sketch of the History of Newbury, Newburyport, and West Newbury, from 1635 to 1845* (Boston, 1845), pp. 245–247.

whom they encountered. Flight was resolved upon. All the horses and vehicles in the town were put in requisition; men, women, and children hurried as for life towards the north. Some threw their silver and pewter ware and other valuables into wells. Large numbers crossed the Merrimac, and spent the night in the deserted houses of Salisbury, whose inhabitants, stricken by the strange terror, had fled into New Hampshire to take up their lodgings in dwellings also abandoned by their owners.

A few individuals refused to fly with the multitude; some, unable to move by reason of sickness, were left behind by their relatives. One old gentleman, whose excessive corpulence rendered retreat on his part impossible, made a virtue of necessity; and, seating himself in his door-way with his loaded king's arm, upbraided his more nimble neighbors, advising them to do as he did, and "stop and shoot the devils." Many ludicrous instances of the intensity of the terror might be related. One man got his family into a boat to go to Ram Island for safety. He imagined he was pursued by the enemy through the dusk of the evening, and was annoyed by the crying of an infant in the after part of the boat. "Do throw that squalling brat overboard," he called to his wife, "or we shall be all discovered and killed." A poor woman ran four or five miles up the river and stopped to take breath and nurse her child, when she found to her great horror that she had brought off the cat instead of the baby!

All through that memorable night the terror swept onward towards the north with a speed which seems almost miraculous, producing everywhere the same results. At midnight a horseman, clad only in shirt and breeches, dashed by our grandfather's door, in Haverhill, twenty miles up the river. "Turn out! Get a musket! Turn out!" he shouted; "the regulars are landing on Plum Island!"—"I'm glad of it," responded the old gentleman from his chamber-window; "I wish they were all there, and obliged to stay there." When it is understood that Plum Island is little more than a naked sand-ridge, the benevolence of this wish can be readily appreciated.

All the boats on the river were constantly employed for several hours in conveying across the terrified fugitives. Through "the dead waste and middle of the night" they fled over the border into New Hampshire. Some feared to take the frequented roads, and wandered over wooded hills and through swamps where the snows of the late winter had scarcely melted. They heard the tramp and outcry of those behind them, and fancied that the sounds were made by pursuing enemies. Fast as they fled, the terror, by some unaccountable means, outstripped them. They found houses deserted and streets strewn with household-stuffs abandoned in the hurry of escape. Towards morning, however, the tide partially turned. Grown men began to feel ashamed of their fears. The old Anglo-Saxon hardihood paused and looked the terror in its face. Single or in small parties, armed with such weapons as they found at hand,—among which long poles, sharpened and charred at the end, were conspicuous,—they began to retrace their steps. In the mean time such of the good people of Ipswich as were unable or unwilling to leave their homes became convinced that the terrible rumor which had nearly depopulated their settlement was unfounded.

Among those who had there awaited the onslaught of the regulars was a young man from Exeter, New Hampshire. Becoming satisfied that the whole matter was a delusion, he mounted his horse and followed after the retreating multitude, undeceiving all whom he overtook. Late at night he reached Newburyport, greatly to the relief of its sleepless inhabitants and hurried across the river, proclaiming as he rode the welcome tidings. The sun rose upon haggard and jaded fugitives, worn with excitement and fatigue, slowly returning homeward, their satisfaction at the absence of danger somewhat moderated by an unpleasant consciousness of the ludicrous scenes of their premature night flitting.

Any inference which might be drawn from the foregoing narrative derogatory to the character of the people of New England at that day, on the score of courage, would be essentially erroneous. It is true, they were not the men to court danger or rashly throw away their lives for the mere glory of the sacrifice. They had always a prudent and wholesome regard to their own comfort and safety; they justly looked upon sound heads and limbs as better than broken ones; life was to them too serious and important, and their hard-gained property too valuable, to be lightly hazarded. They never attempted to cheat themselves by under-estimating the difficulty to be encountered or shutting their eyes to its probable consequences. Cautious, wary, schooled in the subtle strategy of Indian warfare, where self-preservation is by no means a secondary object, they had little in common with the reckless enthusiasm of their French allies or the stolid indifference of the fighting machines of the British regular army. When danger could no longer be avoided, they met it with firmness and iron endurance, but with a very vivid appreciation of its magnitude. Indeed, it must be admitted by all who are familiar with the history of our fathers, that the element of fear held an important place among their characteristics. It exaggerated all the dangers of their earthly pilgrimage, and peopled the future with shapes of evil. Their fear of Satan invested him with some of the attributes of Omnipotence, and almost reached the point of reverence. The slightest shock of an earthquake filled all hearts with terror. Stout men trembled by their hearths with dread of some paralytic old woman supposed to be a witch. And when they believed themselves called upon to grapple with these terrors, and endure the afflictions of their allotment, they brought to the trial a capability of suffering undiminished by the chloroform of modern philosophy. They were heroic in endurance. Panics like the one we have described might bow and sway them like reeds in the wind; but they stood up like the oaks of their own forests beneath the thunder and the hail of actual calamity.

It was certainly lucky for the good people of Essex County that no wicked wag of a Tory undertook to immortalize in rhyme their ridiculous hegira, as Judge Hopkinson did the famous Battle of the Kegs in Philadelphia. Like the more recent Madawaska war in Maine, the great

Chepatchet demonstration in Rhode Island, and the "Sauk fuss" of Wisconsin, it remains to this day "unsyllabled, unsung"; and the fast-fading memory of age alone preserves the unwritten history of the great Ipswich fright.

The Palatine Light

. . . LOOKING from McSparran Hill, Block Island is plainly to be seen in all its breadth, some twenty miles to the south, with Montauk Point, the eastern extremity of Long Island, lying some few leagues to the westward of it. From this point, too, if unbroken tradition can be relied upon, there was formerly seen occasionally at night the "Palatine ship" all in flames, hovering about the island, where the legend asserts a ship freighted with emigrants and their effects from Germany in the first half of the eighteenth century was purposely—as some said—run on shore by her captain and crew, for the sake of plunder, whilst others said that the vessel was decoyed one dark stormy night by means of false lights arranged by the islanders with like intent. I remember hearing, when quite young, of an islander by the name of ——, who was generally well and in his right mind except at the season of the year when the Palatine ship was wrecked, and after being stripped of everything of value was set on fire by the land pirates and burned with all the crew and passengers on board. At this particular season this old man, it was said, always became madly insane, and would rave about seeing a ship all ablaze, with men falling from her burning rigging and shrouds, and ever and anon shrink in horror from the spectres of two women, whose hands he cut off or disabled by blows from a cutlass, as they sought to cling to the gunwale of the last boat that left the burning ship and all on board to their fate that not one might remain alive to bear witness of the terrible catastrophe and crime. Whether the legend is true or false I know not, though I do know that many Block Islanders, in my early days, firmly believed that the burning Palatine ship was often seen near the island.

My father became possessed, by will of his uncle, Rowland Robinson, of two or more farms on Block Island, which he leased for some years, and finally sold to several different purchasers. This gave occasion for some of the leading and most intelligent men, as well as others from Block Island, to visit our house in Narragansett, and sometimes pass the night. Of course I was always curious to hear about the old Palatine ship, and I

From *Recollections of Olden Times:* Rowland Robinson of Narragansett and His Unfortunate Daughter, With Genealogies of the Robinson and Hazard Families of Rhode Island, by Thomas R. Hazard, "Shepherd Tom," in His Eighty-First and Eighty-Second Years, Also Genealogical Sketch of the Hazards of the Middle States, by Willis P. Hazard, of Westchester, Pa., pp. 127–129. Entered according to Act of Congress, in the year 1879, by John P. Sanborn, in the Office of the Librarian of Congress, at Washington, D.C. Newport, Rhode Island.

do not remember an instance wherein these several visitors did not bear testimony to the verity of the phenomenon. On one occasion I remember asking the late George Sheffield, who had just arrived at our house from Block Island, what he thought the weather would be, to which he replied that it would continue fair, but directly hesitated, and said to Shedrick Card—a venerable old patriarch, who happened to accompany him—, "Mr. Card, the old Palatine loomed up high last night, didn't she?" Mr. Card answered in the affirmative, when the other rejoined, addressing his words to me, "I was mistaken; it will be stormy soon." It was evident that neither of these men, both of whom were very intelligent, had the least doubt of their having seen the ship all in flames the night before, and that her *bona fide* appearance was no more than an ordinary occurrence.

Since the conclusion of these papers in printed form, I have received a very interesting letter from Mr. Benjamin Congdon, who, I remember, lived many years ago in a house that stood north of the Walcott farm and west of the road in Point Judith. Mr. Congdon is now in his ninetieth year and was considered by all who knew him in Rhode Island to be a man of unusual intelligence and probity. I make the following extracts from his letter which is dated "Napoli, Cattaraugus Co., New York, March 4, 1878."

"In 1800, my elder brother attended Robert Rogers' Academy in Newport. I was then twelve years old. My father had a school kept in a small house, on our farm, for a number of years, by the late Thomas Perry, who kept the best school I was ever in. Mr. Perry afterwards moved to Westerly, and was chosen cashier of the Washington Bank, which position he retained until his death, when his son Charles succeeded him, who, I think, remains cashier of the same bank still, now seventy years since his father first assumed the same position. I can recollect well when Washington's second term expired, in 1797; when John Adams became President, followed by Jefferson, and then Madison, who was President during the War of 1812. About the burning Palatine ship you speak of in your interesting papers, I may say that I have seen her eight or ten times or more. In those early days nobody doubted her being sent by an Almighty Power to punish those wicked men who murdered her passengers and crew. After the last of these were dead she was never more seen. We lived when I was young, in Charlestown, directly opposite Block Island, where we used to have a plain view of the burning ship."

The Dancing Mortar

THIS, though somewhat intermixed with another legend, has its own individuality. Like every *ignis fatuus* it has its foundation in a reality. The

---

From *Block Island,* I. A Map and Guide; II. A History (Abridged), by Rev. S. T. Livermore, pp. 89–92. Copyright, 1882, by S. T. Livermore. Hartford, Connecticut: Press of The Case, Lockwood & Brainard Company.

real seems to be this,—that when the ship *Palatine* stopped at Block Island and left her diseased and dying inmates, she either then or on her return from the West Indies left on the Island logs or blocks of lignum-vitae, from which the Islanders, then destitute of mills, made mortars for crushing their corn. Two of those mortars are now in existence, the one here described having been deposited by the writer in Rhode Island Hall of Brown University.

To test the authenticity of this legend of the Dancing Mortar, several of the oldest and most trustworthy Islanders were consulted concerning it separately, without informing one of the statements of the other. This was in the year 1876. Mrs. Margaret Dodge, eighty-six years old, of remarkably clear memory; Mr. Anthony Littlefield, and his wife, each eighty-four years old; Mr. and Mrs. John Ball, both over seventy; Mrs. Caroline Willis, eighty-one; and others, all agreed that this mortar was from the ship *Palatine*. It was well known to have been kept and owned at the house once owned and occupied by the venerable Simon Ray, where several of the unfortunate passengers of the *Palatine* were hospitably received, and near which house are theii graves. There it remained long after the Ray family had passed away, and his house was occupied by another family.

For a considerable period after this change, the old Ray house was said to be haunted. But few, perhaps, of the present readers know how much this means, unless they are familiar with the old stories of chimney ghosts and such "hobgoblins" as Bunyan had in mind when he wrote the Pilgrim's Progress. In and around that house such sights and sounds were said to have been seen and heard as ordinary nerves protest against repeating in an attempted description. In comparison with them the modern fabrications of spiritualism and the tricks of ventriloquists are puerile.

The Dancing Mortar, as a part of the furniture of that house so powerfully haunted, naturally shared in the mysterious endowments of its surroundings. Before contemplating some of its strange freaks, a view should be had of it in its present condition.

It is of lignum-vitae, fourteen inches high, about ten inches in diameter, and is nearly as heavy as would be the same bulk of stone, it is so hard. It would hold about four quarts. The grains of its fiber are diagonal, for the most part, and so interwoven as to prevent it from cracking by hard usage or from age. For a considerable time it was used as a splitting-block, and now bears the marks of the axe on its weather-worn, gray, and shabby exterior, made so by a half century's exposure to the storms of summer and winter. Its interior, which used to receive the corn and the pestle, now looks "aged and gray," and it is hoped the rosette of moss which it wore when placed in its modern and more classic home will long remain as an ornament of one of the relics of antiquity.

In its younger days it did its dancing, according to the legend, when the old house where it was had the reputation of being mightily haunted. Then, they say, while the inmates were conversing on common topics, or musing over the hauntings of the house, this mortar would begin to move, untouched by human hand, until it threw itself from its standing position upon its side, striking with a *thud* upon the floor. This in itself was sufficient to alarm the spectators. But this was only the first preparation for dancing. Its next move was to roll from one side of the room to the other, by some invisible impulse. At this the amazement of the inmates can better be imagined than described. We can picture to ourselves the lively times in that room, lighted by a wood fire in the evening, as men, women, and children dodged here and there to escape the touch of that haunted, rolling mortar, lest they too should be infected with its witchery. After this rolling came its final antics, for the occasion. These, after a little respite, consisted of righting itself up again on end. Then came the *dancing,* as without visible springs, or the touch of visible hands, it bounded from the floor to the joists and floor overhead, and thus went up and down between the floors, varying its position from one part of the room to another. Admitting this to be so, what could have been more natural than for those inmates, at the beginning of that lonely, mysterious mortar waltz, to have danced a "quickstep" hurriedly out of the doors and windows!

One of the half dozen aged witnesses concerning this legend incidentally suggested, though unintended, a key to its solution. "La! yes," said she, "I've hear'n tell about that mortar when I was a child; it was at the house of Mr. T. D——, *the old opium eater.*" There, in his brain, probably, the house haunting and the mortar dancing legend originated.

This mortar has been well known for over a century. More than fifty years ago its old home, the Simon Ray house, was taken down, and a part of it was put into the new house, about one hundred yards distant, then built and now owned by the aged and highly esteemed Raymond Dickens, who from his youth has been intimately acquainted with this mortar. He knew it when used for a splitting block. But for some reason, perhaps on account of its waywardness in former days, it was refused a place in the new dwelling, and, as if to keep it quiet ever after, it was placed in a fence wall, on its side, with heavy stones on it, and there, for nearly fifty years, it did penance until liberated by the writer in 1876, and was honored with its present home,—

"Where Fame's proud temple shines afar."

MYSTERIOUS CREATURES

The Reverend Samuel Peters' Contributions to the Natural History of Connecticut

Caterpillars and Wild Pigeons [1]

In 1768 the inhabitants of Connecticut River were as much alarmed by an army of caterpillars as those of Windham were at the frogs; and no one found reason to jest at their fears. These worms came in one night and covered the earth, on both sides of the river, to an extent of three miles in front and two in depth. They marched with great speed, and eat up everything green for the space of one hundred miles, in spite of rivers, ditches, fires, and the united efforts of 1,000 men. They were, in general, two inches long, had white bodies covered with thorns, and red throats. When they had finished their work they went down to the river Connecticut, where they died, poisoning the waters, until they were washed into the sea. This calamity was imputed by some to the vast number of logs and trees lying in the creeks, and to cinders, smoke, and fires, made to consume the waste wood for three or four hundred miles up the Connecticut River; while others thought it augurated future evils, similar to those of Egypt. The inhabitants of the Verdmonts [Vermont] would unavoidably have perished with famine, in consequence of the devastation of these worms, had not a remarkable Providence filled the wilderness with wild pigeons, which were killed by sticks as they sat upon the branches of the trees, in such multitudes that 30,000 people lived on them for three weeks. If a natural cause may be assigned for the coming of the frogs and caterpillars, yet the visit of the pigeons to the wilderness in August has been necessarily ascribed to the interposition of infinite Power and Goodness. Happy will it be for America, if the smiling providence of Heaven produces gratitude, repentance, and obedience amongst her children!

The Whapperknocker [2]

The whapperknocker is somewhat larger than a weasel, and of a beautiful brown colour. He lives in the woods on worms and birds; is so wild

[1] From *The Rev. Samuel Peters' LL.D. General History of Connecticut . . .* to Which Are Added Additions to Appendix, Notes, and Extracts from Letters, Verifying Many Important Statements, by Samuel Jarvis McCormick, pp. 131–132. Copyright, 1877, by D. Appleton and Company. New York.

A good deal of the natural lore, as well as the professed history, of the *General History of Connecticut,* by Samuel Peters, seems to be the product of the myth-making imagination. This history was first published in London in 1781, and an American edition . . . was published in New Haven in 1829. Apparently Peters was determined to be interesting, even to the extent of cracking credibility.—George Philip Krapp, *The English Language in America* (New York, 1925), I: 109.

[2] *Ibid.*, pp. 182–183.

that no one can tame him, and, as he never quits his harbour in the day-time, is only to be taken by traps in the night. Of the skins of these animals —which are covered with an exceedingly fine fur—are made muffs, at the price of thirty or forty guineas apiece; so that it is not without reason the ladies pride themselves on the possession of this small appurtenance of female habiliment.

The Cuba [3]

The cuba I suppose to be peculiar to New England. The male is of the size of a large cat; has four long tushes sharp as a razor; he is very active in defending himself, and, if he has the first blow, will spoil a dog before he yields. His lady is peaceable and harmless, and depends for protection on her spouse, and, as he has more courage than prudence, always attends him to moderate his temper. She sees danger, and he fears it not. She chatters at him while he is busy preparing for battle, and, if she thinks the danger is too great, she runs to him and clings about his neck, screaming her extreme distress; his wrath abates; and by her advice, they fly to their caves. In like manner, when he is chained, and irritated into the greatest rage by an impertinent dog, his lady, who is never chained, will fly about his neck and kiss him, and in half a minute restore him to calmness. He is very tender of his family, and never forsakes them till death dissolves their union. What further shows the magnanimity of this little animal, he never manifests the least anger toward his lady, though I have often seen her extremely loquacious, and, as I guessed, impertinent to him. How happy would the rational part of creation become if they would follow the example of these irrational beasts! I the more readily suppose the cuba to be peculiar to New England, not only from my never having yet seen the creature described, but also on account of its perverse observance of carnival and neglect of *carême*.

The Dew-Mink [4]

. . . The dew-mink, so named for its articulating those syllables, is black and white, and the size of an English robin. Its flesh is delicious. . . .

The Humility [5]

. . . The humility is so called because it speaks the word humility, and seldom mounts high in the air. Its legs are long enough to enable it to outrun a dog for a little way; its wings long and narrow; body maigre and of the size of a blackbird's; plumage variegated with white, black, blue,

---

[3] *Ibid.*, pp. 183–184.
[4] *Ibid.*, p. 186.
[5] *Ibid.*, p. 186.

and red. It lives on tadpoles, spawn, and worms; has an eye more piercing than the falcon, and the swiftness of an eagle; hence it can never be shot, for it sees the sparks of fire even before it enkindles the powder, and by the extreme rapidity of its flight gets out of reach in an instant. It is never known to light upon a tree, but is always seen upon the ground or wing. These birds appear in New England in summer only; what becomes of them afterwards is not discovered. They are caught in snares, but can never be tamed.

The Whippoorwill [6]

The whippoorwill has so named itself by its nocturnal songs. It is also called the Pope, by reason of its darting with great swiftness from the clouds to the ground and bawling out Pope, which alarms young people and the fanatics very much, especially as they know it to be an ominous bird. However, it has hitherto proved friendly, always giving travellers and others notice of an approaching storm by saluting them every minute by Pope! pope! It flies only a little before sunset, unless for this purpose of giving notice of a storm. It never deceives the people with false news. If the tempest is to continue long, the augurs appear in flocks, and nothing can be heard but Pope! pope! The whippoorwill is about the size of a cuckoo, has a short beak, long and narrow wings, a large head, and mouth enormous, yet is not a bird of prey. Under its throat is a pocket, which it fills with air at pleasure, whereby it sounds forth the fatal word Pope in the day, and Whip-her-I-will in the night. The superstitious inhabitants would have exorcised this harmless bird long ago, as an emissary from Rome and an enemy to the American Vine, had they not found out that it frequents New England only in the summer, and prefers the wilderness to a palace. Nevertheless, many cannot but believe it a spy from some foreign court, an agent of antichrist, a lover of persecution, and an enemy of Protestants, because it sings of whipping and of the Pope, which they think portends misery and a change of religion.

Belled Snakes [7]

. . . The belled or rattle-snakes are large, and will gorge a common cat. They are seldom seen from their rocky dens. Their bite is mortal if not speedily cured; yet they are generous, and without guile; before they bite they rattle their bell three or four times, but after that their motion is swift and stroke sure. The Indians discovered and informed the English of a weed, common in the country, which, mixed with spittle, will extract the poison.

---

[6] *Ibid.*, pp. 186–187.

[7] *Ibid.*, pp. 188–189.

TREE-FROGS[8]

The toads and frogs are plenty in the spring of the year. The tree-frogs, whippoorwills, and whooping owls serenade the inhabitants every night with music far excelling the harmony of the trumpet, drum, and jews-harp.

The tree-frog cannot be called an insect, a reptile, or one of the winged host; he has four legs, the two foremost short, with claws as sharp as those of a squirrel; the hind-legs five inches long, and folding by three joints. His body is about as big as the first joint of a man's thumb. Under his throat is a wind-bag, which assists him in singing the word I-sa-ac all the night. When it rains, and is very dark, he sings the loudest. His voice is not so pleasing as that of the nightingale; but this would be a venial imperfection, if he would but keep silence on Saturday nights, and not forever prefer I-sa-ac to Abraham and Jacob. He has more elasticity in his long legs than any other creature yet known. By this means he will leap five yards up a tree, fastening himself to it by his fore-legs, and in a moment will hop or spring as far from one tree to another. It is from the singing of this tree-frog that the Americans have acquired the name of Little Isaac. Indeed, like a certain part of them, the creature appears very devout, noisy, arbitrary, and phlegmatic, and associates with none but what agree with him in his ways.

Cotton Mather's Snake Stories

COTTON MATHER sent the Royal Society two good snake stories in 1712. They are reported, with some changes in form, in the Philosophical Transactions [No. 339 (for April–June, 1714), xxix, 68]. I give them from a copy of the original letter.

A Traveller in this Countrey mett and killed a *Rattlesnake;* but suffered the Angry *Snake* to give a Bite before he died unto ye lower end of the Switch, with ye lashes of which he had first spoiled his leaping. He rode on, & a fly disturbing him on one of his Temples, he rubb'd ye place, wth ye upper end of the Switch in his hand, unto which ye poison below had so permeated, that ye Head of ye poor Man Swell'd immediately, and (as I remember) he died upon it. . . . At Cape *Fear*, one of or people Sporting with a *Rattlesnake*, provoked him, & suffered him to

[8] *Ibid.*, p. 189.

From *Letters of Samuel Lee and Samuel Sewall Relating to New England and the Indians,* edited by George Lyman Kittredge, p. 174. Reprinted from *The Publications of the Colonial Society of Massachusetts,* Vol. XIV. Cambridge: John Wilson and Son, University Press. 1912.

bite ye edge of a Good Broad Ax; whereupon, immediately ye Colour of the Steeled Iron changed, & at the first blow he gave, when he went after this to use his Axe, ye discoloured part of ye Bitten Iron, broke off without any more ado. I know not whether I have now Sprung a New Game, for the Gentlemen, that are hunting after ye Liquor *Alkahest*.[1]

The New England Sea-Serpent

On August 18th, 1817, the Linnean Society of Boston formed a committee [2] "for the purpose of collecting any evidence which may exist respecting a remarkable animal, denominated a *Sea Serpent,* reported to have been seen in and near the Harbour of Gloucester."

* * * * *

The Committee's report was published as a small pamphlet [3] (now very scarce) in December, 1817. It contained, *inter alia,* the sworn depositions of twelve witnesses.[4] Before giving extracts from these, it seems worth while to reproduce the very excellent rules which the Committee laid down to govern its investigations.

"*Boston, Aug.* 19, 1817.

"The Committee appointed by the Linnean Society . . . have concluded on the following method of proceeding in the execution of their commission.

I. The examination to be confined to persons professing actually to have seen the animal in question.

II. Such persons to be examined as may be met with by either of the Committee, or by Hon. Lonson Nash of Gloucester, who is to be requested by a letter addressed to him from the Committee to undertake this service.

III. All testimony on the subject to be taken in writing, and after being deliberately read to the person testifying, to be signed by him, and sworn to before a magistrate. The examinations to be separate, and

---

[1] Letter of Nov. 27, 1712 (addressed to Richard Waller, the Secretary of the Royal Society). In the archives of the Society. From a copy kindly lent me by our associate Mr. Frederick Lewis Gay. The alkahest, or universal solvent, was passionately sought after in the seventeenth and eighteenth centuries.—G. L. K.

From *The Case for the Sea-Serpent,* by Lieut.-Commander R. T. Gould, pp. 29–32, 53–60. New York: G. P. Putnam's Sons. 1934.

[2] John Davis, Jacob Bigelow, and Francis C. Gray.—R. T. G.

[3] REPORT/of a/COMMITTEE/of the/LINNEAN SOCIETY OF NEW ENGLAND/relative/to a large marine animal/supposed to be/A SERPENT,/seen near Cape Ann, Massachusetts,/in/August 1817.//BOSTON:/published by Cummings and Hilliard,/No. 1, Cornhill.//Univ. Press . . . Hillard and Metcalf./1817.

Small 8vo., gray paper cover. 10½" x 6½". 52 pp., 2 plates.—R. T. G.

[4] Their names, reminiscent of Widecombe Fair, were: Amos Story, Solomon Allen, Eppes Ellery, Wm. H. Foster, Matthew Gaffney, James Mansfield, John Johnston, Wm. B. Pearson, Sewall Toppan, Robert Bragg, Wm. Somerby, and Elkanah Finney. —R. T. G.

the matter testified by any witness not to be communicated until the whole evidence be taken.

IV. The persons testifying to be requested first to relate their recollections on the subject, which being taken down, the following questions to be proposed, if not rendered unnecessary by the statement given:

QUESTIONS

1. When did you first see this animal?
2. How often and how long at a time?
3. At what times of the day?
4. At what distance?
5. How near the shore?
6. What was its general appearance?
7. Was it in motion or at rest?
8. How fast did it move, and in what direction?
9. What parts of it were above the water and how high?
10. Did it appear jointed or only serpentine?
11. If serpentine, were its sinuosities vertical or horizontal?
12. How many distinct portions were out of water at one time?
13. What were its colour, length, and thickness?
14. Did it appear smooth or rough?
15. What were the size and shape of its head, and had the head ears, horns, or other appendages?
16. Describe its eyes and mouth.
17. Had it gills or breathing holes, and where?
18. Had it fins or legs, and where?
19. Had it a mane or hairs, and where?
20. How did its tail terminate?
21. Did it utter any sound?
22. Did it appear to pursue, avoid, or notice any thing?
23. Did you see more than one?
24. How many persons saw it?
25. State any other remarkable fact."

* * * * *

One creature only was seen. It frequented Gloucester harbour from August 10th (or, possibly, a few days earlier) to August 23rd, after which it proceeded northward, being seen *en route* on August 28th, and in Long Island Sound on October 3rd and 5th. It was observed by many persons simultaneously, for periods ranging from a few minutes to two hours and upwards, and at distances varying from a few feet to a mile.

It was seen at all times of the day, sometimes in rapid motion, sometimes at rest. When moving, it appeared to curve its back in vertical undulations; when at rest, its back seemed, at times, to be undulating, and at others smooth. It presented the appearance of an enormous serpent, of a black or dark-brown colour, its body (so far as this could be seen) having a diameter of something under three feet, tapering slightly towards the extremities. Its length was variously assessed at from seventy to one hundred and twenty feet. Its skin appeared smooth to most of the witnesses, but rough to two.

The head was generally described as like a serpent's. Three witnesses deposed to seeing a long tongue projected almost vertically from the mouth. One witness only spoke of seeing the eye, bright and resembling that of an ox. No legs, fins, gills or mane were observed. There was great unanimity of opinion as to the monster's extreme lateral flexibility.

It appeared to take little notice of surrounding objects, human beings, and even gunshots. It was not heard to utter any sounds. On two occasions it was seen, or believed to be seen, lying partly on the shore and partly in the water.

It is, I think, difficult for any person of unbiased mind to read through the depositions without being struck by their weight and general agreement. Something of the latter, no doubt, must be regarded as artificial. Had the witnesses made entirely independent statements, one would not expect to find them all deposing, with only the slightest of verbal changes, that they had seen "a strange marine animal," which they "believed to be a serpent." One imagines that this formula was submitted to them—in substitution, possibly, for some much more terse and vigorous description—by Mr. Lonson Nash; and that they accepted it as sufficiently conveying their meaning. Broadly speaking, one imagines that while Nash probably acted up to the spirit of his instructions, directing "the examinations to be separate, and the matter testified by any witness not to be communicated until the whole evidence be taken," he performed (perhaps unconsciously) the functions of a compiler and editor, bringing the various accounts into a slightly misleading state of general uniformity—uniformity of language, be it noted, not of fact. I do not suggest that he took any liberties with the reported facts—his comments on Allen's evidence are sufficient proof that he did not.

The evidence afforded by the depositions is, as already remarked, entitled to very serious consideration. Unfortunately, the Committee went out of their way to stultify the valuable work which they had performed. Not content with merely collecting testimony—a task which they had accomplished most admirably—they cast about for a hypothesis which should explain this, and be incorporated in their report. Such an hypothesis, accordingly, will be found appended to the depositions; and a very singular one it is.

About a month after the "strange marine animal" had quitted Gloucester harbour, a small black snake of somewhat curious appearance was found by two boys on the beach at Loblolly Cove.[1] Alarmed, they summoned their father. This brave fellow attacked the savage reptile—which

[1] On the east side of Cape Ann peninsula.—R. T. G.

was fully three feet long—with a pitchfork, and ultimately slew it. It was bought by a resident named Beach, who presented it to the Committee; apparently on the slender chance that its appearance might in some way be connected with the monster recently seen in the harbour. It appears that the local pothouse-pundits were firmly of opinion that the latter had visited Gloucester's shores to deposit its eggs thereon.

The Committee received the snake, and the suggestion, with great gravity. They examined and dissected the carcase, and were delighted to find that its back exhibited a series of small humps, or bunches. Nothing further, surely, was necessary. Devoting some four pages of their report to a minute comparison of the snake's anatomy with the reported characteristics of the "strange marine animal," they concluded as follows:

"On the whole, as these two animals agree in so many conspicuous, important and peculiar characters, and as no material difference between them has yet been clearly pointed out, excepting that of size, the Society will probably feel justified in considering them individuals of the same species, and entitled to the same name, until a more close examination of the great Serpent shall have disclosed some difference of structure, important enough to constitute a specific distinction."

Holding this remarkable opinion, they christened their newly-acquired specimen *Scioliophis Atlanticus,* and appended to their report an anatomical description of it, illustrated by two plates. By so doing, they made a rod for their own backs; since European naturalists, headed by H. M. D. de Blainville,[1] immediately pointed out to them that their juvenile sea-serpent was nothing more than a common black snake (*Coluber constrictor*) in a diseased condition. Moreover, since the Committee had gone out of their way to assert a close connection between their small, common land-snake and the huge sea-creature seen off Gloucester, it is scarcely surprising that those competent to form an opinion should have concluded that persons capable of so egregious a blunder in a simple point of identification were not the safest guides to accurate information regarding a strange and huge creature of unknown species which they had not personally examined.

For good reason, therefore, scientific men in general received the Committee's report with a "calmness bordering on indifference." The vulgar, on the other hand, were at no loss to suggest, in pretty plain language, that the Gloucester monster was a myth, and that those who professed to have seen it were drawing the long bow. This, of course, was almost inevitable. The story was strange and improbable; it rested on the assertions of a comparatively small number of persons living in the same town; and it provided their less-favoured neighbours with a most excellent means of poking fun at Gloucester credulity and vaunting their own superior perspicacity and common sense. In consequence, the sober tales of the Gloucester witnesses were, in no long time, distorted, parodied and (to a great

[1] *Journal de Physique* . . . , Vol. LXXXVI (Paris, 1818).—R. T. G.

extent) laughed out of court. Practical jokers sent in marvellous reports of apocryphal "sea-serpents"; not supporting—or, indeed, designed to support—the slightest examination. The Press, with one or two honourable exceptions, followed on the same side—after its fashion. And about a year after the "sea-serpent's" last appearance off Gloucester an event occurred which, designedly or not, helped materially to throw ridicule on the whole matter.

I am uncertain whether it should be regarded as a malicious hoax, a misfired practical joke, or an honest blunder. Personally, I incline to the second hypothesis. Here are the facts, as related by Colonel Perkins many years afterwards: [1]

". . . As it happened, a circumstance took place which did not do much credit to the actors in it, but which served to fortify the unbelief of our southern brethren. Believing that the possession of the sea-serpent would be a fortune to those who should have him in their power, many boats were fitted out from Cape Ann and other places in the neighbourhood of his haunts, armed with harpoons and other implements, and manned with persons used to the whale fishery, in hopes of getting near enough to him to fasten their harpoons in his side.

"Among others a Captain Rich . . . of Boston, took command of a party, which was fitted out at some expense, and went into the bay,[2] where they cruised along shore two or three days without seeing the serpent. With a view, however, to keeping the joke for themselves, they . . . spread a report that they had caught the serpent, or what had been taken for one, and that he was to be seen at a place [3] mentioned in the advertisement.[4]

"Thousands were flocking to see this wonder, when it was found to be no other than a large horse macquerel,[5] which (though a great natural curiosity, weighing sometimes 600 or 700 pounds) very much disappointed those, who had been induced to visit it. Those who had declared their disbelief of the existence of the Sea-serpent amongst themselves were delighted to find their opinions were confirmed, and gave themselves great credit for their judgment and discrimination. The report spread from Boston to New Orleans, that what had been thought by some persons to be a sea-serpent had proved to be a horse macquerel, and even those who had been believers now supposed that those who had reported that they had seen the serpent had either misrepresented or had been themselves deceived. As no report of the snake having been seen after the capture of the macquerel was made, during that year, Captain Rich had the laugh with him, until circumstances, which have transpired since, have borne rather against him."

---

1 *Boston Daily Advertiser,* 25, xi. 1848.—R. T. G.
2 Massachusetts Bay.—R. T. G.
3 At Boston.—R. T. G.
4 In the *Boston Daily Advertiser,* and other local papers, 3, ix. 1819.—R. T. G.
5 Or tunny [tuna].—R. T. G.

It is fair to add, though, that Captain Richard Rich protested in print, and immediately, against the general impression that he had tried to perpetrate a silly hoax. Writing in the *Boston Weekly Messenger* of September 17th, 1818, he contended that he had repeatedly observed, in the course of his cruise in Massachusetts Bay, the appearance of a creature similar to that seen off Gloucester the year before—that he had finally captured it—and that it had proved to be a tunny. He continues:

". . . If I am asked—how is it possible for a Fish like this to produce such a wonderful appearance, I can only answer: 'His peculiar movement and his velocity produced a greater deception than I ever saw before, and the describing his body as being like kegs fastened together, struck me so forcibly, that had I not followed it up and discovered the deception, I should have given my testimony to the long list already given, of the existence of a Sea Serpent on our coast.'

"I now take my leave of the public, hoping they will do me the justice to say that I used no deception.

"RICHARD RICH."

I have a strong impression that the public took no such action. The discrepancies between Rich's assertions—and his tunny—and the Gloucester depositions are more than Appella himself could stomach.

As Perkins notes, the dime-show staged by Rich put an end, for a time, to the reports of sea-serpents off the New England coast. Rich's joke, if it were a joke, had obviously fallen exceedingly flat; the public was no longer amused by hoaxes, and these in their turn had effectually discredited, in advance, any further similar reports. . . .

Moby-Dick

FOR some time past, though at intervals only, the unaccompanied, secluded White Whale had haunted those uncivilized seas mostly frequented by the Sperm Whale fishermen. But not all of them knew of his existence; only a few of them, comparatively, had knowingly seen him; while the number who as yet had actually and knowingly given battle to him, was small indeed. For, owing to the large number of whale-cruisers; the disorderly way they were sprinkled over the entire watery circumference, many of them adventurously pushing their quest along solitary latitudes, so as seldom or never for a whole twelve-month or more on a stretch, to encounter a single news-telling sail of any sort; the inordinate length of each separate voyage; the irregularity of the times of sailing from home; all these, with other circumstances, direct and indirect, long obstructed the spread through the whole world-wide whaling-fleet of the special individualizing tidings

From *Moby-Dick:* or the Whale (1851), by Herman Melville, Chapter XLI, in *The Works of Herman Melville*, Standard Edition, Vol. VII, pp. 222–228. London, Bombay, Sydney: Constable and Company, Ltd.

concerning Moby-Dick. It was hardly to be doubted, that several vessels reported to have encountered, at such or such a time, or on such or such a meridian, a Sperm Whale of uncommon magnitude and malignity, which whale, after doing great mischief to his assailants, had completely escaped them; to some minds it was not an unfair presumption, I say, that the whale in question must have been no other than Moby-Dick. Yet as of late the Sperm Whale fishery had been marked by various and not unfrequent instances of great ferocity, cunning, and malice in the monster attacked; therefore it was, that those who by accident ignorantly gave battle to Moby-Dick; such hunters, perhaps, for the most part, were content to ascribe the peculiar terror he bred, more, as it were, to the perils of the Sperm Whale fishery at large, than to the individual cause. In that way, mostly, the disastrous encounter between Ahab and the whale had hitherto been popularly regarded.

And as for those who, previously hearing of the White Whale, by chance caught sight of him; in the beginning of the thing they had every one of them, almost, as boldly and fearlessly lowered for him, as for any other whale of that species. But at length, such calamities did ensue in these assaults—not restricted to sprained wrists and ankles, broken limbs, or devouring amputations—but fatal to the last degree of fatality; those repeated disastrous repulses, all accumulating and piling their terrors upon Moby-Dick; those things had gone far to shake the fortitude of many brave hunters, to whom the story of the White Whale had eventually come.

Nor did wild rumors of all sorts fail to exaggerate, and still the more horrify the true histories of these deadly encounters. For not only do fabulous rumors naturally grow out of the very body of all surprising terrible events,—as the smitten tree gives birth to its fungi; but, in maritime life, far more than in that of terra firma, wild rumors abound, wherever there is any adequate reality for them to cling to. And as the sea surpasses the land in this matter, so the whale fishery surpasses every other sort of maritime life, in the wonderfulness and fearfulness of the rumors which sometimes circulate there. For not only are whalemen as a body unexempt from that ignorance and superstitiousness hereditary to all sailors; but of all sailors, they are by all odds the most directly brought into contact with whatever is appallingly astonishing in the sea; face to face they not only eye its greatest marvels, but, hand to jaw, give battle to them. Alone, in such remotest waters, that though you sailed a thousand miles, and passed a thousand shores, you would not come to any chiselled hearth stone, or aught hospitable beneath that part of the sun; in such latitudes and longitudes, pursuing too such a calling as he does, the whaleman is wrapped by influences all tending to make his fancy pregnant with many a mighty birth.

No wonder, then, that ever gathering volume from the mere transit over the widest watery spaces, the outblown rumors of the White Whale did in the end incorporate with themselves all manner of morbid hints, and half-formed foetal suggestions of supernatural agencies, which eventually invested Moby-Dick with new terrors unborrowed from anything that visibly appears. So that in many cases such a panic did he finally strike, that few who by those rumors, at least, had heard of the White Whale, few of those hunters were willing to encounter the perils of his jaw.

But there were still other and more vital practical influences at work. Not even at the present day has the original prestige of the Sperm Whale, as fearfully distinguished from all other species of the leviathan, died out of the minds of the whalemen as a body. There are those this day among them, who, though intelligent and courageous enough in offering battle to the Greenland or Right Whale, would perhaps—either from professional inexperience, or incompetency, or timidity, decline a contest with the Sperm Whale; at any rate, there are plenty of whalemen, especially among those whaling nations not sailing under the American flag, who have never hostilely encountered the Sperm Whale, but whose sole knowledge of the leviathan is restricted to the ignoble monster primitively pursued in the North; seated on their hatches, these men will hearken with a childish fireside interest and awe, to the wild, strange tales of Southern whaling. Nor is the pre-eminent tremendousness of the great Sperm Whale anywhere more feelingly comprehended, than on board of those prows which stem him.

And as if the now tested reality of his might had in former legendary times thrown its shadow before it; we find some book naturalists—Olassen and Povelson—declaring the Sperm Whale not only to be a consternation to every other creature in the sea, but also to be so incredibly ferocious as continually to be athirst for human blood. Nor even down to so late a time as Cuvier's, were these or almost similar impressions effaced. For in his Natural History, the Baron himself affirms that at sight of the Sperm Whale, all fish (sharks included) are "struck with the most lively terrors," and "often in the precipitancy of their flight dash themselves against the rocks with such violence as to cause instantaneous death." And however the general experiences in the fishery may amend such reports as these; yet in their full terribleness, even to the bloodthirsty item of Povelson, the superstitious belief in them is, in some vicissitudes of their vocation, revived in the minds of the hunters.

So that overawed by the rumors and portents concerning him, not a few of the fishermen recalled, in reference to Moby-Dick, the earlier days of the Sperm Whale fishery, when it was oftentimes hard to induce long practised Right whalemen to embark in the perils of this new and daring warfare; such men protesting that although other leviathans might be hopefully pursued, yet to chase and point lances at such an apparition as the Sperm Whale was not for mortal man. That to attempt it, would be inevitably to be torn into a quick eternity. On this head, there are some remarkable documents that may be consulted.

Neverthless, some there were, who even in the face of these things were ready to give chase to Moby-Dick; and a still greater number who, chancing only to hear of him distantly and vaguely, without the specific details of any certain calamity, and without superstitious accompaniments, were sufficiently hardy not to flee from the battle it offered.

One of the wild suggestings referred to, as at last coming to be linked with the White Whale in the minds of the superstitiously inclined, was the unearthly conceit that Moby-Dick was ubiquitous; that he had actually been encountered in opposite latitudes at one and the same instant of time.

Nor, credulous as such minds must have been, was this conceit altogether without some faint show of superstitious probability. For as the secrets of the currents in the seas have never yet been divulged, even to the most erudite research; so the hidden ways of the Sperm Whale when beneath the surface remain, in great part, unaccountable to his pursuers; and from time to time have originated the most curious and contradictory speculations regarding them, especially concerning the mystic modes whereby, after sounding to a great depth, he transports himself with such vast swiftness to the most widely distant points.

It is a thing well known to both American and English whale-ships, and as well a thing placed upon authoritative record years ago by Scoresby, that some whales have been captured far north in the Pacific, in whose bodies have been found the barbs of harpoons darted in the Greenland seas. Nor is it to be gainsaid, that in some of these instances it has been declared that the interval of time between the two assaults could not have exceeded very many days. Hence, by inference, it has been believed by some whalemen, that the Nor' West Passage, so long a problem to man, was never a problem to the whale. So that here, in the real living experience of living men, the prodigies related in old times of the inland Strello mountain in Portugal (near whose top there was said to be a lake in which the wrecks of ships floated up to the surface); and that still more wonderful story of the Arethusa fountain near Syracuse (whose waters were believed to have come from the Holy Land by an underground passage); these fabulous narrations are almost fully equalled by the realities of the whaleman.

Forced into familiarity, then, with such prodigies as these; and knowing that after repeated, intrepid assaults, the White Whale had escaped alive; it cannot be much matter of surprise that some whalemen should go still further in their superstitions; declaring Moby-Dick not only ubiquitous, but immortal (for immortality is but ubiquity in time); that though groves of spears should be planted in his flanks, he would still swim away unharmed; or if indeed he should ever be made to spout thick blood, such a sight would be but a ghastly deception; for again in unensanguined billows hundreds of leagues away, his unsullied jet would once more be seen.

But even stripped of these supernatural surmisings, there was enough in the earthly make and incontestable character of the monster to strike the imagination with unwonted power. For, it was not so much his uncommon bulk that so much distinguished him from other sperm whales, but, as was elsewhere thrown out—a peculiar snow-white wrinkled forehead, and a high, pyramidical white hump. These were his prominent features; the tokens whereby, even in the limitless, uncharted seas, he revealed his identity, at a long distance, to those who knew him.

The rest of his body was so streaked, and spotted, and marbled with the same shrouded hue, that, in the end, he had gained his distinctive appellation of the White Whale; a name, indeed, literally justified by his vivid aspect, when seen gliding at high noon through a dark blue sea, leaving a milkyway wake of creamy foam, all spangled with golden gleamings.

Nor was it his unwonted magnitude, nor his remarkable hue, nor yet his deformed lower jaw, that so much invested the whale with natural terror, as that unexampled, intelligent malignity which, according to specific accounts, he had over and over again evinced in his assaults. More than all, his treacherous retreats struck more of dismay than perhaps aught else. For, when swimming before his exulting pursuers, with every apparent symptom of alarm, he had several times been known to turn round suddenly, and, bearing down upon them, either stave their boats to splinters, or drive them back in consternation to their ship.

Already several fatalities had attended his chase. But though similar disasters, however little bruited ashore, were by no means unusual in the fishery; yet, in most instances, such seemed the White Whale's infernal aforethought of ferocity, that every dismembering or death that he caused, was not wholly regarded as having been inflicted by an unintelligent agent.

The Whistling Whale

THE ship *Milton,* an old New Bedford Whaler, while cruising in the Northern Gulf, discovered a whistling whale, which they killed. When the headsman placed his feet in his spout holes to cut off his head, he found a harpoon running transversely, which had produced the whistling. By the stamp on the harpoon, it was found that the whale had worn this ornament fourteen years. He yielded one hundred and eighty barrels of oil. A tongue has been known to yield twenty-seven barrels of oil.

Mr. Mittin's Triton

ONE Mr. *Mittin* related of a *Triton* or *Mereman* which he saw in *Cascobay,* the Gentleman was a great Fouler, and used to goe out with a small Boat or Canow, and fetching a compass about a small Island, (there being many

---

From *Truro—Cape Cod, or Land Marks and Sea Marks,* by Shebnah Rich, p. 113. Second Edition, Revised and Corrected. Copyright, 1883, by D. Lothrop and Company. Boston. 1884.

From *An Account of Two Voyages to New-England,* Made during the years 1638, 1663, by John Josselyn, Gent., p. 23. Boston, Massachusetts: Published by William Veazie. 1865.

small Islands in the Bay) for the advantage of a shot, was encountered with a *Triton,* who laying his hands upon the side of the Canow, had one of them chopt off with a Hatchet by Mr. *Mittin,* which was in all respects like the hand of a man, the *Triton* presently sunk, dying the water with his purple blood, and was no more seen.

HAUNTS AND SPECTERS

The Harbor Boys of Block Island

In addition to the troubles from the mother colony and from the British during the revolution the Island was kept in almost constant alarm by a class of persons known as *Refugees.* They were deserters mainly from both armies, and were perfect desperadoes, going singly, or in bands, unprincipled and cruel in their demands. . . .

. . . A galley of these roughs, according to tradition, nine in number, four oarsmen on a side, and a helmsman, approached the Island for plunder. They attempted to land at the Old Harbor Landing, near the spring of the Spring House. They probably intended to land in the night. The burning flames of oil upon Beacon Hill are supposed to have signaled their approach in that kind of a boat then called a "Shaving Mill." But with the darkness of that evening came also a heavy sea from the southeast. The boat was now tossed to and fro like a shaving upon the waves. The armed Islanders inferred the intended point of landing, and there secreted themselves behind rocks and boulders to give the invaders a warm reception. But the darkness grew dense; the seas rolled higher as the wind increased; the surf dashed fearfully against the rocky shore; and only occasional dim views could be had of the "Shaving Mill," until nothing was visible upon sea or land, and nothing was heard amid the angry tones of the sea but the suppressed words passing from one to another on the alert for the enemy, until a strong determined voice upon the deep was heard thundering out the command—"Row! boys, row for your lives!" The *Refugees* were approaching the shore! But as soon as they were near enough to be struck by the surf their "Shaving Mill" went to pieces, and the last ever known of them was their drowning cry—"Help! Help!" piercing the darkness, and reaching only the ears of those whom they intended to rob. From that ill-fated crew originated the weird legend of the "Harbor Boys," whom the Islanders for a hundred years suppposed to be the ghosts of the drowned refugees still hovering about the Old Harbor landing, and repeating in dark

From *Block Island,* I. A Map and Guide; II. A History (Abridged), by Rev. S. T. Livermore, pp. 61, 62–63. Copyright, 1882, by S. T. Livermore. Hartford, Connecticut: Press of The Case, Lockwood & Brainard Company.

stormy nights there the old command—"Row! boys, row!" and the cries—"Help! Help!" The writer has conversed with men who say they have heard these mysterious voices there, and these ghostly voices are spoken of by the old inhabitants as the "Harbor Boys." Why not imagine these ghosts to be the crew of the fire ship that used to glide about Sandy Point, and which some one named after the Palatine?

The Screeching Woman

It was said that, during the latter part of the seventeenth century, a Spanish ship, laden with rich merchandise, was captured by pirates and brought into the harbor of Marblehead. The crew and every person on board the ill-fated ship had been murdered at the time of the capture, except a beautiful English lady, whom the ruffians brought on shore near what is now called Oakum Bay, and there barbarously murdered her. The few fishermen who inhabited the place were absent, and the women and children who remained could do nothing to prevent the crime. The screams of the victim were loud and dreadful, and her cries of "Lord, save me! Mercy! Oh! Lord Jesus, save me!" were distinctly heard. The body was buried where the crime was perpetrated and for over one hundred and fifty years on the anniversary of that dreadful tragedy the screams of the poor woman were repeated in a voice so shrill and supernatural as to send an indescribable thrill of horror through all who heard them.

The Legend of Apple Island

The Apple Island legend is a tragic one. Some ten years before Marsh landed there for the first time, it is said that a beautiful young girl, a descendant of one of the royal governors, was missed from home, and a few weeks later her lifeless body was recovered from the waters off Apple Island. Since a band of robbers was living on the Island at that time, the young girl's sweetheart at once suspected that the men were the cause of his lady's death. Nothing was heard from him for weeks, until a friend finally disclosed that he had gone to the Island and joined the robber band in order to find out the details of the girl's death.

From *The History and Traditions of Marblehead* (Third Edition), by Samuel Roads, Jr., pp. 37–38. Copyright, 1880, by Samuel Roads, Jr. Marblehead: Press of N. Allen Lindsey & Co. 1897.

From *The Islands of Boston Harbor,* Their History and Romance, 1626–1935, by Edward Rowe Snow, p. 207. Copyright, 1935, by Edward Rowe Snow. Andover, Massachusetts: The Andover Press.

The elm, landmark for over a century in Boston Bay, was cut down in 1938 by hoodlums.—E. R. S., *The Romance of Boston Bay* (Boston, 1944), p. 92.

One day a fisherman was sailing by the Island, and as was usually the case, looked at the tall elm which still stands at the top of the Island to get his bearings. From the lower limb of the elm there hung a body! Knowing about the robber band, he did not dare to go ashore, but on reaching Boston he notified the authorities who dispatched armed men to the spot. When the body was cut down, it was found to be that of the young man who had tried to avenge his sweetheart's death. There was not a robber left on the Island, and they never again returned to the scene of their double crime. The ghosts of the two were said to be still walking up and down the shores and around the great elm in 1900, but not for these 35 years have they been either seen or heard.

The Lady in Black

EVERY island has its legends, but perhaps the most famous of them all concerns the Lady in Black at Fort Warren.

The legend of this famous Lady in Black has been whispered at Fort Warren for many, many years, until now there are quite a few who believe in the existence of this lady of the black robes. I herewith offer the reader the legend without the slightest guarantee that any part of it is true.

During the War between the States, hundreds of prisoners were captured by Burnside at Roanoke Island. Among the group incarcerated at Fort Warren in the corridor of dungeons was a young lieutenant who had been married only a few weeks before. He succeeded in getting a message to his young wife by the underground railroad, giving complete directions as to where he was and how she could reach him. Being very much in love, she obtained passage on a small sloop, and landed in Hull a few weeks later. She quickly located the home of a Southerner in that town and was fitted out with a pistol and dressed in men's clothing.

Choosing a dark, rainy night, the lady rowed across Nantasket Road and finally landed on the beach at George's Island. Slipping noiselessly by the sentries, she reached the ditch under the Corridor of Dungeons. After giving a prearranged signal, she was hoisted up to the carronade embrasure and pulled through the opening. As soon as husband and wife had exchanged greetings, they made plans for the future. The prisoners decided to dig their way out of the dungeon into the parade ground and immediately set to work. Unfortunately for their plans, a slight miscalculation brought their tunnel within hearing of Northern soldiers stationed on the other side of the wall. Colonel Dimmick was notified and the whole scheme was quickly exposed. The brave little woman, when cornered, attempted to fire at the Colonel, but the gun was of the old fashioned pepper box type and exploded, killing her husband.

Colonel Dimmick had no alternative but to sentence her to hang as a

Ibid., pp. 72–74.

spy. She made one last request,—that she be hanged in women's clothing. After a search of the Fort, some robes were found which had been worn by one of the soldiers during an entertainment, and the plucky girl went to her death wearing these robes.

At various times through the years the ghost of the Lady in Black has returned to haunt the men quartered at the Fort. Two winters ago three of the soldiers were walking under the great arched sally port at the entrance to the Fort, and there before them, in the fresh snow, were five impressions of a girl's shoe leading nowhere and coming from nowhere. Only last summer a certain sergeant from Fort Banks was climbing to the top of the ladder which leads to the Corridor of Dungeons when he heard a voice warning him, saying: "Don't come in here!" Needless to say, he did not venture further.

There actually are on record court-martial cases of men who have shot at ghost-like figures while on sentry duty, and one poor man deserted his post, claiming he had been chased by the lady of the black robes.

For many years the traditional poker game was enjoyed in the old ordnance storeroom, and at ten o'clock one night a stone was rolled the entire length of the storeroom. As all the men on the Island were playing poker, no explanation could be found. When the same thing happened the next time that the men played poker in the evening, the group at the card table decreased appreciably. By the end of the month the ordnance storeroom was deserted, and since that time, if any of the enlisted men wish to indulge in this pastime, they choose another part of the Island. The ghost of the "Lady in Black" was of course blamed for the trouble.

Nix's Mate

THE legend of Nix's Mate, although a story without foundation, should be remembered. Late on a summer's day in 1689 as darkness descended on the waters of Massachusetts Bay, Captain Nix was guiding his ship into Boston Harbor. He anchored off what is now Nix's Mate Island. During the night screams were heard coming from the vessel, and in the morning the captain was found murdered. Accused of the crime, the mate was convicted by a Puritan jury, and sentenced to be hanged from the nearby island. The next morning, when they took him ashore to be executed, Nix's Mate asked permission to make a final statement. He declared that as proof of his innocence the island would some day wash away.

We cannot deny that the island did wash away, leaving a small area around which the present seawall was built in 1805, but there are reasons why the legend is false. The British Admiralty laws were very strict, so

---

From *The Romance of Boston Bay,* by Edward Rowe Snow, pp. 121–122. Copyright, 1944, by Edward Rowe Snow. Boston, Massachusetts: The Yankee Publishing Company.

that any trial would have to be recorded, and any hanging of necessity had to take place between the rise and fall of the tide in Boston proper. There is no record either of the trial or the hanging. In addition, Nix's Mate Island was so called at least forty years before the first marine execution took place in the colony.

A letter from Richard Burbeck to Nicholas Merrit in Marblehead, written around 1700, explains the mystery of the name. William Coddington, a passenger on the *Jewel,* one of Winthrop's fleet, asked the Dutch pilot about an island near which they were anchored. At the time the waves were making a great noise as they madly dashed against the island cliffs. Burbeck's story follows:

> Dirke Stone was on the deck of the *Jewell,* and Master Coddington, one of the passengers, ask'd Dirke, as Dirke did thinke, about the noise. And Dirke told him the name of the noise in Dutch. And so when Master Coddington saide, "What do you Dutch call that?" Dirke said "Nixie Shmalt; I do not know how to spell it, but it meaneth the Wail of the Water Spirits . . ." But Master Coddington thought it was the name of the Island, and set it down on a map he had "Nix his Mate Island."
>
> And after that, in order to account for the name, Dirke did saie that your Massachusetts people had made up a fairy Tale about a Captain Nix and hys mate, and a Kyling and a Hanging and a Sheriff and a neckespeche which was a prophecy.

The Watcher of the Isles of Shoals

I HAVE before me a weird, romantic legend of these islands, in a time-stained, battered newspaper of forty years ago. I regret that it is too long to be given entire, for the unknown writer tells his story well. He came to the Shoals for the benefit of his failing health, and remained there late into the autumn of 1826, "in the family of a worthy fisherman." He dilates upon the pleasure he found in the loneliness of the place, "the vast solitude of the sea; no one who has not known it can imbibe the faintest idea of it." "From the hour I learned the truth," he says, "that all which lives must die, the thought of dissolution has haunted me;—the falling of a leaf, a gray hair, or a faded cheek, has power to chill me. But here in the recesses of these eternal rocks, with only a cloudless sky above and an ocean before me, for the first time in my life have I shaken off the fear of death and believed myself immortal."

He tells his strange story in this way: "It was one of those awfully still mornings which cloud gazers will remember as characterizing the autumn months. There was not a single vapor-wreath to dim the intense blue of the

---

From *Among the Isles of Shoals,* by Celia Thaxter, pp. 177–183. Entered according to Act of Congress, in the year 1873, by James R. Osgood & Co., in the Office of the Librarian of Congress, at Washington. Boston.

sky, or a breath to ruffle the almost motionless repose of the great deep; even the sunlight fell seemingly with stiller brightness on the surface of it." He stood on a low, long point fronting the east, with the cliffs behind him, gazing out upon the calm, when suddenly he became aware of a figure standing near him. It was a woman wrapped closely in a dark sea-cloak, with a profusion of light hair flowing loosely over her shoulders. Fair as a lily and as still, she stood with her eyes fixed on the far distance, without a motion, without a sound. "Thinking her one of the inhabitants of a neighboring island who was watching for the return of a fishing-boat, or perhaps a lover, I did not immediately address her; but seeing no appearance of any vessel, at length accosted her with, 'Well, my pretty maiden, do you see anything of him?' She turned instantly, and fixing on me the largest and most melancholy blue eyes I ever beheld, said quietly, 'He *will* come again.'" Then she disappeared round a jutting rock and left him marvelling, and though he had come to the island (which was evidently Appledore) for a forenoon's stroll, he was desirous to get back again to Star and his own quarters after this interruption. Fairly at home again, he was inclined to look upon his adventure as a dream, a mere delusion arising from his illness, but concluded to seek in his surroundings something to substantiate, or remove the idea. Finding nothing,—no woman on the island resembling the one he had met,—and "hearing of no circumstance which might corroborate the unaccountable impression," he resolved to go again to the same spot. This time it blew half a gale; the fishermen in vain endeavored to dissuade him. He was so intensely anxious to be assured of the truth or fiction of the impression of the day before, that he could not refrain, and launched his boat, "which sprang strongly upon the whitened waters," and, unfurling his one sail, he rounded a point and was soon safely sheltered in a small cove on the leeward side of the island, probably Babb's Cove.

Then he leaped the chasms and made his way to the scene of his bewilderment. The sea was rolling over the low point; the spot where he had stood the day before, "was a chaos of tumult, yet even then I could have sworn that I heard with the same deep distinctness, the quiet words of the maiden, 'He *will* come again,' and then a low, remotely-ringing laughter. All the latent superstition of my nature rose up over me, overwhelming as the waves upon the rocks." After that, day after day, when the weather would permit, he visited the desolate place, to find the golden-haired ghost, and often she stood beside him, "silent as when I first saw her, except to say, as then, 'He *will* come again,' and these words came upon the mind rather than upon the ear. I was conscious of them rather than heard them,—it was all like a dream, a mysterious intuition. I observed that the shells never crashed beneath her footsteps, nor did her garments rustle. In the bright, awful calm of noon and in the rush of the storm there was the same heavy stillness over her. When the winds were so furious that I could scarcely stand in their sweep, the light hair lay upon the forehead of the maiden without lifting a fibre. Her great blue eyeballs never moved in their sockets, and always shone with the same fixed, unearthly gleam. The motion of her person was imperceptible; I knew that she was here, and that she was gone."

So sweet a ghost was hardly a salutary influence in the life of our invalid. She "held him with her glittering eye" till he grew quite beside himself. This is so good a description I cannot choose but quote it: "The last time I stood with her, was just at the evening of a tranquil day. It was a lovely sunset. A few gold-edged clouds crowned the hills of the distant continent, and the sun had gone down behind them. The ocean lay blushing beneath the blushes of the sky, and even the ancient rocks seemed smiling in the glance of the departing day. Peace, deep peace was the pervading power. The waters, lapsing among the caverns, spoke of it, and it was visible in the silent motion of the small boats, which, loosening their white sails in the cove of Star Island, passed slowly out, one by one, to the night-fishing." In the glow of sunset he fancied the ghost grew rosy and human. In the mellow light her cold eyes seemed to soften. But he became suddenly so overpowered with terror that "kneeling in shuddering fearfulness, he swore never more to look upon that spot, and never did again."

Going back to Star he met his old fisherman, who without noticing his agitation, told him quietly that he knew where he had been and what he had seen; that he himself had seen her, and proceeded to furnish him with the following facts. At the time of the first settlement, the islands were infested by pirates,—the bold Captain Teach, called Blackbeard, being one of the most notorious. One of Teach's comrades, a Captain Scot, brought this lovely lady hither. They buried immense treasure on the islands; that of Scot was buried on an island apart from the rest. Before they departed on a voyage, "to plunder, slash, and slay," (in which, by the way, they were involved in one awful doom by the blowing up of a powder magazine), the maiden was carried to the island where her pirate lover's treasure was hidden, and made to swear with horrible rites that until his return, if it were not till the day of judgment, she would guard it from the search of all mortals. So there she paces still, according to our story-teller. Would I had met this lily-fair ghost! Is it she, I wonder, who laments like a Banshee before the tempests, wailing through the gorges at Appledore, "He will *not* come again"? Perhaps it was she who frightened a merry party of people at Duck Island, whither they had betaken themselves for a day's pleasure a few summers ago. In the centre of the low island stood a deserted shanty which some strange fishermen had built there several years before, and left empty, tenanted only by the mournful winds. It was blown down the September following. It was a rude hut with two rough rooms and one square window, or rather opening for a window, for sash or glass there was none. One of our party proposed going to look after the boats, as the breeze freshened and blew directly upon the cove where we had landed. We were gathered on the eastern end of the island when he returned, and, kneeling on the withered grass where we were grouped, he said suddenly, "Do you know what I have seen? Coming back from the boats, I faced the fish-house, and as I neared it I saw some one watching me from the window. Of course I thought it was one of you, but when I was near enough to have recognized it, I perceived it to be the strange countenance of a woman, wan as death; a face young, yet with a look in it of infinite age. Old! it was older than the Sphinx in the desert! It looked as if it had been watching and waiting for me since the beginning of time. I walked straight into the hut. There wasn't a vestige of a human being there; it was absolutely empty." All the warmth and brightness of the summer day could hardly prevent a chill from creeping into our veins as we listened to this calmly delivered statement, and we actually sent a boat back to Appledore for a large yacht to take us home, for the wind rose fast and "gurly grew the sea," and we half expected the wan woman would come and carry our companion off bodily before our eyes.

The Blue Rock of Chappaquiddick

On a dark and stormy night an unknown vessel dropped anchor in the surf, which is forever beating at the foot of Wasque Bluff, where "the sea rolls like moving mountains on the shore, and the surf breaks in a terrible manner," and a mysterious personage landed in a small boat with a strong box and six sturdy ruffians, who trooped inland to where stood a lone bluish-colored rock. Here a deep hole was dug and the chest placed therein. Then the sailors stepped back and stood with bowed, uncovered heads while the stranger drew from his bosom a small green package which, with a muttered invocation to the father of pirates, he threw on the box, when instantly with crash and roar a blinding, lurid flame of pale green shot out of the hole, and for a moment lit up all the country round. The blackness of the stormy night succeeded, and when the sailors recovered from their confusion and prepared to fill the hole, lo! no hole was there; only the scorched and blackened earth. Then the little procession silently filed off into the gloom, returning whence it came, not a sound having been uttered from the time the boat's keel first grated on the sands. The lone spectator of this frightful scene, the only white man on the island, arose from his hiding place in the grass and fled, but he handed the story of that night's horrid work down to later generations, who have sought for the treasure in vain.

The experiences of such of the treasure seekers as have dared to tell them have been quite as terrible as were those of the peeping Tom who saw the pirates bury their gold. Two such adventurers agreed to meet one night at the rock, the hour being that when "the ghost from the tomb

From *The Story of Martha's Vineyard*, from the Lips of Its Inhabitants, Newspaper Files and Those Who Have Visited Its Shores, Including Stray Notes on Local History and Industries, Collected and Arranged by C. G. Hine, pp. 25–27. Entered, according to Act of Congress, in the year 1908, by C. G. Hine, in the Office of the Librarian of Congress, Washington, D. C. New York: Hine Brothers.

affrighted shall come, call'd out by the clap of the thunder." The first to arrive leaned up against the great stone and, being tired with his tramp, was fast falling to sleep, when a noise came to him from off the waters (for the haunted spot is close by the shore of Cape Poge Pond) and, opening wide his eyes in astonishment, he saw "a great big old ship," with all sails set, standing straight in toward the rock. No man was at the wheel, nor a soul in sight, yet she dodged the shoals and shallows like some old fisherman, and just as she must have grounded, down came every sail, and the vessel drifted gently in until her keel touched lightly on the sandy shore.

Then a mysterious plank ran out of itself and, with a horrible yell, the hatch was thrown off, and on the instant the deck was swarming with skeletons. " 'Twas an all-fired dark night, but it seemed as if them critters carried their light with them, for I could see 'em plain enough," says the treasure hunter. Now they come filing down the plank, bearing a dead body, and begin to dig, but the earth seemed to come up of itself, for almost instantly there was a deep hole and the spades were striking something that gave back the ring of metal, which a peep showed was a big iron pot with lid half off, and filled to the brim with gold and silver. On the top of this the corpse is tumbled and the hole is being filled when, for the first time the skeletons catch sight of the intruding human, who has been scared so stiff that he could not run, and they came for him "as thick as bees," grabbing him with intent to put him in the hole to keep company with the corpse. But if his legs would not work his lungs would, and he gave such a ghastly screech that even the ghosts were frightened and dropped him so that his head fell with a bang against the rock. When he "ris to his feet" not a phantom was in sight, the ship was gone and all signs of digging obliterated. Our adventurer had had enough, however, and when his companion arrived all was dark and lonely. The deserted one, however, was not the kind to take such treatment quietly, and when next the two met he gave his terrified friend such a drubbing that in order to justify his run away he was compelled to tell his experiences, and so the facts, which would otherwise have been lost, have been preserved for posterity.

Others have tried, and even reached the pot, but always is there a horrible flash and a cave in, shadowy forms of threatening aspect and the blackness of darkness, with the hole leveled and no sign of digging to show for the night's labor. Some there be who claim that a stranger whose heel prints showed a curious cleft did secure the pot, and transported it and himself to unknown parts on a mysterious vessel that had been hovering on the horizon for days, and it may be so, for recent digging fails to cause any unusual disturbance, except possibly in the backs and muscles of the diggers.

Black Bellamy's Shipwreck

No SHIPWRECK is more remarkable than that of the noted pirate Bellamy, mentioned by Governor Hutchinson, in his history. In the year 1717, his ship, with his whole fleet, were cast on the shore of what is now Wellfleet, being led near the shore by the captain of a snow,[1] which was made a prize the day before, who had the promise of the snow as a present, if he would pilot the fleet in Cape Cod harbor; the captain suspecting the pirate would not keep his promise, and that, instead of clearing his ship, as was his pretence, his intention might be to plunder the inhabitants of Provincetown. The night being dark, a lantern was hung in the shrouds of the snow, the captain of which, instead of piloting where he was ordered, approached so near the land, that the pirates' large ship, which followed him, struck on the outer bar; the snow, being less, struck much nearer the shore. The fleet was put in confusion; a violent storm arose: and the whole fleet was shipwrecked on the shore. It is said that all in the large ship perished in the waters except two. Many of the smaller vessels got safe on shore. Those that were executed were the pirates put on board a prize schooner before the storm, as it is said. After the storm, more than an hundred dead bodies lay along the shore. At times, to this day, there are king William and queen Mary's coppers picked up, and pieces of silver, called cob-money. The violence of the seas moves the sands upon the outer bar; so that at times the iron caboose of the ship, at low ebbs, has been seen.[2]

For many years after this shipwreck, a man, of a very singular and frightful aspect, used, every spring and autumn, to be seen travelling on the Cape, who was supposed to have been one of Bellamy's crew. The presumption is that he went to some place where money had been secreted by the pirates to get such a supply as his exigencies required. When he died, many pieces of gold were found in a girdle, which he constantly wore. Aged people relate that this man frequently spent the night in private houses, and that, whenever the Bible or any religious book was read, or any family devotions performed, he invariably left the room. This is not improbable. It is also stated that, during the night, it would seem as if he had in his chamber a legion from the lower world; for much conversation was often overheard which was boisterous, profane, blasphemous, and

---

From *Massachusetts Historical Collections,* Being a General Collection of Interesting Facts, Traditions, Biographical Sketches, Anecdotes, &c., Relating to the History and Antiquities of Every Town in Massachusetts, with Geographical Descriptions, by John Warner Barber, pp. 57–58. Entered, according to Act of Congress, in the year 1839, by Dorr, Howland & Co., in the Clerk's Office of the District Court of Massachusetts. Worcester: Dorr, Howland & Co.

[1] A three-masted vessel, with its third and smallest mast just abaft and close to the mainmast, carrying a trysail.—J. W. B.

[2] 3d vol. Coll. Mass. Hist. Soc., p. 120.—J. W. B.

quarrelsome in the extreme. This is the representation. The probability is, that his sleep was disturbed by a recollection of the murderous scenes in which he had been engaged, and that he, involuntarily, vented such exclamations as, with the aid of an imagination awake to wonders from the invisible regions, gave rise, in those days, to the current opinion that his bedchamber was the resort of infernals.*

The Whaling-Boat in the Sky

. . . WHEN Captain Southack sailed out to capture the pirate Bellamy . . . , the sea, lashed by the storm, forced a passage through the Cape along the very line chosen later for the Orleans Canal, and the captain sailed with a whaleboat through from the Bay to the Atlantic Ocean. Those who would cast a doubt on the authenticity of this trip need only confer with any native of Orleans, man or child. For every one knows that when a storm is brewing a mirage is plainly visible in the sky. Then it is that we can see again Captain Southack's whaling-boat sailing once again across the meadows of Orleans,—following the old route which legend grants him, from the Bay to the Atlantic Ocean,—and disappearing in pursuit of the pirate ship!

The Devil-Doomed Sand-Man

HARRY MAIN [1]

IN ANOTHER place, down by the river side, the house where Harry Main lived is pointed out to the visitor. He having thus a local habitation, the legend concerning him is no vagabond tradition. Harry Main is the Wandering Jew of Ipswich, around whom darkly hangs the shadow of an unpardonable crime and its fearful doom. It is said that he had been by turns a pirate, a smuggler, and a wrecker, who followed the wicked trade of building fires on the sands, in order to decoy vessels among the breakers, where they were wrecked, and their crews perished miserably. For these crimes, at his death he was doomed to be chained on Ipswich Bar, the scene of his former murderous exploits, and everlastingly to coil a cable of sand there. When the cable broke, his demoniacal yells of baffled rage could be heard for miles around; and when those fearful sounds announced

* Alden's Coll. Epitaphs, vol. iv.

From *Cape Cod, New & Old,* by Agnes Edwards, p. 104. Copyright, 1918, by Agnes Edwards Pratt. Boston and New York: Houghton Mifflin Company.

[1] From *A Book of New England Legends and Folklore, in Prose and Poetry,* by Samuel Adams Drake, New and Revised Edition, pp. 274–276. Copyright, 1883, 1901, by Samuel Adams Drake. Boston: Little, Brown and Company. 1910.

the rising gale, mothers would clasp their babes to their breasts, while the men shook their heads and said, "Old Harry's growling again!" His name was long the bugbear used to frighten refractory children into obedience, while the rote on the bar, heard in storms, still audibly perpetuates the legend, with its roar.[1]

The old people living on Plum Island used to say that Harry Main's ghost troubled them by wandering about the sand-hills on stormy nights, so that they were afraid to venture out of doors after dark. Indeed the town itself, in its palmy days, was so full of ghostly legends, that certain localities supposed to be haunted, were scrupulously avoided by the timid ones, who had a mortal dread of being accosted by some vagabond spectre with its tale of horror.

Harry Main's house—for we must remember that he had one—was ransacked, and every rod of the garden dug up for the money that he was supposed to have buried there; but nothing rewarded the search. Other places, too, have been explored with the same result, in quest of Kidd's hidden treasures. One good man dreamed three nights in succession that vast sums were buried in a certain hill in the town. He could see the very spot. Haunted by the realism of the dream, he determined to test the matter for himself; and one dark night, just as midnight struck, he took his spade, his lantern, and his Bible, and started on his weird errand. Upon reaching the spot he recognized it as the same that he had seen in his dream. He immediately fell to work. After plying his spade vigorously a while, it struck against some hard object. He now felt sure of his prize. Scraping the earth away with feverish haste, he came to a flat stone having a bar of iron laid across it. This he eagerly grasped with one hand, and was about to turn the stone over with the other when he was suddenly surrounded by a troop of cats, whose eyeballs blazed in the darkness. The digger felt his hair slowly rising on end. A cold sweat stood on his brow. Brandishing the bar aloft, he cried out, "Scat!" when these vigilant guardians of the treasure vanished in a twinkling, leaving the crestfallen money-digger standing up to his middle in cold water, which had poured into the hole, when he broke the spell by speaking. Half drowned, and wholly disgusted, he crawled out of it. The iron bar, however, remained tightly clutched in his hand. He carried it home, and I was assured that upon going to a certain house in Ipswich I might see the identical door-latch which a smith had made out of this bar for a souvenir of the night's adventure.

Old Trickey [2]

Trickey was a fisherman, and as rough and unruly of disposition as the wildest sea he ever rode out. He lived at the mouth of York River, but just where, no one seems to know; but there were Trickeys in Kittery. He

---

[2] From *Maine Pioneer Settlements: Old York*, by Herbert Milton Sylvester, pp. 311–313. Copyright, 1906, and 1909, by Herbert M. Sylvester. Boston: W. B. Clarke Co. 1909.

was as prickly and irritable as the saltiest brine; and his ugliness and generally disreputable character for wickedness and malevolence were nowhere to be questioned. All these made of him a privileged character, who, without let or hindrance, wrought in the devil's vineyard after his own inventions.

After he died it was said that on account of his misdeeds done in the body, the devil condemned him to stay about the region of Bra'boat Harbor, and he was supposed to haunt the vicinity constantly. The curse was upon him, and his doom was to bind and haul sand with a rope until the devil was satisfied. Curse as he would, and fume and fret, it was useless until his task was done. The devil had exacted so much sand, and so much he would have, so old Trickey got at his work. When the storm began to gather and the sand dunes inshore grew in size and number, when the brew of the gale wet the nose of Cape Neddock, the wraith of old Trickey would come shrieking along over the marshes and then he was at his Sisyphus-like labor, when the air was filled with his wailing cries, "More rope! More rope! More sand! More sand!" and there he wrought amid the rack of the storm. As the dusk deepened, the figure of old Trickey grew and grew, until racing inland with his load of sand he strode over the cabin roofs to disappear until the coming of the next gale. In the morning, the sands had shifted strangely, and as the sun shot its light across them, the village folk could not but observe the tremulousness of the atmosphere above them. It was old Trickey struggling with the devil over the scene of his labors of the night before, and after dark these sands were as much to be avoided as the graveyard a little way up the hill.

Nowadays, when the fogs roll in, and the sea and sky are one, and the winds begin to rise, and the growl of the surf on the harbor bar grows louder, the fisher folk say, "Old Trickey is binding and hauling sand to-night! God save the fishing-smacks from harm!"

The old jail at York is now used as a museum for such antiquities as the people there are able to keep from taking wings and flying away. Among the treasures there shown is the Bible once owned by Trickey, a cherished curiosity and an eerie thing, if what one may hear is to be taken without salt. It is said there is a spell upon it. It is ancient enough, and its joints are stiff and dry. As one opens it, the binding is somewhat reluctant in its yielding, and like many books made to-day it will not stay opened, but flies back with a vicious snap; and some say they cannot push its black covers apart; and so, it must be haunted, or "cursed." If old man Trickey had used it more frequently himself the old tome would have been more pliable, doubtless. However, it is an interesting relic, and as one fumbles at its discolored leaves, the story of its owner of long years ago smacks of reality, and out of the moaning of the sea and the wailing of the wind is readily conjured the tortured and maddened outcries of this devil-doomed sand-man.

Ocean-Born Mary

No state has more tales of witches and ghosts with which to while away the winter evenings than New Hampshire. And of all the tales of New Hampshire ghosts, I like best the story of Ocean-Born Mary. I like it so much that I made a visit to the haunted house in which folks say her ghost still walks, and I heard her story from the lips of eighty-year-old Mrs. Roy who lives there.

I arrived at the house, which is on the side of a steep mountain south of the village of Henniker, just at twilight. Mrs. Roy was in the yard gathering herbs, but she kindly led me through the old green doorway built many years before the American Revolution. We sat in the front room, the eagle room, she calls it, because someone, possibly Ocean-Born Mary herself, painted above the fireplace long ago an American eagle with a band of sixteen stars above him. There she told me the story while the light left the New Hampshire hills and the room grew gray and dark and the white-spindled old stairway to the second story creaked mysteriously.

In the year 1720 Mrs. Roy said, a group of emigrants from Londonderry, Ireland, took ship for America, expecting to join relatives and friends living in Londonderry, New Hampshire. As they were nearing the Massachusetts coast a sinister-looking frigate flying no flag bore down upon their unarmed boat, fired a gun across her bows, forcing her to heave to. Then, while the crew stood helpless, white and silent, and the emigrants kneeled on the deck in prayer for deliverance, a boat put out from the stranger bearing sunburned men. They clambered aboard the emigrant ship, terrified the passengers and crew with their weapons, and bound them securely.

Their leader, whom they called Captain Pedro, was a tall dark man who said little. Though he looked Spanish he talked perfect English when he ordered his captives to prepare for immediate death. As he spoke, a faint cry came from below deck, and he suddenly wheeled about and hastened down the companionway. In a cabin below he came upon a mother and her newborn girl baby. He said to her: "Madam, if I may be allowed to name this little girl after my own mother, I will not harm this ship or its passengers." The mother gladly gave consent, and the pirate captain said: "Her name shall be Mary."

Then he went back on deck and ordered all the captives released and his own men into their boat. In a few moments he was on his way back to the frigate. Just as the emigrants were rejoicing over their good fortune, however, they were again panic-stricken by the captain's return. He carried with him a bolt of grayish green tapestry silk, exquisitely embroidered

---

From *The Hurricane's Children*, Tales from Your Neck o' the Woods, by Carl Carmer, pp. 29–37. New York and Toronto: Farrar & Rinehart, Inc.

in a flower pattern. He strode down to the mother's cabin. "For your little daughter's wedding dress," he said, and returned to his boat.

The emigrants landed safely, but soon thereafter in Boston Ocean-Born Mary's father died. Then the mother took the little girl into New Hampshire hills. More than a score of years went by, and Ocean-Born Mary was a wife and herself the mother of four boys. She was six feet tall now, with red hair, very white skin, and green eyes. All over the state people talked of her beauty. And many grieved for her when she was left a widow with her four small sons to bring up.

But Captain Pedro had never forgotten the girl named for his mother. He was getting old now and longed for a more peaceful life—somewhere distant from the scenes of his criminal career. And so he came to Henniker to build a peaceful refuge from his own past and to be near his mother's namesake. He brought with him black slaves and his ship's carpenters and a few of his pirate crew. They chose a spot completely out of sight of any human dwelling and there they built a stately Colonial house with high handrailings on the stair like those on the bridge of the captain's ship and a sloping floor in the rear rooms like the slanting surface of a deck. Then he invited Ocean-Born Mary to come to live in the house, take care of him in his old age, and bring up her sons there. She accepted and became a fitting and beautiful mistress of the stately house. The captain presented her with a coach-and-four, and neighbors smiled to see her riding in it with her four tall sons. One day the captain returned from the seacoast with an enormous wooden chest. At midnight he and one of his pirate men staggered out of the high side door of the house carrying it on their shoulders, and Ocean-Born Mary heard the sound of shovels in the earth, then a low groan, and silence. The captain came back to the house alone and no one ever saw his pirate helper again.

It was over a year later that Ocean-Born Mary came home from a drive in her coach one late afternoon to find the house deserted. But in the orchard behind the house she found the body of the captain. He had been run through with a sailor's cutlass. She had her slaves bring the body into the house and there she supervised the captain's burial under the eight-by-three-foot stone slab in front of the big kitchen hearth—just as he had directed her to do in case of his death.

Ocean-Born Mary lived on in the old house. Her sons, grown to be men and all of them over six-foot-eight, left her to fight against the British king in the American Revolution. When they returned they took houses of their own. But Ocean-Born Mary lived on alone in the big house until 1814, when she died at the age of ninety-four.

The house was long unoccupied after that. Then people began to talk about the strange things that went on there. They still do. They say that strange lights appear in the windows at midnight. Some curious folks who went there at twilight claimed that they saw a very tall woman of great beauty walking down the high-railinged stair. Others say that on warm spring nights just after darkness has followed the twilight, a coach-and-four drives up to the old entrance and a tall woman steps out and hurries into the house. Immediately after that there come, from the old orchard back of the house, fearful groans as of a man in mortal pain.

Mediums and other people who claim supernatural power frequently visit Mrs. Roy in the old house. Some of them say that surely there is something of mysterious interest under the eight-by-three stone slab in the kitchen. I asked Mrs. Roy why she didn't have the slab lifted to see if the bones of the captain are there. She said that it would cost a hundred and fifty dollars and she thought that so much money as that would buy a lot of things more useful to her than a skeleton. One of the mediums not long ago said that she had summoned up the captain's spirit and talked to it. She said that she told the captain Mrs. Roy was a nice lady and that he ought to let her know somehow where his treasure is buried—but the captain just said: "I buried it. Let her *find* it."

When I heard all this for the first time I thought somebody had just made up a fancy story for me that had few words of truth in it. But now that I have seen a piece of Ocean-Born Mary's wedding gown—the gray-green silk embroidered in a flower pattern—and the strange eight-by-three hearthstone that looks like the top of a coffin with a hole drilled in the middle of it—and the house itself looking dark and haunted in the late twilight—and listened to Mrs. Roy—I'm not sure where truth ends and fancy begins. At any rate, many folks in New Hampshire love to tell this story on winter evenings before their birch-log fires, or on their porches on summer evenings when the stars are very bright above the mountaintops.

The Ghosts of Georges Bank

HER decks and spars aglitter in the moonlight, the new schooner *Charles Haskell* was like a queen enthroned as she sat chocked on the ways at Essex. At that time—December, 1869—Story's boatyard was already more than a hundred years old; and all the miracles which that institution could perform with white oak and tall spruce had been lavished on the new craft. Yes, like a queen she was, and the moon over the bay that night was giving her a train of pure gold—and none too good for her!

The boatyard was through with her now. Everything those magicians could do for her had been done. Rigging and a suit of sails, ground tackle and gear—give her these, with an able crew, and she was ready for sea. Give her as she deserved of these, and she would be the match of any sea she met, of any gale that blew. Yes, even of Georges Bank in the winter!

A worker walked through the deserted boatyard that night down to the

---

From *In Great Waters,* The Story of the Portuguese Fishermen, by Jeremiah Digges, pp. 104–105, 107–108, 109–110, 112–121. New York: The Macmillan Company.

ways, and climbed aboard the new schooner for one last look. He inspected the deck and then started down the forecastle companion. His foot slipped. Next morning, they found a man aboard the *Charles Haskell,* a man lying at the foot of the companion ladder—dead of a broken neck.

The skipper for whom the *Charles Haskell* was built refused her. She was perfect, he said. She was a beauty. She was everything they said she was. But no contract on earth could make him take her; because for his business, he said, she was now disqualified.

His business was winter-fishing on Georges Bank.

* * * * *

There have been in this fishery any number of forebodings, premonitions of tragedy, placed on record by virtue of their weird fulfillment. What part of such a "premonition" is really afterthought I do not know; nor do I care, for what interests me is not whether these things actually took place as related, but the fact that they were *said* to have taken place.

One such instance was set down in the journal of Captain J. Wenzell of the Gloucester schooner *Sachem.* She had been fishing on Brown's Bank, but on September 7, 1871, ran up to cruise Georges. That night John Nelson, cook, went aft and begged the skipper to "get off Georges Bank." Making no bones about it, he explained that he had just waked from a dream. He had seen "women, dressed all in white, and standing in the rain." Twice before, cook said, he had had this same dream, and each time he had been shipwrecked. "For God's sake, skipper, get off Georges Bank!"

A little later it breezed up. At one-thirty A.M. the *Sachem* was hove to under close-reefed foresail. Then, from the forecastle, one of the men yelled that the vessel was filling. Captain Wenzell went below and found six inches of water. Pumps were manned, bucket bailing was got under way, and cook was ordered to provision a boat. Believing the leak was under the port bow, the captain wore around and hove to on the other tack, in the hope that this might bring the leak out of water.

But nothing was effective against cook's "women dressed all in white." With a strong breeze blowing, the *Sachem* signaled the Gloucester schooner *Pescador,* and shortly afterward, at great risk to both crews, the men were got off the leaking vessel.

At two o'clock the *Sachem* rolled on her side, settled by the bow, and went down.

* * * * *

Although tragedy on Georges Bank has been a continued story, even beyond the motorization of the fleet and into the present, with its wireless, Coast Guard cutters, planes, and other aids to mariners, the dread of a winter's gale on those grounds today is nothing like what it was in the days of sail. Then disaster lay in "going adrift"—parting the cable and running, wholly out of hand, to almost certain collision, and in that case, certain death.

The Georges fleet was a large one. Fishing ports from Cape Cod down to Newfoundland were represented among the craft there, and frequently from the rigging a man could count between two and three hundred sail. Where one vessel had good luck, others flocked to be "on the fish." And the result was that the fleet usually bunched itself over a few small spots on the bank.

In good weather this was well enough; but it multiplied the risks many times in a storm. For if the gale should overtake a schooner in those days, all her crew could do was to snug down, pay out a good string to the anchor, and hope for the best while they tried to ride it out. From then on, if anything less than the best happened, it happened first to that all-important part of their equipment, the ground tackle; the anchor would drag, or the cable part under the strain.

A single vessel, once set adrift in those crowded waters, was sure to spread destruction. If she struck another, both went down. But usually, before this happened, several vessels lying in her path had cut their own cables and gone adrift themselves, to get out of her way. Cutting cable was a last resort, but on each craft a man stood ready with the axe. And as each was forced to cut loose, by so much more were the others in the fleet endangered. Thus death went snowballing over Georges Bank on such a night.

* * * * *

Taking Georges Bank into account for what it was, and for what it meant to these men, it may be easier to understand the refusal of the skipper to accept that beautiful new schooner, the *Charles Haskell.* A man had died on board, while the craft was still on the ways. And that was an omen—a sure sign she was unfit for the Georges Bank winter fishery. But a year passed, and another Gloucester skipper did take her out. And now, let us go back to her story.

"Yes, sir, gentlemens," Joe Enos said in his remote, singsong manner while he tossed the lead out after the snoods, "we get a breeze o' wind tonight, yes, sir, gentlemens!"

Hand-lining for cod forty miles west of Georges North Shoal, the *Haskell's* crew were doing some fast fishing at the moment. But, busy as they were, a couple of the boys paused to glance at "the Portygee." Joe, the only Portuguese on board, didn't have a great deal to say, but already on this first trip of the new schooner he had proved himself an able fisherman; when he did talk the others listened, and when he took the trouble to mention "a breeze o' wind" the chances were that it was going to be no ordinary weather.

"What makes you think so, Portygee?" George Scott asked.

"You see the way the fish bite now?" Joe shook his head. "Fish don't take the hook like this—only when we got a breeze o' wind by 'm by. Yes, sir, gentlemens, a breeze o' wind!"

Faster and faster, the fat cod were being hauled aboard. Within five or six miles of one another, more than a hundred vessels could be seen from the deck of the *Charles Haskell,* and on each the scene was the same.

Around noon the wind hauled to east-northeast, and from then on rose steadily. At three o'clock Captain Clifford Curtis ordered the *Haskell's* crew to haul in their lines.

"All right, boys! Heave in strads and give her cable!"

The crew took off the "strads"—pieces of rope bound around the cable to prevent chafing in the hawsepipe—gave her eighty more fathoms of the string, and stradded her up again. Then they took in the foresail, putting a double reef in it before they furled it, so as to have it ready for hoisting in case they should go adrift. The fishing vessel of that day carried no triangular storm trysail, such as is used for steadying the modern power-driven vessel; instead, for the same purpose, three reefs were taken in the mainsail, a rig that was termed "balanced-reefed mainsail."

By nine o'clock that night, Joe Enos's "breeze o' wind" had become a full-fledged hurricane. On Georges Bank, at the time, were 290 vessels; and with the wind continuing from the east-northeast, the deadly North Shoal lay under the lee of the fleet.

On board the *Charles Haskell,* as on other vessels, all hands were called on deck. Captain Curtis stationed himself at the cable, axe in hand. From his post he could see the lights of one unlucky schooner after another, passing by like a ghastly parade through the sleet—vessels that had already broken adrift.

Within an hour, the *Haskell* herself was dragging anchor but before she had slipped far from her berth, the hook fouled something on the bottom and brought her up short. There she hung, giving and tautening by turns, when suddenly the men at the forward lookout yelled warning. Directly over the schooner's bowsprit, looking as if it were almost atop her, a light was riding.

Captain Curtis brought down his axe, the *Haskell* bounded off like a catapulted stick and silently the stranger swept by.

"Up with the foresail! You, Portygee, keep her due west!"

Joe Enos nodded understanding. It was the skipper's idea to get to the leeward of the fleet if he could, and at the same time work beyond the North Shoal; for between collision and running aground on that shoal, there was precious little to choose.

After half an hour of running, they raised another light, this time on the weather bow. Captain Curtis, thinking the vessel was riding at her anchor, called out:

"Hard up the helm!"

But the other fellow, coming bow-on, also had his wheel hove up hard. Too late the skipper discovered that he, too, was running adrift. There was no chance then to pay off; and from a wave-crest the *Haskell* crashed into the other craft, cutting her down just abaft the port rigging. The stranger was split nearly to the mainmast.

As the figures of passers-by on a dark street are caught by a flash of lightning and "stopped" for the instant, so the crew of the unknown vessel appeared to those aboard the *Haskell.* One or two could have jumped aboard from where they stood, but none moved. And in the next instant, vessel and crew had vanished.

The *Haskell's* main boom and main rigging on the starboard side had carried away in the crash. The bowsprit had broken off, but was still hanging there, thudding against the planking and threatening to bash in the bow. The men cut this stick free, and in order to keep the mast from starting, made a line fast to the jibstay, passed it through the hawsepipe, and then under the windlass.

When the wreck was cleared, Joe Enos went below. No one aboard the *Haskell* expected her to stay afloat. No vessel stayed afloat when this happened. But down in the forecastle, Joe found George Winters, pointing and laughing hysterically, and screaming, "She's dry! She's dry! I tell you, there ain't a drop in her!"

Joe wouldn't believe it. He took up the trap in the forecastle floor. There was no water underneath! Then he ran to tell the skipper. Captain Curtis had the men try the pump. Below deck, the *Charles Haskell* was dry as a bone!

"Graças a Deos!" said Joe Enos. Then he turned to the skipper. "Those poor fellers! I see the faces, captain—one, two mens. *Ai,* the faces!"

Captain Curtis nodded, and for a moment turned away and looked into the sleet. Then he asked Joe:

"Did you see what vessel she was?"

Joe didn't know. Neither did anyone else on board the *Charles Haskell.*

When they had returned to Gloucester, they learned that nine vessels had gone down on Georges that night. Wrecks of six had been witnessed by others standing by, or accounted for by the few survivors from among the crews. The craft which the *Charles Haskell* had rammed and sunk was one of the remaining three: schooners *A. E. Price* and *Martha Porter* of Gloucester, and the *Andrew Johnson*[1] of Salem. Captain Curtis knew the skippers of all three; but which it was that his own vessel had wrecked, he supposed he would never learn.

The *Charles Haskell* was run up on the flats near her owner's wharf, repaired, and refitted. While she was there, thousands came to look at her. Old fishermen could scarcely believe the story that she had survived a collision on Georges Bank; yet there she was, and what she did no other vessel had ever done in the history of Georges; nor would any be likely to do it again!

So said the old fellows; but they also shook their heads and told Captain

---

[1] Cf. W. H. Bishop, "Fish and Men in the Maine Islands," *Harper's New Monthly Magazine,* Vol. LXI (September, 1880), No. 364, pp. 506–507: "She [the *Haskell*] broke loose from her moorings in a gale on George's, and tore into and sank the *Andrew Johnson,* with all on board. For years after, the spectres of the drowned men were reputed to come aboard the *Hascall*[*sic*] at midnight and go through a dumbshow of fishing in regular form over the side, so that no crew could be got in Gloucester to sail her, and she would not have brought sixpence in the market."

Curtis that if 'twas them a-skipperin' her, they'd go find another berth. After what *she'd* done, they wouldn't want none of *her*, by God! Ten good men of Gloucester—or was it Salem—walking the water somewhere out there on Georges Bank!

Captain Curtis didn't laugh at the old men; on the contrary, he turned upon them, excited, angry.

"We ain't got no blood on our hands!" he said.

Nevertheless, Miles Joyce and James Allen wouldn't ship on her for another trip, and the skipper had to find men for their places. Joe Enos, Scotty, and the rest stuck by him.

They were glad they did; for on her next trip out, she ran straight down to Georges, sailing it like a queen, and for the next few days, did some beautiful fishing.

There was nothing curious in the fact that all the men wanted the early watches. They always did that. And when it came to setting the watch, the skipper followed the custom of the time, calling the men around him to "thumb the hat." The crew stood in a circle, each man holding to the brim of the hat, thumb up. The skipper looked away, reached over, touched a thumb, and then counted ten from that one, going around the hat clockwise. The owner of the tenth thumb got first watch, and the business was repeated to determine who his watchmate should be, for the period from eight o'clock to ten. Then it was gone through again for the next two, and so on. There was nothing peculiar in the fact that Scotty and George Winters felt relieved when they were picked for first watch the night they arrived on Georges.

But the sixth day's work was over, fish stowed, crew long since asleep, when Harry Richardson and Joe Enos took their watch on deck. Shortly after twelve o'clock, while Joe was nodding over the wheelbox, he felt a frantic thumping at his side. He started, awoke, and faced his watchmate.

Shaking, unable at the moment to speak, young Harry Richardson pointed forward. Joe straightened up and stared over the wheel. In the starlit bow of the *Charles Haskell* he saw a little group of men.

"What's a matter them fellers?" Joe asked. "What's a matter they don't turn in?"

"Portygee," Harry Richardson softly croaked, "look at 'em again! Look at 'em! Them—*them ain't our boys*!"

Joe squinted, started forward, and after a couple of steps, stood still. The little knot of figures had grown! From somewhere, more had appeared! He could see that. And then he could see a man climb in over the rail, coming up from the starboard side. And another. Out of the waters of Georges Bank, men—figures, shadows in the shape of men—were boarding the schooner. Things of the imagination, yes; mere apparitions seen there in the starlight—but seen, Joe suddenly realized, not by one pair of eyes, but two!

Joe Enos stood still and watched. Then he turned to Harry.

"I go wake the skipper," he whispered.

As he turned, the younger man clutched at his arm. "No, you don't! You don't leave this deck, Portygee! Not with me up here, you don't!"

It didn't matter to Joe *who* went for the skipper. Still staring at the bow, he was about to tell Harry to go when the men—the things up there in the bow—started to move.

"Look!" Joe said. "They come aft!"

Silently they were stationing themselves at the regular "berths" along the deck, baiting hooks, and heaving gossamer lines over the side. And as Joe watched, it became apparent that these beings, whatever they were, were paying no attention to himself and Harry Richardson. The waters from which they had arisen were calm tonight, peaceful, beneficent; in nothing was there harm.

"All right," Joe said at last to Harry Richardson. "We stay here. We don't say nothing, you and me. By 'm by, Scotty and O'Neill got the watch. We wait and see, no?"

And so the two men stayed at the wheelbox while fishermen fished for shadows, and out of the starshine, hauled up their subtile catch.

Three minutes after Joe Enos had called the new watch and settled himself in his bunk, there was a yell from the deck. He heard the thud of boots above him, pounding aft. Then all hands were called.

When Joe went up again, the crew of the *Charles Haskell* was gathered around the cabin companionway. The figures along the deck were still obviously tending their lines, still heaving over splashless leads and slatting airy shapes into the barrels.

"I see 'em!" Captain Curtis was saying to one of the men as Joe came near. "Ain't I got eyes? But I tell you, there's no blood on our hands!" Over and over he said it, and in his voice there was a strange mingling of anger and appeal.

"There's fair wind tonight for home, skipper," somebody said.

"Me, I ain't staying out here another night," another put in. "Not me—if I have to swim it back!"

Captain Curtis was for sticking it out, and in the argument voices rose —until one or another of the men glanced forward, and then all spoke in low tones again. For this there was no need. The *Charles Haskell's* extra hands turned now and then to one another, and smiled as their lips moved soundlessly; but for all else that went on aboard the vessel, they seemed to have deaf ears, sightless eyes.

The skipper, alone in his stand, gave in at last.

"All right, boys. Get in the anchor. We're going home."

Gingerly the men went about their work. It was slow. There was much hesitating, much backing away, for now the strangers were hauling in their lines, their work finished. But when they had gone through the motions of leaving everything shipshape, one by one they filed to the bow, stepped over the rail, and walked into the darkness of Georges Bank.

Twenty-four hours later, during the same watch, the *Charles Haskell* again was manned with the silent fishermen. But she was homeward bound now. She had passed the twin lights of Thacher's Island, and under a good breeze, was bowling past the welcome glimmer of sidelights carried on vessels from the home port.

In the small watches of the morning, she brought Eastern Point Light nearly abreast. Then the captain gave the order to bear about for Gloucester Harbor, and took the wheel himself.

At that moment, each of the strangers turned, looked aft at Captain Curtis, and then went to join his shipmates up in the bow. While the *Haskell's* men were trimming the sails, these others stood there, watching. Then from among them one stepped out, walked aft as far as the fore-rigging, and gazing intently at the helmsman, slowly shook his head. But the schooner was running fast for the mouth of Gloucester Harbor, and the skipper held her to her course. And so the lone figure mounted the rail, beckoned to his fellows, and was gone over the side. The others followed. And the last the *Haskell's* crew saw of them, they were slowly marching through the dawn—*towards Salem!*

We may think what we will of the things men say they've seen. We may explain these nightly visitors of the *Charles Haskell* into being, or we may explain them away. Whatever we care to make of them will be of no more substance than the ghost-fishes they themselves slatted into empty barrels.

But what men *do* because of the things they've "seen"—well, here is another matter. And the fact does remain that from the morning she arrived home from her second trip to Georges Bank, the schooner *Charles Haskell* was taboo in Gloucester. Captain Curtis could not find a crew for her. With good fishing in prospect, and not too many berths open for the men who gathered daily in Rogers Street, one might think that a dozen men could be found for the crew from among those hundreds who were looking for berths, crowd of motley temperament, men of many faiths and none.

Not a dozen, not five, not two, could be induced to ship on the *Charles Haskell.* But one—Joe Enos, the "Portygee"—did tell Captain Curtis he was willing to try it once more. And Joe was willing because, he said, now he understood. He knew what to do.

"Next time," Joe told the skipper, "we go to Georges, we fish, we set sail. But we don't take the vessel back to Gloucester, Cap'n! When we come back, we go to Salem. We take them fellers home first!"

But the captain, man of a colder, more practical race than Joe Enos's, did not understand; and for months the *Charles Haskell* lay idle at a Gloucester wharf. Finally, rather than keep her at a dead loss, her owners sold her off to a group in Digby, Nova Scotia.

Whether the wanderers of Georges Bank ever came on board the *Charles Haskell* again, I do not know. The next time I could find the schooner mentioned was in this little item in the ship-news column of the *Provincetown Beacon,* March 11, 1893:

On Thursday last, sch. *W. B. Keene,* was at Lewis Wharf, having on board a box belonging to a hand-horn of the type used by fishing vessels for giving fog warning. On the box, which had been newly split and but a few days in the water, was painted the name, "Charles Haskell." The *Keene* is fresh-haddocking this season on Georges Bank.

The Ghost of Mrs. Sam Blood

THERE is a fine old brick tavern still standing in a New England seaboard town, and now doing service as a rather disreputable road house. It is a building rigidly square, set due north, south, east, and west, with four long, narrow doors opening over broad doorstones to the four ends of the earth. A long tail of summer and winter kitchens, a washroom, brew-house, smoke-house, wood-rooms, sheds, barns, piggeries, pigeon-houses, hen-houses, once stretched a hundred feet or more adown the road, part of which is now torn down. Each joint of the tail helped loyally in olden times to furnish good cheer to the traveller. The great square rooms of the main house are amply furnished; one was a taproom, and in each second-story room still are two double beds, save in the corner room next the kitchen tail of the house, where stands nailed firmly to the floor of the room a somewhat battered oaken table. A little open staircase in the corner of this room leads down to the working end of the house, and was used in olden days to carry supplies to the upper table from the lower kitchen.

It has been many a year since good cheer was spread on that broad oaken board, though at one time it was the favorite dining place of a choice brotherhood of old salts, called the Mariners' Club, who gathered there when on shore to tell tales of wild privateering, and of sharp foreign trade, and to plan new and profitable ventures. Many of these Mariners' Clubs and Marine Societies existed in seaport towns at that golden time in New England's marine commercial history.

This room was the scene about seventy-five years ago of a somewhat unusual expression of feminine revolt—that is, both the expression and the revolt were unusual. One of the most constant frequenters of the tavern, the heaviest eater and deepest drinker, the greatest money-spender at these Mariners' dinners, was one Captain Sam Blood, who ran a large coasting brig, which made but short trips to Atlantic seaports. Thus he was ever on hand for tavern fun. He had a large and rather helpless family which he kept somewhat in retreat on a gloomy farm two miles inland; his mother old and feeble, yet ever hard-working; a large number of untidy children, and, worst of all, a sickly wife, a tall, gaunt woman who whined, and whined, and ever whined from her patch-covered couch, over the frequent desertions of her spouse to the tavern-table, and his wilful waste of money,

---

From *Stage-Coach and Tavern Days,* by Alice Morse Earle, pp. 419–426.

while she could never leave the house. One night a specially good dinner was set in the Mariners' room, roast and boiled meats, pies and puddings, a grand array of full pitchers, decanters, and bottles; the assembled group of old salts were about to ascend from the taproom to seat themselves comfortably at the round table for solid work, when a terrible crash and scream were heard, each seeming louder than the other, and before the startled eyes of the landlord and his guests, as they rushed up and into the room, there were all the steaming dishes, all the streaming bottles, with table-cloth and plates in a disorderly hopeless wreck on the floor. "Who could have done it?" "There he goes," shouted one captain, as he ran to the window; and, surely enough, a slender man in nautical garb was seen striking out from under the sheltering walls of the ell-kitchens and sheds, and running desperately across the snowy fields. Full chase was given and the marauder finally captured; he was swung roughly around with oaths and blows, when sudden silence fell on all. It was Sam Blood's wife in Sam Blood's togs. "I'll settle for this dinner," said Sam Blood, blackly.

On his next voyage Mrs. Blood sailed with the captain. With the usual ethical inconsistencies which prevail in small communities, Mrs. Sam Blood the despoiler attracted more attention and sympathy than Mrs. Sam Blood the poor, hard-working, sickly wife; it was the universal talk and decision of all the women in town that the captain's wife needed a change of scene; and she had to take it in that ironical form decreed to the wives of old-time ship-owners, in a voyage of uncertain length and certain discomfort on a sailing vessel, with no woman companion and the doubtful welcome of the male members of the crew. Off she went to Savannah. At that port she was no better, cried all the time (the first mate wrote home), and seemed little like the woman of spirit who had wrecked the Mariners' dinner. The captain decided to go with a cargo to South America to see how the tropics would serve the ailing woman. His old home crew shipped back to Boston, not caring for the trip far south, and a crew of creoles and negroes was taken on the supplemental trip.

When Captain Blood and his schooner at last came into port at home, he landed with sombre countenance, a mourning widower, and soon was properly clad in trappings of woe. Mrs. Sam Blood was no more. Her husband stated briefly that she had died and was buried at sea off the island of Jamaica. A discreet and decent term of mourning passed, and Mrs. Blood, as is the way of the living—and of the dead—was quite forgotten. Once more the Mariners' Club was to have a dinner, and once more the table in the Mariners' room was spread with good cheer and ample drink. Captain Blood, in somewhat mitigated bereavement, was among the thronging guests who lingered over a final stomach-warmer at the bar. The landlord ran out of the room and roared down the main stairs that dinner was ready, and even as he spoke, crash! smash! came a din from the Mariners' room, and there was all the dinner and all the broken bottles with the table-cloth and the upset table on the floor. It was a very unpleasant reminder to Sam Blood of a very mortifying event, and his friends sympathized with him in silence. This time no miscreant could be found in house or on farm, but the landlord suspected a discharged and ugly servant, who might have run down the little corner staircase, as Mrs. Blood had before him.

The ruined dinner was replaced by another a week later. The guests were gathered, the landlord was bearing a last roast pig aloft, when smash! crash! came again from the Mariners' room. Every one in the house rushed up in tremendous excitement: the table-cloth was off, table upset, bottles smashed. An ominous silence and a sense of the uncanny fell on all in the room; some glanced askance at Sam Blood. More than one sharp-eyed old salt noted that the great, hairy, tattooed hands of the widower shook amazingly, though his face was the calmest of all the bronzed, weather-beaten figure-heads staring around.

There has never been a meal served from that table since, though many a meal has been spread on it. The landlord, a stubborn man of no nonsense and no whims, grimly nailed the legs of the table to the floor, and proceeded to set the suceeding dinner on the bare boards. It mattered not, cloth or no cloth, every dinner small or great was always wrecked. Watchers were set, enjoined not to take their eyes from the table, nor themselves from the room. Something always happened, an alarm of fire, a sudden call for help, an apparent summons from the landlord—this but for a single moment, but in that moment smash! crash! went the dinner.

Captain Blood lived to a rather lonely and unpopular old age, for he was held responsible for the decay and dissolution of the Mariners' Club; and unjustly enough, for Neptune knows it was no wish of his. When occasional dinners and suppers were given by nautical men in wholly mundane rooms in other taverns, with no spiritual accompaniments,—that is, in the form of ghosts,—the captain was left out. Men did not hanker for the companionship of a man who left port with a wife and came home with a ghost. He has been dead for decades, and is anchored in the old Hill graveyard, where he sleeps the quiet sleep of the righteous; and the name and virtues of Elvira, his beloved wife, are amply recorded on his tombstone. But her ghost still walks, or at any rate still wrecks. I don't like ghosts, but I really should like to meet this lively and persistent Yankee wraith, clad in the meek and meagre drooping feminine attire which was the mode in the early part of this century, or perhaps tentatively mannish in peajacket and oilskins as in her day of riot of old. I really wish I could see the spry and spiteful spirit of Mrs. Sam Blood, with her expression of rampant victory as she twitches the table-cloth off, and wrecks the bottles, and says in triumphal finality, "I'll settle for this dinner"; thus gaining what is ever dear to a woman, even to the ghost of a woman—the last word.

Moosilauke's Ghost Doctor

I REMEMBER a night when the Dartmouth boys served a big hot supper, then settled us down for close harmony and wild tales of witches seen by early climbers in the moonlit mist on the rocks, and of Moosilauke's famous ghost of the doctor who bought a home near the base and used the cats and dogs of his neighbors for research work in anatomy. "Anatomy, my eye!" cried the early settlers. With the help of the Devil, he was searching for the lost elixir of youth; and when his gaunt cloaked figure now and then appeared, they vowed it was to steal babies that he came out of his infamous home. So one bleak December day, when a baby was missing from a farm, they came in a mob and burned his house; and on finding no baby or doctor there, the mob went after him up Moosilauke, where a hunter claimed to have seen him that day. Though most were driven back by a storm, the few who reached the top that night caught a glimpse of him on a high ledge silhouetted against the clouds, his long cape flying in the gale and one lean hand holding to his lips the elixir of youth eternal made from his baby victim's blood! Since then he has often been heard or seen up there, for with that damned elixir, like the Wandering Jew, he cannot die!

Tim Felt's Ghost

CONNECTED with the Ireland Parish district of the city of Holyoke, Mass., is a famous ghost story, which runs as follows: In the old days there lived on "Back Street" a Mr. Felt. One fall he sowed a field of rye. The rye came up well, and in the spring was looking green and thrifty. He was therefore the more disturbed at the frequent visits of Neighbor Hummerston's geese to the said field.

Mr. Felt had a quick temper, and this sort of thing was too much for him. He caught the whole flock one day, killed them, and then wended his way to Deacon Hummerston to inform him what he had done, and where his geese were to be found.

This and other acts showed his hasty temper and savage disposition, and brought him into disrepute among his neighbors. He often cruelly beat his horses and cattle, and there were times when he served the members of his family in the same way.

He had a son, Timothy by name, a dull-witted fellow, who was slow

---

From *The Great White Hills of New Hampshire,* by Ernest Poole, p. 384. Copyright, 1946, by Ernest Poole. Garden City, New York: Doubleday & Company, Inc.

From *What They Say in New England,* A Book of Signs, Sayings, and Superstitions, collected by Clifton Johnson, pp. 249–252. Copyright, 1896, by Lee and Shepard. Boston.

of comprehension, and in his work made many mistakes. This was a frequent cause of anger to his father, who on such occasions would strike Tim to the earth with whatever implement he happened to have in hand,—a hoe, a rake, or a pitchfork, perchance. These attacks sometimes drove Tim from home; but, after a few days' absence, necessity would bring him back again. At last, however, he disappeared, and was seen no more; and a little later the Felts moved West.

In building the New Haven and Northampton canal, a great deal of limestone was used. On Mr. Felt's farm was a ledge of this rock, and the company soon had to quarry there. The overseer was a rough, ill-tempered fellow; and it was not long before he had trouble with his workmen, and they all left him. That brought work to a standstill, and the overseer was at his wit's end to find some way out of his difficulty.

One night, shortly after the men left, the overseer, on his way home from the corner store, quite late, saw a dark figure standing on the limestone ledge, outlined against the sky. The overseer stood still, his frightened gaze riveted on the stranger. Presently he broke the silence by asking, "Who are you? and what is your business?"

The spectre replied, "My name is Timothy Felt, and my bones are under where I stand. I was killed by my father four years ago, and if you will blast this rock you will find my bones."

This story ran through all the country round, and created great excitement. Every day, for some time afterwards, loads of people, not only from Ireland Parish, but from towns quite distant, wended their way thither, inquiring the way to the "ghost place"; and when night came on people would make a long detour rather than pass the spot, and run the risk of meeting Tim's uneasy spirit. Money was raised to continue the quarrying until Tim's skeleton should be brought to light, but no bones were found; and after the overseer had gotten out what stone he wanted, the work lagged and was discontinued.

Was this humbug or not? A certain old lady used to say:—

"Where folks believe in witches, witches air;
But when they don't believe, there are none there."

In this case there was wide belief that Tim was murdered, and that his ghost did really appear.

The Ghost of Hannah Mason

On the post-road in southern New Hampshire stands an old house, which according to its license was once "improved" as a tavern, and was famous for its ghost and its Roses. The tavern was owned by a family of two brothers and two sisters, all unmarried, as was rather a habit in the Mason family; though when any of the tribe did marry, a vast throng of children

From *Old-Time Gardens,* Newly Set Forth, by Alice Morse Earle, pp. 473–478. Copyright, 1901, by The Macmillan Company. New York. 1902.

quickly sprung up to propagate the name and sturdy qualities of the race. The men were giants, and both men and women were hard-working folk of vast endurance and great thrift, and, like all of that ilk in New England, they prospered and grew well-to-do; great barns and outbuildings, all well filled, stretched down along the roadside below the house. Joseph Mason could lay more feet of stone wall in a day, could plough more land, chop down more trees, pull more stumps, than any other man in New Hampshire. His sisters could bake and brew, make soap, weed the garden, spin and weave, unceasingly and untiringly. Their garden was a source of purest pleasure to them, as well as of hard work; its borders were so stocked with medicinal herbs that it could supply a township; and its old-time flowers furnished seeds and slips and bulbs to every other garden within a day's driving distance; but its glory was a garden side to gladden the heart of Omar Khayyam, where two or three acres of ground were grown over heavily with old-fashioned Roses. These were only the common Cinnamon Rose, the beloved Cabbage Rose, and a pale pink, spicily scented, large-petalled, scarcely double Rose, known to them as the Apothecaries' Rose. Farmer-neighbors wondered at this waste of the Masons' good land in this unprofitable Rose crop, but it had a certain use. There came every June to this Rose garden all the children of the vicinity, bearing milk-pails, homespun bags, birch baskets, to gather Rose petals. They nearly all had Roses at their homes, but not the Mason Roses. These Rose leaves were carried carefully to each home, and were packed in stone jars with alternate layers of brown or scant maple sugar. Soon all conglomerated into a gummy, brown, close grained, not over alluring substance to the vision, which was known among the children by the unromantic name of "Rose tobacco." This cloying confection was in high repute. It was chipped off and eaten in tiny bits, and much treasured—as a love token, or reward of good behavior.

The Mason house was a tavern. It was not one of the regular stopping-places on the turnpike road, being rather too near the town to gather any travel of teamsters or coaches; but passers-by who knew the house and the Masons loved to stop there. Everything in the well-kept, well-filled house and barns contributed to the comfort of guests, and it was known that the Masons cared more for the company of the traveller than for his pay.

There was a shadow on this house. The youngest of the family, Hannah, had been jilted in her youth, "shabbed" as said the country folks. After several years of "constant company-keeping" with the son of a neighbor, during which time many a linen sheet and tablecloth, many a fine blanket, had been spun and woven, and laid aside with the tacit understanding that it was part of her wedding outfit, the man had fallen suddenly and violently in love with a girl who came from a neighboring town to sing a single Sunday in the church choir. He had driven to her home the following week, carried her off to a parson in a third town, married her, and brought her to his home in a triumph of enthusiasm and romance, which quickly fled before the open dislike and reprehension of his upright neighbors, who abhorred his fickleness, and before the years of ill health and ill temper of the hard-worked, faded wife. Many children were born to them; two lived, sickly little souls, who, unconscious of the blemish on their parents' past, came with the other children every June, and gathered Rose leaves under Hannah Mason's window.

Hannah Mason was called crazy. After her desertion she never entered any door save that of her own home, never went to a neighbor's house either in time of joy or sorrow; queerer still, never went to church. All her life, her thoughts, her vast strength went into hard work. No labor was too heavy or too formidable for her. She would hetchel flax for weeks, spin unceasingly, and weave on a hand loom, most wearing of women's work, without thought of rest. No single household could supply work for such an untiring machine, especially when all labored industriously—so work was brought to her from the neighbors. Not a wedding outfit for miles around was complete without one of Hannah Mason's fine tablecloths. Every corpse was buried in one of her linen shrouds. Sailmakers and boat-owners in Portsmouth sent up to her for strong duck for their sails. Lads went up to Dartmouth College in suits of her homespun. Many a teamster on the road slept under Hannah Mason's heavy gray woollen blankets, and his wagon tilts were covered with her canvas. Her bank account grew rapidly—she became rich as fast as her old lover became poor. But all this cast a shadow on the house. Sojourners would waken and hear throughout the night some steady sound, a scratching of the cards, a whirring of the spinning-wheel, the thump-thump of the loom. Some said she never slept, and could well grow rich when she worked all night.

At last the woman who had stolen her lover—the poor, sickly wife—died. The widower, burdened hopelessly with debts, of course put up in her memory a fine headstone extolling her virtues. One wakeful night, with a sentiment often found in such natures, he went to the graveyard to view his proud but unpaid-for possession. The grass deadened his footsteps, and not till he reached the grave did there rise up from the ground a tall, ghostly figure dressed all in undyed gray wool of her own weaving. It was Hannah Mason. "Hannah," whimpered the widower, trying to take her hand,—with equal thought of her long bank account and his unpaid-for headstone,—"I never really loved any one but you." She broke away from him with an indescribable gesture of contempt and dignity, and went home. She died suddenly four days later of pneumonia, either from the shock or the damp midnight chill of the graveyard.

As months passed on travellers still came to the tavern, and the story began to be whispered from one to another that the house was haunted by the ghost of Hannah Mason. Strange sounds were heard at night from the garret where she had always worked; most plainly of all could be heard the whirring of her great wool wheel. When this rumor reached the brothers' ears, they determined to investigate the story and end it forever. That night their vigil began, and soon the sound of the wheel was heard.

They entered the garret, and to their surprise found the wheel spinning round. Then Joseph Mason went to the garret and seated himself for closer and more determined watch. He sat in the dark till the wheel began to revolve, then struck a sudden light and found the ghost. A great rat had run out on the spoke of the wheel and when he reached the broad rim had started a treadmill of his own—which made the ghostly sound as it whirred around. Soon this rat grew so tame that he would come out on the spinningwheel in the daytime, and several others were seen to run around in the wheel as if it were a pleasant recreation.

The old brick house still stands with its great grove of Sugar Maples, but it is silent, for the Masons all sleep in the graveyard behind the church high up on the hillside; no travellers stop within the doors, the ghost rats are dead, the spinningwheel is gone, but the garden still blossoms with eternal youth. Though children no longer gather rose leaves for Rose tobacco, the "Roses of Yesterday" bloom every year; and each June morn, "a thousand blossoms with the day awake," and fling their spicy fragrance on the air.

The Murdered Traveler

Just as almost every town on Cape Cod has a sea-serpent story, Berkshire abounds with tales of missing travelers. At every second town, some unfortunate wayfarer has disappeared, never to be seen again. Of all these legends, the most gruesome is the tale of the traveler who haunted the tavern in Savoy.

One black night when the rain poured down the mountains and the thunder sounded like the trumpets of Judgment Day, a lone traveler stopped for the night at the tavern in Savoy Hollow. He was never seen thereafter. The landlord, accused of robbing and murdering his guest, sobbed out an indignant denial. Since there was no proof of death, nothing could be done; but from that day on the tavern was haunted. Travelers fled in terror when they saw bloodstains on the stairs—bloodstains that could not be washed away or even covered. The specter of the murdered man, hollow-eyed and gory, appeared in an upstairs window, mutely warning wayfarers to shun the dubious hospitality of the tavern. To make matters worse, a short time after the traveler vanished, a man working in a hay field nearby mysteriously broke his neck. For years afterward his spirit was said to haunt the vicinity, moaning and groaning mournfully. No tavern could survive the attentions of two spooks like these, and at last it closed its doors. One would not suspect so bloodcurdling a chapter in the annals of Savoy, the peaceful hamlet which never housed a lawyer nor paid the bills of more than one "home" doctor.[1]

---

[1] From *The Berkshire Hills,* Compiled and Written by Members of the Federal Writers' Project of the Works Progress Administration for Massachusetts, pp. 255–256. Copyright, 1939, by The Berkshire Hills Conference, Inc. New York: Duell, Sloan and Pearce.

In West Stockbridge you will hear a Berkshire version of the murdered traveler story, variations of which occur all over New England. On a night when a violent storm was raging, with plenty of thunder and rain, an unknown traveler from New York State stopped at a West Stockbridge tavern for supper. After he had paid his bill from a large roll of money, inquired the way to Stockbridge, and departed "on the edge of the evening," he was never seen alive again. There were other strangers in the inn that night, two "evil-looking" men, who cast covetous eyes at the bank roll. But there seemed no cause for alarm until in the spring the melting snow surrendered the body of the traveler. The spot is on Mass 102 about a mile south from the junction of that highway and Mass 41 on the road to Stockbridge. Near a small ravine by a brook on the right of the road, near the town, is his burial place, or so it is said. The melancholy tale is recorded by William Cullen Bryant in "The Murdered Traveler."

When Spring to woods and wastes around
 Brought bloom and joy again
The murdered traveler's bones were found
 Far down a mountain glen.

They little knew, who loved him so,
 The fearful death he met,
When shouting o'er the desert snow,
 Unarmed and hard beset. . . .

Nor how, when strangers found his bones,
 They dressed the hasty bier,
And marked his grave with nameless stones
 Unmoistened by a tear.

Fruitless attempts have been made to identify the murdered traveler of West Stockbridge. Quite a few local families would like to have him as an ancestor—a companion, perchance, for the skeleton in the closet.[2]

The Bridge That Wasn't There

A MR. VAN RENSSELAER, a young gentleman from Albany, came one evening into an inn, kept by a Mr. Root, just at the eastern end of the bridge [in Great Barrington]. The inn-keeper, who knew him, asked him where he had crossed the river. He answered, "On the bridge." Mr. Root replied, that that was impossible, because it had been raised that very day, and that not a plank had been laid on it. Mr. Van Rensselaer said that it could not be true, because his horse had come over without any difficulty or reluctance; that the night was indeed so profoundly dark as to prevent

[2] *Ibid.*, pp. 101–102.

him from seeing anything distinctly; but that it was incredible, if his horse could see sufficiently well to keep his footing anywhere, that he should not discern the danger, and impossible for him to pass over the bridge in that condition. Each went to bed dissatisfied, neither believing the story of the other. In the morning, Mr. Van Rensselaer went, at the solicitation of his host, to view the bridge, and, finding it a naked frame, gazed for a moment with astonishment, and fainted.[1]

Not far from the year 1806, Mr. Charles Stevens, who lived on East Hill, made a horse-back journey to Massachusetts, passing down on his way from home over the high bridge across the Winooski about three-fourths of a mile below Daggett's Mills village. During his absence the bridge had been stripped of all the plank, preparatory to replanking or putting in some new string-pieces. While the bridge was in this dismantled condition—which condition was wholly unknown and unsuspected by Mr. Stevens—he reached home, on his return from his journey, at a late hour on an unusually dark night, totally unconscious that he had passed through any peril in passing over the river, which was only a mile or two from his house.

"Which way did you come?" asked his family.

"The way I went, of course."

"No, you couldn't, for the river is roaring high, and there is not a single plank on the bridge."

"Yes, I did come the same way and over the same bridge, and you can't beat me out of it."

Here was a complete issue, and neither party being in the least disposed to yield, they the next morning, in company with a neighbor, a Mr. Parker, repaired to the bridge, and to their amazement discovered, by the tracks on the ground and the calk marks of the animal's shoes on the timber, that the horse, after selecting the broadest hewn string-piece, had mounted it and passed so quietly and safely over it to the other side that the rider was not made aware, in the great darkness of the night, that he was undergoing the dangerous transit.

We have seen published, we think, later accounts of similar feats performed in the darkness of night by horses bearing their unconscious riders in safety over bridge timbers; but of the truth of such accounts there is much room to doubt, and it is not impossible that this one, which is as true as it was remarkable, and which soon passed into one of the wide-

---

[1] From *Massachusetts Historical Collections,* Being a General Collection of Interesting Facts, Traditions, Biographical Sketches, Anecdotes, &c., Relating to the History and Antiquities of Every Town in Massachusetts, with Geographical Descriptions, by John Warner Barber, p. 73. Entered, according to Act of Congress, in the year 1839, by Dorr, Howland & Co. In the Clerk's Office of the District Court of Massachusetts. Worcester.

Related by Dr. Dwight.—J. W. B.

spread traditions of the country, may have been the only original of all such reported stories.[2]

At the Sign of Sir Charles

LATE on a November night in the early part of this century the landlord and half a dozen teamsters sat drinking deep in the taproom of the Buxton Inn. These rough travellers had driven into the yard during the afternoon with their produce-laden wagons; for a heavy snow was falling, and it was impossible wheeling, doubtful even whether they could leave the inn in forty-eight hours—perhaps not for a week. Their board would not prove very costly, for they carried their own horse-provender, and much of their own food. Some paid for a bed, others slept free of charge round the fire; but all spent money for drink. It was a fierce storm and a great fall of snow for the month of the year—though November is none too mild any year in New England. Though this snow was too early by half to be seasonable, yet each teamster was roughly merry at the others' expense that he had not "come down" on runners.

With dull days of inaction before them there was no need for early hours of sleep, so all talked loud and long and drank boisterously, when suddenly a series of heavy knocks was heard at the front door of the inn. Bang! bang! angrily pounded the iron knocker, and the landlord went slowly into the little front entry, fumbled heavily at the bolt, and at last threw open the door to a fine young spark who blustered in with a great bank of snow which fell in at his feet, and who was covered with rolls and drifts of snow, which he shook off debonairly on all around him, displaying at last a handsome suit of garments, gold-laced, and very fine to those country bumpkins, but which a "cit" would have noted were somewhat antiquated of cut and fashion.

He at once indicated and proved his claim to being a gentleman by swearing roundly at the landlord, declaring that his horses and servant were housed ere he was, that they had driven round and found shelter in the barn before he could get into the front door. He could drink like a gentleman, too, this fine young fellow, and he entered at once into the drinking and singing and story-telling and laughing with as much zest as if he had been only a poor common country clown. At last all fell to casting dice. The stakes were low, but such as they were luck all went one way. After

[2] From *History of the Town of Montpelier,* from the Time It Was First Chartered in 1781 to the Year 1860, Together with Biographical Sketches of Its Most Noted Deceased Citizens, by D. P. Thompson, pp. 157–158. Entered according to Act of Congress, in the year 1860, by Daniel P. Thompson, in the Clerk's Office of the District Court for the District of Vermont. Montpelier: E. P. Walton, Printer.

From *Stage-Coach and Tavern Days,* by Alice Morse Earle, pp. 426–429. Copyright, 1900, by The Macmillan Company. New York and London.

two hours' rounds the gentleman had all the half-dollars and shillings, all the pennies even, in his breeches pocket; and he laughed and sneered in hateful triumph. Sobered by his losses, which were small but his all, one teamster surlily said he was going to sleep, and another added, " 'Tis high time." And indeed it was, for at that moment old Janet, the tavern housemaid, came in to begin her morning round of work, to pinch out the candles, take up part of the ashes from the chimney-hearth, fill the kitchen pots and kettles, gather in the empty bottles and glasses; and as she did so, albeit she was of vast age, she glanced with warm interest at the fine figure of fashion slapping his pockets, sneering, and drinking off his glass. "Why, master," she said, staring, "you do be the very cut of Sir Charles off our sign-board." "Let's see how he looks," swaggered the young blade; "where's a window whence we can peep at him?" All trooped to a nigh window in the tavern parlor to look at the portrait of Sir Charles Buxton on the swing-sign, but to no avail, for there was yet but scant light without, and they peered out only on thick snowdrifts on the window panes. But when they reëntered the kitchen, lo! their gay companion was gone. Gone where? Back on the sign-board, of course. All who heard the oft and ever repeated wonder-tale would have scoffed at the fuddled notions of a drunken group of stupid teamsters, but the dollars and shillings and pennies were gone too—the devil knows where; and who was to pay the score for the double bowl of punch and the half-dozen mugs of flip Sir Charles Buxton had ordered while the dicing was going on, and a large share of which he had drunk off with all the zest of flesh and blood? Besides, Janet had seen him, and Janet's eye for a young man could never be doubted.

PROPHETIC CURSES

Chocorua's Curse

And Chocorua is the only mountain whose peak is crowned with a legend. Would that the vigorous pen which has saved for us many of the fragmentary traditions of the early Indian life in New England, and set them to the music of such terse and vigorous lines as "The Bridal of Pennacook," "Mogg Megone," and "The Funeral Tree of the Sokokis," had enshrined thus the story of Chocorua's Curse, and in this way given the mountain added glory in the landscape of New Hampshire! Mr. Whittier has not told it in verse; but our readers will be glad that we can give it to them in such vivid prose as the following, by Mrs. Child:—

From *The White Hills; Their Legends, Landscape, and Poetry,* by Thomas Starr King, pp. 145–149. Entered according to Act of Congress, in the year 1859, by Crosby, Nichols and Company, in the Clerk's Office of the District Court of the District of Massachusetts. Boston: Crosby and Ainsworth. 1866.

"A small colony of hardy pioneers had settled at the base of this mountain. Intelligent, independent men, impatient of restraint, they had shunned the more thickly-settled portions of the country, and retired into this remote part of New Hampshire. But there was one master-spirit among them who was capable of a higher destiny than he ever fulfilled.

"The consciousness of this had stamped something of proud humility on the face of Cornelius Campbell,—something of a haughty spirit, strongly curbed by circumstances he could not control, and at which he seemed to murmur. He assumed no superiority; but, unconsciously, he threw around him the spell of intellect, and his companions felt, they knew not why, that he was 'among them, but not of them.' His stature was gigantic, and he had the bold, quick tread of one who had wandered frequently and fearlessly among the terrible hiding-places of nature. His voice was harsh, but his whole countenance possessed singular capabilities for tenderness of expression; and sometimes, under the gentle influence of domestic excitement, his hard features would be rapidly lighted up, seeming like the sunshine flying over the shaded fields in an April day.

"His companion was one calculated to excite and retain the deep, strong energies of manly love. She had possessed extraordinary beauty, and had, in the full maturity of an excellent judgment, relinquished several splendid alliances, and incurred her father's displeasure, for the sake of Cornelius Campbell. Had political circumstances proved favorable, his talents and ambition would unquestionably have worked out a path to emolument and fame; but he had been a zealous and active enemy of the Stuarts, and the restoration of Charles II. was the death-warrant of his hopes. Immediately flight became necessary, and America was the chosen place of refuge. His adherence to Cromwell's party was not occasioned by religious sympathy, but by political views too liberal and philosophical for the state of the people; therefore, Cornelius Campbell sought a home with our forefathers, and, being of a proud nature, he withdrew with his family to the solitary place we have mentioned.

"A very small settlement in such a remote place was, of course, subject to inconvenience and occasional suffering. From the Indians they received neither injury nor insult. No cause of quarrel had ever arisen; and, although their frequent visits were sometimes troublesome, they never had given indications of jealousy or malice. Chocorua was a prophet among them, and, as such, an object of peculiar respect. He had a mind which education and motive would have nerved with giant strength; but, growing up in savage freedom, it wasted itself in dark, fierce, ungovernable passions. There was something fearful in the quiet haughtiness of his lips; it seemed so like slumbering power—too proud to be lightly roused, and too implacable to sleep again. In his small, black fiery eye, expression lay coiled up like a beautiful snake. The white people knew that his hatred would be terrible; but they had never provoked it, and even the children became too much accustomed to him to fear him.

"Chocorua had a son, nine or ten years old, to whom Caroline Campbell had occasionally made such gaudy presents as were likely to attract his savage fancy. This won the child's affections, so that he became a familiar visitant, almost an inmate of their dwelling; and, being unrestrained by the courtesies of civilized life, he would inspect everything, and taste of everything which came in his way. Some poison, prepared for a mischievous fox, which had long troubled the little settlement, was discovered and drunk by the Indian boy, and he went home to his father to sicken and die. From that moment jealousy and hatred took possession of Chocorua's soul. He never told his suspicions; he brooded over them in secret, to nourish the deadly revenge he contemplated against Cornelius Campbell.

"The story of Indian animosity is always the same. Cornelius Campbell left his hut for the fields early one bright, balmy morning in June. Still a lover, though ten years a husband, his last look was turned towards his wife, answering her parting smile; his last action a kiss for each of his children. When he returned to dinner, they were dead—all dead! and their disfigured bodies too cruelly showed that an Indian's hand had done the work!

"In such a mind grief, like all other emotions, was tempestuous. Home had been to him the only verdant spot in the desert of life. In his wife and children he had garnered up all his heart; and now that they were torn from him, the remembrance of their love clung to him like the death-grapple of a drowning man, sinking him down into darkness and death. This was followed by a calm a thousand times more terrible—the creeping agony of despair, that brings with it no power of resistance.

'It was as if the dead could feel
The icy worm around him steal.'

"Such, for many days, was the state of Cornelius Campbell. Those who knew and reverenced him feared that the spark of reason was forever extinguished. But it rekindled again, and with it came a wild, demoniac spirit of revenge. The death-groan of Chocorua would make him smile in his dreams; and, when he waked, death seemed too pitiful a vengeance for the anguish that was eating into his very soul.

"Chocorua's brethren were absent on a hunting expedition at the time he committed the murder, and those who watched his movements observed that he frequently climbed the high precipice, which afterwards took his name, probably looking out for indications of their return. Here Cornelius Campbell resolved to effect his deadly purpose. A party was formed, under his guidance, to cut off all chance of retreat, and the dark-minded prophet was to be hunted like a wild beast to his lair.

"The morning sun had scarce cleared away the fogs, when Chocorua started at a loud voice from beneath the precipice, commanding him to throw himself into the deep abyss below. He knew the voice of his enemy, and replied, with an Indian's calmness, 'The Great Spirit gave life to Chocorua, and Chocorua will not throw it away at the command of the white man.' 'Then hear the Great Spirit speak in the white man's thunder!' exclaimed Cornelius Campbell, as he pointed his gun to the precipice. Chocorua, though fierce and fearless as a panther, had never overcome his dread of firearms. He placed his hands upon his ears, to shut out the stunning report; the next moment the blood bubbled from his neck, and he reeled fearfully on the edge of the precipice. But he recovered himself, and, raising himself on his hand, he spoke in a loud voice, that grew more terrific as its huskiness increased, 'A curse upon ye, white men! May the Great Spirit curse ye when he speaks in the clouds, and his words are fire! Chocorua had a son, and ye killed him while the sky looked bright! Lightning blast your crops! Winds and fire destroy your dwellings! The Evil Spirit breathe death upon your cattle! Your graves lie in the war-path of the Indian! Panthers howl and wolves fatten over your bones! Chocorua goes to the Great Spirit,—his curse stays with the white man!'

"The prophet sank upon the ground, still uttering inaudible curses, and they left his bones to whiten in the sun. But his curse rested on that settlement. The tomahawk and scalping-knife were busy among them; the winds tore up trees, and hurled them at their dwellings; their crops were blasted, their cattle died, and sickness came upon their strongest men. At last the remnant of them departed from the fatal spot to mingle with more populous and prosperous colonies. Cornelius Campbell became a hermit, seldom seeking or seeing his fellow-men; and two years after he was found dead in his hut."

During many years the cattle in the town of Burton, now called Albany, at the base of Chocorua, were afflicted with a strange disease. Science has discovered that the trouble is in the water, which contains a weak solution of muriate of lime. The disease of the cattle was for years attributed to Chocorua's dying curse. Whether that curse sank into the mountain and poisoned with muriate of lime the springs from which the Burton cows were to drink, or the muriate of lime at the base generated the story of the sachem's imprecation on the summit, let us not too curiously inquire. Let us only recall the fact with gratitude that, since science has provided a remedy for the suffering cattle in common soapsuds, the superstitious dread has nearly disappeared. Some charming cultivated intervales in the village of Albany now add to the beauty of the prospect from the battered crest of the mountain, and intimate, either that the sachem's wrongs have been expiated, or that his dusky spirit is appeased.

Rogers' Rangers and the Silver Image of St. Francis

The Sack of St. Francis[1]

In the month of September, 1759, the army of Sir Jeffrey Amherst was in cantonments at Crown Point. A picked corps of American rangers, commanded by Robert Rogers, was attached to this army. One day an aide-de-camp brought Rogers an order to repair forthwith to head-quarters, and in a few moments the ranger entered the general's marquee.

"At your orders, general," said the ranger, making his salute.

"About that accursed hornet's-nest of St. Francis?" said the general, frowning.

"When I was a lad, your excellency, we used to burn a hornet's-nest, if it became troublesome," observed Rogers, significantly.

"And how many do you imagine, major, this one has stung to death in the last six years?" inquired General Amherst, fumbling among his papers.

"I don't know; a great many, your excellency."

"Six hundred men, women and children."

The two men looked at each other a moment without speaking.

"At this rate," continued the general, "his Majesty's New England provinces will soon be depopulated."

"For God's sake, general, put a stop to this butchery!" ejaculated the exasperated ranger.

"That's exactly what I have sent for you to do. Here are your orders. You are commanded, and I expect you to destroy that nest of vipers, root and branch. Remember the atrocities committed by these Indian scoundrels, and take your revenge; but remember, also, that I forbid the killing of women and children. Exterminate the fighting-men, but spare the non-combatants. That is war. Now make an end of St. Francis once and for all."

Nearly a hundred leagues separated the Abenaqui village from the Eng-

[1] From *The Heart of the White Mountains*, Their Legend and Scenery, by Samuel Adams Drake, pp. 259–265. Entered according to Act of Congress, in the year 1881, by Harper & Brothers, in the Office of the Librarian of Congress, at Washington. New York. 1882.

The St. Francis Indians occupied this [Swanton] area hundreds of years before the white men came, and prior to 1700 built a chapel under the guidance of the French Jesuits, which was the first church erected in the territory that is now Vermont. These Indians participated in many depredations against the whites, most terrible of which was the Deerfield Massacre, 1704, at which time they stole the Deerfield Bell to use in their chapel at Swanton for many years. After France lost this new country to England, the Indians moved their beloved chapel stone by stone to St. Hyacinth on the Yamaska River. It was the repeated and bloody raids made by the St. Francis warriors that led in 1759 to the daring drive of Rogers' Rangers against the village of St. Francis, in which the Rangers attacked in Indian fashion, killing and burning without mercy to wipe out the entire settlement.—*Vermont*, A Guide to the Green Mountain State (Boston, 1937), p. 277. For the Bell legend see p. 372 below.

lish; and we should add that once there, in the heart of the enemy's country, all idea of help from the army must be abandoned, and the rangers, depending wholly upon themselves, be deprived of every resource except to cut their way through all obstacles. But this was exactly the kind of service for which this distinctive body of American soldiers was formed.

Sir Jeffrey Amherst had said to Rogers, "Go and wipe out St. Francis for me," precisely as he would have said to his orderly, "Go and saddle my horse."

But this illustrates the high degree of confidence which the army reposed in the chief of the rangers. The general knew that this expedition demanded, at every stage, the highest qualities in a leader. Rogers had already proved himself possessed of these qualities in a hundred perilous encounters.

That night, without noise or display, the two hundred men detailed for the expedition left their encampment, which was habitually in the van of the army. On the evening of the twenty-second day since leaving Crown Point a halt was ordered. The rangers were near their destination. From the top of a tree the doomed village was discovered three miles distant. Not the least sign that the presence of an enemy was suspected could be seen or heard. The village wore its ordinary aspect of profound security. Rogers therefore commanded his men to rest, and prepare themselves for the work in hand.

At eight in the evening, having first disguised himself, Rogers took Lieutenant Turner and Ensign Avery, and with them reconnoitred the Indian town. He found it the scene of high festivity, and for an hour watched unseen the unsuspecting inhabitants celebrating with dancing and barbaric music the nuptials of one of the tribe. All this marvellously favored his plans. Not dreaming of an enemy, the savages abandoned themselves to unrestrained enjoyment and hilarity. The *fête* was protracted until a late hour under the very eyes of the spies, who, finding themselves unnoticed, crept boldly into the village where they examined the ground and concerted the plan of attack.

At length all was hushed. The last notes of revelry faded on the still night air. One by one the drowsy merrymakers retired to their lodges, and soon the village was wrapped in profound slumber—the slumber of death. This was the moment so anxiously awaited by Rogers. Time was precious. He quickly made his way back to the spot where the rangers were lying on their arms. One by one the men were aroused and fell into their places. It was two in the morning when he left the village. At three the whole body moved stealthily up to within five hundred yards of the village, where the men halted, threw off their packs, and were formed for the assault in three divisions. The village continued silent as the grave.

St. Francis was a village of about forty or fifty wigwams, thrown together in a disorderly clump. In the midst was a chapel, to which the inhabitants were daily summoned by matin and vesper bell to hear the holy father, whose spiritual charge they were, celebrate the mass. The place was enriched with the spoil torn from the English and the ransom of many miserable captives. We have said that these Indians had slain and taken, in six years, six hundred English: that is equivalent to one hundred every year.

The knowledge of numberless atrocities nerved the arms and steeled the hearts of the avengers. When the sun began to brighten the east the three bands of rangers, waiting eagerly for the signal, rushed upon the village.

A deplorable and sickening scene of carnage ensued. The surprise was complete. The first and only warning the amazed savages had were the volleys that mowed them down by scores and fifties. Eyes heavy with the carousal of the previous night opened to encounter an appalling carnival of butchery and horror. Two of the stoutest of the rangers—Farrington and Bradley—led one of the attacking columns to the door where the wedding had taken place. Finding it barred, they threw themselves so violently against it that the fastenings gave way, precipitating Bradley headlong among the Indians who were asleep on their mats. All these were slain before they could make the least resistance.

On all sides the axe and the rifle were soon reaping their deadly harvest. Those panic-stricken, half-dazed wretches who rushed pell-mell into the streets either ran stupidly upon the uplifted weapons of the rangers or were shot down by squads advantageously posted to receive them. A few who ran this terrible gauntlet plunged into the river flowing before the village, and struck boldly out for the opposite shore; but the avengers had closed every avenue of escape, and the fugitives were picked off from the banks. The same fate overtook those who tumbled into their canoes and pushed out into the stream. The frail barks were riddled with shot, leaving their occupants an easy target for a score of rifles. The incessant flashes, the explosions of musketry, the shouts of the assailants, and the yells of their victims were all mingled in one horrible uproar. For two hours this massacre continued. Combat it cannot be called. Rendered furious by the sight of hundreds of scalps waving mournfully in the night-wind in front of the lodges, the pitiless assailants hunted the doomed savages down like blood-hounds. Every shot was followed by a death-whoop, every stroke by a howl of agony. For two horrible hours the village shook with explosions and echoed with frantic outcries. It was then given up to pillage, and then to the torch, and all those who from fear had hid themselves perished miserably in the flames. At seven o'clock in the morning all was over. Silence once more enveloped the hideous scene of conflagration and slaughter. The village of St. Francis was the funeral pyre of two hundred warriors. Rogers had indeed taken the fullest revenge enjoined by Sir Jeffrey Amherst's orders.

From this point our true history passes into the legendary.

While the sack of St. Francis was going on a number of the Abenaquis took refuge in the little chapel. Their retreat was discovered. A few of their assailants having collected in the neighborhood precipitated themselves toward it, with loud cries. Others ran up. Two or three blows with the butt of a musket forced open the door, when the building was instantly filled with armed men.

An unforeseen reception awaited them. Lighted candles burnt on the high altar, shedding a mild radiance throughout the interior, and casting a dull glow upon the holy vessels of gold and silver upon the altar. At the altar's foot, clad in the sacred vestments of his office, stood the missionary, a middle-aged, vigorous-looking man, his arms crossed upon his breast, his face lighted up with the exaltation of a martyr. Face and figure denoted the high resolve to meet fate half-way. Behind him crouched the knot of half-crazed savages, who had fled to the sanctuary for its protection, and who, on seeing their mortal enemies, instinctively took a posture of defence. The priest, at two or three paces in advance of them, seemed to offer his body as their rampart. The scene was worthy the pencil of a Rembrandt.

At this sight the intruders halted, the foremost even falling back a step, but the vessels of gold and silver inflamed their cupidity to the highest pitch; while the hostile attitude of the warriors was a menace men already steeped in bloodshed regarded a moment in still more threatening silence, and then by a common impulse recognized by covering the forlorn group with their rifles.

Believing the critical moment come, the priest threw up his hands in an attitude of supplication, arresting the fatal volley as much by the dignity of the gesture itself, as by the resonant voice which exclaimed, in French, "Madmen, for pity's sake, for the sake of Him on the Cross, stay your hands! This violence! What is your will? What seek ye in the house of God?"

A gunshot outside, followed by a mournful howl, was his sole response. The priest shuddered, and his crisped lips murmured an *ave*. He comprehended that another soul had been sent, unshriven, to its final account.

"Hear him!" said a ranger, in a mocking undertone; "his gabble minds me of a flock of wild geese."

A burst of derisive laughter followed this coarse sally.

In fact, they had not too much respect for the Church of Rome, these wild woodsmen, but were filled with ineradicable hatred for its missionaries, domesticated among their enemies, in whom they believed they saw the real heads of the tribes, and the legitimate objects, therefore, of their vengeance.

"Yield, Papist! Come, you shall have good quarter; on the word of a ranger you shall," cried an authoritative voice, the speaker at the same time advancing a step, and dropping his rifle the length of his sinewy arms.

"Never!" answered the ecclesiastic, crossing himself.

A suppressed voice from behind hurriedly murmured in his ear, *"Écoutez: rendez-vous, mon père: je vous en supplie!"*

"Jamais! mieux vaut la morte que la miséricorde de brigands et meurtriers!" ejaculated the missionary, rejecting the counsel also, with a vehement shake of the head.

"Grand Dieu! tout, donc, est fini," sighed the voice, despairingly.

The rangers understood the gesture better than the words. An officer, the same who had just spoken, again impatiently demanded, this time in a higher and more threatening key,

"A last time! Do you yield or no? Answer, friar!"

The priest turned quickly, took the consecrated Host from the altar, elevated it above his head, and, in a voice that was long remembered by those who heard it, exclaimed,

"To your knees, monsters! to your knees!"

What the ranger understood of this pantomime and this command was that they conveyed a scornful and a final refusal. Muttering under his breath, "Your blood be upon your head, then," he levelled his gun and pulled the trigger. A general discharge from both sides shook the building, filling it with thick and stifling smoke, and instantly extinguishing the lights. The few dim rays penetrating the windows, and which seemed recoiling from the frightful spectacle within, enabled the combatants vaguely to distinguish each other in the obscurity. Not a cry was heard; nothing but quick reports or blows signaled the progress of this lugubrious combat.

This butchery continued ten minutes, at the end of which the rangers, with the exception of one of their number killed outright, issued from the chapel, after having first stripped the altar, despoiled the shrine of its silver image of the Virgin, and flung the Host upon the ground. While this profanation was enacting a voice rose from the heap of dead at the altar's foot, which made the boldest heart among the rangers stop beating. It said,

"The Great Spirit of the Abenaquis will scatter darkness in the path of the accursed Pale-faces! Hunger walks before and Death strikes their trail! There wives weep for the warriors that do not return! Manitou is angry when the dead speak. The dead have spoken!"

The torch was then applied to the chapel, and, like the rest of the village, it was fast being reduced to a heap of cinders. But now something singular transpired. As the rangers filed out from the shambles the bell of the little chapel began to toll. In wonder and dread they listened to its slow and measured strokes until, the flames having mounted to the belfry, it fell with a loud clang among the ruins. The rangers hastened onward. This unexpected sound already filled them with gloomy forebodings.

The Disastrous Retreat [2]

Rogers had fallen upon St. Francis and completed his work expeditiously, because he realized the fact that three hundred French and Indians were already on his trail and every day drawing nearer. Worn out and exhausted from their forced march of twenty-two days—obliged as they were again

[2] From *Indian Legends of the White Mountains*, by J. S. English, pp. 64–73. Copyright, 1915, by Rand Avery Supply Company. Boston.

to face the forbidding forest with scarcely any rest, the lot of the Rangers was no easy one. The cool October blast chilled them to the marrow. Ignorant of the country, it was with difficulty that they made any progress at all. The French and Indians, well provisioned, were but a few miles in their rear, and so great was their confusion that for three days the Rangers wandered aimlessly in a dense swamp. On the fourth day they again struck the trail in the rear of their pursuers. They now decided upon a desperate measure of hope. The pangs of famine had already reached them; their provisions had been lost in the swamp, and fearful of attracting the enemy by hunting for food, they were obliged to endure. It was determined to separate into nine parties and agreed that whatever body met the enemy, for the protection of their companions, would give battle. A short while after separation repeated firing proclaimed the fact that the enemy had been encountered by one party, and the sacrifice had been made; but too great was the sin of the Rangers to expect atonement at such a paltry price. The blood of three hundred men, women, and children cried out for vengeance, and Rogers' Rangers were yet destined to pay the penalty for the sack of St. Francis. Ere the shores of Memphremagog were reached, famine had so reduced what remained of the band of two hundred that they were scarcely able to drag their emaciated forms along. Fearful of an ambuscade, they were ever on the watch for an unseen foe, and their moccasins and powder horns had long since been boiled to furnish sustenance.

Bradley, who had been foremost in the work of butchery, was the first to reach the Connecticut River at Upper Coos, eighteen days after his departure. From here he lost his course and wandered over the mountains, seeking shelter in a cave where a year afterwards his parched bones and skull were found by a party of hunters and, scattered about, silver brooches and wampum plunder from St. Francis.

General Amherst had despatched Lieutenant Stevens with provisions to meet the stragglers, but he had missed them and returned. The commands under Lieutenant Philips and Sergeant Evans suffered horribly. Day after day with throats parched from lack of water, not a morsel of food passing their lips, the men under Lieutenant Philips plodded on. He saw them one by one drop by the wayside, some too weak to utter even a cry; others with glassy eyes bulging from their sockets, and skin so drawn and parched as to be almost transparent; in their delirium, uttering agonizing cries and bitter imprecations, and haunted by the curses of the dying victims of St. Francis, they would shriek and start at the imaginable advent of a foe.

At last ready to sink from hunger they determined to kill an Indian prisoner and feast on human flesh and blood, but it happened that on that very day a muskrat was killed, and the Indian's life was spared. Still more terrible were the sufferings of Sergeant Evans' men. Their only nourishment for days and weeks was birch bark and roots. Delirious in their suffering, they came upon the dead bodies of their late companions. They sat down to a feast of human flesh. Like ravenous beasts they tore the flesh from the bones, built a fire, and when they had gorged themselves on this human diet, filled their knapsacks with steaks cut from the dead bodies.

Lieutenant George Campbell in command of another party was four days without food of any kind when they discovered three human bodies floating down the river. The bodies were scalped and horribly mutilated, yet the famished Rangers pounced upon them like so many wolves, and, not even waiting to build a fire, devoured the raw flesh.

Major Rogers, who had throughout his trying march never lost his wonderful nerve, also reached this section. He collected the Rangers who had safely arrived thus far and alone started down the river in search of assistance. He constructed a crude raft, floated down the river, and, after a hazardous journey, procured help. Canoes were built, and in ten days, true to his pledge, Major Rogers returned with the promised succor to his surviving Rangers.

The people of Coos found many relics and eloquent signs of this ill-fated expedition, and to this day tell tales which have been transmitted from Indians. They firmly believed in the prophetic curses which followed the sacrilege at the chapel and the pillaging of the silver statue and the sacred vessels.

On the Connecticut River near the head of the Fifteen Miles Falls, a party of nine Rangers secured the services of an Indian guide who agreed to conduct them through the "Great Pass" (the Notch) of the mountains to the settlement. This party had the silver image, weighing eight pounds, stolen from the church. The guide led them to Israel's River in Jefferson, N. H., through the pathless forests along the shores of the stream to the deep, snow-laden gorges at the foot of the White Hills. Pretending to fear the wrath of the Manitou if he dared enter the forests of the sacred Agiochook, the Indian made a rude birchbark map and gave it to one of the Rangers, at the same time apparently accidentally scratching his hand with the poisonous fangs of a rattlesnake. Plodding with desperate efforts through the deep snow, braving as best they could the cold storm, they continued their journey but a short way when the poison of the rattlesnake did its work. The Ranger became mad and in the violence of his delirium he rushed to the top of a high precipice and flung himself into the depths below. The survivors, weak from their long and perilous march, with scarcely sufficient strength to carry themselves, concluded to bury their plunder in a cave on the mountain, where the superstitious horror of the Indian would prevent his entering, thus protecting their treasure and their lives.

Deceived by the false chart of their treacherous guide, they wandered in a circle for several days, suffering extreme cold and hunger. One by one they succumbed to the fatigue and cold. Several years afterward some hunters found a barkless spot on a pine tree at the entrance to a wild ravine on which were many partially obliterated characters engraved by some rude tool. Near this were some rusty buttons, decayed cloth, a small copper kettle and the metallic parts of a gun. At the foot of a steep bank, six rusty gun barrels were found and what resembled the relics of a pile of knapsacks. An old hunter, exploring for this hidden treasure, sought shelter from a terrible storm in a cave, where in the farthest corner he discovered several stones forming a pile. Beneath was found a hatchet heavily incrusted with rust, also a roll of birch back covered with the wax of wild bees. In the roll was found an Indian-tanned fawn skin on which were many mysterious hieroglyphics.

In 1815, the golden candlesticks were found near Lake Memphremagog, but no trace has ever been heard of the silver statue. Once, however, a number of years ago a lonely hunter wandered far into the mountains and when nightfall came, he was close to the summit of Mt. Adams. During the night a terrific storm arose; thick black clouds rolled over the mountains, the lightning flashed, thunder boomed and the wind raged and howled in a terrible manner.

The clouds broke, and there suspended over a deep chasm was the skeleton form of an Indian. Then the voice of the storm ceased, and from the deep abyss below came the screams of lost spirits; the mountain mist rolled back, the voices stopped and supreme quietness reigned, while before the astonished vision of the hunter appeared a great stone church. Within the church was an altar brilliantly lighted; the glow from the candles illumined the whole interior—the golden candlesticks, crucifixes and statues on the altar dazzled in their splendor, and from a sparkling censer rose curling wreaths of incense. Around the altar appeared a tribe of savages kneeling in profound silence; then the church spire, church and altar vanished, and down the steep mountain trailed the long line of savages in solemn silence. Before all, as if borne by some heavenly spirit, floated the glittering statue of silver, which, as it penetrated into the deep shadows, changed into the form of the St. Francis Friar; then, sparkling again, the image of the Blessed Virgin shone for a moment and disappeared in the side of a mountain ledge.

Such is the story of St. Francis, the sack and the massacre, and the hardships of the return journey by Rogers' Rangers being a true narrative of one of the bloodiest events ever perpetrated by civilized beings on their fellowmen. The prophecy and unnatural happenings are but legendary accounts handed down by settlers and savages.

The Legend of the White Deer of Onota

THERE is hardly a country where a deer ever trod in which there does not linger some legend of one or more of these graceful animals, either wholly or in part of a supernatural whiteness. It is a fancy which seems to spring

From *Taghconic; The Romance and Beauty of the Hills,* by Godfrey Greylock (Joseph Edwards Adams Smith), pp. 184–189. Copyright, 1879, by J. E. A. Smith. Boston: Lee and Shepard; New York: Charles T. Dillingham; Pittsfield: S. E. Nichols.

spontaneously in the rich soil of a woodman's imagination. The "White Doe of Rylston," and Bryant's "White-footed Deer," will occur to every one, as instances of the use to which these forest tales have been put in poetry. Traditions of a similar character are said to exist in many tribes of American Indians, and among others, those of the Housatonic valley.

A gentleman tells me that in the old witch times—long after the Salem delusion ended—there were no firmer believers in that sort of supernaturalism than the people who lived about Lake Onota; one of whom was his own grandfather, of whom he relates the following anecdote:

Coming in one day from an unsuccessful day's hunting, he was surprised to see a white deer stooping down to drink at Point Onota—the little cape which extends into the lake at its south end. Instantly his rifle was at his shoulder; but before he could pull the trigger, his dog howled, and the startled deer fled into the wood. The marvellous story of the white deer of the Mohegans at once occurred to him, and it entered into his head that his dog was bewitched; or rather that an old hag who lived in "The North Woods"—a section on the north-western side of the lake—had assumed his form; which, among other freakish powers, she had the perilous reputation of being able to do. With never a doubt, therefore, that he was all the while belaboring the witch, our disappointed hunter whaled his poor hound till the woods howled again with his piteous cries.

This done, he posted away in hot haste to the cabin of the old crone, and demanded that she should show him her back—never doubting that he would find upon it the marks of the stripes he had inflicted upon his miserable beast. Of course the old woman was in a tempest of wrath when she learned the errand of her visitor; and it is believed that he made a retreat more discreet and rapid than valiant, under a sudden shower of blows from that notorious article of household furniture which was supposed to serve its mistress the double purpose of a broom by day and an aerial steed by night, and which now answered another very excellent turn.

Another gentleman, to whom I mentioned this anecdote, tells me an aboriginal legend of this same White Deer.

"Long before the Englishman set foot in the Housatonic valley," he said, "the Indians used to notice a deer, of complete and spotless white, which came often, in the summer and autumn months, to drink at Onota. Against this gentle creature, no red man's arrow was ever pointed; for, in their simple faith, they believed that with her light and airy step she brought good fortune to the dwellers in the valley. 'So long,' the prophecy ran, 'so long as the snow-white doe comes to drink at Onota, so long famine shall not blight the Indian's harvest, nor pestilence come nigh his lodge, nor foeman lay waste his country.' In the graceful animal, the tribe recognized and loved their good genius. He among them who dared to harm her would have met swift punishment as a sacrilegious wretch and traitor."

Thus protected by the love of her simple friends, year after year, soon as the white blossoms clothed the cherry, the sacred deer came to drink at her chosen fountain; bringing good omens to all, and especially to the maiden who first espied her, glittering brightly among the foliage. Finally she brought with her a fawn, if possible, of more faultless purity and grace than herself; and that year more than the usual plenty and happiness reigned around the lake. Not long after this, the first French and Indian war broke out, and a young French officer—Montalbert by name—was sent to incite the Housatonic Indians to join in the league against the English colonies.

In his sacred character as an ambassador, he was welcomed to their lodges, had a seat at their council fire, and listened eagerly to their wild and marvellous tales. Among others, he heard the story of the White Deer; and, however incredulous of her sanctity, sufficiently admired the description of her beauty. Among those reckless and ambitious adventurers who set up the standard of France in Canada, it was a passion to carry away some wonderful trophy of the forest domain, to lay at the feet of their sovereign. Even the persons of the savages had thus been presented at the Court of Versailles, and royal favor had not been niggard in rewarding the donors of the more unique and costly trophies of barbaric splendor.

It was for such reasons that an uncontrollable desire to possess the skin of the White Deer took possession of Montalbert. He already enjoyed, in imagination, the reward which could not fail him who brought so rare and beautiful a peltry to the splendid Louis.

Not fully aware of the veneration which the Deer received from the natives, he first offered liberal rewards to the hunter who should bring him the coveted spoil. For half the proffered price, the chiefs would, perhaps, have alienated their fairest hunting-grounds; but the proposition to destroy their sacred Deer was received with utter horror and indignation. It was gently hinted to Montalbert that a repetition of the offer might ensure him the fate he designed for the Deer.

But the Frenchman was not of a nature to be so baffled. He had noticed that one of the native warriors—Wondo, by name—was already debased by the use of the white man's fire-water, of which Montalbert possessed a large supply. Concealing his purposes for a time, the adventurer sought out this Wondo, and shortly contrived to foment the poor fellow's appetite to such a degree that he became the absolute slave of whoever had it in his power to minister to his desires.

When the hunter was thought to be sufficiently besotted, Montalbert ventured to propose to him a plan to secure the skin of the White Deer. Depraved as he had become, Wondo at first recoiled from the thought, but appetite at length prevailed and he yielded to the tempter.

Years of unmolested security had rendered the Deer so confident in the friendship of man that, when at last treachery came she proved an easy victim. Before conscience could awaken in the sacrilegious hunter, the gentle animal was taken and slain, and the ill-gotten fur was in the possession of the white man.

No sooner had Montalbert secured his prize than, concealing it in his baggage, he set out for Montreal; but the legend hints that he never reached the French border, and the beautiful skin of the Indians' sacred deer never added to the splendors of French royalty.

Among the natives, the impious slaughter was not suspected until the fire-water of the slayer was expended, and a returning consciousness compelled him to confess his deed of horror, and to meet the speedy vengeance which atoned for it.

Long and earnest were the supplications which the frightened natives sent up to the Great Spirit, that He would avert from the tribe the punishment due to such a crime; but its prosperity never again was what it had been, and its members slowly wasted away.

MIRACLES AND HOLY LEGENDS

St. Elmo Sees Them Through

"I AIN'T the one to believe in no furriner's miracles. You know that. But what I seen, I seen. And I say that vessel never should have stayed afloat by rights, never *would* have, without it was just a plain and simple miracle!"

They were yarning in the Master Mariners' clubrooms. While rubber-shod feet kept up a constant shuffle through the metropolis-in-little that was Gloucester's main street, the select group of skippers up here in "the Rooms" spent their evenings ashore in the dignified piracy of cutthroat whist or "swacker," and occasionally in making statements of "fact," plain and fancy, which nobody dared question.

Just now Captain Frank Hall, Captain Joe Mesquita, and half a dozen others had tilted back for a session, and old Captain Bob McEachern was getting under way on the subject of St. Elmo's fire—those eerie lights that sometimes appeared out of nowhere on a vessel's rigging.

Queer balls of fire, they were, which showed at the masthead or the bowsprit or the tips of the booms; but only once in a great while, in the worst part of the heaviest gales, and not always then. Sailors had given them the name "corposant" (*corpo santo*—saint's body) but Captain Bob added that professors and high-toned people like that said 'twas only brush electricity that come to roost somehow on the ironwork of the rigging.

"P'r'aps so, p'r'aps so," Captain Bob conceded. "But in the gale of '73, when we seen that Frenchman rolling in the trough, with everything

---

From *In Great Waters,* The Story of the Portuguese Fishermen, by Jeremiah Digges, pp. 171–173. Copyright, 1941, by Josef Berger. New York: The Macmillan Company.

carried away but the split stump of her bowsprit, I watched two of them lights dancing along the hull, and it didn't look like no electricity to me.

"I yelled down to the captain that we had a Frenchman afire almost alongside. He come on deck, and a feller named Louis Veneau, which we'd shipped in Judique, Nova Scotia, come up too when he heard it was a French vessel.

"The minute the Judiquer looked at her, he give a laugh like he was tickled to death. The skipper stared at him and said he didn't see nothing funny in it—them poor devils with their vessel afire and in such a gale, and with their craft already the saddest-looking wreck you ever seen! And what kind of a man was he, to be laughing when it was a crew of Frenchmen—his own people—that was dying out there on the Queero? But the Judiquer just grinned.

"'No fire, no fire!' he says. 'That vessel, she safe, Captain, she safer as we are!'

"Well, the Judiquer had always seemed to me like a good, level-headed sort of a feller, so when my watch was over I went below to see what 'twas that had throwed him off ballast like that. He told me the light I'd seen on that vessel was St. Elmo's fire. She was from Brittany, and St. Elmo is them fellers' patron saint. When that kind of fire shows on a vessel, they know their saint has come to watch over her, and they quit worrying then, no matter what shape she's in. St. Elmo will see her through.

"I told him I still didn't see no reason to laugh. Even if that craft wasn't afire, she was in such desperate bad shape that all the saints in the catalogue wasn't going to save her. I'd never seen a gale like this one, and that vessel was just about the completest wreck that ever had the nerve to show herself out of water on Queero bank.

"Through the night it blowed harder and harder. I didn't know whether we was going to see daylight ourselves, and we had one of the best sea boats out of Gloucester. For that other craft, there wasn't a chance in a thousand to keep afloat through them next twenty-odd hours of gale!

"But she did. Yes, sir, so help me God, we sighted her again the next night, and we took off her crew and towed the wreck to Canso! Eighteen of 'em, there was, and they was in pretty bad shape. But after he'd jabbered with 'em awhile, the Judiquer told me there wasn't none of 'em really worried through the worst of the blow, because when they seen that fire on their wreck, they knew St. Elmo was going to see 'em through. Their saint had hoisted his colors on their craft. They knew there was going to be a miracle, and—well, there was!"

Joseph's Boat

THE Reverend Joseph Metcalfe "viaged" from Falmouth to Dedham. Before he embarked on this perilous journey he visited Caleb Gifford to announce a welcome legacy and discuss the purchase of a boat. The Reverend Joseph, father of one son and ten daughters, never before had enjoyed money to spend. Generously he relinquished £60 in arrears on his salary, a stipend that the new little town of Falmouth had not been able to pay.

Joseph informed Caleb that he always had wanted a boat, "in which," said the eager, innocent dominie, "to take mine ease on the deep." Caleb regarded him with astonishment not unmingled with fear. The Reverend Joseph was as sea-going as a buttercup. Moreover, Caleb was shocked: a minister "taking his ease!" What had ease to do with parsons, or with boats, "worritin' critters" necessary to some pursuits but never allied to pleasure. Joseph exhibited his legacy, "figgers wrote down on a paper"; and Caleb decided, if Parson Metcalf was ready to pay good shillings and pence, that he was not one to let another man "horn in" on the trade.

The minister returned from Dedham and the collecting of his legacy, one Saturday afternoon. While passing through the town of Boston he had purchased a new wig, and "covered" with this, he made his appearance at Caleb Gifford's door. Caleb led him down to the shore where an apple-cheeked dory bobbed at its mooring, a craft that had known far better days, but Caleb saw no sense in wasting seaworthy timber on "Parson's folly."

As Mr. Metcalfe looked at this boat pride shone in his eye. He scanned the horizon where the sun was reddening the "minnew ripples" of the fairway. On such a calm night, in such a boat, a man might voyage far.

When he returned to the parsonage, he found three goodwives waiting. A pressing problem of moral delinquency occupied their minds. Were coloured flowers vanitous? Were coloured flowers worldly? And what about plucked posies? Might flowers appear in church or did their gaudy hues suggest the adornment of godless women? The Reverend Metcalfe, genial soul, who had just come into his world's estate, was in no mood to

---

From *The Narrow Land, Folk Chronicles of Old Cape Cod,* by Elizabeth Reynard, pp. 301–303. Copyright, 1934, by Elizabeth Reynard. Boston and New York: Houghton Mifflin Company.

Kittredge and Freeman tell the story of the wig. The scrap from his diary was given to me as "copied." I have been unable to find the diary. The story of Joseph's Boats seems to have no written source, rests entirely upon O[ral]. T[radition]. The death of Joseph Metcalfe, the night after the great storm, is "apocryphal." Apparently, he was taken ill then, but did not die until in the winter. According to Falmouth records, deceased Dec. 24, 1723.—E. R., *ibid.*, p. 326.

I have heard them called Joseph's gardens, these retired dories which are filled with earth and made to serve as flower-boxes, but the particular Joseph who was in command of this craft of many colors remained unknown until Elizabeth Reynard's book, *The Narrow Land,* tracked him down in Falmouth—Jeremiah Digges, *Cape Cod Pilot* (Provincetown and New York, 1937), pp. 199–200.

chasten nor condemn the radiant gifts of earth. Flowers, he opined, were a sign of God and might be plucked in posy bunches. With this reply the three women departed, unconvinced, but with their minds distracted by the minister's new wig.

They spread word of Parson's adornment and by Meeting Hour of the next day, Sunday, the whole village goggled at the dominie's "Boston Vanitie." The Reverend Metcalfe took a text about Joseph who was a fisherman, but felt no deepening response in his auditors although he was vaguely conscious of his flock's unwavering gaze. In the "nooning," before second service, the secular status of flowers came up for a reconsideration and then Joseph discovered that the problem hinged, not on posy-bunches, but on his own garden plot. It was thought he spent overmuch time there, time that might be far better expended on parish visits or sermon-making. At heart devoutly humble, eager to please his congregation, he would, he declared, abandon his garden; devote to his people all hours—except those, he added quickly, in which he looked forward to "meeting his Maker at sea." This was news to the parish. Caleb, desiring no competition, had abstained from mentioning his negotiations with the minister. Joseph, his round face beaming with pride, made known his purchase; then settled the matter of posy-bunches by appointing a *Ladies Delegation* to search the Bible for "light." He would call, he said, "on Monday-morrow" at the house of Deacon and Goodwife Jenkins, there to study the "Bible-findings" and reach a final conclusion.

The next afternoon as he set forth, he turned to look back at his posy-plot. Summer roses were "taking the brease" and the "hiehocks" swayed. His practised eye caught a gleam of weeds sprung up during his visit to Boston. He stopped to right a sagging moss rose; then straightened, remembering his promise. Weeds were to choke these flowers of his; the dry earth wither them to dust.

Joseph walked slowly down the lane and paused at the Deacon's door. Goodwives in the greatroom gabbled so fast that they did not see him. No longer intent on their Bible-findings, they were wagging their tongues, every garrulous one of them, about his "Vanitie Wig." "Not expressed in fancy, neat, not gaudy," he had felt very pleased with this purchase that covered his scanty hair. He spoke aloud from the doorway, effectively silencing chatter. Would the goodwives be better pleased if he ceased to wear any wig? They turned in confusion but answered his question frankly. "No wig? Scand'lous! An insult to the sacred office!" Would they prefer that he put on his old wig "mouldy and gnawed by silver boterflies"? The goodwives' souls revolted. "Then let us alter the new one until it ceases to offend." This solution met prompt response. Joseph removed his Boston wig and handed it to Goodwife Jenkins who clipped the lush and sinful locks, then passed it on to Goodwife Hatch who clipped it yet more closely. "Cut out of plumb, galleywest," a product of erratic fervour, it soon lost "unaformacie" as each one of the *Ladies Delegation* snipped and pulled to her taste. The last goodwife, returning the peruke, remarked that to wear any wig at all was to break the Second Commandment. Joseph could stand no more. The wig, said he, was now so unlike "anything that is in Heaven above or in the earth beneath, or in the water under the earth," that to it no law of God nor man could rightly be applied.

He clapped the relic on his head and sorrowfully returned to his home. There he found three Elders waiting in the matter of the sea-going boat. They stared, puzzled, at his galleywest wig, then stated their business plainly. God willing, the three Elders stood ready to supply Joseph, his one son and his nine surviving "datters," with adequate servings of fish. The parson hastened to reassure them declaring that he did not desire nor expect to fish from his dory; all that he wanted was *a sea-going boat in which to take his ease.* The Elders looked at one another. Then they reminded Joseph that ministers should not be seeking ease; that the sea was a restless, fluctuant platform; that certain poor widows might benefit much by the money expended for the boat.

Joseph promised the Elders to dispose of his "legacie purchas" and in the evening he walked down-lane to notify Caleb. At the foot of the lane, in a little harbour, the dory tugged at her mooring. Joseph removed his moccasins and waded in to get her. He laid his hand on her side; he touched her thwarts and rowlocks. She rubbed her nose against his coat and Joseph looked across-Sound toward the shadow of "Mayhew's Island" where a sloop rode and the sun descended over the "minnew ripple."

During the night a violent tempest, a "thund'rous storme" long remembered, swept the whole South Shore. Houses were blown from their cellars; trees toppled; were shunted inland; ships were wrecked in the Sound. All night Joseph prayed for the safety of his people, for their stock, their crops, their shipping. Toward dawn, he heard a sharp knock at his door. He rose from his knees to answer the summons. Holding his lanthorn high he peered into the darkness, drew his hand over his eyes, then looked out again. A long heavy object leaned against the doorstone. In the storm the sea-going boat had journeyed the length of the lane.

The good minister entered his study and wrote in his commonplace book:

> August, 1723—
>
> I have bin tempted to persue the sea sence I was borne. Yit may natt be. Yett have I pruf of the Lord's haboring no wrath, for this nite in storme cam to me my bote that fain would live on land.

In the morning Joseph rode out to care for his stricken people. When he returned at nightfall his "datters" had shoved the dory into the front yard. Blown sand completely covered the parson's flower garden. But some kind hand rescued his uprooted rose trees and thrust them for safe keeping into the sea-going boat. Absent-mindedly Joseph straightened the dory, straightened the plants that were placed in her, and covered the roots with soil. Tuesday-morrow he would bid his daughters deliver them to some goodwife who had lost her flowers in the storm.

While he slept, exhausted by his long day of "service," death crept in for a bedfellow and "embraced the Reverend Joseph Metcalfe, aged forty-two." In the morning when the Deacons came, the roses were blooming in the sea-going boat that stood in a sandy yard.

The dory was old; her timbers rotten. Caleb did not haul her back to the shore. Instead he stood and "looked on her," and thought how Joseph had loved posies; how he had never used his legacy.

And after the funeral other men "looked on her" and returned to beautify her by the planting of "slips." Even the three doubting goodwives brought some godless pansies.

"Joseph's Boat" the townsmen called the dory, and every summer they filled and seeded her; for they had not known until he left them how much they thought of Joseph Metcalfe, who preached short sermons and gave long counsels, who managed to "rear up" one son and nine daughters with almost no money at all.

Old dories were plentiful; the good brown earth was scarce. Never had flowers flourished so gaily, thrived in droughts, preserved their soil, as they had in Joseph's boat. Towns where good topsoil was lacking adopted the strange device. Other boats were dragged on shore, filled with earth, planted with "greenerie." When sailors came home from sea these skiffs were "striped up good."

In the Burying Acre in Falmouth, no tombstone has ever been placed over Joseph's body; but Joseph's Boats are in every town, and on the due-date of the "thund'rous storme" the Reverend Metcalfe is said to return to inspect his *land-going* dories.

Mary's Flower

Or you might hear a legend like that of how the gray moss that covers the dunes and blooms with a yellow flower happens to be called "Mary's flower" by the Portuguese. A fisherman took his wife and baby to live in one of the deserted shacks up at Helltown. He was so poor he didn't have a power dory and still used sail. As he didn't return, food grew low and there was only enough flour left for one loaf of bread for his wife and baby.

One night there was a terrible storm and the woman heard a knocking on the door and hastened to open it. It was a woman with a baby wrapped in a shawl. The fisherman's wife warmed her visitors before the fire and gave them the last of the bread and used the last bit of coffee.

The next morning was beautiful. The woman said good-by and started off across the gray moss of the dunes, the baby in her arms. Then a wonderful thing happened. The gray moss bloomed under her feet in golden

From *Time and the Town, A Provincetown Chronicle,* by Mary Heaton Vorse, pp. 165–166. Copyright, 1942, by Mary Heaton Vorse. New York: The Dial Press.

flowers, and as she went away in the mist, the fisherman's wife could see a shining halo around her head, so she knew she had been visited by the Blessed Virgin, who had come to comfort her in her husband's absence, and that her husband would soon return.

The Three Hinckley Roses

In Barnstable, long ago, lived the Three Hinckley Roses, Hannah, Samuel, and Elisabeth who was the Smallest Rose. They had blue eyes and the two girls wore a "french fringe" of brown hair cut across their foreheads. Sammy, their brother, was capped with shining curls. The three, not far separated in age, were like "three steps of a gradual stairway," and they were seldom separated, from the time when they rocked as "cradlemites" until Hannah, the eldest, outgrew her trundle, in the year when the Boston plague came along the Bay to Barnstable.

Hannah, the first to be smitten with disease, was put to bed in the West Front Room. The two younger children were sent in to "comfort Sister." A few mornings later, Samuel awoke with his small back aching, his eyes blinded and dizzy, his throat "wondrous soar." Then Elisabeth, the Smallest Rose, began to be frightened. Hannah and Samuel were having the plague and she was left out. This "tortience-baby," the youngest, some folk said the plainest, since her hair was a little more lank than Hannah's, her eyes a little less blue, was always struggling to share every adventure of her older sister and brother to whom she was Cape-loyal and sometimes much of a nuisance.

She was the last one over the fence and never would be helped. She secretly ate Sammy's porridge for him when he could not have plum-cake until his porridge was consumed. She also ate his plum-cake as well as her own whenever he became lost in day-dreams from which he bitterly awakened to the discovery of his loss. She borrowed Sister Hannah's sampler and stitched it to "supprize Sister." Mistress Hinckley, mother of the three, pulled the false stitches out, while Hannah looked on in superior wisdom and Elisabeth loudly wept.

When she developed the plague and was not very ill of it, she accepted the suffering as part of life with Brother Sam and Sister Hannah. Then one wintry day, the two older children took a turn for the worse, and good

---

From *The Narrow Land, Folk Chronicles of Old Cape Cod,* by Elizabeth Reynard, pp. 178–180. Copyright, 1934, by Elizabeth Reynard. Boston and New York: Houghton Mifflin Company.

O[ral]. T[radition]. In the Boston Public Library, a broadside, signed M. T., laments the deaths of Hannah, Samuel, and Elisabeth. The elegy does not follow the oral tradition; Hannah, apparently, dying first, and no mention made of the final exhortation made by Elisabeth. For another story, typical of the "pious deaths" of Cape children, see the account of Priscilla Thornton of Yarmouth, in Cotton Mather's *Magnalia Christi Americana* (Hartford, 1820. 1st Amer. from Lond. ed.), Vol. II, pp. 418–419.—E. R., *ibid.*, p. 322.

Mr. Walley, the minister, came to prepare Hannah and Sammy for Heavenly Judgment. He told them exactly what to say, how to talk to the angels, why they must not be afraid. Elisabeth listened with eyes wide; later she put her hands on the great man's knee and asked what should she do. He pinched her cheek and answered that such problems were not for those who must live in a "World of Sorrows."

After the minister had gone, Hannah and Samuel grew excited about going to Heaven. Hannah's eyes became shiny. She did not see her younger sister. Instead she beheld angels to whom she gave good welcome, and beseeched them for kind mercy. Sammy shook his small fists and started a battle with "Satane's impes," big ones, under his bed. Elisabeth, to reassure him, removed the trundle and crawled under the poster, but found only a lost white button and linsey-lint from his plague-jacket.

The grown people knelt in prayer. Mrs. Ruth Bourne who knew about plague rode over from Sandwich and sat with Hannah's hand in hers. She kept stroking the child's forehead, then held her by the wrist and listened, with her head on one side like a bright-eyed robin. Mistress Hinckley told Elisabeth that soon she must say good-bye to Sister Hannah, and perhaps to Brother Sam.

In the afternoon a weathergall (rainbow) shone over the ocean, like a handle to a great blue basket. The weathergall was taken as a "sign." Later, sunsucker clouds turned a shadowy crimson. Elisabeth was sent into the East Front Bedroom to sleep in the big bed usually occupied by her father and mother. Neither of them seemed to remember that sober-light was descending. They kept candles brightly burning and stayed with Samuel and Hannah.

Elisabeth crept into the bed in the East Front Room. No one came to tuck her in, nor heated the sheets with a warming pan. In the West Room, Hannah breathed queerly. The minister remained there with Elder Chipman and others. Samuel shifted and moaned. Suddenly, in the darkness, Elisabeth began to shake. They could not go to Heaven without her, Sister Hannah and Brother Samuel, she to stay in a World of Sorrows while Hannah talked with Deathwatch Angels and Sammy fought like a warrior. She had no angels to "speak her faire"; she had no devils to fight. The Good Lord would reward Hannah with soft wings and a halo; Sammy would get him a crown and a golden sword for his service; and she would not be there to see, left in a World of Sorrows. Her heart thumped a queer summons, like the Meeting House Drum.

She crawled out of bed. In her white nightdress she ran into the lighted West Room where Hannah and Samuel were lying on the goose-feather mattress of the pineapple poster. Grown folk knelt beside them. Radiant, smiling, she swayed for a moment, then lifted her arms and delivered to the watchers a swift exhortation:

"Behold! Hannah talketh with Angels!
Behold! Sammy battleth with Devils!
But Elisabeth walketh with God!"

She toppled forward on her face, this Smallest Rose who had no care at all, no ministerial guidance, yet who was the first to walk with God of the Three Hinckley Roses.

The Miracle of the Ice

An old Frenchman said to me: I will tell you the story of the old stone church that still stands on the cliffs at the village of St. Simeon. It has a history and it was built about two hundred years ago. Before that time there was a little wooden church in the village of St. Simeon and the curé had in vain urged the inhabitants of the village to build a large stone church. This village, situated at the edge of the sea, was not, at that time, populated by religious people, as most of the inhabitants were sailors and hunters who were inclined to scoff at anything that they could not feel, and they had but little faith in the church. These sailors and hunters lived a very evil life. When not on board a ship or trapping in the forest, they spent their time in drinking, carousing, and fighting. Many were the bloody battles that were fought, in the taverns, between the sailors and the hunters. So you see, my child, why these ungodly people were not interested in what the curé said about building a church.

Two days before Christmas all of the hunters, sailors, and settlers moved into town in order to properly celebrate Christmas. There was much fighting and carousing in the taverns, and at this season the village of St. Simeon was as crowded and as gay as the town of Quebec. The weather was cold. Mon Dieu, it was very cold! It was one of the coldest days of the year. The snow creaked sharply underneath the feet of the people going up and down the street. The next morning, a strange sight presented itself to the people of St. Simeon. The river was not to be seen. It was a mass of ice stretching from shore to shore. This was a sight not often seen as this part of the St. Lawrence River is full of salt water that comes in from the Atlantic ocean. The people rushed down to the beach to see the sight. A short ways out, on the ice, were seen many small black dots which moved. The more venturous of the men walked out on the ice to learn what these black dots were. As the men went further out on the ice, they saw that these dots were thousands of seals which had drifted into the St. Lawrence river on the ice-floes. The men ran back to the shore and the news quickly spread through the village.

Now this was fine news for these French Canadians, as seal skins and the fat of a seal were worth plenty of money in those days. All the men of the parish armed themselves with clubs, knives, axes, and any weapon that would serve to take the life of a seal. Thus armed, they ran out to

---

From "French-Canadian Folklore," Woonsocket, Rhode Island. Manuscripts of the Federal Writers' Project of the Works Progress Administration for the State of Rhode Island.

the seals while their wives and children stood upon the shore watching, with greedy eyes, their men-folks gather the easy booty. When the men reached the seals, the massacre began. The seals were helpless to prevent their slaughter and soon the ice was covered with blood. The butchery went on for hours as each man tried to kill as many seals as he could. The day was drawing to a close when the supply of seals began to thin out and then the men started to carry the dead seals away. But in the excitement of killing no man knew just which seals he had killed and the men now began to dispute with one another over possession of each seal.

It would seem as if the devil had entered into them and made them crazy. There were enough seals for every one but each man wanted them all. They quarreled and soon the quarreling turned into fighting. The daylight had vanished. It was very dark upon the ice and it must have been terrible, for the children and the wives, to see the dark forms of the men fighting on the blood-washed ice while the dead seals lay about, more than a thousand of them, like the dead on a battlefield.

Suddenly a cry like a moan arose from the women who were watching their men from the shore. The wind had changed and the ice along the shore was breaking up, leaving a widening stretch of black icy water between the ice-floe and the shore. The men, out on the ice, realized what was happening. They stopped fighting and cried, "Run for your life! The ice is drifting out to sea!" They abandoned their sleds, axes, and seals and ran to the edge of the ice. Some of the strongest swimmers plunged into the water and swam ashore, but as the strip of water was becoming wider every second most of the men were trapped upon the ice-floe. More than two hundred men remained upon the drifting ice. Heartbreaking cries came from the shore as the wives saw their husbands drifting out to sea, while the men on the ice cried out and implored God, whom they had never served, to save them.

Driven by the wind, the ice-floe drifted out toward the sea and was rapidly breaking up. The women, mad with grief, rushed to the little wooden church and started praying before the altar. The curé stood in front of the altar, in the light of lanterns which the villagers had brought. With hands uplifted and with his face turned toward the sea, he prayed for a miracle. He asked God to let the men on the ice-floe once more see their families and promised that he would do all in his power to see that these men lived a good Christian life in the future. He said to the women, "Kneel, my children, let us pray. I am going to give them absolution." The kneeling crowd, sobbing as if their hearts would break, prayed for the safe return of their men. A last despairing cry was heard from the men, then all was quiet, and the people in the church heard only the beating of the waves upon the rock. When the moon came up and its light fell across the river nothing was to be seen but the dark water with a few pieces of ice floating around. The ice-floe had broken up. There was no longer any hope. All were lost.

The curé and his parishioners never stopped praying and after it had seemed as if everything was lost, their devotion was rewarded. The wind changed and the astonished people saw the ice-floe with their men coming back. It seemed to be impelled by some miraculous force, like an unseen hand driving it back toward the shore. The women went wild with joy as the ice-floe grounded upon the shore. Soon every one was safe on shore. Even their sleds, axes, and seals had not been lost. There was no fighting this time over the division of the seals as there was too much joy in the hearts of the men because of their safe return.

The next day was Christmas. It was a very pious congregation that attended church that day. The church was filled to overflowing with those who had come to give thanks for the miracle that had saved their lives. It was a miracle such as God alone could accomplish. After Christmas all the people of the parish joined together and built the stone church that still stands to-day. Since that time the people of St. Simeon have been noted for their devotion to the church and to God.

The Legend of the Bell of Saut St. Louis

FATHER NICHOLAS, the French priest, having assembled a considerable number of Indians, who had been converted to the Catholic faith, had established them in the village which now bears the name of the Saut St. Louis, upon the River St. Lawrence.

The situation of the village is one of the most magnificent which the banks of that noble river presents, and is among the most picturesque which the country contains.

The church stands upon a point of land which juts into the river, and its bell sends its echoes over the waters with a clearness which forms a striking contrast with the iron bells which were formerly so common in Canada, while the tin-covered spire of the church, glittering in the sunlight, with the dense and gloomy forests which surround it, give a character of romance to this little church, and the legend of its celebrated bell.

Father Nicholas having, with the aid of the Indians, erected a church and a belfry, in one of his sermons explained to his humble auditors that a bell was as necessary to a belfry as a priest to a church, and exhorted them to lay aside a portion of the furs that they collected in hunting, until enough was accumulated to purchase a bell, which could only be procured

---

From *The Forest Arcadia of Northern New York,* Embracing a View of its Mineral, Agricultural, and Timber Resources, pp. 176–186. Entered, according to Act of Congress, in the year 1864, by T. O. H. P. Burnham, in the Clerk's Office of the District Court of the District of Massachusetts. Boston and New York.

Be it historical or legendary, the tale of the "Crusade of the Bell" is too interesting to be omitted from Colonial Sagas.—Marion Harland, *Colonial Homesteads and Their Stories* (New York, 1912), p. 384. See the Rev. John Williams, *The Redeemed Captive, Returning to Zion* (1706), for an account of the Deerfield massacre, the trek to Canada, and his captivity.

by sending to France. The Indians exhibited an inconceivable ardor in performing this religious duty, and the packet of furs was promptly made out, and forwarded to Havre, where an ecclesiastical personage was delegated to make the purchase. The bell was accordingly ordered, and in due time forwarded, on board the Grand Monarque, which was on the point of sailing for Quebec.

It so happened that after her departure one of the wars which the French and the English so often waged sprung up, and in consequence the Grand Monarque never attained her destined port, but was taken by a New England privateer, brought into the port of Salem, where she was condemned as a lawful prize, and sold for the benefit of her captors.

The bell was purchased by the village of Deerfield, upon the Connecticut River, for a church then about being erected by the congregation of the celebrated Rev. John Williams.

When Father Nicholas received news of the misfortune, he assembled his Indians, related to them the miserable condition of the bell, retained in purgatory in the hands of heretics, and concluded by saying, that it would be a most praiseworthy enterprise to go and recover it.

This appeal had in it, as it were, a kind of inspiration, and fell upon its hearers with all the force of the eloquence of Peter the Hermit in preaching the Crusades.

The Indians deplored together the misfortune of their bell, which had not hitherto received the rite of baptism; they had not the slightest idea of a bell, but it was enough for them that Father Nicholas, who preached and said mass for them in their church, said that it had some indispensable use in the services of the church.

Their eagerness for the chase was in a moment suspended, and they assembled together in groups, and seated on the banks of the river, conversed on the unhappy captivity of their bell, and each brought forward his plan, which he deemed most likely to succeed in effecting its recovery.

Some of their number, who had heard a bell, said that it could be heard beyond the murmur of the rapid, and that its voice was more harmonious than that of the sweetest songster of the grove, heard in the quiet stillness of evening, when all nature was hushed in repose.

All were melancholy, and inspired with a holy enthusiasm; many fasted, and others performed severe penances, to obtain the deliverance of the bell, or the palliation of its sufferings.

At length the day of its deliverance approached; the Marquis de Vaudreuil, governor of Canada, resolved to send an expedition against the British colonies of Massachusetts and New Hampshire. The command of this expedition was given to Major Hertel de Rouville, and one of the priests of the Jesuit college at Quebec was sent to procure the services of Father Nicholas to accompany the expedition.

The Indians were immediately assembled in the church, the messenger was presented to the congregation, and Father Nicholas, in a solemn discourse, pointed to him as worthy of their veneration, from his being the bearer of good tidings, who was about departing for his return to Quebec, to join the war. At the end of the discourse the whole audience raised, with one voice, the cry of war, and demanded to be led to the place where their bell was detained by the heretics.

The savages began to paint themselves in the most hideous colors, and were animated with a wild enthusiasm to join the expedition.

It was the depth of winter when they departed to join the army of M. de Rouville, at Fort Chambly. Father Nicholas marched at their head, with a large banner, surmounted by a cross, and as they departed from their village their wives and little ones, in imitation of women of the Crusades, who animated the warriors of Godfrey of Bouillon, sang a sacred hymn, which their venerated priest had selected for the occasion. They arrived at Chambly, after a march of great hardship, at the moment the French soldiers were preparing to start on their march up Lake Champlain.

The Indians followed in their rear, with that perseverance peculiar to their character. In this order the Indians remained, following in silence, until they reached Lake Champlain, where all the army had been ordered to rendezvous. This lake was then frozen, and less covered by the snow than the shores, and was taken as a more convenient route for the army. With their thoughts wrapped up in the single contemplation of the unhappy captivity of their bell, the Indians remained taciturn, and during this pensive march exhibiting no symptoms of fatigue or fear, no regret for their families or homes, and they regarded with equal indifference, on the one hand, the interminable line of forest, sometimes black from dense evergreens, and in others white from loads of snow; and, on the other, the bleak lines of rocks, and deserts of snow and ice, which bordered their path.

The French soldiers, who suffered dreadfully from fatigue and cold, regarded with admiration the agility and cheerfulness with which the Indians seemed to glide over the yielding surface of the snow on their snowshoes.

The quiet endurance of the proselytes of Father Nicholas formed a striking contrast with the irritability and impatience of the French soldiers.

When they arrived at the point where now stands the city of Burlington, the order was given for a general halt, to make more efficient arrangements for penetrating through the forest to Massachusetts.

In leaving this point De Rouville gave to Father Nicholas the command of his Indian warriors, and took the lead of his own himself, with compass in hand, to make the most direct course for Deerfield. Nothing which the troops had thus far suffered could compare with what they now endured on this march through a wild country, in the midst of deep snow, and with no supplies beyond what they could carry.

The French soldiers became impatient, and wasted their breath in curses and complaints at the hardships they suffered; but the Indians, animated by a zeal which sustained them above the sense of hardships, remained steadfast in the midst of fatigue, which increased with the severity of their sufferings. Their custom of travelling in the forest had qualified them for these hardships, which elicited the curses and execrations of their not less brave but more irritable companions.

Some time before the expedition arrived at its destination the priest Nicholas fell sick from over-exertion. His feet were worn by the labor of travelling, and his face torn by the branches, which he neglected to watch, in his eagerness to follow the troops.

He felt that he was engaged in a holy expedition, and recalling to mind the martyrdom of the saints, and the persecutions which they endured, he looked forward to the glory reserved for his reward for the sufferings which he might encounter in recovering the bell.

On the evening of February 20th, 1704, the expedition arrived within two miles of Deerfield, without being discovered. De Rouville here ordered his men to rest and refresh themselves a short time, and he here issued his orders for attacking the town.

The surface of the snow was frozen, and crushed under the feet, but De Rouville, with a remarkable sagacity, adopted a stratagem to deceive the inhabitants and the garrison. He gave orders in advancing to the assault his troops should make frequent pauses, and then rush forward with rapidity; thus imitating the noise made in the forest by the irregular blowing of the wind among branches laden with ice. The alarm was at length given, and a severe combat ensued, which resulted in the capture of the town, and the slaughter and dispersion of the inhabitants and the garrison.

The attack occurred in the night, and at daybreak, the Indians, who had been exhausted by the labors of the night, presented themselves before Father Nicholas in a body, and begged to be led to the bell, that they might by their homage prove their veneration for it. Their priest was greatly affected by this earnest request, and De Rouville and others of the French laughed immoderately at it, but the priest wished not to discourage them in their wishes, and he obtained of the French chief permission to send one of his soldiers to ring it in the hearing of the Indians.

The sound of the bell in the stillness of a cold morning, and in the midst of the calmness of the forest, echoed clear and far, and fell upon the ears of the simple Indians like the voice of an oracle. They trembled, and were filled with fear and wonder. The bell was taken from the belfry, and attached to a pole in such a manner that four men could carry it, and in this way it was borne off with their plunder in triumph, the Indians glorying in the deliverance of this miraculous wonder. But they shortly perceived it was too heavy a burden for the rugged route they pursued and the yielding nature of the snows over which they travelled. Accordingly, upon arriving at the point on the lake where they had left it, they buried their cherished treasure, with many benedictions of Father Nicholas, until the period should arrive when they could transport it with more convenience.

As soon as the ice had disappeared, and the bland air of spring had returned, giving foliage to the trees, and the fragrance and beauty of flowers to the forests, Father Nicholas again assembled at the church his Indian converts, to select a certain number of the tribe, who, with the assistance of a yoke of oxen, should go and bring in the dearly prized bell.

During this interval, all the women and children of the Indian village, having been informed of the wonderful qualities of the bell, awaited its arrival with eagerness and impatience, and regarded its advent as one of those events which but rarely mark the progress of ages. As the time approached when the curious object should arrive, they were assembled on the banks of the river, and discoursing upon the subject, when far off, in the stillness of the twilight, there was heard from the depths of the forest a sound, which, from being feeble and scarcely audible, became every moment louder. Every one listened, when presently the cry arose, "It is the bell!" "It is the bell!" and in a moment after the oxen were seen emerging from the wood, surrounded by a group of Indians, and bearing the precious burden on a pole between them. They had hung upon the beam and around the bell clusters of wild flowers and leaves, and the oxen were adorned with garlands of flowers. Thus marching in triumph, Father Nicholas entered his village, more proud of his success, and received with more heartfelt joy, than a Roman general returning in triumph from the conquest of nations.

From this triumphal march, in the midst of the quiet of the evening, which was broken only by the murmur of the rapid softened by the distance, arose the shouts of rejoicing as the cortege entered the village, and the idol bell was deposited in the church. Every one gratified his eager curiosity by examining the strange and musical metal, and the crusade had been crowned with unqualified success.

In due time it was raised to its place in the belfry, and has ever since, at the accustomed hours, sent its clear tones over the broad bosom of the St. Lawrence, to announce the hour of prayer and the lapse of time; and although its tones are shrill and feeble beside its modern companion, they possess a music, and call up an association, which will long give an interest to the church of the Saut St. Louis, at the Indian village of Caughnawaga.

II. THE POWERS OF DARKNESS

Go tell Mankind, that there are Devils and Witches.—COTTON MATHER

. . . If anything happened out of the common, the devil was in it. So say many to-day. . . . The persistent life of such local traditions as these [haunts of the Devil] fully attests to the belief of former generations of men in the active agency of the Evil One in human affairs.—SAMUEL ADAMS DRAKE

William Dean Howells used to come up here and he told me that, when things went wrong for months on end, old [New Hampshire]

hill farmers used to say, "The Witch is in it." And by this they meant some dark heavy power of fate inexorably pressing down.
—Ernest Poole

1. Monster or Gentleman?

The coming of the Devil to New England might have been reckoned among remarkable providences inasmuch as it enabled the leaders of church and state to prove that God is greater than the Devil and that in exterminating the devilish sect of witches they (the leaders) were the chosen instruments of God. But in New England the Devil behaved much as he did everywhere else. He assumed divers animal shapes (according to his wont), from a blue boar (obviously copied from a tavern sign) to a skipping deer; he left giant footprints (rarely in the shape of a cloven foot) in numerous rocks; and he lent his name to rocks, caves, glens, and other natural objects, "whose singularity would seem to suggest more than mortal occupancy."

The Devil found himself at home in the New World. For one thing, he encountered there many devil-worshipers among the Indians, or at least many whites believing that Indians (like all pagans) were devil-worshipers.[1] As a matter of fact, the Indians "knew nothing, till the English told them, either of purgatory, or of the Devil," as Edward Augustus Kendall has said, in relating the "facetious tradition" of Purgatory, a chasm at Middletown, Rhode Island, where the Indian Devil is supposed to have killed a squaw and thrown her into Purgatory.[2] At the same time, it is true that the Indians had their trickster-heroes and mischief-makers, distinguished for their devilish craft and cunning, such as the Ojibwa Manobozho, whose exploits Longfellow, following Schoolcraft, attributed to the Iroquois Hiawatha, and the giant Maushope, commemorated in many Martha's Vineyard landmarks (the Devil's Den, the Devil's Bridge, the Devil's Head and Pillows) and in the Devil's Ash Heap, or Nantucket.

But whatever the place of the Devil in Indian religion and mythology, the Indian practice of magic, through powpows or wizards, had an important bearing on New England witchcraft in that it was a "constant reminder of the possibility of danger from witchcraft." [3]

If the Devil often met his match in New England, that was because there were many Yankees like Jonathan Moulton, of whom it was said that "neither man nor devil could get the better of him in a trade." However, General Moulton, like Tom Walker (another avaricious Yankee who tried to cheat the Devil out of his due and failed),[4] was in this instance too

---

[1] According to Trumbull, the Indians of New England "paid their principal homage to Hobbamocho. They imagined that he was an evil spirit, and did them mischief; and so, from fear, they worshipped him, to keep him in good humor."—Rev. Henry White, *The Early History of New England Illustrated by Numerous Interesting Incidents* (Boston, 9th ed., 1841), p. 312.

[2] See "Purgatory" below.

[3] George Lyman Kittredge, "Notes on Witchcraft," American Antiquarian Society *Proceedings*, N. S., Vol. XVIII (April, 1907), p. 196.

[4] See "The Devil and Tom Walker," *A Treasury of American Folklore* (New York, 1944), pp. 731–740.

smart for his own good. In "The Devil and Daniel Webster" Stephen Vincent Benét has told the story of one sharp Yankee who beat the Devil —a story without known traditional source, which may yet become folklore.

To Jabez Stone, in Benét's story, the devil appeared as a "soft-spoken dark-dressed stranger," wearing handsome black boots and a cane and driving a handsome buggy. This is in the older tradition of the devil as a gentleman, belying the many monstrous shapes that he assumes in New England witchcraft and sorcery. When the Devil came to make a contract with Jonathan Moulton, he was "dressed from top to toe in black velvet," and for Goody Hallett's benefit he was "dressed in fine French bombasset." Even when he exhibited himself to the bewitched Mercy Short in 1692,[1] "having the Figure of a Short and a Black Man . . . not taller than an ordinary Walking-Staff," with straight hair and a cloven foot, he wore a high-crowned hat as a concession to the gentlemanly tradition.

2. Dancing to the Devil's Fiddle

In his dealings with witches the Devil was his other monstrous self. Thus at the Devil's Hop Yard, at Chapman Falls, one mile outside of Millington, Connecticut, where "on stormy nights the old hags were wont to congregate . . . and cast spells and mumble incantations as they stirred their potions" in circular pot-holes in the rock, "His Satanic Majesty himself would sometimes attend these meetings, a lurid glow from his body lighting up the dismal scene. His customary seat was at the very edge of the precipice, where, with tail laid over his shoulder as a scepter, he would majestically direct the exercises."[2]

Such mumbo-jumbo was part of the folklore of witchcraft, which outlasted, as it antedated, the witchcraft delusion in New England. The history of the latter (probably the greatest single piece of work of the Devil in this region) differs from the witchcraft of folklore as mass-hallucination differs from sporadic beliefs. But the witchcraft cases also belong to folklore through their use of all the trappings and paraphernalia of black magic, possession, transformation, and divination. The "spectral evidence" which served to convict many an innocent victim was full of familiar witchcraft phenomena, based on erroneous perception, "expectant attention," and deliberate lies. Yet some of those accused of being witches must have believed themselves to be or had the reputation of being possessors of extraordinary powers, such as the power to assume invisibility, change shape, and afflict enemies with physical or mental illness, disease or destruction of cattle or crops, storms, etc. Favorite types of New England witches are the storm-raising witch[3] and the witch-weaver.

In French-Canadian legends of the *loup-garou* witchcraft plays into the

[1] Cotton Mather, *A Brand Pluck'd Out of the Burning* (1693), reprinted in *Narratives of the Witchcraft Cases, 1648–1706,* edited by George Lincoln Burr (New York, 1914), p. 261.

[2] W. Harry Clemons, "The Legends of Machimoodus," in *The Connecticut Magazine,* Vol. VII (Series of 1902–1903), No. 5, p. 454.

[3] A combination of the storm-breeder and the Flying Dutchman motifs is to be seen in William Austin's legend of "Peter Rugg, the Missing Man." See *A Treasury of American Folklore* (New York, 1944), pp. 742–750.

hands of religion. Condemned for neglect of religious duties to "leave their human form at stated intervals and do as the Devil directs them," the *loups-garous* can be restored to human form only by drawing blood from them.

If the Devil was hard on New England, that was only to be expected, since New England was hard on the Devil, employing every means, fair or foul, at its disposal to fight and outwit him and his familiars.

B. A. B.

THE DEVIL IS IN IT

Jonathan Moulton and the Devil

THE legendary hero of Hampton is General Jonathan Moulton. He is no fictitious personage, but one of veritable flesh and blood, who, having acquired considerable celebrity in the old wars, lives on through the medium of a local legend.

The General, says the legend, encountered a far more notable adversary than Abenaki warriors or conjurers, among whom he had lived, and whom it was the passion of his life to exterminate.

In an evil hour his yearning to amass wealth suddenly led him to declare that he would sell his soul for the possession of unbounded riches. Think of the Devil, and he is at your elbow. The fatal declaration was no sooner made—the General was sitting alone by his fireside—than a shower of sparks came down the chimney, out of which stepped a man dressed from top to toe in black velvet. The astonished Moulton noticed that the stranger's ruffles were not even smutted.

"Your servant, General!" quoth the stranger, suavely. "But let us make haste, if you please, for I am expected at the Governor's in a quarter of an hour," he added, picking up a live coal with his thumb and forefinger, and consulting his watch with it.

The General's wits began to desert him. Portsmouth was five leagues—long ones at that—from Hampton House, and his strange visitor talked, with the utmost unconcern, of getting there in fifteen minutes! His astonishment caused him to stammer out,—

"Then you must be the—"

"Tush! what signifies a name?" interrupted the stranger, with a deprecating wave of the hand. "Come, do we understand each other? Is it a bargain, or not?"

At the talismanic word "bargain" the General pricked up his ears. He had often been heard to say that neither man nor devil could get the better

---

From *A Book of New England Legends and Folk Lore,* in Prose and Poetry, by Samuel Adams Drake, New and Revised Edition, pp. 322–328. Copyright, 1883, 1901, by Samuel Adams Drake. Boston: Little, Brown, and Company. 1910.

of him in a trade. He took out his jack-knife and began to whittle. The Devil took out his, and began to pare his nails.

"But what proof have I that you can perform what you promise?" demanded Moulton, pursing up his mouth and contracting his bushy eyebrows, like a man who is not to be taken in by mere appearances.

The fiend ran his fingers carelessly through his peruke, when a shower of golden guineas fell to the floor and rolled to the four corners of the room. The General quickly stooped to pick up one; but no sooner had his fingers closed upon it, than he dropped it with a yell. It was red-hot!

The Devil chuckled; "Try again," he said. But Moulton shook his head and retreated a step.

"Don't be afraid."

Moulton cautiously touched a coin; it was cool. He weighed it in his hand, and rung it on the table; it was full weight and true ring. Then he went down on his hands and knees, and began to gather up the guineas with feverish haste.

"Are you satisfied?" demanded Satan.

"Completely, your Majesty."

"Then to business. By the way, have you anything to drink in the house?"

"There is some Old Jamaica in the cupboard."

"Excellent! I am as thirsty as a Puritan on election-day," said the Devil, seating himself at the table, and negligently flinging his mantle back over his shoulder, so as to show the jewelled clasps of his doublet.

Moulton brought a decanter and a couple of glasses from the cupboard, filled one, and passed it to his infernal guest, who tasted it, and smacked his lips with the air of a connoisseur. Moulton watched every gesture. "Does your Excellency not find it to your taste?" he ventured to ask; having the secret idea that he might get the Devil drunk, and so outwit him.

"H'm, I have drunk worse. But let me show you how to make a salamander," replied Satan, touching the lighted end of the taper to the liquor, which instantly burst into a spectral blue flame. The fiend then raised the tankard to the height of his eye, glanced approvingly at the blaze,—which to Moulton's disordered intellect resembled an adder's forked and agile tongue,—nodded, and said, patronizingly, "To our better acquaintance!" He then quaffed the contents at a single gulp.

Moulton shuddered; this was not the way he had been used to seeing healths drunk. He pretended, however, to drink, for fear of giving offence; but somehow the liquor choked him. The demon set down the tankard, and observed, in a matter-of-fact way that put his listener in a cold sweat: "Now that you are convinced I am able to make you the richest man in all the province, listen! Have I your ear? It is well! In consideration of your agreement, duly signed and sealed, to deliver your soul"—here he drew a parchment from his breast—"I engage, on my part, on the first day of every month, to fill your boots with golden elephants, like these before you. But mark me well," said Satan, holding up a forefinger glittering with diamonds, "if you try to play me any trick, you will repent it! I know you, Jonathan Moulton, and shall keep my eye upon you; so beware!"

Moulton flinched a little at this plain speech; but a thought seemed to strike him, and he brightened up. Satan opened the scroll, smoothed out the creases, dipped a pen in the inkhorn at his girdle, and pointing to a blank space, said, laconically, "Sign!"

Moulton hesitated.

"If you are afraid," sneered Satan, "why put me to all this trouble?" and he began to put the gold in his pocket.

His victim seized the pen; but his hand shook so that he could not write. He gulped down a mouthful of rum, stole a look at his infernal guest, who nodded his head by way of encouragement, and a second time approached his pen to the paper. The struggle was soon over. The unhappy Moulton wrote his name at the bottom of the fatal list, which he was astonished to see numbered some of the highest personages in the province. "I shall at least be in good company," he muttered.

"Good!" said Satan, rising and putting the scroll carefully away within his breast. "Rely on me, General, and be sure you keep faith. Remember!" So saying, the demon waved his hand, flung his mantle about him, and vanished up the chimney.

Satan performed his part of the contract to the letter. On the first day of every month the boots, which were hung on the crane in the fireplace the night before, were found in the morning stuffed full of guineas. It is true that Moulton had ransacked the village for the largest pair to be found, and had finally secured a brace of trooper's jack-boots, which came nearly up to the wearer's thigh; but the contract merely expressed boots, and the Devil does not stand upon trifles.

Moulton rolled in wealth; everything prospered. His neighbors regarded him first with envy, then with aversion, at last with fear. Not a few affirmed that he had entered into a league with the Evil One. Others shook their heads, saying, "What does it signify?—that man would outwit the Devil himself."

But one morning, when the fiend came as usual to fill the boots, what was his astonishment to find that he could not fill them. He poured in the guineas, but it was like pouring water into a rat-hole. The more he put in, the more the quantity seemed to diminish. In vain he persisted; the boots could not be filled.

The Devil scratched his ear. "I must look into this," he reflected. No sooner said, than he attempted to descend; but in doing so he found his progress suddenly stopped. A good reason. The chimney was choked up with guineas! Foaming with rage, the demon tore the boots from the crane. The crafty General had cut off the soles, leaving only the legs for the Devil to fill. The chamber was knee-deep with gold.

The Devil gave a horrible grin, and disappeared. The same night Hampton House was burned to the ground, the General only escaping in his shirt. He had been dreaming he was dead and in hell. His precious guineas were secreted in the wainscot, the ceiling, and other hiding-places known only to himself. He blasphemed, wept, and tore his hair. Suddenly he grew calm. After all, the loss was not irreparable, he reflected. Gold would melt, it is true; but he would find it all,—of course he would,—at daybreak, run into a solid lump in the cellar,—every guinea. That is true of ordinary gold..

The General worked with the energy of despair, clearing away the rubbish. He refused all offers of assistance; he dared not accept them. But the gold had vanished. Whether it was really consumed, or had passed again into the massy entrails of the earth, will never be known. It is only certain that every vestige of it had disappeared.

When the General died and was buried, strange rumors began to circulate. To quiet them, the grave was opened; but when the lid was removed from the coffin, it was found to be empty.

Another legend runs to the effect that upon the death of his wife under —as evil report would have it—very suspicious circumstances, the General paid his court to a young woman who had been the companion of his deceased spouse. They were married. In the middle of the night the young bride awoke with a start. She felt an invisible hand trying to take off from her finger the wedding-ring that had once belonged to the dead and buried Mrs. Moulton. Shrieking with fright, she jumped out of bed, thus awaking her husband; who tried in vain to calm her fears. Candles were lighted and search made for the ring; but as it could never be found again, the ghostly visitor was supposed to have carried it away with her. This story is the same that is told by Whittier in the "New Wife and the Old."

Jack-the-Ripper

In the days when Dyer Brook was an active logging center, some of the villagers believed that if a man went seven nights at the same hour to the same place, the Devil would appear and talk with him on the seventh night. There is a tale to the effect that a log driver called Jack-the-Ripper carried out the conditions, and held converse with Satan who warned him to stay off the logs the following day to avoid an accident. Ignoring the warning, Jack jumped carelessly from log to log, working his way to the center of the drive. As he did so, a streak of red fire in the form of a pickaxe flamed up between the logs, a reminder of the warning. He went hastily ashore. From then on Jack was thought by his neighbors to be in league with the Devil. When his axe chopped, another was always heard in accompaniment. He was often heard conversing with a voice

From *Maine,* A Guide "Down East," Written by Workers of the Federal Writers Project of the Works Progress Administration for the State of Maine, pp. 293–294. Copyright, 1937, by Everett F. Greaton, Executive Secretary, Maine Development Commission. Boston: Houghton Mifflin Company.

whose owner was invisible. Once he drove his axe into the hard trunk of a tree with such force the handle split. When he reached out to grasp the handle again, it became whole in his hands. Conclusive proof to residents of Dyer Brook that Jack-the-Ripper had acquired supernatural powers came when, after the combined efforts of several woodsmen had failed, Jack, single-handed, though unobserved, cleared a camp site of a huge tree that had blown across it during a storm.

The Devil and the Card-Players

In a Connecticut village four men were visiting together one evening. At length one of them proposed that they should have a game of cards. They were aware of the wickedness of card-playing, and knew very well how scandalous the proposal was. Nevertheless, after a little argument, they agreed to play for a short time. On a stand in the corner of the kitchen was a candle whose flame had eaten nearly down to the socket. Said one of the men, "We'll just play till the candle burns out. There can't be much harm in that, I'm sure."

"Very good," said the others; "we'll stop when the candle burns out."

They played one game, two games, three games, and still the candle burned. The candle burned, and game followed game until morning came, and the first rays of daylight startled the four players.

Then they knew that Satan himself had been their companion through the night. Who but the Devil would have kept that candle burning for so many hours for such a purpose?

Cheating the Devil

A farmer who had no money wanted a barn. Indeed, he wanted the barn very badly. The man had just a shed or two back of his little house, and it did not seem to him he could get along without a barn much longer possibly. Now, the Devil knew very well how the man was feeling; and one day he went to the man, and said he'd build him a barn. So they fixed up a bargain between them. For putting up the barn the Devil was to have the man's soul when he died; but the work must be done before the first rooster crew in the morning, or the bargain was off. All that night the man heard the Devil hammering and hammering away up the hill a little ways, where he was building the barn. A while before daylight the man got up, and went out the back door to where he had a slab shed he kept his hens in. He stopped before the door, and made an imitation of crowing, and the old

---

From *What They Say in New England,* A Book of Signs, Sayings, and Superstitions, collected by Clifton Johnson, p. 237. Copyright, 1896, by Lee and Shepard. Boston.

Ibid., pp. 241–242.

rooster answered him. That knocked the bargain all to pieces, and the Devil got well cheated that time. The man got his barn free; but being of the Devil's building I don't suppose it was a very good one, or lasted very long.

How Old Sarah Bunganuck Fought the Devil

. . . You see, old Sarah she was one of the converted Injuns, and a good old critter she was too; worked hard, and got her livin' honest. She made baskets, and she made brooms, and she used to pick young wintergreen and tie it up in bunches, and dig sassafras and ginsing to make beer; and she got her a little bit o' land, right alongside o' Old Black Hoss John's white-birch wood-lot.

Now, I've heerd some o' these 'ere modern ministers that come down from Cambridge college, and are larnt about every thing in creation, they say there ain't no devil, and the reason on't is, 'cause there can't be none. These 'ere fellers is so sort o' green!—they don't mean no harm, but they don't know nothin' about nobody that does. If they'd ha' known old Black Hoss John, they'd ha' been putty sure there was a devil. He was jest the crossest, ugliest critter that ever ye see, and he was ugly jest for the sake o' ugliness. He couldn't bear to let the boys pick huckleberries in his paster lots, when he didn't pick 'em himself; and he was allers jawin' me 'cause I would go trout-fishin' in one o' his pasters. Jest ez if the trout that swims warn't the Lord's, and jest ez much mine as his. He grudged every critter every thing; and if he'd ha' hed his will and way, every bird would ha' fell down dead that picked up a worm on his grounds. He was jest as nippin' as a black frost. Old Black Hoss didn't git drunk in a regerlar way, like Uncle Eph and Toddy Whitney, and the rest o' them boys. But he jest sot at home, a-soakin' on cider, till he was crosser'n a bear with a sore head. Old Black Hoss hed a special spite agin old Sarah. He said she was an old witch and an old thief, and that she stole things off'n his grounds, when everybody knew that she was a regerlar church-member, and as decent an old critter as there was goin'. As to her stealin', she didn't do nothin' but pick huckleberries and grapes, and git chestnuts and wannuts, and butternuts, and them 'ere wild things that's the Lord's, grow on whose land they will, and is free to all. I've hearn 'em tell that, over in the old country, the poor was kept under so, that they couldn't shoot a bird, nor ketch a fish, nor gather no nuts, nor do nothin' to keep from starvin', 'cause the quality folks they thought they

---

Cf. "The Devil's Bridge" below.

From *Oldtown Fireside Stories,* by Harriet Beecher Stowe, pp. 195–199. Entered, according to Act of Congress, in the year 1871, by James R. Osgood & Co., in the Office of the Librarian of Congress, at Washington. Boston. 1872.

owned every thing, 'way down to the middle of the earth and clear up to the stars. We never hed no sech doin's this side of the water, thank the Lord! We've allers been free to have the chesnuts and the wannuts and the grapes and the huckleberries and the strawberries, ef we could git 'em, and ketch fish when and where we was a mind to. Lordy massy! your grandthur's old Cesar, he used to call the pond his pork-pot. He'd jest go down and throw in a line and ketch his dinner. Wal, Old Black Hoss he know'd the law was so, and he couldn't do nothin' agin her by law; but he sarved her out every mean trick he could think of. He used to go and stan' and lean over her garden-gate and jaw at her an hour at a time; but old Sarah she had the Injun in her; she didn't run to talk much: she used to jest keep on with her weedin' and her work, jest's if he warn't there, and that made Old Black Hoss madder'n ever; and he thought he'd try and frighten her off'n the ground, by makin' on her believe he was the Devil. So one time, when he'd been killin' a beef critter, they took off the skin with the horns and all on; and Old Black Hoss he says to Toddy and Eph and Loker, "You jest come up tonight, and see how I'll frighten old Sarah Bunganuck."

Wal, Toddy and Eph and Loker, they hedn't no better to do, and they thought they'd jest go round and see. Ye see 'twas a moonlight night, and old Sarah—she was an industrious critter—she was cuttin' white-birch brush for brooms in the paster-lot. Wal, Old Black Hoss he wrapped the critter's skin round him, with the horns on his head, and come and stood by the fence, and begun to roar and make a noise. Old Sarah she kept right on with her work, cuttin' her brush and pilin' on't up, and jest let him roar. Wal, Old Black Hoss felt putty foolish, 'specially ez the fellers were waitin' to see how she took it. So he calls out in a grum voice,—"Woman, don't yer know who I be?"

"No," says she quite quiet, "I don't know who yer be."

"Wal, I'm the Devil," sez he.

"Ye be?" says old Sarah. "Poor old critter, how I pity ye!"[1] and she never gin him another word, but jest bundled up her broom-stuff, and took it on her back and walked off, and Old Black Hoss he stood there mighty foolish with his skin and horns; and so he had the laugh agin him, 'cause Eph and Loker they went and told the story down to the tavern, and he felt awful cheap to think old Sarah had got the upper hands on him.

Wal, ye see, boys, that 'ere's jest the way to fight the Devil. Jest keep straight on with what ye're doin', and don't ye mind him, and he can't do nothin' to ye.

---

[1] A similar story is told of Cynthia Gross and the Devil by Elizabeth Reynard, in *The Narrow Land* (Boston, 1934), p. 200.

The Loup-Garou

. . . NAOW, wait till Ah'll goin' tol' you baout de loup garou. Ah dat was so bad ting, it mek me scare for tink of it ever sen Ah 'll leetly boy an' de hol' mans an' de hol' hwomans tol' of it. Den we 'll seet an' squeeze de fire, an' be scare fer look behin' of us, fer see de shadder creep, creep on de floor an' jomp on de wall, fer fred it be de loup garou.

* * * * *

. . . dey was dev' more as anyting. . . . Dev', dev'. Some tam dey was mans jes lak anybodee, and den dey was be wolfs, oh, more wusser as wolfs. Dey ketch dead mans in graveyards an' heat it, dey ketch live mans, an' heat it. Oh, dey was awfuls. Ah b'lieve dey ant gat some more in Canada, naow, but in de hol' tam dey had it. One tam, mah gran'-gran'mudder, he'll gat so hol' he'll mek off hees min's hee 'll die, an' mah gran'fader he 'll was go fer pries' in de naght, an' long, long way t'rough de hwood, an' he drivin' long on hees traine, can' hear no nowse 'cep' de snow scroonch, scroonch under de runner an' de hoss feet of it. Wal, seh, mah gran'pere was drovin' long, ant tink for much, 'cep' for hurry fas'. He 'll was goin' on smooze road t'rough de hwood wen hees hoss was beegin fer go slow an' he 'll can' mek it go fas', all he 'll wheep it. De hoss jes' pull hard lak he 'll draw more as two ton load an' sweat so he 'll smoke lak stimboat an' melt de snow on de road wid de drop of de sweat.

Bambye mah gran'pere look behin' of it, an', seh, he 'll see great beeg, beeg black dawg, mebby wolf, he do' know if it ant prob'ly, wid hees fore-foots off de graound an' can' pull back some more.

Mah gran'pere was mad, an' scare more as he 'll was mad, an' he stroke dat ting wid hees whip, an' dat ting jomp raght on de traine an' put hees before feet on mah gran'pere shoulder of it, so heavy, he mos' squeese him. Mah gran'pere feel of hees knife fer cut at it, cause ef you drew bleed of de loup garou he 'll turn mans raght off an' go away.

But he can' fin' hees knife, an' he 'll ant know what he 'll do. De hoss was scare an' run lak hol' hurricanes, 'cause de loup garou gat hees behin' foots off de graound an' can' pull back some more.

Mah gran'pere feel dat hell ting's hot bress froze hees neck, an' hees hairs bresh hees face lak needle, an' he 'll shut off hees heye, so he can' see dat awfuls yallar heye clost hees hown, an' he give up for tink he dead, jes' as de hoss run in de pries' gate, an' he holler an' de pries run aout an' say some word quick an' laoud an' de loup garou be mans raght off so quicker as you mek some wink an' run off in de hwood.

My gran'fader was so scare it was took more as mos half pant of de pries' whiskey-en-esprit to brought it to.

From *Danvis Folks*, by Rowland E. Robinson, pp. 181–183. Boston and New York: Houghton Mifflin Company.

The Devil and the Loups-Garous

MANY years ago a man named Jean Dubroise lived in the village of St. Denis. He mocked the church and said that the Bon Dieu was non-existent. The crops grown upon his land were the finest in that part of Canada and in the winter his trap-line caught the largest number of animals with the finest fur. His house, barn, and fences were kept in repair and his neighbors could not account for this as he was never seen to do any work. It was told that from his house and farms strange wild noises issued and none of the villagers would set foot on his land at night. Even in the daytime, when a villager had to pass Jean Dubroise's house, he would cross himself and hurry away.

Alphonse Gaulin, returning home late one night from a dance where he had a few drinks of whisky, said, "What care I for the Devil? I go for a walk where I please and if the Devil come near me I give him a fine licking." So saying, Alphonse cut across Jean Dubroise's land as a short cut home. When he arrived near the house, he heard a horrible noise which came from the north and seemed to be something coming fast, like a railroad train. This was queer, as there was no railroad anywhere near this farm. The nearer it came, the greater the noise. It came straight at Alphonse, who was now thoroughly frightened, and saying his act of contrition he threw himself flat upon the ground, the while he promised the Bon Dieu that if he escaped alive he would always attend church and stop drinking and swearing. The noise had grown louder and at the height of about thirty feet over his head passed a great canoe. He could hear a snarling, a howling, a clanking of chains and evil noises of all kinds, like pieces of iron being shaken up in a kettle. The noise was so loud that his ears rang for ten minutes after the great canoe had passed.

The canoe came down to the ground near the door of Jean Dubroise's house, and Alphonse, from his hiding place, could see a huge man, who was sitting in the back of the canoe dressed in red from head to toe, swing a whip and lash the occupants of the canoe, the while shouting, "Come, get out of the canoe. There is much work to be done before morning." About twenty small elf-like creatures jumped out of the canoe and started plowing the land under the direction of the Devil and of Jean Dubroise, who had come out of the house. Now Alphonse knew the whole story. Jean Dubroise, who had mocked the priests and the church, had sold his soul to the Devil for burning and the Devil was paying him by working his farm every night with about twenty loups-garous. These were living men who, for not having attended to their religious duties, were compelled to leave their human form at stated intervals and do as the Devil directs them. They had to serve the Devil for various lengths of time. One who had not

---

By Edward Rousseau, Woonsocket, Rhode Island. Manuscripts of the Federal Writers' Project of the Works Progress Administration for the State of Rhode Island.

received communion for five years would have to serve the Devil for five years. Another who had not gone to confession for ten years would have to serve that length of time before he would be free of the Devil's spell.

Alphonse Gaulin was afraid to move and, lying on the ground, he watched the twenty loups-garous doing the farm work. They kept on working until just before dawn the Devil ordered them into the canoe and away the canoe dashed through the sky. Alphonse then rushed home and told his neighbors of what he had witnessed. While some of his neighbors thought that what he had seen was the Devil who came out of a whisky bottle, others believed and urged him to go to the curé and tell his story. He went to the parish house and told his story to the curé who promised to put an end to the Devil's coming to the village of St. Denis. The next day, while Jean Dubroise was away from his farm, the men of the parish, with the curé leading them, marched to the farm and upon arriving there the curé said Mass and then he sprinkled holy water all over the farm.

That night all the men of the parish and the curé hid themselves near the farmhouse of Jean Dubroise. Just before midnight they heard the Devil's canoe approaching. They were afraid, but knowing that the power of Bon Dieu was greater than that of the Devil, none moved from their hiding places. The canoe slid to earth and the Devil stepped out. When the foot of the Devil touched the earth he gave a great shout that shook the trees, for as every one knows the Devil is afraid of holy water. He shouted, raged, and tore up the ground. Thinking that Jean Dubroise had told the curé of his visits, he rushed to the house and, grabbing Jean, he hurried back to the canoe. Every time that the Devil's foot touched the ground terrifying groans of agony came from his lips. He threw Jean Dubroise into the canoe, jumped in himself, and then in a blast of flame that scorched the ground for many yards, the Devil, Jean Dubroise, and the canoe disappeared.

All this time the twenty loups-garous were wandering around with no one to direct them and as even a child knows, the only way to restore human form to these poor men is to draw blood from them. The men of the parish rushed upon the loups-garous and with knives cut them slightly so that the blood would flow. Almost immediately the loups-garous changed to human form and the men of St. Denis were astonished to find that they were friends who had been bewitched by the Devil. There was joy in St. Denis that day and a great feast was prepared. After eating, all of the people went to Mass and from that time on no man of St. Denis has mocked either the church or the curé nor has any one neglected his religious duties.

Why Purgatory Was Made

MANY years ago in the village of St. Ours lived a man by the name of Victor. Now Victor was a cunning good-for-nothing who wished to live without working and tried to cheat every one. All day long he would gamble with cards, even on Sunday. One day when his luck was bad, he lost all of his money.

That evening a stranger came to Victor's house and asked Victor to play cards with him. Victor explained to the stranger that he had lost all of his money playing cards and had nothing left to bet. The stranger replied, "If you will give your soul to me for burning, I'll give you this ring, and as long as you wear it, you will never lose when playing cards." Victor then knew that he was talking to the Devil but thought that this was a good bargain, as by winning at cards he would have plenty of money without working. So he agreed and the Devil said, "Here is the ring and when I need your soul I'll come and get you."

Victor put on the ring and went down to the Inn to play cards. For about three years Victor won every time that he played cards. He was very happy, as he had plenty of money. But one day the Devil suddenly appeared and said, "I have kept my promise. Now I want you to keep yours. On next Monday I will come for you, as I need your soul." Then the Devil disappeared, leaving Victor regretting that he had made such a bargain.

The next day Victor, trying to think of a way to cheat the Devil, was walking along the road when he met the Bon Dieu and St. Peter, who were traveling from village to village. St. Peter noticed the expression on Victor's face and said, "My son, what is the matter? Come, tell us. Maybe we can straighten things out for you." Victor told him of the trouble he was in and the Bon Dieu, who wanted to spite the Devil, said, "I will show you how you may cheat the Devil, but you must never gamble with other men, as you cannot lose, and that would be cheating." Victor promised that if he was delivered from the Devil's power, he would never play cards again and that he would go to work. So the Bon Dieu said, "Throw away the Devil's ring and when he comes for you play him a game of cards. You cannot lose, as I will put a charm upon you."

On Monday when the Devil came for him, Victor said, "Sit down and let us play a game of cards. If I lose, I'll go with you. If I win, I'll stay here." The Devil, seeing that Victor no longer wore the magic ring and believing that he himself would win, replied, "All right, if I don't beat you I'll go back to Hell alone." They played, but the Devil, unable to overcome the charm of the Bon Dieu, lost, and in a puff of smoke disappeared.

From "French-Canadian Folklore," Woonsocket, Rhode Island. Manuscripts of the Federal Writers' Project of the Works Progress Administration for the State of Rhode Island.

Now that Victor no longer feared the Devil, he soon forgot his promise to the Bon Dieu, and instead of going to work he continued to gamble, and for many years Victor led an evil life. One day the Bon Dieu said to St. Peter, "Do you know that we have forgotten Victor and all this time he has been a gambler? He has broken his promise to me. You must go and get him." St. Peter said, "I am very busy now, so you had better send Death for him."

So Death was sent down to earth and he brought Victor to the gates of paradise. St. Peter would not let him in but told him to go and see his friend the Devil. Victor went to the Devil's abode far, far down below, but the Devil would not let him in, saying, "I won't have you here. You cheated me when you were on earth. Get out." Victor went back to the gates of paradise and said, "Now listen, great St. Peter, the Devil won't have me and I've got to sleep somewhere. Let me just hide behind the gates of paradise." St. Peter and the Bon Dieu discussed the matter and agreed to let Victor in if he promised never again to either gamble or to cheat any one. Victor promised and St. Peter let him in and told him to sit on a small white cloud behind the gates of paradise.

For a long time Victor remained quiet and had nothing to say. But this became wearisome, and at last Victor pulled out his cards and asked a neighbor, seated on a larger cloud above him, if he would like to play. "We will play for an exchange of places," said Victor, and he won the game. After he had moved to the second cloud, he said to his neighbor next above, "Would you like to play for each other's places?" Again Victor won, for the charm that the Bon Dieu had given him, long ago, was still powerful. This went on until Victor found himself seated beside the Great Throne. "Bon Dieu," said Victor, "will you play a little game with me for each other's place?" But the Bon Dieu said, "You are lucky to be here. Twice have you broken your promise to me and this time I'll put you where you will never again have any one to play cards with."

So the Bon Dieu made a place that was not as bad as Hell nor as good as Heaven and he called it Purgatory. It was a place of darkness and silence where a man's soul, by suffering, is purified from venial sins, and the man's soul is then admitted into Heaven. Victor was sent to Purgatory, where for many years he must suffer for the sins that he committed while on earth. Since that time every man who on earth is a gambler is sent to Purgatory when he dies so that he may suffer for his sins.

The Devil's Hole

You know, my children, that there was not always a church at Sorel. A very long time ago, in the time of my great-grandfather, there was a

By William Leclair, Woonsocket, Rhode Island. Manuscripts of the Federal Writers' Project of the Works Progress Administration for the State of Rhode Island.

curé only at Saint Michel. At that time in order to go to the Easter celebration, to get married, or to have children baptised, it was necessary to go to Saint Michel. You can see that this was very inconvenient and it was very annoying when the roads were bad as they usually were, mud and mire most of the year.

But of course there were not many people in the parish then. Two or three families on the hill and a few dozen at the foot of the hill. But besides these there were many poor people who were moving into the woods and clearing the land so that they could farm. These people built little log houses and were very poor and had no live stock. Mon Dieu, there was hardship then for these poor people. You do not know what it is to take the forest land and make it ready for the plow. The stumps that had to be pulled out and the stones piled up! The curé from Saint Michel came to Sorel every fortnight to say mass in a little wooden chapel which stood where the chapel for the dead now stands. Then one fine day the news came to the people of Sorel that they were to have a curé of their own. I do not need to tell you that this caused great joy. But Mon Dieu, it is a wonder that the poor curé who came to take charge of the parish did not die. There was no church, no house for the priest. He was obliged to ask shelter from a farmer. Then the people built him a kind of house, a very poor one where the poorest people to-day would scarcely live. But Monsieur le Curé was very happy. He was not proud, this good Monsieur le Curé. All priests are good, my children, but this one was a saint, a true saint. Some time after his arrival it was decided to build a church. But Monsieur le Curé did not know how to get the stone carted that was necessary for the building. There were few horses in the country then, just enough for the spring sowing and other work. There was always work to be done.

So one night when Monsieur le Curé was thinking how the stone might be drawn, he heard a voice call his name. "I felt a great fear," he said. It called a second time. Then he felt his fright pass away. "I am in a state of grace," he said to himself. "I have nothing to fear." And he replied, "In the name of God, who are you and what do you want?" Then he saw a beautiful White Lady appear before him. "Do not be afraid, François," she said, "I am the Holy Virgin. To-morrow morning when you arise you will find a horse tied before your door. Use him to cart the stone for your church. You may give him a heavy load to carry for he is very strong. But one precaution must be taken. Never take off his bridle. His bridle is holy and if taken off he will disappear forever." The apparition vanished, then Monsieur le Curé fell asleep.

In the morning the sun lit up his room and he awoke with a start. He recalled the vision of the night but he thought he had been dreaming. He knelt to say his morning prayers, when suddenly outside he heard the pawing of a horse. He cast his eyes towards the garden and was surprised to see, tied there, a magnificent black horse. Two or three times he passed his hand over his eyes to make sure that he was awake. At last he went out to the garden and put his hand on the horse's neck to assure himself that he was not dreaming. The horse trembled but did not stir a foot. The vision that he had during the night had come true. At five o'clock the workmen arrived to begin their day's labor. "My friends," said the curé, showing them the horse, "some one has lent me this animal to cart the stone for the church. He seems to be a good horse but he is a bit wild. You will have to be careful and especially don't unbridle him to let him drink or eat, because if you do he will run away." "What's the name of the horse, Monsieur le Curé?" asked Louis Jarrett. "Oh, yes, let's see," said the priest. Then after some moments of reflection he replied, "Call him Old Nick. I will entrust him to you, Louis." Louis answered, "Ah well, I'll see to him, Monsieur le Curé. All the same that's a queer name for a horse, Old Nick. But no matter, if he is not possessed by the devil it will be all right." "As for that," said the curé smiling, "I can answer for it."

Then they harnessed Old Nick to the cart to carry the stones. They put on the ordinary load, but Old Nick went off with that load as though it was air. The curé, who was watching, told them not to worry but to put on a heavier load. This did not seem to tire the horse at all. They then got another cart twice the size of the first, then loaded it up as high as a load of hay. The wheels cracked, but Old Nick pulled the load easily. What a horse this Old Nick was! Black as jet, not a white hair on him, and four strong legs. Besides that, a fine black beautiful arched neck. Oh, but he was a fine horse! A little touchy, it was true, and he had a wicked mouth. The curé told them to look out for his mouth and to keep away from him. Since they did not unbridle him, that was easy. From time to time Monsieur le Curé would ask Louis, "Well, my Louis, how do you like Old Nick?" Louis would always reply, "Damn fine horse, Monsieur le Curé."

Louis was always the one to drive this horse, but one day he could not come and Batisse Champlain replaced him. Batisse was a good fellow and a great worker, but he thought that he was more cunning than any one else. And boastful too. To hear him talk you would believe that only his things were worth anything. His horse—words could not describe him. His cow—she was a spring and her milk was cream. His pigs—they got fat by only lying in the sun. His dog knew more than most people and his wife made the best pancakes in the country. Besides all this he was a horse-jockey—Mon Dieu, such as one did not see often. For a long time he had been watching Old Nick and criticizing Louis behind his back. So when he found himself with this splendid horse to drive he was much pleased. One would have thought that it was his very own. It was "my horse" here and "my Old Nick" there. One could hear nothing but his clack. Louis had warned him not to unbridle the horse to let him drink, but Batisse had replied, "Don't you worry, my Louis, I know horses. This is not the first I have bridled and if I wish to unbridle him, the devil take me if I can't put his bridle back on again."

All that day Batisse enjoyed himself. They were drawing stone from the other side of the river. It was the middle of the day and very hot. When crossing the river, Batisse, who was thirsty, stopped the horse right in the middle and drank out of the hollow of his hand. Then he tried to get his horse to drink but the horse did not seem to want to do so. Batisse thought, "It's on account of his bridle. Just as if it was sensible not to unbridle a horse to let him drink! What do priests know about horses? Poor Old Nick, I'm going to take off his bridle, for I'm sure he is thirsty."

He put his hand on the horse's mane to hold him, then unbuckled the throat-strap, then gently took out the bits and removed the bridle. In a flash Old Nick darted away at full speed, leaving harness and cart in the river. Batisse had fallen fifteen feet away and was struggling in the water. Old Nick was running up the road as fast as he could go when Monsieur le Curé, who was taking the blessed sacrament to a sick person, saw him. Monsier le Curé placed himself in the middle of the road and as Old Nick drew near he made a great sign of the cross. Then the horse reared up and, leaving the road entirely, he flew straight north on to a rock which overhangs the river. There was a frightful noise, the rock split from top to bottom, making a cleft six feet wide, and Old Nick disappeared into a deep cavern in the rock. It is now called the "Devil's Hole." Monsieur le Curé was much vexed at the loss of Old Nick, not that he liked him so much, for Monsieur le Curé knew too well what sort of a horse he was, but without him it made the work of finishing the church much harder for the people.

Old Nick, who was really the devil, was much insulted when he was made to draw stones for the building of a church. Therefore he promised himself that he would have his revenge by playing vile tricks and casting spells upon the people of Sorel. So for years and years not a Christian could drive his wagon past the "Devil's Hole" without some damage being done. Sometimes a tug or a whiffletree broke; at other times the horse stumbled and went lame, or else the wagon was stopped by a wheel breaking. For many, many years never would a horse pass the place without pricking up his ears and trembling as though he perceived some frightful thing which no human could see. At night moans and the clanking of chains were heard. At other times there was seen coming out of the cavern a black beast like a wolf, with a terrible mouth spouting flames. A curious thing was that when Monsieur le Curé carried past the Bon Dieu, nothing happened. This proved that it was the devil. As is well known, the devil cannot come near the blessed sacrament.

And it was all the fault of Batisse. Damn! It was quite clear. If he had listened to the curé this would not have happened. All the curés of the parish had for many years done their best to cause these sorceries to cease. They had prayed, they had hung crosses and medals in the "Devil's Hole," together with blest palms, candles, and all kinds of holy things. They had blest the rock on all sides. Nothing did any good. But people said,

"God is stronger than the devil. It will come to an end some time." But the sorceries still went on. Then one night a priest, new to the parish, saw in a dream the Holy Virgin, who said, "If you wish to deliver your parishioners from the evil deeds of the demon, have a cross erected on the rock." Early the next morning the curé began to carry out the desire of the Holy Virgin. He spoke to the chief men of the parish and every one was set to work. Some brought cut stone, others fine beams of pine, others cedar logs, and others lime, pegs, and iron nails. Soon there was to be seen upon the rock a beautiful cross which the pious people of Sorel still keep in place.

To consecrate the cross there was a great retreat in the parish. The preaching was done by Monseigneur Maillot. The Monseigneur sprinkled the cross and the people with holy water and at the same time he said prayers in Latin. He next preached the most eloquent of his sermons. Almost every one wept. At the end he made the men promise not to drink or swear any more. He blessed us all once more, and intoned the Te Deum in a solemn voice while the procession went back to the church. Since then the devil has not dared to come out of his cavern.

How the Black Horse Was Beaten

Sam Hart, of Woburn, was well known in the Bay State in the later years of the eighteenth century, for he was a lover of swift horses, a fearless rider, a layer of shocking wagers, and a regular attendant at fairs, races, and other manner of doubtful enterprises. He had one mare that he offered to pit against any piece of horse-flesh in the country, and he bragged about her, in season and out, making of her his chief topic of conversation and prayers, after the manner of men who drive fast horses. While taking the air on his door-step on a summer evening he was visited by a bland and dignified stranger whose closely shaven jowls, sober coat, cocked hat, and white wig made him look like a parson, but whose glittering black eyes did not agree with his make-up. This gentleman had called to brag about his black horse, that would beat anything on legs, as he wished to prove by racing him against Hart's mare. He offered odds of three to one, with his horse into the bargain, and he would give the mare ten rods start. The race was to begin at Central Square and the black horse must catch the mare by the tail with his teeth before Woburn Common was reached.

Sam accepted this challenge in an instant, and next morning the village emptied itself upon the street to see the fun. The word was given. There was a cry and a snap of the whip, and away went the coursers, tearing over the earth like a hurricane. The mare was supple, longwinded, and strong, yet the big black was surely gaining. His breath seemed actually

From *American Myths and Legends,* by Charles M. Skinner, Vol. I, pp. 78–80.

to smoke, so hot was his pace. Sam began to suspect what sort of being this was behind him, and instead of ending the run in the way prescribed he made for the Baptist church. It was impossible to pull up sharply with such a headway, and the chase went three times around the building at a furious gallop before Sam could steer the mare close enough to the church door to be on holy ground. Fire sprang from the black horse's nostrils. It singed the mare's tail and the horizontally streaming coat-tails of her rider. Then the black horse went down upon his haunches, and Sam, pulling up with difficulty, dismounted. The Devil, who had been riding the black, was out of his saddle first. Said he: "You have cheated one whose business is cheating, and I'm a decent enough fellow to own up when I'm beaten. Here's your money. Catch it, for you know I can't cross holy ground, you rascal; and here's my horse; he'll be tractable enough after I've gone home, and as safe as your mare. Good luck to you."

A whiff of sulphur smoke burst up from the road and made Sam wink and cough. When he could open his eyes again the Devil was gone. He put the black horse into his stable, and had him out at all the fairs and functions, winning every race he entered. Still, the neighbors doubted the blessing of the Devil, for they used to say that the black was still the Devil's horse, and that money won by racing—especially when it was won on a sure thing—would weigh the soul of its owner down to the warm place when he died.

THE WITCH IS IN IT

Captain Paddock and Crook-Jaw

"Old Yarmouth" included what is now the town of Dennis . . . which was set off and incorporated in 1793. When Ichabod Paddock lived there, it was the East Parish of Yarmouth, and so to Yarmouth is given the credit for sending one of its native sons to Nantucket, a bit of New England history which to this day gives Yarmouth a chuckle and is somewhat embarrassing to the island. For, in 1690, Nantucket, which now prides itself upon being one of the world's greatest ex-whaling centers, sent for Ichabod Paddock "to instruct the people in the art of killing whales."

Of Captain Paddock's fabulous proficiency in his "art," the whalers of both the island and the Cape have heard accounts. Expurgating as I go, I can give one version of a high point in the old whalemaster's career.

After years of slaughtering the great cows and bulls alike, Ichabod had at last met his match in the form of a giant battle-scarred "crook-jawed

---

From *Cape Cod Pilot*, by Jeremiah Digges, with Editorial and Research Assistance of the Members of the Federal Writers' Project, pp. 80–84. American Guide Series, Federal Writers' Project, Works Progress Administration for the State of Massachusetts. Copyright, 1937, by Poor Richard Associates. Provincetown and New York: Modern Pilgrim Press and the Viking Press.

sparm bull," a monster who would make two hundred barrels of oil if he'd make a thimble. Time and again Captain Paddock had let fly at old Crook-Jaw from the small-boat, but never once had he made fast. Come at him anywhere, stem, stern or amidships, and your iron would either glance off like a dull axe on green pine, or shatter into a cloud of horse-nails.

A few years of the chase after Crook-Jaw, and the captain wearied of this business of wasted heaves and lost irons. He jammed his two good jaws together and vowed through his teeth he'd find out what kind of black conjury was upon the critter if it was the last thing he did at sea.

One day shortly afterwards he raised Crook-Jaw lolling in the choppy waters of Handkerchief Shoal, sound asleep and snoring like a sated sinner on Sabbath-day leave. Heaving to about a mile to leeward, Ichabod pulled off his long-leggers and plunged overboard. Straight up to the whale he swam, and then he waited. Half an hour he waited, treading water, and at last he got what he was waiting for. Crook-Jaw opened his great mouth and yawned. Wider, wider, like a cavern a-stretch in the quaking of the earth, went the whale's mouth, until the huge jaws stood apart so that a cart upon wheels might have gone into it. Then, arching like a porpoise, in dove Ichabod.

It was parlous close for air inside the whale, but once down below, the captain thought he saw a light, split-aglimmering, and started aft towards it. Sure enough, on squeezing through, he came into a snug lamp-lit cabin where, on opposite sides of the table, two people were sitting at cards. One was a betaking young wench with hair the color of Eastham corn, plum-blossom skin, and a hitherly glance in the five-fathom green of her eyes. The other was the Divil.

As Ichabod entered, the Divil slammed his cards on the table, and sparks singed their edges and sent little wisps of blue smoke curling upward.

"Divil take me!" he swore absent-mindedly. "Again I lose the hand!" And getting to his feet he kicked over his chair and vanished in a huff.

"I'm very sorry, ma'am," Ichabod said. "I didn't come purposing to break up the game."

The girl laughed, and her voice was the ripple-wash of harbor waters on the bows of a shallop.

"The game was over," she told him.

"Your friend was mortal put out," Ichabod remarked. "Could a body inquire what the stakes might be?"

"Captain Paddock, *you* were the stakes!" And she stopped laughing and raised the brows above her green, green eyes, and added softly, "You might oblige me, sir, by bearing witness that I won."

And so it happened that Ichabod was quite given up for lost by his crew aboard the vessel; but at the coming of dawn they saw the waters of Handkerchief Shoal set a-dance by the arms of a returning figure, and Ichabod climbed wearily aboard.

Now, during the course of his little "gam," it had become evident to the captain that the green-eyed woman of Crook-Jaw had not spent all her life inside the whale's body; either that, or Ichabod himself had not been the first to venture through those gaping jaws. Hence, his queasy conscience being eased on certain essentials, the next evening, at the coming of sober-light, he pulled off his long-leggers and again plunged overboard, and was seen no more by his bewildered crew until the following morning.

This happened continuously until the vessel had to make in for a new fit-out, and again continuously, until the next fit-out. Ichabod was losing both his reputation as a whaler and a certain instinctive trust in which he had been held at home. He was also losing considerable of his usual color, and his men decided he had gone clean batchy.

The next time he came ashore, his good wife, a handsome creature not yet thirty, made him a gift—a shiny new whaling iron—which pleased Ichabod but also caused him a little pang, as a reminder of business which had been so long neglected. He was somewhat less pleased, when he went to sea again, to hear her insist that his father-in-law go with him.

A few days later, old Crook-Jaw spied the captain's vessel just outside the surf at Monomoy, and by this time the whale had come to regard Ichabod as a friend and guest, entitled to a certain amount of civility. He stood by, and Ichabod, standing on deck beside his father-in-law, watched him. When the old man began to exclaim at the size of the creature, and to beg Ichabod to lower for him, he could not properly refuse. Over they went in the small-boat, and with a mighty heave the whalemaster sent his new iron whistling through the air at Crook-Jaw. He was confident that the whale would understand, and there would be no harm done, but to his astonishment, this time he made fast! The beast churned and thrashed the water, and finally died. When they cut him up, all that Ichabod Paddock found inside, where his cozy cabin had been, was a strand of seaweed which had bleached to the color of Eastham corn, a shell of plum-blossom pink, and two round sun-squalls, of pure emerald green.

As for the explanation of the killing of Crook-Jaw, I have not heard whether Ichabod's wife ever confessed to him what she had done. But the shiny "iron" she had given him as a present was made of pure silver—the only metal that could pierce the heart of a witch.

The Sea Witch of Billingsgate

I HAVE heard that it is witch-haunted, this ground on both sides of the town line as you enter Wellfleet from the south.

Although several witches have been mentioned as haunters of the place, investigation reveals only one with proper credentials—the Sea Witch of Billingsgate—but she has a number of exploits to her credit. They pop up through several centuries of local lore, suggesting almost as many lives

Ibid., pp. 192–198, 204–205.

for this creature as for the cat who was one of her ever-present "familiars."

Her main interest appears to have been in the marine phase of the business—contriving for the souls of lost sailors and such—but she has taken many a flyer among landlubbers too. Wherever she may show, you can spot her by her heels. They were a weakness with her, those high red heels, and she affected them even at the risk of being frequently betrayed. Also, if business should ever take her abroad o' nights again, you will know her by her familiars running alongside—a cat and a gray goat with one glass eye.

Frankly, the chances are against meeting her. She has become inactive over these half-dozen decades just past. For one thing, business at sea has fallen off; and then, these Portuguese people have brought over effective countercharms from the Old Country. We know now that if any witch should start cutting up didoes around our house, we can drive her away once and for all by sticking pins in the heart of a calf and dropping the heart down the chimney.

But the science of preventive conjury was unknown here in the heyday of the Sea Witch of Billingsgate. Some said she was a red girl, some said she was white. In her time, it is clear, she was both. Having heard something of the talents of these creatures, I would not begrudge her a Scot's plaid.

But her color or her form at a given time depended on the soul that was "betaken" by her at the moment. The notion that there was more than one witch operating in the territory is grossly unfair to the Lower Cape towns. It is a libel, an old wives' tale. And I should firmly refuse to believe anything—except, of course, that there was a Sea Witch of Billingsgate, and that her familiars were a cat and a gray goat with one glass eye.

Among the poor souls that were "betaken" was pretty little Goody Hallett of Eastham. Goody was only fifteen, and no more knowful of the black arts than a babe in swaddlecloth.

One spring night in 1715, Goody was seduced; and the following winter she was apprehended, lying in a barn, with a dead baby in her arms. She was at once whisked into the village, seized up to Deacon Doane's fine new whipping-post and given a lashing as a sort of preliminary to the real punishment that awaited the outcome of her trial for murder. Pending that, she was clapped into Eastham Gaol.

The poor girl asked only that she be allowed to die, and while the town fathers were inclined to oblige her in this, a little writhing first, they thought, might serve as a valuable warning to others of the godless younger generation of their day. The gaoler was cautioned against bringing Goody any victuals that wanted cutting with a knife.

One afternoon, while the girl was beating wildly against the bars of her cell window, a stranger sauntered up to the wall and stood looking in at her. He was dressed in fine French bombasset, and he carried a gold-tipped cane. Something about his gaze quieted Goody and kept her spell-moored. One of the iron cell bars stood between their faces. He reached out, took it lightly between his thumb and finger, and flicked it away—clean out of the window-frame—as if it were no more than a stray bit of ryestraw. Then he smiled and slowly shook his head.

"Ah, these stiff-necked hymn-bellerin' Yankees! I tell ye, sometimes they make me feel like the rawest greeny ever went on the account!"

The words meant nothing to little Goody Hallett, but in the man's voice there was something smooth and wisterly, something that tautened the spell.

"Now, my girl," he went on, flicking another bar out of the window, "I'm going to play ye fair and square, cross my—er, by yer leave. Ye're young, but ye've showed old enough, sartin, for the employment I can get ye. Ye can forget all this, child," and with a gesture, he tossed away still another bar from the window. "Yer life's still before ye. 'Tis all in the future—yes, hmm!"

Soothingly, softly, he went on talking to her, but once he had led up to it properly, he made no bones about who he was. And as he spoke, from time to time he punctuated his remarks by taking out the bars from the window, until all were gone, and Goody Hallett's way to freedom lay clear. Also, the while he spoke, the girl felt bitter against those who had not let her die; and beguiled into vengeful thoughts, she listened and nodded.

At last he took a paper from his waistcoat.

"Can ye write, Goody? Well, no matter. A mark's as good. Just put it there, where the line's broken into small grains." He touched a gold quill to his tongue, and as Goody took the quill, she observed that the tip glistened scarlet. She was about to make the mark when he caught her arm.

"What! Tricks, is it? So soon?" His eyes were suddenly like fiery drills, and his fingers bruised her. But after a moment, he smiled again. "Young, aye! I forget ye're but a child, Goody Hallett. Go on and make yer mark; but if it's to be two lines, ye'll oblige me to make 'em slantindicular, like an X—not any other way."

Goody understood. And that night she disappeared from Eastham Gaol, and before her case could come up in General Court, the town of Eastham found that locks and bars could not hold Goody Hallett. No one seems to have thought of using silver "darbies" on her wrists—which would have done the trick—or else no one in Eastham was willing to give Deacon Doane's gaoler the loan of the silver. At any rate, Goody was finally "warned out" of Eastham town; and so she crossed into Billingsgate, where she lived in a lorn hut on the poverty-grass meadow, and where etarnal-strange capers were cut each night before cock-crow.

It is said that she, like Ichabod Paddock's lady-friend, took up quarters in a whale, and that she went cruising about, with a ship's light hung to the creature's tail, luring unwary mariners on the shoals. She dealt also in tempests, dabbled a bit in hurricanes, and now and then singled out some skipper who caught her fancy, to take him out at night, whisk him from the deck of his ship, bridle him and ride him up and down Cape Cod, and then send him back before morning, worn and creak-j'inted from the cruel exertions. Now and then she selected a strong, good-looking young fo'mast hand for other kinds of "divarsion." For Goody, in her later years, had become a deep-dyed sinner, whom you would never have taken for the blossoming maid, once the pride of the hymn-singing Halletts of Eastham town.

Now, it has been said that the man who ruined Goody on that moonlit occasion under an old apple tree in 1715 was Black Bellamy himself. But I suspect that the tale grew of the fact that the pirate happened to be in Eastham in that year, and was wrecked two years later in the waters hard by. I have no doubt that Goody had a hand in brewing the April hurricane that brought on disaster to Bellamy's ship, the *Whidah*. But if she did, she was merely cooperating with her employer as she had done in a long string of other shipwrecks in the territory.

As the record shows, Sam Bellamy was a simple, blustering windbag of a fellow, and a furriner at that; and I doubt if he was capable of the uncommon finesse it wanted, to trick the prettiest girl in a Cape Cod town. It wants a mite of doing to win one of these creatures, and in the version which I have heard of Goody's first fall, it seems to me the native touch was present.

The last official appearance of the Sea Witch of Billingsgate was as an Indian, living in the north end of town. On the record she is set down as Delilah Roach, and Delilah is described by the historians as the "sole survivor of the tribe of Nausets."

Well, Delilah herself insisted on having it that way. When the suspicion got around town that she was the Sea Witch, she marched right into the town clerk's office, to straighten the thing out—the way she wanted it straightened. And the town clerk, though he knew very well that Delilah's late husband, Simon Roach, had been the last *real* Indian, was not the man to cross Delilah. Her black eyes burned with the Unholy Powers as she stood over his table and commanded him to write, and as she commanded, so it was written. Delilah Roach was set down as the "last Indian." And as she flounced out of the office, the town clerk stole a glance at her. Beneath the hem of her skirt, which just missed sweeping the floor, his eye caught a brief spot of scarlet, now on the left side, now on the right.

Other townsfolk, even to the selectmen themselves, knew the importance of avoiding a "black conjury"; and in 1802, it was voted in town meeting "to repair the Indian's house and make her comfortable."

The Merwoman and the Finback Whale

LONG JOHN, a finback whale, lived in the sea not far from Lost Island, and while all other whales were caught by the Truro Seed-Corners, Long John, harpoon shy, succeeded in escaping. Likewise he evaded the charms of the merwoman of Lost Island who coaxed him with fish coddle, kelp cakes, and flattery. The big finback curvetted, blew and when temptation came too near, dived under the island, coming up on the opposite shore. Mischief twinkled in his small eyes, flickered along his tail. When the merwitch begged for a ride on his back, Long John blew bubbles at her, chuckled, and departed.

Contrary is the nature of woman whether with heels or a fishtail. The boon denied her becomes heart's desire; and the merwitch soon lost interest in flipperdancing, in sewing frills on kelp bonnets; even forgot to contemplate mirrored pools where her mica scales, her green hair, her fish-shaped eyes, her square white teeth gleamed back at her pleasantly. Once she had delighted in manipulating a ship's pump that fell top-side-turvy in the sea-bottom. Instead of sucking water up, the pump sucked water down. But as Long John continued to flout her, even this toy became neglected. She spent her days fashioning a greenweed harness of Sargossa-sea-rope, herringbone stitched, barnacle tufted. With this, if she succeeded in catching John, she intended to bridle him smartly.

What with tears, bribes and a thwart temper, that merwoman grew to be a deepsea nuisance. Lobsters and crabs sighed when they thought about her, for her singing never meant happiness; nor did she render, as they well knew, any tidewater psalms. Also they ruefully recalled the time when she tried to make them hold Long John by sitting on his horizontal tail. One, two, three, jump! they all caught hold at once. Then they took a ride, dizzying, dazzling, spun up, spun down, spun over and roundabout, until one by one they lost hold and sank into the mudbottom. A long claw-walk it proved, back to the shores of Lost Island where the merwoman sat, scowling.

One moonlight night the water-witch swam up-coast to Truro. Out on a Coomb sat Ichabod Paddock, the great whalemaster, who was later sent from the mainland to teach frail-minded Islanders (of the Vineyard and Nantucket) how to catch a fish. Ichabod was spread over the edge of Truro Coomb, looking for a ship due to bring him death-money from England. He heard a faint ripple, saw cockled silver, and the merwoman looked up and smiled.

From *The Narrow Land, Folk Chronicles of Old Cape Cod*, by Elizabeth Reynard, pp. 286–289. Copyright, 1934, by Elizabeth Reynard. Boston and New York: Houghton Mifflin Company.

An expurgated sailor's yarn. O[ral]. T[radition]. Obviously related to the Indian tale of Squant the Sea-woman. Ichabod Paddock was a real whale master. See Shebnah Rich, *Truro*, etc., p. 111.—E. R., *ibid.*, p. 325.

"Howdy-due," said Ichabod.

"Ev'nin'," said the merwoman. Then she tucked down to business and told him how Long John was living at Lost Island. She would give, she declared, a rope of pearls to the man who killed that whale. Ichabod had no pearl-hanker; especially with death-money due by ship from England! As it was, he feared the minister might nominate him Deacon, or Miranda Paddock might stop his going to sea. He thanked the mer-lady courteously, but declined her offer.

Then she promised him corals and assorted treasure chests, even to the "twelve foot copperbox" known to be full of gold bars, sunken off Monomoy. Ichabod was chary. The gems, he suspected, would all be flawed ones, and as for the gold, she did not look to him like a girl that gives away money.

Next the sea-woman proffered love. She held out white arms, looked "thwartships at him with a slant-eye," sang a mer-chanty. Ichabod felt "langerfied" yet he remembered how she was constructed, both legs locked up in a fishtail. Being a practical man, Ichabod declined love.

After that she pestered him until he could sympathize with the worn look on the faces of Lost Island crabs. So, man-fashion, he decided to get himself some peace by granting her desire and something more besides. "Tell Long John," said he to her, "that Ichabod Paddock, master whalesman, will never draw harpoon against him if he will take you on his head and ride you once around-Cape."

The merwoman hurried back to Lost Island. She took two squid-hound bass as witnesses to Ichabod's statement; and when Long John heard of the whaleman's promise, he was relieved of a long-concealed terror. Before Ichabod could change his mind, the great finback permitted the merwoman to bridle him with a weed rope. "Git aboard," said he to her, "there's a cozy little berth up for'ard." Graceful as a lily, her green hair flying, her mica scales a-glitter, the merwoman sat his bows, and so busy was she unpacking her dittybag that she did not notice how Long John winked his eye at the lobsters.

Up-coast, past Nauset beach, they floated; Long John docile as a shrimp. Now and then he even tacked, pretending that he was a frigate. The moon rose up. The sea-witch sang. Long John would not "jine chorus." At the Peaked Hill Bars he put down his helm and came about into the broad Bay, swimming the length of it toward the harbour opposite Sandwich. "Good measure, John," applauded the merwoman who was usually soft-tongued when the ducks were flying her way. Suddenly the finback took to swimming under water, straight toward shore. Then he rose and spouted high, a jet handsome as the "fountings of Vair Sally." Up, up, up with the spout shot the merwoman. She stopped whale-riding. She went sky-riding, sailing plumb to landward, over dunes, over roofs, over Sandwich town. "Look to your cock-beavers," sang out the goodmen seeing no cloud but receiving a salt-wetting. The whole sky flashed with moon-glitter and out of it dropped one silver splinter that fell like a meteor into Sandwich Pond.

There the merwoman has lived ever since, bottled up, out of mischief. Sulkier and sulkier she grows since no one takes her back to Lost Island. She is nothing but a pale ghost now, the shining mica of her scales gone dune-white with age. She skulks low in the pond-bottom, sometimes singing a mer-song, feeble and woe-silly. Her brains were always "noddlin' ones" and have not improved with time.

Long John spouts off the sunken reefs of Lost Island. He is pale anyway, so age has scarcely changed him. He squirmed out of the greenweed harness, back in Sandwich Bay. Great ropes of it line the shore, a broken and shabby weed. Any man may own a piece of the merwoman's bridle.

How Old Betty Booker Rode Skipper Perkins Down to York

THESE two skippers, Mitchell and Perkins, were both Kittery salts, but of the two Skipper Perkins was the worst curried. Old Betty Booker wanted some fish, and she suggested her need to the skipper, "Bring me a bit o' hal'but, skipper, when you git in ——."

"Show me your sixpence, ma'am," was the thrifty reply.

And with an ill-boding scowl, and a shake of—

"Her wicked head, with its wild gray hair,
And nose of a hawk, and eyes like a snake,"

she watched the skipper sail away. The sea beat him up and down. The gale tore his sails, and the fish sheered away from his trawls. His men got sick, and his schooner came home poorer than she went. Then it got bruited about that Betty Booker was making a witch-bridle for the skipper, and was going to ride him down to York some wild night, whereat, the skipper, when it came to his ears, got into a mortal terror. He was sure to be at home, always, before dusk; and his doors were barred double, and he quaked and shivered and shook until the sun came up. Finally Betty sent the skipper word that the first stormy night she would ride him to York.

Then he waited for the storm, and the storm came. The rain drove across Chauncey's Creek in blinding sheets; the winds wrenched and tore at the trees along shore, shaking the gables of the houses. Folk huddled about their slow fires with so much wet coming down the chimneys, and whispered awesomely that the witches were out.

Skipper Perkins not only barred his door double, but he piled all the movable furniture in his rooms against it, and then he waited for Betty Booker; nor was she long in coming. An unearthly wail came down the

---

From *Maine Pioneer Settlements: Old York*, by Herbert M. Sylvester, pp. 317–320. Boston: W. B. Clarke Co.

wind, and there was a scratching of a hundred witch-claws on his door, and above all sounded the cracked notes of Betty Booker's voice,—

"Bring me a bit o' hal'but, skipper!"

But the skipper piled the furniture higher against the door, and pushed against it with all his strength.

"Bring me a bit o' hal'but, skipper!"

With the cry of the hag, the gale rose higher, and with rougher buffetings it smote the old door that was built to look out on the sea; and then it began to open so the skipper felt a spatter of rain on his face. He heard the wild chatter of the witches, but he still held to his pushing, until he felt himself sliding along the rough floor. He made a leap for his bed, winding himself about in its coverings; the door flew open and in trooped the witches. They pounced upon the skipper, and stripped him to his skin; and while he cowered in his fear, old Betty bridled him and got upon his back, while the other witches climbed upon hers, and off they raced through the gale to York Harbor. When he lagged, they pricked him with their claws to make him go the faster; and so they rode him as long as they wished, to get him back to Kittery before cock-crow, more dead than alive.

"Don't say sixpence, skipper, to a poor old woman again," was Betty Booker's parting admonition, as she and her familiars vanished into the mists of the darkest part of the night.

After that the skipper took to his bed, where for three weeks he nursed his wounds and told his story to his neighbors.

In one of the old houses at Kittery, a part of which was being torn down not long ago, an old witch-bridle was found between the lathing and the outside boarding. It was made of the hair of the tail of a horse, strands of tow, and the inside bark of the yellow birch. A woman who happened to be present knew what it was, and seizing it with the tongs threw it into the fire. That there were such things seems to be well authenticated.

There were witches in York, but they seem to have been of the harmless sort, who never raised anything but a heavy gale to break down the corn or topple over a chimney. One hears about black Dinah and her "weather-pan." Black Dinah lived in York, and her hut stood on a rock at the intersection of three roads, and it overlooked the old mill-dam on York River. Her warming-pan when she put it over the fire was productive of great atmospheric disturbances. It was a Pandora's box of the whole gamut of tempestuous phenomena,—flooding rains, hurricanes, and even earthquakes. She was here in York as early as 1770, and was an object of avoidance by the credulous. Easter Booker was her contemporary in York. She slept at night with her head in Kittery and her feet in York. Emery speaks of her as bearing a striking resemblance to the biblical portrait of Lucinda, the Endor woman of Saul's acquaintance. In later years Easter Booker disappeared and was never afterward seen. She may have been the Betty of the Skipper Perkins yarn; but that does not matter much. The yarn holds its dye just the same.

Old Deb and Other Old Colony Witches

"AFTER you pass Carver Green on the old road from the bay to Plymouth," said one of these women, "you will see a green hollow in a field. It is Witches' Hollow, and is green in winter and summer, and on moonlit nights witches have been seen dancing in it to the music of a fiddle played by an old black man. I never saw them, but I know people who saw witches dancing there. In a small house near the hollow, a little old woman lived who was a witch; she went by the name of Old Betty, and she danced on the green with the devil as a partner. There was an old man who lived in that neighborhood by himself; he was kind to Betty, giving her food and firewood. After a while he got tired of her and told her she must keep away. One day he caught her there and put her in a bag, and locked the bag in a closet, and put the key in his pocket, and went away to his work. While he was gone, she got out of the bag and unlocked the door. Then she got his pig, dog, cat, and rooster, put them into the bag, put the bag in the closet and hid herself. When the man came home the animals in the bag were making a dreadful noise. 'Ah, ha! Old Betty, there you are!' said the man. He took the bag and dashed it on his doorstone, and the old woman laughed and cried out, 'You hain't killed Old Betty yet!' "

Another story told by the old women was of two witches who lived in Plymouth woods, near the head of Buzzard's Bay, who never went out in the daytime; but in the evening twilight they walked out "casting spells." They cast a spell on a boy, compelling him to follow them home. Putting him to bed in a lower room, they went up a ladder into the loft. At midnight the boy saw them come down the ladder, go to the oven, and take out a quahog shell. Each witch rubbed it behind her ears and said "Whisk!" when each flew up the chimney. The boy got up and rubbed the shell behind his ears; immediately he went up the chimney and found himself standing outdoors beside the witches, who were sitting astride black horses in the yard. On seeing the boy one of them dismounted, went into the house and returned with a "witch bridle" and a bundle of straw. She flung the bridle over the straw, and out of it came a pony. The boy was put on the pony's back, and away the three cantered across a large meadow, until they came to a brook. The witches cleared the brook at a leap; but the boy, when he cleared it, said to his pony, "A pretty good jump for a lousy calf!" Those words broke the spell; the pony vanished, the boy stood alone with the bridle and the straw. He now ran after the witches, and soon he came to an old deserted house in which he heard the sound of fiddles. He peeped in a window and saw a black man fiddling, and the two witches and other old women dancing around him. Frightened, he ran down the

---

From *The Old Colony Town and Other Sketches*, by William Root Bliss, pp. 104–112. Copyright, 1893, by William Root Bliss. Boston and New York: Houghton Mifflin Company.

road until he came to a farmhouse. He knocked on the door, was admitted, and the next day the farmer carried him to his parents.

The old women who told the witch stories said that their grandmother had been personally acquainted with two witches, in the last century. One of these was named Deborah Borden, called at that day "Deb Burden," who was supposed to have caused a great deal of mischief in Wareham, Rochester, and Middleboro. It was thought to be necessary for farmers to keep in her good graces lest she should cause a murrain to come upon cattle, lest the rye refuse to head, and the corn to ear. She was a weaver of cloth and rag carpets. Woe to the unlucky housewife who worried Deb or hurried her at her looms! I will let one of the sisters relate her story of this sorceress. It is not probable that the relator had ever heard of Robert Burns' story of Tam O'Shanter and his gray mare Meg; but a running brook filled the same place in that story and in this:—

"Once my grandmother had a web of cloth in Deb's looms, so she sent my mother and a girl named Phebe after it. The two girls were just as intimate as finger and thumb. They went to Deb's house and told her what my grandmother said, and it made her mad, 'cause she didn't like to be hurried. Near her back door was a tree full of red apples, and Phebe, said, 'Won't you please give me an apple?' and Deb said, 'Drat you! No, I won't!' My mother wasn't afraid, so she took an apple for Phebe and one for herself, and she said to Deb:—

" 'I ain't afraid of ye, ye old witch!'

" 'Ye ain't?' Deb screamed; 'then I'll make ye afraid afore ye git home!'

"They had a piece of woods to go through; in the middle of it there was a pair of bars, and on the other side of the bars there was a brook. Suddenly they heard a roaring and they saw a black bull coming. 'Oh!' said Phebe, 'Captain Besse's bull has got out and he will get us'; so they ran for the bars. They got through them and across the brook, when the bull leaped the bars and stopped on the edge of the brook and roared; then my mother knew it was old Deb Burden who was in the bull to frighten the girls, because the brook stopped the critter. Witches can't cross running water, you know.

"The girls reached home dreadfully frightened, and told what had happened. 'Never mind,' said my grandfather; 'I'll fix Debbie!' When she brought home the cloth, he came into the house and slipped behind her as she sat by the fire, and put a darning-needle through her dress and fastened her to the chair. Well, she sot; and every once in a while she said, 'I must go'; but she couldn't stir; she would be still for a while and then say, 'Why, I must go and tend my fire'; but she couldn't stir no more'n a milestone; and he kept her in the chair all day, and then he pulled out the needle and let her go. 'Scare my gal agin, ye old witch!' he said. You know witches can't do anything when steel is nigh, and that was the reason the darning-needle held her.

"Once Deb came to Thankful Haskell's in Rochester, and sot by the fire, and her daughter, fourteen year old, was sweeping the room, and she put the broom under Deb's chair. You can't insult a witch more than that, 'cause a broomstick is what they ride on when they go off on mischief. Deb was mad as a March hare, and she cussed the child. Next day the child was taken sick, and all the doctors gin her up, and they sent for old Dr. Bemis of Middleboro; he put on his spectacles and looked at her, and said he, 'This child is bewitched; go, somebody, and see what Deb is up to.' Mr. Haskell got on his horse and rode to Deb's house; there was nobody in but a big black cat; this was the devil, and witches always leave him to take care of the house when they go out. Mr. Haskell looked around for Deb, and he saw her down to the bottom of the garden by a pool of water, and she was making images out of clay and sticking in pins. As quick as he saw her he knew what ailed the child; so he laid his whip around her shoulders good, and said, 'Stop that, Deb, or you shall be burnt alive!' She whimpered, and the black cat came out and growled and spread his tail, but Mr. Haskell laid on the whip, and at last she screamed, 'Your young one shall git well!' and that child began to mend right off. The black cat disappeared all of a suddint and Mr. Haskell thought the earth opened and took him in."

"Moll Ellis was called the witch of Plymouth," said the other sister, taking up the story-telling. "She got a grudge agin Mr. Stevens, a man my grandfather worked for, and three years runnin' she cast a spell on the cattle and horses, and upsot his hay in a brook. My grandfather drove and Stevens was on the load, and when they came to the brook the oxen snorted, and the horses reared and sweat, and they all backed and the hay was upsot into the brook. One day Stevens said, 'I'll not stand this; I'll go and see what Moll Ellis is about.' So he went up to her house, and there she lay on her back a-chewin' and a-mutterin' dretful spell words, and as quick as Stevens saw her he knew what ailed his cattle; and he walked right up to the bed, and he told Moll, 'If you ever upset another load of hay I'll have you hung for a witch.' She was dretful scart, and promised she never would harm him again. When she was talking, a little black devil, that looked just like a bumblebee, flew into the window and popped down her throat; 't was the one she had sent out to scare the cattle and horses. When Moll died, they couldn't get the coffin out the door because it had a steel latch; they had to put it out the window."

The Witch-Weaver

One of these Narragansett women-weavers was a witch. She would sit for hours bending over her loom, silent, peering into it and not doing a single row. This angered the dames for whom she worked, but they said nothing, lest they get her ill-will. Suddenly she would sit up and start her

---

From *In Old Narragansett,* Romances and Realities, by Alice Morse Earle, pp. 46–50.

treadle; bang! bang! would go her batten as fast as corn in a corn-popper; and at night, after she had gone home, when her piece was still set in the loom, the family would waken and hear the half-toned clapping of the loom, which someone was running softly to help the witch out in her stint, probably the old black man. So, behold! at the end of the week more cloth appeared on the cloth-beam, more linen was ready for bleaching, and more rolls of carpet were woven than could be turned out by any man-weaver in the province. So whether it was hitching up with the devil or not, she always had employment in plenty; and her fine linen table-cloths were in every bridal outfit, and her linen web used in many a shroud throughout Narragansett.

She never ate with the family of her employer as did every other worker in house or on farm, nor was it evident that she brought food with her. The minister suspected she ate nocake, which she could easily hide in her pockets. She never asked for water, nor cider, nor switchel, nor kill-devil, nor had anyone ever seen her drink. Debby Nichols once saw a bumble-bee fly buzz-buzz out of her mouth as she wove in the minister's loom-loft. But the minister said it was only a hornet flying past her—the garret was full of them. But, sure enough, at that very hour Joe Spink fell from his horse on the old Pequot trail from Wickford and broke his leg. Joe said a big bumble-bee had stung the horse on the nose and made him rear and plunge. Joe had high words with the witch over some metheglin he had tried to buy from her the previous week, for she brewed as well as she wove. The minister said that if metheglin had been the only drink Joe ever bought he wouldn't have fallen from his horse, and that it wasn't the first bee Joe had had in his bonnet.

One day some careless darkies in a kitchen set on fire a hank of tow that was being hetchelled by the chimney-side. The sudden blaze extended to a row of freshly ironed sheets, then to a wool-wheel, and soon a dense smoke and darting flames filled the room. All ran out of the house, some for water, some for buckets, some for help, and no one thought of the witch in the loom-loft. The bang and rattle of her work made her ignorant of the noise and commotion below, and as the smoke entered the loft she thought, "But that chimney do smoke!" Finally a conviction of danger came to her and she made her way down the loft-ladder and through the entry with difficulty to the open air.

"Where's the cat?" was her abrupt greeting to the shame-faced folk who began to apologize spasmodically for their neglect to alarm her. "I saw her an hour ago on the spare bed in the fore room"—and back into the house rushed the witch, to return in a few moments with Tabby safely in her arms. This act of course deserved scant praise. Everyone murmured that there was probably some good reason for doing it, that everyone knew witches and cats had close relations, that the house didn't burn down anyway, and probably she knew it wasn't going to.

One night a neighbor met her, breathing heavily, her hand at her side, hobbling haltingly homeward. He told his wife he guessed the witch was pretty sick. She told the minister's wife that the witch was getting her deserts. The latter in turn told her husband, and during a ministerial visit the next day he discoursed profitably on the probable illness and the unsanctified life of that misguided woman. The minister sat long in the front room sipping sangaree, but the hard-working little tailoress in the kitchen overheard his moralizing and his story. And when goose and shears were laid aside, and her day's work was over, she hurried through the winter gloaming, across the ice-crusts of three fields, to the witch's door. No light shone from the window, either of evil or domestic significance; but the tailoress pulled the latch-string and pushed open the door, and by the light of her hand-lantern found the witch in the chilled house cold and dead.

The following August a band of wondering, marauding boys, with alternate hesitation and bravado, entered the tenantless house. The windows had all been broken by missiles thrown by witch-hating passersby, and the spring rains and summer suns had freely entered the room. And lo! the witch's bed, on which she died—a sack full of straw of mouse-barley, with occasional spikes of grain attached—had sprouted and grown through the course hempen bed-tick, and was as green and flourishing as the grass over her unmarked grave.

Tom Dunn's Dance on Rag Rock

Rag Rock, in which Wabanowi had his long sleep, was a home of sprites and demons down to the nineteenth century. Thomas Dunn knew this, and on ordinary nights he would have taken all manner of long cuts around it, for he had no fondness for things not of this world, whether they were ghosts or gospels. But on the night of his dance, having been to a husking-bee where he had "kept his spirits up by pouring spirits down," and having found so many red ears that he was in a state of high self-satisfaction, for he had kissed his pretty partner twenty times, he spunked up and chanced it straight across the hill. As he approached he saw a glow among the trees and heard a fiddle going—going like mad. He buffeted his way through the thicket to see who of his towns-people were holding a picnic in the moonshine and dancing to such sacrilegious music; for there was dancing; he could hear the shuffle of feet. In a minute he had reached the edge of a glade lighted by torches and found there a richly dressed and merry company tripping it with such spirit as he had never seen before. He dearly liked to shake a leg in a jig or reel, and a chance like this was not to be withstood. He entered the ring, bowing and all a-grin, and was welcomed with a shout. On a hummock of moss sat a maid without a partner, a maid whose black eyes snapped with mischief, whose cheeks and lips were rosy,

---

From *American Myths and Legends*, by Charles M. Skinner, Vol. I, pp. 69–73. Copyright, 1903, by J. B. Lippincott. Philadelphia and London.

and whose skirt, raised a trifle higher than common, showed a pair of marvellous neat ankles. The invitation in her smile and sidelong glance were not to be resisted. Tom caught her by the waist, dragged her to her feet, and whirled off with her into the gayest, wildest dance he had ever led. He seemed to soar above the earth. After a time he found that the others had seated themselves and were watching him. This put him on his mettle, and the violin put lightning into his heels. He feated it superbly and won round on round of applause. He and the girl had separated for a matter of six feet and had set in to dance each other down. As he leaped and whirled and cracked his heels in the air in an ecstasy of motion and existence, Tom noticed with pain that the freshness was leaving his partner's face, that it was becoming longer, the eyes deeper and harder. This pain deepened into dismay when he saw that the eyes had turned green and evil, the teeth had projected, sharp and yellow, below the lip, the form had grown lank and withered. He realized at last that it was the demon crew of the hill with which he was in company, and his heart grew so heavy that he could barely leap with it inside of him, yet leap he must, for he was lost unless he could keep up the dance till sunrise or unless a clergyman should order him to stop—which was not a likely thing to happen. So he flung off his coat, hat, vest, and tie and settled into a business jog. The moon was setting. In two hours he would be free, and then—a cramp caught him in the calf, and with a roar of "God save me!" he tumbled on his back.

The cry did save him, for a witch cannot endure to hear the name of God. He saw a brief vision of scurrying forms, heard growling, hissing, and cursing in strange phrases, realized for a second that a hideous shape hung threatening over him, was blinded by a flame that stank of sulphur, then he saw and heard no more till daylight. If he was drunk, and imagined all this, how can one explain the two portraits of the witch he danced with? They were etched in fire on the handle of his jack-knife, one as she appeared when he met her, the other as she looked when his eyes were closing. A fever followed this adventure. After he had regained his health Tom took to himself a wife, joined the church, forsook all entertainments, drank tea, and became a steady workman. He recovered his peace of mind, died a deacon, and was rewarded by having a cherub with a toothache sculptured on his gravestone.

Killing the Witch

Old Meg [1]

We can easily bring the age of credulity as far forward as the middle of the last century, by means of a local legend in which mediaeval super-

[1] From *A Book of New England Legends and Folk Lore, in Prose and Poetry,* by Samuel Adams Drake, New and Revised Edition, pp. 259–260. Copyright, 1883, 1901, by Samuel Adams Drake. Boston: Little, Brown, and Company. 1910.

stition respecting witches survives in full vigor. The test of the silver bullet recalls the weird incantation scene in "Der Freischütz," and all the demon lore associated with the gloomy depths of the Hartz.

There was a reputed witch by the name of Margaret Wesson, and familiarly known by the name of "Old Meg," who once resided in Gloucester. After having been for many years the object of superstitious curiosity and dread to the inhabitants of the Cape, she at length came to her end in the following strange and mysterious manner. At the time of the celebrated victorious siege of Louisburg by the Colonial troops in 1745, two soldiers of the Massachusetts line belonging to Gloucester happened to have their attention drawn to the movements of a crow that kept hovering over them. They threw stones, and then fired their muskets at it, but could neither touch nor terrify it; the bird still continued flying round them and cawing horribly in their ears. At length it occurred to one of them that it might be Old Meg. He communicated his suspicions to his comrade; and as nothing but silver was believed to have any power to injure a witch, they cut the silver buttons off from their uniform coats and discharged them at the crow. The experiment succeeded. At the first shot they broke its leg; at the second it fell dead at their feet. When they returned to Gloucester, they learned that Old Meg had broken her leg while walking by the fort in that place at the precise time when they had shot and killed the crow five hundred miles distant; after lingering for a while in great agony she died. And now comes the singular part of the story; for upon examining her fractured limb, the identical silver buttons which the soldiers had fired from their muskets under the walls of Louisburg were extracted from the flesh. The story of Old Meg was long familiarly told in Gloucester, although the credulity which once received it as solemn truth has nearly, if not quite, passed away, says the Reverend Charles W. Upham, who makes the statement so lately as 1832. It has, however, been reproduced among the sober records of fact contained in Mr. Babson's "History of Gloucester."

Granny Mott [2]

Near 1740, there lived in Hopkinton (then Westerly) an old woman called Granny Mott, who had a reputation of being a witch. It is told that she would ride a smooth-shod horse upon the ice with the greatest speed. She once came to the house of Thomas Potter to procure work. Mr. Potter's son Stephen was playing about the floor, when one of the older children whispered to him to stick an awl in the old woman's chair. She sat

[2] From *Westerly (Rhode Island) and Its Witnesses,* for Two Hundred and Fifty Years, 1626–1876, Including Charlestown, Hopkinton, and Richmond, Until Their Separate Organization, with the Principal Points of Their Subsequent History, by Rev. Frederic Denison, A. M., pp. 165–166. Entered according to Act of Congress, in the year 1878, by Frederic Denison, in the Office of the Librarian of Congress, at Washington, D. C. Providence: Published by J. A. & R. A. Reid.

immovable for hours, until the family became convinced of her character, and removed the awl. Ever after, when she visited the house, she would stand or sit upon a chest or bed, however many chairs might be near. One of her neighbors was much annoyed by a flock of heath-hens, the head one of which would fly close around him, and bid defiance to his oft-repeated shots. He finally cut a silver button from his coat, and loaded his gun, and thus brought down the troublesome bird. He soon heard that Granny Mott was sick unto death; she was attended by her daughter, who refused all assistance in preparing the body for interment, and permitted others simply to bury her. This secrecy was employed to prevent persons from discovering the wound inflicted by the silver button.

Molly Bridget [3]

. . . Portsmouth had another witch—a tangible witch in this instance—one Molly Bridget, who cast her malign spell on the eleemosynary pigs at the Almshouse, where she chanced to reside at the moment. The pigs were manifestly bewitched, and Mr. Clement March, the superintendent of the institution, saw only one remedy at hand, and that was to cut off and burn the tips of their tails. But when the tips were cut off they disappeared, and it was in consequence quite impracticable to burn them. Mr. March, who was a gentleman of expedients, ordered that all the chips and underbrush in the yard should be made into heaps and consumed, hoping thus to catch and do away with the mysterious and provoking extremities. The fires were no sooner lighted than Molly Bridget rushed from room to room in a state of frenzy. With the dying flames her own vitality subsided, and she was dead before the ash-piles were cool. . . .

The Witch Sheep

In Reality [1]

At the time of the great storm before alluded to, my father had a small flock of sheep which was placed under the care of old Benny Nichols, so often referred to in these papers. Among these sheep were two ewes of the

---

[3] From *An Old Town by the Sea,* by Thomas Bailey Aldrich, pp. 72–73. Copyright, 1883 and 1893, by T. B. Aldrich. Boston and New York: Houghton, Mifflin and Company. 1894.

[1] From *Recollections of Olden Times:* Rowland Robinson of Narragansett and His Unfortunate Daughter, With Genealogies of the Robinson and Hazard Families of Rhode Island, by Thomas R. Hazard, "Shepherd Tom," in His Eighty-First and Eighty-Second Years; Also Genealogical Sketch of the Hazards of the Middle States, by Willis P. Hazard, of Westchester, Pa., pp. 81–82. Entered according to Act of Congress, in the year 1879, by John P. Sanborn, in the Office of the Librarian of Congress, at Washington, D. C. Newport, Rhode Island.

creeper or otter sheep, so called, it is supposed, from the peculiar shortness of their legs. One of these sheep lay drifted under a snow-bank twenty-one days. The place where it lay was discovered by old Benny, from chancing to notice a small hole in the snow not bigger than his finger, called "a breathing hole," that was made, as is usually the case, by the warm breath of the sheep underneath. When taken out the poor thing was almost naked, having eaten off its own wool as far as it was within reach. Old Debby Nichols—Benjamin's wife—fed the sheep, at first very cautiously with a little warm milk, gradually increasing the quantity until it got strong enough to digest its ordinary food. When restored to health, the old woman dressed the naked sheep in a suit of clothes made out of old ragged garments of her husband's. It was several days, however, before the flock would permit its approach in so unsightly a garb. My father gave me these two creeper sheep, and their two years' fleeces, together with one fleece from their progeny, constituted the sole capital with which I engaged in the woolen manufacturing business, in 1814, when I was in my seventeenth year.

In Romance [2]

In the darkness of Christmas morning, in the year 1811, old Benny Nichols could not sleep. He was not thinking of Santa Claus nor of Christmas gifts; he was watching for the first gray dawn which marked his regular rising hour, and he tossed and turned, wondering why he was so wakeful, until at last he rose in despair and lighted a candle to discover how long he had to wait ere daybreak. To his amazement he found the hands of the old clock pointing to the hour of nine, and as he stood shivering, candle in hand, staring at the apparently deceitful, bland face the clock raised its voice and struck nine, loudly and brassily, as if to prove that its hands and face told the truth. Benny then walked quickly to the window, and saw that the apparent darkness and length of the night came from a great wall of snow which covered the entire window and which had nearly all fallen since the previous sunset.

Keenly awake at once when he recognized the lateness of the hour, the old man wakened his wife Debby, and bade her "hurry up and git somethin' to eat. It's nine o'clock, and we've had the wust snowstorm ye ever see, and me a-layin' here in bed, and them new sheep a-walkin' into the sea and gittin' drownded!"

Benny was a weazened-faced, dried-up old man, who was the shepherd of a large Narragansett farm which lay between Pender Zeke's Corner and the bay. He knew well the danger that came to sheep in a heavy snowstorm. He had seen a great flock of a hundred timid, shrinking creatures retreat and cower one behind the other to shelter themselves from the fierce beating of the wind and sleet, until, in spite of his efforts, all were edged

---

[2] From *In Old Narragansett, Romances and Realities,* by Alice Morse Earle, pp. 105–119. Copyright, 1898, by Charles Scribner's Sons. New York.

into the sea and lost, save a half-dozen whose throats were cut by him with a jack-knife to save the mutton. Without waiting for any warm food, he cautiously opened the door to dig himself out.

"Ye can't go out, Benny Nichols, in them shoes," said Debby, firmly. "I told ye long ago they was half wore out—here, put on yer Sunday long-boots."

This suggestion was a bitter one to prudent Benny, who expected to have those boots for Sunday wear for the next ten years, just as he had for the past ten; and he knew well what a hard day's work he had before him, and how destructive it would prove to shoe-leather. But Debby was firm, and, seizing the great boots from the nail on which they hung, she poured out the flax-seed with which they were always kept filled when they were not on Benny's feet. The old man pulled them on his shrivelled legs with a groan at Debby's extravagance, and then proceeded to dig out a path in the snow. Benny had not seen such a snow-storm since the great "Hessian snow-storm" in the winter of 1778, when so many Hessian soldiers perished of cold and exposure. When he reached the surface and could look around him, he saw with satisfaction that the snow and wind had blown during the previous night *away* from the water, hence his sheep would hardly be drowned. He quickly discovered a strange-shaped bank of snow by the side of one of the great hay-ricks, so common throughout Narragansett, and he shrewdly suspected that some of his sheep were underneath the great drift. When carefully searched with a rake-stale this proved to be the case, and when he shovelled them out all in the mound were alive and well. In a snow-drift, by the side of a high stone wall, he found the remainder of his flock, save one, a fine little ewe of the creeper breed, the rarest and most valued of all his stock. As sheepsheds at that time were unknown in Narragansett, the loss of sheep was great in the Christmas storm, and many cattle were frozen in the drifts; and one shepherd noted two weeks later that the hungry cattle he foddered never touched a full lock of hay that he had thrown on the top of a little hillock of snow near his rick. So he thrust at it with his hay-tines, and in so doing he lifted off a great shell of snow-crust, and there peered out of the whiteness the bronze, wrinkled face of the old squaw Betty Aaron, who was sitting bolt upright, frozen stiff and dead, her chin resting on both hands, her elbows on her knees. Hence Benny was justly proud of his rescued flock, though he mourned the one sheep that was lost, and blamed himself for sleeping so late, saying, he "wouldn't have minded spilin' his roast-meat boots if he could have found the creeper."

On the fourteenth day of January Benny Nichols chanced to see in the snow, by the side of a hay-rick which stood a mile away from his home, a small hole about half an inch in diameter,, which his practised eye recognized at once as a "breathing-hole," and which indicated that some living thing had been snowed in and was lying underneath. He broke away the covering of icy crust, and to his amazement saw a poor creature of extraordinary appearance, which he at first hardly could believe was his own lost creeper sheep. She was alive, but alas! in such a sorry plight.

The hungry sheep, in her three weeks' struggle against starvation, had eaten off every fibre of her own long wool that she could reach, and she lay bare and trembling in the cold air, too weak to move, too feeble to bleat either in distress or welcome. Old Benny wrapped the half-dead creature in the corner of his cloak and carried her home to Debby, who fairly shed tears at the sight of the poor naked skeleton of a sheep. Tenderly did the kind woman wrap the frozen ewe in an old flannel petticoat and feed her with warm milk, a few drops only at first, and then with much caution until the sheep was able to digest her ordinary food. In a week the creeper seemed as strong as ever, quickly gained the lost flesh, and could bleat both loud and long. And with returning health she grew active and mischievous, and was constantly thrusting her long black nose into the most unexpected and most unsuitable places, to the great distress of careful Debby, who longed to put her out of doors.

But the sheep's lost wool could not grow as quickly as did the fat on her ribs, and she could not be thrust out thus, naked and bare, in the winter air, so Debby decided to make for the little creature a false fleece. For this purpose she took an old blue coat which had once been worn by her son, and cut off the sleeves until they were the right length to cover the ewe's forelegs. She then sewed at the waist of the coat two sleeves from an old red flannel shirt; these were to cover Nanny's hind legs. And when Debby drew on the gay jacket and buttoned it up over the sheep's long backbone with the large brass coat-buttons, there never was seen such a comical, stunted, hind-side-foremost caricature of what is itself a caricature—an organ-grinder's monkey.

When Benny carried the gayly dressed Nanny out to the enclosed yard, it was hard to tell which exhibition of feeling was the keenest—poor, unconscious, and absurd Nanny's delight in her freedom and her eager desire to take her place with her old companions, or the consternation and terror of the entire flock at the strange wild beast which was thus turned loose among them.

They ran from side to side, and crowded each other against the paling so unceasingly and so wildly, that Benny carried the unwilling ewe back to the kitchen.

At nightfall, however, Benny again placed Nanny in the open field with the sheep, thinking that they would gradually, throughout the darkness, become used to the presence of her little harlequin jacket, and allow her to graze by their side in peace.

That night two cronies of Benny's came from a neighboring farm to talk over that ever-interesting topic, the great snowstorm, and to buy some of his lambs. The three old men sat by the great fireplace in the old raftered kitchen in the pleasant glow from the blazing logs, each sipping with unction a mug of Benny's famous flip, while Debby rubbed with tallow the sadly stiffened longboots that had been worn in the Christmas snow. Suddenly a loud wail of distress rang in their ears, the door was thrust violently open, and in stumbled the breathless form of the tall, gaunt old negress Tuggie Bannocks. She was a relic of old slavery times, who lived on a small farm near the old Gilbert Stuart Mill, on Petaquamscut River. They all knew her well. She had bought many a pound of wool from Benny to wash and card and spin into yarn, and she always helped Debby in that yearly trial of patience and skill—her soap-making. The old negro woman had double qualifications to make her of use in this latter work: her long, strong arms could stir the soap untiringly for hours, and then she knew also how to work powerful charms—traditional relics of Voodooism—to make the soap always turn out a success.

Tuggie Bannocks sank upon the table by the fire, murmuring: "Tanks be to Praise! Tanks be to Praise!" and closed her eyes in speechless exhaustion. Debby took a half-crushed basket of eggs from the old woman's arm, drew off her red woollen mittens, and rubbed briskly her long cold claws of hands. Benny had a vague remembrance of the old-time "emergency" saying, "feathers for fainters," and seized a turkey's wing that was in daily use as a hearthbrush, thrust it into the flames, and then held the scorching feathers under the old negress's nose until all in the room were coughing and choking with the stifling smoke.

Spluttering and choking at the dense feather-smoke, Tuggie gasped out: "I ain't dead yit—I specks I shall be soon, dough—kase I seen de ole witch a-ridin'—I'se most skeered to death" (then in a fainter voice)—"gib me a mug of dat flip." Startled, Benny quickly drew a great mug of home-brewed beer and gave it a liberal dash of Jamaica rum and sugar, then seized from the fire the red-hot "loggerhead" and thrust it seething into the liquid until the flip boiled and bubbled and acquired that burnt, bitter flavor that he knew Tuggie dearly loved. The old woman moaned and groaned as she lay on the table-top, but watched the brewing of the flip with eager eye, and sat up with alacrity to drink it.

With many a shuddering sigh and many a glance behind her at the kitchen door, and crossing her fingers to ward off evil spirits she began: "Ye know, Miss Nickkels, I telled ye I was witch-rid by ole Mum Amey, an' dis how I know I was. Ye see I was a-goin' to wuk a charm on her first off—not to hurt her none, jess to bodder her a leetle—an' I jess put my project on de fire one night, an' it jess a-goin' to boil, an' in come her ugly, ole grinnin' black face at de door, an' say she a-goin' to set wid me a spell." Mum Amey was a wrinkled half-breed Indian of fabulous age and crabbed temper, a "squaw-nurse," who was, of course, not half as black as negro Tuggie. "She walk ober to de chimbly to light her pipe an' ask me what I a-cookin', an' I say Ise a-makin' glue, cause Ise afeard she see de rabbit's foot in de pot, an' I say it all done, an' yank de pot offen de crane so she can't see into it. An' ob course when I take de project offen de fire afore it's wukked, it break de charm; an' wuss still, I can't nebber try no project on her no more. Ole Mum Amey larf, an' say, a-leerin' at me, dat pot ob glue won't nebber stick nothin' no more. An' ebber sence dat night I ben witch-rid. Mornin's when I wakes up I sees marks ob de bit in de corners ob my mouf, where Mum Amey ben a-ridin' me all ober Boston Neck an' up de Ridge Hill till I so tired and stiff I can't hardly move. Ise ben pinched in de night an' hab my ha'r pulled. An' my butter won't come till I drops a red-hot horseshoe in de cream to dribe her out. One day I jess try her to see ef she a witch (dough I know she one, 'cause I see her talkin' to a black cat); I drop a silber sixpence in her path, an' jess afore she get to it she turn an' go back, jess I know she would. No witch can't step ober silber. An' now, Benny Nickkels, I know for shore she's a witch, I see her jess now in de moonlight a-chasin' an' ridin' your sheep; an', shore's yer bawn, yer'll find some on 'em stone dead in de mornin'—all on 'em, mebbe!"

Benny looked wretched enough at this statement. Dearly as he loved his sheep and ready as he was to face physical discomfort and danger in their behalf, he was too superstitious to dare to go out in the night to rescue them and brave the witch.

"How did she look, Tuggie? And what did she do?" whispered awe-struck Debby.

"Oh, she was mons'ous fearsome to see! Witches don't nebber go in deir own form when dey goes to deir Sabbaths. She was long an' low like a snake. She run along de groun' jess like a derminted yeller painter, a-boundin', an' leapin', an' springin', a-chasin' dem pore sheeps—oh, how dey run! Wid her old red an' blue blanket tied tight aroun' her—dat's how I knowed her. An' she had big sparklin' gold dollars on her back—wages ob de debbil, I 'specks. Sometimes she jump in de air an' spread her wings an' fly awhile. Smoke an' sparks come outen her mouf an' nos-trums! Big black horns stick outen her head! Lash her long black tail jess like de debbil hisself!"

At this dramatic and breathless point in Tuggie's flip-nourished and quickly growing tale, credulous Debby, whose slow-working brain had failed to grasp all the vivid details in the black woman's fervid and imaginative description, interjected this gasping comment: "It must ha' been the devil or the creeper."

Benny jumped from his chair and stamped his foot, and at once burst into a loud laugh of intense relief, and with cheerful bravado began to explain animatedly to his open-mouthed cronies that of course anyone could see that Tuggie's sheep-chasing witch was only the creeper sheep in her new fleece, and he offered swaggeringly to go out alone to the field to bring the ewe in to prove it.

The old negress sprang to her feet, insulted and enraged at the jeering laughter and rallying jokes, and advanced threateningly toward him. Then, as if with a second thought, she stopped with a most malicious look, and in spite of Debby's conciliatory explanations and her soothing expressions "that it might have been Mum Amey after all," she thrust aside Benny's proffered mollification of a fresh mug of flip, seized her crushed basket, stalked to the door, and left the house muttering, vindictively: "High time to stop such unrageous goin's-on—dressin' up sheeps like debbils—scarin' an ole woman to death an' breakin' all her aigs! Ole Tuggie Bannocks ain't forgot how to burn a project! Guess dey won't larf at witches den!"

And surely enough—as days passed it could plainly be seen that the old negress had carried out her threat—for the chimney was "conjured"—was "salted." On windy nights the shepherd and his wife were sure they could hear Tuggie dancing and stamping on the roof, and she blew down smoke and threw down soot, and she called down the chimney in a fine, high, shrieking voice: "I'll project ye, Benny; I'll project ye." And she burnt the cakes before the fire, and the roast upon the spit, and thrice she snapped out a blazing coal and singed a hole in Debby's best petticoat, though it was worn wrong side out as a saving-charm. And Benny could see, too, that the old ram was bewitched. The remainder of the flock soon became accustomed to the sight of Nanny's funny false fleece, but he always fled in terror at her approach. He grew thin and pale (or at any rate faded), and he would scarcely eat when Nanny was near. Debby despairingly tried a few feeble counter-charms, or "warders," but without avail. When sheep-shearing time came, however, and Nanny, shorn of her uncanny fleece and clothed in her own half-inch snowy wool, took her place with the other short-clipped members of the flock, he ceased to be "witch-rid"—the "project," the "conjure" was worked out. He grew fat and fiercely brave, and became once more the knight of the field, the lord of the domain, the patriarch, the potentate of his flock.

The story of Tuggie Bannocks' fright and her revengeful "project" spread far and wide on every farm from Point Judith to Pottawomat, and was told in later years by one generation of farmers to another. And as time rolled on and Nanny reared her lambs and they her grand-lambs, the creeper sheep were known and sold throughout Narragansett by the name of witch-sheep.

The Man Who Could Send Rats

After supper when my [New Hampshire] landlady had finished doing the dishes and had sat down to sew, we heard a rat in the walls. That reminded her of a chopper who several years ago came to the house to board a few days after he got through the winter in the woods, "and he say he can make the rats go just where he please—send them any place he want; and I say, 'You a nice man—doin' such things!'

"But he say, 'That's all right. It come very handy knowing to do that sometimes'; and I tell him I don't think much of man sending rats round.

From *New England and Its Neighbors,* written and illustrated by Clifton Johnson, pp. 30–32. Copyright, 1902, by The Macmillan Company. New York. 1912.

Well, he been long time in camp, and his clothes much dirty, and he want me to wash for him, and I say, 'No, you hire some other people what does washing here.' But he was a Frenchman and didn't want to spend nothings—these French, they come from Canada, you know, and they brings everything they will need and don't want to spen' one cent. They want to take they money all back to Canada. Then he ask will I let *him* do the wash, and so I did.

"When he ready to go home, an' we settle, he don't want pay fifty cent a day, and he say, 'You wouldn't charge so much to a poor workingman,' and I say, 'I would. You heat enough for two mans together, and I got have the price what I always have.' He want to pay twenty-five cents, but I won't take only my reg'lar price.

"So he went away, and that same day a lot of railway mens come, and the house was full up; and in the night we could not none of us sleep, the rats made so much noise. It was like any one move a trunk and throw a table on the floor—make jus' as much noise as that—and no one believe that was rats. The boarders, they want know the next morning if we hear that terrible noise—that scratch and bang—and they ask if we have ghosts. We never hear any rats before and we think that Frenchman, he go away mad and he mus' make the rats of all the peoples round here come down our place. We didn't have no cat. Every cat we use to have would get fits, and some day we find it turnin' round and grab on the wall and fall on the floor; and we think the cat might jump up on the cradle and scratch the baby, and we get frightened when the cat have fits, and we kill all the time. One of the boarder, he say he heard if you steal a cat, it keep well and never have that sickness same what all the before cats had. So I say, 'If you to steal a cat have a chance, I wish you to goodness would.'

"He kind of keep lookout for cats that day and he found one on the sidewalk 'bout two mile from here; and the boarders say we fed those other cats too much meat, so we didn't any more, and we had that cat eight or nine years and we got it yet. Soon as we got it that cat begun catch rats. It catch mos' as fifteen a day and it wouldn't never eat that rats once. It catch them all night and it not through catching the next morning, but it so tired then it would not kill, but bring them to the kitchen and leave them run round, and we have to take the broom. That make the boarders laugh.

"The next fall that Frenchman come again. It mos' night, and he go to the barn, but I know him as he pass the window. My husband he milking and he not in the dark remember the man. If he have he take a stick and break his neck. The man he ask if he can get board, and my husband he say, 'My wife manage all that.' So the man come and ask me. He have a bag on his back and it been rain hard and he all wet. He say he can't go any farther; and I say, '*You* the man what send the rats any place you want to. We got lots of rats that night you left. I guess you got you bag full of rats again. No, I not keep you.'

"He never sayed anythings, but jus' walk away down the road."

The Man Who Made Weather

One of these earlier local characters, whose story borders on the marvelous, was an old man, called "Uncle Kaler," who lived on Loudon Hill. Uncle Kaler had Finnish blood in his veins and was reputed to be a "wizard." By his magical art, Uncle Kaler could make amulets that would bring good luck to the sailor, love philters for despairing swains and forlorn damsels, and efficacious potions to cure the cattle that were bewitched. This weird enchanter could also make good weather or bad weather to order, although he sometimes overdid the matter, as the following tradition shows.

Uncle Kaler lived in an old house just below the millbrook, and the road from Cobbossee to the Hook ran close by his door. One warm misty evening in May, Uncle Kaler heard some horses speeding up the hill and stopping at his door. He opened it, and a man's voice came in from the darkness: "Is this Mr. Kaler?"

"It is, at your service."

"Well, my name is ——, and this lady with me is Miss —— of Pownalboro. We are on our way to Hallowell to be married. Her relatives don't like the match and are after us hot foot. Listen!"

Away down the river could be heard the long-drawn bay of hounds.

"You hear, old man! Now our horses are about used up, and if something isn't done they will overtake us; then there will be murder. You have the reputation of being a windjammer and wizard. Here are a hundred Spanish milled dollars for the worst weather you have got, and if it does the business, another hundred when I come back."

The old man made no reply, but went to a chest and taking out a small leather bag gave it to the stranger, saying, "Go back a little on the road, cut open the bag, squeeze out its contents, throw the bag away, then come back and resume your journey."

The man did as he was told, and returning in a short time said: "If you have played us false, something will happen to you."

"Rest easy," said Uncle Kaler. "Hark!" and away in the southwest was heard a low grumbling like distant thunder. It increased and deepened momentarily till it seemed as if a cyclone was tearing through the forest.

"What is it?" asked the stranger.

"A cloud-burst in the hills. It will be a sharp hound who follows your track in five minutes. Go in peace, and good luck go with you, from a man who can make good luck."

Away they dashed through the gathering storm and darkness, speeding to happiness, or the contrary, as the case may be with married people.

From *Old Hallowell on the Kennebec,* by Emma Huntington Nason, pp. 290–292. Copyright, 1909, by Emma Huntington Nason. Augusta, Maine. 1909.

From "Van Ho," Loudon Hill.—E. H. N.

Under the roaring thunder, and nearly deafened by the roar and crash of the raging torrent he had conjured, the old man went into the house saying to himself: "I am afraid I made that bagful too strong, but I don't know as I am sorry, for it would never do to have the young people caught."

The next morning the day broke clear and beautiful; but where, the day before, a peaceful little brook had flowed through a green pasture, and the little mill had clattered merrily grinding the few grists the neighbors brought, there was now a fearful gorge gullied down to the bedrock and choked up with uprooted trees and brush; the mill was gone and the big boulder that formed a part of its foundation had been swept away far out into the river, and now forms that impediment to navigation known as Mill Rock. If anyone will take notice at low tide they will see quite a large point stretching out into the river from the mouth of the brook; it is the debris of the cloudburst.

The Fatal Glass Eye

AND why shouldn't a man use his wooden leg to brain an enemy? Wouldn't it be his natural weapon? Not a word. Of course it would. I mind a shipmate of mine, a savage from New London, down on the ship's articles as cook, but a handy man and willing, with only one arm, having had the other burned away in the bight of an out-running line with a big bull sperm at the other end. He had a wooden stump with three steel hooks at the end, kept always shiny and neat and very thefty he was with 'em either in the galley or aloft. I saw him once ungut a Lascar in Liverpool Lou's place in Sydney as tidy as you like. Could he have done such with the hand the devil gave him? He could not.

But I wanted to tell you about Liverpool Jarge, no connection with Lou. Jarge was a one-eyed man, the other having been knocked out by a bucko mate with a belaying pin. A little man he was and steady and soft-tempered like myself, and we shipped together six voyages, no less. Jarge had two hobbies: One was his tattooing and the other was his glass eyes. Ashore with his pay, Jarge wouldn't get decently drunk. Not him. He'd head in at the nearest tattoo professor and have some decoration put on him. Covered he was from neck to heel with beautiful birds and snakes and women and Christ on the cross done by a Jap between his shoulders to keep the devils off. I mind the day I climbed three pair of stairs to a tattooer's room in Whitechapel, and Jarge had his last empty spot, the size of a dollar, filled in with what the man said was a likeness of the evil eye. And Jarge cried because he was all filled up and hadn't any more white skin left, leastways not that would take ink. Talking of the eye, one thing led to another, and the professor took us down to a glass blower a

---

From *Liverpool Jarge, Yarns,* by Halliday Witherspoon, Yarn 10. Copyright, 1933, by Square Rigger Co. Boston.

floor below, and there was where Jarge got the glass eye habit. The glass blower was a Hungarian foreigner and an artist if I do say it, what with gawdy birds and full-rigged ships done out of spun glass and a line of fancy glass eyes on the side all done by himself. Jarge had been wearing an old eye he'd picked up somewhere in 'Frisco that didn't match, and when the man offered to make him a beautiful one of red with a white star in the middle for a pound he ordered it, very much taken with the idea and pleased as Punch. Next day he went back and ordered two more, one blue with a kind of a white snake, and one green with a yellow cross, the whole coming to three pound ten.

I didn't see Jarge for five years after that. We happened to meet next in London again and he had a collection of eyes, a dozen or more, three or four for every time ashore, and said he was the pride of the forecastle every ship he sailed on. I went up with Jarge while he placed his regular order, but the novelty was off and he was hard to please. So the glass man offers to make a genuine evil eye, the tattooed one being no good whatever, covered up with a shirt. And that pleased Jarge. And the man said he would make the eye hollow and fill it with a deadly poison. And that pleased Jarge, too, because he said anyone might get where he'd want to commit suicide and all he'd have to do was bite the eye and die quick. We signed aboard the same ship, the Dunreagh Castle, for Australia, and the day before we sailed Jarge got his eye and it was a work of art if I do say it. It was built in rings of different colors running down to a little red spot in the centre and was hollow and filled with a white liquid and very theftily sealed with a thin glaze of glass behind. When you looked at it hard, the rings ran together and the red spot stuck out and fair gave you the creeps. It cost the amazing sum of two pound ten which Jarge paid cheerfully.

Well, we hadn't cleared the Straits before Jarge had tried the eye on every man in our watch and the carpenter and the cook and the boy and they all, barring the boy, told him to lay off or they'd brain him. All but a little Cockney named Bell and known as Ding Dong. He fair shrivelled up and near went mad. And that pleased Jarge.

Jarge kept putting the eye on Ding Dong until he thought he was bewitched. The other men told him to steal the eye and he tried it, but Jarge was too thefty for him. And Ding Dong got to believe the only way to lift the spell was to get the eye. You wouldn't believe the lengths he went, even to trying to scoop the thing when Jarge was asleep, he having taken to wearing it all the time. It got after a while so Jarge got to hate the Cockney and believe in the eye himself and hoped to kill Ding Dong with it before the voyage was over if he had luck. Which he did at Port Said. We were laying there in the roadstead and Jarge was aloft sitting on a foot rope scraping a spar when something fetched loose and down come Jarge 40 foot head first on a teak deck and scrunched his nob like an eggshell. His eye rolled out and Ding Dong grabbed it up and the mate came running up and Ding Dong popped the eye in his mouth. In about a minute he falls on the deck and gave a couple of shivers and died. There was a good deal of mystery about it. The mate figured Jarge must have hit Ding Dong in the fall. I knew better. He'd bitten into the eye. But I said nothing. So you see a glass eye can be just as fatal as a wooden leg.

III. PLACE LORE

Local names . . . may always be regarded as records of the past, inviting and rewarding a careful historical interpretation.

—Isaac Taylor

. . . the anecdotes told to explain names are by their nature suspect; much like folk-etymologies, they are often ex post facto *concoctions, attempts to rationalize the name.*

—Frederic G. Cassidy

. . . the village street and the lonely farm and the hillside cabin became positively richer objects under the smutch of imputation; twitched with a grim effect the thinness of their mantle, shook out of its folds such crudity and levity as they might, and borrowed, for dignity, a shade of the darkness of Cenci-drama, of monstrous legend, of old Greek tragedy, and thus helped themselves out for the story-seeker more patient almost of anything than of flatness.

—Henry James

1. "A Local Habitation and a Name"

Interest in local names, as in local history generally, springs from local pride and a desire to know one's past. And Yankees are endowed with more than their share of both place-consciousness and curiosity. The former is echoed in such fervid formulations as "I have never ceased to feel my pulse quickened at the mention of the name of Westfield," [1] and the latter in the rural New Englandism, "I want to know!" [2]

In their zeal for local history, Yankees have accumulated a vast amount of local traditions, including place lore. As distinct from local legends (such as the foregoing legends of haunts, specters, witches, and the Devil), place lore proper is the lore of topographical features, landmarks, place-names, settlement, environment, local objects and traits, local rivalries, and everything else that comes under the head of *genius loci.* Much of this lore is buried in the work of local historians, antiquarians, travel and guidebook writers, local colorists, memoirists, and other chroniclers and observers of the local scene. On the family bookshelf the town or country history (generally sold by agents and by subscription) occupied a place next to the Bible and the almanac; and in the continuity of oral tradition,

[1] *The Westfield Jubilee* (Westfield, 1870), p. 27.

[2] Samuel McChord Crothers, *The Gentle Reader* (Boston, 1903), p. 136.

handed down from father to son, as well as in the living memory of old-timers, local tradition was gospel, gossip, and guesswork.

Just as Yankees have insisted on their right to be "characters," especially "Yankee characters," so they have insisted on the right of every locality to its characteristic traditions. And where recorded history has failed to provide them, unwritten history or pseudo-history has been quick to supply *ex post facto* accounts.

But even apocryphal explanations of history, including the history of place-names, have indirect historical value, inasmuch as they "sometimes furnish under the guise of fiction useful clues to the real facts" and (in the case of place names), "whether fact or fiction, frequently shape and control their forms and fortunes."[1] Outside of history, such explanations, as Reverend Livermore said of the legend of the *Palatine* Light, afford considerable gratification of the taste for the marvelous.

In the study of place-names Americans have the advantage of being close to the beginnings and so to the documentary sources. Thus in the accounts of early voyagers, as when Captain Gosnold tells us how he named Cape Cod (which narrowly escaped being "Shoal Hope"), we see geography as well as history in the making. In after-the-fact explanations of place-names, a guess is occasionally right, but more often history is written or rewritten to suit the whims of romantic or facetious fancy.

At the root of many fanciful derivations is the need of making the unfamiliar familiar, according to the process of folk-etymology. This process results, on the one hand, in the garbling of Indian and foreign names into what sounds like the nearest English equivalent, and, on the other, in outlandish coinages or outrageous fabrications based on an assumed etymology. Other place-name stories originate in casual or accidental names, arising "either from an immediate circumstance attending the giving of the name, a happening, an object present, a natural feature of the landscape, or from memory association with other places or names."[2]

Among the more specious and spurious place-name stories Indian or pseudo-Indian fancies run a close second to the haunts of the Devil, in persistence and in mediocrity. For the folklorist they have the interest of migratory legends (*e.g.*, the Lovers' Leap and Pocahontas motifs)—a species of traveling local legend which always turns up like a bad penny. They also have the historical interest of period-pieces, since in both their style and their content, they reflect the taste of a past generation—a generation that apparently attempted to make amends for exterminating the Indian by romanticizing him, only to continue to kill him off by suicide, as if the only good Indian was an Indian who died for love. Indian legends also appealed to the taste for the exotic, seen, in another direction, in the naming of towns for places like Peru.

2. "More Patient Almost of Anything than of Flatness"

Although place-names serve as a focus for all the "recorded incidents and the floating traditions" that hold local associations for Yankees, other

[1] Robert L. Ramsay, Foreword to Frederic G. Cassidy's *The Place-Names of Dane County, Wisconsin,* Publication of the American Dialect Society Number 7 (April, 1947), p. 5.

[2] George Philip Krapp, *The English Language in America* (New York, 1925), Vol. I, p. 188.

place traditions occupy the borderland between history and folklore which is pseudo-history or pseudo-folklore. At various points these stories touch on the lore of local characters, tall tales, and customs. But their identification with a particular locale and the details of local color give them a special local flavor and a special appeal to local pride or prejudice.

Local bias creeps into origin legends like the Devil's Ash Heap, with their "deliberate slur born of malice"; into stories of neighborhood feuds, with their resultant splits and secessions; and into controversies over the relative merits of Narragansett and Boston brown bread and Massachusetts (or New England) and Rhode Island (or Manhattan) clam chowder. Some of these innuendoes and slanders are born of actual town rivalries, as between Windsor and Hartford, while others are simply in the nature of invidious comparison, as in Cape Cod rivalries.

Finally, since a good yarn knows no limitations of time or place, local rivalry reaches the point where several localities claim their version to be the original one.

B. A. B.

THE ART OF NAMING PLACES

There Are No Peruvians in Peru

. . . Not only has it pleased the good people of New England to decorate their towns with every name that is of note, in ancient or in modern, in profane or in sacred history, but they have often applied these names in immediate contempt of things; calling north, south; towns, shires; and hills, vales. A day's ride will carry a man from Middlesex to Jericho, and thence to Athens, Corinth, Hyde Park, Peru, Jamaica, Georgia, Bristol, China, Guildhall, *Vershire,* Scotland, Mount Tabor, Babylon, Bedlam, Padanaram and Cheapside. It is an even chance, but on reaching Mount Tabor, he finds a plain; and so of the other denominations; except, indeed, that he may be sure of wit and elegance in Athens, and splendid luxury in Corinth. He shall find Ash*ford* upon a hill; Dan*bury* and Marl*borough* where there is no *borough;* and Cumberland where the *Cymbri* was never heard of. Even names of original composition are equally destitute of meaning; there is no *borough* in New England, unless all its towns be boroughs, in fact though not in name; and yet we read of Dewey's*burgh* and Green's*borough*.

Hapless he, whose imagination is mocked with the name of his native village, far left under the canopy of other skies! When the sun rises, he sets forth, half promising himself to behold the dark and ivied battlements of its church, empurpled by the evening ray. Evening descends, and

---

From *Travels through the Northern Parts of the United States, in the Year 1807 and 1808,* by Edward Augustus Kendall, Esq., Vol. I, pp. 117–121. New York: Printed and published by I. Riley. 1809.

he is told that he has performed his journey; but, the church, the copse, the gardens and the cottages, where are they?

Nor is it enough that he reconciles himself to the new association, and learns that there may be a Delhi without palaces or pagodas, without baths or palm-trees, but with wide acres of stumps and trunks of trees, naked, gray and black; and here and there a hut of logs. This is not enough. The name returns upon him thrice in a day; he travels from Pekin in the morning, and he sleeps at Pekin at night. But the Pekin of the morning was a sea-port or a mountain; and the Pekin of the night is a cluster of saw-mills. Every state, and sometimes every county, recurs to the same names.

In the earlier periods of the colonies, the license was somewhat less extravagant; because, though names were arbitrarily borrowed and imposed, yet there was some motive, some sentiment, directing the choice; and names of places are rational, when they have reference to a historical fact, as much as when they are purely geographical. The name of a founder, or of the birth-place or residence of a founder, may be fairly given, upon principles of natural pride, or natural affection; and a kindred motive often led the first colonists of New England to name their towns after the birth-places of former residences of their favorite clergy. But, now, little of this sort is regarded. There are no Peruvians in Peru, nor Chinese in China, nor aldermen nor giants in the glens and forests of Guildhall. It is matter of fact, that the choice is often made on no other principles than that a name sounds prettily on the ear. Persons, appointed on committees for naming towns, have told me, that their resource had been, to turn over a gazetteer, and cull from the alphabet a few well sounding names. The lists had been then submitted to the town-meeting, and the choice effected.

In a town in Maine, I was informed, that a different name from that which that town now bears, had been at first imposed by vote of the town-meeting; but, a principal inhabitant, who arrived a little too late, on promising his neighbors a cask of rum, procured the vote to be rescinded, and his own name to be received. Towns often change their names.

I heartily join in the regrets of those who wish that the Indian names of places had been more generally preserved; and this, not from any idle preference of a foreign language to my mother tongue, nor from any particular admiration of the sounds; but, from the agreement which those names possessed with the places they denoted. The savage has no temptation to that spirit of mean mimicry which so often disfigures lettered society; and he must call things by their right names, or it is in vain that he calls them by any. When he speaks of *the bend of river,* he means the bend of a river, and not a forest, a lake nor an island. It is the same when he speaks of an island, of a cataract, or of the basin at the cataract's foot. Such is the description of the Indian names that are still retained; and description, as being almost peculiar to these names, stamps them almost exclusively with the character of *classic,* in the whole nomenclature that embraces them. The rest exhibit a senseless heap; and if the reader turn with impatience from its barbarism, let him at least pity the pen that here commits it to paper!

Yankee Flavor

DURING the eighteenth century, by some alchemy, the Puritan was transmuted into the Yankee. Separated from the other colonies by the bottleneck of the Dutch-speaking Hudson Valley, the New Englanders went their own ways. They still said *brook* and *notch*. The Maine people developed the use of *stream*. At first perhaps this denoted the water flowing from a certain pond or lake, so that Mopang Stream was said in distinction from Mopang Pond; it came, however, to mean any flowing water, between a brook and a river in size. The usage spread into northern New Hampshire and Vermont, and emigrants took it westward into the Adirondacks. *Intervale* was another northern word. Zadock Thompson, Vermont historian, explained it with rare exactitude:

> It may be derived from *inter*—within, and *vallis*—a vale, or valley; and in its specific signification, it denotes those alluvial flats, lying along the margins of streams, which have been, or occasionally are, overflowed.[1]

Another word arose from the frustrating process of attempting to lay out right-angled plots upon a spherical earth. The surveyors were sometimes left with a wedge-shaped piece of land lying between the boundaries of two towns and not included in either. Most of these were too small and badly shaped to be incorporated in their own right. Some were annexed to the adjoining towns, but others still remain as Coburn Gore, or Million Acre Gore, possessing individuality neither by the lay of the land nor by legislative act, but as mere left-overs.

New England was little affected by *-burgh* and *-ville*. As everywhere, the majority of the town-names were commonplace, but the legends and folk-tales attaching to a few of them do much to show the nature of the people. The accuracy of a tradition may always be questioned, but the very persistence of one shows the quality of the folk-mind and suggests that, even if merely invented for one town, it may well have functioned at the naming of another.

In 1781 the citizens of a small community in Maine petitioned for incorporation, and sent their minister, the Reverend Seth Noble, to Boston on this errand. As the clerk was filling out the papers, Mr. Noble stood by, in true Yankee fashion, quietly humming a tune to himself. When the clerk suddenly asked him, "What's the name?" he absent-mindedly thought of

---

From *Names on the Land,* A Historical Account of Place-Naming in the United States, by George R. Stewart, pp. 205–209. Copyright, 1945, by George R. Stewart. New York: Random House.

[1] For further discussion of the word, see "Interval(e)," below.

the tune, not the town, and replied "Bangor." The naming from a hymn-tune became a repeated folk-tale. Even one of the greatest of New Englanders gave it circulation: "named at a pinch from a psalm tune," as Mr. Emerson wrote, disparagingly.

Two years after Bangor, the town of Littleton in New Hampshire took its name. It continued the Connecticut tradition of the name manufactured from parts of others, here the two chief landowners, Moses Little and Tristram Dalton.

Illogically, as the religious fervor of the Puritans declined, Biblical names grew more numerous. Perhaps they began to seem less holy. Goshen and Canaan and Sharon might even be good for advertising, vaguely suggesting rich valleys flowing with milk and honey. Bozrah in Connecticut may also have brought to mind good pasturage from the mention of its sheep by the prophet Micah. On the other hand, its inhabitants braved the full-fledged threat of Jeremiah, 49, 13:

> I have sworn by myself, saith the Lord, that Bozrah shall become a desolation, a reproach, a waste, and a curse.

As the story runs, however, the name sprang from still another quotation. In 1786 the district applied for incorporation and asked to be called Bath. The rustic who presented this petition was dressed in some parti-colored homespun so strange as to cause someone to quote the query of Isaiah, 63, I:

> Who is this that cometh from Edom, with dyed garments from Bozrah?

And so the Assembly, in acknowledgment of an apt quotation, rejected Bath, and substituted Bozrah.

The re-naming of a certain town in Vermont shows that such affairs did not always pass without heat. It had been granted as Wildersburgh in 1780, but the name became unpopular. A town-meeting to replace it met in 1793. Various names were proposed, but the running was soon limited to two. Captain Joseph Thomson strenuously contended for Holden, in honor of the town in Massachusetts which had been his former home. Mr. Jonathan Sherman was equally vehement for Barre, because he had come from Barre, also in Massachusetts. The argument was so hot that someone proposed a settlement by combat. The champions readily agreed.

The meeting then adjourned to a new barn-shed with a floor of rough hemlock planks. Space was cleared, and a pole was leveled waist-high. The combatants were to fight with their fists across this pole; but if one should knock the other down, he might follow up his advantage in any way he could.

Like two ancient warriors, they squared off—Thomson to lay on for Holden; Sherman, for Barre. Thomson was the more powerful; Sherman, the more lithe. After a little sparring, Thomson with a mighty blow knocked Sherman to the floor, and then leaping upon him began to pummel his head and face. But the supple Sherman squirmed so elusively that many of Thomson's blows merely barked his own knuckles on the hemlock floor. And all the while Sherman was working his own fists adroitly from beneath. Suddenly Thomson groaned, and his blows grew weak. Sherman, throwing him off, sprang to his feet and claimed the victory by shouting in exultation, "There, the name is Barre, by God!"

This particular story was transmitted through the village doctor, an eyewitness. He may even be called a participant because, next day, he had to use his professional skill to extract from the victor's back and buttocks the hemlock splinters they had collected while he was writhing on the plank floor.

Less authenticated but even more illustrative of the folk-mind is the naming of Canton. Realists may point out that by 1798 the China trade had made Yankees familiar with the name of the most frequented far-eastern port, and also that *canton* was used in France and Switzerland to mean a district. According to the tale, however, Canton was named at the instance of a prominent citizen, who maintained that his Massachusetts town was antipodal to the Chinese city. Actually, such an opinion was startlingly wrong. No two places in the northern hemisphere could be antipodal. Even if Canton was thought to be the corresponding opposite spot in the northern hemisphere, the calculation was still 1,300 miles in error. The name, however, rapidly became popular.

Canton in Ohio was settled by New Englanders in 1805, and the name has spread to twenty-three states. Several of them tell the same story to explain their naming. The very perversity of the story is almost an argument for it. It seems just what a crotchety Yankee of 1798 would be likely to maintain. Moreover, the folk-mind is never scientifically exact. American children (and probably most American adults) still believe firmly that if they dug straight down through the earth, they would come out in China. Actually, they would emerge in the southern part of the Indian Ocean, west of Australia.

Names of the New England States

THE name of each of the six New England States originated as follows:

MASSACHUSETTS derived its name, as is supposed, from the blue appearance of its hills; the word in the Indian language, according to Roger Williams, signifying *Blue Hills*.[1]

From *The Early History of New England,* Illustrated by Numerous Interesting Incidents, by Rev. Henry White, p. 303. Entered according to an Act of Congress, in the year 1841, by Rev. Henry White, in the Clerk's Office of the District Court of New Hampshire. Ninth edition. Boston: Sanborn, Carter, Bazin & Co.

[1] [Captain John] Smith wrote Massachuset as an Indian town. Though Smith may not have known it, the meaning is fairly clear, being the tribal name Mass-adchuseuck, "big-hill-people," which in English ears was blended with the name of the place,

CONNECTICUT derives its name from the river by which it is intersected, called by the natives Quonectacut. This word, according to some, signifies *the long river;* it has, however, been stated by others, that the meaning of the word is *River of Pines,* in allusion to the forests of pines that formerly stood on its banks.

As early as 1644, the Island of Rhode Island, on account of a fancied resemblance to the Isle of Rhodes, was called by that name, and by an easy declension it was afterwards called Rhode Island. This is supposed to be the origin of the name of the state of RHODE ISLAND.

NEW HAMPSHIRE derived its name from the county of Hampshire in England, the residence of Mason, to whom a patent embracing a considerable part of the state was given.

The provincial name of MAINE,[1] according to Williamson, was probably chosen in compliment to the queen of England, who had inherited a province of the same name in France.

VERMONT derived its name from the range of green mountains, which pass through it. *Verd* signifying green, and *mont,* mountain.

Nicknames of the New England States

Connecticut enjoys quite a number of sobriquets by which it is popularly known. Sometimes it is called the *Blue Law State* from the unenviable fame acquired by the first regulations of the government of New Haven Plantation, known as the Blue Laws. The valuable quarries of freestone, to which the State is largely indebted for its revenue, have procured for it the name of the *Freestone State,* while at other times it appears as the *Nutmeg State,* from the famous speculation in wooden spices, immortalized by Sam Slick, or, as a facetious native prefers to explain it, "because you will have to look for a grater!"

Mass-adchu-ut, "at-big-hills." Smith made of the Indian word an English plural to indicate the tribe, and so came Massachusetts.—George R. Stewart, *Names on the Land* (New York, 1945), pp. 37–38.

[1] In a New England charter of 1620 the lawyers wrote "the country of the Maine Land," words which suggest a general description rather than a name. Two years later, however, a charter was granted to two old sea-dogs of the Royal Navy, Sir Ferdinando Gorges and Captain John Mason, and in it the word had certainly ceased to be a description. Dated on August 10, 1622, the charter declared that "all that part of the mainland" the grantees "intend to name The Province of Maine." Some have thought that this name arose because of the greater number of islands off that northern coast, which made men have more reason to speak of "the main." Others have tried to connect it with the Province, or County, of Maine in France. But again, *main* as equaling *chief* or *important* would have been of good omen, if a little boastful. Moreover, about 1611 Captain Mason had served in the Orkneys, and must have known the name as used there.—*Ibid.*, pp. 41–42.

Maine obtains its name as the *Pine-Tree State* from the extensive pine-forests which cover its central and northern parts, while the occupation they afford to a large number of inhabitants, engaged in felling and rafting the trees, and in converting them into singles, boards, and the like, has made it also known as the *Lumber State.*

Massachusetts, known as the Colony of Massachusetts Bay before the formation of the present Union, still continues to be called the *Bay State.*

New Hampshire, originally so called by the early settlers, who wished to perpetuate the memory of the county from which many had emigrated, is now known as the *Granite State,* its mountains being largely composed of that material.

Rhode Island, the smallest State in the Union, is therefore affectionately called *Little Rhody.*

Vermont is generally, by simple translation of the original name given by the French settlers, called the *Green Mountain State,* the principal ridge of mountains within its boundaries being known by that name.

The Naming of Cape Cod

THE fifteenth day we had againe sight of the Land, which made ahead, being as wee thought an Iland, by reason of a large sound that appeared Westward betweene it and the Mayne, for comming to the West end thereof, we did perceive a large opening, we called it Shole-hope. Neere this Cape we came to Anchor in fifteene fadome, where wee tooke great store of Codfish, for which we altered the name, and called it Cape Cod. Here wee saw sculs of Herrings, Mackerels, and other small fish in great abundance. This is a low sandie shoare, but without danger, also wee came to Anchor again in sixteene fadome, faire by the Land in the latitude of 42 degrees. This Cape is well neere a mile broad, and lieth North-east by East. The Captaine went here ashoare and found the ground to be full of Pease, Strawberies, Hurtberies,[1] &c., as then unripe; the sand also by the shoare somewhat deepe, the firewood there by us taken in was of Cypresse, Birch, Wich-hazell and Beech. A young Indian came here to the captaine armed with his Bow and Arrows, and had certaine plates of Copper hanging at his Eares; hee shewed a willingnesse to help us in our occasions.

From "The Relation of Captaine Gosnol[d]'s Voyage to the North Part of Virginia, Begunne the Sixe-and-Twentieth of March, Anno 42 Elizabethae Reginae, 1602, and Delivered by Gabriel Archer, a Gentleman in the Said Voyage," in *Hakluytus Posthumus or Purchas His Pilgrimes* . . . (1625), IV, reprinted in *Forerunners and Competitors of the Pilgrims and Puritans,* edited for the New England Society of Brooklyn by Charles Herbert Levermore, Vol. I, pp. 45–46. Brooklyn, New York: Published for the Society. 1912.

[1] Whortleberries.—C. H. L.

Why the White Mountains Are Called "White"

He [Darby Field],[1] however, found "store of Muscovy glass" and some crystals, which, supposing them to be diamonds, he carefully secured and brought away. These glittering masses, congealed, according to popular belief, like ice on the frozen regions of the [White] mountains, gave them the name of the Crystal Hills—a name the most poetic, the most suggestive, and the most fitting that has been applied to the highest summits since the day they were first discovered by Englishmen.

* * * * *

It is not precisely known when or how these granite peaks took the name of the White Mountains. We find them so designated in 1672 by Josselyn, who himself performed the feat of ascending the highest summit, of which a brief record is found in his "New England's Rarities." One cannot help saying of this book that either the author was a liar of the first magnitude, or else we have to regret the degeneracy of Nature, exhausted by her long travail; for this narrator gravely tells us of frogs which were as big as a child of a year old, and of poisonous serpents which the Indians caught with their bare hands, and ate alive with great gusto. These are rarities indeed.

The first mention I have met with of an Indian name for the White Mountains is in the narrative of John Gyles's captivity, printed in Boston in 1736, saying:

> These White Hills, at the head of Penobscot River, are by the Indians said to be much higher than those called Agiockochook, above Saco.

The similitude between the names White Mountains and Mont Blanc suggests the same idea, that color, rather than character, makes the first and strongest impression upon the beholder. Thus we have White Mountains and Green Mountains, Red Mountains and Black Mountains, the world over. The eye seizes a color before the mind fixes upon a distinctive feature, or the imagination a resemblance. It is stated, on the authority of Schoolcraft, that the Algonquins called these summits "White Rocks."

From *The Heart of the White Mountains, Their Legend and Scenery,* by Samuel Adams Drake, pp. 118, 119–121. Entered according to Act of Congress, in the year 1881, by Harper & Brothers, in the Office of the Librarian of Congress, at Washington. New York. 1882.

[1] The first white man to ascend Mount Washington.—In . . . 1642 one Darby Field, an Irishman, with some others, traveled to an high mountain, called the White Hills, an hundred miles, or near upon, to the west of Saco. It is the highest hill in these parts of America. . . . There was a great expectation of some precious things to be found, either on the top or in the ascent, by the glistering of some white stones. Something was found like crystal, but nothing of value.—Rev. William Hubbard, *A General History of New England from the Discovery* to MDCLXXX (Boston, 1815, 1848), p. 381.

Mariners, approaching from the open sea, descried what seemed a cloud-bank, rising from the landward horizon, when twenty leagues from the nearest coast, and before any other land was visible from the masthead. Thirty leagues distant in a direct line, in a clear midsummer day, the distant summits appeared of a pearly whiteness; observed again from a church steeple on the seacoast, with the sky partially overcast, they were whitish-gray, showing that the change from blue to white, or to cool tones approximating with white, is due to atmospheric conditions. The early writers succeed only imperfectly in accounting for this phenomenon, which for six months of the year at least has no connection whatever with the snows that cover the highest peaks only from the middle of October to the middle of April, a period during which few navigators of the sixteenth and seventeenth centuries visited our shores, or, indeed, ventured to put to sea at all.

Names in the White Mountains

WHAT a pity that the hills could not have kept the names which the Indian tribes gave to them! The names which the highest peaks of the great range bear were given to them in 1820, by a party from Lancaster. How absurd the order is! Beginning at "The Notch," and passing around to Gorham, these are the titles of the summits which are all seen from the village just spoken of: Webster, Clinton, Pleasant, Franklin, Monroe, Washington, Clay, Jefferson, Adams, Madison. What a wretched jumble! These are what we have taken in exchange for such Indian words as Agiochook, which is the baptismal title of Mount Washington, and for words like Ammonoosuc, Moosehillock, Contoocook, Pennacook, Pentucket. Think, too, of the absurd association of names which the three mountains that rise over the Franconia Notch are insulted with—Mount Lafayette, Mount Pleasant, and Mount Liberty! How much better to have given the highest peaks of both ranges the names of some great tribes or chiefs, such as Saugus, Passaconaway, Uncanoonuc, Wonnalancet, Weetamoo, Bomazeen, Winnepurkit, Kancamagus,—words that chime with Saco, and Merrimack, and Sebago, and Connecticut, and Ossipee, and Androscoggin.

Even the general name, "White Mountains," is usually inapplicable during the season in which visitors see them. All unwooded summits of tolerable eminence are white in the winter; and in the summer, the mountains of the Washington range, seen at a distance in the ordinary daylight, are pale, dim green. The first title, "Crystal Hills," which the white explorers gave them, it would have been better to have retained. But how much richer is the Indian name "Waumbek!" The full title they applied to them

---

From *The White Hills; Their Legends, Landscape, and Poetry*, by Thomas Starr King, pp. 28–30. Entered according to Act of Congress, in the year 1859, by Crosby, Nichols and Company, in the Clerk's Office of the District Court of the District of Massachusetts. Boston: Crosby and Ainsworth. 1866.

was Waumbek-Methna, which signifies, it is said, "Mountains with snowy foreheads." Yet not a public house in all the mountain region bears the name of Waumbek, which is so musical, and which might be so profitably exchanged for Alpine House, or Glen House, or Profile House, or Tip-Top House. We are surprised, indeed, that the appellation "Kan Ran Vugarty," signifying the continued likeness of a gull, which it is said one Indian tribe applied to the range, has not been adopted by some landlord as a title to a hotel, or in some village as the name of a river, on account of its barbarity.

Would this be worse than to give the name "Israel's River" to the charming stream, fed from the rills of Washington and Jefferson, which flows through the Jefferson meadows, and empties into the Connecticut? The Indian name was Singrawac. Yet no trace of this charming name is left in Jefferson or Lancaster. Think of putting "Mount Monroe," or "Mount Clay," or "Mount Franklin," or "Peabody River," or "Berlin Falls," or "Israel's River," into poetry. The White Mountains have lost the privilege of being enshrined in such sonorous rhythm and such melody as Longfellow has given to the Indian names in his lines. . . .

The Christening of Vermont

It is from the Green Mountains that the country has received the name of *Vermont*. Of what is strangely called its baptism, as strange an account has been given, by the hand by which it was conferred. The narrative that I subjoin belongs to the history of Vermont, and is perhaps not uncharacteristic; and it is concluded with a criticism on a modern departure from what is represented to be the true orthography and pronunciation:

"Verd-mont was a name given to the Green Mountain, in October, 1763, by the Rev. Dr. Peters, the first clergyman who paid a visit to the thirty thousand settlers in that country, in the presence of Colonel Taplin, Colonel Willes, Colonel Peters, Judge Peters and many others, who were proprietors of a large number of townships in that colony. The ceremony was performed on the top of a rock standing on a high mountain, then named Mount Pisgah, because it *provided* to the company, *a clear sight of Lake Champlain at the west, and of Connecticut River at the east;* and overlooked all the trees and hills in the vast wilderness at the north and south.

"The baptism was performed in the following manner and form, *viz:* Priest Peters stood on the pinnacle of the rock, when he received a bottle

---

From *Travels through the Northern Parts of the United States, in the years 1807 and 1808*, by Edward Augustus Kendall, Esq., Vol. III, pp. 237–240. New York: Printed and published by I. Riley. 1809.

of *spirits* from Colonel Taplin; then, haranguing the company with a short history of the infant settlement, and the prospect of its becoming an impregnable barrier between the British colonies in the south, and late colonies of the French in the north, which might be returned in the next century to their late owners, for the sake of governing America by the different powers of Europe, he continued, 'We have here met on the rock Etam, standing on Mount Pisgah, which makes a part of *the everlasting hill,* the spine of Africa, Asia and America, holding together the terrestrial ball, and dividing the Atlantic from the Pacific Ocean, to dedicate and consecrate this extensive wilderness *to God manifested in human flesh,* and to give it a new name, worthy of the Athenians and ancient Spartans; which new name is *Verd-mont,* in token that her mountains and hills shall be ever green, and shall never die.'—And then poured the *spirits* around him, and cast the bottle on the rock Etam. The ceremony being over, the company descended Mount Pisgah, and took refreshment in a log-house, kept by Captain Otley, where they spent the night with great pleasure. After this, Priest Peters passed through most of the settlements, preaching and baptizing for the space of eight weeks; in which time he baptized nearly twelve hundred children and adults.

"Since Verdmont became a state, in union with the thirteen states of America, its general assembly have seen proper to change the spelling of *Verd*-mont, Green Mountain, to that of *Ver*-mont, Mountain of Maggots. Both words are French; and, if the former spelling is to give place to the latter, it will prove, that the state had rather be considered as a mountain of worms, than an ever-green mountain." [1]

After learning, from the inventor himself, that he formed the name *Vermont* or *Verdmont* from the French language, we can pay no attention to the derivation of a topographer, who gives us a Latin etymology, "*Ver Mons*, Green Mountain"; [2] but, when we find a complaint instituted, of a departure from the original meaning of the word, such as involves a departure from its signification, we are naturally struck with the circumstance, that the word never was compounded and applied in any accurate form. Green Mountain, in the singular, and not Green Mountains, was the name intended to be translated; and this is to be accounted for by the fact, that the mountains, of which only the southernmost part was known to the first settlers, were usually so spoken of—*the mountain.* But, for the name Green Mountain, *Ver Mons* is not Latin, and *Verd Mont* is not French.

---

[1] *A History of the Rev. Hugh Peters, A.M. &c.* By the Rev. Samuel Peters, LL.D. New York. 1807.—E. A. K.

[2] *American Gazetteer.*—E. A. K.

South Kingstown, Rhode Island, Place Nicknames

The boys of South Kingstown conceived a great liking for nicknames, and carried it to extreme degrees, so much so that every family, and almost everybody had one of these cognomens attached. As a sample of their aptness this way we give the names of the places in the town, with the boy's name attached, as a piece of curiosity:

Harley's Mill—Biscuit City.
Wells' Carding Mill—The Little Punch Bowl.
Usquepaug—Old Mumford's.
Point Judith—Pirate's Paradise.
Tower Hill, on hill—Sodom.
Tower Hill, under hill—Gomorrah.
Watson's Corner—Rum Corner.
Kingston Hill—Hornet's Nest.
Wakefield—Old Mill.
Peacedale—Wool Slusher.
Rocky Brook—Nigger Swamp.
Bridgetown—Buckey-town.
Narragansett Pier—Mushroom City.
Curtis' Corner—Sot's Hole.
Perryville—Backside.
South Ferry—Sailor's Rest.
Mooresfield—God's Anger.
Tuckerstown—The Wilderness.

Haunts of the Devil

In almost every New-England village the personality of Satan has been acknowledged by calling by his name some particular rock or cave, or other natural object whose singularity would seem to suggest a more than mortal occupancy. "The Devil's Punch-bowl," "The Devil's Wash-bowl," "The Devil's Kettle," "The Devil's Pulpit," and "The Devil's Den," have been designations that marked places or objects of some striking natural peculiarity. Often these are found in the midst of the most beautiful and romantic scenery, and the sinister name seems to have no effect in lessening its attractions. . . .

From *The Narragansett Historical Register,* A Magazine Devoted to the Antiquities, Genealogy and Historical Matter Illustrating the History of the Narragansett Country, or Southern Rhode Island, edited by James N. Arnold, Vol. I (January, 1883), No. 3, p. 233. Entered according to Act of Congress, in the year 1882, by the Narragansett Historical Publishing Company, in the Office of the Librarian of Congress, Washington. Hamilton, Rhode Island.

From *Oldtown Fireside Stories,* by Harriet Beecher Stowe, pp. 190–191. Entered, according to Act of Congress, in the year 1871, by James R. Osgood & Co., in the Office of the Librarian of Congress, at Washington. Boston. 1872.

The Naming of Auburn

Before the post office was established, mail was brought from Worcester by a post rider who announced his arrival by the blast of a horn. From 1831 to 1840, stages from Worcester to Norwich stopped at the Tavern with the mail. At this time letters did not carry stamps; the amount charged was marked at the corner and collected by the postmaster on delivery. Thus mail was often held for weeks before being claimed. Almost as soon as the mail route was established, Ward began to experience difficulty in the delivery of mail. The similarity of the names of Ward and the more western town of Ware was so marked that the mail of the two towns was constantly getting mixed. A town meeting was held on November 14, 1836, to see what steps should be taken to insure more prompt delivery of business letters, to say nothing of personal mail and love letters.

Joseph Stone was elected chairman with Thomas Merriam, Alvah Drury, Israel Stone, Jr., and Hervey Bancroft. The committee reported at the adjourned meeting on November 28, 1836, and "recommended to the town (though not literally within the commission) to choose a Committee to prepare or cause to be prepared, a petition to the General Court, for the purpose aforesaid. . . .

The petition was granted and reads as follows:

Ch. 14

COMMONWEALTH OF MASSACHUSETTS

In the year One thousand eight hundred and thirty seven. An Act to change the name of the Town of Ward.

Be it enacted by the Senate and House of Representatives in General Court assembled, and by the authority of the same, as follows: The name of the town of Ward in the County of Worcester is hereby changed to the name of Auburn, and said town shall henceforth be known and called by the said last mentioned name, anything in the Act whereby the said town was incorporated to the contrary notwithstanding.

House of Representatives February 15, 1837
Passed to be enacted
Julius Rockwell, Speaker
In Senate February 16, 1837
Passed to be enacted
Horace Mann, President

February 17th, 1837.
Approved,
Edward Everett.

A *Historical Sketch of Auburn, Massachusetts,* From the Earliest Period to the Present Day, with Brief Accounts of Early Settlers and Prominent Citizens, Written and Compiled by the Federal Writers' Project of the Works Progress Administration for the State of Massachusetts, pp. 21, 22–23. Sponsored by the Auburn Centennial Committee. 1937.

There has been considerable speculation as to why the name of Auburn was selected. The most commonly accepted explanation is that the name was suggested by Oliver Goldsmith's poem, *The Deserted Village.* The poetic phrase, "Auburn, Sweet Village of the Plain" does not, however, describe Auburn, Massachusetts, with its rolling hills and valleys, and it seems safe to assume that the name was derived from another source. Joseph Stone, chairman of the naming committee, is said to have been the one to propose "Auburn." Stone was the great-great-grandson of Simon Stone, who, in 1636, settled on the banks of the Charles River in Watertown. The land remained in the Stone family until 1825, when a section of it, called Stone's Woods, was sold by David Stone and the heirs of C. Stone to George W. Brimmer, who was attracted by its natural beauty. The tract was a favorite spot of the Harvard College students, who called it "Sweet Auburn." Mr. Jacob Bigelow, secretary of the newly incorporated Horticultural Society of Boston, happened to visit the land with Mr. Brimmer, and proposed that the whole lot be purchased for a cemetery under the auspices of the Society. Accordingly, in 1831, the land was sold and Mount Auburn Cemetery established. A religious ceremony was held on Saturday, September 24, 1831, at which several members of the Stone family were present. Thus, it is probable that Auburn received its name from this lovely tract of land.

These Haddams

Mark Twain, in speaking of the way New Englanders mix up the names of their towns, tells the following:

"They tell a story of a stranger who was coming up the Connecticut river, and was trying his best to sleep; but every now and then the boat would stop and a man would thrust his head into the room. First he sang out "Haddam!" and then "East Haddam!" and then "Haddam Neck!" and then "North Haddam!" and then "Great Haddam!" "Little Haddam!" "Old Haddam!" "New Haddam!" "Old Haddam!" "Irish Haddam!" Dutch Haddam!" "Haddam-Haddam!" and then the stranger jumped out of bed, all excited, and says: "I'm a Methodist preacher, full of grace, and forty years in service without guile! I'm a meek and lowly Christian, but blast these Haddams. I wish the devil had 'em, I say!"

Which Dover?

Repetition of place names, which is of frequent occurrence in New England, is sometimes confusing. Once in his youth my father and one of his

---

From an old newspaper clipping scrapbook in the editor's possession.

From *It's an Old New England Custom,* by Edwin Valentine Mitchell, p. 227. New York: The Vanguard Press, Inc.

brothers became lost while driving home from a dance at Curtis's Grove in Medfield, Massachusetts, to Framingham. Their horse did not know the way any better than they did. After spending the dull watches of the night wandering around back-country roads, they at length came to a house. In answer to their summons, a man put his head out of an upper window and asked what they wanted at such an hour.

"What town is this?" inquired my father.

"Dover," was the answer.

"Dover, Maine, or Dover, New Hampshire?" asked the brother.

"Dover, Massachusetts, you damn fool!" came the disgusted reply.

Lake Charcogg-Etc.-Maugg

. . . THE name came through many transmigrations. The first deed in which the pond is named goes back to 1681—a deed giving to Governor Winthrop the "land lying all along and from end to end upon the westerly side of Chapnacongoe Pond toward Connecticut." Littlefield, the historian, says Chapnacongoe Pond was intended for Chabanakongkomuin, now known as Webster Lake. One must remember that in those early days the Indians had no written language, so that the matter of spelling was beyond their purview. Roger Williams' key to the Indian language and the translation of the Bible by John Eliot was the first orderly arrangement of the Indian tongue. When I was a boy we called the name of the lake "Junkermug." This you see is a phonetic spelling such as the Indians themselves often used. When the name was reduced to print it took its first expression in a form which has been maintained from that day to this, and which certainly has every claim to stand by itself unchanged. Keith's map which was in vogue in the early part of the last century had the name of the lake, Chaubunagungamaugg, so you will see that the abbreviation which took place on the last part of the name of the lake is without authority. That name eliminated "Chaubuna" without any reason whatever. In Kinnecut's *Indian Names of Worcester County,* we have Charchamonchogego and Charbunabungamaug. So you will see that if you wish to perpetuate the name which has back of it the full assent of the antiquarian and the students of the Indian tongue, the name must be written "Charcoggagoggmanchaugagoggchabunagungamaugg." . . .

From *Black Tavern Tales,* Stories of Old New England, by Charles L. Goodell, pp. 82–83. Copyright, 1932, by Charles L. Goodell. Brooklyn, New York: Willis McDonald & Co.

How Lexington in Old Kentucky Was Born

IN THE far-away South, some weeks after the Battle of Lexington, a party of hunters clad in buckskin,—armed with flintlocks, hatchets, and scalping-knives, lest they encounter the redskin varmints in these impenetrable canebrakes or the trackless forests,—supped on "jerk" and parched corn. By a clear spring, they had resolved to pitch their tents and make a settlement, and what should they name this luxuriant wilderness? Strange news came on the wing: "King George's troops had called Americans 'rebels' and shot them down at Lexington on the 19th of April!" Every other name was flung aside, and *Lexington* in old Kentucky was born.

The Origin of "Hoosic"—A Satire

ON THE borders of the stream now called by the name of Hoosick, as tradition saith, there formerly dwelt a good old lady, of rather a gossiping disposition, and who was possessed of an insatiable curiosity to learn, and an unconquerable desire to be the first to communicate, all the wonderful news in the vicinity. Among other things, she was prodigiously fond of hearing of all the lamentable cases of sickness far and near, and seemed to live on the pains and aches, the "gripes and grumbles" of her fellow creatures. With this fondness for the sad and horrible, she never failed to run out when the doctor was passing, and bawl out loud as she could—"*Doctor, who's sick?*" This she repeated so often, that at length the man of medicine grew tired of her importunities, and invented a hundred stories of improbable cases, with which he amused himself and ridiculed the old woman's love of the marvellous, but which she swallowed with the same avidity as she did her catechism.

At one time he told her he had been to see a patient who had the mortal borborigums, and that he had cured him completely by taking out his "insides" and washing them in soap suds and vinegar.

"Is it possible, doctor!" exclaimed the old woman. "Well, I hope the man will have a clean conscience after this."

At another time the doctor told her he had called to see a child that was born without any tongue.

From *Old Paths and Legends of New England,* Saunterings Over Historic Roads with Glimpses of Picturesque Fields and Old Homesteads in Massachusetts, Rhode Island, and New Hampshire, by Katharine M. Abbott, p. 66 n. Copyright, 1903, by Katharine M. Abbott. New York and London: G. P. Putnam's Sons. 1904.

From *Wehman's Idle Hours with the Humorists,* Brimful of Fun about Yankee Yarns, Western Sports, Boarding-House Hash, Rich College Scrapes, Wild Widows' Wit, and Tall Tales of Sailors and Marines, p. 27. New York: Published by Henry J. Wehman. [n. d.]

"Oh me!" cried the old lady. "How will the poor thing ever talk!—is it a boy or a gal, doctor?"

"A girl," he replied.

"Ah, well," said she, "I ain't a bit afeared then but what it will talk well enough."

On a third occasion he told her he had been to visit a woman who was bitten by a rattlesnake. He said the patient was a great snuff taker, and as she was one day picking up blackberries, the snake, which was concealed among the briers, being highly enraged at the smell of the snuff, sprang from his lurking place and seized the woman by the end of the nose.

"Oh lord!" ejaculated the sympathizing listener, and giving her own nose a thorough wipe, "didn't it kill the woman?"

"No, by Jove," returned the doctor, "but it killed the snake."

But to return to the etymology. The doctor from being so often questioned by the old lady, "Who's sick?" at last began to call the neighborhood of her residence *Who's Sick;* and when asked by his own neighbors, "Which way are you riding to-day, doctor?" he would reply jocularly, "I'm going to *Who's sick.*" This appellation was at first caught from the doctor and familiarly used by his neighbors, and afterwards by those more remote; and thus not only the neighborhood of the inquisitive old lady, but in process of time the whole stream and the valley on its borders, came by a slight alteration in its spelling, to be called by the name of *Hoosick.*

AFTER THE FACT

Origin of the Name of Wickford

We give four traditions of the origin of the name of this [Rhode Island] place, and beg leave to say here there is no truth in the matter worthy of any historical importance, but is merely fiction, and given to show how far some traditions are from the truth.

I. It is said to have come from Mr. Lodowick Updike who used to own the land upon which the place is built. It was formerly an island, and the place where entrance was made was called the ford; then Wick's ford, (referring to Mr. Updike who was commonly called "Wick," and "Old Wick"). From *Old Wick's ford,* and *Wick's ford,* it is claimed came this name.

II. A sick lady, on her way from New York to Boston, stopped there to

---

From *The Narragansett Historical Register,* A Magazine Devoted to the Antiquities, Genealogy and Historical Matter Illustrating the History of the Narragansett Country, or Southern Rhode Island, Vol. I (January, 1883), No. 3, edited by James N. Arnold, pp. 214–215. Entered according to Act of Congress, in the year 1882, by the Narragansett Historical Publishing Company, in the Office of the Librarian of Congress, Washington. Hamilton, Rhode Island.

rest, and going out one morning for a walk she found a spring bubbling out from under a stone which greatly interested her, and she said it put her in mind of a similar spring that she used to visit in her childhood, in her native town, Wickford, England.

III. Roger Williams and Richard Smith were in conversation one evening and Mr. Smith was remarking how apt was Mr. Williams' name to his settlement, (Providence,) to which Mr. Williams suggested he (Smith) should have a name also to his settlement. Mr. Smith remarked that it would be a grand idea, and that he had thought much upon it but had come to no definite conclusion. There was present at this interview a lady, a guest of Mr. Smith, and Mr. Williams suggested that perhaps the lady could help Mr. Smith out of his dilemma. On being thus appealed to she laughingly said: "We are all very fond of our native town, and so am I of mine, which is Wickford, England." The gentlemen were very gallant and concluded that would make a very pretty name, and in this way was the name adopted.

IV. The teamers who drew ship timber down to the Point, (now Baker's wharf,) complained how bad the ford was at night. (The ford by the way was in the road close to where Mr. Shippee's blacksmith shop now is.) In order to remedy this they furnished a lamp, which consisted of a wick drawn through an iron ring and elevated to burn, the other end drawing from an open vessel of grease or oil in an open pot, which contrivance was called a "Kill Devil." One Whitman used to gather the oil for the lamp at the ford. In time it came to be spoken of as the ford at the wick, or the wick's ford, in time running into Wickford.

Point Judith

About two centuries ago a vessel was driving toward the coast in a gale, with rain and mist. The skipper's eyes were old and dim, so he got his daughter Judith to stand beside him at the helm, as he steered the vessel over the foaming surges. Presently she cried, "Land, father! I see land!" "Where away?" he asked. But he could not see what she described, and the roar of the wind drowned her voice, so he shouted, "Point, Judith! Point!" The girl pointed toward the quarter where she saw the breakers, and the old mariner changed his course and saved his ship from wreck. On reaching port he told the story of his daughter's readiness, and other captains, when they passed the cape in later days, gave to it the name of Point Judith.[1]

. . . I used to hear when a boy that "Point Judith point" was so called because it was first discovered by an old negro woman named Judith on

[1] From *Myths & Legends of Our Own Land,* by Charles M. Skinner, Vol. II, p. 35. Copyright, 1896, by J. B. Lippincott Company. Philadelphia & London.

board ship in a fog. The captain could not see the land with his spy-glass, and so he said to the old darky to point out the direction in which she saw it. Said he, "Point, Judy, point," and so when the captain saw it he put it down on his chart by that name, which has since been converted into "Point Judith," or "Pint Judy." Per contra, my brother Joseph tells me that Josiah Quincy, of Boston, during whose mayoralty the Cochituate water was introduced into the city and the great reservoir built near the capital, once told him that Point Judith was named after a relation of his, "Judith Quincy," who married a Mr. Hull and went at a very early date to live on Point Judith. . . .[2]

Mount Hope

BETWEEN the southernmost point of the peninsula called Bristol Neck, and a northern projection of Rhode Island, is Bristol Ferry, of which the width is about three quarters of a mile. On the east side of the peninsula is a mountain, (almost the only one in the republic,) called Mount Hope, and Mount Haup. If the derivation is really from an Indian name, it is probably *Montaup*. A point of land on Long Island is called *Montaug*. The summit of Mount Hope terminates in a single peak; and this the Indians describe by *monad*, in which is the first syllable of *Montaup*: hence *Monadnoc*, the name of two mountains on the Connecticut; *monad nac*, one or a single peak. Mount Hope is celebrated, in the history of New England, for the death of Philip, the chief of the Narragansett Indians.

Squantum

A DERIVATION of the name, as grotesque and far-fetched as it is absurd, was at a later period found in the ubiquitous Lover's-leap legend. An Indian woman was supposed to have put an end to herself by springing from the bold crag which forms the peninsula's eastern extremity, and is still known as Squaw Rock. (See *Memorial History of Boston*, i. 64.)

---

[2] From *Jonny-Cake Papers of "Shepherd Tom,"* Together with Reminiscences of Narragansett Schools of Former Days, by Thomas Robinson Hazard, With a Biographical Sketch and Notes by Rowland Gibson Hazard, pp. 306–307. Copyright, 1915, by Rowland G. Hazard. Boston: Printed for the Subscribers.

From *Travels Through the Northern Parts of the United States, in the Years 1807 and 1808*, by Edward Augustus Kendall, Esq., Vol. II, p. 5. New York: Printed and published by I. Riley. 1809.

From *Three Episodes of Massachusetts History*, The Settlement of Boston Bay, The Antinomian Controversy, A Study of Church and Town Government, by Charles Francis Adams, p. 21. Copyright, 1892, by Charles Francis Adams. Boston and New York: Houghton, Mifflin and Company. 1903.

Thence the name Squaw's Tumble, corrupted into Squantum. Even John Adams, writing in 1762, speaks of "the high, steep rock from whence the squaw threw herself who gave the name to the place."

Moose Hillock or Moosilauke?

THIS orthography [Moosilauke] is of recent adoption. By recent I mean within thirty years. Before that time it was always Moosehillock. Nothing is easier than to unsettle a name. So far as known, I believe there is not a single summit of the White Mountain group having a name given to it by the Indians. On the contrary, the Indian names have all come from the white people. That these are sometimes far-fetched is seen in Osceola and Tecumseh; that they are often puerile, it is needless to point out. Moosehillock is probably no exception. It is not unlikely to be an English nickname. The result of these changes is that the people inhabiting the region contiguous to the mountain do not know how to spell the name on their guide-boards.[1]

The Amonoosuc joins the Connecticut at the foot of a hill or lofty promontory, to the east of which is one of the principal mountains in New Hampshire, called Moose Hillock, on which, from the opposite side of the Connecticut, snow is said to have been seen as late as the thirtieth day of June, and as early as the thirty-first day of August. Though it appears difficult to understand, unless as comparing it with the White Mountains, why this majestic mountain should have been called a *hillock,* still it may be the most probable interpretation of the name, that it was originally known as a hill or hillock inhabited by the moose-deer or elk; but some, by spelling it Mooseheeloc, give a different turn to the name. In the vicinity of this mountain, I met with persons who asserted that it is called Moose Hillock, not as abounding in moose-deer, but as being a great mountain; the Indians, according to them, regarding it as great among mountains, as the moose-deer is great among beasts, and hence using the term in a figurative sense.—I confess myself disposed to regard the name as wholly English, and not Indian, and as being most properly written Moose Hillock; but, if it can be shown that *Mooseheeloc* is the more proper orthography, then the word must be wholly Indian, and may have a signification different from all the foregoing.[2]

---

[1] From *The Heart of the White Mountains,* Their Legend and Scenery, by Samuel Adams Drake, p. 267n. Entered according to Act of Congress, in the year 1881, by Harper & Brothers, in the Office of the Librarian of Congress, at Washington. New York. 1882.

[2] From *Travels Through the Northern Parts of the United States,* in the Years 1807 and 1808, by Edward Augustus Kendall, Esq., in Three Volumes, Vol. III, pp. 190–191. New York: Printed and published by I. Riley. 1809.

Lemon Fair River

The [Lemon Fair] river's name is said to have grown out of an Indian massacre that occurred on the banks of the stream; the settlers referred to it as "the lamentable affair," and through constant usage this was shortened to Lemon Fair. A variant is the legend which traces the name to "leman fair," the old English phrase for "mistress fair."[1]

. . . Impossible stories are told to explain it, but it is still called Lemon Fair River, and the most likely explanation is that the strange name is only a Vermonter's attempt to render Les Monts Verts.[2]

STORIES IN PLACE-NAMES

Bride Brook

A stream which was the original west boundary of New London [, Connecticut,] was the scene of a very odd incident toward the end of winter in 1646. A young Saybrook couple wished to be married, and as the magistrate in their own place was away they sent word to Governor John Winthrop at New London that they would ride thither to have him perform the ceremony. He concluded to ride to meet them. Both he and the wedding party got as far as the boundary stream, and found it in flood and the ice broken up. They could not cross, but the marriage took place just the same. The governor on his side of the stream pronounced them man and wife, and they on the other side promised to love, honor, and obey. Since then the stream has been called "Bride Brook."

---

[1] From *Vermont:* A Guide to the Green Mountain State, written by Workers of the Federal Writers' Project of the Works Progress Administration for the State of Vermont, p. 317. American Guide Series. Copyright, 1937, by the Vermont State Planning Board. Boston: Houghton Mifflin Company.

[2] From *Names on the Land:* A Historical Account of Place-Naming in the United States, by George R. Stewart, p. 167. Copyright, 1945, by George R. Stewart. New York: Random House.

From *New England, A Human Interest Geographical Reader,* by Clifton Johnson, pp. 192–193. Copyright, 1917, by The Macmillan Company. New York and London.

Dragon Point

THIS [Connecticut] place was formerly called Dragon, from a sandy point of that name, about forty rods below the bridge, on the eastern side of the river. The tradition is, that at the time of the first settlement of New Haven this point was a place of resort for seals, who lay here and basked themselves in the sun. At that time these animals were called *dragons,* hence the name Dragon Point.

Hatchet Harbor and Providence Hill

THE Regicides, Goffe and Whalley, had a number of places of concealment in the limits of this town; the most noted of which is called the *Lodge,* or *Hatchet Harbor,* about seven miles from New Haven. It was situated (says Dr. Stiles, in his history of the Judges) at a spring in a valley. "A little northward of it was an eminence, called the *Fort* to this day, from whence there was an extensive and commanding prospect, and a full view of New Haven Harbor to the S. E., seven miles off. From this they could see the vessels passing in and out of the harbor. When they came to this abode is uncertain;—it was in the summer, and they left it and removed to Milford, August, 1661, after having resided in and about New Haven for near half a year, from the 7th of March to the 19th of August, 1661." "On a tract about a mile square, and lying four miles N.W. of Sperry's [farm], there are four hills or eminences, between which are vallies and intercurrent brooks. . . . On the northern declivity of one of these hills, issues a small perennial spring, between two trees, a walnut and chestnut, now three and four feet in diameter, and judged to be two hundred years old, standing twenty-two feet apart. This fountain is stoned as if with design, and probably remaining as the Judges left it. Tradition says that when they come to this spring, one of them said 'Would to God we had a hatchet'; and immediately finding a hatchet, left there probably by the Indian hunters, they cut down boughs and built a temporary harbor, from this circumstance called Hatchet Harbor to this day." . . . "On an eminence west of this, by the side of a ledge of rocks twenty feet high, was built a cave, or convenient lodgment, ten feet long and seven wide, regularly stoned. I find the walls (says Dr. Stiles) now remaining, though somewhat

---

From *Connecticut Historical Collections,* Containing a General Collection of Interesting Facts, Traditions, Biographical Sketches, Anecdotes, &c., Relating to the History and Antiquities of Every Town in Connecticut, with Geographical Descriptions, by John Warner Barber, p. 159. Entered according to the Act of Congress, in the year 1836, by John W. Barber and A. Willard, in the Clerk's office, of the District Court of Connecticut. New Haven and Hartford.

Ibid., pp. 273–274.

broken down. It was covered with trunks of trees, which remained, though much rotten and decayed, till within forty years ago: indeed I saw some of the rudera, rafters, or broken relics, limbs and trunks of trees, still lying in the cavity. This was undoubtedly their great and principal lodge, and in a very recluse and secreted place. There is a beautiful spring six rods from it." . . . About 100 rods north, "on Deacon Peck's farm, lies another hillock or eminence, called to this day, and in the records so early as 1675, 'Providence Hill'; between which and Fort Rock's Hill, is a valley and brook. Between these two hills runs the dividing line of the towns of Milford and New Haven. The tradition is, that it acquired its name thus. While the Judges resided at the lodge on the southern hill, they apprehended themselves discovered and pursued, while walking on the tops of the hills,—and the Indians always burned rings or tracts on those summits, to give a clear view for hunting deer. Supposing themselves discovered, they took to the bush, and to deceive their pursuers, ranged a north course between the hills, and giving them a false scent, turned off to the westward, and came round the hill to their old place in security. On account of this deliverance, they called this northwest hill, *Providence* Hill."

Purgatory

On the shore, to the eastward of Newport, [Rhode Island,] and in the town of Middletown, is a chasm in the rocks, to which is given the name of Purgatory. The elevation of the rocks, from the surface of the water, is about forty feet, and the greatest breadth of the chasm, about twelve. Its length is perhaps seventy feet. At its mouth, which is open to the sea, when the winds blow, or the tide rises, the waves continually break; and, as there is no outlet at the opposite extremity, they also continually return. The counter-currents detain within the chasm any floating substance that happens to be received there, driving it by their motion to and fro; and this phenomenon (certainly a very humble one) has given rise to the name of Purgatory. But, invention and romance have ventured a little further, in distinguishing this marvellous spot; and a place is shown, on the irregular surface of the rocks above, where *the devil killed a squaw,* (or Indian woman,) and, dragging her to the summit, thence *threw her into Purgatory.*

To what source we are indebted for this facetious tradition, it has not happened to me to learn; or which of the two has had the larger share in its putting together, the superstitions of the Indians, or the superstitions of their English successors. The Indians knew nothing, till the English told them, either of purgatory, or of the devil; and why, when the settlers

---

From *Travels through the Northern Parts of the United States, in the Years 1807 and 1808,* by Edward Augustus Kendall, Esq., Vol. II, pp. 11–13. New York: Printed and published by I. Riley. 1809.

imparted their derision of the one, and their fear of the other, a poor Indian woman should have become the vicitim of both, it may not be easy to discover. The devil, (that is, Satan,) or the devils, (that is, the other fallen angels,) undoubtedly attended the settlers to New England, and showed them, in their asylum, many of the usual devil's tricks; but whether the tragedy in question took place before or after the arrival of the latter, is not particularly related.

Wolf Bog

. . . I WILL just here say that when I was a boy, I used to hear a good deal about a wolf that came to his death in what is to this day called the "Wolf Bog," on the north border of Peace Dale [, Rhode Island]. The story ran after this wise: A big gray wolf gave chase to an old slab-sided, long-bodied, sharp-nosed sow of what was then called the land-shark breed, which kind of swine the late William French, of Kingston, always contended made the best pork and hams of any breed of swine, which I, too, think is the fact. Just before the old sow reached the edge of the aforesaid bog, the wolf grabbed her with his teeth, by the end of her tail, which caused the terrified creature to increase her speed so marvelously that, as old Jim Newberry, who was cutting wood near by, said, neither the sow nor the wolf could be separately discerned with the naked eye, they somewhat resembling a streak of lightning as they passed along, only rather quicker in motion; so quick, in fact, that the terror-stricken old sow in her heedless course plunged directly through a maple tree two feet in diameter that stood in her way, dragging the gray wolf after her more than half his length, when he was caught by the rebound of the maple just forward of his hips and so held secure until Jim Newberry (whom I used to know) came forward and dispatched him with his wood axe. This story may be rather tough for people of contracted minds to swallow, much less digest; but yet it would seem to rest on a foundation, else why has the boggy swale where the wolf came to his end always to this day been known as the *wolf bog*? . . .

Hardscrabble

. . . OLD Kit Robinson, in passing by John's house, just held up his horse a moment to inquire of old *Miss* Gould (John's wife, not *Mrs.* if

From *The Jonny-Cake Papers of "Shepherd Tom,"* Together with Reminiscences of Narragansett Schools of Former Days, by Thomas Robinson Hazard, With a Biographical Sketch and Notes by Rowland Gibson Hazard, pp. 346–347. Copyright, 1915, by Rowland G. Hazard. Boston: Printed for the Subscribers.

Ibid., pp. 231–232.

you please, the latter term being applied in those primitive times only to "quality folk"), how her husband (then out at work by the day) expected ever to be able to pay for the *three parts* stone lot and one part moss (he heard he had lately contracted for), situated on the other side of the road. In answer the old woman told one by one some dozen or more ways by which her husband expected to get the money, each and all of which were shown by old Kit to be fallacious in turn. Whereupon old Miss Gould, now driven to her wits' end, after two or three hesitating sighs, drew a long breath and remarked, that at any rate she thought they would get along somehow or another "in the scrabble," and pay for their lot, upon which old Kit Robinson rejoined, that he feared it would prove a "hard scrabble" for John, from which saying not only old John Gould's new purchase, but a large, rocky, stony, and mossy district of country, lying on the south side of the Little Rest road opposite "Old Brit," came to be known as "Hardscrabble." . . .

Abram's Rock

THE turnpike runs near Abram's Rock in Swansea village, [Massachusetts,] and from its top you view the two bays and measure the feat which Abram, the half-breed Indian deserter, was forced to perform. Philip gave him Hobson's choice between death at the stake and three leaps from the summit of his rock where he lived in its natural room, "Abram's kitchen." It is said that after the first two successful leaps he became too confident and struck the branch of a tree and perished.

Rhyme of the Elizabeth Islands

ON CUTTYHUNK ISLE, off Dartmouth shore, [Massachusetts,] Gosnold built his warehouse on a rocky islet in the fresh-water pond, separated from the salt bay only by a narrow beach. *Elizabeth,* Gosnold named his woodland island; and wherever you may alight on the charming shores of Buzzard's Bay,—at Nonquitt, Falmouth, Mattapoiset, or New Bedford—you are not eligible to maritime inner circles until you can repeat the rhyme of the Elizabeth Islands:

Nashawena, Pesquinese, Naushon, Nonameset,
Cuttyhunk, Penekees, Onkatonka, Wepecket

From *Old Paths and Legends of New England,* Saunterings Over Historic Roads with Glimpses of Picturesque Fields and Old Homesteads in Massachusetts, Rhode Island, and New Hampshire, by Katharine M. Abbott, pp. 399–400. Copyright, 1903, by Katharine M. Abbott. New York and London: G. P. Putnam's Sons. 1904.

Ibid., p. 419.

The Devil's Den

At Gay Head [, Martha's Vineyard,] is the Devil's Den, which, notwithstanding the terror of its name, has nothing formidable in its appearance. It is a depression in the hill in the form of a bowl, except that it is open on the side next the sea, through which it is not difficult to descend to the strand. It is about 400 yards around, and 100 feet deep. If it was on the top of a mountain it might be called a crater. In this cavity, according to an Indian traditionary fable, many years before the English came to Martha's Vineyard, a giant, or tutelar deity, named Maushope, resided. Here he broiled the whale on a fire made of the largest trees, which he pulled up by the roots. Though a malignant spirit has now taken possession of his den, yet the first occupier was a benevolent being, and he kindly supplied the Indians with whales and other fish. After separating Noman's Land from Gay Head, metamorphosing his children into fishes, and throwing his wife on Saconet Point, where she still remains a misshapen rock, he went away, nobody knew whither. Perhaps the report that volcanic flames have been seen to ascend from the Devil's Den is as fabulous as the story of Maushope, as they have never been observed by any of the well-informed inhabitants. It has been suggested that the above story of the giant might have originated by the Indians finding fossil skeletons of large marine animals at that place, and from supposing the lignite which there abound to be the remains of his fires.

Corn Pond

On the way to 'Sconset, [Nantucket,] there is a small swamp hole by the roadside. Once when the Cap'n was driving two gentlemen out from town their conversation turned to feet, and each told the other how he suffered from corns. "Well, now," said the old joker, "that's lucky. You've come to jest the right place. There's a pond a little way ahead that they call Corn Pond. There's some medicinal property in the water there that jest cures corns; but it's a funny thing, somehow or other, if you take the water

---

From *Massachusetts Historical Collections,* Being a General Collection of Interesting Facts, Traditions, Biographical Sketches, Anecdotes, &c., Relating to the History and Antiquities of Every Town in Massachusetts, with Geographical Descriptions, by John Warner Barber, pp. 149–150. Entered, according to Act of Congress, in the year 1839, by Dorr, Howland & Co. In the Clerk's Office of the District Court of Massachusetts. Worcester.

From *The Nantucket Scrap Basket,* Being a Collection of Characteristic Stories and Sayings of the People of the Town and Island of Nantucket, Massachusetts, Second Edition, Revised, Expanded and Rearranged by William F. Macy, p. 72. Copyright, 1916, by William F. Macy and Roland B. Hussey. Copyright, 1930, by William F. Macy. Boston and New York: Houghton Mifflin Company.

away it seems to lose its virtue. So people come out here and sit on the bank and soak their feet. They say it does wonders for 'em." The old Cap'n was so serious that the strangers were much impressed and asked him if he would be willing to wait while they took a treatment. Nothing loth, the Swiftsure came to anchor, the passengers removed their shoes and stockings and sat on the mossy bank with their feet dabbling in the water for an hour or more while Cap'n B. rested his horses and placidly smoked his pipe. Whether it was the Cap'n or the passengers who revealed the joke was never known, but to this day that particular pool is known to the old-timers as "Corn Pond."

Jack Siah's Rock

ONCE there was a man named Jack Siah. He came to Dennis [, Massachusetts,] on a Christmas morning, drifting slowly shoreward, clinging to a broken spar. He was naked to the waist, dark and very tall. In his ears were golden hoops. On his broad chest ships were sailing—stars and anchors on his arms. He was a queer fellow and would have nothing to do with anyone, but lived sole alone on the beach. He built a cabin below the old Point Bluff, and lived on clams and wild fowl. He made his clothing from sealskins, and his fish lines from wild flax. And he would sit all day on a big rock, waiting for nibbles.

One morning the village boys found his cabin empty and told folks Jack had gone away. . . . And that afternoon an Indian caught a squid-hound. When he landed the monster in his boat, he saw that there was a second line in its mouth. The Indian pulled on it, and discovered that it stretched to sea. He took off his sealskin coat, and tugged and tugged. And when he had pulled it in, there was Jack Siah, with the line tied to his toe!

He must have grown sleepy, and tied it while he napped, thinking that a bite would waken him. The squid-hound had grabbed the bait, and given the line such a pull that Jack slid from the rock into the sea. And all day long the squid-hound dragged him about, dead as a doornail. Ever since then the rock on which he sat has been called Jack Siah's Rock.

Pomp's Lot

NORTHEASTERLY from the house of Leonard P. Rich [in Truro, Massachusetts,] is a wood-lot that keeps alive the memory of "Pomp," who was an African of the pure Congo species, purchased or stolen according to the

From *And This Is Cape Cod!*, by Eleanor Early, p. 61. Copyright, 1936, by Eleanor Early. Boston and New York: Houghton Mifflin Company.

From *Truro—Cape Cod, or Land Marks and Sea Marks*, by Shebnah Rich, p. 25. Copyright, 1883, by D. Lothrop and Company. Boston.

gospel of the times, by the captain of a whaleman from Truro, and on arrival sold to Jonathan Paine. Pomp performed his duties as a slave faithfully, but he was never fairly happy or content. He indulged in the homesick passion which the negro feels, and with his countrymen, believed in metempsychosis, or transmigration of soul.

One day when the longing for kith and kin and home was deep in his heart, he took a jug of water, a loaf of bread and a rope, and went into a thick wood-lot belonging to his master. Selecting a high tree, the stump of which may yet be seen, he placed his jug of water and loaf of bread at the foot of the tree, to sustain him over the journey, and placing the rope around his neck, took his departure for Afric's sunny fountains. Many days after, his body was found hanging to the tree; his soul had gone to the God who gave it, in whose merciful hands we leave him.

Squaw Rock

THE wigwam of Ahauton is said to have stood near the site where Hon. Charles H. French [of Canton, Massachusetts,] erected his stone house in 1854, a part of the material of which was blasted from an immense rock which stood out from the surrounding field and had been known to the former generation as "Squaw Rock." The tradition is that the squaw of William Ahauton, of Pecunit, after having lived for ten years in great love with her husband, was condemned at a hearing before Justice Daniel Gookin, in October, 1688, for conduct unbecoming a wife and mother. It was decided to spare her life, but that the said Ahauton "shall on the twenty-ninth instant stand on the gallows, after the lecture in Boston, weth a roape around hir neck one hower, and that the marshall-general shall cause hir to be took down, returned to prison, and commited to the Indian constable, who on a public day, by order of Capt. Gookin, shall severely whip hir, not exceeding thirty stripes." The punishment was duly inflicted; and, unable to bear the disgrace attending it, upon her return home she dashed out her brains by jumping head-foremost from this rock.

Defiance

A THIRD mill was built [in Dalton, Massachusetts,] in 1824 by Thomas Carson, David's son. Year after year the wooden dams above his structure

From *History of the Town of Canton, Norfolk County, Massachusetts*, by Daniel T. V. Huntoon, p. 23. Published by the Town. Cambridge: John Wilson and Son. University Press. 1893.

From *The Berkshire Hills*, Compiled and Written by Members of the Federal Writers' Project of the Works Progress Administration for Massachusetts, p. 237. Copyright, 1939, by The Berkshire Hills Conference, Inc. New York: Duell, Sloan and Pearce.

were washed away during the spring freshets. Carson commissioned a well-known engineer of the day to build a dam "that would stay." The natives, distrusting the ability of the "outsider," predicted the dam wouldn't last through the next spring. "I defy the Devil himself to wash it away!" shouted the engineer. His rash challenge made such a profound sensation in the town that both the dam and the mill were named "Defiance" from that day on. Not a badly chosen name, as it turned out, for the dam weathered the springs floods of forty years and was replaced only when a larger one became necessary.

Joe Keiler's Farm

A WAG named Keiler, owning property adjacent to the lake, once tried to make a sale of Pontoosuc [Lake, Pittsfield, Massachusetts,]—winter-bound as the lake was at the time—to a New York gentleman who mistook its snow-covered level expanse for highly desirable land set in a singularly attractive locality amid the encircling hills. The deed of sale was drawn up, but for some reason or other the transaction was never consummated. Possibly the would-be purchaser tried to see just how deep he would have to dig in order to place his cellar. The lake was called "Joe Keiler's Farm" for many a day.

Peru, Massachusetts

WHEN the village [of Partridge Field] was renamed in 1806, townsmen explained, "Like Peru in South America, we are in the mountains, and though there is no gold and silver under the rocks, our town favors hard money and begins with a P." Two years before, the western district of Peru had been set off, and, along with additions of land from neighboring grants, incorporated as the town of Hinsdale.

Bash-Bish

YOU may have read—or, at any rate, whether you have read it or not, it is true—that, at a very early date, there was a Swiss colony of iron-makers upon Mount Washington [, Massachusetts]. Miss Sedgwick asserts that

---

Ibid., p. 85.

Ibid., p. 251.

From *Taghconic; The Romance and Beauty of the Hills*, by Godfrey Greylock, (Joseph Edwards Adams Smith), pp. 222–223. Copyright, 1879, by J. E. A. Smith. Boston: Lee and Shepard; New York: Charles T. Dillingham; Pittsfield: S. E. Nichols.

they gave the name of Bash-Bish to the cascade—that being the patois of their canton for a small waterfall. But I have my doubts as to that: first, because two or three Swiss gentlemen of whom I made inquiry were not aware of anything of the kind; and, secondly, because Dr. O'Callaghan, the New York historian, once pointed me to an old vocabulary of the language of some western Indian tribes—in Illinois, I think—in which Bash-a-Bish is given as signifying a water-fall. Still Miss Sedgwick may be correct, as she had visited in Switzerland, and was the intimate friend of the historian, Sismondi, and his family. A resident of one canton in Switzerland is not necessarily familiar with the patois of another, and makers of Indian vocabularies are a long way from infallible, as I grieve to know.

But, however it may have been with regard to Bash-Bish, Miss Sedgwick is certainly good authority for the assertion that the Swiss colony gave the name of Mount Rhighi to the locality where they settled, in honor of the famous mountain they had left behind. She was a descendant of the most prominent of the early settlers of southern Berkshire, and was likely to be well informed in regard to its history.

Mingo Beach

As you go from Beverly to Manchester [, Massachusetts,] you will see the justly celebrated Mingo Beach about which there still echoes the tradition of Robin Mingo—a slave who had been promised his freedom on the day that the ebbing tide should leave a dry passage between Mingo's Beach and a rocky promontory called Becky's Ridge. He waited patiently for this great event, and then, one morning in 1773 when the receding tide did actually leave a dry passage, the kindly neighbors ran to tell him of the news. Awed and half terrified by the strange significance, they found the black man had indeed attained his freedom on that day, for he was lying dead—a smile upon his lips.

The Singing Beach

But Manchester's peculiar attraction is that beach of ruddy sand—a warm tawny pink—which, when a carriage drives over it or people tread on it, gives forth a crisp note, something like snow under foot in dry cold weather. This odd formation of the atoms which makes them triturate together in keen musical vibration has poetically christened it the Singing Beach, a wonder of the world and a never failing source of entertainment.

From *The Romantic Shore*, by Agnes Edwards, pp. 77–78. Copyright, 1915, by Agnes Edwards Rothery. Salem, Massachusetts: The Salem Press Company.

Ibid., p. 79.

Old Orchard Beach

THOMAS ROGERS, one of the earliest settlers here, who lived near Goose Fare Brook, planted an orchard, from which the beach takes its name. The Indians burned Rogers' house to the ground soon after their repulse at Phillips' garrison; but his orchard continued for a century longer to blossom among the ruins of his homestead,—an eloquent reminder of what it cost in the old days to be a pioneer.

Boon Island

ACCORDING to tradition, in April, 1682, the "Increase," a trader between Plymouth and Pemaquid, was wrecked on an offshore island, its only survivors, three white men and one Indian, existing as best they could on the rocky shores. They were nearly ready to give up hope of rescue when one day in May they saw smoke rising from the summit of Agamenticus. This smoke was that of the burnt offerings of hundreds of Indians from all over Maine, converts of Aspinquid, who was a disciple of John Eliot; they had brought deer, moose, fish, and even rattlesnakes to sacrifice in the flames to the memory of their departed leader. Heartened by the smoke that indicated the presence of people on the mainland, the castaways gathered driftwood and themselves built a huge fire which attracted rescuers from the mainland. In gratitude for their salvation, it is said, the men named the island Boon. Boon Island Light was erected here in 1811.

Mount Desert Island

THE same day [September 5th, 1604] we passed also near to an island about four or five leagues long, in the neighborhood of which we just escaped being lost on a little rock on a level with the water, which made an opening in our barque near the keel. From this island to the main land on the north, the distance is less than a hundred paces. It is very high

---

From *The Pine-Tree Coast,* by Samuel Adams Drake, p. 122. Copyright, 1890, by Estes & Lauriat. Boston. 1891.

From *Maine:* A Guide "Down East," written by Workers of the Federal Writers' Project of the Works Progress Administration for the State of Maine, p. 205. Copyright, 1937, by Everett F. Greaton, Executive Secretary, Maine Development Commission. Boston: Houghton Mifflin Company.

From "Journal of Samuel de Champlain," in *Forerunners and Competitors of the Pilgrims and Puritans,* edited for the New England Society of Brooklyn by Charles Herbert Levermore, Vol. 1, pp. 98–99. Brooklyn, New York: Published for the Society. 1912.

and notched in places, so that there is an appearance to one at sea, as of seven or eight mountains extending along near each other. The summit of the most of them is destitute of trees, as there are only rocks on them. The woods consist of pines, firs, and birches only. I named it Isle des Monts Déserts.* The latitude is 44° 30′.

The Maine Islands

THESE islands [of Casco Bay, Maine,] are sometimes called the Calendar Isles because an official English report of 1700 said, "Sd. Bay is covered from storms that come from the sea by a multitude of Islands, great and small, there being (if one may believe report) as many islands as there are Days in a yr."[1]

Casco Bay is said to contain *three hundred and sixty-five* islands. The same number of islands is attributed to many other bodies of water; and, in the several instances, we sometimes find geographers gravely remarking, that they are not sure that the number is quite accurate, or that any actual enumeration has been made: it does not occur to them, that the specification of this number is only a periphrasis of the proverbial expression—*as many as there are days in the year.*[2]

He remarked a quaint and vigorous play of imagination in the naming of the islands.** He began to note here, and continued to find on his travels in plenty, such titles as, the Ship, the Barge, the Whale-Boat, the House, the Basket, the Junk of Pork, Little Spoon and Big Spoon, the Ram, the Gooseberry, the Great Duck and Little Duck, the Brown Cow. Then there was a numerous human family of an eccentric sort: the Hussey, the Orphan, the Brothers, the Sisters, and the Old Man and Old Woman—

* "Possibly with a punning reference to the man who had sent him on the voyage." —*Maine:* A Guide "Down East" (Boston, 1937), p. 281.

It may be the perils of the fog, and rock, and mountain aspect, from the sea—all were suggestive of utter uninhabitableness, or depopulation—hence, an island of mountain wastes, uninhabitable, was the foremost and uppermost thought in the mind of the geographer in writing his narrative.—From an old newspaper clipping scrapbook in the editor's possession.

[1] From *Maine:* A Guide "Down East," Written by Workers of the Federal Writers' Project of the Works Progress Administration for the State of Maine, p. 211. Copyright, 1937, by Everett F. Greaton, Executive Secretary, Maine Development Commission. Boston: Houghton Mifflin Company.

[2] From *Travels through the Northern Parts of the United States, in the Years 1807 and 1808*, by Edward Augustus Kendall, Esq., Vol. III, p. 149. New York: Printed and Published by I. Riley. 1809.

** Cf. Edwin Valentine Mitchell, *Maine Summer* (New York, 1939), pp. 37–41.

in short, a suggestion of every shape or trait from common life to which a resemblance could be forced by the liveliest fancy.[3]

. . . Such intriguing farmyard names of some of them—such as Lower Goose and Upper Goose, the Goslings, Sow and Pigs, Ram, Cow, Horse, Little Bull Ledge, Big Hen and Little Hen, Dog's Head, Turnip, Gooseberry, Clapboard, Goose Nest, Junk of Pork, and Pound of Tea, so named they say because that was the basis of a swapping deal made by a canny Yankee fisherman.[4]

Sea-Gull Cliffs

FROM these creatures the locality has taken the name of Sea-Gull Cliffs.

It seems that these gulls were in danger of extermination until the people of the island awoke to the necessity of preserving them as one of its attractions. In the first place, some thoughtless person introduced foxes to the island. These animals soon drove the gulls to retreats inaccessible either to man or beast. Then came the caprice for wearing the snow-white breasts and wings on ladies' bonnets. This brought a swarm of eager hunters down upon the gulls, and soon drove them to make their rookeries still farther out, so that few remained in their old haunts. At this stage the law was invoked for their protection, much to the amusement of the lawmakers, be it said, who could not see why such a useless thing as a gull should be made to occupy their serious attention.

"I will tell you why, gentlemen," said the champion of the gulls of Grand Manan. "We islanders get our living by fishing. Now for one thing, the gulls show us where fish are schooling, for they fish as well as we; and so where we see gulls sailing about the water we steer our boats. We don't want them killed off, because, dumb creatures though they are, their instinct helps us to live."

By this time the provincial legislature had settled itself to listen.

"For another thing, gentlemen," the spokesman for the gulls went on, "our men are often caught out in the bay in a fog; and when that happens, the screams the gulls set up if a boat or a vessel comes near the cliffs—for you must know, gentlemen, that a gull can see enough farther than a

[3] From "Fish and Men in the Maine Islands," by W. H. Bishop, in *Harper's New Monthly Magazine,* Vol. LXI (August, 1880), No. 363, p. 338. Entered according to Act of Congress, in the year 1880, by Harper and Brothers in the Office of the Librarian of Congress, at Washington. New York.

[4] From *I Discover Maine,* Little-Known Stories about a Well-Known State, by Herbert G. Jones, pp. 51–52. Copyright, 1937, by Curtis Stuart Laughlin. Portland: The Machigonne Press.

From *The Pine-Tree Coast,* by Samuel Adams Drake, p. 378. Copyright, 1890, by Estes and Lauriat. Boston. 1891.

man—often does us a good turn in a bad place, by letting us know where we are. We don't want the gulls destroyed, because they help to keep us from death by shipwreck. That's all I have to say."

The bill was passed without further speech-making.

Hockamock Head

. . . HOCKAMOCK HEAD, the gray and craggy headland on the inside passage between Boothbay Harbor and Bath, Maine, received its name from a baroque incident which occurred there in colonial times. Near it was a small settlement which was attacked and burned by the Indians. On the appearance of the savages, the settlers abandoned their homes and fled along the promontory, where the cliffs and steeps made a series of natural defenses. As they raced across the neck toward their stronghold, the Indians pursued them hotly.

"A Scotchman," says a Maine historian, "less fleet of foot than his fellows from age or corpulence, his head protected by a wig of antique size and fashion, brought up the lagging rear, and soon fell within grasp of the pursuing red man, whose outstretched hand laid hold of the flowing wig for a head of hair which promised a magnificent trophy to the scalping knife. But to the surprise and consternation of the savage, the periwig clave to his hold, while the apparently headless body still ran on, leaping from steep to steep, utterly indifferent to what he had left behind. The astonished savage, believing he had been running a race with a devil, suddenly stopped, and dropping the wig in superstitious horror, turned to fly in the opposite direction, crying to his comrades, 'Hockamock! Hockamock! The devil! The devil!'"

Bug Hollow

"BUG HOLLER" was located in outer Broadway [Brewer, Maine]. The story connected with it is that in the early days a crew of men was walking to a lumbering operation in or around Glenburn. Most of the men were new in this section and some of them were direct from Ireland. A brook, which crossed the road near where Bean's store now is, had low, swampy shores for some distance on both sides. As the men walked along the road, several large mud turtles were startled from their sleep and started crawling to the brook. One of the Irishmen, never seeing one before, hollered to the other men, "Come quick, for God's sake, and see these bugs." Thus the name "Bug Holler."

From *It's an Old New England Custom,* by Edwin Valentine Mitchell, pp. 250–251. Copyright, 1946, by Edwin Valentine Mitchell. New York: The Vanguard Press, Inc.

By John Lamson, Brewer, Maine. Manuscripts of the Federal Writers' Project of the Works Progress Administration for the State of Maine.

Coos

Moose Hillock [, New Hampshire,] towers over the Connecticut below the Fifteen-Mile Falls, by which latter all further navigation of the river is precluded. Above and below the Fifteen-Mile Falls, on the Connecticut, are tracts of country, called respectively the Upper and the Lower *Coos* or *Cohoss;* which term implies, according to some, a fall in a river; according to others, a bend in a river; and, according to a third party, a parcel of meadowland; but the true interpretation is pineland, the word being derived from the Indian *cohâ* or *coä;* a pine-tree. Some Indians, of this part of the Connecticut, still remain at Saint-François, where they call themselves *Cohâssiac.*—Such is the origin of the name *cohass, cohoss* or *coös;* but, the pine-trees having been removed, their place is occupied by meadow; while, at the same time, the lands lie on bends of the river, and are contiguous to the Fifteen-Mile Falls:—hence, the diverse explanations.

* * * * *

The explanation of the word *cohoss,* which is here applied to two tracts of country on the Connecticut, is not to be extended to the word *cohoes* or *cohoez,* a name given to a cataract on the Mohawk River, in the ancient country of the Six Nations or Iroquois. *Cohoes* has been supposed to be formed of sounds imitating the noise of falling water; but the name really belongs to the basin at the foot of the cataract, considered simply as a *receptacle.* It implies, in the Mohawk dialect of the Iroquois, a place to which canoes, or anything floated away by the stream, will be carried, and where therefore it is reasonable to look for them. *Cohoos* and *cohoes* are therefore words belonging to two different languages.

Nancy's Brook

I have heard it said by the people of Portsmouth, that when children were at play and happened to fall out with each other, the worst punishment they

---

From *Travels through the Northern Parts of the United States, in the Years 1807 and 1808,* by Edward Augustus Kendall, Vol. III, pp. 191, 194n. New York: Printed and Published by I. Riley. 1809.

From *The History of the White Mountains from the First Settlement of Upper Coos and Pequaket,* by Lucy, Wife of Ethan Allen, Crawford, pp. 107–110. Entered, according to Act of Congress, in the year 1845, by Lucy Crawford, in the Clerk's Office of the District Court of New Hampshire. White Hills. 1846.

One cascade, however, about half a mile from the former residence of old Abel Crawford, is more honored by the sad story associated with it than by the picturesqueness of the crags through which it hurries for the last mile or two of its descending course. It is called "Nancy's Brook"; and the stage-drivers show to the passengers the stone which is the particular monument of the tragedy, bearing the name "Nancy's Rock."

Here, late in the autumn of the year 1778, a poor girl, who lived with a family in Jefferson [New Hampshire,] was found frozen to death.—Thomas Starr King, *The White Hills* (Boston, 1866), p. 184.

could inflict upon their mates was to wish them up to the White Hills, as that was considered the worst place in the world by them. Perhaps their minds had been affected by the story of Nancy, who perished in the woods in attempting to follow her lover. She had been at work in Jefferson for Colonel Whipple, when the heart of this honest girl was won by a servant of his; and as he was going in the fall to Portsmouth, he promised to take her along with him, and after they should arrive there, he would make her his wife. She was honest herself and thought him to be also; and he had contrived every means to please her in all their domestic concerns which they were engaged in, while under the control of the Colonel, and she had entrusted him with her money, which had been paid her for her labor, and she went to Lancaster to make preparations for the intended journey; while she was preparing, her lover went away with the Colonel and left her behind. She was immediately informed of his treachery, and was determined to pursue him. There had been a deep snow and there was no road—nothing, but spotted trees, besides the tracks of the Colonel and her false lover to follow. When she arrived at Jefferson she was wet with snow which had collected upon her clothes, and was wearied. The men that were there tried to persuade her not to go any further, setting forth the many difficulties she would have to encounter, and likewise the danger she would be exposed to in such an undertaking, through a howling wilderness of thirty miles, without fire or food. All these entreaties did not move her, or alter her determination; for such was her love either for the man whom she had placed her affections upon, or the money she had placed in his hands, that she was inflexible; and having a great opinion of her own ability, in her imagination she thought as they had only been gone some hours, and would probably go no further than the Notch that night, and would probably camp there, she might, by travelling all night, overtake them before they started in the morning.—In this she was disappointed; they had left before she arrived; but from every appearance the fire had not gone out. It may be inquired how it was known that the fire had not gone out there? When a fire is made in the woods, it is made of very large wood, cut and rolled together, and then left to burn, as was evidently the case here, and there will be brands left at each end of the fire. These brands she had put together, and they burnt out as the ashes plainly showed for themselves, when the men found them. She was tired and worn out with fatigue and hunger, having taken nothing with her to eat on the way. Yet her passion was not abated, and she still persevered, thinking she could overtake them. She went on and got a distance of twenty-two miles when the men, thinking she was in earnest, followed her. —When she set off in the afternoon, they thought she would not go far before she would come back, and they waited until late in the evening, expecting every moment to hear the sound of her footsteps at the door; but in vain did they imagine this. They pressed on and found the fire in the situation just described, which made them think she found fire to warm her benumbed limbs. Here they rested only a short time and then proceeded and found her just after crossing a brook, in a sitting position, with her clothes frozen upon her—having wet them while crossing the brook, and her head was resting on her hand and cane which had been her support through the woods, and she was frozen to death.

This place is near my father's and has ever since, from that circumstance, borne the name of Nancy's Brook, and Nancy's Hill. . .

The reader would perhaps like to know what became of her lover. Shortly after hearing of this, his own conscience was smitten and he became frantic and insane, and was put into the hospital, where he in a few months after, died in a most horrible condition. This is a true story, as I have heard it told by those who were knowing to the facts, as related in the above statement.

Moses' Rock

Near the center of the town [Shelbourne, New Hampshire,] is a steep, precipitous ledge, named Moses' Rock. It is sixty feet high and ninety long, very smooth, and rising in an angle of fifty degrees. Tradition says that a hunter once drove a moose over the steep descent, and his dog, in close pursuit, followed close at his heels, both mingling together in one common mass at the foot. During the early survey of the town, the best lot of land in the township was offered to the man who would climb this ledge. One Moses Ingalls, stripping off his shoes, accomplished the daring feat, running up its smooth front like a cat. This circumstance gave it its name.

Joe English Hill

Joe English Hill in New Boston [, New Hampshire,] stands out above all others in both height and interest with its southern side some two or three hundred feet in height and nearly perpendicular. As you ride along the base and scan the upright mass of shelving rock, you unconsciously wonder what powerful upheaval of nature rent such precipices in the bowels of the earth and threw them up into such a gigantic pile. The incident

From *Incidents in White Mountain History:* Containing Facts Relating to the Discovery and Settlement of the Mountains, Indian History and Traditions, A Minute and Authentic Account of the Destruction of the Willey Family, Geology, and Temperature of the Mountains; Together with Numerous Anecdotes Illustrating Life in the Back Woods, by Rev. Benjamin G. Willey, p. 246. Entered, according to Act of Congress, in the year 1855, by Benjamin G. Willey, in the Clerk's Office of the District Court of the District of Massachusetts. Boston: Published by Nathaniel Noyes. 1856.

By Derry Women's Club. From *New Hampshire Folk Tales,* compiled by Mrs. Moody P. Gore and Mrs. Guy E. Speare, pp. 21–23. Copyright, 1932, by New Hampsire Federation of Women's Clubs.

from which the hill took its name is in this wise:—in 1705 or 1706 there was an Indian living in these parts noted for his friendship for the English settlers upon the lower Merrimack.

He was an accomplished warrior and hunter, but following the counsels of Passaconaway, and Wonalancet, continued steadfast in his partiality for the whites. From this fact the Indians gave him the name, "Joe English." In the course of time, the Indians, satisfied that Joe gave information of their hostile designs toward the English, determined to kill him at the earliest opportunity. Accordingly, one day just at twilight, finding Joe upon one of the branches of the "Squag" hunting, they commenced an attack upon him. He escaped from them, two or three in number, and ran directly for this hill in the southeastern part of New Boston. Quick as thought, Indian like, he concluded that in a long race the chances were against him and he must use strategy. Going up the hill he slackened his pace until his pursuers were almost upon him, that they might become more eager. When near the top, he started with greater rapidity and the Indians raced him, straining every nerve. As Joe came upon the brink of the precipice, he leaped behind a jutting rock and waited. A moment passed, the hard breathing and light footsteps of his pursuers were heard, but in another moment, with screeches and yells, their dark forms were rolling down the steep rocks, to be food for the hungry wolves at the base. Henceforth the hill was called "Joe English" and well did his friendship deserve so enduring a monument.

Joe English was the grandson of the Sagamore of Agawam (now Ipswich) whose name was Wasconnomet. Later he came to his death in consequence of his fidelity to the whites. He was acting as guide to Lieut. Butterfield and a party of three, between Dunstable and Chelmsford, when he fell into an Indian ambuscade. Joe was the object of pursuit and toward him they directed their energies. A hard race ensued, and he had nearly gained the thick woods when the Indians, despairing of taking him alive, fired upon and disabled him. They expressed their pleasure, saying, "Now Joe, we got you; you no tell English again we come." "No," retorted Joe, "Cap'n Butterfield tell that at Pautucket." "Ugh," exclaimed the Indians, the thought just striking them that the soldiers would soon be upon them.

There was no time for delay and a hatchet was buried in the head of the prostrate Indian. Thus died Joe English, the white man's faithful friend. Later the legislature of Massachusetts made a grant of land to his wife and two children because, "He died in the service of his country."

Bungy-jar

"BUNGY-JAR" or the "bungy-bull a-bellowing" is often heard on a perfectly clear day on Sugar Hill [, New Hampshire]. It is a curious natural

---

By Ola G. Veazie. Manuscripts of the Federal Writers' Project of the Works Progress Administration for the State of New Hampshire.

phenomenon. When the south wind starts to blow through Kinsman Notch, it sounds something like surf beating on a shore that cannot be seen. It increases in intensity until a storm has blown up. Fog will sooner or later come through the Notch. It starts like a thin veil and will gradually thicken up and the weather will not clear until the fog ceases to roll over the tops of the mountains and settles off level. This level will be the snow-line in the winter time. There will be snow-chimneys when the south wind is just starting to blow and the natives can tell the difference between the storm fog and the snow fog. "When the fog runs up the mountain, rain runs down the hill" is an old saying which the natives have found to be true. Most summer people, however, look for the end of a storm when the fog starts up the mountain.

"Bungy-jar" gets its name in an interesting manner. In the very earliest days many settlers entered Franconia and Easton through Kinsman Notch and the south as it was more direct than through the Profile Notch or Littleton. Roads were opened there first. Many of these settlers located for a year or so in Benton and Easton but the land was more fertile farther down the valleys and many moved along after a short stay. The ones who stayed said of those who moved along that they "bunged out" and soon that district became known as "Bungy Corner" and hence the name "Bungy-jar."

One time a native of Sugar Hill moved to an adjoining town but came back for a visit. He was asked if he liked his new location and replied, "No, I long to hear the roar of Kinsman and see the devil pump fog out of Lincoln."

Waterloo

WATERLOO [, New Hampshire,] . . . takes its name from the village of the same name in central New York,[1] although there is a traditional explanation that in the fall of 1815, just after the close of the second war with Great Britain, there was a "raising" in the hamlet around the Great Falls. All men and boys of the village and the surrounding region were assembled to put up the frame of the John P. Colby house. About that time the mail carrier arrived on horseback at the post office. "What's the news?" somebody shouted. "Old Bonaparte has been beat by the British at Waterloo,

---

From *New Hampshire,* A Guide to the Granite State, written by Workers of the Federal Writers' Project of the Works Progress Administration for the State of New Hampshire, p. 436. The American Guide Series. Copyright, 1938, by the Secretary of State, State of New Hampshire. Boston: Houghton Mifflin Company.

[1] Two New Hampshire deputy sheriffs chased a fugitive from New Hampshire into New York and captured him at Waterloo. So impressed were the deputies with the beauty of the village of Waterloo lying at the foot of Seneca Lake that they not only brought back their man but also the name of the place where they caught him.—Edwin Valentine Mitchell, *It's an Old New England Custom* (New York, 1946), p. 247.

and he is dead beat too." On hearing it, Philip Colby is said to have remarked, "Too bad the British licked him, but the world will remember him; so hurrah for Waterloo!"

Lost River

THERE is a tradition that some 50 years after [Asa] Kinsman hewed his way through the Notch [that bears his name], two boys, Royal and Lyman Jackman, went fishing there. Suddenly, according to Royal, Lyman disappeared "as though the earth had opened and swallowed him." He had dropped down a dozen feet through a hole into a waist-high pool. Badly frightened but unhurt, he was fished out by Royal. Many years afterward, Royal came back to North Woodstock to visit, and with a group of boys found his way through the woods to the present Cave of Shadows. This, the old man declared, was where he and his brother found "the lost river." The name is more probably derived from the fact that the Moosilauke River has a way of losing itself here and there beneath huge rocks, riven by frost action from the side of the mountain to the north and tumbled down the riverbed.

Peru, Vermont

SOMETIME between December 1803 and February 1804 the name of the town was changed from Bromley to Peru. It is said the change was made because Bromley, so far as it had any reputation abroad, was noted for being a poverty-stricken place, and few would go there to settle; but the name of Peru being associated with the wealth of the South American Province, conveyed an entirely different impression. And indeed, very soon after the change, people began to come into the place, and for a time the town increased quite rapidly. It is thought by some, even now, that Peru is a poor township of land; true, there is no great wealth here, but there have been 16 years (not consecutive) during which no "poor" have been upon the town. Truly, here, if anywhere, has been answered the prayer of Agur, "Give me neither poverty nor riches."

Ibid., p. 411.

From "Peru," by Miss Nancy M. Haynes, in *The Vermont Historical Gazetteer: A Magazine, Embracing a History of Each Town, Civil, Ecclesiastical, Biographical and Military*, edited by Abby Maria Hemenway, in Three Volumes, Vol. I, p. 208. Entered according to Act of Congress, in the year 1859, by Abby Maria Hemenway, in the Clerk's Office of the District Court of the District of Vermont. Burlington, Vermont: Published by Miss A. M. Hemenway. 1867.

INDIAN AND PSEUDO-INDIAN

Lovers' Leap

Both the most picturesque and the least substantiated of these legends is the Pocahontaslike story that is supposed to have given the name of Lovers' Leap to the western precipice of the gorge below Waramaug's palace [near New Milford, Connecticut]. According to the story, one summer day in the years before the whites had come up to Weantinock to settle, the great chief's daughter Lillinonah discovered a paleface youth lost and hungry in the forest. She took him to her father, pleaded for and saved his life, and when the first snow flew obtained the chief's consent to their marriage. The boy said he must return to his people for a little while, but that he would return shortly. The winter dragged through and he did not return. By May, Lillinonah was in a dangerous decline, and Waramaug decreed that she should marry a certain promising young sagamore. On the wedding day, Lillinonah's maidens decked her in her finest beads and feathers, but just before the ceremony she slipped down to the river and, pushing out in her little canoe below the falls of Metichawan, headed downstream toward the canyon and the great rapids thundering through it with the power of the spring flood. When she was already in the gorge and nearing the heavy whirl of waters that would be her doom, her true white lover appeared on the cliff above, leaped down the hundred-foot precipice, and so joined her in the arms of the Great Spirit.

The Canoe of the Two Sisters

Washining and Washinee[1] were the beautiful daughters of an old and tyrannical chief who claimed the land between the Housatonic and the Hudson: suitors travelled from far council-fires, but none were accepted. War was made on the chief by a hostile tribe, but the Weatogue band were crafty, and the young leader was captured and condemned to death by torture. Each of the sisters secretly fell in love with the captive brave, and brought him food. They begged their obdurate father to set him free; finally, wild with grief, the sisters confessed to each other their secret. The

---

From *The Housatonic, Puritan River,* by Chard Powers Smith, pp. 107–108. Copyright, 1946, by Chard Powers Smith. New York and Toronto: Rinehart & Company, Incorporated.

From *Old Paths and Legends of the New England Border:* Connecticut, Deerfield, Berkshire, by Katharine M. Abbott, pp. 352–354. Copyright, 1907, by Katharine M. Abbott. New York and London: G. P. Putnam's Sons.

[1] Salisbury's glorious Twin Lakes—Panaheconnok and Hokonkamok, or Washining and Washinee, the "Laughing Water" and the "Smiling Water."—*Ibid.*, p. 352.

evening arrived before the fateful day of torture and no reprieve. Then the dusky maidens pushed off their frail canoe into the moonlit waves and sprang into the lake together. They say that when the moon is at the full an empty canoe is seen floating, it may be on Washining, it may be on Washinee; if you gaze long it will fade away, and the stillness is broken only by the hoot of the night-owl.

Carbuncle Pond

FROM Coventry [, Rhode Island,] comes the Legend of Carbuncle Pond. Years ago when that particular region was claimed by Narragansett and Mohegan alike, there lived on Carbuncle Hill a great snake. Its species was unknown, but its size was enormous and in the center of its head was a large gem—a carbuncle—deep red, glowing with the brilliancy and radiance of a great fire. Whenever it moved about at night, its coming was announced by the glow of the gem, and even by day its light could be seen in a crimson flood in the darkness of the woods. Efforts of the Indians to capture the snake were unsuccessful until, shortly before the coming of the first white men, a large party of Indians surprised the reptile, and after a terrific battle killed it and secured the carbuncle. Tradition relates that at the scene of the battle a large rock was cleft in twain by the snake's tail. The carbuncle served the Indian tribe as a talisman and warning of danger for many years. When the white men came and heard the story of this wonderful gem, they longed to possess it and arranged an expedition against the Indians for that purpose. They attempted a surprise attack, but their advance was announced by the increased glow of the stone, and the Indians were prepared. After a battle which decimated the Indians, the chief alone was left standing; but when the white men tried to take the carbuncle from him he drew back his arm and gave it a mighty throw. It landed with a great splash in the middle of the pond and was lost forever.

The Origin of Nantucket

CONCERNING the discovery of Nantucket by the Indians, they had the following fabulous tradition, which was related to the early English settlers.

In former times, a great many moons ago, a bird, extraordinary for its size, used often to visit the south shore of Cape Cod, and carry from thence in its talons a vast number of small children. Maushope, who was

From *Rhode Island*, A Guide to the Smallest State, written by Workers of the Federal Writers' Project of the Works Progress Administration for the State of Rhode Island, pp. 106-107. American Guide Series. Copyright, 1937, by Louis W. Cappelli, Secretary of State for the State of Rhode Island and Providence Plantations. Boston: Houghton Mifflin Company.

an Indian giant, as fame reports, resided in these parts. Enraged at the havoc among the children, he on a certain time waded into the sea in pursuit of the bird, till he had crossed the sound and reached Nantucket. Before Maushope forded the sound, the island was unknown to the red men. Maushope found the bones of the children in a heap, under a large tree. He then, wishing to smoke a pipe, ransacked the island for tobacco, but finding none, he filled his pipe with poke, a weed which the Indians sometimes used as a substitute. Ever since the above memorable events, fogs have been frequent at Nantucket and on the Cape. In allusion to this tradition, when the aborigines observed a fog rising, they would say, "There comes old Maushope's *smoke*." This tradition has been related in another way: that an eagle having seized and carried off a papoose, the parents followed him in their canoe till they came to Nantucket, where they found the bones of their child, dropped by the eagle. There is another Indian tradition that Nantucket was formed by Maushope, by emptying the ashes from his pipe after he had done smoking.—The two tribes on the island were hostile to each other. Tradition has preserved a pleasing instance of the effect of love. The western tribe having determined to surprise and attack the eastern tribe, a young man of the former, whose mistress belonged to the latter, being anxious for her safety, as soon as he was concealed by the shades of night, ran to the beach, flew along the shore below the limit of high water, saw his mistress a moment, gave the alarm, and returned by the same route before day-break; the rising tide washed away the traces of his feet. The next morning he accompanied the other warriors of the tribe to the attack: the enemy was found prepared, and no impression could be made on them. He remained undetected till, several years after, peace being restored between the two tribes, and the young man having married the girl, the truth came to light.[1]

While Moshop was the first inhabitant of Martha's Vineyard of whom there is any authentic record, these same records concerning him plainly show that the land was well peopled in his time, as witness the following:—

Moshop was as kind hearted and wise as he was great and good, and to him all those in trouble came for counsel and advice. So it came to pass that a certain maiden whose poverty prevented her union with the youth of her choice came to the Great Chief. The fathers of the young people were petty chiefs and equal in rank, but the one was poor, the other rich,

---

[1] From *Massachusetts Historical Collections,* Being a General Collection of Interesting Facts, Traditions, Biographical Sketches, Anecdotes, &c., Relating to the History and Antiquities of Every Town in Massachusetts, with Geographical Descriptions, by John Warner Barber, pp. 447–448. Entered, according to Act of Congress, in the year 1839, by Dorr, Howland & Co., in the Clerk's Office of the District Court of Massachusetts. Worcester.

and the wealthy father would not permit his son to take a poor girl to wife.

The lovers, after talking the situation over, concluded that their only help lay in Moshop, and the girl, as the best pleader, was chosen to bear the petition. Then watching her opportunity when the chief, her father, had gone on a long hunt, the girl started on her journey to Aquinnah, and toiling up its steep slopes, for the heights in those days were 500 feet or more above the sea, she came into the presence. She was much frightened to see the great man loom so tall above her, but he spoke gently and she finally found courage to tell her story, receiving a prompt promise of aid.

It was appointed that the two lovers should meet the Giant on Sampson's Hill, Chappaquiddick, and there they came. While discussing the matter and canvassing every possible expedient, the elder took out his pipe and began to smoke. Now you must know that the pipe was in accord with the size of the man, and that it took many bales of tobacco to fill it, so that when he was through and proceeded to knock the ashes out into the sea there arose a tremendous hissing sound and great clouds of smoke and vapor which filled the whole region with a dense fog.

There was method in all this on the part of Moshop, but the lovers, who did not appreciate it, only thought he was a poky old giant and very slow to suggest a remedy for their very real woes. Imagine then their astonishment when, as the fog lifted, they beheld a beautiful island in the sea, gilded by the rising sun.

Thus was Nantucket born to meet the wants of a pair of Vineyard lovers. The marriage portion being now provided, the hard hearted parent relented and there was nothing to longer delay the ceremony which Moshop himself performed, and after celebrating the nuptials at his royal mansion in a fitting manner, he dismissed the pair to their new domain with his blessing.

So in Nantucket we have the authentic proof that the great Moshop once lived, and while it may gall our little neighbor to know that it was never intended in the original order of things and was merely created to fill a sudden emergency, it yet seems best to give the facts without bias.

Some there be who call Nantucket "The Devil's Ash Heap," but the reader can readily see that this is a deliberate slur born of malice and all manner of uncharitableness. The facts are as above stated.[2]

[2] From *The Story of Martha's Vineyard,* from the Lips of Its Inhabitants, Newspaper Files and Those Who Have Visited Its Shores, Including Stray Notes on Local History and Industries, Collected and Arranged by C. G. Hine, pp. 211–213. Entered, according to Act of Congress, in the year 1908, by C. G. Hine, in the office of the Librarian of Congress, Washington, D. C. New York: Hine Brothers.

The Devil's Bridge

Moshop is said to have originally held sway on the mainland where, after a fierce battle and the loss of nearly all his braves, he was defeated and forced to fly. Then he came to Aquinnah, and in a well watered place called the Den he made his home. The Devil's Den is a hollow in the edge of the cliff about 100 feet deep, and several hundred feet south of the lighthouse. It is claimed by some to be the crater of an extinct volcano.

To this dwelling he brought his lovely Squant, now Ol' Squant, and their twelve beautiful daughters. Standing at his door he would catch a whale, or other great fish, by the tail and swing it up to his hearthstone where a fire always burned, constantly replenished by large forest trees which he pulled up by the roots for the purpose.

When the whales failed to approach near enough Moshop would throw great rocks into the sea on which to approach his victim—hence the Devil's Bridge.

Moshop appears to have been a kindly disposed old fellow and a hard worker when it was necessary. The following legend tells how he was outwitted and his work brought to naught by the cunning of an old woman. Those living on the Vineyard wished to secure easy access to the island of Cuttyhunk, and begged Moshop to build a bridge across, while the Cuttyhunkers, who were satisfied with their home trade, and desired not the intrusion of foreigners, as earnestly begged him not to build; thus was he torn between two opinions, until finally his home friends prevailed and he consented, the only stipulation being that he was to begin at sunset and stop at cockcrow, whether the bridge was finished or not. This, however, would give ample time.

Then were they of Cuttyhunk much alarmed and exercised, being wholly unable to devise any means to stay his hand until an old woman came forward and said that if watch was kept and she informed when Moshop began, she would stop him. Her friends thought her crazy, asking how a poor, weak woman could stop such a great giant, when the strength of all the men of Cuttyhunk could not prevail against him. But she persisted, and they finally agreed. Thus a sharp watch was kept every sunset until finally Moshop was seen to approach the shore with a great rock in his hands and, as the sun took his evening dip in the western waters, to throw it far out into the Sound.

Then came rocks in a shower, some as large as the greatest wigwams, and the bridge began rapidly to grow. All Cuttyhunk was soon on the beach, watching by the dying light of day the terrific pace at which Moshop worked, and it was only when it became too dark to see that they bethought them of the old woman and ran to her with cries and taunts, asking what she was going to do about it, but she dismissed them to their homes.

Ibid., pp. 209–211.

Then went she in unto her cock, and passing a bright light before his eyes caused him to awake with the thought of dawn in his mind, whereupon he lustily began to crow and Moshop was, by the bargain he had made, compelled to stop his work. But the rocks remain even unto this day, and many a good ship has gone to pieces on the Devil's Bridge.

The Siren of Narragansett Bay

THERE lived, many summers ago, a set of giants on the islands of Narragansett, who were of great power and strength. Among these giants, one was called Moshup, who had a reputation of being very cruel when in anger. This report was corroborated by the following anecdote. One day, while in his lodge, something occurred to enrage Moshup, at which he caught up his wife, who stood near by, and hurled her through the air. She dropped upon Seaconet Point; but, singular to relate, survived the fall, and for many years was heard singing low, melancholy songs, while she sat alone overlooking the bay. These songs were so sweet and seductive that many a fisherman moored his canoe and sought the singer, when he was always obliged to pay her tribute. Many moons passed, and the siren sat upon the shore, singing her songs; but finally, one morning, it was noticed that her song had ceased. Great curiosity was felt among the people; one, who had been very much enamored with her, went to the place where she usually was found. Alas! she had been transformed into a rock.

The Legend of Scargo Lake

SCARGO LAKE, to the eastward, figures in an ofttold Indian legend. So long ago that no tree-rings can number the years, Princess Scargo was the darling of her chieftain-father, Sagam of the Nobscussets. His favorite squaw, so the story goes, died in giving birth to the princess, and Sagam, stricken and bewildered, vowed that the innocent baby should never have to ponder the dark riddle of death, never have to face the intimacy of loss as he had faced it.

From *Indian Myths,* or Legends, Traditions, and Symbols of the Aborigines of America, Compared with Those of Other Countries Including Hindustan, Egypt, Persia, Assyria, and China, by Ellen Russell Emerson, pp. 438–439. Copyright, 1884, by Ellen Russell Emerson. Boston: James R. Osgood and Company.

From *Cape Cod Pilot,* by Jeremiah Digges, with Editorial and Research Assistance of the Members of the Federal Writers' Project, pp. 94–96. American Guide Series, Federal Writers' Project, Works Progress Administration for the State of Massachusetts. Copyright, 1937, by Poor Richard Associates. Provincetown and New York: Modern Pilgrim Press and the Viking Press.

One day, among the gifts the distant tribes sent to Scargo, arrived one which snared her fancy as no other—a golden bowl carved from a pumpkin; water inside, and in the water, "little perch and dainty trout."

When the fish got bigger, Scargo made a little pool. They grew in number; then there came a dry summer. The streams failed, the pool dwindled, and some of the Princess's pets, "with gills wide opened, turned them on their sides to die."

The little girl had never heard of the thing called dying. But somehow she knew. Her grief was intolerable to Sagam. He called for signal fires, and drew to him all his warriors, squaws, even the papooses, for a mighty powwow. The tribe, he said, must dig a fishpond—one that would be so wide and so deep it would never fail—as broad across, in fact, as an arrow's flight.

The Princess picked the brawniest brave in the tribe to draw the bow, and stood him so that dart should have fair wind.

Scargo watched the arrow's falling,
Placed a shell on either side,
Cheated some on east and west lines,
Got it longer than 'twas wide.

For weeks in the broiling sun, the squaws toiled on, and the braves grunted. At last, in the autumn, it was finished; a great heap of sand, Scargo Hill, stood beside it. And the rains of October filled the lake to its brim. Of her beloved fish the Princess had saved a few.

Now she placed them in the pond,
Watched them as they swam away,
There they are, or their descendants,
Swimming to this very day.

And on quiet summer evenings,
At the far side of the lake,
Calling gently, "Scargo, Scargo!"—
Then the echoes will awake.

The legend has been told in several forms, but most published versions of it draw upon a long anonymous poem that was published in the *Cape Cod Magazine* in January, 1922, from which the above passages are quoted. The poem concludes:

Where the shadows lie the deepest
Loving couples often pause.
They are listening to the echoes,
'Tis the grumbling of the squaws.

Santuit Pond

Long ago, before the Crockers or any other English folk lived here, a giant trout came into the South Sea. This was old Mish-que—in the language of the Indians, "great red fish." He was a thousand years off the coast of the Nausets, and another thousand years in the waters of the Monomoyicks, and how many thousands of years he had spent near the Mattakeesets, or the Nobscussets or the Payomets, nobody knew. But now, certainly, Mish-que was getting on, and no fish knew it better than he. He had peopled the ocean with his kind, his mission in life was done. In his old age he desired quiet water, and most of all, solitude; and there was a spot he remembered, a placid, lonely harbor on the Bay, across-Cape. But it was a bad thing, to be in the South Sea and suddenly to remember the waters of the Bay—and to be as old as Mish-que; it was disheartening to think of the long swim, all the way around, through the stormy waters to the far tip of the Cape and then across-Bay. Mish-que hesitated. And while he was swimming back and forth and pondering the situation, an Indian girl watched him from the beach at Popponesset.

"Old Mish-que!" she said. "Go find the quiet water, where you belong now. You are as bad, my friend, as some of our braves in the tribe, who never know when they are *san-quoi*!" And because san-quoi meant old, and because the young girl was thinking of a thing that had happened, she laughed.

"I am not like your old men in the tribe," Mish-que answered stiffly. "If I could get to the quiet water, I would go there."

The girl thought of the short way to the calm waters—overland. "Come, old fish!" she cried suddenly, and beckoned inshore. When Mish-que obeyed, she jumped astride his back and headed him up the beach. Mish-que struggled hard over the sand, on through the fields and the woods, leaving a great gully behind him. The girl whispered and urged him on, but before he was half-way across-Cape, his strength failed him. He spied a pond, made for it, and dove in. The laughing girl of Popponesset was carried in with him, and neither girl nor fish was ever seen again. The pond is called Santuit—"place for the aged"—and from it now runs a river to the South Sea, the Santuit River.

The Bride of Winnepurkit

It was to these same [Lynn, Massachusetts,] woods that Winnepurkit, the Sagamore of Saugus, brought his bride. She was the dusky daughter

Ibid., pp. 343–344.

From *The Romantic Shore*, by Agnes Edwards, pp. 19–20. Copyright, 1915, by Agnes Edwards Rothery. Salem, Massachusetts: The Salem Press Company.

of Passaconaway, the chief and wizard of the Merrimac county. Passaconaway sent his daughter to her future husband with braves and nobles and fitting ceremony, for they were both mighty chiefs and proud to honor one another. When, after a brief season in the wigwam village of Saugus, the bride announced her desire to return home to visit her father, Winnepurkit sent her back with as distinguished an escort of warriors as had accompanied her before. But when, however, the lady was ready to return and her father sent word to Winnepurkit to arrange again for the body guard, the young husband refused, declaring it beneath his dignity to send his men to bring back what was already his own. It was her father's place to furnish escort. The Chief of the Merrimac retorted that he had sent her once with pomp, and that if she were worth coming she was worth sending for. She was the squaw of the noble Winnepurkit and not the daughter of the famous Passaconaway. The wrangle continued for some time: the father was perfectly willing to keep his daughter but his dignity forbade him to bestow her twice in the same grandeur. The husband wanted his squaw but his reputation forbade his sending for what was already his own. And while the two chiefs quarrelled interminably, the little wife hung dangling between them, until one night she loosed a canoe and fled down the river to her husband's tribe. But only the broken canoe, empty and wave tossed, reached Saugus the following night.

The Legend of Sweet Waters

AN INDIAN legend clings to these mineral springs of Sweet Waters [Bedford Springs, Massachusetts]. The forest tribe had captured a young pioneer, bound him to a tree intending to put him to death; Sweet Water, the beautiful daughter of the chief Mancomee, snatched the burning brand from the fagots crying: "The Great Spirit is angry, the pale-face shall not die, unless Sweet Water dies with him." Mancomee heard the Great Spirit and bade a warrior unbind the captive, who eventually married Sweet Water, becoming a counsellor of the tribe.

The Spirit Profile of White Swan

IN THE pool two hundred feet below [the Bash Bish Falls, Massachusetts,] according to an Indian legend, is to be seen the "spirit profile" of the beau-

---

From *Old Paths and Legends of New England,* Saunterings Over Historic Roads with Glimpses of Picturesque Fields and Old Homesteads in Massachusetts, Rhode Island, and New Hampshire, by Katharine M. Abbott, p. 73. Copyright, 1903, by Katharine M. Abbott. New York and London: G. P. Putnam's Sons. 1904.

From *The Berkshire Hills,* Compiled and Written by Members of the Federal Writers' Project of the Works Progress Administration for Massachusetts, p. 186. Copyright, 1939, by The Berkshire Hills Conference, Inc. New York: Duell, Sloan and Pearce.

tiful Indian maiden, White Swan, the daughter of a witch who lived beneath the falls. The girl was married to a handsome young brave whom she loved dearly. Because she proved childless, her husband after some years took another wife. White Swan began to pine and brood by the falls, often gazing for hours into the water below. To the despairing maiden came one day the voice of her mother, whom she had never known, calling to her from beneath the cataract. With an answering cry of joy, she plunged over the cliff, to drown just as her husband came through the forest. He leaped after her in a vain attempt at rescue. Next day the brave's body was found, but his bride had disappeared. They say the lovely maiden and her mother still live behind the falls, and on moonlight nights White Swan smiles in the clear pool.

The Tragedy of Monument Mountain

Bryant, whom Walter Prichard Eaton considers "as much a poet of the Berkshires as Wordsworth of the Lake Country," wrote his version of the tragedy on Monument Mountain, the height north of town [, Great Barrington, Massachusetts]. The mountain had been named from a rock cairn which stood beside an Indian trail. According to the poet, the cairn commemorates the fearful punishment of an Indian girl who had fallen in love with her cousin. For such transgression of tribal laws, the penalty was death, death at the foot of the towering cliffs.

. . . But when the sun grew low
And the hill shadows long, she threw herself
From the steep rock and perished. There was scooped,
Upon the mountain's southern slope, a grave;
And there they laid her, in the very garb
With which the maiden decked herself for death.
With the same withering wild flowers in her hair
And o'er the mound that covered her, the tribe
Built up a simple monument, a cone
Of small loose stones. Thenceforward, all who passed,
Hunter, and dame, and virgin, laid a stone
In silence on the pile. It stands there yet.
And Indians from the distant West, that come
To visit where their fathers' bones are laid,
Yet tell the sorrowful tale, and to this day
The mountain where the hapless maiden died
Is called the Mountain of the Monument.

* * * * *

There is another version than his of the
Tale about these reverend rocks,
A sad tradition of unhappy love,
And sorrows borne and ended, long ago.

Ibid., pp. 161–162.

According to a wilder account than Bryant's plaintive verse, a condemned Indian maiden was hurled from the lofty peak by her tribesmen. She saved herself by catching desperate hold on a long branch of an old pine tree, whose roots had found lodgment in a cleft in the rocks. The branch lowered with her weight but held firm, and as she clung to it, her screams echoed through the mountain stillness. For two days and nights she clung to the old pine until, just before the dawn of the second day, a fierce storm burst forth. Neither driving rain nor howling wind could drown out the girl's renewed shrieks. As the storm lulled a moment, her last plea for mercy rose to her tribesmen gathered on the mountain summit. While they gazed in horror, a bolt of lightning struck the tree and tore it from its anchorage in the cliff. The tree and the maiden spiraled downward in horrifying plunge, disappearing in the darkness. Long the Mahicans searched, but found no trace of tree or maiden. In memory of her whom the Great Father had taken in this weird manner the awestricken Indians fashioned a rude cairn. Strangers visiting the spot added their tribute of more stones, gradually forming the crude monument that now gives the mountain its name.

Some people think the cairn is one of many altars in New England erected to an unknown god to whom the Indians brought symbolic offerings.* A plausible story is that Konkapot, the chief of the Mahicans, declared that a monument should mark the boundary of land agreed upon in a treaty between his tribe and the Mohawks, by which the Mahicans were to have as their hunting grounds all the area within a day's journey of the pile.

Whatever the truth may be, THE CAIRN, a pyramid six or eight feet in diameter at the base, was fashioned before white settlers looked upon the Housatonic Valley. The curious may find it on the trail opposite the Squaw Peak Cabins on US 7.

Legends of the White Mountains

THE GREAT FLOOD [1]

THE first mention of the White Mountains in print, occurs in John Josselyn's New England's Rarities Discovered, printed in 1672, a book now chiefly memorable as furnishing the earliest account of our plants; and this writer, in his Voyages, printed a year or two later, gives us the best part of the mythology of our highest hills. The story, as Josselyn tells it, is curious enough; and its resemblance to one of the most venerable of Caucasian traditions should seem to suggest some connection of the people

* See "Halfway Rock and other Sacrifice Rocks" below.

[1] From *The White Hills; Their Legends, Landscape, and Poetry,* by Thomas Starr King, pp. 34–35. Entered according to Act of Congress, in the year 1859, by Crosby, Nichols and Company, in the Clerk's Office of the District Court of the District of Massachusetts. Boston: Crosby and Ainsworth. 1866.

which transmitted it, with the common Asiatic home of the bearded races. "Ask them," says Josselyn, "whither they go when they dye, they will tell you pointing with their finger to Heaven beyond the white mountains, and do hint at *Noah's* Floud, as may be conceived by a story they have received from Father to Son, time out of mind, that a great while agon their Countrey was drowned, and all the People and other Creatures in it, only one *Powaw* and his *Webb* foreseeing the Floud fled to the white mountains carrying a hare along with them and so escaped; after a while the *Powaw* sent the *Hare* away, who not returning emboldened thereby they descended, and lived many years after, and had many Children, from whom the Countrie was filled again with *Indians*." * The English name of our mountains, which had its origin, perhaps, while as yet they were only known to adventurous mariners, following the still silent coasts of New England, relates them to all other high mountains, from *Dhawala-Giri,* the White Mountain of the Himmalayah, to *Craig Eryri* or Snowdon of Wales; but it is interesting to find them also, in this legend, in some sort of mythical connection with traditions and heights of the ancient continent, the first knowledge of which carries us back to the very beginnings of human history.

The Great Carbuncle

According to the Indians, on the highest mountain, suspended from a crag overlooking a dismal lake, was an enormous carbuncle, which many declared they had seen blazing in the night like a live coal. Some even asserted that its ruddy glare lighted the livid rocks around like the fire of a midnight encampment, while by day it emitted rays, like the sun, dazzling to look upon. And this extraordinary sight they declared they had not only seen, but seen again and again.

It is true that the Indians did not hesitate to declare that no mortal hand could hope to grasp the great fire-stone. It was, said they, in the special guardianship of the genius of the mountain, who, on the approach of human footsteps, troubled the waters of the lake, causing a dark mist to rise, in which the venturesome mortal became bewildered, and then hopelessly lost. Several noted conjurers of the Pigwackets, rendered foolhardy by their success in exorcising evil spirits, so far conquered their fears as to ascend the mountain; but they never returned, and had, no doubt, expiated their folly by being transformed into stone, or flung headlong down some stark and terrible precipice.

This tale of the great carbuncle fired the imagination of the simple settlers to the highest pitch. We believe what we wish to believe, and, notwithstanding their religion refused to admit the existence of the Indian demon, its guardian, they seem to have had little difficulty in crediting the

* Josselyn's Voyages, p. 135. "The Indians gave them the name of *Agiocochook.*" Belknap, N. H. iii. p. 31. There are one or two other, so called, Indian names.—T. S. K.

reality of the jewel itself. At any rate, the belief that the mountain shut up precious mines has come down to our own day; we are assured by a learned historian [Sullivan, *History of Maine*] of fifty years ago that the story of the great carbuncle still found full credence in his.[2]

It has been supposed by some that there were valuable mines somewhere about the mountains. I have searched for these also, but found none. I recollect a number of years ago, when quite a boy, some persons had been up on the hills and said they had found a golden treasure, or carbuncle, which they said was under a large shelving rock, and would be difficult to obtain, for they might fall and be dashed to pieces. Moreover, they thought it was guarded by an evil spirit, supposing that it had been placed there by the Indians, and that they had killed one of their number and left him to guard the treasure, which some credulous, superstitious persons believed, and they got my father to engage to go and search for it; provided themselves with every thing necessary for the business and a sufficient number of good men and a minister well qualified to lay the evil spirit, they set out in good earnest and high spirits anticipating with pleasure how rich they should be in coming home laden with gold; that is, if they should have the good luck to find it. They set out and went up Dry River, and had hard work to find their way through the thickets and over the hills, where they made diligent search for a number of days, with some of the former men spoken of for guides, but they could not find the place again, or anything that seemed to be like it, until worn out with fatigue and disappointment, they returned; and never since, to my knowledge, has any one found that wonderful place again, or been troubled with the mountain spirit.[3]

The Legend of the Old Man of the Mountains[4]

When in the Glacial Age the ice had gouged that vast rift through our range, the sun through untold centuries shone down and clothed in green the bleak naked mountain pass. Pine forests grew and through them wandered deer and wildcat, bear and moose. Hunting them, the red men came and up at the head of the Notch they saw a great stone face frowning

---

[2] From *The Heart of the White Mountains, Their Legend and Scenery*, by Samuel Adams Drake, pp. 115–116. Entered according to Act of Congress, in the year 1881, by Harper & Brothers, in the Office of the Librarian of Congress, at Washington. New York. 1882.

[3] From *The History of the White Mountains from the First Settlement of Upper Coos and Pequaket*, by Lucy, Wife of Ethan Allen, Crawford, pp. 106–107. Entered, according to Act of Congress, in the year 1845, by Lucy Crawford, in the Clerk's Office of the District Court of New Hampshire. White Hills. 1846.

[4] From *The Great White Hills of New Hampshire*, by Ernest Poole, p. 342. Copyright, 1946, by Ernest Poole Garden City, New York: Doubleday & Company, Inc.

down from its cliff in the clouds. They worshiped * him as a god and prayed to him to protect their homes from the Mohawks who raided from the west, and they left this legend of how he responded to their appeals. When a band of Mohawk warriors had burned and massacred down below and been driven back by the Pennacooks, they returned up the long winding Notch trail and exhausted slept through the night. At sunrise they spied that great face frowning on them from the clouds. "It is the Manitou!" they cried. As they fell on their faces, darkness came, and out of thunder and lightning they heard the dreaded Manitou say:

"You have made war on your brothers and your hands are stained with blood! You have dared to enter this place of the Great Spirit unsummoned, and the penalty is death!"

As they lay trembling on the ground, lulled by a strange spellbinding song, they fell asleep and turned to stone and became the boulders found there still.

Metallak Island

ONE of the best of the Indian stories centering around this [Lake Umbagog] region [of New Hampshire] is that concerning Metallak, last chief of the Coosucs. Son of a chief, Metallak grew tall and slender as a sapling, became versed in the ways of the woods, and was the pride of his people. In the course of time he took to his wigwam the fairest of the maidens of the tribe and built his home on the waters of the Ameroscoggin (Androscoggin). Years went by. Metallak became the mighty chief of his tribe and his name became a synonym for fearlessness. Then the dark frown of the Great Spirit fell upon his people. One by one his mighty warriors sickened and died until only Metallak remained. His children left him for the lure of the white man's ways. At last the health of the bride of his youth failed her and she too died. Placing her body in a canoe, the lone chief guided his frail bark with its precious freight down the long reaches of the Ameroscoggin, through treacherous rapids and whirlpools, to the island which now bears his name. Here he buried her and built a hut near-by, where in solitude he lived for years. In 1846, hunters found the old chief blind and nearly dead from starvation. They carried him to Stewartstown, where he died a few years later, but his memory still lingers around the waters of this section.

---

* Although the Profile was probably recognized by the Indians, little credence is placed to-day in the tradition of their making it an object of worship.—*New Hampshire,* A Guide to the Granite State (Boston, 1938), p. 326.

From *New Hampshire:* A Guide to the Granite State, written by Workers of the Federal Writers' Project of the Works Progress Administration for the State of New Hampshire, p. 374. American Guide Series. Copyright, 1938, by The Secretary of State, State of New Hampshire. Boston: Houghton Mifflin Company.

Squaw Cove

Squaw Cove, [New Hampshire,] an arm of the lake, took its name from a block of granite with the appearance of a woman on one side of its ledges. The block has been removed, but the legend associated with it lingers. An Indian leader, Waunega, had long been widowed when he fell in love with the young and graceful Suneta, whose home was across the lake, where her father was a powerful sachem of an allied tribe. Suneta loved young Anonis, but her father favored his friend and ally, Waunega.

After the marriage feast, Waunega and Suneta paddled across the lake to the bride's new home. Anonis was not at the marriage ceremony, but during a fearful storm in the night Suneta suddenly felt the touch of a hand on her face and heard Anonis whisper to come with him.

When the old Waunega, awakened by the storm, missed his bride and went in search of her, a flash of lightning revealed the lovers in a canoe. Waunega discharged an arrow at his rival, who tumbled into the water. Suneta swam to a ledge, imploringly calling on the Great Spirit; but Waunega cried, "May the lightning blast her! Let the Manitou make of her an example to coming time." Hardly were the words out of his mouth when a crash of lightning and thunder made the mountains and rocks tremble. Terrified at the effect of his own words, Waunega plunged into the water and perished. When morning dawned, there was a semblance of her figure on the rock where Suneta had clung.

LOCAL COLOR AND LOCAL RIVALRY

How the Windsor Skipper Outwitted His Hartford Rivals

No great volume of trade ever returned to Windsor, [Connecticut,] although ships continued to anchor in the Little River after the bridge across the Great threw the balance of water traffic to Hartford. Among tales of the bitter rivalry between the two at that period is one relating a Windsor checkmate in the game. Although the new bridge possessed a draw the channel below was always blocked with the craft of the rival companies. The captain of the Windsor ship coming down one day to find his way thus barred ordered the bridge-keeper to open. The other demurred, saying it was useless as the craft from up-river could not get through the mass of shipping further down. "You attend to your business

---

Ibid., p. 316.

From *Connecticut Trilogy*, by Marguerite Allis, with Drawings by the Author, pp. 26–27. Copyright, 1934, by Marguerite Allis. New York: G. P. Putnam's Sons.

and I'll attend to mine," said the Windsor skipper, or words to that effect. The draw was raised and, sailing slowly through, he waited until he was in the middle of the span and there cast over his anchor. One imagines the hullabaloo that went up from either side as the ox-carts and the horse-vans collected. The stalled captain was chagrined; he was mortified; he was grieved; he was very, very sorry, but what could he do? Somebody, of course, had to do something; so the Hartford rivals moved their craft and freed the channel. It is well they did, for a stubborn Yankee is very stubborn indeed and the sailor from up-river might have stayed there "until hell froze over."

The Ghost Train

THE year 1891 saw another straw grasped at—this time an adventure in publicity. The New England Limited, still using New Haven track from Willimantic to New Haven, was painted all white with gilt lettering from stem to stern, with the exception of the locomotive, and became the White Train, a name that lingers in the memories of some who have forgotten all else about the New York & New England—all else, perhaps, save another nickname which presently attached to that train; for as its pale, sinuous length streaked across the Connecticut countryside through the dusk, it had so eerie an effect that it came to be popularly known as the Ghost Train. Its running time was presently reduced from six hours to five hours and forty minutes. Rudyard Kipling, then sojourning in Vermont, was intrigued by it and found in it the idea for a short story which he entitled "007."

* * * * *

But very shortly after that, on October 20, 1895, the White Train disappeared: it was too much trouble to keep it clean. . . .

The Giant Kingfisher

RECENTLY, scientists have puzzled over the appearance of large schools of sockeye salmon in Twin Lakes, two bodies of water at the edge of the Raggie [1] country. The sockeye is native only to Alaska and Oregon, and Conservationists of neither State nor Federal government have found them

From *Steelways of New England*, by Alvin F. Harlow, pp. 209, 213. Copyright, 1946, by Alvin Fay Harlow. New York: Creative Age Press, Inc.

From *They Found a Way*, Connecticut's Restless People, by Iveagh Hunt Sterry and William H. Garrigus, pp. 117–119. Copyright, 1938, by Iveagh Sterry Hunt and William H. Garrigus. Brattleboro, Vermont: Stephen Daye Press.

[1] The "Raggies," known as the "lost people" of Connecticut, are a stranded population living along the lower slopes of Mt. Riga, Salisbury.

east of the Rockies, except here. No one has ever tried to stock Twin Lakes, yet the sockeye is here. This discovery was so important that the Associated Press wires carried the news, but the Raggies just smiled. They have been nourished by these "golden trout" for several years, and they have the answer to the riddle in one of their folk-tales.

Kingfishers, the Raggies say, often do their own stocking of woodland ponds and lakes. They have sensitive knowledge of changes in fish life in a pond and, when there seems to be danger of a certain species weakening, the kingfishers bring in minnows from other waters, thus introducing new blood and improving the quality.

One early spring day, according to the Raggies, a giant kingfisher flew over the Twin Lakes. This bird was so big that the sun was darkened, the chickens went to roost at high noon, and the owls at Owlsbury came out and made the day hideous with their cries. Only the bravest of the Raggies dared to look at this great bird, but the few that did, reported that he seemed to be very weary, and that his beak was splintered and worn stubby at the end. He lit in a giant oak tree, over near the cranberry bog, and the tree bent like a huckleberry bush under his weight. A native kingfisher flew over and the two birds seemed to carry on some sort of a conversation. Snatches of this bird language were overheard by a half-witted boy who smiled wisely, when he was questioned, but offered little information. About all anybody could get out of him was, "There'll soon be good fishin' in the lakes!"

Many moons later, according to legend, this foreign kingfisher returned and stayed much longer. Many local birds were very busy helping him. Old Man Wilcox was picking cranberries that day, and, being broke and consequently sober, he is confident that he saw several "golden trout" dropped into the silvery waters of Twin Lakes by the flock of fisher birds.

Before another year had passed the Raggies were snagging a plentiful supply of sockeye salmon, although it was not until several years later that such fish were caught by outsiders. The huge kingfisher was never seen again but berry-pickers reported the discovery of a great swath of fallen timber, up Bear Mountain way, and claimed to have seen scattered blue and white feathers "with quills as thick as a man's wrist." As Bear Mountain is the highest point of land in Connecticut, the big bird may have miscalculated his altitude and crashed in a fog, as he winged his way back to Alaska for another payload of sockeyes.

Micah Rood Apples

IN WESTERN Florida they will show roses to you that drop red dew, like blood, and have been doing so these many years, for they sprang out of

From *Myths & Legends of Our Own Land,* by Charles M. Skinner, Vol. II, pp. 35–37.

the graves of women and children who had been cruelly killed by Indians. But there is something queerer still about the Micah Rood—or "Mike"—apples of Franklin, Connecticut, which are sweet, red of skin, snowy of pulp, and have a red spot, like a blood-drop, near the core; hence they are sometimes known as bloody-hearts. Micah Rood was a farmer in Franklin in 1693. Though avaricious he was somewhat lazy, and was more prone to dream of wealth than to work for it. But people whispered that he did some hard and sharp work on the night after the peddler came to town—the slender man with a pack filled with jewelry and knickknacks—because on the morning after that visit the peddler was found, beneath an apple-tree on Rood farm, with his pack rifled and his skull split open.

Suspicion pointed at Rood, and, while nothing was proved against him, he became gloomy, solitary, and morose, keeping his own counsels more faithfully than ever—though he never was disposed to take counsel of other people. If he had expected to profit by the crime he was obviously disappointed, for he became poorer than ever, and his farm yielded less and less. To be sure, he did little work on it. When the apples ripened on the tree that had spread its branches above the peddler's body, the neighbors wagged their heads and whispered the more, for in the centre of each apple was a drop of the peddler's blood: a silent witness and judgment, they said, and the result of a curse that the dying man had invoked against his murderer. Micah Rood died soon after, without saying anything that his fellow-villagers might be waiting to hear, but his tree is still alive and its strange fruit has been grafted on hundreds of orchards.

Jemima Was Queer

JEMIMA [Wilkinson], an eccentric lady with a mind of her own, died sometime between 1770 and 1790. Her Ledyard neighbors dutifully gathered about the coffin to pay their last respects to the departed vixen. The weeping was loud and insincere, as a friend lifted the lid of the coffin to let relatives and friends gaze a last time on the face of one whom they were not sorry to see pass on to another world. Jemima, however, had other plans. As the coffin lid was raised, the slender lady arose from the pine box and announced to the startled congregation that she would do the preaching herself that day! Claiming that she had passed through the gates of a better world and had been sent back to earth as a second Redeemer, the impassioned Jemima preached that the day of her resurrection was to mark the regeneration of the world.

When the news spread throughout the surrounding countryside, work was set aside; farmers hitched up their wagons and with their entire families rode into town to see for themselves the living proof of a miracle

---

From *Connecticut,* A Guide to Its Roads, Lore and People, by Workers of the Federal Writers' Project, Works Progress Administration for the State of Connecticut, pp. 366–367. Boston: Houghton Mifflin Company.

in their midst. For some time Jemima's exhortations attracted large congregations, until her neighbors began to whisper that "Jemima always had been queer." Then she and a few converts moved on to fresh fields in Tioga County, Pa., where an enthusiastic sect of "Jemimakins" gathered around her standard. Impelled to spread their tenets, the entire colony later moved to New York State, carrying Jemima through the woods in a resplendent chariot drawn by her proselytes.

Settling in Yates County, they called their first community "The City of Jerusalem." When a post office was needed and a shorter name for it seemed desirable, they chose Penn Yan, for the two factions who made up the congregation, the Pennsylvanians and the Yankees. Thus a Connecticut woman preacher named a New York State town.

The Cow and the Cotton Factory

From the year 1800 to 1815, Connecticut, Massachusetts, and especially Rhode Island people *run wild* about building small Cotton Factories. Farmers that had a small brook running through their farms, especially if it had much fall, felt as though they must erect a small factory on it, go to spinning cotton yarn, and "get rich."

A factory of this class was erected on a small stream that empties into the South-west Branch of the Pawtuxet, in the southerly part of Crompton village [, Rhode Island,] in 1816. It was called the "Flat-top Factory," owing to its having a flat roof. This factory had but little water, especially in a dry time, but it had a fall of over thirty feet. This stream was made by the union of two small brooks, one rising in the south-westerly part of the town of Warwick, the other three quarters of a mile east of it, uniting near the Flat-top pond. They form the small stream that drives the machinery in that factory. The whole length of the stream is not much over one and a half miles from its source to its mouth. This factory has changed owners often. It was built by Jonathan Tiffany. A few years after [it] was bought by Oliver Johnson, who soon took for a partner John Wood. They put in power looms, run it a few years and prospered. John Higgins and others then bought and run it. After them Joseph James and John Card ran it and made yarn. The mill was burnt some three times during fifty years and rebuilt. Jonathan Tiffany built a small factory for spinning cotton yarn on the east brook that helps form the Flat-top stream, which had more than thirty-four feet fall. One day when the machinery was running full speed, all at once the wheel almost stopped.

From "Further Reminiscences of the Valley of the Pawtuxet River and Its Branches," by Noah J. Arnold, in *The Narragansett Historical Register,* A Magazine Devoted to the Antiquities, Genealogy and Historical Matter Illustrating the History of the State of Rhode Island and Providence Plantations, A Historical Magazine for the People, Vol. 7 (July, 1889) No. 3, edited by James N. Arnold, pp. 248–249. Copyright in the office of the Librarian of Congress at Washington, D. C. Providence, Rhode Island: The Narragansett Historical Publishing Company.

The help ran out to see what the matter was. *They found a cow drinking the water that ought to run on to the wheel.* When the cow quenched her thirst, the wheel started up again full speed.

The Manager's White Gloves

. . . In the latter sixties, boat lines were running to New York not only from Stonington but from three ports around Narragansett Bay—Providence, Bristol and Fall River. The rivalry reached a high pitch, and rates at times were cut to the bone. Band concerts were given on the wharves at Providence and Bristol before the departure of the boats, and the Merchants Line at Providence went the others one better by serving tea on the wharf, with the manager in white kid gloves—a fresh pair every day—as host. As the story was told to us—and you may take it or leave it—his stripping off those white gloves, rolling them up and throwing them into the harbor was the signal for the boat to cast off.

Newport "Gentlemen" and "Bullies," "Brats" and "Rats"

. . . They used to have glorious fights, too, them days. Newport was then divided into four boys' quarters; the "up-town boys" owning the north-east part of Newport, the "over-to-The-Point boys" the north-western part of the town, called then, as now, The Point; the "Long-wharf boys" living on the Long Wharf, and the "down-town boys" in the southern part of the town. Free Mayberry (still living) was the bully of The Point boys; Jim Shaw, of the up-towners; Ned Allen, of the Long-Wharfers; and Green Carr, of the down-towners. There used to be a ditty song with four lines in those days in vogue that was a favorite among all the boys except the "Long-Wharfers." The words, when the lines were repeated by the "over-to-the-Point Boys," of which I was one, ran thus :

"The up-town bullies,
The down-town brats,
The over to the Point gentlemen
And the long-wharf rats."

From *Steelways of New England,* by Alvin F. Harlow, p. 230. Copyright, 1946, by Alvin Fay Harlow. New York: Creative Age Press, Inc.

From *The Jonny-Cake Papers of "Shepherd Tom,"* Together with Reminiscences of Narragansett Schools of Former Days, by Thomas Robinson Hazard, With a Biographical Sketch and Notes by Rowland Gibson Hazard, pp. 263–264. Copyright, 1915, by Rowland G. Hazard. Boston: Printed for the Subscribers.

As sung by the up-town boys:

"The over to the Point bullies,
The down-town brats,
The up-town gentlemen,
And the long-wharf rats."

Again, as sung by the down-towners:

"The up-town bullies,
The over to the Point brats,
The down-town gentlemen
And the long-wharf rats."

The reason why the Long-wharf boys did not like the song was, because the rats could not be made to fit any other quarter of the town than the Long Wharf where they belonged. Consequently the "gentlemen" could never become the distinguishing burden of the song when applied to the Long Wharf. In those blessed days, all that was necessary to get up a regular row was for the boys of any quarter of the town to parade of an evening in another quarter singing the song with the "gentlemen" line applied to themselves, whereupon the bully of the invaded quarter would summon his forces and fist fight the insolent foe until one side or the other cried "Nuff," when the combatants would cease, often with bloody noses on both sides almost without exception. . . .

Narragansett Rhineinjun Bread Versus Boston Brown Bread

Even before the Boston brown bread had become utterly worthless by the introduction of Western corn meal, made often of damaged corn, and tasteless Western rye to match, I remember bringing home with me, after a visit to that city, a loaf of the famous material, that my children might compare its quality with our family bread. They were all delighted at the prospect of tasting the famous luxury they had heard so much of; but after the first mouthful, not one of them seemed disposed to take a second. After breakfast I took the loaf and placed it in the trough for an old Berkshire sow to eat, that I knew was very fond of our Rhineinjun bread, a piece of which I used almost daily to treat her with. The old creature—which had not been fed that morning—dove her nose greedily into it; but at the first taste she dropped the morsel, and regarding me askance, with a suspicious and sinister expression in her eye, she hastened to a stagnant, muddy pool in the corner of the yard, and rinsed her mouth.

Ibid., p. 28.

The Crime and Punishment of Captain William Carter

Sometime during the winter of 1741, two travelers stopped late in the afternoon at the house of a widow Nash, who lived in one of the six old houses before alluded to, which I think is yet standing near a small rivulet on the east side of the old post-road, about one mile from Dockray's corner [, Narragansett]. Mrs Nash had the kindness to dress their hair, and playfully remarked to the smaller of the two whilst so engaged, that if he was murdered she could identify his person by a round black lock of hair that marked his head.

About sunset the two men proceeded on their journey with the avowed intention of reaching Franklin Ferry that night and passing over to Newport in the morning.

It subsequently came to light that one of the men, whose name was Jackson, had started from Virginia with a horse load of deer-skins which he intended to convey to Boston, and that he was joined on the way by a Captain William Carter, an old privateersman of Newport, Rhode Island, who had been shipwrecked somewhere on the coast south of the Chesapeake, and was making his way home on foot. After leaving Mrs. Nash's, and when passing over the southern portion of Tower Hill in the evening, it also appeared that Carter knocked Jackson from his horse by hitting him on the back of the head with a stone. Jackson, however, recovered himself and ran to an old uninhabited house near by—which was the only semblance of a habitation within a mile and more of the spot—where he was pursued and beaten to death by Carter, who then proceeded on his way with Jackson's horse and pack, having previously dragged his victim nearly a mile down the hill to a salt water estuary called Pettaquamscutt Cove, and shoved the corpse under the ice, from whence it was fished up some days after by a man whilst jabbing for eels with a spear and identified by Mrs. Nash as the stranger with the *black spot* on his head, to whom she had unconsciously spoken so ominously.

The place where Jackson was first knocked down by Carter is still marked by a stone at the base of the road wall directly west of the exact spot, with the figures "1741" engraven on it. This stone is not far from the junction of the road and the north line of the lot on which the late Nicholas Austin some years ago erected a house on the very same site where the ruins of the old "Carter and Jackson chimney" since my remembrance stood.

From *The Recollections of Olden Times:* Rowland Robinson of Narragansett and His Unfortunate Daughter, With Genealogies of the Robinson and Hazard Families of Rhode Island, by Thomas R. Hazard, "Shepherd Tom," in His Eighty-First and Eighty-Second Years; Also Genealogical Sketch of the Hazards of the Middle States, by Willis P. Hazard, of Westchester, Pa., pp. 23–25. Entered according to Act of Congress, in the year 1879, by John P. Sanborn, in the Office of the Librarian of Congress, at Washington, D. C. Newport, Rhode Island.

Boston as Seen from New York

THE Bostonian is strongly impressed with the idea that his city is the particular nucleus of all that there is great on this side of the Atlantic. He looks upon other American towns as small planetary bodies revolving about the centre of Boston Common, and deriving most of their light, heat, and strength from Cambridge University, Fanueil Hall, and Boston Harbor. He affects a wonderful degree of kinship with the English; and keeps up the connection by sharp shirt collars, short-waisted coats, and yellow gaiters. He is apt to put himself upon English stilts to look down upon the rest of the American world, which he regards complacently through an English eye-glass. He does not so much pity the rest of the American world, as he patronizes and encourages. His literary tastes being formed in the focus of western learning, are naturally correct and profound. He squats himself upon the Boston formulas of judgment, from which nothing can shake him, and puts out his feelers of opinion, as you may have seen a lazy, bottle-tailed bug try his whereabouts, without once stirring, by means of his glutinous and many-jointed antennae.

He likes to try you in discussion, in the course of which it will be next to impossible to tell him anything that he did not previously know; and you will prove a rare exception, if he does not tell you many things that you never knew before—unless, indeed, you have been in Boston. His stock of praises is uncommonly small, and principally reserved for home consumption; things are done *well*, only in Boston; though they are sometimes *creditably* done in other parts of the world.

His superiority in arts, letters, science, and religion, of which he will endeavor strenuously to convince one, is attributable partially to education, but mainly to his being a Bostonian. Whatever idea, or system of ideas, whether in politics, arts, or literature, which had not its beginning, or has not had its naturalization in Boston, is a fungous growth upon the great body of American opinion, which must of necessity wither and perish.

The Bostonian entertains the somewhat singular notion that whatever he has never observed, is not worth observing; and that the very few matters of fact and fancy scattered about the country, which are unbeknown to Bostonians, are not worth their knowing. This gives him under all ordinary circumstances a self-possession, and dignity of address which is quite remarkable. He does not conceive it possible that classical scholarship should thrive at all, out of sight of the belfry of the old South Church; and such chance citations from classic authors, as may appear on pages printed in other parts of the country, he considers filched in some way out of Boston books. He regards all those making any profession of learning,

---

From *The Lorgnette:* or, Studies of the Town, by An Opera Goer, Fifth Edition, Vol. I, pp. 232–235, 236. Entered, according to Act of Congress, in the year 1850, by Stringer & Townsend, in the Clerk's Office of the District Court for the Southern District of New-York. 1851.

out of his own limits, very much as an under pedagogue will eye a promising boy of the "first form" who occasionally hears recitations.

He plumes himself specially on his precision and exactness; you will never see a Bostonian with the lower button of his waistcoat uncaught, and he is uniformly punctual to his dinner hour. Vivacity he condemns from principle—and the best of all principle, which is—Boston principle. Even in religion, he does not recognize the hot zeal of earnest intention, nor does he run toward the lusts of ceremonial. He is coy to acknowledge even the *personnel* of a Divine Mediation; his dignity does not like to admit a superior between himself and the Highest. The comparative chilliness of the Unitarian faith suits the evenness of his temper; and when he casts loose from this unique doctrine, which is to many a pure and holy faith, he runs inevitably into the iciness of Pantheism. * * * * *

. . . He is, like the Virginian, usually of an "old family"; whoever heard of any other sort of families in the Old Dominion, or the "Cradle of Liberty?"

The S.S. Pierce Pung

THE story is told—and how could it be anything but true—of a little Beacon Hill lass who had been permitted to take a wintry walk to the Charles River esplanade, but who had been told specifically not to hitch a ride, in the manner of the proletariat, on that sort of sleigh which in Yankee parlance is called a pung.

Back came the girl to her home. Her dress was wet and her stockings disheveled.

"Well, for Heaven's sake, what have you been doing?" asked Mama.

The child hung her head. Then she sobbed out, "I hooked a ride."

"You naughty girl . . . ," began the fond parent.

"But, Mama, it was an S. S. Pierce pung!"

Why Boston Streets Are Crooked

THERE has been much speculation and a great deal of fun made in regard to the crooked and narrow streets of Boston, and they have been the subject of good-natured banter from wits of all ages, which we have borne with equanimity. There are even some to-day who in all seriousness will say, "My grandmother always said that Boston was laid out by the cows";

From *New England Comes Back*, by Lawrence Dame, with an Introduction by Stewart H. Holbrook, pp. 84–85. Copyright, 1940, by Random House, Inc. New York.

From *The Crooked & Narrow Streets of the Town of Boston, 1630–1822*, by Annie Haven Thwing, p. 7. Copyright, 1920, by Marshall Jones Company. Boston.

and the old conundrum that the streets of Boston were crooked because Boston was never dead enough to be laid out, is still with us.

Cape Cod Rivalries

ANOTHER pair of towns that do not always see eye to eye are Chatham and Harwich, as close together on the map as geography can get them, but miles apart in other respects. A Chatham man speaks of his Harwich neighbors as if they lived in trees and held on with their feet, while the Harwichean comes back at his detractor with tales like the following. A schooner, the Nancy M. Foster, of Digby, so he says, got aground on Shovelful Shoal, about twenty years ago. There was quite a sea running, enough to start her pounding badly, and since she was old, her seams opened up until she was half full. The crew didn't like the looks of things and went over the side, heading for the beach on planks and hatch covers and hen-coops—whatever they could find handy. One of them made pretty good weather of it, took the sea like a duck, and kept his plank headed bow on for the shore until he got close enough to see what was there. What he saw set him thinking: about a hundred hard-looking customers, waiting for him at the water's edge. An awful thought occurred to him.

"What town is this?" he hollered.

"Chatham," they yelled back.

"Good-bye," says he, and put his plank about and headed out to sea.

And so it goes: Provincetown has its fun with Truro; Truro's pride takes a fall before Orleans; and Harwich, perhaps in envy, tells stories about Chatham. An old philosopher of Provincetown, who has watched three generations of Cape men, gives the conclusion of the whole matter when he says that he can tell as soon as he talks to a man what town he comes from: a Truroer, so he says, slouches along with a hangdog air, a regular countryman. Wellfleeters are blow-hards; they stick out their chests and talk big, when, come to find out, they haven't ten cents to their names. Easthamers are just the opposite; they walk around with a face a mile long and growl about hard times, when really they have long bank accounts; and you can tell a Barnstable man because he is always looking for a high time and will never refuse a drink.

From *Mooncussers of Cape Cod,* by Henry C. Kittredge, pp. 17–18. Copyright, 1937, by Henry C. Kittredge. Boston and New York: Houghton Mifflin Company.

How the Cranberry Came to Cape Cod

A SIGNIFICANT tale narrates how during an argument with the Rev. Richard Bourne the Indian pow-pow lost his temper and, chanting a bog-rhyme, mired Bourne's feet in quicksand. They then agreed to a contest of wits which lasted 15 days, during which Bourne was kept from thirst and starvation by a white dove which placed a succulent "cherry" in his mouth from time to time. Unable to cast a spell upon the dove, and exhausted from his own lack of food, the medicine-man finally fell to the ground and Bourne was free. In the meantime one "cherry" brought by the dove had fallen into the bog and had grown and multiplied. Thus the cranberry came to Cape Cod.

Scrabbletown

THE [wrecking] stories we heard dealt only with one town and with one section of that town. And they were told to us when we were boys, so my memory of them is rather vague. Cap'n Ben, that old friend of ours, told them. In his youth, the lower end of Chatham, the end which is now called "down in the village," was nicknamed "Scrabbletown." Kipling, in *Captains Courageous,* has one of his Gloucester fishermen call to the crew of a Chatham schooner alongside his own: "Ye Scrabble-towners, ye Chatham wreckers! Git aout with your brick in your stockin'."

We do not know to what the "brick in your stockin' " may have referred, but, according to Cap'n Ben, "Scrabbletown" was the derisive name given by outsiders to Chatham village in the old-time yarns about wrecking as a business. There was—this is Cap'n Ben again—a group of daredevil spirits in Scrabbletown who made a living by piloting vessels over or around the shoals, by helping them off those shoals when they had grounded there, or, when they could not be floated, of salvaging, for liberal commissions, or saving and selling—or keeping—goods and chattels which they carried.

Cap'n Ben used to say that his father said the whole of Scrabbletown was in the wrecking game. Even some itinerant members of the clergy. One of Ben, Senior's, yarns, as told to his son, dealt with a revival meeting held in one of the halls there. That evening the preacher was a local product

---

From *Massachusetts,* A Guide to Its Places and People, written and compiled by the Federal Writers' Project of the Works Progress Administration for the State of Massachusetts, p. 594. American Guide Series. Copyright, 1937, by George M. Nutting, Director of Publicity, Commonwealth of Massachusetts. Boston: Houghton Mifflin Company.

From *Cape Cod Yesterdays,* by Joseph C. Lincoln, pp. 235–237. Copyright, 1935, by Joseph C. Lincoln and Harold Brett. Boston: Little, Brown & Company.

who preached occasionally but whose worldly profession was that of a wrecker. He was in the middle of a fervent discourse when a small boy came up the aisle with a note in his hand. The preacher took the note, read it, and then requested the members of the congregation to bow their heads in silent meditation for a moment. He waited until all heads were bowed and every eye, except his own, closed. Then he tiptoed from the pulpit and darted from the building by the back door. The note was from his partner in the wrecking business and informed him that a schooner was ashore on a shoal back of the outer beach and had set lighted signals for help. He meant to be, and was, with his partner, the first to reach the stranded vessel and make a trade with the skipper for floating her.

Provincetown and the Devil

PROVINCETOWN from its earliest days has been freer, richer in life than its neighbors. Back in 1727 Truro asked to be severed from Provincetown because of the goings-on there. Provincetown gloried in this separation and laughed to itself. Truro sitting discreetly in the folds of her moors looked down her nose at Provincetown and still does. The Cape early wrote, in legend, its opinion of the folk on Land's End.

Captain Jeremiah Snaggs lived up the Cape and he did not die in the odor of sanctity. The story is he tried to escape the devil by various devices. He dodged the devil in Barnstable, he eluded him in a hollow tree in Orleans, he escaped from him in Wellfleet by putting a jack-o-lantern which looked like him in a tree, but in Provincetown the devil caught up with him.

"Well," said Captain Jeremiah, "you caught me fair and squar'. Whar do we go from here?"

"Go?" said the devil. "Nowhar. Ain't we to Provincetown?"

How Provincetown Is Split

THE town itself is split into the East End and the West End. Way-up-along is to the westward, Down-along to the eastward. The road Up-along has two sharp turns caused by Lancy, who when the front road was laid out declared they'd have to saw right through him before they could saw through his salt-works.

From *Time and the Town, A Provincetown Chronicle,* by Mary Heaton Vorse, p. 76. Copyright, 1942, by Mary Heaton Vorse. New York: The Dial Press.

Always the flight ends in Provincetown, and the conclusion is the same; but different Captains and different towns are used for the starting-point. Probably of late origin.—Elizabeth Reynard, *The Narrow Land* (Boston, 1934), p. 326.

Ibid., pp. 81–82.

"Well," said one of the selectmen, "get your saw," but Lancy stood firm and so the road has two perilous turns.

East End and West End used to fight each other in mighty battles. Boys from the East End used to come in bands to rescue a lone East End boy beaten up by the West End gang. Up in the honeycomb of back streets to the westward there is an almost unbroken Portuguese colony, where many an old man and woman speak but little English, and dark-skinned beautiful children line the streets.

The miles that separate east from west are long miles. My next-door neighbors had living with them an aged relative whom I knew only as Miss Philomena and whom I saw as a delicate, aged profile against a window. When she died, Mrs. Higgins said,

"Poor thing, she was lonely here. She didn't get to see her friends often, so far from them."

"Where did she live?"

"Oh, she was from the westward," Mrs. Higgins said. It was as though she spoke of a prairie woman planted in the Eastern seaboard.

Today, with cars, "the westward" is more accessible to us, but the East End and the West still have each its own specific flavor and the old rivalries are not yet dead.

Why Provincetown Houses Are like Ships

Provincetown men are not landsmen. Almost without exception they have at one time or another "followed the sea." Certainly their forebears have. Provincetowners have spent so much of their time on the sea in ships that they look upon houses as a sort of land ship or a species of houseboat and therefore not subject to the laws of houses.

Every man who owns a boat or a vessel overhauls it, alters it, tinkers with it. That is why all Provincetown people tinker with their houses and keep adding to them perpetually. The people here are seafaring folk and that is why carpentry on houses is never done and why the houses do not stay upon their foundations after the fashion of those in other towns but go wandering up roadways or sandy dunes.

Many a ship's timber has gone into Provincetown houses. Some have been partly constructed from the fine knees of old vessels and the magnificent timbers of dead ships. Frederick Waugh's studio was made that way and the interesting Flagship owes much of its uniqueness to Pat's beachcombing. This likeness of Provincetown houses to ships explains some of their architectural peculiarities. In many an old house the door opens on a narrow entry. The stairs mount sheer. They are not really stairs but a companionway. There are upper chambers where the small windows are like portholes, as though built for security against the weather rather than for light.

Ibid., pp. 89–90, 91.

When the Winslows bought a piece of property near us and went to build a new house there, the question was what to do with the old house. The carpenter was a Provincetown man and he was not for a moment perplexed. He rolled the old house out into the bay and there he anchored it. A storm came up and for two days the distracted house rocked and curtsied. Its shutters and doors blew open and the blank windows and the yawning door looked like a doleful screaming mouth.

One day Tony Avellar shouted to me, "Want to come and tow a house over to Beach Point?"

He hitched his gas boat to the house and slowly we chugged and bobbed across the Bay, where men rolled the house across the beach, and there it became a garage.

* * * * *

It would not be fair to Provincetown not to speak of what you might call the "barn and fishhouse architecture." For most of these little unpretentious dwellings have been done over with so much ingenuity and love that they fit into Provincetown's old-time charm far more closely than some of the new houses which have been built "Down-along." Back of my own house is now one of the pleasantest dwellings in town—a long white house with blue shutters and pleasant bricked paths leading to a studio. A few years ago this was an ugly barn.

In the fishhouses on the shore the big room that was used for storing tackle and mending nets is transformed into a living room of ample size. Dormer windows make pleasant bedrooms of the loft formerly used for storing sails and gear and nets. Add a picket fence with a bright flower garden on each side, and you find what was formerly a mere "store" transformed into a pleasant habitation.

Fishhouse Stories

If you stopped inside the fishhouse you would hear stories of miraculous catches, of strange creatures seen—stories like that of Louis Tindrawers and his dory mate, Lopez, who were separated from their vessel by fog, and when the fog lifted the vessel was gone. They rowed for two days and two nights and finally came upon the back side, thinking themselves in hard luck, only to find they were the only ones left alive of their crew and that their vessel had been cut down by a steamer in the fog.

* * * * *

There is the story of the vessel that sounded her foghorn for twenty-four hours and heard no answering sound of conch. When the fog lifted not a dory was to be seen, yet these dories, attached to one another, triumphantly made Provincetown Harbor. They had been picked up by a Gloucester-

Ibid., pp. 165, 173–174.

man, put overboard at Race Point, and they rowed into harbor after having been given up for lost.

There is the tale of the young fisherman who was courting the same girl that his Old Man courted. He got the consent of the girl but the Old Man got the consent of her father. The lovers parted in tears. The girl did not dare go against her father's wishes. But the young suitor, overboard in a fog, made harbor first and when the vessel made port, after her trip, the Old Man weeping crocodile tears over the loss of his rival, the girl had vanished with the young suitor.

Some of the stories have a sourer ending, like that of the widow who had already spent the life-insurance money and was outraged at her husband's reappearance, going back to her folks to stay.

And the story of the man and his wife who got on none too well. They got on so badly indeed that each had consoled himself surreptitiously with another love. Finally the husband was lost at sea, the widow married again and put up a fine tablet, LOST AT SEA, in the cemetery. But there was quiet gossip that he had not been lost at all but had shared with her the life insurance and had settled down elsewhere and married his sweetheart, under another name, and that once a year he and his old wife met in Boston and went "on a time" to commemorate his death.

Fishermen's Races

THE stories of the fishermen's races in Gloucester are great stories of magnificent sailing; the race that brought the Lipton Cup to Provincetown is a great story. But the real stories and those that will never be recorded are those of the races to market.

The legend here in Provincetown is that the great highliners, like Captain Gaspy of the *Valerie* and Santos and Marion Perry and Joe King (Antoine Joaquin Sousa) of the *Jessie Costa* or Manuel Enos of the *Annie Perry*, never hove to in their race from the George's Banks. They left their fishing grounds with a "keep 'er full and drive 'er." Drive her they did. A coastwise steamer came to anchor in Provincetown Harbor reporting, "Had a fishing boat pass me sailing underwater."

They sailed their vessels with water swirling around the waist of the helmsman. They kept on canvas until the water came around the helmsman's neck. They tied their halyards aloft so they couldn't shorten sail. Fishermen claimed a good Provincetown boat sailed better when her cabin house was "most draggin'." They said that a vessel like the *Annie Perry* couldn't sail at all if her rail came up for air. There are stories of Gloucester boats winning races with "their sail just level with the water and their crew sitting on the keel."

Ibid., pp. 168–169.

Weymouth Herring

FROM the sportsman's point of view, Weymouth [, Massachusetts,] is a "capital" town; Whitman's Pond and Weymouth Great Pond are wild duck's haunts. On sunny days in April, Weymouth Back River is no longer a river of water, but of herring; the fish are literally shovelled out. Weymouth smelts are "choice," and it is not an uncommon affair to see a clever cat catching a tomcod in Fore River. The old ditty runs:

"Cohasset for beauty,
Hingham for pride;
If not for its herring
Weymouth had died."

Secession in Abington

SOUTH ABINGTON (Whitman), [Massachusetts,] with its chimneys so huge that a child can sit on each end of the log in the cavernous fireplaces and look up in the sky, became after a time a separate parish, through an odd church controversy. The tempest arose over the choice of a chorister leader; and one Sabbath, to the astonishment of the pastor and congregation, two leaders and two choirs appeared in the galleries. A hymn was sung by each to a different tune at the same time. Confusion reigned, and the pastor's wife fainted. An attorney took the names of the delinquents as disturbers of the peace,—such was the power of the church in colonial town-government. The discord not abating, South Abington (Whitman) seceded and built her own meeting-house. . . .

Philosopher's Stone

ONE of the oddest of Ware's industrial experiences had to do with an alleged silver mine on the Greenwich road not much more than two miles

---

From *Old Paths and Legends of New England*, Saunterings Over Historic Roads with Glimpses of Picturesque Fields and Old Homesteads in Massachusetts, Rhode Island, and New Hampshire, by Katharine M. Abbott, p. 350. Copyright, 1903, by Katharine M. Abbott. New York and London: G. P. Putnam's Sons. 1904.

Ibid., p. 369.

From *Historic Hampshire in the Connecticut Valley*, Happenings in a Charming Old New England County from the Time of the Dinosaur Down to About 1900, by Clifton Johnson, pp. 212–213. Copyright, 1932, by The Northampton Historical Society. Springfield, Massachusetts: Milton Bradley Company.

At a still earlier period, when physical science was rarely studied, even by the learned, divining by the *hazel rod,* and by the *stone in the hat,* which made the universe transparent, taught sapient divines, as well as astute laymen, that beneath the surface treasures vast were within their grasp, and could be easily obtained.—John S. Barry, *A Historical Sketch of the Town of Hanover, Mass.*, (Boston, 1853), p. 31.

from Ware Village. About 1816 strange rumblings were heard coming from a ledge there, and the local settlers went to consult Parson Hosca Ballou of North Dana, who had won a reputation as a soothsayer. They told him that straw placed on the ledge soon burst into a blaze with no apparent cause, and that rumblings from the rock made dishes rattle in their houses.

The clergyman had what he called a philosopher's stone. He placed it in his soft hat, which he drew down over his face, and said he saw wonderful workings of nature, and that the ledge contained vast deposits of what seemed to be silver. As a result 18 Ware farmers formed a company, bought the property, and in a crude sort of way worked the mine for several years, chiefly by hacking away at the face of the ledge. Once a peddler made an offer of $1500 for their mine, which they rejected. Again they visited their reverend soothsayer, and after he had consulted his philosopher's stone he informed them there was enough wealth in the ledge to make their children's children immensely rich. So they puttered at the ledge a while longer, and then quit. Their deed read that the mine was to be their property "forever as long as grass grows and water runs, provided it shall be worked." As it no longer was worked, of course it reverted to the former owners.

The Bugs That Ate Their Way Out of a Table

In 1806, a strong and beautiful *bug* eat out of a table made from an apple-tree, which grew on the farm of Maj. Gen. Putnam, in Brooklyn, Connecticut, and which was brought to Williamstown [, Massachusetts,] when his son, Mr. P. S. Putnam, removed to that town. It was cut down in 1786, sixty-five years after it was transplanted, and if the tree was then fifteen years old, it was 80 years old when cut down. As the *cortical* layers of the *leaf* of the table are about *sixty,* and extend within about *five* of the heart, as the inner ones are quite convex, about fifteen layers have been cut off from the outside. In 1814, a third bug made his way out, the second having appeared two or three years before. The *last* bug came forth from nearest the heart, and 45 cortical layers distant, on the supposition of its age, from the outside. The tree had now been cut down 28 years. Of course, the egg must have been deposited in the wood *seventy-three* years before. This bug eat about three inches along the grain, till it emerged into the light. The eating of the insect was heard for weeks before its appearance. These *facts* were given by Mr. Putnam, in whose possession the table still remains, and were first published in the *Repertory* at Middlebury, Vt., in 1816. One

From *Massachusetts Historical Collections,* Being a General Collection of Interesting Facts, Traditions, Biographical Sketches, Anecdotes, &c., Relating to the History and Antiquities of Every Town in Massachusetts, with Geographical Descriptions, by John Warner Barber, pp. 108–109. Entered, according to Act of Congress, in the year 1839, by Dorr, Howland & Co. In the Clerk's Office of the District Court of Massachusetts. Worcester.

Source: *History of Berkshire,* p. 39.—J. W. B.

of the bugs, preserved for some time by the Rev. Dr. Fitch, "was about an inch and one fourth long, and one third inch in diameter; color, dark glistening brown, with tints of yellow."

Luther Maddocks and His Whale

A FAVORITE tale of the fishermen along the harbor here [Boothbay Harbor, Maine] is of Luther Maddocks and his whale. In 1885 Maddocks decided that the exhibition of a whale at a Grand Army of the Republic reunion in Portland would be profitable. Capturing a 60-foot humpbacked whale, he towed it at high tide over a scow he had ingeniously weighted to a reef with rocks. When the tide receded, Maddocks removed the rocks, bailed out the water, and waited for another tide to lift his load. He towed his catch into Portland Harbor, and, after a heated argument with the mayor, won the right to exhibit it, realizing $800 by the venture. He then sold the carcass for $150 to a company that wanted the hide and blubber. The company, having profited by the venture, sent the remains out to sea where it sank. Unfortunately, gas had begun to generate in it, and it soon floated inshore, to the annoyance of the inhabitants, who towed it out again. But the remains floated back in. The performance was repeated several times, though it was once lashed temporarily to a rocky islet. At length it came ashore at Old Orchard Beach, where another Yankee decided to profit by it; he exhibited the foul bulk as a "sea-serpent" and special excursions were made from various points to view it. The directors of a Middle West museum that was building up a collection eventually heard about it and purchased the bones.

The Rats and Cats of Haskell Island

. . . A SERIES of strange events took place on this fertile island [Haskell Island, Maine] about sixty years ago, when it became overrun by rats. An old lobsterman named Humphrey, who had built a shack on the shore, seemed to live amicably enough with the rats, even though they continually stole the fish from his bait barrel. But when winter came on, Humphrey's friends warned him of the danger of living alone with only rats for company. Nevertheless he persisted in staying. One day, Harpswell fishermen noticed that no smoke was rising from the chimney of the little shack and they could see no one stirring on the island, so they rowed out to investigate. When they opened Humphrey's door, they were met by a squealing

---

From *Maine:* A Guide "Down East," written by Workers of the Federal Writers' Project of the Works Progress Administration for the State of Maine, pp. 266–267. American Guide Series. Copyright, 1937, by Everett F. Greaton, Executive Secretary, Maine Development Commission. Boston: Houghton Mifflin Company.

Ibid., pp. 390–391.

swarm of rats. Driving them away, the men entered the cabin—to find that the old lobsterman had been eaten in his bunk. The horrified citizens of Harpswell and the neighboring islands armed themselves with sticks and clubs and converged upon Haskell Island. When they left they were satisfied that every rodent there had been exterminated. Yet next spring the rats were as numerous as ever.

But it was not long before Harpswell residents again saw smoke rising from the chimney of the hut where Humphrey had lived. Two young fishermen, Wallace and Bruce Mills from North Harpswell, had set up an establishment on Haskell, bringing with them for companionship and protection a dozen or more very husky cats. The war began. At first the cats had the worst of it, but they lived to emerge triumphant. They were almost as prolific as the rats; and, fed on fish and cared for by the Mills boys, they and their progeny grew to a size and strength unheard of among mainland cats. It was not long before the last rat met his fate. But not only the rats disappeared—Haskell, once a paradise of songbirds, became silent except for nightly yowls. The cats increased in number, and Wallace and Bruce were kept more than busy catching enough fish to feed them. With the young men they were docile enough, but any visitor who attempted to land on the island would be met by several hundred spitting and clawing furies.

One day a prospective purchaser from the city approached Haskell; here in this green and pleasant spot he saw an ideal place to build a summer home. But he did not land on the island; in fact, he left rather hurriedly. The owner of the island told Wallace and Bruce that something would have to be done. They were only squatters, and they and their cats had no legal right to usurp the island. But the boys would do nothing. Finally, however, they arose one morning to find an army of dead cats stretched before the shack. Someone had come in the night and poisoned them. The Mills boys were broken-hearted. They disappeared, and no one knew where they went. But never since has a cat been seen on Haskell Island—or a rat.

The River That Ran Blood

In 1775, says Sullivan, in his "History of Maine," the Saco was found to swell suddenly, and in a singular manner. As there had not been rain sufficient to account for this increase of volume, people were at a loss how to explain the phenomenon, until it was finally discovered to be occasioned by a new river having broken out of the side of the White Mountains.

When this river issued from the mountains, in October, 1775, a mixture

---

From *The Heart of the White Mountains, Their Legend and Scenery,* by Samuel Adams Drake, p. 153. Entered according to Act of Congress, in the year 1881, by Harper & Brothers, in the Office of the Librarian of Congress, at Washington. New York. 1882.

of iron-ore gave the water a deep red color, and this singular, and to them most startling, appearance led the people inhabiting the upper banks of the Saco to declare that the river ran blood—a circumstance which these simple-minded folk regarded as of evil omen for the success of their arms in the struggle then going on between the Colonies and Great Britain.

Captain Clough and Marie Antoinette

. . . In 1793 the captain [Samuel Clough, of North Edgecomb, Maine, captain of a merchantman that frequently visited France] became engaged in an enterprise, the details of which are somewhat obscure. According to romantics, he was moved by the unfortunate situation of the imprisoned Queen of France to attempt her rescue with the aid of her friends; it seems clear, however, that he was merely hired by them to carry her to America on the "Sally" when they had managed to effect her release. Some of her personal belongings and various articles that her friends thought might make her home in exile more comfortable and furnish it in a style befitting her rank were smuggled aboard the Yankee ship. The plan, however, like others with the same purpose, failed; the queen was beheaded and Captain Clough set sail hastily to escape possible punishment for his share in the enterprise. In the meantime the captain had written to his wife to give her warning of the guest she might expect to have for a time, carefully trying to reconcile her to the dismaying idea of sheltering royalty. He doubtless found his home polished and shining when he at last arrived—without the queen.

The captain stored the queen's possessions in his home; some thought this was because of a personal devotion to her, but it seems more likely that his Yankee conscience made him uneasy about his right to dispose of the goods that had come into his possession in such an irregular manner. Gradually, as time passed and no one came to claim the cargo, the furnishings came into use in the large, plain, square house, now standing in North Edgecomb. Many stories are told of their later uses and wanderings. It is said that a satin robe, worn by the King of France on state occasions, was in time made into a dress by Mrs. Clough. A Wiscasset clockmaker discovered in the interior of an old clock a plate inscribed in French indicating that the timepiece had been presented by the maker to the queen on the Dauphin's birthday. Other mementoes are at the Metropolitan Museum of Art in New York; a few articles still remain in the Clough House.

From *Maine:* A Guide "Down East," written by Workers of the Federal Writers' Project of the Works Progress Administration for the State of Maine, pp. 264–265. American Guide Series. Boston: Houghton Mifflin Company.

Coon Cats and Rabbit Cats

It is claimed for the coon cats that they are distinctly a Maine development, and romantic legends are cited to account for their introduction to Maine. One of these legends is to the effect that a Maine shipmaster, Captain Samuel Clough, who is chiefly remembered for his connection with the royalist plot to rescue Marie Antoinette from prison and transport her to Maine, brought home a strange, oriental cat on one of his China voyages; and this Asiatic cat mating with the common American domestic cat produced the coon cat.. Others say that a cat in the town of China, Maine, had a clandestine affair with a raccoon, and the coon cat was a result of this romance. This legend, however, ignores the fact that the raccoon is a canine and not a feline. The broad head and luxuriant tail of the cat undoubtedly suggested its resemblance to a raccoon, and the name resulted from this fancied resemblance.

A legend similar to that of the cat and the raccoon is told of the so-called rabbit cat of Maine, the tailless Manx cat, which has hindquarters and long hind legs strikingly like those of a rabbit. Its movements, too, are rabbit-like, and under certain circumstances it is easy to see how one of these cats could be mistaken for a rabbit. They are very common in Maine. The sea captains who brought them here, either directly from the Isle of Man or more probably from Liverpool or other near-by ports on the mainland, may have purchased a few in Leadenhall Market, London, where a brisk trade used to be done selling cats to shipmasters, especially the masters of rat-infested ships. As for the legend that the rabbit cat is part rabbit, there is nothing to it. A rabbit is a rodent. Yet the only person I know who has aelurophobia is affected by rabbits in the same way as by cats.

How the Shoalers Walk and Stand

Nearly all the Shoalers have a singular gait, contracted from the effort to keep their equilibrium while standing in boats, and from the unavoidable gymnastics which any attempt at locomotion among the rocks renders necessary. Some stiff-jointed old men have been known to leap wildly from broad stone to stone on the smooth, flat pavements of Portsmouth town, finding it out of the question to walk evenly and decorously along the straight and easy way. This is no fable. Such is the force of habit.

From *Maine Summer*, by Edwin Valentine Mitchell, pp. 70–71. Copyright, 1939, by Coward-McCann, Inc. New York.

From *Among the Isles of Shoals,* by Celia Thaxter, pp. 73–74. Entered according to Act of Congress, in the year 1873, by James R. Osgood & Co., in the Office of the Librarian of Congress, at Washington. Boston.

Most of the men are more or less round-shouldered, and seldom row upright, with head erect and shoulders thrown back. They stoop so much over the fish-tables—cleaning, splitting, salting, packing—that they acquire a permanent habit of stooping.

What the Shoalers Don't Know

THE people along the coast rather look down upon the Shoalers as being beyond the bounds of civilization. A young islander was expressing his opinion on some matter to a native of Rye, who answered him with great scorn: "You don't know nothin' about it! What do *you* know? *You* never see an apple-tree all blowed out." A Shoaler, walking with some friends along a road in Rye, excited inextinguishable laughter by clutching his companion's sleeve as a toad hopped innocently across the way, and crying: "Mr. Berraye, what kind of a bug do you call that? D——d if I ever see such a bug as that, Mr. Berraye!" in a comical terror. There are neither frogs nor toads at the Shoals. "Set right down and help yourselves," said an old fellow at whose door some guests from the Shoals appeared at dinner-time. "Eat all you can. I ain't got no manners; the girl's got the manners, and she ain't to hum."

A Town Divided

FOR many years [at Naples, Maine,] there has been strong political feeling between the Republican and Democratic parties. The feeling is not as intense as it once was, but nevertheless the antagonism is quite marked. Many years ago the feeling was so intense that there were two community flag poles, one for the Democrats and the other for the Republicans. A doctor was hired to administer to the needs of the people; and as he was an active worker in the Democratic party, the Republicans hired a practitioner of their views: hence two doctors. The churches were built with two front doors, and the Democrats sat on one side of the church and the Republicans sat on the other side. This feeling was even carried into education, and school houses were built with two front doors. The children of Republican parents entered one door and sat on that side of the room, the other side of the room being given over to the Democrats. To cap the climax, a superintendent of schools was hired who was a rabid Democrat. This did not suit the Republicans, and they hired a superintendent of their own political views. Each superintendent hired a teacher for each grade, and

---

Ibid., p. 78.

Naples, Maine. Manuscripts of the Federal Writers' Project of the Works Progress Administration for the State of Maine.

here arose a situation that became alarming. These grades had two teachers each, who taught in the same room the children of these political fanatics. The situation became so bad that the Maine legislature had to step in and settle the difficulty in 1904, and enact special legislation to govern the case. The strange feature of the whole thing is that the whole town took sides and the upheaval was not the work of any small group. While the natives grin sheepishly and tell about the affair, the listener can sense the tense feeling that still exists.

Moving a Town down a Hill

NEWFANE, the shire town of Windham County, [Vermont,] is a real pretty village down in a valley off the West River. It has the county courthouse and the Grange and some other nice white clapboard buildings, and you'd think it had been there since the settlers took the land away from the Indians. It has, too— since just a few years before gramp was born. The place where Newfane is now used to be called Fayetteville; Newfane was right up on top of Newfane Hill. You'd probably call Newfane Hill a mountain; it's pretty steep, even for these parts. Newfane was built up there for protection from the Indians, and it would pretty near take a medium tank to attack the old site now.

Finally, in 1825, they decided the Indians wasn't going to bother them no more, and it really was a pretty smart climb up Newfane Hill, specially in mud time. So they took apart the courthouse and all the rest of the buildings, and drawed them down to Fayetteville by ox team, and set them up around the green like you see them now. Every so often, somebody tries to move the shire town from Newfane to Brattleboro, but I don't think they'll ever succeed. It used to be one of my neighbor John Gale's hobbies to stop them.

Ephraim Wright and the Underground Railroad

WE READ in history that Vermont was the first state in the Union to prohibit slavery. . . .

From the day when the name of the state was first adopted, no slave had been taken away from Vermont against his will. The fugitive who set foot upon her soil was safe, if not free.

From "Grandpa Was Quite a Fellow," by Walter Needham, as recorded by Barrows Mussey, *Saturday Evening Post*, Vol. 219 (Nov. 9, 1946), No. 19, p. 108.

From *Folklore of Springfield*, by Mary Eva Baker, pp. 62–66. Springfield, Vermont: Publishers, The Altrurian Club of Springfield, Vt. 1922.

Her north roads and her south roads were her underground railroads. There were Democrats who would send their teams to carry fugitives northward; while they themselves walked to a convention to shout for Douglas (the Democratic candidate for the presidency, in favor of slavery) and resolve that slavery must not be interfered with in states where it existed by law.

It is interesting to trace the underground railroad through this part of the state. Noah Safford, who lived near the foundry in a house that has been recently moved to Olive Street, [Springfield, Vermont] while spending winters in the south selling straw-cutters of his own manufacture, saw enough of slavery to make him vow eternal vengeance upon it. From that time his home was one of the most important stations where the fugitives were always safe—sometimes it might be weeks in the attic, again it might be only a few days in the barn.

His daughter, Mrs. Rebecca (Safford) Holmes, remembered when a little girl hearing teams drive up in the night and saw food carried to the barn in the morning; the following night she heard the sound of wheels again as fugitives were taken to the next station, which was usually Judge Pingree's office in Perkinsville. This office was a station where slaves were secreted, fed, and lodged, then sent to Col. Thomas Powers in Woodstock; from there to Deacon and Mrs. Morris' home in Strafford, which is just over the line in Orleans county. Judge Pingree had a very ingenious place for secreting these slaves. A movable panel by the fireplace gave entrance to a small closet, which was so arranged that none were ever discovered.

Ephraim Wright, a fugitive, remained with Mr. Safford for several years and was much afraid of being recaptured. One day he went to the store and came running back, asking to be hidden; for he saw, or thought he saw, what looked like his old master. It is said of him that he was as white as it is possible for a colored man to be.

This story is also told of him: From that time on he always walked with his head partially turned over his shoulder, that he might see anyone approaching from behind. One of the neighbors, meeting him one day, asked him what he should do if he saw his master coming. Ephraim replied, "I think I should fight."

He was a very large and powerful man, who had little fear from other men physically.

Ephraim Wright later married a fugitive girl who came here on the underground railway, escaping to Canada. The house, owned at the present time by Mrs. Will Nourse on South Street, was built for them. Ephraim and his wife became good citizens and, with their three children, united with the Congregational Church. He was the village barber for some time.

IV. HISTORICAL TRADITIONS

Not everything orally transmitted is mere *legend; there is traditional history as well as traditional folklore.*—J. FRANK DOBIE

Some legends, unquestionably, are historically true, and many others are elaborations on historical fact. And a few no doubt are pure invention, concocted for sheer amusement or for some reason in the mind of the inventor.—STEWART H. HOLBROOK

To some extent, mythology is only the most ancient history and biography. So far from being false or fabulous in the common sense, it contains only enduring and essential truth, the I and you, the here and there, the now and then, being omitted. . . . We moderns, on the other hand, collect only the raw materials of biography and history, "memoirs to serve for a history," which itself is but materials to serve for a mythology. . . . Who knows what shape the fable of Columbus will at length assume, to be confounded with that of Jason and the expedition of the Argonauts. And Franklin,—there may be a line for him in the future classical dictionary, recording what that demigod did, and referring him to some new genealogy. "Son of —— and ——. He aided the Americans to gain their independence, instructed mankind in economy, and drew down lightning from the clouds."
—HENRY D. THOREAU

1. TRADITION AND HISTORY

THE relation of tradition to history is not and probably never will be clearly understood. Still more difficult to explain is the mixture of the two in historical traditions. These include (1) legends of doubtful exploits of historical personages and (2) traditions (of varying degrees of reliability) of historical events which for one reason or another have become a part of national tradition. The events related in historical traditions need not have happened but they should be such as are believed to have happened.

The difference between historical traditions and local traditions (which also involve history) is the difference between the "now and then" and the "here and there." Both kinds of traditions may belong to a "family of stories or beliefs." Just as migratory legends become attached to various places, so they become attached to various persons, since a good yarn knows no limitations of time, place, or character. The migratory type of historical tradition is generally known as an historical legend, because, as A. H. Krappe wisecracks, they are not historical at all. A case in point is the stories of Lorenzo Dow. Historical traditions, proper, on the other hand, are "isolated stories or beliefs," following John Fiske's distinction, and conforming more or less to his definition of these as "untrustworthy traditions of doubtful events."[1] Unlike unhistorical historical legends, then, they may be semi-historical or pseudo-historical; and, as part of national tradition, they may become an historical force.

At the same time historical traditions are no less credible than history itself, which must necessarily contain a large amount of conjecture. Ordinarily, however, we expect the former to involve a greater proportion of untruth because of the well-known unreliability of oral or popular tradition. But they are generally so convincing as to inspire the comment, "Well, if it didn't happen that way, it *ought* to have happened." So no matter how persistently and legitimately historians may pick holes in the story of Priscilla and John Alden, the popular imagination will stubbornly continue to cherish it as one of its prized possessions, according to the following reasoning:

> Some of it is true, and I expect you to believe that part, but some of it is extremely untrue and I expect you to disbelieve that part. The trouble is that the true portion is harder to believe than the untrue portion; and, after all, the untrue portion may be true, because witnesses could only testify they'd never seen such things happen, and one's not having seen things happen doesn't keep them from happening.[2]

2. The Bardic Tradition

It is almost impossible to conceive of an historical character or event about which there has not grown up a body of legend or apocryphal anecdote. The natural affinity and attraction between history and legend points to a time before written history when the two were virtually indistinguishable. In this stage the bard, as singer or story-teller, is both historian and poet, "not always clearly differentiated from the medicine man and the soothsayer."[3] The special magic of the bard (like that of the good historian[4]) consists in giving us the sense of history (and literature) in the making. In the same way, tradition is both prophetic and creative.

Because of their prophetic and symbolic character, historical traditions—in songs and slogans as well as stories—are an integral part of a national tradition and of the heroes and other sacred symbols embodying it. That is because these traditions help, if not to interpret, to shape history, or, at least, "to remind us of the happenings that occasioned them."[5] Because these traditions also serve to illustrate traits of character and ideals, they easily pass into fable and illustrative anecdote. Not all anecdotes are folklore, but a good deal of folklore (as well as history) may be said to be in its anecdotage.

---

[1] *Myths and Myth-Makers* (Boston, 1898), p. 15.

[2] Frost Woodhull, "Folklore Shooting," *Southwestern Lore,* Publications of the Texas Folklore Society Number IX (Austin and Dallas, 1931), p. 1.

[3] Ludwig Lewisohn, *The Story of American Literature* (New York, 1939) p. xx.

[4] Cf. Samuel McChord Crothers: ". . . the great historian is one who has a certain prophetic gift. . . . He identifies himself so thoroughly with the age of which he writes that he always seems to be at the beginning of an era peering into the yet dim future."—"That History Should Be Readable," *The Gentle Reader* (Boston, 1903), p. 199.

[5] Henry F. Woods, *American Sayings* (New York, 1945), p. vii.

Likewise on account of their symbolic value, historical traditions are the materials of poetry. And working in this rich vein, in the tradition of the "national poet,"[1] Longfellow and Whittier, particularly the former, have succeeded in stamping historical traditions indelibly upon the imagination of Americans, especially young Americans, and at the same time in stamping these traditions with the qualities of the American imagination. And this because as much as in spite of the liberties that a poet like Longfellow has taken with history[2] (as in "Paul Revere's Ride," "The Courtship of Miles Standish," and "Evangeline") and even mythology (as in "The Song of Hiawatha"). For, by poetic license, poetry and folklore have a way of fitting history to the requirements of the imagination, or poetic truth, tantamount to rewriting and perhaps distorting history but also (in rare prophetic moments) to *making* it.

3. The Yankee as Hero: Legend and Myth

As hero or demigod, the Yankee does not stack up so well as, say, the Westerner. This may be due to the fact that in its insistence on the sacred right of the individual to be a character, New England may have bred eccentrics rather than heroes. Heroes have a way of transcending the merely personal, as well as the purely local, just as they have a way of transcending history, because their function is to embody certain ideal traits. And when we look at Yankee heroes, we are apt to be struck by the fact that so many of them are heroes in a state of arrested development, or mere eccentrics.

As a "peculiar people," the Yankees are not heroic. For personal peculiarity or idiosyncrasy is the bane of the hero. Not every odd character, of course, can even boast of being a true eccentric (like Timothy Dexter), since the latter must be a person whose "oddities must be his chief claim to attention, and he must be known, more or less, throughout the nation."[3] The very greatness of his eccentricity, however, gives the Yankee eccentric a certain heroic stature.

Even when they rise above the limitations of mere eccentricity, Yankee heroes still tend to be local rather than national heroes. Thus Yankee leaders like John Adams and even Daniel Webster fail to attain the heroic stature of Washington and Lincoln, whereas Franklin and Paul Revere come nearer to appealing to the national (and popular) imagination. The fact is that the national hero, the culture-hero, requires a large proportion of myth as well as legend. Whereas legend simply explains or transforms history, myth explains or transforms nature and human nature. In his rôle of culture-bringer or culture-carrier, the hero appears as a demigod. And the only demigod among Yankees is the trickster-hero, the generic and ubiquitous Yankee peddler, trickster, and showman hero, from Sam Slick to P. T. Barnum, from Jack Downing to (even) Ethan Allen, whose tricks are tricks of the trade. As a "practical wag," Barnum, like Franklin, exemplifies and teaches the Yankee "art of getting on," and the more

---

[1] Cf. "Longfellow Our National Poet," *Proceedings of the Massachusetts Historical Society,* February, 1907, pp. 564–582.

[2] *Ibid.*

[3] Edmund Lester Pearson, *Books in Black or Red* (New York, 1923), p. 157.

practical than heroic Yankee virtues of common sense, thrift, faculty, or "know-how," and handiness, as a means to security, self-respect, comfort, power, and prestige.

The Yankee peddler also possesses the heroic trait of restlessness. For the heroic spirit belongs to a "time of migrations," "a society cut loose from its roots." For the same reason the Yankee skipper and merchant-adventurer appeals to hero-worship. And the Yarmouth whalemaster, Captain Ichabod Paddock, who taught Nantucketers the "art of killing whales," is somewhat of an exception among Yankee heroes in his combination of the rôles of culture-hero and adventurer with a touch of the Casanova.

But in spite of the mobility of the Yankee peddler and the Yankee skipper, a mobility which belongs to their time and which existed for the sake of moving and placing things rather than in movement for its own sake, and in spite of the readiness with which Yankees have left home to "New Englandize" the country, their genius is for staying put and digging in. To them even pioneering was a job rather than (as exploration was for the Connecticut Yankee John Ledyard) a gallant adventure.

For all these reasons, then, the Yankee mythus is plebeian and prosaic—workaday. It all boils down to the importance of work in the New England creed—an importance recognized by its place in the Puritan trinity of "Faith in God, faith in man, and faith in work." In commenting on the dry, unpoetic character of New England history as essentially a history of work, Lowell says: "So much downright work was perhaps never wrought on the earth's surface in the same space of time as during the first forty years after the settlement. But mere work is unpicturesque and void of sentiment." [1] And throughout New England history and folklore, we hear, not the horns of elfland faintly blowing, but the "noise of axe and hammer and saw, an apotheosis of dogged work, where, reversing the fairy-tale, nothing is left to luck, and, if there be any poetry, it is something that cannot be helped—the waste of the water over the dam." [2]

B. A. B.

FABLES AND SYMBOLS

Priscilla and John Alden

In Tradition [1]

In a very short time after the decease of Mrs. Standish [January 29th, 1621], the captain was led to think, that, if he could obtain Miss Priscilla

[1] *Among My Books,* (Everyman's Library), p. 181.
[2] *Ibid.*, p. 180.

[1] From *Massachusetts Historical Collections,* Being a General Collection of Interesting Facts, Traditions, Biographical Sketches, Anecdotes, &c., Relating to the History and Antiquities of Every Town in Massachusetts, with Geographical Descriptions, by John Warner Barber, p. 500. Entered, according to Act of Congress, in the year 1839, by Dorr, Howland & Co. In the Clerk's Office of the District Court of Massachusetts. Worcester.

Source: Alden's *A Collection of American Epitaphs* . . . , III.—J. W. B.

Mullins, a daughter of Mr. William Mullins, the breach in his family would be happily repaired. He, therefore, according to the custom of those times, sent to ask Mr. Mullins' permission to visit his daughter. John Alden, the messenger, went and faithfully communicated the wishes of the captain. The old gentleman did not object, as he might have done, on account of the recency of Captain Standish's bereavement. He said it was perfectly agreeable to him, but the young lady must also be consulted. The damsel was then called into the room, and John Alden, who is said to have been a man of most excellent form with a fair and ruddy complexion, arose, and, in a very courteous and prepossessing manner, delivered his errand. Miss Mullins listened with respectful attention, and at last, after a considerable pause, fixing her eyes upon him, with an open and pleasant countenance, said, *Prithee, John, why do you not speak for yourself?* He blushed, and bowed, and took his leave, but with a look which indicated more than his diffidence would permit him otherwise to express. However, he soon renewed his visit, and it was not long before their nuptials were celebrated in ample form. From them are descended all of the name, Alden, in the United States. What report he made to his constituent, after the first interview, tradition does not unfold; but it is said, how true the writer knows not, that the captain never forgave him to the day of his death.

In History [2]

Tradition states that Capt. Standish, after the death of his wife, proposed a matrimonial alliance with Miss Mullens, the daughter of William Mullens, and that John Alden was engaged as the messenger to announce his wishes. But the lady, it seems, not so much enamored with the military renown of Standish as by the engaging address of the youthful advocate, dexterously hinted her opinion to that effect; by which course an end was put to all hope on the part of the distinguished military leader of the Pilgrims.

Without intending to discredit this ancient tradition, which has so long held its claim undisputed in the families descended from Alden and Chilton, there seem to be sufficient grounds for entering a protest against the unbounded license assumed by fiction, originating from various quarters, both in a verbal and written form, in relation to this amusing incident of early times. The following facts are therefore stated as aids to truth in the matter. Rose, the wife of Standish, died Jan. 29th, and William Mullens, the father of Priscilla, Feb. 21, 1621. Edward Winslow married the widow of Wm. White, May 12, 1621, it being the first marriage which occurred after the landing. John Alden and Miss Mullens were probably married in the spring of 1622, or the preceding fall.

Bearing in mind these facts, it seems hardly *credible* that Standish, so

[2] From *Pilgrim Memorials, and Guide to Plymouth,* by Wm. S. Russell, pp. 22–23. Entered according to Act of Congress, in the year 1855, by Wm. S. Russell, in the Clerk's Office of the District Court of the District of Massachusetts. Boston: Crosby, Nichols, Lee and Company. 1860.

soon after the decease of his beautiful and excellent wife,—for such tradition assures us she was,—that within a month, "nay, not so much," he should propose a renewal of the matrimonial bonds, so suddenly severed, in the saddest hour of even Pilgrim experience. It is gratifying in this case that tradition and the facts of history may pleasantly harmonize under the guidance of rational probabilities, leaving us to infer that no leave was asked of Mr. Mullens, in person or by proxy, to visit his daughter; but that the embassy of Alden was to the maiden herself, some time after; that, as no cattle were imported into the colony till the year 1623, of course no animal of that species was here found, to be "covered" with a "handsome piece of broadcloth"; that, as the town of Barnstable was not settled till the year 1639, some eighteen years subsequent, when all the parties were happily settled in the same neighborhood in old Duxbury; therefore the bridal party and the novel cavalcade, which figure so largely in the story, on proceeding to and returning from the nuptial ceremonies of the *transported* lovers, are matters assignable to some after period, when time and circumstances rendered them entirely suitable and appropriate. We are justified in assuming that a "flirtation" actually occurred at the commencement of "good old colony times," and that *Cupid* and *Mars* were in open conflict—that Miss Mullens was irresistibly attractive in person, manners and character, since a military hero was *fairly* conquered, never before known to surrender, being severely but not mortally wounded; as a certain skilful lady, who came over in the ship Ann, in the year 1623, and became his second wife, was able to effect a perfect cure.

The Tinker and the Fencing-Master

. . . A TINKER with a cheese under his arm and a kettle of blacking in the hand, stopped at a tavern in a village in Massachusetts, where a French Fencing Master was teaching the art of fencing. He was challenging any one to try with him. Several did so and so expert was he, that he would soon disarm them. Presently the Tinker with his swab stick and his cheese under his arm took the floor and said he would try him. Although he disdained such a competitor as this tinker, yet to make sport for the company at the tinker's expense, he consented to try him. They went at it, but with all his skill he could not touch the tinker. Presently the tinker caught the fencing master's sword in his cheese and blacked one of his cheeks with the end of his swab stick, and the laugh turned on him instead of the tinker.

From "Further Reminiscences of the Valley of the Pawtuxet River and Its Branches," by Noah J. Arnold, in *The Narragansett Historical Register,* A Magazine Devoted to the Antiquities, Genealogy and Historical Matter Illustrating the History of the State of Rhode Island and Providence Planations, Vol. 7 (July 1889), No. 3, edited by James N. Arnold, p. 238. Copyright in the office of the Librarian of Congress at Washington, D. C. Providence, Rhode Island: The Narragansett Historical Publishing Company.

He sweat and grew mad and exerted himself to the utmost to overcome the tinker. The next moment the tinker blacked the other cheek! The fencing master was now in a rage and threatened to kill him, but the tinker said coolly "don't you attempt that, for if you do, you are the dead man." The fencing master's sword dropped, and he said: "You are either Goffe, Whalley,[1] or the Devil, for there are no others in the world that can fence with me," and he was right, for it was one of these men, in the disguise of a tinker that stood before him.

The Angel of Hadley

DURING Philip's war, in 1676, Hadley was attacked on the morning of the 12th of June, by about seven hundred Indians. "In the preceding night, they approached the town, laid an ambuscade at the southern extremity, and advanced the main body towards the other, and at day-light the attack was commenced with great spirit; but the English, turning out, received them at the palisades. The Indians gained possession of a house at the north end of the street, and fired a barn, but were in a short time driven back with loss. The attack was renewed on other points, and the Indians, though warmly opposed, appeared determined on carrying the place; but a discharge of a piece of ordnance checked their fury and their ambuscade failing of their object, which was to attack the people who might be driven from the village, they drew off. Major Talcott, at Northampton, hearing the attack, hurried on, passed the river, and, joining the Hadley forces, precipitated the Indians into the woods. Only two or three men were lost by the English; the enemy's was not ascertained." "When the people were in great consternation, and rallying to oppose the Indians, a man of vener-

[1] They were two of Oliver Cromwell's ablest generals in the revolution in England, which dethroned and then beheaded Charles I, King of England. Their names were Goffe and Whalley, and [they] were reputed to be the best swordsmen in Europe. They were members of the Court that tried the king and voted the sentence of death upon him. After the restoration of Charles II, all those who were alive that were members of that Court had to flee from England to such places of refuge as they could find, or they would have been put to death. Goffe and Whalley came to this country, and kept secreted as well as they could.—N. J. A.

Cf. John Warner Barber, *Massachusetts Historical Collections* (Worcester 1839), p. 324, who places this episode, between the judge, disguised as a rustic, and a fencing-master, in Boston.

From *Massachusets Historical Collections,* Being a General Collection of Interesting Facts, Traditions, Biographical Sketches, Anecdotes, &c., Relating to the History and Antiquities of Every Town in Massachusetts, with Geographical Descriptions, by John Warner Barber, pp. 325–326. Entered, according to Act of Congress, in the year 1839, by Dorr, Howland & Co. in the Clerk's Office of the District Court of Massachusetts. Worcester.

Source: *Hoyt's Indian Wars,* p. 135.—J. W. B.

Cf. "The Gray Champion," by Nathaniel Hawthorne.

able aspect, differing from the inhabitants in his apparel, appeared, and, assuming command, arrayed them in the best manner for defence, evincing much knowledge of military tactics, and by his advice and example continued to animate the men throughout the attack. When the Indians drew off, the stranger disappeared, and nothing further was heard of him. Who the deliverer was, none could inform or conjecture, but by supposing, as was common at that day, that Hadley had been saved by its guardian angel. It will be recollected that at this time the two judges, Whalley and Goffe, were secreted in the village, at the house of the Rev. Mr. Russell. The supposed angel, then, was no other than Gen. Goffe, who, seeing the village in imminent danger, put all at risk, left his concealment, mixed with the inhabitants, and animated them to a vigorous defence. Whalley, being then superannuated, probably remained in his secluded chamber."

Lovel and the Indians

THERE is no doubt that farmer Lovel had read ancient history or he would not have been so ready in the emergency that befell him one time in the last century. He had settled among the New Hampshire hills near the site that is now occupied by the village of Washington and had a real good time there with bears and Indians. It was when he was splitting rails on Lovel Mountain—they named it for him afterward—that he found himself surrounded by six Indians, who told him that he was their prisoner. He agreed that they had the advantage over him and said that he would go quietly along if they would allow him to finish the big chestnut log that he was at work on. As he was a powerful fellow and was armed with an axe worth any two of their tomahawks, and as he would be pretty sure to have the life of at least one of them if they tried to drive him faster than he wanted to go, they consented. He said that he would be ready all the sooner if they would help him to pull the big log apart, and they agreed to help him. Driving a wedge into the long split he asked them to take hold, and when they had done this he knocked out the wedge with a single blow and the twelve hands were caught tight in the closing wood. Struggle as the savages might, they could not get free, and after calmly enjoying the situation for a few minutes he walked slowly from one to the other and split open the heads of all six. Then he went to work again splitting up more chestnuts.

From *Myths & Legends of Our Own Land,* by Charles M. Skinner, Vol. I, pp. 207–208. Copyright, 1896, by J. B. Lippincott Company. Philadelphia & London.

This ruse is attributed to many Indian-fighters, including Ford (Katharine M. Abbott, *Old Paths and Legends of New England,* New York, 1903, p. 113) and Weare (or Wyer) (Manuscripts of the Federal Writers' Project of the Works Progress Administration for the State of Maine).

Sarah Hanson's Song

ONCE, while on their way to Canada through these mountains, a war-party of Indians, fresh from a successful foray on the sea-coast, halted with their prisoners on the banks of a stream whose waters stopped their way. For weeks these miserable captives had toiled through trackless forests, through swollen and angry torrents, sometimes climbing mountains on their hands and knees—they were so steep—and at night stretching their aching limbs on the cold ground, with no other roof than the heavens.[1]

The captives were a mother, with her new-born babe, scarcely fourteen days old, her boy of six, her two daughters of fourteen and sixteen years, and her maid. Two of her little flock were missing. One little prattler was playing at her knee, and another in the orchard, when thirteen red devils burst in the door of their happy home. Two cruel strokes of the axe stretched them lifeless in their blood before her frenzied eyes. One was killed to intimidate, the other was despatched because he was afraid, and cried out to his mother. There was no time for tears—none even for a parting kiss. Think of that, mothers of the nineteenth century! The tragedy finished, the hapless survivors were hurried from the house into the woods. There was no resistance. The blow fell like a stroke of lightning from a clear sky.

This mother, whose eyes never left the embroidered belt of the chief, where the reeking scalps of her murdered babes hung; this mother, who had tasted the agony of death from hour to hour, and whose incomparable courage not only supported her own weak frame, but had so far miraculously preserved the lives of her little ones, now stood shivering on the shores of the swollen torrent with her babe in her arms, and holding her little boy by the hand. In rags, bleeding, and almost famished, her misery should have melted a heart of stone. But she well knew the mercy of her masters. When fainting, they had goaded her on with blows, or, making a gesture as if to snatch her little one from her arms, significantly grasped their tomahawks. Hope was gone; but the mother's instinct was not yet extinguished in that heroic breast.

But at this moment of sorrow and despair, what was her amazement to hear the Indians accost her daughter Sarah, and command her to sing them a song. What mysterious chord had the wild, flowing river touched in those savage breasts? The girl prepared to obey, and the Indians to listen. In the heart of these vast solitudes, which never before echoed to a human voice, the heroic English maiden chanted to the plaintive refrain of the river the sublime words of the Psalmist:

From *The Heart of the White Mountains, Their Legend and Scenery,* by Samuel Adams Drake, pp. 126–128. Entered according to Act of Congress, in the year 1881, by Harper & Brothers, in the Office of the Librarian of Congress, at Washington. New York. 1882.

[1] Captivity of Elizabeth Hanson, taken at Dover, New Hampshire, 1724.—S. A. D.

"By the rivers of Babylon, there we sat down, yea, we wept, when we remembered Zion.

"We hanged our harps upon the willows in the midst thereof.

"For there they that carried us away captive required of us a song; and they that wasted us required of us mirth."

As she sung, the poor girl's voice trembled and her eyes filled, but she never once looked toward her mother.

When the last notes of the singer's voice died away, the bloodiest devil, he who murdered the children, took the babe gently from the mother, without a word; another lifted her burden to his own shoulder; another, the little boy; when the whole company entered the river.

Cotton Mather's Advice to Ben Franklin

WHEN I was a boy, I met with a book entitled "Essays to Do Good," which I think was written by your father [Cotton Mather]. It had been so little regarded by a former possessor that several leaves of it were torn out, but the remainder gave me such a turn of thinking as to have an influence on my conduct through life, for I have always set a greater value on the character of a *doer of good* than on any other kind of reputation; and if I have been, as you seem to think, a useful citizen, the public owes the advantage of it to that book.

You mention your being in your seventy-eighth year. I am in my seventy-ninth. We are grown old together. It is now more than sixty years since I left Boston, but I remember well both your father and grandfather, having heard them both in the pulpit, and seen them in their houses. The last time I saw your father was in the beginning of 1724, when I visited him after my first trip to Pennsylvania. He received me in his library, and on my taking leave showed me a shorter way out of the house through a narrow passage, which was crossed by a beam overhead. We were still talking as I withdrew, he accompanying me behind, and I turning partly towards him, when he said hastily, "Stoop, stoop!" I did not understand him till I felt my head hit against the beam. He was a man that never missed any occasion of giving instruction, and upon this he said to me, "You are young and have the world before you. *Stoop* as you go through it, and you will miss many hard thumps." This advice, thus beat into my head, has frequently been of use to me, and I often think of it when I see pride mortified and misfortunes brought upon people by their carrying their heads too high.

Letter of Benjamin Franklin to Rev. Samuel Mather, from Passy, May 12, 1784. From *Franklin's Boyhood in Boston,* Old South Leaflets, No. 161, pp. 19–20 (Vol. VII, pp. 223–224). Published by the Directors of the Old South Work, Old South Meeting House. Boston.

Old Put's Wolf

In the year 1739, he [Gen. Putnam] removed from Salem to Pomfret, an inland fertile town in Connecticut, forty miles east of Hartford; having here purchased a considerable tract of land, he applied himself successfully to agriculture.

The first years on a new farm are not, however, exempt from disasters and disappointments, which can only be remedied by stubborn and patient industry. Our farmer, sufficiently occupied in building an house and barn, felling woods, making fences, sowing grain, planting orchards, and taking care of his stock, had to encounter, in turn, the calamities occasioned by a drought in summer, blast in harvest, loss of cattle in winter, and the desolation of his sheep-fold by wolves. In one night he had seventy fine sheep and goats killed, besides many lambs and kids wounded. This havoc was committed by a she wolf, which with her annual whelps, had for several years infested the vicinity. The young were commonly destroyed by the vigilance of the hunters, but the old one was too sagacious to come within reach of gunshot; upon being closely pursued she would generally fly to the western woods, and return the next winter with another litter of whelps.

This wolf at length became such an intolerable nuisance that Mr. Putnam entered into a combination with five of his neighbors to hunt alternately until they could destroy her. Two by rotation were to be constantly in pursuit. It was known that having lost the toes from one foot, by a steel trap, she made one track shorter than the other. By this vestige, the pursuers recognized in a light snow the route of this pernicious animal. Having followed her to Connecticut River and found she had turned back in a direct course towards Pomfret, they immediately returned, and by ten o'clock the next morning, the blood-hounds had driven her into a den, about three miles distant from the house of Mr. Putnam. The people soon collected with dogs, guns, straw, fire and sulphur to attack the common enemy. With this apparatus several unsuccessful efforts were made to force her from the den. The hounds came back badly wounded and refused to return. The smoke of blazing straw had no effect; nor did the fumes of burnt brimstone, with which the cavern was filled, compel her to quit the retirement.

Wearied with such fruitless attempts, which had brought the time to ten o'clock at night, Mr. Putnam tried once more to make his dog enter, but in vain; he proposed to his Negro man to go down into the cavern

---

From *The Life & Heroic Exploits of Israel Putnam, Major-General in the Revolutionary War,* by Colonel David Humphreys, pp. 8–12. Entered, according to the Act of Congress, in the year 1833, by Ezra Strong, in the Clerk's Office of the District Court of the Southern District of New York. New York. 1835.

and shoot the wolf: the Negro declined the hazardous service. Then it was that the master, angry at the disappointment, and declaring that he was ashamed to have a coward in his family, resolved himself to destroy the ferocious beast, lest she should escape through some unknown fissure of the rock. His neighbors strongly remonstrated against the perilous enterprise; but he, knowing that wild animals were intimidated by fire, and having provided several strips of birch-bark, the only combustible material which he could obtain, that would afford light in this deep and darksome cave, prepared for his descent. Having accordingly, divested himself of his coat and waistcoat, and having a long rope fastened round his legs, by which he might be pulled back, at a concerted signal, he entered head foremost with the blazing torch in his hand.

The aperture of the den, on the east side of a very high ledge of rocks, is about two feet square; from thence it descends obliquely fifteen feet, then running horizontally about ten more, it ascends gradually sixteen feet towards its termination. The sides of this subterraneous cavity are composed of smooth and solid rocks, which seem to have been divided from each other by some former earthquake. The top and bottom are also of stone, and the entrance in winter, being covered with ice, is exceedingly slippery. It is in no place high enough for a man to raise himself upright, nor in any part more than three feet in width.

Having groped his passage to the horizontal part of the den, the most terrifying darkness appeared in front of the dim circle of light afforded by his torch. It was silent as the house of death. None but monsters of the desert had ever before explored this solitary mansion of horror. Cautiously proceeding onward, he came to the ascent, which he slowly mounted on his hands and knees until he discovered the glaring eyeballs of the wolf, who was sitting at the extremity of the cavern. Started at the sight of fire, she gnashed her teeth, and gave a sullen growl. As soon as he had made the necessary discovery, he kicked the rope as a signal for pulling him out. The people at the mouth of the den who had listened with painful anxiety, hearing the growl of the wolf, and supposing their friend to be in the most imminent danger, drew him forth with such celerity that his shirt was stripped over his head and his skin severely lacerated. After he had adjusted his clothes, and loaded his gun with nine buck-shot, holding a torch in one hand and the musket in the other, he descended the second time. When he drew nearer than before, the wolf assuming a still more fierce and terrible appearance, howling, rolling her eyes, snapping her teeth, and dropping her head between her legs, was evidently in the attitude and on the point of springing at him. At this critical instant he levelled and fired at her head. Stunned by the shock, and suffocated with the smoke, he immediately found himself drawn out of the cave. But having refreshed himself, and permitted the smoke to dissipate, he went down the third time. Once more he came within sight of the wolf, who appearing very passive, he applied the torch to her nose, and perceiving her dead, he took hold of her ears, and then kicking the rope still tied round his legs, the people above with no small exultation dragged them both out together.

Yankee Doodle

. . . [It was] Colonel Thomas Fitch, [of Norwalk, Connecticut,] whose shabbily dressed troops, which he led from here to the French and Indian War, inspired a British army surgeon, Dr. Shuckburgh, to write the derisive "Yankee Doodle." According to local tradition, Elizabeth Fitch, on leaving the house to bid good-bye to her brother, was dismayed by the ill-assorted costumes of the "cavalry." Exclaiming, "You must have uniforms of some kind," she ran into the chicken yard, and returning with a handful of feathers announced, "Soldiers should wear plumes," and directed each rider to put a feather in his cap. When Shuckburgh saw Fitch's men arriving at Fort Crailo, Rensselaer, New York, he is reputed to have exclaimed, "Now stab my vitals, they're macaronis!" sarcastically applying the slang of the day for fop, or dandy, and proceeded to write the song, which instantly caught popular fancy.[1]

. . . The British army lay encamped in the summer of 1755, on the eastern bank of the Hudson, a little south of the city of Albany. . . . In the early part of June the eastern troops (Colonial) began to pour in, company after company, and such a motley assemblage of men never before thronged together on such an occasion. It would . . . have relaxed the gravity of an anchorite to have seen the descendants of the Puritans making through the streets of our ancient city to take their station on the left of the British army, some with long coats, some with short coats, and some with no coats at all. . . . Their march, their accoutrements, and the whole arrangement of their troops furnished material of amusement to the wits of the British army. Among the club of wits that belonged to the British army there was a physician attached to the staff, by the name of *Doctor Schackburg,* who combined with the science of the surgeon the skill and talents of a musician. To please Brother Jonathan he composed a tune, and, with much gravity, recommended it to the officers as one of the most celebrated airs of martial musick. The joke took, to the no small amusement of the British Corps. Brother Jonathan exclaimed that it was a "nation fine," and in a few days nothing was heard in the Provincial camp but "Yankee Doodle!"[2]

---

[1] From *Connecticut,* A Guide to Its Roads, Lore and People, written by Workers of the Federal Writers' Project of the Works Progress Administration for the State of Connecticut, p. 267. American Guide Series. Copyright, 1938, by Wilbur L. Cross. Boston: Houghton Mifflin Company.

[2] From *Farmer & Moore's Literary Journal* (1824). Cited in *Our American Music,* Three Hundred Years of It, by John Tasker Howard, p. 120. Copyright, 1929, 1930, and 1931, by John Tasker Howard. New York: Thomas Y. Crowell Company.

The Boston Tea Party

December 18*th* [1773]. However precarious our situation may be, yet *such* is the present calm composure of the people that a stranger would hardly think that ten thousand pounds sterling of the East India Company's *tea* was destroy'd the night, or rather evening before last, yet its a serious truth; and if your's, together with ye. other Southern provinces, should rest satisfied with *their* quota being stor'd, poor Boston will feel the whole weight of ministerial vengeance. However, its the opinion of most people that we stand an equal chance now, whether troops are sent in consequence of it or not; whereas, had it been stor'd, we should inevitably have had 'em, to enforce the sale of it.—The affair was transacted with the greatest regularity and despatch. Mr. Rotch finding he exposed himself not only to the loss of his ship but for ye. value of the tea in case he sent her back with it, *without a clearance from the custom house,* as ye. Admiral kept a ship in readiness to make a seizure of it whenever it should sail under *those circumstances;* therefore declin'd complying with his former promises, and absolutely declar'd his vessel should not carry it, without a *proper* clearance could be procur'd or he to be indemnified for the value of her:—when a general muster was assembled, from this and all ye. neighboring towns, to the number of five or six thousand, at 10 o'clock Thursday morning in the Old South Meeting house, where they pass'd a *unanimous* vote that the *Tea* should go out of the *harbour* that afternoon, and sent a committee with Mr. Rotch to ye. Custom house to *demand* a clearance, which the collector told 'em was not in his power to give, without the duties being first paid. They then sent Mr. Rotch to Milton, to ask a pass from ye. Governor, who sent for answer, that "consistent with the rules of government and his duty to the King he could not grant one without they produc'd a previous clearance from the office."—By the time he return'd with this message the candles were light in [the] house, and upon reading it, such prodigious shouts were made, that induc'd me, while drinking tea at home, to go out and know the cause of it. The house was so crouded I could get no farther than ye. porch, when I found the moderator was just declaring the meeting to be *dissolv'd,* which caused another general shout, out doors and in, and three cheers. What with that, and the consequent noise of breaking up the meeting, you'd thought that the inhabitants of the infernal regions had broke loose. For my part, I went contentedly home and finish'd my tea, but was soon inform'd what was going forward: but still not crediting it without ocular demonstration, I went and was *satisfied.* They muster'd, I'm told, upon Fort Hill, to the

---

From *Letters of John Andrews, Esq., of Boston, 1772–1776,* compiled and edited from the Original Mss., with an Introduction, by Winthrop Sargent, pp. 12–13. Reprinted from the Proceedings of the Massachusetts Historical Society. Cambridge: Press of John Wilson and Sons. 1866.

number of about two hundred, and proceeded, two by two, to Griffin's wharf, where Hall, Bruce, and Coffin lay, each with 114 chests of the *ill fated* article on board; the two former with *only* that article, but ye. latter arriv'd at ye. wharf only ye. day before, was freighted with a large quantity of other goods, which they took the *greatest* care not to injure in the least, and before *nine* o'clock in ye. evening, every chest from on board the three vessels was knock'd to pieces and flung over ye. sides. They say the actors were *Indians* from *Narragansett*. Whether they were or not, to a transient observer they appear'd as *such,* being cloath'd in Blankets with the heads muffled, and copper color'd countenances, being each arm'd with a hatchet or axe, and pair pistols, nor was their *dialect* different from what I conceive these geniusses to *speak,* as their jargon was unintelligible to all but themselves. Not the least insult was offer'd to any person, save one Captain Conner, a letter of horses in this place, not many years since remov'd from *dear Ireland,* who had ript up the lining of his coat and waistcoat under the arms, and watching his opportunity had nearly fill'd 'em with tea, but being detected, was handled pretty roughly. They not only stripp'd him of his cloaths, but gave him a coat of mud, with a severe bruising into the bargain; and nothing but their utter aversion to make *any* disturbance prevented his being tar'd and feather'd.

Should not have troubled you with this, by this Post, hadn't I thought you would be glad of a more particular account of so *important a transaction,* than you could have obtain'd by common report; and if it affords my brother but a *temporary* amusement, I shall be more than repaid for the trouble of writing.

The Young Rebels

Sunday, January 29th (1775). . . . Shall close this by giving you a small anecdote, relating to some of our school lads—who as formerly in this season improv'd the Coast from Sherburn's hill down to School street. General Haldiman, improving the house that belongs to Old Cook, his servant took it upon him to cut up their coast and fling ashes upon it. The lads made a muster, and chose a committee to wait upon the General, who admitted them, and heard their complaint, which was couch'd in very genteel terms, complaining that their fathers before 'em had improv'd it as a coast for time immemorial, &ca. He order'd his servant to repair the damage, and acquainted the Governor with the affair, who observ'd that it was impossible to beat the notion of Liberty out of the people, as it was rooted in 'em *from their Childhood.*[1]

---

[1] *Ibid.*, pp. 85–86.

Near the centre of the [Boston] Common is a stone-rimmed body of water known as the Frog Pond. The old-time Boston boys used to slide down hill on to this pond, and they heaped up the snow to make a steeper descent. Just before the Revolution, the English soldiers who were camped on the Common destroyed the slides again and again while the boys were gone to school. The boys protested in vain to the soldiers, and then went to their general and complained. He asked who sent them.

"Nobody sent us, sir," one of them replied. "Your soldiers have spoiled our snow-slides and broken the ice where we skate. When we complained to them, they called us young rebels, and told us to help ourselves if we could. Now we will bear it no longer."

The general turned to an officer and exclaimed, "Good heavens! the very children draw in a love of liberty with the air they breathe."

Then he assured the boys that if any of the soldiers molested them again, they would be severely punished.[2]

The Original Brother Jonathan

When General Washington, after being appointed Commander of the Army of Revolutionary War [June 15th, 1775,] came to Massachusetts to organize it, and make preparations for the defence of the country, he found a great want of ammunition and other means necessary to meet the powerful foe he had to contend with, and great difficulty to obtain them. If attacked in such condition, the cause at once might be hopeless. On one occasion, at that anxious period, a consultation of the officers and others was held, when it seemed no way could be devised to make such preparations as were necessary. His Excellency Jonathan Trumbull, the elder, was then Governor of the State of Connecticut, on whose judgment and aid the general placed the greatest reliance, and remarked: "We must consult 'Brother Jonathan' on the subject." The general did so, and the governor was successful in supplying many of the wants of the army. When difficulties arose, and the army was spread over the country, it became a by-word, "We must consult Brother Jonathan." The term Yankee is still applied to a portion, but "Brother Jonathan" has become a designation of the whole country, as John Bull is for England.

---

[2] From *New England, A Human Interest Geographical Reader,* by Clifton Johnson, pp. 66–67. Copyright, 1917, by The Macmillan Company. New York and London.

From *The American Joe Miller:* A Collection of Yankee Wit and Humour, Compiled by Robert Kempt, p. 116. Entered at Stationers' Hall. London: Adams and Francis. 1865.

A Loyal Tory of Hancock

TRADITIONS and tales from the past are Hancock's chief contribution to the history of Berkshire. Her glory was at its peak during the years when the "Berkshire Boys" marched up the long valley to Bennington, and Tories received short shrift from the patriots.

A loyal Tory of Hancock, Richard Jackson, was accused of high treason against the Colonies when he was captured on his way to join the British near Bennington. Making no pretense of being other than a Royalist, ready to fight for his king, he was taken to the jail at Great Barrington to await trial in Springfield. The jail was dilapidated and the guard lax, so that any prisoner could have escaped with ease. But Jackson's integrity was beyond question. Local tradition has it that he appealed to the sheriff.

"Let me go free that I may work and earn something."

"But—but—" stammered the sheriff, who respected Jackson, though he felt that this request was a little unorthodox.

"Have no fear, Sheriff, I shall come back at night," and he added grimly, "When it's time for me to be hanged, I'll be there."

Morning after morning Jackson was let out, did his day's work, and was safely locked up again at night. Finally in May it became the sheriff's duty to take him to Springfield. But seeing that his jailer was loath to leave his plowing and planting, Jackson suggested that he make the trip alone.

The sheriff, accustomed by this time to his prisoner's unusual requests, agreed, and his charge set off alone to trudge miles through the woods to his trial and execution, for there was no apparent hope of acquittal. In the woods of Tyringham he was overtaken by the Hon. Mr. Edwards, who was on his way to a meeting of the Executive Council in Boston.

"Whither are you bound?" asked Edwards. "To Springfield, sir, to be tried for my life," was the calm rejoinder.

Without disclosing his own identity, Edwards soon learned his companion's story. Pondering, he went on to Boston, while Jackson stopped in Springfield, was duly tried, and condemned to death. Meantime, the Executive Council, which at that time exercised power of release over those condemned to death, was listening to petitions for pardon. After all these had been read, Edwards asked the Council if a pardon was not to be granted to Mr. Jackson of Hancock. Earnestly addressing the assembly, Edwards told the story of Jackson's loyalty not only to his king, but to the laws and regulations of the Colony in so far as they implied no disloyalty to his English sovereign. The members of the Council hesitated, scarcely believing their ears, but when the story was proved true, they unanimously agreed

---

From *The Berkshire Hills*, Compiled and Written by Members of the Federal Writers' Project of the Works Progress Administration for Massachusetts, pp. 51–52. New York: Duell, Sloan and Pearce.

that such a man as Jackson ought not to be sent to the gallows. An unconditional pardon was immediately made out and the loyal Tory returned to his family and farm in Hancock.

The early town records of Hancock lead one to wonder what kind of reception awaited Jackson after he cheated the noose. The town was militantly patriotic in Revolutionary times. Her sons served their country valiantly and as a rule Royalists received little tolerance from the Town Fathers. . . .

The Satisfied Redemptioner

Both before and after the Revolution, the poorer class of emigrants, in the lack of ready money, secured a passage to this country through shipping companies specially organized for that purpose, by signing a negotiable obligation for the amount of their passage ticket, whereby they were "bound to service for a term of years,"—more or less, according as the persons were single or had families. This class of persons was included in the famous rendition clause of the Constitution of the United States, Art. IV, Sect. 11, 3. They were familiarly known as "Redemptioners."

One of these was "held to service" by a planter in Westerly [, Rhode Island,] who had duly bought his paper. After serving very cheerfully and happily in his new relation for a season, he took occasion to express to his master or employer his entire satisfaction with his situation, and seriously averred that he wished his written obligation extended through his life. He was disquieted and depressed with the idea that he should finally, on the expiration of his service, be obliged to plan and toil for himself in a land of strangers. The farm to him was an Eden, and his employer was a father. He therefore proposed to have his obligation made perpetual in a new writing.

The appropriate paper for his life service, at his request, was duly prepared and presented for his signature. On taking the pen to sign the instrument, he hesitated, saying that he did not understand how the obligations of the old and new papers harmonized, as the time in the new in part overlapped the time in the old. Explanations were in vain. Finally the master proposed to destroy the old paper and thus clear the way. This was satisfactory. The old instrument was thrown under the forestick. The redemptioner again took his pen, but again hesitated. He seemed to be in a brown study. The employer inquired for the reason of his embarrassment. Was the paper satisfactory? Was it not just what he himself had proposed and dictated? It was allowed that the instrument was exactly

---

From *Westerly (Rhode Island) and Its Witnesses,* for Two Hundred and Fifty Years, 1626–1876, Including Charlestown, Hopkinton, and Richmond, Until Their Separate Organization, with the Principal Points of Their Subsequent History, by Rev. Frederic Denison, A.M., pp. 143–144. Entered according to Act of Congress, in the year 1878, by Frederic Denison, in the Office of the Librarian of Congress, at Washington, D. C. Providence: Published by J. A. & R. A. Reid.

what he had desired. "But," said the redemptioner, "I was thinking of some advice that my father once gave me. He gave me good counsel, and I only wish I had followed it more closely. He once said to me, 'My son, never sign your name to a paper of any kind.' As I have signed one paper, but have just got rid of it, I think I shall not sign another. So, sir, I kindly bid you a good-by." The redemptioner walked away a free man, and left the employer counting up his wits.

The Yarn-Beam Cannon

HARD on the heels of the Revolution came Shays' Rebellion. The Berkshire farmers, oppressed by heavy taxes, hard times, and the almost worthless post-Revolutionary currency, understood better than the "city folks" in Boston the real purpose of Daniel Shays' uprising. Lee was in particularly hard straits. In the winter of 1787, a battle more comic than tragic took place between the Shaysites and the government troops under General Patterson, drawn up on a hill in East Lee. Uniformed troops these, with polished rifles and menacing cannon. Opposite, across Greenwater Brook, were lined up the ragged and hungry rebels. They had only a few old-fashioned muskets, little ammunition, and no cannon. But someone had an inspiration. "Bring out Mother Perry's yarn-beam," he cried; "we'll make it look like a cannon to scare the sheep across the way." Quickly the ponderous piece of weaving machinery, looking remarkably like a cannon, was mounted on a pair of ox-cart wheels. A ramrod and other military gadgets were flourished for the benefit of the enemy. Peter Wilcox roared the order, "Fire," and a blazing tarred rope was brandished like a fuse. Before the flames could damage Mother Perry's property, General Patterson's troops were in flight. In a twinkling, the hill they had occupied was bare.

Skipper Ireson's Ride

ON SUNDAY, the 30th of October [1808], the schooner Betty, commanded by Skipper Benjamin Ireson, arrived from the Grand Banks. Shortly after their arrival, the crew reported that at midnight on the previous Friday,

---

From *The Berkshire Hills,* Compiled and Written by Members of the Federal Writers' Project of the Works Progress Administration for Massachusetts, pp. 137–138. Copyright, 1939, by The Berkshire Hills Conference, Inc. New York: Duell, Sloan and Pearce.

From *The History and Traditions of Marblehead,* (Third Edition), by Samuel Roads, Jr., pp. 292–295. Copyright, 1880, by Samuel Roads, Jr. Marblehead: Press of N. Allen Lindsey & Co. 1897.

when off Cape Cod lighthouse, they passed the schooner Active, of Portland, which was in a sinking condition; and that the skipper had refused to render any assistance to the unfortunate men on board the wreck. The excitement and indignation of the people upon the reception of this news can be better imagined than described. Two vessels, manned by willing volunteers, were immediately dispatched to the scene of the disaster, with the hope of their arrival in time to save the shipwrecked sailors. But their mission was a failure, and they returned with no tidings of the wreck. The resentment of the people was still further provoked when, on the following day, the sloop Swallow arrived, having on board Captain Gibbons, the master of the ill-fated schooner. He corroborated the story told by the crew of the Betty, and stated that the Active sprang a leak at about eleven o'clock on Friday night. An hour later the Betty was spoken, "but contrary to the principles of humanity," she sailed away without giving any assistance. On Saturday, Captain Gibbons and three of the passengers were taken off the wreck by Mr. Hardy of Truro, in a whale boat. Four other persons were left on the wreck, but the storm increased so rapidly that it was found impossible to return to their rescue. Captain Gibbons was placed on board the revenue cutter Intent, and afterward went aboard the sloop Swallow, in which he came to Marblehead.[1]

This statement by one who had so narrowly escaped a watery grave made a deep impression upon the fishermen, and they determined to demonstrate their disapproval of Skipper Ireson's conduct by a signal act of vengeance. Accordingly on a bright moonlight night, the unfortunate skipper was suddenly seized by several powerful men and securely bound. He was then placed in a dory, and, besmeared from head to feet with tar and feathers, was dragged through the town, escorted by a multitude of men and boys. When opposite the locality now known as Workhouse Rocks, the bottom of the dory came out, and the prisoner finished the remainder of his ride to Salem in a cart. The authorities of that city forbade the entrance of the strange procession, and the crowd returned to Marblehead.

Throughout the entire proceeding, Mr. Ireson maintained a discreet silence, and when, on arriving at his own home, he was released from custody, his only remark was: "I thank you for my ride, gentlemen, but you will live to regret it."

His words were prophetic. When too late to make reparation for the wrong they had committed, the impulsive fishermen realized that they had perpetrated an act of the greatest injustice upon an innocent man.

At this late day, when for years his memory has been defamed throughout the land, and the fair name of the women of Marblehead has been sullied by the fictitious story of one of our best New England poets, it is but just that the true history of the affair should be written. Skipper

[1] See *Boston Centinel, Essex Register*, and *Salem Gazette*, November, 1808.—S. R., Jr.

Ireson was not more to blame than his crew and, it is believed, not at all. When the wreck was spoken and the cry of distress was heard, a terrific gale was blowing. There was a consultation on board the Betty as to the course to be pursued, and the crew decided not to endanger their own lives for the sake of saving others. Finding that they were resolute in their determination, Skipper Ireson proposed to lay by the wreck all night, or until the storm should abate, and then go to the rescue of the unfortunate men. To this they also demurred, and insisted upon proceeding on their homeward voyage without delay. On their arrival in Marblehead, fearing the just indignation of the people, they laid the entire blame upon the skipper. This version of the affair is generally accepted as true; and, for the credit of the town, be it said that it is one of the few incidents in its entire history that its citizens have any reason to regret.[1]

[1] Immediately upon the publication of the first edition of this book, Mr. Whittier sent the author a letter in which he gracefully acknowledged himself mistaken as to the facts in the case. He also gave directions that the letter should be published with the poem in subsequent editions of his works. The letter, herewith printed, is published with his permission.

OAK KNOLL, DANVERS, 5 mo, 18, 1880.

MY DEAR FRIEND: I heartily thank thee for a copy of thy *History of Marblehead*. I have read it with great interest and think good use has been made of the abundant material. No town in Essex County has a record more honorable than Marblehead; no one has done more to develop the industrial interests of our New England seaboard, and certainly none have given such evidence of self-sacrificing patriotism. I am glad the story of it has been at last told, and told so well. I have now no doubt that thy version of Skipper Ireson's ride is the correct one. My verse was founded solely on a fragment of rhyme which I heard from one of my early schoolmates, a native of Marblehead.

I supposed the story to which it referred dated back at least a century. I knew nothing of the participators, and the narrative of the ballad was pure fancy. I am glad for the sake of truth and justice that the real facts are given in thy book. I certainly would not knowingly do injustice to any one, dead or living.

I am very truly thy friend,
JOHN G. WHITTIER.

—S. R., JR.

The "Chant of Flood Oirson," as it has been called, [the "fragment of rhyme" referred to by Whittier] was current in the town years before Whittier wrote, and ran in this wise:—

Old Flood Oirson for his hord hort
Was tor'd and further'd and coried in a cort,
A becos he left five men on a wrack
Was tor'd and further'd all over his back!

The true story was first published some twenty years ago by the late Rev. Charles T. Brooks, minister and poet, in a newspaper, by way of introduction to his verses, *A Plea for Flood Ireson,* written as an offset to Whittier's poem. . .

Poor Ireson sailed another voyage as skipper, the following year, but never after. Later in life he followed the dory-fishing in the bay, and used to peddle his catch in a handcart through the streets. Although the best townspeople soon after the affair became entirely satisfied that he had suffered unjustly, and treated him with respect, his

Mrs. Bailey's Petticoat

THEY tell a story here [in Groton, Connecticut,] of the war of 1812 worth relating: One day Commodore Hardy in the "Ramilies" and Sir Hugh Pigott in the "Orpheus" hove in sight, and the people came to the conclusion that New London was to be attacked. Major Smith at once manned Fort Griswold with volunteers from the vicinity, while the women and children fled into the interior. At the last moment the Major found he had no wadding for his cannon, and sent out a squad in search of flannel for that purpose. Unfortunately all the houses and stores were closed, and they could secure none. Returning, they met on the street Mrs. Anna Bailey, who, on hearing their story, dropped her flannel petticoat, and told them to give it to the British at the cannon's mouth. The officers and garrison were greatly elated by the lady's spirit, and Hardy would no doubt have fared ill had he attacked. When the danger was over, Commodore Decatur gave a grand ball, at which Mrs. Bailey was the heroine of the occasion. Later her fame spread throughout the country, and she was visited by Lafayette, Monroe, Jackson, and other notables. "Mother Bailey" died in 1851 aged ninety-two years.

John Adams Tries Ditching

WHEN I was a boy, I had to study the Latin grammar, but it was dull, and I hated it. My father was anxious to send me to college, and therefore I studied grammar till I could bear it no longer, and, going to my father, I told him I did not like study, and asked for some other employment. It was opposing his wishes, and he was quick in his answer. "Well, John," said he, "if Latin grammar does not suit, you may try ditching; perhaps that will. My meadow yonder needs a ditch, and you may put by Latin, and try that." This seemed a delightful change, and to the meadow I went.

---

life was wrecked; and he drifted aimlessly till his death, only a year or two before the appearance of Whittier's ballad. His name was Benjamin Ireson; "Flood," not "Floyd," as Whittier gives it, being a nickname.—Edwin M. Bacon, *Historic Pilgrimages in New England* (Boston, 1898), pp. 210–211, 212.

From *In Olde Connecticut*, Being a Record of Quaint, Curious and Romantic Happenings There in Colonie Times and Later, by Charles Burr Todd, pp. 104–105. Copyright, 1906, by The Grafton Press. New York.

From *Massachusetts Historical Collections,* Being a General Collection of Interesting Facts, Traditions, Biographical Sketches, Anecdotes, &c., Relating to the History and Antiquities of Every Town in Massachusetts, with Geographical Descriptions, by John Warner Barber, p. 480. Entered, according to Act of Congress, in the year 1839, by Dorr, Howland & Co. In the Clerk's Office of the District Court of Massachusetts. Worcester.

But I soon found ditching harder than Latin, and the first forenoon was the longest I ever experienced. That day I eat the bread of labor, and glad was I when night came on. That night I made some comparison between Latin grammar and ditching, but said not a word about it. I dug the next forenoon, and wanted to return to Latin at dinner; but it was humiliating, and I could not do it. At night, toil conquered pride, and I told my father —one of the severest trials of my life—that if he chose I would go back to Latin grammar. He was glad of it; and if I have since gained any distinction, it has been owing to the two days' labor in that abominable ditch.

Daniel Webster and the Scythe

DURING one of the college vacations, he and his brother returned to their father's in Salisbury. Thinking he had a right to some return for the money he had expended on their education, the father put scythes into their hands and ordered them to mow. Daniel made a few sweeps, and then, resting his scythe, wiped the sweat from his brow. His father said, "What's the matter, Dan?" "My scythe don't hang right, sir," he answered. His father fixed it, and Dan went to work again, but with no better success. Something was the matter with his scythe—and it was again tinkered. But it was not long before it wanted fixing again; and the father said in a pet, "Well, hang it to suit yourself." Daniel with great composure hung it on the next tree; and putting on a grave countenance said, "It hangs very well; I am perfectly satisfied."

Daniel Webster and the Woodchuck

DANIEL and his brother Ezekiel caught a woodchuck which had been doing mischief in the Webster garden. Zeke was about to kill it when their father interfered saying: "You two boys can be lawyers while I'll be judge and will hear you plead your case." Zeke's plea was: "The woodchuck does no good. A worthless animal. Has eaten our peas and beans, thus depriving us of our food. If he goes free, he will continue to destroy things we need." Daniel said, "Although only a woodchuck, it is one of God's creatures, just as we are. It desires to live, just as we do. We have plenty of peas

---

From *The New-England Almanac,* for the Year of Our Lord 1833, by Anson Allen, Philo., p. 32. Hartford: Published and Sold by Andrus and Judd.

From *Marshfield, 70°–40′ W: 42°–5′ N, The Autobiography of a Pilgrim Town,* Being an Account of Three Hundred Years of a New England Town; founded by the Pilgrims; Lived in and Developed by the Royalists; Adopted by Daniel Webster & Beloved by Many of the Ancestors of Those Who Today Make It Their Home, 1640–1940, p. 203. Copyright, 1940, by Marshfield Tercentenary Committee. Marshfield, Massachusetts.

and beans. Look at the poor fellow! How he must suffer with his leg in a trap! A severe penalty for what he has done or will do. We have a large farm and can afford to give a little woodchuck something to eat." "Enough," cried the judge, "Zeke, you let that woodchuck go."

The Sacred Codfish

Poised high aloft in the old hall of the Massachusetts House of Representatives, riding serenely the sound waves of debate, unperturbed by the ebb and flow of enactment and repeal or the desultory storms that vexed the nether depths of oratory, there has hung through immemorial years an ancient codfish, quaintly wrought in wood and painted to the life.

Humble the subject and homely the design; yet this painted image bears on its finny front a majesty greater than the dignity that art can lend to graven gold or chiselled marble. The sphere it fills is vaster than that through which its prototype careered with all the myriad tribes of the great deep. The lessons that may be learned of it are nobler than any to be drawn from what is only beautiful; for this sedate and solitary fish is instinct with memories and prophecy, like an oracle. It swims symbolic in that wider sea whose confines are the limits set to the activities of human thought. It typifies to the citizens of the Commonwealth and of the world the founding of a State. It commemorates Democracy. It celebrates the rise of free institutions. It emphasizes progress. It epitomizes Massachusetts.

To the sober student of the world's past this historic codfish is fraught with ripe significance. A few details as to the origin and vicissitudes of this material emblem may shed some light on its serious purpose and high mission.

This old codfish has kept its place under all administrations, and has looked upon outgoing and incoming legislative assemblies, for more than one hundred years. It does not appear under what precise circumstances this familiar representation assumed its position; but it is an assured fact that the identical image which hangs to-day in the hall recently occupied by the lower branch of the Great and General Court came there from the old State House at the head of State Street, when the archives were transferred in 1798. That it was suspended in the old State House since 1784 appears from the following entry in the Journal of the House of Representatives of Wednesday, March 17, 1784:—

"Mr. Rowe moved the House that leave might be given to hang up the representation of a Cod Fish in the room where the House sit, as a memorial of the importance of the Cod-Fishery to the welfare of this Commonwealth,

---

From *A History of the Emblem of the Codfish in the Hall of the House of Representatives,* Compiled by a Committee of the House, pp. 11–13, 17–20, 34–36. Boston: Wright and Potter Printing Co., State Printers. 1895.

as had been usual formerly. The said motion having been seconded, the question was put, and leave given for the purpose aforesaid."

And so the emblem was suspended, and, as Mr. Rowe was a man of peculiar public spirit and patriotism, it is probable that he paid for the carving of the fish and all the expenses incident thereto, even those connected with its "hanging up in the room where the House sit," out of his own pocket.

* * * * *

There is a dim tradition that in the primitive House of Assembly of the Province there hung a codfish which was the gift of Judge Samuel Sewall, author of the famous "Diary."

Judge Sewall died in 1729. His published remains make no mention of this traditional fish, and it is difficult to imagine that a man of his loquacious verbosity would have omitted to chronicle his munificence, either in his diary or his letters.

The expression, "as had been usual formerly," in the original motion of Mr. Rowe, apparently refers to this prehistoric creature of tradition, which hung in the old State, or Town, House. When this structure was burned, Dec. 9, 1747, the codfish doubtless went up in the whirl of smoke which still clouds its history to the peering vision of the antiquarian. The new Old State House (which stands to this day at the head of State Street) was erected in the succeeding year; and, at whatsoever date the old-time emblem was restored to its original place of honor, it is clear that it flourished there in all its pristine glory as early as 1773; for, in an old bill of that year, presented by Thos. Crafts, Jr., to the Province of Massachusetts Bay, for painting the State House, and which, from all that can be learned, has not been disputed, appears the item:—

To painting Codfish, ... 15 Shillings.

At some indeterminate time subsequent to the painting of the codfish by Thomas Crafts, Jr., it disappeared from the State House and was doubtless destroyed, for the closest historical research fails to shed any light upon the time, manner or cause of its disappearance, or to disclose any further reference to it whatever. Mayhap some burly British trooper, quartered in the improvised barracks of the old State House, took umbrage at the spick and span elegance of the newly painted emblem of colonial independence and thrift. Such a one may have torn the cherished symbol from the wall whence it had offered aid and comfort to the rebel patriots, with its assurance of the material wealth accessible to the embryonic State, and, in the spirit of vandalism so prevalent at that age, used it to replenish his evening camp fire. Whatever may have been its fate in that epoch of political upheaval, no record was left to tell the tale.

There seems good reason to believe that this missing fish, or its successor, which has come down to us, was carved by one John Welch, a Boston patriot. Welch was born Aug. 11, 1711. He was a well-known citizen, and lived on Green Lane in West Boston. In 1756 he was a captain in the Ancient and Honorable Artillery Company. He, too, was one of the signers of the famous petition or memorial, charging the officers of the Crown with appropriating to their own use money belonging to the Province. The descendants of John Welch have always insisted that he carved the State House codfish of to-day. His great-great-grandson, Capt. Francis Welch, is now living in Brookline, at the age of eighty-six, and he has recently stated that the truth of this assertion has always been recognized among the family traditions. It has been handed down from father to son uncontradicted for at least three generations. Captain Welch's father repeatedly told him that he heard the story from the lips of his grandfather, and never expressed the least doubt in regard to it.

Conceding the authenticity of this tradition, a question remains as to which of the two codfishes was the handiwork of John Welch. Welch died Feb. 9, 1789; so that, if he carved the fish now in the State House, he must have been in his seventy-fourth year. This seems unlikely, whereas he might easily have wrought the codfish Thomas Crafts painted; and it is quite probable that, in the growing vagueness of domestic tradition, the identity of the two may have been confounded. In that chaotic revolutionary period which left to us no record of the loss or destruction of the object of Thomas Crafts' artistic attention, the Welch family may easily have lost trace of it, and have taken it for granted that the older emblem is the actual symbol of to-day.

It has been said by some one that the old codfish has never been taken down since it was first suspended in the then new State House in 1798; but Capt. Thomas Tucker, the venerable doorkeeper of the House, can tell another story. Within his own recollection the old emblem has twice been lowered, and he furthermore says that the codfish did not always occupy its present vantage ground. It used to hang from a point in the ceiling directly over the Speaker's desk, but in the fifties it was shifted to the rear of the chamber. In 1867, for a brief space, the fish was missing from its accustomed haunt; but it soon returned, brighter than before, in a new coat of submarine motley. Again, in 1874, while the chamber was being renovated, the codfish was taken down to be repainted; and at the time Captain Tucker measured it, finding its length to be four feet and eleven inches. He also noted that it was carved from a solid block of wood. Since that time, a period of twenty-one years, the sacred emblem has not been profaned by mortal touch.[1]

* * * * *

Years before the statesmen of the period had decided to make public acknowledgment of the indebtedness of the colony to the codfish, and had voted to adorn the assembly chamber with a wooden representation thereof, individuals and private corporations were eager to pay tribute to

[1] The subsequent "stealing" of The Sacred Codfish by Harvard students excepted.

the codfish, and vied with one another in their anxiety to make the recognition as conspicuous as possible. As early as 1661 the codfish appears upon the corporate seal of the Plymouth Land Company, proprietors of lands on the Kennebec River. In 1743 Col. Benjamin Pickman of Salem, who was one of the most prominent men of the colony, erected the Mansion House in that town, and decorated the end of every stair in his spacious hall with a carved and gilded codfish. Some of the journals of the day recognized it. On the front of the "Salem Gazette" for 1768 appears a coat of arms, consisting of a shield, supported by two Indians, and bearing the dove and olive branch. The crest above this shield is an unmistakable codfish.

Official notice of the obligation owed to the people of the colony had been taken, and the emblem inserted in some of the court seals, among others, upon the seal affixed to the processes issued from the famous Court of Oyer and Terminer, which tried and condemned the witches in 1692. The origin of the seal seems to have been traced as far back as 1686, when it was used by the Court of Quarter Sessions of the Peace and the Inferior Court of Common Pleas, as well as in the melancholy instances referred to above. The seal bears the word "Essex," elegantly carved in cipher, with what passes for the dove and olive branch above it, and an unmistakable codfish below.

Again, the seal of the "Middle Circuit Court of Common Pleas" shows the codfish. In the margin of the seal is the word "Massachusetts," with the style of court, and on its face "Fiat Justitia," under which motto agriculture, commerce and the fisheries are respectively represented by the sheep, the anchor and the codfish. This court was established in 1811, by an act dividing the Commonwealth into six circuits, each having a chief justice and associates. The "Middle Circuit" comprised Essex, Middlesex and Suffolk.

The Commonwealth paid tribute to this source of her earliest prosperity in other directions. In 1755 a two-penny internal revenue stamp of the colony bore the impress of the codfish, surrounded with this striking and significant legend: "Staple of the Massachusetts." This stamp may be seen, says Felt, upon a contract for building the draw of the old North bridge at Salem, which draw, being raised at the approach of Leslie's Regulars, twenty years later, became the bulwark of the liberties of America.

The currency of the colony at a later date bore the same impress on several of its issues. In the years 1776 and 1778 many of the coins, from three-pence upwards, seem to have been thus embellished. In an old collection of American currency the following denominations bear the tutelary fish upon their face: In 1776, $3, $5, $8, $11, also 3*d*, 6*d*, 8*d*, 9*d*, 1*s*, 1*s* 6*d*, 2*s*, 3*s*, 4*s*, and 4*s* 6*d*; in 1778, 4*d*, 1*s* 6*d*, 2*s*, 3*s*, 4*s*, and 4*s* 6*d*.

Thus it appears that the use of the codfish as a symbol of the progress and pre-eminence of Massachusetts was no novel or unaccustomed departure. The homely emblem is closely identified with the greatness of the

State. It might almost be said that its crescent outlines are graven on every page of its history.

Tradition invests our codfish with the grandeur gathered from the days when "there were giants" in Massachusetts. It speaks to us of all the old Bay State was and is. Patriotism protects it from the cavil of the cynic and the gibe of the unthinking. It typifies the world-old simplicity of those who go down to the sea in ships; the goodly, Godly race, whom the stately scriptural story has immortalized; whose sturdy virtues the Saviour himself distinguished in the choice of Peter, the apostolic fisherman; and whose singular achievements on sea and land, in the arts alike of peace and war, have glorified the annals of the Commonwealth.

ROGUES, ECCENTRICS, AND HEROES

Captain Kidd Legends in New England

Kidd in Narragansett [1]

Here, up on the northern tip of Conanicut Island, lived Kidd's friend Captain Pain, whose eventful life is another skeleton of what Kidd's might have been—from privateering *against* pirates in the West Indies and some plundering of his own along the Florida coast, to citizenship in Rhode Island, where he served on the grand jury, became captain of a company of militia, was admitted as a freeman of the colony, and ultimately became one of the founders of Trinity Church in Newport. Captain Pain's adventurous days were ten or fifteen years behind him when Kidd came to his house in 1699 to disturb his now not dishonest repose. Pain deposed before two officials at Newport on September 26, 1699, that he could not remember the day or the month, but sometime "Last Spring" Kidd had "run up the Bay w'th his Sloops as high in ye Bay as my house and sent his boate on Shore to desire me Company aboard wch I did. . . . After some tyme hee desired mee to secure some things for him. But I refused aleadging my house would bee Searcht and I could not doe it." Nevertheless he did, and his house was searched—in vain—and we may assume he returned ultimately to the old farmhouse on Conanicut, part of which still stands. The Earl of Bellomont thought of him as an old pirate, and though not successful in the search of his house, the Earl was reasonably satisfied from the intercepted letter already mentioned that he had some of Kidd's gold and had escaped with more. So might we today and so did the Earl report it. This is the basis for the quiet understandable belief that Kidd had

[1] From *Pirate Laureate:* The Life & Legends of Captain Kidd, by Willard Hallam Bonner, pp. 130–131. Copyright, 1947, by The Trustees of Rutgers College in New Jersey. New Brunswick, New Jersey: Rutgers University Press.

deposited goods somewhere in Narragansett Bay. It was early written into the Colonial records.

The Narragansett legend attached to Kidd a familiar piece of villainy in buried treasure lore. This was the murder of a man, a helper it may be assumed, and the burial of his body along with the chest of money for the double purpose of keeping the location a secret and of casting a protective spell. Thirty years after the Revolution one Thomas B. Hazard, a reputable citizen of Peace Dale, saw from the house of his friend Greene of Warwick Neck the shore "covered with people digging in the sand along the beach in all directions." He tells us that a week before, a box holding a skeleton had been washed out by the tide. The people were digging for Kidd's money. Kidd had been "often at Newport and was finally hung there on Gravelly Point" with twenty-seven others, all on one gallows. The skeleton, says Hazard, was that of a man killed and buried to protect it. The Kidd fever endured around Newport where the Captain, it was said, had often been seen, and where such excitement would naturally be nourished by the ill repute of Rhode Island as a favorite harboring and retiring place for those who would go no more a-roving.

Kidd Hoaxes [2]

In the *Fairy Queen* Spenser pictures little errors feeding on the blood of their dam Error. So legends beget legends, and the Kidd legends of buried treasure beget hoaxes. Very early there were claimants, impersonators, and jesters. Watson reported that a Jersey wag hoaxed the credulous in 1699 during the excitement incurred by the visit of Shelly and Kidd by declaring he had buried money on Cape May. In 1699 an arrogant, disfigured freebooter, John James, captain of the *Providence Galley*, a strong ship of twenty-six guns and one hundred and thirty men, fired upon an English man-of-war in Linnhaven Bay, Virginia, and declared to the captain of a Bristol merchantman whom he later pursued, "I am Captain Kidd." In 1704 Samuel Lowman, Collector of the Port of Lewes, then in Pennsylvania, presented a claim against the government for expenses entailed in curtailing the illegal trade in 1700 with the *Pirate*, a ship said to be commanded by Captain Kidd. Also in 1704 one John Corso presented a false claim for £30,000, saying he had been robbed by Captain Kidd.

The most spectacular hoaxes, however, came later. First there was the famous letter found in a field near Palmer, Massachusetts, sixty rods from the Boston road in the year of the California Gold Rush, 1849. Two boys, who were cousins named Shaw, came upon the letter sealed in a bottle and lodged beneath a rock in a cave. This paper looked old and was written in an antique hand full of supposed antique misspellings. It purported to be written in some distress from Boston in 1700/1 and was signed "Robert Kidd." It read in part as follows:

---

[2] *Ibid.*, pp. 143–148.

To John Bailey, Esq., New York. Sir: I fear we are in a bad situation. We are taken for pirates and you must come to Boston as soon as you get this. . . . If I do not see you, I will tell you where my money is, for we have plenty of that if it will do us any good it is . . . buried on . . . Conant's Island in Boston Harbor on the northwest corner of the Island in two chests containing from fifteen to twenty thousand pounds sterling in money Jewels and Diamonds. They are buried about four feet deep with a flat stone on them and a pile of stone near by. There is no one that knows where it is but me now living as Dick Jones and I hid it when part of my men were in Boston and the rest asleep one night; it is about sixty rods up the side hill. . . . I want you to see Col. Slaughter and John Nichols Esq. and James Bogard and Captain Houson and Edward Teach and all that can do me any good. . . . They think I have got the money buried down at Plymouth or down that way somewhere, they don't think it is so near to Boston. . . . Come quickly, if I am gone for England, secure money or diamonds and follow. It will buy a great many people. . . . Keep dark. . . . They keep me well here, this from your friend

Robert Kidd.

A postscript repeats his request to hurry, speaks again of the general locations of the money, and urges Bailey to keep dark.

There was a solemn reading of this letter to Palmer folk in one of the Shaw homes; and the publicity it created was prolonged by a quarrel between the fathers of the boys, Samuel Shaw and Gardner Shaw, over the possession of it, the paper at last being lodged in a bank vault for safekeeping. One man sued the other, and when the case came to court Samuel confessed to forging it. The two young discoverers had by that time followed the lure of other gold to California. The excitement must have lasted at least a year. The boys found the letter in February, 1849, and in the next year Gardner Shaw published in Palmer a life of Kidd and an account of this "discovery," *The Life, Trial, and Execution of the Famous Pirate Capt. Robert Kidd . . . Also, the letters of Kidd's wife to Lord Bellomont, and the famous Kidd Letter, Recently found, enclosed in a bottle, in a ledge of rocks in the town of Palmer, Mass.* This work does not hint that the Kidd letter is a hoax and purports to be the first full account of Kidd, though it is well garnished with error, local legend, and three spurious documents.

Gardner Shaw tells two local tales, one of which could easily have been suggested by the hoax, the other possibly being a source of the hoax itself. An old gentleman of West Warren, Massachusetts, a neighboring town, recollected his father as saying that a man once stopped at his tavern several days and made a search in the vicinity for a letter which he once attempted to carry from Boston to New York, and which he concealed among some rocks near Quabog. The other is a more conventional type of legend. One of Kidd's company, a Negro named James Marks, died in Warren in 1802 at the advanced age of 115. People now living, wrote

Shaw, remember him and recall his saying that he was twelve years old when Kidd was arrested in Boston, and that he himself was spared because of his tender years. He and a white boy "assisted Kidd in burying a chest of treasures on Long Island, and . . . after the hole was dug and the chest lowered to the bottom, Kidd said to the boys 'which one of you will take care of this money when I am dead and gone?' The white boy instantly answered, 'I.' At the same moment Kidd severed his head from his body and tumbled him into the hole with the chest. This old man frequently accompanied money diggers to Long Island . . . but he was unable to identify the spot."

It would be interesting to speculate what suggested to Samuel Shaw the idea of a Kidd hoax at all. Tales like these may have been common near Palmer. In addition there were the more generally known reports of the salvage operations in the Hudson four and five years earlier, and there was the excitement of the gold rush in California.

Most flourishing was the famous Astor hoax. This was perpetrated in an after-dinner mood by a prosperous Chicago manufacturer and banker, Franklin H. Head, in 1894, for the amusement of the family of Frederick L. Olmsted, famous landscape architect of Brookline, Massachusetts. The Olmsted family were the real or supposed owners of Deer Island in the mouth of the Penobscot River in Maine. Head's hoax was done with such an air of legal exactness that it has been successfully hoaxing people ever since, especially people willing to believe anything of the famous Astor millions. From time to time notices of it have appeared in newspapers and magazines, and the Olmsted family have been so disturbed with inquiries that they have had to print a circular in self-defense, explaining the now fifty-two-year-old hoax. I have one of them before me, sent in December, 1939, to the librarian of the Grosvenor Library of Buffalo. It is identical with the "Commentary" appearing at the end of "Captain Kidd and the Astor Fortune" in *Forum Magazine* (July, 1931), possibly the last public printing of this interesting document.

According to the tale told, the year 1801 saw the sudden increase in wealth of two people, John Jacob Astor, fur trader, and Jacques Cartier, a French-Canadian employee of Astor who lived along the Penobscot and bought furs from the Indians. In 1801 the latter bought a few acres on Deer Isle from Cotton Mather Olmsted, the original owner, and retired from work forever to live at ease with his Indian wife, indulging only in such pastimes as hunting, fishing, and drinking whisky. Simultaneously, John Jacob Astor's deposits in a Manhattan bank leaped from $4,011 to over $500,000. Drafts and credits to Astor from a London dealer in precious stones amounted to $1,300,000 in the next two years. Checks written to Cartier for small amounts in settlement for furs leaped to $5,000.

Mr. Frederick L. Olmsted in 1894, according to the story, was led to formulate a theory that Cartier had found in a cave on the shore of Deer Isle, substantiated by markings and excavations, the buried treasures of Captain Kidd; that he had delivered the treasure chest to Mr. Astor and received $5,000 for it; and that the treasure really belonged to the Olmsteds inasmuch as it was discovered on their land and not on Cartier's, which was only a few acres in the middle of the island. Mr. Olmsted continued his investigations, recovering Kidd's chest, which fitted perfectly the excavated imprints in the Deer Isle cave and was traced through a Brooklyn junk dealer to the Astor house, identifying the gems sold by Astor to be Kidd's plunder, discovering that a card handed by Kidd to his wife near the end of his confinement in prison with the mysterious numeral 44106818 upon it showed the exact latitude and longitude of Deer Isle, and ascertaining that Kidd left no descendants to claim the fortune. Then he proceeded against the Astor family for a handsome settlement, ranging from one to five million dollars and the Astor real estate in New York City. The Astors refuted all such claims, and Mr. Olmsted went to the courts with the possibility of obtaining some settlement by one of several speciously legal methods. The case hung fire in 1894 "owing to delays at proceedings at law," and thus Mr. Franklin H. Head "summarized" *A Remarkable Lawsuit.*

In this manner have the Long Island rumors picked up by Watson a hundred years ago come to a logical refinement in our times. Though the editor of *Forum* hoped to "lay this ghost for all time," it may be safely assumed that such disclaimers are impotent before such formidable ghosts.

Kidd's Tomb [3]

. . . [In Boston] is King's Chapel, where the British officials and loyalist gentry worshipped in colonial days. Close to each of these buildings is an ancient cemetery with its lowly gray stones. Some say that in the King's Chapel churchyard the notorious pirate, Captain Kidd, lies buried. Before his reputation became as black as it did later, he was employed by the colonial governor of New England and certain others to go on a voyage to catch pirates. After a while rumors came that he had himself turned pirate. However, in a few years he appeared in Boston and delivered to the governor the treasure he had acquired in capturing various ships. This included 1111 ounces of gold, 2353 ounces of silver, 57 bags of sugar, and 41 bales of goods.

Orders came from England for his arrest, and he was locked up in Boston Jail. This was in 1699. The prison was a gloomy building with thick stone walls, ponderous oaken doors, and dark passages; and the keys that the jailer carried at his girdle weighed from one to three pounds each. Captain Kidd was later sent to London, where he was tried and hung. How his body happens to be in King's Chapel churchyard is not explained, but the statement is made that if a person will visit his tomb there at midnight, tap on it three times, and ask in a whisper, "Captain Kidd, for what were you hung?" the pirate will answer nothing.

---

[3] From *New England, A Human Interest Geographical Reader,* by Clifton Johnson, pp. 67–68. Copyright, 1917, by The Macmillan Company. New York and London.

Kidd's Ghost [4]

A SHORT distance south of the town [of Northfield, Massachusetts] is Clark's Island, which has a curious legend of Captain Kidd. We are told that the pirate sailed up to this secluded spot, and he and his men brought on shore a heavy iron chest full of gold and jewelry and other precious loot. They dug a deep hole and lowered the chest into it. Then, in what was considered the proper old-fashioned pirate way, one of the crew was selected by lot, killed, and his body placed on top of the loose earth that had been thrown into the hole. His ghost was supposed to haunt the vicinity, and to forever guard the riches from audacious treasure-seekers.

From time to time, in the darkness of night when the gales howled, persons are said to have seen sailing up the stream a phantom ship, manned by a spectral crew, and commanded by a black-bearded ghost with the familiar features of Captain Kidd. Opposite the island the anchor was let go, and Kidd in a boat rowed by four sailors went ashore. After satisfying himself that the plunder was safe he returned to the ship and sailed down the river.

Some people doubt the whole story and ask how Captain Kidd ever navigated his ship up there past the rocky falls.

Lambert's Gold

THE settlers in Maine, like all the other settlers in New England, indulge an unconquerable expectation of finding money buried in the earth. The money is supposed to have been buried by pirates; but the discovery of its burial-place is hoped for only from dreams. Where dreams have conveyed some general information of the place, then mineral-rods are resorted to, for ascertaining the precise spot at which to put the spade and pick-axe into the ground; and then charms and various observances, to defeat the watchfulness of the spirits that have the treasure in charge. The superstition, as may be supposed, sometimes enables sharpers to prey upon those that yield to it.

It is only three years since the entire neighbourhood of Noridgewoc was thrown into confusion by a fraud, of which this was the basis. One Lambert and his sons were the impostors, and half the country were the dupes. Lambert was one of those debauched inhabitants that I have described. He had two or three well-grown sons; and the young men, like their

[4] *Ibid.*, p. 129.

From *Travels through the Northern Parts of the United States, in the Years 1807 and 1808,* by Edward Augustus Kendall, Esq., Vol. III, pp. 84–104. New York: Printed and published by I. Riley. 1809.

father, were lumberers, and in a very abject condition of life. On a sudden, both the father and his sons discovered some appearance of property; and though they continued to live in the hovel that they had previously occupied, they bought good horses and good clothes, and, renouncing all pretensions to labour, rode the country, spending their time in the different public-houses, where they were not only ready to pay for themselves, but to treat their friends. All this, say some of the neighbours, would have been attributed to the gains of successful house-breaking, but that no house was known to have been then lately broke open, and therefore another explanation was to be sought for. The parties themselves, only by half words, confessed that they had found—a chest of money.

A hint of this sort, on being permitted to escape, obtained the readiest ear; and the remainder of the story was instantly made and vouched for by the country round. Lambert was pronounced to be one of those fortunate persons, who, born under a certain planetary aspect, are endowed with various and extraordinary powers; and he was soon found to possess enchanted mineral-rods, which had grown in the mystic form, and been cut at the proper age of the moon.

The discovery not only accounted for every actual appearance of wealth, but induced a belief in more; and the old man, or his sons, at length acknowledged, in a whisper, and as a secret, that the funds were inexhaustible. Nothing was now talked of but Lambert and his gold; and every day gave birth to new histories of the chest that had been found, and of its immeasurable contents. At the public houses, and at the *stores,* law, divinity, politics, and methodist-preachers were forgotten; and all the conversation, the discussions and the bets, arose out of this one source.

Traffic is the passion of all the peasantry of New England. To buy, to sell, to exchange, or, as they term it, to *swap,* are the pursuits in which they wish to be constantly engaged; and, above all things, to make any bargain by which they are to receive, in any proportion, hard money or cash: to give and receive credit is also the soul of their undertakings. Of these dispositions and habits it was the business of Lambert to take advantage. Every man was ready to drive his yoke of oxen to Lambert's door, or to leave in Lambert's *barn* his horse, saddle and bridle, so that he could but walk home with Lambert's note of hand for the purchase-money in his pocket. Lambert was to have credit, because, for one reason or other, (different reasons being given at different times,) the principal bulk of his wealth was not yet forthcoming.

The delusion lasted for some months, and its effects were of the most extensive and most baleful nature. One of its first evils was to give new food to the credulity of the multitude, and a fresh excitement to the inclination, constantly lurking in its mind, to depend for a living upon digging for money-chests, rather than upon daily and ordinary labour. The belief in the existence of these buried money-chests, and the consequent inclination to search for them, is imbibed in infancy; and there wants nothing but the slightest occasion to awaken both. The story of Lambert's success led to the recollection of every thing connected with these treasures. They have been dug for in all parts of the United States; and, as the history further goes, they have not unfrequently been found. More, however, are supposed still to remain concealed; and, upon the smallest prospect of discovery, the farm and every other rational pursuit are neglected for its accomplishment. Of the public feelings and reasonings on this subject, I am able to cite a picture, from the pen of an eyewitness of Lambert's affair, and one that has been long and well acquainted with the settlers of the upper Kennebec:—" 'But,' says the multitude, 'there is more money to be found in the earth; there were more pirates than one.' The mineral-rods are called for again. All hands are digging in search of money, to the neglect of tilling their lands, and securing their crops. Days and nights are spent by many persons, in digging up old swamps and deserts, sixty, seventy and eighty miles from *navigation*. Doleful sighs and dismal noises are heard;—the chest moves in the earth, almost out of their very hands!—They are disappointed, become insolent and saucy, neglect economy and industry, and every benefit to society; and moral habits decay, wherever these ideas prevail:—for 'What a stupid clown must he be,' say they, 'who will toil all day for a dollar, or for what he can raise on his farm, while a chest of money can be dug up in one night, and he become rich at once.' "

But, beside the habits of indolence and profitless adventure, to which this transaction led, there were serious losses of property and a general derangement of affairs. We have just seen in what relation the settlers stand to the store-keeper or country-merchant. The farmer is commonly in debt to the merchant to an amount exceeding the value of his whole property. The merchant considers the farm, the crops, the oxen and the utensils of his debtor as his own; but reckons upon the industry of the farmer, and on the security of the property; and, so long as he is satisfied with these, he reckons on his outstanding debts as on money put out to use, and from which he is to derive yearly interest. What, therefore, is the situation of the merchant, when he sees the farmer, tempted by the offer of a good price in cash, parting with his farm, his horses, his cattle, and everything that the sharper will condescend to take: Shall he attempt to secure himself, by laying hold on the property that remains? But the settlers are always prepared to oppose by physical force the process of law: "The populace," says the writer already quoted, "are always ready to rise in *mutiny*, if any creditor undertakes to compel payment.—'My property shall not be sold,' says one—and drives his stock into the woods." These infatuated settlers had parted with every thing to Lambert and his sons, and not only relied upon the payments to be made them for what they sold, but even neglected their labour, because the same persons promised them loans, and even gifts, without limitation!

Meanwhile, attempts were made to undeceive the people, and lead them to a closer examination of the story. Some were persuaded to ask Lambert why the money was not yet produced; and, having done so, they brought for answer, these, that it was kept back in the fear of its being claimed by the United States, and those, that the gold had been found in ingots, and had been sent to the mint of the United States to be coined into money; but no disagreement in the parts of a story ever undeceived the credulous any where, nor did it here. Other suspicious circumstances presented themselves, but were passed over with the same ease. It happened, in innumerable instances, that the oxen and other things that Lambert purchased on his notes, he sold in the sight of their former owners, at a lower price.

One of the dupes was an unfortunate man, who had been worth a little farming-stock, to the amount of five hundred dollars, and who had transferred the whole to Lambert, expecting, not only to be paid his five hundred dollars, but to be accommodated with a large loan, of which he was much in need. His creditor, who saw with no small dissatisfaction his dealings with Lambert, and who was very little amused with his prospects of future indemnification, urged him, while it was yet time, to demand some other proof, than the mere word of Lambert, that the funds were actually existing. Lambert had sometimes said, that a part of the ingots was in his cellar; and the debtor, made at length uneasy, and depending, for his ruin or prosperity, upon Lambert's veracity and honesty, took his wife with him and went to satisfy himself of facts. Having represented to Lambert the suspicions that were abroad, the anxiety of his particular situation, and, at the same time, his unshaken confidence in the money-chest; and his wife having added, with less ceremony, that they were come to see the ingots with their own eyes, Lambert undertook to gratify them by the most irrefragable testimony. For this purpose, he took the husband and wife into a dark cellar, where, with rapture, they beheld several well filled sacks. Lambert went still further, and not only bade them lift the sacks, to try their weight, but even took out of one of them what he called an ingot, and tearing off, at one corner, the paper that covered it, showed them, by the help of a candle, a portion of yellow metal. His visitors desired no more; but returned home, rejoicing in their own security, and advising all their friends to prevail on Lambert to buy not only their stock, but their farms too. It was in vain that the unbelieving objected, that what they had been shown might be no other than a brass candlestick.

The month of September, in the year 1804, had been fixed upon by Lambert, and his sons, for the time of general payment, and the time when they would lend or give to all that would borrow or receive. Before September arrived, the family quitted the country: however, one of the young men occasionally visited it, and, at length, a particular day was fixed on for the day of fruition. The money was to be brought in a waggon, and a dinner for seventy persons was ordered in Noridgewoc, where every one that would was invited to assist.

Before the day arrived, all the Lamberts were missing; but this was a source rather of satisfaction than of uneasiness, because they were supposed to be employed in fetching the money from Providence, where it was said to have now arrived from the mint. On the day itself, their friends went out in a party to meet them on the road; but, alas! neither waggon, nor money, nor Lamberts were to be seen.

A short period produced some tidings; but the tidings were no other than these, that Lambert and one of his sons had escaped from justice into the British province of New Brunswic [*sic*] and that one or two of his other sons were in gaol, at Castine, on the Penobscot. The cause of the reverse of fortune was gradually developed.

The purpose of all this scheme of imposture was that of turning into money a quantity of counterfeit bank-notes. The prime movers were inhabitants of New Hampshire, and they reckoned among their number some names in credit with the world. The bank designed to have been defrauded was the Portland Bank. A New Hampshire justice, who, during the progress of the imposture, exhibited himself in Maine, haranguing in public houses upon the reasonableness of the belief in money-chests, and dreams, and mineral-rods, was soon ascertained to be an accomplice. Before the notes were perfectly ready for circulation, the design upon the Portland Bank was discovered, and its execution frustrated, by the government of New Hampshire. The connection of the counterfeiters in New Hampshire with the impostors in Maine was at this time unknown.

New Hampshire, therefore, contained the mint from which the Lambert's money was to come. The more purchases that Lambert and his sons could make, the greater the amount of counterfeit notes was to be exchanged for real value. All Lambert's debts were to be punctually paid, but paid in counterfeit notes. The discovery of a money-chest was the story intended to account for the wealth of a man like Lambert.

It was upon this foundation that Lambert had confidently promised to produce his money in the month of September, that he had afterward fixed a day, and that himself and his sons actually set out to fetch it; but, in the interim, the notes, and some of the counterfeiters, were seized upon in New Hampshire, and, after this event, the impostors had nothing left but flight. They travelled along the sea-coast of Maine, in their way to New Brunswic; but, at a public-house in the neighbourhood of Castine, they stole a silver watch, and three spoons that had been put into their glasses. An alarm being spread, they were stopped at the ferry on the Penobscot, and lodged in gaol. The law allowing, however, of bail, in some cases where it were wiser to refuse it, bail for criminals being purchasable in the United States, and the penalty of the bail-bond being of small amount, a part of the gang, by giving up their horses and saddles, regained their liberty, and continued their journey into New Brunswic.

The amount of losses, upon this occasion, in the county of Kennebec, which county comprehends the upper part of the country of the Kennebec, was estimated at from twelve to fifteen thousand dollars. Of the infatuation of the people, and the practicability of raising this sum by the means described, an episode, in the history of Lambert's imposture, furnishes the fullest evidence. In this instance, I suppress all names.

A farmer of the better sort, resident on Sandy River, was one of the warmest enthusiasts, not only in Lambert's cause, but in the belief in money-chests. He had parted with chattels to Lambert, to the amount of two or three hundred dollars, and he was prepared to part with as much more, when two of his neighbours, who were among the few that resisted the tide, conceived the project of chastising his credulity.

They commenced the execution of the project at the place of general rendezvous, the *store*. The farmer being present, but a little distance from the counter, one of the conspirators opened a side conversation with the keeper of the *store*, (to whom he gave a hint of his purpose,) observing carelessly, that Lambert's good fortune was by no means of that incredible or even extraordinary description which some people represented it to be: "Money-chests," he continued, "are buried not only in one or two places, but in many." The farmer, at the first mention of Lambert's name, had drawn nearer to the counter, and he would have drawn nearer still, but that the conspirator gradually lowered his voice, and gave his conversation an air of privacy and secrecy. He advanced, however, as near as he decently could, and while he affected not to listen, drank in every word that was uttered:—"We go on," said the conspirator, "toiling like fools; digging the ground for the sake of a few potatoes, and neglecting the treasures that have been left in it by those that have been before us! For myself, I confess it, to my mortification, that I have been toiling all my life, to make a paltry living, and neglecting, all the while, the means that have long been in my hands of make a sudden and boundless fortune. I have been ploughing, or lumbering, or trading with the Indians, or hunting deer or sables,[1] or setting traps for beaver or muskrats, when, with the smallest penetration, I might have been the owner of a money-chest."—Here the farmer lost all government in himself, and almost jostled the elbow of the foolish beaver-hunter; but the other only affected an extreme unwillingness to be over heard, and now scarcely spoke above a whisper: "I have papers," said he, "that were left me by my grandmother, and, among others, one in which there is an account of a money-chest buried at a certain spot. The account is as plain as the sun at noon day; and yet I have been stupid enough to turn it over, many and many is the time, and never to discover its meaning, till lately, that they have talked about Lambert's chest."

Enough was now said. The conspirator left the *store*, but he was closely followed by the farmer: "What was that you were talking about," was the first question?—"Nothing in particular," was the answer; but the farmer was not to be so silenced: "You were talking about a money-chest," returned he: "No";—"Yes; it does not signify denying it; I heard you!"—"What, did you hear any thing that I said? I am sorry for it!"

"I'll tell you what," said the farmer, "you and I have long been neighbours and friends, and it is not neighbourly to make a secret of this matter with me. You have papers that show where a money-chest is hidden, and

[1] In Maine, the *marten* is called a *sable*.—E. A. K.

you know me well enough to tell me all about it. I don't want to take any advantage of you, not I!"

His neighbour long declined the communication; but, at length, with much apparent reluctance, agreed to make it. He then explained to his eager auditor, that the principal paper consisted in an ancient plan of a certain place on the banks of Hudson's River, where the spot, at which a money-chest lay buried, was distinctly marked, together with all the accessories that would enable a man to place his very foot upon it.—The next thing was to see the papers;—but the papers were not yet in existence. The day, on which the conversation took place, was Saturday;—a sight of the papers was promised at a few days' distance;—the farmer was frequently at his neighbour's house, impatient of the delay;—his neighbour affected to be too busy to think of looking for them;—at length, however, they were found;—that is, they were manufactured.

The farmer no sooner saw them, than he was all amazement at the conduct of his neighbour, who had so long neglected to avail himself of information the most intelligible and complete. But, he was now wholly bent upon acquiring possession of the papers himself, and to this end it was not long before he offered his farm in exchange.

The offer was rejected. His neighbour said, that though he had hitherto neglected the chest, he did not mean to neglect it always, and that he would not part with it for any consideration whatever. The farmer persevered in his attempt to effect a bargain. He went to a common friend, (one that was in the plot to ridicule him,) and earnestly represented the value of his farm, which he estimated at three thousand dollars; a deed of this farm he carried in his pocket, and was willing to give for the papers, with a warranty of the title. The value of the farm he did not pretend to say was equal to that of the money-chest; but, then, he insisted, that it was an advantageous offer for his neighbour, all things considered: "He is a poor man," said he, "and has always been poor; he was never worth a farm, but has been content to sleep in the woods, hunt, and sell a few furs. He has no means of going to Hudson's River, and encountering all the expense of digging for the chest. A farm, that is worth three thousand dollars, will be as much a fortune to him, as the chest to me. On the whole, I make him a very fair offer; I don't want to *jockey* him; and you, that are his friend, ought to advise him to deal with me."

The common friend declined the interference: "Our neighbour," said he, "promises himself great things from his papers; and though your farm, to him may be worth as much as the papers are, he will be very apt to think that we want to impose upon him. For my part, therefore, I shall let him take his own course."

The farmer persisted; and it was at length agreed, that in exchange for his farm, he should be admitted to half the property in the papers. The possessor readily allowed, that he had not funds of his own for going to Hudson's River.

When this bargain was completed, the farmer surrendered his whole mind to the contemplation of his good fortune. Hudson's River was to be visited with very little delay; but, in the interim, it was suggested by his copartner, that it would be well to take Lambert with them, in order to assist with his mineral-rods. The farmer thought the papers too plain to need this assistance, but nevertheless agreed.

His friend next advised, that before Lambert should be engaged, and carried to Hudson's River, at an inevitable expense, some trial of the infallibility of the rods, when in his hands, should be made. The thought appeared to the farmer to spring from a very obstinate scepticism; but he nevertheless agreed even to this. With his friends, therefore, he set out, to solicit from Lambert an exhibition of the rods, in the act of pointing to buried metal.

The mysteries of the mineral-rods are many. The rod, or as, with some propriety, they are called the rods, consist in two divergent branches of witch-hazel. They must be shoots that grow in a pair from the main stem or branch. Thus growing, they diverge on either side, making angles with the main stem in the centre. The main stem is cut away, and they then form a pair of divergent rods, of one substance, and united at the common root. It is the natural property of such an instrument, dependent on its configuration, to move spontaneously, when held in the hand; because it is difficult for the hand to grasp with equal force the two limbs of which it is composed, and because that which is the least confined of the two will tend, by its own weight, to escape from the hand, and in so tending will act as a lever upon the opposite limb, and consequently impart motion. That the rods may be susceptible of the attraction of metals, they must be cut in a certain quarter of the moon, and must be held by a person of an approved horoscope.

The farmer and his friend visited Lambert. The farmer carried twenty dollars in specie in his pocket; and the test, proposed to Lambert, was this, that money being buried, his rods should point to it, before the faces of his guests, and subject to their scrutiny.

A single dollar was judged to be sufficient to try the rods; for, such is the delicacy of their tact, that the weakest power is sufficient to determine them. The dollar was buried at the foot of a tree; Lambert produced his rods; their points wandered for a few moments; then betrayed a decided attraction to the dollar; quivered a little, but soon made a fixed point. —Matters were now arranged for Lambert's journey; the farmer returned his dollar into his pocket, and then set out with his friend, on his way home, with a heart more delighted than before.

His friend, however, now thought, that the jest had been carried far enough; and, on the journey, completely undeceived him. The farmer extolled the virtues of the mineral-rods; but his friend led to think deeper upon the question.

The credulous spectator, whenever it is undertaken to examine the mystery of the rods, confines his whole attention to the hand of the operator. If he can discover nothing there, to justify a suspicion that the rods are pointed by aid of artifice, he is satisfied. In burying money, to be discovered by the rods, he makes no secret of the place at which it is buried; but only looks to the rods, to see whether they will point to it, and to the hand of the operator, to see that there is no fraud. All, therefore, that distinguishes an operator from another man, is his skill or slight of moving the rods at pleasure, and moving them imperceptibly. In vulgar hands, they are awkward and unmanageable. In the hands of an adept, they are moved in an artist-like manner; and it is then, that in vulgar technology, they are said to *work* well.

The farmer was first asked this question by his friend, by way of reply to his praises of the rods: "When you buried the dollar at the foot of the tree, had you not nineteen dollars left in your pocket?"—"Yes."—"Do you recollect where you stood, while the rods were *working*? Do you recollect that you stood a little on one side of the tree, but on a line advanced a few feet before it, and that therefore the rods passed you, to reach the tree?"—"Yes."—"How, then, do you account for it, that the rods were attracted by the single dollar at the foot of the tree, rather than by the nineteen dollars in your pocket? that is, how do you account for it, that the rods did not point to your pocket, rather than to the foot of the tree?"

This discourse shot a new light into the mind of the farmer; and now his friend discovered to him the whole extent of his delirium: "Neighbour," said he, "myself and **** have almost reason to be ashamed of the length to which we have carried this folly; and you ought to be ashamed ever to show your face in the world any more! The whole is a contrivance to laugh at you: there is no money-chest on Hudson's River: my grandmother left me no papers; and those papers, for which you have so much wished to exchange the deed of your farm, were drawn by myself and ****, after I promised that you should see them."—

My informant added, that the farmer, who put a few questions at the beginning of this fearful explanation, was presently absorbed in stupid silence; that he discovered, in several instances, during the remainder of his journey, a total absence of mind; and that he was scarcely himself for some days after.

Tom Cook, the Leveler

IN THE year 1741 the little child of Cornelius Cook, the blacksmith of Westborough, Massachusetts, and of his wife Eunice, lay very close to death. As was the custom of the day, the good old parson, Dr. Parkman, and his deacons prayed earnestly over the boy, that the Lord's will be done; but his mother in her distress pleaded thus: "Only spare his life, and I care

From *Stage-Coach and Tavern Days,* by Alice Morse Earle, pp. 381–384. Copyright, 1900, by The Macmillan Company. New York and London.

not what he becomes." Tom Cook recovered, and as years passed on it became evident by his mischievous and evil deeds that he had entered into a compact with the devil, perhaps by his mother's agonized words, perhaps by his own pledge. The last year of this compact was at an end, and the devil appeared to claim his own as Tom was dressing for another day's mischief. Tom had all his wits about him, for he lived upon them. "Wait, wait, can't you," he answered the imperative call of his visitor, "till I get my galluses on?" The devil acquiesced to this last request, when Tom promptly threw the suspenders in the fire, and therefore could never put them on nor be required to answer the devil's demands.

Tom Cook became well known throughout Massachusetts, and indeed throughout New England, as a most extraordinary thief. His name appears in the records of scores of New England towns; he was called "the honest thief"; and his own name for himself was "the leveller." He stole from the rich and well-to-do with the greatest boldness and dexterity, equalled by the kindness and delicacy of feeling shown in the bestowal of his booty upon the poor and needy. He stole the dinner from the wealthy farmer's kitchen and dropped it into the kettle or on the spit in a poor man's house. He stole meal and grain from passing wagons and gave it away before the drivers' eyes. A poor neighbor was ill, and her bed was poor. He went to a thrifty farm-house, selected the best feather bed in the house, tied it in a sheet, carried it downstairs and to the front door, and asked if he could leave his bundle there for a few days. The woman recognized him and forbade him to bring it within doors, and he went off with an easy conscience.

* * * * *

Tom Cook was most attractive in personal appearance; agile, well formed, well featured, with eyes of deepest blue, most piercing yet most kindly in expression. He was adored by children, and his pockets were ever filled with toys which he had stolen for their amusement. By older persons he was feared and disliked. He extorted from many wealthy farmers an annual toll, which exempted them from his depredations. One day a fire was seen rising from the chimney of a disused schoolhouse in Brookline, and Tom was caught within roasting a stolen goose, which he had taken from the wagon of a farmer on his way to market. The squire took him to the tavern, which was filled with farmers and carters, many of whom had been his victims. He was given his choice of trial and jail, or to run a gantlet of the men assembled. He chose the latter, and the long whips of the teamsters paid out many an old score of years' standing.

George White, Horse Thief

In the early years of this century there existed in eastern Massachusetts an organized band of thieves. It is said they were but one link in a chain

Ibid., pp. 388–393.

of evil night-workers which, with a home or shelter in every community, reached from Cape Hatteras to Canada. This band was well organized, well trained, and well housed; it had skilful means of concealing stolen goods in innocent-faced cottages, in barns of honest thrift, and in wells and haystacks in simple dooryards. One mild-mannered and humble house had a deep cellar which could be entered by an ingeniously hidden broadside door in a woodshed; into this cave a stolen horse and wagon or a pursued load of cribbed goods might be driven, be shut in, and leave no outward sign. Other houses had secret cellars, a deep and wide one beneath a shallow, innocuous storage place for domestic potato and apple bins, and honest cider barrels. In a house sheltering one of these subterranean mysteries, a hard-working young woman was laboriously and discreetly washing clothes when surprised by the sheriff and his aids, who wisely invaded but fruitlessly searched the house. Nothing save the simplest household belongings was found in that abode of domesticity; but in later years, after the gang was scattered, a trap-door and ladder were found leading to the sub-cellar, and with chagrin and mortification the sheriff remembered that the woman's washing tubs stood unharmed upon the trap-door during the fruitless search.

* * * * *

The leader of this band of thieves was an ingenious and delightful scamp—one George White. He was hard to catch, and harder to keep than to catch. Handcuffs were to him but pleasing toys. His wrists were large, his hands small; and when the right moment came, the steel bracelets were quickly empty. Locks and bolts were as easily thrust aside and left far, far behind him as were the handcuffs. At last he was branded on his forehead H. T., which stands for horse thief; a mean trick of a stupid constable who had scant self-confidence or inventiveness. Curling lovelocks quickly grow, however, and are ill in no one's sight; indeed, they were in high fashion in similar circles in England at that time, when various letters of the alphabet might be seen on the cheeks and brow of many a gay traveller on the highway when the wind blew among the long locks.

Term after term in jail and prison were decreed to George White when luck turned against him. Yet still was he pardoned, as he deserved to be, for his decorous deportment when behind bars; and he had a habit of being taken out on a writ of *habeas corpus* or to be transferred; but he never seemed to reach his journey's end, and soon he would appear on the road, stealing and roistering. The last word which came from him to New England was a letter from the Ohio Penitentiary, saying he was dying, and asking some of his kin to visit him. They did not go, he had fooled them too often. Perhaps they feared they might put new life into him. But the one time they were sure he lied he told the truth—and his varied career thus ended.

Flying once along a Massachusetts highway on a stolen horse, George White was hotly pursued. At the first sharp turn in the road he dismounted in a flash, cut the horse a lash with his whip, altered the look of his garment with a turn of his hand, tore off his hat brim and thus had a jaunty cap, and started boldly back on foot. Meeting the sheriff and his men all in a heat, he fairly got under their horses' feet, and as they pulled up they bawled out to know whether he had seen a man riding fast on horseback. "Why, yes," he answered ingenuously, "I met a man riding as though the devil were after him." They found the horse in half an hour, but they never found George White.

He once stole a tavern-keeper's horse, trimmed the mane, thinned out the tail, and dyed the horse's white feet. He led the renovated animal in to the bereft landlord, saying innocently that he had heard his horse was stolen, and thought he might want to buy another. He actually sold this horse back to his owner, but in short time the horse's too evident familiarity with his wonted stable and yard and the fast-fading dye revealed the rascal's work. To another tavern-keeper he owed a bill for board and lodging, which, with the incongruity of ideals and morals which is often characteristic of great minds, he really wished to pay. The landlord had a fine black horse which he had displayed to his boarder with pride. This horse was kept temporarily in a distant pasture. White stole the horse one night, rode off a few miles, and sold it and was paid for it. He stole it again that night from the purchaser, sold it, and was paid. He stole it a third time and returned it to the pasture from whence it never had been missed. He then paid his boardbill as an honest man should.

Dexter's Profitable Blunders

ACCORDING to his own account, TIMOTHY DEXTER was born in Malden, Mass., Jan. 22, 1747. After having served as an apprentice to a leather dresser, he commenced business in Newburyport, where he also married a widow, who owned a house and a small piece of land, part of which, soon after the nuptials, was converted by him into a shop and tanyard for his own use.

By application to his business, his property increased, and the purchase of a large tract of land near Penobscot, together with an interest which he bought in the Ohio Company's purchase, eventually afforded him so much profit as to induce him to buy up public securities at forty cents for the pound, which securities soon after became worth twenty shillings on the pound. By these and other fortunate business transactions, he prospered so greatly, that property now was no longer the sole object of his pursuit; he exchanged this god of idolatry for that of *popularity*. He was charitable to the poor, gave liberal donations to religious societies, and handsomely rewarded those who wrote in his praise. His lordship—a self-conferred title—about this time acquired his peculiar taste for style and splendor, set up an elegant equipage, and, at great cost, adorned the front of his mansion with numerous figures of illustrious personages.

Some of his lordship's speculations in trade have become quite as celebrated for their oddity as those of Rothschild for their . . . cunning. He once anxiously inquired of some merchants, whom he knew, how he should dispose of a few hundred dollars. Wishing to hoax him, they answered, "Why, buy a cargo of warming pans, and send them to the West Indies, to be sure." Not suspecting the trick, he at once bought all the warming pans he could find, and sent them to a climate where—there was every reason to suppose—ice would be far more acceptable. But "Providence sometimes shows his contempt of wealth, by giving it to fools." The warming pans met with a ready sale—the tops being used for strainers, and the lower parts for dippers, in the manufacture of molasses.

With the proceeds of his cargo of warming pans, Dexter built a fine vessel; and being informed by the carpenter that *wales* were wanting, he called on an acquaintance, and said, "My head workman sends me word that he wants 'wales' for the vessel. What does he mean?" "Why, whalebones, to be sure," answered the man, who, like everybody else, was tempted to improve the opportunity of imposing upon Dexter's stupidity. Whalebones were accordingly bought; but, finding that Boston could not furnish enough, he emptied New York and Philadelphia. The ship-carpenters, of course, had a hearty laugh at his expense; but, by a singular turn of fortune, this blunder was also the means of increasing his wealth. It soon after became fashionable for ladies to wear stays completely lined with whalebone; and as none was to be found in the country, on account of his having thus so completely swept the market, it brought a golden price. Thus his coffers were a second time filled by his odd transactions.[1]

How Did Dexter make his money Inw ye says bying whale bone for staing for ships in grosing three houndred & 40 tuns bort all in boston salum and all in Noue york under Cover oppenly told them for my ships thay all Lafed so I had at my one prise I had four Couning men for Rouners thay founed the horne as I told them to Act the fool I was foull of cash I had Nine tun of silver on hand at that time all that time the Creaters more or Less Lafing it spread very fast heare is the Rub in fifty Days thay smelt A Rat found whare it was gone to Nouebry Port speklaters swarmed Like hell houns to be short with it I made seventy five per sent one tun and halfe of silver and over one more spect Drole A Nouf I Dreamed of worming pans three Nits that thay would doue in the west inges I got not more than fortey two thousand put them in Nine vessels for difrent ports that tuck good hold——I cleared sevinty nine per sent——the pans thay mad yous of them for Coucking very good master for Coukey blessed

---

[1] From *Cyclopaedia of Commercial and Business Anecdotes* . . . , edited by Frazar Kirkland, Vol. I, pp. 20–21. Entered, according to Act of Congress, in the year 1864, by D. Appleton and Company, in the Clerk's Office of the District Court of the United States for the Southern District of New York. New York and London.

good in Deade missey got Nise handel Now bourn my fase the best thing I Ever see in borne days I found I was very luckkey in spekkelation I Dreamed that the good book was Run Down in this Countrey Nine years gone so low as halfe prise and Dull at that the bibbel I means I had the Readey Cash by holl sale I bort twelve per sent under halfe prise thay Cost forty one sents Each bibels twenty one thousand I put them into twenty one vesels for the westinges and sent A text that all of them must have one bibel in Every familey or if not thay would goue to hell and if thay had Dun wiked flie to the bibel and on thare Neas and kiss the bibel three times and Look up to heaven Annest for giveness my Capttens all had Compleat orders heare coms the good Luck I made one hundred per sent & Littel over then I found I had made money A Nuf I hant speck A Lated sence old times by gouerment secourties I made or cleared forty seven thosands Dolors that is the old A fare Now I toald the all the sekrett Now be still Let me A Lone Dont wonder Now more houe I got my money boaz [2]

T DEXTER

Sam Hyde, Proverbial Liar

THERE are few, we imagine, who have not heard of this personage; but; notwithstanding his great notoriety, we might not be thought *serious* in the rest of our work, were we to enter seriously into his biography; for the reason, that from his day to this, his name has been a by-word in all New England, and means as much as to say the *greatest of liars.* It is on account of the following anecdote that he is noticed.

Sam Hide was a notorious cider-drinker as well as liar, and used to

[2] From *A Pickle for the Knowing Ones:* or Plain Truths in a Homespun Dress, by Timothy Dexter, Esq., pp. 20–21. Second Edition with Large Additions. Newburyport: Printed for the Author. 1805.

From *The Book of the Indians,* by Samuel G. Drake (Boston, 1841), Book I, pp. 21–22. Cited in *The Old Farmer and His Almanack,* by George Lyman Kittredge, pp. 241–243. Copyright, 1904, by Horace E. Ware. Boston: William Ware and Company.

"To lie like Sam Hyde" is still a New England saying, though, like so many old saws, it is going out of use as the population becomes more mixed. He is said to have been an Indian, and here is his biography as it stands in S. G. Drake's Book of the Indians. If it is not true, it is all the more appropriate in view of Sam's talent for mendacity. . . . We must take this narrative for what it is worth. Drake cites no authority, and one regrets to find that the Dedham archives contain no record of Sam Hyde's death, whether in 1732 or in any other year. The deer story is told of "one Tom Hyde, an Indian famous for his cunning," in Freeman Hunt's anonymous book of American Anecdotes, which was published in 1830. Hunt dates it "some years anterior to the independence of the United States," and says that the white man whom Hyde tricked was an innkeeper at Brookfield, Massachusetts. Drake's account of Sam's ambition to kill twenty of his foes seems to be adapted from a passage in Hubbard's Indian Wars.—G. L. K., *ibid.*, pp. 241, 243.

travel the country to and fro begging it from door to door. At one time he happened in a region of country where cider was very hard to be procured, either from its scarcity, or from *Sam's* frequent visits. However, cider he was determined to have, if lying, in any shape or color, would gain it. Being not far from the house of an acquaintance, who he knew had cider, but he knew, or was well satisfied, that, in the ordinary way of begging, he could not get it, he set his wits at work to lay a plan to insure it. This did not occupy him long. On arriving at the house of the gentleman, instead of asking for cider, he inquired for the man of the house, whom, on appearing, *Sam* requested to go aside with him, as he had something of importance to communicate to him. When they were by themselves, *Sam* told him he had that morning shot a fine deer, and that, if he would give him a crown, he would tell him where it was. The gentleman did not incline to do this, but offered half a crown. Finally, *Sam* said, as he had walked a great distance that morning, and was very dry, for a half crown and a mug of cider he would tell him. This was agreed upon, and the price paid. Now *Sam* was required to point out the spot where the deer was to be found, which he did in this manner. He said to his friend, *You know of such a meadow,* describing it—Yes—*You know a big ash tree, with a big top by the little brook*—Yes—*Well, under that tree lies the deer.* This was satisfactory, and Sam departed. It is unnecessary to mention that the meadow was found, and the tree by the brook, but no deer. The duped man could hardly contain himself on considering what he had been doing. To look after *Sam* for satisfaction would be worse than looking after the deer, so the farmer concluded to go home contented. Some years after, he happened to fall in with the Indian; and he immediately began to rally him for deceiving him so; and demanded back his money and pay for his cider and trouble. *Why,* said *Sam, would you find fault if Indian told truth half the time?*—No—*Well,* says *Sam, you find him meadow?*—Yes—*You find him tree?*—Yes—*What for then you find fault* Sam Hide, *when he told you two truth to one lie?* The affair ended here. *Sam* heard no more from the farmer.

This is but one of the numerous anecdotes of *Sam Hide,* which, could they be collected, would fill many pages. He died in Dedham, 5 January, 1732, at the great age of 105 years. He was a great jester, and passed for an uncommon wit. In all the wars against the Indians during his lifetime, he served the English faithfully, and had the name of a brave soldier. He had himself killed 19 of the enemy, and tried hard to make up the 20th, but was unable.

The Old Darnman

Of all the eccentric characters New England has produced, none ever inspired such a feeling of sympathy and tenderness as the Old Darnman.

To the present generation he is quite as mythical a figure as the Wandering Jew or Rip Van Winkle; but, fortunately, there are a few octogenarians still living who either heard of him from their parents or who themselves recall him as a vivid personality, hurrying along Connecticut highways and byways. Then, too, many people whose lives touched his during his wanderings of much more than half a century have left behind them frequent allusions to the Darnman, in both letters and other documents.

Apparently his real history was never fully known and with his passing in the late Eighteen Hundreds it was irrevocably lost. But piecing all these fragments together, one gleans that this pathetic old character had a regular itinerary in Massachusetts and Connecticut which lasted about six months and that those whom he honored by accepting their hospitality always looked forward to his coming around the time he was supposed to be due.

If he arrived in time for dinner, he remained over night, but was off before breakfast. If he was too late for dinner, he would accept no food until the morning meal. After morning prayers, through which he stood with bowed head, eyes closed, and hands folded reverently on his breast, he would express his thanks for the hospitality accorded him and take his departure. Nor could any amount of persuasion induce him to remain for another night or another meal.

While he did not say so, it was evident that he did not wish to impose on the hospitality of his friends, nor to wear out his welcome; hence his respect for the precedent he established.

His most outstanding eccentricity, which gave rise to his name as the Darn Coat, the Darned Man, or the Darnman, was his request for a needle and thread to mend his garments the moment he entered a house. Then he would slip off his coat or vest and sometimes his trousers, sit down quietly in an inconspicuous place, and proceed to make needed repairs. Now and then, where he was well acquainted, he would ask for a skillet and a little oil which he would heat and rub into his well-worn boots. There were never any holes in them, for he kept them patched and in as good condition as possible.

By Louise E. Dew Watrous, Clinton, Connecticut. Manuscripts of the Federal Writers' Project of the Works Progress Administration for the State of Connecticut.

I first heard of the Darnman through an uncle of my husband, a Mr. Charles Dolph of Centerbrook, Conn., who passed away the summer of 1936, aged 94. As he used to see the Darnman when he was a boy, it must have been around 1850. All I know is what Mr. Dolph told me, and also an aged man in the town of Clinton—a man who now has paralysis and cannot see visitors.—L. E. D. W.

To describe the Darnman is difficult, for his personality was so elusive. He was tall and must have had a well-knit, fine physique in his youth. Even in his old age, when he had grown wan and spectral, he still carried himself with stately dignity.

It was apparent to every one from his bearing and attire that he was to the manner born. He wore a suit of the finest navy-blue broadcloth. The long coat was not unlike a swallow-tail or dress-coat of to-day and it was double-breasted. A long brocaded vest hung down below the coat in front, and from the old-fashioned watch pocket there dangled a gold fob which gave him the appearance of a dandy. His trousers were close-fitting and had straps at the bottom. Topping his long-limbed figure was a bell-crowned tall hat, probably once white, but metamorphosed by the elements, the dust of years, and time to a dingy smoke gray.

During all the sixty years or so he journeyed up and down the valley, from shore town to shore town, and back up through Windham County again, he wore the same garments, always scrupulously clean, but each year a little more threadbare and shabby. As the years passed, his shoulders became slightly bent, his eyes sunken and his cheeks pale and wan. But his blue eyes retained the same bright piercing look.

An old Connecticut Yankee of ninety, whose mind is still alert, recalls the Darnman distinctly. He says that when he was a boy of ten or thereabouts in Civil War times, an uncle in Windham County wrote his parents about the Darnman. He had appeared unexpectedly, so spring was almost there. He had asked for a needle and thread the moment of his arrival. Aunt Sarah had offered to mend the rent in his coat for him, but he had refused with a deprecatory "Thank you, Madame, but I must refuse. These are my wedding clothes and they are sacred. My bride will be here soon. . . ."

A few weeks later, the old gentleman says, he saw the Darnman hurrying along through the village. He knew him by his picturesque attire that was so reminiscent of Uncle Sam as depicted by so many artists. The small boy, curious to know more of the Darnman's movements, followed him for some distance. As always, he walked with head bent, and hands clasped in front of him, apparently oblivious to all else. Presently, he turned off at the shore-road and went down to the beach where the children were sailing their toy boats. They stopped playing and watched him, but there were no cat-calls or stones thrown as was sometimes done when odd characters passed through the town. There was something about the pathetic face and drooping shoulders that inspired them with a feeling of awe.

Without looking either to the right or the left, the Darnman paid no attention to the children, but walked past them down to the sands. Picking up a razor-back clam shell, he began digging in the sands. After a time, the children crept closer to watch him, but he kept right on at his task. Finally, the village boy ventured to ask him if he had lost something.

"Yes, my little man," was the low reply and the words came with stately courtesy, "I have had the great misfortune to lose a gold ring . . . a wedding ring . . . like the one I wear." He held up the third finger of his left hand where a gold ring gleamed brightly in the sunset, then went on: "Only the ring I have lost is tiny and beautiful. It belonged to my bride. If you should find the little gold band, will you not be so good as to take care of it until I come again?"

The boy, now much older than the Darnman was then, says that he promised to do so, and so convinced was he that the Darnman had actually lost a ring, long hours were spent digging in the sands for it.

The Darnman passed through this village-by-the-sea, many times after that, and the boy's family, like the uncle in Windham County, always kept a room ready for him. If it was not yet dark when the gentle old man had reverently finished mending his garments, he and the boy used to go and hunt for the bride's lost ring.

Years passed. The boy grew up. The old Darnman still paid his visit to the village wearing the same worn garments, asking for a needle and thread to mend them, the moment he arrived. But his fingers trembled now, and the pathetic look in his face and eyes had deepened. "My bride is so long in coming . . . ," he would whisper sadly to himself as he darned and mended, and oiled his ancient boots, now covered patch upon patch. But his manner still set him apart as a gentleman.

There was only one thing about which he was at all particular and that was his tea. He was a connoisseur. "Madame," he would begin with stately courtesy, "the bouquet is sadly lacking in this beverage. Would you mind if I show you how to brew me a cup, or better still, permit me to brew my own tea?"

Those who had become acquainted with him during all these years, whom he favored with his few confidences, gathered from the few remarks he made from time to time that he had passed through some great emotional shock and that it had upset his mental equilibrium. He was not crazy, but his mind was disordered and out of tune.

One evening he sat on the porch with a family where he had often accepted sanctuary. He was unusually quiet and abstracted. Presently, he rose and went out to sit in the moonlight under the tall elm he so loved, and where his sick spirit always seemed to find repose. A glorious June moon was shining through the branches of the tree. He kept glancing up at the glowing orb and whispering: "My bride will come tonight. Surely she will not disappoint me. . . . Come, my beloved little bride. . . ."

Suddenly, through the stillness there was the sound of carriage wheels on the hilltop. Voices. One was the rippling laughter of a girl. The old Darnman rose quickly and walked down to the picket-fence. At the gateway he paused for an instant. He rushed out to the road. Instead of stopping, the horse was urged on.

"Here I am, my little bride," the old Darnman cried in an agony of fear. "Long have I been waiting, do not pass me by. . . ." And he held out his arms.

At this instant, the horse became frightened at the sudden apparition, and lurched forward. Before the driver could control the animal, the carriage had knocked the old man down and passed over his body. Loving hands carried him into the house, but he died that night.

When they came to lay him away, instead of the shroud the undertaker brought, the women folk shook their heads, and said: "No, he wouldn't feel at home in that garment. We will clean, press, and mend his own."

The old Darnman was laid to rest in his own wedding clothes—the ones in which he'd wandered up and down Connecticut highways and byways for more than sixty years in search of his bride.

According to popular beliefs, the Darnman was Frank Howland, a direct descendant of John Howland, the Mayflower Pilgrim. Young Howland's father came from Cape Cod. When a young man, Frank had a strong physique and a brilliant, well-balanced mind. He planned to go to Yale and fit himself for the law. Owing to overstudy and carelessness, he was stricken down with a fever, which nearly proved fatal. His strong constitution pulled him through. After some months, when he had regained his strength, he accepted an offer to teach in a school near New London.

It was while there he met the daughter of a sea-captain who won his heart. They became betrothed and the girl went to New York for her trousseau. On her way back, the vessel she was on sank in a storm and Frank Howland never saw her again. A funeral service was held for her in her home-city, but young Howland was unable to attend. The shock of her drowning had been so great that reason was tottering.

When he finally regained his poise, his mind was a blank of all that had happened except that the lovely girl to whom he had plighted his troth had gone to the city for her wedding trousseau. When she failed to return, he donned his wedding suit and fared forth to find her, continuing his search until the day of his death sixty years or so later.

This in brief is the story of the old Darnman, one of Connecticut's most eccentric and beloved characters of an earlier day.

The Old Leather Man

THE Old Leather Man got his name from the clothes he wore. Winter and summer he was dressed from head to foot in leather. Cap and vest, bulky coat, breeches, clumsy shoes and pack were all made of old boot tops laced together. People said that he was a Frenchman who had been wealthy in his own country until he had speculated in leather and lost his fortune and his bride. Thereafter he exiled himself and dressed in leather to be constantly reminded of the cause of his downfall.

Whatever the reason for his coming, from 1860 to 1889 he was a

---

Manuscripts of the Federal Writers' Project of the Works Progress Administration for the State of Connecticut.

familiar sight in eastern Connecticut and western New York. His route lay along the Connecticut River, through the shore towns, up the Hudson to Poughkeepsie and across through Thomaston and Farmington to the Connecticut River again, and always went in the same direction. At regular stopping places he accepted food but he always spent the night in a cave or shelter.

Two or three years after he had first been seen going by one place in Woodbridge, he turned into the yard and, coming up onto the porch, knocked at the door. When it was opened he smiled shyly and said in a low, guttural voice, "Something to eat, please," accompanying his words by the action of carrying food to his lips. "Ta," he said when food was given to him.

After his first stop, the Leather Man came regularly every forty-one days, usually arriving between four and five o'clock. There was a good deal of curiosity about him, and when "Leather Man's day" fell on a Saturday, as many as sixteen neighbors might gather to see him. They would sit behind the closed blinds of the living room marvelling at his neatness, watching him as he sat on the ell-porch eating. When he had finished, he would take a piece of clean brown paper from his pack and wrap up whatever food remained. If the weather were very cold, he might come into the house, but as soon as he had eaten, he always went to one of his shelters for the night.

How much he understood was an open question. He would sometimes do as he was asked, but he almost never spoke. People tried addressing him in various languages without getting any response. One woman spoke to him in the French of Canada as she was giving him some food. He said nothing, but his eyes snapped so angrily and took on such a wicked look that she never tried again.

The Leather Man was usually mild and gentle and people treated him with kindness; even the children did not molest him. Sometimes they gave him pennies. He would smile and thank them courteously, but later they would find their coins on the gate posts. After he had gone, the boys used to visit his shelter. They never found anything but the ashes of his fire and perhaps a few tin cans he had used for cooking, put neatly in a corner.

One wintry day in March, 1889, the Leather Man failed to appear. At first it was decided that the snow had delayed him, but when he failed to turn up for several days, a party set out through the snow to look for him. He was found dead in a cave with the long-cold ashes of his fire beside him. His grave is in Rye, N. Y.

Crazy Lorenzo Dow

Not many years since, there was a famous preacher of the old Puritan school in one of the New England States, who used to play such pranks in the pulpit as our Rowland Hill is said to have done, and as a contemporary now occasionally indulges in at the Tabernacle, only the Rev. Lorenzo Dow was the more daring performer of the three. On one occasion he took a text from Paul, *"I can do all things."* The preacher paused, took off his spectacles, laid them on the open Bible, and said, "No, Paul, you are mistaken for once; I'll bet you five dollars you can't, and stake the money." At the same time putting his hand into his pocket, he took out a five-dollar bill, laid it on the Bible, took up his spectacles again, and read, *"Through Jesus Christ our Lord."* "Ah, Paul!" exclaimed Dow, snatching up the five-dollar bill, and returning it to his pocket, "that's a very different matter; the bet's withdrawn." [1]

There was a story going the rounds of the papers in Vermont of Lorenzo Dow raising the devil. One day while he was at the dinner table at our house in Hardwick, mother asked him about it. Lorenzo replied that the circumstances were as follows: In traveling through the northern part of Vermont, he was belated one night in a blinding snow-storm. He went for the only light he could discover, and found it came from a small log-house. After repeated knockings at the door, a woman opened it. He asked accommodations for the night. She said her husband was gone, and she could not possibly accommodate a stranger. But he plead with so much earnestness, she concluded to take him in. He immediately went to bed, without removing his clothing, in a little corner, separated off from the room where the family lived by a partition of rough boards, with cracks between, covered with paper pasted over, which was torn off in many places, and anything going on in the opposite room could be easily seen. It soon appeared this woman was not alone, but had a paramour. Late in the night on came her husband, drunk as usual, and demanded admittance, hallooing and cursing at the top of his voice, his wife all the while trying to stop him, but before opening the door, she secreted her pal in a cask of tow in the room. When admitting her husband, she tried to silence him by telling him that Lorenzo Dow was in the other room, and if he was not still he would wake him up. Well, says the husband, I understand he can raise the devil, and now he has got to *do it.* Notwithstanding all the appeals of his wife, the husband pounded on the door, calling on Dow to come out. At last Dow pretended to be roused out of a sound sleep (although he had been awake all the time); rubbing his eyes and yawning, he came out. The man insisted on Dow's raising the devil, and would not take *no* for an answer. Well, if you insist on it, said Dow, I will do it, but when *he* comes, it will be in a flame of fire, and you must set the doors wide open, so he will have plenty of room. The man opened his door, and Dow, taking the candle, touched the tow in the cask. In an instant the cask was

---

[1] By John Camden Hotten. From Introduction to *The Complete Works of Charles F. Browne*, Better Known as "Artemus Ward," pp. 27–28. London: John Camden Hotten.

wrapped in flame, and the man inside jumping out, all on fire, ran up the street like the very devil, all of a light blaze, tearing through the snow at the rate of 2:40. The husband was so frightened, for once it made a sober man of him.[2]

In Vermont, in passing through a dense woods one day to fill an appointment, he saw two men chopping wood. He mounted on a large stump, and said "Crazy Dow will preach from this stump 6 months from to day, at 2 o'clock, P. M." Six months from that time an immense audience was assembled, and Dow in going to the place saw a man in great distress looking for something. Dow enquired what the matter was. The man replied that he was poor, and that some one had stolen his axe, and that he felt the loss very much. Lorenzo told him if he would go to the meeting he would find his axe. Before getting to the place of service, Dow picked up a stone and put it in his pocket. After the delivery of a powerful sermon, Dow said—"There is a man here who has had his axe stolen, and the thief is here in this audience, and I am going to throw this stone right to his head," —drawing back his hand as though in the act of throwing the stone. One man ducked his head. Dow went up to him and said—"You have got this man's axe!" And so he had, and went and brought it and gave it to him.[3]

At another time, while preaching in Mississippi, some rowdies were thrusting a knife into a beautiful beaver hat of his, at some distance from the stand. He turned to them and addressed them thus:—The laws of society condemn you; the laws of your country condemn you; moreover the laws of God condemn you. The word condemned means damned. 1st. You are villains. 2d. You are condemned villains, that is you are damned villains. 3d. God condemns you by His law; that is He damns you. Hence, you are *God damned villains!* [4]

---

[2] By Lewis Joseph Bridgman (nephew of Lorenzo Dow), in "Montpelier," *Vermont Historical Gazetteer,* A Local History of All the Towns in the State, Civil, Educational, Biographical, Religious, and Military, Vol. IV, collated and published by Abby Maria Hemenway, p. 372. Copyright secured to Miss Hemenway. Montpelier, Vermont: Vermont Watchman and State Journal Press. 1882.

For the genealogy and geographical distribution of this story, which is common in European folklore and which is told of Lorenzo Dow with locales varying from New York and Delaware to the Oxfordshire border of Warwickshire, see Emelyn E. Gardner, *Folklore from the Schoharie Hills* (Ann Arbor, 1937), pp. 314–317.

The same story is told of Rev. Matthew Clark, of Londonderry, New Hampshire (*The Scotch-Irish in America,* Cincinnati, 1890, p. 143) and the English divine, Charles H. Spurgeon.

[3] *Ibid.*, p. 366.

[4] *Ibid.*, p. 374.

Johnny Appleseed's Childhood in the Connecticut Valley

Stebbins Park in Springfield, Massachusetts, commemorates John Chapman, the famous "Johnny Appleseed," with an attractive little monument,[1] the inscription on which declares in part that Johnny "spent his boyhood in this pleasant valley [the valley of the Connecticut River] or somewhere near by. Here he received inspiration for his life work of spreading westward his gospel of beauty and service."

About the inspiration one cannot be sure now, of course, for any boy's inspirations are elusive matters after a century and a half, particularly when that boy was John Chapman, who was not brought up to keep a journal or letterbooks, who probably never thought of recording memoirs, and whom folks found very reticent, at least in his old age, about saying anything at all concerning his beginnings. But about the setting for John Chapman's boyhood, the Stebbins Park memorial is probably correct. The aged Johnny Appleseed left distinct impressions among the farmers who remembered him in Ohio and Indiana in the eighteen-thirties and forties that he had come from the vicinity of Springfield.[2] That fact was reinforced by the knowledge that certain half-brothers and -sisters had come from there. In later years an erroneous statement in D. A. R. records that John's father, Nathaniel Chapman, had been born in Springfield seemed to clinch the matter.

It is no wonder, therefore, that after Johnny Appleseed's death in 1845, when tales about him began to spread beyond the Middle West, they found easy foothold in the Connecticut Valley, and by the first quarter of the 1900's had flourished there in typical Appleseed-myth fashion. John's father had owned several farms in the neighborhood of Springfield, it was said. Though the boy's mother had died when he was an infant, a kindly aunt had cared for him until the father, a hero of the Revolution, had found a second wife. The home was a log cabin in a spot by a stream, overlooking the Connecticut River—the primitiveness of this pleasantly idyllic abode contrasting illogically with the supposed Chapman acreage. The father, a woodworker, turned out bowls and dishes which the boy John helped peddle in Springfield. There was, of course, a beautiful and inspiring apple tree in the front yard. The boy grew up a dreamer. He would wander off to the hills and woods, where he would stay for days with his Bible, reading aloud to the foxes, the shy fawns, and the chipmunks. One day, however, he came home to find that his father, while fishing for shad at South Hadley

---

From "A Boyhood for Johnny Appleseed," by Robert Price, in *The New England Quarterly,* Vol. XVII (1944), No. 3, pp. 381–382, 391–393.

[1] Erected by the Springfield Garden Club, 1936, in the three-hundredth anniversary year of the founding of Springfield.—R. P.

[2] See a typical account in Henry Howe, *Historical Collections of Ohio* (Cincinnati, 1908), II, 484–487.—R. P.

Falls, had been swept over and drowned. At the age of eighteen, he was alone in the world, but already filled with the vision of his lifework on the Western frontier.[1]

Although, like most other episodes in the Appleseed myth, this one from the Connecticut Valley deserves to stand intact, as biography it is without a single supporting fact. In the early 1930's, members of the Springfield Garden Club uncovered the record of John's father's second marriage and residence, not in Springfield, but in neighboring Longmeadow. This clue led to discovery of the records of his earlier marriage in Leominster and of the birth of Johnny Appleseed there in 1774. Beginning with these findings, Miss Florence Wheeler, librarian in Leominster, was able to piece out, after remarkable detective work, the whole story of John Chapman's New England family origins.[2]

* * * *

[His half-sister] Persis [twenty years his junior] used to say, another writer has maintained, that John had always been extremely fond of outdoor sports and natural scenery, that as a boy he liked nothing better than listening to the birds or watching the stars, and that he enjoyed wandering off on long hunting trips. When he was only ten or eleven, she said, he would run away from home and spend two or three days at a time in the woods. "The father had never been known to lay hands on John."[3] One cannot be sure now how much of any such statement was due to rationalization in a family to whom John Chapman was always an unsolved riddle.

If his real schoolhouse was the outdoors, he did not have to wander far to practise his lessons. The road past the Chapman door ran directly down to the river on the one hand and into the woods on the other. He was well taught, for instance, in the ways of water. It is no myth that the Johnny Appleseed of maturity was well-nigh amphibious. Although it may stretch credulity to believe that he really did float down the Allegheny peacefully asleep on an ice floe, there is no doubt of his having been comfortably adept either in the water or on it. Astride logs, in canoes or dugouts, on rafts or flatboats, wading, swimming, paddling, poling, he was to spend much of his lifetime navigating the waterways of the West. He had a fine skill in matching wits with water, and it must have been acquired early, quite possibly on the Connecticut. The road past the Chapmans' led not only boys but most of Longmeadow's householders down to the river, for much of their living came from it. John Chapman would have grown up a part of this activity.

Such easy surmises, of course, prove nothing. More substantial, though

---

[1] A resumé of numerous accounts.—R. P.

[2] Florence E. Wheeler, "John Chapman's Line of Descent from Edward Chapman of Ipswich," *Ohio Archaeological and Historical Quarterly* (January, 1939), XLVIII, 28–33.—R. P.

[3] James Lattimore Himrod, *Johnny Appleseed* (Chicago, 1926), p. 8.—R. P.

indirect, indications of Johnny Appleseed's early connections with the Connecticut Valley may be found in later events. John Chapman is said (on semi-historical grounds) to have appeared first as a frontier nurseryman, some time prior to 1797, in the Wilkes-Barre, Pennsylvania, section of the Susquehanna Valley.[1] Many Connecticut Valley people are known to have migrated to that region upon the opening up of lands there from 1795 on. Young Chapman could logically have followed a natural flow of settlement. In 1805, Captain Nathaniel Chapman moved his family from Longmeadow to Ohio, settling in the neighborhood of the new town of Marietta. It is known that his oldest son, John, although already a wanderer for several years, maintained contacts with his father and half-brothers both before and after that move, contacts sufficiently close to suggest that he must have known the household in Longmeadow with a considerable degree of intimacy.[2] That he ever lived in the Nathaniel Chapman residence on the "Way to the Woods" in Longmeadow cannot now be proved. That he knew the Connecticut Valley and thought of it as his boyhood home seems beyond a doubt.

Paul Revere: A Hero in Search of a Legend

MOST American heroes of the Revolutionary period are by now two men, the actual man and the romantic image. Some are even three men—the actual man, the image, and the debunked remains. For a very brilliant analysis of these fates see Dixon Wecter's *Hero in America.* Paul Revere has not suffered so much from the debunkers (but see Stark's *Loyalists in Massachusetts* for a good try. He is even represented in that book with a full beard and a leer). Although it has been rumored that he never took his ride and it is now well known that he engraved (but did not draw his pictures), about the worst that has been said of him is that he was really a "middle-aged goldsmith on a stout plough horse"—which is not very bitter. His reputation divides into pre- and post-Longfellow periods. The *Tales of the Wayside Inn* was published in 1863—when the pressure of the Civil War had created a demand for popular heroes. The story of his gallant ride filled a need. How much was known about it before that time? The earliest biographical sketch I have found of him (except the obituary notices) is in the *New England Magazine* (1832)—fourteen years after his death. The unknown author seems to have known him personally. Here is the first account of his running away to the West Street Church, Doctor

[1] J. S. Schenck and W. S. Rann, *History of Warren County, Pennsylvania* (Syracuse, New York, 1887), 153–154.—R. P.

[2] Storrs, Genealogical Appendix, 26; W. M. Glines, *Johnny Appleseed by One Who Knew Him* (Columbus, Ohio, 1922).—R. P.

Church adding the poem to the "Recinders" caricature, etc. He speaks of him as a "messanger" and quotes almost completely his own account of the nineteenth of April as it had already been published by the Massachusetts Historical Society. Twenty years later, "The Massachusetts Charitable Mechanics Association" published their "Annals." Its frontispiece is a steel engraving of Revere and he has by far the longest of the biographies. He is accepted as the outstanding mechanic of his day and place, and "he was several times sent by the Provincial Congress to the Continental Congress on confidential business." For his most famous ride the reader is referred to the Massachusetts Historical Society Proceedings. In 1855, May Street was renamed Revere in his honor. He was not forgotten in Boston, although already dead for over thirty years.

But in Snow's *History of Boston* (1825) he is not mentioned. In S. G. Drake's *History and Antiquities of Boston* (1856) he is mentioned many times—but not his ride. Yet it had already caught the popular imagination. . . . the first known attempt to put this ride into romantic form, by "Eb. Stiles," [was] written in 1795. In 1835, Joseph Warren's sister wrote a child's life of General Warren. It is a dialogue between a mother, "Mrs. M.," and her two children, whose well-timed questions help Mama tell her story. Mrs. M. says, "Col Revere was one of his messangers. I think he was sent to Lexington"; and she describes his escape from the British officers on Charlestown Neck. "I think he was a brave man, do not you, Mama?" says the priggish little William. "I fear I should have turned back when I saw the soldiers coming."

"Mrs. M.: 'He certainly was a very brave man.'"

The same year that the "Mechanics" published their factual account of his life, the town of Acton completed their battle monument and the Reverend John Pierpont delivered a six-page poem. This ran in part,

> . . . The foremost Paul Revere
> At Warrens bidding, has the gantlet run,
> Unscathed, and dashing into Lexington,
> While midnight wraps him in her mantle dark
> Halts at the house of Reverent Mr. Clark.

It would seem that Paul Revere's ride had already taken a legendary form—a poem in search of a poet. If Longfellow had followed Revere's own account (already published at least twice), it is unlikely he would have made the mistake of placing Revere on the wrong side of the Charles and bringing him all the way to Concord, although this was a mistake already made by "Eb. Stiles." He may have vaguely known all his life something of this story, for it was already being simplified and put into romantic form. His diary for 1860 suggests (at least) that he got it from a mysterious "Mr. H."; "April 5, Go with Sumner to Mr. H. of the North End who acts as guide," showing the sights of the North End—Copp's Hill, etc., and then "Old North." "We climb the tower to the chime of bells, now the home of innumerable pigeons. From this tower [as the "guide" probably told him] were hung the lanterns as a signal that the British troops had left Boston for Concord." "Mr. H." probably also told him how Revere waited "on the opposite side." "April 6. . . . Paul Revere's ride begun on this day." (Nor had he done much research.) "April 19. I wrote a few lines in 'Paul Revere's Ride,' this being the day of his achievement."

Dixon Wecter, in commenting on the sudden burst of Paul Revere's fame, says: "Silver made by Revere grew rapidly in value, until a good piece fetched $5,000; it was rumored that the late J. P. Morgan offered Mrs. Marston Perry $100,000 for Revere's famous 'Sons of Liberty' punch bowl. His engravings and caricatures were cherished. The folk mind, upon learning that Paul Revere made false teeth and that George Washington wore false teeth, invented the well-known statement that Revere made a set of dentures for the master of Mt. Vernon."

On the hundredth anniversary of the Battle of Lexington, lanterns were hung in the steeple of Christ's Church. Paul Revere's fame had, in twelve years, swept the country. Samuel H. Newman, the son of Robert Newman, "walked out of the vestry with his lighted lanterns, and down the crowded aisle, and up into the tower . . . the excited people made the house rock with their response as if the cannons of Concord and Lexington were even then rending the air."

But Longfellow, so responsible for the excitement, wrote of that day: "Bad day for me; neuralgia raging. In the evening my girls drive over to Prospect Hill to see the lighting of Paul Revere's lanterns in the belfry of Old North Church."

Exploits of Ethan Allen

His Legend [1]

Ethan Allen was a legendary character long before his death, and the legends about him multiplied for the next half-century or so; then production dropped. All the legends now current have probably seen service for more than a century, and many of them go back to the times of the man himself.

Some legends, unquestionably, are historically true, and many others are elaborations on historical fact. And a few no doubt are pure invention, concocted for sheer amusement or for some reason in the mind of the inventor. In the latter category doubtless belongs the hardy old story of Ethan at the bedside of his dying daughter, one of those by his first wife. It goes that the child *knew* that she was going to die, and further that she knew her profane father to be a gross Infidel. During her last gasps this

[1] From *Ethan Allen*, by Stewart H. Holbrook, pp. 266–269, 143. Copyright, 1940, by The Macmillan Company. New York.

precocious infant said to Ethan, "Father, now that I am going to leave you, in what should I put my faith—mamma's religion, or your Nature?" The Great Infidel is supposed to have cried gently a moment, then to have told daughter to die in the faith of her mother.

Better authenticated is another child story, told to Zadock Thompson, the Vermont historian, in 1841 by T. Bradley of Williston, Vermont, who had it direct from Dr. Baker, first president of the Vermont Medical Society. Dr. Baker had been called to a home where a child was suffering from worms. General Allen and two parsons were present. Ethan walked up and down the room. "I wish," he said, "all the worms which were ever permitted to torment an innocent being were in my body all at once."

"What would you do with so many?" inquired one of the parsons.

"Do?" cried Ethan. "Do? I'd take a dose of hellfire and destroy them."

Then, there is the famous white-horse story. In a discussion with St. John de Crèvecoeur, Ethan once said that if the transmigration of souls were a fact, he hoped to return to his Vermont hills in the form of a great white stallion, when he would snort, whinny, and range all over the claim. A Colonel Graham, who came to live in Rutland, Vermont, in 1785, has been quoted as saying, "I have often heard General Allen affirm that he should live again under the form of a large white horse." Just such an animal has been seen a number of times since 1789.

That Ethan could and did bite nails into bits and spit them out with the force of buckshot has never been doubted by any true Vermonter.

A signal used at night by the Green Mountain Boys was three mournful hoots of an owl. Ethan was so good at this call that on one or more occasions he was attacked by large male owls, jealous of some lady owl in the neighborhood. Another time when Ethan was hurrying through the woods a huge catamount leaped onto his back. It was the last time that catamount leaped anywhere. Reaching up and behind his head, Ethan grabbed the big animal around the neck, heaved it forward and to the ground, then strangled it where it lay, without once removing his hands. When he arrived at Cephas Kent's tavern in Dorset that night, he excused his delay. "The goddam Yorkers," he said, "have trained and set varmints against me, God damn their miserable Tory souls."

Not a legend but simply a favorite Big Story often told of Ethan Allen and Seth Warner, to illustrate their differences in character, is revealing. The two were fishing from a boat on Lake Champlain, when Seth's powder-horn fell into the water.

"What'll I do?" complained Seth.

Ethan didn't reply but dived overboard at once. The cautious Warner waited some minutes, then he too dived in. Down deep on the bottom he found Ethan. He was trying to pour Seth's powder into his own horn.[1]

The straight hunting stories told on the man would make a sizeable monograph. A favorite has him shooting the horns off a buck deer at one

[1] Cf. "Jonathan's Hunting Excursion," p. 235 above.

hundred yards, with a smoothbore. Another has him killing a mean and wounded bear by ramming his powderhorn down the animal's throat.

The best of the real estate stories brings in Ira. The property at Charlotte, Vermont, of an exiled Yorker was to be sold for Vermont by the sheriff to the highest bidder. The speculating Allens had tried to keep the coming sale secret, but news leaked out and a number of speculators showed up. The Allen boys didn't like the look of so much potential competition, and the sheriff, at Ethan's order, and on some pretext, announced that the sale would be put off "until one o'clock tomorrow." The crowd went away, planning to return at one the next afternoon. But promptly at one o'clock next morning the sheriff and the two Allens were back on the ground. The sheriff asked for bids. Out of the dark came Ethan's bid—one dollar for house, barn, and a hundred acres. Ira bid two dollars. "Sold," said the sheriff, "to the short man in the coonskin cap."

It seems strange, or possibly it is significant, that no legendary tales concerning extramarital adventures have been told of Ethan Allen. Certainly it was not respect for the Seventh Commandment that kept him "moral" in the generally accepted sense; nor was it a case of inability, as witness eight children, the last of them posthumous. His contemporary enemies called him almost every name conceivable except that fine old English compound word used to describe a man of vast adulteries. He must have been essentially a monogamist.

But the stories of his drinking prowess are without end and, except for the rattlesnake incident, will not be repeated here. Ethan did not like rattlers, which in old times were found in certain regions of southern Vermont. On a hot day in August he was making a long trip afoot with Remember Baker. Up late the night before, the men became sleepy and lay down for a nap in a rocky glen. Sometime later Baker was roused by a noise and woke to gaze horrified at the spectacle of Colonel Allen asleep, while on his broad chest was coiled a huge rattler, all of five feet long. It struck Ethan again and again, on the neck, the arm, the hand, but did not rouse him. Baker jumped up, grabbed his gun and advanced to poke the snake away.

At his approach Baker was startled to see the snake glide off the man and onto the ground, its head weaving from side to side and its body making contortions strange even in a reptile. Baker held his blow, watching fascinated, while the snake stopped and turned to gaze at him, cross-eyed. The snake then gave forth a mighty "Burrp!" and collapsed into sound sleep. "Drunk, by Jesus!" exclaimed Remember Baker, who was an acute if not a pious man.

When Colonel Allen awoke he complained bitterly to Baker about "these eternal, damnable, bloodsucking mosquitoes" which had bitten him while he slept.

Long a favorite story, and dignified in print for more than a century, is the one about Ethan and the dentist of Sunderland. A woman, suffering terribly from toothache, had approached the dentist, then became frightened at his devilish gear used for extraction. Colonel Allen urged her to submit to the grim business. "I'll show you, madam," he said, "that losing a tooth is nothing." Thereupon he sat in a chair and had the dentist extract a perfectly sound tooth, by way of demonstration. "I didn't feel it," he lied gallantly, and the lady took courage.

* * * * *

. . . A man, too, had to mix a modicum of rum with his ink, and on a number of evenings, so legend has it, Ethan returned home from Bennington slightly under the weather.

Whether his wife Mary had a hand in it isn't known, but one night a group of his friends decided to frighten him into sobriety. Wrapping themselves in white sheets, they hid under a bridge on the outskirts of Arlington. Ethan came trotting along on his horse. Suddenly the horse snorted and shied at an army of ghosts in the road. Ethan reined the animal. "Hallo!" he shouted. "If you're angels of light, I'm glad to meet you. And if you're devils, then come along home with me. I married your sister."

What He Said at Ticonderoga: A Variant [2]

An amusing illustration of one of these persistent and popularly cherished fictions has recently come to the knowledge of the writer. According to all histories of the United States, Ethan Allen demanded from the British commander the surrender of Ticonderoga "In the name of the Great Jehovah and the Continental Congress." Prof. James D. Butler, of Madison, Wisconsin, has informed me that his grandfather Israel Harris was present and had often told him that Ethan Allen's real language was, "Come out of here, you d——d old rat."

Hunting Exploits [3]

At Landlord Fay's in Bennington they said he could mix the best drinks and tell the best stories of anybody who came to town, and in the woods he had a reputation for traveling fast and killing many deer. There is a story, Brother Ira used to tell, beginning:

He was fond of hunting game in his youth, run after deer tired them down or turned them by often firing on them so as to kill them by night. I remember to have heard him tell that one day in Poultney he came across a company of Deer and killed one which he dressed hung up the Skin and Meat then to preserve that from the Ravens hung his hat on it and went on. He soon killed another deer; with that he left a short hunting Jaccoat

---

[2] From *Lord Timothy Dexter*, by William Cleaves Todd, in *The New-England Historical and Genealogical Register*, Published Quarterly by the New-England Historical Genealogical Society for the year 1886, Vol. XL, p. 380 n. Boston: Published at the Society's House.

[3] From *Ethan Allen*, by John Pell, pp. 34–35. Copyright, 1929, by John Pell. Boston and New York: Houghton Mifflin Company.

and went on; killed another deer—with that left his Frock and went on and killed another—with that left his Breeches then pursued the deer and killed another—took the skin about him and went to his camp.

Another time late in the fall after being much fatigued and raining in the after part of the day so that he had not a dry thread about him got bewildered and lay out all night; the weather cleared off extremely cold—it was out of his power to make any fire—his clothes began to freeze on him—he knew not what course to take—an extensive wilderness on one side—in this situation—he thought it most prudent to mark out a path in a circle in which he could keep himself awake by going round not daring to sit down lest he should fall asleep and perish this I have often heard him say was among the greatest hazards of his life and required the greatest exertion both of body and mind to preserve life till day being much fatigued by travelling all day without victuals benumbed with the cold became sleepy . . . of Every exertion he repeatedly fell in the snow; this would so far bring him to his senses that he would spring on his feet in a few minutes fall again; when daylight came he came more to himself and after travelling a short time came fully to his senses—his clothes were froze except shirt to his skin—before noon he reached a house where he got some refreshment!

Chastising Yorkers [4]

He went about with a small band of followers (Yorkers called them rioters and the Bennington mob) stirring up the settlers to resist the encroachments of their unwelcome landlords. When he came upon surveyors running lines in the forest, he set up a "Judgment Seat" under some huge, old pine tree, tried them on the spot, and often had them stripped and whipped, calling the punishment "Chastisement with the Twigs of the Wilderness." Both the settlers and Yorkers respected him, and stories of his prowess and strength began to get about among the people. They said he could seize by his teeth, and throw over his head, bags containing each a bushel of salt, as fast as two men could bring them round to him; that he had grasped two enemies, one in each hand, and, lifting them off the ground, held them out at arms' length, and beat them together till they cried for mercy; and that he had engaged alone with a York sheriff and his posse of six men, leaving them all sprawling on the ground. Ethan probably invented stories and told them to the credulous settlers whom he visited in their solitary cabins, but others were based on the experiences of his victims. John Munro, an old offender, was taken, tried, and ordered to be whipped on his naked back. He was tied to a tree and flogged till he fainted; on recovering, he was whipped again till he fainted; he revived and underwent a third lashing till he fainted; his wounds were then dressed and he was banished from the district of the New Hampshire Grants.

---

[4] *Ibid.*, pp. 35–37.

Once Ethan captured two New York sheriffs. He locked them in separate rooms on the same side of a house, and during the night tied an effigy to the limb of a tree outside their windows. At dawn he awakened one prisoner after the other, and told him to look out of the window to see his companion swinging from a tree. Each was allowed to escape believing he had just missed a terrible death, a conviction which lasted until he met the other on the streets of Albany.

Dr. Samuel Adams, of Arlington, openly declared himself a partisan of New York. His neighbors tried advice and warnings. The Doctor armed himself with a brace of pistols, and proclaimed his opinions more loudly and decidedly than ever. He announced his full determination to defend himself to the best of his ability against any person who should approach him with unfriendly design.

When the case was reported to Ethan, he sent a squad of Green Mountain Boys to capture the contumacious doctor. They caught him unawares as he was leaving his house. When the prisoner had been tried and convicted, Ethan sentenced him to be tied in a chair, hoisted up the sign-post of Stephen Fay's tavern at Bennington (a twenty-five-foot gallows surmounted by a stuffed catamount grinning toward New York), and left there for an hour. Afterwards, the Doctor returned to Arlington, but insisted on his opinion no more.

He Eats Iron[5]

I was confined in the manner I have related, on board the Gaspee schooner, about six weeks, during which time I was obliged to throw out plenty of extravagant language, which answered certain purposes, (at that time) better than to grace a history.

To give an instance, upon being insulted, in a fit of anger I twisted off a nail with my teeth, which I took to be a ten-penny nail; it went through the mortise of the bar on my handcuff, and at the same time I swaggered over those who abused me; particularly a Doctor Dace, who told me that I was outlawed by New York, and deserved death for several years past; was at last fully ripened for the halter, and in a fair way to obtain it: When I challenged him, he excused himself in consequence, as he said, of my being a criminal; but I flung such a flood of language at him that it shocked him and the spectators, for my anger was very great. I heard one say, damn him, can he eat iron? After that a small padlock was fixed to the handcuff, instead of the nail, and as they were mean-spirited in their treatment to me; so it appeared to me, that they were equally timorous and cowardly.

[5] From *A Narrative of Colonel Ethan Allen's Captivity* . . . containing his Voyages and Travels . . . , written by himself and now published for the information of the Curious in all Nations, p. 10. Philadelphia: Printed. Boston: Reprinted by Draper & Folsom. 1779.

A Conjurer by Passion [6]

Among the great numbers of people, who came to the castle to see the prisoners, some gentlemen told me that they had come 50 miles on purpose to see me, and desired to ask me a number of questions, and to make free with me in conversation. I gave for answer, that I chose freedom in every sense of the word: Then one of them asked me what my occupation in life had been? I answered him, that in my younger days I had studied divinity, but was a conjurer by passion. He replied that I conjured wrong at the time that I was taken; and I was obliged to own, that I mistook a figure at that time, but that I had conjured them out of Ticonderoga. This was a place of great notoriety in England, so that the joke seemed to go in my favour.

Ethan and the Olives [7]

Notwithstanding his bombast, Allen had much shrewdness, but, unfortunately, the profanity of his clever sayings often neutralized the fun. The extreme simplicity of his tastes made him an object of amusement to the English at New York (where he was released on parole when brought from Halifax). Dining one day with a party at the commander-in-chief's, some olives were on the table, to which he helped himself with the rest, and, seeing they were very small, he put three or four in his mouth at once. This induced a general smile, and his wry faces induced his host to ask how he liked them. "Why, Sir William," he said, "I dare say it's a matter of taste, but I think your green gages are ra-a-ther bitter."

A Hero and a Hanging [8]

The people had arranged a sort of triumph for Ethan. He was their Caesar, the hero of Ticonderoga, the martyr of Montreal: he had liberated them from the tyranny of New York, captured the King's fort, suffered in a prison ship, crossed the sea, and dined with George Washington. Depressed by the dreary hardships of war, poverty, and winter, discouraged by the failure of Congress to recognize their State, they rejoiced at the return of their old leader. If there was anything that the new State movement needed at that moment, it was a figurehead, a colorful leader, a pageant—it was Ethan. Crowds gathered at Landlord Fay's to welcome

---

[6] *Ibid.*, p. 15.

[7] From *Retrospections of America, 1797–1811,* by John Bernard, edited from the Manuscript by Mrs. Bayle Bernard, with an Introduction, Notes, and Index by Laurence Hutton and Brander Matthews, p. 115. Copyright, 1886, by Harper & Brothers. New York. 1887.

[8] From *Ethan Allen,* by John Pell, pp. 139–141. Copyright, 1929, by John Pell. Boston and New York: Houghton Mifflin Company.

him home, cannon were fired that evening as well as the next morning, the "flowing bowl" was passed about, and "rural felicity sweetened with friendship" glowed in every countenance. In fact, the festivities lasted for several days, and it was arranged that they should culminate with a public hanging, the first ever held in Bennington.

The culprit was a man named David Redding. He had been detected in communicating with the enemy and finally in carrying off a number of guns from David Robinson's house which was being used as an arsenal. He was convicted of "enemical conduct" and sentenced to be hanged the 4th of June.

At almost the last moment Redding's attorney, John Burnham, convinced the Council that the law required twelve jurors in a capital case, whereas his client had been convicted by a jury of six. The Council granted a reprieve of a week so that a legal trial might be held. But it was too late to prevent a multitude from assembling on the appointed day to witness the execution. When the people heard of the reprieve, they felt that Redding had somehow cheated them out of a spectacle and threatened to lynch him. The situation looked dangerous until a commotion in a certain part of the crowd attracted its attention to Ethan, who was pressing forward shouting, "Attention the whole!" Mounting a stump he waved his cocked hat until the people were silent and then announced in a thunderous voice the reasons for the delay, and advised the people to go home and return at the same time a week later, concluding, with an oath, "You shall see somebody hung at all events, for, if Redding is not then hung, I will be hung myself." This magnanimous offer quieted the angry mob which dispersed after a few more cheers for its hero. The magic of Ethan's words had saved the day again. In gratitude the Council appointed him State's Attorney for the retrial, and, with very little exertion of magic, he procured a conviction from twelve patriotic jurors.

On the appointed day the Assembly recessed from noon to five, so that its members might attend the performance. The gallows had been erected in a field across the road from Landlord Fay's. Before a gaping mob the victim was led from the saddle room of the tavern shed (there was no jail) to his doom, and his last agonies were exhibited to the accompaniment of cheers for America, Vermont, and Ethan.

For many years a rumor persisted among certain old women of Bennington "that Doctor Jonas Fay had the anatomy of Redding locked up in his house, and that he could never make the bones come together right," which, they considered, plainly showed that Redding ought not to have been hanged. But it more probably indicated that Jonas ought not to have been a doctor. This year he was the father of twin sons whom he named Ethan Allan and Heman Allen Fay, out of regard for the brothers.

Ethan and Fanny Wall[9]

Stephen Bradley had built a house facing the street (there was only one street in Westminster: there still is), just north of the court-house. It was one of those fine, square, solid houses which has all the best furniture in a best room which nobody ever uses. It had in fact so many rooms that Stephen had to take in boarders.

Crean Brush, an Irish lawyer and adventurer, had accumulated sixty thousand acres of Vermont land before he committed suicide in Boston. His estate, divided in thirds, was left to his wife, his daughter (by a former marriage), and his stepdaughter. His wife (now married to Patrick Wall, her third husband and second Irishman) and Fanny, her daughter, came to Westminster to locate their lands, and lodged in some of Stephen Bradley's spare rooms.

Fanny's father, Captain Montresor, was a French officer of the British army. From him she had inherited delicate features, a sensitive, vivacious nature: from her stepfather, Brush, twenty thousand acres.

Fanny's mother was a forceful woman. I believe she survived all three husbands. She forced her child to marry, at sixteen, a British officer named Buchanan. It is said that he loved her tenderly, but that she was repelled by his affection. She bore him a son, but the child never saw its father, for he was killed in action before his son was born.

At twenty-four, Fanny was a widow, an heiress, and a beautiful girl. In the histories she is always referred to as "a dashing woman." With her forceful mother and a wardrobe of New York clothes, she dashed into Westminster, into Brush's acres, into Stephen Bradley's spare rooms, and simply overwhelmed the natives. They talked about her "imperious manner," and waited, cold winter days, to see her dash by in a fresh-painted "pung."

The Assembly met. Ethan came to town. Stephen gave parties. Ethan did not serve on committees. The Yorkers kidnapped Luke Knoulton. Ethan put on his uniform, mounted his charger, looked ferocious, and frightened the Yorkers away.

There was in this town a tavern-keeper named John Norton, one of those unfathomable fellows who seem to understand people's secrets without being told and to attract customers by telling them the disparaging truth. To Fanny he said: "If you marry General Allen, you will be queen of a new state." And she replied: "If I should marry the devil, I'd be queen of Hell."

On the morning of the 9th of February, 1784, while Stephen Bradley was entertaining the judges of the Superior Court at breakfast, he heard the bells of a sleigh stopping at his door, and a moment later saw Ethan entering the room. The judges invited him to join them, but he replied

[9] *Ibid.*, pp. 242–245.

that he had breakfasted at Norton's and, while they were finishing, would step across the hall and see the ladies.

Fanny, dressed in a morning gown, was standing on a chair arranging a china closet when Ethan opened the door. With a cracked decanter in her hand, she turned around on the chair and greeted the intruder by telling him that people didn't make calls so early in the morning. He explained that military duties had brought him to Westminster and that he was on his way to Sunderland. So, he added, "If we are to be married, now is the time." She put the decanter back on the shelf, descended from the chair, and then replied: "Very well, but give me time to put on my Joseph." *

A few minutes later, they crossed the hall and found the judges, still sitting at the breakfast table, smoking their long pipes. With Fanny on his arm, Ethan walked up to his old friend Moses Robinson and said: "Judge Robinson, this young woman and myself have concluded to marry each other and to have you perform the ceremony." "When?" asked Moses, somewhat surprised. "Now," replied Ethan; continuing: "For myself I have no great opinion of such formality, and from what I can discover, she thinks as little of it as I do. But as a decent respect for the opinions of mankind seems to require it, you will proceed." Moses said: "General, this is an important matter. Have you given it serious consideration?" "Certainly," Ethan replied, glancing at Fanny. "But I do not think it requires much consideration."

The ceremony then proceeded until Moses asked Ethan whether he promised to live with Fanny "agreeable to the laws of God." At this Ethan stopped the proceedings. Then, looking out of the window, he exclaimed: "The law of God as written in the great book of nature? Yes. Go on." When the ceremony was completed and Fanny's trunk and guitar case were stowed in the back of the sleigh, Ethan wrapped his bride in the big bear rug and they drove off across the mountains.

Drunk or Sober [10]

. . . One night, it seems, he came home tight. When Fanny rebuked him, he denied the charge. The next morning she remarked, "I will find out whether you come home drunk or sober." Thereupon she drove a nail—pretty well up—in the wall of the bedroom, saying: "When your watch is hanging on that nail in the morning, I shall know that you came home sober." Ethan agreed—of course—but he found it rather a difficult job to prove his good behavior by this severe test. Sometimes the nail would dodge him and the watch ring hit one side. When he tried again,

* A name given in the eighteenth century to a lady's riding habit or great-coat buttoned down the front, and with a broad cape. It is said to have been named in allusion to Joseph's coat of many colors.—Alice Morse Earle, *Costume of Colonial Times* (New York, 1894), p. 144.

[10] *Ibid.*, p. 261.

the floor would give way or his knees get out of joint, but he would stick to it until the ring was hooked. If Fanny had anything to say in the morning, he would point his finger at the watch, saying: "You see, I came home sober last night."

Ethan and the White Horse [11]

A story got about that Ethan believed in the transmigration of souls. He had told his friends that he expected to live again in the form of a large white horse. Evidently death seemed far away when he suggested the idea, half humorously, half wondering. Perhaps subconsciously he remembered having seen, some October morning, a great white stallion standing on one of those high Vermont hills, with arched neck, mane and tail stirred by the awakening breeze, snorting a little and pawing the damp earth, while he surveyed the lake of white mist below him, the rows of blue hills, ranged, like the seats of some gigantic stadium, beneath a prismatic canopy. Such a picture must have touched this earthy man whose life was spent amongst those hills, riding and hunting, fighting and plotting for them and their peculiar people. Recurring unexpectedly in the imagination the image seemed prophetic, visionary. But, of course, Ethan didn't take even visions quite seriously.

My Name Is Allen [12]

. . . This was the same Ethan Allen who, a few years later, when New York had put a price on him dead or alive as leader of the Green Mountain Boys, rode into Albany alone, entered the tavern frequented by the politicians, ordered a bowl of punch, drank it all, set it down, faced the room, put his fists on his hips and said, "Now then, my name is Allen. Who wants that reward?" . . .

Ethan Allen Crawford, Giant of the Hills

NOBLE Ethan Crawford! we must pause a few moments before the career of this stalwart Jötunn of the mountains, in the story of whose fortunes the

[11] *Ibid.*, p. 269.

[12] From *The Housatonic,* Puritan River, by Chard Powers Smith, p. 260. Copyright, 1946, by Chard Powers Smith. New York and Toronto: Rinehart & Company, Incorporated.

From *The White Hills;* Their Legends, Landscape, and Poetry, by Thomas Starr King, pp. 223–228. Entered according to Act of Congress, in the year 1859, by Crosby, Nichols and Company, in the Clerk's Office of the District Court of the District of Massachusetts. Boston: Crosby and Ainsworth. 1886.

. . . In 1819 the first rough path was cut through the forest on the side of the Mount

savageness and hardships of the wilderness and the heroic qualities they nurse are shown in one picture. He was born in 1792. His early childhood was passed in a log hut a few miles from the Notch; and in his manhood, after a fire in 1818 had burned the comfortable house on the Giant's Grave,[1] he lived again in a log house with but one apartment and no windows. In 1819, he had built a rough house of a larger size, with a stone chimney, in which during the cold spells of winter, more than a cord of wood would be burned in twenty-four hours. He tells us that he never owned a hat, mittens, or shoes until he was thirteen years old; yet could harness and unharness horses in the biting winter weather with bare head, hands, and feet, "and not mind, or complain of the cold, as I was used to it." As to what is called comfort in the lowlands, he found that

> Naught the mountain yields thereof,
> But savage health and sinews tough.

He grew to be nearly seven feet in height, and rejoiced in a strength which he would show in lifting five hundred weight into a boat; in dragging a bear that he had muzzled to his house, that he might be tamed; or in carrying a buck home alive, upon his shoulders. What a flavor of wild mountain life, what vivid suggestions of the closest tug of man with nature, —of raw courage and muscle against frost and gale, granite and savageness, do we find in his adventures and exploits;—his leaping from a load of hay in the Notch when a furious gust made it topple, and catching it on his shoulder to prevent it from falling over a precipice; his breaking out the road, for miles, through the wild winter drifts; his carrying the mail on his back, after freshets, to the next settlement, when a horse could not cross the streams; his climbings of Mount Washington with a party of adventurers, laden like a pack-horse, without suffering more fatigue than ordinary men would feel after a level walk of ten miles; his returns from the summit bearing some exhausted member of a party on his back; his long, lonely tramps, on snow-shoes, after moose, and his successful shooting of a pair of the noble beasts, two miles back of the Notch, about dark, and sleeping through the cold night in their warm skins, undismayed by the wolf howls that serenaded him!

Washington range to the rocky ridge. Ethan Allen Crawford, who lived on the Giant's Grave, marked and cleared this path in connection with Abel Crawford, his father, who was living eight miles below the Notch. A few years after, Ethan spotted and trimmed a footpath on the side of Mount Washington itself, along essentially the same route by which carriages are driven now from the White Mountain House to the Cold Spring. And it ought not to be forgotten that it was by Ethan Crawford, that the first protection for visitors was built under the cone of Mount Washington. It was a stone hut, furnished with a small stove, an iron chest, a roll of sheet lead, and a plentiful supply of soft moss and hemlock boughs for bedding. The lead was the cabin-register on which visitors left their names engraved by a piece of sharp iron. Every particle of this camp and all the furniture, was swept off on the night of the storm by which the Willey family were overwhelmed.—T. S. K., *ibid.*, p. 222.

[1] An Indian burial mound.

The tribe of bears in a circumference of twenty miles knew him well. Many a den he made desolate of its cubs by shaking them, like apples, from trees into which they would run to escape him; then tying his handkerchief around their mouths he would take them home under his arms to tame them. Many a wrestle did he have with full grown ones who would get their feet in his traps. Scarcely a week passed while he lived among the mountains which was not marked by some encounter with a bear.

With the wolves also, he carried on a war of years. So long as he kept sheep he could not frighten the wolves into cessation of hostilities. The marauders showed the skill of a surgeon in their rapine and slaughter. Ethan found, now and then, a sheepskin a few rods from his house with no mark upon it except a smooth slit from the throat to the forelegs, as though it had been cut with a knife. The legs had been taken off as far as the lowest joint; all the flesh had been eaten out clean, and only the head and backbone had been left attached to the pelt. When the feat was accomplished, the wolves would give him notice by a joint howl, which the Washington range would echo from their "bleak concave," so that all the woods seemed filled with packs of the fierce pirates. Once in a December night four wolves made a descent upon his sheep, which fled among the carriages near the house, for safety. Ethan went out in his night-dress and faced them in the bright moonlight. He had no weapon, and so they rose on their haunches to hear what he might have to say. He harangued them, to little purpose for some time, and at last "observed to them that they had better make off with themselves," with the intimation that an axe or gun would be soon forthcoming. They then turned about and marched away, "giving us some of their lonesome music." But Ethan found, the next morning, that they had enjoyed his hospitality, by digging up carcasses of bears back of the stable, and gnawing them close to the bone.

He thinned the sables from the region by his traps. The banks of the neighboring brooks he depopulated of otters. Yet he had an affection for all the creatures of the wilderness, and loved to have young wolves, and tame bucks, and well-behaved bears, and domesticated sable, around his premises; while the collecting of rare alpine plants from the snowy edges of the ravines on the ridge, where Nature had "put them according to their merits," was "a beautiful employment, which I always engaged in with much pleasure." But his most remarkable adventures were his contests with the wild-cats, the fiercest animals which the mountains harbored. The hills that slope towards the Ammonoosuc were cleared by him of these furious freebooters, that made great havoc with his geese and sheep. His greatest exploit was his capture of one of these creatures in a tree within the Notch, by a lasso made of birch sticks, which he twisted on the spot. He slipped it over the wild-cat's neck, and jerked the animal down ten feet. The noose broke. He repaired it instantly, fastened it once more around the creature's head, pulled him down within reach, and after a severe battle, killed him. He seems to have possessed a magic fetter, like that which the dark elves of the Scandinavian myths wove to bind the wolf

Fenris, and which was plaited of six things into a cord smooth and soft as a silken string: the beards of women, the noise of a cat's footfall, the roots of stones, the sinews of bears, the spittle of birds, and the breath of fish.

What extremes in Ethan's experience! He entertained many of the wisest and most distinguished of the country under his rude roof, and was gratefully remembered for his hospitality, and his faithful service in guiding them to the great ridge. He would come home from a bear-fight, to find in his house, perhaps, "a member of Congress, Daniel Webster," who desired his assistance on foot to the summit of Mount Washington. *There* was a couple whose talk would have been worth hearing! Ethan says that they went up "without meeting anything worthy of note, more than was common for me to find, *but to him things appeared interesting.* And when we arrived there, he addressed himself in this way, saying: 'Mount Washington, I have come a long distance, and have toiled hard to arrive at your summit, and now you give me a cold reception. I am extremely sorry, that I shall not have time enough to view this grand prospect which lies before me, and nothing prevents but the uncomfortable atmosphere in which you reside.'" How accurately Ethan reported the address, we cannot certify; but as the rostrum was the grandest, and the audience the smallest, which was ever honored with a formal speech by the great orator, the picture should not be lost. The snow from a sudden squall froze upon the pair as they descended the cone. The statesman was evidently interested in his guide, for Ethan says that, "the next morning, after paying his bill, he made me a handsome present of twenty dollars."

And Ethan's life was perpetually set in remarkable contrasts. From struggles with wild-cats in the forests of Cherry Mountain, to the society of his patient, faithful, pious wife, was a distance as wide as can be indicated on the planet. Mount Washington looked down into his uncouth domicile, and saw there

Sparta's stoutness, Bethlehem's heart.

Lucy taught him how to meet calamity without despair and repining. When his house burned down, and left him with no property but one new cheese and the milk of the cows, his wife, though sick, was not despondent. When his debts, caused by this fire, pressed heavy, and he staggered under difficulties as he never did under the heaviest load in the forest, she assured him that Providence had some wise purpose in their trouble. When his crops were swept off, and his meadows filled with sand by freshets, Lucy's courage was not crushed. He knocked down a swaggering bully, once, on a musterfield in Lancaster, and was obliged to promise Lucy that he would never give way to an angry passion again. When death invaded their household, and his own powerful frame was so shaken by disease and pain, that a flash of lightning, as he said, seemed to run from his spine to the ends of his hair, his wife's religious patience and trust proved an undrainable cordial. And after he became weakened by sickness, if he staid out long after dark, Lucy would take a lantern and go into the woods to search for him. He was put into jail at last in Lancaster for debt. Lucy wrote a pleading letter to his chief creditor to release him, but without effect. This says Ethan, "forced me, in the jail, to reflect on human nature, and it overcame me, so that I was obliged to call for the advice of physicians and a nurse." Other forms of adversity, too, beset him,—opposition to his public-house when travellers became more plentiful, which destroyed his prospects of profit; the breaking of a bargain for the sale of his lands; foul defamation of his character to the postoffice authorities in Washington, from whom he held an appointment. Broken in health, oppressed by pecuniary burdens, and with shattered spirits, he left the plateau at the base of Mount Washington for a more pleasant home in Vermont, accompanied by Lucy, whose faith did not allow her to murmur. But he experienced hard fortune there, too, and returned to die, within sight of the range, an old man, before he had reached the age of fifty-six years.

Since the breaking up of his home on the Giant's Grave, the mountains have heard no music which they have echoed so heartily as the windings of his horn, and the roar of the cannon which he used to load to the muzzle, that his guests might hear a park of artillery reply. Few men that have ever visited the mountains have done more faithful work or borne so much adversity and suffering. The cutting of his heel-cord with an axe, when he was chopping out the first path up Mount Washington, was a type of the result to himself of his years of toil in the wilderness; and his own quaint reflection on that wound, which inflicted lameness upon him for months, is the most appropriate inscription, after the simple words, "an honest man," that could be reared over his grave: "So it is that men suffer various ways in advancing civilization, and through God, mankind are indebted to the labors of men in many different spheres of life." . . .

"Ave" Henry, Lumber Baron

J. E. Henry is undoubtedly the most colorful character that Northern New Hampshire has ever produced. He was born in Littleton and was engaged in lumbering on an extensive scale and most successfully from a financial viewpoint. He came from a poor family but was a natural trader, and it is said of him that he was always ready to "sugar anything off" that could be sold at a profit. He firmly believed that the time to sell anything was when someone else wanted it. His advice to his boys, "Make money, honestly if possible, but make money," is a key to his character. He worked hard himself and brought his children up to work early and late, for he said that if he did not put them to work the devil would.

He frequently ran afoul of the law and was generally in a lawsuit. One time when a young man he saw the sheriff coming across the field and

---

By Ola G. Veazie. Manuscripts of the Federal Writers' Project of the Works Progress Administration for the State of New Hampshire.

knew that the only thing he owned that could be attached was two hogs. The law allowed him one live one and one dressed; so he rushed out of the house with a butcher knife and stuck one of them and, when the sheriff arrived, looked up at him and said, "I beat you that time, didn't I?" This was during the time that he lived on a farm in Pattenville.

"Ave" Henry, as he was always called, bought out a small mill at Zealand (just above Twin Mountain village) with two other men as partners, but soon bought them out. They are reported to have logged much of the Zealand country before they purchased it and then paid only a nominal sum for the land.

When he decided to put in a log railroad seven miles in length, he ordered the rails to be delivered at a certain time in the early summer. The rails failed to arrive, but he had engaged a large crew to lay them and so set the crew to work in the woods. When the rails arrived, he sued the company for not getting them there in time and finally got $50,000 damages plus the rails for nothing. In the meantime the crew had piled up a great many logs beside the track while they were supposedly idle waiting for the rails.

There was quite a good-sized village at Zealand with a store, post-office, large barns, and a number of houses, school, and railroad station. To-day an old iron water tub beside the road is the sole remainder of a once prosperous settlement.

Mr. Henry was very strict about liquor and would not have any around a camp that belonged to him. It was in the days when it could be delivered through the mails. One night two men were expecting a case, and two other men had learned that it had been ordered and was expected on a certain train. The men went to the post-office for it and started down the track toward their quarters with it. The other two men dressed up as Mr. Henry and his son. Mr. Henry always wore a fur coat and the son a fur cap, and these two were seen coming toward the men with the case of whiskey. They started to run but were hampered by the weight of the liquor. The other two men took after them and soon they were forced to abandon their load and run so as not to be recognized. This was what the two men had wanted and so of course they got the case of liquor. Mr. Henry heard about it and said that if they were smart enough to work a trick like that he would make an exception and let them keep it.

One time the Henrys moved to Boston for an indefinite stay but returned in a few weeks. Asked why he returned, Mr. Henry said that he enjoyed being a big pig in a small puddle rather than competing with other big pigs in a big one.

He approved of keeping in debt, for he claimed that the only way to keep interested in making money was to buy something that you wanted before you could pay for it and then have to struggle to make enough to pay for it. When he moved to Lincoln and bought a large acreage and mill there, it cost a lot more than he had, but it seemed worthwhile to him to go into debt in order to get it.

He succeeded in buying all of the land around Lincoln except one small building lot which a man by the name of Pat McGuire owned and would not sell. One day Pat met Mr. Henry on the street, and it is reported that he had indulged in more than one drink before meeting him. He walked up to Mr. Henry and said, "You and I own the whole of Lincoln, don't we, Mr. Henry?"

One time a new stable boy was hired to take care of the team that Mr. Henry used personally and was an excellent team. The first day he worked they drove a long distance and were on the road many hours; so the man cared for them as quickly as possible and went directly to bed. The next day they did not use the team much, and the fellow again did not take very good care of them. About ten o'clock Mr. Henry went to his room and woke him up. He asked him if he liked his job, if the team was good, if they bit him, kicked him, or were at all vicious. The fellow answered by highly praising the team as there was a stranger present and he thought that perhaps the stranger was interested in buying them. Then Mr. Henry said, "Well, if it is as good a team as you claim it to be, you had better get up and go and take better care of them."

One day Mr. Henry saw a woodsman searching the snow for something and at once was all curiosity and asked him what he was looking for. The man answered, "A chain, but I can't seem to find it." When he went to the office to settle up in the spring, he found he was charged with the loss of a logging chain. He asked what that meant as he had never lost one. Mr. Henry reminded him of the time he was searching for one and could not find it. The man began to laugh and told him that it was a watch chain that he had been looking for.

Henry found a K. of P. charm and insisted on wearing it although he was not a member of that order. His son had sponsored the lodge and told him it was against the rules for him to have such a charm. He replied, "Haven't I paid for all of their paraphernalia? I guess I can wear this pin if I want to." A good many of the help belonged, and one day a man got fired and complained to Mr. Henry that he was fired because he had not seen fit to join. He then proceeded to lay off everyone who did belong and to hire those who did not.

A good many men were hired through an employment agency in Boston but had to make their own way to Lincoln. One day too many of them arrived for his needs, and so when another came into the office and asked for a job he said, "I'll give you a job. Count the ties from here to Boston." He meant, of course, that he had no job open for him. The man, however, took him literally and counted the railroad ties to Boston. He reported back in due time with the number of ties. Mr. Henry checked with railroad officials and found that the man was approximately right and so paid him for his time.

A certain man who lived near Lincoln was a constant source of annoyance to Mr. Henry. He tried hard to get rid of the man by buying him out but did not succeed. One time he laid a deep plot to bother the poor man. He pretended to become friendly with him and asked him to keep a sickly shoat for him. The man owned a very good one and after a week or so he (Henry) sent the sheriff after his shoat which he claimed the man had taken without his permission. The sheriff took the big one as Mr. Henry claimed it was his. The other man had no proof and so lost the big one for a poor one.

A Frenchman down the valley sold him a pile of pulpwood, and he would only pay him for 50 cords, although both knew that there was considerable more there. The Frenchman had no other market for the wood; so had to take what was given. As soon as he bought it, he set it on fire and started by team for Plymouth to insure it. He insured and collected for 200 cords. Later the Frenchman heard of the amount that he had insured it for and went to him for pay for the other 150 cords. He protested, but, when the Frenchman threatened to tell the sheriff about it, had to come across with the amount demanded.

Driving out of the woods one spring day, Henry overtook one of his men and gave him a ride. The man was carrying a large bag which aroused Henry's curiosity. The man told him that it contained spruce gum which was worth $1.50 per pound. When they were settling up, he called for the bag and had it weighed and charged the man $1.50 per pound for the contents and also for the time it would take to pick it. The man had gathered it on Sundays, and as he had happened to run across it and not really spent any of the company's time on it at all, he was very indignant about it but could do nothing. This action was highly characteristic on Henry's part.

Another of his favorite tricks was to get the men going into the woods to leave their watches or jewelry with him in his office for safe-keeping. Then if they did not make good, and many of them would come out of the woods owing the company more than they had made, he would keep the watches, etc. It is even reported that he would sometimes claim he lost them, and one man back in the woods recognized his watch which another had bought on his way in and which Henry, claiming he did not know the owner, had sold.

A man sluiced a horse and Henry charged him $60.00 for the horse. He only had about $20.00 coming to him. His brother was present when he told Henry that he would quit and asked him if he would keep back his pay also. Henry got up close to the brother and grabbed his gold watch and said, "Yes, and this too."

Henry was often heard to brag that no one ever made a cent working for him. He forced all to trade at the company store where very high prices were charged for everything. For instance, if eggs were selling at 18¢, the company store would ask 28¢ for them.

A family came there with two horses and a cow. They were persuaded to leave the cow at Lincoln while they went back into the woods. In the spring they came out to settle up and then learned that they could not have the cow, for she had "dried up and eaten her head off" and so would have to be kept to pay for her board. They were in debt to the company after working hard all winter and were allowed to take only one of their pair of horses with them.

Hired girls at the Henry home were expected to work every minute and amongst other things had to split the dry wood for kindling, feed the pigs, milk cows, and in their spare time braid rugs and sew. They received $3.00 per week and the Henrys could never understand why they had difficulty in keeping help. One time they discovered that a girl had a pair of silk stockings and brought her into court as they were sure that she had stolen them from Mrs. Henry. She proved that her family, who were quite well to do, had given them to her. She also had to prove that some silver found in her trunk had also been given her by her family.

One time Henry had a warrant served on a certain woman for letting her hens out so that they got in a neighbor's garden. He was overly interested in the neighbor and was quite surprised when he found that they were the neighbor's own hens and she had been afraid to tell him they were hers.

He used to have potatoes planted on both sides of the road so close that teams could not pass and then watch and, if anyone turned out and touched a potato plant, have them arrested for trespassing.

There was an old cemetery beside the road which had been there before he came to Lincoln. When he started to put in some water works for the town, he started to go through the cemetery rather than go around it. Neighbors protested and stopped him but he could not see why it was not all right to go through as he said, "Why, they're all gone, aren't they?" referring to the bodies in the old graves.

Usually Mr. Henry was very meticulous in his dress and wore a white shirt and a diamond stud in his tie, but whenever he got up in the morning and put on a certain old faded blue cap and an old coat, everyone knew that he was on the war-path and that they had better not cross him that day or they would be fired.

When G. L. Johnson wanted to put the Elbow Lake branch of his railroad from Johnson Village into the end of the lake where he had another mill, he secured the money from Henry. Johnson had a certain number of years to return logs in lieu of money to Henry. The price of lumber dropped sharply and so he returned them all the first year, causing Henry to lose several dollars per thousand. Henry claimed that Johnson was the only man who ever got the best of him on a large deal.

"All I care about a dollar is to see it tick" was a frequent statement of "Ave" Henry.

In 1884 Henry bought a large ranch at Tintah, Minnesota, which is twelve hours' ride west of Minneapolis. Cattle and wheat were raised there and, as he started things on his usual scale, he soon had a small village with a post-office and school on his property. Many of his help came from New Hampshire. One time he was there and refused to pay the help. It was not that he did not have the money but that he got angry about something and was trying to punish the whole crowd. They seized him and strung him up. He promised to pay if they would let him down. They did and then he found some reason for not immediately complying. They strung him up again and left him until he was nearly dead. They finally let him down and he paid. They told him never to show himself in that community again under penalty of death. He never did. He gave the ranch to his daughters and never went there again.

Barnum's Road to Riches

The Brick Man [1]

I THOROUGHLY understood the art of advertising, not merely by means of printer's ink, which I have always used freely, and to which I confess myself so much indebted for my success, but by turning every possible circumstance to my account. It was my monomania to make the Museum the town wonder and town talk. I often seized upon an opportunity by instinct, even before I had a very definite conception as to how it should be used, and it seemed, somehow, to mature itself and serve my purpose. As an illustration, one morning a stout, hearty-looking man, came into my ticket-office and begged some money. I asked him why he did not work and earn his living? He replied that he could get nothing to do and that he would be glad of any job at a dollar a day. I handed him a quarter of a dollar, told him to go and get his breakfast and return, and I would employ him at light labor at a dollar and a half a day. When he returned I gave him five common bricks.

"Now," said I, "go and lay a brick on the sidewalk at the corner of Broadway and Ann Street; another close by the Museum; a third diagonally across the way at the corner of Broadway and Vesey Street, by the Astor House; put down the fourth on the sidewalk in front of St. Paul's Church, opposite; then, with the fifth brick in hand, take up a rapid march from one point to the other, making the circuit, exchanging your brick at every point, and saying nothing to any one."

"What is the object of this?" inquired the man.

"No matter," I replied; "all you need to know is that it brings you fifteen cents wages per hour. It is a bit of my fun, and to assist me properly you must seem to be as deaf as a post; wear a serious countenance; answer no questions; pay no attention to any one; but attend faithfully to the work and at the end of every hour by St. Paul's clock show this ticket at

[1] From *Struggles and Triumphs:* or, Forty Years' Recollections of P. T. Barnum, Written by Himself (Biography Complete to April, 1872.), pp. 121–123. Entered according to Act of Congress, in the year 1871, by P. T. Barnum, in the Office of the Librarian of Congress, at Washington. Entered also at Stationer's Hall, London, England. Buffalo, New York: Warren, Johnson, & Co. 1873.

the Museum door; enter, walking solemnly through every hall in the building; pass out, and resume your work."

With the remark that it was "all one to him, so long as he could earn his living," the man placed his bricks and began his round. Half an hour afterwards, at least five hundred people were watching his mysterious movements. He had assumed a military step and bearing, and looking as sober as a judge, he made no response whatever to the constant inquiries as to the object of his singular conduct. At the end of the first hour, the sidewalks in the vicinity were packed with people all anxious to solve the mystery. The man, as directed, then went into the Museum, devoting fifteen minutes to a solemn survey of the halls, and afterwards returning to his round. This was repeated every hour till sundown and whenever the man went into the Museum a dozen or more persons would buy tickets and follow him, hoping to gratify their curiosity in regard to the purpose of his movements. This was continued for several days—the curious people who followed the man into the Museum considerably more than paying his wages—till finally the policeman, to whom I had imparted my object, complained that the obstruction of the sidewalk by crowds had become so serious that I must call in my "brick man." This trivial incident excited considerable talk and amusement; it advertised me; and it materially advanced my purpose of making a lively corner near the Museum.

It Pays to Advertise [2]

While I expended money liberally for attractions for the inside of my Museum, and bought or hired everything curious or rare which was offered or could be found, I was prodigal, in my outlays to arrest or arouse public attention. When I became proprietor of the establishment, there were only the words: "American Museum," to indicate the character of the concern; there was no bustle or activity about the place; no posters to announce what was to be seen;—the whole exterior was as dead as the skeletons and stuffed skins within. My experiences had taught me the advantages of advertising. I printed whole columns in the papers, setting forth the wonders of my establishment. Old "fogies" opened their eyes in amazement at a man who could expend hundreds of dollars in announcing a show of "stuffed monkey skins"; but these same old fogies paid their quarters, nevertheless, and when they saw the curiosities and novelties, in the Museum halls, they, like all other visitors, were astonished as well as pleased, and went home and told their friends and neighbors and thus assisted in advertising my business.

For other and not less effective advertising,—flags and banners, began to adorn the exterior of the building. I kept a band of music on the front balcony and announced "Free Music for the Million." People said, "Well, that Barnum is a liberal fellow to give us music for nothing," and they

[2] *Ibid.*, pp. 131–132.

flocked down to hear my outdoor free concerts. But I took pains to select and maintain the poorest band I could find—one whose discordant notes would drive the crowd into the Museum, out of earshot of my outside orchestra. Of course, the music was poor. When people expect to get "something for nothing" they are sure to be cheated, and generally deserve to be, and so, no doubt, some of my out-door patrons were sorely disappointed; but when they came inside and paid to be amused and instructed, I took care to see that they not only received the full worth of their money, but were more than satisfied. Powerful Drummond lights were placed at the top of the Museum, which, in the darkest night, threw a flood of light up and down Broadway, from the Battery to Niblo's, that would enable one to read a newspaper in the street. These were the first Drummond lights ever seen in New York, and they made people talk, and so advertise my Museum.

To the Egress [3]

On that Fourth of July, at one o'clock, P.M., my Museum was so densely crowded that we could admit no more visitors, and we were compelled to stop the sale of tickets. I pushed through the throng until I reached the roof of the building, hoping to find room for a few more, but it was in vain. Looking down into the street it was a sad sight to see the thousands of people who stood ready with their money to enter the Museum, but who were actually turned away. It was exceedingly harrowing to my feelings. Rushing down stairs, I told my carpenter and his assistants to cut through the partition and floor in the rear and to put in a temporary flight of stairs so as to let out people by that egress into Ann Street. By three o'clock the egress was opened and a few people were passed down the new stairs, while a corresponding number came in at the front. But I lost a large amount of money that day by not having sufficiently estimated the value of my own advertising, and consequently not having provided for the thousands who had read my announcements and seen my outside show, and had taken the first leisure day to visit the Museum. I had learned one lesson, however, and that was to have the egress ready on future holidays.

Early in the following March, I received notice from some of the Irish population that they meant to visit me in great numbers on "St. Patrick's day in the morning." "All right," said I to my carpenter, "get your egress ready for March 17"; and I added, to my assistant manager: "If there is much of a crowd, don't let a single person pass out at the front, even if it were St. Patrick himself; put every man out through the egress in the rear." The day came, and before noon we were caught in the same dilemma as we were on the Fourth of July; the Museum was jammed and the sale of tickets was stopped. I went to the egress and asked the sentinel how many hundreds had passed out?

---

[3] *Ibid.*, pp. 138–141.

"Hundreds," he replied, "why only three persons have gone out by this way and they came back, saying that it was a mistake and begging to be let in again."

"What does this mean?" I inquired; "surely thousands of people have been all over the Museum since they came in."

"Certainly," was the reply, "but after they have gone from one saloon to another and have been on every floor, even to the roof, they come down and travel the same route over again."

At this time I espied a tall Irish woman with two good-sized children whom I had happened to notice when they came in early in the morning.

"Step this way, madam," said I politely, "you will never be able to get into the street by the front door without crushing these dear children. We have opened a large egress here and you can pass by these rear stairs into Ann Street and thus avoid all danger."

"Sure," replied the woman, indignantly, "an' I'm not going out at all, at all, nor the children aither, for we've brought our dinners and we are going to stay all day."

Further investigation showed that pretty much all of my visitors had brought their dinners with the evident intention of literally "making a day of it." No one expected to go home till night; the building was overcrowded, and meanwhile hundreds were waiting at the front entrance to get in when they could. In despair I sauntered upon the stage behind the scenes, biting my lips with vexation, when I happened to see the scene-painter at work and a happy thought struck me: "Here," I exclaimed, "take a piece of canvas four feet square, and paint on it, as soon as you can, in large letters—

☞ TO THE EGRESS."

Seizing his brush he finished the sign in fifteen minutes, and I directed the carpenter to nail it over the door leading to the back stairs. He did so, and as the crowd, after making the entire tour of the establishment, came pouring down the mainstairs from the third story, they stopped and looked at the new sign, while some of them read audibly: "To the Aigress."

"The Aigress," said others, "sure that's an animal we haven't seen," and the throng began to pour down the back stairs only to find that the "Aigress" was the elephant,[1] and that the elephant was all out o' doors, or so much of it as began with Ann Street. Meanwhile, I began to accommodate those who had long been waiting with their money at the Broadway entrance.

[1] Alluding to "seeing the elephant," or seeing all that is to be seen and being disappointed; a current phrase.

John L. Sullivan, the Strong Boy of Boston

• His Size and Strength [1]

As I am the only one [of my family] who has been noticed for size or strength, people have sometimes been curious to know from whom mine come, particularly as my father was a small man, being only five feet three and one half inches, and never weighing more than one hundred and thirty pounds. My mother was a fair size, weighing about one hundred and eighty pounds, and some have given the credit to her. One writer, after I had grown in reputation as an athlete, said: "Sullivan derived all his great physical strength from his mother, who in her youth was considered a woman of remarkable physical and mental powers." Whatever there may be in this, it should be borne in mind that my uncles and the other relatives of my father in Ireland were all large men, and were known in their section of the country by a Celtic word which might be translated as the "big Sullivans."

* * * * *

I was always a big fellow, weighing two hundred pounds at the age of seventeen, and I had the reputation for more than my proportionate share of strength.

I remember one time of a horse car getting off the track on Washington Street, and six to eight men trying to lift it on. They didn't succeed, and so I astonished the crowd by lifting it on myself. I used to practise such feats as lifting full barrels of flour and beer or kegs of nails above my head, but I gave up those things as I found that men who did feats of strength made themselves too stiff for any good boxing. I could lift a dumb-bell with the best, but I do not use more than a two-pounder as it is nimbleness and skill that a boxer needs.

It was on account of these feats that I first got the name of "Strong Boy." There was a light boxer named Fairbanks that I called "Billy-go-lightly," and he replied by calling me "John, the Strong Boy."

Now that I have touched on the subject of nicknames, I may as well give a little list of titles that have been given to me after various victories in the ring, not with the idea that I endorse them myself; but that—

A little nonsense, now and then,
Is relished by the wisest men.

"The Boston Hercules." "Knight of the Fives." "The hard-hitting Sullivan." "The Boston Miracle of huge muscles, terrific chest, and marvelous strength." "The king of the ring." "The youthful prince of pugilists."

---

[1] From *Life and Reminiscences of a 19th Century Gladiator,* by John L. Sullivan, pp. 21–22, 28–30. Copyright, 1892, by Jas. A. Hearn & Co. Boston: Jas. A. Hearn & Co. London: Geo. Routledge & Son., Ltd.

"The magnificent Sullivan." "Boston's philanthropic prize-fighter." "Young Boston giant." "The finest specimen of physical development in the world." "The terrific Boston pugilist." "Triphammer Jack." "Spartacus Sullivan." "The king of pugilists." "Monarch of the prize ring." "The scientific American." "Hurricane hitter." "Mighty hero of biceps." "His fistic Highness." "Champion of champions." "Boston's pet." "Boston's pride and joy." "The cultured slugger." "Sullivan the Great." "The Napoleon Bonaparte of sluggers." "King of fistiana." "Sullivan the wonder." "The champion pounder." "Professor of bicepital forces." "Prize-fighting Caesar." "The Hercules of the ring." "The Goliath of the prize ring." "America's invincible champion." "A champion who never knew defeat."

How He Knocked Out Jake Kilrain [2]

The fight took place at Richburg, in the State of Mississippi. The Kilrain party, as well as my own, took a special train on the Queen and Crescent R. R., on Sunday the 7th of July (1889). They were guests of Charles Rich, while I was quartered at the house of Mr. Smith, who was foreman for Mr. Rich.

The battle was fought on the estate of Charles Rich. Kilrain was seconded by Charles Mitchell, the bombastic sprinter, and Mike Donovan, of the New York Athletic Club, and John Murphy of Boston was bottle holder. I was seconded by Mike Cleary and William Muldoon, and had for bottle holder Dan Murphy. After all the preliminaries had been arranged, Kilrain won the toss for corners and selected the southeast. I had the opposite corner. The referee was John Fitzpatrick, a well-known politician of New Orleans, and at the writing of this book mayor of that city. The timekeeper for the Kilrain party was Bat Masterson, of Denver; and for me, Thomas Costello, of Cleveland, officiated. Finally, we were assigned our corners. The order to get ready was given. Kilrain advanced to the center of the ring and I met him, and each man placed one thousand dollars in the referee's hand on himself to win. The bet being made, we were ordered back to our corners, and we received the call and orders of the referee to step to the middle of the ring, shake hands, and return to corners. The referee said, "Get ready," and "Time." The hostilities commenced then, and without a blow being struck Kilrain won first fall by throwing me with a cross buttock, ending the round. On going to my corner I remarked, "If that is his game, I will fool him," and on time being called for the second round Kilrain attempted the same thing, but I was ready for him and threw him heavily to the ground, fooling him and giving Mitchell the laugh. This spoiled Kilrain's chances of wrestling and he gave up in despair.

Time being called for the third round, we both advanced to the centre

[2] *Ibid.*, pp. 208–212, 221.

of the ring and on Kilrain running around his corner, I caught him, hitting him a right-hand punch under the heart, following it up with a left-hand punch on the top of the head, injuring my left hand slightly, and virtually, if I do say it myself, winning the fight right there and then, and ending the round by knocking Kilrain down. In the succeeding rounds, there being seventy-five of them, Kilrain either went down to avoid punishment, or was knocked down with my blows, right and left handed. His tactics were pursued in endeavoring to tire me out, and were according to the advice of his seconds. Mitchell, in particular, gave him lessons in his method of dodging me when I fought him in France.

Now, from the best of my remembrance, I think it was in the middle of the fight that I took a drink of cold tea in which a little whisky had been put. Joe Coburn, thinking there was not enough whisky put in, left his seat, and coming to the corner, put in more whisky than I could hold. There being too much liquor in the tea, and my stomach being in such a good condition, I threw it right off. My opponent's friends, seeing this, said,—

"Go at him, Jake; you have got him."

I said, "Come on."

Kilrain said, "Give it up, John; I have got you."

I said, "Come on and fight."

With the encouragement of his seconds, he came close enough to me to be knocked down, thus ending the round. From that time, Donovan, who was one of Kilrain's seconds, played between the two corners of the ring, keeping Kilrain between himself and Mitchell, and I had to fight him out of his corner repeatedly; Donovan acting like the umpire of a baseball game, rather than like a second in a fight. During this fight, it was Kilrain's intentions, through the advice of his seconds, to keep in the ring by repeatedly falling or being knocked down, it being the only resort or hope he had of winning this fight. He was carried to his corner by his seconds during all the rounds. I walked to my corner, and being asked by my seconds to sit down on a chair provided for me, refused, saying:—

"What is the use of sitting down? I have to get up again," and I remained standing in my corner, talking with my seconds and friends.

When asked to go on and finish Kilrain, I laughed and said,—

"Let me stay. They say a man who can hold me half an hour can lick me. I will show these fellows that I can stay and make as long a fight as anybody else, if that is what they call fighting."

I did this more to satisfy the newspaper men who had styled me a hurricane fighter and not a stayer. I proved conclusively in this fight that I could stay as long as I liked, and could have finished this man at any time, as the fight was all my own. I was fighting an hour and twenty minutes when I was asked by Muldoon how I felt.

I said, "I never felt better in my life. How long have we been fighting?"

Muldoon said, "About an hour. How long can you stay, John?"

"Until to-morrow morning, if it is necessary," I replied.

This was all in the sun at one hundred and twenty degrees. Kilrain resorted to all the tricks imaginable. He had spiked me and tore my right shoe wide open, so that the blood oozed through the shoe on to the grass. I found no fault about this, and never made it known to his seconds or to anybody else at the time. Every one could see what Kilrain's game was. In throwing him later, in one of the rounds, Kilrain, in falling, threw his foot up and caught me with his spike, tearing my tights open. Upon which I turned to the referee, and said,—

"Make that man fight fairly."

The referee warned him not to let that occur again. He was finished five rounds before they threw the sponge up, and I was more scared than anybody for fear that I had killed him, as in each fall that he had made during the last five rounds it looked as if his neck had been broken.

In the third round, after the right-hand punch, on being taken to his corner, he said,—

"My God, I am licked. He is too strong, too powerful, and can hit too hard."

Before he had entered the ring that morning, he had told a prominent physician, Dr. J. A. Dougherty, of Philadelphia, who had been engaged by the Kilrain party to look after and attend to him in case of his being injured in the fight, that he felt so strong that he thought he could punch a hole through the wall. The doctor examined him before allowing him to enter the ring, found his pulse to be normal, and his condition in every other respect to be of the first order. These are facts that are well known, and can be substantiated by Dr. John A. Dougherty, who is a well-known member of the Athletic Club, located near the Schuylkill, in Philadelphia. The same doctor, who had attended him after the fight, found that he was severely punished and hurt internally, and has since told me that it looked as if Kilrain would never get over the beating that I had given him. He stated to me that he had given him a number of grains of morphine and drams of brandy, injected hypodermically to alleviate his suffering after this defeat. It is a well-known fact that he stated to several of his friends that it was the mistake of his life to ever have allowed himself to be so foolishly led into making a match with me.

* * * * *

It actually cost me eighteen thousand six hundred and seventy dollars * to get out of this fight. What it cost Kilrain, I do not know, but on account of my being victor, and having a reputation for "throwing money away," they made me settle in good shape.

---

* Referring to his subsequent arrest and trial "for breaking the laws by fighting in the state of Mississippi."

Daniel Webster, Sportsman

To HIS guns he gave names after the fashion of most old hunters. He had his "Mrs. Patrick," his "Learned Selden," his "Wilmot Proviso," and several others. His trout rod, with which he used to fish about Sandwich and Marshfield Rivers, was "Old Killall," made for him by the notorious John Trout. It was with this rod in his hand, as he waded Marshfield River, that he composed a portion of his Bunker-Hill oration, as he writes in his biography. His son, Fletcher Webster, remembered the occurrence well.

No one enjoyed the incidents of shooting and fishing more than he. He liked to commune with plain people, living in out-of-the-way places, whom he encountered; and occasionally he would derive more amusement from the men he met than from the fish he caught. His son Fletcher has left the following account of a fishing excursion on the Cape:—

"I was taken along with him, to make trial of a certain brook of which we had heard, but had never visited, the name of which I have forgotten. It was some eight or ten miles from Sandwich. We drove through the pine woods, and at last reached the stream. It ran through an open meadow, near which, on the rising ground, stood the owner's house. My father drove up to the fence, and, finding the occupant there, very civilly asked permission of the old man to fasten his horse for an hour or two. This was readily granted. He knew the man's name, which, I think, was Baker, with whom he commenced a conversation by some trivial remark about the weather, and received a similar reply. As he was preparing his rod and line, the conversation proceeded.

"WEBSTER. 'Well, Mr. Baker, with your leave, we thought we would like to try and take a trout in your brook.'

"BAKER. 'Oh, yes, sir, very welcome to.'

"WEBSTER. 'I have heard that there was very good fishing in it, Mr. Baker.'

"BAKER. 'Well, a good many folks have been here, and taken a good many trout out sometimes.'

"WEBSTER. 'We must try and see what we can do this morning. Where do they usually begin to fish?'

"BAKER. 'Oh, I'll show you.'

"The old man accompanied my father to the brook, and pointed out the spot. It was where the brook was thickly overhung with alders, and the ground was very miry. Father sank into the mud half-way up his leg.

"WEBSTER. 'Rather miry here, Mr. Baker.'

"BAKER. 'Yes, that's the worst on't.'

"After throwing several times, and catching his hook in the alders:—

From *Reminiscences and Anecdotes of Daniel Webster,* by Peter Harvey, pp. 283–285, 292–293. Entered according to Act of Congress, in the year 1877, by Little, Brown, and Company, in the Office of the Librarian of Congress, at Washington. Boston.

"WEBSTER. 'These alders are rather in the way, Mr. Baker.'

"BAKER. 'I know it. That's the worst on't.'

"The mosquitoes now began to bite most annoyingly: one hand was busy all the time slapping them off the face and the other hand.

"WEBSTER. 'These mosquitoes are pretty thick and very hungry, Mr. Baker.'

"BAKER. 'I know it. That's the worst on't.'

"Now the heat in the low ground, without a breath of air, had become intense. My father wiped his forehead and rested a moment.

"WEBSTER. 'It is very hot down here in these bushes, Mr. Baker.'

"BAKER. 'I know it. That's the worst on't.'

"My father resumed his fishing, and after an hour's struggle with the heat, the bushes, the mire, and the mosquitoes:—

"WEBSTER. 'There seem to be no fish here, Mr. Baker.'

"BAKER. 'I know it. That's the worst on't.'

"There was no resisting this. My father put up his rod and departed; but he laughed all the way home at the 'worst on't,' and always took pleasure in recalling the occurrence to mind."

* * * * *

Soon after Mr. Webster went to Marshfield, he was one day out on the marshes, shooting birds. It was in the month of August, when the farmers were securing their salt hay. He came, in the course of his rambles, to the Green Harbor River, which he wished to cross. He beckoned to one of the men on the opposite bank to take him over in his boat, which lay moored in sight. The man at once left his work, came over, and paddled Mr. Webster across the stream. He declined the payment offered him, but lingered a moment, with Yankee curiosity, to question the stranger. He surmised who Mr. Webster was, and with some hesitation remarked:—

"This is Daniel Webster, I believe."

"That is my name," replied the sportsman.

"Well, now," said the farmer, "I am told that you can make from three to five dollars a day, pleadin' cases up in Boston."

Mr. Webster replied that he was sometimes so fortunate as to receive that amount for his services.

"Well, now," returned the rustic, "it seems to me, I declare, if I could get as much in the city, pleadin' law cases, I would not be a-wadin' over these marshes this hot weather, shootin' little birds!"

The Enigma of Silent Cal

"You Got to be Mighty Careful" [1]

"How does it feel to be President of the United States?"

He weighed the question for nearly a quarter of a minute.

[1] From *Yankee Lawyer,* The Autobiography of Ephraim Tutt, [by Arthur Train], pp. 306–309. Copyright, 1943, by Ephraim Tutt. New York: Charles Scribner's Sons.

"Well," he said finally, "you got to be mighty careful."

He was a long way from Windsor County, Vermont, but . . . Cal Coolidge had expressed his entire philosophy in those six words—"You got to be mighty careful!"

* * * * *

It is only to be expected that an effort should have been made for political reasons to gloss over his peculiarities and picture him as a sort of Yankee Will Rogers with a dry wit that showed itself in pithy sayings. Well, I knew Cal for over half a century. I never heard him say anything that I regarded as witty, and many of the remarks that were heralded as examples of Coolidge humor he meant seriously. He had a perverse streak that led him to do and say eccentric things which he did not intend to be funny at all. I think the truth of the matter to be that he was a thin-lipped, cautious New Englander, and since the Americans as a whole did not understand him they had to invent another and somewhat more appealing figure. I sat near him that night at the Gridiron Club dinner and for two hours he neither cracked a smile nor uttered a word. He did not enjoy the jokes at his expense and on the way back to the White House he remarked that "all that tomfoolery" was a waste of money.

* * * * *

. . . These [White House] breakfasts were so notoriously dismal that those who were invited would resort to every imaginable excuse to avoid coming. In one instance eight senators declined in a row. I found out afterwards that a meal at which a public official had been a guest could be charged to "public entertaining." Cal was certainly economical. During his incumbency the White House bought the supplies for its kitchen and pantry from the Piggly-Wiggly and Sanitary Grocery Chain.

I never could tell whether economy or eccentricity was the controlling element in some of his acts. For example, he never allowed any one to sit in the same automobile with him when he went to church. . . . Did Cal wish to savor his importance by riding in solitary state? It seems hardly likely. Did he consider that the White House chauffeurs had too easy a time? Possibly. Or did he regard the garage and its contents as something which he was entitled to use and wished to make the most of the privilege while it lasted? Probably a mixture of all three or some other mysterious factor of which he was unaware himself. Did he perhaps in small ways like to exercise power, as when, pointing to the Stuart portrait of John Adams which he could see from the state dining room as it hung on the wall of the Red Room, he said, according to Ike Hoover: "I'm tired of seeing that old bald head. Have some hair put on it." *

Ike told me that out in South Dakota near the presidential lodge among the Black Hills the local inhabitants released fifteen hundred trout in the stream nearby, keeping them within bounds with nets. Cal fished with

---

* In point of fact the picture was touched up with turpentine so that it did look as if it had some hair.—E. T.

worms, but he wore white gloves and the hook was baited and the fish grudgingly removed by the secret service men. Once a stranger caught some trout just in front of the Coolidge Camp. Cal sent one of the men to take them away from him, saying: "They are my fish." Grace made such fun of his wearing the white gloves that he eventually replaced them with a darker shade. Whether he fished because the trout were there and he thought he might as well have them, or because it seemed like good publicity, I don't know.

Cal may have been too careful. He had been president six years and there was the threat of a third term issue being raised if he ran in 1928, but he was canny enough to know, as William Allen White had said, that he represented "something definite in the American heart." I am aware of the strong evidence that has been adduced to prove that, when he issued his statement in August, 1927, "I do not choose to run for president in 1928," he had made up his mind not to do so.* But with my knowledge of his character I am personally of the opinion that he chose his words carefully to see what the reaction would be and never really intended his declaration to be taken as it was. It was in the nature of a "trial balloon." I believe that he was bitterly disappointed at the result, for he was the logical Republican candidate; and that in the end he was humiliated and angry at not being re-nominated and would not have been disturbed had Hoover lost the election.

His Apparent Irrelevance

. . . The Yankee is deeply appreciative of human shortcomings, but he often deceives the stranger by the apparent gravity of his remarks. Since the stranger does not understand the workings of the Yankee's mind, he fails to follow him, and hence does not recognize his apparently irrelevant remark as a humorous criticism. I believe President Coolidge to be a true Yankee in this respect. A recent writer in a popular magazine, I think, completely underestimates the humorous undercurrent of Mr. Coolidge's thinking. He certainly is not stupid, as this writer implies. You may recall the incident of the Pennsylvania senator and the "rubbers." After the senator's earnest and somewhat lengthy statement of a plea for some local cause, the President is reported to have observed his visitor's wet shoes, and instead of uttering the expected opinion on the issue to have remarked that he *ought not to be out without rubbers on a day like this.* From my own experience with New Englanders I should have taken this as my *answer.* Analyzed, the President's mind may have worked in this fashion: "This man is very amusing. He is asking my aid on a matter that

* See Cyril Clemens and Athern P. Daggett, "Coolidge's 'I Do Not Choose to Run': Granite or Putty?", *The New England Quarterly,* Vol. XVIII (June, 1945), No. 2, pp. 147–163.

[2] From "Maine Dialect," by E. K. Maxfield, *American Speech,* Vol. II (November, 1926), No. 2, p. 82.

is really trifling, quite beneath my attention. He hasn't even sense enough to wear rubbers. I can't do anything about his petition. His lack of judgment in coming to me is expressed by his failure to keep his feet dry." Hence the remark which the magazine editor explains as "slow" thinking. I think a Northern Yankee would have seen the point.

His Silence [3]

Known very favorably as Silent Cal, Coolidge said nothing publicly because of one of two possible reasons: Either he had no ideas on public affairs, which seems reasonable; or he was too timid to voice them. But in private Coolidge was garrulity itself. Philip Parrish, newspaperman of Portland, Oregon, once went to what he fondly thought would be an interview with President Coolidge, but for two hours Mr. Parrish was harangued on everything from trout fishing to the cost of cigars and, though he tried diligently, never once managed to get in a question.

His Laconic Style [4]

Now and then in our time the humor of New England will hint of some dour ancestral strain, when it becomes sharp and cold as a frost-etching on a window pane. Calvin Coolidge had more than a little of this harsh wit. During his governorship he spoke one day in a tent near Pittsfield, campaigning for Congressman Treadway. An old lady came up to him afterwards and said tremulously, "I came fifty miles to hear you, Mr. Coolidge, and I stood up all through your speech."

"So did I," said Mr. Coolidge.

Many anecdotes widely quoted as examples of New England humor were never humorously intended. They are bits of wisdom compressed into epigram, the fruit of solitary meditation behind the plow. Mr. Coolidge shared with other Vermonters this trick of condensation in clipt dialect. Dwight Morrow told me two such bits of Coolidgeana. He overheard his son-in-law urging the President to go up in a plane. "Why, Mr. President," urged Colonel Lindbergh, "it's the safest mode of passenger transportation! In two hundred thousand passenger miles only one casualty."

"Very little comfort for the casualty," said Mr. Coolidge.

Dwight said that he was spending a week end at the White House and on Sunday morning called across the hall from his bedroom, "Cal, what time is church?"

The answer came back, "E-leven o'clock."

"What time do we start?"

"Seven minutes to e-leven from upstairs."

---

[3] From *Lost Men of American History,* by Stewart H. Holbrook, p. 338 n. Copyright, 1946, by Stewart H. Holbrook. New York: The Macmillan Company.

[4] From *As Much As I Dare,* A Personal Recollection, by Burges Johnson, pp. 30–31. Copyright, 1944, by Ives Washburn, Inc. New York.

One might pleasantly remember his reply, delivered in the [Massachusetts] House, to a colleague dissimilarly minded upon a bill under discussion, a colleague who spoke windily and at length, prefacing each period and each argument with the affirmative statement, "It is." Calvin, when he had risen to refute, had said, clearly but dejectedly, as though the talk had wearied him: "Mr. Speaker: It isn't"—and had sat down.[5]

A prominent Washington society woman was sitting next to the President at a smart party.

"Oh, Mr. President," she said gushingly, "you are so silent. I made a bet to-day that I could get more than two words out of you."

"You lose," the President replied.[6]

Mrs. Coolidge says that her husband presented her with an old brown bag when they returned from their wedding trip. In it were fifty-two pairs of socks with holes in them.

"Calvin Coolidge!" she exclaimed. "Did you marry me to get your socks darned?"

"No—but I find it mighty handy," he said.

When they moved to a place of their own, Mrs. Coolidge bought a book called *Our Home Doctor*. It would be a good thing, she thought, to have around, with a new baby in the house. But she knew that she might be reproved for her extravagance, so she left it on the table in the sitting room, and waited for her husband to say something. A few days later she noticed a paper in it:

"Don't see any receipt here for curing suckers," she read. "C. C."

There are a hundred anecdotes that newspaper people tell about Coolidge and his mean ways. There is one about two reporters who went to his room in the Parker House, and found Tom W. there. Coolidge unlocked a bureau drawer, and produced a pint of Rye, and poured them each a drink. Tom sat on the side of the bed, and didn't get one.

"You forgot Tom," said one of them.

"Tom's had his," said the Governor, and put the bottle back where it came from. . . . So, with much retelling, the legends live. But few tell the truth about the man, and all his grim and ancient virtues.

For fourteen years, Coolidge commuted in a day coach from Northampton to Boston, which is about a hundred miles. On Saturday nights when

---

[5] From *The Legend of Calvin Coolidge,* by Cameron Rogers, p. 129. Copyright, 1928, by Doubleday, Doran & Company. Garden City, New York.

[6] From *Coolidge Wit and Wisdom,* 125 Short Stories about "Cal," compiled by John Hiram McKee, p. 43. Copyright, 1933, by John Hiram McKee. New York: Frederick A. Stokes Company.

the Governor went home for supper, they had baked beans and brown bread, and Mrs. Coolidge often cooked a ham for Sunday.

Years later, Coolidge exclaimed, "Those White House hams! They worried me. A big one would be brought to the table. Mummer would have a slice, and I'd have a slice. Then the butler would take it away, and what happened to it after that, I never found out."

One night there was a State dinner at the White House, and the President went to the kitchen for a look around.

"Don't see why we have to have six hams," he said.

"But, Mr. President, there will be sixty people," explained the housekeeper. "And Virginia hams are so small! We can't serve more than ten people with one ham."

"Seems an awful lot of ham to me," muttered the President.

Shortly after this, the housekeeper departed. And the Coolidges sent to Boston for Ellen Riley—a New Englander.

"Wilful waste," said Miss Riley, "makes woeful want"—and she made a nice pea soup on a ham bone.[7]

On a certain Sunday morning Mrs. Coolidge did not accompany her husband to church. Upon his return she asked:

"Hear a good sermon?"

"Yes."

"What did the minister preach about?"

"Sin."

"What did he have to say about it?"

"He's agin it."

The story goes that on the occasion of his first meeting President Calvin Coolidge, Will Rogers offered to wager that he could make the President laugh. His friends were willing to let him try it, but were doubtful of his success.

"Mr. President, this is Mr. Rogers, Will Rogers."

Mr. Rogers took the hand of the President quietly, and looking him in the eye, said, "What is the name, please?"

One of the Washington correspondents attempted to sound President Coolidge on the subject of prohibition.

"Instead of answering your question, I'll tell you a story," countered the President.

---

[7] From *A New England Sampler*, by Eleanor Early, pp. 282–283, 292–293. Copyright, 1940, by Waverly House. Boston.

"Frankie dropped in to tell his mother that he was going to his uncle's house for dinner.

" 'I suppose Mary is also going,' said his mother, referring to a grown-up cousin.

"Frankie evidently thought the question too personal, for, after a moment of deep thought, he replied: 'I don't know; I just go round minding my own business.' "[8]

He had been asked to plant a tree in honor of something-or-other. Surrounded by the general staff and the entire diplomatic corps, he perfunctorily turned over the sod with a golden trowel and stood back bored, while the seedling was imbedded. All looked towards the President, including the massed bands of the Army and Navy, waiting until he should make his speech of dedication. Nothing happened: Cal just stood there in stony silence. At length, when the situation had become awkward, Chief Justice Taft stepped to his side and whispered:

"Please say a few words, Mr. President!"

Cal puckered his mouth. Looking down his nose at the upturned earth he remarked solemnly:

"That's a good angleworm!"[9]

At one of the White House press conferences various reporters were vainly firing their questions at Calvin Coolidge.

"Have you anything to say about Prohibition?"

"No."

"Have you anything to say about the World Court?"

"No."

"About the farm situation?"

"No."

"About the forthcoming senatorial campaign?"

"No."

The meeting broke up and the reporters began to file out of the room.

"And," called the President, "don't quote me."[10]

---

[8] From *Master Book of Humorous Illustrations,* Compiled and Edited by Leewin B. Williams, pp. 90–91. Copyright. 1938, by Whitmore & Smith. Nashville: Abingdon-Cokesbury Press.

[9] From *Yankee Lawyer,* The Autobiography of Ephraim Tutt (by Arthur Train), p. 7. Copyright, 1943, by Ephraim Tutt. New York: Charles Scribner's Sons.

[10] From *Thesaurus of Anecdotes,* A New Classified Collection of the Best Anecdotes from Ancient Times to the Present Day, edited by Edmund Fuller, pp. 25. Copyright, 1942, by Crown Publishers. New York.

"Kitty": Yankee Pedagogue

His lectures were the best show in Harvard. For years English 2, Mondays, Wednesdays, and Fridays at 11 a.m., was given in the same classroom on the second floor of old Harvard Hall. Promptly on the hour Professor Kittredge arrived and shut the door; any one who was outside then never got in. A late-comer who opened the door and peeked timidly in met such a withering glare from the platform that he faded away.

Professor Kittredge mounted the platform at once, and began to speak without prelude, beginning where he had left off in the previous lecture. A sound track of his lectures would give no hint of a two-day interval between them. He spoke without notes, pausing now and then to shoot a question at a name taken at random from the class list before him. He rarely got an answer. A few minutes before the end of the period he would turn about, still talking, and collect his green book-bag, his hat and coat. Still talking, he put on his coat, took the hat and bag, and stalked down the aisle. Still talking, he grasped the door knob. With his last syllable he turned the knob, opened the door, and slipped out, and at the same instant the bell rang, announcing the end of the period. His timing was infallible.

His sense of academic etiquette was rigid and his manner was that of a top sergeant. Anybody who coughed during his lecture was banished. He told his classes: "Before the lecture I cough. After the lecture I cough. But during the lecture I do not cough, and neither shall you." Once, however, he did cough halfway through a lecture. He drew himself up, remarked, "I am sorry, gentlemen, I cannot go on," and walked out. He believed that hats should be worn only out of doors, and he used to lurk behind a pillar in the lobby of the Widener Library with his stick and knock them from the heads of the thoughtless.

From the New York *Herald-Tribune.* Reprinted in *Harvard Alumni Bulletin,* Vol. 44 (October 18, 1941), No. 2, p. 59.

In the undergraduate world Mr. Kittredge was one of the figures about whom legends grew, and tales, even as in his once beloved folklore. He was arrogant, he was impatient of dullness and stupidity, he had a temper that could flare, and a tongue that could lash, and—when real need of any sort arose amongst his youngsters—he was the very soul of kindness and help. Shakespeare and Chaucer mean to thousands today something which they could never have meant without his great courses which dealt with them. His books constitute one of his monuments, but his supreme monument is the recollection, in thousands of minds, of those courses, and of a vivid and dynamic —and sometimes redoubtable—figure on the platform.—John Livingston Lowes, *The American Scholar,* Autumn, 1941, cited in *Harvard Alumni Bulletin,* Vol. 44 (October 4, 1941), No. 1, p. 19.

Jane E. Howard, Assistant to the Editor of the *Harvard Alumni Bulletin,* has kindly furnished me with the following list of references to George Lyman Kittredge (1860–1941) in the pages of the *Bulletin:* Vol. 38, pp. 591, 646, 984, 1009; Vol. 39, pp. 145, 188, 275; Vol. 42, pp. 5, 147, 697, 705, 784, 829, 865, 941, 1230; Vol. 43, p. 345; Vol. 44, pp. 18, 22, 23, 60, 313, 381; Vol. 45, pp. 275–278; Vol. 46, p. 274.

He was a terror to candidates for the Doctor of Philosophy degree. In the ordeal of the three-hour oral examination he would floor not only the candidate but the other examiners, his fellow faculty members, with his searching questions on abstruse points. . . .[1]

When he gave his last lecture at Harvard on May 1, 1936, about 300 students crowded Harvard 6. This was perhaps three or four times the enrollment of the course and twice the normal capacity of the room, but his lectures always had been popular (students who were not taking his courses used to drop in often) and Harvard was determined to give him a good send-off. The lecture was on "The Winter's Tale," and the professor went through it as casually as if it were not an occasion. But he did not stroll to the door as usual. He remained on the platform until the bell rang.

"We'll stop here," he said.

A thunder of applause broke and he stood with bowed head for a minute or two. Then he motioned silently for the aisle to be cleared and passed down and out of the door into the Yard.

---

[1] When asked if he was a Ph.D., he would say, "Who could examine me?" or, "I make them." (*Harvard Alumni Bulletin*, Vol. 44, October 4, 1941, p. 23.)

PART THREE

BELIEFS AND CUSTOMS

New England was the child of a superstitious mother.

—SAMUEL ADAMS DRAKE

I stand by the old thought, the old thing, the old place, and the old friend.

—JAMES RUSSELL LOWELL

When questioned, they rarely go further than to say, that they do so because they have been taught that it is right to do it, or because their fathers did so before them: if they add anything to this, it is, that they expect blessings from the observance of the practice, and evils from the neglect.

—EDWARD AUGUSTUS KENDALL

I, Tattaru,
Tell you
To tell Tatterier
That sits by the fire
That Tatterrags is dead.

—A VERMONT INCANTATION

I. THE POWER OF FAITH

Why do you conjure up a thousand frightful monsters to torment yourself, when there are enough of real evils? Some seem to think there is a ghost in every gust of wind. Away with such vain illusions of the imagination. Strange it is that a courage, that never startles at real dangers, should shrink at even the thought of an empty chimera! Signs and omens and prognostics continually fill the mind of some. . . . What power has superstition!

—ROBERT B. THOMAS, The Farmer's Almanack, 1830

Signs! Signs everywhere for the man who knew his acres and their heavens, and one must learn to read them all aright.

—MARION NICHOLL RAWSON

I beleave in ghosts,—only a little,—just enuff to keep up an assortment.—JOSH BILLINGS

There will be Weather this Week tho' I say nothing about it.

—NATHANIEL AMES, Almanack for 1731

1. EVANESCENT CLUES

ALTHOUGH the fairy faith is dead, as Whittier points out, and "never had much hold upon the Yankee mind," superstition will never die. Nor is it conceivable that, like the fairies, it will pack up and leave New England for a more congenial clime. We shall always have superstition because most superstition is the obsolete science of yesterday. Like children's games, which were once the pastimes of adults, signs, warnings, divination, taboos, charms, countercharms, and folk cures are part of the wreckage of culture, which has sunken from a higher to a lower level and been pushed to the periphery of society and to the back of our minds. In the process of downward transmission, superstition, like myth, has decayed, and survives chiefly in scraps of belief concerning good and bad luck.

More than the relics of an earlier stage of culture, superstition also represents a kind of empirical knowledge and prelogical or alogical thinking. While resting its case on faith, superstition likes to adduce evidence of its faith from experience—erroneous observation, hearsay, resemblances mistaken for causes—evidence that proves nothing except that superstition, like myth, sees what it wants to see and believes what it wants to believe.

The evidence of superstition consists of signs and warnings. Whether unusual natural phenomena, visions, or simply intuitions, signs and omens are forewarnings of something that is going to happen or (as in the case of wraiths) a telepathic signal that something has happened. All of us have hunches or a sixth sense, but only a few of us are gifted with "second sight."

The most common signs are weather signs, which survive in rural New England as in other rural areas as a traditional tool of the farmer; but the unpredictability of New England weather gives them special bearing and importance in this region. The weather also dominates the life of seafaring and fishing folk; and the hold of superstition upon sailors and fishermen is explainable in terms of their need of a superior kind of intelligence or wisdom to keep them safe.

> Knowledge and intelligence was theirs; and theirs also that extra sense . . . , call it intuition or instinct or even genius, that subconscious sense or faculty—whatever we care to call it—in sea-born men which makes it safe for them to do the thing that other men say cannot be

On the sea intuition also takes the form of a "nose for fish," the "fisherman's greatest gift," according to Mary Heaton Vorse. Like a nose for fish, weather lore and folk medicine are a synthesis of empirical knowledge and "some evanescent clue" which some men are able to perceive before it is gone.

> done.[1]

2. The Power of Sympathy

Besides mystical faith—faith in intuition—superstition involves the "willing suspension of disbelief that constitutes poetic faith." Superstition is also poetic in its symbolism, its ablity to see a pattern of analogy and sympathy in things apparently unrelated. Analogy—the principle that "like produces like"—is especially notable in folk cures, with its doctrines of "like cures like" and the "hair of the dog that bit you."

An aspect of analogy or sympathy which once played an important part in pseudo-medicine, and which survives in folk rhymes like the one beginning "Monday's child is fair of face," has to do with planetary influences, physiognomy, etc. Many almanacs (not including, however, Robert B. Thomas's *Old Farmer's Almanack*) featured prominently the Man of the Signs—the "figure of a man, surrounded by the twelve Signs of the Zodiac, each referred to some part of his body by means of a connecting line or a pointing dagger," indicating that "Each sign of the zodiac 'governed' an organ or part of the body, and, in selecting a day to treat any ailment, or to let blood, it was necessary to know whether the moon was or was not in that sign." [2]

The Man of the Signs, or the Moon Man, is himself a perfect symbol of the Power of Superstition, which sees a man as determined by mystic influences and tied to the universe by thousands of imperceptible lines radiating this influence. This sympathetic relationship of man and the universe is the ultimate source of the faith, intuition, and analogy of superstition. One of the strongest influences on man is custom. And even among hard-

---

[1] James B. Connolly, *The Book of the Gloucester Fishermen* (New York, 1927), p. 286.

[2] George Lyman Kittredge, *The Old Farmer and His Almanack* (Boston, 1904), p. 54.

headed New Englanders, where superstition is made of sterner stuff than the poetry of fairy faith, folk beliefs survive as folkways or expedients, with a power of custom all the greater because of the strong hold of the past on New England.

B. A. B.

SIGNS AND WARNINGS

St. Elmo's Fire

. . . ABOUT 8 of the clock at night, a flame settled upon the main mast, it was about the bigness of a great Candle, and is called by our Seamen St. *Elmes* fire, it comes before a storm, and is commonly thought to be a Spirit; if two appear they prognosticate safety: These are known to the learned by the names of *Castor* and *Pollux,* to the *Italians* by St. *Nicholas* and St. *Hermes,* by the *Spaniards* called *Corpos Santos.*[1]

. . . Those pale flames that we beheld burning from the spikes of the lightning-rod, I suppose were identical with the St. Elmo's fire that I have since seen described as haunting the spars of ships in thunder-storms. And here I am reminded of a story told by some gentlemen visiting Appledore sixteen or eighteen years ago. They started from Portsmouth for the Shoals in a whaleboat, one evening in summer, with a native Star-Islander, Richard Randall by name, to manage the boat. They had sailed about half the distance, when they were surprised at seeing a large ball of fire, like a rising moon, rolling toward them over the sea from the south. They watched it eagerly as it bore down upon them, and, veering off, went east of them at some little distance, and then passed astern, and there, of course, they expected to lose sight of it; but while they were marvelling and speculating, it altered its course, and suddenly began to near them, coming back upon its track against the wind and steadily following in their wake. This was too much for the native Shoaler. He took off his jacket and turned it inside out to exorcise the fiend, and lo, the apparition most certainly disappeared! We heard the excited account of the strange gentlemen and witnessed the holy horror of the boatman on the occasion; but no one could imagine what had set the globe of fire rolling across the sea. Some one suggested that it might be an exhalation, a phosphorescent light, from the decaying body of some dead fish; but in that case it must have been taken in tow by some living finny creature, else how could

---

[1] From *An Account of Two Voyages to New-England,* Made during the years 1638, 1663, by John Josselyn, Gent., p. 8. Boston, Massachusetts: Published by William Veazie. 1865.

it have sailed straight "into the teeth of the wind"? It was never satisfactorily accounted for, and must remain a mystery.[2]

Death Warnings

THIS allusion to graveyards naturally suggests a bit of folk-lore still current in some out-of-the-way corners. Some women lay claim—and the claim is not restricted to superannuated crones as of old—that no death can occur unless they have had "a warning," as they term it. Exactly what the nature of this warning may be, or how manifested, I have yet to learn; but I do know that full faith is accorded to those professing this gift of second sight. Among seafaring people the belief is also more or less current that a sick person will not die till the tide ebbs.

The Death Watch

FOR more than a hundred years a certain kind of wood tick, which made a curious little drumming sound with its head, added to the superstitious fears of our fathers. It was called the death watch, and though it was often in the walls the sick who heard it felt sure that death was near. But if the sound ceased, everyone made haste to repeat these encouraging words:

> "The omen is broken, the danger is over,
> The insect will die, and the sick will recover."

Telling the Bees

RESPECTING bees, one very old superstition among others is, as I can strictly affirm, still cherished, surviving, apparently, through that peculiarity of the mind which, the event being uncertain, elects to give it the

---

[2] From *Among the Isles of Shoals,* by Celia Thaxter, pp. 136–138. Entered according to Act of Congress, in the year 1873, by James R. Osgood & Co., in the Office of the Librarian of Congress, at Washington. Boston.

From *The Pine-Tree Coast,* by Samuel Adams Drake, p. 112. Copyright, 1890, by Estes & Lauriat. Boston. 1891.

From *In Old South Hadley* by Sophie E. Eastman, p. 30. Copyright, 1912 by Sophie E. Eastman. Chicago: The Blakely Printing Company.

From *A Book of New England Legends and Folk Lore, in Prose and Poetry,* by Samuel Adams Drake, New and Revised Edition, pp. 314–315. Copyright, 1883, 1901, by Samuel Adams Drake. Boston: Little, Brown and Company. 1910.

benefit of the doubt rather than to discard it as a childish and meaningless custom. This is the common belief that bees must be made acquainted with the death of any member of the family, otherwise these intelligent little creatures will either desert the hive in a pet, or leave off working and die inside of it. The old way of doing this was for the goodwife of the house to go and hang the stand of hives with black, the usual symbol of mourning, she at the same time softly humming some doleful tune to herself. Another way was for the master to approach the hives and rap gently upon them. When the bees' attention was thus secured, he would say in a low voice that such or such a person—mentioning the name—was dead. This pretty and touching superstition is the subject of one of Whittier's "Home Ballads."

The Wraith in the Storm

THE number of persons who have testified to having seen the apparitions or death wraiths of dying or deceased friends is already large, as the records of various societies for psychical research bear witness. These phenomena are not in their nature forewarnings of something that is about to happen, but announcements of something that already has happened. They therefore can have no relation to what was formerly known as "second sight."

In spite of all that our much-boasted civilization has done in the way of freeing poor, fallible man from the thraldom of superstition, there is indubitable evidence that a great many people still put faith in direct revelations from the land of spirits. In the course of a quiet chat one evening, where the subject was under discussion, one of the company who had listened attentively, though silently all the while, to all manner of theories, spiced with ridicule, abruptly asked how we would account for the following incident which he went on to relate, and I have here set down word for word:—

"My grandparents," he began, "had a son whom they thought all the world of. From all accounts I guess Tom was about one of the likeliest young fellows that could be scared up in a day's journey. Everybody said Tom was bound to make his mark in the world, and at the time I speak of he seemed in a fair way of doing it, too, for at one and twenty he was first mate of the old *Argonaut* which had just sailed for Calcutta. This would make her tenth voyage. Well, as I am telling you, the very day after the *Argonaut* went to sea, a tremendous gale set in from the eastward. It blew great guns. Actually, now, it seemed as if that gale would never stop blowing.

"As day after day went by, and the storm raged on without intermission,

---

From *The Myths and Fables of To-Day*, by Samuel Adams Drake, pp. 224–228. Boston: Lee and Shepard.

you may judge if the hearts of those who had friends at sea in that ship did not sink down and down with the passing hours. Of course, the old folks could think of nothing else.

"Let me see; it was a good bit ago. Ah, yes; it was on the third or four night of the gale, I don't rightly remember which, and it don't matter much, that grandfather and grandmother were sitting together, as usual, in the old family sitting-room, he poring over the family Bible as he was wont to do in such cases, she knitting and rocking, or pretending to knit, but both full of the one ever present thought, which each was trying so hard to hide from the other.

"Dismally splashed the raindrops against the windowpanes, mournfully the wind whined in the chimney-top, while every now and then the fire would spit and sputter angrily on the hearth, or flare up fitfully when some big gust came roaring down the chimney to fan the embers into a fiercer flame. Then there would be a lull, during which, like an echo of the tempest, the dull and distant booming of the sea was borne to the affrighted listener's ears. But nothing I could say would begin to give you an idea of the great gale of 1817.

"Well, the old folks sat there as stiff as two statues, listening to every sound. When a big gust tore over the house and shook it till it rocked again, gran'ther would steal a look at grandmother over his specs, but say never a word. The old lady would give a start, let her hands fall idly upon her lap, sit for a moment as if dazed, and then go on with her knitting again as if her very life depended on it.

"Unable at length to control her feelings, grandmother got up out of her chair, with her work in her hand, went to the window, put aside the curtain, and looked out. I say looked out, for of course all was so pitchdark outside that nothing could be seen, yet there she stood with her white face pressed close to the wet panes, peering out into the night, as if questioning the storm itself of the absent one.

"All at once she drew back from the window with a low cry, saying in a broken voice: 'My God, father, it's Tom in his coffin! They're bringing him up here, to the house.' Then she covered her face with her hands, to shut out the horrid sight.

" 'Set down 'Mandy!' sternly commanded the startled old man. 'Don't be making a fool of yourself. Don't ye know tain't no sech a thing what you're sayin'? Set down, I say, this minnit!'

"But no one could ever convince grandmother that she had not actually seen, with her own eyes, her dear boy Tom, the idol of her heart, lying cold in death. To her indeed it was a revelation from the tomb, for the ship in which Tom had sailed was never heard from."

The Girl in the Fog

Captain Cook would tell stories of wrecks and rescues and legends. One was the story of the coast guard who, when on his rounds, saw a girl "loomin' out of the fog." He was surprised to see anyone so far from the town. The next night he was on patrol he met her once again. This time she seemed so beautiful he realized that he had fallen in love with her and begged her to meet him again. She smiled at him in a dubious fashion and answered,

"I'll meet you again, soon," and vanished in the fog.

Within a few nights there was a wreck of a Portuguese vessel from the Western Islands. There, on the deck, a child in her arms, was the girl whom he had met in the fog. She recognized him and waved to him.

As the surfboat came alongside "on the heave of the wave," she threw the child to him. Then she jumped, but missed the boat and was swirled away in the churning sea. Then he realized that it had been her spirit he had seen and that she had given him the child in trust. The child proved to be an orphan and he adopted the little girl and brought her up.

The Black Newfoundland Dog

Fog imperils the vessels as well as the dories. Most Provincetown trawl-fishermen can tell you the story of the black Newfoundland dog.

Old "Cheeny" Marshall, who was drowned on the banks when his dory capsized in April, 1937, told this story to me. Cheeny was just a boy, a "salt-passer" on one of the old hand-liners, when—so help him God! it happened.

The vessel is well out to sea, off Newfoundland. She has not sighted a sail all day, when suddenly, out of a sea calm and smooth as an oil slick, up pops the great black dog. Cheeny lifts him over the rail and lets him lie, half dead, on the deck. The dog has webbed feet.

"Heave him overboard!" shouts one old-timer. "He's the divil!"

But the lad pleads for him, keeps him, takes care of him, puts him in his own bunk. And finally comes the day when the "soup" settles thick over the Devil's Graveyard, in the Bay of Fundy. The helmsman is steering blindly. The dog, standing in the bow, suddenly barks a warning. The

---

From *Time and the Town,* A Provincetown Chronicle, by Mary Heaton Vorse, p. 57. Copyright, 1942, by Mary Heaton Vorse. New York: The Dial Press.

From *Cape Cod Pilot,* by Jeremiah Digges, with Editorial and Research Assistance of the Members of the Federal Writers' Project, pp. 239–240. American Guide Series, Federal Writers' Project, Works Progress Administration for the State of Massachusetts. Copyright, 1937, by Poor Richard Associates. Provincetown and New York: Modern Pilgrim Press and the Viking Press.

helmsman—Cheeny Marshall himself—puts her hard over. And the vessel veers in time to clear by inches the massive bows of a steamer looming out of the mist! It happened, Cheeny Marshall assured me over and over—so help him God!

The Haunted Ship

As REGARDS haunted ships, the following incident, taken down as literally as I could transcribe it at the time, from the lips of a seafaring friend, speaks for itself:—

"'Twas some dozen year ago, may be less, may be more—beats all how time travels when you've turned the half-century post—I was aboard of the old *Paul Pry*—queer name, now, warn't it? We was a lyin' in Havana harbor, all snug, about a mile from shore. Well, the mate he was on watch. In port, you know, ships always keep slack watch. Our'n was light, nothin' in her, hold all swep' out clean that very day, 'cause we was to begin takin' in sugar and molasses in the mornin'. All hands were off in the ship's boat visitin' another ship—all 'cept the steward. The old man, he was ashore.

"I'm slow, but you just hold your hosses. All to once't the mate thought he heern somebody walkin' back'ards and for'ards plumb down in the hold. He walked to the open hatch and called down, 'Who's there?' No answer. He listened. No sound. Thinkin' it might possibly have been the steward getting his firewood, the mate went for'ard to the steward's room to see if it was so, and found him fast asleep in his bunk. That settled it. Nobody aboard but them two.

"The mate he said nothin' to nobody, but got a lantern and slipped quietly down the ladder into the hold, determined to find out who was skylarkin' there, for I tell you the mate he was a game one all the time, and don't you b'leeve he warn't!

"He hunted high and low, from the forepeak to the run, but not a soul was to be seen anywhere; but just as soon as he stood still he would hear those myster'ous footsteps go trampin' fore and aft, fore and aft, as plain as day, right by him, where he stood.

"By this time the mate had got pretty well worked up, I want you to know, so he just gin one kinder skeered look around him, and then hustled himself off up that ladder just a leetle mite faster than he came down, wonderin' to himself what it all could mean, and thinkin' all sorts of things to once't.

"Then he went and woke up the steward, and both on 'em went and listened fust at one hatch, then at t'other, and sure enough that consarned tramp, tramp, tramp, was a-goin' on agin just the same as before. Then

---

From *The Myths and Fables of To-day*, by Samuel Adams Drake, pp. 188–191. Boston: Lee and Shepard.

they pulled on the hatches. But, Lor' bless you, it warn't no use. Them critters down below had the bulge on 'em every time.

"The mate he said nothin' 'cept to the old man, who looked as black as a new-painted deadeye with the lanyards unrove when he heerd it; but somehow it leaked out among the crew before we sailed, and one or two ran away and laid low till the ship was clean out of the harbor.

"It was gen'lly b'leeved fore and aft that them there footsteps was a warnin'. Hows'ever, the thing quieted down some in a day or two, so nothin' more was heerd of the walkin' match down below; but on the third day out, I think it was, we was struck by one of them northers, and in spite of all we could do we was drove ashore on a reef off the Bermudys, where the *Paul Pry* brought up all standin', and there she left her old bones. The wreckers they came and took off the crew, and fetched 'em all safe into Nassau. Now if that ship warn't haunted, I miss my guess. You can't most always tell about them things, I know; but ef it was skylarkin', all I've got to say is, it was a purty neat job, and don't you forget it."

The Cradle Will Rock

"My aunt, Lois Toothacre, that lives down by Middle Bay," said Miss Ruey, "used to tell about a dreadful blow they had once in time of the equinoctial storm,—and what was remarkable, she insisted that she heard a baby cryin' out in the storm—she heard it just as plain as could be."

"Laws a-mercy," said Mrs. Pennel, nervously, "it was nothing but the wind,—it always screeches like a child crying; or maybe it was the seals; seals will cry just like babes."

"So they told her,—but no; she insisted she knew the difference,—it *was* a baby. Well, what do you think, when the storm cleared off, they found a baby's cradle washed ashore sure enough!"

"But they did n't find any baby," said Mrs. Pennel, nervously.

"No, they searched the beach far and near, and that cradle was all they found. Aunt Lois took it in—it was a very good cradle, and she took it to use, but every time there came up a gale, that ar cradle would rock, rock, jist as if somebody was a-sittin' by it; and you could stand across the room and see there wa' n't nobody there."

"You make me all of a shiver," said Mrs. Pennel.

This, of course, was just what Miss Ruey intended, and she went on:—

"Wal', you see they kind o' got used to it—they found there wa' n't no harm come of its rockin', and so they didn't mind; but Aunt Lois had a sister Cerinthy that was a weakly girl, and had the janders. Cerinthy was one of the sort that 's born with veils over their faces, and can see

---

From *The Pearl of Orr's Island, A Story of the Coast of Maine,* by Harriet Beecher Stowe, pp. 47–49. Copyright, 1862, and 1890, by Harriet Beecher Stowe. Boston and New York: Houghton, Mifflin and Company. 1891.

sperits; and one time Cerinthy was a-visitin' Lois after her second baby was born, and there came up a blow, and Cerinthy comes out of the keepin'-room, where the cradle was a-standin', and says, 'Sister,' says she, 'who's that woman sittin' rockin' the cradle?' and Aunt Lois says she, 'Why, there a'n't nobody. That ar cradle always will rock in a gale, but I've got used to it, and don't mind it.' 'Well,' says Cerinthy, 'jist as true as you live, I jist saw a woman with a silk gown on, and long black hair a-hangin' down, and her face was pale as a sheet, sittin' rockin' that ar cradle, and she looked round at me with her great black eyes kind o' mournful and wishful, and then she stooped down over the cradle.' 'Well,' says Lois, 'I a'n't goin' to have no such doin's in my house,' and she went right in and took up the baby, and the very next day she jist had the cradle split up for kindlin'; and that night, if you 'll believe, when they was a-burnin' of it, they heard, jist as plain as could be, a baby scream, scream, screamin' round the house; but after that they never heard it no more."

The Dead Ship of Harpswell

AT TIMES the fisher-folk of Maine are startled to see the form of a ship, with gaunt timbers showing through planks, like lean limbs through rents in a pauper's garb, float shoreward in the sunset. She is a ship of ancient build, with tall masts and sails of majestic spread, all torn; but what is her name, her port, her flag, what harbor she is trying to make, no man can tell, for on her deck no sailor has ever been seen to run up colors or heard to answer a hail. Be it in calm or storm, in-come or ebb of tide, the ship holds her way until she almost touches shore.

There is no creak of spars or whine of cordage, no spray at the bow, no ripple at the stern—no voice, and no figure to utter one. As she nears the rocks she pauses, then, as if impelled by a contrary current, floats rudder foremost off to sea, and vanishes in twilight. Harpswell is her favorite cruising ground, and her appearance there sets many heads to shaking, for while it is not inevitable that ill luck follows her visits, it has been seen that burial-boats have sometimes had occasion to cross the harbor soon after them, and that they were obliged by wind or tide or current to follow her course on leaving the wharf.[1]

. . . Many years ago, so we read, a tea-clipper homeward bound for Wiscasset was nearing the coast after dark. There was no fog and the lights of approaching vessels could easily be seen. The man on lookout felt no uneasiness at his post when suddenly as if out of nowhere, without

[1] From *Myths & Legends of Our Own Land*, by Charles M. Skinner, Vol. I, pp. 190–191. Copyright, 1896, by J. B. Lippincott Company. Philadelphia & London.

any warning of bells or lights, the sharp bow of a full rigged ship loomed up hardly a ship-length in front.

"Hey! what the blazes are you trying to do?" roared the mate, enraged at this unheard of violation of the right of way. But no voice answered his challenge and without any sign of life on board the ghostly ship swung by with all her sails set to a spanking breeze. She bore directly across the bow of the clipper which just grazed her stern in passing.

"There's something rotten on board there," said the mate.

"Aye," said the Captain, "there's something rotten there right enough. Swing your helm to port and get after her," he ordered.

"Aye, aye, sir," came the response of the helmsman as he changed his course to follow the strange craft only to see it mysteriously disappear, a misty shape in the night.

"The Phantom Ship," muttered the crew as, chilled with fear, they scurried for home away from the ghastly spot.[2]

Rooster Talk

In one of the old New England towns there lived in days of yore a youth named William Smith. William lived at the lower end of the chief village street. Near the upper end of the same street lived a young woman with whose charms William was so smitten that his calls on her were not only frequent but protracted.

One night when he had made one of these calls, he sought his home at the magic hour when, in such towns as had steeple clocks, the bells tolled twelve. William had not gone down the street far when he was startled by the crow of a rooster. But the remarkable thing was that he clearly detected beneath its rough notes these words, "The woman rules here." There was no doubt about what the rooster said, for it immediately repeated the words, and even more clearly, "The woman rules here."

While William walked along pondering this strange statement, he heard the voice of a second rooster at the next house below. It said, "The man rules here. The man rules here."

It was plain to William that he was being let into some of the family secrets of the village. All through the street the roosters greeted him as he passed along. At some of the houses it was the man that was chief, at some the woman. William certainly had food for reflection, but it is not related that he ever made any use of this knowledge which came to him so strangely.

---

[2] From *I Discover Maine,* Little-Known Stories about a Well-Known State, by Herbert G. Jones, pp. 61–62. Copyright, 1937, by Curtis Stuart Laughlin. Portland: The Machigonne Press.

From *What They Say in New England,* A Book of Signs, Sayings, and Superstitions, collected by Clifton Johnson, pp. 253–254. Copyright, 1896, by Lee and Shepard. Boston.

In this connection I may mention that some say if you listen to roosters calling back and forth you can hear this conversation.

Rooster at first house. "The women rule here."

Rooster at second house. "And so they do here."

Rooster at third house. "And so they do everywhere."

A grown person, when a rooster crows, will sometimes imitate its call, and work a child's name into the sound. Then he says to the child, "Didn't you hear the rooster calling you?"

The Accusing Ghost

. . . THE old-time, respectable ghost of our fathers, . . . like the ghost in Hamlet, made his unwelcome appearance only to subserve the ends of justice. This practical generation hardly realizes, we think, how lately the ghost was accepted in that character, or how trustworthy his evidence was deemed by the purveyors of public intelligence. On turning over the files of the *New England Weekly Journal* of December 1, 1729, we came across the following ghost story, here reproduced *verbatim:*—

"Last week, one belonging to Ipswich came to Boston and related that some time since he was at Canso in Nova Scotia, and that on a certain day there appeared to him an apparition in blood and wounds, and told him that at such a time and place, mentioning both, he was barbarously murdered by one, who was at Rhode Island, and desired him to go to the said person and charge him with the said murder, and prosecute him therefor, naming several circumstances relating to the murder; and that since his arrival from Canso to Ipswich the said apparition had appeared to him again, and urged him immediately to prosecute the said affair. The abovesaid person having related the matter was advised and encouraged to go to Rhode Island and engage therein, and he accordingly set out for that place on Thursday last." [1]

The Dark Day

THE 19th of May, 1780, was a remarkable dark day. Candles were lighted in many houses; the birds were silent and disappeared, and the fowls retired to roost. The legislature of Connecticut was then in session at Hartford. A very general opinion prevailed, that the day of judgment was at

---

From *The Myths and Fables of To-day,* by Samuel Adams Drake, pp. 202–204. Copyright, 1900, by Samuel Adams Drake. Boston: Lee and Shepard.

[1] The rule, as laid down by Cotton Mather in *More Wonders* was this: "When there has been a murder committed, an apparition of the slain party accusing of any man, although such apparitions have oftener spoke true than false, is not enough to convict the man of that murder; but yet it is a sufficient occasion for Magistrates to make a particular inquiry," etc.—S. A. D.

hand. The House of Representatives, being unable to transact their business, adjourned. A proposal to adjourn the Council was under consideration. When the opinion of Colonel Davenport was asked, he answered, "I am against an adjournment. The day of judgment is either approaching, or it is not. If it is not, there is no cause for an adjournment; if it is, I choose to be found doing my duty. I wish therefore that candles may be brought." [1]

May 19, 1780.—This was the *dark* day. By ten o'clock, A.M., it had the appearance of night. Pomp, a negro in Medford, became frightened, and, going to his master, said, "Massa, the day of judgment has come: what shall I do?" "Why, Pomp, you'd better wash up clean, and put on your Sunday clothes." Pomp, perceiving that his master was not frightened, began to produce proofs. "Massa, it *has* come; for the hens are all going to roost." "Well, Pomp, they show their sense." "And the tide, massa, in the river, has stopped running." "Well, Pomp, it always does at high water." "But, massa, it feels cold; and this darkness grows more and more." "So much the better, Pomp; for the day of judgment will be all fire and light." Pomp concluded not to wash up, but wait. [2]

LUCK, DIVINATION, AND CONJURATION

The Dream Line

IT WAS the sun-cured salt-fish that was the favorite article of diet in the islanders' households, while very little account was made of the fresh. The young people had some merry customs of their own with it. They represented that if a certain particularly salt strip in the centre, called the "dream line," were eaten before going to bed, the girl or the young man one was to marry would be indicated by appearing in a vision and handing him or her a glass of water.

---

1 Quoted from Timothy Dwight, in *Connecticut Historical Collections,* Containing A General Collection of Interesting Facts, Traditions, Biographical Sketches, Anecdotes, &c., Relating to the History and Antiquities of Every Town in Connecticut, with Geographical Descriptions, by John Warner Barber, p. 407. Entered according to the Act of Congress, in the year 1836, by John W. Barber and A. Willard, in the Clerk's Office, of the District Court of Connecticut. New Haven and Hartford.

2 From *History of the Town of Medford, Middlesex County, Massachusetts,* from Its First Settlement, in 1630, to the Present Time, 1855, by Charles Brooks, pp. 488–489. Boston: Published by James M. Usher. 1855.

From "Fish and Men in the Maine Islands," by W. H. Bishop, in *Harper's New Monthly Magazine,* Vol. LXI, (August, 1880), No. 363, p. 351. Entered according to Act of Congress in the year 1880, by Harper and Brothers, in the Office of the Librarian of Congress at Washington. New York.

Flower Oracles

Here we picked great bunches of yellow-eyed bird-foot violets, or made bouquets of dandelion "curls." Buttercups held under each other's chins usually cast a yellow shadow and proved that we "loved butter." Fortunes were told by means of "white weed" petals, but I could never decide whether "rich man, poor man, beggar man, thief, doctor, lawyer, merchant, chief," referred to four or eight possible husbands, and "chief" in my mind, was always associated with scalplock and tomahawk. When three puffs of breath failed to blow all the tufted seeds from a dandelion globe, the shout arose, "Your mother wants you!" If the drop of juice pressed with thumb nail to the top of one grass stalk "took off" the drop from the one held against it, then your "wish would come true."[1]

. . . There was a love divination by Lilacs which we children solemnly observed. There will occasionally appear a tiny Lilac flower, usually a white Lilac, with five divisions of the petal instead of four—this is a Luck Lilac. This must be solemnly swallowed. If it goes down smoothly, the dabbler in magic cries out, "He loves me"; if she chokes at her floral food, she must say sadly, "He loves me not." I remember once calling out, with gratification and pride, "He loves me!" "Who is he?" said my older companions. "Oh, I didn't know he had to be somebody," I answered in surprise, to be met by derisive laughter at my satisfaction with a lover in general and not in particular. It was a matter of Lilac-luck-etiquette that the lover's name should be pronounced mentally before the petal was swallowed.[2]

Apple Divinations

The following rhyme, used in New England at the beginning of the present century, remains unchanged in a single word, except the omission of the last three lines.

Apples formerly were an essential part of every entertainment in the country; in the winter season, a dish of such always stood on the side-board. As the hours went by, a foaming dish of eggnog would be brought in, always with a red-hot poker inserted, for the purpose of keeping up the proper temperature. It was then that the apple, having been properly

---

[1] From *In Dover on the Charles,* A Contribution to New England Folk-Lore, by Alice J. Jones, p. 37. Copyright, 1906, by Alice J. Jones. Newport, Rhode Island: The Milne Printery.

[2] From *Old Time Gardens,* Newly Set Forth, by Alice Morse Earle, pp. 150–151. Copyright, 1901, by The Macmillan Company. New York and London. 1902.

named, with a fillip of the finger was divided, to decide the fate of the person concerned according to its number of seeds.

One, I love,
Two, I love,
Three, I love, I say,
Four, I love with all my heart,
And five, I cast away;
Six, he loves,
Seven, she loves,
Eight, they both love;
Nine, he comes,
Ten, he tarries,
Eleven, he courts,
Twelve, he marries;
Thirteen wishes,
Fourteen kisses,
All the rest little witches.[1]

It is interesting to note the folk customs of Old England which have lingered here, such as domestic love divinations. The poet Gay wrote:—

I pare this Pippin round and round again,
My shepherd's name to flourish on the plain.
I fling th' unbroken paring o'er my head,
Upon the grass a perfect L. is read.

I have seen New England schoolgirls, scores of times, thus toss an "unbroken paring." An ancient trial of my youth was done with Apple seeds; these were named for various swains, then slightly wetted and stuck on the cheek or forehead, while we chanted:—

"Pippin! Pippin! Paradise!
Tell me where my true love lies!"

The seed that remained longest in place indicated the favored and favoring lover.[2]

Halfway Rock and Other Sacrifice Rocks

From the most remote time, the notion of making propitiatory offerings, either to a beneficent or malevolent power, to insure success in a hazardous adventure, seems to have been common to all peoples in all ages. Thus, among the ancients it was the blind goddess Fortuna who was to be propitiated; with the American Indians it was the evil spirit, Hobomock, whose malevolence was to be turned aside. . . .

On the Sasanoa River, one of the mouths of the Kennebec, in Maine, there is a fine promontory which goes by the name of Hockomock Head, in consequence of the legend related of it by Champlain, to whom, more

[1] From *Games and Songs of American Children,* collected and compared by William Wells Newell, p. 109. Copyright, 1883, 1903, by Harper & Brothers. New York and London.

[2] From *Old Time Gardens,* Newly Set Forth, by Alice Morse Earle, pp. 205–206. Copyright, 1901, by The Macmillan Company. New York and London. 1902.

than to any other writer, we are indebted for a knowledge of the manners and customs of the Aborigines of the New England coast. It should be said that the navigation of the Sasanoa is sometimes rendered difficult, and even dangerous, by the rapidity of its current, its tortuous windings, its eddies, and its falls, not so easily overcome when Champlain ascended it, as to-day. He moreover tells us that each of his Indian guides left an arrow at the bold headland, as an offering to its guardian spirit whose weird name it bears.

* * * * *

Whether the fisherfolk of Marblehead derived any of their superstitious beliefs from the Indians or not, we do not undertake to say. But some three miles out to sea, and midway between Boston Light and Cape Ann, a stark and solitary rock lifts its dingy brown back above the waves, when it is not smothered in foam or shut in by thick fogs. Half-Way Rock is, therefore, a veritable rock of danger. This may, perhaps, explain why fishermen, outward-bound, were long in the habit of tossing copper coins upon this rock, as they passed it, to bring them good luck on the voyage. If this rock did not stand with these rude minds for the symbol of some unseen, elemental power, why not throw their coins anywhere else? [1]

Two Sacrifice Rocks are on the side of the road leading from Plymouth to Sandwich. One of them may be six feet high, and the other four; and both are of ten or twelve feet in length: and they differ in nothing, as to their figure, from the masses of granite and other rock, which are scattered over the surface of all the adjacent country. All that distinguishes them is the crowns of oak and pine branches which they bear, irregularly heaped, and of which some are fresh, some fading, and some decayed. These branches the Indians place there, from motives which they but obscurely explain, and for doing which their white neighbors therefore generally suppose that they have no reason to give. When questioned, they rarely go further than to say, that they do so because they have been taught that it is right to do it, or because their fathers did so before them: if they add anything to this, it is, that they expect blessings from the observance of the practice, and evils from the neglect.

But to whom is this worship offered? To a *manito;* and by *manito,* through the religious prejudices of the whites is usually understood *a devil.* . . .[2]

---

[1] From *A Book of New England Legends and Folk Lore in Prose and Poetry,* by Samuel Adams Drake, pp. 233, 234. Copyright, 1883, 1901, by Samuel Adams Drake. Boston: Little, Brown, and Company. 1910.

[2] From *Travels through the Northern Parts of the United States in the Years 1807 and 1808,* by Edward Augustus Kendall, Esq., Vol. II, pp. 49–50. New York: Printed and Published by I. Riley. 1809.

Sailor's Superstitions

One curious characteristic of the sailors is their faith in superstitions. In particular, they have an ineradicable belief in "Jonahs." A person or thing that causes a poor voyage is a Jonah. If a single new man joins a crew and there is a small catch of fish that cruise, he is a Jonah. One man is known to have hoodooed three schooners thus in a twelve-month. Very strange instances are related of ships "losing their luck" when a certain man sailed on them, and regaining it when he left.

If a cake of ice is accidentally dropped overboard when a vessel is preparing for a fishing trip the voyage will be fortunate; but if the hatch should fall into the hold there will result some dire disaster. Scarcely less serious is the trouble that will follow if, when the hatch is taken off, it is turned bottom up. In such a case there is sure to be a good deal of excitement and apprehension on board.

If you watch a ship out of sight you will never see it again.

It is unlucky to have an umbrella brought on board.

It is unlucky to drive nails on Sunday.

Whistle for a breeze when it is calm; and if you would have the wind fair stick a knife in the after side of the main-mast.

If a bee or a small bird comes on board it brings good luck; but ill luck results when a hawk, owl, or crow alights in the rigging.

A horseshoe nailed to the mast is a protection against witches.

Have nothing to do with a man who comes on board with a black valise, and don't ship with him; for he is sure to be a Jonah.

Sunday sail, never fail,
Friday sail, ill luck and gale.

This last saying has lost much of its old-time influence, and Friday is a not unusual sailing-day if the weather is favorable.

Lucky and Unlucky Ships' Names

Shipmasters are admittedly very superstitious folk. I once knew of a ship being named for a certain well-known cotton mill, because the said mill had always proved a lucky investment to its owners. Another instance came to my knowledge where a master, himself part owner, consulted a clairvoyant, about naming his new ship. When the applicant timidly suggested the name of *Pocahontas,* it was promptly rejected with the remark:

From *Highways and Byways of New England,* including the States of Massachusetts, New Hampshire, Rhode Island, Connecticut, Vermont, and Maine, Written and Illustrated by Clifton Johnson, pp. 166–168. Copyright, 1915, by The Macmillan Company. New York and London. 1916.

"She was nothing but an old Indian woman. What do you want to name your vessel after her for? Call her the *Eagle Wing*." And *Eagle Wing* it was.

By way of reënforcing beliefs of this particular kind, we find a newspaper writer saying, it is supposed in all sincerity, as otherwise his offence would be unpardonable: "Don't let us call any of the new ships for Uncle Sam's navy after the state of Maine. For my part, nothing would induce me to go aboard a new *Maine* or a new *Portland*. Like that watch of Captain Sigsbee, which has gone down into the ocean three times, the last plunge being caused by the explosion of the *Maine*, a superstitious person would prefer to be left at home." Whether or not the navy bureau shall listen to this plea, and change the name proposed for one of the new battleships, we fear that an ineffaceable stigma will hereafter rest upon these two names in the minds not alone of seafaring folk, but of the whole generation to whom the twin horrors which these names recall are so familiar.[1]

It would seem the most natural thing in the world that the vessels engaged in this [ice] traffic should bear such high-sounding and suggestive names as the *Ice-King*, or the *Ice-Monarch*, or even the *Iceberg*, instead of those of their owners, or their owners' wives and daughters, which seem so puerile and commonplace. Speaking of this to a large taker of marine risks, he replied, quite off-hand, that nobody would think of taking a risk on a ship having the word "ice" in any part of its name, because such names are considered unlucky.[2]

Ship Figureheads

You will wonder who was the most noted woodcarver. I should say that it was Joseph True, for his work, more than any of the others has been handed down. He was a particular friend of us both, and we were always welcome visitors with him. It was from him I learned many legends of the sea, many romantic tales which the quaint imagination of the old salts had woven around the relics of the past. He used to say that it was only natural that sailors during the long and tiresome voyages around the Horn or the Cape of Good Hope should attach undue importance to the influence

[1] From *The Myths and Fables of To-day*, by Samuel Adams Drake, pp. 82–83. Copyright, 1900, by Samuel Adams Drake. Boston: Lee and Shepard.

[2] From *The Pine-Tree Coast*, by Samuel Adams Drake, p. 193. Copyright, 1890, by Estes & Lauriat. Boston. 1891.

From *Memories of Old Salem*, Drawn from the Letters of a Great-Grandmother, by Mary Harrod Northend, pp. 86–88. Copyright, 1917, by Moffat, Yard and Company. New York.

which they believed the figureheads exerted on good and bad luck. Indeed some of them went so far as to attribute superhuman qualities to the wooden man or woman that adorned the prow, and woe betide the voyage if the figurehead received damage in any way.

One of the sailors had told him a story of what once happened in the Indian Ocean when the Captain of a full-rigged ship threatened a mutinous crew with a punishment he probably would never dare have inflicted. Those were the days of pirates and the crew, determining to become pirates themselves, had fastened the Captain and first mate into the cabin, but, armed only with knives, they could make little resistance to the fire of muskets opened on them from the cabin windows. Attracting the crew by a well-planned ruse to the starboard side of the vessel, the Captain, carrying a pail of black paint, and a paint brush, rushed from his hiding place toward the bowsprit. Quickly the crew darted after him with eyes blazing and knives uplifted in the sunlight, when, stopping in horror, they saw that the Captain was about to give the beautiful white-draped figure of a woman that surmounted the prow a coat of black paint. Dropping on their knees, they promised submission if only he would relinquish his fatal purpose.

To such tales of the sea we listened, our blood thrilling with excitement, till the old woodcarver, noting our disorder, would calm us by quiet talk. He showed us a bust of the Apostle Paul which he had been asked to make for the ship *St. Paul,* owned by one Stephen Phillips. This bust rode proudly on the prow for many years, when, for some unaccountable reason, probably because in need of repairs, it was removed just before the ship started for Manila. When the sailors discovered their loss they were very uneasy. John Hancock, the second mate, went as far as to say he refused to ship, giving as a reason his premonition that the vessel without its mascot would never return—which proved true. For many years I loved to look at this particular bust. It stood in front of an old shop, but it has recently been removed to other quarters.

They Talk about Fish

LISTEN in to any knot of men talking together on the wharves or loafing on the steps of the bank or congregating to the westward in the Sandbar Club. They talk about one thing—fish. They talk about fish and the prices of fish. They talk about their recent catches, the disasters that are the fate of fishermen. The older men talk of the days of fabulous catches. There are a few among the old men who have been whaling. They are getting as rare as Civil War veterans. There are plenty who've been banking. Many of them who are now dragging or seining or dory fishing have known

From *Time and the Town, A Provincetown Chronicle,* by Mary Heaton Vorse, p. 85. Copyright, 1942, by Mary Heaton Vorse. New York: The Dial Press.

the glorious days of the fresh fishermen, the hundred-foot, two-masted schooners. But whatever form of fishing these men have known, or what vessels they go out in today, they've all gambled their lives for fish and they've all known the adventure of danger.

"Fish are queer people. Don't let anyone tell you different," Captain Kendrick told me. "No one but God can fathom their ways. Take bluefish. Up to 1890 bluefish was a big catch hereabouts. Ain't been none but a sprinklin' sence." Nor to this day have the bluefish ever returned. Some essential food they sought has vanished. Why? No one knows. We are surrounded by mystery when it comes to fish.

So men talk less trivially than elsewhere, if not less bawdily. For when they talk of fish they talk also of life and death and danger and heroism and mystery.

A Nose for Fish

A NOSE for fish is still a fisherman's greatest gift. A captain will sense that there are fish nor'ard and he will up anchor and follow this hunch. A nose for fish is like second sight, or it's perhaps a synthesis of a knowledge of weather, of the habits of fish, of some evanescent clue, come and gone too quickly for a man's brain to record it. Yet it's as real as two times two. Year after year a captain with a nose for fish will come in, his gunwales awash, when his less gifted competitors come in empty.

Fish Lore

FOR a few days every summer the tuna come to Provincetown Harbor and whole boatloads of them are sometimes brought in. Here they are called the "horse-mackerel," and they are in fact a species of mackerel. They weigh from 100 to 1000 pounds.

A trip in the trapboats is exciting when the horse-mackerel are running. To watch one of the men "gaff" a five hundred pounder over the gun'ls, with a quick heave, is worth getting up at any time of night. The fishermen say if you get the blood of the horse-mackerel in a cut, it will poison you. I tried this, but perhaps my hands were too clean. They will tell you, too, of the trapman who saw his great horse-mackerel slipping away from him, stripped off his coat and jumped astraddle, riding the fish around

---

Ibid., pp. 169–170.

From *Cape Cod Pilot,* by Jeremiah Digges, with Editorial and Research Assistance of the Members of the Federal Writers' Project, pp. 243–245. American Guide Series, Federal Writers' Project, Works Progress Administration for the State of Massachusetts. Copyright, 1937, by Poor Richard Associates. Provincetown and New York: Modern Pilgrim Press and the Viking Press.

Provincetown harbor until, like a bronco-buster, he had him tamed, then had a special saddle made for him and carried the mail 'cross-Bay to Boston.[1]

When you buy a fish, look him in the eye. If his gaze is bright and unblurred, he has not been away from home long. If his gills are bright red, that is another sign he is fresh. But if his eye is dull and sunken, he probably has been witnessing the destruction of his race over a long spell in the hold of a beam-trawler. Professional fish buyers will also have a look at what they call the napes, but the eyes and gills will tell you the story.

Cod and haddock are "firm fish," which keep fresh longer than "soft fish," such as whiting or herring. America, great among nations, nevertheless has no sole. Boston calls flounder "lemon-sole," and a hotel calls almost anything "fillet of sole." Usually it is selling you flounder. Fishermen like "yellowtails" better than the more expensive kinds of flounder. They say it isn't so dry. "Black backs" also are flounder, and halibut is one of the same family's rich relatives. Fish dealers say the public "won't take a mackerel west of Pittsburgh," but whiting is popular in the west. Frozen whiting are sent by carloads from Provincetown to St. Louis, for the "fish sandwich" stands in that territory. They used to call it "Jack salmon" out west, until the law intervened in favor of just plain "whiting."

Say "Minister"

THE man with the ear-rings had picked up a piece of shell and was attempting to drop it from the height of his shoulder through a crack in the wharf. He failed to accomplish his purpose though he tried again and again.

"Mr. Klunn, if you want to drop that shell through thar, just mention the minister," advised Cap'n Benson.

He had hardly spoken when Mr. Klunn let the shell fall, and it slipped straight through the crack. "I godfrey!" exclaimed the Cap'n, "I did it for you. I never known that to fail. When I been whaling, and we was cutting up the whale, you couldn't sometimes strike a j'int. You'd try and try and you couldn't strike it, and then you'd stop and say 'Minister!' and it was done already—you'd hit the j'int right off."

[1] Cf. Jeremiah Digges, "Bowleg Bill," in *A Treasury of American Folklore* (New York, 1944), pp. 196–199.

From *New England and Its Neighbors,* written and illustrated by Clifton Johnson, p. 328. Copyright, 1902, by The Macmillan Company. New York and London. 1912.

Passing the Curse

IF YOU know how to "pass a curse," you can get as much free fish as you can eat. All you need do is go to the wharf in Provincetown and ask for it. If the men refuse you, you "pass the curse" on them. Then, the next time they go out, they will get no fish. But it's not quite as simple as it sounds; for you must know the ancient ways of passing curses—plain and fancy—and certainly no fisherman will teach you those.

Clam Bake Ovens Do Not Bake Well Twice

IN RIDING through this picturesque and historic country he had noticed many black clambake holes, or stone ovens, in the same orchards, under the cool trees. He had asked, "Why do the people need more than one clam oven?" and received, as has been shown, the usual answers, that these ovens "do not bake well twice."

Why the Flounder Has a Wry Mouth and Two Colors

THE French fishermen account for the distorted mouth of the flounder by the following legend: St. Christopher, a martyr of the third century, one day took it into his head to bless the fishes and to preach to them. All the inhabitants of the deep came and listened with attention and respect except the flounder, who derided the holy man by making faces at him. The Saint, indignant at the insult, cursed the whole brood, and condemned them forever after to exhibit themselves with mouths awry.

In the course of ages the rebuke thus given by Saint Christopher seems to have wrought a change in the character of the flounder, for a Greek legend, still current at Constantinople, ascribes the discordant color of the two sides of the fish to the fact that when the Turks conquered Constantinople in 1453, some priests at a church near the Silivria gate were frying flounders for dinner just as the Infidels entered the city, and were among the first victims of the massacre. The fish, filled with pious respect for

---

From *Cape Cod Pilot*, by Jeremiah Digges, with Editorial and Research Assistance of the Members of the Federal Writers' Project, p. 242. American Guide Series, Federal Writers' Project, Works Progress Administration for the State of Massachusetts. Copyright, 1937, by Poor Richard Associates. Provincetown and New York: Modern Pilgrim Press and the Viking Press.

From *In Old New England,* The Romance of a Colonial Fireside, by Hezekiah Butterworth, p. 151. Copyright, 1895, by D. Appleton and Company. New York.

From *A Summer Cruise on the Coast of New England,* by Robert Carter, pp. 197–198. Copyright, 1864, by Crosby and Nichols; 1888, by Cupples and Hurd. Boston. Cupples and Hurd, Publishers.

the Church, expressed their horror at the sacrilegious deed by jumping out of the frying-pan into a neighboring stream, whence they made their way to the sea, completely cooked on one side. In token of the miracle, the entire species has ever since exhibited the mark of the fire, generally on the right side; though, now and then, an eccentric individual displays it on the left side.

Snake Lore

"THE way a snake catches birds and frogs and things is not by chasing and grabbing them, but by charming them. It just gets its eyes on their eyes, and runs its tongue out and in, and then the bird can't move if it wanted to. The snake keeps that up a while, and then he can take his own time about doin' the swallerin'. You have to be kind o' careful yourself about not bein' charmed, specially by black snakes. I know there was some of the children out berrying one time, and Sarah Hill came near bein' charmed. They thought she was comin' along all right, when they noticed she warn't with 'em. They ran back then, and Sarah was standin' still lookin' right into a bush. They told her to come along, and she didn't say a word. Then they tried to pull her away; but she said, 'Don't,' because she saw such beautiful sights. Well, there was a black snake in that bush, and she was bein' charmed by it. Little more'n she might a got bit."

When a snake proposes to charm you, it looks you straight in the eye in such a sinister and unwinking way that you are fascinated and paralyzed.

I was told the story of a boy who was charmed one day. His companions found him looking at a snake and making a strange kind of noise. He did not come to himself until they killed the snake, and broke the spell.

An old farmer told me that one morning when he was out mowing his attention was attracted by a bird fluttering around a bush in a queer kind of way. "It was makin' sort of a mournful noise, and flutterin' round and round close to the bush. I went along up to the bush to see what the matter was. Then I see there was an adder in there watching of it, and its nest was in that bush. The snake was charming it; for I no sooner give the bush a little shake and took the snake's attention, than away the bird went as quick as a flash.

"I s'pose most any kind of a snake will charm birds and such things; but I don't s'pose these striped snakes are powerful enough to charm people. Black snakes and rattlers will, though. My uncle got charmed once. He was goin' along through the woods with my father when he stopped and was gettin' left behind. My father called to him to come along; but he didn't pay no attention—just kep' lookin' at somethin'. My

---

From *What They Say in New England, A Book of Signs, Sayings, and Superstitions,* by Clifton Johnson, pp. 96–101, 102–103. Copyright, 1896, by Lee and Shepard. Boston.

father see he was gettin' charmed by a snake. So he went back and give him a yank, and then they killed the snake. He said he wanted to come when father called him, but he couldn't. He said that he saw everything that was pretty,—all the colors he ever thought of and more too, and they seemed to be right in the snake's eyes."

Many still believe that in drinking from brooks one runs the risk of swallowing a young snake, which is liable to grow in the stomach, and become large and troublesome. In support of this idea, it is related that once there was a certain child that took large quantities of food, in particular a great deal of milk, yet became more and more emaciated. One night when the child was sitting at the table with a bowl of milk before it, of which it had not eaten, a great snake put its head out of the child's mouth. Apparently it was hungry, had scented the milk, and came up out of the child's stomach to get it. The child's father was by, and he gripped the snake by the neck, and pulled it out. It was four feet long.

Some say that instead of a bowl of milk on the table, it was a pailful on the kitchen-floor fresh from the cow.

Another telling of the story has it that a woman swallowed the snake. As it grew she was in great distress, so that finally she could not eat. At length her friends laid her down with her stomach on a chair, and put a basin of steaming hot food on the floor before her. That brought out the snake, and the woman got well.

It is bad enough to have a snake in your stomach, but you are even worse off if you meet with one of these hoop-snakes. Let one of those chase you, and you are a goner. They ain't afraid of a man no more'n nothin', and they can run faster'n any horse goin'. The way the snake does is to pick its tail up in its mouth, and then whirl over and over like a hoop. His tail is sharp-pointed and hard like a spike. When he catches up with you, he just takes his tail out of his mouth, and jabs it into you. Oh, I tell you, you'd better swallow a dozen snakes rather'n get one o' these hoop-snakes after you.

It is said that when a hoop-snake strikes a man it "blasts" him. I suppose that means he is paralyzed, turns black, shrivels up, and like enough blows away. When one of these hoop-snakes strikes its tail into anything wooden,—a hoe-handle, for instance,—it shivers the wood into splinters, just as if it had been struck by lightning.

Another snake you want to beware of is the "black racer snake." It is said that he has a bluish tinge, and that he will chase a man whenever he gets sight of one.

* * * * *

"I've hearn 'em tell about how that there was a little girl once that always used to eat her dinner out-doors when it was good weather. She'd get her plate full, and then she'd go off out back o' the barn somewhere, and nobody didn't know what she went off like that for. So after a while her folks followed her; and she went along out there by a stone wall and set down, and she rapped on her plate, and out there come a big rattlesnake, and went to eatin' off the plate with her. And when the snake got over on to her side of the plate too much, she'd rap him with her spoon, and push him away, and say, 'Keep back, Graycoat, on your own side.' Her folks didn't like to have her eatin' with a snake that way, and they sent her off to stay somewhere else. When she was gone, they went and killed the snake. Bimeby the little girl come home again, and then she found out her snake was killed. Arter that she kind o' pined away and died.

"I've hearn 'em tell about that a good many times, and I s'pose that's a pretty true story."

A Letter to the Rats

Conjuring Rats [1]

In New England, as well as in other parts of the United States, it is still believed, by certain persons, that if a house is infested with rats, these can be exiled by the simple process of writing them a letter, in which they are recommended to depart, and make their abode in another locality. The letter should indicate precisely the habitation to which they are assigned, and the road to be taken, and should contain such representations of the advantages of the change as may be supposed to affect the intelligence of the animal in question. This method of freeing a house from its domestic pests is well known, but is commonly regarded as a jest. As in most such cases, however, what is supposed to be mere humor is, in fact, the survival of a perfectly serious and very ancient usage. This custom, still existing in retired places, is illustrated by the following document, the genuineness of which may be relied on.

The country house of a gentleman, whose permanent home was in Boston, being infested by rats, the owner proposed to use poison; but the caretaker, who was in charge of the empty house, represented that there was a better way, namely, to address an epistle to the creatures; he prepared a letter, of which the following is a reproduction.

**** Maine, October 31, 1888

Messrs. Rats and Co.,—Having taken quite a deep interest in your welfare in regard to your winter quarters I thought I would drop you a few lines which might be of some considerable benefit to you in the future seeing that you have pitched your winter quarters at the summer residence of **** No. 1 Seaview Street, I wish to inform you that you will be very much disturbed during cold winter months as I am expecting to be at work through all parts of the house, shall take down ceilings, take up floors,

[1] From "Conjuring Rats," by William Wells Newell, *The Journal of American Folk-Lore,* Vol. V (January–March, 1892), No. XVI, pp. 23–24. Copyright, 1892, by the American Folk-Lore Society. Boston and New York: Houghton, Mifflin and Company.

and clean out every substance that would serve to make you comfortable, likewise there will be nothing left for you to feed on, as I shall remove every eatable substance; so you had better take up your abode elsewhere. I will here refer you to the farm of **** No. 6 Incubator Street, where you will find a splendid cellar well filled with vegetations of (all) kinds besides a shed leading to a barn, with a good supply of grain, where you can live snug and happy. Shall do you no harm if you heed to my advice; but if not, shall employ "Rough on Rats."

Yours, ****

This letter was greased, rolled up, and thrust into the entrance of the rat-holes, in order that it might be duly read, marked, and inwardly digested; the result being, as the owner of the house was assured, that the number of the pests had been considerably diminished.

The reader cannot but admire the persuasive style of the Yankee farmer, and the judicious mixture of argument, blandishment, and terror, exhibited in the document; while in the choice of the barn of a neighbor, recommended as a desirable place of abode, is shown a shrewdness worthy of its reward.

Aunt Weed's Rat Letter [2]

It was found tucked away in a crevice in the cellar wall, after the old house in East Sandwich was "gone in ruins." It was a piece of paper, good old paper made from linen rags, or it would not have remained intact and the writing on it legible after long years in that interstice between granite block and granite block of the potato pit. It was damp, of course, even in that inner cellar far from the bulkhead door; it had been damp even before the roof leaked and the floors began to sag. The piece of paper, apparently a second sheet of a folded over note, had weathered successfully under those unfavorable conditions some forty years' immuration, the last ten of which the house was unoccupied.

Since it has come into possession of Mrs. Leon Currier, the great-great-niece of the Mrs. Abigail Weed who wrote it, it has had a certain local currency as "Emmy's Rat Letter." It now hangs, framed, in Mrs. Currier's parlor. It has for fellows there other relics of old times, an inlaid candle stand, fanback windsors, a Currier and Ives of Lincoln, the most generous flip glass I ever saw, a Washington and Lafayette pitcher in blue and white, a pewter wafer box and a sugar shaker in soft paste Staffordshire known in the family as "Mrs. Phillpotts." It has been widely copied, and it has been photographed, but I cannot discover that any one in recent years has tried the efficacy of its formula by inserting a copy in cellar or chamber

[2] From *New Hampshire Neighbors,* Country Folks and Things in the White Hills, by Cornelius Weygandt, pp. 191–194. Copyright, 1937, by Henry Holt and Company, Inc. New York.

or corn loft. Perhaps they feel that what banished, three generations ago, the gentle creatures of dark mole gray known as black rats, would fail in this day and generation with the predatory brown rats that have supplanted them.

Inasmuch as the exorcism is written with a dearth of punctuation and capitalization, and as it has a word or two of unfamiliar or uncertain meaning, I cannot reproduce it exactly as it was written. I must print it so that its meaning can be followed as it is read, and I must add a little exegesis. It is dated "Sandwich May the 9th 1845." It reads as follows:

"I have bourn with you till my patience is all gone. I cannot find words bad enough to express what I feel, you black devils you are, gnawing our trace corn while we are asleep! And even when we are awake you have the audacity to set your infernal jaws to going. Now, spirits of the bottomless pit, depart from this place with all speed! Look not back! Begone, or you are ruined! If you could know as much as I do, you never would take another thing from here. I will keep nothing to myself. You shall hear the whole. We are preparing water [to] drown you; fire to roast you; cats to catch you; and clubs to maul you. Unless you want your detested garments dyed in fire and brimstone, you satans, quit here and go to Ike Nute's! This is for cellar rats. Please give notice to those in the chamber. There are many of us in the garret plotting against you, when our eyes are open all but one poor female who is affraid of life. But the rest is not affraid I can tell you. There is our bill, and I leve if they get hold of you [you] would think you're in wire cage. A hint to the wise is sufficient. To the bigest and most inventive rat.

Mrs. Weed."

It is necessary, perhaps, to explain that "trace corn" is seed corn bound together in a long string by the plaiting together of the husks turned back from the ears. Twenty such strung ears make a "trace." "Leve" is the old word of the countryside for "believe." The chamber is the low attic over the ell of the one-story house, as the garret is the high attic over the main part of that house. One-story house proper and ell, together with garret and chamber, make the story-and-a-half house typical of New England.

A re-reading of the exorcism tells us the writer is playful as well as earnest. She is making game at the same time that she is half hoping the letter will rid her home of rats. She is laughing at herself for writing the charm and trusting there is enough power in it to induce her to feel the thrill of making magic. Light from her family on her personality and character make clearer, perhaps, certain of the letter's phrases. She was a prim and exact little person who was, as she says in the letter, "affraid of life." Her great-grandniece says she was timorous about everything from mice to tramps. Mistress Abigail lost her husband and returned with her daughter to her childhood's home where she lived with her brothers William and Steven Cogan.

As I read it first I could not but wonder if the hocus-pocus of it was veiled language threatening reprisals against some one who was vilifying the old lady or some of her family. "To the bigest and most inventive rat" would so well suit a fabricator of lies. I have dismissed any such interpretation. I think it is a charm, an exorcism to rid the house of black rats. Written apparently on the back of a sheet from an old letter which was saved, no doubt, because it had little writing on it, for scrap paper, it has not the importance of a document written on unused paper. It is not to be taken too seriously. I say this, not because charms and incantations are taboo to Puritanism. They are not, as the world knows. There was witchcraft in Sandwich, New Hampshire, as well as in Salem, Massachusetts, plenty of it when witchcraft was in season. I say the exorcism is not to be taken too seriously because of the mockery with which it is written. The writer had a sense of humor. She was play-acting in writing it, but many a play-actor has convinced herself that her rôle was real life. I believe that she had by her in some old almanac, that repository of strange odds and ends, some sort of incantation against rats; or that she remembered the phrases of some evangelist tearing into the Devil. I believe she was half satiric, half serious in what she wrote, that it is a mock exorcism as well as an exorcism. It has affiliations with well-known charms, even to those in Anglo-Saxon days. Whatever your interpretation of Aunt Weed's Rat Letter, it drives you to own that there were complexities as well as simplicities in back-country life three generations ago.

It should perhaps be added that it is the tradition of the countryside that the rats did leave the cellar of the old lady's house after she put in it the letter to them, and that they did go, as she exorcised them, to Ike Nute's.

Driving a Witch Out of the Soap

IN LATER years two pounds of potash in dark-colored pieces were purchased at the store and put into the melted fat. This potash was dangerous stuff to handle. A man in Scituate, while breaking some pieces for his wife to use, made a piece fly into his eye and he lost his sight. Into the melted grease the lye was poured a little at a time, some one stirring the hot mass continuously for all one day and a part of the next with a long stick. The stick, usually of apple tree, was a sort of mascot, for good luck in soap making was not at everybody's bidding. Too much or too little lye or some unknown defect would easily spoil the soap. This uncertain behavior gave rise to witch stories, and a certain woman in Beechwood was accused of bewitching people's soap. To drive her out of the soap a black-

From *A Narrative History of the Town of Cohasset, Massachusetts,* by E. Victor Bigelow, p. 234. Copyright, 1898, by E. Victor Bigelow. Published under the Auspices of the Committee on Town History. 1898.

handled butcher knife was once stabbed into the soap, and the soap-maker claimed that it cut off the witch's ear, so that she wore a shawl over her head ever afterwards to conceal the wound.

Shaking the Witches Off

"As to witches," said my uncle Richard, gravely, "I don't know. Whether the denunciations of them in Holy Writ are intended to apply to any actually supernatural power possessed by them, or only to the pretence of it,—and both are mischievous in their effect on the popular mind,—I shall not undertake to say. It is certain that the poor old women who are thus stigmatized seem to have little power to help themselves in this world, or, if real tamperers with the powers of darkness, any enjoyable expectations from the other. But this I do know, that I was riding, not many days since, with my lawyer, a man of considerable acuteness, though a little eccentric at times, coming from K——'s Island, where we had been on some business; and as we neared the turn of the causeway to the main road, he pulled up the chaise, jumped out, and placing himself on a broad flat rock by the road-side, began violently to dance up and down and to shake his clothes. 'Good Heavens!' cried I, 'are you mad?' 'Oh, no,' said he, resuming his seat, 'but my mother always told me, that whenever I was coming away from K——'s Island, I must stand upon that rock and shake the witches off!'"

The Fairies Who Didn't Stay

FAIRY faith is, we may safely say, now dead everywhere,—buried, indeed, —for the mad painter Blake saw the funeral of the last of the little people, and an irreverent English Bishop has sung their requiem. It never had much hold upon the Yankee mind, our superstititions being mostly of a sterner and less poetical kind. The Irish Presbyterians who settled in New Hampshire about the year 1720 brought indeed with them, among other strange matters, potatoes and fairies; but while the former took root and flourished among us, the latter died out, after lingering a few years in a very melancholy and disconsolate way, looking regretfully back to their

From *Old New England Traits,* edited by George Lunt, pp. 167–168. Entered, according to Act of Congress, in the year 1873, by George Lunt, in the Office of the Librarian of Congress, at Washington. New York: Hurd and Houghton. Cambridge: The Riverside Press.

From *Prose Works of John Greenleaf Whittier,* Vol. II, pp. 237–240. Entered according to Act of Congress, in the year 1866, by John Greenleaf Whittier, in the Clerk's Office of the District Court of the District of Massachusetts. Boston: Ticknor and Fields.

green turf dances, moonlight revels, and cheerful nestling around the shealing fires of Ireland. The last that has been heard of them was some forty or fifty years ago in a tavern house in S——, New Hampshire. The landlord was a spiteful little man, whose sour, pinched look was a standing libel upon the state of his larder. He made his house so uncomfortable by his moroseness that travellers even at nightfall pushed by his door and drove to the next town. Teamsters and drovers, who in those days were apt to be very thirsty, learned, even before temperance societies were thought of, to practise total abstinence on that road, and cracked their whips and goaded on their teams in full view of a most tempting array of bottles and glasses, from behind which the surly little landlord glared out upon them with a look which seemed expressive of all sorts of evil wishes, broken legs, overturned carriages, spavined horses, sprained oxen, unsavory poultry, damaged butter, and bad markets. And if, as a matter of necessity, to "keep the cold out of his stomach," occasionally a wayfarer stopped his team and ventured to call for "somethin' warmin'," the testy publican stirred up the beverage in such a spiteful way, that, on receiving it foaming from his hand, the poor customer was half afraid to open his mouth, lest the red-hot flip iron should be plunged down his gullet.

As a matter of course, poverty came upon the house and its tenants like an armed man. Loose clapboards rattled in the wind; rags fluttered from the broken windows; within doors were tattered children and scanty fare. The landlord's wife was a stout, buxom woman, of Irish lineage, and, what with scolding her husband and liberally patronizing his bar in his absence, managed to keep, as she said, her "own heart whole," although the same could scarcely be said of her children's trousers and her own frock of homespun. She confidently predicted that "a betther day was coming," being, in fact, the only thing hopeful about the premises. And it did come sure enough. Not only all the regular travellers on the road made a point of stopping at the tavern, but guests from all the adjacent towns filled its long-deserted rooms,—the secret of which was, that it had somehow got abroad that a company of fairies had taken up their abode in the hostelry and daily held conversation with each other in the capacious parlor. I have heard those who at the time visited the tavern say that it was literally thronged for several weeks. Small, squeaking voices spoke in a sort of Yankee-Irish dialect, in the haunted room, to the astonishment and admiration of hundreds. The inn, of course, was blessed by this fairy visitation; the clapboards ceased their racket, clear panes took the place of rags in the sashes, and the little till under the bar grew daily heavy with coin. The magical influence extended even farther; for it was observable that the landlord wore a good-natured face, and that the landlady's visits to the gin-bottle were less and less frequent. But the thing could not, in the nature of the case, continue long. It was too late in the day and on the wrong side of the water. As the novelty wore off, people began to doubt and reason about it. Had the place been traversed by a ghost or disturbed by a witch they could have acquiesced in it very quietly; but this outlandish belief in fairies was altogether an overtask for Yankee credulity. As might have been expected, the little strangers, unable to breathe in an atmosphere of doubt and suspicion, soon took their leave, shaking off the dust of their elfin feet as a testimony against an unbelieving generation. It was, indeed, said that certain rude fellows from the Bay State pulled away a board from the ceiling and disclosed to view the fairies in the shape of the landlady's three slatternly daughters. But the reader who has any degree of that charity which thinks no evil will rather credit the statement of the fairies themselves, as reported by the mistress of the house, "that they were tired of the new country, and had no pace of their lives among the Yankees, and were going back to Ould Ireland."

WEATHER LORE

Signs and Seasons

THE skunks were coming in early from the woods and renting houseroom under the barns for the winter. The coats of the foxes were heavy. Up under the walnut tree the nuts were falling by the bushel. Down along Warren's brook the muskrat homes were going up in great number and size, from three to seven feet long and from two to three feet high. There would be a long hard winter.

Out in the barnyard the hens were "curling up and picking," so it was soon going to rain. It was the end of the second quarter of the moon so tonight there would be a change in the weather. This line storm of March was clearing warm, so it would be warm in The Town for the next six months, or at least there would be an early spring. The last three days of January or June or August or any other month had been rainy, the next month then would be too rainy for much outdoor work. Dame Messer, the great hill east of the Pond, was wearing her nightcap of fog, it would be a long time before the storm was over. The Pond was roaring tonight, it would soon be yielding under a big thaw. Cobwebs on the morning grass meant a clear pleasant day, if one would but notice their ecstasy of lace. Sundogs were showing their broken rainbows over old Tory hill in Langdon, so the winter day would be very cold, or the summer day very hot. Signs! Signs everywhere for the man who knew his acres and their heavens, and one must learn to read them all aright.[1]

There are all sorts of ways to prophesy the weather when you go fishing. In Boston there was "Old Solitaire," a one-legged gull who frequented the wharves for years, and whose presence always meant a hard blow ahead.

[1] From *New Hampshire Borns a Town,* by Marion Nicholl Rawson, pp. 138–139. Copyright, 1942, by E. P. Dutton & Co., Inc. New York.

In Provincetown, when you see the gulls flying high over the harbor, be ready for a bad blow within a matter of hours. And if you look across the water, at the Truro shore, and the land looms high, you have another sure sign of heavy weather.

Your rheumatism should warn you of an easterly; but if it is hazy and a yeller-eyed sou'wester is in prospect, you may suffer no more than a wetting through the neck of your oil jacket.

There are ways, too, of looking still further ahead. When the oysters bed deep at Wellfleet, there will be a hard winter, and Provincetown Harbor will fill up with pack ice in February—floes so wide there won't be enough open water for a duck to light on, and so thick only the flatfish can navigate below. But if a chicken's gizzard comes away easily from the inner skin, look for an "open winter"; and if a school of herring is raised in January, stow your overcoat for another year—especially if the ducks start laying ahead of schedule and the willows on the swamp banks bud too soon.[2]

Prognostics of the Weather

Animals, by some peculiar sensibility to electrical or other atmospheric influence, often indicate changes of the weather, by their uneasy motions and habits; for instance, asses bray more than ordinary, and shake their ears, before rain.

When the ass begins to bray,
We surely shall have rain that day.

Again,

When the donkey blows his horn,
'Tis time to house your hay and corn.

Swine will be restless, grunt loudly, squeal and jerk up their heads, before high winds. Moles will cast up their hills before rain. Horses will stretch out their necks, sniff the air, and assemble in the corner of the field, before rain. Rats and mice will be restless and squeak much. Foxes and dogs will growl and bark more than usual, and dogs will grow sleepy and dull, and eat grass, before showery weather, and cats will lick their bodies and wash their faces. Cattle will leave off feeding, and chase each other in their pastures. Sheep will spring about the meadows, more than usual. The change from fair weather to foul makes all animated nature restless and uneasy.

Ants.—Bustle and activity in the ant-hills may be regarded as a sign

[2] From *Cape Cod Pilot,* by Jeremiah Digges, with Editorial and Research Assistance of the Members of the Federal Writers' Project, pp. 240–241. American Guide Series, Federal Writers' Project, Works Progress Administration for the State of Massachusetts. Copyright, 1937, by Poor Richard Associates. Provincetown and New York: Modern Pilgrim Press and the Viking Press.

of rain. Before a storm, these curious insects appear all in motion together, and carry their eggs about from place to place. If they clear their holes and pile the dirt high before eleven in the morning, it seldom fails to be fair the rest of the day.

* * * * *

BATS flitting about late in the evening, in spring and autumn, foretell a fine day on the morrow.

BEES, when they remain in their hives, or fly but a short distance from them, foretell showers and rainy weather.

BEETLES flying about late at evening foretell a fine day on the morrow.

BIRDS are particularly sensitive as to changes of the weather. The gull, seemingly one of the most stupid of birds, will fly inland, on the approach of a storm, long before it appears, and will fly out to sea again when fair weather is coming. Swallows fly low before the approach of a storm, and high when fair weather is upon us. When the blue jay comes near the houses and screams, foul weather is at hand. The peacock will squall, the guinea-hen call "come back," the cock crow upon the fence less than usual, the quail call out "more wet," and be more noisy than he is wont. The crow will "caw," the owl screech, the water-fowl scream and plunge into the water, the thrush will sing loud and long, and most of the bird tribe will pick their feathers, plume themselves, and fly to their nests, before stormy weather, seeming anxious to avoid trouble.

BLUE SKY.—When there is a piece of blue sky seen on a rainy morning, big enough, as the proverb says, "to make a Dutchman a pair of breeches," we shall probably have a fine afternoon.[1]

BUTTERFLIES, when they appear early, are sometimes forerunners of fine weather. The first kind that appears in spring is called the Sulphur Butterfly,—his wings being yellow; the next, called the tortoise-shell butterfly, appears later; and still later, the white, or cabbage butterfly.

* * * * *

CANDLEMAS DAY.—(Feb. 2d.)

If Candlemas Day be fair and bright,
Winter will have another flight;

[1] From *The (Old) Farmer's Almanack,* Calculated on a New and Improved Plan, for the Year of Our Lord 1855, by Robert B. Thomas, p. 46. Entered, according to Act of Congress, in the year 1854, by Jenks, Hickling & Swan, in the Clerk's Office of the District Court of the District of Massachusetts. Boston.

From Actual Observation—Alphabetically Arranged. Collected from Various Sources, and Prepared for this Almanac.

Instead of repeating the Weather Table, inserted on this page for several years, and which may be referred to in previous numbers of the Almanac, we have thought it would be more acceptable to our readers to give an alphabetical list, to be continued from year to year, until completed, of Prognostics of the Weather, from the experience of actual observers. We should be very glad to have our farming friends aid us in this plan, by forwarding their own observations.—R. B. T.

But if Candlemas Day be cloudy and rain,
Winter has gone, not to come again.

Chickens, when they are more noisy than usual, are said by some to prognosticate rain.

Chickweed.—When open in the morning, fair weather may be expected; when closed, rain. It is called, like the pimpernell, the poor man's weather-glass, or barometer. As long as they continue to unfold and display themselves, the whole day may be depended on. If, however, the flowers withdraw into their green envelope, the pedestrian need wish no better hint to take his umbrella in his walk.

* * * * *

Christmas.—The clemency of the season at Christmas is a blessing to the poor, whatever it be to the coal-merchants. We may fear, however, for its effects on health, if there be truth in the old adage:

When Christmas is white
The graveyard is lean;
But fat is the graveyard
When Christmas is green.

* * * * *

Cobwebs.—If on the grass early in the morning, they indicate fair weather that day.

Corn Husks.—If these adhere closely and are more difficult to pull apart than usual, it is a sign of a hard winter.[2]

Colors of various shades in the sky and clouds are tokens of different phenomena, or changes. Much red, says Forster, always forbodes wind or rain. . . . Sometimes, however, much red indicates a fine day, if the morning be gray. The following lines of the poet are familiar to most of our readers.

An evening red and a morning gray,
Will set the traveller on his way;
But an evening gray and a morning red,
Will pour down rain on the pilgrim's head.

A greenish color of the sky near the horizon often shows that we may expect more wet weather. The most beautiful greenish tints are seen in autumn, and in that season the purple of the falling haze is often a sign of a continuation of fine weather.

* * * * *

Crows.—These utter a peculiar cry before rain, different from their usual voice.

* * * * *

---

[2] From *The (Old) Farmer's Almanack,* Calculated on a New and Improved Plan, for the Year of Our Lord 1856, by Robert B. Thomas, p. 46. Entered, according to Act of Congress, in the year 1855, by Hickling, Swan & Brown, in the Clerk's Office of the District Court of the District of Massachusetts. Boston.

Dandelions.—When these blow out full, early in the morning, expect fair weather that day.

* * * * *

Fish.—When fish bite readily, and gambol near the surface of streams or ponds, it is an indication that foul or wet weather is near.[3]

Flies.—These and various sorts of volatile insects, become more troublesome, and sting and bite more than usual, before, as well as in the intervals of, rainy weather, particularly in autumn. This remark applies to several kinds of flies. Horse-flies are more troublesome before the fall of rain.

Flowers.—Many of these are excellent indicators of approaching changes by their opening and shutting, and other motions. We wish some observing friend would note these, and give us the result. For instance, the evening primrose opens at sunset and closes at daybreak.

Linnaeus has enumerated forty-six flowers that possess sensibility to the weather. He divides them into three classes. 1. Meteoric flowers, which less accurately observe the hour of folding, but are expanded sooner or later, according to the cloudiness, moisture, or pressure of the air. 2. Tropical flowers, that open in the morning, and close before evening, every day; their hour of expanding becoming earlier or later, as the length of the day increases or decreases. 3. Equinoctial flowers, which open at an exact hour of the day, and, for the most part, close at another determinate hour.

* * * * *

Frogs, by their clamorous croaking, indicate rainy weather; as does, likewise, their coming abroad in great numbers of an evening; but this sign applies more obviously to toads.[4]

Geese are not such "geese" as we think them; their movements are impelled and controlled by strong and almost unerring instincts. When washing, or taking wing with a clamorous noise and flying to water, they portend rain. Geese are excellent guards against fire or thieves, always watchful, and giving notice by their noise of any unusual movements about them. When wild geese are observed to migrate southward or westward in greater numbers than usual in autumn and winter, they are said to indicate hard weather; when to the northward, warmer weather. In gen-

[3] From *The (Old) Farmer's Almanack,* Calculated on a New and Improved Plan, for the Year of Our Lord 1857, by Robert B. Thomas, p. 46. Entered, according to Act of Congress, in the year 1856, by Hickling, Swan & Brown, in the Clerk's Office of the District Court of the District of Massachusetts. Boston.

[4] From *The (Old) Farmer's Almanack,* Calculated on a New and Improved Plan, for the Year of Our Lord 1858, by Robert B. Thomas, p. 46. Entered, according to Act of Congress, in the year 1857, by Hickling, Swan & Brewer, in the Clerk's Office of the District Court of the District of Massachusetts. Boston.

eral, the early appearance of flocks of geese or other wild fowls in the south foreshows a severe winter. A curious illustration of their instinct is seen in their flight, which is wedge-shaped, the leader cleaving the air for those who follow, and at stated intervals falling in the rear, and his place being supplied by another, who pursues the same course; which proceeding will at once be seen to facilitate as much as possible the flight and preserve the strength of the flock.

GENTIANELLA.—This dark and lovely plant is said to "open its blue eyes to greet the mid-day sun, but to close its petals against the approach of a shower."

GNATS.—When these bite keenly and fly near the ground, we look for wind or rain; when they fly in a vortex in the beams of the setting sun, they forebode fair weather; when they frisk about more widely in the open air at eve, they foreshow heat; and when they assemble under trees and bite more than usual, they indicate rain.

GOATS-BEARD.—This plant, called also salsify and oyster-plant, will not unclose its flowers in cloudy weather. From its habit of closing its flowers at noon it has received the common name of "Go-to-bed-at-noon," and in many districts of England the farmers' boys are said to regulate their dinner-hour by the closing of the goats-beard.

GOSSAMER, as it is called, being the fine web of a certain species of spider, floating in the air in abundance and lodging on the trees or rigging of vessels, and on other objects, affords a sign of fine settled weather in autumn, as does the much covering of the ground and herbage by the woof of the spiders in general.

* * * * *

HAWKWEED.—Most plants of this tribe open their flowers at morning, but go to sleep, or close them, in the afternoon, especially if rain is near.[5]

Signs in the Sea's Rote

I HEAR the sea, very strong and loud at the North, which is not unusual after violent atmospheric agitations, and when the wind has lulled. They call this the "rote," or "rut," of the sea. Either expression is correct. The Latin *rota* is the root of both words. The "ruts" in the road are the result of rolling, or the repeated and successive pressure of blows of the wheel. Rotation means repetition as well as succession. To learn a thing by *rote*, is to possess the mind of it by repeated readings or hearings. The *rote* or *rut* of sea, therefore, means only the noise produced by the action of the

[5] From *The (Old) Farmer's Almanack,* Calculated on a New and Improved Plan, for the Year of Our Lord 1859, by Robert B. Thomas, p. 46. Entered according to Act of Congress, in the year 1858, by Hickling, Swan & Brewer, in the Clerk's Office of the District Court of the District of Massachusetts. Boston.

surf, the successive breaking of wave after wave on the shore; and the beach means precisely the smooth shore, beaten by this eternal restlessness of the ocean. There is another expression for the same thing, sometimes used instead of "rut" or "rote"; I hear our people speak of the "cry of the sea," not an unapt phrase to signify the deep, hollow-sounding, half-groaning, or loud wailing voice of the ocean, uttered as if in resentment of its violent disturbance by the winds. As an indication of wind and weather, the rote of the sea is generally understood to signify either that the wind has recently left the quarter whence the rote is heard, or else is soon to spring up in that quarter.[1]

The air here was tremulous with the steady roll of the surf. To an untrained ear, this sound of the sea is the sound of the sea. But to those who follow the sea, or live by its shores, the dash of the breakers against the rocks would never be mistaken for the long roll upon the beach. This noise of the rote is also an infallible sign of a change of wind or weather; for the quarter out of which it comes to your ears is that from which the wind will blow before many hours. In thick weather, pilots feel their way among the crookedest passages, safely guided only by the echo from the shores or sound of the surf. "I speak of pilots who know the wind by its scent, and the wave by its taste, and could steer to any port between Boston and Mount Desert, simply by listening to the peculiar sound of the surf on each island, beach, and line of rocks along the coast." [2]

CURES

Simples and Benefits

. . . THE young doctor learned about simples and benefits, the efficacy of herbs, that a plaster of onions would save a lung patient, that grease rubbed on the soles of the feet was sovereign for heading off colds in the head and the "prevailing distemper," that salt pork was sovereign for almost every disease, especially when a slab of it was worn about the throat, or over an

---

[1] Quoted from Daniel Webster. In *Marshfield, 70°–40′ W: 42°–5′ N, The Autobiography of a Pilgrim Town,* Being an Account of Three Hundred Years of a New England Town; Founded by the Pilgrims; Lived in and Developed by the Royalists; Adopted by Daniel Webster & Beloved by Many of the Ancestors of Those Who Today Make it Their Home, 1640–1940, p. 214. Copyright, 1940, by Marshfield Tercentenary Committee. Marshfield, Massachusetts.

Cf. Henry David Thoreau, *Cape Cod* (Boston, 1896), Vol. I, pp. 129–130.

[2] From *The Pine-Tree Coast,* by Samuel Adams Drake, p. 116. Copyright, 1890, by Estes & Lauriat. Boston. 1891.

From *New Hampshire Borns a Town,* by Marion Nicholl Rawson, p. 140. Copyright, 1942, by E. P. Dutton & Co., Inc. New York.

infected part. A rush to the cobwebby cellar and the pork barrel saved many a life, the heavy brine killing all of the germs which might have accrued to barrel or pork during its cellar months. Tea was good for sore eyes, mashed-up potato or butter for burns, mud for bee stings, kerosene on a feather for a sore throat, a pin run through a wart would be its finish, whiskey with honey and butter for bronchial gruntings, cornmeal and honey for a sty, a brew of tobacco to deaden pain, and so on and on. What was good in The Town was just as good over in Marlow or Keene.

Roots and Herbs

An old character, Chucky Reuben used to help Mother gather her roots and herbs. He wuz a Cobe, but there bein' two Charles Cobes—descent of Ed and Reuben; distant rel'tives—we diff'rentated 'em that way: Charles Ed and Chucky Reuben.

I dunno how Mother got to know so much about nature remidies, but she doctered all our fam'ly and half the neighbers of her time.

In helpin' her scour the fields and woods for medicine greejentses, Chucky took in (and made up), consid'able "root-'n-yarb l'arnin'," as he called it, and after Mother passed on, he confided to me, that if he had his rights, he'd have a shingle hung out and tote a docter's satchel 'round, "a-treatin' folks cons'itutions."

"Lis'n," he'd say, "I kin fix what ails ye! Rheumatiz? Chaw some Canady thistle root, like I do. Knocks the creaks an' aches right out-a ye! Never have no more toothache neither. Fever? Chaw the peth of March turnip root. Chills? Try the Thompsonian treatment: red-pepper tea an' dry pepper in yer stockin's."

"Fidgets? Steep some dried skullcap or archangel leaves fer a nerveen. A cold? Lobelia tea mixed with West Injie m'lasses will throw it off (a-vomitin' ye), an' fer a cough: take jingshang or spike-root tea, or a cough syrup made of the squeezin's of fir-balsom blisters, or jest water, syrupied with brake root peth."

(Dunno but I'd ought-a hang out a shingle myself—the way I'm reelin' this off.) But Chucky'd run on jest so: "A puffball mushroom to stop bleedin', yaller dock or burr dock b'iled in hard cider is good fer biles (modified with wicky-up),"—and so on, no end.

Mother took pains a-brewin' her herbs and roots, but Chucky—bein' shif'less—carried his 'round in his pockets, and jest chawed 'em raw—and lived to be nigh ninety.

From *Village Down East,* Sketches of Village Life on the Northeast Coast of New England before "Gas-Buggies" Came, from Conversations with Zackery Adams, Duck Trap Cove, Maine, by John Wallace, p. 62. Copyright, 1943, by Stephen Daye Press, Inc. Brattleboro, Vermont.

Tonics and Family Rites

SOMETIMES instead of baskets they [the Indians] sold medicines, various salves and tonics. In the disposal of these I think they were more successful. Baskets were after all luxuries, whereas a beneficial mixture, made exclusively as they always averred from the herbs of the fields and tested as to its efficacy upon any number of Indians, might prove in the long run less dear than even infrequent doctor's bills. Moreover, since the nature of man is ever to seek release from major or minor bodily ills and likewise seldom to be averse to the delineation of them, these wandering herbalists did no little business especially among the outlying districts.

My mother stoutly set her face against their remedies. She felt that we, as more enlightened town dwellers, should not be led away by them. But my father grievously disappointed her by purchasing each spring from a very tall and old Indian, who claimed to be a Penobscot chief, a great bottle labeled "Kickapoo Indian Sagwaw." This concoction, which was black and syrupy, emitted a really delectable smell. With each yearly acquisition my father alternately sniffed the contents and read the ingredients, which with commendable if not complete honesty were printed upon the label beneath the feathered head of an Indian chief.

"Horehound, anise, checkerberry, sarsaparilla, camomile, wormwood"—thus he would enumerate to my mother as he laughed at her misgivings. "Herbs made for the service of man."

But she remained obdurate until three unopened bottles had collected on the shelf in the cellarway. What influence finally proved her undoing, I do not know. Perhaps it was her innate thrift, for my father's relative extravagance caused her no little anxiety. At all events, one March morning she began to alternate the Sagwaw with the sulphur and molasses, which with the coming of spring was always dealt out to us on the principle of three mornings in succession followed by a skipping of the three ensuing.

This consumption of sulphur and molasses was a rite familiar to rural New England and needs neither introduction nor description to middle-aged and elderly New England readers. The two ingredients were mixed in a large bowl to the consistency of a heavy paste. In our large family we ranged ourselves before breakfast in a line and received, each from the same big spoon, a mouthful, which in the phraseology of to-day would be termed "capacity." The taste was not unpleasant, although the double nature of the dose sometimes made swallowing a long and complicated process. Much easier and more agreeable in every way was the Sagwaw, which, though it was perhaps a trifle bitter, savored of spring woods and disappeared with ease.

Whether we received any benefits from either of these tonics beyond

---

From *A Goodly Heritage,* by Mary Ellen Chase, pp. 78–80. Copyright, 1932, by Henry Holt and Company, Inc. New York.

the sense of family solidarity which they engendered I cannot say. Certain it is that we received no harm. I am sure, too, that my nephews and nieces, who are beset by baby specialists, carrots, orange juice, and spinach, present no better appearance of health than did we in our day. It is at least a matter of some regret that they will never know that family rite, instituted by sulphur and molasses, alleviated by Kickapoo Indian Sagwaw, and carrying in its long wake such resultant humor in reminiscence.

Meetin' Seed

IN THE herb garden grew three free-growing plants, all three called indifferently in country tongue, "meetin' seed." They were Fennel, Dill, and Caraway, and similar in growth and seed. . . . Their name was given because, in summer days of years gone by, nearly every woman and child carried to "meeting" on Sundays bunches of the ripe seeds of one or all of these three plants, to nibble throughout the long prayers and sermon.

It is fancied that these herbs were anti-soporific, but I find no record of such power. On the contrary, Galen says Dill "procureth sleep, wherefore garlands of Dill are worn at feasts." A far more probable reason for its presence at church was the quality assigned to it by Pliny and other herbalists down to Gerarde, that of staving the "yeox or hicket or hicquet," otherwise the hiccough. If we can judge by the manifold remedies offered to allay this affliction, it was certainly very prevalent in ancient times. Cotton Mather wrote a bulky medical treatise entitled *The Angel of Bethesda*. It was never printed; the manuscript is owned by the American Antiquarian Society. The character of this medico-religious book may be judged by this opening sentence of his chapter on the hiccough:—

> The Hiccough or the Hicox rather, for it's a Teutonic word that signifies to sog, appears a Lively Emblem of the battle between the Flesh and the Spirit in the Life of Piety. The Conflict in the Pious Mind gives all the Trouble and same uneasiness as Hickox. Death puts an end to the Conflict.

Parson Mather gives Tansy and Caraway as remedies for the hiccough, but far better still—spiders, prepared in various odious ways; I prefer Dill.

Peter Parley said that "a sprig of Fennel was the theological smelling-bottle of the tender sex, and not unfrequently of the men, who from long sitting in the sanctuary, after a week of labor in the field, found themselves tempted to sleep, would sometimes borrow a sprig of Fennel, to exorcise the fiend that threatened their spiritual welfare."

Old-fashioned folk kept up a constant nibbling in church, not only of these three seeds, but of bits of Cinnamon or Lovage root, or, more com-

---

From *Old Time Gardens,* Newly Set Forth, by Alice Morse Earle, pp. 341–343. Copyright, 1901, by The Macmillan Company. New York and London. 1902.

monly still, the roots of Sweet Flag. Many children went to brooksides and the banks of ponds to gather these roots. . . .

Plantain

A TOAD was seen fighting with a spider in Rhode-Island; and when the former was bit, it hopped to a plantain leaf, bit off a piece, and then engaged with the spider again. After this had been repeated sundry times, a spectator pulled up the plantain, and put it out of the way. The toad, on being bit again, jumped to where the plantain had stood; and as it was not to be found, she hopped round several times, turned over on her back swelled up, and died immediately. This is an evident demonstration that the juice of the plantain is an antidote against the bites of those venomous insects.

Snake Ball

SYLVESTER WOODBRIDGE, [Southampton] merchant, advertised in 1793, "Satin, West India rum, snake balls, etc." He closes with an invitation to all indebted to him "to make immediate payment, as the day of patience with them will soon expire, when the law will bite-and-sting."

A snake ball was a small piece of stone or bone or other substance which is placed on the bite of a poisonous snake to absorb or charm away the poison. The common people believed in this means of cure.

From *The Farmer's Almanack,* Calculated on a New and Improved Plan, for the Year of Our Lord, 1798, No. VI, by Robert B. Thomas. Boston: Printed by Manning & Loring, for John West, Proprietor of the Copy-Right.

The essential element in the story of the duel between the Toad and the Spider lies in the doctrine that animals know what is good for them, and in particular that they instinctively seek curative herbs when they have suffered an injury. This doctrine is universal.—George Lyman Kittredge, *The Old Farmer and His Almanack* (Boston, 1904), pp. 119–120.

From *Historic Hampshire in the Connecticut Valley,* Happenings in a Charming Old New England County from the Time of the Dinosaur Down to about 1900, by Clifton Johnson, p. 223. Copyright, 1932, by The Northampton Historical Society. Springfield, Massachusetts: Milton Bradley Company.

II. THE FORCE OF CUSTOM

. . . on the southern coast of Rhode Island, the fabled Atlantis . . . the soft, balmy breezes from the Gulf Stream . . . impart to the grain that genial softness, that tempting fragrance and delicious flavor, that caused the Greeks of old to bestow upon Narragansett corn meal the name of Ambrosia.

—THOMAS ROBINSON HAZARD

How blessed are we to live in a more charitable and enlightened age, to enjoy the comforts and conveniences of modern times, and to realize that the world is continually growing wiser and better.—P. T. BARNUM

Many hands make light work.—OLD PROVERB

Reminiscences and not history is the intended basis of this book.

—JOSEPH C. FARNHAM

1. THE GOOD OLD DAYS

ALICE MORSE EARLE's unhappy experience with flip, made, as related below, according to Old Put's recipe, was sufficient to cure her of "any overweening longing for the good old times." This atavistic yearning for the past, especially the past of one's childhood, on which a "rare epic glamor" is wont to rest, is one of the oldest and most persistent of old New England customs. From the beginning Yankees have sought to perpetuate or cling to the past—in place-names sacred with historical or ancestral associations; in zealously cultivated family and local history and traditions; in grandfather worship; and in countless survivals, symbols, and shibboleths treasured for their emotional and association value. Not the least powerful of these links and ties with a glorified past are local and old-time customs, whose memory is preserved in antiquarian reminiscences and in nostalgic antique-collecting.

When Dorothy Canfield Fisher writes that "Vermont represents the past, is a piece of the past in the midst of the present and future,"[1] she is testifying to the force of custom which binds one generation to another and to the power of survival which the folklife of New England possesses amidst change and decay.

A strong sense of the past as a Golden Age usually goes hand in hand with strong local pride in a Land of Milk and Honey. And in one of the most ardent and zestful of New England local patriots, "Shepherd Tom" Hazard, contempt for the degeneracy of modern times is mingled with praise of Narragansett dishes as the food of the gods. But if the *Jonny-Cake Papers* are a delightful monument to the glory that was Narragansett and the grandeur that was Washington and Newport Counties, *Recol-*

[1] *Vermont: A Guide to the Green Mountain State* (Boston, 1937), p. 4.

lections of Olden Times proves that Thomas Robinson Hazard was also something of a social historian. And it is only by seeing lost arts and passing institutions in their social context and historical perspective that one can avoid the pitfalls of merely antiquarian and provincial enthusiasm.

2. Co-operation and Ritual

When we examine the functional basis of New England customs (some of which were local and others merely pioneer folkways), we see that they served the purposes mainly of co-operation and ritual—both characteristic of primitive and folk society. Mary Ellen Chase points out that chores—a foundation stone of Yankee household economy—are distinguished from jobs by their co-operative and voluntary character.

> One was paid for a job but never for a chore. The performance of the former connoted agreement and consent; the performance of the latter, participation and partnership.[1]

In the same way, bees and change-work were chores on a community or neighborhood basis; and in exchanging chores with one's neighbors, one not only proved the truth of the old adage that "Many hands make light work" but also laid oneself open to the danger (pointed out by Robert B. Thomas) that "many go more for the sport than to do any real good" and "it tends to lounging and idleness, and neglect of business; for we cannot always have our neighbours at work with us."[2]

When co-operative labor takes on the nature of a celebration, as in the case of "raisings," the element of ritual is added to that of sociability and amusement. The rhymes used at raisings ("Here is a fine house! It stands high on dry land") are reminiscent of Anglo-Saxon charms. Ritual and symbolism also enter into handicrafts and folk arts as an aesthetic element superimposed upon utility. Quilt patterns, even to their very names, preserve symbolic memories of personal experiences and historical events as well as memorials of the living and the dead. The old New Hampshire needlewoman who went in for basket patterns said that "When I'm making patchwork, I think of all the baskets I've had. . . . I do like baskets." Even local foods and food-making take on the aspect of a ritual, in the hands of a high priestess like Shepherd Tom's Phillis.

The addition of sociability and ritual to home and local industries is all the more inevitable and important in early New England and other pioneer societies in view of the sheer amount of labor and drudgery to be performed. And the adjustment of work to individual talent and skill increased not only the dignity but the virtuosity of labor so that whittling Yankees become not only inventive but creative Yankees. Life, in New England, however, was never wholly divorced from purpose, as illustrated by Samuel Goodrich's story of the Yankee in straits and the wealthy Quaker, who kept him busy pounding on a log with the head of an ax. The Yankee quit in disgust, saying: "I'll be hanged if I'll cut wood without seeing the chips fly!"[3]

---

[1] *A Goodly Heritage* (New York, 1932), p. 43.

[2] *The Old Farmer's Almanack,* October, 1808, and June, 1821, cited by George Lyman Kittredge, *The Old Farmer and His Almanack* (Boston, 1904), pp. 169, 179.

[3] *Recollections of a Lifetime* (New York and Auburn, 1857), Vol. I, pp. 96–97.

In games and pastimes, finally, ritual seems to be an end in itself. But in so far as children in their amusements inherit or imitate adult interests and activities, even playing at work may have a pedagogic as well as a symbolic value. And this may be the crowning achievement of folk culture and folk art—that whether at work or at play, the folk succeeds in combining the two in ingenious forms and fashions, especially in the far-from-simple good old days.

B. A. B.

OLD NEW ENGLAND DISHES

St. Pompion

To THE other bountiful companion food of corn, pumpkins, the colonists never turned very readily. Pompions they called them in "the times wherein old Pompion was a saint." Johnson, in his "Wonder-Working Providence," reproved them for making a jest of pumpkins, since they were so good and unfailing a food—"a fruit which the Lord fed his people with till corn and cattle increased." [1]

> We have pumpkins at morning and pumpkins at noon,
> If it were not for pumpkins we should be undone.[2]

Pompions, and what Higginson called squantersquashes, Josselyn squontersquoshes, Roger Williams askutasquashes, Wood isquoukersquashes—and we clip to squashes—grew in vast plenty. The Indians dried the pompions on strings for winter use, as is still done in New England farm communities. Madam Knight had them frequently offered to her on her journey—"pumpkin sause" and "pumpkin bred." "We would have eat a morsel ourselves, but the Pumpkin & Indian-mixt bread had such an Aspect." Pumpkin bread is made in Connecticut to this day. For pumpkin "sause" we have a two-centuries-old receipt, which was given by Josselyn, in 1671, in his *New England Rarities,* and called by him even at that day "an Ancient New England Standing-dish."

> The Housewives manner is to slice them when ripe and cut them into Dice, and so fill a pot with them of two or three Gallons and stew

---

From *Customs and Fashions in Old New England,* by Alice Morse Earle, pp. 150–153. Copyright, 1893, by Charles Scribner's Sons. New York.

[1] The chiefest Corne they planted before they had Plowes was Indian Graine, whose increase is very much beyond all other, to the great refreshing of the poore servants of Christ, in their low beginnings. All kinde of Gardens Fruits grew very well, and let no man make a jest at Pumkins, for with this fruit the Lord was pleased to feed his people to their good content, till Corne and Cattell were increased.—Edward Johnson, *The Wonder-Working Providence of Sion's Saviour in New England* (Edited by J. Franklin Jameson, New York, 1910), p. 85.

[2] This well-known couplet is cited by Barber in his *Massachusetts Historical Collections* (Worcester, 1839), p. 195, in a humorous song dealing with the early settlers' hardships.

them upon a gentle fire the whole day. And as they sink they fill again with fresh Pompions not putting any liquor to them and when it is stir'd enough it will look like bak'd Apples, this Dish putting Butter to it and a little Vinegar with some Spice as Ginger which makes it tart like an Apple, and so serve it up to be eaten with fish or flesh.

This must be a very good "sause," and a very good receipt when once it is clear to your mind which of them—the housewives or the pompions—sink and are to fill and be filled in a pot, and stirred and stewed and put liquor to.

In an old book which I own, which was used by many generations of New England cooks, I find this "singular good" rule to make a "Pumpion Pye":

Take about halfe a pound of Pumpion and slice it, a handful of Tyme, a little Rosemary, Parsley and Sweet Marjoram slipped off the stalkes, and chop them smal, then take Cinamon, Nutmeg, Pepper, and six Cloves and beat them, take ten Eggs and beat them, then mix them, and beat them altogether, and put in as much Sugar as you think fit, then fry them like a froiz, after it is fryed, let it stand til it be cold, then fill your Pye, take sliced Apples thinne rounde-wayes, and lay a row of the Froiz and layer of Apples with Currans betwixt the layer while your Pye is fitted, and put in a good deal of sweet butter before you close it, when the pye is baked take six yelks of Eggs, some White-wine or Vergis, and make a Caudle of this, but not too thicke, cut up the Lid and put it in, stir them wel together whilst the Eggs and Pompions be not perceived and so serve it up.

I am sure there would be no trouble about the pompions being perceived, and I can fancy the modest half-pound of country vegetable blushing a deeper orange to find its name given to this ambitious and compound-sentenced concoction which helped to form part of the "simple diet of the good old times." I have found no modern cook bold enough to "prove" (as the book says) this pumpion pie; but hope, if any one understands it, she will attempt it.

Josh Billings on Pumpkin Pie

Punkin pi iz the sass ov Nu England. They are vittles and drink, they are joy on the haff-shell, they are glory enuff for one day, and are good kold or warmed up. I would like to be a boy again, just for sixty minitts, and eat miself phull ov the blessed old mixtur. Enny man who dont luv punkin pi, wants watching cluss, for he means to do sumthin mean the

---

From *Old Probability, Perhaps Rain—Perhaps Not,* by "Josh Billings," with 250 Comic Illustrations, 1875, p. 12. Entered, according to Act of Congress, in the year 1879, by G. W. Carleton & Co., in the Office of the Librarian of Congress, at Washington. New York: G. W. Carleton & Co.; London: S. Low & Co.

fust good chance he kan git. Giv me all the punkin pi i could eat, when i waz a boy, and i didn't kare whether sunday-skool kept that day or not. And now that i hav grown up to manhood, and hav run for the legislature once, and only got beat 856 votes, and am thoroly marrid, thare aint nothing i hanker for wuss, and kan bury quicker, than two-thirds ov a good old-fashioned punkin pi, an inch and a halff thik, and well smelt up, with ginger and nutmeg. Punkin pi iz the oldest American beverage i kno ov, and ought to go down to posterity with the trade mark ov our grandmothers on it; but i am afrade it wont, for it iz tuff even now to find one that tastes in the mouth at all az they did 40 years ago.

Cranberry Pie

If your acquaintance with a cranberry pie has been made in a restaurant or hotel dining-room, I do not blame you for not cultivating it. The average restaurant or bakeshop cranberry pie is a sad affair. It is flat and shallow, filled with berries stewed to a soggy paste, and the strips of crust checkerboarding the top are pallid and unhealthy-looking. It reminds one, as much as anything, of a bit of beach at low tide, the filling representing stranded seaweed and the strips of crust the sand. As to taste—well, it is invariably either too sickishly sweet or too puckeringly sour. It is just another one of those things helping to strengthen one's conviction that this world is going to the dogs.

But a real cranberry pie—a homemade, home-baked cranberry pie, prepared by a Cape Cod kitchen-artist of the old school, is different, gloriously different. The berries in such a pie are not cooked beforehand to the consistency of sticky cement and then plastered over the lower crust with a trowel. No, indeed! Mother, and Grandmother also, used to make a cranberry pie that came to the table fat and puffy and inviting. It was baked in a deep dish and when cut it streamed juice, just as does a properly constructed blueberry pie. The triangular sections on our plates were islands set in red seas. We could—and often did—eat the pie with a spoon.

I should like to give you the recipe for that kind of pie, but, alas, I cannot. I haven't it to give. In my youth we were interested in the completed product, not in the process of manufacture, and the formula, so far as our family is concerned, is lost. One thing I do remember, however: the berries were not mashed and stewed to a pulp; they were, each one, cut in half with a chopping knife. . . .

I have a dim memory that, in our house at that time, a cranberry pie was sweetened with brown sugar. Old-fashioned brown sugar, the moist, lumpy kind. In Grandmother's youth it was, of course, sweetened with molasses. And over at Great-uncle Silas's, in his little house on the North Shore, molasses was still used.

From *Cape Cod Yesterdays,* by Joseph C. Lincoln, pp. 88–89. Copyright, 1935, by Joseph C. Lincoln and Harold Brett. Boston: Little, Brown & Company.

Narragansett Jonny-Cake

White Indian meal is very nice, as all Rhode Islanders know, but we should like to ask Thomas R. Hazard how much his cost him in his farming days?—*Providence Journal,* January 16, 1879.

And where, let me ask in turn, did the Journal learn that white Indian meal is very nice? Not certainly outside of Washington and Newport counties, for nowhere else on the globe was the real article ever to be found. The Southern epicures crack a good deal about hoe-cakes and hominy made from their white flint corn, the Pennsylvanians of their mush, the Boston folks of their Boston brown bread, whilst one Joel Barlow, of New Haven, or somewhere else in Connecticut, used to sing a long song in glorification of New England hasty pudding; but none of these reputed luxuries are worthy of holding a candle to an old-fashioned Narragansett jonny-cake made by an old-time Narragansett colored cook, from Indian corn meal raised on the southern coast of Rhode Island, the fabled Atlantis, where alone the soft, balmy breezes from the Gulf Stream ever fan the celestial plant in its growth, and impart to the grain that genial softness, that tempting fragrance and delicious flavor, that caused the Greeks of old to bestow upon Narragansett corn meal the name of Ambrosia, imagining it to be a food originally designed and set apart by the gods exclusively for their own delectation.

But alas, since the introduction of coal fires, cooking stoves, common schools, and French and Irish bedeviling cooks, the making and baking of a jonny-cake has become one of the lost arts. And yet I can remember when its preparation and completion deservedly stood at the very acme of the fine arts of Rhode Island. My grandfather used to have in his kitchen an old cook by the name of Phillis, originally from Senegambia, or Guinea, who probably made as good a jonny-cake in her day as any other artist known, whether white or black, or in short, as was ever made outside of heaven. Her process, so far as I could gather from observation, was as follows:—premising that she always insisted on having white Narragansett corn, ground at what is now called Hammond's Mill, which is situated on the site of the elder Gilbert Stuart's snuff mill, just above the head of Pettaquamscutt pond or lake.

* * * * *

. . . after Phillis had sifted the meal for her jonny-cake, she proceeded to carefully knead it in a wooden tray, having first scalded it with boiling water, and added sufficient fluid, sometimes new milk, at other times pure water, to make it of a proper consistence. It was then placed on the jonny-

---

From *The Jonny-Cake Papers of "Shepherd Tom,"* together with Reminiscences of Narragansett Schools of Former Days, by Thomas Robinson Hazard, with a Biographical Sketch and Notes by Rowland Gibson Hazard, pp. 17–18, 28–30. Boston: Printed for the Subscribers. 1915.

cake board about three-quarters of an inch in thickness, and well dressed on the surface with rich sweet cream to keep it from blistering when placed before the fire. The red oak jonny-cake board was always the middle portion of a flour barrel from five to six inches wide. This was considered an indispensable requisite in the baking of a good jonny-cake. All the old-time colored cooks, without exception, hold that the flour barrel was first made for the express purpose of furnishing jonny-cake boards, and that its subsequent application to the holding of flour was merely the result of an afterthought. Be this as it may, no one I feel certain ever saw a regular, first-rate, old-time jonny-cake that was not baked on a red oak board taken from the middle part of the head of a flour barrel. The cake was next placed upright on the hearth before a bright, green hardwood fire. This kind of fire was indispensable also. And so too was the heart-shaped flat-iron that supported it, which was shaped exactly to meet every exigency. First the flat [iron]'s front smooth surface was placed immediately against the back of the jonny-cake to hold it in a perpendicular position before the fire until the main part of the cake was sufficiently baked. Then a slanting side of the flat-iron was turned so as to support the board in a reclining position until the bottom and top extremities of the cake were in turn baked, and lastly, the board was slewed round and rested partly against the handle of the flat-iron, so as to bring the ends of the cake in a better position to receive the heat from the fire. After a time it was discovered that the flat-iron, first invented as a jonny-cake holder, was a convenient thing to iron clothes with, and has since been used for that purpose very extensively. When the jonny-cake was sufficiently done on the first side, a knife was passed between it and the board, and it was dextrously turned and anointed, as before, with sweet, golden-tinged cream, previous to being placed again before the fire.

Such, as I have described, was the process of making and baking the best article of farinaceous food that was ever partaken of by mortal man, to wit, an old-fashioned jonny-cake made of white Rhode Island corn meal, carefully and slowly ground with Rhode Island fine-grained granite mill-stones, and baked and conscientiously tended before glowing coals of a quick green hardwood fire, on a red oak barrel-head supported by a flat-iron. With proper materials and care, a decent jonny-cake can be baked on a coal stove, though by no means equal to the old-time genuine article, for the simple reason that wood fires in open fireplaces have become, as a general rule, things of the past, and good, careful, painstaking cooks extinct.

Corn Dishes

People living in cities can know but little of the exquisite flavor of the early red-cobbed sweet-corn, or of the later white-cobbed evergreen, for the reason

---

Ibid., pp. 50–51, 53–59 *passim*, 61–62.

that the market is supplied with ears of corn gathered some hours before it is eaten. Old Phillis' method of boiling green-corn was first to set her pot of water boiling, drawn fresh and sparkling from the bubbling well, whilst she took the outside husks from the ears of corn just gathered by old mill-boy, fresh from the stalk in the green-corn patch, back of the barn, leaving a few of the inside husks on the outside of each ear, and then plunging them instanter into the boiling water before the sweetness had departed. How many ears of Phillis' corn, prepared after this fashion, a small boy could eat with a fair amount of sweet, fragrant, aromatic butter, I cannot say, for although Phillis always boiled a bushel pot full of green-corn at once, I could never manage to get enough fully to satisfy my appetite. As for the green sweet-corn, when nicely roasted before a green hardwood fragrant fire, I used to think when a small boy that I could have eaten at least two bushels of it could I have got all I wanted. So, too, with succotash, the Indian for dried sweet-corn and beans, which my grandmother used to always caution me about eating too much of, as she had once known a naughty boy who burst asunder in the middle from having eaten too heartily of the tempting dish. . . .

* * * * *

Then again there was the Indian baked pudding made of ambrosia, milk, and eggs, with a trifle of Muscovado sugar or Portorique molasses. I can remember when I could eat near upon a six-quart pan of this delicious viand and then cry for more. Still again there was the huckleberry and blackberry baked and boiled pudding, and the green fox-grape boiled pudding, none of your tasteless catawba or Isabella insipids, all eaten with luscious brown sugar sauce. . . .

* * * * *

Then again, there was the hasty pudding, not the half-cooked knotty stuff of modern days, but nice faithfully stirred, well-boiled pudding without any two particles of ambrosia sticking together in it. Phillis used to say there was "nothing an airth she 'spised so as lumpy, half-raw, half-burned hasty pudding." People nowadays don't know how to eat hasty pudding and milk. A spoon should be dipped into the milk before it lifts the pudding, to keep it from sticking, which should then be dropped into the porringer of milk, so as each mouthful shall remain separate.

When cold, Phillis used to fry her hasty pudding in the nicest fresh butter, which made it a dish, as she said, fit to set before a king. . . .

* * * * *

Then again, there was the never-absent dish in good families of old, milk porridge, a luxury of surpassing excellence when rightly concocted and cooked, that must be reckoned among the lost arts in these hurrying, money-getting and universal thievery, food-spoiling and food-bolting days. Many a time have I sat by when a boy, watching old Phillis as she made this delicious beverage. First, she boiled the water, always drawn fresh, buoyant, and sparkling from the well; none of your poison leaden pipe, or wooden pump, dead and alive wells, or water works, but a real old-fashioned well, every stone of which was coated with life-given green moss, with a frog or two seated near the bottom, which was ever vitalized and kept alive and fresh by the plunges and splashings of the old oaken bucket hanging at the end of the pole of a big, long well-sweep, balanced at the further end with a pile of stones. Into the boiling water she carefully sifted through the fingers of her left hand the flour of ambrosia, if for the sick, and if for common purposes the second sifting, which she stirred with a pudding-stick, held in her right hand, so artistically, that no two grains of the meal were ever known to adhere together. Phillis used to carry a magnifying glass of some twenty-five hundred or as many thousand horse-power, I disremember which, with which she from time to time surveyed the boiling compound, nor did she commence adding the rich new milk until every separate minute particle of the ambrosia had become transparent and sufficiently expanded in dimensions to enable her to discern the image of her own nose fully reflected therefrom. So exquisite was this compound that I have known one pint porringer of Phillis' milk porridge to work a complete and instant cure of the blues, and that of the worst kind. In fact, the old woman used to tell a story of Sol Smith, who once stopped in my grandfather's kitchen to warm, whilst on his way to hang himself on the limb of a sour apple tree in our lower orchard, about some love affair, just as she was finishing off a pot of porridge. Phillis said he looked so woe-begone-like that she gave him a porringer of her porridge, which was not more than half finished, when he took a rope with a noose braided on one end out of his pocket and threw it to Phillis to mend her clothes-line with as he said, accompanied with the remark that Almira might marry as many other fellows as she wanted to, and he wouldn't mind, so long as he could get "such porridge as them was." In such high esteem was the milk porridge of the olden time held by Narragansettees that since my memory they always spoke of it in the plural number. No ordinary man or woman in Narragansett ever said in those days, "Please give me a little more of that porridge," but, "Please give me a few more of them porridge."

Then again, there was the samp—coarse hominy pounded in a mortar—and the great and little hominy, all Indian dishes fit to be set before princes and gods. But what shall I say of the hulled corn of old? None of your modern tasteless western corn, hulled with potash, but the real, genuine ambrosia, hulled in the nice sweet lye made from fresh hard oak and maple-wood ashes. I remember when a bowl or porringer of hulled corn and milk was a thousand times more relished by me than any dish I can now find at any hotel in the United States. Narragansett hulled corn and beans was in those days ten thousand times as good, as I remember, as the best pork and beans ever cooked in Boston town of that day, or in Boston city of the present dishonest, defaulting age. Then again, there was the great Indian dish called no-cake, in which was concentrated such inexpressible sweetness and life-sustaining power that the aborigines of New England, when hunting or on the warpath, could carry forty days' provisions each on their backs without inconvenience.

The No-cake family, the last survivors of the famous Narragansett Indians, have recently, I think, with one exception, become extinct in Washington county, where the scanty remnants of the tribe were located, on the Indian reserve in Charlestown.

No-cake was made of pounded parched Indian corn. Curious enough, I can remember when the eating of no-cake and milk was considered somewhat a test in Narragansett of good breeding. To be eaten gracefully no-cake must be placed very carefully on the top of the milk, so as to float, and a novice, in taking a spoonful of it to his mouth, is very liable to draw his breath, when the semi-volatile substance enters his throat in advance of the milk and causes violent strangling or sneezing. An expert in the art places the spoonful of milk with the no-cake floating upon the top, carefully into his mouth, and mixes them together without drawing his breath until he swallows. I well remember the old no-cake mortar that used to stand in my grandfather's kitchen, upside down when not in use, so as to serve for a seat. I think it would hold half a gallon of parched corn, or more, which was pounded with a heavy double-headed pestle, for lack of one made of stone, as used by the Indians. This mortar was made of unsplittable wood, known as gumwood or horn-beam, the heart of which is absolutely without grain running in any direction. Old Tom Griswold once described horn-beam, after burying every wedge at the woodpile in a short log without cracking it, as being made of "double and twisted lignum vitae sawdust, spun cross-banded, wove kairsy, cussed at both ends, and damned in the middle."

* * * * *

Corn biscuit, or pound cake, another Indian meal luxury, used to be made with one pound of butter, one pound of sugar, ten eggs, and a pint of new milk, with enough ambrosia to mould it into thin cakes. Then there was the whitpot, differing but little from the common baked Indian pudding, except that it is mixed very thin, and baked very slowly and a great while, so that the milk, eggs, and molasses form a jelly throughout the whole pudding. . . .

Narragansett Fried Smelts and Broiled Eels

. . . PHILLIS, after taking from the chest her modicum of meal, proceeded to bolt it through her finest sieve, reserving the first teacupful that fell for the especial purpose of powdering fish before their being fried. This brings to my recollection the vast difference there was in the old-fashioned way of frying fish, especially smelts, from that now in vogue in Providence, Bos-

Ibid., pp. 24–27.

ton, and such like outlandish places, at least so far as hotels and restaurants are concerned. There smelts are nowadays, without preparation, simply thrown pell-mell into a pan with raw hog's lard of questionable purity, which they absorb before it is half cooked, imparting thereby a greasy, slippery savor to the dear little fish too horrible to mention or abide. On the contrary, Phillis used always to keep a kettle of pure leaf lard, from corn-fed hogs, thoroughly boiled, set apart for the especial purpose of frying smelts during their season. These were always obtained each morning from the Saucatucket smelt weir, and delivered to her alive and flipping, the kettle of lard being on the fire boiling all the time. Each delicate little fish was, after being washed, rolled carefully in the meal until every hair breadth of it from the tip of its head to the end of its tail was coated in the flour of ambrosia; then taking the caudal extremity of each smelt between her thumb and finger, she dropped it head foremost into the boiling kettle, and there left it until it was thoroughly done and crisp. No epicure who has never tasted smelts cooked by that method knows anything of what a smelt is, nor after having once tasted of such can he ever be induced to put into his mouth one of the vile things bearing the name, that has been, minus the meal, half fried in less than half-cooked hog's lard, thereafter.

It is said by some that the Narragansett smelt, cooked in the only proper way, was in pagan times one of the two relishes or condiments that the gods alone indulged in whilst reveling in jonny-cake made of Narragansett white corn meal, the other being Pettaquamscutt eels caught in the months of January and February with spears thrust into the mud beneath the ice, where they lie. The glorious excellence of these eels, prepared in the old-time way, I am sure no poet—not even Homer or Byron, with all their glowing powers of description—can portray, much less a simple writer of prose. The method was as follows: A basket of fat, yellow-breasted eels being brought fresh from the frozen river, were first saturated with a handful of live wood ashes. This loosened the coating of slime so that they were readily cleansed. Next the head was taken off, and the eel split down the entire length of the back. They were then washed in clean sea water and hung up the kitchen chimney, with its wide, open fireplace, for one night only. Next morning the eels were cut in short pieces and placed on a gridiron, flesh side next to sweet-smelling, glowing coals, made from green oak, walnut, or maple wood. When sufficiently broiled on that side, they were turned on the gridiron and a small slice of fragrant butter, made from the milk of cows fed on honey-laden white clover and aromatic five-fingers, put on each piece of eel. By this time the family were seated at the breakfast table in the great-room, waiting impatiently for the all-but-divine luxury, the exquisite aroma of which penetrated every nook and cranny of the house. In due time it appears, on a China plate, you may say; by no means! but on the identical gridiron, hot and luscious, with little transparent globules of dew-like nectar sparkling on each piece. Every guest or member of the family helps himself from the hot gridiron, which is then returned to the glowing coals, and again and again replenished until the appetite is surfeited or the supply of eels exhausted; probably the latter, as I never heard of but one instance wherein a fatal surfeit was produced by the dainty dish, which was the case of one of the kings of England, who died from eating too enormously of broiled eels, speared under the ice at the mouth of the river Humber. I am aware that history charges his death to gormandizing on stewed lamprey eels—a transparent mistake—as no man could be tempted to indulge his appetite exorbitantly on eels of any kind—stewed or fried, but only on yellow-breasted eels, speared under the ice and prepared and cooked after the Narragansett mode.

There used to be an old man in Narragansett by the name of Scribbins, who was a great favorite of my grandfather because of his simplicity and honesty. When a small boy, I remember Scribbins's breakfasting at our house, one winter morning, when we had broiled eels. The old man helped himself from the gridiron seventeen times, a steady smile playing over his features every moment that passed between the first and last mouthful. He then looked my grandfather—Uncle Toby like—blandly and steadily in the face, and significantly nodding his head sideways in the direction of the kitchen door, remarked: "Them's eels, them is."

Nantucket Quahaugs

THE savory and hearty meal was further supplied, or we may say "topped off," with amazing quantities of a species of animal called by the islanders

---

From *Miriam Coffin,* or The Whale-Fishermen, by Joseph C. Hart, Chapter IV, in *Spun-Yarn from Old Nantucket,* edited and published by H. S. Wyer, pp. 46–48. Copyright, 1914, by Henry S. Wyer. Nantucket: The Inquirer and Mirror Press.

In the Cape vocabulary, as in the bright lexicon of youth, occur certain words that trap the stranger. Quahaug is the worst offender. Let us at once solve the mystery of its pronunciation by saying that if you call it "co-hog" you will be talking the language of the native fishermen. When the Government was about to purchase the Canal in 1926, it was necessary for the congressman from the Cape to turn tutor, and tell his colleagues in Washington about this nationally unknown bivalve and its relation to the waterway.

Of all this linguistic effort which it causes, the quahaug is sublimely ignorant, for it shuts itself out from the world in a fashion that few living creatures can command. If you think that a clam or an oyster has a retiring disposition, you should try to open one of the mollusks with which we are for the moment concerned. Almost adamantine is its refusal to yield entrance to its abode. The shell is extraordinarily hard, and all doors are bolted to any amateurish approach. Only an expert knows the trick of admission. It was the blue portion of the interior of this shell from which the Indians made their "suckanhock," or black money, worth twice the white wampum that passed with them as coin of the realm.

While it is true that the adult quahaug is scarcely known away from the Massachusetts coast, its children are widely famous on metropolitan menus as "little neck" clams. The man who reaches down into the sea to harvest them uses a still different name, "cherrystones." . . . Wellfleet Harbor is commonly regarded as the largest quahaug grounds in the country, 2500 acres being devoted to this industry, with a

the "Pooquaw," and sometimes by the other Indian name of "Quohog." These are found in great numbers on the sandy shores of the island; and, but for their great plenty in the northern parts of America, they would be esteemed a delicious luxury.

Lest we may not be well understood while we speak of the inimitable quohog, and, by our obscurity, engender doubts of its inexhaustible abundance, it may be well to inform the gentle reader and enlighten his understanding. Its aboriginal name, and that which it still holds in the oldest parts of America, is just as we have written it down. Nevertheless, the *quo-hog* hath neither bristles nor tail, nor is it a quadruped, as its name would seem to import; but it is in truth a species of shell-fish, which naturalists, in the plenitude of their lore, denominate *bivalvular.* It is grievous further to say, in explanation, that its original and sonorous name, and that by which it is still known in Nantucket, has been made to yield, by the pestilent spirit of innovation in the middle states, to the flat, insipid, and unsounding title of—the clam! Spirit of the erudite Barnes, the conchologist—spirits of Sir Joseph Banks, and Sir Humphrey Davy—spirit of the learned Mitchell—could you not, in the course of your long and well-spent lives, hit upon a more expressive and euphonious jaw-cracker for the persecuted quohog, than the abominable name of *clam?*

The manner of cooking the quohog in the most palatable way at the *Squantums* of Nantucket, as oracularly given out by the knowing Peleg Folger, was resorted to on this occasion [of the sheep-shearing], to eke out the foregoing meal. Even unto this day, some of the eastern people adopt the same method to "stap the vitals" of the quohog at their "roast-outs" or forest junketings. As to the peculiar mode of cooking, we adopt the argument of Peleg, even as he learnedly discussed the matter while arranging a bed of the aforesaid bivalvular shell-fish on the morning of the shearing. Imprimis—The quohogs were placed upon the bare ground, side by side, with their mouths biting the dust. The burning coals of the camp-fires, which had done the office of boiling and broiling, were removed from under the cross-trees, where hung the pot and tea-water kettle, and applied plentifully to the backs of the quohogs. In a few minutes after the application of the fire, the cooking was declared to be at an end, and the roasting of the quohogs complete. The steam of the savory liquor, which escaped in part without putting out the fire, preserved the meat in a parboiled state, and prevented it from scorching, or drying to a cinder, and the whole virtue of the fish from being lost. The ashes of the fire were effectually excluded by the position in which the animal was placed at the beginning; and the heat as completely destroyed the tenacity of the hinge which connected the shells.

---

yearly shipment of 2,000 barrels. A group of Finns do most of the dredging, with a fleet of about thirty converted catboats, powered with gasoline engines. They steer the same course in and out of the bay that a picturesque predecessor of theirs once steered, Captain Baker of Wellfleet and the West Indies. . . .—Arthur Wilson Tarbell, *Cape Cod Ahoy!* (Boston, 1932), pp. 181–183.

"And now," said Peleg, "take a few on thy platter; remove the upper shell, and apply a lump of fresh butter and a sprinkling of pepper and salt." Our blessings on thee, Peleg Folger. The morsel, if taken hot, might be envied by an eastern emperor, whose palate is pampered by bird-nest delicacies; or by the exquisite gourmand of any nation. But in America, who eats a clam or a quohog? None but the wise—and that includes a majority of the people;—the fashionable, never—more's the pity.

New England *versus* Manhattan Clam Chowder

THERE is a terrible pink mixture (with tomatoes in it, and herbs) called Manhattan Clam Chowder, that is only a vegetable soup, and not to be confused with New England Clam Chowder, nor spoken of in the same breath. Tomatoes and clams have no more affinity than ice cream and horse radish. It is sacrilege to wed bivalves with bay leaves, and only a degraded cook would do such a thing.

Representative Cleveland Sleeper of Maine recently introduced a bill in the State legislature, to make it an illegal as well as a culinary offense to introduce tomatoes to clam chowder. And immediately a chowder battle ensued—with high-class chefs asserting that a tomato and clam should never meet, and the low maestros of Manhattan advocating their unholy union.

Anyone who wants tomato soup can have it; but Manhattan Clam Chowder is a kind of thin minestrone, or dish water, and fit only for foreigners. In Boston we like our chowders rich and creamy, and this is how we make them:

First you must have:

A quart of clams (from Duxury, if possible)
A quarter of a pound of salt pork
Four potatoes
Two onions
A quart of milk
A quarter of a pound of butter
Plenty of Common Crackers
Salt and pepper
A kernel of garlic (if you like garlic)
And a jar of cream (if you want a very rich chowder)

Cut the pork up in small pieces and try it out. Strain the fat, and sauté the chopped onions gently, until they are golden-yellow. Fried onions won't give people indigestion, unless they (the onions) are brown or black. Heat the clams in their own juice until the edges turn up (this will take

From *a New England Sampler,* by Eleanor Early, pp. 349–351. Copyright, 1940 by Waverly House. Boston.

only a couple of minutes). Dice and parboil the potatoes. When the clams are cool enough to handle, some people squeeze the dark part from their little bellies. This is done with the thumb and forefinger, and is not as surgical as it sounds. The necks are of no value except to the clam, and might as well be removed. Personally, I eat clams *as is*. But for company, I pinch their bellies and cut off their necks.

Pour everything together and add the milk and butter. Split half a dozen Common Crackers and float on the top, with a spot of butter on each. Spear the garlic on a toothpick, and let that float too. The toothpick will locate it, when you want to take it out.

* * * * *

A proper chowder should marinate on the back of the stove for an hour or more while the ingredients become thoroughly familiar with one another. The cream should be added at the last.

Rhode Island Clambakes

IT HAS been said that the chief contribution of the Indians to the New England pioneers was the clambake.

All along the shore line from Maine to Connecticut are found heaps of buried shells of the soft shell clam-heaps marking the old gathering places where the tribes assembled for their feasts of shellfish. For the Indians of all the New England tribes went down to the shore in summer for clambakes, just as the New England farmers did later. And the Indians enjoyed their bakes just as much.

While the white man has elaborated the bake, its essentials and the method of making it remain unchanged from those which the Red Man enjoyed. In the Indian clambake the clams, fish and corn were all cooked in the steam from the clams and from rockweed spread on hot stones; this was covered over to confine the steam. In the centuries since the first white man tasted the delectable results of this rude open-air cooking he has not improved on it.

The Indian and then the farmer went to the shore, dug his clams in flats exposed at low tide, found stones in the fields, and with them made his bake. Later, some of the country churches began making an annual

---

By Horace G. Belcher, in *The Yankee Cook Book,* by Imogene Wolcott, pp. 23–26. Copyright, 1933, by Coward-McCann, Inc. New York.

The number of inland dwellers who come to New England each summer with the idea that it [a clambake] is something to be dished up in a café or hotel like a boiled dinner is surprisingly large.

A middle-aged, well-dressed man was recently given a seat in the main dining-room of a well-known Boston Hotel. Pushing away the menu, he looked up expectantly.

"Please bring me a clambake," he said.

"Clambake, sir?" repeated the astonished waiter.

"Certainly. That's what I'm ordering. One of your famous New England clambakes I have read so much about!"—I. W., *ibid.*, p. 57.

bake as a summer outing and several of these bakes are continued to this day. The annual bake of the Hornbine church of Rehoboth, just over the Massachusetts line from Rhode Island, and of the Liberty Church in famous old "South County" in Rhode Island, served in groves adjacent to the church, still draw crowds of city folk every year. The Antiquarian Society bake, another Rehoboth fixture, used to draw 1500 or more, served in relays in a great tent; it is now reduced to about one third of that number. The Frenchtown bake, another annual Rhode Island feature in what is popularly known as South County, although its official name is Washington County (formerly King's), is a popular one. And there are others. Many a political career has been boosted by speeches at some of these bakes.

Each bake has its own bakemaster who serves year after year, sometimes for half a lifetime. He supervises its preparation from the building of the fire to the placing of the clams and the rest of the bake. His judgment fixes the time for the opening bake and to him goes credit for its success. Bake-making is an art not given to every one, and a good bakemaster is much sought after and proud of his skill.

But these country bakes came only once a year, and Rhode Islanders and their visitors pined for an opportunity to enjoy this feast whenever they felt like it. The fame of the Rhode Island bake spread and with it a demand. And so in the latter part of the last century and in the earlier years of the present, the shores of upper Narragansett Bay were dotted with clambake resorts where bakes were served daily. These resorts were reached by big fleets of Bay steamboats running out of Providence, and in their heyday many excursions were run to them from neighboring states.

The automobile has driven the sidewheel passenger steamboat of a more leisurely period from Narragansett's waters. Where once stood Field's Point, whose chowder was famous, is now a Providence municipal dock. But two of these old clambake resorts—Rocky Point and Crescent Park, both near Providence—still serve bakes daily in the summer, and the secret of the Field's Point chowder has not been lost.

The Clambake Club at Newport is an adjunct to Bailey's Beach where Society bathes; and the Squantum Association and the Pomham Club, both just outside Providence, serve weekly bakes to their members. Squantum, where Presidents and titled guests have dined, has another famous clam chowder, still made as it was when this exclusive organization was founded during the time that Grant ran for re-election. Guest registers of Squantum and Pomham contain the names of many of the nation's most distinguished men. But their bakes differ only in detail and in their elaboration from the public bakes and wherever you may get your bake you will find it made in the same way.

Opinions may differ as to whether a clam chowder should be made with milk or should include tomatoes: two propositions good for an argument wherever chowder and bakes are known, but no one ever disputes the old Indian method of making a bake.

The Rhode Island bake is made with soft-shell clams preferably about two inches long. On a layer of stones, each about the size of a man's head, is built a fire of cordwood, which is allowed to burn until the stones are heated white hot. Then the embers are removed with six-tined potato diggers and pitchforks, the stones are swept clean of ashes, and a thick layer of rockweed, a marine growth found along the shores of Rhode Island, is thrown on the hot stones. A good fire will have the stones white hot and ready in about an hour. At clambake resorts the stones are heated on a cement platform.

In rapid succession the ingredients of the bake are placed on the steaming rockweed whose salty moisture cooks them and whose flavor permeates them. First the clams, then another layer of rockweed, then white and sweet potatoes still in their skins, sweet corn covered with a thin layer of husks, fish in cloth or paper bags (bluefish by preference although mackerel will do), small sausages or buckworsts similarly wrapped, lobsters or chickens or both, although strictly speaking the chicken does not belong in a Rhode Island bake.

Then the whole is covered with a thick wet canvas which is kept wet during the baking. The steam from the moisture of the clams and the rockweed permeates, "tenderizes," and flavors everything. This steam is carefully confined, for the edges of the canvas are kept covered with rockweed and held down with stones. Even then, the mouth-watering odor of the bake escapes during the forty-five minutes or more it takes to cook the bake.

On the tables you will find sliced cucumbers, sliced tomatoes, sliced raw onions, brown bread, white bread, butter, pepper, salt, vinegar, pepper-sauce, small pitchers of melted butter. The first course is clam chowder, which may be made with soft-shell clams alone, or of the hard-shell clam, which here is known by its Indian name of quahog, or of both. In most cases your clam-chowder is made from quahogs, but the best chowder is from equal portions of both soft- and hard-shell clams, flavored with the quahog liquor and with the results of trying out minced salt pork.

With the chowder are served hot clam-cakes or clam fritters, delectable concoctions of dough containing chopped quahogs which give them an incomparable flavor. Dropped from a spoon, the cakes, which take odd, irregular shapes, are fried in deep fat to a golden brown. Properly made, they are light, and eaten hot, they fairly melt in your mouth. A clam-cake in the left hand and a spoonful of chowder thickened with pilot bread (a flaky hard cracker of nutty flavor) in the right is the proper procedure, repeated to taste; and there is something wrong with your appetite if you do not have a second helping of chowder from the big tureen set on the table. At private bakes chowder, clam-cakes, and little-necks (young quahogs about the size of a half-dollar) are served for luncheon, the bake being opened in the late afternoon, five or six o'clock.

When the bake is opened, tin dishes holding two quarts of clams are served to each guest. You spread the clam shells apart with your fingers, remove the covering of the clam snout, take the clam by the snout, and dip it in a small dish in which you have placed a quantity of hot melted butter with a little vinegar or perhaps a dash of pepper-sauce. Then you eat the clams with the exception of the snout, which is tough. The taste is something to remember.

Between times you may drink a cup or so of the clam broth, which you will find fit for the gods and a stomach-settler. After the hot clams come more hot clams—and all the other good things that were in the bake. If the bake is properly made, you will find you can eat clams until the cows come home. When you feel you cannot eat another mouthful, watermelon or, if you are especially fortunate, baked Indian pudding made of Indian meal, molasses, and milk and baked long in a slow oven is brought on. And at the clambake clubs the bake ends with clear coffee. It is a meal you will never forget—and if you do your duty by the bake you will not need another meal that day.

Josh Billings on the Briny Codfish

The codfish iz the fruit ov the oshun, which accounts for their being so salt. They are good eating for a wet day; they are better than an umbreller to keep a man dry. They want a good deal ov freshning before they are eaten, and want freshning a good deal afterwards.

If i can have plenty ov codfish for breakfast, i can generally manage tew make the other two meals out of cold water.

Daniel Webster's Fish Chowder

TAKE a cod of ten pounds, well cleaned, leaving on the skin. Cut into pieces one and a half pounds thick, preserving the head whole. Take one and a half pounds of clear, fat salt pork, cut in thin slices. Do the same with twelve potatoes. Take the largest pot you have. Try out the pork first, then take out the pieces of pork, leaving in the drippings. Add to that three parts of water, a layer of fish, so as to cover the bottom of the pot; next a layer of potatoes, then two tablespoons of salt, 1 teaspoon of pepper, then the pork, another layer of fish, and the remainder of the potatoes.

Fill the pot with water to cover the ingredients. Put over a good fire. Let the chowder boil twenty-five minutes. When this is done have a quart

---

From *Old Probability, Perhaps Rain—Perhaps Not,* by "Josh Billings," with 250 Comic Illustrations, July, 1871. Entered, according to Act of Congress, in the year 1879, by G. W. Carleton & Co., in the Office of the Librarian of Congress, at Washington. New York: G. W. Carleton & Co.; London: S. Low & Co.

From *The Yankee Cook Book,* by Imogene Wolcott, pp. 8–9. Copyright, 1939, by Coward-McCann, Inc. New York.

of boiling milk ready, and ten hard crackers split and dipped in cold water. Add milk and crackers. Let the whole boil five minutes. The chowder is then ready to be first-rate if you have followed the directions. An onion may be added if you like the flavor.

Herring Sticks

THE Herring Brook attracted us youngsters throughout three quarters of the year, but it was in May or early June that it became of general interest to all, grownups as well as children. Then the herring run was on.

The Cape Cod herring is, as every one knows, an alewife.[1] According to the dictionary, the name was "perhaps jocularly given or, perhaps, derived from the Indian." It, the same dictionary, also adds that the alewife is "a poor food fish." Well, maybe, but Cape Codders did not use to think so. Either that, or they were accustomed to poor food, an alternative which, I am sure, no Codder will admit. In at least one of the towns—and no doubt in many others—each child born within township limits was entitled to so many herring—alewifes of course—each year. This was an old law dating back to early Colonial times. Herring was an accepted part of the community food supply.

When the run was on, the brook was literally packed with herring. . . .

About a hundred feet from the foot of the fall, where the brook ran between boulders and the channel was narrowest, was a section with plank gates which raised and lowered in grooves. Ordinarily, in the herring season these gates were kept closed and the water forced to flow through another and wider section, walled and floored with plank and also fitted with gates at each end. Once daily, at "shut-down" time, these latter gates were closed and those of the regular channel opened. The surplus water in the artificial channel drained away through holes in the lower gate and the herring were left high and dry, trapped in a wooden box.

* * * * *

There were far more herring taken during the running season than the townspeople could use, of course, and many were shipped to the city. But a surprising number were taken care of locally. Some were eaten fresh—Grandmother used to say, "I do relish a nice fresh herring with my breakfast"—but many more were salted and smoked. Before salting or smoking, they were strung on sticks.

The sticks were for the most part whittled from cedar—we are quite sure cedar was the wood used. Made from the old split-cedar rail fences that used to be so common. You see very few of these old rail fences

From *Cape Cod Yesterdays,* by Joseph C. Lincoln, pp. 67–69, 71–74. Boston: Little, Brown and Company.

[1] And you pronounce it "ell-y," in case you don't know.—Robert P. Tristram Coffin, *Kennebec, Cradle of Americans* (New York, 1937), p. 202.

nowadays. In our boyhood they were plenty. We used to make our bows and arrows from cedar rails. The herring sticks were pointed at both ends and whittled thin enough to pass through the gills of the fish. A dozen were strung on a stick. All along the Cape roads the lettered signs on the fences used to read, "Herring 10 Cents a Stick." Occasionally we see those signs now, but not very often.

Against the rafters of practically every barn, and in many sheds and outbuildings, those sticks of herring used to hang. You could smell them before you opened the door. During the summer they were often hung out of doors in the sunshine, festooning the eaves of barns and sheds. You could smell them there, too. That is one characteristic of a herring which salting or drying does not remove, but rather accentuates—the smell. The memory of an old-time Cape Cod kitchen at breakfast hour would not be complete without the odor of fried herring. Call him an alewife if you will, but, like the rose by another name, it does not change his aroma.

* * * * *

But when I state, as I did earlier in this chapter, that the herring used to be a regular and important part of Cape Cod's food supply, I do not exaggerate. They not only ate them on land but carried them on fishing vessels as part of the regular rations. A good friend of ours, now dead, more is the pity—a comrade with whom we camped and fished and sailed times without number—was an old sea captain. In his youth, however, he had gone "mackereling" aboard Captain Ote Young's little fore-and-aft schooner. . . .

This Captain Young, so our friend said, had the reputation, spread by the unlucky foremost hands who had sailed with him, of being a "poor provider." He was a first-rate skipper and fisherman, but he fed his crews in meager fashion. . . .

* * * * *

According to our friend, an acquaintance of his sailed with the Captain on another trip in the same schooner. On this cruise, so the narrator avowed, the sole supply of "hearty" on board were three sticks of salt herring. If you are a confirmed Cape Codder, you know that "hearty" means, or used to mean, "meat victuals."

The herring lasted four days and the schooner did not return to port until the afternoon of the sixth day. When the yarn was sprung upon its innocent victim, there was always a pause at this point. And then the said victim, having been allowed time to think it over, was supposed to, and usually did, ask this question:

"But if there were no more herring, what did you and the rest of the crew eat during those last two days?"

"Oh," with sad solemnity, "we chewed the sticks."

Lobster Stew

Save every part of the hot lobsters you have taken apart, except the shells, the colon, and the sack of the stomach with its "lady." Take all the clotted blood. And especially every drop of the liquid spared by the shellers. The proportion of solid to liquid will be about 50–50. For this is no ordinary stew, no curtain-raiser to a feast. It is the whole business. The man who gets outside of two bowls of this pottage is through with eating for some hours, and he is a nobler man. Perhaps two sour pickles. Maybe two rounds of pilot bread. But no other fringes to this feast. This stew is all in all.

Begin with the tomally [liver]. Sauté it in about an equal quantity of new butter, and in an old-fashioned thick iron kettle, for seven minutes, say. Then add the lobster meat, the blood, the juice. Add no salt, no pepper. There is the whole sea full of salt this lobster has drawn on artistically, and all the spices of the deep are in him. Hs is all-spice already. Add not a drop of water, on peril of your soul. But add more melted butter. At the end, this stew is pure gold on top and Kingdom Come below. Leave the kettle on a very hot fire. Say, ten minutes. Then push it back on the stove, let it cool down slightly. Then gently—O, gently, gently!—pour in milk, a trickle poured continuously, and stir as you do. About a cupful of rich cream can go in to advantage, at great risk I say it, for this is one of my helpmate's little nuances that I do not mean to let slip out. Stir constantly, for you do not want to have a curdled ruin to your masterpiece. When the stew blossoms out suddenly into a rich salmon pink under your spoon, you can know you have achieved fame. You are done. Why green tomally blossoms out pink I do not know. But it does. That is the last hallmark of excellence.

Set the kettle off the stove to cool. The cooling is as important as everything else. For every hour that passes increases the flavor, not in arithmetic, but in geometric progression. But once the fragrance of the dish goes through the house, there is little likelihood of there being many hours or even minutes to the aging. Short of standing over the kettle with a shotgun, my wife has found it practically impossible to age her nectar for more than five or six hours. That is enough, though, to give her the reputation of being the artist in lobsters she so deservedly is.

My wife always heats the stew up when she finally has to serve it, of course.

From *Mainstays of Maine,* by Robert P. Tristram Coffin, egged on by Ruth P. Coffin, pp. 11–12. Copyright, 1944, by the Macmillan Company. New York. Originally printed in *Gourmet,* May, 1943.

Josh Billings on Baked Beans

Next to rhy bread, beans hav been called by the poets, and philosphers the cumfort, and staff ov life. The bean iz all food, thare iz no more waste in them, than thare iz in a pint ov cold water, when a man iz auphull dry. Beans are all colors, and most shapes, flat, round, oblong, square, and 3 cornered, and a quart ov them put into a pot, and biled 2 hours, will meazzure a gallon, and a haff, when they cum out. This makes them a better dividend paying seed than enny thing we kno ov. Beans are az old az Esau, he sold out for bean porridge. Beans gro on the jump, and thare aint but phew things that kan beat a bean klimbing a pole. I luv beans, but dont hanker for them. But beans, and me wont quarrell. Baked beans are a grate necessity in Nu England, and not to hav a platter ov them for Sunday dinner, iz lookt upon thare az being stuck-up to the neighbors. One ov the old blue laws ov Massachusetts waz, *"thou shalt eat baked beans on Sunday."* I kan remember now ov eating baked beans, and rhy, and injun bread every Sunday, when i waz a boy, and luving it, bekauze i waz obliged to.

Scootin'-'Long-the-Shore

Mrs. Mae Bangs Twite, Oak Bluffs, Martha's Vineyard, Mass., says this plain but appetizing combination of potatoes and onions rejoices in the name of Scootin'-'Long-the-Shore because for years upon years Cape Cod fishermen prepared this meal while at their work. Mrs. Twite has often heard her grandmother ask her "granddad" what they should have for lunch. Always his comeback was, "Well, Mother, make it Scootin'-'Long-the-Shore."

Down in Maine a similar recipe is popular. Potatoes are sliced as thin as possible, and thrown into cold water while salt pork is tried out. Pork is removed from pan and potatoes fried slowly for about 30 minutes, stirring frequently. Sometimes an onion is added. When the potatoes are done, the salt pork is placed on top. This dish is known as Very Poor Man's Dinner.

From *Old Probability, Perhaps Rain—Perhaps Not,* by "Josh Billings," with 250 Comic Illustrations, December 1876. Entered, according to Act of Congress, in the year 1879, by G. W. Carleton & Co., in the Office of the Librarian of Congress, at Washington. New York: G. W. Carleton & Co.; London: S. Low & Co.

From *The Yankee Cook Book,* by Imogene Wolcott, p. 111. Copyright, 1939, by Coward-McCann, Inc. New York.

New England Boiled Dinner

The "boiled dinner" to which, on hotel menus, the descriptive words "New England" are still universally appended, was, as a matter of fact, the universal *pièce de résistance* of the comfortable but uncultivated householder of olden times. It was prepared in a single great pot, the meat being put in first, and then—at intervals properly calculated to turn the whole thing out cooked, just as it should be, the minute the big clock in the corner should strike the hour of noon—were added potatoes, beets, squash, turnip, and cabbage, with very likely a bag of Indian pudding into the bargain. Such a dish was a meal of itself, neither dessert nor bread being regarded as necessary to its completeness.

Muslin Toast

Muslin toast was a favorite supper dish, prepared with nicety and precision. A rye short cake, the full size of the griddle iron, was browned to a delicate crisp, on each side, the thin crust deftly flayed from the hot side, the denuded surface returned to the griddle, and the crust placed in the waiting basin of hot, thickened and salted milk. This process was repeated until the upper crust of the cake was reached and ready to be "dipped."

Old Bachelor's Doughnuts

An old Maine recipe called "Old Bachelor's Doughnuts" has the following curious wording.

"Pour hog's lard in an old-fashioned iron fry pan; heated till she sputters will do the trick. Then take a deep yellow dish and put in one cup of sugar, and if eggs don't cost over 2 cents each, put in one and the yolk of another, and put the white away until eggs are worth more. Then add one cup of cow's milk without anything in it except about a big spoonful of cream and a little salt and nutmeg, then add two teaspoons of tartar and one and a little over of soda in some flour. Then take a big spoon and

---

From *Social Life in Old New England,* by Mary Caroline Crawford, pp. 260–261. Copyright, 1914, by Little, Brown and Company. Boston. 1915.

From *In Dover on the Charles,* A Contribution to New England Folk-Lore, by Alice J. Jones, pp. 50–51. Copyright, 1906, by Alice J. Jones. Newport, Rhode Island: The Milne Printery.

From *The Yankee Cook Book,* by Imogene Wolcott, pp. 140–141. Copyright, 1933, by Coward-McCann, Inc. New York.

give her Hail Columbia for about 20 seconds. Next find a good clean place to roll them out. Fry one at a time, cut out with a four-quart pail cover, and cut the hole with a pint dipper with handle busted, and if you are looking for a housekeeper, take one of the doughnuts, hold it up to the window, and call in the first maiden lady who comes in sight, and kiss her through the hole, and she is yours."

Nantucket Wonders

. . . WHAT were they? Simply doughnuts made in a certain prescribed regulation form—cut out round, jagged across and separated at the center two or three times, but not cut through to the edge; made in that way the fat, while they were frying, passed between those jagged cuts, with the result of crisp, deliciously browned cross-pieces, so that the "wonder" easily broke into such separate sections, or bars, and was peculiarly appetizing.

. . . The ordinary ring doughnut, with hole in the center, in lusciousness could in no wise approximate unto them. Surely the "wonder" was—may I not say is?—the king of doughnuts. I have often in these later years "wondered" if the "wonder" was known as a "wonder" anywhere but at Nantucket. I am inclined to think that it is a name for a doughnut solely indigenous to my native town. Here in my adopted city of Providence I have produced occasional merriment by calling a doughnut, no matter the form in which it was made, a "wonder." The name is a "quaint" belonging exclusively to the town where it is used, is a "laconic" of its inhabitants, and is of "lore" exclusively their own—at least, I believe so.

Skully-Jo

. . . PROVINCETOWN youngsters used to carry around bits of a delicacy known as "skully-jo," which was a kind of dried fish, cured until it was very hard, and . . . they munched on this as children of other places ate candy—only it was said of skully-jo that the longer you chewed on it, the more you had. And if you ever lost or mislaid it, you could buy a new piece almost anywhere in town—including the hardware store.

From *Brief Historical Data and Memories of My Boyhood Days in Nantucket*, by Joseph E. C. Farnham, pp. 180–181. Providence: Joseph E. C. Farnham. 1923.

From *In Great Waters, The Story of the Portuguese Fishermen*, by Jeremiah Digges, pp. 56–57. Copyright, 1941, by Josef Berger. New York: The Macmillan Company.

"Biled Cider Apple Sass"

IN NEW ENGLAND what the "hired man" on the farm called "biled cider apple sass" took the place of apple butter. Preferably this was made in the "summer kitchen," where three kettles, usually of graduated sizes, could be set over the fire; the three kettles could be hung from a crane, or trammels. All were filled with cider, and as the liquid boiled away in the largest kettle it was filled from the second and that from the third. The fresh cider was always poured into the third kettle, thus the large kettle was never checked in its boiling. This continued till the cider was as thick as molasses. Apples (preferably Pound Sweets or Pumpkin Sweets) had been chosen with care, pared, cored, and quartered, and heated in a small kettle. These were slowly added to the thickened cider, in small quantities, in order not to check the boiling. The rule was to cook them till so softened that a rye straw could be run into them, and yet they must retain their shape. This was truly a critical time; the slightest scorched flavor would ruin the whole kettleful. A great wooden, long-handled, shovel-like ladle was used to stir the sauce fiercely until it was finished in triumph. Often a barrel of this was made by our grandmothers, and frozen solid for winter use. The farmer and "hired men" ate it clear as a relish with meats; and it was suited to appetites and digestions which had been formed by a diet of salted meats, fried breads, many pickles, and the drinking of hot cider sprinkled with pepper.

Salt Horse

THE cabin fare was the same as ours except that they had sugar for coffee and butter on their white bread (soft-tack) with a few delicacies thrown in. We had salt beef and pork, good of the kind, but the cabin was furnished with the choice cuts. The beef came in three-hundred-pound casks and was soaked in brine well saturated with saltpeter. When taken from the cask it was as red as a flannel shirt. It was put into a wooden oval cask, holding about forty gallons, larger at the bottom than the top to keep it from capsizing. The wood was usually scraped and oiled on the outside and bound with brass hoops, which were polished bright, and this piece of deck furniture, called a "harness-cask," was used exclusively for soak-

---

From *Old Time Gardens,* Newly Set Forth by Alice Morse Earle, pp. 213–214. Copyright, 1901, by the Macmillan Company. New York and London. 1902.

From *The Making of a Sailor* or Sea Life Aboard a Yankee Square-Rigger, by Frederick Pease Harlow, pp. 147–149. Publication Number Seventeen of The Marine Research Society. Copyright, 1928, by The Marine Research Society. Salem, Massachusetts.

ing out salt meat by covering it with salt water. The meat was allowed to soak for a day or so before it was fresh enough to cook.

It was customary at this time, when a cask of salt beef was opened, to let the steward first pick out the choice pieces, for the cabin, and leave the lean pieces for the crew. These were called by the sailors "old horse" and were thrown into the "harness-cask" only as the cook needed them. The name of "old horse" is ancient history. Richard H. Dana in his "Two Years before the Mast" says, "There is a story current among seamen that a beef-dealer was convicted, at Boston, of having sold an old horse for ship's stores, instead of beef, and had been sentenced to be confined in jail until he should eat the whole of it, and that he is now lying in Boston jail." He also quotes the rhyme all sailors knew in my time, "Old horse! Old horse! what brought you here?" This would seem to show that the name is purely American.

Another writer claims the words to be of Welsh extraction of years ago. The fact that Dana mentions the "harness-cask" would indicate that it was used years before he went to sea and he sailed from Boston, around the Horn to California in the brig *Pilgrim,* in the year 1834.

The "harness-cask" no doubt obtained its name from throwing the scraps of the old salt beef to be soaked out in a tub and it is easily understood how these scraps could have been called the horse's harness. Even in my day I have heard some old sailor with a grouch, when the evening meal was brought in, stab at a particularly uninviting dry piece of salt beef, with his fork or sheath-knife, in a vicious manner and with an oath that would arrest the attention of us all, hold it above the pan and reverently proceed to recite the well-known rhyme:

Old horse! old horse! what brought you here?
From Sacarap' to Portland pier
I carted stone for many a year.
I labored long and well, alack,
Till I fell down and broke my back.
They picked me up with sore abuse
And salted me down for sailor's use.
The sailors they do me despise,
They pick me up and damn my eyes,
They eat my flesh and gnaw my bones
And throw the rest to Davy Jones.

. . . The salt beef is not noted for its moisture and usually was as dry as a chip; but with salt pork, which we were allowed three times per week and is quite a delicacy, the beef was eatable. It takes a little time to get used to salt beef and at first it takes the skin off the roof of your mouth, but as with your hands in hauling ropes, your mouth soon becomes calloused and the sailor can digest anything he can swallow.

Whaleship's Menu

It would be a mistake to fail to preserve here the menu known to whalemen in the early days. It will intensify our respect for our forbears, who as lads were eager to risk the loss of all the comforts of home to sail on long voyages, knowing full well what conditions they would be compelled to meet. The mess table of those days was in strong contrast to what is served Jack in these days of tinned food-stuffs, and the "tar" of to-day is better looked after in every particular, through better national and international laws bearing upon his protection.

In the old days *Lobscouse* was a prominent feature of the menu of a whaleship. It was a stew of soaked hard-tack, pork fat, or "top o' the pot" (grease left after boiling "salt horse"—beef), or any sort of "slush" (sailor's term for grease), boiled with molasses and water.

Potato scouse was the same as above, excepting that potatoes were substituted for hard-tack.

Dandy funk. This appears to have been a dish of class on shipboard, made of powdered hard-tack, molasses, and water and baked in the oven—evidently a sort of pudding.

Salt horse (salted beef) was served twice a week, as was boiled salt pork.

Duff, boiled in a cloth, was on the menu twice weekly, and one day of the seven gingerbread was served.

Scalded yellow meal with molasses was served daily, and occasionally salt fish and potatoes.

Whale scraps were occasionally eaten, and porpoise meat, and sometimes fresh fish found place on the festive board; and when they were trying out a whale, advantage was taken of the abundance of hot fat to do more or less frying in the try-pots.[1]

To the whaleman, salt beef was always "meat," while pork was pork. As some preferred one and some the other, a sailor would frequently offer to swap his "meat" for his mess-mate's pork, or vice versa. Whalemen used to say they varied their diet by having salt horse and hard-tack one meal, and hard-tack and salt horse the next, and so on.

From *The Nantucket Scrap Basket,* Being a Collection of Characteristic Stories and Sayings of the People of the Town and Island of Nantucket, Massachusetts, Second Edition, Revised, Expanded, and Rearranged by William F. Macy, pp. 146–148. Copyright, 1916, by William F. Macy and Roland B. Hussey; 1930, by William F. Macy. Boston and New York: Houghton Mifflin Company. 1930.

[1] If a whaling man is lucky, he gets aboard a ship where the captain's wife is aboard. When the blubber is being "tried out," she often gives the crew a treat by frying a batch of doughnuts in the hot fat of the tried-out blubber.—Imogene Wolcott, *The Yankee Cook Book* (New York, 1939), p. 143.

Flip

FLIP was a dearly loved drink of colonial times, far more popular in America than in England, much different in concoction in America than in England, and much superior in America—a truly American drink. . . .

The earliest date that I find flip named in New England is 1690. From that year till the middle of this century there never was a day, never a minute of the day, and scarce of the night, that some old Yankee flip drinker was not plunging in a loggerhead, or smacking his lips over a mug of creaming flip.

In the *New England Almanac* for 1704 we read under December:—

> The days are short, the weather's cold,
> By tavern fires tales are told.
> Some ask for dram when first come in,
> Others with flip and bounce begin.

American flip was made in a great pewter mug or earthen pitcher filled two-thirds full of strong beer; sweetened with sugar, molasses, or dried pumpkin, according to individual taste or capabilities; and flavored with "a dash"—about a gill—of New England rum. Into this mixture was thrust and stirred a red-hot loggerhead, made of iron and shaped like a poker, and the seething iron made the liquor foam and bubble and mantle high, and gave it the burnt, bitter taste so dearly loved. A famous tavern host of Canton, Massachusetts, had a special fancy in flip. He mixed together a pint of cream, four eggs, and four pounds of sugar, and kept this on hand. When a mug of flip was called for, he filled a quart mug two-thirds full of bitter beer, added four great spoonfuls of his creamy compound, a gill of rum, and thrust in the loggerhead. If a fresh egg were beaten into the mixture, the froth poured over the top of the mug, and the drink was called "bellows-top."

Let me not fail to speak of the splendid glasses in which flip was often served—I mean the great glass tumblers without handles which, under the name of flip glasses, still are found in New England homes. They are vast drinking-vessels, sometimes holding three or four quarts apiece, and speak to us distinctly of the unlimited bibulous capacities of our ancestors. They are eagerly sought for by glass and china collectors and are among the prettiest and most interesting of old-time relics.

English flip is not so simple nor so original nor so good a drink as American flip. It might be anything but flip, since it is compounded in a sauce-pan, and knows naught of the distinctive branding of flip, the seething loggerhead. If it contained no spirits, it was called "egg-hot."

A rule for flip which seems to combine the good points of the American

---

From *Stage-Coach and Tavern Days,* by Alice Morse Earle, pp. 108–111, 112–114.

and English methods uses ale instead of home-brewed. It may be given "in the words of the Publican who made it":—

> Keep grated Ginger and Nutmeg with a fine dried Lemon Peel rubbed together in a Mortar. To make a quart of Flip: Put the Ale on the Fire to warm, and beat up three or four Eggs with four ounces of moist Sugar, a teaspoonful of grated Nutmeg or Ginger, and a Quartern of good old Rum or Brandy. When the Ale is near to boil, put it into one pitcher, and the Rum and Eggs, etc., into another: turn it from one Pitcher to another till it is as smooth as cream. To heat plunge in the red hot Loggerhead or Poker. This quantity is styled One Yard of Flannel.

* * * *

Other names for the hospital loggerhead were flip-dog and hottle. The loggerhead was as much a part of the chimney furniture of an old-time New England tavern and farmhouse as the bellows or andirons. In all taverns and many hospitable homes it was constantly kept warm in the ashes, ready for speedy heating in a bed of hot coals, to burn a mug of fresh flip for every visitor or passer by. Cider could be used instead of beer, if beer could not be had. Some wise old flip tasters preferred cider to beer. Every tavern bill of the eighteenth century was punctuated with entries of flip. John Adams said if you spent the evening in a tavern, you found it full of people drinking drams of flip, carousing, and swearing. The old taprooms were certainly cheerful and inviting gathering-places; where mine host sat behind his cagelike counter surrounded by cans and bottles and glasses, jars of whole spices and whole loaves of sugar; where an inspiring row of barrels of New England rum, hard cider, and beer ranged in rivalry at an end of the room, and

> Where dozed a fire of beechenlogs that bred
> Strange fancies in its embers golden-red,
> And nursed the loggerhead, whose hissing dip,
> Timed by wise instinct, creamed the bowl of flip.

These fine lines of Lowell's seem to idealize the homely flip and the loggerhead as we love to idealize the customs of our forbears. Many a reader of them, inspired by the picture, has heated an iron poker or flip-dog and brewed and drunk a mug of flip. I did so not long ago, mixing carefully by a rule for flip recommended and recorded and used by General Putnam—Old Put—in the Revolution. I had the Revolutionary receipt and I had the Revolutionary loggerhead, and I had the old-time ingredients, but alas, I had neither the tastes nor the digestion of my Revolutionary sires, and the indescribable scorched and puckering bitterness of taste and pungency of smell of that rank compound which was flip will serve for some time in my memory as an antidote for any overweening longing for the good old times.

LOST ARTS AND PASSING INSTITUTIONS

Barnum Recalls the Good Old Days

My friends: Among all the varied scenes of an active and eventful life, crowded with strange incidents of struggle and excitement, of joy and sorrow, taking me often through foreign lands and bringing me face to face with the king in his palace and the peasant in his turf-covered hut, I have invariably cherished with the most affectionate remembrance the place of my birth, the old village meeting house, without steeple or bell, where in its square family pew I sweltered in summer and shivered through my Sunday-school lessons in winter, and the old school-house where the ferule, the birchen rod and rattan did active duty, and which I deserved and received a liberal share [of]. I am surprised to find that I can distinctly remember events which occurred before I was four years old.

I can see as if but yesterday our hard-working mothers hetcheling their flax, carding their tow and wool, spinning, reeling, and weaving it into fabrics for bedding and clothing for all the family of both sexes. The same good mothers did the knitting, darning, mending, washing, ironing, cooking, soap and candle making, picked the geese, milked the cows, made butter and cheese, and did many other things for the support of the family.

We babies of 1810, when at home, were dressed in tow frocks, and the garments of our elders were not much superior, except on Sunday, when they wore their "go-to-meeting clothes" of homespun and linsey-woolsey.

Rain water was caught and used for washing, while that for drinking and cooking was drawn from wells with their "old oaken bucket" and long poles and well sweeps.

Fire was kept over night by banking up the brands in ashes in the fireplace, and if it went out one neighbor would visit another about daylight the next morning with a pair of tongs to borrow a coal of fire to kindle with. Our candles were tallow, home-made, with dark tow wicks. In summer nearly all retired to rest at early dark without lighting a candle except on extraordinary occasions. Home-made soft soap was used for

---

From *Barnum,* by M. R. Werner, pp. 10–13. Copyright, 1923, by Harcourt, Brace and Company, Inc. Garden City, New York.

The character of his early environment in Bethel, Connecticut, was admirably summed up by Barnum when he was seventy-one years old. He presented a bronze fountain eighteen feet high, "the design a Triton of heroic size, spouting water from an uplifted horn," to the inhabitants of his birthplace. The town was decorated with flags and bunting, and the police and fire companies, with apparatus and bands of music, greeted their native son, their returned hero, the conqueror of Success. Barnum made this speech, which is inserted here because it tells with characteristic altiloquence more of his early life than anything he ever wrote, or which ever could be written by another.—M. R. W., *ibid.*, p. 10..

washing hands, faces, and everything else. The children in families of ordinary circumstances ate their meals on trenchers, wooden plates. As I grew older our family and others got an extravagant streak, discarded the trenchers and rose to the dignity of pewter plates and leaden spoons. Tin peddlers who traveled through the country with their wagons supplied these and other luxuries. Our food consisted chiefly of boiled and baked beans, bean porridge, coarse rye bread, apple sauce, hasty pudding beaten in milk, of which we all had plenty. The elder portion of the family ate meat twice a day—had plenty of vegetables, fish of their own catching, and occasionally big clams, which were cheap in those days, and shad in their season. . . .

Our dinners several times each week consisted of "pot luck," which was corned beef, salt pork and vegetables, all boiled together in the same big iron pot hanging from the crane which was supplied with iron hooks and trammels and swung in and out of the huge fireplace. In the same pot with the salt pork, potatoes, turnips, parsnips, beets, carrots, cabbage, and sometimes onions, was placed an Indian pudding, consisting of plain Indian meal mixed in water, pretty thick, salted and poured into a home-made brown linen bag which was tied at the top. When dinner was ready the Indian pudding was *first* taken from the pot, slipped out of the bag and eaten with molasses. Then followed the "pot luck." . . .

There were but few wagons or carriages in Bethel when I was a boy. Our grists of grain were taken to the mill in bags on horseback, and the women rode to church on Sundays and around the country on week days on horseback, usually on a cushion called a pillion fastened behind the saddle, the husband, father, brother, or lover riding in front on the saddle. The country doctor visited his patients on horseback, carrying his saddle-bags, containing calomel, jalap, Epsom salts, lancet, and a turnkey, those being the principal aids in relieving the sick. Nearly every person sick or well was bled every spring.

Teeth were pulled with a turnkey, and a dreadful instrument it was in looks, and terrible in execution. . . .

I remember seeing my father and our neighbors put through military drill every day by Capt. Noah Ferry in 1814, for the war with Great Britain of 1812–15. . . .

My uncles, aunts, and others, when I was a child, often spoke about ravages of Indians from which their ancestors had suffered, and numbers of them remembered and described the burning of Danbury by the British in 1777. . . .

Esquire Tom Taylor sometimes wore white-topped boots. He was a large, majestic-looking man, of great will-force, and was considered the richest man in Bethel. Mr. Eli Judd was marked second in point of wealth. Every year I took twelve dollars to Esquire Tom Taylor to pay the interest on a two hundred dollar note which my father owed him. I also annually carried four dollars and fifty cents to Eli Judd for interest on a seventy-five dollar note which he held against my father. As these wealthy men quietly turned over each note filed away in a small package till they found the note of my father, and then indorsed the interest thereon, I trembled with awe to think I stood in the presence of such wonderfully rich men. It was estimated that the richer of them was actually worth three thousand dollars!

Esquire Tom Taylor made quite a revolution here by one act. He got two yards of figured carpet to put down in front of his bed in the winter, because the bare board floor was too cold for his feet, while he was dressing. This was a big event in the social life of that day, and Esquire Tom was thought to be putting on airs which his great wealth alone permitted.

When I was but ten years old, newspapers came only once a week. The man who brought us the week's papers came up from Norwalk, and drove through this section with newspapers for subscribers and pins and needles for customers. He was called Uncle Silliman. I can remember well his weekly visit through Bethel, and his queer cry. On coming to a house or village he would shout, "News! News! The Lord reigns!" One time he passed our schoolhouse when a snow storm was prevailing. He shouted: "News! News! The Lord reigns—and snows a little."

Everybody had barrels of cider in their cellars and drank cider-spirits called "gumption." Professors of religion and the clergy all drank liquor. They drank it in all the hat and comb shops, and the farmers had it at hay and harvest times. Every sort of excuse was made for being treated. A new journeyman must give a pint or quart of rum to pay his footing. If a man had a new coat he must "sponge" it by treating. Even at funerals the clergy, mourners, and friends drank liquor. At public vendues the auctioneer held a bottle of liquor in his hand and when bidding lagged he would cry "a dram to the next bidder," the bid would be raised a cent, and the bidder would take his boldly and be the envy of most of the others.

The public whipping post and imprisonment for debt both flourished in Bethel in my youthful days. Suicides were buried at crossroads. How blessed are we to live in a more charitable and enlightened age, to enjoy the comforts and conveniences of modern times, and to realize that the world is continually growing wiser and better.

I sincerely congratulate my native village on her character for temperance, industry, and other good qualities.

And now, my friends, I take very great pleasure in presenting this fountain to the town and borough of Bethel as a small evidence of the love which I bear them and the respect which I feel for my successors. the present and future citizens of my native village.

Corn Lore

Samp was often pounded in olden times in a primitive and picturesque Indian mortar made of a hollowed block of wood or a stump of a tree, which had been cut off about three feet from the ground. The pestle was a heavy block of wood shaped like the inside of the mortar, and fitted with a handle attached to one side. This block was fastened to the top of a young and slender tree, a growing sapling, which was bent over and thus gave a sort of spring which pulled the pestle up after being pounded down on the corn. This was called a sweep and mortar mill.

They could be heard at a long distance. Two New Hampshire pioneers made clearings about a quarter of a mile apart and built houses. There was an impenetrable gully and thick woods between the cabins; and the blazed path was a long distance around, so the wives of the settlers seldom saw each other or any other woman. It was a source of great comfort and companionship to them both that they could signal to each other every day by pounding on their mortars. And they had an ingenious system of communication which one spring morning summoned one to the home of the other, where she arrived in time to be the first to welcome fine twin babies.

* * * * *

We ought to think of the value of food in those days; and we may be sure the governor and his council thought corn of value when they took it for taxes and made it a legal currency just like gold and silver, and forbade any one to feed it to pigs. If you happen to see the price of corn during those years down to Revolutionary times, you will, perhaps, be surprised to see how much the price varied. From ten shillings a bushel in 1631, to two shillings in 1672, to twenty in 1747, to two in 1751, and one hundred shillings at the opening of the Revolution. In these prices of corn, as in the price of all other articles at this time, the difference was in the money, which had a constantly changing value, not in the article itself or its usefulness. The corn had a steady value; it always furnished just so much food, and really was a standard itself rather than measured and valued by the poor and shifting money.

* * * * *

Many games were played with the aid of kernels of corn: fox and geese, checkers, "hull gull, how many," and games in which the corn served as counters.

The ears of corn were often piled into the attic until the floor was a foot deep with them. I once entered an ell bedroom in a Massachusetts

From *Home Life in Colonial Days,* by Alice Morse Earle, pp. 131–132, 138, 139–141. Copyright, 1898, by the Macmillan Company. New York and London. 1919.

farmhouse where the walls, rafters, and four-post bedstead were hung solid with ears of yellow corn, which truly "made a sunshine in a shady place."

Some of the preparation of corn fell upon the boys; it was their regular work all winter in the evening firelight to shell corn from the ears by scraping them on the iron edge of the wooden shovel or on the fire-peel. My father told me that even in his childhood in the first quarter of this century many families of moderate means fastened the long-handled frying-pan across a tub and drew the corn ears across the sharp edge of the handle of the pan. I note in Peter Parley's reminiscences of his childhood a similar use of a frying-pan handle in his home. Other farmers set the edge of a knife blade in a piece of wood, and scraped on the back of the blade. In some households the corn was pounded into hominy in wooden mortars. . . .

When the corn was shelled, the cobs were not carelessly discarded or disregarded. They were stored often in a leanto or loft in the kitchen ell; from thence they were brought down in skepes or boxes about a bushel at a time; and after being used by the children as playthings to build "cob-houses," were employed as light wood for the fire. They had a special use in many households for smoking hams; and their smoke was deemed to impart a specially delightful flavor to hams and bacon.

One special use of corn should be noted. By order of the government of Massachusetts Bay in 1623, it was used as ballots in public voting. At annual elections of the governors' assistants in each town, a kernel of corn was deposited to signify a favorable vote upon the nominee, while a bean signified a negative vote; "and if any freeman shall put in more than one Indian corn or bean he shall forfeit for every such offence Ten Pounds."

Bees, Change-Work, and Whangs

. . . SOMETIMES a logging-bee was made to clear a special lot for a neighbor, and a band of wood-choppers worked all day together. It was cheerful work, though the men had to stand all day in the snow, and the thermometer was below zero. But there was no cutting wind in the forest, and the exercise kept the blood warm. Many a time a hearty man would drop his axe to wipe the sweat from his brow. Loose woolen frocks, or long-shorts, two or three over each other, were warm as are the overlapping feathers of a bird; a few had buckskin or sheepskin waistcoats; their hands were warmly covered with home-knit mittens. In later days all had heavy well-greased boots, but in the early years of such pioneer settlements, as the towns of New Hampshire and Vermont, all could not afford to wear boots. Their place was well supplied by heavy woolen stockings, shoes, and

Ibid., pp. 416–417.

an over-covering of old stockings, or cloth soaked in neat's-foot oil; this was deemed a positive preventive of frozen feet.

It was the custom both among men and women to join forces on a smaller scale and have a little neighborly visiting by what was called "change-work." For instance, if two neighbors both were to make soap, or both to make apple-butter, or both to make up a rag carpet, instead of each woman sitting at home alone sewing and fitting the carpet, one would take her thimble and go to spend the day, and the two would sew all day long, finish and lay the carpet at one house. In a few days the visit would be returned, and the second carpet be finished. Sometimes the work was easier when two worked together. One man could load logs and sled them down to the sawmill alone, but two by "change-work" could accomplish the task much more rapidly and with less strain.

Even those evil days of New England households, the annual house-cleaning, were robbed of some of their dismal terrors by what was known as a "whang," a gathering of a few friendly women neighbors to assist one another in that dire time, and thus speed and shorten the hours of misery.

Raisings

"Here is a fine house! It stands high on dry land.
The owner is rich, and a very fine man.
At home he is honored, and abroad it's the same;
May he still keep increasing in honor and fame.
This house it stands square, and in a fair view
Of a river, fine meadows and neighbors a few.
The timber is square, and is well put together;
May God bless the owner, forever and ever!"

THIS was the toast proposed by Kimball Fletcher in 1835, when Parker Tabor's frame house was raised near the river in old Indian Stream Republic, now the town of Pittsburg, which lies just under the Canadian border.

In New Hampshire, as elsewhere in pioneer America, a "raising" brought out all the neighbors for miles around. Every available able-bodied man came to lift the heavy timbers when the master-builder gave the signal and cried, "Heave O heave!" The women gathered to serve the mammoth noon meal and early supper; the boys, accompanied by their dogs, scampered around everywhere, carrying tools and water to the workmen and running errands for the women.

Unless there was a bad accident like the one which happened in 1773

From *Hands That Built New Hampshire,* The Story of Granite State Craftsmen Past & Present, compiled by Workers of the Writers' Program of the Work Projects Administration in the State of New Hampshire, pp. 25–27. Brattleboro, Vermont: Stephen Daye Press.

when the Wilton meetinghouse was raised and one of the center beams supporting the frame broke and pitched timber, axes, board saws, and fifty men to the ground, raisings were gala occasions for the whole countryside. During the day there were intervals of relaxation from the hard work of lifting the great sills, plates, posts, and beams, when the young men held races and wrestled while their elders smoked and gossiped and watched the fun. Everybody had access to the hard cider and to the West India rum, which was furnished by the town if a public building was raised or by the host when a house was put up.

Liquid refreshments usually helped out even in the raisings of meetinghouses. In Mont Vernon, when the church was framed in the late eighteenth century, the building committee was instructed to provide one barrel of rum, two barrels of cider, and "one quarter of sugar" for the workmen. Tradition also tells us that the lack of rum at the raising of the Sandown meetinghouse, completed in 1774, was responsible for the first labor strike in New Hampshire. The supply ran out just as the workmen were about to put on the roof; so the men refused to work for half a day while a messenger was sent down to Newburyport for another half-barrel.

But in some communities there was opposition to so much drinking at raisings. The master builder, William Abbot of Boscawen, framer of churches at Somersworth, Cornish, Wentworth, Unity, Thornton, Henniker, and West Concord, took an active part in temperance reform. When the question of buying liquor for the raising of the West Concord meetinghouse came up in 1820, Mr. Abbot opposed it vigorously. He was told that there was always drinking at raisings and that it would be impossible to get workmen without rum.

"If there are not enough temperance men in Concord, I'll try and get them elsewhere," answered. "Send me down twelve good men," he told Thomas Coffin of Boscawen. There were so many volunteers that nearly one hundred men arrived to raise the meetinghouse, without rum.

The high point of a raising came after the body of the frame was actually up, the beams put in place, and the rafters placed in position, a pair at a time. Then the final task of pinning the ribs, to which the shingles were to be fastened, was divided between two crews, both ready for a merry contest to see which team would get its allotment of ribs placed first. The honor of setting the ridgepole and naming the building went to the victors, so the rivalry between the teams was great. When the last nail had been pounded down, two men from the winning team, each one with a bottle in his hand, clambered out on the ridgepole. Reaching the center of their high perch, up they stood, one of them facing the south, and the other, the north.

"This is a fine frame and deserves a good name!" one man cried, following a recognized custom of the North Country.

"Oh, yes! Oh, yes!" chanted the crowd below him. "What shall we call it?"

The man facing the north answered by giving a very humorous or elaborate name; and when his companion sang out "Oh, yes!", each of them took a long drink from his bottle.

An eye-witness of a barn-raising held in Coös County in the mid-nineteenth century says that, in this particular instance, one of the pseudo godparents was a sailor who added an original note to the customary procedure by reciting at the top of his lungs:

"The owner is a cooper, a jolly old soul,
We'll drink all his rum, but leave the ridgepole."

Sailors were particularly popular at raisings, for they dared to climb to and height and to perform all kinds of daring feats. They stood on the ridgepole or hung down by their heels as they drank the toast and christened the building, according to their own doggerel:

"Some oak and some pine,
Some coarse and some fine,
Some old and some new,
Hand on the bottle and that will do."

The Cider-Mill

Abijah Crombie's cider-mill was somewhat off the main road, upon a bank that sloped toward the river. . . .

* * * * *

On account of its situation upon the slope, the mill had two stories in front, and one in the rear. Carts were driven in from the lane to unload apples at the upper level, and then taken around to receive barrels of cider at the lower. The mill might have been called a shed without hurting anybody's feelings. Many of the sheathing boards and shingles were split, or warped, or loose; and little of a burglar's art would have been required to open the rickety doors, fastened by wooden latches and pins. The building had never been painted, and its rough sides had the tone of soft gray, which is so pleasing in pictures, and so melancholy in fact.

The upper story was a receptacle for apples, from whence they were poured through an inclining trough into the grinding mill below. The visitor who entered upon the lower level saw a pair of upright wooden cylinders, placed near together, and revolving in opposite directions, so as to crush the apples drawn in between them. Teeth upon one cylinder fitted into holes in the other, to facilitate the crushing. The power was supplied by a horse traveling in a small circle, and moving the lever which turned the motor-wheel. The machinery was of the rudest sort, wholly of wood,

From *Quabbin,* The Story of a Small Town, with Outlooks upon Puritan Life, by Francis H. Underwood, pp. 238, 239–240. Copyright, 1892, by Lee and Shepard. Boston. 1893.

but easily managed, and efficient. The pomace fell into a large shallow vat (presumably clean), and was scooped out by wooden shovels when a form was made up to be pressed. The form was simply arranged. A sheaf of clean straw was spread out evenly upon a platform, which was grooved with channels, and placed directly beneath a large perpendicular screw depending from a solid frame. Upon the layer of straw the pomace was spread like a boy's jam; that is to say, considerably more jam than bread. Then a second even layer was spread at right angles to the first; then more pomace and more straw, until the pile reached a height of two or three feet. A coping board was placed upon the top, and blocks were laid upon it. Then the great screw was turned with long wooden levers, and brought down upon the blocks, very gently at first, so that the pile might retain its consistency, then harder, until the last drops of juice had trickled out.

If the apples were carefully picked over, excluding those that were rotten or wormy; if all parts of the mill, including cylinders, channels, vats, shovels, and straw, were scrupulously clean; and if the barrels were well-seasoned and sweet, the cider was certain to be pure and palatable. There were many *ifs*.

Sugaring Science

LIKE I said, they generally start sugaring operations along the first week in March; they begin to wash the buckets. Nowadays they get the buckets out of the sugarhouse and scald them. In grandpa's time they didn't have sugarhouses, to begin with, and at first they didn't even keep buckets from year to year, but made wooden trenchers.

They would cut down a white birch or some other tree with soft wood, and split the tree in half. They would adz out a hollow in the flat side and chop off that section, and then adz out another hollow and chop that off. So the trenchers was a sort of rough oblong chopping bowls, as you might say. They didn't hang them on the trees, but just propped them up on the ground where the sap was handy.

When they got their trenchers made or their buckets tightened up and cleaned and distributed around by the trees, they could start tapping. The Indians used to cut a gash in the tree just as if they was making turpentine. Gramp had got a little beyond that; he used a tapping iron.

A tapping iron looks like a big gouge chisel, and it was used the same way—you simply drove it into the tree at a right angle. Then you put in a steel sap spout. They've come back to metal spouts again now; the oldest and the newest spouts is metal, and the wooden ones that you occasionally see come from the time in between.

From "Grandpa Was Quite a Fellow," by Walter Needham, as recorded by Barrows Mussey, *Saturday Evening Post,* Vol. 219 (Nov. 9, 1946), No. 19, pp. 93–94, 96.

The auger to bore a hole for tapping is newer, too; the old-time blacksmiths couldn't make an auger, where they could make a tapping iron. The big old three-quarter-inch augers with a wooden cross handle go along with the wooden spouts. You will find a great many old trees around here that have been bored with an old T-handled three-quarter-inch auger. Now, of course, they only use a half or three-eighths bit, with the small metal spout.

The old steel spouts was made by the blacksmith out of worn-out scythe blades. The blacksmith would cut off the heavy rim on the back to make nails with, and bend the thin part into spouts. That was just one sign of how precious metal was in gramp's time. That was why the blacksmith was such a big man in the community.

The steel spouts they drove into the cut made by the tapping iron. The wooden spouts was whittled out of staghorn shoemake. I've made them myself. You take a piece that is about right for size, and whittle it around to fit a hole the size of your auger. You cut away half of the spout on top, and just left the end that went into the tree round. Then you run a hot iron through the pith and burned out a hole for the sap to flow through.

The science of tapping a tree is something that not many people know. The only results you get from tapping comes from the sap growth, the outer growth. You could bore a hole clear to the center of the tree, and you wouldn't get no more sap than if you just bored two inches under the bark. There is only two inches' depth of sapwood on a tree. You can bore as much deeper as you're a mind to, and all you will do is hurt the tree.

The trees don't seem to be damaged any by tapping. Some of the old holes in a big tree will be ten inches under the bark. Wherever you bore, it makes a kind of an elliptical dead place, and that spot always stays in the tree forever, and the hole doesn't fill up; it grows over, but it won't fill up. You cut any old maple, and you will find the holes far underneath the bark.

In deciding where to tap a tree, you pick out a place that has new growth. It's very hard to tell without you study it, but if you look at the tree, there will be new cracks or openings in the bark. As the tree expands, the bark doesn't expand with it, but keeps splitting open; that is why they are shaggy. If you look around carefully, you will find where the new growth shows on the bark.

The next part of the science is to set your buckets on the side where there is the most limbs or the biggest limbs. The sap goes to the limbs, so you always look up a tree as well as at the bark. You look for the new growth on the side where the limbs will draw the sap. The ideal is to get more or less on the southeasterly exposure, but you tap on any side if the new growth and limbs is right.

Once a tree has been tapped, you mustn't tap directly in line with the old hole, above it or below it. If you tap below it, you will get sap, but it's injurious to the tree. If you tap above it, you won't get any sap. Just move out of line to one side, and it won't matter. The height doesn't matter in itself; you just want a convenient level for handling the buckets.

Well, you tap your trees and you hand your buckets. Then you come back to the weather and the season, the same as gramp done every day of his life. They've got their evaporators and their central-reservoir gathering systems and their state grading nowadays, but the weather is still the only thing that will make the sap run.

To get a good run of sap, it should freeze hard at night and thaw day-times. For a good sap day there must be a west wind and bright sunshine; it is unusual that sap will run on a south wind.

When the snow goes and the frost gets out of the ground, the minute the buds begin to swell on the tree, the sirup starts to take on a leathery taste. It's like the difference between Scotch and straight whisky. What little sap runs after that is called the bud run; that sugar is generally just sold for tobacco sweetening. The quality of the sap varies from year to year too. Some years it's good and some years it's quite sandy. And some years it's sweeter than other years, so you get more sirup for the same amount of sap.

In a bad year, the sap won't hardly run at all, to do you any good; in a very good year, it may run as long as four weeks. It isn't usually steady. It will run a day or two, and you'll have a freeze-up and it will stop entirely. Then it will start again and run two or three days more. As long as it freezes at night, you're all right; you don't get the buddy taste. During some of these extra runs, the sap may even run all night, and the buckets will be full again in the morning. Then the buckets may start to sour, and instead of drawing sap away, you have to draw water to the buckets and wash them.

Gramp would go around and collect in the morning, and again in the afternoon. Nowadays they use a big gathering tub on a sledge or even run the sap straight from the trees down metal gutters to a reservoir. In gramp's time, you just lugged the buckets in by hand, and they got pretty heavy along toward night, especially if the snow was deep. The modern buckets hold around fourteen to fifteen quarts. The old ones was a lot more awkward, but they had two of the staves on opposite sides prolonged at the top, with a stick running between them for a handle. A lot of people in gramp's time used wooden sap yokes—pieces of wood hollowed out to fit over your shoulders, with a semicircle cut out for the neck and a piece sticking out from the shoulder at each end. You would take two of your wide-bottomed wooden buckets, and hang them by cords on the ends of the yoke, and go to a tree. You could collect from one tree to another until your two buckets was full or, if the ones on the tree was full, you would just swap buckets and go back. In those days you wouldn't pretend to gather a great ways off. Sometimes you see a sap yoke made of two bows fastened together at the ends, with two straps across in between for your shoulders, but I think those mostly come from Canada.

Before the time of the gathering tub, they would just go around and collect the sap, come back and pour it in a big kettle over a fire of maple chunks, and leave it to boil while they went back for more sap. When things got more permanent, they used what they called a sap pan—just an ordinary big iron pan maybe eight feet long and two or three feet wide. That's all I ever knew of gramp's using. After that come the evaporator. There's different kinds of evaporators, but the idea is about the same in all of them. The Bellows Falls evaporator, for example, is a sap pan with crosswise partitions. Each partition connects at one end with the wall of the pan, and at the other end it doesn't. The openings are at alternate ends, so that the cold sap flows in over the fire on the front end, and zigzags through these partitions until it gets to the back end, which has a partition with a gate. You lift up the gate and fill the back end. You shut the gate and start watching your thermometer; the back end boils slowly because it's so far away from the fire, and when you get to the temperature of sirup or sugar—the sugar temperature is higher, of course—you draw the liquid off through a felt strainer into your cans or tubs or whatever you're putting it up in.

In the old days they used to use part of the run to make sap beer. They put the sap in a barrel and let it ferment, just the same as you make cider. I never knew of grandpa's making sap beer, which may be why I never cared much for it. I don't think it's a very appetizing drink myself, but if you go back into the hills around Wardsboro at the right time, you will still get some sap beer, in case you want to try it.

Gramp's sirup was a black molasses, of course, but like I said, he would boil it on down to sugar, and pour it into crocks or tubs. He made wooden sugar tubs specially, and he would pour the liquid sugar right in and let it harden in the tub. When they wanted some sugar, they'd just go in there and crack some out. Sometimes they might melt it. If they wanted it fine, they would pound it up. Ordinarily, they used it in lumps just as they pounded it out, for cooking or in their tea. They didn't drink coffee much in those days, anyway. For sweetening, they put it on the stove and heated it, because when it was melted you could measure it. They melted it for pancakes, too.

Sugaring off is a big occasion around here. The young folks will come in for a party, with doughnuts and coffee and sour pickles. They bring in tubs of snow. They boil the sirup down until it will wax—a little past what the cookbook calls the soft-ball stage—and then they pour it on the snow. It cools right away into sheets or strips, not particularly sticky, and you can pick it straight off the snow with a fork and eat it. The pickles is to cut the sweetness, so as you can eat more sugar.

In the old days they used to sugar off sometimes on the kitchen stove, and they would hang a piece of fat salt pork from the stove shelf. When the sirup got to boiling up, it would hit that salt pork and would flatten right out.

After white sugar got to be common, and maple sugar was something special, it was mostly sold as cake sugar. I remember when they sold a five-pound box of cake sugar for a dollar. That box would probably cost you around six dollars now, if you could find it. I helped put the cakes up in nice clean white basswood boxes with pinked paper. My job was pinking the paper with a toothed iron.

When I was in Indiana I met a girl at Huntington who had what she called maple sugar and pecan nuts, a kind of black stuff. I told her she didn't know what maple sugar was, and I sent her out a box of the best maple sugar I could find. She wouldn't give in, though; she said that was maple candy.

Late years they think they have to have stirred sugar—a very recent invention. You cook it to the temperature marked for stirred sugar on your sugar thermometer, and while it's cooling you beat it with a wooden paddle. It's like warm butter, and never hardens; it grains, but the grains are very fine from being beaten, and that makes it white. It makes a pretty good spread or a frosting, but it don't taste much like maple to me.

Another thing they do in making these little candy hearts and leaves and shapes like that, they dip them in hot sirup while they're fresh. That glazes them and keeps the inside from ever hardening.

Well Digging

Water on the farm is like the seasons—you don't think about it until after you've bought your first farm and spent a dry summer there. Gramp found plenty of water, but then, of course, he knew where to go and dig. Once he found water, if it wasn't a big spring, he would have to dig a well. That was a two-man job after he got down a little way. The hole to start with would be quite large, depending on how deep they thought they was going, but generally ten or twelve feet across. When it got down to where they had trouble throwing the dirt over and out, they started another hole in the center or to one side, a smaller size, and dug down again. They would throw the dirt onto the shelf, and the next man would relay it up; they throwed it up with long spades. Possibly they might have to make as many as two shelves. Most wells are not much over twenty feet deep; you hear of forty-foot wells, but I never see one. Around here, twenty-five feet is a good well. If they didn't begin to strike water in twenty feet, I don't know what they would have done—dig somewhere else, most likely.

Laying up a well was an art all to itself, like building stone walls, only the stones for laying a well was selected. They had to be of about a uniform size and triangular shape. Gramp would lay the well with the pointed ends of the stones toward the center of the well. That made the circular form, and then, when the dirt pressed against them from behind, they could never fall in. It's very seldom you see an old well that has caved.

As gramp went up, somebody would shovel down the dirt and odd-shaped

Ibid., p. 107.

rocks against the outside of the stone well. They worked the dirt in and packed it down as they went along, and, when they got through, the well was there for good.

Building a Stone Wall

GRAMP was really more of a hand with the cobblestones that come up out of the field. They was something the seasons brought out on the farm. The land hereabouts is strewed with these round, smooth stones left by the ice sheets, supposedly. They are various kinds but mostly a granite formation that was rolled in here.

They would plow once the best they could to free the stones some. They would just dig out the small ones with a spade. For the big ones they would have to use the oxen and a stoneboat. They would dig around them, and then flip a chain over the stone with what they called a rolling hitch. It was quite a trick to make the hitch stay on various different shapes of stone, because no two were alike. It looked simple, but I can't even tell you what a rolling hitch is like without I see the stone you're going to hitch on to. Anyway, with a proper rolling hitch, the oxen could pull the stone right out of the ground and onto the stoneboat.

A stoneboat is merely a large plank toboggan, except the front end is not turned up so high. The planks was sawed special, nosed up at the end, so that the front would run three inches or so from the ground. At the sawmill the planks was sawed straight to a certain point, and then put on the carriage at a diagonal and sawed the rest of the way, so the nose turned up.

The stone walls both fenced in the fields and cleared them out. In preparation for the wall, they would plow the loam where the wall was going, and shovel it out more or less to the subsoil. Then they would draw the stoneboat along beside this trench, and roll the big ones in for foundation stones. Quite often they would wall off a ten-acre lot, forty rods one way and forty rods the other. Sometimes it was only haphazard.

After gramp had rolled the big stones off into the ditch and placed them to suit him, he would draw the boat beside of it. As fast as the boat comes along he would take off the small stones that a man could pick up, and he'd throw them right on the wall, and build it straight ahead just as easy as you please. He worked so fast you might have thought he was just throwing them in at random, yet when he got through, the wall was as solid as if it was one rock.

Ibid., p. 99.

The Hired Man

If the Nineties in a New England town were years of weakness in many ways, and foretold the apparent decay of a strong civilization, it was in those very years that a fine institution flourished. Back in those last decades of the nineteenth century, and until almost 1920, there lived in the small Yankee town an unique kind of person, the Hired Man. No civilization or group of folkways save our own could have produced him, and ours could not have existed without his help. Van Wyck Brooks does not know him, O'Neill disdains him, and Frost is only condescending. Nevertheless, this half-forgotten man is as important as any other constructive member of the community. He was not genteel; he was not cultured or social-minded, but he was of the town and the ways of life that built and sustained it. Now, alas, he is out of the picture, gone with the Saybrook Platform, witches, the heath hen, and stern dominies.

There will always be plenty of mercenary yokels who work out on farms, but they are not the hired men I knew thirty years ago. Some were neat, dapper sports who drove a fast horse; others were dirty and always broke. They might be married or single, moral and staid and even church members, or mighty swearers and drinkers with whom no hired girl was safe. About half of them were unimaginative fellows who plodded through a life of hard work; the others labored just as hard and became legendary figures who added zest and color to sedate rural life. Most of them dreamed of how they would farm it for themselves if they had a chance, and a few did get their own places in time; the others died in an ell chamber or a rented room. But no matter what they were like, they were more than just laborers who took wages; they *helped* on a farm, not just worked out.

Those hired men I knew were the best exponents of the social-contract theory the world has ever produced. They knew that of their own free will and accord they had signed an agreement with the men who paid them, an agreement which, through long years of hiring and being hired, had so developed that now it took into consideration the demands of farms, farmers, and helpers, and was more binding than any piece of paper with seals and signatures.

A good hired man might tell his boss to go to hell, but he would not quit in such farm crises as haying or threshing. Changing jobs was no disgrace; in fact, an independent fellow liked to show what he was made of by so doing, but he would not quit because an employer set too fast a pace of work. Mind you, I said, "Set too fast a pace." In other words, the boss was doing as much as he demanded. A hired man could lie all he wanted to about some matters, but he must tell the truth about what happened on the place in the way of crops, cattle, and buildings. He must never steal

---

From *Town Meeting Country*, by Clarence M. Webster, pp. 162–164. Copyright, 1945, by Clarence M. Webster. New York: Duell, Sloan & Pearce.

from the farm, and an employer's family was sacrosanct unless a Mrs. Potiphar was too insistent and Potiphar himself none too moral. All these things a good hand did or did not do, not because he was paid so much money, but because he was helping that family and that farm.

The employer lived up to his share of the contract or he lost a good worker. For instance, a hired man was accepted as part of the family; he usually ate with the folks, called them by their first names, and was listened to when he gave advice. There must be food enough to keep a worker in body and spirit, and he was capable of saying a few words about too much salt pork or dried codfish. As I have said already, a good boss got out and set the pace at working if he were physically capable of doing so. If slight and almost frail, he had to earn the praise of "tryin' his damnedest t' keep up." A farmer could pay as low wages as the market allowed, and he expected a hired man to work overtime in case of emergency, but on the other hand he helped out that hired man if the latter were sick or needed money. Thirty years ago New England farmers had to be gentlemen before they could get along with their help and be given those words of accolade: "A goddam good man to work for."

After the contract of service between the hired man and his boss was drawn, the hired man had to think of his relations to the town. Very seldom, in fact almost never, was he a candidate for any office, but he paid his taxes, went to caucus and town meeting, and voted with more or less thoughtful deliberation. He was not a town father or elder statesman like the man he worked for, and he knew he probably never would be but, just the same, he felt that he was a real part of the town and was helping to make it a better place to live in.

Men like these have almost disappeared. A few of the toughest, bibulous, profane old rascals are still doing chores for their keep on little hill farms, but in another decade the last of them will have been buried by the town, and from our land will have gone another proof that a man can fill a humble role in life and still retain the comforting feeling that he is just as good as the other fellow.

Weaving and Spinning Lore

In the American colonies hand-weaving was . . . a universal industrial art. In no part of the country has the industry lingered longer than in old Narragansett. In many old New England towns single hand-looms can be found, some in running order, and with owners capable of running them to make rag-carpets. Others are still standing, cob-webbed and dusty, in attic lofts, lean-to chambers, woodsheds, or barns, with no one to set the

---

From *In Old Narragansett,* Romances and Realities, by Alice Morse Earle, pp. 26–27, 29–30, 34–35, 41–45, 46. Copyright, 1898, by Charles Scribner's Sons. New York.

piece or fill the shuttles. In Narragansett I know a score of old looms in good running order, though, save in one instance, set only for weaving rag-carpets; in many cases the owners, who do not make weaving a trade, will not "start them up" for weaving less than a hundred yards of carpeting. This is a long strip for a room in a cottage or farm-house, so neighbors frequently join together in ordering these carpets, and in company send vast rolls of the filling, which is made of inch-wide strips of cloth of all colors and materials sewed in long strips. Within a few years these old hand-looms have been used for weaving rag-portières made of silk strips.

Weaving was a very respectable occupation. It is told that the regicide Judge Whalley lived to great old age in Narragansett—one hundred and three years—and earned his living by weaving. The son of the Congregational minister at Narragansett, Dr. Torrey, was a weaver. The province was full of weavers. Miss Hazard gives the names of many in her *College Tom.* With all the spinning-jennies for spinning a vast supply of thread and yarn, there were no power-looms in Narragansett till 1812. Hand-looms made up all the yarn and thread that were produced. The prince of Narragansett weavers was Martin Read. In 1761 he was baptized in St. Paul's Church as "Martin Read, an adult, the Parish Clerk." He was a devoted lover of the church and was sexton for many years. . . .

* * * * *

. . . He wove coverlets, blankets, broadcloth, flannel, worsted, linen, tow-cloth, and calamanco. This last was a glossy woolen twilled fabric, sometimes woven in a pattern in the warp. James Fontaine, a Huguenot weaver, says it was made of a fine double-twisted worsted. It was much used for the nightgowns and banians [1] worn by substantial citizens of the day, and for women's winter gowns.

Other goods made by Weaver Reed were duroy, durant, and crocus, a coarse tow-stuff for servants' wear. This word, crocus, still may be heard in Virginia, and perhaps elsewhere in the South, where it was more and longer used than in Narragansett.

Martin Read lived near the old church he so dearly loved, and a sightly spot it was for a home. Still standing beside the church foundation, the site where the church first stood, is the deserted house in which Martin Read lived and wove and whistled and sung. On the road near his home lives to-day the last of the old-time weavers [Weaver Rose], one who can weave woolen and linen stuffs. Hand-weaving is not with him an accidental industrial makshift, but his every-day occupation and means of livelihood. He learned to weave from one of Martin Read's apprentices.

* * * * *

The old-time cotton and wool bed-spreads or coverlets, seen of old on every four-post bedstead, he now sells for portières and bathroom rugs, as well as for bed and couch spreads. They are woven in simple geometric

[1] A morning gown such as is worn by the Banians.—Alice Morse Earle, *Costume of Colonial Times* (New York, 1894), p. 51.

patterns, just as in the times of the ancient Britons, when the wools of the weft were dyed with woad and broom. The patterns are nearly all over a century old. He has a worn pattern-book with bewildering rules for setting the heddles for over fifty designs. Quaint of name are the patterns: "chariot-wheels and church-windows" is a bold, large design; "church-steps," a simpler one; "bachelors' fancy," "devil's fancy," "five doves in a row," "shooting-star," "rising sun," "rail fence," "green veils" offer little in their designs to give reason for their names. "Whig rose," "Perry's Victory," and "Lady Washington's fancy" show an historical influence in naming. "Orange-peel" is simply a series of oblong hexagons honeycombed together. "All summer and all winter" was similar. "Bricks and blocks" is evenly checkered. "Capus diaper" is a more complicated design for weaving damask linen, taking five harnesses. Floral names are common, such as "Dutch tulip," "rose in bloom," "pansies in the wilderness," "five snow-balls," etc.

* * * * *

Had the weaving been the only portion of the work done in the farm-house it would seem an important addition to the round of domestic duties, but every step in the production of clothing was done at home, as expressed by Miss Hazard of her great-grandfather's household in Narragansett: "From the shepherd who dagged the sheep, the wool-comber who combed the wool, the spinners who spun, the weavers who wove, all in regular order till the traveling tailor made the clothes up, and Thomas Hazard went to meeting in a suit made from wool of his own growing." The "all-wool goods, yard wide," which we so glibly purchase to-day meant to the Narragansett dame the work of months from the time the fleeces were given to her deft fingers. After daglocks, bands, feltings, tarred locks, were skilfully cut out, the white locks were carefully tossed and separated, and tied in net bags with tallies, to be dyed. The homely saying, "dyed in the wool," indicated a process of much skill. Indigo furnished the blue shades, madder and logwood the red. Sassafras, fustic, hickory, and oak bark furnished yellow and brown. It will be noted that the old-time dyes were all vegetable. After the dyeing mixed colors could be made by spreading in layers and carding them over and over again. In carding wool, the cards should be kept warm and the wool very slightly greased with rape-oil or "swines'-grease." At last the wool was carded into light rolls and was ready for the wheel.

An old writer says, "The action of spinning must be learned by practice, not by relation." The grace and beauty of wool-spinning, ever sung by the poets, need not be described. Stepping lightly backward and forward, with arms at times high in the air, now low at the side, often by the light only of the fire, the worker, no matter what her age, seemed the perfection of the grace of motion; and the beauty of the occupation makes the name of spinster (the only title by law of every single woman) a title of honor and dignity.

The preparation of flax was infinitely more tedious and more complicated.

From the time the tender plant springs up, through pulling, spreading, drying, rippling, stacking, rotting, cleaning, braking, swinging, beetling, ruffling, hetchelling, spreading, and drawing, there are in all over twenty dexterous manipulations till the flax is ready for the wheel, the most skilful manipulation of all, and is wrapped round the spindle. Flax thread was spun on the small flax-wheel. "Lint on the wee wheel, woo' on the muckle." It was reeled into skeins on a clock-reel, which ticked when the requisite number had been wound, when the spinner stopped and tied the skein. A quaint old ballad has the refrain:

And he kissed Mistress Polly when the clock-reel ticked.

These knots of linen thread had to be bleached before they were woven. They were soaked in water for days, and constantly wrung out; they were washed again and again in the brook; they were "bucked" with ashes and hot water in a bucking-tub; they were seethed, soaked, rinsed, dried, and wound on bobbins and quills for the loom. In spite of all this bleaching, the linen web, when woven, would not be white, and it afterward went through twoscore more processes of bucking, possing, rinsing, drying, and grassing. In all, forty bleaching manipulations were necessary for "light linens." Thus, at least, sixteen months had passed since the flax-seed had been sown, during which the good-wife had not "eaten the bread of idleness."

* * * * *

The old-time preparatory work of the weaver is much simplified for this Narragansett weaver in modern times, by the use of machine-spun threads and yarns. The warp of these bed coverlets is of strong twine or thread, while the weft is of various woolen yarns or zephyrs or crewels, bought at mills. These latter are aniline-dyed, and in no artistic sense equal the old indigo, hickory, sassafras, or madder home-dyed wools of yore. These skeins of yarn are prepared for use by spreading them on a reel or swifts, and winding the yarn off on quills in a quilling-wheel, which is somewhat like a simplified spinning-wheel.

Besides these weavers who worked in their own homes, making their own wool into cloth to sell, or weaving the thread and yarn brought to them by their neighbors, there was a distinct class of traveling weavers, who went from house to house working for a few shillings a day and their "keep." They often were quaint and curious characters; frequently what were known as "natural preachers"; that is, either mystic or fanatic souls who tried to supplement or supersede the religious teaching of the community by itinerant preaching. Such teachers and preachers have ever flourished in Narragansett since the day of Samuel Gorton and his associates. . . .

* * * * *

. . . There were few women-weavers among them, especially for linen-weaving, which was hard work. Occasionally some sturdy woman, of masculine muscle and endurance, was a weaver.

Samplers

THE word sampler, the "ensempler" of Chaucer's day, referred originally to the fact that these pieces were a means of recording needlework stitches for future reference. All seventeenth-century samplers, both English and American, had this purpose. They were made by experienced needleworkers, and the stitches worked on them were elaborate and intricate in design. Like English samplers of the period, American specimens were rich with drawnwork, cutwork, and lace stitches which the owners intended to use in the adornment of bed curtains, petticoats, and other household and personal finery. Few of them are in existence today. An exhaustive search conducted by the Society of the Colonial Dames of Massachusetts in 1921 revealed only seven American samplers of the years of 1600–1700. One of these is the well-known Anne Gower sampler (actually made in England), embroidered by the first wife of Governor John Endicott of Massachusetts Bay Colony. None of the seven was of New Hampshire origin.

These early samplers were worked on the narrow, coarse linens produced on the hand looms used at the time. The embroidery threads were linen or loosely woven silk strands, usually no coarser than present-day sewing silks. "Sam-cloths," as they were called, could be easily rolled up, tucked into a bag or an apron pocket, and then brought out at an instant's notice when the needleworker wished to study a stitch or to add a new one to her collection. Sometimes they were a yard long and only eight to twelve inches wide. Even after wider linen became available, they held to this convenient, longer-than-wide form during the years when samplers were used simply for pattern purposes.

The oldest New Hampshire sampler of which we have record was worked by Mary Wingate of Hampton, probably in 1719,[1] and is nearly

---

From *Hands That Built New Hampshire,* The Story of Granite State Craftsmen Past and Present, compiled by Workers of the Writers' Program of the Work Project Administration in the State of New Hampshire, pp. 176–179, 180–181. Copyright, 1940, by Francis P. Murphy, Governor of New Hampshire. Brattleboro, Vermont: Stephen Daye Press.

[1] The oldest sampler I have ever seen is in the collection of antique articles now in Pilgrim Hall at Plymouth. It was made by a daughter of the Pilgrims. The verse embroidered on it reads:—

> Lorea Standish is My Name.
> Lord Guide my Heart that I may do thy Will,
> And fill my Hands with such convenient skill
> As will conduce to Virtue void of Shame,
> And I will give the Glory to thy Name.

—Alice Morse Earle, *Home Life in Colonial Days* (New York and London, 1919), p. 266.

twice as long as it is wide. Besides the pattern stitches, it is ornamented with designs of animals and birds and has two sets of alphabets. Another example of these longer-than-wide samplers is one made in 1731 by Lydia Hart. It is owned by the New Hampshire Historical Society.

Besides the rows of stitches with colorful names, like trellis stitch, holly stitch, fern stitch, queen stitch, and fisher stitch, all of which John Taylor immortalized in verse in 1640, samplers were adorned with alphabets and numerals, as patterns to mark household linens and to keep track of the number of pieces turned out. They were also embellished with embroidered portrayals of "Flowers, Plants, and Fishes, Beasts, Birds, Flyes, and Bees," as Taylor, in "Needle's Excellency," pointed out three hundred years ago:

> There's nothing near at hand, or farthest sought,
> But with the needle may be shaped and wrought.

Many of the motifs were executed in that oldest form of needlework decoration, the cross-stitch, which is still one of the best liked of stitches. Arranged in double lines, blocks, and borders, the tiny crosses make perfect frames to enclose embroidered verses and pictures. After 1740 few samplers were made which did not include such frames.

On a sampler embroidered in 1729 by Polly Eppes of Francestown, and now owned by Mrs. Orpha Durgin of Manchester, the border appears only as a frame around the verse, but it anticipates the general use of borders by a number of years. This piece of New Hampshire needlework, next in age to the Wingate sampler, is worked on two layers of linen. On it Polly inscribed this couplet:

> This needle work of mine doth tell
> That the child hath learned well.

When the sampler advanced from the sam-cloth stage to a status where it was displayed as a certificate of merit for ability in needlecraft, the name of the work, the date it was finished, and an inscription, became part of the design. Many of the inscriptions of eighteenth and nineteenth century work were moral mottoes, often designed to instruct the young needlewoman in the precepts of daily living. Mrs. Mary Thompson of Troy says she was brought up on the principle expressed in a verse on her grand-

---

Other sampler rhymes:

Mary Jackson is my name,
America my nation,
Boston is my dwelling place,
And Christ is my salvation.

Dorothy Lynde is my Name
And this Work is mine
My Friends may have
When I am Dead and laid in Grave
This Needlework of mine can tell
That in my youth I learned well
And by my elders also taught
Not to spend my time for naught.
(In Old South Church, Boston)

—Alice Morse Earle, *Child Life in Colonial Days* (New York, 1899), pp. 332, 333.

mother's sampler, and that she, in turn, impressed the thought upon her own children. When one of them started to complain of another's wrong-doing, Mrs. Thompson quoted the first line and asked the child to complete the quatrain which little Ruth Aked embroidered in 1811:

How soon our watchful eyes can view
The smallest faults which others do
Yet to our own we're ever blind
And very few or none we find.

The stanza worked by Sarah K. Little in 1827 is more sombre in its feeling and quite similar to the melancholy lines which were inscribed on samplers made during the years when the followers of Jonathan Edwards were hurling their threats of damnation at the New England people. Fourteen-year-old Sarah embroidered a design of pink roses and green leaves with feathery edges on her sampler, but she enclosed in a black-bordered frame the following verse:

As summer flowers fall to rise no more
As billows rise and die upon the shore
So generations live and pass away
They sleep in silence till the Judgement Day.

This sampler hangs in the Manchester Historic Association Building.

Even more lugubrious is the inscription on a sampler owned by Mrs. Eaton Sargent of Nashua:

Let me in life prepare to die
That I may live with God on high,
With Saints and Angels let me be
And dwell with them eternally.

The saddest note of all the words enclosed in the beautifully embroidered border is found in these words: "Elizabeth Gage wrought this in 1822 in the 10th year of her age."

Among the definite changes which took place in the evolution of the American sampler during the eighteenth century was the decrease in the ages of their makers. The samplers of the seventeenth century were embroidered by mature women; by the 1780's they had become the prerogative of girls around thirteen years of age and younger. Every well-brought up daughter of the family made at least one, to show that she had served her apprenticeship in an important branch of work which for centuries has been allotted to womankind.

* * * * *

The period between the close of the Revolutionary War and the beginning of the Civil War was the great era of American sampler-making. Nineteenth-century samplers are distinguished for their original designs, which include birds of a coloring and shape Audubon never catalogued, and animals of strangely mixed characteristics. Pictorial samplers portraying Biblical scenes, like the tempting of Adam and Eve, and the spies returning from the Land of Canaan, or showing representations of patriotic symbols, public buildings, and dwelling houses, were all popular.

Death, never far distant from the minds of early New England settlers, left a definite imprint on needlework designs. Memorial samplers,

> Each with its urn and stiffly-weeping tree
> Devoted to some memory long ago
> More faded than their lines of worsted woe, [1]

often were worked at girls' schools as a part of the assigned courses in needlework for all young gentlewomen. . . .

* * * * *

Genealogical samplers, which appeared just before the Revolutionary War, read like pages from the family Bible, and provide a valuable historic record of births, marriages, and deaths. . . .

Quilting

For many years patchwork, like sampler-making, was part of every young girl's education. According to Lucy Larcom, almost every New England girl learned to make patchwork at school while she was learning the alphabet.

Patchwork bedcovers were divided into two groups: the "comforter," made with a thick interlining, and the quilt, in which the interlining was much lighter. The top and under covers of the "comforter" were held together by strands of worsted pulled through them and the interlining and then tied or "tacked" together, while the coverings of quilts were fastened by means of fine patterns done in running stitches.

Quilting was an art in itself, and needleworkers were proud of their ability in this line. Sometimes they "quilted by the eye"; again they used the edge of a saucer or pan to make patterns of scallops or circles. Sometimes a string was chalked and stretched tautly across the quilt top. It was then snapped to impress the lines of the design on the fabric. A Nashua woman says that one of her earliest recollections was watching her grandmother mark a quilt in this manner. "Snap it again, Grannie!" she always cried as her grandmother completed each step of the marking process.

[1] James Russell Lowell.

Ibid., pp. 183–185, 186, 187–189.

Another method of marking patterns was by means of carved wooden blocks which were heavily chalked and then pressed firmly against the upper side of the coverlet. Mrs. R. P. Peabody, a native of the Androscoggin valley town of Shelburne, wrote in 1882 that in her girlhood pressed quilts were part of every bride's marriage outfit. She recalled a number of pressed quilts of unusual beauty made by her mother's friends. One was bright green, lined with straw color, and quilted in inch squares with blue thread; another was blue, quilted in little fans; a third was quilted in feather work with a border of sunflower leaves, and then cross-quilted in straight lines. The patterns for these, like most others made in this vicinity, were pressed and marked by Mrs. Ezekiel Evans, who was famous in those days for her designs.

In the nineteenth century, needlewomen who were expert quilters were the queens of the quilting bees. All the women in the neighborhood were invited to these social gatherings, which combined business and pleasure, to quilt or tack the patchwork tops made by the hostess during the winter. Probably no other festival is more fundamentally a part of early American folklore than is the quilting bee. Customary thrift and industry imposed traditional restrictions on gaiety unless it was for a practical purpose, but a day busily spent over a quilting frame provided that justification. The men folks came to the bee, the village parson rendered thanks for all material benefits, and then merriment reigned. The hostess prepared stewed chicken, smoked hams, beans and Indian pudding baked in brick ovens, pies, cakes, jams, preserves, and pickles. After the evening meal, in communities where such amusement was permitted, the floor was cleared for games and dancing.

* * * * *

The terms "pieced" quilt and "patchwork" quilt have become synonymous through common usage, despite the fact that to *piece* means to *join by seams* and to *patch* means to *sew a smaller piece of goods onto a larger one.* Strictly speaking, the appliquéd quilt belongs in the latter category.

The pieced variety is the more common, and nearly all the quilts made in America before 1750 were of this type. The pieced squares of geometrical figures, based on the square, the rectangle, the diamond, the circle, and the hexagon, were made by sewing together vari-colored pieces of cloth, usually combining an equal number of light and dark pieces. Quiltmakers were proud of the fine stitches they used in joining these myriad bits of fabric. A quilt of this kind, composed of four triangular pieces in the inch block pattern, the whole containing 42,568 pieces, was completed by a young girl of Bow when she was only ten years of age. It, too, was displayed at the New Hampshire Historical Society exhibition of 1939.

In making appliquéd or laid-on quilts, flowers, leaves, wreaths, and similar motifs were cut from colored fabrics and sewed with small stitches to a neutral background. The one well-known deviation from these two standard groups is the crazy quilt, in which odds and ends of cloth were put together hit-or-miss "crazy fashion," and which was probably the earliest type of American-made quilt. In its simplest form it was designed to use up scraps of worn-out clothing; the more elaborate type, which was very popular in the late nineteenth century, consisted of "boughten" pieces of cloth and was adorned with featherstitching, herringbone, and other examples of line stitches.

* * * * *

Every quilt block, from the simple pieced-up "four-square" and "nine-square" to the intricate laid-on "Rising Sun," has its own individual name. To the imagination of our feminine ancestors, we are indebted for the variety given the designs of their handicraft. Living experiences, involving history, religion, politics, romance, and nature, were reproduced through the creations of their fingers, and christened "Log Cabin," "Star of Bethlehem," "Tree of Life," "Jacob's Ladder," "Rose of Sharon," "Whig Rose," "Yankee Pride," "Fifty-Four Forty or Fight," "Lincoln's Platform," "Air Castle," "Lovers' Links," "Orange Peel," and other picturesque names.

Variations of the "Log Cabin," "Star," and "Basket" designs are perhaps the most popular with modern quiltmakers. One elderly New Hampshire needlewoman confided to a visitor that there was "an awful lot of sameness" in her quilts because she loved the basket pattern. She said: "When I'm making patchwork, I think of all the baskets I've had. One I used to put apples in, shiny red Mackintoshes, one for flowers, and then my old work basket—I sort of miss my old work basket, it got lost someway. But I do like baskets."

One of the most ornate designs ever used by American quiltmakers is the "American Eagle," which was applied to many forms of arts and crafts during the first part of the last century. Mrs. Mabel F. Ames of Somersworth displayed a quilt decorated with this symbol at the Rochester Fair in 1939. The quilt was made approximately one hundred and fifty years ago. In the center, narrow red, green, and gold bands, shaped like elongated leaves, form a circle. These are enclosed in a narrow band of crosswise stitches, arranged to form a sort of frame to the first picture. Around this circle are placed four eagles with heads and tails of green, bodies of deep gold color, and spreading red wings. A four-inch band of needle scrollwork, finished with a band of red, encircles the four eagles. The quilt is finished with a narrow band of green.

Like the sampler, a quilt was often used as a memorial piece. Friends and neighbors of the deceased would reverently open her scrap bag and stitch together bits of dress materials she had worn into a "Memory Quilt," reminiscent of her life and the qualities which endeared her to them.

A near relative to the "Memory Quilt" is the "Memorial" coverlet. At first the names were interchangeable, but later the term "Memorial" came to mean the work of living persons to perpetuate their memory for posterity. An illustration of this type of bedcovering is found in the rooms of the Milford Historical Society at "Lullwood," ancestral home of Colonel Oliver W. Lull. It is made of unbleached cotton, each block bearing the embroidered name of some person prominent in the life of the community. The writing was all done in the same fine hand, that of the late Mrs. Arthur W. Howison, during the first World War. The embroidery is beautifully executed, and the brilliant colors of the material make the quilt a valuable memento of which the town is very proud.

Out of the autograph album with its varying sentiments both wise and maudlin, emerged the "Album" quilt, each block bearing an embroidered text or verse and signed by the donor. Sometimes the inscription, written in indelible ink in a bold masculine hand, gave evidence that men were not averse to joining in these testimonial tokens. To be the recipient of an "Album" quilt was considered a distinguished honor.

Similar to the "Album" was the "Friendship" coverlet, often more interesting than beautiful because of the latitude allowed in both design and coloring. The finished product was a medley of patterns and fabrics, since each block, including material and workmanship, was the contribution of some friend.

* * * * *

The names of New Hampshire quiltmakers are legion. Many of them are elderly women who, as a pastime for unaccustomed leisure, revert to a form of handicraft which they learned in their childhood. One of them said recently, "Yes, indeed, I sewed patchwork from the time I was five years old. Used to have to piece so many blocks as a stint before I could play. And I couldn't hurry it either for if it wasn't done just so, I had to rip it out and do it all over again. . . .

The Art of the Hooked Rug

THE earliest written directions that I have been able to find in regard to making hooked rugs were published under "Editorial Chit-chat" in *Peterson's Magazine* for October, 1876. The rugs were called rag-carpets, but the name was misapplied. The article stated, "The prettiest and newest way of using rags is to make them into rugs. These rag-carpet rugs and carpets are becoming quite the fashion again. They not only outwear all others, but richer combinations of color, and more original ones, can be obtained than in bought carpets generally. The ground for these is made of course canvas, known as 'Burlaps,' such as is used for packing bags. The pattern is roughly outlined on the burlap, and the rags, which are cut into little bits about half an inch wide (the length is of no consequence) are drawn through the meshes of the canvas with a large crochet-needle on the wrong side, leaving loops to stand up on the right side. This, of course, forms loops on the wrong side also; but these are only just long enough to secure the rags. No fastening is needed, as they must be drawn through tightly enough to keep them in place without it. Every three or four

---

From *Homespun Handicrafts*, by Ella Shannon Bowles, pp. 200–201. Copyright, 1931, by Ella Shannon Bowles. Philadelphia & London: J. B. Lippincott Company.

meshes of the canvas will generally do; but practice will soon show the right distance. Sometimes the pile of the right side is cut, but oftener not. This is now quite a domestic branch of industry in New England, where the farmers' wives employ the long winter evenings in this work. It is also being introduced into charitable institutions. The work is not difficult to be learned. Some prefer a frame to stretch the burlaps on; others do it best without. The rugs are, many of them, really beautiful and command a good price. The prettiest are those in Arabesque patterns, which resemble Persian mats. Of two now before us, one has a light-gray border, with a Greek pattern in a darker shade; the centre is deep blue, with a Greek device in black in the middle; the other is blue with a scarlet star in the middle, gray border with smaller blue and scarlet stars. These are very simple but effective patterns. The taste and ingenuity of the worker can readily supply a variety of designs. These rugs must not be confounded with the old-fashioned rag-carpet which was woven, and woven generally without reference to color."

How to Make a Birch Splint-Broom

CHEPA ROSE was one of those old-time chapmen known throughout New England as "trunk pedlers." Bearing on his back by means of a harness of stout hempen webbing two oblong trunks of thin metal,—probably tin, —for forty-eight years he had appeared at every considerable farmhouse throughout Narragansett and eastern Connecticut, at intervals as regular as the action and appearance of the sun, moon, and tides; and everywhere was he greeted with an eager welcome.

Chepa was, as he said, "half Injun, half French, and half Yankee." From his Indian half he had his love of tramping which made him choose the wandering trade of trunk pedler; his French half made him a good trader and talker; while his Yankee half endowed him with a universal Yankee trait, a "handiness," which showed in scores of gifts and accomplishments and knacks that made him as warmly greeted everywhere as were his attractive trunks.

He was a famous medicine-brewer; from the roots and herbs and barks that he gathered as he tramped along the country roads he manufactured a cough medicine that was twice as effective and twice as bitter as old Dr. Greene's; he made famous plasters, of two kinds—plasters to stick and plasters to crawl, the latter to follow the course of the disease or pain; he concocted wonderful ink; he showed Jenny Greene how to bleach her new straw bonnet with sulphur fumes; he mended umbrellas, harnesses, and tinware; he made glorious teetotums which the children looked for

---

From *Home Life in Colonial Days,* by Alice Morse Earle, pp. 300–304. Copyright, 1898, by The Macmillan Company. New York and London. 1919.

as eagerly and unfailingly as they did for his tops and marbles, his ribbons and Gibraltars.

One day he came through the woods to John Helme's house carrying in his hand a stout birchen staff or small tree-trunk, which he laid down on the flat millstone imbedded in the grass at the back door, while he displayed and sold his wares and had his dinner. He then went out to the dooryard with little Johnny Helme, sat down on the millstone, lighted his pipe, opened his jackknife, and discoursed thus:—

"Johnny, I'm going to tell you how to make an Injun broom. Fust, you must find a big birch-tree. There ain't so many big ones now of any kind as there useter be when we made canoes and plates and cradles, and water spouts, and troughs, and furnitoor out of the bark. But you must get a yallow birch-tree as straight as H and edzactly five inch acrost. Now, how kin ye tell how fur it is acrost a tree afore ye cut it off? I kin tell by the light of my eye, but that's Injun larnin'. Lemme tell you by book-larnin'. Measure it round, and make the string in three parts, and one part'll be what it is acrost. If it's nine inch round, it'll be three inch acrost, and so on. Now don't you forgit that. Wal! you must get a straight birch-tree five inch acrost where you cut it off, just like this one. Then make the stick six foot long. Then one foot and two inch from the big end cut a ring round the bark; wal! say two inch wide just like this. Then you take off all the bark below that ring. Then you begin a-slivering with a sharp jackknife, leetle teeny flat slivers way up to the bark ring. When it's all slivered up thin and flat there'll be a leetle hard core left inside at the top, and you must cut it out careful. Then you take off the bark above the ring and begin slivering down. Leave a stick just big enough for a handle. Then tie this last lot of slivers down tight over the others with a hard-twisted tow string, and trim 'em off even. Then whittle off and scrape off a good smooth handle with a hole in the top to put a loop of cowhide in, to hang it up by orderly.

"Yes, Johnny, I've got just enough Injun in me to make a good broom; not enough to be ashamed of and not enough to be proud of. But you mustn't forgit this; a moccasin's the best cover a man ever had on his feet in the woods; the easiest to get stuff for, the easiest to make, the easiest to wear. And a birch-bark canoe's the best boat a man can have on the river. It's the easiest to get stuff for, easiest to carry, the fastest to paddle. And a snowshoe's the best help a man can have in the winter. It's the easiest to get stuff for, the easiest to walk on, the easiest to carry. And just so a birch broom is the best broom a man or at any rate a woman can have; four best things and all of 'em is Injun. Now you just slip in and take that broom to Phillis. I see her the last time I was here a-using a mizrable store broom to clean her oven—and just ask her if I can't have a mug of apple-jack afore I go to bed."

If this scene had been laid in New Hampshire or Vermont instead of Narragansett, the Indian broom would have been no novelty to any boy or house-servant. For in the northern New England states, heavily wooded with yellow birch, every boy knew how to make the Indian brooms, and every household in country or town had them. There was a constant demand in Boston for them, and sometimes country stores had several hundred of the brooms at a time. Throughout Vermont seventy years ago the uniform price paid for making one of these brooms was six cents; and if the splints were very fine and the handle scraped with glass, it took nearly three evenings to finish it. Indian squaws peddled them throughout the country for ninepence apiece. Major Robert Randolph told in fashionable London circles about the year 1750 that when he was a boy in New Hampshire he earned his only spending-money by making these brooms and carrying them on his back ten miles to town to sell them. Girls could whittle as well as boys, and often exchanged the birch brooms they made for a bit of ribbon or lace.

The Horse and Buggy Age in New England

The Carriage Line

. . . Here and there in New England were carriage shops that specialized in building vehicles to order. There was no city of any size that did not have its fashionable carriage-maker who could build anything in the way of a vehicle, from a racing sulky—the name, by the way, is derived from the fact that the driver wishes to be alone—to a Russian droshky. An advertisement of one of these carriage-builders mentions the following vehicles as among those he stood ready to make to order:

Barouches	Physicians' Phaetons
Broughams	Pony Phaetons
Cabriolets	Road Wagons
Coaches	Rockaways
Coupe Rockaways	Rockelets
Coupes	Rumble Phaetons
Depot Wagons	Skeleton Wagons
Dog Carts	Sulkies
Buggies	Surreys
Ladies' Phaetons	T. Carts
Landaulets	Village Carts
Landaus	Vis-a-vis
Light Rockaways	Victorias
One-Man Wagons	Wagonettes
Canopy-Top Phaetons	Extension-Top Phaetons

From *The Horse & Buggy Age in New England,* by Edwin Valentine Mitchell, pp. 25–26, 39–42, 67–71, 79–80.

The Harness Line

As for the small retail harness shops, which once flourished everywhere but are now extinct, no better idea of them can be conveyed than by quoting from an advertisement of one in which is given a list of the stock in trade it carried. The advertisement is from a New England city directory for the year 1860.

Harnesses, Trunks, Saddles & Collars.

Our Stock Consists of the Following Goods.

TRUNKS

Buggy, Phaeton, Tandam, Trotting, Droskie, Coach, Hack, Draft.

HARNESS

Sole Leather, Ladies' Dress, Ladies' Hat, Ladies' French, Single, Double, Folio and Valises.

SADDLES

Ladies' Quilted, Ladies' Plain, Gents' Somerset, Gents' Plain, Boys' Pilchs, Girls' Pilchs, English Saddles, Mexican Saddles.

WHIPS

Buggy, Phaeton, Hack, Ladies' and Gents' Riding Whips.

BITS

Pelham, Buxton, Single Snaffles, Double Snaffles, Arch and Port, Military, Embossed, Steel Curb.

HORSE CLOTHING

Summer, various patterns, Winter, various patterns, Knee Caps, Ear Nets, Neck, Flank and Body Nets, Rollers, Surcingles.

Also Brushes, Combs and Curry Combs.
Russet Round and Flat Riding and Driving Bridles.
Fancy Leather Riding Bridles, Plated Martingales.
Hand Pieces, Holders, Buttons, Children's Chaises, Dusters, Mats.
Pole Straps, Rubber Clothing, Sleigh Bells, Halters.

Collars and Interfering Boots made to fit the most difficult leg or neck. Repairing, Oiling, &c.

No Stitching Machines used in this Establishment.

The last line is significant. Most of the small harness shops did not have sewing machines, which cost about $650 apiece, and the harness-makers appealed to the prejudices of people in favor of hand work by advertising that no machine stitching was done in their shops. Custom-made harness was a hand job anyway and so was most repair work. Mending harness was a major part of the business of the small harness shops. One of these shops which I remember was a small bow-windowed place which stood next door to a wood engraver's and had the following admonition across its front in gilt letters: "A Stitch in Time Saves Nine." It was a very apt slogan for a harness-maker. Cheap, ready-made harness, costing, say, from thirteen to seventeen dollars for a single set and proportionately more for a double set, needed constant attention. It was poor economy to buy it. It did not last and was sometimes the cause of accidents. I was a witness to a runaway caused by defective harness. A grocery team was going down a hill, when suddenly the backstrap broke, the wagon ran against the horse's legs, and the animal bolted, smashing the wagon and injuring itself. When it came to buying harness, the best was none too good.

A fine set of custom-made single harness could be had for fifty dollars and a set of double harness for one hundred and fifty dollars. This included silver mountings instead of brass, with your initial or monogram on the blinkers. There were as many conventions and niceties of detail to be observed in harnessing horses correctly as there were in matters of personal dress. The proper shape for the blinkers, for example, on a set of driving harness was square or with only slightly rounded corners. D-shaped, horseshoe shaped, and round blinkers were usually seen only on cab, grocery, and cart horses. Similarly, buckles were also square or slightly rounded on the edge, save in the case of harness used for sporting purposes, when horseshoe-shaped buckles were permissible. In sporting outfits the collars might be faced with tan leather, otherwise the proper facing was black. And the pattern of the harness depended on the kind of vehicle with which it was to be used. A heavy harness designed for drawing a brougham was not the thing to use with a light carriage.

The wise owner put the cart before both the horse and the harness. He decided first what kind of a carriage he would keep, bought the right size and kind of horse to go with it, and then ordered harness that was appropriate for both horse and carriage. The man who threw himself on the mercies of a first-rate harness-maker pursued the wisest course.

Whip-Making

Whip-making involved many different operations. A straight carriage whip of good grade had a center composed of rawhide and rattan. This hide was tanned, dried, and twisted, and run through a machine which cut and shaped it. Around the rawhide, which was about the thickness of a pen or pencil, eight pieces of previously prepared rattan were glued and bound in place until the glue dried. The glued strip of rawhide and rattan was then rounded and tapered by machinery and passed along to an experienced whip-maker, whose job it was to take out the "jumps." Holding the partly finished whip by the handle, the whip-maker tested it to see if it bent evenly. If it did not, the whip had a "jump" in it, which the whip-maker took out with a plane. An expert workman knew instantly by the feel of a whip exactly where the "jumps" were, and by a few deft applications of his plane here and there quickly eliminated them.

To give a good whip the proper weight and balance a piece of iron called the "load" was placed in the butt. The large whip companies used as much as a hundred tons of iron a year for loading butts.

When a whip had been shaped and tested it was, if it was of reasonably good grade, given a covering of rubber, which made it waterproof. It was then sent to the plaiting machine for its final outer covering. After that it was filled and given several coats of varnish, and the mountings—buttons, ferrules, etc.—were added, and, last of all, the snapper. One factory specialized in whip-mountings, making them for all the whip manufacturers, and it is perhaps worth noting that there was even a company in Westfield [1] that made whip-sockets for the carriage trade.

Some of the fancy whips had elaborate mountings with chased buttons or head-mounts and as many as sixteen ferrules of nickel, silver, or gold. Rubber caps were sometimes used on the butts, though most whips had simply buttons of japanned metal. Hand-plaited leather buttons and ferrules were also used. There was as much variety in the mountings as there was in the styles of the whips.

The snaps or snappers were made separately and put on by hand in all the better grade whips. They were of cotton, silk, half and half, or buckskin, and were hand braided or machine made according to the quality of the whips on which they were used. Attaching them was a simple operation, because in plaiting a whip a loop was made at the end of the lash through which the snapper was slipped and secured. A feature of the more expensive whips was the imported handmade English snappers. The snappers on the cheap whips were not made separately, but were all of a piece with the plaiting, an attenuated extension of the lash. They were known as Boston snaps, while the others—the loose snappers—were called Philadelphia snaps.

Most of the rawhide and rattan used in making whips came from India, as did also the water buffalo hide that was used. One whip company stated in its catalogue, "our rawhide centers cannot be equalled by anybody. We tan our own hides and make our own centers, and use nothing but the best commissariat hides, bought from the English army, cured in the best manner possible, imported direct by us, and use no slaughters, derbungas, or deads, which are inferior stock." This statement was made in connection with a line of rawhide whips, one of which was called the Madras Rawhide, another the Burma Rawhide, and still another the Ceylon Rawhide. "We invite the closest examination," the statement continues," and do not fear the knife if you wish to cut the whips open." What person whose youth was spent during the horse and buggy age does not remember cutting up old horse-whips just to see what they were made of? And what man of middle age does not recall using an old whip stock for beating carpets?

Whalebone made excellent whips, but was more generally used during the earlier years when it cost only thirty or thirty-five cents a pound than it was later. It rose in value until toward the close of the horse and buggy period it was ten dollars a pound. Despite the high price, many carriage

---

[1] This Massachusetts city, known as the Whip City and once producer of ninety per cent of the world's supply of horse-whips, has only one factory today as against forty at the turn of the century.

whips continued to be made of whalebone, but they were only one-third, one-half, or seven-twelfths bone. Bone track whips, chiefly in the three and three-quarter foot size, are still made in Westfield.

"The whalebone comes from San Francisco and is cut in New York," one of the old whip manufacturers who is still on the job told me recently. "There are no bone cutters in Westfield now and there's only one man in New York who knows how to cut whalebone for whips."

Nobody knows how many different style whips were made in Westfield. A great variety of materials in all kinds of combinations was used, and the different classes of whips showed many variations in length, color, mountings, and other details of manufacture. The last catalogue of the United States Whip Company, issued some years ago, lists one hundred and forty styles, but actually some two hundred were carried in stock, and this was after the decline had set in. The salesmen of this company carried about sixty sample whips to show to the trade. Their samples included such whips as "Giant Cracker. Full Stock Imported Java. Loaded." "Blue Belton. Combination of Steel Wire and Finest Manila Reed." "Dictator. Solid Rawhide Center." "Park Pride. Warranted Waterproof. One-half Whalebone." "Rough and Ready. Rawhide from Snap Through Cap. Double Wire Undercover." "The Flail. Eel Skin Lined," etc. These were the straight whips, and there were many with long drooping lashes, the drop tops, as they were called, in a variety of styles, including carriage, cab, coach, and express drop tops. The Franklin Whip Company of Westfield imported holly wood stocks and specialized in making long-lashed English whips. The longest whips were the harvester whips, made expressly for use in driving the great teams of horses employed on the harvesting machinery in the West. These whips had ten- or eleven-foot stocks of bamboo or hickory, with lashes four or five feet long. Literally hundreds of different style whips were manufactured by the Westfield factories.

The best-selling whips were the twenty-five and fifty-cent carriage whips, followed by the better grade of whips at a dollar, a dollar and a half, and two dollars. Some whips sold for as little as five or ten cents, others for as much as twenty or twenty-five dollars. There was really no limit to what you could pay for a fancy whip. A whip with a carved ivory handle cost the purchaser for the handle alone at the rate of a dollar an inch. The handle ranged anywhere from eight to eighteen inches in length. Many whips were made with the owner's name woven into the handle. This gave work to a number of women, but to-day there is only one woman in Westfield who knows how to do this, and she is seldom called upon to do the weaving for a name whip.

All the manufacturers sold racks for the display of whips in shops and stores. These racks were either straight, cross, or circular and were usually of the type that was suspended from the ceiling or wall, the whips hanging from them by their snaps. It ruined a whip to keep it standing against a wall.

Sleigh Bells

Many different patterns were used in sleigh-bell making. The commonest were the globe, band, and rim bells, which were either single- or double-throated; that is, the bells had a single slit in them to let out the sound, or two slits cut across each other at right angles. The bells were given a simple polishing, or a silver-white finish, or were plated with nickel, brass, silver, or gold. The Bevin Brothers [1] made twenty different sizes of common sleigh-bells, ranging in diameter from seven-eighths of an inch to three and three-quarter inches. Strung together in clusters of a dozen, they were sold by the pound as loose bells or were wired or riveted to neck straps, body straps, or martingale straps. The number of bells on a strap depended on the size of the bells used. A body strap might have as many as sixty small bells, or a fewer number of larger bells of a single size, or assorted sizes. The price of a strap of sleigh-bells ran from a dollar to eighteen dollars, depending on the quality of the harness leather used and also the quality of the bells with which it was equipped.

The best sleigh-bells were cast from pure bell metal composed of tin and copper, the core of the bell being embedded in the sand when the mold was made. The cheap bells were stamped out of steel or brass.

The difference between the two classes of bells in both tone and volume of sound was made plain to me when Mr. Gordon Bevin, who showed me over the old sleigh-bell factory, jingled first a strap of stamped bells and then a strap of cast bells. The cast bells had a sweeter tone which carried farther than that of the stamped bells.

This difference was also noticeable in the chimes, the open-mouthed bells made to attach to the shafts of sleighs. Chimes were hung in metal frames on top of the shafts or were suspended underneath. They came in many different shapes—tea-bell, hand-bell, gong, band, bevel, beaded, dome, Swiss, etc. The Swiss chimes were cup-shaped. The fanciest were the Russian saddle chimes, which, as the name implies, were not made for the shafts or poles but for attaching to the saddles. Hame chimes were similar to the saddle chimes, except that they were made to be fastened to the hames of the collars rather than to the saddles. Sometimes body straps of ordinary sleigh-bells were made with chimes at the top. Then there were the featherweight speeding chimes designed expressly for fast driving where light chimes were required. The bells were small and occupied a position so close to the under side of the shaft that there was no danger of the horse cutting himself while racing or in case of an accidental fall.

---

[1] Of East Hampton, Connecticut, where William Bevin got his start as apprentice to William Barton, pioneer American sleigh-bell maker.

Coast Traders

We knew and cherished with no little covetousness the stories of the "traders," which had gladdened the hearts of children of an earlier generation. A trader was a vessel from Boston or New York which earned the livelihood of its captain, or perchance of its owner, by carrying annually into the smaller harbors of the coast every kind of ware imaginable and selling its multifarious cargo at prices which the village stores could not meet. Blue Hill children of the sixties and seventies had waited months for the arrival of this floating junk-shop, scanning the sea from every hill and headland for an unfamiliar sail. According to the older people among us, its captain was invariably an accommodating soul, who was not in the least averse to interpreting as coin of the realm any stray bits of old iron, in exchange for which he would proffer oranges and great Boston apples, gorgeously striped candies, dates, figs, and nuts. Moreover, he carried in his hold, for those who had been most thrifty and parsimonious of their small savings, doll buggies and pop-guns, and for the despair of fathers and mothers, who could be lured to the wharf, bolts of cloth and shiny new shoes with voluptuous and alluring tassels.

Sometimes in those days, we understood, still with envy that progress had cheated us of so much greater excitement, Blue Hill had supplied her own traders. An obliging captain, with a weather eye out for his own pocket, sailing light from Boston or New York, Philadelphia or Norfolk, would gladly undertake the filling of commissions in those centers and bring home a sundry cargo. . . .

These shopping sea-captains must, indeed, have been men of gregarious instincts and of great good nature. A slip of paper much torn and obviously incomplete, dated in 1859, gives a partial list of commissions to be fulfilled and suggests the ardous undertaking of the purchaser:

For J. Candage, a hoss harness

For Messrs. Holt, Horton, Candage, & 3 Hinckleys tobaco, both chewing & smoking

For J. C.—a new hat, my own size with 2 cravats & ties

For the minister, one cane, snake's head prefered, not to cost over $1

For Sylvester C., a good quantity nails, all sizes, & 12 brass handles

For Coggin family, to invest $20 in white flour and raisins, also nuts of sorts, also toys such as marbles, tops, & a book of pictures

For Miss Clara Wood, stuff for weding dress with threads & silks for sewing same & white lace for triming

For Mrs. Duffy, 1 bolt flowered calico at lowest price, blue & white prefered, also buttons, also wools for kniting socks in bright shades, also pink roses for bonet brims

---

From *A Goodly Heritage,* by Mary Ellen Chase, pp. 163–166.

For Horton boys, 2 large pocket knives
For H. Henderson, 6 steel traps suitable for rabits or foxes
For little Osgood girl, a doll with black hair, blue eyes, big as possible for $1
For Mrs. Grindle, one singing bird in cage, for the church gift.

Even we in the nineties knew at first hand something of this sort of supply and demand. When I was in the neighborhood of twelve, my father, together with three other men of the village, bought a quarter share in a two-masted schooner called *The Gold Hunter*. Rumor had it that their act was largely one of charity since the captain and owner had fallen on evil days by the decline of the coast trade. But whatever its cause, the effect brought delighted satisfaction to four large families. . . .

Bean's Maine Hunting Shoe, Etc.

. . . It was because his feet got tired and sore on hunting trips, in the period when he was managing a store, that he got the idea which founded his business. As an experiment, one day, he left off the heavy lumberman's boots which hunters customarily wore in the Maine woods, and went out hunting with only a pair of ordinary rubbers over three thicknesses of stockings. These kept his feet warm, dry and comfortable, but he felt the need of some kind of support around the ankles, so he took the rubbers to Dennis Bibber, the local cobbler, and got him to sew some leather tops on them. This became The Maine Hunting Shoe with which Bean first went into the mail-order business.

The Yankee ingenuity which thus produced the first leather-topped rubber shoes has also enabled Bean to develop many other items which had never occurred to more orthodox manufacturers. The duck-hunting coat, for instance, which he praised so highly to the general, would have been just another ordinary sheepskin-lined coat if he had not added his special touch—he had it made with sheepskin cuffs that would turn down and serve as a muff. This, he points out, makes it possible to keep the hands warm, and still have them ready for instant use when the ducks appear, without having to pull off cumbersome mittens. Ideas like that obviously come only from shooting—and failing to shoot—ducks; and Bean spends a substantial part of each year hunting and fishing. . . .

* * * * *

One of the first items that L. L. added to his line, after the shoe, was, naturally enough, stockings to go with it. Emma Tooney, up in Unity, had knitted him a pair, and he liked them, so he arranged with her to knit some more, and put them in his catalogue. Before long, most of Emma's

From "The Discovery of L. L. Bean," by Arthur Bartlett, *The Saturday Evening Post*, Vol. 219 (December 14, 1946), No. 24, pp. 31, 92, 95, 97.

friends and neighbors were knitting for Bean, too, and they still couldn't keep up with the demand. L. L. had to add machine-knit socks and stockings to the hand-knit ones, but he still tried them out himself before he would offer them. Even now, when his stock ranges all the way from fish-hooks to tents, L. L. considers an item salable only if it is something that he would choose for his own use, and gets people in the plant and other Freeporters to help him test things before committing himself to them. He likes to be able to say, of a pocket fish knife, for instance: "The hook disgorger which locks open is the best I have ever tried." But if he can't try everything himself, he makes sure that somebody else has, as in the case of a fire kindler listed in a recent catalogue: "One of our employees has just reported that he started 3 fires in the woods, where the snow was ten inches deep, with one half 6¢ package."

About the time he was adding Emma Tooney's stockings to his list, L. L. decided he had never had a hunting coat with enough pockets in it, so he had one made with a total of seven pockets, including a double back that made the most capacious pocket of all—plenty of stowage space, at last, for shells, lunch, pipe, tobacco, license, and game. And noticing, some years later, that he was having trouble lighting matches in wet woods, he had a match-scratching device incorporated in the coat—a little piece of abrasive stitched inside where it would keep dry. Bothered another year by the difficulty of keeping minnows alive and lively on fishing trips, he figured out a combination minnow cage and canvas bait pail, so that he could put the minnows in the cage and the cage in the water-filled bucket, and the water would ooze out through the canvas just enough to keep it damp and cool, like Pharaoh's water jars, instead of getting hot, like a metal pail, and enervating the fish. Again, thinking he would like to carry an extra fly-rod tip along without having to worry about one more loose piece of equipment, he hit upon the idea of putting a hollow handle on a landing net, so the fly-rod tip would fit into it.

As business increased and customers began to ask for other standard outdoor articles, Bean widened his offerings. If he decided that a sharpening stone was a handy thing to have on an outing—and if he could make a satisfactory deal for sharpening stones that he liked—he included them in his catalogue; and so with field glasses, flashlights, and hundreds of other impedimenta. Eventually, he was even offering Bean's Special Pipe Tobacco, since, as he says in the catalogue, "most hunters and fishermen smoke," and Bean's Business Man's Shirt to wear going and coming on outing trips.

Still L. L. sells only what he likes, and likes everything he sells, and wants every one to know it. The catalogue may give credit to "a Tribe of State-of-Maine Indians" for Bean's Pack Basket, and point out that Bean's Maine Woods Compass is "made for us by the most reliable company we know of," but they are still "Bean's." In one recent eighty-page catalogue, the name appeared no less than 317 times, in one way or another. The only item ever listed in a Bean catalogue with its non-Bean origin definitely identified is the Hudson's Bay Company blanket, which L. L. liked so well that he wanted to sell it even if he couldn't completely adopt it.

* * * * *

It is the catalogue, however, through which most of Bean's customers discover him and become addicted to him. It is a remarkably graphic and accurate extension of his small-town, down-East personality. L. L. wrote every word of it himself for years, and although he now permits others to draft portions of it, he invariably rewrites and revises it so completely that their copy becomes his. In the process, he often does considerable violence to academic English, but he becomes personally and unmistakably present on almost every page. "I am very anxious," he writes, "that all my customers who do both duck hunting and stream fishing try a pair of these boots." Or: "This is the shirt I personally use on all my hunting and fishing trips." Or, in the equally identifiable plural: "We do not know of a warmer, more nearly waterproof fabric."

When materials were plentiful, L. L. always urged his customers to send for free samples. To test the material of Bean's Bird Shooting Pants, for instance, he suggested: "Send for free samples and scratch with pin to show brier resistance." And of Bean's Double and Twist Hunting Pants, he urged: "Be sure to send for free sample as the color is much more conservative than shown by cut."

He always tucks in plenty of good advice: "A white handkerchief is dangerous for a hunter to use. They have been the cause of many shooting accidents. A red or blue handkerchief is much safer." This, admittedly, is a selling point for Bean's Red and Blue Handkerchiefs, but often his advice is in favor of curtailed buying. "We have made a survey of hundreds of brook-trout flies to determine how many we could eliminate," he notifies those fishermen who are always stocking up on new varieties. "We have decided that nine flies in two sizes are all that are necessary and in many cases four or five will answer nicely."

Ride and Tie

THIS was a clever, economical mode of journeying in good old times, when we could boast of rigid honesty among men. It was done after this wise. If John and James, two young farmers, both wanted to go to Boston at the same time—having but one horse between them, and neither chaise nor buggy, John would first mount the saddle and ride on, while James set off on foot. Having rode a few miles, John made fast the bridle to a post or tree, and then became the pedestrian in his turn. James coming up, took his turn to ride a bit, and in this way of *ride* and *tie* they effected

From *The Old Farmer's Almanack,* Calculated on a New and Improved Plan, for the Year of Our Lord 1855, by Robert B. Thomas, p. 23, September. Entered, according to Act of Congress, in the year 1854, by Jenks, Hickling & Swan, in the Clerk's Office of the District Court of the District of Massachusetts. Boston.

their journey with ease and safety. Dobbin stood perfectly safe and secure with the saddle-bags across him, holding the cold junk and bread and cheese on one side, and a stone to balance on the other. Such a thing as thieving was not thought of, any more than in the famous good moral reign of the excellent King Alfred of England. Say, my friend, how would such a project answer now, when a man must watch his coat hanging up in his own entry, to have it safe against pilferers! Alas, for the degeneracy of the times!

Sleighing Rules of the Road

THERE were no sidewalks along Main Street for some years after it was laid out, and pedestrians had to take to the road. Mr. Hadley, in the new "History of Concord," says that the Rev. Dr. McFarland, when pastor of the North Church, was wont at the coming of the first sleighing of each year to promulgate a rule from the pulpit in these words: "Persons who drive in sleighs will please keep to the right, and let those who are afoot have the middle of the road."

Chebobbins

AFTER there had been a heavy fall of snow and the roads were well broken, the time was always chosen where any logging was done to haul logs to the sawmill on ox-sleds. An interesting sled was used which had an interesting name—chebobbin. One writer called it a cross between a tree and a bobsled. It was made by a close and ingenious adaptation of natural forms of wood, which made excellent runners, cross-bars, etc.; they were fastened together so loosely that they readily adjusted themselves to the inequalities of the wood-roads. The word and article are now almost obsolete. In some localities chebobbin became tebobbin and tarboggin, all three being adaptations in nomenclature, as they were in form, of the Indian toboggan or moose-sled,—a sledge with runners or flat bottom of wood or bark, upon which the red men drew heavy loads over the snow. This sledge has become familiar to us in the light and strong Canadian form now used for the delightful winter sport of tobogganing.

On these chebobbins great logs were hitched together by chains, and dragged down from the upland wood-lots. Under these mighty loads the

---

From *Wayside Jottings,* or Rambles Around the Old Town of Concord, New Hampshire, and Its Suburbs, by Howard M. Cook, pp. 31–32. Concord, New Hampshire: Edson C. Eastman. 1910.

From *Home Life in Colonial Days,* by Alice Morse Earle, pp. 415–416. Copyright, 1898, by The Macmillan Company. New York and London. 1919.

snow-tracks got an almost icy polish, prime sledding for country sleighing parties. . . .

Stranger's Fire

THE distance from village to town was so great before the railway entered five years ago, and in spring the mud of the rude, rutty roads so heavy, that Rehobothites with good old-fashioned hospitality kept a "Stranger's fire." An old lady, now of Providence, said:

"I was often aroused at night by the clicking of the latch and whispers of weary, chilled farmers with loads of woods. My hospitable uncle would call out 'Open the fire,' and, after refreshing themselves from the great mug of cider which stood by the andirons, the unseen visitors would cover the fire and away they'd go, and presently others would appear and open the fire."

Pillow Bears and Feather Voyages

LIVE-GEESE feather-beds were an object of considerable emulation, and moved the social barometer much as would now a solid silver service. The frequent visits of the fishermen to Belle Isle and Labrador (pronounced by the fishermen Larbadore) afforded excellent opportunity to secure the genuine article. The sack that left home filled with straw, returned with the downy store for bed-pillows, the latter called pillow bears, and apostrophized by the old people as pille'bers. Fifty years ago or less, high beds were as fashionable as now the other extreme. The boys used to joke about rigging a jury-mast and rattle down the shrouds to climb into bed.[1]

Josiah and Edward [Childs] bought the small estate of John Logge, (a part of Elder Cobb's great lot), which they divided, and each had a house thereon. Both were coopers and small farmers, and displayed more taste for horticultural and floricultural pursuits than was common in those days. Both, in early life, went on *feather voyages,* a term which few, at the present time, will understand. About a century ago, vessels were fitted out for the coast of Labrador to collect feathers and eider down. At a certain season of the year some species of wild fowl shed a part of their wing

From *Old Paths and Legends of New England,* Saunterings Over Historic Roads with Glimpses of Picturesque Fields and Old Homesteads in Massachusetts, Rhode Island, and New Hampshire, by Katharine M. Abbott, pp. 406–408. Copyright, 1903, by Katharine M. Abbott. New York and London: G. P. Putnam's Sons. 1904.

[1] From *Truro—Cape Cod, or Land Marks and Sea Marks,* by Shebnah Rich, pp. 339–340. Second Edition, Revised and Corrected. Copyright, 1883, by D. Lothrop and Company. Boston. 1884.

feathers, and either cannot fly, or only for a short distance. On some of the barren islands on that coast, thousands of those birds congregated. The crews of the vessels would drive them together, kill them with a short club or a broom made of spruce branches, and strip off their feathers. Millions of wild fowl were thus destroyed, and in a few years, their haunts were broken up by this wholesale slaughter, and their numbers so greatly diminished that feather voyages became unprofitable and were discontinued.[2]

Filling Boots with Flaxseed

THIS was in the days when shoddy was unknown, and cloth was made to wear rather than to sell, and when "go-to-meeting" boots passed from generation to generation in the same way. It was a custom with many farmers, as soon as they returned from "meeting," to fill these last named expensive articles of wear with beans or flax-seed and hang them up on pegs until some extraordinary occasion or "meetin' day" called for their use again. The use of flax-seed was finally pretty much abandoned, be cause of a mischievous boy, on occasion of his father's whipping him one day, hitting the old man's suspended boots now and then a sly rap with the broom-handle for several days in succession, in consequence of which, when his father took them down on the next Sunday, he found both split at the toes, through the pressure of the slippery flax-seed.

Pay

TRADING and shopping then were very different operations from what they are now. The word *pay* was used to denote whatever was employed as currency or medium of exchange. Suppose a farmer went to buy a pair

---

[2] From *Genealogical Notes of Barnstable Families,* Being a Reprint of the Amos Otis Papers, Originally Published in The Barnstable Patriot, revised by C. W. Swift, Largely from Notes Made by the Author, Vol. I, p. 187. Entered according to Act of Congress, in the year 1885, by F. B. Goss, in the Office of the Librarian of Congress, at Washington. Barnstable, Mass.: F. B. & F. P. Goss, Publishers and Printers. 1888.

From *Recollections of Olden Times:* Rowland Robinson of Narragansett and His Unfortunate Daughter, with Genealogies of the Robinson and Hazard Families of Rhode Island, by Thomas R. Hazard, "Shepherd Tom," in His Eighty-First and Eighty-Second Years, Also Genealogical Sketch of the Hazards of the Middle States, by Willis P. Hazard, of Westchester, Pa., p. 60. Entered according to Act of Congress, in the year 1879, by John P. Sanborn, in the Office of the Librarian of Congress, at Washington, D. C. Newport, Rhode Island.

From *History of the Town of Medford, Middlesex County, Massachusetts,* from Its First Settlement, in 1630, to the Present Time, 1855, by Charles Brooks, pp. 406–407. Boston: Published by James M. Usher. 1855.

of oxen, how would the colloquy proceed? Somewhat thus:—Neighbor A.: "I want to buy your two-year-old steers: what do you ask for them?" "I will sell; but what's your *pay*?" Answer: "Flax at 1*s*. 4*d*., butter at 12*d*., winter wheat at 8*s*., and the rest in paper at 17*s*. per ounce of silver." This is satisfactory; and so they trade. A dialogue between two merchants, in the purchase of a ship, would be something like this:—Mr. S.: "What will you take for your bark 'Columbus'?" Mr. T.: "You know that depends on the *pay*." Mr. S.: "My pay is, double-johns at £4.16*s*., moidores at 36*s*., pistoles at 22*s*., the rest in old-tenor bills at the rate of 45*s*. for 6*s*. of specie, and middle tenors at 11*s*. 3*d*. for 6*s*." Mr. T.: "Well, that's all right; and you may have her for £237,—pay down." So the bargain closes. When a boy went to buy a penknife, whose cash price was 12*d*., the following conversation ensued:—Boy: "I want a good penknife, sir." Shopkeeper: "Is your pay ready?" "Yes, sir." "What is it?" "It's *pay*." "Well, then, the price is 24*d*." The boy then asks, "What will it be in *pay* as money?" Answer: "16*d*." "What will it be in hard money?" "12*d*." If a young lady went to purchase a dress, and, having looked and chosen, she asked the price, she was answered by the usual question, "What's your pay?" She answers: "Part in pillar-pieces at 6*s*. each, part in 'pieces-of-eight' at 4*s*. 6*d*., and the rest in cobb money at 6*s*. 8*d*. ounce."

Powder-Horns

On his powder-horn the rustic carver bestowed his best and daintiest work. Emblem both of war and of sport, it seemed worthy of being shaped into the highest expression of his artistic longing. A chapter, even a book, might be filled with the romantic history and representations of American powder-horns; patriotism, sentiment, and adventure shed equal halos over them. Months of the patient work of every spare moment was spent in beautifying them, and their quaintness, variety, and individuality are a never-ceasing delight to the antiquary. Maps, plans, legends, verses, portraits, landscapes, family history, crests, dates of births, marriages, and deaths, lists of battles, patriotic and religious sentiments, all may be found on powder-horns. They have in many cases proved valuable historical records, and have sometimes been the only records of events.

Jagger-Knives

The "jagger-knife" by which those [Nantucket] "wonders" were scored may be more or less known; but such as was used, and are used in my

---

From *Home Life in Colonial Days,* by Alice Morse Earle, pp. 320–321. Copyright, 1898, by The Macmillan Company. New York and London. 1919.

From *Brief Historical Data and Memories of My Boyhood Days in Nantucket,* by Joseph E. C. Farnham, pp. 181–182. Providence: Joseph E. C. Farnham. 1923.

native town, I think are exclusive to localities from whence hailed and sailed the whale-ship. Unique in construction they surely are. They were made "aboard-ship" from ivory, and were deftly wrought from the tooth of the sperm whale. Each consisted of a revolving wheel set into a slot or groove at the end of a handle. The handle, sometimes made straight, sometimes slightly circular in form, was about four or five inches in length, and the wheel about an inch or an inch and a half in diameter.

Those wheels, fashioned smooth and round, had an edge cut like a "frill" so as to get the jagged effect when used for scoring dough. Each section or part of this peculiar knife, "made at sea," was artistically executed. The wheel revolved on a metal pin, fastened at each end outside of the slot in the handle to hold it in place. With much time on their hands while at sea, no whales in sight, sailors were nevertheless busy, and many articles made by them on ship-board manifested rare skill and workmanship, and these "jagger-knives" represent such to a marked degree, for the varying genius of the "sailor-mechanic" was aptly shown in their construction.[1]

In different artistic shapes have I seen them, and I could minutely describe the make of many of them. Just one by way of illustration. The handle of one I have in mind was delicately smoothed, concaved from the center to represent the arm of a child, the end finished in a closed hand or closed fist, and the fingers were delicately and perfectly formed; drilled in slightly from each side of that closed hand a hole was made in which was placed a neatly made ring, also of ivory, sprung in, which swung a little rigidly in its place. I have tried to minutely describe the sailor-made "jagger-knife," not that native Nantucketers required any such description, but rather because some eyes may read this sketch who never heard of such an affair.

Noggin and Piggin

. . . No home in central New Hampshire in old days was considered completely equipped if it had not "a noggin for milk and a piggin for soap." A piggin is a small piece of cooperage with one stave left high for a handle, a miniature in short of that sort of sap bucket that has one stave left high, with a hole in that stave so the bucket may be hung on the tap inserted in the auger hole bored into the tree. Through this tap the maple sap seeps through and drops into the bucket The piggin has sometimes, too, a hole

---

[1] Jagger-knives were an ingenious and beautiful form of scrimshaw, or "carving or decorating whales' teeth, walrus' tusks or bones," etc., especially engraving teeth. See A. Hyatt Verrill, *The Real Story of the Whaler* (New York, 1923), pp. 191–194.

From *New Hampshire Neighbors,* Country Folks and Things in the White Hills, by Cornelius Weygandt, pp. 111–112.

in its high stave, so that it may be hung above the sink in a place handy for use.

A noggin I have is of two-quart size. It is six inches in diameter. Its staves are four and a half inches high. It would, perhaps, be more exact to speak of its stave, for all its twenty-one and a half inches of circumference seem of one piece of wood save where the piece carrying the handle is inserted. If you call this handle's base a stave, there are two staves. To get the pitch necessary to the diminishing diameter of the noggin from top to bottom, the lower end of the broad stave has had narrow gores cut out of it by a very sharp knife. This gives its lower sides a shivered effect. All the noggin is so brown with the use of years it is difficult to say of what wood it is made. The wide stave, I shall venture to guess, is of brown ash, as are the hoops, two at top and two at bottom, and each a half an inch wide. The bottom and handle seem to be of pine.

Its lightness is a part of the noggin's efficiency. One of its uses, according to the talk of the countryside, was to carry out to barn or pasture, or wherever the cow happened to be, when milk fell short in the house. The woman of the house would run out with the noggin, and crouch down by bossy. With the noggin held in one hand she would use the other to milk the sup she wanted for this or that into the noggin.

Cat Holes

. . . OF THE hardiest of Tom Fool stories is that of the two holes at the bottom of the barn door, the larger one for the old cat, the smaller for the kitten. My own eyes have seen two instances of the two holes side by side in a door that admitted to an undivided interior.

. . . One wondered were there occasions when it would be desirable to keep the old cat out, but to let the kitten in. . . .

* * * * *

. . . A more plausible explanation of the two cat holes, but one that hardly accounts for their difference in size, is suggested by a story Mrs. Robert Frost loves to tell. Asked why he had five cat holes cut at the bottom of his barn door for his five cats, all grown tabbies and toms, the old farmer replied: "When I says 'scat,' I means 'scat!' "

The single cat hole is, of course, in instances a necessity, but I have known it to be made in barn doors when there were other easy ways of entrance for puss into the barn, an open space between the timbers of the overshot second story, a pane of glass out of a low window, a slit for ventilation in the stone end of the barn. The cat hole, though, is, I think, in a sense an institution, a something dictated by tradition to be made in the doors of well-conducted barns, at least in places of not too severe winters.

Ibid., pp. 259, 260–262.

The farther north you go, the fewer cat holes there are in barn and stable doors. . . .

* * * *

There are, though, in our section of New Hampshire, indoor cat holes to compensate in a measure for the dearth of the commoner variety in barn doors. Such indoor cat holes are rare, but not unique, as I thought when I saw the first series of them. This series is in the attic of a farmhouse under the west scarp of the Ossipees. The cat holes are thought to be part of the original equipment of the house, the three of them in the floor of the chamber and the one between the chamber and the grain loft of the barn. Here, of course, house and woodshed and barn are all one building. Two of the cat holes in the floor still have in place the caps to cover them. The cat holes, circular and of six-inch diameter, were designed to let puss into the spaces between four great floor timbers that ran the whole width of the house. The three are in a row, about four feet apart. Each had been cut out with a compass saw, and a square piece of wood nailed to the circular piece cut out of the floor. When in place, the upper layer of the cap projected above the floor. That top part was beveled on its edges, but there must be, even at that, many a stumble over the caps. If they were left out an ankle sprained might easily have been the result. The fourth cat hole, between this chamber and the corn loft, was very necessary to give puss access to this granary so sought by mice and rats.

Boarding Around

It was the custom in those days [in Suffield, Connecticut,] for the teacher to "board around." The arguments for the practice were two and conclusive. It was cheaper than any other plan. It enabled the teacher to get acquainted with the home life of his pupils. Whatever a man might have thought of it at the time, it is certainly a pleasant thing to look back on.

If the session was to be ninety days and there were thirty pupils, of course it meant three days for each. It was quite an event to have the teacher to board and suitable preparations must be made. So it was customary for him to send word a day or two beforehand that he was coming. Very often word came back for him "to wait a few days as they had not killed their hogs yet." He was reasonably sure of a plenty of fresh pork, sausage, and feather beds. Once when the teacher was up quite late helping one of his pupils, a seventeen year old lass, to solve some problems in the double "Rule of Three," he suddenly realized how late and how cold it was. He hurried to his room and undressing as quickly as possible jumped into bed. Here he made the acquaintance of a warming pan full of live

---

From "Old Slave Days in Connecticut," by Judge Martin H. Smith, in *The Connecticut Magazine,* Vol. X (January–March, 1906), No. 1, pp. 113–114.

coals. There was not room enough for both of them in bed, and as a result, quicker than can be told, they were sprawling on the floor. The kind hostess had tried to warm his bed, but forgot to tell him of it. As a result she warmed both the bed and the teacher. After all there were some very pleasant features in this "boarding-round," and many a life-long friendship came of it. But woe to the bashful man that tried it. If it did not cure him of bashfulness his case was past hope.

Letter Writing

LETTER writing was a very serious affair to many folks in The Town, especially the "backing" of the double-fold sheets which were simply folded and sealed with a red wax wafer, with no thought yet of an envelope. Three sides could be covered with writing but the fourth must be left empty for the address, which was called the "backing."

"Uncle says when you back your letters you should put the town's name in a large fair hand."

Even after the 1860's had brought envelopes the old expression was still in use. "George, this is the last envelope you backed for me before you left for the war."

Because postage was so high and the earlier letters must be confined to the one sheet, many letters were dizzy affairs with the first part written over crisscross by the latter part, and again some letters were so little more than "I take my pen in hand," and inquiry after the health of each member of the addressed family, that the complaint would come back: "Don't send so much clean paper," or ". . . so much waste space paid for!" Secret missives were written in old Bossy's milk to be scorched into visibility in front of the receiver's hearthfire. Gaiety began to enter the postal ranks when tiny paper wafers of glossy black, carrying some message from Cupid, were affixed to the heated wax wafer. "When this you see remember me, though many a mile we distant be." One would have a picture of a broken gate: "I'm quite unhinged."

Visiting and Advertising Cards

"HERE's somethin' else." Mr. Botsford reaches into the bookcase, brings forth a small box, from which he removes the cover. "Visitin' cards," says he. "It used to be an old habit to swap these cards with your friends. Not

---

From *New Hampshire Borns a Town,* by Marion Nicholl Rawson, p. 232. Copyright, 1942, by E. P. Dutton & Co., Inc. New York.

From "Connecticut Clockmaker," as told by Arthur Botsford, Thomaston, Connecticut, to Francis Donovan, in *Living Lore of New England.* Manuscripts of the Federal Writers' Project of the Works Progress Administration for the State of Connecticut.

leave 'em when you called at someone's home, understand, just swap 'em." He takes the cards out, one by one, recalling old friends whose names are printed, or in some cases handwritten. "Papers used to be full of advertisements for these cards. Here's one should interest you. Used to be the custom to hand one of these to a girl when she was comin' out of church."

The card bore this message: "Escort card. Fair Lady, will you allow me the pleasure of escorting you home? If so, keep this card, if not return it. Yours respectfully," with a space for the gallant's signature.

"Used to have lozenges, too," says Mr. Botsford, "with some sentimental message printed on 'em. You'd hand one to a girl you was sweet on. Another great thing was advertisin' cards. Did I mention them before? Kids used to collect 'em and paste 'em in big books, like scrap books. It was a great fad back in the seventies. Older people used to collect 'em too. You go in any drug store, in them days, and the counters would be piled high with these big books. You got the cards from the merchants. Come on out in the woodshed and I'll show you some."

We repair to the woodshed, where Mr. Botsford digs out two old books, turns the pages. "See what I mean?" The cards are an interesting sidelight on the vast changes in advertising methods coincident with the dawn of the motor age. Every conceivable subject was covered by them. They ran the gamut from the sublime to the ridiculous, dwelt on matters political and matters amorous, touched such widely diversified subjects as religion and warfare—advocated temperance and advertised liquor. In virtually no instance was the sponsor's product, or goods, prominently mentioned, and on some of them the merchant's name was in such small print as to almost escape attention.

"There's a good story about them advertising cards. You remember how old Mr. Lemmon, the druggist, used to stutter. When he first came to town here and went to work in the drug store, there was another fellow used to stutter just as bad, name was Fred Birch.

"Birch went into the store one day, and he says, 'G-g-g-g-imme, s-s-s-some advertisin' c-c-c-ards.' Lemon says, "You g-g-g-get the h-h-hell outa here.' Thought he was mockin' him, you see.

"All the merchants handled them cards. Sometimes they'd give you one or two, sometimes, if they was in a good humor, they'd give you a whole stack of 'em.

"Cards came in cigarette packages later, the kids took to collectin' them. And some of them gave out printed flags of all countries. Idea was to get as many different flags as you could, and then the girls would make sofa pillows out of them.

"Times change. In the old days, there was so little to do, now it's all different. The kids now have a million things they can do."

Keeping Awake in Church

In summer the coolness of the audience-room with its window-blinds was grateful, but many hard-working men furtively dozed, suspiciously nodded with sudden, periodic jerks, and sometimes openly snored. To be sleepy during sermon-time was the universal failing. It was the custom on warm Sundays to carry sprigs of caraway, or dill, or coriander, to nibble at when the eyelids inclined to droop. The efforts to ward off slumber were frequently amusing. A man would often be seen straightening up with a surprised look when his wife gave his elbow a nudge. One old man had what appeared to be an automatic alarm. The top of his head was bald, and the long, thin hair at the sides was brought up and braided in a central line from crown to forehead, and, along with it, a something that looked like a shoestring. When he nodded, the ends of the string fell in his eyes, whereupon he waked and restored the equilibrium. Twenty times in the course of a sermon his head fell, and as often the dangling ends of string restored him to consciousness and propriety.

Deaconing the Psalm

It was customary with our early ancestors to appoint an individual from the church to read the psalm, two lines at a time; after which reading, the whole congregation sang the two lines. The reading was so commonly done by a deacon, that this mode of announcing the psalm was called "deaconing" it. The scarcity of psalm-books was the origin of this custom; and, when they became so common as to be left in the meeting-house through the week, the proposition to discontinue the "deaconing" of the psalm was made, and it met with quick opposition from the deacons and readers. The habit continued till the Revolution. . . .

From *Quabbin, The Story of a Small Town with Outlooks Upon Puritan Life,* by Francis H. Underwood, pp. 166–167. Copyright, 1892, by Lee and Shepard. Boston. 1893.

From *History of the Town of Medford, Middlesex County, Massachusetts,* from Its First Settlement, in 1630, to the Present Time, 1855, by Charles Brooks, pp. 259–260. Boston: Published by James M. Usher. 1855.

For the origin and abolition of the custom of "lining out" (fought by musicians), see Alice Morse Earle, *The Sabbath in Puritan New England* (New York, 1893), pp. 213–217. Cf. "Lining Out the Hymn," p. 184 above.

The Meetinghouse Bell

THE meetinghouse was nearly square, with a turret for a bell rising from the center of the roof. A small bell was bought and paid for with wheat the same year that the building was finished. The bell rope hung down in the broad aisle.

Henry Clarke, who died in 1675, left in his will money "for a bigger bell that may be heard generally by the inhabitants." The next year the town voted that the new bell should be rung each night at nine o'clock. This "nine o'clock bell" was long a regular institution in the New England towns. It was universally understood to be the signal for bedtime. Custom and courtesy alike demanded that any visitors who had dropped in to call should prepare immediately to depart; and the comment often was made, "It is nine o'clock—time for honest men to go home, and for rogues to go about their business."

Of course, in the case of a ball or an evening party, or of young couples who were "sitting up," the participants did not feel obliged to be "tied to the bell-rope." The ringing ended with a number of light, quick taps to show the day of the month. For some reason or other the sound of the Hadley nine o'clock bell was very disturbing to Dr. Reuben Bell's dog. He began howling at its first stroke and kept up his dismal protest until the ringing ceased.

During the summer, the bell was rung in the middle of the day at 12 o'clock. This was largely for the benefit of workers on the meadows, and the sound was joyful music to man and beast, for it meant an hour of rest after a long morning of laborious toil.

It used to be the custom to ring what was known as the "passing bell" when a person died in the community. Nine strokes at half-minute intervals announced the death of a man; six that of a woman; and three that of a child. After a short pause, a series of rapid strokes gave the age of the deceased in years. All activities of people within hearing of the bell stopped at its first peal, and everybody waited to get the full announcement. It usually revealed to them, without the need of any questioning, what family was bereaved and where kindly help was needed.

Stove and Anti-Stove Factions

. . . FELT, in his *Annals of Salem,* asserts that the First Church of Boston was the first New England congregation to have a stove for heating the

---

From *Historic Hampshire in the Connecticut Valley,* Happenings in a Charming Old New England County from the Time of the Dinosaur Down to about 1900, by Clifton Johnson, pp. 89–91. Copyright, 1932, by The Northampton Historical Society, Northampton, Mass. Springfield, Massachusetts: Milton Bradley Company.

From *The Sabbath in Puritan New England,* by Alice Morse Earle, pp. 96–100. Copyright, 1891, by Charles Scribner's Sons. New York. 1893.

meeting-house at the time of public worship; this was in 1773. This statement is incorrect. Mr. Judd says the Hadley church had an iron stove in their meeting-house as early as 1734—the Hadley people were such sybarites and novelty-lovers in those early days! The Old South Church of Boston followed in the luxurious fashion in 1783, and the *Evening Post* of January 25, 1783, contained a poem of which these four lines show the criticising and deprecating spirit:—

Extinct the sacred fire of love,
Our zeal grown cold and dead,
In the house of God we fix a stove
To warm us in their stead.

Other New England congregations piously froze during service-time well into this century. The Longmeadow church, early in the field, had a stove in 1810; the Salem people in 1815; and the Medford meeting in 1820. The church in Brimfield in 1819 refused to pay for a stove, but ordered, as some sacrifice to the desire for comfort, two extra doors placed on the gallery-stairs to keep out draughts; but when in that town, a few years later, a subscription was made to buy a church stove, one old member refused to contribute, saying, "good preaching kept him hot enough without stoves."

As all the church edifices were built without any thought of the possibility of such comfortable furniture, they had to be adapted as best they might to the ungainly and unsightly great stoves which were usually placed in the central aisle of the building. From these cast-iron monsters, there extended to the nearest windows and projected through them hideous stove-pipes that too often spread, from every leaky and ill-fastened joint, smoke and sooty vapors, and sometimes pyroligneous drippings on the congregation. Often tin pails to catch the drippings were hung under the stove-pipes, forming a further chaste and elegant church-decoration. Many serious objections were made to the stoves besides the aesthetic ones. It was alleged that they would be the means of starting many destructive conflagrations; that they caused severe headaches in the church attendants; and worst of all, that the *heat warped the ladies' tortoise-shell back-combs*.

The church reformers contended, on the other hand, that no one could properly receive spiritual comfort while enduring such decided bodily discomfort. They hoped that with increased physical warmth, fervor in religion would be equally augmented—that, as Cowper wrote,—

The churches warmed, they would no longer hold
Such frozen figures, stiff as they are cold.

Many were the quarrels and discussions that arose in New England communities over the purchase and use of stoves, and many were the meetings held and votes taken upon the important subject.

"Peter Parley"—Mr. Samuel Goodrich—gave, in his *Recollections,* a very amusing account of the sufferings endured by the wife of an anti-stove deacon. She came to church with a look of perfect resignation on the Sabbath of the stove's introduction, and swept past the unwelcome intruder with averted head, and into her pew. She sat there through the service, growing paler with the unaccustomed heat, until the minister's words about "heaping coals of fire" brought too keen a sense of the over-whelming and unhealthful stove-heat to her mind, and she fainted. She was carried out of church, and upon recovering said languidly that it "was the heat from the stove." A most complete and sudden resuscitation was effected, however, when she was informed of the fact that no fire had as yet been lighted in the new church-furnishing.

Similar chronicles exist about other New England churches, and bear a striking resemblance to each other. Rev. Henry Ward Beecher in an address delivered in New York on December 20, 1853, the anniversary of the Landing of the Pilgrims, referred to the opposition made to the introduction of stoves in the old meeting-house in Litchfield, Connecticut, during the ministry of his father, and gave an amusing account of the results of the introgression. This allusion called up many reminiscences of anti-stove wars, and a writer in the *New York Enquirer* told the same story of the fainting woman in Litchfield meeting, who began to fan herself and at length swooned, saying when she recovered "that the heat of the horrid stove had caused her to faint." A correspondent of the *Cleveland Herald* confirmed the fact that the fainting episode occurred in the Litchfield meeting house. The editor of the *Hartford Daily Courant* thus added his testimony:—

> Violent opposition had been made to the introduction of a stove in the old meeting-house, and an attempt made in vain to induce the society to purchase one. The writer was one of seven young men who finally purchased a stove and requested permission to put it up in the meeting-house on trial. After much difficulty the committee consented. It was all arranged on Saturday afternoon, and on Sunday we took our seats in the Bass, rather earlier than usual, to see the fun. It was a warm November Sunday, in which the sun shone cheerfully and warmly on the old south steps and into the naked windows. The stove stood in the middle aisle, rather in front of the Tenor Gallery. People came in and stared. Good old Deacon Trowbridge, one of the most simple-hearted and worthy men of that generation, had, as Mr. Beecher says, been induced to give up his opposition. He shook his head, however, as he felt the heat reflected from it, and gathered up the skirts of his great coat as he passed up the broad aisle to the deacon's seat. Old Uncle Noah Stone, a wealthy farmer of the West End, who sat near, scowled and muttered at the effects of the heat, but waited until noon to utter his maledictions over his nut-cakes and cheese at the intermission. There had in fact been *no fire in the stove,* the day being too warm. We were too much upon the broad grin to be very devotional,

and smiled rather loudly at the funny things we saw. But when the editor of the village paper, Mr. Bunce, came in (who was a believer in stoves in churches) and with a most satisfactory air warmed his hands by the stove, keeping the skirts of his great-coat carefully between his knees, we could stand it no longer but dropped invisible behind the breastwork. But the climax of the whole was (as the Cleveland man says) when Mrs. Peck went out in the middle of the service. It was, however, the means of reconciling the whole society; for after that first day we heard no more opposition to the warm stove in the meeting-house.

With all this corroborative evidence I think it is fully proved that the event really happened in Litchfield, and that the honor was stolen for other towns by unveracious chroniclers; otherwise we must believe in an amazing unanimity of church-joking and sham-fainting all over New England.

Disciplining the Congregation

A RATHER unconventional and eccentric preacher in Newbury awoke one sleeper in a most novel manner. The first name of the sleeping man was Mark, and the preacher in his sermon made use of these Biblical words: "I say unto you, mark the perfect man and behold the upright." But in the midst of his low, monotonous sermon-voice he roared out the word "mark" in a loud shout that brought the dozing Mark to his feet, bewildered but wide awake.

Mr. Moody, of York, Maine, employed a similar device to awaken and mortify the sleepers in meeting. He shouted "Fire, fire, fire!" and when the startled and blinking men jumped up, calling out "Where?" he roared back in turn, "In hell, for sleeping sinners." Rev. Mr. Phillips, of Andover, in 1755, openly rebuked his congregation for "sleeping away a great part of the sermon"; and on the Sunday following an earthquake shock which was felt throughout New England, he said he hoped the "Glorious Lord of the Sabbath had given them such a shaking as would keep them awake through one sermon-time." Other and more autocratic parsons did not hesitate to call out their sleeping parishioners plainly by name, sternly telling them also to "Wake up!" A minister in Brunswick, Maine, thus pointedly wakened one of his sweet-sleeping church-attendants, a man of some dignity and standing in the community, and received the shocking and tautological answer, "Mind your own business, and go on with your sermon."

The women would sometimes nap a little without being discovered. "Ye women may sometimes sleepe and none know by reason of their enormous

---

From *The Sabbath in Puritan New England,* by Alice Morse Earle, pp. 70–71, 83, 87–88, 314–315. Copyright, 1891, by Charles Scribner's Sons. New York. 1893.

bonnets. Mr. Whiting doth pleasantlie say from ye pulpit hee doth seeme to be preaching to stacks of straw with men among them."

* * * * *

A minister about to preach in a neighboring parish was told of a custom which prevailed there of persons who lived at a distance rising and leaving the house ere the sermon was ended. He determined to teach them a lesson, and announced that he would preach the first part of his sermon to the sinners, and the latter part to the saints, and that the sinners would of course all leave as soon as their portion had been delivered. Every soul remained until the end of the service.

* * * * *

Another clergyman was irritated beyond endurance by the stamping, clattering feet, a *supplosio pedis* that he regarded as an irreverent protest and complaint against the severity of the weather, rather than as a hint to him to conclude his long sermon. He suddenly and noisily closed his sermon-book, leaned forward out of his high pulpit, and thundered out these Biblical words of rebuke at his freezing congregation, whose startled faces stared up at him through dense clouds of vapor. "Out of whose womb came the ice? And the hoary frost of heaven, who hath gendered it? The waters are hid as with a stone, and the face of the deep is frozen. Knowest thou the ordinance of heaven? Canst thou set the dominion thereof on the earth? Great things doth God which we cannot comprehend. He saith to the snow, Be thou on the earth. By the breath of God frost is given. He causeth it to come, whether for correction, or for his land, or for mercy. Hearken unto this. *Stand still,* and consider the wondrous works of God." We can believe that he roared out the words "stand still," and that there was no more noise in that meeting-house on cold Sundays during the remainder of that winter.

* * * * *

Another arbitrary clergyman, having had an altercation with some unruly singers in the choir, gave out with much vehemence on the following Sunday the hymn beginning,—

"And are you wretches yet alive
And do you yet rebel?"

with a very significant glower towards the singers' gallery. In a similar situation another minister gave out to the rebellious choir the hymn commencing,—

"Let those refuse to sing
Who never knew our God."

A visiting clergyman, preaching in a small and shabby church built in a parish of barren and stony farm-land, very spitefully and sneeringly read out to be sung the hymn of Watts' beginning,—

"Lord, what a wretched land is this,
That yields us no supplies!"

But his malicious intent was frustrated and the tables were adroitly turned by the quick-witted choirmaster, who bawled out in a loud voice as if in answer, "Northfield,"—the name of the minister's own home and parish, —while he was really giving out to the choir as was his wont, the name of the tune to which the hymn was to be sung.

Bundling

NOTWITHSTANDING the modesty of the females is such that it would be accounted the greatest rudeness for a gentleman to speak before a lady of a garter, knee, or leg, yet it is thought but a piece of civility to ask her to *bundle;* a custom as old as the first settlement in 1634. It is certainly innocent, virtuous and prudent, or the Puritans would not have permitted it to prevail among their offspring, for whom in general they would suffer crucifixion. Children brought up with the chastest ideas, with so much religion as to believe that the omniscient God sees them in the dark, and that angels guard them when absent from their parents, will not, nay, cannot, act a wicked thing. People who are influenced more by lust, than a serious faith in God, who is too pure to behold iniquity with approbation, ought never to *bundle.* If any man, thus a stranger to the love of virtue, of God, and the Christian religion, should *bundle* with a young lady in New England, and behave himself unseemly towards her, he must first melt her into passion, and expel heaven, death, and hell, from her mind, or he will undergo the chastisement of negroes turned mad—if he escape with life, it will be owing to the parents flying from their bed to protect him. . . . I am no advocate for temptation; yet must say, that *bundling* has prevailed 160 years in New England, and, I verily believe, with ten times more chastity than the sitting on a sofa. I had daughters, and speak from near forty years' experience. *Bundling* takes place only in cold seasons of the year—the sofa in summer is more dangerous than the bed in winter. About the year 1756, Boston, Salem, Newport, and New York, resolving to be more polite than their ancestors, forbade their daughters *bundling* on the bed with any young men whatever, and introduced a sofa to render courtship more palatable and Turkish. Whatever it was owing to, whether to the sofa, or any uncommon excess of the *feu d'esprit*, there went abroad a report that this *raffinage* produced more *natural consequences* than all the *bundling* among the boors with their *rurales pedantes,* through every village in New England besides.

From *The Rev. Samuel Peters' LL.D. General History of Connecticut* . . . to Which Are Added Additions to Appendix, Notes, and Extracts from Letters, Verifying Many Important Statements, by Samuel Jarvis McCormick, pp. 224–229. Copyright, 1877, by D. Appleton and Company. New York.

In 1776, a clergyman from one of the polite towns, went into the country, and preached against the unchristian custom of young men and maidens lying together on a bed. He was no sooner out of the church, than attacked by a shoal of good old women, with, "Sir, do you think we and our daughters are naughty, because we allow of *bundling*?" "You lead yourselves into temptation by it." They all replied at once, "Sir, have you been told thus, or has experience taught it you?" The Levite began to lift up his eyes, and to consider of his situation, and bowing, said, "I have been told so." The ladies, *una voce,* bawled out, "Your informants, sir, we conclude, are those city ladies who prefer a sofa to a bed; we advise you to alter your sermon, by substituting the word *sofa* for *bundling,* and on your return home preach it to them, for experience has told us that city folks send more children into the country without fathers or mothers to own them, than are born among us; therefore, you see, a sofa is more dangerous than a bed." The poor priest, seemingly convinced of his blunder, exclaimed, *"Nec vitia nostra, nec remedia pati possumus,"* hoping thereby to get rid of his guests; but an old matron pulled off her spectacles, and, looking the priest in the face like a Roman heroine, said, *"Noli putare me haec auribus tuis dare."* Others cried out to the priest to explain his Latin. "The English," said he, "is this: Woe is me that I sojourn in Meseck, and dwell in the tents of Kedar!" One pertly retorted, *"Gladii decussati sunt gemina presbyteri clavis."* The priest confessed his error, begged pardon, and promised never more to preach against bundling, or to think amiss of the custom; the ladies generously forgave him, and went away.

It may seem very strange to find this custom of bundling in bed attended with so much innocence in New England, while in Europe it is thought not safe or scarcely decent to permit a young man and maid to be together in private anywhere. But in this quarter of the old world the viciousness of the one, and the simplicity of the other, are the result merely of education and habit. It seems to be a part of heroism, among the polished nations of it, to sacrifice the virtuous fair one, whenever an opportunity offers, and thence it is concluded that the same principles actuate those of the new world. It is egregiously absurd to judge of all countries by one. In Spain, Portugal, and Italy, jealousy reigns; in France, England, and Holland, suspicion; in the West and East Indies, lust; in New England, superstition. These four blind deities govern Jews, Turks, Christians, infidels, and heathen. Superstition is the most amiable. She sees no vice with approbation but persecution, and self-preservation is the cause of her seeing that.

* * * * *

I should not have said so much about bundling, had not a learned divine[1] of the English church published his travels through some parts

[1] Dr. Andrew Burnaby, *Travels through the Middle Settlements in North America, in the Years 1795 and '60* (London, 1775).

of America, wherein this remarkable custom is represented in an unfavorable light, and as prevailing among the *lower class* of people. The truth is, the custom prevails among all classes, to the great honor of the country, its religion, and ladies. The virtuous may be tempted; but the tempter is despised. Why it should be thought incredible for a young man and young woman innocently and virtuously to lie down together in a bed with a great part of their clothes on, I cannot conceive. Human passions may be alike in every region; but religion, diversified as it is, operates differently in different countries.

Upon the whole, had I daughters now, I would venture to let them *bundle* on the bed, or even on the sofa, after a proper education, sooner than adopt the Spanish mode of forcing young people to prattle only before the lady's mother the chitchat of artless lovers. Could the four quarters of the world produce a more chaste, exemplary and beautiful company of wives and daughters than are in Connecticut, I should not have remaining one favorable sentiment for the province. But the soil, the rivers, the ponds, the ten thousand landscapes, together with the virtuous and lovely women which now adorn the ancient kingdoms of Connecticote, Sassacus, and Quinnipiog, would tempt me into the highest wonder and admiration of them, could they once be freed of the skunk, the moping-owl, rattlesnake and fanatic Christian.

Courting-Sticks

LUKE MONTAGUE, a stalwart bachelor of 27, brought to South Hadley one of the famous courting-sticks. It was very useful on winter nights when there was only the single fire in the house and the whole family must be present at the wooing. The lovers heeded the conventions by sitting primly apart from each other, yet by means of the courting-stick, which was a hollow tube about five feet long, could whisper back and forth without their conversation being audible to those about them.

Courting with Stones

VERY ancient tradition says that the method of courtship at the Isles of Shoals was after this fashion: If a youth fell in love with a maid, he lay

---

From *Historic Hampshire in the Connecticut Valley,* Happenings in a Charming Old New England County from the Time of the Dinosaur Down to About 1900, by Clifton Johnson, pp. 165–166. Copyright, 1932, by The Northampton Historical Society. Springfield, Massachusetts: Milton Bradley Company.

From *Among the Isles of Shoals,* by Celia Thaxter, p. 58. Entered according to Act of Congress, in the year 1873, by James R. Osgood & Co., in the Office of the Librarian of Congress, at Washington. Boston.

in wait till she passed by, and then pelted her with stones, after the manner of our friends of Marblehead; so that if a fair Shoaler found herself the centre of a volley of missiles, she might be sure that an ardent admirer was expressing himself with decision certainly, if not with tact! If she turned, and exhibited any curiosity as to the point of the compass whence the bombardment proceeded, her doubts were dispelled by another shower; but if she went on her way in maiden meditation, then was her swain in despair, and life, as is usual in such cases, became a burden to him.

Bride Stealing

THE sport of stealing "Mistress Bride," a curious survival of the old savage bridals of many peoples, lingered long in the Connecticut valley. A company of young men, usually composed of slighted ones who had not been invited to the wedding, rushed in after the marriage ceremony, seized the bride, carried her to a waiting carriage, or lifted her up on a pillion, and rode to the country tavern. The groom with his friends followed, and usually redeemed the bride by furnishing a supper to the stealers. The last bride stolen in Hadley was Mrs. Job Marsh, in the year 1783. To this day, however, in certain localities in Rhode Island, the young men of the neighborhood invade the bridal chamber and pull the bride downstairs, and even out-of-doors, thus forcing the husband to follow to her rescue. If the room or house-door be locked against their invasion, the rough visitors break the lock.

The Devil's Fiddle

. . . [THE horning or skimmerton] generally comes upon the midnight clear, this still-virile welcome home of the bride and groom, and along with the jugs of cider which are shoved up on the hayrick along with the neighbors, or horners, is the Devil's Fiddle, famous in one town in New Hampshire, where it has driven out all humbler efforts at noise. The originator of this agent of torment, a man beloved in his village, gives us his own version of the hornings which he has enjoyed, and always to the accompaniment of plenty of good cider.

"We used to hitch up my old white horse and another in a team, hitch 'em to a haybody, put the old Devil's Fiddle on and go to let the young couple know we were glad for them and wanted to pay them some atten-

---

From *Customs and Fashions in Old New England,* by Alice Morse Earle, p. 77. Copyright, 1893, by Charles Scribner's Sons. New York.

From *Little Old Mills,* by Marion Nicholl Rawson, pp. 322–324. Copyright, 1935, by E. P. Dutton & Co., Inc. New York.

tion. You could hear the old fiddle for miles. They'd invite us in and treat us on cider and cigars. Sometimes we took along an old circular saw. They'd run a stick through it and two men hold the ends and then somebody'd begin to hammer it, and it certain did make an uncommon awful noise. Some folks thought they could make more noise on an old plough share, but give me an old circular saw.

"Then I got thinkin' it would be nicer for the bride if we took some of the girls along. Of course I said always I wouldn't take the fiddle out at all if they didn't behave good—like gentlemen, you know, not get drunk. And so now sometimes more girls than men go long."

There was a difference between the fiddle of the pre-girl era and that in use today. The "old fiddle" was a huge wooden box, six feet long and three across and deep, with its edges resined. The bow was a "two by four" sixteen feet long. One man stood in the box to keep it steady and the others drew the bow across the edges, and the noise which came forth "would shake a house, honest." The "new" fiddle is an improved product, needing even more cider to make it work musically, harboring a still more raucous sound, especially when it begins its music without warning at the door of a neighbor just across the mowing. This box is only four feet four long, two deep and three across. The edges are resined but the bow is a mere stripling of some six feet and one by two inches in thickness. Here the changes occur. Two telephone wires run through two holes in each end, and two movable boards—like bridges on a violin—pull the wires taut and make it howl. Upon this double taut wire hang two banged-up but still voluble tin oil cans with stones in them, which, when the bow begins to saw across resined edge and wires, dance up and down and along the strings, rattling their stones and groaning in chorus with the rest.

Shift Marriages

THESE ungallant and extremely inconvenient ceremonies are not American inventions or Yankee notions, but an old English custom, being in brief the marriage of a woman, usually a widow, clad only in her shift, to avoid hampering her newly made husband with her old debts. All through New England, in New York and Pennsylvania, this custom was known until this century. In Narragansett it was comparatively common. The exact form of the *sacrifice* (for sacrifice it was of modesty to the new husband's cupidity) and notions about it varied in localities. Let me give a marriage-certificate of a shift-marriage which took place on this very cross-roads where the three towns meet: [1]

> On March 11th, 1717, did Philip Shearman Take the Widow Hannah Clarke in her Shift, without any other Apparel, and led her

From *In Old Narragansett,* Romances and Realities, by Alice Morse Earle, pp. 54–58, 59. Copyright, 1898, by Charles Scribner's Sons. New York.

[1] North Kingston, South Kingston, and Exeter, Rhode Island.

across the Highway, as the Law directs in such Cases and was then married according to law by me.

WILLIAM HALL, *Justice.*

It is not specified in this certificate that this grotesque proceeding took place at night, but, out of some regard for decency, and to avoid notoriety, such was usually the case.

There is an ancient registration book of births, deaths, and marriages at the handsome new Town Hall at South Kingston, R. I. There is an entry within it of a shift-marriage:

> Thomas Calverwell was joyned in marriage to Abigail Calverwell his wife the 22. February, 1719–20. He took her in marriage after she had gone four times across the highway in only her shift and hair-lace and no other clothing. Joyned together in marriage by me.
>
> GEORGE HAZARD, *Justice.*

This was but two years after the marriage of Widow Clarke, and the public parade may have taken place on the same spot, but there is a slight variation, in that the fair Abigail's ordeal was prolonged to four times crossing the road. The naming of the hair-lace seems trivial and superfluous with such other complete disrobing, but it was more significant than may appear to a careless reader. At that date women wore caps even in early girlhood, and were never seen in public without them. To be capless indicated complete dishabille. A court record still exists wherein is an entry of a great insult offered to the town constables by an angry and contemptuous woman. She threatened to pull off her head-gear and go before them, "only in her hair-lace and hair, like a parcel of pitiful, beggarly curs that they were." So the abandon of only a hair-lace comported well with Abigail Calverwell's only a shift.

Hopkinton is another Narragansett town, in the same county. In 1780 David Lewis married at Hopkinton, Widow Jemima Hill, "where four roads meet," at midnight, she being dressed only in her shift. This was to avoid payment of Husband Hill's debts. Ten years later, in a neighboring town, Richmond, still in the South County, Widow Sarah Collins appeared in the twilight in a long shift, a special wedding-shift covering her to her feet, and was then and thus married to Thomas Kenyon.

Westerly, still in the same Naragansett county, had the same custom and the same belief.

> To all People whom It May Concern. This Certifies that Nathanell Bundy of Westerly took ye Widdow Mary Parmenter of sd. town on ye highway with no other clothing but shifting or smock on ye Evening of ye 20 day of April, 1724, and was joined together in that honorable Estate of matrimony in ye presence of
>
> JOHN SANDERS, *Justice.*

JOHN COREY.	MARY HILL.
GEORGE COREY.	PETER CRANDALL.
	MARY CRANDALL.

The use of the word smock recalls the fact that in England these marriages were always called smock-marriages.

* * * *

Another husband who thus formally lent wedding-garments to a widow-bride was Major Moses Joy, who married Widow Hannah Ward in Newfane, Vt., in 1789. The widow stood in her shift, within a closet, and held out her hand through a diamond-shaped hole in the door to the Major, who had gallantly deposited the garments for Madam to don before appearing as a bride. In Vermont many similar marriages are recorded, the bride not being required to cross the highway. One of these unclad brides left the room by a window, and dressed on the upper rounds of a ladder, a somewhat difficult feat even for a "lightning-change artist." In Maine the custom also prevailed. One half-frozen bride, on a winter's night in February, was saved for a long and happy life by having the pitying minister, who was about to marry her, throw a coat over her as she stood in her shift on the king's highway. In early New York, in Holland, in ancient Rhynland, this avoidance of debt-paying was accomplished in less annoying fashion by a widow's appearing in borrowed clothing at her husband's funeral, or laying a straw or key on the coffin and kicking it off.

* * * *

It has been asserted that these shift-marriages were but an ignorant folk-custom, and that there never was any law or reason for the belief that the observance procured immunity from payment of past debts. But it is plainly stated in many of these Narragansett certificates that it was "according to the law in such cases." The marriages were certainly degrading in character, and were gone through with only for the express purpose of debt evasion, and they must have been successful. The chief actors in these Narragansett comedies were, from scant negative testimony of their life and the social position of their families, not necessarily of limited means. Any man of wealth might not, however, wish to pay the debts of his matrimonial "predecessor," as the first husband is termed in one case.

CALENDAR CUSTOMS

Thanksgiving

Its History[1]

Thanksgiving, commonly regarded as being from its earliest beginning a distinctive New England festival, and an equally characteristic Puritan holiday, was originally neither.

The first New England Thanksgiving was not observed by either Plym-

[1] From *Customs and Fashions in Old New England,* by Alice Morse Earle, pp. 216–220, 221, 222. Copyright, 1893, by Charles Scribner's Sons. New York.

outh Pilgrim or Boston Puritan. "Gyving God thanks" for safe arrival and many other liberal blessings was first heard on New England shores from the lips of the Popham colonists at Monhegan, in the Thanksgiving service of the Church of England.

Days set apart for thanksgiving were known in Europe before the Reformation, and were in frequent use by Protestants afterward, especially in the Church of England, where they were a fixed custom long before they were in New England. One wonders that the Puritans, hating so fiercely the customs and set days and holy days of the Established Church,* should so quickly have appointed a Thanksgiving Day. But the first New England Thanksgiving was not a day of religious observance, it was a day of recreation. Those who fancy all Puritans, and especially all Pilgrims, to have been sour, morose, and gloomy men should read this account of the first Thanksgiving week (not day) in Plymouth. It was written on December 11, 1621, by Edward Winslow to a friend in England:

> Our harvest being gotten in our governor sent four men on fowling that so we might after a special manner rejoice together after we had gathered the fruits of our labors. They four killed as much fowl as with a little help beside served the company about a week. At which times among other recreations we exercised our arms, many of the Indians coming amongst us, and among the rest their greatest king Massasoyt with some ninety men, whom for three days we entertained and feasted, and they went out and killed five deer which they brought and bestow'd on our governor, and upon the captains and others.

As Governor Bradford specified that during that autumn "beside waterfoule ther was great store of wild turkies," we can have the satisfaction of feeling sure that at that first Pilgrim Thanksgiving our forefathers and foremothers had turkeys.

Thus fared the Pilgrims better at their Thanksgiving than did their English brothers, for turkeys were far from plentiful in England at that date.

Though there were but fifty-five English to eat the Pilgrim Thanksgiving feast, there were "partakers in plenty," and the ninety sociable Indian visitors did not come empty-handed, but joined fraternally in provision for the feast, and probably also in the games.

These recreations were, without doubt, competitions in running, leaping, jumping, and perhaps stool-ball, a popular game played by both sexes, in which a ball was driven from stool to stool or wicket to wicket.

During that chilly November week in Plymouth, Priscilla Mullins and John Alden may have "recreated" themselves with this ancient form of croquet—if any recreation were possible for the four women of the colony, who, with the help of one servant and a few young girls or maidekins,

---

* The Churchmen derisively referred to Thanksgiving Day as St. Pompion's (Pumpkin's) Day.

had to prepare and cook food for three days for one hundred and twenty hungry men, ninety-one of them being Indians, with an unbounded capacity for gluttonous gorging unsurpassed by any other race. Doubtless the deer, and possibly the great turkeys, were roasted in the open air. The picture of that Thanksgiving Day, the block-house with its few cannon, the Pilgrim men in buff breeches, red waistcoats, and green or sad-colored mandillions; * the great company of Indians, gay in holiday paint and feathers and furs; the few sad, overworked, homesick women, in worn and simple gowns, with plain coifs and kerchiefs, and the pathetic handful of little children, forms a keen contrast to the prosperous, cheerful Thanksgivings of a century later.

There is no record of any special religious service during this week of feasting. The Pilgrims had good courage, stanch faith, to thus celebrate and give thanks, for they apparently had but little cause to rejoice. They had been lost in the woods, where they had wandered surbated,** and been terrified by the roar of "Lyons," and had met wolves that "sat on thier tayles and grinned" at them; they had been half frozen in their poorly built houses; had been famished, or sickened with unwonted and unpalatable food; their common house had burned down, half their company was dead—they had borne sore sorrows, and equal trials were to come. They were in dire distress for the next two years. In the spring of 1623 a drought scorched the corn and stunted the beans, and in July a fast day of nine hours of prayer was followed by a rain that revived their "withered corn and their drooping affections." In testimony of their gratitude for the rain, which would not have been vouchsafed for private prayer, and thinking they would "show great ingratitude if they smothered up the same," the second Pilgrim Thanksgiving was ordered and observed.

In 1630, on February 22d, the first public thanksgiving was held in Boston by the Bay Colony, in gratitude for the safe arrival of food-bearing and friend-bringing ships. On November 4, 1631, Winthrop wrote again: "We kept thanksgiving day in Boston." From that time till 1684 there were at least twenty-two public thanksgiving days appointed in Massachusetts—about one in two years; but it was not a regular biennial festival. In 1675, a time of deep gloom through the many and widely separated attacks from the fierce savages, there was no public thanksgiving celebrated in either Massachusetts or Connecticut. It is difficult to state when the feast became a fixed annual observance in New England. In the year 1742 were two Thanksgiving Days.

* * * * *

---

* A man's garment something of the nature of a doublet and also spelt mandilian. It was first worn in France in the sixteenth century, and was for many years a soldier's wear, and was frequently sleeveless. . . . Mandillions were among the articles of clothing given to each Bay and Piscataway planter. The mandillions of the New England colonists were fastened with hooks and eyes, and lined with cotton.—Alice Morse Earle, *Costume of Colonial Times* (New York, 1894), pp. 154–155.

** Sore-footed.

The early Thanksgivings were not always set upon Thursday. It is said that that day was chosen on account of its reflected glory as lecture day. Judge Sewall told the governor and his council, in 1697, that he "desir'd the same day of the week might be for Thanksgiving and Fasts," and that "Boston and Ipswich Lectures led us to Thorsday." The feast of thanks was for many years appointed with equal frequency upon "Tusday com seuen-night," or "vppon Wensday com fort-nit." Nor was any special season of the year chosen: in 1716 it was appointed in August; in 1713, in January; in 1718, in December; in 1719, in October. The frequent appointments in gratitude for bountiful harvests finally made the autumn the customary time.*

* * * * *

Though in the mind of the Puritan, Christmas smelled to heaven of idolatry, when his own festival, Thanksgiving, became annual, it assumed many of the features of the old English Christmas; it was simply a day of family reunion in November instead of December, on which Puritans ate turkey and Indian pudding and pumpkin-pie, instead of "superstitious meats" such as a baron of beef, boar's head, and plum-pudding.

Many funny stories are told of the early Thanksgiving Days, such as the town of Colchester calmly ignoring the governor's appointed day and observing their own festival a week later in order to allow time for the arrival, by sloop from New York, of a hogshead of molasses for pies. . . .

Its Customs [2]

It was the practice of some of this class to knock at the doors of those thought to be better off, on the evening before, begging "something for Thanksgiving"; and, by way of a joke, the children of comfortable neighbors and friends would often array themselves in cast-off bizarre habiliments, and come in bands of three or four to the houses of those whom they knew, preferring the same request. Ordinarily, the disguise was readily detected. Sometimes the little mimics would come in, and keep up the show and the fun for a while; but for the most part their courage failed them at the threshold, and they skurried away, shouting for glee, almost before they got any answer to their mock petitions. It was a queer fancy,

* [In 1680] the form of recommendation indicates that the autumnal Thanksgiving had gained recognition as an annual festival. . . . During the Revolution Thanksgiving became national, the Congress annually recommending a day to be set apart for this purpose. In 1862–3, President Lincoln recommended special days for Thanksgiving, and since the Civil War the practice has assumed the regularity of official routine, and may be regarded as a national institution.—Charles Ledyard Norton, "Thanksgiving Day, Past and Present," *The Magazine of American History*, Vol. 14 (December, 1885), No. 6, pp. 560–561.

[2] From *Old New England Traits*, edited by George Lunt, pp. 105–107. Entered, according to Act of Congress, in the year 1873, by George Lunt, in the Office of the Librarian of Congress, at Washington. New York: Hurd and Houghton. Cambridge: The Riverside Press.

thus to simulate poverty; but kings have sometimes done so. Did not James of Scotland find amusement in roaming through a portion of his domain, as a "gaberlunzieman?" Yes—and even composed a famous ballad to celebrate his exploits in this humble way. In the evening, we had a lively company, regaled with nuts, apples, and cider; and my grandmother, who indulged in the old-fashioned practice, that is for females, of smoking a pipe, sat in the chimney-corner, where a genial wood-fire was brightly blazing, for coal was then a thing unknown in family consumption, duly furnished with the implement, and sometimes called out to us,—"A-done, children, a-done," when in anywise annoyed by us, and occasionally would sing us an old song, of which I remember only "Robert Kid" and "A galliant ship, launched off the stocks, from Old England she came," etc.; and, often when a storm was raging without, repeating to us the rhymes,—

> "How little do" (pronounced doe) "we think, or know,
> What *the* poor sailors undergo."

Christmas Eve on Beacon Hill

EVERY Christmas Eve Boston's Beacon Hill turns back the pages of history and offers an enchanting scene.

From the brilliantly illuminated State House to Charles Street, from aristocratic Beacon Street right over the Hill into the slum districts, old houses beam holiday tidings to all and hospitality reigns.

Caroling groups stream up and down the Hill past Bullfinch mansion fronts which are gaily illuminated with vari-colored lights. Good fellowship flourishes as luxuriantly as Yuletide greetings. At Louisburg Square, the focal point of the celebration, guests toast each other with eggnog.

Householders come to their doors as the carolers halt outside. With them, as a gesture of democracy, the servants are permitted to stand. A few homes invite small groups of carolers to enter and warm themselves before the open fire. The custom of Beacon Hill carols was originated by Frederick W. Briggs, of Newtonville, Mass., in 1895 after spending a merry and musical evening in an English town. In recent years some 150,000 Christmas Eve celebrators have joined the wandering minstrels in celebrating Joyous Yuletide on the Hill.

Menin Jesu in Provincetown

CHRISTMAS to New Year's is our great moment, and the loveliest of all local customs was *Menin Jesu,* the little Jesus, brought by the Portuguese

From *The Yankee Cook Book,* edited by Imogene Wolcott, pp. 328–329. Copyright, 1939, by Coward-McCann, Inc. New York.

From *Time and the Town,* A Provincetown Chronicle, by Mary Heaton Vorse, p. 51. Copyright, 1942, by Mary Heaton Vorse. New York: The Dial Press.

from the Western Islands. The older Portuguese people once kept open house from Christmas to New Year's. Every window in their houses had a candle behind it. A home ablaze with lights meant that everyone was welcome, whether or not he knew the host. Indeed, the most welcome and honored guests were the strangers.

In the front room was a pyramid of graduated shelves. One candle on top, on the next shelf two saucers of sprouted wheat; on the next, two candles; on the next, four saucers of sprouted wheat, and so on. These represented the Resurrection and the Light. At the bottom was a crèche of little figures brought from the Western Islands. To everyone who came was given a tiny cordial glass of homemade wine—beach plum, elderberry, or dandelion—and a tiny cake.

The Avellars and ourselves used to go at Christmas through the western part of town, seeing down a dark lane, under willow trees, houses brilliant with light. In the distance there was the sound of music and singing. The ships' bands of Portuguese instruments, from the great vessels, went from house to house, saluting the *Menin Jesu*. In some houses they would have both the *Menin Jesu* and a Christmas tree—the Christmas tree, with its presents, looking materialistic and Teutonic beside the sprouted wheat and the lights. Little by little the custom of *Menin Jesu* has vanished. Only a few very old people still celebrate it.

Hallowe'en

. . . HALLOWE'EN was not much remembered in Boston at this time, outside of a few English families associated with Christ Church.

These families had loved to keep the remembrance of the old superstitions, and to pretend to believe that the dead return to their late habitations on that one night of the year, and mingle with the people as they used to do. They filled great tubs with water and floating apples, and tried to secure the apples with their teeth, and so bobbed their heads into the water. They hung sticks from the ceiling, with a burning candle on one end of them and an apple on the other, and twisted them, and tried to catch the apple in their teeth, and received smutches from the candle. They threw apple parings over their shoulders that these might form the initial letters of their lovers' names. They combed their hair before looking-glasses in lonely chambers that their future husbands might appear and look over their shoulders. They told ghost stories of castle life in old England, and sang ballads, the same as people now read Burns's Hallowe'en, or Poe's Black Cat, or William Morris's tale of the Northern knight who visited Elsie with "his coffin on his back." The gift of pieces of cake on which were rings or sibyl-like poems and prophecies ended the merriment at midnight.

From *In Old New England, The Romance of a Colonial Fireside,* by Hezekiah Butterworth, p. 89. Copyright, 1895, by D. Appleton and Company. New York.

The Fourth of July

On the Fourth of July here the boys fired the old cannon which for immemorial years had voiced the patriotism of the eager lads of the town. It was a primitive cannon cast by farmers in a sand mould of their own and guiltless of art. It was usually fired by touching the red-hot end of a scythe to the powder at the vent. In order to make it "speak" it was the custom to follow the powder with dry paper and then "ram home" wet paper and fill the cannon to the muzzle with green grass or soaked rags. When such a charge was touched off, the charge went one way, the cannon another and the boys another.

In the passing of the years the touch-hole, or vent, had become worn and enlarged so that occasionally there was a back fire and most of the powder went out at the vent. It was therefore necessary that the vent should be tightly covered. It was an important and distinguished task to be allowed to thumb the vent. If this was carefully done the danger of a premature discharge was reduced to the minimum. On one never-to-be-forgotten Fourth of July morning, Bill undertook to thumb that hole. The iron was so hot that he moved his thumb a little, when off went the cannon. This time the boy and the cannon went the same way. When his comrades picked Bill up his face was as black as a negro's and he was blind. They took him to our barn and called the doctor. The powder had imbedded itself in his face, his eyebrows and lashes were gone, and it seemed a miracle that he was ever able to see. But for years the powder marks were plain upon his face and a certain amount of respect was accorded by his comrades, and by myself to this day, to one who had survived being shot by a cannon!

All raids against the peace and order of the town were planned in dark hours on The Common or in the horse shed bordering it. The glorious Fourth was rung in at midnight by Church and Academy bell, and when every boy had satisfactorily blistered his hands at the rope there was a lull in the tintinnabulation and the boys made ready for strategy and war. An ancient strong man is said to have borne off the gates of Gaza and our boys emulated his example by removing every gate in town that could be broken or torn from its place. There was a tradition that a certain itinerant pastor's rooster would walk into the house on the morning of April first and roll on his back, sticking up his legs to be tied and ready for the journey to the next appointment. The gates around town must have had the same state of mind on the Fourth of July. However faithfully they had swung back and forth to welcome the coming and speed the parting guest, off they went themselves in the darkness of Independence Day. Most of them would be hidden in the tall grasses of the meadow not to be discovered until the mower struck them with his scythe in late July or August.[1]

[1] From *Black Tavern Tales, Stories of Old New England,* by Charles L. Goodell, pp. 44–46. Copyright, 1932, by Charles L. Goodell. Brooklyn: Willis McDonald & Co.

The worst day in the year for horses was the Fourth of July. No one who could help it drove a horse in town on that day. . . .

Frightening horses by tossing lighted firecrackers near them was considered legitimate sport. If your horse bolted in consequence of a firecracker exploding under its feet, you got little sympathy. You should have known better than to take your horse out on the Fourth. So most people stayed home and ate watermelon and ice cream, and if they wanted to hear the Independence Day oration and witness the balloon ascension, or if in the evening they wished to attend the band concert and fireworks exhibition in the park, they went in public conveyances or walked.

How milkmen hated the day! There was no better kind of wagon to figure in a runaway than a milk cart filled with cans and bottles. Daring indeed was the milkman who drove his route on the Fourth of July without a helper to hold his horse while he ran round to back doors to deliver milk. . . .[2]

The First Forefathers' Day

As OUR public anniversary celebrations [Forefathers' Day, December 11] originated with this association, some account of its origin will doubtless be interesting to the reader. It was formed in 1769, as will be seen from the following extracts, copied from the records which are now in existence.

January 16, 1769.—We whose names are underwritten, having maturely weighed and seriously considered the many disadvantages and inconveniences that arise from intermixing with the company at the taverns in this town, and apprehending that a well-regulated club will have a tendency to prevent the same, and to increase not only the pleasure and happiness of the respective members, but, also, will conduce to their edification and instruction, do hereby incorporate ourselves into a society, by the name of the *Old Colony Club.* For the better regulation of which we do consent and agree to observe all such rules and laws as shall from time to time be made by the Club. Dated at our Hall, in Plymouth, the day and year above written.

Isaac Lothrop
Pelham Winslow
Thomas Lothrop
John Thomas
Edward Winslow, Jr.
John Watson
Elkanah Cushman

[2] From *The Horse & Buggy Age in New England,* by Edwin Valentine Mitchell, p. 174. Copyright, 1937, by Coward-McCann, Inc. New York.

From *Pilgrim Memorials, and Guide to Plymouth,* by William S. Russell, pp. 120–123. Entered according to Act of Congress, in the year 1855, by Wm. S. Russell, in the Clerk's Office of the District Court of the District of Massachusetts. Boston: Crosby, Nichols, Lee and Company. 1860.

For a traditional "Forefathers' Dinner" (featuring succotash) see *Mrs. Lincoln's Cook Book* (Boston, 1895), pp. 284–285.

December 18.—At a meeting of the Club, voted, that Friday next be kept by this Club in commemoration of the landing of our worthy ancestors in this place; that the Club dine together at Mr. Howland's and that a number of gentlemen be invited to spend the evening with us at the Old Colony Hall.

Old Colony Day. First Celebration of the Landing of our Forefathers.—Friday, December 22. The Old Colony Club, agreeably to a vote passed the 18th instant, met in commemoration of the landing of their worthy ancestors in this place. On the morning of the said day, after discharging a cannon, was hoisted upon the hall an elegant silk flag, with the following inscription, *"Old Colony,"* 1620. At eleven o'clock, A. M., the members of the club appeared at the hall, and from thence proceeded to the house of Mr. Howland, inn-holder, which is erected upon the spot where the first licensed house in the Old Colony formerly stood; at half after two a decent repast was served, which consisted of the following dishes, viz.:

1. a large baked Indian whortleberry pudding; 2. a dish of sauquetach (succatach, corn and beans boiled together); 3, a dish of clams; 4, a dish of oysters and a dish of codfish; 5, a haunch of venison, roasted by the first jack brought to the colony; 6, a dish of sea-fowl; 7, a dish of frost-fish and eels; 8, an apple pie; 9, a course of cranberry tarts, and cheese made in the Old Colony.

These articles were dressed in the plainest manner (all appearance of luxury and extravagance being avoided, in imitation of our ancestors, whose memory we shall ever respect). At four o'clock, P. M., the members of our club, headed by the steward, carrying a folio volume of the laws of the Old Colony, hand in hand, marched in procession to the hall. Upon the appearance of the procession in front of the hall, a number of descendants from the first settlers in the Old Colony drew up in a regular file, and discharged a volley of small arms, succeeded by three cheers, which were returned by the Club, and the gentlemen generously treated. After this, appeared at the private grammar-school, opposite the hall, a number of young gentlemen, pupils of Mr. Wadsworth, who, to express their joy upon this occasion, and their respect for the memory of their ancestors, in the most agreeable manner joined in singing a song very applicable to the day. At sunsetting a cannon was discharged, and the flag struck. In the evening the hall was illuminated, and the following gentlemen, being previously invited, joined the Club, viz.:

Col. George Watson	Capt. Thomas Davis
Col. James Warren	Dr. Nathaniel Lothrop
James Hovey, Esq.	Mr. John Russell
Thomas Mayhew, Esq.	Mr. Edward Clark
William Watson, Esq.	Mr. Alexander Scammell
Capt. Gideon White	Mr. Peleg Wadsworth
Capt. Elkanah Watson	Mr. Thomas Southworth Howland

The President, being seated in a large and venerable chair, which was formerly possessed by William Bradford, the second worthy governor of the Old Colony, and presented to the club by our friend Dr. Lazarus Le Baron, of this town, delivered several appropriate toasts.* After spending the evening, in an agreeable manner, in recapitulating and conversing upon the many and various advantages of our forefathers in the first settlement of this country, and the growth and increase of the same, at eleven o'clock in the evening a cannon was again fired, three cheers given, and the Club and company withdrew.

Guy Fawkes' Day

Guy Fawkes' Day, or "Pope's Day," was observed with much noise throughout New England for many years by burning of bonfires, preceded by parades of young men and boys dressed in fantastic costumes and carrying "guys" or "popes" of straw. Fires are still lighted on the 5th of November in New England towns by boys, who know not what they commemorate. In Newburyport, Mass., and Portsmouth, N. H., Guy Fawkes' Day is still celebrated. In Newcastle, N. H., it is called "Pork Night." In New York and Brooklyn, the bonfires on the night of election, and the importunate begging on Thanksgiving Day of ragged fantastics, usually children of Roman Catholic parents, are both direct survivals of the ancient celebration of "Pope's Day." [1]

. . . Portsmouth, N. H. . . . enjoys, I think, the special distinction of being the only place in this hemisphere where Guy Fawkes and the Gunpowder Plot are still appropriately celebrated.

---

* 1. To the memory of our brave and pious ancestors, the first settlers of the Old Colony.

2. To the memory of John Carver, and all the other worthy Governors of the Old Colony.

3. To the memory of that pious man and faithful historian, Mr. Secretary Morton.

4. To the memory of that brave man and good officer, Captain Miles Standish.

5. To the memory of Massasoit, our first and best friend, and ally of the Natives.

6. To the memory of Mr. Robert Cushman, who preached the first sermon in New England.

7. The union of the Old Colony and Massachusetts.

8. May every person be possessed of the same noble sentiments against arbitrary power that our worthy ancestors were endowed with.

9. May every enemy to civil or religious liberty meet the same or a worse fate than Archbishop Laud.

10. May the Colonies be speedily delivered from all the burdens and oppressions they now labor under.

11. A speedy and lasting union between Great Britain and her Colonies.

12. Unanimity, prosperity, and happiness to the Colonies.

---

[1] From *Customs and Fashions in Old New England,* by Alice Morse Earle, p. 229. Copyright, 1893, by Charles Scribner's Sons. New York.

The anniversary is known as "Pope Night," and the observances have dwindled to hornblowing and the carrying about of pumpkin-lanterns by the boys. The origin of the celebration is quite forgotten.[2]

Nantucket Sheep Shearing

. . . THE moors, or "commons," as they are popularly called, are especially adapted for sheep-grazing, both in a positive and negative sense—the short, dry herbage making particularly fine mutton, and the soil seeming incapable of raising anything else. Hence, from the earliest days, sheep have been a specialty of Nantucket, and a source of wealth rivaling the whale. To thoroughly elucidate the sheep question is reserved for some Macaulay, Carlyle, or Mackenzie of the future, for it involves not only the chief land-industry of this remarkable island, but its chief political economy, its municipal struggles, its angry passions, its still smoldering feuds, its family quarrel decently guarded from the stranger's eye. Suffice it to say that the moors were once owned in common, any man using them for grazing ground as he would; and subsequently they were nominally divided into shares, each shareholder having the right to graze a fixed number of sheep without boundaries. There were several favorite pastures for these flocks, one of them lying just outside the part of the village called Newtown; and here a gate was placed across the road to keep what was called the Town Flock from coming in and devastating the gardens by night. Beside this gate also stood the only gallows ever erected in Nantucket, and here the solitary execution took place; the culprit was an Indian, taken red-handed in the act of murder, and whether the gallows was a salutary terror to the sheep as well as the Indians is not mentioned in history.

The Indians soon died out, but the sheep increased and multiplied until they were counted by thousands; and for a century or so an idyllic and pastoral Shearing Feast was kept by the entire population, who, on the first Monday in June, migrated to the ponds near the western end of the island, where the sheep had been previously driven up and penned. Miacomet Plain, with its chain of ponds—one of them still called Washing Pond—then became for three days an encampment of tents and booths, where busy matrons and merry girls cooked such savory dishes as were at that time dear to the island epicure, or set forth those daintier viands prepared at home. The fathers, husbands, brothers, and sweethearts mean-

[2] From "Contributions to the New England Vocabulary," by Frederic D. Allen, in *Dialect Notes,* Vol. I (Part I, 1890), p. 18 and note. Boston: Published by the American Dialect Society.

From *Nantucket Scraps,* Being the Experiences of an Off-Islander, in Season and out of Season, among a Passing People, by Jane G. Austin, pp. 233–236. Copyright, 1882, by James R. Osgood and Company. Boston. 1883.

time washed the sheep, lightening their labor with a great deal of rough play and many practical jokes among themselves, and returned them to the pens to dry until next day, when the shearing began; and let us be glad Mr. Bergh was not obliged to watch its progress, since seldom did a sheep escape his shearer's hands without one or more patches of tar to show where the scissors had gone deeper than the fleece. The next thing was to rebrand each animal with its owner's initial or emblem; and then the shearing was over, and the encampment broke up, the lads and lasses finishing out the holiday with a surreptitious dance in town—for these were the days of Quaker supremacy, when dancing, music, cards, and most modes of amusement were strictly forbidden. But like most efforts to suppress human nature, these laws were only fully honored by those who had no longer the temptation to break them; and the young Quakers danced, sang, and frolicked in their generation very much as their too-liberal descendants do to-day.

Town Meeting Day

THAT second Tuesday in March was and still is the Big Red Letter Day of the old New England towns—Town Meetin' Day! To the children of the early 1800's it meant a gift of gingerbread in the homecoming pockets of their fathers; to the older folks it meant the great expression of democracy where each man might have his say on town affairs, make his vote in his own voice, and if on the wrong side of the question learn to take his defeat like a man, quite sold to the idea that the greater number should win. . . .

* * * * *

In 1845 Angelina Kidder of Mill Hollow, in the East Part, wrote to her brother: "Father is as merry as possible. I wish they would have town meeting every week if it would always have such a good effect on his spirits. He is moderator." So it was then and so it has been ever since, Town Meeting an event of fair import and a raiser of the spirits of every one, from the youngest to the oldest. And if one might but be "Moderator" —there was nothing more for which to long.

Then, after our forefathers had found that the beautiful red but poisonous Love Apple was a perfectly edible tomato, it became the custom to see that the saved and dried tomato seeds from the summer before were planted in their seed box on the window sill—always on Town Meetin' Day!

From *New Hampshire Borns a Town*, by Marion Nicholl Rawson, pp. 54, 67. Copyright, 1942, by E. P. Dutton & Co., Inc. New York.

For accounts of the present-day Town Meeting, see Charles Edward Crane, *Winter in Vermont* (New York, 1941), pp. 292–296; Louise Dickinson Rich, *We Took to the Woods* (Philadelphia, 1942), pp. 298–306; and Clarence M. Webster, *Town Meeting Country* (New York, 1945), pp. 228–235.

PASTIMES AND GAMES

Chimney-Corner Story-Telling

IN THOSE days we had no magazines and daily papers, each reeling off a serial story. Once a week, "The Columbian Sentinel" came from Boston with its slender stock of news and editorial; but all the multiform devices —pictorial, narrative, and poetical—which keep the mind of the present generation ablaze with excitement, had not then even an existence. There was no theatre, no opera; there were in Oldtown no parties or balls, except, perhaps, the annual election, or Thanksgiving festival; and when winter came, and the sun went down at half-past four o'clock, and left the long, dark hours of evening to be provided for, the necessity of amusement became urgent. Hence, in those days, chimney-corner story-telling became an art and an accomplishment. Society then was full of traditions and narratives which had all the uncertain glow and shifting mystery of the firelit hearth upon them. They were told to sympathetic audiences, by the rising and falling light of the solemn embers, with the hearth-crickets filling up every pause. Then the aged told their stories to the young,—tales of early life; tales of war and adventure, of forest-days, of Indian captivities and escapes, of bears and wild-cats, and panthers, of rattlesnakes, of witches and wizards, and strange and wonderful dreams and appearances and providences.

In those days of early Massachusetts, faith and credence were in the very air. Two-thirds of New England was then dark, unbroken forests, through whose tangled paths the mysterious winter wind groaned and shrieked and howled with weird noises and unaccountable clamors. Along the iron-bound shore, the stormful Atlantic raved and thundered, and dashed its moaning waters, as if to deaden and deafen any voice that might tell of the settled life of the old civilized world, and shut us forever into the wilderness. A good story-teller, in those days, was always sure of a warm seat at the hearthstone, and the delighted homage of children. . . .

The Debating Society

PERHAPS chief among our most pleasurable concerns was a debating club, known as the Webster-Hayne Society. Throughout the academy and even

---

From *Oldtown Fireside Stories,* by Harriet Beecher Stowe, pp. 1–3. Entered, according to Act of Congress, in the year 1871, by James R. Osgood & Co., in the Office of the Librarian of Congress, at Washington. Boston: James R. Osgood & Company. 1872.

From *A Goodly Heritage,* by Mary Ellen Chase, pp. 268–270. Copyright, 1932, by Henry Holt and Company, Inc. New York.

throughout the village the loyalty accorded to this organization was intense. Debates were held once a fortnight between opposing teams of two each; and since it was the aim of the club to be inclusive rather than selective in the choice of its speakers, opportunity was widespread for this legitimate means of self-expression. Our subjects were many and varied, and it was an unalterable rule that we should *draw* both for them and for the side we were to support. Thus it was conceivable that I, who would have liked to defend the heroism of the American Indian, or the pre-eminence of sailing vessels over steamships, might be compelled to denounce the Monroe Doctrine or the Assassination of Julius Caesar. The preceptor of my day, who was responsible for this rule as well as for the list of suggested subjects, maintained that by this method of assignment we were trained in the necessary virtue of adaptability; and my father, who was for years a patron of the society, entirely agreed with him.

We usually wrote our arguments and then committed them to memory, although gifted ones among us might prefer to speak "off-hand." The rebuttal which followed the debate proper always called for some spontaneous denouncing of our rivals, which, in the heat of the controversy, we found not too difficult in spite of a large and interested audience. A letter of commendation from my father, written from Augusta a few days following my spirited denunication of Napoleon as a monster to civilization, is one of my treasured possessions as is also a notebook which lists our subjects of one winter term:

Resolved, that the American Indian was, on the whole, an heroic rather than a dastardly figure in history.

Resolved, that the system of taxation under the Roman Empire was unjust to the provinces.

Resolved, that the study of Greek is valuable to the student in Blue Hill Academy.

Resolved, that the Annexation of Texas was unjustifiable.

Resolved, that the rural life of Maine affords advantages above that of the urban.

Resolved, that *Ivanhoe* is a greater and a more interesting novel than *The Last of the Mohicans.*

Sleigh Riding

Among the amusements of New England, sleigh-riding has always held a distinguished place. It is one of the principal winter pastimes; is entered

From *The Life and Adventures of Dr. Dodimus Duckworth,* A.N.Q., to which is added, The History of a Steam Doctor, by The Author of "A Yankee among the Nullifiers" (Asa Greene), Vol. II, pp. 157–158, 159–160. Entered, according to Act of Congress, in the year 1833, by Asa Greene, in the Office of the Clerk of the District Court of the United States for the Southern District of New York. New York: Published by Peter Hill.

into with a great deal of zest; and is altogether a social amusement. Sleigh-riders are generally divided into two classes—the married and the single. These form separate companies. The young do not choose to be restrained by the gravity of the old; and the old do not like to be annoyed by the flirtations of the young. Such is the natural conclusion; but it is shrewdly hinted by the single ones that gravity, on these occasions, finds little place even among married people; that, in fact, they carry their merriment to a pitch never ventured upon by the single; and that it is the old who dread the restraints of the young, rather than the young of the old.

* * * * *

The mere business of riding in a sleigh is not the sole object on these occasions; but a dance, or frolic of some kind, is connected with it. If the party consists of young persons, dancing is usually the order of the night; if of married ones, some other amusement—such as blindman's buff, changing partners, forfeits, and the like—is not unfrequently substituted; and grave papas and mamas, throwing aside their sober parental character, for the time being, assume that of frolicsome children.

The order of a sleigh-ride is this: All the members of the party convene at some given point, from whence they start in company, and drive in a sort of procession, or long line of vehicles, to some other point at a convenient distance—usually some tavern out of town, provided with a large hall, where dancing, or other amusements may be carried on. A supper is bespoken, and wines and other liquors are expected to be forthcoming, if called for. Here all is joy, sport, and hilarity. Dull care is given to the winds; and life and merriment succeed. Sambo has his fiddle new strung, and his bow new rosined for the occasion; and sitting on a platform in one corner, while he makes all feet obedient to the motion of his elbow, fancies himself a greater man than Solomon in all his glory. Or if some other amusement take the place of dancing, then mirth, life, and frolic, move round the circle; and the infliction of sportive penalties, the redemption of forfeits, and the romping and playing of grown-up children occupy the festive hours.

The amusements being over, the party return in the same regular order in which they went forth. It is not to be supposed, however, because they move in a line, that their procession is slow and solemn, like that of a funeral; or stately and exact, like that of a regiment on the line of march. On the contrary, they move briskly and merrily along at a swift trot—the sleighs gliding one after another, as though they slid upon nothing—and the bells musically chiming, to the great animation both of steed and rider. But there is, nevertheless, an order even here—a rule, enacted for the preservation of the property, the life, and character of those concerned. The enactment is this—that there shall be no running of horses during the ride; and that whoever drives his steed faster than a trot, shall forfeit and pay a certain sum of money, to be expended for the benefit of the party; and moreover shall be held and deemed to have drunk more than becomes a respectable man, or than the occasion itself requires.

Husking Bees or Frolics

HUSKING. The act of stripping off husks from Indian corn. In New England it is the custom for farmers to invite their friends to assist them in this task. The ceremonies on these occasions are well described by Joel Barlow, in his poem on Hasty Pudding:

> For now, the cow-house fill'd, the harvest home,
> Th' invited neighbors to the *Husking* come;
> A frolic scene, where work, and mirth, and play,
> Unite their charms, to chase the hours away.
> * * * * *
> The laws of *husking* every wight can tell;
> And sure no laws he ever keeps so well:
> For each red ear a gen'ral kiss he gains,
> With each smut ear, she smuts the luckless swains;
> But when to some sweet maid a prize is cast,
> Red as her lips, and taper as her waist,
> She walks around, and culls one favor'd beau,
> Who leaps, the luscious tribute to bestow.
> Various the sport, as are the wits and brains
> Of well-pleas'd lasses and contending swains;
> Till the vast mound of corn is swept away,
> And he that gains the last ear, wins the day.—Canto 3.

Cattle Show

Now for the cattle-show and the premiums! At daybreak all are on the move, and wide awake for the grand exhibition. Fat beeves and working cattle, fill-pail milkers, Ayrshire bulls, bellowing calves, snorting grunters, with wagon-loads of fat cheeses, and boxes of rich butter, bearing the stamp of super-excellence, carefully put on by my honest aunt Tabitha. See what mammoth squashes, and other fruits in abundance! Here come the groups of fair damsels, crowding into the hall, to see the various handiwork. Carpets, mats, rugs, bedspreads, needle-work and knitting-work, of every kind and description! But come; let us away to the ploughing match; that is what takes the rag off, and is something to the purpose. Twelve teams,—no drivers. Keep steady helm, boys, and mind your eye! How true they lay the sod! The committee will have their match to settle who

From *Dictionary of Americanisms,* by John Russell Bartlett, p. 186. New York: Bartlett and Welford, 1848.

From *The Old Farmer's Almanack,* Calculated on a New and Improved Plan, for the Year of Our Lord 1852, p. 25, October. Entered, according to Act of Congress, in the year 1851, by Jenks, Hickling & Swan, in the Clerk's Office of the District Court of the District of Massachusetts. Boston.

does the best. Off yonder are the working cattle, drawing their ponderous loads of stone; hard and heavy they tug and tug. See how they haw, gee, go ahead, and back astern! no lashing, no bawling, and their teams move as regular as a platoon of soldiers!

County Fair

THE best place to see neo-Puritans really at play was at the county fairs held every fall. The fair-going addict had plenty of attractions to choose from. I've forgotten which one opened the season in early September, but the Stafford Springs event in the middle of October was the last. Sturbridge, Oxford, Willimantic, Norwich, Putnam, Rockville, Palmer, Woodstock, and other towns had at one time or another a fair of their own. But the oldest and most typical of all was the one at Brooklyn, Connecticut.

There was the place where you best caught the real Yankee land as it completely relaxed for one day in the year. Over in Massachusetts there was the famous Brockton Fair where prizes were magnificent and the exhibits awe-inspiring. At Hartford in Charter Oak Park famous harness racing could be enjoyed, the Willimantic track was a sporty half-mile, and Sturbridge had its noted drivers. Brooklyn could not match such attractions; nevertheless, people seemed to feel that it had something the other fairs lacked. For one thing, it was a nice home affair that respected the old ways and exhibited a mode of life that was sound even while it pleased. You met everybody at Brooklyn Fair. You heard a woman say, "Why, I ain't seen her since last Fair day." And a man remark, "When I run into him at th' Fair he told me. . . ." Plenty of people went to the other fairs, but they never seemed to meet old friends the way they did at Brooklyn. As far as I can figure out, that Fair was a sort of catalytic which helped bring to a fine, satisfying blend all the sedate pleasures of a quiet, sensible people, who, nevertheless, could take a day off in the fall and spend a dollar or two and perhaps win a few blue ribbons and the accompanying cash prize.

There were three days to the Fair, Opening, Cattle, and Horse. The first was more or less given over to arranging exhibits in the buildings, although the Midway had started, and there were harness races in the afternoon. The second day was the big one, for then the cattle were on exhibit and were judged. On the third, the horses were shown, and there were some good races. Schools were let out for the Big Day, and only the sternest fathers dared to keep their families home. Even Sam Hunt, famous among thrifty men for his more-than-thrift, bestowed one-half of a dollar on each of his seven children, sorrowfully accepting the fact that, as he said, "There goes a lot of damned good money I've worked hard for, but th' little cusses sorta look forward t' Brooklyn Fair."

From *Town Meeting Country*, by Clarence M. Webster, pp. 159–161. New York: Duell, Sloan & Pearce.

By ten o'clock in the morning every one was there, even Lester Gull, who walked the eight miles barefoot and put on his shoes at the gates. Up against the rails of the half-mile track were hitched the teams. Fancy rubber-tired buggies and black pacers, smart spans of horses and the canopy-topped surrey, farm horses hitched to lumber wagons with boards for seats. Ever since dawn the farmers had been driving their cattle toward Brooklyn, and now the long sheds were filled with calves, bulls, milch cows, hogs, and sheep. A man could spend quite a while, happily wandering from one stall or pen to another, commenting freely on each exhibit and telling a friend that he had a boar or yearling heifer better than any he'd seen yet. Over in the Main Exhibition or the Food and Fancy Work buildings the women folks were happy. Over the hum of voices rose the cry of the sideshow barker, the crack of the buggy whip wielded by the sporty vendor, and the occasional roar of the Wild Man from Borneo down in his pit.

In the afternoon the grandstand was full, and the crowd stood three deep against the rails. Next to the judges' stand was the platform where a band played when acrobats were not performing. The races were gallantly listed as 2/05 pace and trot, 2/13 trot, but if any horse made 2/20 he was very suspect indeed. This was the time when the young bloods had their big moment of the year, and the fellow who entered a horse and even drove it himself was a real hero.

When the last heat was trotted, tired celebrators piled into their carriages and express wagons and started home. Brooklyn Fair was over for the year, and there were chores to do. Most families in my town went to at least one or other fair during the fall, and a few reckless men took in four or five, but on the whole it was considered very bad form to waste too much time in this way. For in pleasure-seeking, as in other habits, the Yankees I knew were men of "measured merriment" and could not enjoy themselves if they broke the bonds of decorum. To them life was not an adventure; rather, it was a nice comfortable affair in which one day a year at Brooklyn Fair fitted neatly, a pleasant, almost gay eight hours, with just a touch of the sportive, even the exotic, but never unrestrained. For in the Indian Summer of a civilization, it is not coltish and wild; its joys are quiet ones.

Cockroach and Bedbug Match

Oh, yes! The cook gave me a lot of insect powder and a squirt-gun to blow into the cracks. I used it once but the bugs ate it all up and came out of their holes licking their chops and looking for more, so I gave up in

From *The Making of a Sailor* or Sea Life Aboard a Yankee Square-Rigger, by Frederick Pease Harlow, pp. 51–52. Publication Number Seventeen of The Marine Research Society. Copyright, 1928, by The Marine Research Society. Salem, Massachusetts.

disgust. You ought to see the arena the cook has on his table. He has made a frame which slips over the edges of his cake-board and placing this on the table, he goes behind the range and catches a cockroach; then, taking a straw from the broom, he runs it up and down in the cracks of the bulkhead, back of your bunk, chasing out the bugs until he secures a lively one. Then placing the two in the center of the board, with their heads together, he sics 'em on. You'd naturally think that the cockroach would eat the bug up, but believe me! the bug is there with bells.

The first time I saw the fight I nearly laughed my head off. I was talking to the cook one Sunday afternoon when I saw him with a straw in his hands poking the bugs about the board. "What have you got there?" I asked. "Come down and see," said he. "How much will you bet on the bed-bug that he can lick the cockroach?" "Oh, I'll bet the cockroach can lick the bed-bug," said I. "All right! It'll cost you twenty-five cents to come in," said the cook. I put up the money and the cook said, "Ready! Go!" keeping their noses pointed together with the straw. The roach finally got mad and jumped on the bug and stuck his beak in, but the bug rolled over on his back and caught a leg of the roach and working himself up under his breast, tried to get a half-Nelson on him. The roach would draw up first one leg and then another in an effort to pry the bug loose and sometimes all his legs would be working at the same time. It was sure a comical sight. His legs seemed too long and there was no way in which he could bring two feet in a position at the same time so as to shake off the bug which held to it like a bulldog holding a shaggy cur by the throat. Finally, getting a vulnerable spot on the roach, he fairly sucked the life out of him and I lost my quarter. If it wasn't so late we'd ask the cook to give us an entertainment this afternoon.

The Gam

If two strangers crossing the Pine Barrens in New York State, or the equally desolate Salisbury Plain in England; if casually encountering each other in such inhospitable wilds, these twain, for the life of them, cannot well avoid a mutual salutation; and stopping for a moment to interchange the news; and, perhaps, sitting down for a while and resting in concert; then, how much more natural that upon the illimitable Pine Barrens and Salisbury Plains of the sea, two whaling vessels descrying each other at the ends of the earth—off lone Fanning's Island, or the far away King's Mills; how much more natural, I say, that under such circumstances these ships should not only interchange hails, but come into still closer, more friendly and sociable contact? And especially would this seem to be a

From *Moby-Dick: or The Whale,* by Herman Melville, Chapter LIII, *The Works of Herman Melville,* Standard Edition, Vol. VII, pp. 301–304. London, Bombay, Sydney: Constable and Company, Ltd. 1922.

matter of course, in the case of vessels owned in one seaport, and whose captains, officers, and not a few of the men are personally known to each other; and consequently, have all sorts of dear domestic things to talk about.

For the long absent ship, the outward-bounder, perhaps, has letters on board; at any rate, she will be sure to let her have some papers of a date a year or two later than the last one on her blurred and thumb-worn files. And in return for that courtesy, the outward-bound ship would receive the latest whaling intelligence from the cruising-ground to which she may be destined, a thing of the utmost importance to her. And in degree, all this will hold true concerning whaling vessels crossing each other's track on the cruising-ground itself, even though they are equally long absent from home. For one of them may have received a transfer of letters from some third, and now far remote vessel; and some of those letters may be for the people of the ship she now meets. Besides, they would exchange the whaling news, and have an agreeable chat. For not only would they meet with all the sympathies of sailors, but likewise with all the peculiar congenialities arising from a common pursuit and mutually shared privations and perils.

Nor would difference of country make any very essential difference; that is, so long as both parties speak one language, as is the case with Americans and English. . . .

So, then, we see that of all ships separately sailing the sea, whalers have most reason to be sociable—and they are so. . . .

. . . What does the whaler do when she meets another whaler in any sort of decent weather? She has a *"Gam,"* a thing so utterly unknown to all other ships that they never heard of the name even; and if by chance they should hear of it, they only grin at it, and repeat gamesome stuff about "spouters," "blubber-boilers," and such like pretty exclamations. . . .

But what is a *Gam*? You might wear out your index-finger running up and down the columns of dictionaries, and never find the word. Dr. Johnson never attained to that erudition; Noah Webster's ark does not hold it. Nevertheless, this same expressive word has now for many years been in constant use among some fifteen thousand true born Yankees. Certainly, it needs a definition, and should be incorporated into the Lexicon. With that view, let me learnedly define it.

GAM. Noun—*A social meeting of two (or more) Whaleships, generally on a cruising-ground; when, after exchanging hails, they exchange visits by boats' crews: the two captains remaining, for the time, on board of one ship, and the two chief mates on the other.*

A Childish Pastime

I MIGHT have mentioned, as one of the amusements of childhood, the throwing of a piece of paper upon the embers of our wood-fire, for we had no coal in those days, and watching the gradual extinguishment of the sparks, likening it to a congregation entering the meeting-house. "There they go in," we would say. "There's the ministers"; and as the final spark disappeared,—"Now, the sexton has gone in and shut the door." I speak of this only as a curious illustration of English ways traditionally surviving in New England. Thus Cowper tells us:—

> So when a child, as playful children use,
> Has burnt to tinder a stale last year's news,
> The flame extinct, he views the roving fire,—
> There goes my lady, and there goes the squire;
> There goes the parson, O illustrious spark!
> And there, scarce less illustrious, goes the clerk!

Horse Chestnut Men

. . . THE small boy of the family brought a cup of boiled chestnuts, and while we munched them, explained how he had picked up eighty-one quarts of nuts so far that year. In his pocket the boy had other treasures. He pulled forth a handful of horse-chestnuts, and told me they grew on a little tree down by the burying-ground.

"The boys up at our school make men of 'em," he said. "They take one chestnut and cut a face on it like you do on a pumpkin for a jack-o'-lantern. That's the head. Then they take a bigger one and cut two or three places in front for buttons, and make holes to stick in toothpicks for legs, and they stick in more for arms, and with a little short piece fasten the head on the body. Then they put 'em up on the stovepipe where the teacher can't get 'em, and they stay there all day. Sometimes they make caps for 'em." He got out his jack-knife and spent the rest of the evening manufacturing these queer little men for my benefit.

From *Old New England Traits,* edited by George Lunt, pp. 225–226. Entered, according to Act of Congress, in the year 1873, by George Lunt, in the Office of the Librarian of Congress, at Washington. New York: Hurd and Houghton. Cambridge: The Riverside Press.

From *The New England Country,* by Clifton Johnson, pp. 61–62. Copyright, 1892, by Clifton Johnson. Boston: Lee and Shepard. 1893.

Fly Away, Jack

A TRICK to amuse children. A person sticks pieces of white paper to the nails of his forefingers. He places his forefingers on the edge of a table with the other fingers closed. He raises his right hand and brings it back, with the middle finger substituted for the forefinger, crying *fly away, Jack.* He does the same with the left and cries *fly away, Gill.* He then restores his forefingers in the same way crying *come again, Jack; come again, Gill.*

Smell Brimstone

A CHILD is asked if he wishes to smell brimstone. He naturally does. He is asked to double his fists and hold them in front of his face. The person then seizes his wrists, rubs his knuckles briskly together to make the brimstone and suddenly hits him in the nose with his own fist.

I Languish

A FEW years later, we forced our mother in a moment of weakness to admit that she too had played kissing games in her youth. She described one called "I Languish"—a game in which two straight chairs were placed back to back, in the center of the room. A boy knelt in one of them and announced, "I languish."

"Who do you languish for?" inquired the encircling company.

"I languish for Susan."

Susan then knelt in the other chair and they kissed. The young man retired and Susan proceeded to languish in her turn. My mother's mother was of pure New England stock, and her father three-quarters Yankee, so my first Puritans must accept seven-eights of the responsibility for that unpuritanic pastime.

From "Cape Cod Dialect Addenda," by George Davis Chase, in *Dialect Notes,* Vol. III (Part V, 1909), p. 420. Publication of the American Dialect Society. New Haven, Connecticut.

Ibid., p. 422.

From *As Much As I Dare,* A Personal Recollection, by Burges Johnson, p. 11. Copyright, 1944, by Ives Washburn, Inc. New York.

Hailey Over

PERHAPS a corruption for hail ye! over! A children's game of ball played as follows: The players choose sides and take positions on opposite sides of a barn. One player throws the ball over the barn, crying out, *hailey over*. Some one of the opposing players tries to catch it, and then tags one of his opponents with the ball. The player tagged has to change sides. The side wins which gains all of the players.

Violet Fights

THE recorder, Mrs. Fanny D. Bergen, writes:

"Armies of blue violets are annually sacrificed by little people in the 'Violet Fights.' Two children provide themselves with a goodly pile of these flowers, which they have purposely plucked with long stems. Each combatant holds his posy by the stem; the two spurs are interlocked; then the children simultaneously jerk the stems, and off comes one or the other violet head. Once in a great while the two heads fall, so evenly matched in resistance are they. Usually, however, one conquers the other; the flowerless stem is replaced by a fresh one from the pile, and the flower battle goes on. Occasionally a soldier is so valiant and successful as to lay low the heads of as many as a hundred or two of his enemies, but sooner or later he, too, is numbered with the beautiful slain. I am glad to have known of a few little girls who were too humane to take part in this ruthless play. The pastime is not only common among children throughout the United States and Canada, but is a familiar childish amusement in Japan, and a friend found that the same play was known to Indian children in the summer encampment at York Beach, Maine. The little red children say that the one whose violet conquers will be a great man. The Onandagas have a name for violets which, interpreted, means 'two heads entangled,' referring to the flower game."

Statues

DURING the long summer evenings until our bedtime at eight or eight-thirty we played with others of the neighborhood in all manner of merry-

---

From "A Word-List from Aroostook," by J. W. Carr and G. D. Chase, in *Dialect Notes*, Vol. III (Part V, 1909), p. 412. Publication of the American Dialect Society. New Haven, Connecticut.

From *Games and Songs of American Children*, collected and compared by William Wells Newell, pp. 251–252. New and Enlarged Edition. Copyright, 1883, 1903, by Harper & Brothers. New York and London.

From *A Goodly Heritage*, by Mary Ellen Chase, pp. 66–68. Copyright, 1932, by Henry Holt and Company, Inc. New York.

makings, usually the noisier the better. But there was one diversion which never palled, serious and silent as it was by contrast. This was the making of ourselves into *statues*. A judge was chosen, usually by counting out, and he thereupon at once retired from the scene while we decided by individuals or by groups what we should personify. The odd thing about this amusement lay in its abstract nature. There was nothing to prevent our choosing to make our forms and our faces into images of well-known persons or representative of famous events. Rather we decided to typify various emotions or states of mind—Joy, Fear, Pity, Hatred, Jealousy, Faith, Rage, Pride, Cruelty, Melancholy, and Grief. Sometimes one strove singly to make oneself into the outward and visible sign of some mental or spiritual mood; sometimes we functioned in small groups, our aim to present an ensemble like the Niobe in one of our history books. When we had finally decided what we were to represent, for which task we were allowed but a few minutes, we communicated this information to the judge, who if material was at hand wrote down the emotion or the state of mind opposite the name of the actor. If no pencil, paper, or slate were easily procurable, the judge relinquished his position in favor of mere guesswork.

Whence this game sprang it is impossible to say. Perhaps, indeed, it was born from gazing upon the reproductions of famous statuary in schoolbooks. It seems to have been of relatively new growth; my mother had never played it. But it was dear to the children of my generation and environment. We always entered upon it with high seriousness, perhaps vaguely realizing that the emotions and passions we attempted to portray were the very stuff and pattern of human life. Melancholy, clasping his knees, his head sunk upon his flannel blouse, remained for long, solemn minutes while the judge criticized, appraised, or attempted to guess what his posture indicated; Faith, gazing heavenward in a blue gingham apron, was too rapt in her contemplation of eternal verities to laugh; Jealousy, called to bed in the very act of stabbing his rival, preferred to incur punishment rather than to abandon his studied, awful formation until all chance of getting first place had been well lost.

Old Witch

A.—Ten girls, a mother, a witch, and eight children—namely, Sunday, Monday, Tuesday, Wednesday, Thursday, Friday, Saturday, and the eldest daughter Sue. The mother, preparing to go out, addresses her children:

Now all you children stay at home,
And be good girls while I am gone;
Let no one in [1]

* * * * *

From *Games and Songs of American Children*, collected and compared by William Wells Newell, pp. 215–216, 217–218. New and Enlarged Edition. New York and London.

[1] A line and a half are wanting.—W. W. N.

Especially you, my daughter Sue,
Or else I'll beat you black and blue.[1]

The witch knocks at the door, and is refused entrance by the children. She beguiles them by promises to admit her, which they finally do. She then holds out her pipe (a bit of stick), which she carries between her teeth, saying to Sue, "Light my pipe!" Sue refusing, she makes the same demand to each child, in the order of the days of the week in which they are ranged. All refuse till she reaches the last, who consents and touches her pipe, whereupon the witch seizes her hand, and drags her out of the house to her "den."

The mother then returns, counts the children, and Sue is questioned and punished. This is played over until each child is taken, Sue last.

When the mother has lost all her children, the witch calls, and invites her to dinner. Upon going to the witch's door, she finds a table set for the meal, and the witch asks her to order a dish to suit her taste. She does so, whereupon the witch produces Sunday, and lays her upon the table, with considerable assistance from Sunday.

A very amusing dialogue now ensues between the witch and the mother. The former urges the mother to eat, with many blandishments, and the mother (recognizing her child) declines, with such excuses as any ingenious child can devise.

The mother, upon pretence of inability to eat the food, calls for another dish, and when the witch leaves the room, hurries the child from the table and places her behind the chair. When the witch returns, she says that she found the dish so good that she ate it all, and calls for another.

Each child is produced in turn, with the same result. When all are arranged behind their mother, she calls for another dish, and when the witch leaves the room to get it, runs home with all her children.

Hartford, Conn.

* * * * *

C.—The name of the witch in this variation is "Old Mother Cripsy-crops," and the game begins by playing No. 89 [*Old Mother Tipsy-toe*]. When the mother goes out, the children call after her, "Old mother, the kettle boils." She answers, "Take a spoon and stir it." "We haven't got any." "Buy one." "We have no money." "Borrow," says the mother. "People won't lend," reply the children.

The witch come in, and entices Sunday away by fine promises. When the mother comes back, she inquires, "Where's my Sunday?" The children

---

[1] "I charge my daughters every one,
To keep good house while I am gone.
You and *you* [points] but especially *Sue*,
Or else I'll beat you black and blue."

From "Nursery Rhymes of England," where it is said to be a game of the Gypsy, who "during the mother's absence comes in, entices a child away, and hides her. This process is repeated till all the children are hidden, when the mother has to find them." —W. W. N.

make some excuse, as, "Perhaps he has gone down cellar," etc. She tells Tuesday to take care of Monday, as she had previously placed Monday in charge of Sunday, and goes out again, when the same scene is repeated, until all the children have been carried off.

The mother now calls at the witch's house, and asks to be let in. The witch refuses, saying, "No, your shoes are too dirty." "But I will take off my shoes." "Your stockings are too dirty." "Then I will take off my stockings." "Your feet are too dirty." "I will cut off my feet." "That would make the carpet all bloody." "But I must see my children, and you have got them." "What should I know about your children? But if you like you may call to-morrow at twelve."

The mother departs, and as soon as she is gone the witch goes to the children and renames them all. One she calls Mustard, another Pepper, another Salt, another Vinegar, etc. Then she turns their faces to the wall, and tells them to give these names if they are asked who they are. The mother calls again at the house of the witch, and this time is admitted. She asks the children what their names are, and they all answer as they were instructed by the witch. She then asks the first child to let her feel his toe. He puts up his foot, and when the mother feels it she says, "This is my Sunday! let your big toe carry you home;" whereupon he runs off. The same process is gone through with all the other children.

D.—To the mother (this time present), in the midst of her children, approaches the witch, who comes limping, leaning on a cane. The dialogue is between mother and witch.

"There's old mother Hippletyhop; I wonder what she wants to-day?"
"I want one of your children."
"Which one do you want?"

The witch names any child of the row.

"What will you give her to eat?"
"Plum-cake" (a different delicacy for each child).

The witch carries off the child, and observes: "Walk as I do, or else I'll kill you." She takes the child home and kills her, then returns for another. When all are gone the mother goes out to look for her children. She goes to the witch's house, and finds all the children (presumed to be dead) against the wall, making the most horrible faces. She points to a child, and asks, "What did [Mary] die of?" "She died of sucking her thumbs" (naming the child's gesture). Suddenly all the children come to themselves, and cry out, "Oh, mother, we are not dead!"

Portsmouth, N. H.

Hoist the Green Sail

They chose captains and sides, and one captain led off his side and hid them somewhere, agreeing on a set of signals, for which they used the names of fruits. Then he would return, and with a stick trace on the ground the course he had taken, for the benefit of the opposing side. "And right there," he would finish, "is where they are." "Oh, I know," the other captain would cry. "Come on!" And immediately they would start on the trail, the first captain following them and crying monotonously at intervals: "Ba-na-a-nas!" or "Aw-w-r-un-jes!" The pursuers would try to confuse him and those in hiding by adding their voices to his. Furthermore it was possible, from the inflection of his voice and from the alternation of the signals, that a wary player should discern whether a certain word meant "stay back" or "come in," and direct his fellows accordingly. Sometimes the searchers would discover their quarry, and run back to the starting-place to claim the victory; sometimes, while wandering aimlessly about, they would hear the disappointing cry of the others at the goal, "Hoist the green sail!"

Games of Boston Boys

Punk

The games played by the boys of Chestnut and the adjacent streets are most pleasantly recalled; among which "I Spy," "The Red Lion," and "Punk" stand out prominently. This last was always popular, the only requisite being a soft ball,—not too soft, however, for obvious reasons, when it is known that the first boy holding it plugged, or "punked," the boy that suited him as a mark. A general scrimmage then ensued for the possession of the ball, and the one securing it promptly "punked" another victim selected from the rapidly scattering boys.

The Locust

The American boy is nothing if not inventive, and anything that can be produced which will make a noise is dear to his heart. One of the earliest of such inventions which I recall was named the "locust," a harmless production, and one that no doubt paved the way for the later abomina-

---

By B. A. Botkin. Played in Dorchester, Massachusetts, about 1910. Quincy children called it "Hist-de-green-sail," without knowing what it meant.

From *Old Boston Boys and the Games They Played,* by James D'Wolf Lovett, pp. 10, 18–19; 29–32, 36–37; 41–47, 137–138. Copyright, 1906, by James D'Wolf Lovett. Boston: Privately printed at the Riverside Press.

tion known as the "Devil's fiddle." The locust was made of an old-fashioned, round wooden match-box, over the open end of which a piece of kid was tightly stretched; a strand or two of horse hair was then passed in and out of this improvised drumhead, and the long ends were made into a loop which ran around in a groove, with a little resin in it, made at the end of a stick. The box was then whirled around rapidly, the result being a sound which almost exactly resembled the note of the insect from which it received its name.

Coasting

Of course the winter sport *par excellence* was coasting, and those Boston boys whose boyhood was at the zenith in the fifties include coasting, as it was then practised, among the lost arts. If any of the youngsters of to-day are inclined to laugh at this statement, let any one of them, athlete though he may be, take a running start of from three to ten yards at full speed with the sled following at the end of its cord, and when sufficient impetus has been acquired, throw it ahead, letting the line fall along the seat, at the same time launching his body, curved bow-wise, forward through the air, alighting breast first, with no apparent effort, jar, or retardment of speed as softly as a falling snowflake, upon the flying sled as it shoots underneath. This would be called a pretty, acrobatic feat to-day, but was too common then to attract special notice. That's the difference.

All coasting in those days was racing, pure and simple. Prominent sleds were as well known among the boys as race horses and yachts are to-day, and on any Saturday afternoon hundreds of spectators might be seen hedging in the "Long Coast," which ran from the corner of Park and Beacon streets to the West Street entrance and as much farther along Tremont Street Mall as one's impetus would carry him. A squad of coasters would be bunched together at the top of this coast, holding their sleds like dogs in leash, waiting for some "crack" to lead off. As he straightened himself and started on his run with the cry of "Lullah!" to clear the way, it was the signal for all to follow, and one after another would string out from the bunch after him, in rapid succession, each keen to pass as many of those ahead as possible, the lesser lights being careful not to start until the "heavyweights" had sped on their way.

The walk back uphill was made interesting by discussing the merits, faults, lines, etc., of the noted sleds, and if, as often happened, invidious comparisons were made between a "South End" and a "West End" sled, a lively and not altogether unwelcome scrap, then and there, was usually the logical outcome.

Sleds (the first-class ones) were made with much care and skill, and cost proportionately. Natural black walnut was a favorite material, finished either with a fine dead polish or a bright surface, varnished with as much care as a coach; the name, if it bore one, was usually a fine specimen of lettering in gold or bright colors. The model was carefully planned, and the lines were graceful and a delight to the eye of a connoisseur. Black enameled leather, bordered by gold or silver headed tacks, made a popular seat, and the "irons," as they were called, were made of the best "silver steel," whatever that meant. They were kept burnished like glass, with constant care and fine emery and oil, and a streak of ashes or a bare spot was avoided as a yacht steers clear of rocks.

The amount of "spring" given to the irons was also a matter of moment, and a nice gradation of the same was thought to have influence on the speed; it certainly added greatly to one's bodily comfort.

"Let's see your irons" was a common request, and the owner thus honored would jerk his sled up on its hind legs, so to speak, wipe off the steel with mitten or handkerchief, and show off the bright surface with much pride.

* * * * *

Steering a first-class sled in those days was not accomplished by sticking out one's leg and digging gullies in the snow with the toe of the boot. Heaven forbid! Those who owned crack sleds knew how to handle and get all the speed possible out of them, and would no more have retarded the speed by employing the above method than a yachtsman would think of steering his boat by towing a spar overboard. The correct form for a coaster who knew the game was to lie on the sled with head well down, feet firmly crossed and knees flexed as far over the back as possible, both hands resting easily upon the same runner near its point; the steering was done by "pulling her head round" in the desired direction, by little short jerks of the runner upon which the hands rested.

Dan Sargent conceived the idea of steering by holding out in front of his sled a second one of diminutive proportions. This, however, could only be done on a steep coast, where no running start was necessary. I saw him try it several times, but it was never adopted. The first step to the "double runner" was two sleds hitched together tandem, and then the long connecting board quickly followed.

Marbles

In the spring, as soon as the frost was out of the ground, many games stood waiting for us. Probably to the boys of to-day "marbles" sounds rather weak, and "Go and play marbles" is a phrase which one often hears hurled at the head of some unsuccessful competitor in field sports. It is true that it cannot be classed among athletics, but it was a much more serious business then than it is to-day, and was played with a good deal of skill. To shoot an "alley" with force and precision, "knuckling down," that is, with the knuckles resting upon the ground, is not so easy and requires much practice.

A boy's stock of marbles was usually carried in a bag with a running string, and consisted of "Alleys," "Jaspers," "Chinees," "Peewees," "Agates," "Bull's Eyes," and several other kinds. A special marble was kept for long shots, which might perhaps have been six feet, and it was remarkable how many times a small marble would be struck at this distance, with only the snap of the thumb.

I wonder if Mr. Rogers, a most courteous and dignified gentleman, whom I often see, remembers his skill at this sport! He was as expert as any boy of whom I can think. He, among many others, used to run a "bank," as we called it,—which consisted of a strip of wood, perhaps twelve or fifteen inches long, with six or eight little arches cut in it, each somewhat wider than a marble, and numbered from one up. This row of arches was held upright upon the ground, and the marksman, a few feet away, would shoot his marble with the object of entering one of the arches; if he succeeded, he was given the number of marbles which corresponded with the number over the arch, while, if he failed, the marble was appropriated by the banker.

Then there was "ring taw" and "three holes," and lots of other names which have been forgotten. These games were good fun, and kept boys out of doors as well as out of mischief.

Kite-Flying

Kite-flying had and always will have a fascination for boys. Few "grown-ups," however, give it any attention at the present day, except in the interest of science. Formerly many gentlemen used to make kites for their children, and meet upon the Common to fly them. The late Dr. Nathaniel B. Shurtleff, once mayor of Boston, the writer's father, and several others made fine kites. Dr. Shurtleff was very skilful in making Chinese kites; I remember several which resembled owls, with large, blinking eyes, and which were most effective in the air. My father once made a bow-kite seven feet high, a piece of rattan forming the bow. It had a "pull" which would have delighted the heart of a politician; one afternoon I was allowed to hold the cross-bar to which the string was attached, but I did not hold it long, as, although I dug both heels into the ground, it drew me along with the utmost ease. Stout gloves were required in letting out and pulling in the string of this kite.

Tops

Tops, of course, had their innings, and some of the older boys used to get theirs turned to order, from hard, fancy woods, such as lignum vitae, rose, box, tulip, leopard, and many other woods. These had long and sharp steel spikes fixed in them, with which we would try to split each other's tops while spinning. Since then I have never seen boys, playing at this sport, throw the tops with their utmost strength, as we used to do.

Stilting

Stilting, too, was a fad for a time, and some got to be quite expert at the game, hopping upon one stilt and shouldering the other. We would in this fashion have jousts, necessarily short-lived, handling the unused stilt as a lance. Games of tag, too, were played upon stilts, and in fact we got to feel pretty much at home upon them.

Tip-Cat

"Tip-cat"[1] was also a popular game. One occasionally sees it played to-day, but not to the extent that it was then. Not content with small soft wood cats, two or three inches in length, we made them of a section of broom handle and about six or eight inches long, using the remainder of the handle for the cat-stick. With the three strokes which were allowed in this game, I have seen a cat of the latter kind sent from the Spruce Street path on the Common over the Public Garden fence. Charlie Troupe, who was a fine player at the old "Massachusetts" game of baseball, made these three strokes; they held the record, and I very much doubt if any cat has ever jumped as far since.

Choosing Sides

The mode of choosing sides was about as follows: one of the two captains would sharply toss a bat, held in perpendicular position, to the other, who would catch it wherever he could. The one who tossed it would then place one of his hands above and touching that of the other, and so on, alternately, until the knob on the end was reached, when the last one would endeavor, by digging his thumb and finger nails down inside the other's grip, to get such a hold upon it as would enable him to swing the bat three times around his head. Failing to do this, the other had his first choice of the players for his side, and then the choosing proceeded alternately and rapidly.

The reader will, no doubt, wonder why a coin was not "flipped" up and the first choice decided in a jiffy. Well, it was a boy's way of deciding; and it afforded some sort of fun, mingled with a mild excitement, as the two neared the top of the bat, to watch the last one try to get a hold upon the rounded knob and with clenched teeth swing the bat around his head.

Games of Nantucket Boys

Cracks and Squares

In my native town, when a boy, we had but few stone sidewalks,—laid in squares, we knew them as "flagstone" sidewalks. The cracks between those

[1] Also known as "peggy."

From *Brief Historical Data and Memories of My Boyhood Days in Nantucket*, by Joseph E. C. Farnham, pp. 65–66, 124–125, 249, 250. Providence: Joseph E. C. Farnham. 1923.

squares of stone we children always avoided by stepping over them, as we, in our innocent, honest belief, used to say if we "step on the cracks" we will "miss our lessons." . . .

Pitching Penny Shells and Leadies

"Pitching penny shells" I think is distinctly peculiar and entirely original to Nantucket. Possibly it may have been a practice elsewhere, but if so, I never heard of it. . . . "Penny shells" were, and presumably now are, abundant about the ocean-washed shores of Nantucket. Many a day in boyhood have I roamed about the south shore gathering and filling my pockets with them. They are simply the shells of a small sea animal, similar in shape to the quahaug or little-neck, varying in size from about the dimensions of one of the old-fashioned copper cents and graduating down to about half that size. . . . They are washed, scoured and bleached by the waves and sand, only a slight black or brownish discoloration appearing on the outer side of some of them. Such were our "penny shells." With a knife-blade stuck in the ground at a fence, or similar background, we used to pitch those shells at that knife as a goal, after the manner of pitching pennies. We also employed them by tossing in the air and letting them fall to the ground on the "heads I win and tails you lose" order. "Heads" was the outside of the shell; "tails" the inner side. . . .

Another of our long-ago games was pitching "leadies." I know not whether this was distinctively and absolutely a Nantucket creation, but I am morally sure that it was far from being universal, and I am quite as certain that it was closely allied to my native heath. Leadies were of our own manufacture. Scores of these I have made in my father's shop, where I had the privilege of using his tools for my boyish pleasures. First was the construction of a mould. This we made from a piece of pine or other soft wood. We carefully fashioned two pieces of wood, each of a size of three or four inches long, perhaps two or two and one-half inches wide and a half or three-quarters of an inch thick. The frame for the mould made ready we would then throw an old-fashioned copper cent into the fire in the little cast-iron cylinder stove, leaving it to become red hot. Removing it we would place it on one side of the mould, about a quarter of an inch from the top, place the other side carefully and evenly over it, then holding it firm in position we would place it in a vise and gradually close it until the two sides of the mould came together. This done we removed the cent, and we had a perfect mould for casting our leadies. In other words we could make the old-fashioned cent, except that it was cast in lead, and was of no use except as a plaything. Then we cut on the inside at the top of each portion of the mould a slight opening which made the run into which we poured the lead. In moulding we held the mould firmly in place by again using the vise. These we pitched up against a knife or other object set up for the purpose the same as we did for the penny-shells. It was a crude process and an equally crude product. I am inclined to the belief that this was quite a Nantucket institution.

Kick Poke

While it was most decidedly more crude, yet the now popular collegiate game of football is not more enthusiastically appreciated than such a game was by us associated boys more than fifty years ago, albeit it was with us not only a more limited enthusiasm, but it was, perforce, a more unique and quite original pastime. Our sport was, as we called it, to "kick poke." With us it certainly was a great game. We did not have the regulation ball, but most essentially a far different one, because we used a hog's bladder. So many hogs were killed in the town, especially in the fall, for numerous citizens, that a plea for a bladder by a boy at the slaughter house was usually graciously granted. Thus many of the boys each had such an unseemly football which, with his fellows, all enjoyed kicking. One of those bladders obtained, we would break the stem from an ordinary clay pipe, insert it into the orifice at the neck of the bladder, and "blow it up." In that homely way we got a prodigious ball, as to size and lightness, and with it in the open had many hours of exhilarating pastime. . . .

* * * * *

A number of the more deft of the boys made from thin leather a quite nicely finished covering within which the bladder was inserted and laced, thus preserving it for more extended active service. . . .

Round Ball

This [Dudley Common] was the place where old-fashioned round ball came into its own, before baseball was heard of. Round ball was of the same athletic family as "barn-tick," "three-old-cat" and "four-old-cat" and synchronous [*sic*] with them. It was played with a soft ball—reasonably soft, if it was thrown with moderate speed. The bases were at the corners of a parallelogram instead of a diamond and it was allowable to hit the base runner with the ball; in which case he was out. There were no fouls behind the catcher. Indeed the most expert stroke was a back-hand hit driving the ball behind the catcher and so opening the whole field to the runner. So it happened that one of the fielders was placed behind the catcher when a back-handed hitter was at the bat. The catcher stood close to the batter and caught off the bat—and—tell it not in Gath—sometimes caught the *bat*.

From *Black Tavern Tales, Stories of Old New England,* by Charles L. Goodell, pp. 43. Copyright, 1932, by Charles L. Goodell. Brooklyn: Willis McDonald & Co.

PART FOUR

WORD LORE

It is only from its roots in the living generations of men that a language can be reinforced with fresh vigor for its needs. . . . True vigor and heartiness of phrase do not pass from page to page, but from man to man. . . .

—JAMES RUSSELL LOWELL

The metaphorical and other odd expressions . . . often originate in some curious anecdote or event, which is transmitted from mouth to mouth, and soon made the property of all.

—JOHN RUSSELL BARTLETT

We were talking about names, one day. Was there ever anything, I said, like the Yankee for inventing the most uncouth, pretentious, detestable appellations, inventing or finding them, since the time of Praise God Barebones?

—OLIVER WENDELL HOLMES

It is curious how we are attracted by the wise, pithy sayings of an unlettered man. It is the contrast between his mind and his culture. We like contrasts and we like metaphors and striking comparisons. The more they are according to nature and everyday life, the better they please the masses. . . . It is an old thought that has been dressed up for centuries, and suddenly appears in everyday clothes.

—CHARLES HENRY SMITH ("Bill Arp")
on Josh Billings

I. YANKEEISMS

. . . country New Englanders use the dialect in all stages of its gradual disintegration, from those who use still a pure "Biglow" vocabulary and pronunciation, to those whose dictionary English is tinged by the mere dying twang of Yankeedom.

—PERCY MACKAYE

. . . the geographic variations in American English are the result of the history of the settlement and of the influence of trade areas and culture areas on the speech of the American people.

—HANS KURATH

Boston has enough of England about it to make a good English dictionary.—OLIVER WENDELL HOLMES

Though this native speech was felt to be vigorously expressive, may even have been felt to be the real speech of New England, yet it was always used with a reluctant admission that the reality was not good enough for the highest purposes. . . . This sense for double personality has existed nowhere else in the country so completely as in New England.—GEORGE PHILIP KRAPP

1. REGIONALISM IN YANKEE SPEECH

FROM the beginning the gen-u-ine Yankee has been tagged with clichés like *snum, tarnal, plaguey nation, tarnation.*[1] Even the dialect of *The Biglow Papers,* which has the authentic Yankee ring and flavor, contains a maximum of colloquialism and a minimum of localism, with a generous proportion of "eye dialect," or humorous misspelling. Because of the long association of Yankee dialect (like all dialect) with humor and caricature, Lowell's discovery and investigation of the linguistic and literary riches of rural New England speech came as a revelation—the revelation that dialect is a matter of character as well as custom, of sense as well as sound.

An' yit I love th' unhighschooled way
Ol' farmers hed when I wuz younger;

---

[1] For more vigorous and elaborate Yankee oaths, compare "Dod blast ye to Helsibub," which, Burges Johnson says, "seems to avoid both hell and Beelzebub, but gains strength from each"; (*As Much as I Dare,* New York, p. 29) also: "Goshfrey mighty dorman," "Flush-to-bung-town," and "Jumped-up flat-footed Sabriny," reported by Ola G. Veazie from New Hampshire (Manuscripts of the Federal Writers' Project). As Johnson explains, "upon the farms of Vermont and New Hampshire, and along the coast and in the forests of Maine, there has been since the days of Ethan Allen an easy fluency in cussing that never sought the least disguise" because "All of that northern territory was first peopled by folk who had fled the Massachusetts and Connecticut clergy and their dour god."

Their talk wuz meatier, an' 'ould stay,
While book-froth seems to whet your hunger;
For puttin' in a downright lick
'twixt Humbug's eyes, ther' 's few can metch it,
An' then it helves my thoughts ez slick
Ez stret-grained hickory does a hetchet.[1]

Lowell's mastery of the speech enabled him to explain as well as demonstrate its uses skilfully. While it was well known that Yankees are distinguished from speakers from other parts of the country by their flat, drawling nasal tone (which Whitman, in *An American Primer,* called "offensive") and by their tortuous vowel-twisting and juggling of *r,*[2] less was known about differences between one Yankee and another and variations in the pronunciation of the same word according to the emphasis. Lowell distinguishes five ways of pronouncing *well* and two ways each of pronouncing *for, too,* and *to.*

A friend of mine . . . told me that he once heard five "wells," like pioneers, precede the answer to an inquiry about the price of land. The first was the ordinary *wul,* in deference to custom; the second, the long, perpending *ooahl,* with a falling inflection of the voice; the third, the same, but with the voice rising, as if in despair of a conclusion, into a plaintively nasal whine; the fourth, *wulh,* ending in the aspirate of a sigh; and then, fifth, came a short, sharp *wal,* showing that a conclusion had been reached.[3]

. . . *for* is commonly *fer* (a shorter sound than *fur* for *far*), but when emphatic it always becomes *for,* as "wut *for*!" So *too* is pronounced like *to* (as it was anciently spelt), and *to* like *ta* (the sound as in the *tou* of *touch*), but *too,* when emphatic, changes into *tue,* and *to,* sometimes, in similar cases, into *toe,* as "I did n' hardly know wut *toe* du!"[4]

The peculiarities and variations of Yankee speech are a matter not only of custom but also of linguistic geography, which is in turn patterned after population history.[5] So Vermont is linguistically as well as historically and geographically split in two by the Green Mountains, its two major speech divisions corresponding to the two major speech areas of New England—roughly, a westward-expanding coastal region and a northward-pushing

---

[1] *The Biglow Papers, Second Series, The Poetical Works of James Russell Lowell* (Boston, 1885), p. 286.

[2] It is said that one of Calvin Coolidge's remarkable achievements was the pronunciation of "cow" in four syllables.—Charles Edward Crane, *Let Me Show You Vermont* (New York, 1937), p. 30.

. . . the Southern English and Eastern American habit of adding superfluous [r], as in *the idear of it,* is frequently misunderstood. This is subject to the same law,—the superfluous [r] is added only when a vowel quickly follows. The Bostonian or Englishman is apt to say *Americar and France,* though he says *France and America* as Westerners do. I recently heard from a native of Boston, "No, this is not the piazza; the piazzar is here."—John S. Kenyon, "Some Notes on American R," *American Speech,* Vol. 1 (March, 1926), No. 6, p. 333.

[3] Lowell, *op. cit.,* p. 221.

[4] *Ibid.,* p. 227.

[5] Cf. Hans Kurath and others, *Linguistic Atlas of New England* and *Handbook of the Linguistic Geography of New England* (Providence, 1939).

trans-Connecticut River hill region. And since the original colonists brought with them the speech habits of their mother provinces (chiefly in the South of England), many typical Yankeeisms may be traced to British sources, such as *ben* (been), *eend* (end), and *yender* (yonder).[1] The following Cornish survivals have been noted on Cape Cod:

> We instance *housen,* for house, quite common among a few of the old people less than fifty years ago; *banger* for very large; *million* for melon; *sheer* for share, as half a sheer; *sight* for a good many, as a sight of 'em; *bagnet* for bayonet; *puss, nuss,* and *wuss,* for purse, nurse, and worse; *chaney* for china; *chimbley* for chimney, and many kindred expressions, some of which still linger, all of which are in use in some parts of Cornwall.[2]

2. Folk Speech and Speech Folklore

The linguistic geography of New England involves not only regionalism of speech but also the curious rivalry between the speech of Boston and that of the hinterland—essentially a conflict between Boston as a state of mind and the Yankee as a type of character. On the one hand, in attempting to set itself up as a national standard, Boston has fought the provinciality of the back country; and, on the other, the back country has clung to many of its vernacular and provincial speech forms as a badge of defiance against the artificial and polite standards of Boston.[3]

The struggle between Biglowese and Bostonese was thus a struggle between idiom and diction, between a living language and a dead language, between folk speech and "talking like a book" (whether schoolmarm English, journalese, or Websterian rhetoric). In spite of its limitations as a literary language, folk speech, as Lowell recognized, contains within itself the power of reviving and invigorating language. Just as dialect links the past with the present of language, so folk speech relates language to the experience of ordinary men—folk words, like proverbs and proverbial phrases, being symbols or signs that bind man to man and that evoke the very "influences of place and kinship and common emotion" that gave them birth.

Not only does folk speech take on something of the time-hallowed, ritualistic quality of the traditional mindskills and handskills of the folk, but local customs, characters, and events are enshrined in many local words and bywords, names and nicknames. The origin of these terms is transmitted in anecdotes and stories that are likewise part of the folklore of speech, as folk speech is part of folklore.

Perhaps the most fertile source of speech folklore is the process of playing upon words, one form of which is folk etymology (previously illustrated in place-names). This consists in the "changing of a strange or more or less learned term into a familiar or partly familiar one, often by substituting,

---

[1] Lowell, *op. cit.,* pp. 214–218 *passim.*

[2] Shebnah Rich, *Truro—Cape Cod* (Boston, 1884), pp. 128–129.

[3] Cf. George Philip Krapp, *The English Language in America* (New York, 1925), Vol. I, pp. 19–45. On page 44, he writers: "Boston is the only city in America in which *boots* is a common equivalent for *shoes, calico* for *unbleached muslin,* and *shop* a common name for *store.*"

adding, or omitting a sound or two."[1] Sometimes the change is only a change in spelling. Thus *jonny-cake* (from journey-cake) is commonly spelt *Johnny-cake*—a spelling which arouses the violent denunication of "Shepherd Tom" Hazard, who attempts to rationalize *jonny* by deriving it from "Brother Jonathan" Trumbull. Other examples of Yankee folk etymology are *kill-er-cure* (killcow), and *intervale* (interval).

Around words with disputed etymologies and fluctuating favorable and unfavorable connotations (like the word *Yankee*) or with changed applications (like *mooncussin'* in its original London slang use and in its various Cape Cod uses) has grown up another species of speech folklore. This consists of the myths, legends, and traditions surrounding words with a folk history if not a folk origin.

B. A. B.

PROVINCIAL SPEECH

Vermont Dialect Areas

VERMONT . . . is divided linguistically as well as historically and geographically into two major sections by the Green Mountains. The western section, which derives its population largely from western Connecticut and has always had fairly intimate contacts with New York State, contrasts in several respects with the eastern, whose settlement is much more diverse, comprising elements from the lower Connecticut valley, eastern and central Massachusetts, and New Hampshire, as well as colonies of Scotch and Scotch-Irish. For instance, the *r* in words like *work, first, father, hammer, bar, beard,* which is pronounced by speakers in western Connecticut and in the entire northern United States west of New England, but is silent in the greater part of eastern New England, is correspondingly present in the speech of western Vermont, but absent from that of eastern Vermont (except for the Scotch and Scotch-Irish sections and a few other communities). The vowel in *calf, glass, pasture, afternoon, bath* is universally pronounced with a flat *a* in western Vermont, while eastern Vermont has many cases of the broad *a*. The so-called "New England short o" in words like *home, stone, coat, road, toad, whole* (pronounced almost like *hum, stun,* etc.) is rather rare in western Vermont, but very common in eastern Vermont; the second syllable of *towel* is pronounced in western Vermont with a short, obscure second vowel or with no vowel at all, but in eastern Vermont has *ill* with a clear vowel.

As for vocabulary, the two sections again show interesting differences. The seesaw is called *seesaw* in all parts of the state, but the word *teeter-totter* (imported from southwestern Connecticut) occurs twice and the

[1] Harold Wentworth, *American Dialect Dictionary* (New York, 1944), p. 225.

From *Let Me Show You Vermont,* by Charles Edward Crane, pp. 34–35.

word *tinter* (from central Connecticut) occurs once in western Vermont, while *tilt* (a Cape Cod word) occurs once in eastern Vermont. The earthworm is called *angleworm,* but several cases of angledog (a central Connecticut word) occur in western Vermont, and several cases of *mud-worm* (a northeastern Massachusetts word) in eastern Vermont. Sour milk is called *lobbered* or *loppered* milk throughout Vermont, but in eastern Vermont the term *bonnyclabber* (originally an Irish word, but now found in many parts of eastern New England) is equally common. The horizontal rain-gutter along the edge of the roof is usually called *eaves trough* in western Vermont, but *eaves spout* in eastern Vermont. The funnel used when pouring liquids into a narrow-necked bottle is called either *funnel* or *tunnel* in western Vermont, but nearly always *tunnel* in eastern Vermont. When a boy slides downhill lying flat on his sled, western Vermonters say he is sliding downhill *belly-bunt* or *belly-bunk,* while eastern Vermonters say he is sliding *belly-bump.* It is clear that in many respects the eastern part of the state is more old-fashioned or more conservative than the western part, but it is interesting to observe that natives of each side of the Green Mountains profess to be greatly amused by the "flatness" of the dialect spoken by the natives on the other side.

The Yankee Twang

The Nasal Tone [1]

The nasal tone in New England, it is said, was caused by the severe climate and the prevalent catarrh; but those were not the sole causes. Catarrh debases speech, both in quality of tone and in distinctness of articulation; but the disease is more prevalent now than formerly, while the general speech is probably less nasal. Australians are said to have nasal voices, and they are not afflicted with catarrh. The New England drawl and the nasal tone were probably derived originally from the meeting-house and the prayer-meetings; both defects became fixed by habit, and, of course, have been greatly heightened by climatic conditions.

The virtue constantly insisted upon in the old times by parents and religious teachers was humility, self-abnegation. In repeating passages of Scripture, or of the Catechism, the tone was subdued. The religious spirit was manifested in awe and reverence, seldom in cheerfulness, and never in exaltation—except in such exaltation as was accompanied with moistened eyes and "tears in the voice." It was "a dying world" in which our fathers lived; the expression of their ideas and feelings would not require the expansive lungs, nor heave the deep chest, of a vigorous and well-developed

---

[1] From *Quabbin, The Story of a Small Town, with Outlooks Upon Puritan Life,* by Francis H. Underwood, pp. 71–73. Copyright, 1892, by Lee and Shepard. Boston. 1893.

man. The *noise,* no less than the manner, of a burly fox-hunter and athlete, would be abhorrent to one whose soul was melted in penitence, and who in his daily devotions *intoned* in dragging minor intervals the prayers that he dared not address to the Dread Majesty of Heaven with steady eyes and manly voice. There was a good deacon in Quabbin whose words, when he prayed, were joined, as by a singer's *portamento,* with *ah* and *er,* and with indescribable sounds, like the final hum of a nasal *m* and *n.* The words were hyphenated, and each sentence was a close-linked, long-drawn chain. Let such usages of speech go on for generations, and the infection will pervade the community. The child will be soothed by a nasal lullaby, and will drawl from the time he leaves his cradle. He will drawl at his lessons, and make catarrhal yells in the playground. As a lover he will drawl to his mistress, and repeat love's litany through the nose. When his duet with her is finished, and his snuffy voice extinct, he will be drawn (slowly) to his grave, to drawl no more.

It appears to be certain that the nasal and drawling tone is in a large measure the result of two and a half centuries of Puritan training; just as the peculiarities of language, including local and obsolete terms, half-articulated contractions, and clipping of words, are the result of the fusion of many illiterate British dialects. The bucolic speech is dying out, for school-teachers are uprooting it, as farmers do thistles, but the tone hangs on, like the scent of musk in Hosea Biglow's "draw."

AN ODD MIXTURE [2]

The American Reader lay open on the teacher's desk. "Hiram, read on page 11, and read good with Expression."

"Little Torm walked along the raw'd through the ha'dwood trees. Yender came marster preacher a'horseback. The poine trees was hidin' b'ar in Torm's young mind and he so laded daown he could not run away. He was not motch afeared of b'ar but he was afeared of Preacher Weatherby."

"Say *much,* not *motch.* Dan'l, you read the next." Tom sat down and Daniel began: "Last Sabbath a week Torm had larfed out loud in Meetin' when a black crow come in the window and the tythin' man had wropped him on the head with his stick. He cal'lated as how the preacher would be worser to meet nor a b'ar nor even a Injin, for larfin' was no manners for chorch. But bein' as how Torm was afoot he must go on and meet the preacher. 'If he don't be layin' on with the switch I'll git me this solather home to Paw come candlelight. Mebbe if I slip behind this here big poplar he will not be a'seein' of me.' But a pa'tridge flew up in Torm's face and he yowled out good and the Preacher seen him. Moral: Good little boys do not larf out in Meetin' and so love to meet their good Preachers."

"You got the sense oncommon good, Dan'l, but you fetched in some of

[2] From *New Hampshire Borns a Town,* by Marion Nicholl Rawson, pp. 264–265. Copyright, 1942, by E. P. Dutton & Co., Inc. New York.

your own words. Say *church,* not *chorch,* and go put that houn'dawg out in the raw'd. He's got fleas."

When the next class came to recite they ranged themselves along the back wall, for now *The North American Spelling Book* was open on the desk. Said Teacher: "Caow," and the first child spelled C O W. Teacher said: "Caounty," and the next child spelled: C O U N T Y. The Teacher said: "Collar, what you wear round your neck, not the person who comes to see you in the evening." There was no chance to spell phonetically here. An odd mixture of flat *ow* slipped in where no *ow's* should be, and *A's* were broadened and darkened where they stood alone, and lightened where they shouldered with an *R.* Yankee twang mated kindly with a most extreme Harvard accent, a combination which would in days ahead lose somewhat of the former, and, oddly enough among the most backroad folks, retain the latter.

Ancient Pronunciation

IN A certain class, the ancient pronunciation of many English words was maintained, doubtless brought by the ancestors of New England families from "home," and transmitted to their descendants; such as *airth* for earth, *fairm* for firm, *sartain* for certain, *pint* for point, en*vy* for envy, *ax* with the broad *â* for ask, *housen* for houses, *his'n* and *her'n* for his and hers, *rare* for rear; as, for instance, the horse *rares* up; and sounding the *l* in would. Common enough names, too, were clipped or contracted in English fashion. Thus, the names of Norwood and Harwood became Norrod in sound and Harrod in spelling; and the name of Currier, whether with any reference or not to the French *Cuir,* for leather, was not long since uniformly pronounced *Kiah,* with the long *ī;* Thurlow was strangely transformed into *Thurrill;* and Pierpont, often formerly spelled Pierpoint, with entire neglect of its derivation, was pronounced *Pearpint,* by old-fashioned people, the first syllable approximating to the original formation of *pierre.*

Kentish Provincialisms in New England

. . . WE RECOGNIZE our old Yankee friends, slick, for sleek or smooth; swath, swarth, a row of grass left on the ground by the mower; grub, for

From *Old New England Traits,* edited by George Lunt, pp. 144–145. Entered, according to Act of Congress, in the year 1873, by George Lunt, in the Office of the Librarian of Congress, at Washington. New York: Hurd and Houghton. Cambridge: The Riverside Press.

From *The Obligations of New England to the County of Kent,* A Paper Read before the American Antiquarian Society as a Part of the Report of the Council, April 29, 1885, by George F. Hoar, pp. 26–27. Worcester, Massachusetts: Press of Charles Hamilton. 1885.

food; bail, the handle of a pail; agen, for against; argufy, for argue; along used as in the phrase, all along of you; bar-way, the passage into a field where the bars are removed; bat, a large stick; biddy, a chicken; bay, the space between two beams; by-gorries and by-gollies, a sort of oath; botch, to do any thing badly; bodily, for entire; bolt, to swallow whole, and fast; bolt-upright; booby-hatch, a clumsy carriage; boosy, drunk; brand-new; buck, the body of a cart or wagon; cess, a tax, cess-pool; cheeses, the seed of the mullen; moonshine, for illicit spirits. . . .

Nantucket Pronunciation of the Points of the Compass

WE HAVE our own names for the points of the compass. Many writers persist in making the sailorman say "nor'east" and "sou'east." None such ever used the words. He does say "nor'west" and "sou'west," but north is "no'the," with a long "o" and a soft "th." Northeast is "no'theast," pronounced the same way (the "no'the" like the verb "loathe"). South is pronounced with the same soft "th" (like "mouth" when used as a verb).

When either north or south is used as an adjective before the noun, however, each takes its ordinary dictionary pronunciation, as a "north wind," or the "south shore." It is only when used without the noun that the long "o" sound in "no'the" and the soft "th" in both words are heard. Thus we say the wind is "out southe," or "about no'the"—never a "no'the wind" or the "southe shore." It is a curious distinction, for which there seems to be no reason except custom itself. Then we have "no-no'theast," and "sou'-southeast," but always "nor'nor'west" and "sou'sou'west." Writers who wish to apply the local color correctly are urged to study these forms carefully, and not slip up, as most of them do, on such simple matters. "Southe" is sometimes used as a verb, when speaking of the moon, as "when the moon southes"; and the word "easting" is sometimes heard.

Contributions to the New England Vocabulary and Idiom

FROM LOWELL'S LEXICON [1]

I SUBJOIN a few phrases not in Mr. Bartlett's book which I have heard. *Baldheaded:* "to go it bald-headed"; in great haste, as where one rushes

---

From *The Nantucket Scrap Basket,* Second Edition, Revised, Expanded, and Rearranged by William F. Macy, pp. 145–146. Copyright, 1916, by William F. Macy and Roland B. Hussey; 1930, by William F. Macy. Boston and New York: Houghton Mifflin Co. 1930.

---

[1] From Introduction to *The Biglow Papers,* Second Series, in *The Poetical Works of James Russell Lowell,* pp. 223–224. Copyright, 1848, 1857, 1866, 1868, 1869, 1876, and 1885, by James Russell Lowell. Boston and New York: Houghton Mifflin Co.

out without his hat. *Bogue:* "I don't git much done 'thout I *bogue* right in along 'th my men." *Carry:* a *portage*. *Cat-nap:* a short doze. *Cat-stick:* a small stick. *Chowder-head:* a muddle-brain. *Cling-john:* a soft cake of rye. *Cocoa-nut:* the head. *Cohees:* applied to the people of certain settlements in Western Pennsylvania, from their use of the archaic form *Quo' he. Dunnow'z I know:* the nearest your true Yankee ever comes to acknowledging ignorance. *Essence-pedlar:* a skunk. *First-rate and a half. Fish-flakes,* for drying fish: O. E.: *fleck (cratis). Gander-party:* a social gathering of men only. *Gawnicus:* a dolt. *Hawkins's whetstone:* rum; in derision of one Hawkins, a well-known temperance-lecturer. *Hyper:* to bustle: "I mus' *hyper* about an' git tea." *Keeler-tub:* one in which dishes are washed. ("And Greasy Joan doth *keel* the pot.") *Lap-tea:* where the guests are too many to sit at table. *Last of pea-time:* to be hard-up. *Lōse-laid (loose-laid):* a weaver's term, and probably English; weak-willed. *Malahak:* to cut up hastily or awkwardly. *Moonglade:* a beautiful word: for the track of moonlight on the water. *Off-ox:* an unmanageable, cross-grained fellow. *Old Driver, Old Splitfoot:* the Devil. *Onhitch:* to pull trigger (cf. Spanish *disparar*). *Popular:* conceited. *Rote:* sound of surf before a storm. *Rot-gut:* cheap whiskey; the word occurs in Heywood's "English Traveller" and Addison's "Drummer," for a poor kind of drink. *Seem:* it is habitual with the New-Englander to put this verb to strange uses, as, "I can't *seem* to be suited," "I could n't *seem* to know him." *Sidehill,* for *hillside. State-house:* this seems an Americanism, whether invented or derived from the Dutch *Stadhuys,* I know not. *Strike* and *string:* from the game of ninepins; to make a *strike* is to knock down all the pins with one ball, hence it has come to mean fortunate, successful. *Swampers:* men who break out roads for lumberers. *Tormented:* euphemism for damned, as, "not a tormented cent." *Virginia fence, to make a:* to walk like a drunken man.

Chiefly from Portsmouth [2]

caught: milk is "caught" when it is slightly burned.

claw out: make excuses, get out of an embarrassment, and the like. [Portsmouth, N. H.] Elsewhere (in New England) "claw off" is said.

fresh: in the phrase "a fresh cook," that is, one who uses little salt. [Portsmouth, N. H.]

heavy-handed (or *heavy*)*:* said of a cook. "She's heavy-handed with salt"—uses much salt. [Portsmouth, N. H.]

light and shut: of the weather. "It lights and shuts," that is, the sun peeps out at intervals. The common New England maxim is "Open and shet's a sign of wet." [Portsmouth, N. H.]

---

[2] From "Contributions to the New England Vocabulary," by Frederic D. Allen, in *Dialect Notes,* Vol. I (Part I, 1890), pp. 18–20. Boston: American Dialect Society.

on the mending hand: convalescent. A common New England phrase.

out: of the wind. Along the seaboard, the wind "is out" or "has got out" when it blows from the sea. The expression is known in Portsmouth, Salem, and Plymouth. I do not think it is common in Boston.

primlico: in the phrase "in primlico order," of furniture, etc. [Portsmouth, N. H.] The opposite of this is:

ride-out: "The chairs are riding out." "The room looks like ride-out." [Portsmouth, N. H.] *

rub the time close: allow little time. "Aren't you rubbing the time too close?" [Portsmouth, N. H.]

rubbers: misfortune, ill-luck. The phrase is, "to meet with the rubbers." [Portsmouth, N. H.]

scooch: crouch. "To scooch down in the corner." In New York City *scouch* . . . is said to be used.

scoocher: to "take a scoocher" is to slide down a snowslope in a squatting position. [Portsmouth, N. H.]

spandy: clean, spick-span, of linen. "Spandy" alone is used; elsewhere "spandy-clean," or "spandy-dandy."

sprawl: life, animation, vigor. "He has no sprawl." Portsmouth and Lowell.

stand in hand: behoove, beseem. "It stands you in hand to be careful." Widely used.

thatchy: said of milk. The milk tastes "thatchy" because the cows eat "thatch." A long, coarse grass, growing in the salt marshes, is known as "thatch" on the New Hampshire and Massachusetts seacoast. If it was ever used for roofing, it is no longer so used. The "thatch" which the New Hampshire cows eat seems to be different from this. It is described as a sort of weed, growing in low places. [Portsmouth, N. H.]

trappatch (trap-hatch): trap-door; rent in clothes. "You've torn a trappatch in your dress." [Portsmouth, N. H.]

From Maine and New Hampshire [3]

Able to set up an' eat a few porriges, adj. phr. Convalescent. Or, in good health. Usually the latter. A common answer to any inquiry regarding a person's health.

accommodatin' as a hog on ice, adj. phr. Extremely disagreeable or unobliging.

---

* This use is explained by the saying common fifty years ago on Cape Cod: "The room looks as if it was ready to ride out; every chair saddled and bridled"; used of a room in great disorder.—George Lyman Kittredge, *ibid.*, p. 79.

---

[3] From "Rural Locutions of Maine and Northern New Hampshire," by George Allen England, in *Dialect Notes,* Vol. IV (Part II, 1914), pp. 67–83. Publication of The American Dialect Society. New Haven, Connecticut: Published by the Society.

bag yer head, v. phr. Retire; pull in one's horns; be more modest. "I cal'late he better *bag his head!*"

bean-water, up on one's, adv. phr. Feeling very lively, strong, frisky. "Gosh! I'm right *up on* my *bean-water* this mornin'!"

big fer y'r boots, gittin' too, v. phr. Getting uppish, self-assertive.

black as zip, or *sip,* adj. phr. Extremely black.

bluer 'n a whetstone, adj. phr. Extremely dejected.

boil-thickened, adj. Referring to a kind of gravy, thickened, while boiling, by flour stirred in.

boozefuddle, n. Liquor.

buffle-brained, adj. Stupid.

bug-bite an' moonshine, interj. Expressive of incredulity or disgust.

bust yer haslet [*harslet*] * *out,* v. phr. A violent threat involving complete evisceration.

carry guts to a bear, he ain't got sense enough to, v. phr. Equivalent of "He doesn't know enough to come in when it rains."

cheeky as a man on the town, adj. phr. Overbearing, "nervy."

choppin'-block, n. In the phrase, "Bate ye two fingers on the *choppin'-block,* an' resk it." A common form of laying a wager.

dead clear to y'r navel, adj. phr. Lifeless.

devil an' Tom Walker. Same as desprit. "He wukked like the *Devil an' Tom Walker.*"

dingclicker, n. An unusually fine or pleasing person or thing. . . .

dingmaul, n. Mythical animal in lumber-camp.

dish, in yer own, prep. phr. Happening to your own self. "How'd ye like t' hev that *in yer own dish?*"

doctor ordered, what the. Something very pleasing, useful, or necessary. "She thought Ezry was jest *what the Doctor ordered.*"

dull, v. i. To make a mistake, miscalculation, or stupid blunder. "When she married that 'ar Bud Hayes, she shore *dulled.*"

dust yer back, v. phr. Wrestle; throw a man. "Fer two cents I'll *dust yer back!*"

fallin' out, him an' wuk has had a. Said of a lazy, shiftless man.

fiddlers in Hell, thick as, adj. phr. Very plentiful.

flamigigs, n. pl. Airs and graces; affectations.

go bag yer head! Angry, scornful, or sarcastic advice.

God's amint, any, or *Any God's immense,* n. phr. A large quantity. "They're *any God's amint* [amount?] o' woodchucks in them woods!"

goolthrite, n. Any small, wizened, puckered object. "She was all puckered up to a *goolthrite,* with the cold."

gormin', adj. Clumsy, stupid.

harker, n. A fine, strong person or thing.

haulin' a hog out'n a scaldin' tub, like, adv. phr. Comparison to denote difficulty.

---

* Viscera.

heaven, as long as John Brown stayed in, adv. phr. No time at all.

hell-bent an' crooked, adv. phr. In a swift, disorderly, excited manner. "He lit out fer hum, *hell-bent an' crooked.*"

Herrin'-choker, n. A Prince Edward's Islander, or native of any of the Provinces "down east."

higher'n his head, don't look no, etc., *fer my Saviour,* v. phr. He fills all the world, for me; satisfies every aspiration and longing.

hook an' bendum, a little, n. phr. Any small, gripping tool.

hotter'n a skunk, hotter'n love in hayin'-time, adj. phr. Extremely intoxicated.

hyker, hyper, [*hiker, hiper*], v. i. To go quickly, to run. "*Hyper out-a thar, now!*" "He more than *hikered!*"

jeeroosely, adj. Mighty, big, enormous.

jill-poke, n. A log stuck in the mud or along the banks of a lake or stream. [*Jell-poke.*]

jorum, n. Jug of liquor.

keezer's ghost! Great keezer's ghost! Ejaculations.

kicked to death by cripples, to be, v. phr. An expression of supreme contempt. "Huh! You'd oughta *be kicked to death by cripples,* you varmint!"

kill-er-cure,[1] *no gret,* n. phr. No great importance. "It hain't *no gret kill-er-cure* ef he comes or don't."

lap salt, know enough to, v. phr. To have common sense. "He don't *know enough to lap salt.*" He is thoroughly stupid.

livin' laws! by the. Form of affirmation.

lollygags, n. pl. Airs, affectations, love-making. "Him an' her was *lollygaggin'* the hull 'tarnal time."

long arms, make, v. phr. To help one's self, at table. "*Make long arms,* everybody!"

longer'n [*taller'n*] *the moral law,* adj. phr. Very long [tall].

lucivee, n. The loup-cervier, or "Injun devil," apparently a half-mythical "specie" of wild-cat.

mad as hops, also *madder'n snakes in hayin',* adj. phr. Very angry.

make a touse, v. phr. To make a row, or fight; "take on."

make brags, v. phr. To brag, boast. "You've allus *made yer brags* you'd go."

make one's haslet curl, v. phr. To surprise or injure one.

mill tail o' thunder, like the, adv. phr. See "Hell-bent an' crooked."

mingie, n. A gnat. Corruption of midge [?].

'mongst the missin', come up, v. phr. To die; to be lost. "Some day he'll come up *'mongst the missin'.*"

mooner, n. Mythical creature in logging-woods.

naked bed, in one's, prep. phr. Down sick.

nimshy, n. A human being, creature, girl, young girl. "She was a smart young *nimshy.*" Rather a laudatory sense.

---

[1] See "Killcow" below.

no bigger'n a pint o' cider; a goolthrite, adj. phr. Very small.

oh-be-joyful. Also, *oh-be-rich-an'-happy.* Hard liquor. "They come home plumb full of," etc.

P.I., abbrev. A Prince Edward's Islander.

pale's dishwater, adj. phr. Very pale.

peg out, v. phr. To get ill; die. "He's all *pegged out.*" "He'll *peg out* 'fore snow flies." Also very tired; same as "beat."

pell-mell fer a cat-race! Also, *pell-mell fer Kitt'ry.* Very fast.

pile out, v. phr. To get up and go to work. "Hank's quite a feller to *pile out.*"

poor's pooduc, also, *poor's poverty in a gale o' wind,* or *poorer'n skimmed whey,* adj. phr. Extremely poor.

prayer-handles, n. pl. Knees.

pumple-footed, adj. Club-footed.

rackergaited, adj. Loose-jointed.

red wagon, hot's a, adj. phr. Very drunk.

salter'n the briny ocean, adj. phr. Very salt.

sand in a rat-hole, don't know enough to pound, v. phr. Very stupid.

settled minister, fatter'n a, adj. phr. Very fat; in good condition.

shirt on a beanpole, n. phr. A bad fit. "It looks like, etc."

shoe taps, up on yer, prep. phr. Feeling fit and fine.

sick abed in the wood-box, adv. phr. In good health. A common answer to any inquiry after one's condition.

side-hill ranger, n. phr. Mythical animal in lumber-woods.

sight by suthin' to see ef he's movin', v. phr. Said of a lazy, indolent person.

slacker'n dishwater, adj. phr. Untidy, dirty, slovenly.

slick's a ram-cat, or *greased pig,* or *school-marm's leg,* adj. phr. Very pleasing, successful, pretty, etc.

slower'n a jill-poke, or *slower'n stock-still,* adj. phr. Extremely slow.

spin a thread, can't, v. phr. Powerless to act. "He *can't spin a thread,* nohow!"

spoon victuals, n. phr. Invalid diet.

starved fit to eat the Lord's supper, or *the Lamb o' God,* adj. phr. Very hungry.

still ez mouse wuk, adj. phr. Extremely quiet.

taller'n a stackpole, adj. phr. Very tall.

thin's vanity, adj. phr. Very thin, said of persons, fabrics, etc.

thinner'n a hayrake, adj. phr. Same as "thin's vanity."

throw up Jonah, also, *throw up yer shoe-taps,* v. i. To be extremely nauseated.

tight's ye can jump fer luck, adv. phr. As fast or hard as you can go, work.

tip-toe Nancy, n. phr. Affected girl, putting on airs.

tunket, n. Hell. "Madder'n *tunket.*"

twitch, v. i. To drag timber from the forest into a road, clearing or "yard."

warm it to anybody or *anything,* v. phr. To strike or work hard. "Warm it to him, Bill!"

wee-waw, adj. Shaky, loose, rickety. "The ole waggin was *wee-wawin'* all over the road."

white hen's chickens, n. phr. Extremely pleasant or desirable persons. "Sue thought Hy was one o' the *white hen's chickens.*"

witherlick, n. Mythical animal, in lumber-camps.

withy, adj. Wiry, tough, strong. "A withy feller."

wroppin' round yer finger, n. phr. Anything of slight value. "Tain't wuth a wroppin' round my finger."

y'r Uncle Dud, n. phr. The narrator. "Y'r *Uncle Dud* [contraction of *Dudley*] seen it, himself!"

STORIES IN WORDS

The Baldwin Apple

SURVEYING one day for the Middlesex Canal near "Butters Row" in Wilmington, Colonel Baldwin was attracted by woodpeckers drilling circles about the trunk of a tree, red with apples. He set a dish of the delectable fruit before his guests at dinner. "What is the name, Colonel?" "It is an unknown species hereabouts," answered their host. "Then a toast to the Baldwin apple!"

The Bofat

ONE of the most unique of these [names] is "the Bofat," the name of a section of the township. Constable Benjamin Bryant had been sent over to this section to collect certain unpaid taxes. Being asked on his return how the settlers in that region were prospering, he replied that they were "as poor as the devil's bofat." Hence the name. A bofat, I need hardly say, is a little corner closet where the family rum was generally kept. The word is evidently a corruption of buffet, to which our ancestors did not give the

From *Old Paths and Legends of New England,* Saunterings Over Historic Roads with Glimpses of Picturesque Fields and Old Homesteads in Massachusetts, Rhode Island, and New Hampshire, by Katharine M. Abbott, pp. 93–94. Copyright, 1903, by Katharine M. Abbott. New York and London: G. P. Putnam's Sons. 1904.

From "In Western Massachusetts," by John W. Chadwick, in *Harper's New Monthly Magazine,* Vol. LXI (November, 1880), No. 366, p. 879. Entered according to Act of Congress in the year 1880, by Harper and Brothers, in the Office of the Librarian of Congress at Washington. New York.

French pronunciation. Indeed, this word buffet seems to tend easily to corruption, the king's "beef-eaters," the yeomen of the guard, being the king's buffetiers, the keepers of the king's buffet.

The Cape Cod Cat

THE Rev. Thomas Crosby came to New England with his father Simon in the ship Susan & Ellen in 1685. Jesse Crosby, a descendant, was born in 1732 and grew up with a family named Lewis in Centerville. He had eleven children, one of whom, Daniel, settled in Osterville. Andrew, a son, lived a short distance along the shore from the Hinckley shipyard in or near Kokachoise, and built small craft with his two sons, Worthington and Horace. As he grew older, Andrew became, with a number of others, interested in Spiritualism. The group spent much time together, and his wife Tirza became a "medium."

At that time most of the small boats used along the Cape were called sharpies, being about twenty feet long and sharp at both ends. Andrew, from his experience and as he claimed, with the help of "spirits," began working on a very different type. He was much scoffed at by other boatmen, who said no boat would sail with the mast up in the eye, with no keel, and that with only one sail it would have no speed. Before he could complete his plan Andrew died and the boys were left to carry on. When difficulties arose on which they needed advice, Tirza, their mother, would hold a "seance" and bring them from their father their mistakes and how to remedy them. In 1850 the "Little Eva," as the new craft was called, was finished, launched, and a curious crowd gathered for her trial trip. Many boats were also waiting to test her speed and found, as an old sea captain remarked, that "She would sail three inches to their one." Another man exclaimed: "She comes about as quick as a cat." That is the story of the origin and naming of the "Cape Cod Cat." Its design remains the same to this day and as a popular pleasure boat it is seen everywhere along our shores.

Cape Cod Turkey

THE origin of the name "Cape Cod turkey" is obscure. It has come to mean cooked fish; what kind doesn't matter unless you are literal. If you are, it means baked stuffed codfish well-larded with salt pork.

From *Barnstable: Three Centuries of a Cape Cod Town,* by Donald G. Trayser, with Articles by Phyllis Bearse, Sarah H. Boult, Louisa Cobb, Richard Cobb, Alfred Crocker, Chester A. Crocker, Ora Hinckley, Elizabeth C. Jenkins, Henry C. Kittredge, A. Lawrence Lowell, Nathaniel B. H. Parker, p. 433. Copyright, 1939, by Donald G. Trayser. Hyannis, Massachusetts: F. B. & F. P. Goss.

From *The Yankee Cook Book,* by Imogene Wolcott, p. 41. Copyright, 1939, by Coward-McCann, Inc. New York.

One explanation of the term centers about Thanksgiving. The traditional food for that day was, and still is, turkey. Turkey meant thankfulness to God for his bounty. However, without the fishing industry the colonists would have had very little to be thankful for. No doubt the term "Cape Cod turkey" was started by some wit, which shows that even in early times life was not all drab.

* * * * *

Then, too, the Irish in and around Boston used the term "Cape Cod turkey" to refer to their Friday meal of fish. Fish, and particularly salt fish, seemed to taste better if it bore the more aristocratic name "Cape Cod turkey."

"Cat" Words

I SHALL never forget . . . in Dublin, New Hampshire, driving through what our delightful Yankee charioteer and guide called "only a cat-road."

This was to me a new use of the word cat as a praenomen, though I knew, as did Dr. Holmes and Hosea Biglow, and every good New Englander, that "cat-sticks" were poor spindling sticks, either growing or in a load of cut wood. I heard a country parson say as he regarded ruefully a gift of a sled load of firewood, "The deacon's load is all cat-sticks." Of course a cat-stick was also the stick used in the game of ball called tip-cat. Myself when young did much practise another loved ball game, "one old cat," a local favorite, perhaps a local name. "Cat-ice," too, is a good old New England word and thing; it is the thin layer of brittle ice formed over puddles, from under which the water has afterward receded. . . .

Comfort Powders

FOR several successive summers a tall thin man with a long beard called at our house. He was the purveyor of what he called "Comfort Powders." These were tiny bits of white paper, folded like medicinal powders. Opened, each revealed a verse of Scripture of a distinctly comforting nature. I remember him, perhaps not so much because of his quieting doses as because of my grandmother's terrible anger when one day we so far forgot ourselves as to laugh at him and to call our taunts behind his attenuated back. . . .

From *Old Time Gardens,* Newly Set Forth, by Alice Morse Earle, pp. 452–453. Copyright, 1901, by The Macmillan Company. New York and London.

From *A Goodly Heritage,* by Mary Ellen Chase, pp. 82–83. Copyright, 1932, by Henry Holt and Company, Inc. New York.

A Dead Horse

A DEAD horse was work you got paid for before you finished it. Say you had a half a case done at the end of the week. Well, you could have the whole case put on the books as done, and you'd get your money for it. But then on the next Monday morning you'd have that empty case to do, and no pay for it. A dead horse sure looked dead on Monday morning.

The foreman would be the one responsible for getting the dead horses done, for he was the one that let the help give them in, often unbeknownst to the owner.

And sometimes a worker, especially a cutter, would skin out, quit his job, and the foreman would be left with a whopper of a dead horse to explain. And say if that dead horse was eight or ten cases, it would be considerable to explain.

If the foreman was the right kind of fellow, though, we always pitched in and done that dead horse for him. That was a help to us too for if we didn't do that, the boss would likely come along and say:

"There'll be no more dead horses in this shop from now on."

We'd do a lot to prevent that 'cause dead horses would be durn handy, when you wanted to buy something special some week and you was short of cash.

But among the cutters there come to be so durn many that skun out on their dead horses, that they come to be pretty hard to get. For cutters in the old days was like the old class of printers. Kind of hoboes. Here today and gone tomorrow. They had the kind of trade that made it easy for them to get a job quick, so they didn't have to stick to one place any longer than it suited them. That made kind of tramps of them.

If your reputation was reliable, though, you could always give in a dead horse. Many is the time I done that when I was short of change some week.

Drail

WHY it is a "drail," we know not. It is, and on Cape Cod it has always been, so far as I can learn. The troller from a boat uses one of those

---

From "The Lynn Shoe Worker," as told by John Healey to Jane K. Leary, in *Living Lore of New England*. Manuscripts of the Federal Writers' Project of the Works Progress Administration for the State of Massachusetts.

From *Cape Cod Yesterdays*, by Joseph C. Lincoln, pp. 188–189. Copyright, 1935, by Joseph C. Lincoln and Harold Brett. Boston: Little, Brown & Company.

Japanese feather baits—the lure with a metal head set with glass eyes and a feathered tail covering the hook—but the genuine heaver and hauler still sticks to his drail. It—the drail—is made of some heavy metal, is bright and shiny and has the hook rigidly set in its after end. I mention the "rigidly" because the hook attached to the feather bait usually swings loose from a ring. Pulled—or "hauled"—through the water, it looks like a rapidly swimming sand eel or "shiner" and the bluefish darts to snap at it. This is an error of judgment on his part.

In former days, the heaver and hauler often covered his drail with an eelskin. The dried skin was pulled over the metal with the tail flopping loosely about the hook. Some old-timers still cover their drails in this way. It is a good bait, especially for striped bass.

Ear-Timers

An ear-timer named "Buddy" Keen or Kerr had a fetish of some kind tacked above his bench. Whether it was a small statue, a doll, or a kind of billiken he had won some place, Mr. Potter wasn't sure. But Kerr was obsessed with the idea that the thing was his lucky piece. He thought it had some definite bearing on his work. Somebody stole it one day and never brought it back, and Kerr became a nervous wreck. He resigned his job a few weeks later and went elsewhere to work, though Mr. Potter says he is still working at his trade and has apparently forgotten the incident.

Ear-timing is a process which seems to be on the way out in clock manufacture. It has been abolished at Seth Thomas, though still a part of the clock-making routine at Ingraham's. Ear-timers must regulate a clock with the use of a metronome, depending, as the name implies, upon their sense of hearing to synchronize the movement with the metronome beat. There seems to be a prevalent impression among clockmakers that ear-timing is likely to develop eccentricities. Because of the tension under which ear-timers work day in and day out, many of them become hard drinkers, according to popular belief. This impression is the nearest approach to a superstition brought to light during the conversation with Mr. Richmond. It may have basis in fact, or it may be that its widespread acceptance has in some cases actually been an evil influence upon credulous ear-timers. Because of the difficulty of training men for this phase of clock-making ear-timing has been one of the highest paid jobs in the industry, with wages reported authentically of as high as one dollar per hour piece-work.

From "Connecticut Clockmakers," by Francis Donovan, in *Living Lore in New England*. Manuscripts of the Federal Writers' Project of the Works Progress Administration for the State of Connecticut.

Gallbuster

One morning when a head wind had us at full disadvantage, and common sailing vessels were passing us like steam boats, I ventured out of the gangway and said, "Mr. Hatch, how does she go along?" He promptly replied, "By the Prophets' nippers, Skipper, when you can see her wake out of the weather hawse-hole, I call it a gallbuster!"

Heave and Haul

Here are two good Cape Cod words for you. Brought ashore from the deep sea, of course. The fo'mast hands on the old "wind-jammers" heaved —or "hove"—the anchor or the lead and hauled the sheet or the bowline.

> Haul on the bowline,
> The *Polly* is a-rollin'.
> Haul on the bowline,
> The bowline HAUL.

So the old chantey goes. Surely it is not necessary to tell you that "bowline" is pronounced "bo-lin." I should not mention it if I had not heard a landlubber—and he was a college professor, at that—pronounce it "bow line," "bow," like the bough of a tree, and "line" like something to catch fish with. It may have been a bow line in the beginning, but it has been a bo-lin since Noah hove short on the Ark's cable—shortly after that, anyhow. If it were not "bo-lin" how could it rhyme with "rollin'?" I ask you.

But down on the Cape, we heave and haul on land, as well as on water. Our small boys "heave" a baseball or a stone. Our horses "haul" a buggy or truck-wagon, or did in the days when there were truck-wagons and buggies. A summer neighbor noticed that a neighbor of his—a retired mackerel seiner—was at work with hammer and saw on the roof of his dwelling. Naturally, being a neighbor, our friend stopped to ask questions. The old mackerelman explained.

"Goin' to put in one of them dormer windows," he said. "Cal'latin' to see if I can't heave a little sunshine into the front upstairs bedroom."

And when we asked a Cape acquaintance as to the professional ability of a dentist who had recently begun practice in the community, the answer was informative and characteristic.

From *Truro—Cape Cod, or Land Marks and Sea Marks,* by Shebnah Rich, p. 433. Second Edition, Revised and Corrected. Copyright, 1883, by D. Lothrop and Company. Boston. 1884.

From *Cape Cod Yesterdays,* by Joseph C. Lincoln, pp. 181–183. Copyright, 1935, by Joseph C. Lincoln and Harold Brett. Boston: Little, Brown & Company.

"They say he's first-rate at his job. Fixes your teeth up fine and don't charge all outdoors for it. But," by way of warning, "you understand he don't do no haulin'."

Meaning that the dentist did not extract teeth.

Yes, we heave and haul almost everything on Cape Cod, but when, early in August, we notice men walking along the edge of the surf at Monomoy Point or on the beach below the lighthouse, men who whirl their right hands in circles above their heads, we know that they are both heaving *and* hauling. We know that the bluefish have "struck on."

For, down our way, in August and September and early October, to "heave and haul" means to cast for bluefish from the beach with a hand line and it does not mean anything else.

Herb Tea

On the corner of Winchester Road (Mystic Street) the troops knocked roughly at the village shoemaker's, asking why the candles burned at this unseemly hour. The gudewife replied that she was making herb tea. The shoemaker's "herb tea" was a concoction afterwards absorbed by the red-coats in the form of solid material, sometimes known as "Yankee bullets," made from the household pewter.

Hubbub

Skull Head was the scene of aboriginal battles, and Nantasket Beach the play-ground of Indian tribes. Three centuries ago, where yonder children are now playing leap-frog, stood a pole hung with beaver skins and wampum; fantastic, swarthy figures are running and playing football to win these trophies; their wild shouts may be heard above the *sawkiss* (great panting) of the ocean. Chiefs who have seen eighty snows look on stoically while the young men strike on the beach a wooden bowl containing five flat pieces of bone, black on one side and white on the other; as the bones bound and fall, white or black, the game is decided; the players sit in a circle making a deafening noise,—*hub, hub,* "come, come," from which it was called hubbub. Their council fires were lighted on Sagamore Hill.

From *Old Paths and Legends of New England,* Saunterings Over Historic Roads with Glimpses of Picturesque Fields and Old Homesteads in Massachusetts, Rhode Island, and New Hampshire, by Katharine M. Abbott, p. 56. Copyright, 1903, by Katharine M. Abbott. New York and London: G. P. Putnam's Sons. 1904.

Ibid., p. 329.

Interval(e)

. . . The term *interval,* though originating with the colonists themselves, has almost ceased to be understood by writers in the United States, and even in New England itself. They are at one time perplexed as to its etymology, and at another as to its application.

One of them, translating Mr. Volney's work on the soil and climate of the United States, is careful to present the word *interval* under a peculiar form:—"The *inter-vales* and banks of rivers"; a refinement of which the intention appears to be, that of refreshing the reader's memory as to a supposed derivation of the word from *inter* and *vallis,* meaning a space between valleys. This etymology I have heard assigned by word of mouth, and it appears to be adopted in the passage cited, because, had the writer supposed the word to come from *inter* and *vallum,* he would certainly have left it *interval,* in the ordinary form. Meanwhile, a moment's reflection will suggest, that a space *between valleys* must necessarily be filled only with mountains.

Again: as to the signification of the term, we find it confounded with the term meadow:—"The lands west of the last mentioned range of mountains," says a native geographer, "boarding on Connecticut River, are interspersed with extensive *meadows* or *intervals,* rich and well watered." [1]

But, if the word *interval* were synonymous with *meadow,* it ought upon no occasion to be employed; and it is only because it is not synonymous that [it] is useful, and deserves to be retained. The elder colonists resorted to it on account of the peculiar disposition of a very great proportion of the surface, over all the country which they colonized.

The *interval,* intended in New England geography, is the *interval* or *space between a river and the mountains* which on both sides uniformly accompany its course, at a greater or less distance from the margin. Hence, *interval-lands* include meadow and uplands, and in general the whole of the narrow valley, through which, in these regions, the rivers flow. Where rivers flow through extensive plains; where, in short, the eye is not constantly tempted to measure the distance between the river and the adjacent mountains, there is no mention of *interval-lands.* Among the interval-lands are to be reckoned the *swales,* or rich hollows, lying behind the uplands, by which latter they are separated from the meadows. These hollows are on levels greatly raised above the meadows, and have not been visited by the floods for ages, but are composed of bog-earth, formed by the long growth and repeated decay of timber, together with their aptness for collecting and detaining water on their surface.

From *Travels Through the Northern Parts of the United States,* in the Years 1807 and 1808, by Edward Augustus Kendall, Esq., Vol. III, pp. 191–194. New York: Printed and published by I. Riley. 1809.

[1] American Universal Geography.—E. A. K.

Jonny-Cake

. . . To DESECRATE the name of Rhode Island's chiefest luxury with an "h" sticking up in the middle of it! This proves Old Cove's entire ignorance of the patriotic derivation of the Christian name Jonny as applied to the far-famed cake, made only in perfection in the South counties of Rhode Island, of soft-feeling, fine, flat meal, ground from pure white floury Rhode Island corn, in Rhode Island granite stone mills. Old Cove, if to the manor of Rhode Island and Providence Plantations born, should have known that the original spelling of the name of the favorite food of the gods was journey-cake, so called, because of the facility with which it could be prepared, to gratify the impatient appetites of those heathen deities, on their annual arrival at the delightful summer resorts or watering-places on the southern shores of the Atlantic, the chief of which were situated where the Narragansett Pier and Newport now stand. This name journey-cake was retained until the close of the War of Independence, about which time, in compliance with the prayers of memorials from the women of Connecticut and Rhode Island to the respective Legislatures of these commonwealths—the term journey, as applied to the favorite food of the gods and of the Yankee nation, was abrogated by sovereign authority, and that of jonny substituted in its place, in honor of Gov. Jonathan Trumbull, the honored and trusted friend of General Washington, who always addressed the sterling patriot with the affectionate pet name of *Brother Jonathan*. . . .

Kennebec Turkey

KENNEBEC turkey! To me and any Kennebec man those words are pure music. I know there is a Yankee joke in this name for herring. It is all of a piece with wind-pudding, which is a word for a dinner consisting of tightening the belt. But there is substance and truth behind the joke. For any Kennebec man would rather have a slab of that dark meat that grows in the sea than one off the best speckled and bearded bird that ever blushed and gobbled on a Vermont hill. And herring is a foundation stone of Maine life and character.

From *The Jonny-Cake Papers of "Shepherd Tom,"* Together with Reminiscences of Narragansett Schools of Former Days, by Thomas Robinson Hazard, with a Biographical Sketch and Notes by Rowland Gibson Hazard, pp. 31–32. Copyright, 1915, by Rowland G. Hazard. Boston: Printed for the Subscribers.

From *Kennebec,* Cradle of Americans, by Robert P. Tristram Coffin, p. 202. Copyright, 1937, by Farrar & Rinehart, Inc. New York and Toronto.

Killcow

In old-fashioned use on Cape Cod and in Cheshire County, N. H., in the phrases: "That's no great killcow," *i.e., that's of no great account, that's no matter;* and "He's no great killcow," *i.e., he doesn't amount to much* (of a person who thinks himself somebody). The word was common in the Elizabethan age. Thus,—"The killcow champion of the three brethren," Nashe, ed. Grosart, II, 184; "This vaine of kilcowe vanitie," Id., III, 37; "It is the kill-cow Dorilaus," Fletcher, Lovers' Progress, iii, 3, *ad fin.*; "the kill-cow Caratach," Fletcher, Bonduca, ii, 3 (where see Weber). In these places it seems to mean a bully, a madcap fighter with a touch of Drawcansir about him. Weber is no doubt right in referring its origin to Guy of Warwick's exploit with the Dun Cow. (Two or three further citations in Nares and in Halliwell. The latter gives "kill-cow: a matter of consequence; a terrible fellow" as a Northumberland word.)

The Minister's Rib Factory

. . . Mount Holyoke College, when it was Mount Holyoke Seminary, used to be called "The Minister's Rib Factory" because it turned out so many wives for ministers and missionaries.

Mooncussin'

> The Moon Curser is generally taken for any Link-Boy; but particularly he is one that waits at some Corner of Lincolns-Inn-Fields with a Link in his hand, who under the pretence of Lighting you over the Fields, being late and few stiring, shall Light you into a Pack of Rogues that wait for the comming of this Setter, and so they will all joyne in the Robbery.
>
> Richard Head's *Canting Academy*, 1673, p. 101.

At haggard sea-corners of old Cape Cod men held lanthorns high in the black nights of the Seventeenth and Eighteenth Centuries. They swung the discs in a wide arc as though directing pilotless ships over Nauset Sea. Many an hemp-and-salt shipmaster mistook these swaying signals for

---

From "Various Contributions," in *Dialect Notes*, Vol. I (Part I, 1890), p. 22. Boston: Published by the American Dialect Society.

From *The Yankee Cook Book*, by Imogene Wolcott, p. 202. Copyright, 1933, by Coward-McCann, Inc. New York.

From *The Narrow Land, Folk Chronicles of Old Cape Cod*, by Elizabeth Reynard, pp. 237–238. Copyright, 1934, by Elizabeth Reynard. Boston and New York: Houghton Mifflin Company.

mastlights of other craft, turned to follow them, and ran on hidden bars. Such misfortune only occurred when no moon whitened the dunes that loom along that water-line, when no decisive starlight sharpened the shadow between tall Clay Pounds to the northward and the foam-sprecklded edges of the sea. 'Mooncussers' was the name bestowed on these human harpies who fed on the spoils of such moonless disaster, who filched a lucrative plunder from the unchartable, shifting shoals of Race Point, Nauset, and Monomoy.

A few wise inhabitants put their hands into their pockets to contribute toward 'Government Beacons,' whereupon certain God-fearing puritans advanced sharp arguments against the 'policy of beaconing,' a device designed to 'injure the wrecking business.' Yet these same puritans risked their lives again and again to rescue sailors as well as cargoes and ribbed hulls and wreck-iron from fishing sloops, snows, pinks, bermudas boats, broad-winged Eastindia Men, deeply laden yawls and ketches that were 'Poundin' up' on the offshore bars. After initial salvage had been completed and flotsam had been gathered from spume-wet beaches, the goodmen buried drowned sailorboys while churchbells rang and prayer-books lay open and salt tears glazed the eyes.

In up-Cape towns such as Sandwich and Barnstable, whose harbours face Baywater, freemen expressed disgust at the 'dirty doings' down Nauset way, to which the wreckmasters of Monomoy and Nauset replied by mentioning 'green grape cankers itchin' the tongues' of envious 'up-Capers.'

With the growing trade of a young nation, so many ships perished along that 'White Graveyard of the Atlantic' that link-boys were not necessary to lure unwary wanderers into a Pack of Rogues. The term *mooncursing* gradually lost its older connotation. With no implication of false lights it was used, in the Nineteenth Century, to indicate all those who practised beachcombing or salvage. But in 1717 the old derisive, condemnatory aspect of the word still clung to it, though without the precise implication of 'luring lights.' So a hostile Cape took pleasure in bestowing the title 'King of the Mooncursers' on Captain Cyprian Southack, brave mariner, skilled map-maker, when he came at the behest of the Royal Governor to court 'fickell salvedge,' after word had reached Boston of the Black Bellamy's death.

Mud Time

One old lady wrote that the roads were the "terabilist" after the spring rains, and today The Town still has her annual spring "mud time"—but now only on the old dirt roads. It is not many years since the schools let

---

From *New Hampshire Borns a Town,* by Marion Nicholl Rawson, p. 96. Copyright, 1942, by E. P. Dutton & Co., Inc. New York.

out for three weeks in March because the "bottoms of the roads had fell out." The children were always jubilant at mud time, shrilling their yearly cry of "Mud time! Six weeks to bare feet."

Munching Drawer

. . . MRS. MAUD ELLIOT remembers the munching drawer in the cabin of her father's vessel, the Independent. Captain Willis L. Case kept in his munching drawer all sorts of good things, fruits, nuts, candy, and various sweets, to which he went when he felt like eating.

The Pilgrims

. . . IN THE history and the saga of the Pilgrims, both curiously tangled tales, surely nothing is more curious than this—that their very name, "the Pilgrims," is little more than a century old, having come into common usage since 1840. Heterogeneous in origin, split even by religious differences, the Pilgrims had no name for themselves as a group. For generations they were known to their descendants merely as the Forefathers, a name preserved in the only holiday officially dedicated to their memory, Forefathers' Day, tardily instituted by Massachusetts in 1895.

* * * * *

To the end of the Revolutionary War the plain people of Plymouth celebrated Forefathers' Day with fitting ceremony each year in Town Square, renamed Liberty Pole Square, but not again till 1793 when the Reverend Chandler Robbins preached a memorial sermon. It was in no way remarkable but for one fact—thumbing through the old church records, particularly those yellowed pages on which Nathaniel Morton had copied long passages from Bradford's now "lost" manuscript,[1] Robbins

---

From *Barnstable:* Three Centuries of a Cape Cod Town, with Articles by Phyllis Bearse, Sarah H. Boult, Louisa Cobb, Richard Cobb, Alfred Crocker, Chester A. Crocker, Ora Hinckley, Elizabeth C. Jenkins, Henry C. Kittredge, A. Lawrence Lowell, Nathaniel B. H. Parker, edited by Donald G. Trayser, p. 320. Hyannis, Massachusetts: F. B. & F. P. Goss. Copyright, 1939, by Donald G. Trayser.

From *Saints and Strangers,* by George F. Willison, pp. 2, 421. Copyright, 1945, by George F. Willison. New York: Reynal & Hitchcock.

[1] It was in 1630, as he himself tells us, that Governor Bradford sat down amid the distractions and burdens of office to begin what he called his "scribled Writings." These were necessarily "peeced up at times of leesure afterwards," for to the day of his death some thirty years later Bradford led a busy and usually bedevilled life at the center of affairs. By 1650, when he laid down his pen, he had piled up a manuscript of 270 folio pages, all patiently inscribed in his own neat hand. His chronicle, simply and modestly entitled *Of Plimoth Plantation,* related in graphic detail the story of the Pilgrims from 1606 to 1647, through the most critical and eventful period of their always eventful career.

* * * * *

came upon the phrase, "they knew they were pilgrimes,"[1] and happily so named them. But not until the 1840's did the phrase begin to make its way into print and become the generally accepted designation of the heterogeneous group long known merely as the First Comers.

But for two hundred years the world was little the wiser for anything that Bradford had written, for his history had a curious history of its own. As Bradford had not written for publication, his manuscript was handed down from father to son for several generations, with little or no appreciation of its unique worth. Some passages were copied into the church records by Nathaniel Morton, Bradford's nephew and secretary of the Old Colony, who also consulted it in compiling his rather dull and sketchy annals of the Forefathers, *New England's Memorial* (1669). Many years later Bradford's history passed into the hands of another early New England chronicler, the Reverend Thomas Prince, who published a few excerpts from it and then placed it on the shelves of the library he had fitted up for himself in the tower of the renowned Old South Church, Boston. Here the manuscript presumably remained until the American Revolution.

During the early years of that conflict the Old South was turned into a stable and a riding academy by the British, and after their evacuation of Boston an inventory of Prince's library revealed that Bradford's chronicle and other priceless old documents were missing. A search for them was made, and hopes of recovering them bounded up in 1793 when a manuscript volume of Bradford's letters suddenly came to light in a grocer's shop at Halifax, Nova Scotia, where its large folio pages were being used to wrap up pickles, soap, cheese, butter, and other small purchases. What little remained of it was rescued and published at Boston the next year, which stimulated more determined search for the other missing treasures. But when decade after decade passed without the discovery of a single clue, they were given up as irretrievably lost and written off as casualties of the Revolution.

But here, as often in the Pilgrim story, chance had yet to speak the last word. In 1855, while thumbing through a book borrowed from a friend, a dull ecclesiastical work published in England almost ten years before, a student of Massachusetts history suddenly came upon several quoted passages attributed to an anonymous manuscript and instantly recognized that they could have been written only by Bradford. This promising lead was quickly followed up, and the long-lost manuscript was soon traced to its dusty hiding place. It was found—of all places—in the library of Fulham Palace, beside the Thames on the outskirts of London, one of the episcopal seats and long the favored summer residence of the bishops of London. How this loot from the Old South came into their possession has never been explained, and delicacy has precluded any too pressing inquiry. In any case, his then Lordship graciously allowed a transcript of *Plimoth Plantation* to be made, and with its publication at Boston early the next year the mists that had so long enshrouded the Pilgrims, blurring their features both as a group and as individuals, began to lift for the first time.

The year 1856 marks, in a real sense, the beginning of Pilgrim history.—G. F. W. *ibid.*, pp. 3, 4–5.

---

[1] . . . "that goodly & pleasante citie which had been their resting place for near 12 years; but they knew they were pilgrimes, & looked not much on those things, but lift[ed] up their eyes to ye heavens, their dearest cuntrie, and quieted their spirits." —G. F. W. *ibid.*, p. 120.

P. I.'s and Frenchmen

. . . STRICTLY speaking, a P. I. is one who hails originally from Prince Edward's Island; but around here it has come to be used loosely to refer to any Canadian who isn't a Frenchman. A Canadian Frenchman is just a Frenchman. If you mean a man from France—and you very seldom do—you say a French Frenchman.

Pot Luck

FROM East Lee is said to have come the phrase "pot luck" as applied to a delectable New England boiled dinner. A town historian, the Reverend L. S. Rowland, speaks of it as . . . the most satisfying dish for the men who spent long hours in outside labor. It is interesting to note that corned beef and cabbage is not, as generally supposed, a dish brought from Ireland by early immigrants. They did not arrive here until about 1850 and "pot luck" was well-known in 1791, in the town of Lee which was settled by Cape Cod people mostly.

This homely dish is still a favorite in Lee. In 1938 the Corned Beef and Cabbage Club was organized in the town for the purpose of "sociability and the enjoyment of good food." The founder has moved away, but if you should lift the lid of the iron pot bubbling on many a range in Lee, you'd sniff the appetizing smell of "pot luck."

Pumpkin-Heads

NEW HAVEN is celebrated for having given the name of "pumpkin-heads" to all the New Englanders. It originated from the "Blue Laws," which enjoined every male to have his hair cut round by a cap. When caps were not to be had, they substituted the hard shell of a pumpkin, which being put on the head every Saturday, the hair is cut by the shell all round the head. Whatever religious virtue is supposed to be derived from the custom,

---

From *Happy the Land,* by Louise Dickinson Rich, p. 77. Copyright, 1946, by Louise Dickinson Rich. Philadelphia and New York: J. B. Lippincott Company.

From *The Berkshire Hills,* Compiled and Written by Members of the Federal Writers' Project of the Works Progress Administration for Massachusetts, pp. 146–147. Copyright, 1939, by The Berkshire Hills Conference, Inc. New York: Duell, Sloan and Pearce.

From *The Rev. Samuel Peters' LL.D., General History of Connecticut* . . . to which are added Additions to Appendix, Notes, and Extracts from Letters, verifying many important statements, by Samuel Jarvis McCormick, pp. 153–154. Copyright, 1877, by D. Appleton and Company. New York.

I know not; but there is much prudence in it: first, it prevents the hair from snarling; secondly, it saves the use of combs, bags, and ribbons; thirdly, the hair cannot incommode the eyes by falling over them; and fourthly, such persons as have lost their ears for heresy, and other wickedness, cannot conceal their misfortune and disgrace.

The Sacred Cod

It is said that fishermen originally believed the cod became "the sacred cod" because it was the fish that Christ used when He multiplied the fish and fed the multitude, and even to-day the marks of His thumbs and forefingers are plainly visible on the codfish. His Satanic majesty stood by and said he, too, could multiply fish and feed multitudes. Reaching for one of the fish it wriggled and slid through his red-hot fingers, burning two black stripes down its side and thus clearly differentiating the haddock with its stripes from the sacred cod. These markings, in actual practice, do distinguish one variety from the other.

Schooner

These were genuine New England vessels. It is stated in the Journal of Moses Prince, a brother of the annalist, under date of 1721, at which time he visited Gloucester, that the first vessel of the class called schooner was built at Gloucester about eight years before, by Andrew Robinson; and late in the same century one Cotton Tufts gives us the tradition with some particulars, which he learned on a visit to the same place. According to the latter, Robinson having constructed a vessel which he masted and rigged in a peculiar manner, on her going off the stocks a by-stander cried out, *"Oh, how she scoons!"* whereat Robinson replied, *"A schooner let her be!"* "From which time," says Tufts, "vessels thus masted and rigged have gone by the name of schooners; before which, vessels of this description were not known in Europe."[1] Yet I can hardly believe this, for a schooner has always seemed to me the typical vessel.

According to C. E. Potter of Manchester, New Hampshire, the very word schooner is of New England origin, being from the Indian *schoon* or *scoot,* meaning to rush, as Schoodic, from *scoot* and *auke,* a place where water rushes. N. B. Somebody of Gloucester was to read a paper on this matter before a genealogical society in Boston, March 3, 1859, according to the Boston Journal, q.v.

From *The Yankee Cook Book,* by Imogene Wolcott, p. 36. Copyright, 1939, by Coward-McCann, Inc. New York.

From *Cape Cod,* by Henry David Thoreau, pp. 239–240. Copyright, 1864, by Ticknor and Fields; 1893, by Houghton, Mifflin & Co. Boston and New York.

[1] See *Mass. Hist. Coll.* vol. ix, 1st series, and vol. i, 4th series.—H. D. T.

Towner

Mr. Richard Paine told the writer that he could remember when there were lookouts at the Pond Landing for whale, and a man was kept constantly on them. When a whale was discovered, the alarm was given by shouting from the lookout, *Towner!* which was quickly taken up, and repeated and repeated with might of lung. And that he had heard on calm days the shout at his father's house, quite two miles distant. I inquired what was the meaning of Towner; he could not tell, but afterwards, when reading Walter Folger's description of Nantucket I found it was an Indian word, and signifies that they have seen the whale twice. I have referred to a similar practice in Cornwall during the pilchard season.

Twitches

. . . A yarding crew consists of three men and a twitch horse. One of the men cuts down the trees and limbs them, one drives the twitch horse, dragging—or "twitching"—the entire trunk of the tree to a cleared space called a yard, where the third man saws it up with a buck saw and piles it.

* * * * *

. . . He was finally discovered about five hundred yards from the tar paper shack where the horses are taken to eat their noon-day meals; or as the man who found him said, "About two and a half good twitches." A good twitch is the distance a horse can drag a full-length pulp log without resting. Distances are frequently measured in twitches or fractions thereof by woodsmen. It's a habit I've got into myself.

Twizzles

Every now and then the men would come across a snarl in their nets that they called a twizzle, and often a good deal of time and patience were required to pick and shake it out. "All sorts of fish make twizzles," Dan said. "Sometimes a little alewife will make one of the meanest sort."

From *Truro—Cape Cod, or Land Marks and Sea Marks,* by Shebnah Rich, pp. 111–112. Second Edition, Revised and Corrected. Copyright, 1883, by D. Lothrop and Company. Boston. 1884.

From *We Took to the Woods,* by Louise Dickinson Rich, pp. 95, 101–102. Copyright, 1942, by Louise Dickinson Rich. Philadelphia and New York: J. B. Lippincott Company.

From *Highways and Byways of New England,* Including the States of Massachusetts, New Hampshire, Rhode Island, Connecticut, Vermont and Maine, Written and Illustrated by Clifton Johnson, p. 263. Copyright, 1915, by The Macmillan Company. New York and London. 1916.

Wangan

I SHOULD explain "wangan." It is an Indian word, and can mean almost anything, like the Latin *res.* It can mean a camp or building. Pond-in-the-River wangan—or Pondy wangan, as the drivers call it—is a long, low shack a third of a mile above us, where the Rapid River crew lives during the drive. There is a sign in the bunk-house that reads, "Wangan open an hour after supper." That refers to the store where the cook sells candy, tobacco, snuff, and clothing. (It really is a big box in the kitchen, and the reason it isn't open all the time is that the cook doesn't want to be bothered in the middle of his baking to hand out and charge against wages a nickel's worth of makings.) The cook may say, "I lost my wangan when the work boat swamped," and that means that his dishes are at the bottom of the lake. Or he may complain, "The wangan's runnin' low," meaning this time that he's short of food. Or a man may take his wangan and fly —leave the job with his little bundle of personal belongings. You can tell only by the context what the word means, and it's a very convenient word to know. I use it myself a lot, in non-[log]driving connections.

Yankee

According to Reverend Gordon [1]

You may wish to know the origin of the term Yankee. Take the best account of it which your friend can procure. It was a cant, favorite word with farmer Jonathan Hastings, of Cambridge, about 1713. Two aged ministers, who were at the college in that town, have told me they remembered it to have been then in use among the students, but had no recollection of it before that period. The inventor used it to express excellency. A *Yankee* good horse, or *Yankee* cider and the like, were an excellent good horse and excellent cider.

From *We Took to the Woods,* by Louise Dickinson Rich, pp. 183–184. Copyright, 1942, by Louise Dickinson Rich. Philadelphia and New York: J. B. Lippincott Company.

Wangan (a boat) appears in Alexander F. Chamberlain's list (1902) of 132 words borrowed from Algonquin dialects. See H. L. Mencken *The American Language: Supplement I* (New York, 1945), p. 171.

---

[1] From *The History of the Rise, Progress and Establishment of Independence in the United States of America,* by William Gordon, Vol. I, p. 324. London. 1789.

According to Mencken [2]

Perhaps the most notable of all the contributions of Knickerbocker Dutch to American is the word *Yankee.* The earlier etymologists, all of them amateurs, sought an Indian origin for it. Thomas Anbury, a British officer who served in the Revolution with Burgoyne, argued in his "Travels" (1789, Ch. II) that it came from a Cherokee word, *eankke,* meaning a coward or slave; Washington Irving, in "Knickerbocker's History of New York" (1809, Ch. VII) derived it (probably only humorously) from *yanokies,* "which in the Mais-Tschusaeg or Massachusetts language signifies silent men"; and the Rev. John Gottlieb Ernestus Heckewelder, a learned Moravian missionary who published "An Account of the History, Manners and Customs of the Indian Nations Who Once Inhabited Pennsylvania and the Neighboring States" in 1822, maintained therein that it was simply a product of the Indians' unhappy effort to pronounce the word *English,* which they converted, he said, into *Yengees.* Noah Webster accepted this guess, but other contemporary authorities held that the word the Indians were trying to pronounce was not *English* but the French *Anglais.* There were, however, difficulties in the way of all forms of this theory, for investigation showed that *Yankee* was apparently first applied, not to the English but to the Dutch. So early as 1683, it was discovered, *Yankey* was a common nickname among the buccaneers who then raged along the Spanish Main, and always the men who bore it were Dutchmen. Apparently it was derived either from *Janke,* a diminutive of the common Dutch given name *Jan,* or from *Jankees* (pronounced *Yoncase*), a blend of *Jan* and *Cornelis,* two Dutch names which often appear in combination. Analogues in support of the former hypothesis are to be found in the use of *dago (Diego)* to indicate any Spaniard (and now, by extension, any Italian), and of *Heinie* or *Fritz, Sandy* and *Pat* to indicate any German, Scotsman or Irishman, respectively; and for the latter there is reinforcement in such familiar back-formations as *Chinee* from *Chinese, Portugee* from *Portuguese, tactic* from *tactics,* and *specie* from *species.* But how did this nickname for Dutchmen ever come to be applied to Englishmen, and particularly to the people of New England, male and female alike? To this day no satisfactory answer has been made. All that may be said with any certainty is that it was already in use by 1765 as a term of derision, and that by 1775 the Yankees began to take pride in it. In the latter year, in fact, John Turnbull spoke of it in his "McFingal" as connoting "distinction." But he neglected to explain its transfer from Dutch pirates to New England Puritans, and no one has done so to this day. During the Civil

---

[2] From *The American Language,* An Inquiry into the Development of English in the United States, by H. L. Mencken, Fourth Edition, corrected, enlarged, and rewritten, pp. 110–111. Copyright, 1919, 1921, 1923, 1936 by Alfred A. Knopf. New York.

Also *The American Language: Supplement I,* by H. L. Mencken, pp. 192–194. Copyright, 1945, by Alfred A. Knopf, Inc. New York.

War, as everyone knows, Yankee became a term of disparagement again, applied by the people of the South to all Northerners. But its evil significance began to wear off after the turn of the century, and when in 1917 the English began applying it to the men of the A.E.F., Southerners and Northerners alike, the former seem to have borne the affliction philosophically. At that time a characteristic clipped form, *Yank,* came into popularity at home, launched by its use in George M. Cohan's war song, "Over There." But *Yank* was not invented by Cohan, for it has been traced back to 1778, and the Confederates often used it during the Civil War. . . .

* * * * *

The etymology . . . adopted in AL4,[1] to wit, that *Yankee* comes from *Jan* and *kees,* signifying *John Cheese,* is not approved by the DAE,[2] but it has the support of Dr. Henri Logeman of the University of Ghent, and it seems likely to stand. In its original form the term was *Jan Kaas,* and in that form it has been a nickname for a Hollander, in Flanders and Germany, for a great many years. In the days of the buccaneers the English sailors began to use it to designate a Dutch freebooter, and in this sense it became familiar in New York. Presently the New York Dutch, apparently seizing upon its opprobrious significance, began to apply it to the English settlers of Connecticut, who were regarded at the time as persons whose commercial enterprise ran far beyond their moral scruples. A little while later it came into general use in the colonies to designate a disliked neighbor to the northward, and there was a time when the Virginians applied it to Marylanders. In the end the New Englanders saw in it a flattering tribute to their cunning, and so not only adopted it themselves, but converted it into an adjective signifying excellence. The DAE's first printed example of *Yankee,* then spelled *Yankey,* is dated 1683, at which time the term still meant a pirate, and was applied as a proper name to one of the Dutch commanders in the West Indies. By the middle of the Eighteenth Century it had come to mean a New Englander, and by the Revolutionary period the English were using it to designate any American. During the Civil War, as everyone knows, the Southerners used it, usually contemptuously, of all Northerners, and in consequence its widened meaning became restricted again, but in World War I it underwent another change, and since then, though they objected at first, even Southerners have got used to being called *Yankees, e.g.,* by the English. The shortened form *Yank* is traced by the DAE to 1778. The adjective *yankee,* signifying good or superior, had a vogue in the Boston area at the beginning of the Eighteenth Century, but soon passed out of use, and has not been found in print for many years. To *yankee,* a verb signifying to cheat, followed a century later, but is also now obsolete. So is *yankee,* as the name of a drink made of whiskey sweetened with molasses, recorded for 1804, but forgotten by the Civil War era.

---

1 *The American Language,* Fourth Edition.

2 Craigie and Hulbert, *A Dictionary of American English.*

Many derivatives are listed by the DAE, *e.g., Yankee-trick,* traced to 1776; *-land,* to 1788; *-ism,* to 1792; *-like,* to 1799; *-phrase,* to 1803; *-notions,* to c. 1851; *-ish,* to 1830; *-dialect,* to 1832; *-peddler,* to 1834; *-made* and *-clock,* to 1839; *-dom,* to 1843; *-grit,* to 1865; *-twang,* to 1866; to *catch a Yankee* (to catch a tartar), to 1811, and *to play Yankee* (to reply to a question by asking one), to 1896. *Yankee Doodle* as the name of a song is traced to 1767. . . .

NAMES AND NICKNAMES

Old Testament Names in New England

IN DISCOURSES and exhortations, references were constantly made to the favor shown by the Creator of all men to "His chosen people." It is not to be supposed that the disciples and apostles were not reverenced, but there was far more heard of Moses, David, and the prophets. The bush that burned and was not consumed was as often in mind as the pathetic symbol of Christ's death and man's redemption. The sonorous names of Semitic warriors and kings were familiar to the lips of the early ministers; the syllables of Ze-rub-ba-bel gurgled like water falling over stones; Jehoiada, Jeroboam, Ahasuerus, Ahab, Hezekiah and Sennacherib, how well they were known! But Augustine, Ambrose, Chrysostom, Clement, Ignatius, Irenaeus, and Polycarp, were never mentioned except once a year, in the course of a thundering attack upon the Scarlet Woman of the Apocalypse.

Baptismal names showed a similar drift. Of course, a few old English names were represented; but most children wore appellations laboriously sought out from the Bible; and they were often ponderous enough to make the toddling wearers top-heavy. The names were not necessarily Hebrew; they might be Greek or Roman; but they had become hallowed by being imbedded in a biblical text. Aquila, Epaphras, and Theophilus flourished, though less frequently than Abijah, Eliphaz, and Ichabod. A father who had been christened Moses had three sons, Moses, Aaron, and Josiah. In Webster's Dictionary there is a list of Scripture names, and, in running them over, about one hundred and eighty were found that were well known in Quabbin and vicinity. Many were beautiful, but more were inharmonious. Ridiculous associations came to be attached to some that were originally noble. In hearing the names Hosea and Ezekiel, one seldom thinks of the majestic prophets, but of "Hosy" the shrewd and comic hero of the Biglow Papers, and of "Zekle" of the Yankee idyl. What young lady in modern society would willingly own to the name of Jemima, Jerusha, or Tabitha? There were twin sisters not many miles from Quabbin named Tryphena and Tryphosa. One bright-eyed matron was named Tirzah;

another, fair and delicate, had been called Zeruiah. What angelic patience must have been required to bear such burdens for life!

In common speech all names were clipped and vulgarized; and among school-boys and young men the actual designations were "Eph," "Bije," "Ez," "Hi," "Rast," "Josh," "Lije," etc. Poets must find it hard to fit these docked and ill-used names into pastoral verse; and even when the line is made, the reader is apt to be disgusted by some unromantic association. Lowell's ballad of "The Courtin'" is almost perfect in beauty; and yet, in some moods, at the mention of "Zekle" and "Huldy" a sense of vulgar comedy comes in to overbear the poetic feeling.

Oddly enough, there was never a man or boy named Paul in Quabbin, or in the region. Was there some half-conscious sympathy with the Judaistic distrust and dislike of the great apostle to the artistic and lettered world? [1]

The names in those old burying grounds are interesting—to me, at least. There is one critic who has objected to the Christian names in my Cape Cod novels and stories. He insists that those names are, for the most part, the author's own invention. There never were, so he maintains, such names on the Cape or anywhere else.

Well, I wish I might conduct that critic through a few of these grave-yards. In one—and I was not "name hunting" either, but merely seeking unusual inscriptions—I casually picked up the following in something less than ten minutes:

"Bashua, widow of Jeptha." "Theophilus, son of Veranus." "Levi and Asenath." "Tamisen." "Diadama." "Bathsheba." "Tryphenia." "Sabra." "Aruna." "Shubel." "Susa."

These, beside the usual assortment of Jedidiahs and Sophronias and Jeremiahs and Calebs and Solomons and Elkanahs and the like.[2]

Providential Names

Like the old Jews, the Pilgrims and Puritans had a providential way of naming their children from local surroundings, or events of time and place. Thus "Peregrine" [White], travelling from one country; "Oceanus," a boy born to Stephen Hopkins, on the ocean. "Reliance," Governor Hinckley's

---

[1] From *Quabbin, The Story of a Small Town, with Outlooks upon Puritan Life,* by Francis H. Underwood, LL.D., pp. 63–64. Copyright, 1892, by Lee and Shepard. Boston. 1893.

[2] From *Cape Cod Yesterdays,* by Joseph C. Lincoln, p. 124. Copyright, 1935, by Joseph C. Lincoln and Harold Brett. Boston: Little, Brown & Company.

From *Truro—Cape Cod, or Land Marks and Sea Marks,* by Shebnah Rich, pp. 75–76. Second Edition, Revised and Corrected. Copyright, 1883, by D. Lothrop and Company. Boston. 1884.

daughter, the wife of Nathaniel Stone, second minister of Boston, born on the day when the English whipped the Narragansetts, was so named by Rev. Mr. Russell as a token of divine favor, and became a popular name not extinct to this day on the Cape. "Love," "Fear," "Patience," and "Wrestling" were some of the names of Elder Brewster's children.

"Seaborn" was a son of Rev. John Cotton, born on the passage. He married a daughter of Governor Bradford. "Resolved," "Humility," "Remember," "Shining," "Desire," and "Faith" were other female names.

"Armemaryvetta," born 1714, was the name of an accomplished daughter of the schoolmaster, Mr. John Rogers, of Sandwich. Scripture names were their delight and duty: the longer and harder, the more religious. "Mahershallalhashbaz (Isaiah viii I), son of William Dyar, born in Newport, 1661.

An old lady who lived in Provincetown, born in Truro, used to thank the Lord that all her family had Scripture names. This was the way she told them:—

Hezekiah, Jedediah, Shebnah, and Eliakim,
Sarah and Mary, Hannah and Penina.

Girls' Names

An interesting subject of thought is found in the Christian names which have been given to children, borne through longer or shorter lives, and finally carved on gravestones. Whence came some of these names, especially as names given to female children? Here are a few out of many which I have copied in various burial-places along the roads. Some are Scriptural, varied in spelling, some noteworthy only for the spelling:

Vesta	Smilinda	Bezaleed
Madona	Theodate	Phileena
Imagene	Mitty	Asenath
Sabrisal	Rozill	Resolved
Alanette	Lima	Comfort
Rocksena	Orlo	Romanzo
Ora	Elmon	Theda
Phene	Ede	Diademia
Arozina	Irena	Coral

While on this subject of names of the dead, here is an illustration of names now in use by the living. In a village inn in New Hampshire I found the printed catalogue of a school located there, and copied in my notebook the following Christian names of young lady students:

Myrtie Ioline	Mary Etta
Una Gertrude	Margaret Marilla

From *Along New England Roads,* by W. C. Prime, pp. 114–115. Copyright, 1892, by Harper & Brothers. New York and London.

Mary Adella	Lora Eliza
Lois Ella	Franca Lydia
Corrie Elbra	Fannie Mae
Daisy Sarah	Minnie Etta
Hattie Rose Pearl	Lizzie Estelle
Myrtie Kate	Mary Loraine
Florence Genevra	Bernette Samantha

Double Christian Names

THERE is one thing more. By the natural expansion of a few families, whole neighborhoods often exhibit a single surname, like that of Wildes or Huff. There may be half a dozen persons of the same Christian name. The surname being dropped among themselves, it has an odd effect to hear them speaking of each other as Miss Mary Clem, Aunt Sally Josh, Aunt Hannah Eben, Aunt Sam Paulina, and so on, all being of one surname. Then the archaic words or idioms in everyday use, of vagrant or unknown origin, would set a college of comparative philology wild with delight.

Portuguese American Names and Nicknames

MANY Portuguese families have American names. A cabin boy would be brought over by some old sea captain and raised as a son of the family. First he would be known, perhaps, as "Snow's Manell," and then he would become known as "Manny Snow," his old name forgotten but his religion kept. Other names became Anglicized. Perriaras or Perez became Perrys, Diaz became Deers.

* * * * *

Almost everyone in Provincetown has a nickname. This custom is said to have come from São Miguel. The nickname often descends from father to son. So Louis Chocolate, whose tan was doubled by tarring nets, has a flock of little Chocolates. Captain Gaspy, one of the highliners of the great fresh fishermen, was known as "Vadee." Mr. Silva of the fish market was called "Begunna." And there is Mrs. Jazz Garters who lives to the westward. John Bull, Tony Fall River, Manny Bigfeet—there is no end to the nicknames. There is the Goddamn family, with Tony Goddamn and Manny Goddamn.

* * * * *

Captain Antoine Joaquin Sousa, who became captain of the *Jessie Costa* in 1911, one of the great Provincetown vessels of that day, was among the

From *The Pine-Tree Coast,* by Samuel Adams Drake, p. 109. Copyright, 1890, by Estes & Lauriat. Boston. 1891.

From *Time and the Town, A Provincetown Chronicle,* by Mary Heaton Vorse, pp. 163, 164, 178. Copyright, 1942, by Mary Heaton Vorse. New York: The Dial Press.

famous captains. He was generally known as "Joe King," because when he first came to America in the whaling vessel he was asked by the mate what his name was.

"Joaquin," he answered.

"Oh yes, Joe King," said the mate, and he was Joe King all his days.

Ships' Names

THE very names of their ships stir the imagination: the Light Foot, the Chariot of Fame, the Chispa, the Rosario, named for the wife of an owner who had been a captain in his day and had loved and won a Spanish beauty. The Whirlwind and Challenger were famous clipper ships; and one man commanded successively the Undaunted, the Kingfisher, the Monsoon and Mogul and Ocean King, and the steamers Zenobia and Palmyra—and Edward Everett. There was the Young Turk and Santa Claus, the Tally Ho, the Expounder and Centaur and Cape Cod; the Agenor and Charmer and Vahalla, the Shooting Star and the Flying Dragon, the Altof Oak, and, quaintly, the Rice Plant; the Oxenbridge and Kedar. Some ships were so famous that when their day was done, they passed down their names to ships of a younger generation than theirs. Masters changed from one ship to another, and discussion as to how this captain and that handled the Expounder or Monsoon on such or such a voyage filled many a long evening of their old age at home.

* * * * *

The captains of these packets that ran out of every town on the north shore of the Cape had their fun racing one another from port to port; it is probable some money was lost or won on the results. Barnstable, even, produced a ballad to immortalize some of the contestants:

"The Commodore Hull she sails so dull
She makes her crew look sour;
The Eagle Flight she is out of sight
In less than half an hour,
But the bold old Emerald takes delight
To beat the Commodore and the Flight."

Other packets had the romantic names of Winged Hunter and Leading Wind; the Sarah of Brewster was as familiar to her people as "old Mis' Paine" or "Squire Freeman." Truro had the Young Tell, the Post Boy and the Modena. . . .

From *Old Cape Cod: The Land, The Men, The Sea,* by Mary Rogers Bangs, pp. 243–244, 275–276. Boston and New York: Houghton Mifflin Company.

Ships' Names on Old Barns

On the way to the Atwood house, watch on the left for the white barn that says HORATIO HALL in great big letters. It is an ancient custom on Cape Cod to place the name of an old boat on the front of a barn.[1] The *Horatio Hall* was a steam vessel, but some of the loveliest clippers ended the same way—their beautiful names on old barns, their figureheads over the doors. Of the great ships that sailed so proudly, that fought typhoons and knew the doldrums, the monsoons, and the roaring forties, there is nothing left but names on barn doors. Once I saw the name of the *Magdalena,* and I thought she must have been a ship of great beauty and a strange doom. And I have seen the *Wanderer*—a black name on a gray board—on an old red barn.

'Sconset House Names

Unique, catchy, original and forcefully cute titles have been given by present owners and occupants to many of the old houses once possessed and occupied as homes by a hardy farmer and fisherman people of days long agone. Similar titles, by inviting, dainty lettering, also grace the exterior of many of the modern built dwellings. All are scrupulously neat and pretty, and the names given to them add alluring charm.

Of those appellations I have record of the following: Takitezie, In and Out, Hatetoquitit, Bigenough, Nonetoobig, High Tide, House of Lords, Seldomin, Castle Bandbox, Ocean Spray, Come Aboard, Loafalot, Solid Comfort, The Pilot House, The Deck House, The After Cabin, Mizzen Top, Nipantucket, Cap'n's Cabin, Fo'castle, Doubledecker, The Breezes, Daisy Cot, Nauticon Lodge, Whick Whack, Waldorf Astoria, Jr., The Anchorage, Flagship, Cosey Corner, Sea Shell, Cap'n's Gig, Thimble Castle, Big Sunflower, Beehive, Vale of Rest, Castle William, Liberty Hall, Hill Top, Martin Box, Columbia Cottage, Blue Bird, Rosemary, The Manor, Bluff View, Eagle Cottage.

That many of these titles are aptly apropos is strikingly evident on perusal; the old island and its once hardy dwellers, in days agone so closely dependent upon marine affairs, are, in that line of service, notably memorialized by several of them.

From *And This is Cape Cod!* by Eleanor Early, p. 150. Copyright, 1936, by Eleanor Early. Boston and New York: Houghton Mifflin Company.

[1] This statement of "an innocent lady observer" amuses Jeremiah Digges (*Cape Cod Pilot,* p. 309). For the Cape Cod custom of salvaging ships' quarterboards, wheels, etc., for souvenirs and ornaments, see Henry C. Kittredge, *Mooncussers of Cape Cod* (Boston, 1937), pp. 96–121.

From *Brief Historical Data and Memories of My Boyhood Days in Nantucket,* by Joseph E. C. Farnham, pp. 28–29. Published by the author. Providence. 1923.

Poor Old Country Railroad

THE Portland & Oxford Central Railroad, running out of Minot, was built in 1850. It had a hard time to meet running expenses. There were no water stops, and the crew had to fill the tender with buckets from brooks, and stump fences furnished the fuel. One cold, sleety winter's day ice formed over the rails and had to be picked off by hand. They were six days in running thirteen miles. One day the engineer was sick and the superintendent tried running the engine. He threw the lever back in the engine house. It kicked and threw the super through the cab window, and then rushed through the engine house wall and out into the pasture. Because of these mechanical escapades and the suggestive initial letters on the cars, the road was nicknamed "Poor Old Country Railroad."

The Hub

A JAUNTY-LOOKING person, who had come in with the young fellow they call John—evidently a stranger—said there was one more wise man's saying that he had heard: it was about our place, but he didn't know who said it. A civil curiosity was manifested by the company to hear the fourth wise saying. I heard him distinctly whispering to the young fellow who brought him to dinner, *Shall I tell it?* To which the answer was, *Go ahead!* Well—he said—this is what I heard:

"Boston State-House is the hub of the solar system. You couldn't pry that out of a Boston man, if you had the tire of all creation straightened out for a crowbar."

Sir—said I—I am gratified with your remark. It expresses with pleasing vivacity that which I have sometimes heard uttered with malignant dulness. The satire of the remark is essentially true of Boston, and of all other considerable and inconsiderable places with which I have had the privilege of being acquainted. Cockneys think London is the only place in the world. Frenchmen—you remember the line about Paris, the Court, the World, etc. I recollect well, by the way, a sign in that city which ran thus: "Hôtel de l'Univers et des États Unis"; and, as Paris *is* the universe to a Frenchman, of course the United States are outside of it. "See Naples and then die." It is quite as bad with smaller places. I have been about lecturing, you know, and have found the following propositions to hold true of all of them:—

From Minot, Maine. Manuscripts of the Federal Writers' Project of the Works Progress Administration for the State of Maine.

From *The Autocrat of the Breakfast-Table,* VI, in *The Writings of Oliver Wendell Holmes,* Vol. I, pp. 125–126. Copyright 1858, 1882, 1886, 1891, by Oliver Wendell Holmes. Cambridge: The Riverside Press. 1891.

1. The axis of the earth sticks out visibly through the center of each and every town or city.

2. If more than fifty years have passed since its foundation, it is affectionately styled by the inhabitants the "*good old* town of"—(whatever its name may happen to be).

3. Every collection of its inhabitants that comes together to listen to a stranger is invariably declared to be a "remarkably intelligent audience."

4. The climate of the place is particularly favorable to longevity.

5. It contains several persons of vast talent little known to the world. (One or two of them, you may perhaps chance to remember, sent short pieces to the *Pactolian* some time since, which were "respectfully declined.")

Boston is just like other places of its size—only, perhaps, considering its excellent fish-market, paid fire-department, superior monthly publications, and correct habit of spelling the English language, it has some right to look down on the mob of cities. . . .

Back Side and Bay Side

"BACK SIDE" and "Bay Side" . . . are terms to remember when you visit Cape Cod. A prim Wellfleet housewife who rents rooms to summer people once confessed to me that she had somehow shocked her guests by a "perfectly civil answer" she had given them. They wanted to know the best place to take a sunbath. And, of course, she told them the best place was on the Back Side.

II. FOLK-SAY

Dialect speech as the embodiment of living, many-sided human nature is perhaps nowhere so closely seen as in a collection of the figurative terms and phrases applied to people and things.

—ELIZABETH MARY WRIGHT

Proverbs are not merely decorations on life. They have life itself in them. They are the bedrock substance of living, built up by many people and many years. They are the beginnings of all literature, the first metaphors and similes, the first comedies and tragedies. They are the first poetry we have. The Kennebec valley is rich in such poetry, a poetry of Yankeedom, tart, sparkling, and full of meat.—ROBERT P. TRISTRAM COFFIN.

From *Cape Cod Pilot*, by Jeremiah Digges, with Editorial and Research Assistance of the Members of the Federal Writers' Project, p. 6. American Guide Series, Federal Writers' Project, Works Progress Administration for the State of Massachusetts. Copyright, 1937, by Poor Richard Associates. Provincetown and New York: Modern Pilgrim Press and the Viking Press.

Ginowine proverbs ar like good kambric needles—short, sharp, and shiny.—JOSH BILLINGS.

1. MYTHOLOGY IN FOLK SPEECH

LOWELL was impressed by two aspects of New England folk speech, which, at first seemingly contradictory, are reciprocal parts of the same process—the process, that is, by which literature and folklore are constantly passing into each other, to their mutual enrichment. On the one hand, Yankee speech usage has behind it the sanction of "antiquity and very respectable literary authority." On the other hand, the "ordinary talk of unlettered men among us is fuller of metaphor and of phrases that suggest lively images than that of any other people I have seen." Folk speech is thus both conservative and creative; and the "germinal element" in language, which gives life to poetry and slang as well as folk speech, is metaphor, including proverbial comparisons.

Among the attributes of this proverbial lore of trope and comparison are two which folk speech shares with poetry and mythology: the "power of rapidly dramatizing a dry fact into flesh and blood," and the "quality of the mind which delights in finding an element of identity in things seemingly the most incongruous." The process by which language interchanges inanimate, animal, and human qualities, in the attempt to explain nature and human nature, is essentially a mythopoeic process.

This process is nowhere better illustrated than in "those comparisons wherein the moods, habits, and actions of men are likened to those of birds, beasts, fishes, and even insects in real or imaginary situations,"[1] as well as to things. Such comparisons are too familiar to need citing, but particularly characteristic (it would seem) of New England are "crazy as a coot," "deader than a pelcher [pilchard]," "happy as a clam," "pious as a barn rat," and (of a mawkish sentimentalist) "softer'n stewed punkin." Among metaphors are "no see 'ems" (the Indian's words for midges), the "old seedfolks" (ancestors), and "soft sawder [solder]" (smooth talk, deception). Examples of irony and hyperbole are: "A pushing individual was 'not backward in going forward' and a disagreeable one had 'winning ways to make himself hated.' . . . A poor marriage was described as 'nothing marrying nothing.' A futile act or speech was '*to* nothing and *for* nothing.' "[2]

For another kind of speech mythology involving folk metaphor we turn to the "odd custom" noted by Jeremiah Digges among the Portuguese fishermen of Cape Cod—"of bestowing nicknames on one another—not in a spirit of levity, but in dead earnest"—so earnestly, in fact, that the nickname replaces the surname of the entire family and "Some have been in use so long that in the course of generations the real family names have become obscured, and legal problems have arisen." "There is the 'Rat

---

[1] Elizabeth Mary Wright, *Rustic Speech and Folklore* (London, 1913), p. 158.

[2] For most of these expressions, see Annie E. Perkins, "Vanishing Expressions of the Maine Coast," *American Speech*, Vol. III. (December, 1927), No. 2, pp. 134–141. "No-see-ems" is also cited by Thoreau in *The Maine Woods* (Boston, 1893), p. 2; while "soft sawder" was made popular by Sam Slick.

family,' for instance; there are the 'Codfishes'—Manuel Codfish, Maria Codfish, and the little Codfishes. . . ."[1] Perhaps the most famous example of this type of surname is the "Goddams," which Captain Joseph Captiva explains thus:

That's 'cause the old lady she couldn't speak English so good and she'd call the children when they was little: "You come here, goddam," "Don't you do that, goddam." So they call 'em the "Goddams."[2]

Nomenclature descriptive of local and group traits, both depreciatory and affectionate, has given rise to an extensive mythology of nicknames of states, towns, neighborhoods, sections of the population, etc.; *e. g.*, the Nutmeg State; Pudding Town and Puddingers (Northampton and its residents, from the custom of eating hasty pudding and milk for Saturday evening supper);[3] Scrabbletown (the lower end of Chatham); Bluenoses (Nova Scotians or New Brunswickers); lard-eaters (Canucks);[4] chowderheads; mooncussers (Cape Codders); codfish aristocracy ("an opprobrious name for persons who have made money in trade," according to Thornton); Boston Brahmins; bean-eaters; lace-curtain Irish; Hoot, Toot, & Whistle, the Hot Tea & Whisky, and the Hog-Tied & Weary (the Hoosac Tunnel & Wilmington R. R., among short line fans).[5]

---

2. Local Bywords and Proverbs

Local bywords are clearly mythological when they involve a mythical character like Sock Saunders, the "guy who hangs around and makes life complicated" for Maine loggers. But the mythology of local characters and customs enters into other bywords which originate in an old story or for which an explanatory story has been invented—it is often difficult to tell which. Sometimes the story has been forgotten and all that is left is the proverb. In this way every community has its proverbial characters as well as its "character" proverbs, of which Ola G. Veazie reports the following examples from New Hampshire:

Any one around Bath who makes a strong and rather queer statement is said to be "equal to Priest Sutherland," as he was a man who made many such statements and who influenced the town greatly during his fifty years as minister there.

"Going back like John Northey's lamb": equivalent to backsliding. (John Northey was an early resident on Sugar Hill.)

"Leaning toward Sawyer's" was said when some one went out of a house sur-

---

[1] *Cape Cod Pilot* (Provincetown and New York, 1937), pp. 232–233.

[2] As told to Alice Douglas Kelly, *Living Lore of New England,* Manuscripts of the Federal Writers' Project of the Works Progress Administration for the State of Massachusetts.

[3] Clifton Johnson, *Historic Hampshire in the Connecticut Valley* (Springfield, 1932), p. 36.

[4] Robert P. Tristram Coffin, *Kennebec, Cradle of Americans* (New York, 1937), p. 193.

[5] Archie Robertson, *Slow Train to Yesterday* (Boston, 1945), p. 24.

reptitiously or as though going for a drink when he should not. A family by the name of Sawyer kept a store where drinks could be purchased many years ago on Sugar Hill.[1]

Other local sayings allude to the character of the place and the people, with jests and gibes about weather, seasons, landmarks, towns, customs, and similar features.

We have two seasons: winter and Fourth of July.[2]

. . . the New England climate consists of "nine months winter and three months late in the fall."[3]

Fogs so thick you could cut 'em up into junks with your jack-knife.[4]

Boston folks are full of notions.

"Go to Poodic!" (An Indian name for a point of land on the Maine coast; equivalent to "Go jump in the bay!")[5]

Here is to the Nutmeg State—who can produce a grater? (A toast.)

A rib was taken off Billerica to make Bedford.[6]

They call a house a house, but a house with a shed is a village. (Of Cape Cod, as observed by travelers.)[7]

Put a bag of coffee in the mouth of hell, and a Yankee will be sure to go after it.[8]

In addition to proverbial characters and local proverbs, New England has its local phrase-makers and folk-sayers. Out of Poor Richard, by way of the comic almanacs, the Yankee aphorism flowers in Josh Billings.

B. A. B.

---

[1] Manuscripts of the Federal Writers' Project of the Works Progress Administration for the State of New Hampshire.

[2] Louise Dickinson Rich, *Happy the Land* (Philadelphia, 1946), p. 251.

[3] Arthur G. Crandall, *New England Joke Lore* (Philadelphia, 1922), p. 15.

[4] "My Summer with Dr. Singletary," *Prose Works of John Greenleaf Whittier* (Boston, 1886), Vol. II, p. 226.

[5] George R. Stewart, *Names on the Land* (New York, 1945), p. 338.

[6] Katharine M. Abbot, *Old Paths and Legends of New England* (New York, 1904), p. 70.

[7] *Massachusetts: A Guide to Its Places and People* (Boston, 1937), p. 326.

[8] George Lunt, *Old New England Traits* (New York, 1873), p. 61. As attributed to Emperor Christophe of Haiti: "Hang up a bag of coffee in hell, and a Yankee would go down and bring it up without being singed." (Samuel S. Cox, *Why We Laugh,* New York, 1876, p. 325.)

SALT OF THE SEA

Nantucket Nauticalisms

THEY never pull, they always "haul"; they do not tie or fasten anything, they "splice" or "belay" it; they do not arrange a thing, they "rig it"; they do not throw anything away, but "heave it overboard"; they "back and fill," they "luff," "tack," "come about" and "square away" on any and all occasions. Before engaging in any venture they first "see if the coast is clear," then, as they proceed, they "keep the weather eye peeled" and always "look out for squalls." Then they "sound it out" until they "fathom" it. If they don't like "the lay of the land" they "give it a wide berth." To be prudent is "to keep an eye to windward," but to be over-prudent to the point of timidity is to be "always reefed down and standing on the inshore tack." To be reckless and take too many chances is to "sail too close to the wind," and to be caught off one's guard is to be "taken aback," meaning to catch the wind on the wrong side of the sails—an exasperating and sometimes perilous experience for a mariner. Anything put by for a rainy day, or any provision against adversity or disaster is "an anchor to windward," while to be gay or foolish is to "carry on" as an inexperienced or reckless navigator may carry on (sail). A telling rebuke of extravagance is the phrase "two lamps burning and no ship at sea." To overcome or to best an opponent is to "take the wind out of his sails." To be ready for anything is to be "always on deck," and so on *ad infinitum*.

Some day, perhaps, if you are an old-time Nantucketer, you "tackle up" the horse and "all rigged out" you "cruise down along." A "mate" recognizes you by "the cut of your jib," and you are "hailed" with the query, "where you bound?" Replying that you are "bound to the south'ard" or to the "east'ard," as the case may be, you are urged to "heave to" or to "come alongside." Complying with the request, you are urged to "drop anchor," and to "come aboard and have a gam"; so you "make fast" and visit for a while, till it's time to "heave your anchor short" and "get under way" for the next "port."

So the conversation goes, not always with the nauticalisms as thick as in the samples given, but always with the salty flavor of the sea. Less now than formerly, perhaps, for the times are changing; but much of it lingers yet in the speech of the older generation. Some of the old expressions are rarely heard nowadays. In former times a Nantucket mother told her children to "splice their patience," and if she went out, one of the older ones had to "tend the kitchen halyards" in her absence.

From *The Nantucket Scrap Basket,* Being a Collection of Characteristic Stories and Sayings of the People of the Town and Island of Nantucket, Massachusetts, Second Edition, revised, expanded, and rearranged by William F. Macy, pp. 6–11. Boston and New York: Houghton Mifflin Company.

Of a light-minded person or one who didn't amount to much they would say, "Well, I guess he'd come over the bar without camels," while the expression applied to an absolutely useless fellow, "he ain't good enough even to take in slack," explains itself. An ill-fitting garment was said to "fit like a purser's shirt on a hand-spike." "God made the food, but the devil made the cook" is a sailor's phrase, often borrowed to describe a poor cook ashore; and the expression "we must take it as it comes from the cook" is, perhaps, another form of the same idea.

A certain Nantucket Quaker mother once denied that she ever used these nautical phrases, and told her children to remind her if they ever caught her doing it. The very next morning she gave one of them some eggs to leave at the house of a relative on the way to school with the words: "Take these into Cousin Phebe's, and tell her I think this squares the yards with us; and thee must scud, for it's almost school time."

Of course not all these expressions are peculiar to Nantucket. Many of them are heard elsewhere along the coast, and even far inland, and many of them, indeed, have become so much a part of the language that they are not recognized as nautical phrases at all.[1] Of such are several already given—notably such terms as "taken aback," to "carry on" or "the lay of the land" and many others, such as mainstay, bulwark, chock full, etc.; but even of these, when their sense is grasped and understood, it must be admitted that their origin is obvious. Even the very common word "landmark," is a sailor's term, meaning a mark on the land by which to steer or lay a course. "Landfall" was land sighted from a ship. Others not recognizable at all, except by the initiated, are constantly used. "A1" or "A No. 1" originated in the classification of wooden ships, being the highest grade in Lloyd's register. "First rate" was originally a naval term, applied to the old wooden line-of-battle ships. "Skyscraper," long before the day of high buildings, was the sailor's name for a ship with very tall masts. Even more surprising, perhaps, will be the statement that the term "bitter end" is a very technical nautical phrase, that being the sailor's name for that part of the cable which is abaft the windlass bitts; so when the cable is let out to the bitter end, that is as far as it is possible for it to go, and it is only in very deep water or when riding out a gale at anchor that this occurs.

"To know the ropes" is obviously of nautical origin. It is said there are only seven "ropes" on a full-rigged ship. Everything else which might be taken for a rope by a land-lubber goes by some other name, as halyards, clewlines, earrings, garnets, sheets, tacks, stays, buntlines, gaskets, etc., to mention only a few. So that to pick the seven "ropes" from all this confusion of nomenclature requires an "A.B." degree in seamanship.

Another common expression, "fagged out," or the "fag end," is undoubtedly of nautical origin, that being the sailor's term for a rope which is untwisted and frayed at the end.

---

[1] Cf. Joanna Carver Colcord, *Sea Language Comes Ashore* (New York, 1945).

A "fake" in its original meaning was a turn in a rope or a cable. Hence to "fake" a rope is to lay it down in coils.

Examples of this nature might be multiplied indefinitely, and it is a fascinating study; but further discussion of the subject is hardly within the scope of this work, even if space permitted. Our language undoubtedly owes much to the sailors, who, while they may not have actually coined many of the words in question, have probably preserved many very old ones which would otherwise have passed into disuse and been forgotten.

"Give a woman all the advice in the world and then she'll go ashore with both anchors on the bows" expresses the contempt of an old Nantucket captain for feminine judgment and capacity.

"The devil would have made a sailor if he'd ever looked aloft" is said of or to a man who gets things snarled aloft by not looking to see that everything is clear; and the first thing he knows everything is "mops and brooms."

"Nothing but hot water and ashes can be thrown to windward" is told to the green-horn, who needs only to try it once to learn the lesson.

Said of a gale off Cape Horn: "It blows so hard it takes two men to hold one man's hair on."

Of a captain in a tight place, from which it would seem next to impossible to extricate himself, the sailors were wont to say: "The old man's 'twixt Heaven and hell without halyard or downhaul."

Of an incredible story: "That yarn doesn't square by its lifts and braces."

Of an over-dressed woman, displaying flounce, ruffle and furbelow: "Here she comes, stud'n's'ls set alow and aloft."

Similarly, of a sailor home from sea, with his pockets full of money rolling down Main street on his sea-legs, with a girl on each arm: "There goes Jack, rolling down to St. Helena, eighteen cloths in the lower stud'n's'l, and no change out of a dollar!"

An old skipper, still hale and hearty, being asked why he quit going to sea, replied: "Well, I thought when I got to the north'ard o' sixty, 'twas time to heave to."

Another, being invited out to dinner, announced on his arrival that he was "ready to fall to any time," as he had "come with a swep' hold."

Still another old salt spoke of "bending on a new necktie."

Captain Stephen Bailey, partaking of an oyster stew at a church supper, called the waitress with, "See here, my lass, can't ye get me some more oysters? These here are a day's sail apart."

It was Captain Bailey who said, "Once you start the standing rigging of a five-dollar bill, there's d——n little left."

Varieties of Nantucket Wind and Weather

THE varieties of weather known to Nantucketers often surprise the inland visitor, who recognizes only two kinds, good and bad. We have fair, good, fine, foul, dirty, nasty, bad, thick, rough, heavy, and several other sorts, including "owlish" and "mirogenous," whatever that may mean. Wind conditions are described as dead calm, stark calm, calm, light, puffy, squally, heavy, single-reef, two-, three-, and close-reef breezes, half-a-gale, gale, hurricane, etc.; or a wind may be described as a six- or eight-knot breeze, and so on. Among those to the manner born, a "tempest" means a thunderstorm.

Nantucketisms

WHEN an old whaleman was asked after his health, his reply was "*Bung up and bilge-free,*" referring to the way casks are stowed in the hold of a ship; but if you happen to hear one say that he was "*pretty nigh fin out,*" you can know that he has been very sick, or that he thought he was, for that expresses the condition of a dying whale when he rolls over on his side, showing a fin above water. The nearest counterpart to this expression we have now is "about all in."

Bungy—"Where you going?" "I'm going to Bungy." What and where is Bungy? The impression seems to be that the reply is a rather saucy one—almost as if to say, "None of your business."

Clip—A Nantucketer would say, "I'll just 'clip' in to Mary's on the way back." One meaning of the verb clip is to move quickly, and as our use of this term implies haste, or a hurried call, it is doubtless derived from that meaning.

Coof, the Century defines as "a lout, a coward." (Scotch.) Originally, the word was without doubt used in a somewhat contemptuous sense, and to the resident of a prosperous urban community of ten thousand people, such as Nantucket was seventy or eighty years ago, visitors from Cape

---

From *The Nantucket Scrap Basket,* Being a Collection of Characteristic Stories and Sayings of the People of the Town and Island of Nantucket, Massachusetts, Second Edition, Revised, Expanded, and Rearranged by William F. Macy, pp. 144–145. Copyright, 1916, by William F. Macy and Roland B. Hussey; 1930, by William F. Macy. Boston and New York: Houghton Mifflin Company. 1930.

From *The Nantucket Scrap Basket,* Being a Collection of Characteristic Stories and Sayings of the People of the Town and Island of Nantucket, Massachusett, Compiled, Edited, and Arranged by William F. Macy and Roland B. Hussey, and Published for the Benefit of "The Sons and Daughters of Nantucket," pp. 17–19, 129–151 *passim,* and 160–169 *passim.* Copyright, 1916, by William F. Macy and Roland B. Hussey. Nantucket: The Inquirer and Mirror Press.

The material has been rearranged and alphabetized in a single word list.

Cod (to whom the term was originally applied) might well have seemed loutish. Gradually the word came to be applied to any off-islander, and lost most of its contemptuous significance, implying only a slight inferiority by reason of the accident of birth [or residence] elsewhere than on the island. It is a good English word, which is the main point.

Diddledees—A curious old word used for pine-needles. This has always been something of a puzzle, but the Century again helps us out: "Diddledees—a shrub in the Falkland Islands and other Antarctic regions used for fuel." As pine-needles have been used as "kindlings" by the Nantucket people for generations past, may it not be that the word was brought from the Antarctic by the whalers? In the absence of any better explanation of the origin of the term, this theory is advanced for what it may be worth.

Down Along—Many Nantucketers, when asked as to where they are bound, reply, "Oh, jest down along." No one has ever been able to locate just where this popular destination is located. The North Shorer, the Upper Main Streeter, or the Chicken Hiller means when he uses it, that he is going down town. The Newtowner gives it the same meaning, but he also uses it to express a port in the opposite direction, as when he heads for home. The Under-the-Banker also uses it to indicate both up town and down town. We have always heard of people who were going there but we never knew any one to arrive. "Up-along" is sometimes heard, but much less frequently.

Flink—"I'm going out on a flink," meaning a good time. May it be a corruption of "fling" sometimes used in a similar sense?

Another common term was *foopaw*. This is said to have been a corruption of the French *faux pas,* and is believed to have been borrowed from the French whalers. To "make a foopaw" of anything was to make a mess of it, to bungle it—as when a harpooner missed his whale, or having succeeded in "getting an iron in," to have the line foul or snarl. That was a dangerous "foopaw to make, as unless the line was cut quickly before the whale "ran" or "sounded," it might mean death to one or more men in the boat.

The expression *gallied* is still current to some extent among the older generation of Nantucketers. It was a whaling term, meaning primarily frightened and excited, and withal uncertain what to do next. Its nearest synonym, perhaps, is the modern word "rattled," though it implies more of fear and fright than the latter term. If a whale became "gallied" before being struck, it required much more skill and caution in the attack than would otherwise be the case.

Gam—A social visit and talk. Originally this term was applied to a school of whales, and its use by the whalemen is doubtless derived from that source. Whaleships meeting at sea often hove to, and the captains would visit back and forth during the time the ships were in company. Under certain conditions the crews were allowed the privilege also. The word was used both as a noun and as a verb, and it is still very frequently heard among Nantucketers. One says, "I met so-and-so today, and we had a grand gam together," or "we gammed for an hour or more."

Greasy Luck—To wish a whaleman greasy luck meant to wish him a good voyage with plenty of oil; hence the Nantucketer uses it in well-wishes to his friends in any proposed venture. To say on parting, "Well, greasy luck to you!" is to say "Bon voyage!"

Huddle—An old-time name for a dance or ball. All the old-timers will recall "Handy's huddles."

It Takes a Voyage to Learn—Equivalent to "experience is the best teacher." This is often quoted as an excuse for mistakes or inefficiency due to inexperience.

Tradition has it that no whaleman was expected to ask the girl of his choice for her hand until he had *killed his whale,* and if she were of the better class of the island maidens, the wedding day was not fixed until he had won a command. *"She married him before he had a ship"* was a reproach which no high-born damsel of spirit would venture to endure.

Meeching—Is another word often noted. The dictionary gives "skulking, sneaking, mean," which is just the sense we give it in Nantucket.

Off—An abbreviation of "off-island," is very frequently heard. One often hears such a remark as "I haven't seen you lately. Have you been Off?" Still more odd is the expression, "When did you come On from Off?"

Old Town Turkey—The Nantucketer's name for any resident of Martha's Vineyard; from the town of Edgartown, which was formerly known as Old Town.

Porch—Applied to an ell kitchen. A summer cottager who instructed the native man-of-all-work to sweep and clean the porch accused him of stupidity when she returned an hour or two later to find her kitchen nicely cleaned, while the veranda remained in the same disorder as when she went out. Each knew what a porch was, but each had something quite different in mind. The word porch is defined as "a covered way or entrance, whether enclosed or unenclosed." In ecclesiastical architecture, where it presumably originated, it describes the covered and usually enclosed entrance built on to a church or cathedral—for all the world, in general outline and appearance, like the ell kitchen of a typical old Nantucket house, succeeding the "lean-to" in the very old ones. The use of the word as applied to a veranda is modern U. S., and more or less local at that. So the Nantucketer may have been nearer right than his employer. The room over this style of kitchen was always "the porch chamber."

"Put that butter within darting distance, will you?" was the request of an old whaleman at the table, bread in one hand and knife in the other, as he scanned the intervening distance.

Rantum Scoot[1]—A term, we believe, peculiar to Nantucket, and very old. It means a day's "cruise" or picnic about the island, usually a drive,

---

[1] Also reported from New York state by Harold W. Thompson in *Body, Boots & Britches* (Philadelphia, 1940), p. 287.

but it might be on foot. The distinctive feature of such an excursion is that the party has no definite destination, but rather a roving commission, in which respect such a trip differs from a "squantum" (which see later). "Rantum" is probably a corruption of random.

Scrap Islander—The name applied to a Nantucketer by the people of Martha's Vineyard.

Scrimshont—A curious word, of which the original is said to have been scrimshaw. The dictionary defines it in effect as any fine or delicate mechanical work, especially the carving on shells or ivory done by sailors. Many fine examples of "scrimshonting" may still be seen in some of the old Nantucket homes, and the Historical Association has some excellent specimens in its collection.

Serve—If a Nantucket woman breaks her broomstick or mop-handle, she fits the pieces together and asks her husband or some other man to "serve" it. If he is a sailor he knows what she means, and he does a wonderfully neat job. He does not need to look in the dictionary, where he might learn that it means "to bind or wind tightly with small cord or marline"; but unless he is a sailor, or has been taught by a sailor, he cannot do it without having at least one of the ends, if not both, showing when the work is finished. It is a fine art when properly done.

Of a particularly fine young woman it was said: *"She deserves an East India cap'n,"* the popular impression being that such worthies were likely to be more than ordinarily prosperous and successful.

Shool—according to the dictionary, means "to saunter about, to loiter idly"—a favorite pastime with the "shooler," who is a well-known character in the local vernacular.

Skimming Slicks—Securing the full limit of return from any effort. A "slick," as used by the islanders, refers to the smooth, oily patches often seen on the sea over a school of blue-fish, mackerel or other surface-feeding fish, and which exudes from the small fish or "bait" on which the school are feeding. The full significance of this term will be recognized if one stops to think of the labor necessary to skim the slick and get all there is in it.

Slatch—A word still in quite common use on the island among the older people. It means "a short gleam of fine weather, an interval in a storm." When caught away from home in a heavy rain, we plan, if possible, to "wait for a slatch" before starting to return. The term is also sometimes used in the sense of a respite from labor, as "I had a slatch in my work, and I thought I'd run over and see you."

Sliver—(pronounced with a long "i")—Ask your city fish man to sliver a flounder, a plaice fish or a scup for you, and there's one chance in ten, if he's not an old fisherman himself, that he will know what you mean; yet the dictionary defines it exactly: "to cut each side of a fish away in one piece from the head to the tail," which is the only proper way to clean either of the fish mentioned, as every Nantucketer knows.

Snivver—Here's a queer word, still used occasionally. One says "I'll be over to your house snivver dinner." The presumption is that the speaker means "as soon as ever I have had my dinner." A good definition would be: immediately after. We have been unable to find any record of the use of this odd term off-island.

Squantum—Doubtless of Indian origin; the Nantucketer's name for a party outing or picnic—differing from a "rantum scoot" (see before) in that a squantum usually implies some definite destination for the cruise.

To *throw a tub to a whale* is to offer a sop to keep any one quiet, said to be a survival of a very ancient custom when approaching a sperm whale suspected of being ugly, or perhaps only "gallied," to throw a cask overboard so it would drift toward the whale to distract its attention while the boat was approaching.

Tivis—To wander aimlessly about.

Top up your boom—Get ready to go; from the custom of hoisting on the topping-lift of a fore and aft sail, before hoisting the sail itself.

Nantucketers never sit at the window or by the window, but always *"under" the window*. There is perhaps no phrase, which is more often noted in our speech than this, and we who use it are often asked to explain or even to demonstrate just how we sit under the window. The answer is, obviously, that as Nantucket windows are usually rather high from the floor, as we sit by or at one of them, we are under them, just as the wall paper or the baseboard, or even the floor, for that matter, is under them—which only goes to prove that whatever may be said of us, we are never in the wrong. Let him who can prove the contrary.

Wadgetty—Fidgety; nervous.

Whittle—There seems to be no good authority for our use of this word, meaning to fuss, to get uneasy; also, sometimes, to tease, to pester. One says, "Well, it's time to go. Mother'll be whittling." What child of a Nantucket mother hasn't been told, when he had exhausted her patience to the point of exasperation by teasing for something, "Oh, stop your whittling!"

Wilcox—Much used in Nantucket formerly, to describe an uneasy, sleepless night. To this day the old folks (and some of the young ones) say: "I couldn't sleep. I wilcoxed all night long." It has been suggested that the term originated with a story of some family named Wilcox who, having an overplus of company one night, slept four or five in a bed, with the natural result that no one slept at all.

Wild as a Tuckernuck Steer—Wild, harum-scarum. Many beef cattle were formerly raised on Tuckernuck, and their antics, when brought into the gay metropolis of Nantucket town, probably gave rise to this expression.

Nantucket Similes and Sayings

THE speech of the older generation of Nantucketers is full of quaint similes, most of which refer to some old story. In some cases the story has been

Ibid., pp. 75–77.

forgotten, while the expression still remains. We have succeeded in collecting a number of these odd sayings with the accompanying stories:

"As Mad as Tucker."

Tucker was one of those gentle souls whose heart was bigger than his brains. His only relation and caretaker was a grandmother to whom he was as deeply attached as his feeble mental capacity would permit. When this poor innocent was seen on the street one day, crying bitterly, the compassionate neighbor hastened to inquire the cause. "I'm so mad," he sobbed. "I'm so mad. Granny's dead and I'm so mad I don't know what to do." The poor fellow could not even distinguish between his emotions, and although not wholly unsympathetic, the Nantucketers could not refrain from their inalienable right to seize upon a joke by using the simile, "As mad as Tucker when his granny died."

"As Weak as Annie Burrill's Tea."

Annie Burrill was so flustered when she entertained the minister that she forgot to put any tea in the teapot, serving him with a nice cup of freshly-boiled water. When asked if his tea was satisfactory, his reply was: "It has no bad taste, madam." Thus the expression became a simile for weakness in her day.

"As Bad as Old Skitzy."

Skitzy remarked one day, "Now, wife, that cheese is all gone, and I've had none of it." "Well, why didn't you eat some?" she asked. "Why, I don't like cheese," answered Skitzy.

"As Handy as Caleb's Cheese."

It is said that Caleb Macy was (unlike Skitzy) so fond of cheese that he kept one hanging by a string in his sitting room, "so's to have it handy"; hence the expression.

"A Poor Gamaliel."

Gamaliel, a poor good-for-nothing, coming home one night, said to his long-suffering wife: "Well, I've sold my horse." "Have you? What did you get for it?" "Why—a cart!" Hence, the expression, "a poor Gamaliel" has a deep significance to the Nantucketer.

"You Haven't Got Dinah Paddock to Deal With."

Dinah Paddock was a weak-minded woman whom the boys delighted to tease, when playing around her door. After she moved away, they began playing the same tricks on her successor, but she soon scattered them, saying: "I'll let you know you haven't got Dinah Paddock to deal with." This became a simile for efficiency for that day and generation.

"Keeping Still like Uncle Jimmy." [1]

In the old days when families laid in the winter's supply of beef and pork in barrels, Uncle Jimmy missed, little by little, the pork from the barrel which stood in the yard. He suspected a certain man, but said nothing.

Fourteen years went by, and one day, in talking of losses, the man whom he had suspected, said: "Uncle Jimmy, you never found out who took that pork, did you?" "No," said Uncle Jimmy, "*not till this day.*" Out of this incident grew the well-known expression, "keeping still like Uncle Jimmy."

"No More Use for Them Than Meader Had for His Teeth."

A man named Meader, living during the war of 1812, applied to his neighbor for the loan of a hammer. Being asked why he wished it, he replied: "To knock out my teeth. I have no need of them, for I can get nothing to eat." Hence the saying among old Nantucketers, "I have no more use for it than Nick Meader had for his teeth."

YANKEE ELOQUENCE

Wit in Yankee Speech

Prosaic as American life seems in many of its aspects to a European, bleak and bare as it is on the side of tradition, and utterly orphaned of the solemn inspiration of antiquity, I cannot help thinking that the ordinary talk of unlettered men among us is fuller of metaphor and of phrases that suggest lively images than that of any other people I have seen. Very many such will be found in Mr. Bartlett's book,[2] though his short list of proverbs at the end seem to me, with one or two exceptions, as un-American as possible. Most of them have no character at all but coarseness, and are quite too long-skirted for working proverbs, in which language always "takes off its coat to it," as a Yankee would say. There are plenty that have a more native and puckery flavor, seedlings from the old stock often, and yet new

---

[1] See "Who Stole the Pork?", p. 60 above.

From Introduction to *The Biglow Papers,* Second Series, in *The Poetical Works of James Russell Lowell,* pp. 224–225. Copyright, 1848, 1857, 1866, 1868, 1869, 1876, and 1885, by James Russell Lowell. Boston and New York: Houghton, Mifflin and Company.

[2] John Russell Bartlett, *Dictionary of Americanisms* (New York, 1848), the 1859 edition of which Lowell reviewed.

varieties. One hears such not seldom among us Easteners, and the West would yield many more. "Mean enough to steal acorns from a blind hog"; "Cold as the north side of a Jenooary gravestone by starlight"; "Hungry as a graven image"; "Pop'lar as a hen with one chicken"; "A hen's time ain't much"; "Quicker'n greased lightnin' "; "Ther's sech a thing ez bein' *tu*" . . .; hence the phrase *tooin' round,* meaning a supererogatory activity like that of flies; "Stingy enough to skim his milk at both eends"; "Hot as the Devil's kitchen"; "Handy as a pocket in a shirt"; "He's a whole team and the dog under the wagon"; "All deacons are good, but there's odds in deacons" (to *deacon* berries is to put the largest atop); "So thievish they hev to take in their stone walls nights"; [1] may serve as specimens. "I take my tea *barfoot,*" said a backwoodsman when asked if he would have cream and sugar. (I find *barfoot,* by the way, in the Coventry Plays.) A man speaking to me once of a very rocky clearing said, "Stone's got a pretty heavy mortgage on that land," and I overheard a guide in the woods say to his companions who were urging him to sing, "Wal, I *did* sing once, but toons gut invented, an' thet spilt my trade." Whoever has driven over a stream by a bridge made of *slabs* will feel the picturesque force of the epithet *slab-bridged* applied to a fellow of shaky character. Almost every county has some good die-sinker in phrase, whose mintage passes into the currency of the whole neighborhood. Such a one described the county jail (the one stone building where all the dwellings are of wood) as "the house whose underpinnin' come up to the eaves," and called hell "the place where they didn't rake up their fires nights." I once asked a stage-driver if the other side of a hill were as steep as the one we were climbing: "Steep? chain-lightnin' couldn' go down it 'thout puttin' the shoe on!" And this brings me back to the exaggeration of which I spoke before. To me there is something very taking in the Negro "so black that charcoal made a chalk-mark on him," and the wooden shingle "painted so like marble that it sank in water," as if its very consciousness or its vanity had been overpersuaded by the cunning of the painter. I heard a man, in order to give a notion of some very cold weather, say to another that a certain Joe, who had been taking mercury, found a lump of quick-silver in each boot, when he went home to dinner. This power of rapidly dramatizing a dry fact into flesh and blood, and the vivid conception of Joe as a human thermometer, strike me as showing a poetic sense that may be refined into faculty. At any rate, there is humor here, and not mere quickness of wit,—the deeper and not the shallower quality. The *tendency* of humor is always towards overplus of expression, while the very essence of wit is its logical precision. Captain Basil Hall denied that our people had any humor, deceived, perhaps, by their gravity of manner. But this very seriousness is often the outward sign of that humorous quality of the mind which delights in finding an element of identity in things seemingly the most incongruous, and then again in forcing an incongruity upon things identical. . . .

[1] And, by the way, the Yankee never says "o'nights," but uses the older adverbial form, analogous to the German *nachts.*—J. R. L.

Humor in Yankee Speech

I REMEMBER a remark made to one of our local merchants by a pert "summer boarder." "I don't see what you people do in the winter when *we* are gone." "Oh," said he, "we jest hibernate."[1] I don't suppose that reply would appear the least funny outside of the locality, but it was chuckled over at many a social function. The laugh was on the "boarder," for her "airs" do not impress the "rubes" as much as she supposes. The real life of the village never begins until cold weather has driven these aliens away. The merchant "tacks on" his prices and "makes" all he can out of their patronage, but is secretly amused at their "duds" and their "goings-on." They wouldn't feel quite so superior if they knew that behind their backs they are "summer complaints."

You may have heard the more apocryphal anecdote of the resident who was asked this same question, implying stagnation in the winter. This native is reported to have said, "Oh, I jest sets and thinks, an' sometimes I jest sets." It at least illustrates the Maine type of humor. Another story is told of an old bachelor who at length "made up to" and "up and married" the village "old maid." "I hear you've taken on a wife, Jed, sence I ben gone," remarks an acquaintance just returned from a "cousining" ("cousining" means a visit to distant relatives). "Ye-es," is the tolerant reply, "a *kind* uv one."

Speaking of old maids, they are usually regarded as jokes in most Maine towns, a reminiscence of the old-time feeling that girls are disgraced if they can't "land" a man. If she behaves herself and "quits strugglin'" she will probably escape notice, but if she attempts to prolong her youth by "running with" the "young fry," she will probably win the title of "the youth's companion," which is the name of a literary "stand-by" in New England.

The lazy man is also a joke. Yankee humor describes him as "bottoming chairs" for an occupation. A man who is too lavish with his energy may be cautioned not to "bust his biler." Your humorist will answer your conventional greeting regarding his health with "Oh, jest staggerin' around." I remember I sprang this unthinkingly upon a western Pennsylvanian once and got an indignant reproof. Another reply is, "Sick abed." A person much given to practical joking is a "case." The term equally applies to a clever child. Either may be said to "act up," also. You get a real slant on the psychology of Maine humor, in the statement, "He ken knock a haouse

---

From "Maine Dialect," by E. K. Maxfield, *American Speech*, Vol. II (November, 1926), No. 2, pp. 82–83.

[1] The question, "What on earth do you do here after the summer people leave?" drew the following reply from Shavy Noyes, of Norway, Maine: "Oh, we jest fumigate." See Arthur Bartlett, "Maine," in *Holiday*, Vol. 2 (August, 1947), No. 8, p. 44.

daoun!" It expresses an amused contempt for the "upstart" braggart, the pronunciation being deliberately exaggerated to contribute to the effect.*

Miscellany

A LADY summoned a jack-of-all-trades to repair her fence. After contemplation he enquired, "Well, marm, will you hev it hen-tight or cow-tight?" "As we haven't any hens, I think cow-tight will do." [Guilford, Conn.]

A dweller on Old Street [Deerfield,] many years before his death had a copper coffin built for himself, declaring emphatically, "I'll be d——d if I go snappin' raound hell in a hemlock coffin."

At Shelburne Falls—formerly Deerfield Northwest—some one remarked that the water in the river was very low. "Yaas," drawled a bystander, "it lacks a quart of being any water in it."[1]

The city fellow was discussing the general wild state of spending and nobody paying with a resident of a small Cape Cod town. The old man listened, agreed and then opined—"Nossir, I don't hold with all these new ideas. I've allus made it a point to never wash more'n I can hang out!"

* * * * *

"He pries up the sun with a crowbar"—said of a man who gets up early in the morning.

"The wind blew straight up and down"—a gale.

"Looking for salt pork and sundown"—when a hired man shirks.

"Slower than a hop toad in hot tar."

"Faster than a cat lapping chain lightning."

"Safe as in God's pocket."[2]

"I wish I had a neck as long as a cart-rut." (New Hampshire.) Praise for good drink.

"He's always a-stern of the lighter." (Nantucket.) Behind the last one.

"There was no more heat in the sun than a yellow dog." (Maine.)

"It's tougher where there's none." (Nantucket.) Upon hearing complaints about a tough steak.

---

* I suppose this vowel-twisting was a direct inheritance from certain counties in England where it can still be noted; but I think to some extent our twisting has been deliberate—a sort of contemptuous effort of the Yankee to show he was not of the aristocracy, but good common folk.—Charles Edward Crane, *Let Me Show You Vermont* (New York, 1937), p. 30.

---

[1] From *Old Paths and Legends of the New England Border:* Connecticut, Deerfield, Berkshire, by Katharine M. Abbott, pp. 111, 193. Copyright, 1907, by Katharine M. Abbott. New York and London: G. P. Putnam's Sons.

[2] From *The (Old) Farmer's Almanack,* Calculated on a New and Improved Plan for the Year of Our Lord 1946, No. 154, by Robert B. Thomas, pp. 44, 45. Copyright, 1945, by Mabel M. Swan. Dublin, New Hampshire: Yankee, Inc.

"He had no more suavity than a swine." (Maine.)

"I just ate chagrin." (Maine.) Embarrassment over a faux pas.[3]

When two Marbleheaders meet, they say to each other, "Down bucket!" or else they say, "To hell I pitch it!" Why they say it, or how they began, the Marbleheaders themselves can't tell you.[4]

. . . I like descriptions of how the smelt ran in Mill Brook, spring before last—"You never see nawthin' like it. Looked like a big snake swimming up the current, they was so thick. Every dip, you'd net half a water-pail full"—and of the stately dance of a male spruce-partridge observed in a little sunny clearing, courting his demure brown hen—"She sat there like a bump on a log, never letting on she see him at all till he got disgusted and moseyed off into the bushes. She come to life then all right and skedaddled right along after him. Just like any woman." . . .[5]

Fog's so durn thick this mornin' you kin hardly spit.

It wuz cold enough to freeze two dry rags together. . . .

. . . 'twould break a snake's back to foller that last furrer.

. . . so homely, 'twould gag ye.

He could sell a fiddle to a one-arm deef an' dumber.

. . . the cussed critter was so tough then, ye c'd hardly stick a fork in his gravy!

Somebody declared once that Will Frisbie must-a been the last one in the back row when the faces wuz handed out.[6]

A keen sense of the humorous, with aptness in illustration, drawn from observation in their own sphere, is another distinguishing trait. I was present at a discussion among some village philosophers, about a wedding

---

[3] From *From Here to Yender,* Early Trails and Highway Life, by Marion Nicholl Rawson, pp. 285, 294, 296, 305. Copyright, 1932, by E. P. Dutton and Company, Inc. New York.

[4] From *Cape Cod Pilot,* by Jeremiah Digges, with Editorial and Research Assistance of the Members of the Federal Writers' Project, p. 311. American Guide Series, Federal Writers' Project, Works Progress Administration for the State of Massachusetts. Copyright, 1937, by Poor Richard Associates. Provincetown and New York: Modern Pilgrim Press and the Viking Press.

[5] From *Happy the Land,* by Louise Dickinson Rich, p. 246. Copyright, 1946, by Louise Dickinson Rich. Philadelphia and New York: J. B. Lippincott Company.

[6] From *Village Down East,* Sketches of Village Life on the Northeast Coast of New England before "Gas-Buggies" Came, by John Wallace, from Conversations with Zackary Adams, Duck Trap Cove, Maine, pp. 12, 18, 46, 52, 92, 114, 182. Copyright, 1943, by Stephen Daye Press, Inc. Brattleboro, Vermont.

recently solemnized in the neighborhood. The groom was described as being as poor as a church-mouse; so that the union of hearts did not promise a golden future. "Oh, never mind," said one of these graybeards; "tew pigs allers doos better'n one."[7]

•

"THE hill farmer," one wisecracker said, "got up so early that often he met himself going to bed."

"There ain't much of any winter here," one of our wisecrackers declared, "except from September to June, but we have dog-gone good sleddin' the rest of the year."[8]

A Vermont "Idioticon"

I HAVE my own "idioticon"—a little privately compiled dictionary of words and phrases used by Vermonters I know, all the way from the Supreme Court bench to the backwoods farm. In a few radio talks I asked my fellow Vermonters what were their favorite expressions and I was surprised at the number of contributions from towns all over northern Vermont. I recognize many that are common to all New England, some that may have become familiar farther west or south, but the fact remains they are relished by Vermonters and therefore part and parcel of our way of speech.

Justice Leighton P. Slack of the Vermont Supreme Court, venerable, but sly in his humor, is a rich mine for the good old phrases. "Slipper-toe" is one of the Judge's old-time expressions for a no-account, and an "old pelter" is his way of describing an old Tartar. And I heard him one day say somebody was "homely enough to stop a down train," and that's a phrase which, if you stop to think of it, has much more significance than "homely enough to stop a clock," "homely as a hedge fence," or "homely as hell is wicked."

To "pestle around," a phrase plucked from the mortar-and-pestle days, was a common expression which I recall from the Black River Valley to describe a hasty, puttering activity. But for being "busy" there are many other phrases which my radio helpers sent in to me. The ironic line "as busy as a man on the town" indicates relief workers were always that way. Several persons sent this: "I've trotted around all day in a bushel," meaning a busy day, evidently, without getting anywhere.

---

[7] From *The Pine-Tree Coast,* by Samuel Adams Drake, p. 74. Copyright, 1890, by Estes & Lauriat. Boston. 1891.

[8] From *The Great White Hills of New Hampshire,* by Ernest Poole, pp. 82, 84. Copyright, 1946, by Ernest Poole. Garden City, New York: Doubleday & Company, Inc.

From *Let Me Show You Vermont,* by Charles Edward Crane, pp. 31–32. Copyright, 1937, by Alfred A. Knopf, Inc. New York and London.

The Vermonter would seem to have a hearty contempt for ignorance, especially of the kind that lacks even common sense, for many expressions are of this run of shad: "Don't know enough to pound sand in a rat-hole," "to go in when it rains," to "pour water out of a boot," to "suck alum and drool." To have rendered any of the foregoing with *doesn't* instead of *don't* would have spoiled it all, for this use of *don't* is the most common grammatical error current in Vermont, possibly defensible as it was sanctioned by the highest classes in the eighteenth century.

I can think of some of my friends who find the future "darker'n a wolf's mouth," "blacker'n a stack of black cats," or "dark as a pocket," and "feel bluer'n a whetstone." There are those who are often found to be "fixing for a spell of sickness" or "enjoying dretful poor health," or "just feeling peakéd."

Vermonters' contempt for a lack of common sense is matched by their contempt for lack of thrift, as reflected in such expressions as: "He don't need it any more than a pig needs a wallet," or "He has no more use for it than for water in his boots," or "He don't need it any more than a dog needs two tails."

I'll turn on a few of the expressions sent in:

"It's a poor back that can't press its own shirt."

"Stands out like a blackberry in a pan of milk."

"He's the whole team and the little dog under the wagon."

"Her house was a regular hurrah's nest."

"Jumped like a cat out of the wood-box."

"He's as straight as a yard of pump-water."

"Her head looks as if it had worn out two bodies."

"Twice around a toothpick and half-way back."

A lady up in Craftsbury Common said of a poor, tired, hungry hired man:—"looking for salt pork and sundown."

A Montpelier woman sent me a list in which was that classic phrase: "independent as a hog on ice" (it ought to go on our state seal), and added: "slow as a hog on ice with his tail froze in."

A woman turned to me in a theater to contribute this as her favorite: "Twenty tailors around a buttonhole."

Seamen's Sermon

THE only preacher I heard in Boston was Mr. Taylor, who addresses himself peculiarly to seamen, and who was once a mariner himself. I found his chapel down among the shipping, in one of the narrow, old, water-side streets, with a gay blue flag waving freely from its roof. In the gallery opposite to the pulpit were a little choir of male and female singers, a

From *American Notes,* for General Circulation, by Charles Dickens, pp. 39–41. London: Chapman and Hall. 1850.

violoncello, and a violin. The preacher already sat in the pulpit, which was raised on pillars, and ornamented behind him with painted drapery of a lively and somewhat theatrical appearance. He looked a weather-beaten hard-featured man, of about six or eight and fifty; with deep lines graven as it were into his face, dark hair, and a stern, keen eye. Yet the general character of his countenance was pleasant and agreeable.

The service commenced with a hymn, to which succeeded an extemporary prayer. It had the fault of frequent repetition, incidental to all such prayers; but it was plain and comprehensive in its doctrines, and breathed a tone of general sympathy and charity, which is not so commonly a characteristic of this form of address to the Deity as it might be. That done he opened his discourse, taking for his text a passage from the Songs of Solomon, laid upon the desk before the commencement of the service by some unknown member of the congregation: "Who is this coming up from the wilderness, leaning on the arm of her beloved!"

He handled his text in all kinds of ways, and twisted it into all manner of shapes; but always ingeniously, and with a rude eloquence, well adapted to the comprehension of his hearers. Indeed if I be not mistaken, he studied their sympathies and understandings much more than the display of his own powers. His imagery was all drawn from the sea, and from the incidents of a seaman's life; and was often remarkably good. He spoke to them of "that glorious man, Lord Nelson," and of Collingwood; and drew nothing in, as the saying is, by the head and shoulders, but brought it to bear upon his purpose, naturally, and with a sharp mind to its effect. Sometimes, when much excited with his subject, he had an odd way—compounded of John Bunyan, and Balfour of Burley—of taking his great quarto bible under his arm and pacing up and down the pulpit with it; looking steadily down, meantime, into the midst of the congregation. Thus, when he applied his text to the first assemblage of his hearers, and pictured the wonder of the church at their presumption in forming a congregation among themselves, he stopped short with his bible under his arm in the manner I have described, and pursued his discourse after this manner:

"Who are these—who are they—who are these fellows? where do they come from? Where are they going to?—Come from! What's the answer?" —leaning out of the pulpit, and pointing downward with his right hand: "From below!"—starting back again, and looking at the sailors before him: "From below, my brethren. From under the hatches of sin, battened down above you by the evil one. That's where you came from!"—a walk up and down the pulpit: "and where are you going"—stopping abruptly: "where are you going? Aloft!"—very softly, and pointing upward: "Aloft!"—louder: "aloft!"—louder still: "That's where you are going—with a fair wind,—all taut and trim, steering direct for Heaven in its glory, where there are no storms or foul weather, and where the wicked cease from troubling, and the weary are at rest."—Another walk: "That's where you're going to, my friends. That's it. That's the place. That's the port. That's the haven. It's a blessed harbour—still water there, in all changes of the winds and tides; no driving ashore upon the rocks, or slipping your cables and running out to sea, there: Peace—Peace—Peace—all peace!"—Another walk, and patting the bible under his left arm: "What! These fellows are coming from the wilderness, are they? Yes. From the dreary, blighted wilderness of Iniquity, whose only crop is Death. But do they lean upon anything—do they lean upon nothing, these poor seamen?"—Three raps upon the bible: "Oh yes.—Yes.—They lean upon the arm of their Beloved"—three more raps: "upon the arm of their Beloved"—three more, and a walk: "Pilot, guiding star, and compass, all in one, to all hands—here it is"—three more: "Here it is. They can do their seaman's duty manfully, and be easy in their minds in the utmost peril and danger, with this"—two more: "They can come, even these poor fellows can come, from the wilderness leaning on the arm of their Beloved, and go up—up—up!"—raising his hand higher, and higher, at every repetition of the word, so that he stood with it at last stretched above his head, regarding them in a strange, rapt manner, and pressing the book triumphantly to his breast, until he gradually subsided into some other portion of his discourse.

I have cited this, rather as an instance of the preacher's eccentricities than his merits, though taken in connection with his look and manner, and the character of his audience, even this was striking. It is possible, however, that my favourable impression of him may have been greatly influenced and strengthened, firstly, by his impressing upon his hearers that the true observance of religion was not inconsistent with a cheerful deportment and an exact discharge of the duties of their station, which, indeed, it scrupulously required of them; and secondly, by his cautioning them not to set up any monopoly in Paradise and its mercies. I never heard these two points so wisely touched (if indeed I have ever heard them touched at all), by any preacher of that kind, before.

A 'Sconseter's Will

Siasconset, May 30th, 1841

I, OBED GARDNER, master mariner, now living at 'Sconset, write down this will.

From *The Nantucket Scrap Basket*, Being a Collection of Characteristic Stories and Sayings of the People of the Town and Island of Nantucket, Massachusetts, revised, expanded, and rearranged by William F. Macy, pp. 158–160. Copyright, 1916, by William F. Macy and Roland B. Hussey, and 1930, by William F. Macy. Boston and New York: Houghton Mifflin Company.

This manuscript will was found in an old sea-chest in a house in Siasconset some years ago.

The will was never presented in court for probate, because the turn of events made it unnecessary. The Nancy Rotch returned and was sold for a good price. Belindy's husband was drowned by the upsetting of his dory on Miacomet Rip. Ezra returned from China, prosperous and anxious to make amends for past shortcomings, and no one was more delighted to see him than Cap'n Obed. When the latter died, it was

Item. I have cruised with my wife, Huldy Jane, since 1811. We signed articles in town before the preacher on Independence Day. I want her and my oldest boy Jotham to be Captain and Mate in bringing to port whatever I leave and to see that every one of the crew gets the lay as writ down on this paper. I put mother in command. I know sheel be Captain anyway, for six months after we started on our life cruise I found out that I was mate and she was master. I don't mean that she ever mutinied, but I no that whenever we didn't agree she always manoovred to work to windward. May be it is all right for she could sail closer to wind than I could and could manage the crew of little ones that she had as much to do with shipping as I did. She always wanted me to do the swearin' when there was any trouble. I no that when she and Jotham break bulk the cargo will be got out as well as I could do it myself.

Item. In 1838 Captain Ichabod Worth got tired of the old Nancy Rotch and wanted to get rid of her so he got me to take a piece of her. When I saw her last she was lyin' at the wharf in Valparaiso more'n half full. I mean she was more'n half full of oil. Mother never liked her. I want Jotham to have that piece as extra pay for what he does in settlin' up my affairs for heel have to steer things while mother is takin' observations, watchin the weather and lookin over things below deck.

Item. I want mother to have the house on Union street until she goes aloft. Then I want it to go to the children in equal lays and if any child dies I want the lay of the parent to go to the parent's young ones. But I don't want my daughter Belindy to have anythin as long as her husband is livin. He is a lubber, but she has been cruisin with him for years. I haven't got anything agin him, but he doesn't no how to navigate the sea of life. I do believe if he wanted to stop a leak board ship it would be just like him to go into the hold with an auger and bore a hole threw the plankin to let the bilge water out into the sea. But Belindy likes him. Thas just like a woman. If I should give the lay out and out to her, I am afraid her husband would manoover to get hold of it. So I want mother and Jotham to put it out at interest, and give what comes out of it to her until her husband ships for a corpse below decks in the grave yard. Then she can take the lay and do what she wants with it.

Item. I dont want my son Ezry to have anything from what I leave. All the children except him was good ones. They looked out for their mother and me. He didn't take after either of us except the time he took after me with a fid and hit me over the starboard eye. He new what was to come and was smart enough to jump into Johnny Gibbs catboat, hawl in the sheet and steer for the continent. When he got to Bedford he shipped as a boat steerer on the old Falcon. I was glad he did. I don't no where he is now but I herd he was master of a steamboat runnin between Canton and

---

at Ezra's suggestion that the whole estate was given to the widow during her lifetime. After her death, at the age of 92, it was divided among the children, but Ezry gave his "lay" to Belindy's oldest boy, who had been named after him.—W. F. M.

Whampoa. I havent got any use for him and I guess he hasnt any use for me. The black eye he gave me is outlawed and I dont now lay anythin up agin him for that.

Item. I want mother and Jotham to settle up things as soon as they can break bulk, and make a fair divide between the children. But don't forget what I have writ down about mother and Belindy. I don't think Belindy's husband will make any fuss about the way I have taken care of her unless she runs head on the shoals of a lawyers office. Then look out for squalls. I hope sheel stand off if she sees a lawyer comin thort her bows.

Item. I want mother to have half of what comes from what is left of my property besides the house in Union street. She deserves it. Every time I was around the Horn she did her duty to the young ones and I want her to have enough to live on until she goes aloft. Then I want her lay to go to the children in equal pieces except that Belindy shall only have what comes from it until her husband dies. If mother wants to marry again thats her business. I never did like to cruise without a mate, and I guess she wouldn't like to either.

Obed Gardner
Master Mariner

Captain Obed Gardner ast us into his porch and opened his locker. He then ast us to take a drink of rum that was fetched to him from Boston by Captain George Swain in his schooner. We done so. It was a masterly warmin to our insides. Then he pulled this paper out of his pea jacket and signed it and said it was his will and he ast us to sign it as witnesses. We done so, then he ast one of us to write down what took place and as they said I was more of a skoller than they, I did so.

Jethro Coffin, 2nd,
Eleasur Paddock,
Shubael Starbuck.

PROVERBS AND SAYINGS

Old English Proverbs

All truths must not be told at all times. A handsaw is a good thing, but not to shave with. A stumble may prevent a fall. Be patient and you shall have patient children. Fair and softly goes far in a day. He who loses money loses much; he who loses a friend loses more; but he who loses his spirits loses all. At a good bargain pause a while. Good words cost nothing, but are worth much. He who says what he likes, hears what he does not like.[1]

[1] From *The (Old) Farmer's Almanack,* Calculated on a New and Improved Plan, for the Year of Our Lord 1871, by Robert B. Thomas, p. 40. Entered, according to Act of Congress, in the year 1870, by Brewer & Tileston, in the Office of the Librarian of Congress, at Washington. Boston.

The frost hurts not weeds.
He that goes barefoot must not plant thorns.
Get thy spindle and thy distaff ready, and God will send the flax.
Wise men are like timber trees in a hedge: here and there one.
There is small choice in rotten apples.
He that handles a nettle tenderly is soonest stung.
There's no tree but bears some fruit.
He that would have the fruit must climb the tree.
He who plants trees loves others besides himself.
If you would enjoy the fruit, pluck not the flower.[2]

The Sayings of Poor Ned

Poor Ned says, He that makes himself an ass, must not take it ill, if men ride him.

A customary railer is the devil's bagpipe, which the world danceth after.
Good dancers have mostly better heels than heads.
Half-witted people speak much and say little.
It is not a sign of humility to declaim against pride.
Man's best fortune, or his worst, is a wife.
One cannot live by selling goods for words.
When poverty comes in at the door, love creeps out at the window.

Aphorisms of Manners

In the lower school the morning religious instruction and exercise were followed by the recital of what we called "Manners." We even used the word in its singular form: The aphorism or injunction for which each was responsible we termed a "manner." For the searching out and the composition of his daily "manner" each child was a law unto himself; perhaps, indeed, it was the one part of the day's inflexible program which can be called entirely self-directing. We culled these "manners" from books, from parents, from memory, or in cases of the eleventh hour from our own heads; there was no rule against reasonable repetition provided the same

---

[2] From *The (Old) Farmer's Almanack,* Calculated on a New and Improved Plan, for the Year of Our Lord 1890, by Robert B. Thomas, p. 39. Entered, according to Act of Congress, in the year 1889, by William Ware, in the Office of the Librarian of Congress, at Washington. Boston.

From *The Old Farmer's Almanac,* 1795. Reprinted in *The (Old) Farmer's Almanack,* Calculated on a New and Improved Plan for the Year of Our Lord 1935, by Robert B. Thomas, p. 49. Copyright, 1934, by Carroll J. Swan. Boston.

From *A Goodly Heritage,* by Mary Ellen Chase, p. 253–254. Copyright, 1932, by Henry Holt and Company, Inc. New York.

child did not too frequently recite the same "manner" or that the same "manner" were not proffered twice on the same morning by two different children.

The philosopher, Epictetus, who objected to the laying down of rules, particularly rules of etiquette, would have been sadly annoyed at the enjoyment we derived and the glibness we displayed in this peculiar exercise. As the teacher called the roll, each child rose, stood by his seat in the prescribed position, and delivered himself of his "manner." Even the littlest were not excused. The subjects of the "manners" varied from the high affairs of ethics to the more practical concerns of decent and decorous living. A few examples will suffice to suggest their limitless scope and range. A serious, frail little girl, whose general make-up denied an ounce of drama, was given to crying out in impassioned tones, "In case of shipwreck, save the women and children first!" A fat little boy in very tight trousers, who has since become one of the financial props of Boston, furnished proof for the once popular contention concerning the New England morning meal by his reminder, repeated as often as possible and always with a suggestion of regret: "Never ask for two pieces of pie at breakfast." The most popular "manner" of a drab, prosy child, who usually remained for weeks on end at the foot of the spelling-class, echoed her mother's widespread talents as a housewife: "In sweeping a room, never forget the corners."

Hi's Got Some Great Sayings

"Yes, there used to be some great sayin's, if I could remember them all. You know Hi Minor don't you, owns the farm up off Two Mile Bridge? Hi's got some great sayin's. One of his favorites is "Just 'cause I say it's so don't make it so."

Then there was the lad who asked could he go fishin' in Hi's trout stream. "Sure you can go," says Hi, "but don't let me catch you."

Famous Sayings and Allusions

"A dead whale or a stove boat."—Motto of old Yankee whalemen.

"After their arrival, they thankfully fell upon their knees, and then fell upon the aborigines."—Ancient writer.

From "Connecticut Clockmaker," as told by Arthur Botsford, Thomaston, Connecticut, to Francis Donovan, in *Living Lore of New England*. Manuscripts of the Federal Writers' Project of the Works Progress Administration for the State of Connecticut.

For many of these sayings see Henry F. Woods, *American Sayings,* Famous Phrases, Slogans and Aphorisms (New York, 1945).

"And this is good old Boston,
The home of the bean and the cod,
Where the Lowells talk to the Cabots,
And the Cabots talk only to God."

—John Collins Bossidy
(Toast, Midwinter Dinner, Holy Cross Alumni, 1910)

"As Maine goes, so goes the country."—Political maxim, 1888.

"Boston is a state of mind."

"Don't fire until you see the whites of their eyes."—Col. William Prescott, 1775.

"Every one talks about the weather, but no one does anything about it."—Charles Dudley Warner (generally attributed to Mark Twain).

"He comes of the Brahmin caste of New England. This is the harmless, inoffensive, untitled Aristocracy."—Oliver Wendell Holmes ("The Brahmin Caste of New England," *Atlantic Monthly*, January, 1860).

"Hitch your wagon to a star."—Ralph Waldo Emerson, "Civilization and Solitude."

"I do not choose to run for President in 1928."—Calvin Coolidge, 1927.

"I only regret that I have but one life to lose for my country."—Nathan Hale, 1776.

"If you don't like the weather, wait a minute."—Mark Twain.

"In the name of the great Jehovah and the Continental Congress."—Ethan Allen, 1775.

"Keep cool with Coolidge."—Campaign slogan, 1924.

"Massachusetts, there she stands."

"No taxation without representation."—James Otis, 1765.

"One, if by land, and two, if by sea;
And I on the opposite shore will be."

—Henry Wadsworth Longfellow, "Paul Revere's Ride."

"Politics makes strange bedfellows."—Charles Dudley Warner.

"There, my boys, are your enemies, redcoats and tories. You must beat them—or Molly Stark is a widow tonight."—John Stark, 1777.

"There's a sucker born every minute."—P. T. Barnum.

"Where there is no vision, the people perish."—Ralph Waldo Emerson, 1863.

Cold Roast Boston

. . . TOM APPLETON * ("the first conversationalist in America," Emerson

* Thomas G. Appleton, the brother of Longfellow's wife and the son of a notable manufacturer . . . with large means and expansive tastes, was a gourmet and also a spiritualist, and a lover of purple and gold and all things edible, visible, touchable, including Persian rugs and downy sofas. A bachelor and a globe-trotter, a yachtsman and a book collector, "Tom" Appleton was the only man who could ride over Holmes and Lowell and talk them down.—Van Wyck Brooks, *New England: Indian Summer* (New York, 1940), p. 17.

testified * was famous for his "cold roast Boston," "mutual admiration society," and "good Americans when they die go to Paris"—a sentence appropriated by Holmes for his Autocrat, and still later by Wilde. . . .[1]

During the years of the Second Empire, Paris had had all the prestige. Americans had praised everything French and were rather inclined to slight everything English. . . . This was the moment of T. G. Appleton's phrase, "All good Americans, when they die, go to Paris." [2]

It was Appleton who said of the [Boston art] museum—the building replaced in 1908—that, if architecture was "frozen music," this was "frozen Yankee Doodle." [3]

Appleton said if it was true God tempers the wind [to the shorn lamb], he wished somebody would tether a shorn lamb on the steps of Park Street Church.[4]

STORIES IN BYWORDS

Better Have Paid Your Washwoman

. . . I REMEMBER that even when the danger was worst, we found room for joking and one of our men cried out, "Better have paid your washwoman!" That is the usual gibe when a man is caught in a stoven boat, for there is a belief among whalers that if you don't pay your washwoman you'll suffer the penalty of getting your boat smashed.

Boston Folks Are Full of Notions

THIS saying, now world-wide, came around in this way. The Narragansett Indians were many of them mechanics. Many are good stone masons and

* Julia Ward Howe, *Reminiscences* (Boston, 1889), p. 432.

[1] From *Amy Lowell*, by S. Foster Damon, p. 101. Copyright, 1935, by S. Foster Damon. Boston and New York: Houghton Mifflin Co.

[2] From *New England: Indian Summer, 1865–1915*, by Van Wyck Brooks, p. 286 and note. Copyright, 1940, by Van Wyck Brooks. New York: E. P. Dutton & Co., Inc.

[3] *Ibid.*, p. 164 n.

[4] From *Yankee from Olympus*, by Catherine Drinker Bowen, p. 191. Copyright, 1943, 1944, by Catherine Drinker Bowen. Boston: Little, Brown and Company.

From *The Gam*, Being a Group of Whaling Stories, by Capt. Charles Henry Robbins, Who Gratefully Acknowledges the Editorial Suggestions of his Friend, Mr. Rollin Lynde Hartt, p. 67. Copyright, 1899, by Lizzie Pope Robbins. New Bedford: H. S. Hutchinson & Company.

From "Notes on Narragansett," by Joseph P. Hazard, in *The Narragansett Historical Register*, A Magazine Devoted to the Antiquities, Genealogy and Historical Matter Illustrating the History of the Narragansett Country, or Southern Rhode Island, Vol. I (January, 1883), No. 3, edited by James N. Arnold, pp. 225–226. Entered according to Act of Congress, in the year 1882, by the Narragansett Historical Publishing Company, in the Office of the Librarian of Congress, at Washington. Hamilton, Rhode Island.

stone cutters. One whose name was pronounced "Bosum sided" was a watch maker, and after he married he set up business at Indiantown, Charlestown. He died about 1830. One was a tinker and used to make annual excursions to Boston in the spring for the purpose of plying his vocation. He went down one spring and returned after a very brief visit. He was silent as to why he did not stay longer. Another of the tribe, happening in Boston, learned that he had been caught stealing, and had been whipped at the cart's tail through the town, and a polite and emphatic invitation given him to leave, which he had thankfully received. Of course when he came home he told his story and the tribe became eager to learn the facts from the culprit himself. On being asked about it he gave no other information than "Boston folks are full of notions."

Combed With a Hatchel

. . . THE *hatchel-combs* consisted of sets of iron teeth inserted in strong boards. A bunch of flax was moistened and pulled between the teeth, in such a way that the short pieces were combed out and only the long, even fibers were left. These, in turn, were tied in *hanks* and were now ready for the flax-wheel. Hatcheling brought a pithy saying into New England conversation, for many a mother, reprimanding her tousled-haired boy, reminded him that his hair "looked as if it had been combed with a hatchel!"

Eighteen Hundred and Freeze to Death

ONE of the worst years Maine ever experienced was 1817. An unusually cold winter was followed by a backward spring, and the weather continued to be so unseasonable that the crops were failures, and the year was long afterward familiarly known as eighteen hundred and freeze to death. Thousands of discouraged farmers sold their property at a great loss and emigrated to Ohio and Kentucky. But within a few years Maine again became prosperous, and many of those who had moved away returned.

Kilroy Was Here

ON DEC. 5, 1941, I started to work for Bethlehem Steel Company, Fore River Ship Yard, Quincy, Mass., as a rate-setter. . . . I started my new

---

From *Homespun Handicrafts,* by Ella Shannon Bowles, p. 45. Copyright, 1931, by Ella Shannon Bowles. Philadelphia and London: J. B. Lippincott Company.

From *New England, A Human Interest Geographical Reader,* by Clifton Johnson, p. 362. Copyright, 1917, by The Macmillan Company. New York and London.

By James J. Kilroy, Halifax, Mass., in *The New York Times Magazine,* Jan. 12, 1947, p. 30.

job with enthusiasm, carefully surveying every inner bottom and tank before issuing a contract. I was thoroughly upset to find that practically every test leader I met wanted me to go down and look over his job with him, and when I explained to him that I had seen the job and could not spare the time to crawl through one of these tanks again with him, he would accuse me of not having looked the job over.

I was getting sick of being accused of not looking the jobs over and one day, as I came through the manhole of a tank I had just surveyed, I angrily marked with yellow crayon on the tank top, where the testers could see it, "KILROY WAS HERE." The following day a test gang leader approached me with a grin on his face and said, "I see you looked my job over."

Mind Your Orts

IN THE vocabulary of this Billerica of ours, and in secluded farming districts of New England, the casual visitor marks occasional quaint phrases now obsolete in England. At the old homestead farm on Thanksgiving day the white-haired house-mother—gentlewoman to her finger-tips—having heaped some twenty plates with turkey and "fixins," seizes the golden opportunity to inculcate a bit of thrift and table manners into the lively mind of her youngest grandson with her mother's early precept: "Look out for your *orts,* sonny, look out for your *orts,* then Grandma'll give you a piece of mince-pie!" The city boy's mother has to translate the queer word to her little son telling him that it means that the *odds and ends* left upon his plate must be duly swallowed. The expressive Yankee exclamation, "Oh dear me, suz!" is, in the original, "Oh dear me, sorrows!"

Oh, Rinehart!

"HEADS out!" was the cry in Walker's day; "Oh, Rineheart!" began later, after a student of that name had repeatedly been shouted to by noisy

---

From *Old Paths and Legends of New England,* Saunterings Over Historic Roads with Glimpses of Picturesque Fields and Old Homesteads in Massachusetts, Rhode Island, and New Hampshire, by Katharine M. Abbott, p. 123. Copyright, 1903, by Katharine M. Abbott. New York and London: G. P. Putnam's Sons. 1904.

From *Three Centuries of Harvard,* 1636–1936, by Samuel Eliot Morison, p. 300 n. Copyright, 1936, by the President and Fellows of Harvard College. Cambridge, Massachusetts. Harvard University Press.

I am indebted to Jane E. Howard, Assistant to the Editor of the *Harvard Alumni Bulletin,* for the following note on Rinehart: "Although the *Bulletin* did print a story on Rinehart, that particular card disappeared some time ago and we have been unable to trace it, even by thumbing through back volumes. At the time the story was

friends. In course of time it has become a sort of Harvard battle-cry, and the word is now used to describe any Yard uproar, in which the calling of Mr. Rineheart's undying name is an inevitable feature. The story is told that a Harvard graduate, pestered by touts in the courtyard of Shepheard's Hotel, Cairo, called "Oh, Rineheart!" and was presently answered in the same kind from four or five windows, whose occupants then helped him to disperse the beggars.

Pick Up Your Feet

A VERY common admonition from one sawyer to another in this country is, "Pick up your feet, will you?" That is probably meaningless to the uninitiate, but a good sawyer resents it very much. It means that his partner is saying that he doesn't mind riding him back and forth with every stroke of the saw, but he does consider it unnecessary to have to drag his feet along the ground, too. It's the obscure local way of telling a man he's bearing down on his end of the saw and it's an implication that he doesn't know his trade.

"Sock Saunders" Sayings

THE only stories that are told are woods gossip. Nobody ever heard of Paul Bunyan. The nearest thing to him is Sock Saunders, who is more of a poltergeist than a hero. If a man drops a picaroon into the river he says, "Well, take it, Sock Saunders!" If he slips on a log, but catches himself in time, he says, "Foxed you that time, Sock Saunders." If he cuts his foot, he explains, "Sock Saunders got me." There are no stories about Sock Saunders. He's just the guy who hangs around and make life complicated.

---

printed I made a note in my own handbook. The correct spelling is 'Rinehart.' The man for whom it was first called is John Brice Gordon Rinehart, '00, LL.B. '03, c/o Jesse Rinehart, RFD 62, Waynesburg, Pa. The [Harvard] Archives have a clipping from the Boston *Sunday Journal* of June 24, 1900, telling of the original episode. . . . We also have a clipping from the New York *Sun,* 9-24-36, naming this same man. I know at the time we made our research we verified it carefully." For a similar battle-cry of University of California students, see "Pedro! Pedro!", by Archer Taylor, *Western Folklore,* Vol. VI (July, 1947), No. 3, pp. 228–231.

From *We Took to the Woods,* by Louise Dickinson Rich, pp. 73–74. Copyright, 1942, by Louise Dickinson Rich. Philadelphia and New York: J. B. Lippincott Company.

Ibid., p. 197.

PART FIVE

SONGS AND RHYMES

There were popular ballads and folk songs . . . sailors' chanties along the coast, ballads of village murders, rockaby songs, sugar-makers' songs, sung by weavers and carpenters, by farm-wives and wandering fiddlers, by hunters, trappers, guides, and lumbermen, snatches and refrains and longer pieces, brought over from the old world or natural outgrowths of the American soil. . . . Catch a "real, green, live Yankee," as Father Taylor liked to say, and you always caught a man who could sing a song, especially on the seacoast.

—VAN WYCK BROOKS

All over New England, from Cape Cod to the Green Hills, the youngsters have kept in their singing games the craft songs and country dances of a forgotten background of the New England colonist.

—ELOISE HUBBARD LINSCOTT

. . . here are tinkling fiddle tunes that have sent thousands of merry feet dancing down the rough pioneering paths of New England—despite lurking Redskin or Puritan divine.

—JAMES M. CARPENTER

The tradition of a folk song begins when some one, for pleasure's sake, sings a song from memory . . . whoever sings a song from memory, let it be Child ballad or Tin Pan Alley ditty, it matters not, becomes a folk-singer. . . . Changes in the text and air of a ballad, often infinitesimal, but at times appreciable even to the layman, will emerge as expressions of the singer's mood for the time being. Some may be permanent, others evanescent. . . . Yet not alone of the solitary type of singer is folk song the possession. Its social aspects appear wherever a group are gathered together, conserving the elements of the primitive "folk"—congeniality, freedom from care, and light-heartedness—hunters and trappers around a camp-fire, it may be, or railway laborers in a box-car on a wet night.

—PHILLIPS BARRY

I. BALLADS AND SONGS

"I'm not what you'd call a regular singer, you know, for I never learned by book nor never saw nothin' writ down, But . . . I've allus sung just 'cause I can't help it. My father was the same way and my grandfather too. Guess you'd call us of the old school of singing."—JAMES ATWOOD to EDITH B. STURGIS

. . . here are songs to suit almost every palate: semipopular songs treasured up by past generations; comical songs; songs of the read-'em-and-weep variety; quaint old minstrels; lumbermen's songs; sea chanteys; songs with a strictly New England flavor—one can all but hear the Yankee nasal twang; and finally, a fair number of child ballads, "the aristrocrats of folk song."
—JAMES M. CARPENTER

1. YANKEE SONGS AND SINGERS

IT IS told of a Yankee singing master that he " 'set up' in a town way down east as a cobbler! On his sign, under the announcement of his profession, as a provider for the wants of the bodily understanding, was the following choice couplet, setting forth [that], as a musician, he did not neglect to provide also for the wants of the mental.

Delightful task! to mend the tender boot,
And teach the young idea how to flute!" [1]

This musical cobbler was typical of the New England singing craftsmen who worked with both hand and brain. The folk music tradition—homespun and rural—fitted into the Yankee pattern of neighborly work and useful pleasure. And wherever the Yankee went, New Englandizing the country, he carried with him, not only the little red schoolhouse and the white meeting-house, but also the old-time songs and the old-time singing that were so closely identified with them. New England psalmody and hymnody were the foundation of our musical culture. But it took the Yankee singing master to break a psalm-singing folk of the "Bay Psalm Book" rote practice of lining-out or deaconing (reading a line before singing it) and to teach rural folk everywhere the art of singing not only by rule but for enjoyment and entertainment as well as for prayer.

At first, it is true, the singing school and society set themselves sternly, with Cotton Mather, against the "foolish Songs and Ballads, which the

---

[1] Augusta Brown, Cincinnati *Musician and Intelligencer,* Vol. II (1848), No. 1, pp. 21 ff. Cited by George Pullen Jackson in *White Spirituals of the Southern Uplands* (Chapel Hill, 1933), p. 20.

Hawkers and Pedlars carry into all parts of the Countrye."[1] But it was not long before singing masters like "Father". Robert Kemp, the retired shoe-dealer of Wellfleet and organizer of the Reading Old Folks Musical Society and the Old Folks Concert Troupe, yielded to the demands of popular taste and gave ballad concerts. It was Father Kemp, too, who included in *Father Kemp's Old Folks Concert Tunes* the "devil's ditty" of "Captain Kidd," thus forging another link in the chain of ballad diffusion.

But the folk song tradition is nothing if not catholic, and there has always been much borrowing back and forth between sacred and secular music. In accordance with the realization of revivalists and hymn-writers like Wesley that "It is a pity that the Devil has all the good tunes," "Captain Kidd" became a favorite hymn tune. By the same token, the folk did not forget their hymnals when they looked for tunes for their ballads; and "Springfield Mountain" was originally sung to "Old Hundred."

Ballad concerts, in which Father Kemp had been preceded by the Hutchinson family and in which the latter had many imitators, such as the Baker family, thus became an important medium of folk song transmission along with the singing school and society; along with the despised book-peddler and his song-sheets and garlands; and along with print and performance generally. For folk song lives not by the oral tradition alone; the folk memory is preserved in carefully compiled and treasured manuscript books and newspaper-clipping scrapbooks of old songs, of which the vest-pocket songster is the commercial equivalent.

The Hutchinsons and other singing families and troupes performed another important service for New England (and American) folk song and folklore. They helped to diffuse, as well as to create, the tradition of the "Yankee song." This was the comic, fabulous, and slightly nostalgic tradition of "Away Down East"—

> a land of notions, of apple sauce and greens
> A paradise of pumpkin pies, a land of pork and beans.

"Yankee land" is our first regional myth of a land of milk and honey, just as the fabulous Yankee is our first hero-legend. And because "Yankee land" combined the Yankee zest for the good earth and its abundance (which includes the ambrosia of Narragansett corn-meal and the nectar of Maine lobster stew) with the golden age of childhood ("I wish I was in Yankee land, And was a boy again, sirs: I'd suck sweet cider thro' a straw, And fish in ev'ry rain, sirs"), and somehow got mixed up with the American "go-ahead" spirit of whittling Yankee "bo-hoys" and spinning Yankee "gals," of Yankee skill and perseverance and "Yankee manufactures," it has been basic to our whole national tradition. To Yankees up and down the land Yankee songs (sung with the "Yankee" Hill nasal twang) were like a letter from the folk back home and a letter to the world, testifying more eloquently than perhaps any other type of folk song or folklore to New England's legacy to the rest of the country, just as the old English and Scottish ballads and ballad-speech testified to the

---

[1] *Reasonableness of Regular Singing, or Singing by Note* (1720). Cited by Williard Hallam Bonner, *Pirate Laureate: the Life and Legends of Captain Kidd* (New Brunswick, 1947), p. 100; which also see (pp. 107–109) for Father Kemp.

British heritage. The tradition of a land where "the girls are pretty and the cattle very fat" also served to offset the tradition of a hard land of snow and mountains and

> the land of Blue Laws where deacons cut their hair
> For fear their locks and tenants [tenets?] will not exactly square,

(in the twitting words of "Michigania").

Curiously, the Yankee peddler does not figure prominently in Yankee songs. The song of "The Connecticut Peddler" is of the imitative street-cry variety, cataloguing the peddler's wares:

> Here are pins,
> Papers and needles and pins,
> Tracts upon popular sins,
> Any of which I will sell you.
>
> And here are the seeds of asparagus,
> Lettuce, beets, onions, and peppergrass
> From the Limited Society,
> Seeds of all kinds and variety.[1]

Somehow all this sounds bookish and spurious and un-comic. The Yankee peddler seems to have flourished not in songs but in anecdotes and yarns, perhaps because Yankee stories are at home on a journey and in the gossipy environment of the village store and tavern; and perhaps also because the cheating miller had already beat the peddler to it as the favorite folk-song rogue.

2. Songs of the Sea and the Woods

The vogue of the sea song (thanks to Charles Dibdin) had already established itself in British popular tradition before the China and India trade, whaling, the War of 1812, the packet-ship and the clipper made the Yankee and the Bostonian synonymous with sea daring and adventure and naval strength. But the Yankee gave the chantey his characteristic stamp of "wooden ships and iron men," of the humor and protest of "Boston":

> We poor sailors standing on the deck,
> With the blasted rain all a-pouring down our necks;
> Not a drop of grog would he to us afford,
> But he damns our eyes with every other word.
>
> And one thing which we have to crave
> Is that he may have a watery grave,
> So we'll heave him into some dark hole,
> Where the sharks'll have his body and the
> devil have his soul.[2]

---

[1] John A. Lomax and Alan Lomax, *American Ballads and Folk Songs* (New York, 1934), pp. 317–318.

[2] *A Treasury of American Folklore* (New York, 1944), pp. 831–832.

The sea and the War of 1812 gave us some of our best songs of freedom, like the swaggering "*Constitution* and the *Guerrière*" and "Ye Parliament of England," the latter with its ringing defiance:

Ye Parliament of England,
You lords and commons, too,
Consider well what you're about,
And what you're going to do;

You're now to fight with Yankees,
I'm sure you'll rue the day
You roused the sons of liberty
In North America.

In these two naval ballads, the Yankee sounded the two characteristic notes of his patriotic songs; the droll bravura of "Yankee Doodle" and the noble challenge of "Chester" (William Billings' song, which, according to John Tasker Howard, "became the 'Over There' of the Revolution"[1]).

The naval songs of the War of 1812 became part of the repertoire of the singing sailor as "forecastle" (recreational) songs and even of the singing lumberjack, whose songs differed from the sailor's in that they were all recreational (bunkhouse) songs. And like the sailor in his forecastle songs, the shanty-boy derived many of his tunes from Irish-come-all-ye's, which suited the double common metre of his verse.

As the shanty-boy followed the lumber industry, his songs traveled from Maine to the Northwest, with resultant changes, adaptations, and additions paralleling the development of imported English and Irish songs. So the history of the Yankee's western migration may be traced in his song history. In New Englandizing the country the Yankee Americanized his songs.

B. A. B.

OLD AND NEW ENGLAND

Cape Ann

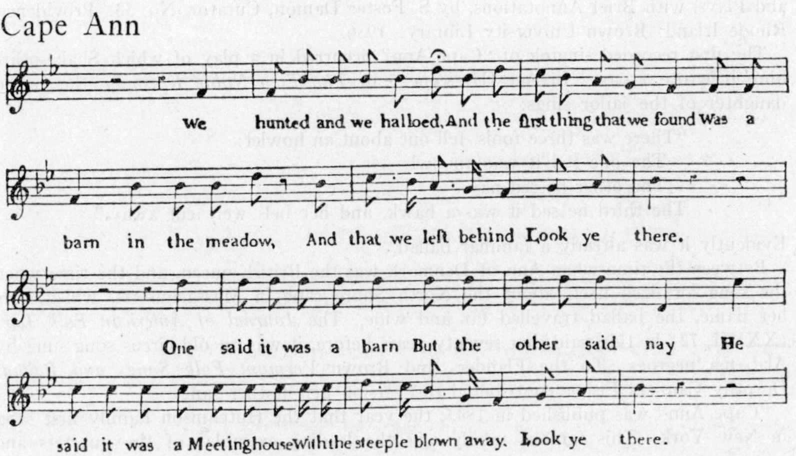
We hunted and we halloed. And the first thing that we found Was a
barn in the meadow, And that we left behind Look ye there.
One said it was a barn But the other said nay He
said it was a Meetinghouse With the steeple blown away. Look ye there.

[1] *Our American Music* (New York, 1931), p. 50.

From *Songs of the Hutchinson Family*, No. 4. New York: Published by Firth & Hall

We hunted and we halloed,
And the first thing that we found,
Was a barn in the meadow,
And that we left behind.
  Look ye there!
One said it was a barn,
But the other said nay;
He said it was a Meetinghouse,
With the steeple blown away.
  Look ye there!

So we hunted and we halloed,
And the next thing we did find,
Was the Moon in the element,
And that we left behind.
  Look ye there!
One said it was the Moon,
But the other said nay;
He said it was a Yankee cheese,
With the one half cut away.
  Look ye there!

So we hunted and we halloed,
And the next thing we did find,
Was a frog in the Mill pond;
And that we left behind.
  Look ye there!
One said it was a frog,
But the other said nay;
He said it was a canary bird,
With its feathers washed away.
  Look ye there!

So we hunted and we halloed,
And the next thing we did find,
Was the light house in Cape Ann;
And that we left behind.
  Look ye there!
One said it was the light house,
But the other said nay,
He said it was a sugar loaf;
With the paper blown away.
  Look ye there!

So we hunted and we halloed,
And the last thing we did find,
Was the owl in the olive bush;
And that we left behind.
  Look ye there!
One said it was an owl,
But the other said nay,
He said it was the Evil One;
And we all three ran away.
  Look ye there!

---

and J. L. Hewitt & Co. [1843.] In *Series of Old American Songs,* Reproduced in Facsimile from Original or Early Editions in the Harris Collection of American Poetry and Plays, with Brief Annotations, by S. Foster Damon, Curator, No. 33. Providence, Rhode Island: Brown University Library. 1936.

The first recorded singing of "Cape Ann" occurred in a play of which Shakespeare himself wrote a part. In Act III, scene 5 of *The Two Noble Kinsman,* the crazed daughter of the jailor sings:

> "There was three fools, fell out about an howlet:
> The one sed it was an owl
> The other he sed nay,
> The third he sed it was a hawk, and her bels were cut away."

Evidently it was already a familiar ballad.

Between the time when Ann of Denmark was the British queen, and the time when the song localized itself about the North Shore cape in Massachusetts, which bore her name, the ballad travelled far and wide. The *Journal of American Folk Lore* (XXVII, 72) in 1908 said that seventy years before, it was an old circus song sung by Alabama negroes. To the Flanders and Brown *Vermont Folk Songs and Ballads* Dorothy Canfield Fisher contributed the version her mother sang.

"Cape Ann" was published in 1843, the year that the Hutchinson Family first sang in New York. This famous family was the leading exemplar of the quartets and quintets that soon were touring the States. Revivers of ballads and composers, as well as vocalists, they did much to spread Yankee culture.—S. F. D.

Old Colony Times

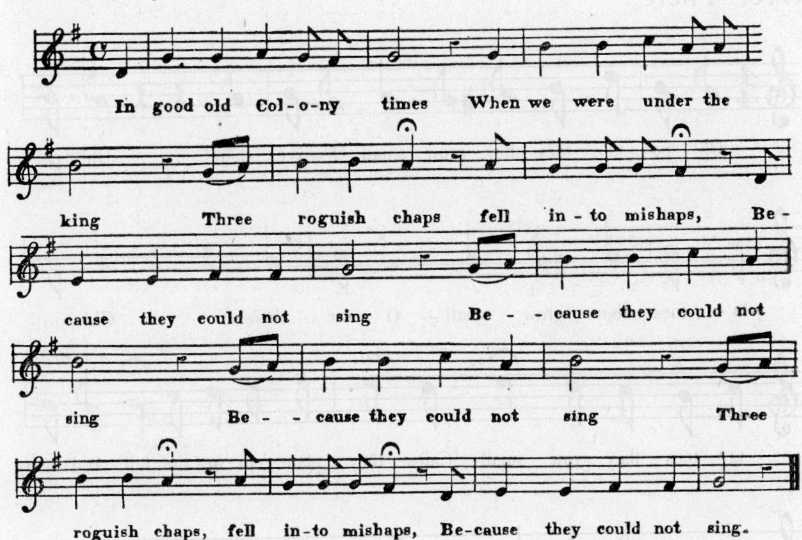
In good old Col-o-ny times When we were under the
king Three roguish chaps fell in-to mishaps, Because they could not sing Be- -cause they could not
sing Be- -cause they could not sing Three
roguish chaps, fell in-to mishaps, Be-cause they could not sing.

In good old Colony times,
When we were under the king,
Three roguish chaps fell into mishaps,
Because they could not sing,
Because they could not sing,
Because they could not sing.
Three roguish chaps, fell into mishaps,
Because they could not sing.

The first he was a Miller,
And the second he was a Weaver,
And the third he was, a little Tailor,
Three roguish chaps together.

Now the Miller he stole corn,
And the Weaver he stole yarn,
And the little Tailor, stole broadcloth for,
To keep these three rogues warm.

The Miller got drown'd in his dam,
The Weaver got hung in his yarn,
And the devil clapp'd his claw on the little Tailor,
With the broadcloth under his arm.

Boston: Published by Parker & Ditson. In *Series of Old American Songs,* Reproduced in Facsimile from Original or Early Editions in the Harris Collection of American Poetry and Plays, with Brief Annotations, by S. Foster Damon, Curator, No. 6. Providence, Rhode Island: Brown University Library. 1936.

This ballad may have preceded even the first attempts at colonization in our country; but the opening lines of this version, sung from Maine to Georgia, and at least as far west as Nebraska, were probably shaped about 1800, when "old colony times" began to seem very remote.

When John Lothrop Motley studied at Göttingen in 1832, he taught this song, one of his favorites, to his fellow student, Bismarck. Over fifty years later, in a speech before the Reichstag on February 6, 1888, Bismarck quoted "Old Colony Times," which he had learned from his "dear deceased friend," Motley. (Orie William Long: *Literary Pioneers,* Cambridge, 1935). This song is sung by the archbishop in Agnes Repplier's *In Our Convent Days;* and in Hardy's *Under the Greenwood Tree* (Pt. IV, ch. 2) it is also to be found, beginning, however, "When Arthur first his court began."

Over There

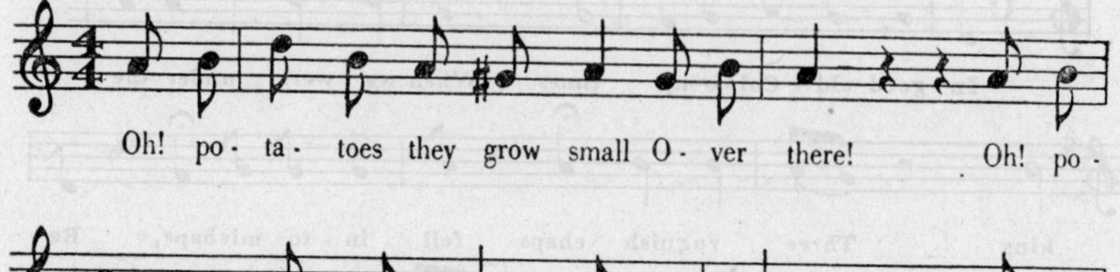
Oh! po - ta - toes they grow small O - ver there! Oh! po -

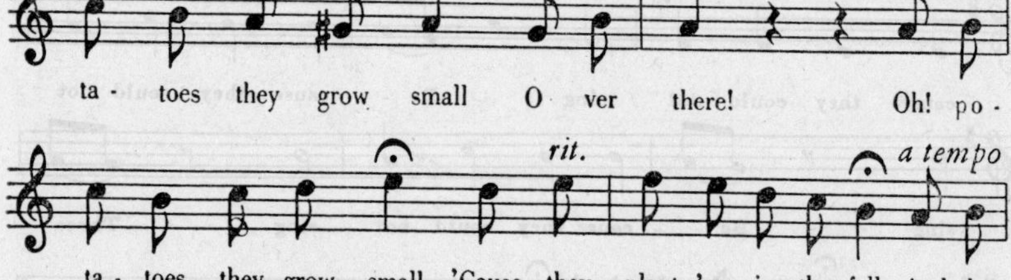
ta - toes they grow small O - ver there! Oh! po -
rit.
a tempo
ta - toes they grow small 'Cause they plant 'em in the fall, And then

eats 'em tops and all O - ver there.

Oh! potatoes they grow small
  Over there!
Oh! potatoes they grow small
  Over there!
Oh! potatoes they grow small,
'Cause they plant 'em in the fall,
And then eats 'em tops and all
  Over there!

Oh! the candles they are small
  Over there!
Oh! the candles they are small
  Over there!
Oh! the candles they are small,
For they dips 'em lean and tall,
And then burns 'em sticks and all,
  Over there!

Where sheep were raised, the "miller" ran a carding mill (see Flanders & Brown's *Vermont Folk Songs,* "The Farmer's Three Sons"). In the colleges, the tune was once much used for less familiar texts (*Journal Am. Folk-Lore,* XXIX, 167; see also XXXV, 350; XLV, 47).—S. F. D.

From *In Old New England,* The Romance of a Colonial Fireside, by Hezekiah Butterworth, pp. 233–234. Copyright, 1895, by D. Appleton and Company. New York. Tune from *"The Wonderful Song of Over There,"* Entered according to Act of Congress in the Year 1844, by J. F. Atwill in the Clerk's Office of the Southern District of New York, in *Series of Old American Songs,* Reproduced in Facsimile from Original or Early Editions in the Harris Collection of American Poetry and Plays, with Brief Annotations, by S. Foster Damon, Curator, No. 42. Providence, Rhode Island: Brown University Library. 1936.

This "wonderful song" is the prototype of "The Cows Fly High" and many another fantasia. How it originated remains a mystery as yet. It will be noted that the tune is not the insidious "Captain Kyd," which has come to replace it too often.—S. F. D.

Oh! I wish I was a geese,
All forlorn!
Oh! I wish I was a geese,
All forlorn!
Oh! I wish I was a geese,
'Cause they lives and dies in peace,
And accumulates much grease
Eating corn!

Oh! they had a clam pie
Over there!
Oh! they had a clam pie
Over there!
Oh! they had a clam pie,
And the crust was made of rye—
You must eat it, or must die,
Over there!

Away Down East

There's a fam-ous fab-led coun-try nev-er seen by mor-tal

eyes, Where the pump-kins aye are grow-ing and the sun is said to

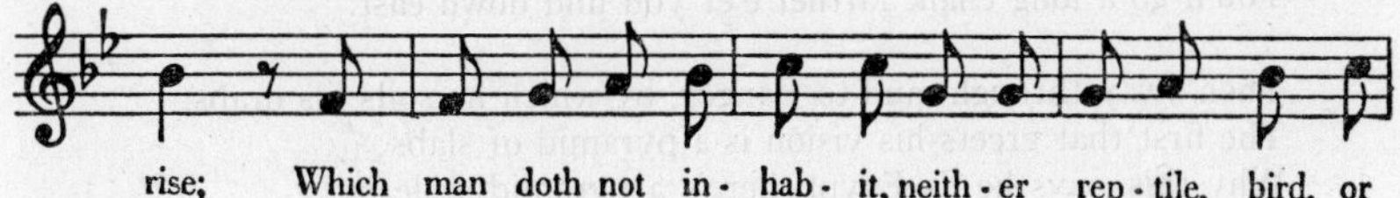
rise; Which man doth not in-hab-it, neith-er rep-tile, bird, or

beast, And this fam-ous fab-led coun-try is a-way down east.

From *Songs of Yesterday*, A Song Anthology of American Life, by Philip D. Jordan and Lillian Kessler, pp. 185–188. Copyright, 1941, by Philip D. Jordan and Lillian Kessler. Garden City, New York: Doubleday, Doran & Co., Inc.

"Down east" is variously interpreted as New England, eastern or northeastern New England, Maine, the easternmost part of Maine, Nova Scotia, and New Brunswick. The following comment is almost a paraphrase of the song:

"The first-comers into New England waters were not more puzzled to find the ancient city of Norumbega than I to reach the fabulous Down East of the moderns. In San Francisco the name is vaguely applied to the territory east of the Mississippi, though more frequently the rest of the republic is alluded to as 'The States.' South of the obliterated Mason and Dixon's line, the region east of the Alleghanies and north of the Potomac is Down East, and no mistake about it. In New York you are as far as ever from this *terra incognita.* In Connecticut they shrug their shoulders and point you about north-north-east. Down East, say Massachusetts people, is just across our eastern border. Arrived on the Penobscot, I fancied myself there at last.

'Whither bound?' I asked of a fisherman, getting up his foresail before loosing from the wharf.

There's a famous fabled country never seen by mortal eyes,
Where the pumpkins aye are growing and the sun is said to rise;
Which man doth not inhabit, neither reptile, bird, or beast,
And this famous fabled country is away down[1] east.

It is called a land of notions, of apple sauce and greens,
A paradise of pumpkin pies, a land of pork and beans;
But where it is, who knoweth? neither mortal man nor beast,
But one thing we're assured of 'tis away down east.

Once a man in Indiana took his bundle in his hand,
And he came to New York city to seek this fabled land;
But how he stares on learning what is new to him at least
That this famous fabled country is farther down east.

Then away he posts for Boston with all his main and might,
And he puts up at the Tremont house, quite sure that all is right;
But they tell him in the morning a curious fact at least,
That he hasn't yet begun to get away down east.

Then he hurries off to Portland with his bundle in his hand,
And he sees Mount-joy, great joy for him for this must be the land;
Poh, nonsense, man, you're crazy, for doubt not in the least,
You'll go a long chalk farther e'er you find down east.

Then away through mud to Bangor, by which he soils his drabs,
The first that greets his vision is a pyramid of slabs;
Why this, says he, is Egypt, here's a pyramid at least,
And he thought that with a vengeance he has found down east.

My gracious, yes, he's found it, see how he cuts his pranks,
He's sure he can't get farther for the piles of boards and planks;
So pompously he questions a Pat of humble caste
Who tells him he was never yet away down east.

But soon he spies a native who was up to snuff I ween,
Who pointing o'er a precipice says don't you see something green.
Then off he jump'd to rise no more except he lives on yeast,
And this I think should be his drink away down east.

'Sir, to you. Down East.'

The evident determination to shift the responsibility forbade further pursuit of this fictitious land. Besides, Maine people are indisposed to accept without challenge the name so universally applied to them of Down Easters. We do not say down to the North Pole, and we do say down South. The higher latitude we make northwardly the farther down we get. Nevertheless, disposed as I avow myself to present the case fairly, the people of Maine uniformly say 'up to the westward,' when speaking of Massachusetts. Of one thing I am persuaded—Down East is nowhere in New England." (Samuel Adams Drake, *Nooks and Corners of the New England Coast,* New York, 1875, pp. 85–86.)

[1] Sometimes pronounced daown.—P. D. J.

And now his anxious mother, whose tears will ever run,
Is ever on the look out to see her rising son;
But she may strain her eyes in vain, I calculate at least,
Her son has set in regions wet away down east.

Yankee Manufactures

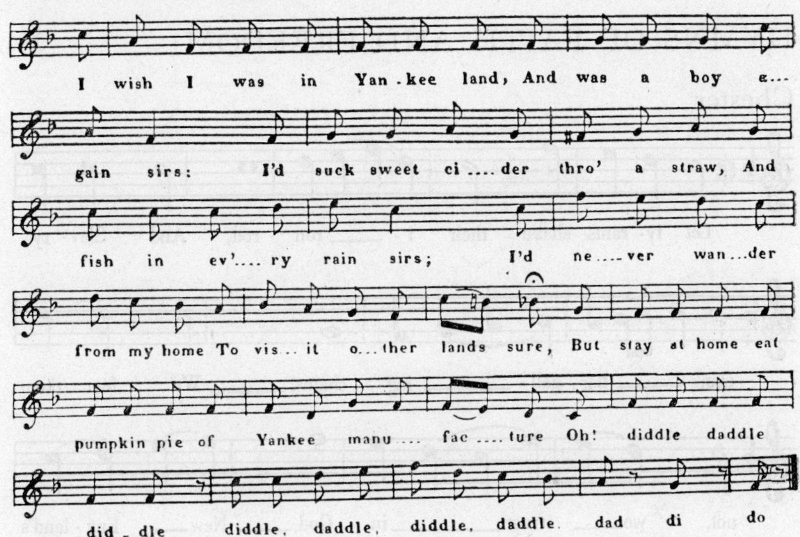

I wish I was in Yankee land,
And was a boy again, sirs:
I'd suck sweet cider thro' a straw,
And fish in ev'ry rain, sirs.
I'd never wander from my home
To visit other lands, sure,
But stay at home, eat pumpkin pie
Of Yankee manufacture.

Chorus:
Oh, diddle, daddle, diddle,
Diddle, daddle, diddle, daddle,
Dad di do.

The people there all go ahead,
They never turn about, sirs,
And when the bo-hoys go on a spree,
Their Mammies know they're out, sirs.

The gals can read and write and spin,
Are modest, chaste, and fair, sure.
No other land has got such gals
As of Yankee manufacture.

I love the Yankees for their skill,
Their perseverance too, sirs.
Their railroads and their telegraphs,
Show what their sons can do, sirs;
And Oregon, like Texas,
The Yankees they will have, sure,
Or Johnny Bull will get some pills,
Of Yankee manufacture.

Now Johnny Bull a lesson got,
Which I hope he has not forgotten,
For Jackson brave at New Orleans
Showed him the use of Yankee cotton.

Ibid., pp. 192–194.

Their Packenham he did brag,
And his army they did blow, sure,
But British balls could not penetrate,
The walls of Yankee manufacture.

There is a spot near Boston town,
They call it Bunker Hill, sir,
Where Johnny Bull with Yankee lead,
Did get his stomach filled, sir.
'Twas there brave General Warren fell,
In freedom's glorious cause, sure,
Yet we had left Great Washington,
Who was of Yankee manufacture.

HYMNS OF FAITH AND FREEDOM

Chester

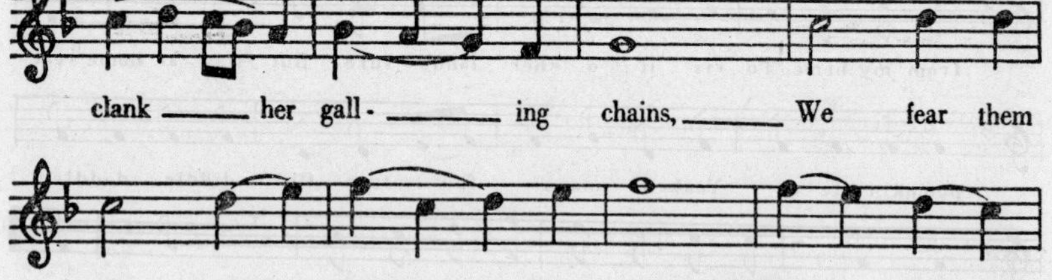

Let tyrants shake their iron rod,
And Slav'ry clank her galling chains,
We fear them not, we trust in God,
New England's God for ever reigns.

Howe and Burgoyne and Clinton, too,
With Prescott and Cornwallis join'd,
Together plot our overthrow,
In one Infernal league combin'd.

When God inspir'd us for the fight,
Their ranks were broke, their lines were forc'd,
Their Ships were shatter'd in our sight,
Or swiftly driven from our Coast.

The Foe comes on with haughty Stride,
Our troops advance with martial noise

From *The Singing Master's Assistant: or Key to Practical Music:* Being an abridgment from "The New England-Psalm Singer," together with several other tunes never before published, composed by William Billings, author of "The New-England Psalm-Singer," p. 12. Boston: Draper and Folsom. 1778.

Their Vet'rans flee before our Youth,
And Gen'rals yield to beardless Boys.

What grateful Off'ring shall we bring,
What shall we render to the Lord?
Loud Hallelujahs let us Sing,
And praise his name on ev'ry Chord.

Free America

That seat of science, Athens,
And earth's proud mistress, Rome;
Where now are all their glories?
We scarce can find a tomb.
Then guard your rights, Americans,
Nor stoop to lawless sway,
Oppose, oppose, oppose,
For North America.

We led fair Franklin hither,
And, lo! the desert smiled;
A paradise of pleasure
Was opened to the world!
Your harvest, bold Americans,
No power shall snatch away!
Huzza, huzza, huzza,
For free America.

From *Heart Songs,* Dear to the American People and by Them Contributed in the Search for Treasured Songs Initiated by the *National Magazine*, pp. 44–45. Copyright, 1909, by The Chapple Publishing Company, Ltd. Boston.

By voice, sword and pen, Joseph Warren contributed to the cause of Independence. In 1772 and 1775, he delivered orations on the Boston Massacre. During the delivery of the second oration, the British soldiery lined the pulpit stairs, but nevertheless it

Torn from a world of tyrants,
  Beneath this western sky,
We formed a new dominion,
  A land of liberty.
The world shall own we're masters here;
  Then hasten on the day:
Huzza, huzza, huzza,
  For free America.

Proud Albion bowed to Caesar,
  And numerous lords before;
To Picts, to Danes, to Normans,
  And many masters more;
But we can boast, Americans,
  We've never fallen a prey;
Huzza, huzza, huzza,
  For free America.

God bless this maiden climate,
  And through its vast domain
May hosts of heroes cluster,
  Who scorn to wear a chain:
And blast the venal sycophant
  That dares our rights betray;
Huzza, huzza, huzza,
  For free America.

Lift up your heads, ye heroes,
  And swear with proud disdain
The wretch that would ensnare you
  Shall lay his snares in vain;
Should Europe empty all her force,
  We'll meet her in array,
And fight and shout, and fight
  For free America.

Some future day shall crown us
  The masters of the main.
Our fleets shall speak in thunder
  To England, France and Spain;
And the nations o'er the oceans spread
  Shall tremble and obey
The sons, the sons, the sons,
  Of brave America.

Ballad of the Tea Party

Tea-ships near to Boston lying,
  On the wharf a numerous crew,
Sons of Freedom, never dying,
  Then appeared in view!
With a rinktum, dinktum, fa la linktum,
  Then appeared in view!

Armed with hammers, axes, chisels,
  Weapons new for warlike deed,
Toward the taxéd, freighted vessels,
  On they came with speed.

Deep into the sea descended
  Curséd weed of China's coast,
Thus at once our fears were ended,
  Rights shall ne'er be lost!

---

was pronounced in defiance of their threats. Not long, it is thought, before his lamented death, he wrote the above ballad.—Joe Mitchell Chapple.

The tune is that of "The British Grenadiers" (16th century).

From *Early American Ballads,* sung by John and Lucy Allison, with Chorus, Keynote Album K-102, Record 535-B, 1. New York: Keynote Recordings, Inc. Leaflet Copyright, 1943, by Keynote Recordings, Inc. Transcribed by Frances Kurland.

Colonial folk turned out many jingles commemorating the so-called Boston Tea Party. This one truly belonged to the people.—J. A.

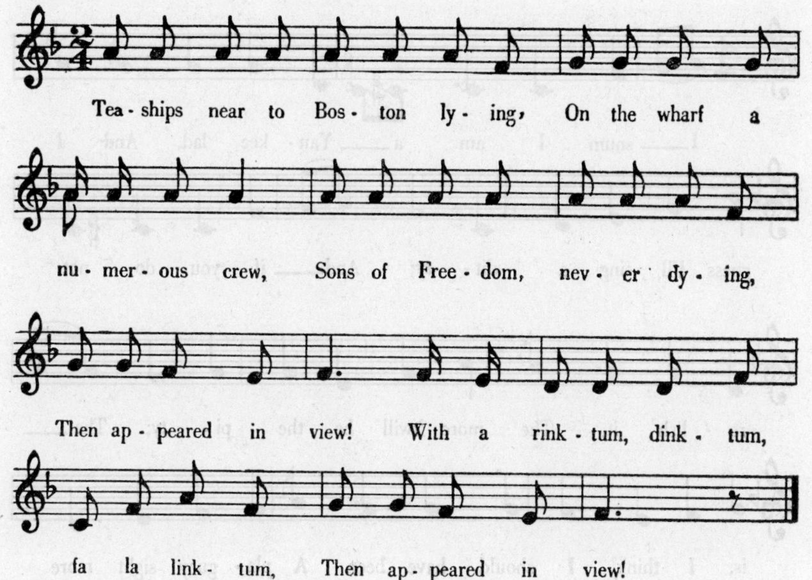
Tea - ships near to Bos - ton ly - ing, On the wharf a
nu - mer - ous crew, Sons of Free - dom, nev - er dy - ing,
Then ap - peared in view! With a rink - tum, dink - tum,
fa la link - tum, Then ap - peared in view!

The Boston Tea Tax

I snum [1] I am a Yankee lad,
  And I guess I'll sing a ditty;
And if you do not relish it,
  There more 'twill be the pity;
That is, I think I should have been
  A plaguey sight more finished man
If I'd been born in Boston town,
  But I warn't 'cause I'm a country-
    man.
Tol-le-lol-de-riddle, tol-le-lol-de-ray,
  But I warn't 'cause I'm a country-
    man.

And t'other day the Yankee folks
  Were mad about the taxes,
And so we went like Injuns dressed
  To split tea chests with axes.
It was the year of seventy-three,
  And we felt really gritty.
The Mayor he would have led the
    gang,
  But Boston warn't a city!

[You see we Yankees didn't care
  A pin for wealth or booty,

From *Ballads of the American Revolution and the War of 1812,* A Program of Early American Songs Taken from the Collection of John Allison, sung by John and Lucy Allison with Sawyer's Minuteman, Victor Album P-11, Record 26458-B, 2. Camden, New Jersey: RCA Victor Division, RCA Manufacturing Company, Inc. Transcribed by Frances Kurland.

Written "in the style of a Yankee colonial wit," this song dates from the 1830's.

Cf. George Stuyvesant Jackson, *Early Songs of Uncle Sam* (Boston, 1933), p. 46: Any character who said "tarnal," "snum," and "plaguey" was a true blue Yankee.

The words of this song have been set by Mr. Allison to a traditional tune. The additional stanzas (in brackets) are from Burton L. Stevenson's *Poems of American History* (Boston, 1908).

[1] Swear, declare, vow; *vum, swow, swan.*—Harold Wentworth, *American Dialect Dictionary* (New York, 1944), p. 575.

I—— snum I am a—— Yan-kee lad, And I
guess I'll sing a dit-ty; And—— if you do not
re-lish it, The more 'twill be the pi-ty; That——
is, I think I should have been A pla-guey sight more
rit.
fin-ished man If—— I'd been born in Bos-ton town, But I
warn't 'cause I'm a coun-try-man. Tol-le-lol-de-rid-dle, Tol-le-
lol-de-ray, But I warn't 'cause I'm a coun-try-man.

And so in State Street we agreed
  We'd never pay the duty;
That is, in State Street 'twould have
  been,
  But 'twas King Street they called it
  then,
And tax on tea, it was so bad,
  The women wouldn't scald it then.
Tol-le-lol, etc.

To Charleston Bridge we all went
  down
  To see the thing corrected;
That is, we would have gone there,
  But the bridge it warn't erected.
The tea perhaps was very good,
  Bohea, Souchong, or Hyson,
But drinking tea it warn't the rage,
  The duty made it poison.
Tol-le-lol, etc.]

And then aboard the ships we went
  Our vengeance to administer,
And we didn't care one tarnal bit
  For any king or minister.
We made a plaguey mess of tea
  In one of the biggest dishes;
I mean we steeped it in the sea
  And treated all the fishes.
Tol-le-lol, etc.

[And then you see we were all found out,
  A thing we hadn't dreaded.
The leaders were to London sent
  And instantly beheaded;
That is, I mean they would have been
  If ever they'd been taken.
But the leaders they were never cotch'd,
  And so they saved their bacon.
Tol-le-lol, etc.

Now heaven bless the president
  And all this goodly nation.
And doubly bless our Boston mayor
  And all the corporation;
And may all those who are our foes,
  Or at our praise have falter'd,
Soon have a change—that is, I mean
  May all of them get halter'd.
Tol-le-lol, etc.]

The Ballad of Bunker Hill

The soldiers from town to the foot of the hill,
  In barges and rowboats, some great and some small,
They pottered and dawdled and twaddled until
  We feared there would be no attack after all.
Let the foeman draw nigh till the white of his eye
Comes in range with your rifles, and then let it fly,
And show to Columbia, to Britain and fame,
How justice smiles aweful when freemen take aim!

The redcoats were ready and all came along,
  The way they marched up the hillside wasn't slow;
We were not a-feared and we welcomed 'em strong,
  Held fire till the word and then laid the lads low.
But who shall declare the end of the affair?
At sundown there wasn't a man of us there;
We didn't depart till we'd given 'em some,
We used up our powder and had to go home!

Ibid., Record 26460-A, 1. Transcribed by Frances Kurland.

On a bright sunny day in June, 1775, three thousand Redcoats were advancing in parade formation up Bunker and Breed's hills to "rout out the peasants." Commanded by General Howe, they came forward steadily, but were met by so terrific a fire that they gave way, retreating in disorder.

Charlestown was set ablaze by cannon fire from the British fleet, and a second time the Redcoats advanced to be driven back. After the third assault, their last charge of powder and ball being spent, the Americans were forced to "go home" as the ballad depicts it, while the battle proved an expensive victory for the British.—J. A.

The words of this song have been set by Mr. Allison to a traditional tune.

Attributed to Edward Everett Hale by Burton L. Stevenson, *Poems of American History* (Boston, 1908), p. 162.

The sol- diers from town to the foot of the hill, In
bar- ges and row- boats, some great and some small, They
pot- tered and daw- dled and twad- dled un- til We
feared there would be no at- tack af- ter all. Let the
foe- man draw nigh till the white of his eye Comes in
range with your ri- fles, and then let it fly, And
show to Co lum- bia, to Bri- tain and fame, How
jus- tice smiles awe- ful when free- men take aim!

Riflemen's Song at Bennington

Why come ye hith - er, Red - coats? Your mind what mad - ness
fills? In our val - leys there is dan - ger, And there's
dan - ger on our hills! Oh, hear ye not the
sing - ing Of the bug - le wild and free? Full
soon ye'll know the ring - ing Of the rif - le from the
tree! For the rif - le (clap, clap, clap, clap, clap) – the
rif - le (clap, clap, clap, clap) In our hands will prove no trif - le!

Ibid., Record 26460-B, 2. Transcribed by Frances Kurland.

When "Gentleman Johnny" Burgoyne advanced on the colonies from Canada, he sent a foraging detachment with a view to raiding the village of Bennington, Vermont, where the Americans had collected horses and stores.

As news of the approaching raiders reached the town, Colonel John Stark organized eight hundred yeomen from the locality. Making their way through a driving rain, "Old Man Stark's Boys" set out to meet the enemy. [On August 16, 1777] Burgoyne's detachment was surrounded on all sides, and within two hours his men were either

Why come ye hither, Redcoats?
Your mind what madness fills?
In our valleys there is danger,
And there is danger on our hills!
Oh, hear ye not the singing
Of the bugle wild and free?
Full soon ye'll know the ringing
Of the rifle from the tree!
For the rifle (clap, clap, clap, clap, clap)—the rifle (clap, clap, clap, clap)
In our hands will prove no trifle!

Ye ride a goodly steed;
Ye may know another master.
Ye forward come with speed,
But ye'll learn to back much faster,
When ye meet our mountain boys
And their leader, Johnny Stark!
Lads who make but little noise,
Lads who always hit the mark!

Had ye no graves at home
Across the briny water
That hither ye must come
Like bullocks to the slaughter?
If we the work must do,
Why, the sooner 'tis begun,
If flint and trigger hold but true,
The quicker 'twill be done.

The *Constitution* and the *Guerrière*

I often have been told
That the British seamen bold
Could beat the tars of France neat and handy, oh!
But they never found their match
Till the Yankees did them catch,
For the Yankee boys at fighting are the dandy, oh!

Chorus:
With a heave ho
And a hey away!

Now the *Guerrière* so bold
On the foaming ocean rolled,
Commanded by Dacres, the grandee, oh!
With a choice of British crew [1]
As a rammer ever drew,
They could beat the French two to one so handy, oh!

---

killed or captured. The buoyant "Riflemen's Song at Bennington," of unknown authorship, depicts the sturdy spirit of the time and place.—J. A.

The words of this song have been set by Mr. Allison to a traditional tune.

Ibid., Record 26462-A, 1. Transcribed by Frances Kurland.

The bragging ballad, "The *Constitution* and the *Guerrière*," is known also by old sailormen as a sea-chanty. The melody is an alteration of the ancient English drinking-song, "A Good Old Glass of Brandy, Oh."—J. A.

This famous single-ship engagement took place on August 19, 1812, off the coast of Nova Scotia. Captain Isaac Hull, commanding the *Constitution,* 44 guns, had sailed from Boston without orders, in the hope of meeting some of the British frigates reported off the coast. In twenty-five minutes the *Guerrière,* 38 guns, Captain R. Dacres, was reduced to a perfect wreck, 78 of her crew being killed and wounded. The *Constitution* had only 7 killed and 7 wounded.—Robert W. Neeser, *American Naval Songs & Ballads* (New Haven, 1938), p. 95 n.

[1] As choice a British crew.

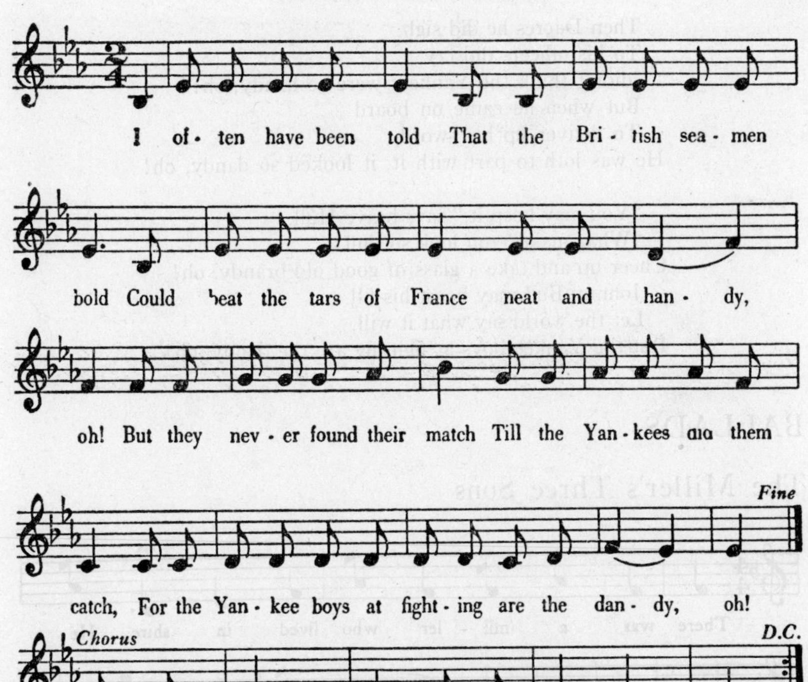
I of - ten have been told That the Bri - tish sea - men
bold Could beat the tars of France neat and han - dy,
oh! But they nev - er found their match Till the Yan - kees did them
Fine
catch, For the Yan - kee boys at fight - ing are the dan - dy, oh!
Chorus
D.C.
With a heave ho And a hey a - way!

This boasting Briton cries,
"Make that Yankee ship your prize,
You can in thirty minutes do it handy, oh!
Or in twenty-five, I'm sure—
If you'll do it in a score,
I will give to you a double share of brandy, oh!"

Cries Hull unto his crew,
"We will try what we can do,
And if we beat the Britons, we're the dandy, oh!"
With that our cannon roared,
Brought the mizzen by the board,
Which doused the royal ensign very handy, oh!

Our gunners aimed so well
That the fore and mainmast fell,
Which made this royal frigate look abandoned, oh!
Dacres says, "We're undone,"
And he fires a lee gun.
Our drummer struck up Yankee Doodle Dandy, oh!

Then Dacres he did sigh,
To his officers did cry,
"I didn't think the Yankees were so handy, oh!"
But when he came on board
To deliver up his sword,
He was loth to part with it, it looked so dandy, oh!

"You may keep it," says brave Hull.
"What makes you look so dull?
Cheer up and take a glass of good old brandy, oh!
Johnny Bull may boast his fill,
Let the world say what it will,
But the Yankee boys at fighting are the dandy, oh!

BALLADS

The Miller's Three Sons

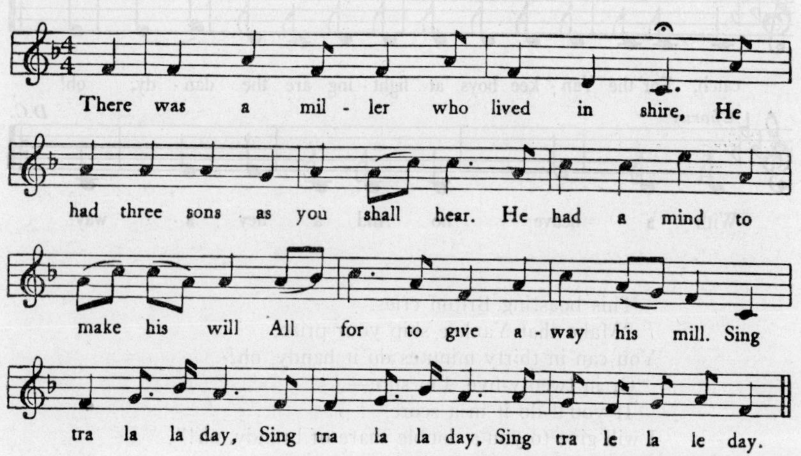
There was a mil - ler who lived in shire, He
had three sons as you shall hear. He had a mind to
make his will All for to give a - way his mill. Sing
tra la la day, Sing tra la la day, Sing tra le la le day.

From *The New Green Mountain Songster,* Traditional Folk Songs of Vermont, Collected, Transcribed, and Edited by Helen Hartness Flanders, Elizabeth Flanders Ballard, George Brown, and Phillips Barry, pp. 11–13. Copyright, 1939, by Helen Hartness Flanders. New Haven: Yale University Press; London: Oxford University Press.

From Mrs. Florence Waters, Brattleboro, Vermont, as sung by her cousin. Mr. Henry Leland, Brownington, Vermont. Melody recorded on the dictaphone by H. H. F. Transcribed by Miss Marguerite Olney.

"Beginning with fibbing but coming speedily to downright lying and peculation, stealing corn from sacks and yielding short measure of adulterated flour, the millers in all ages were accused of licentious freedom or betrayal toward the superabundant sex, and too frequently resorted to murder" (Ebsworth, *Roxburghe Ballads,* VIII, 610).

There was a miller who lived in shire,
He had three sons as you shall hear.
He had a mind to make his will
All for to give away his mill.

Chorus:
Sing tra la la day,
Sing tra la la day,
Sing tra le la le day.

The old man called his oldest son,
Saying, "My son, my glass is run,
And if to you my will I'll make,
Come tell me how much toll you'll take."

"Father, O father, my name is Dick,
From every bushel I'll take one peck,
From every bushel that I grind,
That I may a good living find."

"You are a fool," the old man said,
"You have not learned the miller's trade.
The mill to you I'll never give,
For by such toll no man can live."

The old man called his second son,
Saying, "My son, my glass is run,
And if to you my will I'll make,
Come tell me how much toll you'll take."

"Father, O father, my name is Ralph,
From every bushel I'll take one half,
From every bushel that I grind,
That I may a good living find."

"You are a fool," the old man said,
"You have not learned the miller's trade.
My mill to you I'll never give,
For by such toll no man can live."

The old man called his youngest son,
Saying, "My son, my glass is run.
And if to you my will I'll make,
Come tell me how much toll you'll take."

"Father, O father, I'm your bonnie boy,
And stealing corn is all my joy,
And if I should a living lack,
I'll take the whole and steal the sack."

"The mill is yours," the old man said,
"You have learned the miller's trade.
The mill is yours," the old man cried,
And closed his sinful eyes and died.

"The Miller's Advice to his Three Sons, in Taking of Toll," to quote the title from a London broadside of *ca.* 1730 reprinted by Ebsworth (*op. cit.*, p. 611), is the oldest, perhaps the original, version of our ballad. There is a ring of reality to the story; we very much suspect the knavish miller was a real person. Probably the song came to this country at an early date; a text printed by Newell, *Games and Songs of American Children* (2d ed., pp. 103–104), locates him in Gosport, presumably the English town of that name. Be that as it may, a closely similar text, sung by an old Shoaler, is printed in Celia Thaxter's *Among the Isles of Shoals*, pp. 81–82. One of the early settlements on the Shoals, now abandoned, was named Gosport.

The ballad is known from both Northern and Southern tradition: Ohio (*JAFL*, XXXV, 391); West Virginia (Cox, *Folk Songs of the South*, pp. 450–454); Kentucky and North Carolina (Sharp, Karpeles, *English Folk Songs from the Southern Appalachians*, II, 221–223). Ebsworth quotes from the broadside: "Tune of the Oxfordshire Tragedy" (cf. Chappell, *Popular Music of the Olden Time*, I, 191). The Ohio melody and the three from the South, printed by Cox and Sharp, Karpeles, are all sets of a single air.—P. B.

Mary of the Wild Moor

One night when the wind it blew cold, Blew bit - ter a - cross the wild
moor, Young Ma - ry she came with her child
Wan - d'ring home to her own fa - ther's door, Say-ing,
"Fa - ther, O pray let me in! Have pit - y on
me, I im - plore; Or the child on my bo - som will
Fine
die From the winds that blow 'cross the wild moor!"

One night when the wind it blew cold,
  Blew bitter across the wild moor,
Young Mary she came with her child
  Wand'ring home to her own father's door,
Saying, "Father, O pray let me in!
  Have pity on me, I implore;
Or the child on my bosom will die
  From the winds that blow 'cross the wild moor!

"O why did I leave my lone cot,
  Where once I was happy and free?
Doomed to roam without friends or a home,
  O, Father, have pity on me!"

But her father was deaf to her cry;
  Not a voice nor a sound reached his ear.
But the watchdog did howl and the village bell tolled
  From the winds that blew 'cross the wild moor.

O what must the father have felt
  When he came to the door in the morn?
There he found Mary dead and her child
  Fondly clasped in its dead mother's arms.

From *Songs from the Hills of Vermont*, Sung by James and Mary Atwood and Aunt Jenny Knapp, Texts Collected and Edited by Edith B. Sturgis, Tunes Collected and Piano Accompaniments Arranged with Historical Notes by Robert Hughes, pp. 36–39. Copyright, 1919, by G. Schirmer, Inc. New York.

"Mary of the Wild Moor" (sung by Mary Atwood), evidently a very popular ballad, has been published with quite a different tune in Barrett's *English Folksongs* (p. 76) and in Kidson's *Traditional Tunes* (p. 77). A version with a tune similar to the present one is found in Helen K. Johnson's *Our Familiar Songs* (pp. 303–304). See also *The Journal of American Folklore*, vol. xxvi, p. 355; and vol. xxix, p. 185. The song has been printed in other song-books and in broadsides.—R. H.

The villagers point out the spot
  Where a willow droops over the door,
Saying, "There Mary perished and
    died
  From the winds that blew 'cross the
    wild moor."

The Shining Dagger

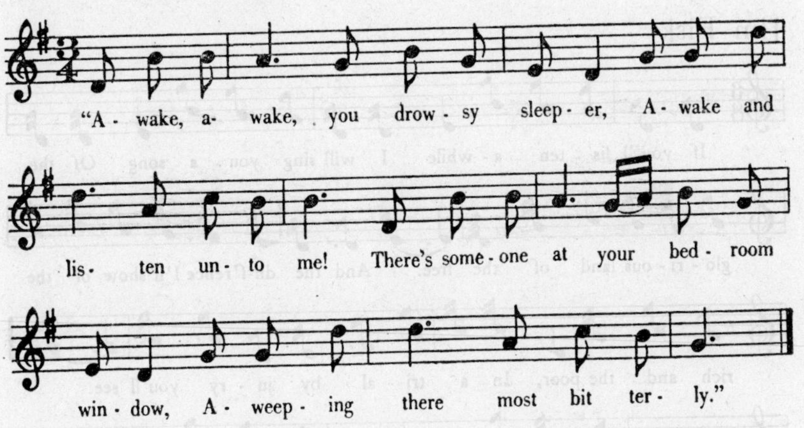
"A - wake, a- wake, you drow - sy sleep - er, A - wake and
lis - ten un - to me! There's some - one at your bed - room
win - dow, A - weep - ing there most bit - ter - ly."

"Awake, awake, you drowsy sleeper,
  Awake and listen unto me!
There's some one at your bedroom
    window,
  A-weeping there most bitterly."

Mary raised her head from her drowsy
    pillow
  To see who calling her might be.
Whom did she spy but her own true
    lover
  A-weeping there most bitterly.

He said, "Mary dear, go ask your
    father
  If you my wedded bride may be.
If he says 'No,' love, return and tell
    me,
  And I no more will trouble thee."

"It is no use to ask my father,
  For he is on his bed of rest,
And by his side is a shining dagger
  To pierce the heart that I love best."

He said, "Mary dear, go ask your
    mother
  If you my wedded bride may be;
If she says, 'No,' love, return and tell
    me,
  And I no more will trouble thee."

"It is no use to ask my mother,
  She too intends to set us free.
So go, my dear, and court some other,
  And I no more will trouble thee."

Then did he seize his own bright dag-
    ger
  And pierced it through his aching
    heart.
"Adieu, adieu, my darling Mary;
  Adieu, adieu, we now must part!"

Ibid., pp. 30–31.

"The Shining Dagger" (sung by James Atwood) shows the admixture of the two ballads, "The Drowsy Sleeper" and "The Silver Dagger." See *The Journal of American Folk-Lore,* vol. xx p. 260; vol. xxx, pp. 338–343, 361–363; Campbell and Sharp, No. 47, pp. 173–175.—R. H.

Then Mary seized the blood-stained
dagger
And pierced it through her lily
breast.
"Adieu, adieu, both father and mother,
My love and I are now at rest.

"Oh, I can climb the tallest tree, love,
And I can reach the highest nest,
And I can pluck the sweetest rose, love,
But not the heart that I love best."

Jim Fisk

If you'll lis - ten a - while I will sing you a song Of the
glo - ri - ous land of the free. And the dif-f'rence I'll show of the
rich and the poor, In a tri - al by ju - ry you'll see.
If you've plen - ty of stamps, you can hold up your head And can
D
go from your own pri - son door, But they'll hang you up high if you've
no friends at all, Let the rich go but hang up the poor.

From *The New Green Mountain Songster,* Traditional Folk Songs of Vermont, Collected, Transcribed, and Edited by Helen Hartness Flanders, Elizabeth Flanders Ballard, George Brown, and Phillips Barry, pp. 213–215. Copyright, 1939, by Helen Hartness Flanders. New Haven: Yale University Press. London: Humphrey Milford, Oxford University Press.

Mr. Josiah S. Kennison of Townshend, Vermont, sang this version of "Jim Fisk" to H. H. F., which was later transcribed by G. B.

Three ballads of James Fisk, Jr., the already semilegendary Prince of Erie, are known. Of the three, the most popular is the one sung by Mr. Kennison. A sheet-music copy, "Jim Fisk, or He Never Went Back on the Poor," published by F. W. Helmick (Cincinnati, Ohio, copyright 1874), is inscribed "written and sung by William J. Scanlon."

A picture, truthful in the main if overvividly drawn, of the real Fisk, may be had in *Jubilee Jim,* by R. H. Fuller [New York, 1928]. Fisk was shot by Edward S. Stokes, and died January 7, 1872. The humor of the myth is that Stokes was actually penniless, subsisting on blackmail, and did murder when court action had cut off his

If you'll listen a while, I will sing you a song
Of the glorious land of the free,
And the difference I'll show of the rich and the poor
In a trial by jury, you'll see.
If you've plenty of stamps, you can hold up your head
And can go from your own prison door;
But they'll hang you up high if you've no friends at all:
Let the rich go, but hang up the poor.

Let me speak of a man who is now in his grave,
A better man never was born.
Jim Fisk he was called, and his money he gave
To the outcast, the poor and forlorn.
We all know he loved both women and wine,
But his heart it was right, I am sure.
[Though he lived like a prince in his palace so fine,
Yet he never went back on the poor.] [1]

Jim Fisk was a man with his heart in his hand,
No matter what people would say.
He done all his deeds, both the good and the bad,
In the broad open light of the day.
With his grand six-in-hand of the Beach of Long Branch
He cut a big gash, to be sure,
But Chicago's great fire showed the world that Jim Fisk
And his wealth still remembered the poor.

---

last source of support. He was tried three times and finally convicted of manslaughter, for which he served four years in the New York State Prison.

Fisk sinned much, both publicly and privately; the song names only his love of women and wine, unconcerned with the social consequences, direct and indirect, of his love for playing with other people's money. Perhaps he saw the value of publicity; at any rate, his dispatch of a trainload of foodstuffs for the relief of the Chicago fire sufferers was a magnificent gesture which the folk imputed to him for goodness. It is a far cry from the hard-hitting and straight-shooting outlaws of romance to the luxury-loving money-changer, yet the way of the folk has placed Fisk in company with Robin Hood, the "good outlaws, who did pore men moch good"; with the Irish Willie Brennan, who "never robbed a poor man upon the king's highway," but gave to the needy what he took from the rich; with Jesse James, "friend to the poor," one who "never would see a man suffer pain." For the "Boston Burglar," on the other hand, the folk has but contemptuous pity; he did nothing great, even of evil. Yet the same folk applauds the pirate Ward, who vows to be king at sea, let who will reign on land. Perhaps the root of it all is grounded in our own infantilism: the outlaw and rebel which, we are told, is latent in all of us, approves successful outlawry, then sheepishly tries to cheat conscience by feigning to discover that such and such a great sinner had his good side; he was, forsooth, "a friend to the poor."

Scanlon's melody has little to recommend it. The ballad is sung in Maine to a different air.—P. B.

[1] These lines from the version given by Carl Sandburg in *The American Songbag* (New York, 1927), p. 419, are substituted for the following here sung by Mr. Kennison:

He'd done all his deeds, both the good and the bad,
In the broad open light of the day.

When the telegram came that the humble that night
  Were starving to death slow but sure,
Then the Lightning Express nobly flew from Jim Fisk
  To feed all the hungry and poor.
Now what do you think of the trials of Stokes
  Who murdered the friend of the poor?
If such men get free, is there any one safe
  To step outside their own door?

Is there one law for the rich and one for the poor?
  It seems so, at least so they say.
If they'd hang up the poor, why shouldn't the rich
  Ought to swing up the very same way?
Never show any favor to friend or to foe,
  To a beggar or prince at your door,
But the millionaire you must hang up also.
  Never go back on the poor.[1]

The Brookfield Murder

Recitative
The Brook-field mur-der has come to light, By a young
man rath-er short of sight. Joe Buzz-ell he hired and
rit.
drove young Cook, To shoot the girl, so it seems to look.

[1] [Fragment remembered later.]
In a trial for murder they have nowaday,
The rich man gets off swift and sure,
With the thousands they pay to the jury and judge,
But you bet they'll go back on the poor.
—P. B.

From *Folk Songs of Old New England,* collected and edited by Eloise Hubbard Linscott, pp. 175–177. Copyright, 1939, by The Macmillan Company. New York.

This song records a local New Hampshire tragedy. It was sung by Mrs. Winifred Allard Piper of Wolfeboro, New Hampshire, which adjoins Brookfield. The third

The Brookfield murder has come to light,
By a young man rather short of sight.
Joe Buzzell he hired and drove young Cook
To shoot the girl, so it seems to look.

She sued for damage which if he'd paid
Would have saved the time while in jail he laid.
But he with murder born in his heart
Soon caused young Susan to depart.

On Monday evening as we tell,
Miss Susan Hanson was known full well,
Sat at her table doing some work,
She little thought death so near did lurk.

The thief and murderer with gun in hand
Beside the house outside did stand.
Discharged his gun through windowpane,
And thus the promised bride was slain.

It was a dreadful shock to the aged mother,
The lamp was lit by the son and brother.
There lay the daughter once so fair
In death cold arms and bloodstained hair.

No farewell words to her friends could say,
But shot dead on the floor did lay.
So young and fair and in life's bloom,
To be hurried away so soon to the tomb.

Come, all young ladies, a warning take,
And shun such reptiles for Susan's sake.
For he who shot this lady gay
Would burn your home while in bed you lay.

---

verse was supplied by Dana Cate of Sanbornville, New Hampshire, who remembers hearing the song as a boy from Warren Stevens, an old man of ninety.

The crime was committed in 1847. According to the story, "Old Pike," a local character, urged Susan Hanson to sue Joseph Buzzell for heart balm when he jilted her. Buzzell was so angry that he hired the half-wit, Charles Cook, to kill his former sweetheart. While at work on the Henry Jones house in Wolfeboro, the wrath of Mr. Buzzell had cooled enough for him to be seized with a change of mind and he thereupon leaped on his horse and galloped for dear life to Miss Hanson's home in Brookfield. It was a matter of some ten miles over "the back road." He arrived too late; Miss Hanson had been done away with.

The case dragged on in the courts for five years before the law finally caught up with the murderer and his accomplice. Only a charge of arson on another case against Cook brought matters to an end. Buzzell was hanged and his accomplice, Cook, imprisoned for life.—E. H. L.

The Pesky Sarpent

On Springfield mountain there did dwell, A comely youth I knew full well, Ri

tu ri nu ri tu di na, Ri tu di na ri tu di na.

On Springfield mountain there did dwell,
A comely youth I knew full well.

Chorus:
Ri tu di nu, ri tu di na,
Ri tu di nu, ri tu di na.

One Monday morning he did go,
Down in the meadow for to mow.

He scarce had mowed half the field,
When a Pesky Sarpent bit his heel.

He took his scythe and with a blow,
He laid the Pesky Sarpent low.

He took the Sarpent in his hand,
And straitway went to Molly Bland.

Oh Molly, Molly here you see,
The Pesky Sarpent what bit me.

Now Molly had a ruby lip,
With which the pizen she did sip.

But Molly had a rotten tooth,
Which the Pizen struck and kill'd 'em both.

From *The Pesky Sarpent,* A Pathetic Ballad, as sung by Mr. Spear. Arranged for the Piano-Forte and respectfully dedicated to the C. B. C.'s by the author. Boston: Published by George P. Reed. [1840.] In *Series of Old American Songs,* Reproduced in Facsimile from Original or Early Editions in Harris Collection of American Poetry and Plays, with Brief Annotations, by S. Foster Damon, Curator, No. 26. Providence, Rhode Island: Brown University Library. 1936.

This ballad is perhaps unique in that the circumstances which inspired it are fully known. (The best account is that by Phillips Barry, running in the *Bulletin of the Folk-Song Society of the Northeast.*)

Mr. Timothy Myrick, son of Lieut. Thomas Myrick of Springfield Mountain (now Wilbraham), Mass., was bitten by a rattlesnake on Friday, August 7, 1761, at Farmington, Mass., and died before he could reach home. He was twenty-two years, two months, and three days old, and "very near the point of marridg" to Sarah Blake. His gravestone is still in existence.

The original ballad was an elegy over this tragic death, which may have been sung at his funeral to the tune of "Old Hundred," in accordance with a custom in western Massachusetts. The author has been named as Nathan Torrey, or Daniel or Jesse Carpenter.

The song succeeded, and traveled far and wide, changing names, dates, and places, and acquiring a number of different tunes. The *Journal of American Folk Lore* is full of variants. About 1836 it began to be sung on the stage; the vogue of the Yankee was then in its prime; and the ancient tragedy became excellent comedy, when stammered or nasalized by George Gaines Spear, Yankee Hill, or Judson Hutchinson—S. F. D.

For a Vermont version of the original ballad, "On Springfield Mountain," see *A Treasury of American Folklore* (New York, 1944), pp. 828–829.

The neighbors found that they were
dead,
So laid them both upon one bed.

And all their friends both far and near,
Did cry and howl they were so dear.

Now all you maids a warning take,
From Molly Bland and Tommy Blake.

And mind when you're in love don't
pass,
Too near to patches of high grass.

Michigania

Come, all ye Yankee farmer boys who would like to change your lot
And spunk enough to travel beyond your native spot
And leave behind the village where pa and ma doth stay,
Come, go with me and settle in Michigania.[1]
For there's your Penobscot way down in parts of Maine
Where timber grows in plenty but not a bit of grain,
And there is your Quaddy and your Piscataqua,
But these can't hold a candle to Michigania.

And there's the state of Vermont, but what a place is that?
To be sure the girls are pretty and the cattle very fat,
But who among her mountains and clouds of snow would stay
While he can buy a section in Michigania?
And there is Massachusetts, once good enough, be sure,
But now she is always lying in taxation and manure.
She'll cause a peck of trouble but deal a peck will pay,
While all is scripture measure in Michigania.

And there's the land of Blue Laws where deacons cut their hair
For fear their locks and tenants [tenets?] will not exactly square,
Where beer that works on Sunday a penalty must pay,
While all is free and easy in Michigania.
And there's the state of New York, the people's very rich;
Among themselves and others have dug a mighty ditch
Which renders it more easy for us to find the way
And sail upon the waters of Michigania.

From the Gernsey Manuscript, in *Ballads and Songs of Southern Michigan,* collected and edited by Emelyn Elizabeth Gardner and Geraldine Jencks Chickering, pp. 5–6. Copyright, 1939, by The University of Michigan. Ann Arbor.

The facts revealed by historical research are stated as follows by George Newman Fuller, *Economic and Social Beginnings of Michigan* (Lansing, Michigan, 1916), p. 469: "It was exceptional for a settler to emigrate directly from his place of birth to Michigan. He was much more likely to have a number of intermediate stopping places; for example, he might be born in England, migrate with his parents to Connecticut, be educated in Vermont, engage in business in New York, and then spend some years on the frontier in Ohio and perhaps return to New York before finally settling in Michigan."—E. E. G., *ibid.*, pp. 4–5 and note. [No tune.]

[1] Pronounced Michiganiay.

What country ever grew up so great in little time,
Just popping from a nursery right into life its prime?
When Uncle Sam did wean her, 'twas but the other day,
And now she's quite a lady, this Michigania.
And if you want to go to a place called Washtenaw,
You'll first upon the Huron; such land you never saw,
Where ship come to Ann Arbor right through a pleasant bay
And touch at Ypsilanti in Michigania.

And if you want to go a little farther back,
You'll find the shire of Oakland, the town of Pontiac,
Which springing up so sudden scared the wolves and bears away
That used to roam about there in Michigania.
And if you want to go where Rochester is there,
And farther still Mt. Clemens looks out upon St. Clair,
Besides some other places within McCombia
That promise population to Michigania.

And if you want to travel a little farther on,
I guess you'll touch St. Joseph where everybody's gone,
Where everything like Jack's bean grows monstrous fast, they say,
And beats the rest all hollow in Michigania.
Come, all ye Yankee farmer boys with metal hearts like me
And elbow grease in plenty to bow the forest tree,
Come, buy a quarter section, and I'll be bound you'll say
This country takes the rag off, this Michigania.

No, Never, No

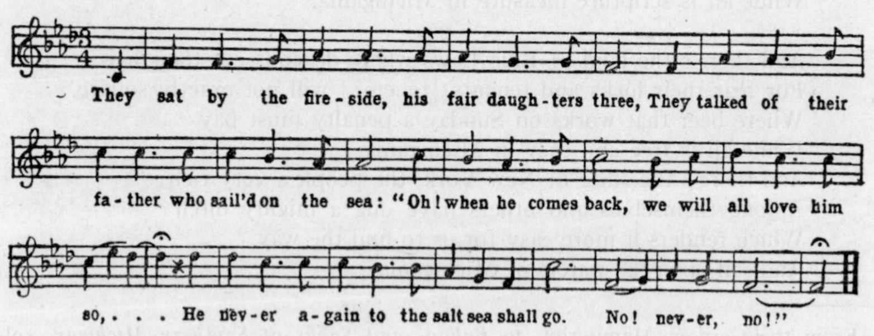
They sat by the fire-side, his fair daugh-ters three, They talked of their
fa-ther who sail'd on the sea: "Oh! when he comes back, we will all love him
so, . . . He nev-er a-gain to the salt sea shall go. No! nev-er, no!"

They sat by the fireside, his fair daughters three,
They talked of their father who sail'd on the sea:
"Oh! when he comes back, we will all love him so,
He never again to the salt sea shall go.
No! never, no!"

Written from memory by Edna Dean Proctor. From *Heart Songs,* Dear to the American People and by Them Contributed in the Search for Treasured Songs Initiated by the *National Magazine,* p. 147. Copyright, 1909, by The Chapple Publishing Company, Ltd. Boston.

"I'll give him this vest all of satin so fine";
"And I'll be his carver when he sits to dine";
"And I'll climb his knee and such kisses bestow
He never again to the salt sea shall go.
No! never, no!"

"O did ye not hear it?" the sisters declare,
"There's surely a spirit that talks in the air;
And whether we speak either loudly or low,
It answers in accents all mournful and slow,
'No! never, no!' "

"It is but the tempest that rages so strong;
The gale will itself waft our father along;
Go look at the vane and see how the winds blow:
He'll bring us gay things for he promised us so."
"No! never, no!"

Prepare ye, fair maidens, prepare ye to weep!
Your father lies cold in the dark-rolling deep;
Look not at the vane nor ask how the winds blow,
His ghost in the storm whispers mournful and slow:
"No! never, no!"

SEA SONGS AND CHANTEYS

The Boston Come-All-Ye

Come, all ye young sailormen, listen to me,
I'll sing you a song of the fish of the sea.

Chorus:
Then blow ye winds westerly, westerly blow,
We're bound to the south'ard, so steady she goes!

Oh, first come the whale, the biggest of all;
He clumb up aloft and let every sail fall.

From *Songs of American Sailormen,* by Joanna C. Colcord, pp. 187–188. Copyright, 1938, by W. W. Norton & Company.

There can be little doubt that the . . . song, although it was sung throughout the merchant service, began life with the fishing fleet. We have the testimony of Kipling in *Captain's Courageous* that it was a favorite within recent years of the Banks fishermen. It is known as "The Fishes" and also by its more American title of "The Boston Come-all-ye." The chorus finds its origin in a Scotch fishing song, "Blaw the Wind Southerly." A curious fact is that Captain Whall, a Scotchman himself, prints this song with an entirely different tune, and one that has no connection with the air of the Tyneside keelmen to which our own Gloucester fishermen sing it. The version given here was sung by Captain Frank Seeley.—J. C. C.

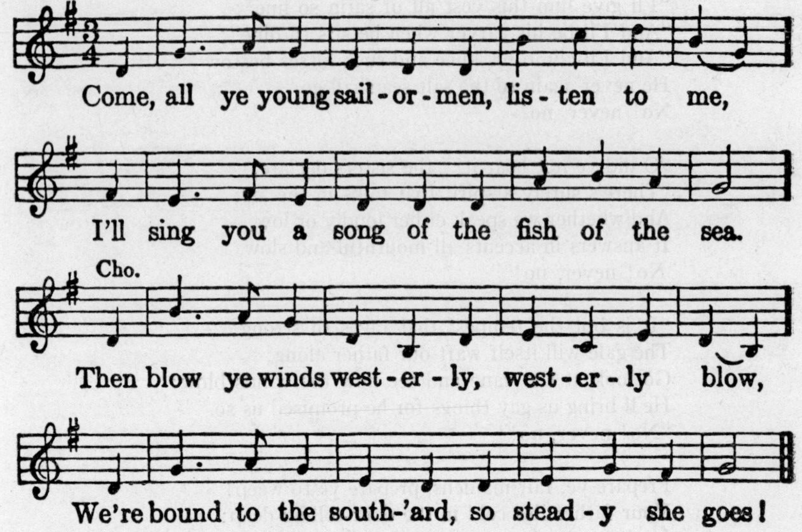
Come, all ye young sail-or-men, lis-ten to me,
I'll sing you a song of the fish of the sea.
Cho.
Then blow ye winds west-er-ly, west-er-ly blow,
We're bound to the south-'ard, so stead-y she goes!

And next come the mack'rel with his stripéd back;
He hauled aft the sheets and boarded each tack.

Then come the porpoise with his short snout;
He went to the wheel, calling "Ready! About!"

Then come the smelt, the smallest of all;
He jumped to the poop and sung out "Topsail, haul!"

The herring come saying, "I'm king of the seas,
If you want any wind, why, I'll blow you a breeze."

Next come the cod with his chuckle-head;
He went to the main-chains to heave at the lead.

Last come the flounder as flat as the ground;
Says, "Damn your eyes, chuckle-head, mind how you sound!"

Blow, Boys, Blow

Solo: A Yankee ship came down the river,
Chorus: Blow, boys, blow!
Solo: Her masts and spars they shine like silver,
Chorus: Blow, my bully boys, blow!

Ibid., pp. 50–52.

A group of famous old shanties had their origin in the packet-trade with Liverpool, which developed soon after the close of the War of 1812. . . .

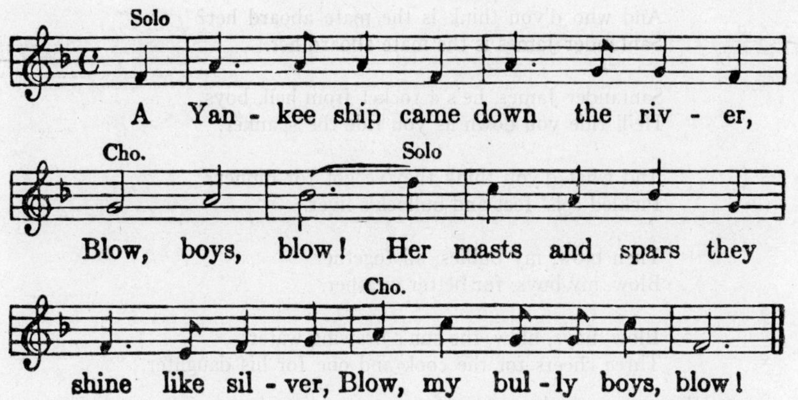
Solo
A Yan - kee ship came down the riv - er,
Cho.
Blow, boys, blow!
Solo
Her masts and spars they
Cho.
shine like sil - ver, Blow, my bul - ly boys, blow!

How do you know she's a Yankee liner?
The Stars and Stripes float out behind her.

(*Or,* How do you know she's a Yankee packet?
They fired a gun, I heard the racket.)

And who d'you think is the captain of her?
Why, Bully Hayes is the captain of her.

Oh, Bully Hayes, he loves us sailors;
Yes, he does like hell and blazes!

"Blow, Boys, Blow" started life as a slaving song, the opening couplet being

A Yankee ship on the Congo River,
Her masts they bend and her sails they shiver.

In this version, the captain is "Holy Joe, the nigger lover," and the mate "a big mulatta come from Antigua." Somewhat later, it was taken over by the "packet-rats" of the Western Ocean, and celebrated the brutalities aboard the Atlantic liners. Doubtless all the well-known masters and mates in that trade have heard themselves picturesquely described in this shanty; but it is Captain Hayes, who was lost in the *Rainbow* in 1848, whose name seems to have survived.

In other versions, the master is said to be "one-eyed Kelly, the Bowery runner," and the ship is recognized as a Yankee clipper "because the blood runs from her scuppers." One couplet, dating evidently from Civil War days, inquires:

What do you think she's got for cargo?
Old shot and shell, she breaks the embargo.

Still another tells of her fate:

Her sails were old, her timbers rotten,
His charts the skipper had forgotten.
She sailed away for London city;
Never got there, what a pity!

But the wildest flights of fancy concerned the bill of fare, which was variously stated to consist of "belaying-pin soup and monkey's liver," "mosquito's heart and sandfly's liver," "hot water soup, but slightly thinner," etc. I have never seen in print the menu here given; but it is what I heard sung aboard ship in the '90's.—J. C. C.

And who d'you think is the mate aboard her?
Santander James is the mate aboard her.

Santander James, he's a rocket from hell, boys,
He'll ride you down as you ride the spanker.

And what d'you think they've got for dinner?
Pickled eels' feet and bullock's liver.

Then blow, my bullies, all together,
Blow, my boys, for better weather.

Blow, boys, blow, the sun's drawing water;
Three cheers for the cook and one for his daughter.

Reuben Renzo

Solo: Roving Reuben Renzo,
Chorus: Renzo, boys, Renzo;
Solo: Roving Reuben Renzo,
Chorus: Renzo, boys, Renzo.

Renzo was no sailor,
He might have been a tailor.

Renzo took a notion,
That he would plough the ocean.

From *Folk Songs of Old New England,* Collected and Edited by Eloise Hubbard Linscott, pp. 144–146. Copyright, 1939, by The Macmillan Company. New York.

Captain Charlton L. Smith of Marblehead, Massachusetts, recalls this chantey from his many years at sea in the sailing ships of the mahogany trade. These ships went out of Liverpool to South America, in the middle of the nineteenth century.

It is a halyard chantey that was popular about fifty years ago and is thought originally to have been one of the songs of the whaling fleet. Whether the name of the hero is a corruption of the Portuguese "Lorenzo" is not definitely established, though it is generally known that the Yankee whalers carried a large number of "Portygee" sailors on their long and dangerous but profitable voyages.

It is probable too that Lorenzo may be a mythical hero, for his rise to the captaincy gave chance for sly digs at officers. No amount of book learning was ever known to make a sailor.

The "limejuice whaler" refers to the custom of rationing lime juice to prevent scurvy on the whaling ships that were so long out of port.—E. H. L.

So he sold his plough and harrow,
And likewise sold his barrow.

And Renzo had a pony,
And sold him to a loidy.

He went to London city,
Where the barmaids are so pretty.

He joined a limejuice whaler,
And tried to be a sailor.

The mate he was a bad man,
He took him to the gangway.

He gave him five and twenty,[1]
And that was a plenty!

But the skipper he was a fine old man,
He took him to his cabin.

And taught him navigation,
And now he ploughs the ocean.

Cape Cod Shanty

Oh, Cape Cod girls they have no combs,
Heave away, heave away!

They comb their hair with codfish bones,
Heave away, heave away!

---

[1] Refers to the number of lashes of the cat-o'-nine-tails, an instrument commonly used for punishing the refractory.—E. H. L.

Cf. the following variant:

O, Johnny was no sailor,
(Renso, boys, Renso.)
Still he shipped on a Yankee whaler,
(Renso, boys, Renso.)
He could not do his duty,
(Renso, boys, Renso.)
And he tried to run away then,
(Renso, boys, Renso.)
They caught and brought him back again,
(Renso, boys, Renso.)
And he said he never would go again,
(Renso, boys, Renso.)

They put him pounding cable,
(Renso, boys, Renso.)
And found him very able,
(Renso, boys, Renso.)
He said he'd run away no more,
(Renso, boys, Renso.)
He only waited to get on shore,
(Renso, boys, Renso.)
So when he put his feet on shore,
(Renso, boys, Renso.)
A-whaling he would go no more,
(Renso, boys, Renso.)

—Capt. Charles Henry Robbins, *The Gam* (New Bedford, 1899), p. 140.

From *The Folk Songs of New England,* sung by Earl Rogers, Musicraft Album 68, Record 334-A, 2. New York: Musicraft Corporation. Transcribed by Frances Kurland.

For a Gloucester version, see Joanna C. Colcord, *Songs of American Sailormen* (New York, 1938), p. 91, who notes of this windlass or capstan shanty: "A 'down-East' variant of this song goes to a simplified and livelier version of the same tune. The words are a rough jest at the expense of sailors who might hail from the fishing towns, and any such towns, from Cape Cod to St. John, were substituted."

For an additional Cape Cod stanza, see Arthur Loesser, *Humor in American Song* (New York, 1942), p. 211:

Oh, Cape Cod roosters never crow,
And crowing hens are all the go.

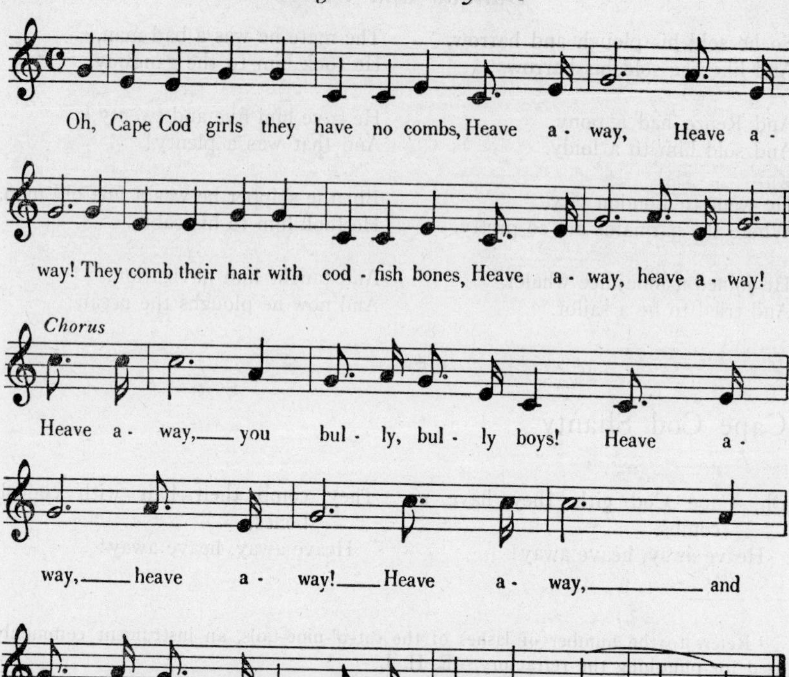
Oh, Cape Cod girls they have no combs, Heave a - way, Heave a -
way! They comb their hair with cod - fish bones, Heave a - way, heave a - way!
Chorus
Heave a - way, you bul - ly, bul - ly boys! Heave a -
way, heave a - way! Heave a - way, and
don't you make a noise, For we're bound for Aus - tral - ia.

Chorus:

Heave away, you bully, bully boys!
Heave away, heave away!
Heave away, and don't you make a noise,
For we're bound for Australia!

Oh, Cape Cod boys they have no sleds,
They slide down hill on codfish heads.

Oh, Cape Cod cats they have no tails,
They blew away in heavy gales.

The Mermaid

'Twas Friday morn when we set sail,
And we were not far from the land,
When the captain spied a lovely mermaid,
With a comb and a glass in her hand.

Chorus:

Oh! the ocean waves may roll,
And the stormy winds may blow,
While we poor sailors go skipping to the tops,
And the landlubbers lie down below, below, below,
And the landlubbers lie down below.

From *The Most Popular Home Songs,* selected and arranged by Gilbert Clifford Noble, pp. 60–61. Copyright, 1906, 1908, by Hinds, Noble & Eldredge. New York.

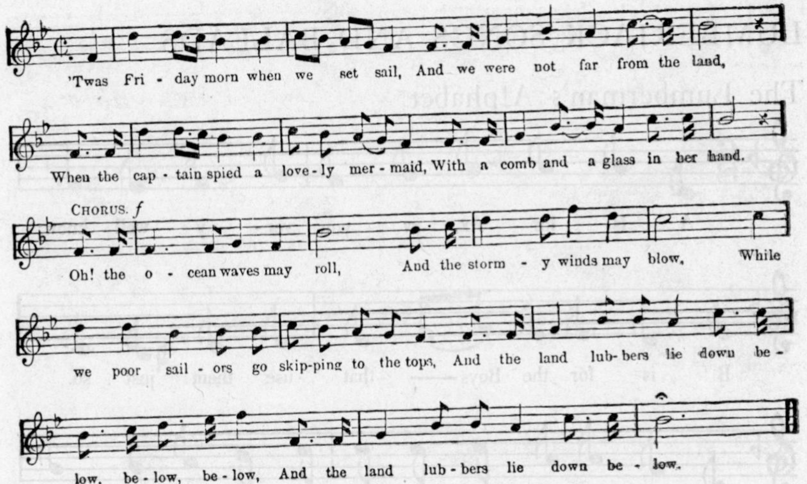
'Twas Fri - day morn when we set sail, And we were not far from the land,
When the cap - tain spied a love - ly mer - maid, With a comb and a glass in her hand.
CHORUS. f
Oh! the o - cean waves may roll, And the storm - y winds may blow, While
we poor sail - ors go skip-ping to the tops, And the land lub-bers lie down be -
low, be - low, be - low, And the land lub - bers lie down be - low.

Then out spake the captain of our gallant ship,
  And a well-spoken man was he:
"I have married me a wife in Salem town,
  And to-night she a widder will be."

Then out spake the cook of our gallant ship,
  And a fat old cookie was he:
"I care much more for my potties and my kets
  Than I do for the depths of the sea."

Then out spake the boy of our gallant ship,
  And a well-spoken laddie was he:
"I've a father and a mother in Boston city,
  But to-night they childless will be."

"Oh! the moon shines bright and the stars give light;
  Oh! my mammy'll be looking for me;
She may look, she may weep, she may look to the deep,
  She may look to the bottom of the sea."

Then three times around went our gallant ship,
  And three times around went she;
Then three times around went our gallant ship,
  And she sank to the depths of the sea.

LUMBERJACK SONGS AND BALLADS

The Lumberman's Alphabet

A is for Ax, as you ver - y well know;

B is for the Boys —— that use them just so.

C is for the Chop - ping that soon will be - gin, And

D is for the Dan - ger we al - ways stand in.

Chorus

Sing Hi, der - ry - o, so mer - ry are we, There's

no one one - half —— as hap - py as we. With a

Hi, der - ry - o, Hi, der - ry - dong. At the

wood - man's shan - ty there's noth - ing goes wrong.

From *Folk Songs of Old New England,* collected and edited by Eloise Hubbard Linscott, pp. 235–237. Copyright, 1939, by The Macmillan Company. New York.

A is for Ax, as you very well know;
B is for the Boys that use them just so.
C is for the Chopping that soon will begin,
And D is for the Danger we always stand in.

Chorus:
Sing hi, derry-o, so merry are we,
There's no one one-half as happy as we.
With a hi, derry-o, hi, derry-dong,
At the woodman's shanty there's nothing goes wrong.

E is for the Echoes that through the woods ring;
F is for the Foreman, the head of the gang,
G is for the Grindstone that swiftly goes round,
And H is for the Handle so smooth and so round.

I is for Iron, with which we mark pine,
And J is for Jolly Boys, all in a line.
K is for the Keen edge our axes we keep,
And L is for the Lice that over us creep.

M is for the Moss that we chink into our camps,
N is for the Needle which mendeth our pants,
O is for Owls that hoot in the night,
And P is for the Pines that we always fall right.

Q is for Quarrels, which we don't have round,
R is for River, where we drive our logs down;
S is for Sled, so stout and so strong,
And T is for the Team to draw it along.

U is for Use, which we put our teams to,
And V is the Valley which we draw our sleds through,
And W is for Woods that we leave in the spring,
And now I have sung all I'm going to sing.
That's all.

While Charles Young of Moultonboro, New Hampshire, was river-driving on the Penobscot River, he learned this song in the lumber camp. In that region he was guide and woodsman for over ten years.

It is said that nearly all the really good tunes and woodsmen's songs were made up by Larry Gorman, one of the most famous fighting lumberjacks of Maine. He was supposed to have come from Prince Edward Island and to have lived near the head-waters of the Penobscot. Many of the men from the provinces were attracted by the good wages paid in the New England woods and crossed and recrossed the border.

There are several variations of this song, the most popular ones unprintable; the earliest known printed version appeared in the *Maine Sportsman,* in February, 1904.

As Charles Young sang the song, the chorus was used after the first, second, third, and last stanzas only; but he remarked that in the woods he'd probably sing the chorus after every verse, to pass the time.—E. H. L.

Jack Haggerty, or the Flat River Girl

I'm a heart-bro-ken rafts-man, from Green-ville I came,
I de-vo-ted my de-par-ture with-out a-ny pain;
From the strong darts of Cu-pid, which have caused me much grief,
My___ heart it is brok-en and I can't find re-lief.
I work on Flat Ri-ver, I earn quite good pay,
I'm stead-fast and___ stead-y, and ne'er played the race;
I'm the boy that stands hap-py on the wide-rol-ling stream,
My thoughts were of An-na, my love's bright-est dream.

I'm a heart-broken raftsman, from Greenville I came;
I devoted my departure without any pain;
From the strong darts of Cupid, which have caused me much grief,
My heart it is broken, and I can't find relief.

From *The Maine Woods Songster*, edited by Phillips Barry, pp. 74–75. Copyright, 1939, by Kate Puffer Barry. The Powell Printing Company. Cambridge, Massachusetts.

For the origin of this song see Geraldine Chickering, "The Origin of a Ballad," *Modern Language Notes*, Vol. L, pp. 465–468. Eloise Hubbard Linscott in *Folk Songs of Old New England*, p. 214, locates Flat River near Greenville, Maine, at the foot of Moosehead Lake. According to Franz Rickaby in *Ballads and Songs of the Shanty-Boy* (Cambridge, 1926) p. 191, "This ballad . . . is native to the Flat River in southern Michigan," which flows through Greenville, Michigan.

I work on Flat Fiver, I earn quite good pay;
I'm steadfast and steady, and ne'er played the race;
I'm the boy that stands happy on the wide-rolling stream;
My thoughts were of Anna, my love's brightest dream.

I'll tell you my troubles without much delay,
'Twas of a fair schoolgirl my heart stole away;
She was a blacksmith's daughter by the Flat River side,
And I always intended to make her my bride.

I dressed her in muslins and the finest of lace,
In the costly linens I did her embrace;
I gave her my wages to keep for me safe;
I refused her nothing I could get in the place.

One day on Flat River a note I received;
She said from her promise herself she'd relieve,
For another true lover, who had long been delayed,
And the next time I saw her, she'd no more be a maid.

To her mother, Jane Tucker, I lay all the blame;
She caused her to desert me and hurt my good name;
She cast off the rigging that I would soon tie,
And left me a wanderer till the day that I died.

Farewell to Flat River, for me there's no rest;
I'll shoulder my peavey [1] and I'll go out West;
I'll start for Baskahegan, some pleasure to find,
And I'll leave my false love on Flat River behind.

Now, come all you young fellows with hearts strong and true,
Don't depend on a woman one bit, or you'll rue;
But if you should meet one with bright chestnut curls,
Just think of Jack Haggerty and the Flat River girl.

The Lumberman's Life

A lumberman's life is a wearisome life,
Although some say it's free from all care;
'Tis a-wielding of an ax from morning until night,
In the middle of the forests drear.

---

[1] The peavey, a short pole with an adjustable hook used in driving logs, was invented in 1858, by Joseph Peavey, a blacksmith of Stillwater Village, Maine.—Eloise Hubbard Linscott.

Ibid., p. 60.

Text and tune from Lamont Forbuss, Monson, Me. Tune transcribed from dictaphone record by Samuel P. Bayard.—P. B., *ibid.*, p. 100.

Also known as "The Shanty-Man's Life." Roland P. Gray, in *Songs and Ballads of the Maine Lumberjacks* (Cambridge, 1924), pp. 55–57, gives a broadside version, "composed and written by Geo. W. Stace, La Crosse Valley, Wis."

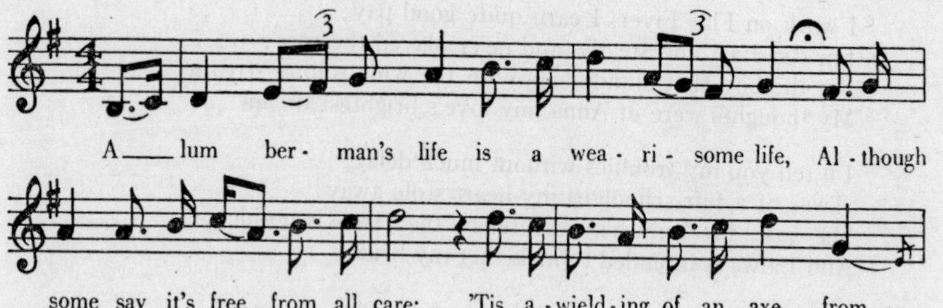
A — lum ber - man's life is a wea - ri - some life, Al - though
some say it's free — from all care; 'Tis a - wield - ing of an axe from —

morn - ing un - til night, In the mid - dle of the for - ests drear.

At four in the morning, the cook he rises up,
  Saying, "Come boys, it is the break of day."
And through broken slumbers, we pass back
  All the long, weary night away.

Sleeping in a shanty so bleak and cold,
  Where the cold winter's winds they do blow,
As soon as the morning stars do appear,
  To the wild woods we must go.

Transported we are from the haunts of all men,
  On the banks of the Bonne Chere stream,
Where the wolves and the owls with their terrifying growls
  Disturb our troubled nightly dream.

Transported from the glass and the charming little lass,
  All enjoyment we've left so far behind,
There is no one here for to wipe away a tear
  When sorrow fills our troubled mind.

When spring has come, then our troubles begin,
  When the water is piercing and cold,
Dripping wet is our clothes, and our limbs are froze,
  And the peavies we can scarcely hold.

The rocky shoals and sands give employment to our hands,
  With a well-bounded raft for to steer,
Every rapid that we run, O we call it the fun,
  We are free from all slavish fear.

The lumbering I'll give o'er, and I'll anchor safe on shore,
  There to lead a quiet, sober life,
No more for to roam, but, contented, stay at home,
  With a kind and loving little WIFE!

Canada I O

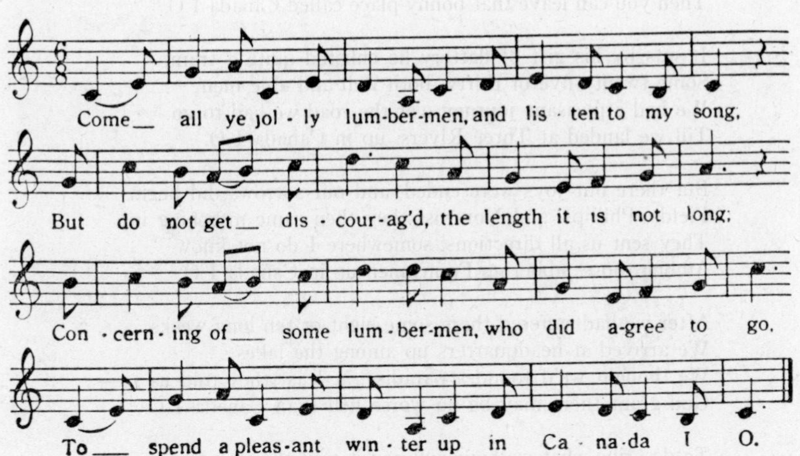

Come all ye jolly lumbermen, and listen to my song,
But do not get discouraged, the length it is not long,
Concerning of some lumbermen, who did agree to go
To spend one pleasant winter up in Canada [1] I O.

It happened late one season in the fall of Fifty-three,
A preacher of the gospel one morning came to me;
Said he, "My jolly fellow, how would you like to go
To spend one pleasant winter up in Canada I O."

To him I quickly made reply, and unto him did say,
"In going out to Canada depends upon the pay.
If you will pay good wages, my passage to and fro,
I think I'll go along with you to Canada I O."

"Yes, we will pay good wages, and will pay your passage out,
Provided you sign papers that you will stay the route;
But if you do get homesick and swear that home you'll go,
We never can your passage pay from Canada I O.

Ibid., pp. 76–77.

The words are by Ephraim Braley, Charlestown, Me., 1854. Tune is "Lord Randall," Type II, come-all-ye variant. Text [previously printed in Eckstorm and Smyth, *Minstrelsy of Maine*, 22–23; *Bulletin of the Folk Song Society of the Northeast*, 6: 11]. Tune [previously printed in FSSNE, 6: 10] from Mrs. Annie Marston, Charlestown, Me. For the history of this song, of which "The Buffalo Skinners" [Lomax, *Cowboy Songs*, pp. 158–161] is an adaptation, see Fannie H. Eckstorm, "Canada I O," in FSSNE, 6: 11–13.—P. B., *ibid.*, p. 101.

[1] Pronounced Canaday.

"And if you get dissatisfied, and do not wish to stay,
We do not wish to bind you, no, not one single day;
You just refund the money we had to pay, you know,
Then you can leave that bonny place called Canada I O."

It was by his gift of flattery he enlisted quite a train,
Some twenty-five or thirty, both well and able men;
We had a pleasant journey o'er the road we had to go,
Till we landed at Three Rivers, up in Canada I O.

But there our joys were ended, and our sorrows did begin;
Fields, Phillips, and Norcross they then came marching in;
They sent us all directions, somewhere I do not know,
Among those jabbering Frenchmen up in Canada I O.

After we had suffered there some eight or ten long weeks,
We arrived at headquarters up among the lakes;
We thought we'd found a paradise, at least they told us so—
God grant there may be no worse hell than Canada I O.

To describe what we have suffered is past the art of man,
But to give a fair description, I will do the best I can.
Our food the dogs would snarl at, our beds were on the snow;
We suffered worse than murderers up in Canada I O.

Our hearts were made of iron and our souls were cased in steel,
The hardships of that winter could never make us yield;
Field, Phillips, and Norcross they found their match, I know,
Among the boys that went from Maine to Canada I O.

But now our lumbering is over and we are returning home,
To greet our wives and sweethearts and never more to roam,
To greet our wives and sweethearts and never more to roam,
Unto that God-forsaken place, called Canada I O.

NURSERY AND HUMOROUS SONGS

Nantucket Lullaby

Hm ——— Hush, the waves are

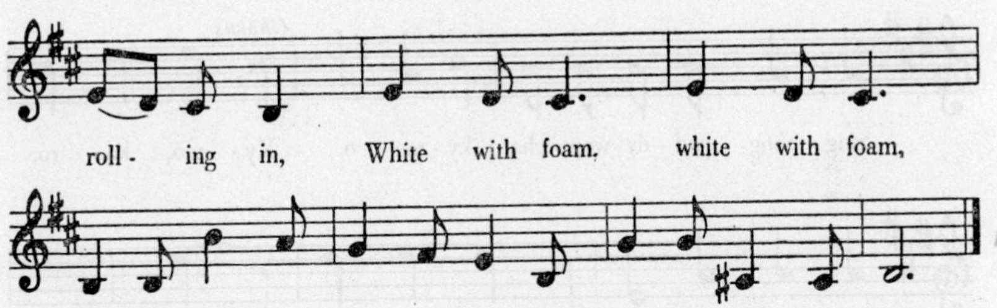
roll - ing in, White with foam, white with foam,
Fa - ther toils a - mid the din, While ba - by sleeps at home.

Hush, the waves are rolling in,
  White with foam, white with foam,
Father toils amid the din,
  While baby sleeps at home.

Hush, the ship rides in the gale,
  Where they roam, where they roam,
Father seeks the roving whale,
  But baby sleeps at home.

Hush, the wind sweeps o'er the deep,
  All alone, all alone,
Mother now the watch will keep,
  Till father's ship comes home.

The Frog in the Spring

There was a frog lived in a spring,
  Singsong paddy woncha kymeo.
He had such a cold that he couldn't
    sing.
  Singsong paddy woncha kymeo.

Chorus:
  Kymo, karo, delto, karo,
    Kymo, karo, kymo.
  Strimstrum, popadiddle,
  There by the rigdum,
    Rigdum bottom in the kymeo!

From *Early American Ballads*, sung by John and Lucy Allison, with Chorus, Keynote Album K-102, Record 533-B, 2. New York: Keynote Recordings, Inc. Leaflet copyright, 1943, by Keynote Recordings, Inc. Transcribed by Frances Kurland.

To words of unknown origin, Lucy Allison made this setting in 1924, and for many years used the song in the folk ballad programs of the Allisons.—J. A.

From *Songs from the Hills of Vermont,* Sung by James and Mary Atwood and Aunt Jenny Knapp, Texts Collected and Edited by Edith B. Sturgis, Tunes Collected and Piano Accompaniments Arranged with Historical Notes by Robert Hughes, pp. 18–21. Copyright, 1919, by G. Schirmer. New York and Boston.

The oldest extant version of "The Frog in the Spring" (sung by Mary Atwood) is "The Marriage of the Frogge and the Mouse," printed with music among the

There was a frog lived in a spring, Sing-song pad-dy won-cha
ky-me-o. He had such a cold that he could-n't sing.
Chorus
Sing-song pad-dy won-cha ky-me-o. Ky-mo, ka-ro,
del-to, ka-ro, Ky-mo, ka-ro, ky- mo,
Strim-strum, pop-a-did-le, There by the rig-dum,
Rig-dum bot-tom in the ky-me-o!

They took him out and put him on the ground,
And he jumped up and bounded around.

"O, Missis Mouse, are you within?"
"O yes, kind sir, I sit and spin.

"There has been here a fine young man,
And I will have him if I can."

He took the mouse where he did dwell.
'Twas in the bottom of the well.

She waded in up to her chin,
And wished she was a maid again.

"Country Passtimes" in Ravenscroft's *Melismata,* 1611. In 1580 a ballad entitled "A Most Strange Wedding of the Frog and the Mouse" was licensed to Edward White at Stationers' Hall; and a song, "The Frog Came to the Myl Dur" (mill door) was sung in Wedderburn's "Complaint of Scotland" as early as 1549. (See Chappell's *Popular Music of the Olden Time,* 1855, vol. i, p. 88.) For a group of related Scottish texts see Maidment's *Scottish Ballads and Songs,* 1859, pp. 153–157; C. K. Sharp's *A Ballad Book,* No. 30; *Journal of the Folksong Society,* vol. ii, p. 225. For English traditional versions see Halliwell's *Nursery Rhymes* (1st ed.), No. 93, pp. 70–72; Rimbault's *Collection of Old Nursery Rhymes,* pp. 26–27; Miss Mason's *Nursery*

Birds' Courting Song

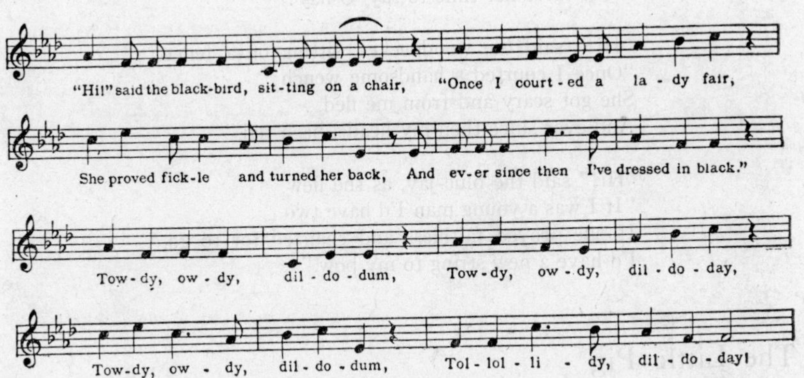
"Hi!" said the black-bird, sit - ting on a chair, "Once I court - ed a la - dy fair,
She proved fick - le and turned her back, And ev - er since then I've dressed in black."
Tow - dy, ow - dy, dil - do - dum, Tow - dy, ow - dy, dil - do - day,
Tow-dy, ow - dy, dil - do - dum, Tol - lol - li - dy, dil - do - day!

"Hi!" said the blackbird, sitting on a chair,
"Once I courted a lady fair;
She proved fickle and turned her back,
And ever since then I've dressed in black."

Chorus:
Towdy, owdy, dildodum,
Towdy, owdy, dildoday,
Towdy, owdy, dildodum,
Tollollidy, dildoday!

"Hi!" said the little leather-winged bat,
"I will tell you the reason that,
The reason that I fly in the night
Is because I've lost my heart's delight."

Rhymes and Country Songs, pp. 8–9; Rimbault's *A Little Book of Old Songs and Ballads*, p. 87; Baring-Gould's *A Book of Nursery Songs and Rhymes*, No. 17, p. 27. There is an Irish version printed in *Notes and Queries*, 1st series, vol. ii, p. 75. American versions have been printed in *The Journal of American Folk-Lore*, vol. xxvi, pp. 134–135; Brockway and Wyman, *Lonesome Tunes*, vol. i, pp. 25–29; Campbell and Sharp, *English Folksongs from the Appalachians*, Nos. 119–120, pp. 317–319. For the version sung by Liston see Davidson's *Universal Melodist*, 1847, vol. i, pp. 166–167. —R. H.

For further notes on the history of the song and British and American variants, see Albert H. Tolman and Mary O. Eddy, "Traditional Texts and Tunes," *The Journal of American Folk-Lore*, Vol. 35 (October–December, 1922), No. 138, pp. 394–399. For the "kymo" type of refrain, see Grace Partridge Smith, "A Vermont Variant of 'The Frog's Courting,'" *ibid.*, vol. 52 (January–March, 1939), No. 203, pp. 125–127.

Ibid., pp. 40–45.

For other versions of *The Birds' Courting Song* (sung by James Atwood) see Campbell and Sharp, pp. 310–311.—R. H.

"Hi!" said the little mourning dove,
"I'll tell you how to regain her love:
Court her night and court her day,
Never give her time to say 'O nay!'"

"Hi!" said the woodpecker, sitting on a fence,
"Once I courted a handsome wench;
She got scary and from me fled,
And ever since then my head's been red."

"Hi!" said the blue-jay, as she flew,
"If I was a young man I'd have two.
If one proved faithless and chanced for to go,
I'd have a new string to my bow."

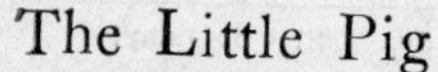

The Little Pig

There was an old woman and she had a little pig,
Um———,
There was an old woman and she had a little pig,
Um———,
There was an old woman and she had a little pig,
He didn't cost much 'cause he wasn't very big,
Um———.

Ibid., 46–49.

For other versions of *The Little Pig* see Halliwell's "Nursery Rhymes," 1st ed., No. 27, p. 18 (6th ed., No. 542, p. 266); M. H. Mason's "Nursery Rhymes and Country Songs," pp. 32–33; Rimbault's "A Collection of Old Nursery Rhymes," No. 34, p. 42. —R. H.

This little old woman kept the pig in the barn,
The prettiest thing she had on the farm.

This little woman fed the pig on clover,
And he laid down and died all over.

The little piggy died 'cause he could n't get his breath,
Now wasn't that a horrible death?

The little old woman she died of grief,
Now wasn't that a great relief.

The little old man laid down and died,
ONE, TWO, THREE laid side by side.

Johnny Sands

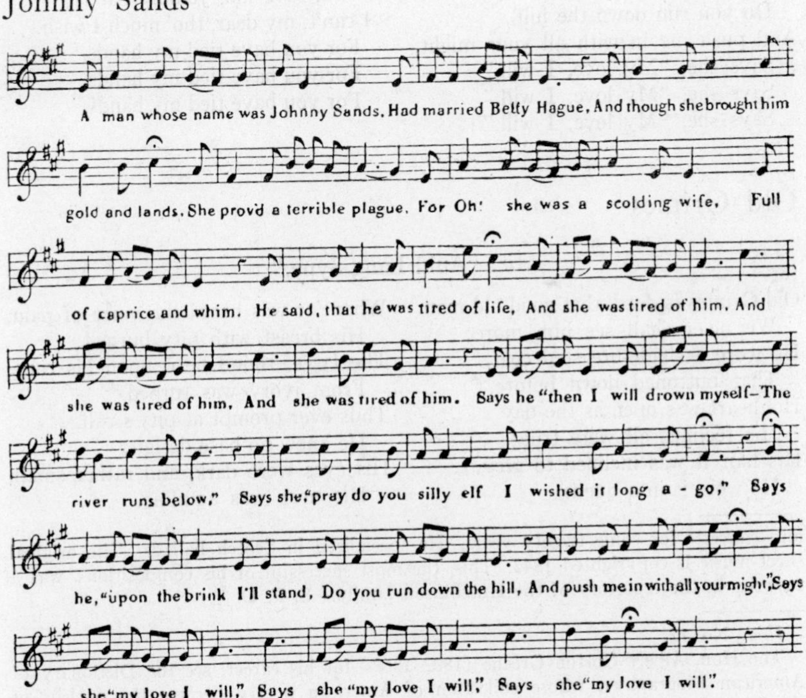
A man whose name was Johnny Sands, Had married Betty Hague, And though she brought him
gold and lands, She prov'd a terrible plague. For Oh! she was a scolding wife, Full
of caprice and whim. He said, that he was tired of life, And she was tired of him. And
she was tired of him, And she was tired of him. Says he "then I will drown myself—The
river runs below," Says she, "pray do you silly elf I wished it long a - go," Says
he, "upon the brink I'll stand, Do you run down the hill, And push me in with all your might," Says
she "my love I will," Says she "my love I will," Says she "my love I will."

From *Series of Old American Songs,* Reproduced in Facsimile from Original or Early Editions in the Harris Collection of American Poetry and Plays, with Brief Annotations by S. Foster Damon, Curator, No. 30. Providence, Rhode Island: Brown University Library. 1936.

This song was founded on a folk tale and in turn has become a folk song, collected by ballad experts. It was written, however, by John Sinclair, who was born in 1790 (probably in Scotland), and began his American career about 1830, singing in operas

A man whose name was Johnny Sands
Had married Betty Hague,
And though she brought him gold and lands,
She prov'd a terrible plague,
For oh! she was a scolding wife,
Full of caprice and whim,
He said, that he was tired of life,
And she was tired of him,
And she was tired of him,
And she was tired of him.

Says he, "Then I will drown myself—
The river runs below,"
Says she, "Pray do you silly elf
I wished it long ago,"
Says he, "Upon the brink I'll stand,
Do you run down the hill,
And push me in with all your might,
Says she, "My love, I will,"
Says she, "My love, I will,"
Says she, "My love, I will."

"For fear that I should courage lack
And try to save my life,
Pray tie my hands behind my back."
"I will," replied his wife.
She tied them fast as you may think,
And when securely done,
"Now stand," she says, "upon the brink
And I'll prepare to run,
And I'll prepare to run,
And I'll prepare to run."

All down the hill his loving bride
Now ran with all her force
To push him in—he stepped aside,
And she fell in, of course,
Now splashing, dashing, like a fish.
"Oh, save me, Johnny Sands."
"I can't, my dear, tho' much I wish,
For you have tied my hands,
For you have tied my hands,
For you have tied my hands."

Old Grimes

Air: "Auld Lang Syne."

Old Grimes is dead, that good old man,
We ne'er shall see him more;
He wore a single-breasted coat,
That buttoned down before.
His heart was open as the day,
His feelings all were true;
His hair it was inclined to grey,
He wore it in a queue.

Whene'er was heard the voice of pain,
His breast with pity burned;
The large, round head upon his cane,
From ivory was turned.
Thus ever prompt at pity's call,
He knew no base design;
His eyes were dark, and rather small,
His nose was aquiline.

---

and concerts for some twenty years. He specialized in Scotch ballads. The original sheet-music is copyrighted 1842. This, the most successful of his compositions, was a favorite in the repertory of the Hutchinson family.—S. F. D.

Ibid., No. 12.

The Hon. Albert Gorton Greene (1802–1868—for his career, see the Dictionary of American Biography), whose collection of American poetry became the nucleus of the Harris Collection, was the author of this ballad, which added a beloved figure to American folklore.

Greene is said to have written the song when only sixteen (at which time he was a sophomore at Brown); another tradition delays the composition until he was studying at the famous Lichfield Law School (1820–22). It was first published anonymously in the *Providence Gazette*, January 16, 1822; Greene acknowledged his authorship of all but the first stanza in a letter to the *Manufacturers' and Farmers' Journal* (Providence) May 16, 1833. He contributed a revised version to Anne Lynch's *Rhode Island*

He lived at peace with all mankind,
In friendship he was true;
His coat had pocketholes behind,
His pantaloons were blue,
But poor old Grimes is now at rest,
Nor fears misfortune's frown;
He had a double-breasted vest,
The stripes ran up and down.

He modest merit sought to find,
And pay it its desert;
He had no malice in his mind,
No ruffle on his shirt.

His neighbors he did not abuse,
Was sociable and gay;
He wore not rights and lefts for shoes,
But changed them every day.

His knowledge, hid from public gaze,
He never brought to view;
He made a noise town-meeting days,
As many people do.
Thus, undisturbed by anxious care,
His peaceful moments ran;
And everybody said he was
A fine old gentleman.

Derby Ram

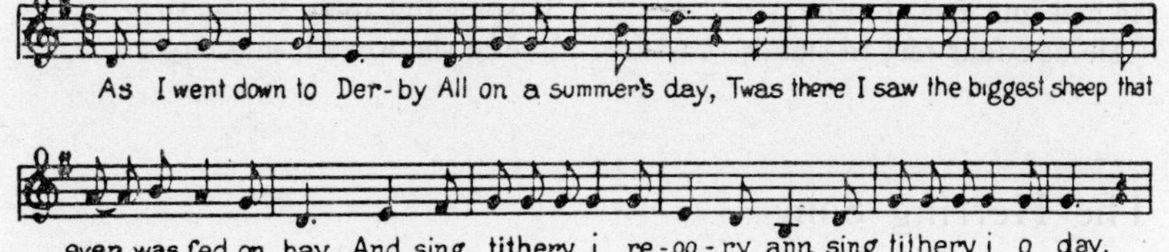

As I went down to Derby,
All on a summer's day,
'Twas there I saw the biggest sheep
'Twas ever fed on hay.

Chorus:
And sing tithery i reoory ann,
Sing tithery i o day.

Book (1841). It was published separately, with illustrations by Augustus Hoppin, in 1867.

The many claimants to authorship while it was still anonymous have been forgotten. There were also several who claimed to be the original Grimes; but as Greene did not write the opening quatrain (it is said to have been an old epitaph), and Goldsmith's "Elegy on Madame Blaize" was obviously its other parent, these claimants also may be dismissed.

A host of imitations at once sprang into existence; Old Grimes was furnished with wives, children, parents, and live-stock, to a surprising extent. One of these, "Young Grimes," was written by Walter (not yet "Walt") Whitman.

The ballad was sung to the tune of "Auld Lang Syne."—S. F. D.

From *A Garland of Green Mountain Song,* edited by Helen Hartness Flanders, piano settings by Helen Norfleet, pp. 24-26. Copyright, 1934, by Helen Hartness Flanders. Number One, Green Mountain Pamphlets. Published as part of the publication program of the Committee for the Conservation of Vermont Traditions and Ideals of the Vermont Commission on Country Life, Arthur Wallace Peach, Agent. Northfield, Vermont.

We have many versions of this spirited song in Vermont. This is transcribed by E. F. as sung by Mr. Eugene Hall (deceased) of Ludlow. The fourth verse was supplied by Mr. E. M. Burdett, formerly of the same lumber camp where it had been learned.—H. H. F.

The wool on the sheep bag, sir,
  It reached unto the sky.
The eagles built their nests there,
  And I heard the young ones cry.

The wool on that sheep belly, sir,
  It dragged unto the ground,
Was sold there in Derby
  For forty-thousand pounds.

The horns on this sheep's head, sir,
  They reached unto the moon.
A man went up in February
  And never came down till June.

He had four feet to walk, sir,
  He had four feet to stand;
And every foot he had, sir,
  It covered an acre of land.

When they killed this sheep, sir,
  It caused an awful flood;
And the man that killed the sheep, sir,
  Was drowned in his blood.

The man that owned this sheep, sir,
  He was immensely rich;
And the man that composed this song, sir,
  Was the lying son of a gun.

The wool on this sheep tail, sir,
  I've heard the weaver say,
It spun full forty yards, sir,
  And she wove it in a day.

The Herring Song

As I was walking down by the sea side,
I saw an old herring floating up with the tide;
He was forty feet long and fifty feet square,
If this ain't a great lie I will sing no more here.

And what do you think I made of his head?
'Twas forty fine ovens as ever baked bread,
Some shovels and pokers and other fine things,—
Don't you think I made well of my jovial herring?

And what do you think I made of his eyes?
'Twas forty great puddings and fifty great pies,
Some mustards and custards and other fine things,—
Don't you think I made well of my jovial herring?

And what do you think I made of his tail?
'Twas forty fine shipping as ever sot sail,
Some long-boats and barges and other fine things,—
Don't you think I made well of my jovial herring?

From "Cape Cod Dialect," by George Davis Chase, in *Dialect Notes,* Vol. II (Part V, 1903), pp. 302–303. Publication of the American Dialect Society. New Haven, Connecticut. Published by the Society.

The . . . *Herring Song* was sometimes used by the men as a cradle song.—G. D. C. No tune. For a Somerset version, with tune, see "The Red Herring," Charles H. Farnsworth and Cecil J. Sharp, *Folk-Songs, Chanteys and Singing Games* (New York, [n.d.]), pp. 46–47.

And what do you think I made of his scales?
'Twas forty fine blacksmiths as ever made nails,
Some carpenters and masons and other fine things,—
Don't you think I made well of my jovial herring?

And what do you think I made of his guts?
Some forty pretty maidens and fifty great sluts,
Some kitchen maids and chamber maids and other fine things,—
Don't you think I made well of my jovial herring?

The Old Man Who Lived in the Wood

There was an old man that lived in a wood, As
you can plain - ly see, Who said he could do more
work in a day Than his wife could do in three. "If
that be so," the old wom - an said, "Why, this you must al -
low, That you shall do my work for a day, While I go drive the plough!"

From *Folk Songs of Old New England,* collected and edited by Eloise Hubbard Linscott, with an Introduction by James M. Carpenter, pp. 248–250. Copyright, 1939, by the Macmillan Company. New York.

Contributed by Phillips Barry, Cambridge, Massachusetts. This ballad is of Scotch origin and is based on a well-known theme in folklore. The oldest version of the story in English goes back to the late fifteenth century. It appeared in James Johnson's *Scots Musical Museum* in 1787. The song is widely known throughout New England. —E. H. L.

There was an old man that lived in a wood,
As you can plainly see,
Who said he could do more work in a day
Than his wife could do in three.
"If that be so," the old woman said,
"Why, this you must allow,
That you shall do my work for a day,
While I go drive the plough!

"But you must milk the tiny cow,
For fear she should go dry;
And you must feed the little pigs
That are within the sty;
And you must watch the bracket hen,
Lest she should lay astray;
And you must wind the reel of yarn
That I spun yesterday."

The old woman took the staff in her hand,
And went to drive the plough;
The old man took the pail in his hand,
And went to milk the cow;

But Tiny hinched and Tiny flinched,
And Tiny cocked her nose;
And Tiny hit the old man such a kick
That the blood ran down his nose.

'T was, "Hey, my good cow," and "Ho, my good cow,"
And "Now, my good cow, stand still.
If ever I milk this cow again,
'T will be against my will."
And when he'd milked the Tiny cow,
For fear she should go dry,
Why, then he fed the little pigs,
That were within the sty.

And then he watched the bracket hen
Lest she should lay astray;
But he forgot the reel of yarn
His wife spun yesterday.
He swore by all the leaves on the tree
And all the stars in heaven
That his wife could do more work in a day
Than he could do in seven!

The Lone Fish-Ball

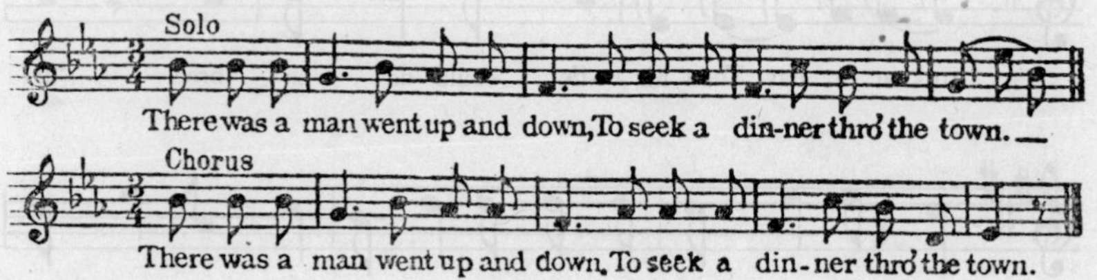

The College Version [1]

Solo: There was a man went up and down,
To seek a dinner thro' the town.

Chorus: There was a man went up and down,
To seek a dinner thro' the town.

---

[1] From *Carmina Collegensia,* edited by H. R. Waite, p. 15. Boston: Oliver Ditson & Company. 1876. Cited in *Read 'Em and Weep,* The Songs You Forgot to Remember, by Sigmund Spaeth, pp. 84–85. Copyright, 1926, by Doubleday, Page & Co. Garden City. 1927.

This song has been adapted by Hy Zaret and Lou Silver under the title "One Meat Ball."

It was one of the earliest and best of those immensely handy community songs in which a soloist presents two short lines, which are immediately repeated after him by the crowd."—S. S.

What wretch is he who wife forsakes,
Who best of jam and waffles makes!

He feels his cash to know his pence,
And finds he has but just six cents.

He finds at last a right cheap place,
And enters in with modest face.

The bill of fare he searches through,
To see what his six cents will do.

The cheapest viand of them all
Is "Twelve and a half cents for two
Fish-balls."

The waiter he to him doth call,
And gently whispers—"One Fish-
ball."

The waiter roars it through the hall,
The guests they start at "One Fish-
ball!"

The guest then says, quite ill at
ease,
"A piece of bread, sir, if you please."

The waiter roars it through the hall,
"We don't give bread with one Fish-
ball."

Moral

Who would have bread with his Fish-
ball
Must get it first, or not at all.

Who would Fish-ball with fixin's eat
Must get some friend to stand a treat.

The History of the Song [2]

In the Boston area, especially among the Harvard elect, American humor in the late fifties, and beyond, centered about a Dr. Holmes-like "Skit" entitled "The Lay of the One Fishball." So fundamentally Harvard was it that as late as 1888, in the college song book of that year, it was the second song in the collection, following "Fair Harvard." Its author was George Martin Lane, Ph.D., Göttingen, 1851; Professor of Latin, Harvard, 1851–1894. That this seeming trifle should outlive all its author's scholarly volumes which for years were of international significance is one of the anomalies of literature.

The poem was first published in 1857, where I do not know. The authentic text, which differs from the song-book version, has been supplied by Charles Eliot Norton, as follows:

THE LAY OF THE ONE FISHBALL

1. There was a man went round the
town,
To hunt a supper up and down;
There was a man, etc.

2. For he had been right far away,
And nothing had to eat all day.

3. He feels his cash to count his
pence,
And all he had was just six cents.

4. "Wretch that I am, it happens
meet,
Why did I leave my Kirkland
Street!

[2] From *The Feminine Fifties*, by Fred Lewis Pattee, pp. 217–220, 221–223. Copyright, 1940, by D. Appleton-Century Company, Inc. New York and London.

5. "None but a fool a wife forsakes,
Who raspberry jam and waffles makes.

6. "If I were now safe out of town,
I'd give my bran-new dressing-gown.

7. "But yet I'll make a start and try
To see what my six cents will buy."

8. He finds at last a right cheap place,
And stealeth in with bashful face.

9. The bill of fare he runneth through,
To see what his six cents will do.

10. The cheapest of the viands all,
Was 12½ for two fishball.

11. The waiter he to him doth call,
And whispers softly, "One fishball."

12. The waiter roars it through the hall,
The guests they start at *"One fishball!"*

13. The waiter brings one fishball on,
The guest he looks abashéd down.

14. The scantness of the fare he sees:
"A piece of bread, now, if you please."

15. The waiter roars it through the hall,
"We don't give bread with one fishball!"

16. Then whoso orders one fishball
Must get bread first or not at all.

17. And who would two with fixins eat,
Should get some friend to stand a treat.

Few facetiae of equal caliber have had such distinguished treatment as this Harvard *jeu d'esprit*. In the opening days of the Civil War it was thrown into the form of an elaborate opera score in Italian by Professor Francis James Child: *Il Pesceballo. Opera Seria: In Un Atto. Musica del Maestro Rossibelli-Donimozarti.* Cambridge, 1862. On the verso of each page was the Italian text and on the recto the poetic translation by James Russell Lowell. The version, made for the Sanitary Commission, was performed several times in Cambridge and Boston, and a goodly sum of money was realized for the use of the soldiers. In 1899 the Caxton Club reissued the little volume in an edition limited to 210 copies with an introduction written by Charles Eliot Norton. Concerning the origin of the ballad he wrote this:

> The theme of the Pesceballo was suggested to him by a local ballad which had had great vogue, written not many years before by his classmate and lifelong friend Lane, the genial and eminent professor of Latin at Harvard. I send you its genuine text. The account of its origin is given in a recent memoir of Mr. Lane by Professor Morgan. He says: "Many fables about the origin of this song have been told, and one was even printed with the song itself; but I know from Professor Lane's lips that it was based upon an adventure of his own. Arriving in Boston one day after a journey, he found himself hungry and with only twenty-five

cents in his pocket. Half that sum he had to reserve to pay his carfare to Cambridge. With the rest he entered a restaurant, "with modest face," and ordered a half portion of macaroni. What followed is described, doubtless with humorous exaggeration, in the ballad itself. During the late Civil War it was worked over into a mock Italian operetta, Il Pesceballo, by Professor Child, with an English version by Professor Lowell!"

Child's Italian version is a rare bit of humor. In a footnote, he explains to mythical Italians who may read the opera the mysteries of the Boston fishball:

> Il Pesceballo *(corruzione della voce inglese Fish-ball) è un prodotto della cucina americana, consistente in una combinazione di stoccofisso con patate, fatta nella forma di pallottole, simili alle nostre polpette, e poi fritta. Msgr. Bedini, nel suo* Viaggio negli Stati Uniti, *c' insegna che la detta pietanza si usa massimamente nella Nuova-Inghilterra, ove, secondo quel venerabile, viene specialmente mangiato a coloazione nelle domeniche.*

* * * * *

Few have known that Lowell, following Child's Italian with extravagant variations, ever wrote a complete opera like this. It must have been done with the pen, somewhat blunted, that had written the *Fable for Critics.* This, for instance, at the crisis moment of the tragedy:

THE STRANGER *in a rich tenor:*

Now, waiter, bring to me the bill of fare.
(*aside*) Ye pangs within, what will not hunger dare?

THE WAITER *in basso profundo:*

Here is the bill of fare, sir,
Of what there is for supper,
Long as the Proverbs of Tupper,—
Command, then, *s'il vous plait*!

Soup, with nothing, twenty coppers,
Roast spring-chicken, three and nime [*sic*],
Ditto biled (but then they're whoppers!)
Fish-balls, luscious, two a dime,
Two a dime, sir, hot and prime, sir,
Fried codfish-balls, two a dime!
There's the bill, and cash procures ye
Any viand that allures ye. . . .
Best of all, though, 's the fish-ball, though,
We have made 'em all the fashion.
Come to try 'em as we fry 'em,—
Presto! liking turns to passion!
There we carry off the banner,
'Taint so easy, neither, that ain't,—

But, you see, we've got a patent,—
Do 'em in the Cape Cod manner,—
That's the way to make 'em flavorous!
Fried in butter, tongue can't utter
How they're brown, and crisp, and savorous!

S. Peace, waiter, for I starve meanwhile,—but hold:
Bring me *one* fish-ball, *one,*—*(aside)* curst lack of gold!
Moment of horror! crisis of my doom!
Led by the dreadful Shape, I sought this room
With half a dime! A slender sum, and yet
'Twill buy one fish-ball! Down, weak pride, forget
Thy happier—but what prate I? Thought of dread
If, with one fish-ball, they should *not* give bread!

W. Here's your *one* fish-ball, sir—*(sarcasticclly)* you ordered *one*?

S. Thanks,—and with bread to match, 'twere not ill done.

W. *(with fury)* With one single fish-ball, is't bread ye are after?
So wild a presumption provokes me to laughter!
So mad a suggestion proves, out of all question,
Howe'er the test shun, you're mad as a hornet!
I trample it, scorn it, so mad a suggestion!
It fills me with fury, it dumbs me with rage!

S. With one dainty fish-ball do *you* bread refuse me?
It's *you* are the madman yourself, sir, excuse me!
My wish was immodest? Of men you're the oddest!
In straight-waistcoat bodiced, go hide ye in Bedlam!
Your fish-balls, *there* peddle 'em! learn to be modest,
And tempt not a stranger half-starving to rage!

Chorus. O'er one paltry fish-ball d'ye make such a rumpus?
For gracious sake, neighbors, we'd rather you'd thump us!

The entrance of the landlady calms the tumult. The opera ends in pure slapstick. . . .

GAME AND DANCE SONGS

Pompey

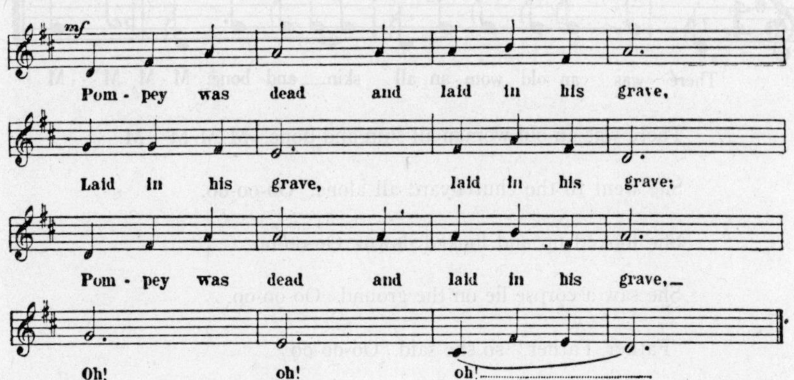
mf
Pom - pey was dead and laid in his grave,
Laid in his grave, laid in his grave;
Pom - pey was dead and laid in his grave,—
Oh! oh! oh!

Pompey was dead, and laid in his grave,
 Laid in his grave, laid in his grave;
Pompey was dead, and laid in his grave,—
 Oh! Oh! Oh!

An apple-tree grew over his head,
Over his head, over his head, etc.

The apples were ripe, beginning to fall.

There came an old woman a-picking them up.

Pompey jumped up and gave her a thump.

It made the old woman go hipple de hop.

If you want any more, then sing it yourself.

From "'Pompey!' A Famous End Song," Words by Mrs. K. B.—Music by W. R. Dehnoff, Arranged by J. J. Freeman. Copyright, 1876, by W. R. Dehnoff. In *Series of Old American Songs,* Reproduced in Facsimile from Original or Early Editions in the Harris Collection of American Poetry and Plays, with Brief Annotations by S. Foster Damon, Curator, No. 50. Providence, Rhode Island: Brown University Library. 1936.

"Pompey" is a child's game of considerable antiquity. The children sing it while enacting the parts of the dead boy, the apple-tree, and the little old woman. The terminal vocalizing is delightfully dramatic.

The ballad experts have found versions all over the United States, the name "Pompey" being variously given as "Old Grimes" (New York and Kentucky), "Old Cromwell" (Cambridge, Mass.), "Old Grampus" (North Carolina and Mississippi), also "Poor Robin," "Old Rover," "Poor Roger," "Poor Johnny," "Poor Tommy," "Sir Roger," "Cock Robin," "Old Tommy," "Old Granddaddy," "Old Pompey," and "Old Kramer." It is said that the song is known as a chantey.

The sheet-music, with "words by Mrs. K. B." and "music by W. R. Dehnoff," is dated 1876.

For references, see W. W. Newell's *Games and Songs of American Children,* p. 100; Louise Pound's *American Ballads and Songs,* pp. 232–233 and 256; Flanders and Brown's *Vermont Folk Songs and Ballads,* p. 182; Louise Pound's *Folk Songs of Nebraska,* p. 57; Mellinger E. Henry's *More Songs of American Southern Highlands,* pp. 94–95;

Old Woman All Skin and Bone

Chantingly
There was an old wom-an all skin— and bone. M-M M--M

There was an old woman all skin and bone. M-M M---M.

She went to the churchyard all alone. Oo-oo-oo.

She looked up and looked down. Oo-oo-oo.

She saw a corpse lie on the ground. Oo-oo-oo.

"Father, Father," so she said. Oo-oo-oo.

"Shall I look so when I am dead?" Oo-oo-oo.

The sexton to her made reply. Oo-oo-oo.

"Yes, my darling, by and by." *Boo!*

---

and the *Journal of American Folk Lore,* Vols. XIII, XXVI, XXXIV, XXXV, XXXIX, XL.—S. F. D.

From *Folk Songs of Old New England,* Collected and Edited by Eloise Hubbard Linscott, With an Introduction by James M. Carpenter, pp. 44–46. Copyright, 1939, by The Macmillan Company. New York.

The children of Dr. and Mrs. Frank Allen Hubbard of Taunton, Massachusetts, who sang and played this game, sometimes reserved it to initiate visiting playmates and newcomers.

The most highly imaginative player usually was chosen for the corpse, for after one really fine screech the game was quite likely to end abruptly with the appearance of a grown-up bringing emphatic requests for less disturbance during the doctor's office hours.

This weird game originally came from Somersetshire and is a dramatization of the belief that the dead return for vengeance on those that disturb them.

Each object and person in the verses is represented by a player chosen by counting out. The one taking the part of the old woman approaches the corpse, which lies at the feet of the sexton. All the players sing as the old woman walks slowly toward the "churchyard," and the eerie, half-moaning chant is broken by the shrill scream of the corpse as it arises suddenly and gives chase to the other players, who add to the effect with shrill cries. If the corpse can catch another player, that one becomes the old woman, the first old woman becomes the sexton, and the game continues.—E. H. L.

Quaker's Courtship

Mad-am, I am come a-courting, Hum, hum, heigh-o hum! 'Tis for pleasure,

not for sport-ing, Hum, hum, heigh-o hum! Sir, it suits me to re-tire, Teedle link tum

D. C.
teedle tum a tee; You may sit and court the fire, Teedle link tum, teedle tum a tee.

"Madam, I am come a-courting—
Hum, hum, heigho hum!
'Tis for pleasure, not for sporting—
Hum, hum, heigho hum!"

"Sir, it suits me to retire,
Teedle link tum, teedle tum a tee;
You may sit and court the fire,
Teedle link tum, teedle tum a tee."

"Madam, here's a ring worth forty shilling,
Thou may'st have it if thou art willing."

"What care I for rings or money?
I'll have a man who will call me honey."

"Madam, thou art tall and slender;
Madam, I know thy heart is tender."

"Sir, I see you are a flatterer,
And I never loved a Quaker."

"Must I give up my religion?
Must I be a Presbyterian?"

"Cheer up, cheer up, loving brother,
If you can't catch one fish catch another."

Hey, Betty Martin!

Hey, Betty Martin, tip-toe, tip-toe,
Hey, Betty Martin, tip-toe fine!

Johnny, get your hair cut, hair cut, hair cut,
Johnny, get your hair cut, hair cut short!

From Games and Songs of American Children, collected and compared by William Wells Newell, pp. 94–95. New and Enlarged Edition. Copyright, 1883, 1903, by Harper & Brothers. New York and London.

In this piece, two children (in costume or otherwise) impersonate a Quaker paying his addresses to a young lady of the world.—W. W. N.

From *Ballads of the American Revolution and the War of 1812,* A Program of Early American Songs Taken from the Collection of John Allison, sung by John and Lucy Allison, with Sawyer's Minute Men, Victor Album P-11, Record 26462-A, 2. Camden,

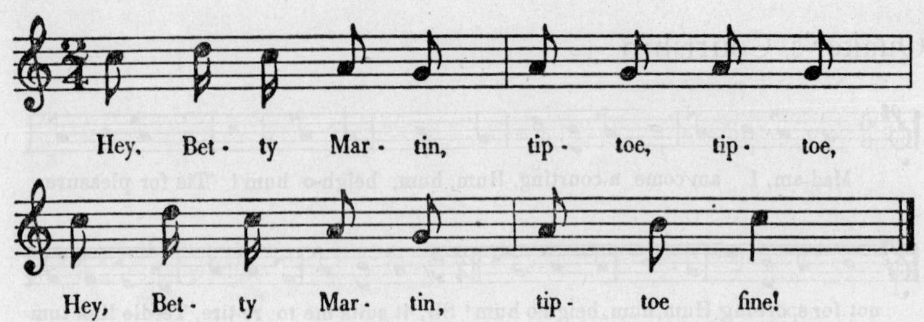
Hey, Bet - ty Mar - tin, tip - toe, tip - toe,
Hey, Bet - ty Mar - tin, tip - toe fine!

Johnny, get your gun and your sword and pistol,
Johnny, get your gun and come with me!

Hey, Betty Martin, tip-toe, tip-toe,
Hey, Betty Martin, tip-toe fine!

Devil's Dream

New Jersey: RCA Victor Division, RCA Manufacturing Company, Inc. Transcribed by Frances Kurland.

. . . this ditty goes back to the War of 1812, and for over a century it has been a favorite march tune with the fifers and drummers of the American army. Iowa pioneers had a version of it as a play-party and dance tune under the title of "Old Brass Wagon."—J. A.

For a different version, from Howe's *Songs and Ballads of ye Olden Times,* describing a Yorkshireman's first visit to London, see Edward Arthur Dolph, *"Sound Off!"* (New York, 1942), pp. 437–439.

Played by Dennis McClure, Willimantic, Connecticut. Dance changes called by Happy Hale, Hinsdale, New Hampshire.

From *Folk Songs of Old New England,* collected and edited by Eloise Hubbard Linscott, with an Introduction by James M. Carpenter, pp. 72–74. Copyright, 1939, by The Macmillan Company. New York.

Square Formation *Four Couples in a Set*

Balance partners eight hands around	8 bars
Swing to the corners	4 "
Head lady swings gentleman on her right.	
Head gentleman swings lady on his left.	
Join hands and circle eight hands around	8 "
Back to place	
First lady leads to the right and swings to the corner	4 "
First lady swings to the third gentleman at the same time the first gentleman swings the lady of the second couple	4 "
Dos-a-dos to the corners	4 "
Allemande left. Then right hand to the partner, and swing	8 "

Repeat, with the second couple progressing through the set as did the first couple.

This is the way Happy Hale sings it:

Here we go eight hands around
First lady leads to the right
Grab that gent and hold him up tight
Up to the next and on your toes
Swing that gent with the big long nose
Up to the next who's standing there
Swing that gent with the curly red hair
Up to the next and swing your own
Now—everybody swing
Dosey dos to the corners all
Dosey dos with your own little doll
Allemande left with the lady on your left
Give right hand to your own little doll
(*Grand right and left*)
Right foot up and left foot down
Hand over hand or you'll never get around
And when you meet her pass her by
Wink at the next as you go by
Kiss the next right on the sly
And swing your own by and by.

The Merry Dance

From *The Country Dance Book,* The Old-Fashioned Square Dance, Its History, Lore, Variations, & Its Callers, Complete & Joyful Instructions, written by Beth

PERHAPS one of the happiest numbers of this [contry] group is the Merry Dance. Everyone seems to like this one no matter which way he believes it should be danced. Of the several versions, we like the one which originated with the Holmes brothers in Stoddard, New Hampshire. They wrote the music for it, too. These boys are contemporary Yankees, and their dance is loyally done in all the surrounding towns. On one occasion not many years ago, the Merry Dance became part of Stoddard's history. It was the night of the "Great Blizzard" (not the Great Blizzard of '88). The snow began to swirl off Pitcher Mountain, and the dancers were forced to stay the night in the town hall. The dance went on as the snow piled up against the windows. Nobody could get home. At the turn of dawn, when the oil lamps were blown out, the orchestra struck up the Holmes brothers' Merry Dance. The dancers stepped this one out until finally the cornetist rebelled. Putting down his instrument, he shouted, "What the hell is this anyway, a dance or a blank-blank overture?" Thereafter the dance was nicknamed the Stoddard Overture. And now, when someone suggests a Stoddard Overture, why don't you ask him if he remembers the night when . . . ?

Contry Formation *Six or Eight Couples in a Set*

First couple cross over, first lady down outside and back with second gent; first gent down the outside and back with second lady at same time	8 bars
Same four join hands, down center four and back	8 "
Cast off, ladies chain	8 "
Half promenade	4 "
Half right and left	4 "

Third and fifth couples start the dance at the same time.

Wild Goose Chase

Contry Formation *Six or Eight Couples in a Set*

First couple cross over before music starts

First and third couples join hands with partners and balance in center toward each other. (Second couple stand like lighthouses)	4 bars

---

Tolman & Ralph Page, pp. 95–96. Copyright, 1937, by The Countryman Press, Inc. New York: A. S. Barnes and Company.

Ibid., pp. 93, 167, 168.

Contry Formation *Six or Eight Couples in a Set*

First couple walk behind second lady and take third couple's place. At the same time third couple walks behind second gent and takes first couple's place. (Second couple still stand like lighthouses)	4 "
These two couples balance again	4 "
First and third couples return in same way to original places	4 "
First couple down center and back	8 "
Cast off, right and left	8 "

(Remember gent is on lady's side, from original crossing over before music began.)

Head couple continue, dancing with fourth, fifth, sixth, etc., couples.

Each head couple cross over before they begin their performance. When they reach the foot of the set they cross over to their respective sides.

* * * * *

Mr. Barrett scoffs at the idea that the dance Wild Goose Chase was so named by Federal soldiers floundering vainly after Jeb Stuart. "Why, old Sewall Page has told me about playing that tune a good many years before the Civil War. Called it Wild Goose Chase, too. Goes something like this . . . ," and after one or two flourishes of the bow, he played it for us. First a simple, direct melody, and then a bow-twisting variation, probably his own, although he didn't say so.

II. RHYMES AND JINGLES

I trust, my friend, you will not gather from this that I condemn rhymes for children. I know that there is a certain music in them that delights the ear of children. Nor am I insensible to the fact that in Mother Goose's Melodies, there is frequently a sort of humor in the odd jingle of sound and sense. There is, furthermore, in many of them, an historical significance, which may please the profound student who puzzles it out; but what I affirm is, that many of these pieces are coarse, vulgar, offensive, and it is precisely these portions that are apt to stick in the minds of children.—Samuel G. Goodrich

. . . the old-fashioned idea was to put into rhyme anything that should be committed to memory; in Yorkshire "nominy" is the name given to this class of verse, an appellation very likely derived from the church formula "in nominee Patris" (in the name of the Father, etc.).—Journal of American Folklore

There is a nationality in districts as well as in countries. . . . This has given rise . . . to an infinite number of phrases expres-

sive of vituperation, obloquy, or contempt, which are applied to the inhabitants of various places by those whose lot it is to reside in the immediate vicinity.—ROBERT CHAMBERS

1. CHILDREN'S RHYMES

FOR all his moralistic objections to their content, or lack of it, Samuel G. Goodrich, the creator of "Peter Parley," hit upon the precise reasons for the appeal of children's rhymes—their jingle and nonsense, their odd humor and bantering wit, and their very impropriety. So even though Boston could not justly claim Elizabeth Vergoose to be the original of that "eponomyous preceptress" of nursery rhymes and tales, as William A. Wheeler attempted to prove in 1870,[1] the New England conscience could not completely ignore the low taste of Yankee youngsters for nursery rhymes any more than it could stamp out the taste of their elders for "devil's ditties." Thus even the rather dreary alphabet in the *New England Primer* surprises us, in the midst of pious and moral platitudes, with a lilting roster of Scriptural names:

Young *O*badias
David, Josias,
All were pious.

And the conclusion—

*Z*accheus he
Did climb the tree
His Lord to see—

was such good nursery-rhyme material that it eventually became incorporated into Negro folk song as "Zaccheus climbed the sycamo' tree [2] and into "Old Dan Tucker":

Old Dan Tucker climbed a tree
Just for his Lord to see.
Limb did break and he did fall,
And he didn't see his Lord at all.[3]

In the same irreverent vein is

Where was Moses when the light went out?
Down in the cellar with his shirt-tail out.[4]

At the same time, since even folk tradition has its didactic side, New England children's rhymes satisfied the demands of morality and faith, or at least of worldly wisdom, in such copybook mottoes as

---

[1] *Mother Goose's Melodies, or Songs for the Nursery* (New York, 1870). See Vincent Starrett, "Much Ado about Mother Goose," in Bookman's Holiday (New York, 1942), pp. 146–166.

[2] See Dorothy Scarborough, *On the Trail of Negro Folk-Songs* (Cambridge, 1925), pp. 200, 286.

[3] See B. A. Botkin, *The American Play-Party Song* (Lincoln, Nebraska, 1937), p. 263.

[4] Melville Johnson, Gorham, Maine, Manuscripts of the Federal Writers' Project of the Works Progress Administration, reports this as a dialogue spoken when a light is blown out by a breeze, with the ending:

He was in the dark with his shirt-tail out.

God is great,
God is good.
So always do
What He thinks you should,

and in such gentle cynicisms as

Needles and pins, needles and pins,
When a man gets married, his trouble begins.

2. Local Rhymes

Mary Heaton Vorse records an interesting example of local adaptation of a children's game in the Provincetown version of "Ring-around-a-rosy," which "has been translated into sea terms."

Ring a ring a rounder,
Daddy caught a flounder,
Oysters, Oysters, Hooray! [1]

Although adaptation is an important part of the process of formula and variation in the transmission of folk rhymes, as in folk sayings, an even more fertile source of local rhymes is the spirit of local rivalry and satire. Local gibes and taunts belong to the class of popular reproaches, which also includes children's teasing and taunting rhymes. The children's taunt and the local gibe are combined in the Newport ditty whose various combinations served to incite the various boys' quarters—the "up-town boys," the "over-to-The-Point boys," the "Long-wharf boys," and the "down-town boys"—against one another.[2]

Here, too, we encounter traditional formulae. Thus, after the pattern of the rhyme about Weymouth and its herring (previously cited),[3] we find:

Amherst for beauty,
Hadley for pride,
But if it hadn't been for huckleberries,
Shutesbury would have died.[4]

And the lines used by Truro and Wellfleet boys and girls to taunt Provincetown youngsters (already given under "The Codfish Shanty") turn up in Gloucester and Bahaman adaptations, the latter reading:

Those Nassau girls ain't got no comb,
O they comb they head with a whipper back bone.[5]

A similar formula is seen in:

The Montague girls are pretty,
And the Howland girls are sweet,

[1] *Time and the Town* (New York, 1942), p. 153.

[2] See pp. 484–485 above.

[3] P. 495 above.

[4] Mrs. Clifton Johnson, South Hadley, Mass., in a letter of July 24, 1947.

[5] "Round the Bay of Mexico," recorded for the Library of Congress by Alan Lomax and Mary Elizabeth Barnicle, *Folk-Music of the United States, 1942* (Washington, D. C.), Album V, No. AFFS 21 A, 2.

But the Passadumkeag girls
Have big feet.[1]

Many nursery rhymes originate in local or historical rhymes, adding a touch of nonsense and word-play to the jest.

As I was dashing down Cutting Hill,
A-cutting through the air,
I saw Charlie Cutting setting
In Oscar Cutting's chair;
And Oscar Cutting was a-cutting
Charlie Cutting's hair.[2]

Finally, the spirit of the nursery rhyme and the local rhyme combined pervades the epitaph, a form of folk rhyme in which New England seems to have excelled. Although the serious epitaph sometimes reaches the level of folk poetry, the humorous (or unconsciously humorous) and the mock epitaph rarely rise above the level of the limerick. Perhaps the most frequently quoted is the following punning epitaph:

Under the sod and under the trees,
Here lies the body of Solomon Pease.
The Pease are not here, there's only the pod—
The Pease shelled out and went to God.[3]

Epitaph humor also includes such stories as the one based on the most common of the traditional epitaphs:

Pause, stranger, ere you pass by—
As you are now, so once was I.
As I am now, soon you will be.
Prepare for death, and follow me.—

It is said of one Cape Cod widow, who had not got on too well with her late husband, that she refused to let the minister spread one of these tributes upon his stone. But something had to be written there, so the usual stock verse was chiseled on it, this too, against her wishes—

As I am now, so you will be,
Prepare for death and follow me.

She went out one dark night and scratched beneath it:

To follow you I'll not consent
Because I know which way you went.[4]

B. A. B.

---

[1] Mrs. Catherine McGinn, Enfield, Me., Manuscripts of the Federal Writers' Project of the Works Progress Administration for the State of Maine, who notes: "Montague was an early name for Enfield."

[2] Bessie Powers Stevens, Georgetown, Me. *ibid.*

[3] Edwin Valentine Mitchell, *It's an Old New England Custom* (New York, 1946), p. 145, who notes: "The descendants of a man at Searsport, Maine, are said to have had so much fun poked at them on account of the . . . epitaph that they had it effaced."

[4] Jeremiah Digges, *Cape Cod Pilot* (Provincetown and New York, 1937), p. 92.

PLAY RHYMES

Counting-Out Rhymes

From Vermont [1]

Inty, minty, dibity fig
Dilah, dalah, dominig,
Ikah, pikah, dominika,
Elika, belika, boo—
Out goes Y O U.

Eenie, meenie, miney mo,
Crack a fenney, finey fo,
Ommanuga, poppatuga,
Rick, stick, dan do.

Entry, mentry, cutery corn,
Apple seed and apple thorn,
Wire, brier, limber lock,
Six geese in a flock.

One zaw, two zaw, zig, zaw, zan,
Bobtail, vinegar, ticklum tan,
Harum, scarum, virgum, marum,
Stringlum, stranglum, back and John.

Eenie, meenie, monie my,
Bassaloney, boney, stry,
Hair, ware, crown, nack,
Alko, balko, we wo wack.

From Massachusetts and New Hampshire [2]

Eena, meena, mona my,
Tuscalona, bona stry,
Tin pan, maska, dary,
Highly, pigly, pig snout,
Crinkly, cranky, you are out.
(New Hampshire.)

One is all, two is all, Zick is all zan,
Bobtail, vinegar, little tol tan,
Harum, scarum, Virginia merum,
Zee, tan, buck.
(New Hampshire.)

Fe, fi, fo, fum,
I smell the blood of an Englishman,
Be he live, or be he dead,
I'll have his bones to make my bread.
(Plymouth.)

Eggs, cheese, butter, bread,
Stick, stock, stone, dead,
Hang him up, lay him down,
On his father's living ground.
(Plymouth.)

Een, teen, feather pip,
Sargo, larko, bump.
(Plymouth.)

Inditie, Mentitie, Petitee, Dee,
Delia, Delia, Dominee,
Oacha, Poacha, Domminnicher,
Hing, Ping, Chee.
(Plymouth.)

Henry, pennery, pit for gold,
Had a louse in his head,
Seven years old.
Seventy, seventy on to that,
This old logy will grow fat,
Hinchiman, pinchiman, make his back smart,
If ever I catch him, I'll sling him to my heart;
Sling, slang, chattery bang—out.
(Plymouth.)

Up on yonder hill,
There's where my father dwells.
He has jewels, he has rings,
He has many pretty things,

---

[1] By Mrs. Rebecca M. Halley, West Newbury, Vermont. Manuscripts of the Federal Writers' Project of the Works Progress Administration for the State of Vermont.

[2] From *Plymouth Memories of an Octogenarian*, by William T. Davis, pp. 208–212. Copyright, 1906, by Bittinger Brothers. Plymouth, Massachusetts.

He has a hammer with two nails,
He has a cat with two tails.
Strike Jack, lick Tom,
Blow the bellows, old man.
(New England.)

One-ery, two-ery, eckeery Ann,
Phillisy, phollisy, Nicholas John,
Queebe, quarby, Irish Mary,
Sinkum, sankum, Johnny go buck.
(Cambridge.)

Ink, mink, pepper stink,
Sarko, Larko, Bump.
(Plymouth.)

Ball-Bouncing Rhymes

Bounce-y bounce-y ball-y,
I called on pretty Polly!
But she's in love with Cholly,
And hasn't time for me!

Teacher, teacher, made a mistake—
She sat down on a chocolate cake!
The cake was soft,
Teacher fell off—
Teacher, teacher, made a mistake!

Gene, Gene, made a machine;
Joe, Joe, made it go;
Frank, Frank, turned the crank,
And his mother came out and gave him a spank
That sent him over the railroad bank!

Red, white, and green!
My father is a machine,
My mother is the steering wheel,
And I'm the gasoline!

Rope-Skipping Rhymes

My father has a horse to shoe,
How many nails do you thing will do?
One, two, three, four, etc.

Fudge, fudge, tell the judge,
Mama's got a baby,
Not a girl, not a boy,
Just a little lady.

Apples, peaches, pumpkin pie,
How many years before I die?

Andy Gump sat on a stump.
He fell off and got a bump.

Susan, Susan, thought she was losin',
So she gave the whole thing up.

Martin, Martin, was only startin',
But he finished and won the cup!

Charlie Chaplin sat on a pin.
How many inches did it go in?
One, two, three, four, etc.

Where are you going, Bill?
Down town, Bill?
What for, Bill?
To pay my gas bill.
How much, Bill?
Ten-dollar bill.

Last night, and the night before,
Twenty-four robbers came to my door.
When I went down to let them in,

From Willimantic, Connecticut. Manuscripts of the Federal Writers' Project of the Works Progress Administration for the State of Connecticut.

Ibid.

They knocked me down with the rolling pin.
Ten ran east, and ten ran west,
And four jumped over the cuckoo's nest.

Shirley Temple walks like this;
Shirley Temple talks like this;
Shirley Temple smiles like this;
Shirley Temple throws a kiss.

Oldsmobile, Chevrolet, Studebaker, Ford—
Now I jump my shining cord.

Ella, Ella, dressed in yellow,
Went downstairs to meet her fellow.
How many kisses did he give?
One, two, three, four, etc.

I come from Chink-a-China,
My home is 'cross the sea.
I send my laundry over,
For fifty cents a week.
So, over, over, over,
You ought to be ashamed
To marry, marry, marry
A boy without a name!

Mississippi lives on shore,
She has children three or four.
Which one shall I marry,
Rich man, poor man, beggar-man, thief,
Doctor, lawyer, merchant, chief.
[*The last two lines are repeated over and over until the jumper misses.*]

Butterfly, butterfly, turn around,
Butterfly, butterfly, touch the ground,
Butterfly, butterfly, show your shoe,
Butterfly, butterfly, twenty-three to do.

Johnny said to Tommy, "How much are your geese?"
Tommy said to Johnny, "Fifty cents apiece."
Johnny said to Tommy, "That's too dear."
Tommy said to Johnny, "Get out of here!"

Lady, lady, turn around.
Lady, lady, touch the ground.
Lady, lady, show your shoe.
Lady, lady, please skidoo!

Mother, mother, I am sick,
Send for the doctor, quick, quick, quick.
How many days shall I live?
One, two, three, etc.

Tenement to let,
Inquire within.
I'll jump out,
And let you jump in.

House for rent,
Furniture in.
As —— moves out,
—— moves in!

Tickling Rhymes

Tickle-y tickle-y
On the knee;
If you laugh,
You don't love me.

If you are an honest girl(boy),
As I suppose you be,
You will neither laugh nor cry
When I tickle you on the knee.

Ibid.

Children's Taunts

——'s It,
And has a fit,
And doesn't know how to get out of it!

Tattle-tale, teacher's pet!
Tell it quick or you'll forget!

Mamma's little condensed-milk baby!

Can't catch me!
Can't catch a flea!

Liar, liar, your pants are on fire,
Your nose is as long as a telephone wire!

Run, Fatty, run! Run for your life!
Here comes Skinny with a butcher knife!
[*Names interchangeable.*]

You think you're cute
With a pimple on your snoot,
A five-cent collar
And a ten-cent suit!

RHYMES FOR OCCASIONS

Incantations and Formulae

Boys try to catch a bat by throwing up the hat and calling:—

Bat, bat, come down my hat,
And when I brew and when I bake,
I'll give you a piece of bat-cake.

Massachusetts.

A swarm of bees in May
Is worth a load of hay.
A swarm of bees in June
Is worth a silver spoon.
A swarm of bees in July
Is not worth a fly.

Westport, Mass.

One crow, sorrow,
Two crows, mirth,
Three crows, a wedding,
Four crows, birth.

Maine.

Children catch a butterfly and hold it in the hand, saying:

Butterfly, butterfly, give me some butter,
And I'll let you go away!

North Cambridge, Mass.

Ibid.

From *Animal and Plant Lore,* Collected from the Oral Tradition of English Speaking Folk, edited and annotated by Fanny D. Bergen, with an Introduction by Joseph Y. Bergen, pp. 56, 57, 58, 59, 60. Copyright, 1899 by The American Folk-Lore Society. Boston and New York: Published for the Society by Houghton Mifflin and Company.

Boys often say while fishing:—

Fishy, fishy,
Come bite my hook,
I'll go captain
And you'll go cook(-ed in the pan).

Maine.

Grasshopper, grasshopper, grasshopper gray,
Give me some molasses to-day I pray,
Or I'll kill you to-day
And bury you to-morrow.

Auburn, Me.

Grasshopper, grasshopper gray,
Give me some molasses
And then fly away.

Central Maine.

Grasshopper, grasshopper green,
Give me some molasses
Or you'll never be seen.

Salem, Mass.

Pick the first brake,
Kill the first snake,
And you will accomplish
What you undertake.

Vermont, 1860.

If you wish to live and thrive,
Let the spider run alive.

Eastern Massachusetts.

On seeing a spider:—

Black, sad,
Brown, glad,
White, good luck attend you.

Guilford, Conn.

The Weather

Rain before seven,
Clear before 'leven.

Red in the morning,
Sailors take warning;

Red at night,
Sailors delight.

Rainbow in the morning;
Sailors take warning;

From *What They Say in New England,* A Book of Signs, Sayings, and Superstitions, collected by Clifton Johnson, pp. 17, 18, 19, 20, 21, 22, 23, 24, 26, 27, 28, 29, 30, 38, 49–50, 51–52, 58, 60, 61, 63, 64, 65, 90, 101, 107, 108, 109, 124, 125, 126, 129, 130, 131, 135, 136, 144, 145–146, 151, 154. Copyright, 1896, by Lee and Shepard. Boston.

Rainbow at night,
Sailors delight;
Rainbow at noon,
Rain very soon.

Fog on the hills,
More water for the mills.

Between twelve and two
You can tell what the day will do.

A sunshiny shower
Won't last half an hour.

When the fog goes up the mountain hoppin',
Then the rain comes down the mountain droppin'.

If the rooster crows when he goes to bed,
He will get up with a wet head.

A mackerel sky
Won't leave the ground dry.

Mackerel scales and mares' tails
Make lofty ships to carry low sails.

A cold, wet May,
A barn full of hay.

When the wind is in the east,
Then the sap will run the least.
When the wind is in the west,
Then the sap will run the best.

Open and shet
Sign of wet.
(That is, you can expect rain when the clouds open and shut.)

When the wind is in the east,
'Tis neither good for man nor beast.

Sun at seven,
Rain at 'leven.

As far as the sun shines in on Candlemas Day,
So far the snow blows in before May Day.

If Candlemas Day be fair and bright,
Winter will take another flight;
If chance to fall a shower of rain,
Winter will not come again.

If Candlemas Day be bright and clear,
Be sure you will have two winters that year.

On Candlemas Day
Half the wood and half the hay.

The old farmer at this time takes a critical survey of his woodpile and haymow; and if there is not in them half what there was at the beginning of winter, he lays plans for their replenishing before the opening of the new season.

Others say,—

Half the pork and half the hay
On Christmas Day.

The Winds

Wind from the east,—bad for man and for beast;
Wind from the south is too hot for them both;
Wind from the north is of very little worth;
Wind from the west is the softest and the best.[1]

[1] From *The Old Farmer's Almanack*, Calculated on a New and Improved Plan, for the Year of Our Lord 1851, by Robert B. Thomas, p. 46. Entered, according to Act

. . . The proverb quoted by Sewall is still current. I have heard the following traditional rhyme on Cape Cod:

When the wind is to the north,
The fisherman he goes not forth;
When the wind is to the east,
'Tis neither good for man nor beast,
When the wind is to the south,
It blows the bait in the fish's mouth;
When the wind is to the west,
Then 'tis at the very best.[2]

Campaign Rhymes

——'s a patriot, noble and true;
—— we never could trust;
—— will guard well the red-white-and-blue;
With —— it will drag in the dust!

(This was a campaign rhyme of the pre-Civil War period, and was given by Mr. Wilbur Davis of Sound Beach, whose ancestors for generations lived in northern Connecticut.)

Coffee and gingerbread hot from the pans
We'll serve to good Republicans.
Fried rats and pickled cats
Are good enough for Democrats.

Shame, shame! Oh, what a shame!
——'s got a baby without any name!

(Back in the good old days, it seems anything went in the heat of a presidential campaign, and it was common to charge the head of the opposition party with at least one illegitmate child!)

—— rides a white horse,
—— rides a mule.
—— is a gentleman,
—— is a fool!

---

of Congress, in the year 1850, by J. H. Jenks and G. W. Palmer, in the Clerk's Office of the District Court of the District of Massachusetts. Boston: Jenks, Palmer & Co.

[2] By George Lyman Kittredge. From *Letters of Samuel Lee and Samuel Sewall Relating to New England and the Indians,* edited by George Lyman Kittredge, p. 177. Reprinted from *The Publications of the Colonial Society of Massachusetts,* Vol. XIV. Cambridge: John Wilson and Son, University Press. 1912.

From Willimantic, Connecticut. Manuscripts of the Federal Writers' Project of the Works Progress Administration for the State of Connecticut.

One, two, three, four, five, six, seven!
All good ——s go to Heaven!
When they get there they will yell,
"All bad ——s go to Hell!"

(One's own party being named in the first blank, of course, and the opposition party in the last.)

One, two, three, four!
Who are we for?
——, ——, ——,
Five, six, seven, eight!
Who do we hate?
——, ——, ——.

(The first row of blanks to be filled in with the name of the shouter's favorite candidate, the last row with the name of his candidate's opponent.)

Sailors' Rhymes

For Occasions [1]

There were his weather rhymes in great store:

Winds that change against the sun
Are always sure to backward run.

And of the barometer:

First rise after a low,
Squalls expect and more blow.

* * * * *

Of winds and clouds:

First the rain and then the wind,
Topsail sheets and halliards mind;
First the wind and then the rain,
Hoist your topsails up again.

Mackerel skies and mares' tails
Make tall ships carry low sails.

When the sun sets behind a cloud
A westerly wind will you enshroud.
When the sun sets clear as a bell,
An easterly wind as sure as hell.

[1] From *Songs of American Sailormen,* by Joanna C. Colcord, pp. 205–207. Copyrigh, 1938, by W. W. Norton & Company, Inc. New York.

Of hurricanes:

June, too soon.
July, stand by.
August, look out you must.
September, remember.
October, all over.

There was his grace before meat, when the beef-kids came in from the galley:

Old horse! old horse! how came you here?
—From Sacarap' to Portland Pier.
I carted stone this many a year,
Until, worn out by sore abuse,
They salted me down for sailors' use.
The sailors they do me despise;
They turn me over and damn my eyes,
Cut off my meat and pick my bones,
And heave the rest to Davy Jones.

And these were the rhymes for turning out the watch, which were sometimes chanted at the forecastle door:

Awake, awake, you weary sleepers,
  Know you not 'tis almost day?
Here while thus you're sleeping,
  God's best hours will pass away.

Show a leg! Show a leg!

In the second rhyme, the terms "larbowlin" and "starbowlin" are old names for the port and starboard watches respectively.

Larbowlins stout, you must turn out
  And sleep no more within;
For if you do we'll cut your clew,
  And let starbowlins in.

RULES OF THE ROAD, AT SEA [2]

Two close-hauled ships upon the sea
To one safe rule must each agree:
The starboard tack must keep his luff,
  The port bear off.

---

[2] From *American Naval Songs & Ballads,* edited by Robert W. Neeser, p. 305. Copyright, 1938, by Yale University Press. New Haven.
Printed in Stephen B. Luce's *Naval Songs* (New York, 1902) pp. 74–76.—R. W. N.

Two steamships meeting:

When both side-lights I see ahead,
I port my helm and show my red.

Two steamships passing:

Green to green, and red to red,
Perfect safety, go ahead.

Two steamships crossing:

If to my starboard red appear,
It is my duty to keep clear,
To act as judgment says is proper,
To port, or starboard, back, or stop her;
But when upon my port is seen
A steamer's starboard light of green,
There's less for me to do or say,
The green is bound to keep away.
All ships must keep a good lookout!
And steamships must stop and go astern;
  If necessary;
Both in safety and in doubt,
Always keep a sharp lookout,
In danger with no room to turn
Ease her, stop her, go astern!

Authors, Titles, and First Lines of Songs

Index of Subjects and Names

Geographical Index

States and Cities

CONNECTICUT

MAINE

MASSACHUSETTS